D1556499

DERHAM ON THE LAW OF SET-OFF

DERHAM ON THE LAW OF SET-OFF

RORY DERHAM
Barrister, New South Wales

OXFORD
UNIVERSITY PRESS

OXFORD

UNIVERSITY PRESS

Great Clarendon Street, Oxford ox2 6dp

Oxford University Press is a department of the University of Oxford.
It furthers the University's objective of excellence in research, scholarship,
and education by publishing worldwide in

Oxford New York

Auckland Cape Town Dar es Salaam Hong Kong Karachi
Kuala Lumpur Madrid Melbourne Mexico City Nairobi
New Delhi Shanghai Taipei Toronto

With offices in

Argentina Austria Brazil Chile Czech Republic France Greece
Guatemala Hungary Italy Japan Poland Portugal Singapore
South Korea Switzerland Thailand Turkey Ukraine Vietnam

Oxford is a registered trade mark of Oxford University Press
in the UK and in certain other countries

Published in the United States
by Oxford University Press Inc., New York

British Library Cataloguing in Publication Data
Data available

Library of Congress Cataloging in Publication Data
Data available

Typeset by Glyph International, Bangalore, India
Printed in Great Britain
on acid-free paper by
CPI Antony Rowe

ISBN 978-0-19-957882-5

1 3 5 7 9 10 8 6 4 2

To Heather, Ryan, Kate and Stephen

PREFACE

A number of important developments have occurred in the law of set-off since the publication of the third edition some seven years ago. Of particular importance are the changes introduced by the Insolvency (Amendment) Rules 2005 in relation to set-off in company liquidation and administration. Curiously, set-off in bankruptcy has not attracted the same attention, notwithstanding that some of the amendments made in relation to company liquidation are equally relevant to bankruptcy. There have also been a multitude of cases in relation to set-off since the last edition, which is to be expected given the breadth of the subject. One may note in particular the decision of the House of Lords in *Secretary of State for Trade and Industry v Frid* [2004] 2 AC 506 (insolvency set-off) and, in the Court of Appeal, *Muscat v Smith* [2003] 1 WLR 2853 (equitable set-off and assignments) and *Re SSSL Realisations (2002) Ltd* [2006] Ch 610 (the rule in *Cherry v Boultbee* and insolvency set-off). In Australia, the High Court in *International Air Transport Association v Ansett Australia Holdings Ltd* (2008) 234 CLR 151 considered the much-discussed decision of the House of Lords in *British Eagle International Air Lines Ltd v Compagnie Nationale Air France* [1975] 1 WLR 758. It came to a different conclusion based upon amendments made to the IATA Clearing House Regulations after the House of Lords' decision. Of significance also is the decision of the Supreme Court of Canada in *Caisse populaire Desjardins de l'Est de Drummond v Canada* (2009) 309 DLR (4th) 323, which recognized that in some circumstances a set-off agreement may constitute a security interest.

Muscat v Smith is significant for at least two reasons. In the first place, it was said in that case that cross-claims available for equitable set-off must lie between the same parties, which imports a requirement of mutuality. This view has since been repeated in the Court of Appeal. Certainly the insolvency set-off section and the Statutes of Set-off require mutuality, and ordinarily it would be necessary for equitable set-off. But, as Australian and Canadian courts have recognized, it is not a strict rule in equity. There have been a number of occasions when set-off has been permitted in equity notwithstanding an absence of mutuality, which is consistent with the inherent flexibility of equitable remedies. The issue of mutuality in relation to equitable set-off is discussed in Chapter 4. The second point concerns the principle that an assignee takes subject to equities. That principle has its foundation in the doctrines of equity in cases where, before the Judicature Acts, an assignment of a debt was recognized only in equity. In order to enforce the debt in a common law action, the assignee had to sue in the name of the assignor and therefore took subject to defences available against the assignor. The principle did not apply in those limited situations, such as in the case of negotiable instruments, where the transferee of a debt could sue in the common law courts in his or her own name and right. In *Muscat v Smith*, however, the Court of Appeal applied the 'taking subject to equities' principle as against a purchaser of leased premises who was entitled to sue for arrears of rent from the period before the sale based on his own title, as opposed to that of the seller as the original landlord. This aspect of *Muscat v Smith* is considered in Chapter 17. The discussion of the case reproduces material first published in an article in the *Law Quarterly Review*.[1] I am grateful to the editor of the *Law Quarterly Review* for permission to reproduce that material.

As in the first three editions, the book considers the principles of set-off from both an English and an Australian perspective.

The law is stated on the basis of the reported law available to me on 15 May 2010. The important judgment of the Court of Appeal in *Geldof Metaalconstructie NV v Simon Carves Ltd* [2010] EWCA Civ 667 in relation to equitable set-off arrived too late for anything other than brief references.

Rory Derham
Tenth Floor St James Hall Chambers
Sydney

---

[1] 'Equitable set-off: a critique of *Muscat v Smith*' (2006) 122 LQR 469.

PREFACE TO THE FIRST EDITION

Set-off is an area of the law that, for some unknown reason, has not proved attractive for academic writers. In the early part of the nineteenth century Babington and Montagu each published monographs on the subject, but since then it has received remarkably little attention. This is surprising given the importance that the business community does attach to the right to set cross-demands against each other, particularly in the event of an insolvency. The avowed aim of this book is to provide an exposition of some of the more important principles of the law of set-off. It had its genesis in a thesis for which the author was awarded the degree of Doctor of Philosophy, and subsequently also a Yorke Prize, at the University of Cambridge. The thesis was entitled 'The Law of Set-off in Bankruptcy and Company Liquidation', and more and less constitutes the material set out in Chapters 2 to 12 of the present book. The first chapter, dealing with equitable set-off and the final chapter, on a surety's right of set-off, have been added in order to expand the scope of the work for the purpose of publication.

The emphasis throughout is on the question of when a right of set-off is available. Questions of pleading and procedure are not dealt with. For these, the appropriate rules of court, and commentaries thereon, should be consulted. Moreover the book is concerned with the *principles* of set-off. It does not purport to provide an exhaustive list of the myriad situations in which the courts in the past have allowed a right of set-off. Rather the aim is to indicate the principles upon which the decided case law is based.

During my period of research at Cambridge I was fortunate to have as my supervisors Professor Gareth Jones, of Trinity College, and Michael Prichard, of Gonville and Caius College. I am grateful to these gentlemen for their advice and assistance. The thesis was examined by Dr Len Sealy, of Gonville and Gaius College, and Professor Roy Goode, of Queen Mary College in London. Their comments and criticisms, and the encouragement they gave me to publish this book, are greatly appreciated. Of course none of these people is in any way responsible for any errors of omission or commission that may be contained in the ensuing pages.

The discussion of the various principles of set-off is based primarily upon English case and statute law, though reference is also made to suitable authorities from Australia and New Zealand. There are also extensive cross-references to the relevant Australian statutory provisions. The law is stated on the basis of the available reported law as at 31 December 1986. However for the second impression of the book cases reported after that date and before 30 September 1988 have been included, but by way of brief reference only in the footnotes. Unfortunately it has not been possible to discuss these cases in any great depth.

R. D.

CONTENTS—SUMMARY

CONTENTS—SUMMARY

CONTENTS

TABLE OF CASES

TABLE OF LEGISLATION, TREATIES, AND CONVENTIONS

UNITED KINGDOM

Primary Legislation

(1603) 1 Jac, c. 15

  s 13 . . . . 6.33, 6.35

(1605) 3 Jac 1, c 15 . . . . 2.35

(1704) 5 & 6 Anne, c. 22

  s 4 . . . . 6.33

(1705) 4 & 5 Anne, c. 17 . . . . 6.37, 6.38

  s 11 . . . . 6.33, 6.38

  s 17 . . . . 6.38

(1705) 7 Anne, c. 25 . . . . 6.38

(1706) 5 & 6 Anne, c. 22 . . . . 6.37

(1708) 7 Anne, c. 25 . . . . 6.38

(1716) 3 Geo I, c. 12 . . . . 6.38

(1718) 5 Geo I, c. 24 . . . . 6.37, 6.38, 6.39

  s 23 . . . . 6.37

  s 25 . . . . 6.37

(1724) 2 Geo I, c. 29 . . . . 6.38

(1726) 13 Geo I, c. 27 . . . . 6.38

(1729) 2 Geo II, c 22 . . . . 2.04

  s 13 . . . . 1.09, 1.11, 2.01, 2.04, 13.131

(1732) 5 Geo II, c. 30 . . . . 6.38, 6.45,
                                   6.62, 9.03

  s 28 . . . . 6.38, 6.39, 9.03

  s 33 . . . . 6.33

  s 45 . . . . 6.37

  s 49 . . . . 6.38

(1735) 8 Geo II, c 24 . . . . 2.04

  s 4 . . . . 2.05

  s 5 . . . . 1.11, 2.05, 2.36, 2.39

(1736) 9 Geo II, c. 18 . . . . 6.38

(1743) 16 Geo II, c. 27 . . . . 6.38

(1746) 19 Geo II, c. 32

  s 2 . . . . 7.27

(1751) 24 Geo II, c. 57 . . . . 6.38

(1758) 31 Geo II, c 25 . . . . 6.38

(1763) 4 Geo III, c. 36 . . . . 6.38

(1772) 12 Geo II, c. 47 . . . . 6.38

(1776) 16 Geo III, c. 54 . . . . 6.38

(1781) 21 Geo III, c. 29 . . . . 6.38

(1786) 26 Geo II, c. 80 . . . . 6.38

(1788) 28 Geo III, c. 24 . . . . 6.38

(1794) 34 Geo III, c 57 . . . . 6.38

(1797) 37 Geo III, c. 124 . . . . 6.38

(1806) 46 Geo II, c. 135 . . . . 6.45

  s 2 . . . . 6.45, 6.62

  s 3 . . . . 6.39, 6.40, 6.45, 6.62

(1824) 5 Geo IV, c. 98 . . . . 6.40

(1825) 6 Geo IV, c. 16 . . . . 6.40, 7.25

  s 47 . . . . 6.45

  s 50 . . . . 6.93, 6.101, 6.136,
                                   7.25, 8.39

  s 56 . . . . 6.40, 6.135, 7.27, 8.39

(1828) 9 Geo IV, c.83

  s 24 . . . . 2.63

(1831) 1 & 2 Will IV, c. 56 . . . . 6.41

  s 22 . . . . 6.33

(1870) 13 Eliz, c. 7

  s 2 . . . . 6.35, 6.37

Access to Justice Act 1999 . . . . . . 2.106, 2.121

EUROPE

Directives

Regulations

Treaties and Conventions

AUSTRALIA

Commonwealth

1

INTRODUCTION

A. The Meaning of Set-off

It is difficult to give a comprehensive definition of set-off without reference to the various **1.01** forms that it can take, but on a general level it can be defined as the setting of money cross-claims[1] against each other to produce a balance. It provides a defence to an action, although, depending on the form of set-off, the issue need not arise in that context. The essence of set-off, in this sense of the word, is the existence of cross-demands.[2] The term 'set-off' is also commonly used in a different sense, to describe a situation in which the damages payable by a defendant to a claimant may be reduced because of a benefit incidentally accruing to the claimant as a result of the defendant's breach.[3] This is not a case of cross-demands, but rather of calculating the true measure of damages. It is not therefore a set-off, in the sense in which that term is used in this book. A similar comment may be made in relation

---

[1] Set-off is concerned with money claims. See *Tony Lee Motors Ltd v M S McDonald & Son (1974) Ltd* [1981] 2 NZLR 281, 288; *Hamilton Ice Arena Ltd v Perry Developments Ltd* [2002] 1 NZLR 309, 311. See also CPR r. 16.6, and para. 3.02 below.

[2] *Re Dalco, ex p Dalco and Deputy Commissioner of Taxation (NSW)* (1986) 17 ATR 906, 913; *Buttrose v Versi* NSW SC, Young J, 14 May 1992. Compare *Bedford Steamship Co Ltd v Navico AG (The Ionian Skipper)* [1977] 2 Lloyd's Rep 273, 279 and *Bitannia Pty Ltd v Parkline Constructions Pty Ltd* (2006) 67 NSWLR 9 at [88].

[3] See e.g. *Nadreph Ltd v Willmett & Co* [1978] 1 WLR 1537; *Ocean Glory Compania Naviera SA v A/S PV Christensen (The Ioanna)* [1985] 2 Lloyd's Rep 164; *Christianos v Westpac Banking Corporation* (1991) 5 WAR 336; *Brown v KMR Services Ltd* [1995] 2 Lloyd's Rep 513, 555; *Longden v British Coal Corporation* [1998] AC 653. When a defendant in an action for detention of goods, who has not been guilty of fraud or negligence, has incurred expenses in good faith with respect to the goods, and the goods have been delivered up to the claimant, who consequently has the benefit of the expenses, the defendant is entitled to have the expenses taken into account in any assessment of damages for detention. See *Peruvian Guano Co Ltd v Dreyfus Brothers & Co* [1892] AC 166; *Hill v Ziymack* (1908) 7 CLR 352; *Halsbury's Laws of England* (4th edn, 1999) vol. 45(2) ('Torts'), 397–8, para. 625. In *Re Baldwin (A Bankrupt), and Tasman Fruit-Packers Ltd, ex p Official Assignee* [1940] NZLR 848, it was held that the value of the interest of a member of a society registered under the Industrial and Provident Societies Act 1908 (NZ) could only be ascertained by deducting the amount of the member's indebtedness to the society. This was independent of any principle of set-off.

to the action for money had and received. The action is based on the principle of unjust enrichment, and it cannot be asserted without the claimant at the same time giving credit for any payments that he or she received from the defendant.[4] The net sum represents the amount of the enrichment, as opposed to the product of bringing together cross-claims. A running account should also be distinguished. A true running account is not within the ambit of the law of set-off[5] because there are not independent cross-demands between the parties requiring to be set off. Rather, there is only one cause of action for the balance.[6]

B. The Importance of Set-off

(1) Insolvency

1.02   The availability or otherwise of a set-off can be be crucial in the event of an insolvency. If there are cross-demands between a creditor and a debtor who has become insolvent, the creditor, in the absence of a set-off, would be obliged to pay the full amount of his or her own debt, and yet be confined to receiving a dividend along with other creditors for the amount of the insolvent's debt. If a set-off is available, however, only the balance remaining after deducting one claim from the other would be payable. Therefore, if the debtor's claim against the creditor exceeds the creditor's claim against the debtor, the creditor in effect would obtain payment in full for his or her claim in the form of a deduction from his or her liability, and would only be obliged to pay the balance. Alternatively, the creditor's claim may be the greater, in which case the creditor would receive payment in full to the extent of his or her liability to the debtor and would be confined to a dividend only in respect of the balance.

(2) Counterclaim

1.03   A set-off also may have advantages in the absence of insolvency. In that context, it is often important to distinguish between set-off and counterclaim.

1.04   A defendant's right to counterclaim against the claimant in the claimant's action originated in the Supreme Court of Judicature Act 1873, s. 24(3).[7] It differs from set-off in that it does not give rise to a defence, but rather it constitutes a procedural device by which the court may consider independent cross-actions in the same proceeding. The cross-actions are

---

[4] *Westdeutsche Landesbank v Islington BC* [1994] 4 All ER 890, 940–1, Hobhouse J commenting (at 941) that: 'As a matter of the principle of unjust enrichment, the defendant has only been enriched in the net sum and the enrichment has only been at the expense of the plaintiff in the net sum.' See also *Dowell v Custombuilt Homes Pty Ltd* [2004] WASCA 171 at [118]. Compare *Roxborough v Rothmans of Pall Mall Australia Ltd* (2001) 208 CLR 516, where the plaintiffs were recouped by means of transactions with third parties.

[5] Compare *Rolls Razor Ltd v Cox* [1967] 1 QB 552, 575; *Opal Maritime Agencies Pty Ltd v Baltic Shipping Co* (1998) 158 ALR 416, 421 (contrast *Opal Maritime Agencies Pty Ltd v 'Skulptor Konenkov'* (2000) 98 FCR 519, 567–8).

[6] *Cottam v Partridge* (1842) 4 Man & G 271, 293–4, 134 ER 111, 120; *Re Armour, ex p Official Receiver v Commonwealth Trading Bank of Australia* (1956) 18 ABC 69, 75; *Re Convere Pty Ltd* [1976] VR 345, 349; *Re Charge Card Services Ltd* [1987] 1 Ch 150, 174.

[7] See now the Senior Courts Act 1981, s. 49(2), and CPR r. 20.4. The Judicature Acts, in introducing a right of counterclaim, did not confer any new right of set-off. See *Hanak v Green* [1958] 2 QB 9, 22.

treated as independent actions for all purposes except execution.[8] In the case of a counter-claim, the courts, particularly in the early years after the Judicature Acts, would sometimes enter only a single judgment for the balance.[9] The usual practice however is to enter separate judgments on both the claim and the cross-claim,[10] but with execution issuing only for the balance.[11] In comparison, since a set-off gives rise to a defence to the claimant's claim, where the claims are of equal value a successful set-off results in a single judgment in favour of the defendant. If the case is one in which the claimant's claim exceeds the defendant's cross-claim and the cross-claim is the subject of a successful plea of set-off, the defendant is entitled to judgment to the extent of the set-off and claimant is entitled to judgment for the balance. Alternatively, the defendant's cross-claim may exceed the claimant's claim. In that circumstance, the defendant should plead his or her claim by way of both set-off and counterclaim. The defendant, if successful, would be entitled to judgment as having defended the claimant's action on the basis of a set-off, and in addition would be entitled to judgment against the claimant for the balance remaining in his or her favour after the set-off.

In an application by a claimant for summary judgment against the defendant,[12] the existence of a cross-claim not amounting to a set-off ordinarily is not sufficient to prevent judgment being entered, although the court in its discretion can stay enforcement on the judgment until the defendant's cross-action has been tried. Under former rules of court, the question whether the court should exercise its discretion to grant a stay depended on a number of factors, such as the degree of connection between the claim and the cross-claim, the strength of the cross-claim, and the ability of the claimant to satisfy any judgment on the cross-claim.[13] It has been suggested that, under the Civil Procedure Rules 1998, the courts may be prepared to grant summary judgment and a delay on enforcement more

1.05

---

[8] *Stumore v Campbell & Co* [1892] 1 QB 314, 317 (Lord Esher MR). See also *Beddall v Maitland* (1881) 17 Ch D 174.

[9] See e.g. *Stooke v Taylor* (1880) 5 QBD 569, 581; *Provincial Bill Posting Co v Low Moor Iron Co* [1909] 2 KB 344, 351; *Chell Engineering Ltd v Unit Tool and Engineering Co Ltd* [1950] 1 All ER 378, 380 (referring to the *Annual Practice* (1948), 410).

[10] *Sharpe v Haggith* (1912) 106 LT 13; *Stumore v Campbell & Co* [1892] 1 QB 314, 317; *McDonnell & East Ltd v McGregor* (1936) 56 CLR 50, 62; *Chell Engineering Ltd v Unit Tool and Engineering Co Ltd* [1950] 1 All ER 378; *Hanak v Green* [1958] 2 QB 9. In New South Wales, compare the Civil Procedure Act 2005, s. 90(2).

[11] *Stumore v Campbell & Co* [1892] 1 QB 314, 317. This practice should not apply when the beneficial ownership of the cross-claims is in different hands in consequence of an assignment of one of the claims. See *John Dee Group Ltd v WMH (21) Ltd* [1998] BCC 972, 976 (CA).

[12] See CPR Part 24.

[13] *The Supreme Court Practice* (1999), 178–9, para. 14/4/14, referring to *A B Contractors Ltd v Flaherty Brothers Ltd* (1978) 16 BLR 8 (CA) and *Drake and Fletcher Ltd v Batchelor* (1986) 83 LS Gaz 1232 (Sir Neil Lawson). See also *State Bank of Victoria v Parry* [1989] WAR 240, 246; *Exmar BV v National Iranian Tanker Co (The Trade Fortitude)* [1992] 1 Lloyd's Rep 169, 177; *Aectra Refining and Manufacturing Inc v Exmar NV* [1994] 1 WLR 1634, 1652; *Benford Ltd v Lopecan SL* [2004] 2 Lloyd's Rep 618 at [27]. For instances in which a stay was refused, see e.g. *Anglian Building Products Ltd v W & C French (Construction) Ltd* (1972) 16 BLR 1 and *Century Textiles and Industry Ltd v Tomoe Shipping (Singapore) Pte Ltd (The Aditya Vaibhav)* [1991] 1 Lloyd's Rep 573. Compare Dillon LJ in *Schofield v Church Army* [1986] 1 WLR 1328, 1334–5, who said that a summary judgment 'ought to be stayed' until after the trial of a counterclaim if the counterclaim is not frivolous, and see also Croom Johnson LJ at 1337. Compare also *L U Simon Builders Pty Ltd v H D Fowles* [1992] 2 VR 189, 196, though that was in the context of a cross-claim that was closely connected with the plaintiff's claim.

frequently than hitherto,[14] but those factors should still be relevant in determining whether to grant a stay. On the other hand, a defendant whom the court considers has a real prospect of establishing a set-off[15] overtopping the claimant's claim ordinarily could expect to be granted leave to defend,[16] either unconditionally or subject to conditions,[17] so that the defendant would not be the subject of an adverse judgment.

(3) Costs

1.06 The distinction between set-off and counterclaim is relevant to the question of costs. Costs are within the discretion of the court, but the general rule is that the unsuccessful party pays the costs of the successful party.[18] Since a set-off gives rise to a defence, it follows that, if the defendant's cross-claim the subject of a successful plea of set-off equalled or exceeded the claimant's claim, the defendant will have successfully defended the action, and accordingly the defendant ordinarily would be entitled to an order for costs for the action.[19] On the other hand, a counterclaim not amounting to a set-off ordinarily results in two judgments, one judgment for the claimant on the claim and a separate judgment for the defendant on the cross-claim. If, therefore, both claim and cross-claim are established, the claimant usually is awarded costs in respect of the claim and the defendant costs in relation to the cross-claim.[20] The circumstances of a particular case may warrant different orders,[21] but those are the *prima facie* positions.

---

[14] *Civil Procedure* (2010) ('White Book') vol. 1, para. 24.2.6.

[15] As opposed to a defence which is merely arguable. See *Doncaster Pharmaceuticals Group Ltd v The Bolton Pharmaceutical Company 100 Ltd* [2006] EWCA Civ 661 at [4].

[16] CPR r. 24.2 (but note the discussion in *Civil Procedure* (2010) ('White Book') vol. 1, para. 24.2.6). See e.g. *Morgan & Son Ltd v S Martin Johnson & Co Ltd* [1949] 1 KB 107; *James Lamont & Co Ltd v Hyland Ltd* [1950] 1 KB 585; *Re K L Tractors Ltd* [1954] VLR 505, 509; *Edward Ward & Co v McDougall* [1972] VR 433; *Mottram Consultants Ltd v Bernard Sunley & Sons Ltd* [1975] 2 Lloyd's Rep 197, 212, 214; *Petersville Ltd v Rosgrae Distributors Pty Ltd* (1975) 11 SASR 433; *General Credits (Finance) Pty Ltd v Stoyakovich* [1975] Qd R 352; *United Dominions Corporation Ltd v Jaybe Homes Pty Ltd* [1978] Qd R 111; *Paynter Ltd v Ben Candy Investments Ltd* [1987] 1 NZLR 257. Compare the proposed order in *Standard Chartered Bank v Pakistan National Shipping Corporation* [1995] 2 Lloyd's Rep 365, 375 (judgment on the plaintiff's claim, with damages to be assessed, and the defendant to be left to advance its cross-claim and, if appropriate, to set it off before a money judgment was entered in favour of the plaintiff). Ordinarily the defendant should quantify the value of his or her set-off to justify leave to defend. Compare *Asco Developments Ltd v Gordon* (1978) 248 E.G. 683.

[17] As in *General Credits (Finance) Pty Ltd v Stoyakovich* [1975] Qd R 352.

[18] See CPR r. 44.3.

[19] *Baines v Bromley* (1881) 6 QBD 691, 694 (Brett LJ); *Baylis Baxter Ltd v Sabath* [1958] 1 WLR 529, 538 (Parker LJ); *Hanak v Green* [1958] 2 QB 9.

[20] *Stooke v Taylor* (1880) 5 QBD 569 (overruling *Staples v Young* (1877) 2 Ex D 324); *Shrapnel v Laing* (1888) 20 QBD 334; *Sharpe v Haggith* (1912) 106 LT 13; *McDonnell & East Ltd v McGregor* (1936) 56 CLR 50, 62; *Chell Engineering Ltd v Unit Tool and Engineering Co Ltd* [1950] 1 All ER 378; *E Reynolds & Sons (Chingford), Ltd v Hendry Brothers (London) Ltd* [1955] 1 Lloyd's Rep 258. Compare para. 5.176 below.

[21] See the matters referred to in CPR r. 44.3. In relation to set-off, see also *Box v Midland Bank Ltd* [1981] 1 Lloyd's Rep 434 and *Hanak v Green* [1958] 2 QB 9, 27. In the case of a counterclaim not amounting to a set-off, where the plaintiff's claim was admitted and the only point that was litigated was the counterclaim, see *Childs v Gibson* [1954] 1 WLR 809, 812–13. Compare *Nicholson v Little* [1956] 1 WLR 829. There may be a special order as to costs in the case of a counterclaim where the issues on the claim and the counterclaim are interlocked. See *Chell Engineering Ltd v Unit Tool and Engineering Co Ltd* [1950] 1 All ER 378, 383 (Denning LJ); *Childs v Gibson* at 815.

(4) Third party interests

The question whether a set-off is available to a debtor can be critical when a third party has **1.07** an interest in the debt, for example as a result of an assignment. An assignee takes subject to defences available to the debtor against the assignor before the debtor received notice of the assignment. This includes the defence of set-off.[22] An assignee does not take subject to a debtor's cross-claim against the assignor if the cross-claim could not have been raised as a set-off in an action by the assignor.[23]

(5) Arbitration

When a person being sued for payment of a debt the subject of a contract with an arbitra- **1.08** tion clause has a cross-claim against the claimant for damages for breach of contract, the question whether the defendant is entitled to a stay of the action on account of the cross-claim has been said to depend on whether the cross-claim gives rise to an equitable set-off.[24] However, a different position has been adopted in England in relation to an application for a stay under s. 9 of the Arbitration Act 1996, as a result of differences in the drafting of s. 9 in comparison to the corresponding provision in earlier legislation. The position under the 1996 Act is that any claim which has been made but not admitted must be taken to be in dispute.[25] When a claim has been referred to an arbitrator, the question whether the arbi- trator has jurisdiction to determine the availability of a set-off against the claim depends on the construction of the arbitration agreement.[26]

An arbitrator may make more than one award, at different times and in respect of different **1.09** aspects of the matters to be determined.[27] In particular, an arbitrator may make an award as to part only of a claim.[28] This power may be exercised in relation to such part of a claim

---

[22] See ch. 17 below.

[23] *Bank of Boston Connecticut v European Grain and Shipping Ltd* [1989] 1 AC 1056, 1105–6, 1109–11. But in Australia compare paras 17.06–17.12 below.

[24] See e.g. *Compania Sud Americana de Vapores v Shipmair BV (The Teno)* [1977] 2 Lloyd's Rep 289; *A/S Gunnstein & Co K/S v Jensen, Krebs and Nielsen (The Alfa Nord)* [1977] 2 Lloyd's Rep 434; *Nova (Jersey) Knit Ltd v Kammgarn Spinnerei GmbH* [1977] 1 WLR 713; *Federal Commerce & Navigation Co Ltd v Molena Alpha Inc* [1978] 1 QB 927, 974; *SL Sethia Liners Ltd v Naviagro Maritime Corporation (The Kostas Melas)* [1981] 1 Lloyd's Rep 18, 27; *Cleobulos Shipping Co Ltd v Intertanker Ltd (The Cleon)* [1983] 1 Lloyd's Rep 586. Compare *Russell v Pellegrini* (1856) 6 El & Bl 1020, 119 ER 1144 (which was followed in *Seligmann v Le Boutillier* (1866) LR 1 CP 681), although Lord Wilberforce in the *Nova Knit* case (and see also *The Alfa Nord*) thought that *Russell v Pellegrini* should only be regarded as correct, if at all, on the basis of the particularly wide arbitration clause there in issue. On other occasions it has been said that *Russell v Pellegrini* should not be followed. See Bramwell B in *Daunt v Lazard* (1858) LJ 27 Ex 399, 400 and Lord Russell of Killowen in *Nova Knit* at 733.

[25] *Halki Shipping Corporation v Sopex Oils Ltd (The Halki)* [1998] 1 Lloyd's Rep 465; *Wealands v CLC Contractors Ltd* [1999] 2 Lloyd's Rep 739; *Collins (Contractors) Ltd v Baltic Quay Management (1994) Ltd* [2005] BLR 63; *Russell on Arbitration* (23rd edn, 2007), 182–3.

[26] *Metal Distributors (UK) Ltd v ZCCM Investment Holdings Ltd* [2005] 2 Lloyd's Rep 37, 43; *Econet Satellite Services Ltd v Vee Networks Ltd* [2006] 2 Lloyd's Rep 423. See also *Norscot Rig Management PVT Ltd v Essar Oilfields Services Ltd* [2010] EWHC 195 (Comm) at [2] (for the arbitration clause) and [16] (iii).

[27] Arbitration Act 1996, s. 47.

[28] Arbitration Act 1996, s. 47(2). On the other hand, an arbitrator is not permitted under the Arbitration Act 1996 to make a provisional order which is subject to a final adjudication unless the parties have agreed to confer that power on the arbitrator. See s. 39.

which undoubtedly is in excess of a cross-claim asserted as an equitable set-off or the subject of a contractual right of deduction.[29]

C. The Forms of Set-off

1.10   There are various forms of set-off.

1.11   In the case of parties neither of whom is bankrupt or is a company in liquidation, a set-off may proceed under the right of set-off derived from the Statutes of Set-off enacted in 1729[30] and 1735[31] if the case is one of mutual debts.[32] Alternatively, a set-off may be available in accordance with the principles developed independently by courts of equity. Set-off in equity is both broader and narrower than set-off under the Statutes. It is broader in that it extends to claims for damages, while it is narrower in that generally it is necessary to show a sufficient connection between the cross-demands. Set-off under the Statutes, on the other hand, does not require any connection between the debts.[33] Further, in the particular case of contracts for the sale of goods with a warranty or for the performance of work pursuant to a contract, a common law principle, known as abatement, may apply, so as to reduce the price payable in the event that there has been a breach of warranty in relation to the goods or a breach of the contract for the performance of the work.[34] These forms of set-off, including the common law principle of abatement, are the subject of discussion in chapters 2 to 5. If one of the parties to the cross-demands is a person who is bankrupt or is a company in liquidation or, in some circumstances in England, administration, the set-off section (or, as it is sometimes called, the mutual credit provision) in the insolvency legislation may apply.[35] Insolvency set-off is discussed in chapters 6 to 8. Chapters 9 to 13 deal with issues relevant to both the Statutes of Set-off and insolvency set-off.

1.12   In addition to those forms of set-off, there are certain rights which are distinct from set-off but which have an analogous effect. Two such rights, combination of bank accounts[36] and the rule in *Cherry v Boultbee*,[37] receive detailed consideration. Combination of bank

---

[29]   *Russell on Arbitration* (23rd edn, 2007), 279 [6-017], referring to *Modern Trading Co Ltd v Swale Building and Construction Ltd* (1990) 24 Con LR 59, *SL Sethia Liners Ltd v Naviagro Maritime Corporation (The Kostas Melas)* [1981] 1 Lloyd's Rep 18 and *Industriebeteiligungs & Handelsgesellschaft v Malaysian International Shipping Corporation Berhad (The Bunga Melawis)* [1991] 2 Lloyd's Rep 271. A decision by an arbitrator that he or she is not satisfied that a set-off is being asserted in good faith and on reasonable grounds does not preclude the party asserting it from continuing to pursue the claim in the arbitration. See *The Kostas Melas* at 27 and *Modern Trading v Swale* at 65.

[30]   (1729) 2 Geo II, c 22, s. 13.

[31]   (1735) 8 Geo II, c 24, s. 5.

[32]   For the position in Australia, see paras 2.63–2.86 below.

[33]   *Axel Johnson Petroleum AB v MG Mineral Group AG* [1992] 1 WLR 270, 272; *Fuller v Happy Shopper Markets Ltd* [2001] 1 WLR 1681, 1690 at [21].

[34]   See paras 2.123–2.134 below.

[35]   Currently the Insolvency Act 1986, s. 323 in the case of bankruptcy. For company liquidation see the Insolvency Rules 1986, r. 4.90, and for administration r. 2.85. In Australia, see the Bankruptcy Act 1966 (Cth), s. 86 and, for company liquidation, the Corporations Act 2001 (Cth), s. 553C.

[36]   See ch. 15 below.

[37]   (1839) 4 My & Cr 442, 41 ER 171. See ch. 14 below.

accounts, as the name suggests, relates to bank accounts, and refers to a bank's right[38] to look upon various accounts held by a customer as combined to produce a single debt. The rule in *Cherry v Boultbee* applies in the situation in which a person who is entitled to receive a distribution from a fund is also obliged to contribute to the fund. It entitles the administrator of the fund to direct the person to satisfy his or her entitlement to a distribution from a particular asset of the fund, in the form of the person's obligation to contribute.

D. Civil Procedure Rules

Set-off is dealt with in r. 16.6 of the Civil Procedure Rules 1998 made pursuant to the Civil Procedure Act 1997.[39] While there are some differences in the drafting, the substance of the rule is the same as the former RSC Ord. 18, r. 17. In relation to the former rule and its predecessors, the courts emphasized that the rule itself did not determine the availability of a set-off,[40] but merely laid down a procedure for claiming the defence outside bankruptcy and company liquidation. In other words, the circumstances in which a set-off was available depended upon the terms of the Statutes of Set-off and the set-off section in the insolvency legislation, and, in other cases, upon an examination of the substantive principles developed by the courts independently of the rules of court.

1.13

It has been suggested that the courts may take the opportunity afforded by the new rule to define set-off differently in the future.[41] There is no reason why this should be the case, however. Like their predecessors, the Civil Procedure Rules relate only to matters of practice and procedure.[42] While the right of set-off, particularly pursuant to the Statutes of Set-off, has procedural aspects to it, it is nevertheless a defence, and because it is a defence it is not a matter of pure procedure.[43] Thus, the scope of the defence can have a substantive effect on the rights of third parties, such as assignees of debts, who take subject to defences available to the debtor against the assignor.[44] Since set-off is not simply a question of practice and procedure, rules of court which are confined to matters of practice and procedure on their own cannot enlarge the defence. Further, it is questioned later whether indeed it is desirable to expand the scope of the defence of set-off where there is no formal insolvency administration.[45]

1.14

---

[38] And also the customer. See para. 15.33 below.

[39] Together with the Senior Courts Act 1981, s. 49(2). See *Re Kaupthing Singer and Fried Lander Ltd* [2009] 2 Lloyd's Rep 154 at [10].

[40] *Re Milan Tramways Co, ex p Theys* (1882) 22 Ch D 122, 126; *Pellas v Neptune Marine Insurance Co* (1879) 5 CPD 34, 40; *Stumore v Campbell & Co* [1892] 1 QB 314, 316–17; *Smail v Zimmerman* [1907] VLR 702; *Hanak v Green* [1958] 2 QB 9, 22; *Bank of Boston Connecticut v European Grain and Shipping Ltd* [1989] 1 AC 1056, 1109; *Griffiths v Commonwealth Bank of Australia* (1994) 123 ALR 111, 124. See also *Westwind Air Charter Pty Ltd v Hawker de Havilland Ltd* (1990) 3 WAR 71, 84; *Hazcor Pty Ltd v Kirwanon Pty Ltd* (1995) 12 WAR 62. Compare the position in Victoria. See paras 2.83–2.85 below.

[41] *Civil Procedure* (2009) ('White Book') vol. 1, para. 16.6.1.

[42] The Civil Procedure Act 1997, s. 1(1), pursuant to which the new Civil Procedure Rules were made, provides that: 'There are to be rules of court . . . governing the practice and procedure . . .', and CPR r. 1.1(1) states that, 'These Rules are a new procedural code . . .'

[43] See paras 2.53–2.57 below.

[44] See ch. 17 below.

[45] See paras 5.163–5.177 below.

E. Applicable Law For Determining The Existence of a Cross-Claim

1.15   The question whether there is a defence to a claim governed by English law is also to be determined by English law. English law in this context includes the rules of private international law, and any foreign law which English law would regard as applicable pursuant to those rules. Therefore, where a defendant asserts a cross-claim against the claimant arising out of a contract which is governed by a foreign law, the question whether there is a cross-claim must be determined by reference to the foreign law.[46]

---

[46] *ISS Machinery Services Ltd v Aeolian Shipping SA (The Aeolian)* [2001] 2 Lloyd's Rep 641, esp. at 644 (Potter LJ), referring to *Meridien BIAO Bank GmbH v Bank of New York* [1997] 1 Lloyd's Rep 437, 446 (Millett LJ).

2

SET-OFF BETWEEN SOLVENT PARTIES: COMMON LAW

A. Early Developments

2.01 Prior to the enactment of the first Statute of Set-off in 1729,[1] there was no general right of set-off available to a defendant in a common law action when he or she was being sued by a solvent plaintiff, as opposed to the assignees of a bankrupt.[2] This denial of a set-off has been explained as being consistent with the adoption by the common law courts of strict rules of pleading and of forms of action, which were designed to reduce the question to be decided by the court as far as possible to a single, well-defined issue. It would have been contrary to that approach to introduce collateral issues through consideration of a cross-claim.[3] There are instances in the late seventeenth and early eighteenth centuries in which equity enforced set-offs of unconnected debts by means of an injunction to restrain the plaintiff in an action at law from proceeding with his or her claim against the defendant until the plaintiff had given credit for his or her own indebtedness to the defendant. Those cases, however, should not be taken as evidence of a general equitable jurisdiction to set off cross-debts. Equitable relief usually was founded upon a custom that the accounts should be balanced,[4] or alternatively an implied agreement to that effect.[5] There is an early decision that seems to indicate a general equitable jurisdiction. In 1699, Sir John Trevor MR in *Arnold v Richardson*[6] ordered that a plaintiff in an action at law for payment of a debt on a bond should bring into account his own indebtedness to the defendant for food and lodging, even though 'there was no Agreement for that Purpose'. The reporter has attributed to the Master of the Rolls a remark that 'a Discount was natural Justice in all cases'. However, the judgment of Sir Joseph Jekyll MR some twenty-three years later in *Jeffs v Wood*[7] suggests that, in the absence of an insolvency, equity at that time ordinarily would look for evidence, however slight, of an agreement for a set-off.

2.02 There were also certain discrete situations in which rights akin to set-offs were recognized by the common law courts.[8] By this it is meant that the common law would allow the defendant in an action to plead the existence of certain facts as a means of reducing the amount which otherwise would be awarded to the plaintiff, when those facts could have formed the basis of a separate action by the defendant against the plaintiff. For example, a bailiff who was entitled to receive rent from the manor could obtain payment by recoupment from his or her obligation to account to the master.[9] Further, if a landlord disseised

---

[1] (1729) 2 Geo II, c 22, s. 13.

[2] For a discussion of the early development of set-off in English and Roman Law, see Loyd, 'The Development of Set-off' (1916) 64 *University of Pennsylvania Law Review* 541 and Tigar, 'Automatic Extinction of Cross-Demands: *Compensatio* From Rome to California' (1965) 53 *California Law Review* 224.

[3] See Loyd, 'The Development of Set-off' (1916) 64 *University of Pennsylvania Law Review* 541, 544, and also Lord Mansfield in *Green v Farmer* (1768) 4 Burr 2214, 2220, 98 ER 154, 157.

[4] See *Curson v African Co* (1682) 1 Vern 121, 23 ER 358.

[5] *Downam v Matthews* (1721) Prec Ch 580, 24 ER 260; *Hawkins v Freeman* 2 Eq Ca Abr 10, 22 ER 8. See also *Sir William Darcy's Case* (1677) 2 Freeman 28, 22 ER 1037; *Jeffs v Wood* (1723) 2 P Wms 128, 24 ER 668.

[6] (1699) 1 Eq Ca Abr 8, 21 ER 833.

[7] (1723) 2 P Wms 128, 24 ER 668.

[8] A number of cases are collected in *Viner's Abridgment* (2nd edn, 1741) vol. 8, 556–7. See also the discussion in Loyd, 'The Development of Set-off' (1916) 64 *University of Pennsylvania Law Review* 541, 544–6.

[9] See *Viner's Abridgment* (2nd edn, 1741) vol. 8, 557, and also the note to *Gybson v Searls* (1607) Cro Jac 176, 178, 79 ER 154, 155, citing 20 Hen 7, pl 5.

the tenant and the tenant then brought a writ of assise against the landlord, the landlord was entitled to deduct from the damages payable any rent which the tenant was required to pay for the period of the disseisin.[10] Similarly, if the holder of a rent-charge disseised the owner of the land, the former's right to receive payment under the charge for the period of the disseisin could be recouped from his or her obligation to pay damages to the owner.[11] The holder of the rent-charge was given this right in order to avoid circuity of action.[12] It should be compared to the right asserted in *Taylor v Beal*[13] in 1591. The case concerned a claim by a landlord for unpaid rent. The tenant gave evidence that the landlord had covenanted to repair the premises but did not do so, and the tenant had expended part of the rent in effecting repairs. Gawdy J accepted that the tenant was entitled to deduct the cost of the repairs from the rent.[14] The tenant's right in this situation was not based upon a desire to avoid circuity of action, but rather Gawdy J said that: 'the law giveth this liberty to the lessee to expend the rent in reparations, for he shall be otherwise at great mischief, for the house may fall upon his head before it be repaired; and therefore the law alloweth him to repair it, and recoupe the rent.'

Customary law provides another instance. According to the custom of foreign attachment, **2.03** if a plaint was entered in the court of the mayor or the sheriff of the City of London against a defendant, and the process was returned *nihil*, and thereupon the plaintiff suggested that another person within London was indebted to the defendant, the debtor was warned, and if the debtor did not deny that he or she was so indebted the debt was attached in the debtor's hands as payment to the plaintiff.[15] The custom apparently contemplated the attachment of a debt owing by the plaintiff him or herself to the defendant,[16] which in effect would have operated as a set-off of the plaintiff's debt against that of the defendant.[17]

B. Statutes of Set-off

(1) Introduction

The Statutes of Set-off were enacted in 1729 and 1735. The title of the first Statute, 'An Act **2.04** for the Relief of Debtors with respect to the Imprisonment of their Persons',[18] suggests that

---

[10] *Coulter's Case* 5 Co Rep 30a, 30b, 77 ER 98 (discussed in Loyd, 'The Development of Set-off' (1916) 64 *University of Pennsylvania Law Review* 541, 545). Only rent owing for the period of the disseisin could be deducted. Arrears of rent owing from before then could not be recouped in this manner. See *Viner's Abridgment* (2nd edn, 1741) vol. 8, 556, citing 9 E 3.8.

[11] See *Viner's Abridgment* (2nd edn, 1741) vol. 8, 556, and *Coulter's Case* 5 Co Rep 30a, 31a, 77 ER 98, 100.

[12] See *Viner's Abridgment* (2nd edn, 1741) vol. 8, 556, and *Coulter's Case* 5 Co Rep 30a, 31a, 77 ER 98, 100.

[13] (1591) Cro Eliz 222, 78 ER 478.

[14] Clench J seems to have sympathized with the proposition, commenting that the tenant 'might well expend the rent in reparations', but he held against the tenant on a question of pleading. Fenner J, however, said that the tenant had to bring a separate action.

[15] See *Comyns' Digest* (5th edn, 1822) vol. 1, 713–14.

[16] See Brandon, *The Customary Law of Foreign Attachment* (1861), 60–1, 143 n s, and *Comyns' Digest* (5th edn, 1822) vol. 1, 716, but compare Bayley J in *Nonell v Hullett and Widder* (1821) 4 B & Ald 646, 106 ER 1073.

[17] The custom has fallen into disuse. See *Halsbury's Laws of England* (4th edn, 1998) vol. 12(1), 180 para. 628 n 13.

[18] (1729) 2 Geo II, c 22, s. 13.

their purpose was to assist debtors who were liable to be sent to debtors' prison for non-payment of debts, although Willes CJ, not long after their enactment, considered that they were designed to avoid circuity of action and multiplicity of suits.[19] The first Statute was a temporary provision intended to last for a period of five years. It provided that:

> [W]here there are mutual Debts between the Plaintiff and Defendant, or if either Party sue or be sued as Executor or Administrator, where there are mutual Debts between the Testator or Intestate, and either Party, one Debt may be set against the other, and such Matter may be given in Evidence upon the General Issue, or pleaded in Bar, as the Nature of the Case shall require, so as at the Time of his pleading the General Issue, where any such Debt of the Plaintiff, his Testator or Intestate, is intended to be insisted on in Evidence, Notice shall be given of the particular Sum or Debt so intended to be insisted on, and upon what Account it became due, or otherwise such Matter shall not be allowed in Evidence upon such General Issue.

2.05   Several questions arose upon the construction of this provision, for example, whether debts of a different nature (i.e. simple and specialty debts) could be set off against each other, and whether in the case of a bond the penalty was to be considered as the debt.[20] Therefore, when the right of set-off conferred by the first Statute of Set-off was made permanent in 1735 by the second Statute (8 Geo II, c 24, s. 4), the Act went on to provide, in s. 5, that mutual debts could be set off notwithstanding that in law they were deemed to be of a different nature, and further that, if either of the debts accrued by reason of a penalty in a bond, the amount to be included in the set-off was the amount 'truly and justly due'.[21]

2.06   The Statutes were repealed in England in 1879 by s. 2 of the Civil Procedure Acts Repeal Act in so far as they applied to the newly founded Supreme Court of Judicature, though it was expressly provided that the repeal was not to affect any 'jurisdiction or principle or rule of law or equity established or confirmed, or right or privilege acquired'.[22] This has been interpreted as preserving the right of set-off originally conferred by the Statutes.[23] In *Glencore Grain Ltd v Agros Trading Co*[24] Clarke LJ (with whose judgment Otton and Kennedy LJJ agreed) suggested that the Statutes of Set-off were replaced by the rules of

---

[19] *Hutchinson v Sturges* (1741) Willes 261, 262, 125 ER 1163; *Pilgrim v Kinder* (1744) 7 Mod 463, 467, 87 ER 1357, 1360. See also *Forster v Wilson* (1843) 12 M & W 191, 203, 152 ER 1165, 1171; *Ex p Cleland, re Davies* (1867) LR 2 Ch App 808, 812–13; *Re Unit 2 Windows Ltd* [1985] 1 WLR 1383, 1387; *Fuller v Happy Shopper Markets Ltd* [2001] 1 WLR 1681, 1690 at [21]; *Coventry v Charter Pacific Corporation Ltd* (2005) 227 CLR 234 at [30]–[31].

[20] See the discussion in *Hutchinson v Sturges* (1741) Willes 261, 125 ER 1163.

[21] See para. 2.36 below.

[22] Civil Procedure Acts Repeal Act 1879, s. 4(1)(b).

[23] *Re Daintrey* [1900] 1 QB 546, 548; *Hanak v Green* [1958] 2 QB 9, 22; *Southern Textile Converters Pty Ltd v Stehar Knitting Mills Pty Ltd* [1979] 1 NSWLR 692, 697–8; *Walker v Department of Social Security* (1995) 56 FCR 354, 374. See also e.g. *Henriksens Rederi A/S v THZ Rolimpex (The Brede)* [1974] 1 QB 233, 246, 252. See now the Senior Courts Act 1981, s. 49(2) and CPR 16.6: *Re Kaupthing Singer and Friedlander Ltd* [2009] 2 Lloyd's Rep 154 at [10]. There was a similar repeal and saving of the right of set-off in relation to courts other than the Supreme Court of Judicature in the Statute Law Revision and Civil Procedure Act 1883 (which in turn was repealed by the Supreme Court of Judicature (Consolidation) Act 1925). See now s. 3 of the Courts and Legal Services Act 1990 (which was substituted for s. 38 of the County Courts Act 1984).

[24] [1999] 2 Lloyd's Rep 410, 417.

court. A more accurate statement would be that the right of set-off conferred by the Statutes has been preserved, but the procedure for giving effect to it is now set out in the rules.[25]

Australia

In Australia, the operation of the Statutes of Set-off varies between the states. The applica- **2.07** tion of the Statutes in Australia is considered later.[26]

(2) When must the set-off be available?

Prior to the Judicature Acts, the courts applied the principle that a set-off under the Statutes **2.08** could only be pleaded in bar to the plaintiff's action if the set-off was available at the commencement of the action, as opposed to when the defence was filed. In other words, at the date of the commencement of the action there had to be a presently existing and payable debt owing by the plaintiff to the defendant.[27] The principle was confirmed in *Richards v James*.[28] The plaintiff in that case became indebted to the defendant after the plaintiff had commenced proceedings against the defendant for payment of a debt. The defendant pleaded that, because of the cross-debt, the plaintiff ought not further to maintain his action. Pollock CB said that: 'The novelty of the plea is supported by no precedent, and there is nothing to warrant us in so construing the statute, so as to enable a defendant to set off a debt which has arisen since the commencement of the action.'[29] Subsequently, Farwell LJ in *Bennett v White*[30] referred to the form of plea for the right of set-off given in the third edition of Bullen and Leake in 1868, in terms that 'the plaintiff, *at the commencement of this suit*, was and still is indebted to the defendant'.[31] He said that it 'was at that time and always has been the proper form'.

Richards v James should no longer apply. After the Judicature Acts, the Supreme Court **2.09** Rules[32] permitted a defendant to rely on a ground of defence which arose after the action was commenced, and in *Wood v Goodwin*[33] Mathew J applied that principle in relation to a defence of set-off. The Rules of the Supreme Court 1965 similarly contained a provision to that effect, in Ord. 18, r. 9. While it has not been reproduced in the Civil Procedure Rules 1998, there is nothing to suggest that the principle itself will not be continued.[34] If, however, a defendant wishes to amend his or her defence after it has been served, the Civil

---

[25] See para. 1.13 above.
[26] See paras 2.63–2.86 below.
[27] *Pilgrim v Kinder* (1744) 7 Mod 463, 87 ER 1357 (plaintiff's debt existing but not payable until after action commenced); *Evans v Prosser* (1789) 3 TR 186, 100 ER 524; *Richards v James* (1848) 2 Ex 471, 154 ER 577. See also *Rogerson v Ladbroke* (1822) 1 Bing 93, 130 ER 39; *Leman v Gordon* (1838) 8 Car & P 392, 173 ER 546; *Dendy v Powell* (1838) 3 M & W 442, 444, 150 ER 1218, 1219; *Lee v Lester* (1849) 7 CB 1008, 1017, 137 ER 399, 403; *Maw v Ulyatt* (1861) 31 LJ Ch 33.
[28] (1848) 2 Ex 471, 154 ER 577.
[29] (1848) 2 Ex 471, 473, 154 ER 577, 578.
[30] [1910] 2 KB 643, 648.
[31] Bullen and Leake, *Precedents of Pleadings* (3rd edn, 1868), 682 (emphasis added by Farwell LJ).
[32] The first such rule was Ord. 21 r. 1 of the Rules of Court set out in the First Schedule to the Supreme Court of Judicature Act 1875.
[33] [1884] WN 17. See also *Toke v Andrews* (1882) 8 QBD 428, 431.
[34] Note in that regard the general language of CPR r. 16.6 in relation to set-off.

Procedure Rules now require the defendant to obtain either the written consent of all the other parties or the permission of the court.[35]

2.10 Farwell LJ's comment in *Bennett v White* (above) was made in a different context, and is therefore distinguishable. The defendant in an action for payment of a debt sought to set off a debt originally due from the plaintiff to a third party, who had assigned it to the defendant. The plaintiff argued that the plea of set-off was bad, since set-off under the Statutes required that the debts originally should have existed between the plaintiff and the defendant. Farwell LJ did not refer to the pleading in Bullen and Leake in order to draw a distinction between debts arising before and after the commencement of the suit, but rather to show that it was not necessary that the plaintiff's debt should have been owing from its inception to the defendant. Of greater concern is *Edmunds v Lloyds Italico SpA*,[36] in which Sir John Donaldson MR referred to *Richards v James* in terms suggesting that it was regarded as still representing the law. The effect of the Supreme Court Rules after the Judicature Acts was not considered, however, and as a matter of policy it is difficult to see why a right of set-off arising after the commencement of the claimant's action should not be able to be relied on as a defence. There is support for that view in Australia,[37] and in New South Wales it was expressly confirmed in the recent re-enactment of the right of set-off conferred by the Statutes in that state.[38] Consistent with that view, Lord Hoffmann commented in passing in *Stein v Blake*[39] that set-off under the Statutes is confined to debts which are liquidated and due and payable 'at the time when the defence of set-off is filed'.[40]

2.11 The view that *Richards v James* no longer represents the law means that a cross-debt which arises after the commencement of the claimant's action may be pleaded as a set-off. This is not inconsistent with the principle discussed later, that a cross-debt owing by a claimant to the defendant must be enforceable at the commencement of the claimant's action in order to be available as a set-off.[41] The issue of enforceability may arise, for example, in relation to a debt which is unenforceable because of the expiration of a time bar. The notion that unenforceability is determined as at the date of the claimant's action has the opposite effect to that which would follow from *Richards v James*. *Richards v James* unduly restricts the availability of the defence. On the other hand, the determination of the enforceability of a pre-existing cross-debt under a statute of limitation as at the commencement of the

---

[35] CPR, Pt 17.

[36] [1986] 1 WLR 492.

[37] Angas Parsons J in *Rex v Ray, ex p Chapman* [1936] SASR 241, 247 noted without adverse comment the views of Farwell LJ in *Bennett v White*, which suggests that the principle in *Richards v James* was thought to be still applicable. On the other hand, Madden CJ in the Victorian Supreme Court in *Ingleton v Coates* (1896) 2 ALR 154 held that the Supreme Court Rules permitted the defendant to plead a set-off in respect of an indebtedness of the plaintiff assigned to him after commencement of the plaintiff's action. Powell J in *McColl's Wholesale Pty Ltd v State Bank of NSW* [1984] 3 NSWLR 365, 381 expressed a similar view in relation to the procedure in force at that time in New South Wales.

[38] Civil Procedure Act 2005 (NSW), s. 21(1). See paras 2.66–2.73 below.

[39] [1996] AC 243, 251.

[40] In *Hoverd Industries Ltd v Supercool Refrigeration and Air Conditioning (1991) Ltd* [1995] 3 NZLR 577, 587 the New Zealand Court of Appeal referred to debts 'which can be ascertained with certainty at the time of pleading'.

[41] See paras 2.46–2.50 below.

claimant's action, rather than the later date when the set-off is pleaded, expands the class of claims which can be set off under the Statutes.

The above discussion relates to a debt of the claimant that arises or becomes due and pay-   **2.12**
able after commencement of the action and before judgment. If the debt arises after judgment, it generally does not provide a ground for restraining the claimant from enforcing the judgment.[42]

(3) Mutuality

The Statutes of Set-off require that the debts be mutual. The concept of mutuality is   **2.13**
considered later.[43]

(4) The requirement of debts

For the Statutes to apply there must be a debt on each side of the account. The debts, and   **2.14**
the transactions giving rise to them, need not be connected in any way.[44] But because of the requirement of 'debts', a claim for the return of goods,[45] or an entitlement to a statutory benefit which does not create a debt enforceable by action,[46] is not susceptible to a defence of set-off under the Statutes.

What is a 'debt'?

The word 'debt' is not used in the strict sense of a claim which could have been the subject   **2.15**
of the old action of debt.[47] Rather, as Cockburn CJ said in *Stooke v Taylor*,[48] the plea of set-off under the Statutes 'is available . . . where the claims on both sides are in respect of liquidated debts, or money demands which can be readily and without difficulty ascertained'.[49] Each of the demands, therefore, must be capable of being liquidated or ascertained with precision at the time of pleading,[50] or, as Lord Hoffmann expressed it in *Stein v Blake*,[51] they must be 'either liquidated or in sums capable of ascertainment without

---

[42] *Maw v Ulyatt* (1861) 31 LJ Ch 33. See para. 2.97 below.

[43] See ch. 11 below.

[44] *Axel Johnson Petroleum AB v M G Mineral Group AG* [1992] 1 WLR 270, 272; *Courage Ltd v Crehan* [1999] 2 EGLR 145, 155; *Fuller v Happy Shopper Markets Ltd* [2001] 1 WLR 1681, 1690 at [21].

[45] *Green v Farmer* (1768) 4 Burr 2214, 98 ER 154.

[46] *Walker v Department of Social Security* (1995) 56 FCR 354. Compare *Saitta v Commissioner of Taxation* (2002) 125 FCR 388 at [5] and [6] in relation to a right to a payment under the Aged Care Act 1997 (Cth). Similarly, it has been said that a liability to repay a preferential payment in a liquidation is not a debt. See *Re Luxtrend Pty Ltd* [1997] 2 Qd R 86.

[47] *Morley v Inglis* (1837) 4 Bing (NC) 58, 71, 132 ER 711, 716; *Victorian WorkCover Authority v Esso Australia Ltd* (2001) 207 CLR 520 at [30]. In relation to the old action in debt, see *Commonwealth Bank of Australia v Butterell* (1994) 35 NSWLR 64, 68.

[48] (1880) 5 QBD 569, 575.

[49] Formerly, it was said that a test for considering whether a plea of set-off was admissible in an action on an agreement was whether the agreement was such that *indebitatus assumpsit* would lie upon it. See Hill J in *Crampton v Walker* (1860) 3 El & El 321, 330–1, 121 ER 463, 466, referring to Tindal CJ in *Morley v Inglis* (1837) 4 Bing (NC) 58, 72, 132 ER 711, 716.

[50] *Morley v Inglis* (1837) 4 Bing (NC) 58, 71, 132 ER 711, 716; *Henriksens Rederi A/S v THZ Rolimpex (The Brede)* [1974] 1 QB 233, 246; *Axel Johnson Petroleum AB v MG Mineral Group AG* [1992] 1 WLR 270, 272; *Courage Ltd v Crehan* [1999] 2 EGLR 145, 155.

[51] [1996] AC 243, 251. See also Hoffmann LJ's earlier comment in *Aectra Refining and Manufacturing Inc v Exmar NV* [1994] 1 WLR 1634, 1649 ('either liquidated or capable of being quantified by reference to

valuation or estimation'. The point is illustrated by *Axel Johnson Petroleum AB v MG Mineral Group AG*.[52] The defendant in an action for payment of a sum certain asserted that the plaintiff had agreed to buy all such oil as the defendant itself bought from a third party, the contract price being the same as the price paid by the defendant to the third party together with a sum of US$ 1.00 per tonne to cover 'local expenses'. The Court of Appeal held that the price payable by the plaintiff under the arrangement was liquidated, and accordingly could give rise to a defence under the Statutes so as to entitle the defendant to leave to defend. It was not necessary that the price should be capable of being computed by reference to the contract without investigation.

2.16 If the quantum of the claim sought to be set off by the defendant can only be ascertained by litigation or arbitration, it will generally be unliquidated, and it makes no difference that an estimate has been made by an expert.[53] On the other hand, a cross-demand may still be regarded as liquidated notwithstanding that the defendant is unable to state at the present time what the precise value of the demand is. It would suffice that, when full particulars are known, the matter simply would be one of addition and subtraction. In a case in Victoria,[54] the defendant in an action on a cheque pleaded that the plaintiffs had been his agents for the sale of tallow, and in breach of their duty as agents they purchased the defendant's tallow themselves and sold it on their own account at enhanced prices without accounting for the difference in price. The defendant alleged that the difference in price amounted to more than the value of the cheque sued upon, though he said that he was not at present able to give further particulars. Although the amount was still uncertain, it was held that the demand nevertheless was pleadable as a set-off, because by its nature it was a liquidated demand.

2.17 If the defendant's cross-claim in its nature is liquidated, a set-off will not be denied simply because the cross-claim is disputed by the claimant as to all or part on grounds that require determination by litigation or arbitration. The defendant in such a case may plead the cross-claim as a defence to an action brought against him or her for payment of a debt, and in an application by the claimant for summary judgment the defendant may be granted leave to defend.[55] As Hirst LJ remarked in *Aectra Refining and Manufacturing Inc v Exmar BV*,[56] when Cockburn CJ in *Stooke v Taylor* spoke of 'money demands which can be readily and without difficulty ascertained', he was referring to ascertainment of the *quantum* of the demand, and not to the amount which might ultimately be held recoverable after all the defences put forward have been considered.

ascertainable facts which do not in their nature require estimation or valuation'), and *Fuller v Happy Shopper Markets Ltd* [2001] 1 WLR 1681, 1690 at [21].

[52] [1992] 1 WLR 270.

[53] *B. Hargreaves Ltd v Action 2000 Ltd* [1993] BCLC 1111 (estimation by a surveyor of the amount claimed in respect of faulty workmanship).

[54] *Woodroffe & Co v J. W. Moss* [1915] VLR 237.

[55] *Aectra Refining and Marketing Inc v Exmar NV* [1994] 1 WLR 1634 (CA), leave to appeal refused [1995] 1 WLR 526.

[56] [1994] 1 WLR 1634, 1647.

Alternative causes of action

If the claim of one of the parties has both a liquidated and an unliquidated component, **2.18**
a set-off may proceed against the liquidated part.[57] Further, if the claimant's claim in truth
is for a liquidated sum, so that prior to the Judicature Acts he or she could have maintained
an action in *indebitatus assumpsit*, the claimant should not be able to deprive the defendant
of a right of set-off by framing his or her claim instead as an action for damages,[58] although
there is authority to the contrary.[59] *Hutchinson v Reid*[60] is not inconsistent with that view.
The plaintiff in that case sold goods to the defendant in consideration of the defendant
agreeing to accept a bill of exchange for the price, the bill to be payable in two months.
The defendant refused to accept the bill whereupon the plaintiff, within the two-month
period, commenced an action. As a defence the defendant pleaded a set-off in respect of a
debt owing by the plaintiff. The defence failed because the plaintiff was not suing for the
price but rather for damages for failure to accept the bill. However, Lord Ellenborough
emphasized in his judgment that the action had been brought within the two-month
period. If the plaintiff had sued after the time of payment, the claim in effect would have
been for the price, in which case Lord Ellenborough indicated that a set-off would have
been available.

Demands closely analogous to debts

Cockburn CJ's formulation of the principle in *Stooke v Taylor*[61] has two aspects. It encom- **2.19**
passes not only liquidated debts but also money demands which can be readily and without
difficulty ascertained. The better view, which was favoured by Hirst LJ in *Aectra Refining
and Marketing Inc. v Exmar NV*,[62] is that this second aspect refers to demands that are
closely analogous to debts and which can be readily ascertained. It encompasses the old
indebitatus counts,[63] including claims in *quantum meruit* and *quantum valebat*, where
work had been performed or goods sold without a price having been agreed.[64] In an appropriate case it may also include a demand that strictly sounds in damages, if indeed it is
ascertainable with precision.[65] An example is a liquidated damages clause. It was settled
in the eighteenth century that the obligation pursuant to a clause in a contract for the

---

[57] *Crampton v Walker* (1860) 3 El & El 321, 121 ER 463.
[58] *Birch v Depeyester* (1816) 4 Camp 385, 171 ER 122; *Crampton v Walker* (1860) 3 El & El 321, 331–2,
121 ER 463, 466–7. This is also consistent with the approach adopted by the Court of Appeal in a different
context in *G. L. Baker Ltd v Barclays Bank Ltd* [1956] 1 WLR 1409.
[59] See e.g. *Colson v Welsh* (1795) 1 Esp. 378, 170 ER 391; *Cooper v Robinson* (1818) 2 Chit 161; *Thorpe v
Thorpe* (1832) 3 B & Ad 580, 584, 585, 110 ER 211, 212–13; *Hill v Smith* (1844) 12 M & W 618, 631, 152
ER 1346, 1351; *Halsbury's Laws of England* (5th edn, 2009) vol. 11 ('Civil Procedure'), 510, para. 653.
[60] (1813) 3 Camp 329, 170 ER 1400.
[61] (1880) 5 QBD 569, 575.
[62] [1994] 1 WLR 1634, 1647, approving of counsel's explanation at 1645.
[63] See *Howlet v Strickland* (1774) 1 Cowp 56, 57, 98 ER 965; *Victorian WorkCover Authority v Esso
Australia Ltd* (2001) 207 CLR 520 at [30].
[64] See the discussion by Farwell LJ in *Lagos v Grunwaldt* [1910] 1 KB 41, 48 in relation to the meaning
of the expression 'debt or liquidated demand', referred to in *Aectra Refining and Marketing Inc. v Exmar NV*
[1994] 1 WLR 1634, 1647.
[65] In *Axel Johnson Petroleum AB v MG Mineral Group AG* [1992] 1 WLR 270, 272 Leggatt LJ said that:
'For set-off to be available at law the claim and cross-claim must be mutual, but they need not be connected.
They need not be debts strictly so called, but may sound in damages.' See also *B. Hargreaves Ltd v Action 2000
Ltd* [1993] BCLC 1111, 1113.

payment of liquidated damages in the event of a breach gives rise to a debt for the purpose of the Statutes.[66] Thus, a sum specified in a shipping contract as being payable by way of demurrage constitutes liquidated damages,[67] and the Court of Appeal in *Axel Johnson* recognized that it could be the subject of a set-off. That view should be compared to *Seeger v Duthie*,[68] in which a claim arising out of a delay in loading a ship was held not to come within the terms of the demurrage clause. Accordingly, it was a claim for unliquidated damages which could not be set off under the Statutes.

2.20 It is not intended to go through the catalogue of cases which illustrate whether various classes of claims are regarded as liquidated for the purpose of the Statutes. However, a question of particular interest to the commercial community is whether a claim on a guarantee or an indemnity may be set off under the Statutes.

Claims on guarantees

2.21 Traditionally, it has been thought that a claim on a guarantee is not susceptible to a set-off.

2.22 The difficulty with a set-off lies in the nature of a guarantor's liability. In *Moschi v Lep Air Services Ltd*[69] Lord Diplock explained that, by the beginning of the nineteenth century, it had come to be accepted in English law that the obligation assumed by a guarantor under the contract of guarantee is to see to it that the debtor performs his or her obligation to the creditor.[70] Accordingly, even if the subject of the guarantee is the payment of a debt, the creditor's remedy against the guarantor lies in damages for breach of contract. Thus, before the Judicature Acts, the creditor's action against the guarantor was in special assumpsit, rather than *indebitatus assumpsit*. Consistent with that view, in *Morley v Inglis*[71] the Common Pleas held that a claim on a guarantee could not be employed by the defendant in a set-off under the Statutes of Set-off, even though the obligation the subject of the guarantee itself was a debt. In particular, Tindal CJ said that the liability was not ascertained because the guarantor's liability for interest and expenses had not been ascertained by a jury.[72] Nevertheless, given the broad meaning that has been ascribed to the word 'debts' in the Statutes,[73] it is suggested that it is unlikely that *Morley v Inglis* would now be followed. In *Axel Johnson*,[74] Leggatt LJ framed the principle in terms suggesting that a liability on a guarantee could be set off under the Statutes if the amount of the liability in respect of which the guarantee was given has been 'established'. But whatever the position in England, *Morley v Inglis* would not represent the law in Australia in light of comments by Mason CJ

---

[66] *Fletcher v Dyche* (1787) 2 TR 32, 100 ER 18. This assumes that the clause is not a penalty.

[67] *President of India v Lips Maritime Corporation* [1988] 1 AC 395.

[68] (1860) 8 CB(NS) 45, 141 ER 1081.

[69] [1973] AC 331, 348–9.

[70] Compare *Trafalgar House Construction (Regions) Ltd v General Surety & Guarantee Co Ltd* [1996] AC 199, 205.

[71] (1837) 4 Bing (NC) 58, 132 ER 711. See also *Crawford v Stirling* (1802) 4 Esp. 207, 170 ER 693; *Williams v Flight* (1842) 2 Dowl NS 11, 16–17. Compare *Bank of Ireland v Martin* [1937] IR 189, 191 (Meredith J), 205 (Fitzgibbon J, on appeal).

[72] (1837) 4 Bing (NC) 58, 72, 132 ER 711, 716.

[73] See para. 2.15 above.

[74] [1992] 1 WLR 270, 272, referring to *Morley v Inglis*.

in the High Court in *Sunbird Plaza Pty Ltd v Maloney*.[75] The Chief Justice said of Lord Diplock's analysis of the nature of a guarantor's liability that, while it may be correct as a matter of history, it does not accord with the modern view, that the guarantor of a debt may be sued for the money sum which the debtor has failed to pay. This should have as a consequence that a set-off would be available in Australia against a guarantor's liability when the subject of the liability is a debt.

There are two cases which support a right of set-off in this situation, though neither provides strong authority. In *National Bank of Australasia v Swan*,[76] Stawell CJ in the Victorian Supreme Court held that a set-off could occur against a guarantor's liability in respect of a debt. However, his Honour based his conclusion on the earlier decision in *Brown v Tibbitts*,[77] which in truth was concerned with an indemnity rather than a guarantee. Moreover, the case may be explained on the basis of the language of the guarantee in issue, by which the defendant promised to pay all advances which were made by the plaintiff to a third party in case of default. This seems to have been a conditional agreement to pay, in the sense discussed by Lord Reid in *Moschi v Lep Air Services*[78] and by Mason CJ in *Sunbird Plaza v Maloney*,[79] so that, when the condition occurred (i.e. default) the guarantor became liable to pay the advances, as opposed to the usual promise of a guarantor to see to it that the principal debtor performs his or her payment obligation. The second case is *The Raven*,[80] in which Parker J seemed to accept that there could be a set-off against a claim under a guarantee.[81] *Morley v Inglis* was not discussed however, and moreover it is not clear from the judgment whether Parker J had in mind set-off under the Statutes or equitable set-off. **2.23**

The above discussion relates to a guarantee of a debt. If the guarantee is in respect of another obligation, breach of which would give rise to a liability in damages, the claim of the person holding the guarantee against the guarantor similarly would be in damages,[82] and accordingly it could not be set off under the Statutes. **2.24**

Indemnities

Indemnities similarly are not free from difficulty. **2.25**

A promise of indemnity is regarded as a promise to hold the indemnified person harmless against a specified loss or expense. Consistent with that view, an action on a contract of indemnity is characterized at common law as an action for unliquidated damages, arising from the failure of the indemnifier to prevent the indemnified person from suffering damage.[83] A classic illustration is a policy of indemnity insurance. Save in the case of a valued **2.26**

---

[75] (1988) 166 CLR 245, 255–6. Deane, Dawson and Toohey JJ agreed with Mason CJ's judgment. See also *Hawkins v Bank of China* (1992) 26 NSWLR 562; *Sandtara Pty Ltd v Abigroup Ltd* (1996) 42 NSWLR 491, 498.
[76] (1872) 3 VR (L) 168.
[77] (1862) 11 CB (NS) 855, 142 ER 1031.
[78] [1973] AC 331, 344–5.
[79] (1988) 166 CLR 245, 256–7.
[80] *Banco Central SA v Lingoss & Falce Ltd (The Raven)* [1980] 2 Lloyd's Rep 266.
[81] See the discussion at [1980] 2 Lloyd's Rep 266, 271–2.
[82] *Sunbird Plaza Pty Ltd v Maloney* (1988) 166 CLR 245, 255.
[83] *Firma C-Trade SA v Newcastle Protection and Indemnity Association* [1991] 2 AC 1, 35–6 (Lord Goff of Chieveley). See also *Ventouris v Mountain (The Italia Express (No. 2))* [1992] 2 Lloyd's Rep 281, 291–2

policy where there has been a total loss,[84] or possibly, according to an Australian decision,[85] in the case of a claim by an insurer under a contract of reinsurance in respect of paid losses,[86] a claim on an indemnity policy for a long time has been regarded as being for unliquidated damages.[87] That remains so even after the loss has been adjusted, because the adjustment is said to be merely evidence of the amount due.[88] Given the nature of a claim on an indemnity, the courts have said that the claim may not be the subject of a set-off under the Statutes.[89] Nevertheless, as Pearson J once remarked,[90] the word 'damages' is used in a somewhat unusual sense in this context and, at least if the loss has been adjusted, it is difficult as a matter of substance to see why a set-off should be denied. The argument that an adjustment is merely evidence of the amount of the loss, so that it may be rebutted, for example by proof of a mistake,[91] is not a convincing reason for disallowing a set-off if the adjustment is accepted by both parties. Further, it has been suggested in Victoria that a claim under a policy of liability insurance in relation to an ascertained liability might not attract the same constraint in relation to set-off.[92]

2.27 In any event, there is no such difficulty when non-indemnity insurance is in issue. The action in this instance is brought to recover a liquidated sum due under the contract, in which case there is no reason for denying a right of set-off under the Statutes against the claim.[93]

(in which Hirst J accepted that Lord Goff's statement of the law in *Firma C-Trade* was of general application); *Re Dixon* [1994] 1 Qd R 7, 18.

[84] *Irving v Manning* (1848) 6 CB 391, 422, 136 ER 1302, 1314 ('liquidated damages'); *Alexander v Ajax Insurance Co Ltd* [1956] VLR 436, 445–6; *Odyssey Re (Bermuda) v Reinsurance Australia* (2001) 19 ACLC 987 at [16].

[85] *New Cap Reinsurance Corporation Ltd v A. E. Grant* (2008) 68 ACSR 176.

[86] See also para. 2.28 below. Compare *Odyssey Re (Bermuda) v Reinsurance Australia* (2001) 19 ACLC 987, discussed in *New Cap Reinsurance Corporation Ltd v A. E. Grant* (2008) 68 ACSR 176 at [103]–[109]. As White J acknowledged in the *New Cap* case at [88] and [103], *Chandris v Argo Insurance Company Ltd* [1963] 2 Lloyd's Rep 65, and possibly *Edmunds v Lloyds Italico & l'Ancora Compagnia di Assicurazioni e Riassicurazione SpA* [1986] 1 WLR 492, may present problems with this view.

[87] *Luckie v Bushby* (1853) 13 CB 864, 138 ER 1443; *Pellas v Neptune Marine Insurance Co* (1879) 5 CPD 34; *William Pickersgill & Sons, Ltd v London and Provincial Marine and General Insurance Co, Ltd* [1912] 3 KB 614, 622; *Jabbour v Custodian of Israeli Absentee Property* [1954] 1 WLR 139, 145; *Chandris v Argo Insurance Company Ltd* [1963] 2 Lloyd's Rep 65, 73–4; *Edmunds v Lloyds Italico & l'Ancora Compagnia di Assicurazioni e Riassicurazione SpA* [1986] 1 WLR 492, 493; *Accident Compensation Commission v C. E. Heath Underwriting & Insurance (Aust) Pty Ltd* [1990] VR 224, 231; *Penrith City Council v Government Insurance Office* (1991) 24 NSWLR 564, 568; *I M Properties Plc v Cape & Dalgleish* [1999] QB 297, 304; *Odyssey Re (Bermuda) v Reinsurance Australia* (2001) 19 ACLC 987; *New Cap Reinsurance Corporation Ltd v A. E. Grant* (2008) 68 ACSR 176 at [87]. Compare *Re HIH Insurance Ltd* [2004] NSWSC 5.

[88] *Luckie v Bushby* (1853) 13 CB 864, 138 ER 1443; *Jabbour v Custodian of Israeli Absentee Property* [1954] 1 WLR 139, 143. Compare *Alexander v Ajax Insurance Co Ltd* [1956] VLR 436, 446.

[89] *Grant v Royal Exchange Assurance Co* (1815) 5 M & S 439, 105 ER 1111; *Castelli v Boddington* (1852) 1 El & Bl 66, 118 ER 361 (affirmed (1853) 1 El & Bl 879, 118 ER 665); *Luckie v Bushby* (1853) 13 CB 864, 138 ER 1443; *Pellas & Co v Neptune Marine Insurance Co* (1879) 5 CPD 34.

[90] *Jabbour v Custodian of Israeli Absentee Property* [1954] 1 WLR 139, 144.

[91] See *Jabbour v Custodian of Israeli Absentee Property* [1954] 1 WLR 139, 145.

[92] *Accident Compensation Commission v C. E. Heath Underwriting & Insurance (Aust) Pty Ltd* [1990] VR 224, 231. Tadgell J suggested that this especially may be the case in Victoria in view of r. 13.14 of the Supreme Court Rules. See paras 2.83–2.85 below.

[93] *Blackley v National Mutual Life Association (No. 2)* [1973] 1 NZLR 668, 672.

A less restrictive approach has also been adopted in relation to an indemnity given for costs **2.28** and expenses incurred.[94] If costs and expenses coming within the indemnity have been both incurred and paid, the courts have accepted that the resulting claim on the indemnity for reimbursement may be the subject of a set-off.[95] Similarly, it has been said that there may be a set-off in the situation in which an indemnity is given to an accommodation acceptor of a bill of exchange, and the acceptor makes a claim on the indemnity for the amount that he or she has had to pay on the bill.[96] If, on the other hand, the sums in question have not been paid, a claim for payment pursuant to the indemnity has been said to be unliquidated so that it cannot be the subject of a set-off,[97] although there is authority in Australia which suggests a more liberal view.[98] If the claim on the indemnity has both a liquidated and an unliquidated component, a set-off under the Statutes may proceed against the liquidated component.[99]

(5) Due and payable

A set-off under the Statutes is only available in respect of cross-debts that are due and **2.29** payable.[100] A debt which is payable *in futuro*,[101] or which is merely contingent,[102] cannot be employed in a set-off.

When a debt is payable on demand, the requirement of a demand is not regarded as creat- **2.30** ing a contingency if the liability in question is primary rather than secondary,[103] unless, it would seem, if the effect of the demand is to change the nature of the liability.[104] This may arise, for example, when a notice turns a liability to pay by instalments into a liability

---

[94] Compare *Cooper v Robinson* (1818) 2 Chit 161.

[95] *Hutchinson v Sydney* (1854) 10 Ex 438, 156 ER 508; *Brown v Tibbitt* (1862) 11 CB(NS) 855, 142 ER 1031. Compare *Attwooll v Attwooll* (1853) 2 El & Bl 23, 118 ER 677, though that case should be understood as turning on a peculiarity of a claim on a penal bond. See Leggatt LJ in *Axel Johnson Petroleum AB v MG Mineral Group AG* [1992] 1 WLR 270, 273–4.

[96] A suggestion to that effect in *Hardcastle v Netherwood* (1821) 5 B & Ald 93, 106 ER 1027 was adopted in later cases. See *Brown v Tibbitt* (1862) 11 CB(NS) 855, 866–7, 142 ER 1031, 1036; *Crampton v Walker* (1860) 3 El & El 321, 121 ER 463.

[97] *Crampton v Walker* (1860) 3 El & El 321, 121 ER 463 (esp. at 329–30, 466 referring to *Hardcastle v Netherwood* (1821) 5 B & Ald 93, 106 ER 1027).

[98] *Kostka v Addison* [1986] 1 Qd R 416 (on the assumption that the clause conferred a true indemnity).

[99] *Crampton v Walker* (1860) 3 El & El 321, 121 ER 463, and see also *Brown v Tibbitts* (1862) 11 CB(NS) 855, 867, 142 ER 1031, 1036. Compare *Cooper v Robinson* (1818) 2 Chit 161.

[100] *Stein v Blake* [1996] 1 AC 243, 251; *Hoverd Industries Ltd v Supercool Refrigeration and Air Conditioning (1991) Ltd* [1995] 3 NZLR 577, 587 ('presently due'); *Fuller v Happy Shopper Markets Ltd* [2001] 1 WLR 1681, 1690 at [21]. Compare *NZ Factors Ltd v Farmers Trading Co Ltd* [1992] 3 NZLR 703, 710. For a discussion of the meaning of 'payable', see *Helou v P. D. Mulligan Pty Ltd* (2003) 57 NSWLR 74.

[101] *Pilgrim v Kinder* (1744) 7 Mod 463, 87 ER 1357; *Smith, Fleming, & Co's Case* (1866) LR 1 Ch App 538 (which was decided before the bankruptcy set-off section was imported into the law of company liquidation); *Rex v Ray, ex p Chapman* [1936] SASR 241, 247; *Hoverd Industries Ltd v Supercool Refrigeration and Air Conditioning (1991) Ltd* [1995] 3 NZLR 577, 587.

[102] *Fromont v Coupland* (1824) 2 Bing 170, 130 ER 271; *Leman v Gordon* (1838) 8 Car & P 392, 173 ER 546. Compare *Agra & Masterman's Bank v Hoffman* (1864) 34 LJ Ch 285, although the injunction to restrain the action at law in that case was granted on the basis of an equitable set-off, as opposed to a set-off under the Statutes.

[103] See Hoffmann LJ, and Dillon LJ in the Court of Appeal, in *M S Fashions Ltd v Bank of Credit and Commerce International SA* [1993] Ch 425, 436, 447–8, and the cases there referred to.

[104] *Esso Petroleum Co Ltd v Alstonbridge Properties Ltd* [1975] 1 WLR 1474, 1483.

to pay the whole at once.[105] A classic example of a secondary liability is a liability under a guarantee. In that case, the requirement of a demand renders the liability contingent upon the making of a demand. But if the guarantee stipulates that the guarantor is to be liable as a principal debtor, the liability is primary, and the debt is not then contingent upon a demand.[106]

2.31   The question as to when the debt must be due and payable was considered earlier.[107] Prior to the Judicature Acts, the courts applied the principle that a set-off could only be pleaded in bar to the plaintiff's action if the set-off was available at the commencement of the action.[108] That should no longer be the case, however. A defendant should be able to plead a set-off in respect of matters arising subsequent to the action,[109] so that it should suffice if the plaintiff's cross-debt is due and payable when the defence of set-off is filed.

(6) Freight and negotiable instruments

2.32   It has been suggested that a defence of set-off under the Statutes of Set-off is not available in an action against the issuer of a negotiable instrument, or against a claim for the payment of freight under a voyage charterparty or a bill of lading. The better view is that there are no such restrictions.[110]

(7) Trustees

2.33   A trustee may hold a debt as trust property, and may have incurred a debt to the debtor in his or her capacity as trustee. The question whether these debts can be set off under the Statutes of Set-off is considered later.[111]

C. The Statutes of Set-off as a Procedural Defence

(1) The procedural nature of the defence

2.34   The Statutes of Set-off provide a defence in the case of mutual debts.[112] That defence is characterized as procedural,[113] and should be contrasted with equitable set-off, which is said to be substantive.[114] But while set-off under the Statutes is commonly referred to as

---

[105] *Esso Petroleum Co Ltd v Alstonbridge Properties Ltd* [1975] 1 WLR 1474, 1483.

[106] *M S Fashions Ltd v Bank of Credit and Commerce International SA* [1993] Ch 425, 436, 447–8.

[107] See paras 2.08–2.12 above.

[108] *Richards v James* (1848) 2 Ex 471, 154 ER 577.

[109] See *Wood v Goodwin* [1884] WN 17.

[110] See paras 5.17–5.22 (freight), and paras 5.35–5.41 (negotiable instruments), below.

[111] See paras 17.124–17.127 below.

[112] See e.g. Parke B in *Graham v Partridge* (1836) 1 M & W 395, 401, 150 ER 488, 490 ('The legislature constituted it a defence . . .'); *Stooke v Taylor* (1880) 5 QBD 569, 575; *Hanak v Green* [1958] 2 QB 9, 16–17; *BICC v Burndy Corporation* [1985] 1 Ch 232, 248 ('cast iron defence of legal set-off'). See also para. 2.39 below. Compare *Benford Ltd v Lopecan SL* [2004] 2 Lloyd's Rep 618 at [10].

[113] See e.g. *Aectra Refining and Manufacturing Inc v Exmar NV* [1994] 1 WLR 1634, 1650–1; *Stein v Blake* [1996] 1 AC 243, 251; *Fuller v Happy Shopper Markets Ltd* [2001] 1 WLR 1681, 1690 at [21] ('procedural device'); *Clambake Pty Ltd v Tipperary Projects Pty Ltd (No. 3)* [2009] WASC 52 at [152]. Compare McCracken, *The Banker's Remedy of Set-off* (3rd edn, 2010), 181–4. *Smit Tek International Zeesleepen BV v Selco Salvage Ltd* [1988] 2 Lloyd's Rep 398, 404–5 is difficult to follow.

[114] See paras 4.29–4.57 below.

a procedural defence, it should nevertheless be appreciated that it is not wholly procedural. Because it is a defence, it also has substantive aspects.[115]

2.35 By a procedural defence, it is meant that the set-off is brought about by a judgment of the court and it has no effect until judgment.[116] In contrast to equitable set-off, prior to judgment the rights consequent upon being a creditor still attach, as do the obligations and liabilities consequent upon being a debtor. For example, the statute (1605) 3 Jac 1, c 15 provided that, if a debtor living within the city of London owed a debt of 40s. or less (other than certain specified debts), it had to be sued for in the court of requests, failing which the plaintiff was not entitled to costs of the action. The courts held that the amount owing had to be measured irrespective of any right of set-off available to the defendant under the Statutes,[117] the reason being that the mutual debts retained their separate identities at the commencement of the action.[118].

2.36 In considering the procedural nature of the defence under the Statutes, two lines of authority should be distinguished. In the first place, in some early cases in which the question of arrest for non-payment of a debt was in issue, it was accepted that the amount for which the creditor could procure the debtor's arrest was limited to the balance only after setting off any mutual debt owing by the creditor to the debtor.[119] The fact that this was so before judgment for a set-off might suggest that, even before judgment, it was thought that only the balance was owing. However, the cases involved the special question of a person's liberty, and on that basis they should be regarded as exceptions to the general principle that set-off under the Statutes is a procedural defence. It is also necessary to explain another line of cases concerning claims on penal bonds. If a bond provided for payment of a penalty in the event of default in the payment of a sum of money, and the defendant, having defaulted in payment to the plaintiff, nevertheless was a creditor of the plaintiff for a greater amount, the plaintiff could not obtain judgment for the penalty.[120] Once again, this might suggest that the mere existence of a cross-debt was regarded as bringing about a reduction in the required payment, so that there was no default and therefore no justification for suing for the penalty. Those cases, however, turned upon a special provision in the second Statute of Set-off[121] that, if one of the debts in a set-off accrued by reason of a penalty contained in a bond or specialty, judgment could be entered 'for no more than shall appear to be truly and justly due to the plaintiff, after one debt being set against the other'. If the plaintiff was indebted to the defendant for an amount which exceeded the amount in respect of which the defendant had defaulted, there was nothing 'truly and justly due to the plaintiff', and the plaintiff was not entitled to judgment for the amount of the penalty.

---

[115] See paras 2.53–2.57 below.

[116] *Stein v Blake* [1996] 1 AC 243, 251; *Clambake Pty Ltd v Tipperary Projects Pty Ltd (No. 3)* [2009] WASC 52 at [152]; *Re Kaupthing Singer and Friedlander Ltd* [2009] 2 Lloyd's Rep 154 at [17].

[117] *Pitts v Carpenter* (1743) 1 Wils KB 19, 95 ER 469; *Gross v Fisher* (1770) 3 Wils KB 48, 95 ER 926.

[118] *Gross v Fisher* (1770) 3 Wils KB 48, 49, 95 ER 926.

[119] *Dronefield v Archer* (1822) 5 B & Ald 513, 106 ER 1278; *Austin v Debnam* (1824) 3 B & C 139, 107 ER 686. Compare the earlier decision in *Brown v Pigeon* (1811) 2 Camp 594, 170 ER 1263.

[120] *Collins v Collins* (1755) 2 Burr 820, 97 ER 579; *Lee v Lester* (1849) 7 CB 1008, 137 ER 399. See also *Rodgers v Maw* (1846) 15 M & W 444, 153 ER 924.

[121] (1735) 8 Geo II, c 24, s. 5.

Concepts inherent in describing the defence as procedural

2.37   The notion that defence of set-off under the Statutes is a procedural defence imports two concepts.

2.38   The first is that one of the parties to mutual debts cannot act unilaterally to bring about a cancellation of the debts through a set-off. For a cancellation of the debts to occur under the Statutes, an order of the court is required.[122] As Brett LJ once remarked:[123] 'the right of set-off only arises where there is an action between parties. It is a statutable remedy which only is given in the case of an action.' The fact that the debts are not set off until judgment is evident from the old form of pleading for set-off under the Statutes, that: 'the plaintiff, before and at the time of the commencement of his suit was and from thence hitherto hath been *and still is* indebted to the defendant.'[124] The plea was bad if it was not stated that the plaintiff 'still is' indebted.[125] It should be compared to a defence that the plaintiff and the defendant had agreed prior to the action that the two debts should be set off. In that circumstance, the defendant would plead accord and satisfaction rather than set-off.[126]

2.39   The second concept is that the Statutes only authorized a set-off in legal proceedings where the set-off was being pleaded as a *defence* in those proceedings.[127] The second Statute[128] provided that 'mutual debts may be set against each other, either by being pleaded in bar, or given in evidence on the general issue . . .'. Both the general issue and a special plea in bar were pleas which denied a cause of complaint.[129] The general issue was a plea which imported an absolute and general denial of what was alleged in the plaintiff's declaration, without offering any special matter whereby it was evaded. A special plea in bar, on the other hand, set forth the particular facts which comprised the defence. Rules made in Hilary Term, 4 Will 4, had the effect that henceforth set-off had to be specially pleaded, and it could not be given in evidence under the general issue.[130] The point remains, however, that those pleas were the only means contemplated in the second Statute for bringing about

---

[122] *Aectra Refining and Marketing Inc v Exmar NV* [1994] 1 WLR 1634, 1650; *Glencore Grain Ltd v Agros Trading Co* [1999] 2 Lloyd's Rep 410, 415–16. Similarly, in the case of an assignment of a debt, notice of the assignment to the debtor does not effect a set-off of the debts. See *Glencore v Agros* at 417–19. Compare Kerr LJ's suggestion in *BICC Plc v Burndy Corporation* [1985] 1 Ch 232, 254–5, that Burndy could have acted unilaterally to bring about a set-off so as to extinguish BICC's claim. The case concerned legal set-off under the Statutes (see Dillon LJ at 247 and Kerr LJ at 256 and 259), and so presumably the comment was intended to apply in that context. The suggestion is incorrect, however.

[123] *Re Anglo-French Co-operative Society, ex p Pelly* (1882) 21 Ch D 492, 507. While *Pelly* concerned a company in liquidation, Brett LJ's reference later in that paragragh to the 'statute of set-off' suggests that he had in mind the Statutes rather than the insolvency set-off section.

[124] See *Chitty's Precedents in Pleadings* (2nd edn, 1847), 390.

[125] *Dendy v Powell* (1838) 3 M & W 442, 150 ER 1218.

[126] *Chitty's Precedents in Pleadings* (2nd edn, 1847), 237–8.

[127] *Stooke v Taylor* (1880) 5 QBD 569, 575 ('The plea can only be used in the way of defence to the plaintiff's action, as a shield, not as a sword', and 'By the terms of the Act the plea must be pleaded in the action'). In *Stein v Blake* [1996] 1 AC 243, 253 Lord Hoffmann said that set-off under the Statutes 'can be invoked only by the filing of a defence in an action'.

[128] (1735) 8 Geo II, c 24, s. 5.

[129] See generally *Blackstone's Commentaries* (1768) vol. 3, 305–6.

[130] *Fidgett v Penny* (1834) 1 C M & R 108, 149 ER 1014; *Graham v Partridge* (1836) 1 M & W 395, 150 ER 488.

a set-off. While the pleas themselves are now obsolete, it is clear that the Statutes only applied where a set-off was pleaded as a defence to an action.

Parker v Jackson *criticized*

In light of those principles, consider the decision in *Parker v Jackson*.[131] The plaintiffs were   **2.40**
the trustees of the will of John Parker. Prior to his death, Parker had mortgaged a property to secure a debt of £700 to Mrs Williams. After Parker's death, his solicitor took a transfer of the mortgage. In addition the solicitor, once again after the death, received a sum of £2,000 constituting the proceeds of an investment made on behalf of the estate. This sum was payable to the plaintiffs as trustees of the estate. The position, therefore, was that the solicitor was a creditor of the estate to the extent of £700 on the mortgage, but at the same time had to pay over £2,000. Subsequently, the solicitor transferred the mortgage to a client. The client as transferee gave notice of the transfer to the plaintiffs, requesting that all interest henceforth should be paid to her. The plaintiffs then brought this action seeking a declaration that the mortgage debt had been discharged, and an order for the delivery up of the mortgage deed and the documents of title. The impetus for this was that the solicitor was insolvent. It would seem that there was no identifiable fund held on trust for the plaintiffs,[132] and because of the solicitor's insolvency a personal claim by the trustees for payment of the £2,000 would not have been satisfied. Equally, if the plaintiffs succeeded in the action and the mortgage was discharged, the transferee would have lost the mortgage and would have been left with a worthless claim against the solicitor. As Farwell J remarked, this was a case in which one of two innocent parties had to suffer. His Lordship held in favour of the plaintiffs. He said that, before the solicitor transferred the mortgage, the plaintiffs as trustees of the estate were entitled to direct the solicitor to apply part of the £2,000 in discharge of the mortgage. He characterized this as a right of set-off.[133] While the plaintiffs did not in fact give a direction to that effect, the transferee nevertheless took subject to the right to do so on the basis of the principle that an assignee takes subject to equities.[134]

If there was no identifiable fund held on trust for the plaintiffs,[135] it would be difficult   **2.41**
to support Farwell J's view that the plaintiffs had a right of set-off which entitled them to direct the solicitor to satisfy the mortgage debt out of the money owing to the estate.

---

[131] [1936] 2 All ER 281.

[132] Compare the explanation of *Parker v Jackson* in *Clairview Developments Pty Ltd v Law Mortgages Gold Coast Pty Ltd* [2007] 2 Qd R 501 at [34], in terms of 'money actually held by the mortgagee and owing to the mortgagor'. However, there was no express finding that a trust was ever established in respect of the £2,000. Farwell J commented in his judgment (at [1936] 2 All ER 281, 287) that the solicitors 'had in their hands, or had as a debt, a sum of something over £2,000 . . .'. The events in question occurred before the Solicitors' Accounts Rules 1935 came into operation on 1 January 1935, which first established the requirement of a trust account for clients' moneys. See *Plunkett v Barclays Bank Ltd* [1936] 2 KB 107, 115–17. Before then, if a separate trust account was not established, a solicitor who received moneys on behalf of a client was regarded simply as a debtor. See *Re Hindmarsh* (1860) 1 Dr & Sm 129, 62 ER 327; *Watson v Woodman* (1875) LR 20 Eq 721. See also *Shand v M J Atkinson Ltd* [1966] NZLR 551, 566.

[133] See the judgment at [1936] 2 All ER 281, 284, 289, 291 ('as in this case the mortgagors had an undoubted right of set-off against the assignor . . . ').

[134] See ch. 17 below.

[135] See above.

Since the claims were unconnected, his Lordship would appear to have had in mind a set-off under the Statutes of Set-off, but the Statutes only provided a procedural defence. They did not permit one party to mutual debts to act unilaterally to bring about a set-off by notice to the other party. The set-off requires a judgment. Indeed, the view expressed by Farwell J sits uneasily with the principle that interest on a mortgage debt continues to accrue, even though there may be a debt for a greater amount owing by the mortgagee to the mortgagor on another account. The mortgagor cannot avoid that result simply by requesting the mortgagee to apply the cross-debt in discharge of the mortgage debt.[136] In *Samuel Keller (Holdings) Ltd v Martins Bank Ltd*[137] Megarry J rejected an argument that a mortgagor can unilaterally discharge the mortgage debt by appropriating to it a damages claim against the mortgagee,[138] and his Lordship emphasized that the position is the same in the case of a liquidated cross-debt:

> Even where there is a claim which is both liquidated and admitted, and it exceeds the mort-gage debt in amount, it may be to the interest of one party or the other, or both, that the mortgage and the mortgage debt should continue in existence. The rate of interest may be attractively high or seductively low; there may be fiscal advantages in keeping the mortgage alive; there may be new projects to be financed which make liquid cash preferable to the satisfaction of mortgage debts; and so on. Nor have I heard any reason why it should be the mortgagor who is to have a unilateral power to discharge the mortgage debt by appropriation without payment.[139]

2.42 The trustees in *Parker v Jackson* therefore would not have been entitled to act unilaterally to bring about a set-off. It has been suggested that the case nevertheless was correctly decided on the ground that the trustees had a *right* of set-off against the solicitor, and the court therefore could give a judgment for a set-off which was binding on the transferees in accord-ance with the usual principles governing set-off against assignees.[140] That suggestion faces two potential difficulties.[141]

2.43 The first is that the plaintiffs were seeking a declaration that the mortgage had been discharged and an order for redemption. The Statutes of Set-off, on the other hand, only authorized a set-off in legal proceedings where the set-off was pleaded as a defence. Since a set-off was not being raised as a defence in *Parker v Jackson*, the case would not appear to have been within the ambit of the Statutes.[142] Nevertheless, there is authority which supports the availability of a set-off in this situation. In *Re Agra and Masterman's Bank (Anderson's Case)*[143] Sir William Page Wood VC appeared to accept that, in an action

---

[136] *Garforth v Bradley* (1755) 2 Ves Sen 675, 678, 28 ER 430, 432; *Fisher & Lightwood's Law of Mortgage* (12th edn, 2006), 887 para. 47.37. See also *Pettat v Ellis* (1804) 9 Ves Jun 563, 32 ER 721, although in any event a set-off under the Statutes was not available in that case.

[137] [1971] 1 WLR 4. On appeal, Russell LJ (at 51) quoted this passage with approval.

[138] See in particular at [1971] 1 WLR 43, 47–8, and Russell LJ on appeal at 51.

[139] [1971] 1 WLR 43, 49.

[140] Wood, *English and International Set-off* (1989), 45. See ch. 17 below in relation to assignments.

[141] This is in addition to any difficulty that would have arisen if the solicitor had held the proceeds of the investment on trust. See ch. 10 below.

[142] In *P. Rowe Graphics Pty Ltd v Scanagraphix Pty Ltd* NSW SC, 6 September 1988, Young J doubted that a declaration is available in the case of a procedural defence such as that provided by the Statutes of Set-off.

[143] (1866) LR 3 Eq 337, 340.

to redeem a security given for payment of a debt, the court can set off an unrelated cross-debt. Further, in *Norrish v Marshall*,[144] which concerned an application for redemption of a mortgage against an assignee of the mortgage, Sir John Leach commented:

> The principle is that, as against an assignee without notice, the mortgagor has the same rights as he has against the mortgagee, and whatever he can claim in the way of set-off, or mutual credit, as against the mortgagee, he can claim equally against the assignee.

This statement would appear to embrace set-off under the Statutes. The point may be made, however, that the issue in the case was one of payment rather than set-off. The mortgagor had paid the mortgagee/assignor before the mortgagor had knowledge of the assignment, and it was held that the assignee took subject to that payment.[145]

Unity Joint Stock Mutual Banking Association v King[146] is distinguishable. Sir John Romilly **2.44** suggested in that case that, where two sons were indebted to their father, and at the same time the sons were entitled to an equitable charge or lien on the father's land on the basis of an equitable proprietary estoppel arising from the expenditure of money on improvements, 'the father would be entitled to set off any sum [owing to him by the sons] against any sum due to them upon the security of this land, and . . . this Court would enforce such right, and cause them to deliver up the land free from any charge upon it'.[147] However, those remarks should be understood in the context of the set-off in issue, which was an equitable set-off permitted in circumstances where the father himself was not indebted to the sons for the expenditure.[148] Since the equitable charge was not security for a debt as such, but rather it was an interest in the land which the court considered that it was appropriate that the sons should have in order to satisfy the equity which arose in their favour as a result of the expenditure of money on improvements, the reasons adduced by Megarry J in *Samuel Keller* for not allowing a mortgagor to appropriate a cross-debt in extinction of the mortgage debt were not applicable.

But there is a second difficulty with the suggestion that the court in *Parker v Jackson* could **2.45** have given a judgment for a set-off in the action before it, and that is that, in the particular circumstances of the case, it is difficult to see how the Statutes of Set-off could have applied in any event. The solicitor's liability to the estate arose after the death, when the proceeds of sale were received, and equally the solicitor obtained a claim after the death when the mortgage was transferred to him. A set-off would not have been available under the Statutes as between the deceased and the solicitor, because the Statutes required that the debts should originally have existed between two living persons.[149] Nor was there a set-off available as between the solicitor and the plaintiffs in their capacity as executors because, while

---

[144] (1821) 56 ER 977, 980, 5 Madd 475, 481.

[145] See the explanation of *Norrish v Marshall* in *Clairview Developments Pty Ltd v Law Mortgages Gold Coast Pty Ltd* [2007] 2 Qd R 501 at [31]. An assignee of a mortgage can only claim what was due from the mortgagor to the assignor mortgagee when the mortgagor first received notice of the assignment. See *De Lisle v Union Bank of Scotland* [1914] 1 Ch 22, 31, 33; *Noia v Bell* (1901) 27 VLR 82.

[146] (1858) 25 Beav 72, 53 ER 563.

[147] (1858) 25 Beav 72, 79–80, 53 ER 563, 566.

[148] See Sir John Romilly's judgment at (1858) 25 Beav 72, 78, 53 ER 563, 565, and also Lord Denning's discussion of the case in *Hussey v Palmer* [1972] 1 WLR 1286, 1290.

[149] See para. 13.131 below.

the receipt of the proceeds of sale by the solicitor could be regarded as a debt owing to the plaintiffs in that capacity,[150] the plaintiffs themselves were not liable for payment of the mortgage debt. There was therefore no mutuality.[151] If, indeed, a set-off had been available to the plaintiffs under the Statutes as against the solicitor, they could have waited until the transferee sued for payment, and then defended the action on the ground that the transferee took subject to their right of set-off.[152] That would have provided adequate protection to the plaintiffs. In the circumstances, however, that course of action would not appear to have been open in *Parker v Jackson*.

(2) Cross-debt must be enforceable by action

2.46 Because the defence of set-off under the Statutes is merely procedural, the cross-debt sought to be set off must be enforceable by action.[153] The point was made earlier in relation to the statutory defence that it should not be necessary that the cross-debt be in existence at the date of the commencement of the claimant's action. It should suffice if the defence is available when the defence of set-off is filed.[154] A corollary of this view is that the cross-debt should be enforceable at that time.[155]

Limitation Act

2.47 A different principle applies in some circumstances under s. 35 of the Limitation Act 1980 in the context of limitation periods. The basic principle is set out in s. 35(1). Essentially, it provides that a 'new claim', in the form of a set-off or a counterclaim,[156] is deemed to be a separate action and to have been commenced on the same date as the original action. *Prima facie*, then, any question as to the expiration of a limitation period for the cross-debt the subject of a proposed set-off should be determined by reference to that date.[157] A similar principle has been adopted in the legislation of other jurisdictions.[158] However, s. 35(3)

---

[150] See *Rees v Watts* (1855) 11 Ex 410, 415, 156 ER 891, 893 in relation to the plaintiff administrator's claim for money had and received by the defendant for the use of the plaintiff as administrator.

[151] The demands would not have been sufficiently closely connected to give rise to an equitable set-off, for which the better view (notwithstanding recent opinions suggesting the contrary) is that mutuality is not always necessary. See paras 4.67–4.83 below.

[152] See ch. 17 below.

[153] *Walker v Clements* (1850) 15 QB 1046, 117 ER 755; *Rawley v Rawley* (1876) 1 QBD 460, 463, 468; *J. & S. Holdings Pty Ltd v NRMA Insurance Ltd* (1982) 41 ALR 539, 554; *Re Elgar Heights Pty Ltd* [1985] VR 657, 665; *Aectra Refining and Marketing Inc v Exmar NV* [1994] 1 WLR 1634, 1650–1 (referring to *Francis v Dodsworth* (1847) 4 CB 202, 220, 136 ER 482, 489); *Glencore Grain Ltd v Agros Trading Co* [1999] 2 Lloyd's Rep 410, 417, 420. See also *Owens v Denton* (1835) 1 C M & R 711, 149 ER 1266; *McDonnell & East Ltd v McGregor* (1936) 56 CLR 50, 57. Nevertheless, a judgment debt may be set off under the Statutes even though enforcement takes place by way of execution. See para. 2.91 below. Compare equitable set-off. See para. 4.51 below.

[154] *Stein v Blake* [1996] AC 243, 251. See paras 2.08–2.11 above.

[155] Compare *Glencore Grain Ltd v Agros Trading Co* [1999] 2 Lloyd's Rep 410, 417, where the Court of Appeal referred to the commencement of the plaintiff's action.

[156] See s. 35(2).

[157] The word 'set-off' in s. 35 encompasses a set-off under the Statutes of Set-off, but not a substantive defence of equitable set-off. See *Westdeutsche Landesbank v Islington BC* [1994] 4 All ER 890, 943–6 (Hobhouse J), and para. 4.52 below.

[158] See e.g. the Limitation of Actions Act 1958 (Vic), s. 30. See also *McDonnell & East Ltd v McGregor* (1936) 56 CLR 50, 55, 57; *Pegasus Leasing Ltd v Cadoroll Pty Ltd* (1996) 59 FCR 152, 162. That principle

goes on to provide for a different approach if the set-off is not an 'original set-off'; in other words, if the person asserting the set-off has previously made a claim in the action, in the sense that he has previously made a claim for some form of relief.[159] Section 35(3) stipulates that, save as provided by s. 33 (which deals with actions in respect of personal injuries or death) or by rules of court,[160] the court shall not allow a claim by way of set-off that is not an original set-off to be made in the course of an action after the expiration of the time limit under the Act which would affect a new action to enforce that claim. Therefore, in the case of a set-off which is not an original set-off, the limitation period is determined by reference to the date when leave to amend is sought so as to include the set-off in the defence.[161]

Unenforceable on other grounds

The courts have held that a set-off under the Statutes may not be based upon a debt which **2.48** is unenforceable, not only because of the expiration of a limitation period,[162] but also because of the operation of moratorium legislation,[163] or because the plaintiff contracted the debt during his or her infancy,[164] or because of the Statutes of Frauds,[165] or because the plaintiff had obtained a discharge under insolvent debtor's legislation.[166] There are two exceptions to the principle, however.

The first exception arises in relation to the statutory provision that a solicitor must deliver **2.49** a bill of costs in the proper form before he or she can bring an action to recover the costs.[167] A solicitor may employ the debt for costs in a set-off even though the requirement has not

---

applies in the case of a cross-claim pleaded as a set-off in the original defence. If it is sought to amend a defence to include a set-off, the operation of the relevant rules of court in relation to amendment of pleadings would also require consideration. See *JFS (UK) Ltd v DWR Cymru Cyf* [1999] 1 WLR 231, 235–6 in relation to the position formerly applying in England. In the *JFS (UK) Ltd* case, the Court of Appeal held that the Limitation Act 1980, s. 35(3) (see below) has widened the court's jurisdiction so that, in an application under the rules to amend a defence, the court in its discretion may allow a new claim which is an original set-off or counterclaim to be made, even though it is founded on a cause of action which is statute-barred. In New South Wales, the Limitation Act 1969, s. 74 deems a claim by way of set-off (as a separate action) to have been brought, as against the person against whom the claim is made, on the earlier of the date on which the person became a party to the principal action and (if it is different) the date on which the person became a party to the claim. Compare also Western Australia, where the Limitation Act 2005 (WA), s. 81 exempts from the operation of that section a counterclaim solely by way of defence.

[159] Compare *JFS (UK) Ltd v Dwr Cymru Cyf* [1999] 1 WLR 231.
[160] See CPR, Parts 17 (Amendments to Statements of Case) and 19 (Parties). The rules of court must comply with certain conditions. See s. 35(4).
[161] Subject to the rules of court. See s. 35(3).
[162] *Remington v Stevens* (1748) 2 Str 1271, 93 ER 1175; *Walker v Clements* (1850) 15 QB 1046, 117 ER 755. See also *Smith v Betty* [1903] 2 KB 317; *Re Morris, Deceased, Coneys v Morris* [1922] 1 IR 136. The comments in *Strachan v Marriott* [1995] 3 NZLR 272, 291–2 in relation to a statute-bar should be considered as having had in contemplation equitable set-off. See para. 4.51 below.
[163] *Rex v Ray, ex p Chapman* [1936] SASR 241.
[164] *Rex v Ray, ex p Chapman* [1936] SASR 241; *Rawley v Rawley* (1876) 1 QBD 460. See also *J. & S. Holdings Pty Ltd v NRMA Insurance Ltd* (1982) 41 ALR 539, 554.
[165] *Salisbury Jones v Southwood and Co* King's Bench Division, Goddard LJ, 9 December 1941, unreported but noted at 193 LT 48.
[166] *Francis v Dodsworth* (1847) 4 CB 202, 136 ER 482.
[167] Solicitors Act 1974, s. 69.

been complied with.[168] In *Rawley v Rawley*[169] Mellish LJ sought to explain this result on the ground that the statute in question merely postponed the remedy of bringing action until a bill of costs was delivered, and left other remedies untouched,[170] although in both Australia and Canada it has been held in other contexts that the principle that the debt sought to be set off must be enforceable by action also applies during any period when the remedy of bringing an action is suspended.[171]

2.50 The second exception arises in relation to an alien enemy. As a matter of public policy, an alien enemy cannot sue as claimant in English courts while the state of hostilities subsists.[172] On the other hand, when an enemy alien is being sued as a defendant, he or she is entitled to appear and be heard in his or her defence.[173] This includes defending an action by way of set-off.[174] Pleading a cross-demand as a set-off is permitted, because it cannot result in an order for payment to the alien enemy.[175] It should be distinguished from counterclaim. An alien enemy is not permitted to counterclaim because it may result in a larger sum being payable to the alien enemy than would be payable by him or her to the claimant.[176] One writer has suggested that the right of an alien enemy to plead a set-off should be confined to the substantive form of equitable set-off considered in Chapter 4.[177] But if the justification for allowing a set-off is that it cannot result in an order for payment to the enemy alien, there is no reason for restricting the availability of the defence to equitable set-off.

(3) Cross-debt must be able to be determined in the plaintiff's action

2.51 Consistent with the notion that set-off under the Statutes of Set-off is a procedural defence, a dispute on the cross-debt sought to be set off must be able to be determined by the court in the claimant's action. Therefore, in an application by a claimant for summary judgment, leave to defend will not be granted on the basis of a set-off under the Statutes if the court in the claimant's action would refuse to try the merits of the case on the cross-debt, for example because the cross-debt is the subject of an arbitration clause or a foreign jurisdiction clause to which the court would give effect.[178] On the other hand, the court has a discretion

---

[168] *Brown v Tibbitts* (1862) 11 CB(NS) 855, 142 ER 1031; *Robinson v Vale* [1905] VLR 405; *Currie v The Law Society* [1977] 1 QB 990, 995. See also *Ex p Cooper* (1854) 14 CB 663, 139 ER 273.

[169] (1876) 1 QBD 460.

[170] (1876) 1 QBD 460, 468.

[171] *Rex v Ray, ex p Chapman* [1936] SASR 241; *Atlantic Acceptance Corporation Ltd v Burns & Dutton Construction (1962) Ltd* (1970) 14 DLR (3d) 175 (though note the criticism of that case in Palmer, *The Law of Set-off in Canada* (1993), 29–30).

[172] *Robinson & Co v Continental Insurance Co of Mannheim* [1915] 1 KB 155, 159.

[173] *Porter v Freudenberg* [1915] 1 KB 857, 883.

[174] *Re Stahlwerk Becker Aktiengesellschaft's Patent* [1917] 2 Ch 272, 273, 275–6.

[175] *Re Stahlwerk Becker Aktiengesellschaft's Patent* [1917] 2 Ch 272, 276.

[176] *Re Stahlwerk Becker Aktiengesellschaft's Patent* [1917] 2 Ch 272, 276.

[177] See Wood, *English and International Set-off* (1989), 755, who refers to this form of set-off as a transaction set-off.

[178] *Aectra Refining and Marketing Inc v Exmar NV* [1994] 1 WLR 1634; *Glencore Grain Ltd v Agros Trading Co* [1999] 2 Lloyd's Rep 410 (esp. at 417). See also Berg, 'Arbitration: Legal Set-off and Enforcing Admitted Claims' [2000] LMCLQ 153.

in such a case to stay execution on a judgment given in favour of the claimant until the cross-debt is determined by the appropriate tribunal.[179]

Unlike set-off under the Statutes, equitable set-off (and, in England, common law abate- **2.52** ment[180]) is regarded as a substantive defence.[181] Because it is not procedural, in the sense in which that expression is used in relation to the Statutes,[182] there is no such objection to the court giving effect to the defence in the face of an arbitration clause or a foreign jurisdiction clause applicable to the cross-claim.[183]

D. Substantive Aspects of the Defence

While set-off under the Statutes is commonly described as a procedural defence, it should **2.53** nevertheless be appreciated that it is not wholly a matter of procedure.[184] It also has substantive aspects.

The fundamental point is that the right of set-off derived from the Statutes is a *defence*. **2.54** In that sense it differs from counterclaim, which merely provides a mechanism by which separate actions may be tried in the same proceedings.[185] Counterclaim is not a defence, and is properly described as being wholly procedural. But because the Statutes provide a defence, the right in question is not wholly a matter of procedure. It can have a substantive effect upon the rights and interests of third parties. For example, an assignee of a debt takes subject to defences, including rights of set-off,[186] which were available to the debtor against the assignor before the debtor received notice of the assignment.[187] This includes the case

---

[179] *Aectra Refining and Marketing Inc v Exmar NV* [1994] 1 WLR 1634, 1652.

[180] See paras 2.123–2.134 below. In Australia there is authority suggesting that abatement is a procedural defence, but the prevailing view in England is that it is substantive. See para. 2.129 below.

[181] See paras 4.29–4.57 below.

[182] See paras 2.34–2.39 above.

[183] *Aectra Refining and Marketing Inc v Exmar NV* [1994] 1 WLR 1634, 1649–50 (referring to *Gilbert-Ash (Northern) Ltd v Modern Engineering (Bristol) Ltd* [1974] AC 689 (esp. at 720, 726)); *Bim Kemi AB v Blackburn Chemicals Ltd* [2001] 2 Lloyd's Rep 93, 96 at [9]. See also *Glencore Grain Ltd v Agros Trading Co* [1999] 2 Lloyd's Rep 410, 416–17.

[184] See also McCracken, *The Banker's Remedy of Set-off* (3rd edn, 2010), 157 *et seq.*

[185] See para. 1.04 above.

[186] See e.g. *Roxburghe v Cox* (1881) 17 Ch D 520, 526 *per* James LJ (an assignee 'takes subject to all rights of set-off and other defences which were available against the assignor'); *White & Tudor's Leading Cases in Equity* (9th edn, 1928) vol. 1, 136; *Edward Nelson & Co Ltd v Faber & Co* [1903] 2 KB 367, 375 *per* Joyce J ('It is a general rule with respect to a chose in action that an assignee takes it subject to all equities – in other words, whatever defence by way of set-off or otherwise the debtor would be entitled to set up against the assignor's claim up to the time of his receiving notice of the assignment . . .').

[187] See ch. 17 below. There are some nineteenth-century cases that have been interpreted in Australia as supporting a proposition that an assignee of a debt may take subject to an unliquidated cross-demand available to the debtor against the assignor, notwithstanding that it would not have given rise to a defence as between those parties, if it arose out of the same contract or transaction as the assigned debt. The point in relation to that interpretation is that it is not generally regarded as sufficient to give rise to an equitable set-off that the cross-demands arose out of the same contract or transaction. The impeachment test for equitable set-off, which still generally applies in Australia (see paras 4.19–4.28 below), requires something more than that. See paras 4.14 and 4.91 below. The proposition inherent in that interpretation, that a cross-demand that is not available as a set-off against an assignor can bind the assignee, was rejected by the House of Lords in *Bank of Boston Connecticut v European Grain and Shipping Ltd* [1989] 1 AC 1056, 1105–6, 1109–11, and it seems incorrect, both historically and as a matter or principle. See paras 17.06–17.09 below.

of a secured creditor pursuant to a crystallized floating charge, because the creditor is regarded in equity as an assignee of any debt owing to the company which comes within the ambit of the charge.[188] Similarly, when an undisclosed principal sues on a contract entered into by the agent, the principal may be met by any defence of set-off under the Statutes that would have been available to the defendant against the agent before the defendant had notice of the agency.[189] The same issue may arise in an action by a party with subrogation rights, for example a subrogated insurer,[190] or where a judgment creditor is seeking to attach a debt owing by a third party to the judgment debtor by way of a third party debt (or garnishee) order, in circumstances where the third party would have had a defence of set-off available in an action brought against him or her by the judgment debtor for payment of the debt.[191]

2.55   If the availability of a defence of set-off can affect the interests of third parties in that manner, the right could hardly be described as wholly procedural.[192] Admittedly, for the purpose of private international law set-off has been said to be a matter of procedure, with the result that it is governed by the *lex fori*.[193] However, this principle should be approached with caution in other contexts, because it has been said that English private international lawyers tended in the past to give a wide meaning to the term 'procedure' in order to evade unsatisfactory choice of law rules.[194] Merely because something has been characterized as a matter of procedure for the purpose of private international law does not mean that it is matter of procedure for all other purposes. For example, *William Cook Pty Ltd v Read*[195] concerned the question whether the power conferred on the Governor in Council by s. 5 of the Justices Act 1958 (Vic) to make rules as to practice and procedure included a power to make rules as to evidence. O'Bryan J in the Victorian Supreme Court held that it did not, even though in private international law the rules of evidence are regarded as a matter of procedure.[196]

2.56   It has been suggested in Australia that, while rights of set-off are procedural in so far as they depend on entry of judgment for their effect, in so far as they operate as 'pleas in bar, they seem to be substantive rights'.[197] Hoffmann LJ (as he then was) made a similar observation in *Aectra Refining and Manufacturing Inc v Exmar NV*.[198] In drawing a distinction between

---

[188] *N W Robbie & Co Ltd v Witney Warehouse Co Ltd* [1963] 1 WLR 1324. See para. 17.100 below.

[189] See paras 13.79–13.99 below.

[190] See *Sydney Turf Club v Crowley* [1971] 1 NSWLR 724, 734 *per* Mason JA. ('When an insurer is subrogated to the rights of the insured against a third party . . . . [the action] is brought in the name of the insured and it is subject to all the defences which would be available if the action had been brought by the insured for his own benefit'), and generally Derham, *Subrogation in Insurance Law* (1985), 122–3.

[191] See paras 17.136–17.145 below.

[192] See Derham, 'Set-off in Victoria' (1999) 73 *Australian Law Journal* 754, 760–4.

[193] *Meyer v Dresser* (1864) 16 CB(NS) 646, 665, 666, 143 ER 1280, 1287–8; *Maspons y Hermano v Mildred Goyeneche & Co* (1882) 9 QBD 530; *Re Vocalion (Foreign) Ltd* [1932] 2 Ch 196, 206.

[194] Dicey, Morris and Collins, *The Conflict of Laws* (14th edn, 2006) vol. 1, 177, and see also McCracken, *The Banker's Remedy of Set-off* (3rd edn, 2010), 159–60 where this point is made in relation to set-off.

[195] [1940] VLR 214.

[196] [1940] VLR 214, 218–19.

[197] *Meagher, Gummow and Lehane's Equity Doctrines and Remedies* (4th edn, 2002), 1066 [37–080]. In *Gertig v Davies* (2003) 85 SASR 226 at [30] Doyle CJ commented that, 'It is not easy to classify a right of set-off as either substantive or procedural . . .'.

[198] [1994] 1 WLR 1634, 1650.

the substantive defence of equitable (or, as it is sometimes called, transaction) set-off,[199] and set-off under the Statutes of Set-off (which he termed independent set-off, and which he referred to generally as having a procedural basis[200]), he said:

> It would not be entirely true to say that transaction set-off was substantive while independent set-off was procedural, because independent set-off does operate as a substantive reduction or extinction of the debt owed to the plaintiff. But it arrives at this result by procedural means.

This thesis is also reflected in Lord Hoffmann's later comment in the House of Lords in *Stein v Blake*,[201] that: 'Legal set-off does not affect the substantive rights of the parties against each other, at any rate until both causes of action have been merged in a judgment of the court.' Thus, the result is substantive, but the means of achieving it are procedural.

Acceleration and termination clauses

Prima facie, Shipton v Casson[202] seems at odds with the procedural nature of the Statutes. **2.57** The plaintiffs and the defendant had agreed that a debt should be payable by instalments, but that, in the event of default in the payment of any one instalment, the plaintiffs could accelerate the debt so that the full amount was payable. The plaintiffs alleged that the first instalment had not been paid in full, and accordingly they sued for the full debt. The defendant pleaded that he had sold some goods to the plaintiffs, and that the plaintiffs' debt for the price could be set off against the unpaid part of the instalment. On that basis, it was said that the instalment should be regarded as having been paid in full, and that the plaintiffs therefore were not entitled to accelerate the debt. That argument succeeded before the King's Bench.[203] But, while one can appreciate the justice of the result, the difficulty is in explaining it.[204] The defendant's right of set-off only entitled him to a defence to an action at law. But this should not have helped the defendant, because the point remained that he had not paid the first instalment on time. Payment of the instalment by way of a set-off would not have occurred until there was judgment for a set-off. On that basis there had been a default, and therefore the plaintiffs *prima facie* should have been entitled to accelerate. A Victorian case suggests an argument that may avoid the rigour of that analysis.[205] In issue in that case was a contract which entitled one party to terminate the contract if the other failed to pay any sum payable to the first party. Byrne J in the Victorian Supreme Court interpreted this as referring to a non-payment of a sum in respect of which the first party could have obtained judgment, so that non-payment in circumstances where the second party had a defence of set-off to an action for payment did not justify termination.

---

[199] See ch. 4 below.

[200] Hoffmann LJ said (at [1994] 1 WLR 1634, 1650) that, 'The procedural basis of independent set-off is reflected in the rule that the mere existence of liquidated cross-claims does not automatically extinguish the smaller debt.'

[201] [1996] 1 AC 243, 251.

[202] (1826) 5 B & C 378, 108 ER 141.

[203] Abbott CJ, Bayley, Holroyd and Littledale JJ.

[204] There would be no such difficulty in the case of a substantive defence of equitable set-off. See paras 4.45–4.47 below.

[205] *Auspac Trade International Pty Ltd v Victorian Dairy Industry Authority* (Vic SC, Byrne J, 30 June 1993, BC9300782 at 69–71). On appeal (Vic SC Appeal Div, 22 February 1994), see BC9406099 at 39.

E. Equitable Remedies

2.58 While the Statutes of Set-off merely provide a procedural defence to an action, so that separate and distinct debts remain in existence until judgment for a set-off, a court of equity may take into account the availability of a right of set-off when considering whether to grant an equitable remedy consequent upon the non-payment of a debt. Prior to judgment for a set-off, when the debts retain their separate identities, an entitlement to a set-off under the Statutes may constitute a ground for refusing the equitable relief sought.[206]

2.59 The point is illustrated by the decision of the Court of Appeal in *BICC Plc v Burndy Corporation*.[207] The plaintiff and the defendant were joint owners of various patents and other rights. The plaintiff was primarily responsible for paying the costs and fees in relation to the rights, subject to a right of reimbursement of one half by the defendant. If the defendant failed to reimburse, the plaintiff could require the defendant to transfer to it all the defendant's interest in the joint rights. The defendant failed to pay an invoice forwarded to it for its share of costs, but asserted that it was entitled to do so on the ground that the plaintiff was separately indebted to it, and therefore it had a right of set-off under the Statutes of Set-off for an amount which exceeded its own liability. The plaintiff then brought this action seeking specific performance of the assignment. Dillon LJ, with whose judgment Ackner LJ agreed, accepted that an equitable set-off available to the defendant would have provided a complete defence to a claim for specific performance, and he said that it should not make any difference that the set-off in issue was pursuant to the Statutes.[208] Kerr LJ adopted a different approach. In his opinion, the availability of a right of set-off to a defendant, whether in equity or under the Statutes, is not a defence *per se* to a claim for specific performance, but rather it constitutes a factor relevant to the exercise of the court's discretion whether to grant the equitable relief sought.[209]

2.60 The question of specific performance is considered in greater detail later.[210] It is suggested that the preferred approach is to have regard to the form of set-off in issue. Equitable set-off, being a substantive defence in equity,[211] should provide a defence to a claim for specific performance. This accords with Dillon LJ's view. But since the availability of a procedural defence under the Statutes does not affect the existence of the debts before judgment, there is attraction in Kerr LJ's opinion that it should simply be a discretionary factor in the determination whether to grant equitable relief.

2.61 *BICC v Burndy* does not stand as authority for the proposition that, because of the availability of the set-off, there had not been default.[212] Rather, given that a claim by the plaintiff

---

[206] In addition to *BICC v Burndy Corporation* (below), see *Dodd v Lydall* (1842) 1 Hare 331, 66 ER 1060 (decree of foreclosure), in which the set-off in issue appears to have been an equitable set-off arising by analogy with the Statutes of Set-off. See para. 3.07 below.

[207] [1985] 1 Ch 232.

[208] [1985] 1 Ch 232, 249.

[209] [1985] 1 Ch 232, 259.

[210] See paras 5.81–5.85 below.

[211] See paras 4.29–4.57 below.

[212] Compare McCracken, *The Banker's Remedy of Set-off* (3rd edn, 2010), 183–4.

for payment would have failed because of the defence of the set-off, it was considered inappropriate that a claim for equitable relief which depended upon non-payment instead should be available.[213]

Forfeiture and possession

In *BICC v Burndy* (above), Dillon LJ accepted that, in the case of leasehold premises, an **2.62** equitable set-off available to the tenant would provide a defence to a claim for forfeiture of the lease and possession of the premises for non-payment of rent, given that a claim for forfeiture and possession depends on the rent being unpaid.[214] In principle, this seems correct. If there is a substantive defence of equitable set-off, equity would not regard the rent as unpaid to the extent of the set-off.[215] But the tenor of Dillon LJ's judgment suggests that he considered that the same result would follow in the case of an entitlement to a procedural defence of set-off under the Statutes.[216] That view is doubtful, because prior to judgment for a set-off the mere entitlement to the set-off does not impugn the proposition that the rent was unpaid.[217] The question would be one of relief against forfeiture.

F. The Statutes of Set-off in Australia

The Statutes of Set-off were originally incorporated into the laws of the various Australian **2.63** jurisdictions[218] and of New Zealand.[219] They are still part of the laws of those jurisdictions,[220] with the exception of New South Wales, where they have nevertheless been re-enacted in a more modern form,[221] and in Queensland, where they have been repealed.[222]

---

[213] See the 'crucial question' framed by Dillon LJ at [1985] 1 Ch 232, 248, and also *Glencore Grain Ltd v Agros Trading Co* [1999] 2 Lloyd's Rep 410, 419. If the court were wrong in relation to specific performance, so that the availability of a right of set-off under the Statutes of Set-off was not a reason for refusing specific performance, Dillon and Kerr LJJ each accepted that it would have been a relevant circumstance to take into account in considering whether to grant relief against forfeiture by way of an extension of time to pay. See [1985] 1 Ch 232, 252 (Dillon LJ), 259 (Kerr LJ).

[214] [1985] 1 Ch 232, 249, 250, referring to *British Anzani (Felixstowe) Ltd v International Marine Management (UK) Ltd* [1980] QB 137. Compare paras 4.131–4.135 and 4.142–4.146 below in relation to a claim for possession by a mortgagee.

[215] See para. 4.30 below.

[216] [1985] 1 Ch 232, 249–251.

[217] See para. 2.38 above.

[218] See e.g. *Day & Dent Constructions Pty Ltd v North Australian Properties Pty Ltd* (1981) 34 ALR 595, 599, 600 (Northern Territory). For New South Wales and Queensland see, respectively, *Stehar Knitting Mills Pty Ltd v Southern Textile Converters Pty Ltd* [1980] 2 NSWLR 514, 522, and *Phillips v Mineral Resources Developments Pty Ltd* [1983] 2 Qd R 138, though note the discussion below of the present position in those states. In the case of South Australia and Western Australia, the incorporation would have resulted from their being 'settled colonies'. For other jurisdictions, see the Imperial Act (1824) 9 Geo. 4, c 83, s. 24. See generally Castles, 'The Reception and Status of English Law in Australia' (1963) 2 *Adelaide Law Review* 1. In the Australian Capital Territory, the operation of the Statutes has been expressly preserved by the Imperial Acts Application Ordinance 1986, s. 5 (together with Sch. 3 Pt 15 and 16).

[219] *Grant v NZMC Ltd* [1989] 1 NZLR 8, 11, and see the Imperial Laws Application Act 1988 (NZ), s. 3.

[220] In Victoria the Statutes were repealed by the Imperial Acts Application Act 1922, s. 7 (and see also the Imperial Acts Application Act 1980), though the legislation had a saving provision similar to that in the English legislation (the Civil Procedure Acts Repeal Act 1879, s. 2) which repealed the Statutes in England. See para. 2.06 above. The current position in Victoria in relation to set-off is considered below.

[221] See below.

[222] See below.

(1) New South Wales

2.64 In New South Wales, the Statutes were repealed by the Imperial Acts Application Act 1969 (NSW). The Statutes have also been repealed in England, by the Civil Procedure Acts Repeal Act 1879, though the English legislation contained a provision which has been interpreted as preserving the right of set-off originally conferred by the Statutes.[223] The New South Wales Act, however, did not have a similar saving provision, so that the operation of the Statutes of Set-off was not preserved in that jurisdiction.[224] On the other hand, the former Pt 15, r. 25 of the Supreme Court Rules (NSW) contemplated that a monetary cross-demand possessed by the defendant against the plaintiff, whether for an ascertained sum or not, could be included in the defence and set off against the plaintiff's claim. In *Stehar Knitting Mills Pty Ltd v Southern Textile Converters Pty Ltd*[225] Hutley and Glass JJA[226] said that Pt 15 r. 25 should take effect according to its literal terms. As a result, it appeared that in New South Wales *any* monetary cross-demand which was due and payable, whether it was liquidated or unliquidated and whether or not it was connected with the plaintiff's claim, could be the subject of a set-off in an action at law.[227] It was not necessary to show mutual debts or, if one of the demands was unliquidated, that the cross-demands were sufficiently closely connected so as to give rise to an equitable set-off.

2.65 In 1984, Pt 15 r. 25 was omitted from the Supreme Court Rules,[228] which had the consequence that the position outlined in *Stehar Knitting Mills* no longer applied. Since the Statutes had been repealed, the only right of set-off available at that time in New South Wales prior to bankruptcy or liquidation was the form of equitable set-off in which there is a sufficiently close connection between the demands.[229]

Civil Procedure Act 2005 (NSW), s. 21

2.66 In 1997 the New South Wales Law Reform Commission received a reference from the Attorney-General requesting the Commission to review the law relating to set-off. This was in response to a request from Justice Handley of the New South Wales Court of Appeal, that consideration be given to rectifying the situation caused by the repeal of the Statutes of Set-off. He suggested that the repeal may have been a mistake.[230] The Commission issued a discussion paper in 1998,[231] and a final report in 2000.[232] It recommended that

---

[223] *Hanak v Green* [1958] 2 QB 9, 22. See para. 2.06 above.

[224] *Stehar Knitting Mills Pty Ltd v Southern Textile Converters Pty Ltd* [1980] 2 NSWLR 514.

[225] [1980] 2 NSWLR 514.

[226] Mahoney JA not considering the issue.

[227] See Glass JA at [1980] 2 NSWLR 514, 523.

[228] Supreme Court Rules (Amendment No. 154) 1984.

[229] *McIntyre v Perkes* (1990) 22 FCR 260, 272; *Sydmar Pty Ltd v Statewise Developments Pty Ltd* (1987) 73 ALR 289, 292; *Roadshow Entertainment Pty Ltd v (ACN 053 006 269) Pty Ltd* (1997) 42 NSWLR 462, 481–2. See also *APM Wood Products Pty Ltd v Kimberley Homes Pty Ltd* (NSW SC, Cole J, 17 February 1989, BC8902896); *Buttrose v Versi* (NSW SC, Young J, 14 May 1992, BC9201877); *Abignano v Wenkart* (1998) 9 BPR 16,765 at 16,772. Compare Burton, 'Negotiability: Set-offs and Counterclaims,' *Directions in Finance Law* (1990), 70, and also *Akki Pty Ltd v Martin Hall Pty Ltd* (1994) 35 NSWLR 470, 479, in which Windeyer J assumed that a right of set-off existed in the case of mutual debts.

[230] New South Wales Law Reform Commission Report No. 94, 'Set-off', February 2000, paras 1.1–1.2.

[231] New South Wales Law Reform Commission Discussion Paper No. 40, 'Set-off, March 1998.

[232] New South Wales Law Reform Commission Report No. 94, 'Set-off', February 2000.

set-off as established by the Statutes of Set-off be reintroduced in New South Wales, but that it be restated in modern legislative form and style.[233] This recommendation was given effect by the enactment of the Civil Procedure Act 2005 (NSW), s. 21.

The purpose of s. 21 was to reintroduce the right of set-off formerly conferred by the Statutes of Set-off as a defence to an action for payment of a debt,[234] but restated in modern legislative form and style. Therefore, like the Statutes, s. 21(1) only permits a set-off in the case of mutual debts. Subsection 21(6) defines a 'debt' as any liquidated claim, which accords with the position under the Statutes. It has been held in relation to the Statutes that the term 'debts' is not confined to claims which could have been the subject of the old action of debt, but extends to 'liquidated debts, or money demands which can be readily and without difficulty ascertained'.[235] It encompasses, for example, claims in *quantum meruit* and *quantum valebat*, where work has been performed or goods sold without a price having been agreed.[236] This should apply equally to s. 21. Further, consistent with the interpretation accorded to the Statutes,[237] it is suggested that a debt which is unenforceable cannot form the basis of a defence under s. 21. **2.67**

For s. 21 to apply the debts must be mutual, which reflects the requirement under the Statutes of Set-off. The question whether mutuality exists in various circumstances has attracted a considerable amount of case law.[238] Essentially, it means that the debts must be between the same parties and be held in the same capacity or interest.[239] **2.68**

Subsection 21(1) permits a defendant to set off a debt owed by the plaintiff to the defendant that was due and payable at the time the defence of set-off was filed.[240] This has two aspects. The first is that a defendant can only set off a debt that is due and payable, which accords with the position under the Statutes.[241] A debt of the plaintiff which is payable *in futuro* or which is merely contingent cannot be included in a defence. The second aspect is that the relevant date for determining the availability of a set-off is the date that the defence is filed. This departs from the principle applied by the courts in England before the **2.69**

---

[233] New South Wales Law Reform Commission Report No. 94, 'Set-off', February 2000, recommendations 1 and 2.

[234] Section 21 refers to a plaintiff and a defendant, which implies that the set-off can only be given effect as a defence to an action for payment. The point was left open in *Australian Beverage Distributors Pty Ltd v Evans & Tate Premium Wines Pty Ltd* (2006) 58 ACSR 22 at [66]–[67] (decision affirmed in part (2007) 69 NSWLR 374), but it is consistent with the Statutes of Set-off. See paras 2.38–2.39 above. In *Williams v Calivil Park Holstein Pty Ltd* [2009] NSWSC 389 (application to set aside a statutory demand), Bryson AJ accepted (at [26]–[27]) that s. 21 did not apply as against a creditor who had a judgment or order for the payment of money. See also *Equity Australia Corporation Pty Ltd v Falgat Constructions Pty Ltd* (2005) 54 ACSR 813 (Macready AJ) (winding-up application).

[235] *Stooke v Taylor* (1880) 5 QBD 569, 575 (Cockburn CJ). See also *Victorian WorkCover Authority v Esso Australia Ltd* (2001) 307 CLR 520 at [30].

[236] *Victorian WorkCover Authority v Esso Australia Ltd* (2001) 207 CLR 520 at [30].

[237] See para. 2.46 above.

[238] See chs 11–13 below.

[239] See para. 11.01 below.

[240] See *Hall v Poolman* (2007) 65 ACSR 123 at [432]–[434] (cross-claim not due and payable when the defence was filed). The reference to the time of filing a defence does not preclude a defence of set-off being raised where, although not contained in a filed form of defence, the defence is litigated at the hearing. See *Equititrust Ltd v Franks* (2009) 258 ALR 388 at [59].

[241] See para. 2.29 above.

Judicature Acts in 1873 and 1875,[242] and accepted more recently in England,[243] that a set-off under the Statutes of Set-off can only be pleaded in bar to the plaintiff's claim if the set-off was available at the commencement of the plaintiff's action.[244] On this view, if the plaintiff became indebted to the defendant after the plaintiff commenced the action, or if a prior debt to the defendant only became payable after the action commenced, it could not be relied on as a defence of set-off. But there are other cases concerned with the Statutes which support a less restrictive view, that the date that the defence is filed should be the relevant date.[245] This is consistent with r. 14.17 of the Uniform Civil Procedure Rules 2005 (NSW), according to which a party may plead any matter even if the matter has arisen after the commencement of the proceedings, and its adoption as the basis for determining the availability of a set-off under s. 21 is to be welcomed.

2.70 Subsection 21(2) confirms that the right of set-off conferred by s. 21 applies to civil proceedings in which one or more of the mutual debts is owed by or to a deceased person who is represented by a legal personal representative. This accords with the first Statute of Set-off, which was expressed to apply where, 'if either party sue or be sued as executor or administrator . . . there are mutual debts between the testator or intestate and either party'.[246]

2.71 Subsection 21(3) provides that the right of set-off conferred by s. 21 does not apply to the extent to which the parties have agreed that debts may not be set off against each other. There was no equivalent provision in the original Statutes of Set-off, but it reflects the courts' acceptance of the view that parties to mutual debts can contract out of the right of set-off conferred by the Statutes.[247] On the other hand, an agreement that debts should not be set off will not be effective if either party becomes bankrupt or, in the case of a company, if it goes into liquidation. The prevailing view is that, unlike set-off under the Statutes, the set-off section in the insolvency legislation[248] is mandatory and cannot be contracted out of.[249]

2.72 Subsection 21(4) appears to be a statutory confirmation of the procedural nature of the defence,[250] but it is infelicitously expressed. It provides that the availability of a defence of set-off under s. 21 does not affect any other rights or obligations of a debtor or creditor 'in respect of mutual debts'. However, the procedural nature of the set-off does not go to the question of the subsistence of rights and obligations in respect of the mutual debts as such. Rather, it concerns the rights and obligations applicable in the case of each debt forming a part of the mutual debts. Nevertheless, the Law Reform Commission discussed the

---

[242] *Richards v James* (1848) 2 Ex 471, 154 ER 577.

[243] *Edmunds v Lloyds Italico SpA* [1986] 1 WLR 492, 495.

[244] See para. 2.08 above.

[245] *Wood v Goodwin* [1884] WN 17; *Ingleton v Coates* (1896) 2 ALR 154; *McColl's Wholesale Pty Ltd v State Bank of NSW* [1984] 3 NSWLR 365, 381; *Stein v Blake* [1996] AC 243, 251. See paras 2.09–2.10 above.

[246] See paras 13.131–13.132 below.

[247] See para. 5.133 below.

[248] Bankruptcy Act 1966 (Cth), s. 86 and, for company liquidation, the Corporations Act, s. 553C.

[249] *National Westminster Bank Ltd v Halesowen Presswork & Assemblies Ltd* [1972] AC 785; *Gye v McIntyre* (1991) 171 CLR 609, 622 ('the traditional and better view'). See paras 6.111–6.112 below.

[250] See paras 2.34–2.45 above.

procedural nature of the statutory set-off in its report,[251] and it would seem to be this concept that s. 21(4) was intended to address. This is consistent with the Commission's expressed desire to restate the law of set-off established by the Statutes.[252] It is also consistent with s. 21(1), which only contemplates a set-off where it is pleaded by way of defence in proceedings between a plaintiff and a defendant. Unless s. 21(4) is understood as confirming the procedural concept, it would make little sense.

The availability of a set-off under s. 21 is expressed[253] to be subject to s. 120 of the Industrial **2.73** Relations Act 1996 (NSW). Section 120 restricts the availability of a set-off to an employer in proceedings against it by an employee for payment of remuneration in certain circumstances where the employer has supplied goods or services to the employee.

(2) Criticism of the *Stehar Knitting Mills* case

Notwithstanding that the *Stehar Knitting Mills* case no longer sets out the position in **2.74** New South Wales, the view expressed in that case, that the Supreme Court Rules themselves could determine when a cross-demand may be set up as a defence,[254] is of general interest, particularly in Queensland where the Statutes of Set-off similarly no longer apply,[255] and in Victoria where it has been suggested that the distinction between set-off and counterclaim has been abolished in the ordinary case.[256] The analysis adopted in *Stehar Knitting Mills* therefore justifies further examination.

The essence of the approach in *Stehar Knitting Mills* was that the Statutes were wholly pro- **2.75** cedural in their operation,[257] in which case it was said that there was no reason why Supreme Court Rules made pursuant to legislation which contained a rule-making power with respect to matters of practice and procedure could not be the source of a similar right. This reasoning is beset with difficulty. In the first place, there is ample authority in England for the proposition that the Judicature Acts, and the Rules of the Supreme Court made pursuant to those Acts and their successors, themselves did not alter the rights of the parties and, in particular, did not confer any new rights of set-off.[258] In the *Stehar Knitting Mills* case

---

[251] New South Wales Law Reform Commission Report No. 94, 'Set-off', February 2000, paras 2.11–2.13.

[252] New South Wales Law Reform Commission Report No. 94, 'Set-off', February 2000, paras 4.23 and 4.24.

[253] Civil Procedure Act 2005 (NSW), s. 21(5).

[254] See para. 2.64 above.

[255] See paras 2.81–2.82 below.

[256] See para. 2.83 below.

[257] See also *Kennedy v General Credits Ltd* (1982) 2 BPR 9456, 9464 (Hope JA, with whose judgment Mahoney JA agreed).

[258] *Halsbury's Laws of England* (5th edn, 2009) vol. 11 ('Civil Procedure'), 503 para. 637; *Re Milan Tramways Co, ex p Theys* (1882) 22 Ch D 122, 126; *Stumore v Campbell & Co* [1892] 1 QB 314, 316–17; *Hanak v Green* [1958] 2 QB 9, 22 *per* Morris LJ ('the Judicature Acts conferred no new rights of set-off'); *Bank of Boston Connecticut v European Grain and Shipping Ltd* [1989] 1 AC 1056, 1109. See also, in Western Australia, *Westwind Air Charter Pty Ltd v Hawker De Havilland Ltd* (1990) 3 WAR 71, 84 *per* Murray J ('reference to the rules does not aid one to understand a full statement of the law' of set-off). In New South Wales, see *West Street Properties Pty Limited v Jamison* [1974] 2 NSWLR 435, 438, and in relation to the Federal Court Rules see *Griffiths v Commonwealth Bank of Australia* (1994) 123 ALR 111, 124. Compare *Edward Ward & Co v McDougall* [1972] VR 433, 436.

Hutley JA sought to distinguish the position in New South Wales from that in England on the ground that, in contrast to New South Wales, the repealing legislation in England preserved the right itself. It is difficult to follow this. If the question was whether the right of set-off in the case of mutual debts survived in New South Wales notwithstanding the repeal of the Statutes, the English position would have been distinguishable. But that was not the question. Hutley and Glass JJA said that the Supreme Court Rules under consideration allowed a cross-demand to be employed in a set-off in circumstances that were considerably broader than the right allowed by the Statutes. It is not clear why the question whether the rules should be interpreted literally so as to allow a right of set-off in those enlarged circumstances should depend upon the survival or otherwise of the right of set-off originally conferred by the Statutes in the limited case of mutual debts.

The defence is not wholly procedural

2.76 Of greater concern is the conclusion that the right of set-off conferred by the Statutes in the case of mutual debts is wholly procedural in its operation. Set-off under the Statutes admittedly is described as a procedural defence.[259] By this it is meant that separate and distinct debts remain in existence until judgment for a set-off, and moreover, as between the parties to the cross-demands, the defence has no effect until judgment. Prior to judgment, the rights consequent upon being a creditor still attach, as do the obligations and liabilities consequent upon being a debtor. It should be distinguished from the form of equitable set-off in which there is a sufficiently close connection between the demands.[260] This is properly described as a substantive defence, in the sense that prior to judgment it is unconscionable for the creditor to assert that moneys are due from the debtor while circumstances exist which support an equitable set-off.[261] But, notwithstanding that distinction, the right of set-off derived from the Statutes is still a defence, and for that reason the point was made earlier that it is not wholly procedural.[262] In particular, it can have a substantive effect on the rights of third parties.[263]

2.77 Meagher, Gummow and Lehane, in expressing reservation about the reasoning in *Stehar Knitting Mills*, commented that, in so far as rights of set-off operate as 'pleas in bar, they seem to be substantive rights'.[264] Similarly, in *Aectra Refining and Manufacturing Inc v Exmar NV*[265] Hoffmann LJ (as he then was) said that set-off under the Statutes of Set-off (which he termed independent set-off[266]) 'does operate as a substantive reduction or extinction of the debt owed to the plaintiff. But it arrives at this result by procedural means.'

---

[259] See paras 2.34–2.52 above.
[260] See ch. 4 below.
[261] See paras 4.29–4.57 below.
[262] See paras 2.53–2.62 above.
[263] See paras 2.54–2.55 above.
[264] *Meagher, Gummow and Lehane's Equity Doctrines and Remedies* (4th edn, 2002), 1066 [37–080]. See also *Gertig v Davies* (2003) 84 SASR 226 at [29]–[30].
[265] [1994] 1 WLR 1634, 1650.
[266] Adopting (at [1994] 1 WLR 1634, 1648) the terminology suggested in Wood, *English and International Set-Off* (1989), 8.

The result is substantive, though the means of achieving it are procedural. But if the result **2.78** is a matter of substance, so should the question of the circumstances in which that result is able to be brought about. Thus, it can be said on the basis of that distinction that a rule-making power limited to matters of practice and procedure would allow the making of rules as to the *means* of achieving a set-off, because that is a question of procedure. On the other hand, the power should not enable the making of rules as to the circumstances in which an extinction of cross-demands by way of set-off can be brought about, because that relates to a matter of substance.[267] This should be so notwithstanding the views expressed in the *Stehar Knitting Mills* case.

Hutley JA in *Stehar Knitting Mills* said that it is only if the rules governing set-off work an **2.79** automatic discharge that they cease to be procedural.[268] But it is not clear why that should be necessary, if the substantive quality of the defence is evident from other factors. Thus, equitable set-off, which is regarded as a substantive defence, does not operate as an automatic extinction of cross-demands.[269]

The right of set-off derived from the Statutes of Set-off is not purely procedural, and on that **2.80** basis it is difficult to support the reasoning in *Stehar Knitting Mills*. The ascertainment of the ambit of the right of set-off ordinarily is not a matter solely of interpreting the rules of court, and it should not make any difference whether in a particular jurisdiction the operation of the Statutes has or has not been preserved.

(3) Queensland

This view as to the nature of the set-off is also relevant to the position in Queensland. **2.81** Rule 173(1) of the Uniform Civil Procedure Rules (Qld) provides that: 'A defendant may rely on set-off (whether or not of an ascertained amount) as a defence to all or part of a claim made by the plaintiff whether or not it is also included as a counterclaim.' It has been suggested that r. 173 may allow any claim to be raised by way of set-off.[270] The suggestion to that effect was made in passing, however, and it does not accurately state the position.

In a number of cases concerned with the rule in force in Queensland before the current **2.82** rule,[271] it was assumed that the principle accepted in England also applied in Queensland, so that the rule itself did not determine when there could be a set-off and regard had to be

---

[267] Earlier in his judgment in *Aectra Refining* (at [1994] 1 WLR 1634, 1649), Hoffmann LJ referred to the Statutes of Set-off, 'whose effect is now to be found in RSC Ord 18, r. 17'. It is unlikely, however, that Hoffmann LJ had in mind that the rule itself was the source of the right of set-off. Ord. 18 r. 17 on its face extended to an unrelated damages cross-claim, but Hoffmann LJ did not suggest that the rule applied in that manner. Indeed, in 1879 Bramwell LJ rejected an argument to that effect in relation to the rule in the 1875 Judicature Act, in *Pellas v Neptune Marine Insurance Co* (1879) 5 CPD 34, 40–1. Similar comments may be made in relation to the current CPR r. 16.6.

[268] [1980] 2 NSWLR 514, 518. See also *Aectra Refining and Manufacturing Inc v Exmar NV* [1994] 1 WLR 1634, 1650.

[269] See para. 4.31 below.

[270] *Piccona v Suncorp Metway Insurance Ltd* (2005) 148 FCR 437 at [29].

[271] Ord. 22, r. 3 SCR (Qld).

had instead to the established principles of set-off.[272] After those cases, however, the Statutes of Set-off were repealed in Queensland, by the Imperial Acts Application Act 1984. The legislation was similar to the corresponding legislation in New South Wales (the Imperial Acts Application Act 1969), in that it did not expressly preserve the principle of set-off originally conferred by the Statutes.[273] As a result, it would appear that in Queensland there is no longer a statutory right of set-off in the case of mutual debts.[274] However, for the reasons given above in relation to New South Wales,[275] and notwithstanding the *Stehar Knitting Mills* case, the repeal without an express preservation of the right should not have the consequence that the rules of court themselves can provide a source of rights of set-off.[276] In any event, r. 173(1) in its terms does not purport to expand the scope of the defence. It does not provide a description of the circumstances in which a set-off is available, but rather it assumes the existence of the right. It simply recognizes a procedure for giving effect to a set-off, by providing that set-off can be relied on as a defence. This is particularly relevant to equitable set-off which, before the Judicature Acts, was given effect by way of an injunction to restrain proceedings at law,[277] but which now, as a result of the Judicature Acts[278] and rules of court such as r. 173(1), can be pleaded directly as a defence in the plaintiff's action.

(4) Victoria

2.83 The view that the Supreme Court Rules do not alter substantive rights is subject to legislation which provides to the contrary. Consider in that regard the position in Victoria.[279] In 1986 the judges of the Victorian Supreme Court made new Supreme Court Rules. Set-off was dealt with in r. 13.14, which allowed a defendant to include in the defence and set off against the plaintiff's claim any claim that the defendant in turn had against the plaintiff for the recovery of a debt or damages.[280] Tadgell J in the Victorian Supreme Court expressed the view that r. 13.14 allowed a cross-claim that would not have given rise to a set-off

---

[272] *Knockholt Pty Ltd v Graff* [1975] Qd R 88 (esp at 90); *General Credits (Finance) Pty Ltd v Stoyakovich* [1975] Qd R 352; *Eversure Textiles Co Ltd v Webb* [1978] Qd R 347 (esp. at 348). See also *Phillips v Mineral Resources Developments Pty Ltd* [1983] 2 Qd R 138.

[273] See para. 2.64 above.

[274] *Forsyth v Gibbs* [2009] 1 Qd R 403 at [4] n 1. In *Walker v Department of Social Security* (1995) 56 FCR 354, 374 (and see also *Cockerill v Westpac Banking Corporation* (1996) 142 ALR 227, 282–3) Cooper J said that there was 'a serious question' whether the 1984 legislation brought about this result.

[275] See paras 2.74–2.80 above.

[276] The principal rule-making power in Queensland relates to 'the practices and procedures' of the court. See the Supreme Court of Queensland Act 1991, s. 118(1)(a). Note however *Forsyth v Gibbs* [2009] 1 Qd R 403 at [4] n. 1, where the position was left open.

[277] See para. 3.01 below.

[278] The Judicature Acts, and the rules of court made under them, related only to matters of procedure and did not alter the rights of the parties. See para. 2.75 above.

[279] See Derham, 'Set-off in Victoria' (1999) 73 *Australian Law Journal* 754.

[280] See now the Supreme Court (General Civil Procedure) Rules 2005, r. 13.14. The 2005 rules were made under the Supreme Court Act 1986 (Vic), s. 25. Set-off under r. 13.14 is only available where there is a proceeding between parties and where the set-off is raised as a defence to a claim made by one party against the other. See *Australian Finance Direct Ltd v Director of Consumer Affairs Victoria* (2006) 16 VR 131 at [127].

according to traditional principles to be included in the defence.[281] In particular, he said that the 1986 rule made 'great inroads' upon the principle that an unliquidated pecuniary claim could not be set off by way of defence unless the defendant's claim impeached the plaintiff's legal demand or equity was on some other basis disposed to intervene.[282] This view is also accepted in the principal commentary on the Victorian Supreme Court rules,[283] and in a number of cases it has been assumed, although without discussion, that r. 13.14 itself confers the defence.[284] The basis of the argument is that the 1986 rules were 'ratified, validated and approved' by s. 41(1) of the Supreme Court (Rules of Procedure) Act 1986. When the Bill for the Act was introduced into Parliament, the Minister in the second reading speech[285] noted that some of the rules arguably changed the substantive law, and he said that, 'It is of particular importance to remove any doubt that this . . . category of rule is within the rule-making power of the judges.' Regard may be had to a second reading speech in interpreting an Act of Parliament,[286] and the question therefore is whether r. 13.14 was one of the rules that was intended to change the substantive law.

The notion that r. 13.14 was intended to have that effect gives rise to a complication. **2.84** According to Tadgell J,[287] r. 13.14 was not intended to be taken wholly literally. For example, he said that the rule should not be interpreted as overturning the principles that a claim for unliquidated damages cannot be pleaded as a defence to a claim upon a bill of exchange[288] or a claim for freight.[289] But that proposition would be far from clear if one were to accept the view that the rule has expanded the scope of the defence. In considering the scope of r. 13.14, the relevant question should be whether it was one of the new rules which, according to the second reading speech for the Supreme Court (Rules of Procedure) Act 1986, was intended to change the substantive law. If it was not, it could hardly be correct to say that the rule has had the effect suggested, because set-off in truth is not a matter

[281] *Moffat v Pinewood Resources Ltd* (Vic SC, 7 April 1989, BC8902914); *MEK Nominees Pty Ltd v Billboard Entertainments Pty Ltd* (1993) V Conv R 54–468 at 65,465. See also *Accident Compensation Commission v C. E. Heath Underwriting & Insurance (Aust) Pty Ltd* [1990] VR 224, 231.
[282] *Moffat v Pinewood Resources Ltd* (Vic SC, 7 April 1989, BC8902914 at 5a). See ch. 4 below in relation to equitable set-off.
[283] Williams, *Civil Procedure Victoria* (looseleaf) vol. 1, para. 13.14.25 ('The rule abolishes the distinction between set-off and counterclaim in the ordinary case'). Compare *L. U. Simon Builders Pty Ltd v H. D. Fowles* [1992] 2 VR 189, 195, in which Smith J left aside the issue of the extent to which r. 13.14 may change the substantive law.
[284] *John Holland Construction and Engineering Pty Ltd v Majorca Projects Pty Ltd* (Vic SC, Hansen J, 27 July 1995, BC9503852 at 12); *Westpac Banking Corporation v Market Services International Pty Ltd* (Vic SC, Batt J, 1 October 1996, BC9604615 at 60); *Novawest Contracting Pty Ltd v Taras Nominees Pty Ltd* [1998] VSC 205 at [22] and [23]. In each of these cases, however, the circumstances in any event would appear to have been such as to give rise to a set-off under established principles (in the case of *John Holland* and *Novawest*, if set-off otherwise had not been excluded by the contract). See also *Main Roads Construction Pty Ltd v Samary Enterprises Pty Ltd* [2005] VSC 388; *AFA Electronics Pty Ltd v Strathfield Group Wholesale Pty Ltd* [2001] VSC 289 at [87] fn 14.
[285] The speech was delivered by Mr Mathews, the Minister for the Arts, in the Victorian Legislative Assembly on 7 May 1986.
[286] Interpretation of Legislation Act 1984 (Vic), s. 35(b).
[287] *Moffat v Pinewood Resources Ltd* (Vic SC, 7 April 1989, BC8902914 at 6–8).
[288] See paras 5.25–5.31 below.
[289] See paras 5.02–5.16 below.

of pure procedure. If, on the other hand, r. 13.14 was intended to alter substantive law, it is not easy from a plain reading of the rule to justify an interpretation that the principles by which an unliquidated cross-demand cannot be pleaded as a set-off against a claim on a bill of exchange or a claim for freight have remained untouched.[290] On the assumption that the rule was intended to operate substantively, there is nothing in its language to suggest that those principles still apply.[291] This suggests that r. 13.14 was not intended to change substantive law. Indeed, Tadgell J also commented that: 'rule 13.14 is after all a rule of procedure, and it would not ordinarily be construed in a way that would abrogate or interfere with substantive rights.'[292] That comment serves to emphasize the point under discussion. Because set-off is a defence, the question of the availability of a set-off is not wholly a matter of procedure.[293] As Hoffmann LJ observed in relation to set-off under the Statutes of Set-off, the set-off operates as a substantive reduction or extinction of the plaintiff's claim, albeit that it arrives at that result by procedural means.[294] This would apply equally to a set-off under rules of court. Therefore, a rule which purported to expand the scope of the defence would constitute an interference with substantive rights, in the same way that a rule which purported to change the principles with respect to bills of exchange and freight would interfere with substantive rights.

2.85 Tadgell J's judgment proceeded on a false assumption, that set-off is simply a rule of procedure. If it is followed, it would raise the question of the effect that the expanded defence could have on the rights of third parties such as assignees.[295] It would be of little assistance to say, as Tadgell J suggested,[296] that the rule ordinarily should not be construed in a way that would abrogate or interfere with the substantive rights, if the conclusion that a cross-claim gives rise to a defence would have that consequence in relation to third party rights. This issue is considered later in the context of assignments of debts.[297]

2.86 Furthermore, for reasons set out later,[298] it is suggested that it is undesirable to expand the defence of set-off to include *any* monetary cross-demand, whether liquidated or unliquidated and whether or not it is connected with the plaintiff's claim.

---

[290] In *L. U. Simon Builders Pty Ltd v H. D. Fowles* [1992] 2 VR 189, 195 Smith J noted the qualifications discussed by Tadgell J, though he declined to express a view on the subject.

[291] Tadgell J's view in relation to bills of exchange and freight should be contrasted with the approach of the courts in New South Wales in interpreting the Common Law Procedure Act 1899 (NSW), s. 79, which provided that matters which were the subject of a cross-action between the parties could by leave of a judge be pleaded by way of set-off. Section 79 was repealed in 1970 by the Supreme Court Act (NSW), but before the repeal the courts accepted that it permitted a damages claim to be pleaded by way of set-off against a claim on a promissory note if the demands arose out of the same transaction. See *Karbowsky v Redaelli* (1914) 31 WN (NSW) 80; *Richardson v Hill* (1922) 22 SR (NSW) 326. The requirement that the demands should have originated in the same transaction followed from a requirement that the courts held was inherent in s. 79 and applied generally. See *Assets & General Finance Co v Crick* (1911) 28 WN (NSW) 91; *Austral Bronze Co Ltd v Sleigh* (1916) 34 WN (NSW) 143.

[292] *Moffat v Pinewood Resources Ltd* (Vic SC, 7 April 1989, BC8902914 at 6a).

[293] See paras 2.53–2.56 above.

[294] *Aectra Refining and Manufacturing Inc v Exmar NV* [1994] 1 WLR 1634, 1650. See para. 2.56 above.

[295] See paras 2.54–2.55 above.

[296] *Moffat v Pinewood Resources Ltd* (Vic SC, 7 April 1989, BC8902914 at 6a).

[297] See paras 17.17 and 17.18 below.

[298] See paras 5.163–5.177 below. This was also the view of the New South Wales Law Reform Commission in its report on 'Set-off', No. 94, February 2000, paras 4.10–4.13, 5.10–5.12.

G. Connected Cross-Demands at Common Law

In *Green v Farmer*[299] Lord Mansfield said: 'Where the nature of the employment, transac-   **2.87**
tion, or dealings, necessarily constitutes an account consisting of receipts and payments,
debts and credits; it is certain that only the balance can be the debt; and by the proper forms
of proceeding in Courts of Law or Equity, the balance only can be recovered.' *Green v
Farmer* was subsequently cited in the third edition of *Halsbury's Laws of England*[300] as
authority for the following proposition: 'Where opposing demands are connected by
originating in the same transaction the balance has always been regarded by the common
law as the debt so that no question of set-off arises . . .'

Lord Denning referred to that passage in *Halsbury* with evident approval in *Henriksens*   **2.88**
Rederi A/S v THZ Rolimpex (The Brede).[301] Indeed, its substance has a long history which
can be traced back to similar statements in early books on set-off, by Babington in 1827[302]
and Montague in 1828.[303] On the other hand, the proposition for which *Green v Farmer*
was cited in the third edition of *Halsbury* was questioned in the fourth edition.[304] In truth,
it is difficult to find evidence which supports a general common law principle that a balance
may be struck, without recourse to the principles of set-off, in a case in which there are
opposing demands which originated in the same transaction. With the exception of *Dale v
Sollett*[305] (see below), the cases to which Babington and Montague referred were instances
in which there was an agreement between the parties for payment of a liability,[306] or alternatively there was a custom by which payment could be effected by way of a deduction.[307]
What Lord Mansfield may have had in mind in *Green v Farmer* is the action for money had
and received,[308] as exemplified by *Dale v Sollett*. Alternatively, he may have contemplated a
running account. However, a running account is not a case of opposing demands. Rather,
it involves a series of debits and credits which gives rise to a single debt for the balance.[309]

There are, nevertheless, certain specific instances in which the common law has recognized   **2.89**
that connected cross-demands may produce a balance outside of the ambit of the established principles of set-off, though these constitute exceptions rather than the rule. One
such case is common law abatement, which may arise in an action for the agreed price of

---

[299] (1768) 4 Burr 2214, 2221.
[300] *Halsbury's Laws of England* (3rd edn, 1960) vol. 34, 396 para. 673 n *(l)*.
[301] [1974] 1 QB 233, 246.
[302] Babington, *The Law of Set-off and Mutual Credit* (1827), 4.
[303] Montague, *Summary of the Law of Set-off* (2nd edn, 1828), 1.
[304] *Halsbury's Laws of England* (4th edn, 1999) vol. 42, 250 para. 421 n 3 (and repeated in the 5th edn,
2009, vol. 11, 511, para. 653 n 3). See also, in New South Wales, *P. Rowe Graphics Pty Ltd v Scanagraphix Pty
Ltd* Young J, NSW SC, 6 Sept 1988.
[305] (1767) 4 Burr 2133, 98 ER 154.
[306] See *Dobson v Lockhart* (1793) 5 TR 133, 101 ER 77; *James v Kynnier* (1799) 5 Ves Jun 108, 31 ER 496;
Sturdy v Arnaud (1790) 3 TR 599, 100 ER 754; *Roper v Bumford* (1810) 3 Taunt 76, 128 ER 31. See also
Le Loir v Bristow (1815) 4 Camp 134, 171 ER 43.
[307] *Bamford v Harris* (1816) 1 Stark 343, 171 ER 492.
[308] This seems to have been the view of Young J in the New South Wales Supreme Court in *McCosker v
Lovett* (1995) 12 BCL 146, 149, 7 BPR 14,507, 14,510.
[309] See para. 1.01 above.

goods sold with a warranty, or of work to be performed pursuant to a contract, in circumstances where the defendant asserts that the goods by reason of non-compliance with the warranty, or the work as a result of failure to perform in accordance with the contract, is diminished in value or is of no value. This defence of abatement is discussed later.[310] Another instance is to be found in a judgment of Lord Mansfield which was handed down the year before his judgment in *Green v Farmer*. In *Dale v Sollett*[311] the King's Bench held that an agent who recovered money on behalf of his principal could deduct from the proceeds an amount sufficient to recompense him for his labour and service in relation to the recovery. This was not by way of a set-off as such, but rather it was characterized as a common law right of deduction.[312] Lord Mansfield explained the result on the following ground:[313]

> This is an action for money had and received to the plaintiff's use. The plaintiff can recover no more than he is in conscience and equity entitled to: which can be no more than what remains after deducting all just allowances which the defendant has a right to retain out of the very sum demanded. This is not in the nature of a cross-demand or mutual debt: it is a charge, which makes the sum of money received for the plaintiff's use so much less.

The action was for money had and received,[314] which is based on the principle of unjust enrichment. It cannot be asserted without the claimant at the same time giving credit for any payments received from the defendant.[315]

H. Judgments

2.90   Questions of set-off typically arise in the situation in which there are two unlitigated cross-claims. It may be the case, however, that one or both of the claims has proceeded to judgment, and the judgment creditor is seeking to rely on the judgment debt as a defence to an action by the judgment debtor to enforce another debt. Alternatively, enforcement of a judgment properly obtained at law may be sought to be stayed on the basis of an unlitigated cross-claim. A third possibility is that a judgment debtor may seek to set off the judgment against a judgment that he or she has obtained in separate proceedings against the judgment creditor. Each of these situations is considered in turn.

---

[310]   See paras 2.123–2.134 below.
[311]   (1767) 4 Burr 2133, 98 ER 112.
[312]   See the discussion in *Re Sutcliffe and Sons Ltd* [1933] 1 DLR 562, 566.
[313]   (1767) 4 Burr 2133, 2134, 98 ER 112, 113.
[314]   The action for money had and received, though of an equitable nature, is a common law action. See *Roxborough v Rothmans of Pall Mall Australia Ltd* (2001) 208 CLR 516 at [96]–[100] (Gummow J), [202]–[203] (Callinan J).
[315]   *Westdeutsche Landesbank v Islington BC* [1994] 4 All ER 890, 940–1 (Hobhouse J); *Dowell v Custombuilt Homes Pty Ltd* [2004] WASCA 171 at [118]. See also *Moses v Macferlan* (1760) 2 Burr 1005, 1010, 97 ER 676, 679. Similarly, the claimant may be required to give credit for expenditure incurred by the defendant which benefited the claimant. See *Ex p Elliott, re Jermyn* (1838) 3 Deac 343, 345; *Dowell v Custombuilt Homes Pty Ltd* at [118].

(1) Pleading a judgment debt as a defence under the Statutes

A judgment for payment of a sum of money gives rise to a debt,[316] and there is longstanding **2.91** authority for the proposition that it may form the basis of a defence of set-off under the Statutes to an action by the judgment debtor for payment of a separate debt owing to him or her by the judgment creditor.[317] The case would be one of mutual debts for the purpose of the Statutes. Moreover, this should apply equally when the judgment arose out of an action for unliquidated damages. When judgment is given the unliquidated claim is replaced by a judgment debt,[318] which should bring it within the ambit of the Statutes. In *Lawrence v Hayes*,[319] Acton and Talbot JJ justified the defendant's right to plead a judgment debt as a set-off against the debt the subject of the plaintiff's claim[320] on the ground that the damages claim on which the judgment debt was based was sufficiently closely connected with the plaintiff's claim so as to give rise to an equitable set-off.[321] But even apart from that ground, the judgment debt should have been able to give rise to a defence under the Statutes.

(2) Stay on enforcement of a judgment on the basis of an unlitigated cross-claim

Subject to the discussion below of equitable set-off, a judgment debtor cannot extinguish **2.92** or reduce the amount of the judgment by setting off an unlitigated simple contract debt owing to him or her by the judgment creditor.[322] However, the question may arise whether an unlitigated cross-claim may provide a ground for staying enforcement of the judgment. In that regard, a distinction must be drawn between a judgment which has been obtained pursuant to the procedure for summary judgment, and a judgment which the claimant obtained after the case went to trial.

Summary judgment is available where it appears that the defendant has no real prospect of **2.93** successfully defending the claim, and there is no other reason why the matter should not be

---

[316] *Hodsoll v Baxter* (1858) El Bl & El 884, 120 ER 739.

[317] *Watkins v Clark* (1862) 12 CB (NS) 277, 142 ER 1149. See also *Baskerville v Brown* (1761) 2 Burr 1229, 97 ER 804; *Russell v May* (1828) 7 LJOSKB 88; *Cochrane v Green* (1860) 9 CB(NS) 448, 142 ER 176; *Lewis v Eliades* [2005] EWCA Civ 1637 (where this was assumed). It has been suggested in Australia that a judgment the enforcement of which had been stayed can be pleaded as a set-off. See *Australian Beverage Distributors Pty Ltd v Evans and Tate Premium Wines Pty Ltd* (2007) 69 NSWLR 374 at [27] and [34], referring to *Pollack v Commissioner of Taxation* (1991) 32 FCR 40, 51. Formerly, if a judgment creditor had taken the body of the judgment debtor in execution pursuant to a writ of *capias ad satisfaciendum*, the judgment creditor could not set off the judgment as a defence to an action brought by the debtor on a cross-demand. See *Taylor v Waters* (1816) 5 M & S 103, 105 ER 989; *Tidd's Practice* (9th edn, 1828) vol. 2, 1029. See also, and compare, *Thompson v Parish* (1859) 28 LJCP 153 (overruling *Peacock v Jeffrey* (1809) 1 Taunt 426, 127 ER 899). However, this principle turned upon a peculiarity of the writ, that the taking of a debtor's body in execution constituted a bar to any other remedy against the debtor during his or her life, which included employing the judgment debt in a set-off.

[318] Compare *Jones v Thompson* (1858) El Bl & El 63, 120 ER 430 and *R v Hopkins* [1896] 1 QB 652.

[319] [1927] 2 KB 111.

[320] The plaintiff was an assignee of a debt, and as such took subject to the defence of set-off available to the defendant against the assignor. See ch. 17 below.

[321] See ch. 4 below.

[322] *Philipson v Caldwell* (1815) 6 Taunt 176, 128 ER 1001; *Hawkins v Baynes and Ireland* (1823) 1 LJOSKB 167; *Re Bank of Hindustan, China and Japan* (1867) LR 3 Ch App 125, 128–9; *Chitty's Practice* (3rd edn, 1837) vol. 1, 140. See also *Newton v Newton* (1832) 8 Bing 202, 203, 131 ER 378.

---

disposed of at trial.[323] In such a case, however, the court in its discretion, and depending on such factors as the degree of connection between the claim and the cross-claim and the ability of the claimant to satisfy any judgment on the cross-claim,[324] may order a stay on enforcement of the judgment.[325] Subject to those discretionary factors, the circumstances in which a stay would be ordered under former rules of court were expressed in various terms, such as that the cross-claim appeared to be so far plausible that it was not unreasonably possible for it to succeed, or that it was impossible to say that the cross-claim had no prospect of success, or that it was by no means frivolous.[326] These were not rigorous tests, and indeed it has been suggested that, under the Civil Procedure Rules, summary judgment and a delay on enforcement might be granted more frequently than hitherto.[327] This approach to the question of a stay has been justified on the ground that a summary judgment is a judgment obtained at the very outset of proceedings before the defendant has had an opportunity to litigate his or her cross-claim.[328] The position is different if the action in respect of which judgment was given had proceeded to trial. In such a case, the defendant will not obtain a stay simply by showing that he or she has an arguable cross-claim.[329] Rather, the defendant must show special circumstances which render it inexpedient to enforce the judgment.[330] The point is illustrated by *Schofield v Church Army*.[331] The appellant had dismissed the respondent from his employment for allegedly stealing money. An industrial tribunal found that the dismissal was unfair, and ordered the appellant to pay him compensation. The respondent obtained an *ex parte* order in the County Court to enforce the tribunal's order, and also a garnishee order *nisi* attaching the appellant's bank account. The amount standing the credit of the account was paid into court, and the respondent applied for an order that the money be paid to him. Meanwhile, the appellant had commenced a civil action against the respondent alleging theft, and opposed the payment to the respondent. The Court of Appeal[332] considered that the question whether the money should be handed over should be determined by the same principles applicable to whether execution on a judgment by writ of *fieri facias* should be stayed under RSC Ord. 47, r. 1. The court may order a stay in that situation if

---

[323] CPR r. 24.2.

[324] See para. 1.05 above.

[325] *Civil Procedure* (2010) vol. 1, paras 24.2.6 and 24.6.3, and see CPR, rr. 3.1(3) and 24.6. In New South Wales, see the Uniform Civil Procedure Rules (2005), r. 13.2.

[326] *Schofield v Church Army* [1986] 1 WLR 1328, 1334–5 (Dillon LJ), referring to Lord Esher and Lindley LJ in *Sheppards and Co v Wilkinson and Jarvis* (1889) 6 TLR 13.

[327] *Civil Procedure* (2010) vol. 1, para. 24.2.6.

[328] *Schofield v Church Army* [1986] 1 WLR 1328, 1335 (Dillon LJ).

[329] *Wagner v Laubscher Bros & Co* [1970] 2 QB 313, 317 (Lord Denning MR). See also *Australian Beverage Distributors Pty Ltd v Evans & Tate Premium Wines Pty Ltd* (2007) 69 NSWLR 374 at [145] in relation to enforcement of a costs order.

[330] *Schofield v Church Army* [1986] 1 WLR 1328, 1335; *State Bank of Victoria v Parry* [1989] WAR 240, 246. Compare *Akki Pty Ltd v Martin Hall Pty Ltd* (1994) 35 NSWLR 470, 479, in which Windeyer J considered that it was likely that a stay would be granted, although that was in the context of a case of mutual debts. Generally, it would take less time for a defendant to establish, and obtain judgment for, a debt owing to him or her, as opposed to prosecuting a damages claim, and in that circumstance the courts may be more sympathetic to a stay.

[331] [1986] 1 WLR 1328.

[332] Dillon and Croom-Johnson LJJ.

the applicant can show special circumstances.[333] In the instant case, there were indeed special circumstances sufficient to support a stay. The industrial tribunal had no jurisdiction to entertain the appellant's allegation of theft as a counterclaim to the respondent's claim for unfair dismissal. Nor was there any suggestion that the appellant had been dilatory in prosecuting its claim. Under the circumstances, it was considered to be inappropriate that the money be paid out before the civil action against the respondent came on for trial.

Equitable set-off

Consider that the cross-demands are such as to give rise to an equitable set-off,[334] either on the basis of equity acting by analogy with the legal right of set-off conferred by the Statutes of Set-off when the demands are mutual having regard to equitable rights,[335] or alternatively when there is a substantive defence of equitable set-off arising from a sufficiently close connection between the demands.[336]   **2.94**

In *Jenner v Morris*,[337] a judgment had been obtained at common law but the assistance of a   **2.95**
court of equity was required to enforce the judgment, and an equitable set-off was allowed to be raised in those proceedings. The plaintiff in that case had recovered judgment against the defendant, and filed a bill in equity for the purpose of enforcing the judgment against a life interest of the defendant in some real estate. The defendant argued as a defence that he had made loans to the plaintiff's wife so that she could purchase necessaries, the wife having been deserted by the plaintiff. While a person who supplied necessaries to a deserted wife could sue the husband at common law, the common law did not recognize a similar right in a person who merely lent money to the wife for the purpose of acquiring necessaries. It was held in *Jenner v Morris* that the lender in that circumstance had a claim in equity against the husband, on the basis that the lender could stand in the shoes of the supplier in respect of the supplier's remedy against the husband, and, further, that the defendant could set off against the judgment the plaintiff's liability to him in equity arising from the advances. In allowing a set-off equity acted by analogy with the legal right of set-off in the case of mutual debts, in that there was a debt due at common law from the defendant to the plaintiff in the form of the judgment, and a debt in equity owing by the plaintiff to the defendant.[338]

More generally, prior to the Judicature Acts, equitable set-offs could be enforced by means   **2.96**
of a common injunction restraining the plaintiff at law from proceeding with the action, or

---

[333] RSC Ord. 47, r. 1(a).

[334] See also the common law case of *Alliance Bank of London and Liverpool v Holford* (1864) 16 CB(NS) 460, 143 ER 1207, in which the demands originated from the one transaction.

[335] See para. 3.07 below.

[336] See ch. 4 below.

[337] (1860) 1 Dr & Sm 218, 62 ER 362; affirmed (1861) 3 De G F & J 45, 45 ER 795.

[338] See the comments by Kindersley VC in other proceedings between the same parties (*Jenner v Morris* (1860) 1 Dr & Sm 334, 336, 62 ER 407, 408) in relation to his earlier decision considered in the text. On appeal from that decision (*Jenner v Morris* (1861) 3 De G F & J 45, 45 ER 795), Lord Campbell commented (at 53–4, 798) that the cross-demands were wholly unconnected. It is therefore clear that a substantive defence of equitable set-off (see ch. 4 below) was not thought to be in issue.

by restraining execution on a judgment obtained by the plaintiff at law.[339] Since the Judicature Acts a defendant in an action at law has been able to plead an equitable set-off as a defence in that action, and an equitable set-off may be given effect after judgment by way of a stay of execution. In Australia there is authority which suggests that a defendant who could have employed a cross-claim as a set-off in the plaintiff's action but failed to do so could be estopped from bringing a later action in respect of it.[340] But apart from the question of estoppel, if a defendant seeks to pursue an equitable set-off in respect of an unlitigated cross-claim after the plaintiff has obtained judgment, it may be necessary, in the post-Judicature Acts system where a cross-claim can be pleaded directly as a defence in the plaintiff's action, for the defendant to show special circumstances in order to obtain a stay of execution.[341] This may be difficult to satisfy if the defendant has not diligently pursued the cross-claim.[342] Other circumstances may militate against a stay. In *Rawson v Samuel*[343] the applicants sought a common injunction to restrain execution on a judgment at law for damages for breach of contract until an account could be taken of amounts due under the contract. Lord Cottenham pointed out that the account would be long and complicated,[344] and it could not be assumed that the balance would be in favour of the applicants. If the balance in fact should be found to be in favour of the plaintiff at law, he said that the plaintiff at law might not be adequately compensated for the delay in enforcing the judgment. Accordingly, the applicants did not have a sufficient equitable ground to support an injunction.

Cross-claim accruing after judgment

2.97   Enforcement of a judgment will not generally be stayed on the basis of a cross-claim that accrued after the judgment.[345] It is not considered reasonable that a subsequently acquired cross-demand should delay the plaintiff from the benefit of his or her judgment until the validity of the cross-demand can be tested.[346] However, this restriction may not apply if the

---

[339] See e.g. *Hamp v Jones* (1840) 9 LJ Ch 258; *Smith v Parkes* (1852) 16 Beav 115, 51 ER 720. See para. 3.01 below.

[340] See paras 5.156–5.159 below. This is not the prevailing view in England, however. See para. 5.155 below.

[341] See para. 2.93 above. Compare *Meagher, Gummow and Lehane's Equity Doctrines and Remedies* (4th edn, 2002), 1066 [37-085] (referring to *Smith v Parkes* (1852) 16 Beav 115, 51 ER 720).

[342] *J. C. Scott Constructions v Mermaid Waters Tavern Pty Ltd* [1983] 2 Qd R 255, 259. Compare *Masterman v Malin* (1831) 7 Bing 435, 131 ER 168, in which the hearing of the cross-claim was ready to proceed, so that there would only have been a 'brief suspension' of the plaintiff's right to obtain the benefit of the judgment.

[343] (1841) Cr & Ph 161, 41 ER 451. See also *Preston v Strutton* (1792) 1 Anst 50, 145 ER 797; *Hill v Ziymak* (1908) 7 CLR 352.

[344] Compare *Clark v Cort* (1840) Cr & Ph 154, 41 ER 449, in which an account was also required to be taken, though apparently it was less complicated than that in *Rawson v Samuel* because Lord Cottenham held that the claim could be the subject of a set-off.

[345] *Whyte v O'Brien* (1824) 1 Sim & St 551, 57 ER 218; *Maw v Ulyatt* (1861) 31 LJ Ch 33. Compare *Gale v Luttrell* (1826) 1 Y & J 180, 148 ER 636; *R (on the Application of Bateman) v Legal Services Commission* [2001] EWHC Admin 797; *Klein v Jeffcoat* [1996] EWCA Civ 686.

[346] See Sir John Leach in *Whyte v O'Brien* (1824) 1 Sim & St 551, 57 ER 218.

demands are otherwise sufficiently closely connected to give rise to a substantive equitable set-off.[347]

(3) Setting off judgments and orders[348]

It has been the practice of the courts since the eighteenth century to allow one judgment or order for the payment of a sum of money to be set off against another.[349] This practice extends to a judgment for debt or damages[350] and to an order for costs,[351] including costs in bankruptcy proceedings[352] and costs ordered to be paid by an appeal court.[353] In Australia, it has been held to apply in the case of a judgment recognizing an entitlement to a share of the proceeds of property ordered to be sold.[354] It is not an objection that one of the judgments had existed at the commencement of the other action, and might have been

2.98

---

[347] See ch. 4 below. Compare *Roadshow Entertainment Pty Ltd v (ACN 053 006 269) Pty Ltd* (1997) 42 NSWLR 462, 489. See, on the other hand, *Alliance Bank of London and Liverpool v Holford* (1864) 16 CB(NS) 460, 143 ER 1207, which was decided at common law, though it is not clear from the report when the cross-claims accrued.

[348] A set-off of costs against costs is permitted by CPR r. 44.3(9). For set-off of judgments and orders in the County Court, or a judgment or order in the County Court against a judgment or order in the High Court, see the County Courts Act 1984, s. 72 and CPR Sch. 2, CCR Ord 22, r. 11. Section 72 was discussed in *Revenue and Customs Commissioners v Xicom Systems Pty Ltd* [2008] EWHC 1945 (Ch). In New South Wales, the Civil Procedure Act 2005, s. 96 sets out a procedure for setting off judgments in the same court (judgments in different Local Courts being deemed to be judgments of the same court). The section does not extend to judgments in the Supreme Court. For judgments in the same proceedings in the Supreme Court, see s. 90(2). Otherwise, judgments may be set off in the Supreme Court pursuant to the court's inherent jurisdiction in accordance with the principles discussed below. On the other hand, the Local Court in New South Wales is a court possessing statutory power and not inherent power. See *Watts v Rodgers* [2005] NSWSC 100 at [25]. Therefore, the power to set off judgments in the Local Court is confined to the power set out in the Civil Procedure Act 2005.

[349] See e.g. *Thrustout v Crafter* (1772) 2 Wm Bl 826, 96 ER 487. Montague, *Summary of the Law of Set-off* (2nd edn, 1828), 4, fn. dates the practice from 23 Geo II (1750), while according to Babington (*The Law of Set-off and Mutual Credit* (1827), 95–6), it became entrenched after 24 Geo II. Prior to then, the courts had refused to allow judgments to be set off. See e.g. *Butler v Inneys* (1731) 2 Stra 891, 93 ER 921; *Tito v Duthie* (1744) 2 Stra 1203, 93 ER 1128.

[350] See e.g. *Howell v Harding* (1807) 8 East 362, 103 ER 382 (debt); *Alliance Bank of London and Liverpool Ltd v Holford* (1864) 16 CB(NS) 460, 143 ER 1207 (debt against debt); *Pringle v Gloag* (1879) 10 Ch D 676 (debt against costs); *Edwards v Hope* (1885) 14 QBD 922, 926 (damages); *Bank of New South Wales v Preston* (1894) 20 VLR 1 (damages); *Goodfellow v Gray* [1899] 2 QB 498 (damages against damages); *Reid v Cupper* [1915] 2 KB 147, 150 (damages); *Puddephatt v Leith (No. 2)* [1916] 2 Ch 168, 173–4; *Anderson v Stasiuk (No. 2)* [1927] 1 DLR 533, 537; *Akki Pty Ltd v Martin Hall Pty Ltd* (1994) 35 NSWLR 470 (debt against costs); *Griffiths v Boral Resources (Qld) Pty Ltd (No. 2)* (2006) 157 FCR 112 at [25] (costs against judgment debt). See also *Flinn v Flinn* [1999] 3 VR 712 at [164] in relation to a non-party.

[351] *Reid v Cupper* [1915] 2 KB 147; *R v Leeds County Court, ex p Morris* [1990] 1 QB 523. See now CPR r. 44.3(9), and in Queensland UCPR 734.

[352] *Re A Debtor, No. 21 of 1950 (No. 2)* [1951] 1 Ch 612. The Divisional Court rejected an argument that costs given in bankruptcy can only be set off against other bankruptcy costs, and held that the petitioning creditor's liability for costs could be set off against the petitioning creditor's judgment debt. See also *Akki Pty Ltd v Martin Hall Pty Ltd* (1994) 35 NSWLR 470; *Griffiths v Boral Resources (Qld) Pty Ltd (No. 2)* (2006) 157 FCR 112.

[353] *Blakey v Latham* (1889) 41 Ch D 518, 523–4; *Wentworth v Wentworth* (NSW SC, Young J, 12 December 1994, BC9403409 at 10) (decision affirmed NSW CA, 21 February 1996, BC9600213); *Whitecap Leisure Ltd v John H Rundle Ltd* [2008] EWCA Civ 1026 at [13]. Compare *Knight v Knight* [1925] 1 Ch 835.

[354] *Sivritas v Sivritas (No. 2)* [2008] VSC 580. See also *Klein v Jeffcoat* [1996] EWCA Civ 686 (set-off of costs against any future sums which may be ordered to be paid on the taking of a partnership account); *Ben Hashem v Ali Shayif* [2009] EWHC 864 (Fam) at [77] and [80] (possible future liability).

pleaded as a defence in that action.[355] There is also authority for the proposition that a judgment the enforcement of which has been stayed can be relied on as a set-off.[356] In order to facilitate a set-off, an order for costs in a proceeding may be made on terms that payment is stayed pending the final determination of the proceeding,[357] and enforcement of a costs order may be stayed pending quantification of other costs orders.[358] The court's power to set off costs against costs is distinct from the taxing master's power under the rules of court, and is not limited by it.[359] In ordering a set-off of judgments or orders,[360] the court is at liberty to impose such terms as it considers reasonable and just.[361]

The nature of the set-off

2.99 It has long been recognized that a set-off of judgments and orders does not depend on the Statutes of Set-off.[362]

2.100 In *Lockley v National Blood Transfusion Service*,[363] the Court of Appeal characterized the set-off as an equitable set-off arising from a close connection between claims.[364] In delivering the court's judgment, Scott LJ said that the 'broad criterion' for determining the availability of the set-off is whether: 'the plaintiff's claim and the defendant's claim are so closely connected that it would be inequitable to allow the plaintiff's claim without taking into account the defendant's claim. As it has sometimes been put, the defendant's claim must,

---

[355] *Barker v Braham* (1773) 2 Wm Bl 869, 96 ER 512.
[356] *Australian Beverage Distributors Pty Ltd v Evans & Tate Premium Wines Pty Ltd* (2007) 69 NSWLR 374 at [34], referring to *Pollack v Commissioner of Taxation* (1991) 32 FCR 40, 51.
[357] See e.g. *R (on the Application of Bateman) v Legal Services Commission* [2001] EWHC Admin 797; *Klein v Jeffcoat* [1996] EWCA Civ 686; *Lockley v National Blood Transfusion Service* [1992] 1 WLR 492. See also the analogous circumstances in *Apostolidis v Kalenik* [2010] VSCA 80. Compare *Maloba v Waltham Forest London BC* [2008] 1 WLR 2079 at [65]–[74]. Compare also *Haydon-Baillie v Bank Julius Baer & Co Ltd* [2007] EWHC 3247 (Ch) at [57]–[64].
[358] *Ryan v South Sydney Junior Rugby League Club* [1975] 2 NSWLR 660; *Wentworth v Wentworth* (NSW CA, 21 February 1996, BC9600213 at 3–4). See also *Denidale Pty Ltd v Abigroup Contractors Pty Ltd (No. 2)* [2007] VSC 552 at [47]–[48]. A set-off of judgments can be given effect by way of a stay of execution. See *In re A Debtor, No. 21 of 1950 (No. 2)* [1951] 1 Ch 612; *Akki Pty Ltd v Martin Hall Pty Ltd* (1994) 35 NSWLR 470, 483; *Krishell Pty Ltd v Nilant* (2006) 32 WAR 540 at [83]. In an appropriate case a set-off may be ordered in relation to costs before the costs have been assessed. See e.g. *Cook v Swinfen* [1967] 1 WLR 457; *Elphick v Elliott* [2003] 1 Qd R 362; *Gertig v Davies* (2003) 85 SASR 226; *Dodds v Premier Sports Australia Pty Ltd (No. 2)* [2004] NSWSC 389 at [40]. For that purpose, the court may stay enforcement of a judgment until costs have been assessed. See *Dodds v Premier Sports Australia Pty Ltd (No. 2)* at [40]. Compare *Landini v New South Wales* [2009] NSWSC 431 at [53]. However, delay in having costs assessed is a factor which may be taken into account by the court in considering whether to exercise its discretion in favour of ordering a set-off. See para. 2.101 below. Payment of a costs order ordinarily will not be stayed pending determination of a separate claim. See *Australian Beverage Distributors Pty Ltd v Evans & Tate Premium Wines Pty Ltd* (2007) 69 NSWLR 374 at [145], and para. 2.93 above.
[359] *Reid v Cupper* [1915] 2 KB 147, 151; *Watkins Ltd v Calcaria* (1985) 78 FLR 417, 429; *Wentworth v Wentworth* (NSW SC, Young J, 12 December 1994, BC9403409 at 4 and 9).
[360] The set-off is not effective or operative until the court so orders. See *Gertig v Davies* (2003) 85 SASR 226 at [27].
[361] *Edwards v Hope* (1885) 14 QBD 922, 927.
[362] *Mitchell v Oldfield* (1791) 4 TR 123, 100 ER 929. See also *Wentworth v Wentworth* (NSW SC, Young J, 12 December 1994, BC9403409 at 4); *Australian Beverage Distributors Pty Ltd v Evans & Tate Premium Wines Pty Ltd* (2006) 58 ACSR 22 at [68] (decision affirmed in part (2007) 69 NSWLR 374).
[363] [1992] 1 WLR 492, 496–7 (Farquharson and Scott LJJ, and Sir John Megaw).
[364] See ch. 4 below.

in equity, impeach the plaintiff's claim.'[365] The concept of impeachment is the traditional foundation of equitable set-off.[366] Applying that principle, Scott LJ said that interlocutory costs which a plaintiff is ordered to pay to the defendant in the progress of an action for trial generally would impeach in equity the right of the plaintiff to recover costs of the action ordered to be paid by the defendant.[367] He said that: 'A set-off of costs against costs, when all are incurred in the prosecution or defence of the same action, seems so natural and equitable as not to need any special justification. I would expect a party objecting to the set-off to give some special reason for that objection.'[368] On the other hand, while Scott LJ accepted that it is not wrong in principle to order that interlocutory costs payable by a person are to be set off against any damages to which that person is or may become entitled in the proceeding, he nevertheless warned that it was 'less obvious that a set-off of costs against damages would always be justified'.[369]

The availability of a set-off in the case of judgments and orders is said to be a matter of the court's discretion.[370] In considering that proposition, Scott LJ drew a distinction between, on the one hand, a set-off of costs against costs and, on the other, a set-off of damages against damages or of costs against damages.[371] He accepted that the former is properly described as discretionary, since all questions regarding costs are subject to the court's discretion.[372] The discretion has been said to be a broad one, encompassing a variety of factors including the public interest, the efficient administration of justice and the conduct of the parties.[373] In particular, the insolvency of one of the parties is a strong consideration in favour of a set-off.[374] The degree of connection between the matters in which costs orders

2.101

---

[365] [1992] 1 WLR 492, 496–7.

[366] See paras 4.02 and 4.03 below.

[367] See also CPR r. 44.3(9).

[368] [1992] 1 WLR 492, 497. In Australia, see also *J. Earle Hermann Ltd v Municipality of North Sydney* (1914) 31 WN(NSW) 166; *Wentworth v Wentworth* (NSW SC, Young J, 12 December 1994, BC9403409 at 9) (decision affirmed NSW CA, 21 February 1996, BC9600213); *Eiros Pty Ltd v St George Bank Ltd* (2008) 68 ACSR 202 at [15].

[369] [1992] 1 WLR 492, 497.

[370] *Currie & Co v The Law Society* [1977] QB 990, 1000; *Edwards v Hope* (1885) 14 QBD 922, 926–7, 928; *Reid v Cupper* [1915] 2 KB 147 (costs against costs); *Puddephatt v Leith (No. 2)* [1916] 2 Ch 168, 173–4; *Knight v Knight* [1925] 1 Ch 835, 838–9, 840; *Re A Debtor, No. 21 of 1950 (No. 2)* [1951] 1 Ch 612, 617–18, 621; *R (on the Application of Burkett) v London Borough of Hammersmith and Fulham* [2004] EWCA Civ 1342 at [44]–[48]; *Revenue and Customs Commissioners v Xicom Systems Ltd* [2008] EWHC 1945 (Ch) at [16]–[25]; *Dadourian Group International Inc v Simms* [2009] EWCA Civ 1327 at [13]. In *Simpson v Lamb* (1857) 7 El & Bl 84, 89, 119 ER 1179, 1181 Lord Campbell CJ said that: 'There is no strict right to such a set-off . . .' In New South Wales, see also *Wentworth v Wentworth* (NSW SC, Young J, 12 December 1994, BC9403409) (affirmed NSW CA, 21 February 1996, BC9600213). The court particularly would favour a set-off if one of the parties has no prospect of paying its debts. See *Revenue and Customs Commissioners v Xicom Systems Ltd* at [18].

[371] [1992] 1 WLR 492, 497.

[372] Referring to the Supreme Court Act 1981, s. 51 (now the Senior Courts Act 1981).

[373] *Miller v Director of Public Prosecutions (No. 2)* [2004] NSWCA 249 at [13]. In the circumstances in issue in *Owen v Ministry of Defence* [2006] EWHC 990 (QB), it was held that it was not just that the claimant's proportionate share of the liability for generic costs be set off against the damages or costs awarded to him in his individual action.

[374] *Wentworth v Wentworth* (NSW SC, Young J, 12 December 1994, BC9403409 at 9) (referring to *Blakey v Latham* (1889) 41 Ch D 518, 521–2 and *Re A Debtor, No. 21 of 1950 (No. 2)* [1951] 1 Ch 612, 620); *Miller v Director of Public Prosecutions (No. 2)* [2004] NSWCA 249 at [28]. See also *Alliance Bank of London and*

have been made, and any delay in having costs assessed, have also been said to be relevant factors.[375] On the other hand, Scott LJ doubted that a set-off of damages against damages or of costs against damages could be described as a discretionary matter.

2.102 Subsequently, a differently constituted Court of Appeal,[376] in *R (on the Application of Burkett) v London Borough of Hammersmith and Fulham*,[377] agreed with Scott LJ as to the discretionary nature of the set-off of costs against costs. But because it is discretionary, the court said that the set-off is of a quite different nature to the defence of equitable set-off. The availability of an equitable set-off has to be decided as a matter of law, not discretion. Cases dealing with equitable set-off, therefore, were said to be irrelevant to the discretionary jurisdiction as to costs. The suggestion that equitable set-off is not discretionary is not entirely accurate. Discretion can be relevant in some circumstances.[378] However, it raises different considerations to a set-off of costs.

2.103 The Court of Appeal's criticism in the *Burkett* case of the proposition that the set-off is an equitable set-off was confined to a set-off of costs against costs. But, notwithstanding that the Court of Appeal on other occasions has referred to the analysis in the *Lockley* case with evident approval,[379] it is also difficult to accept that a set-off of judgments and orders in contexts other than costs against costs is an equitable set-off.[380] In the first place, equitable set-off is a defence to an action to enforce payment of a debt or other monetary obligation, the defence operating in equity as a complete or partial defeasance of the plaintiff's claim.[381] A set-off of judgments and orders, on the other hand, is not a defence in that sense. Essentially, it is a procedural device[382] which determines the amount for which execution may issue, and which may provide a ground for a stay of enforcement. Secondly, the practice of setting off judgments and orders was developed in the common law courts (as opposed to courts of equity) long before the Judicature Acts.[383] It is true that the availability

---

Liverpool Ltd v Holford (1864) 16 CB(NS) 460, 462, 143 ER 1207, 1208 in relation to cross-judgments other than for costs.

[375] *Wentworth v Wentworth* (NSW CA, 21 February 1996, BC9600213 at 3–4); *Miller v Director of Public Prosecutions (No. 2)* [2004] NSWCA 249 at [7]–[8]. See also *Elphick v Elliott* [2003] 1 Qd R 362 at [18]–[20] in relation to delay.

[376] Brooke, Buxton and Carnwath LJJ.

[377] [2004] EWCA Civ 1342 at [44]–[48].

[378] See paras 4.58–4.62 below.

[379] *Klein v Jeffcoat* [1996] EWCA Civ 686; *Gorman v Carter* [1998] EWCA Civ 1038. It has been approved in Queensland. See *Elphick v Elliott* [2003] 1 Qd R 362 at [14]–[17], though compare *Emanuel Management Pty Ltd v Foster's Brewing Group Ltd* (2003) 178 FLR 1 at [1466]. In Victoria, see *Danidale Pty Ltd v Abigroup Contractors Pty Ltd (No. 2)* [2007] VSC 552 at [45]–[47]. The reasoning of Laddie J in *Penwith District Council v V P Developments Ltd* [2005] 2 BCLC 607 at [20]–[26] (on the assumption, at [26], that the company would secure an award in its favour) is consistent with the analysis in the *Burkett* case.

[380] See *Revenue and Customs Commissioners v Xicom Systems Ltd* [2008] EWHC 1945 (Ch) at [15] (costs against judgment for unpaid tax). In Australia, see *Australian Beverage Distributors Pty Ltd v Evans & Tate Premium Wines Pty Ltd* (2006) 58 ACSR 22 at [68]–[70] (decision affirmed in part (2007) 69 NSWLR 374); *Griffiths v Boral Resources (Qld) Pty Ltd (No. 2)* (2006) 157 FCR 112 at [24].

[381] See the *Burkett* case [2004] EWCA Civ 1342 at [45], and para. 4.30 below.

[382] Compare *Gertig v Davies* (2003) 85 SASR 226 at [29].

[383] See e.g. *Thrustout v Crafter* (1772) 2 Wm Bl 826, 96 ER 487 (King's Bench: costs against debt and costs); *Mitchell v Oldfield* (1791) 4 TR 123, 100 ER 929 (King's Bench); *Glaister v Hewer* (1798) 8 TR 69, 101 ER 1271 (King's Bench: damages and costs against damages and costs) *Howell v Harding* (1807) 8 East

of the set-off has been described as an 'equitable' jurisdiction.[384] However, that expression was used in the sense of justice and fairness, as opposed to the jurisdiction of the Court of Chancery.[385]

The true basis of the set-off is the court's inherent jurisdiction.[386] Its purpose is to prevent **2.104** absurdity or injustice,[387] and to do that which is fair.[388] It has long been accepted that the inherent jurisdiction is not confined to judgments in the same action,[389] or the same

---

362, 103 ER 382 (King's Bench: costs against debt and costs); *Simpson v Hanley* (1813) 1 M & S 696, 105 ER 259 (King's Bench: damages and costs against debt and costs); *Bourne v Benett* (1827) 4 Bing 423, 130 ER 831 (Common Pleas: damages); *Bridges v Smyth* (1831) 8 Bing 29, 131 ER 311 (Common Pleas).

[384] *Edwards v Hope* (1885) 14 QBD 922, 926; *Reid v Cupper* [1915] 2 KB 147, 149; *Kostka v Addison* [1986] 1 Qd R 416, 420; *JPA Design and Build Ltd v Sentosa (UK) Ltd* [2009] EWHC 2312 (TCC) at [27]. See also *Simpson v Lamb* (1857) 7 El & Bl 84, 89, 90, 119 ER 1179, 1181; *Bank of New South Wales v Preston* (1894) 20 VLR 1. In *Barker v Braham* (1773) 2 Wm Bl 869, 872, 96 ER 512, 513 Blackstone J in the Common Pleas described it as an 'equitable remedy', while Lord Kenyon in the King's Bench in *Mitchell v Oldfield* (1791) 4 TR 123, 100 ER 929 referred to it as 'an equitable part of [the court's] jurisdiction'.

[385] See e.g. *Reid v Cupper* [1915] 2 KB 147, 149; *Krishell Pty Ltd v Nilant* (2006) 32 WAR 540 at [83]; *Griffiths v Boral Resources (Qld) Pty Ltd (No. 2)* (2006) 157 FCR 112 at [24]. See also *Australian Beverage Distributors Pty Ltd v Evans & Tate Premium Wines Pty Ltd* (2006) 58 ACSR 22 at [68]–[70] (decision affirmed in part (2007) 69 NSWLR 374). In the same way, Lord Mansfield in *Moses v Macferlan* (1760) 2 Burr 1005, 1012, 97 ER 676, 680–1 referred to the common law action for money had and received as a 'kind of equitable action, to recover back money, which ought not in justice to be kept', and as being based upon 'ties of natural justice and equity'. Nevertheless, the action is a common law action. See *Re Mason* [1928] 1 Ch 385, 393 and *Roxborough v Rothmans of Pall Mall Australia Ltd* (2001) 208 CLR 516 at [96]–[100] (Gummow J), [202]–[203] (Callinan J).

[386] *Mitchell v Oldfield* (1791) 4 TR 123, 100 ER 929 ('the general jurisdiction of the Court over the suitors in it'). In *Izzo v Philip Ross & Co* High Court of Justice Chancery Division, 31 July 2001 Neuberger J referred to 'a discretion in the court to allow set-off under its inherent jurisdiction', and said that, 'the power to set off judgment debts or orders arises from the court's inherent jurisdiction: it is not a case of normal equitable or common law or statutory set off'. A similar view has been accepted in Australia. See *Wentworth v Wentworth* (NSW CA, 21 February 1996, BC9600213 at 3) ('The court's general control of its own processes . . .'); *Australian Beverage Distributors Pty Ltd v Evans & Tate Premium Wines Pty Ltd* (2006) 58 ACSR 22 at [68]–[70] (decision affirmed in part (2007) 69 NSWLR 374); *Gertig v Davies* (2003) 85 SASR 226 at [23] and [24]; *Sivritas v Sivritas (No. 2)* [2008] VSC 580 at [22]. See also *Emanuel Management Pty Ltd v Foster's Brewing Group Ltd* (2003) 178 FLR 1 at [1466]. In Queensland compare *Elphick v Elliott* [2003] 1 Qd R 362 at [14]–[16], but see *Team Dynamik Racing Pty Ltd v Longhurst Racing Pty Ltd* [2008] QSC 36.

[387] *Edwards v Hope* (1885) 14 QBD 922, 926.

[388] *Reid v Cupper* [1915] 2 KB 147, 149; *Krishell Pty Ltd v Nilant* (2006) 32 WAR 540 at [83].

[389] *Edwards v Hope* (1885) 14 QBD 922, 926 ('distinct actions'), 927 ('cross judgments in the same action or in different actions and in the same or in different courts'); *Reid v Cupper* [1915] 2 KB 147 (costs against costs); *Ryan v South Sydney Junior Rugby League Club Ltd* [1975] 2 NSWLR 660 (costs against costs); *Australian Beverage Distributors Pty Ltd v Evans & Tate Premium Wines Pty Ltd* (2006) 58 ACSR 22 at [68] (decision affirmed in part (2007) 69 NSWLR 374). See e.g. the following cases, in which the report does not disclose any connection between the matters the subject of the judgments: *Mitchell v Oldfield* (1791) 4 TR 123, 100 ER 929 (debt and costs (to the extent that the set-off was not defeated by the solicitor's lien)); *Glaister v Hewer* (1798) 8 TR 69, 101 ER 1271 (damages and costs against damages and costs); *O'Connor v Murphy* (1791) 1 H Bl 657, 126 ER 375 (costs against costs); *Bridges v Smyth* (1831) 8 Bing 29, 131 ER 311 (damages); *Bristowe v Needham* (1844) 7 Man & G 648, 135 ER 261 (although a set-off was denied on another ground); *Simpson v Lamb* (1857) 7 El & Bl 84, 119 ER 1179 (damages and costs against costs); *Bank of New South Wales v Preston* (1894) 20 VLR 1 (debt and costs against damages and costs); *Goodfellow v Gray* [1899] 2 QB 498 (damages against damages); *Eiros Pty Ltd v St George Bank Ltd* (2008) 68 ACSR 202 at [16]–[20] (costs in different proceedings, and see at [18]–[19] in relation to the Victorian Supreme Court Rules). See also *Barker & Co v Hemming* (1880) 5 QBD 609, 612 (costs in different actions); *Re A Debtor, No. 21 of 1950 (No. 2)* [1951] 1 Ch 612 (judgment debtor's costs in setting aside a receiving order under the Bankruptcy Act 1914 set off against the judgment debt); *Preston v Nikolaidis* (NSW SC, Young J, 25 July 1996, BC9603594)

court,[390] without it being suggested that the claims nevertheless must be closely connected as for an equitable set-off.[391] Further, in so far as the Court of Appeal in the *Lockley* case was reticent to accept that a set-off of costs against damages would always be justified, it is nevertheless the case that the courts have been prepared to order a set-off of costs against a judgment for damages and costs, or of costs against a judgment for debt and costs,[392] or of costs against any future sums which may be ordered to be paid on the taking of a partnership account between the parties.[393] In truth, the distinction between damages and costs was not an important issue in the cases in which the jurisdiction was developed.[394]

2.105 In so far as r. 44.3(9) of the Civil Procedure Rules expressly provides for a set-off of costs against costs, it simply reflects the court's inherent power,[395] and it does not limit that power in other respects.[396]

Mutuality

2.106 A set-off of judgments and orders generally will not be permitted if the judgments and orders, although between the same parties, nevertheless are in different rights, as where one

('The ordinary rule is that where there are costs owing and payable by two parties, even in different pieces of litigation, that there is a set-off, unless there are strong reasons to the contrary'); Babington, *The Law of Set-off and Mutual Credit* (1827), 95 ('To assist the parties in the recovery of costs, and do justice between them, they are allowed to deduct or set off the costs, or debt and costs in one action against those in another'). Compare *Pringle v Gloag* (1879) 10 Ch D 676, 680; *Izzo v Philip Ross & Co* High Court of Justice Chancery Division, Neuberger J, 31 July 2001. Compare also *Throckmorton v Crowley* (1866) LR 3 Eq 196, 199 and *Collett v Preston* (1852) 15 Beav 458, 51 ER 615, which concerned the effect of a solicitor's lien, for which see below. Different considerations also applied when the debtor's body had been taken in execution. See *Taylor v Waters* (1816) 5 M & S 103, 105 ER 989 and *Thompson v Parish* (1859) 5 CB (NS) 685, 141 ER 276.

[390] *Puddephatt v Leith (No. 2)* [1916] 2 Ch 168, 174; *Simpson v Hanley* (1813) 1 M & S 696, 105 ER 259; *Bridges v Smyth* (1831) 8 Bing 29, 131 ER 311; *Bristowe v Needham* (1844) 7 Man & G 648, 649, 135 ER 261; *Simpson v Lamb* (1857) 7 El & Bl 84, 119 ER 1179. In Australia, see *Kostka v Addison* [1986] 1 Qd R 416, 420; *Konstandopoulos v Giammaria* [2004] NSWSC 1010; *Australian Beverage Distributors Pty Ltd v Evans & Tate Premium Wines Pty Ltd* (2006) 58 ACSR 22 at [68] (decision affirmed in part, see (2007) 69 NSWLR 374); *Griffiths v Boral Resources (Qld) Pty Ltd (No. 2)* (2006) 157 FCR 112 at [25].
[391] Compare *Alliance Bank of London and Liverpool Ltd v Holford* (1864) 16 CB(NS) 460, 463, 143 ER 1207, 1208, where it was emphasized that the subject of the judgments related to the same transaction. Compare also the former rules of court in relation to a solicitor's lien, for which see para. 2.118 below.
[392] See e.g. *Lang v Webber* (1815) 1 Price 375, 145 ER 1434 (costs against damages); *Thrustout v Crafter* (1772) 2 Wm Bl 826, 96 ER 487 (set-off against judgment for debt and costs); *Howell v Harding* (1807) 8 East 362, 103 ER 382 (interlocutory costs set off against a judgment for debt and costs); *Bank of New South Wales v Preston* (1894) 20 VLR 1 (judgment for debt and costs against a judgment for damages and costs); *Knight v Knight* [1925] 1 Ch 835 (costs of appeal set off against an entitlement to funds paid into court); *Gertig v Davies* (2003) 85 SASR 226 at [23] (costs against damages in the same action); *Dodds v Premier Sports Australia Pty Ltd (No. 2)* [2004] NSWSC 389 at [40] (costs against damages in the same proceeding); *Shine v English Churches Housing Group* [2004] EWCA Civ 434 at [136]–[138] (damages against interlocutory appeal costs); *Franses v Al Assad* [2007] EWHC 2442 (Ch) at [86]–[91]. See also *Goldsborough Mort & Co Ltd v Quin* (1910) 10 CLR 674.
[393] *Klein v Jeffcoat* [1996] EWCA Civ 686. See also *R (on the Application of Bateman) v Legal Services Commission* [2001] EWHC Admin 797; *Sivritas v Sivritas (No. 2)* [2008] VSC 580 (order for costs set off against the defendants' share of the eventual proceeds of sale of property ordered to be sold).
[394] See *Watkins Ltd v Calcaria Pty Ltd* (1985) 78 FLR 417, 432–3.
[395] See *Gertig v Davies* (2003) 85 SASR 226 at [23] in relation to the South Australian rules of court.
[396] *Reid v Cupper* [1915] 2 KB 147; *State Bank of New South Wales v Preston* (1894) 20 VLR 1, 3; *Ryan v South Sydney Junior Rugby League Club Ltd* [1975] 2 NSWLR 660, 664; *Wentworth v Wentworth* (NSW SC, Young J, 12 December 1994, BC9403409 at 11). See also paras 2.117 and 2.118 below in relation to the interpretation of the former Ord. LXV, r. 14.

of the parties is a trustee in relation to one judgment but in the other is interested in his or her own right.[397] Even before the Judicature Acts, the common law courts would take notice of a trust and deny a set-off on this ground.[398] Conversely, the common law courts in the exercise of their 'equitable' jurisdiction would look behind the parties on the record and allow a set-off of judgments if, having regard to the parties truly interested in the judgments, it was considered just that a set-off should occur.[399] This applied, for example, where A was a judgment creditor of B on one claim, and A had agreed to indemnify C against a judgment obtained by B against C on another claim, so that A was the party who as a matter of substance had the burden of the second judgment.[400]

The principle that cross-judgments should be held in the same right does not preclude a set-off in the situation in which one of the parties died after obtaining judgment.[401] Further, where A has a judgment against B and C, and B has a separate judgment against A, the courts have been prepared to set off the judgments on an application by B,[402] the reason being that execution can be levied against the assets of both B and C.[403] If, however, B has become bankrupt, and the separate action against A was brought by B's trustee in bankruptcy for the benefit of his or her general body of creditors, a set-off of the judgments will not generally be permitted in circumstances where a set-off is not available in relation to the underlying cross-claims under the set-off section in the insolvency legislation.[404]

2.107

---

[397] *David v Rees* [1904] 2 KB 435, 443, 445–6; *Bristowe v Needham* (1844) 7 Man & G 648, 135 ER 261. See also *John Dee Group Ltd v WMH (21) Ltd* [1998] BCC 972, 976. The position of the Legal Services Commission, as a funder of litigation through the provision of legal aid under the Access to Justice Act 1999, does not affect mutuality. See *R (on the Application of Burkett) v London Borough of Hammersmith and Fulham* [2004] EWCA Civ 1342 at [51]–[56]. In relation to legal aid, see paras 2.121–2.122 below.

[398] *Bristowe v Needham* (1844) 7 Man & G 648, 135 ER 261.

[399] See e.g. *O'Connor v Murphy* (1791) 1 H Bl 657, 126 ER 375; *Standeven v Murgatroyd* (1858) 27 LJ Ex 425. For a recent illustration in Queensland, see *Team Dynamik Racing Pty Ltd v Longhurst Racing Pty Ltd* [2008] QSC 36. Compare *Currie & Co v The Law Society* [1977] 1 QB 990 and *Adamson v Ede* [2008] NSWSC 1184 at [28] and [50]–[51] in relation to situations where the benefit of a judgment was assigned to the debtor on another judgment for the purpose of facilitating a set-off.

[400] *Schoole v Noble, Lett and Byrne* (1788) 1 H Bl 23, 126 ER 15; *O'Connor v Murphy* (1791) 1 H Bl 657, 126 ER 375; *Bourne v Benett* (1827) 4 Bing 423, 130 ER 831; *Standeven v Murgatroyd* (1858) 27 LJ Ex 425.

[401] *Bridges v Smyth* (1831) 8 Bing 29, 131 ER 311.

[402] *Roberts v Biggs* (1754) Barnes 146, 94 ER 848; *Mitchell v Oldfield* (1791) 4 TR 123, 100 ER 929; *Dennie v Elliott* (1795) 2 H Bl 587, 126 ER 719; *Ryan v South Sydney Junior Rugby League Club Ltd* [1975] 2 NSWLR 660, 663 (costs against costs); *Krishell Pty Ltd v Nilant* (2006) 32 WAR 540 at [82]–[85] (joint and several). Compare *Tatlers.com.au Pty Ltd v Davis* [2007] NSWSC 835 at [40]–[41], where (in the example) the set-off was sought by C and not by B, and *Campbell v Turner (No. 2)* [2007] QSC 362. In *Izzo v Philip Ross & Co* High Court of Justice Chancery Division, 31 July 2001 Neuberger J accepted (referring to *Dennie v Elliott* and *Mitchell v Oldfield*) that a costs order against a firm of solicitors and a separate costs order in favour of one of the partners in the firm could be set off, although a set-off was denied on another ground. See also *Bourne v Benett* (1827) 4 Bing 423, 130 ER 831, 1 Moo & P 141, in which there was the additional element that one of the defendants against whom judgment was given had agreed to indemnify the other defendants against the judgment, so that he was principally liable *inter se*. It was held that the judgment should be set off against a separate judgment obtained by that defendant against the plaintiff. In allowing the set-off, Park J emphasized this additional element, although the earlier cases referred to above suggest that a set-off may have been available in any event.

[403] *Loughan v O'Sullivan* [1922] 1 IR 103, 109. See also para. 12.21 below (joint and several debts).

[404] See paras 2.111–2.112 below.

Assignment

2.108 In the case of an assignment of a debt, there is a general equitable principle that an assignee takes subject to 'equities', which includes rights of set-off available to the debtor against the assignor.[405] The cut-off date for the application of the principle is the date that the debtor receives notice of the assignment. An assignee takes subject to a defence of set-off which accrued to the debtor against the assignor before the debtor had notice, whereas an assignee generally does not take subject to a set-off which accrued to the debtor after the debtor received notice.[406] There is an exception in the case of cross-demands which are sufficiently closely connected to give rise to an equitable set-off. In that situation, an assignee takes subject to an equitable set-off whether it arises before or after notice.[407] But generally the date of notice is the cut-off date.

2.109 An analogous principle has been applied in the case of an assignment of a judgment.[408] Cross judgments or orders in existence before notice of an assignment of one of them may give rise to an 'equity' to which the assignee takes subject.[409] Therefore, if a judgment debtor had a cross-judgment against the judgment creditor before the judgment debtor had notice that the judgment against him or her had been assigned to a third party, the third party assignee may take subject to the judgment debtor's prior equity.[410] But where the judgment debtor obtained a cross-judgment in a separate action against the assignor after the judgment debtor had notice of the assignment, there was no prior equity at the date of notice. In that circumstance, the Court of Queen's Bench in *Simpson v Lamb*[411] accepted that the rights of the assignee ordinarily would prevail.[412]

2.110 The taking subject to equities principle in the context of costs orders was referred to in *R (on the Application of Burkett) v London Borough of Hammersmith and Fulham*.[413] One of the parties to litigation was funded by the Legal Services Commission. It was argued that costs awarded to the funded person were owed to the Commission, rather than to the person, with the consequence that those costs could not be set off against another costs order obtained by the other party to the litigation against the funded person. The Court of Appeal rejected the argument on the ground that the costs order was made in favour of the

---

[405] See ch. 17 below.

[406] See paras 17.13–17.15 below.

[407] See para. 17.32 below.

[408] In relation to a situation where the benefit of a judgment was assigned to the debtor on another judgment for the purpose of facilitating a set-off, see *Currie & Co v The Law Society* [1977] 1 QB 990 and *Adamson v Ede* [2008] NSWSC 1184 at [28] and [50]–[51].

[409] See *Anderson v Stasiuk (No. 2)* [1927] 1 DLR 533 and *Watts v Rodgers* [2005] NSWSC 100 (see the statement of the facts at [7]–[9]).

[410] *Bank of New South Wales v Preston* (1894) 20 VLR 1; *Anderson v Stasiuk (No. 2)* [1927] 1 DLR 533. See also *Goodfellow v Gray* [1899] 2 QB 498 (charging order).

[411] (1857) 7 El & Bl 84, 89–90, 92, 119 ER 1179, 1181, 1182 (assignment after verdict and before judgment was obtained). See also *Knight v Knight* [1925] 1 Ch 835 (charging order); *Izzo v Philip Ross & Co* High Court of Justice Chancery Division, Neuberger J, 31 July 2001. In *Simpson v Lamb*, however, the assignee was the solicitor conducting litigation on behalf of the assignor, and it was said to be against public policy for the solicitor to purchase the subject of the suit before judgment. Therefore, the set-off prevailed.

[412] The discussion of the priority between the assignment and the set-off was *obiter* since the court went on to hold that the assignment was void.

[413] [2004] EWCA Civ 1342 at [57]–[59].

funded person, not the Commission, and therefore the position of the Commission did not preclude a set-off. As an alternative ground, the Court of Appeal considered that, even if the Commission could have asserted a right of its own to the costs the subject of the order, its position would have been similar to that of an assignee, and on that basis it would have taken subject to the set-off available to the other party. This point was made without reference to the date of the supposed assignment, but presumably the other party would have been aware of the position of the Commission from the outset. Therefore, if there were an assignment, it presumably would have occurred before any right to a set-off had accrued, in which case the Commission, being in a position similar to that of an assignee, *prima facie* should not have taken subject to the set-off. The Court of Appeal's comments favouring the set-off should be considered in the context of the particular circumstances in issue, which concerned costs orders made in the same proceeding. Those costs orders were closely connected and, similar to the position that applies in the case of an equitable set-off where there are closely connected cross-claims,[414] there is attraction in the view that an assignee should take subject to a set-off in relation to the orders whether the orders were made before or after the assignment.[415]

Bankruptcy

When one of the parties to cross-judgments or orders is bankrupt, Lord Ellenborough **2.111** expressed a 'strong disinclination' to permit a set-off in circumstances where the bankruptcy set-off section did not apply to the claims the subject of the judgments. This was in a situation where A had a judgment against B and C for money paid to their use, and B had a separate judgment against A for mesne profits. B had become bankrupt, and the separate action against A was brought by A's trustee in bankruptcy. Since the underlying cross-claims would not have been set off under the set-off provision in the Bankruptcy Act because of lack of mutuality,[416] Lord Ellenborough held that the cross-judgments could not be set off under the court's inherent jurisdiction.[417] He distinguished earlier authority,[418] which suggested that a set-off was available in that situation under the court's inherent jurisdiction notwithstanding the apparent lack of mutuality, on the ground that, in the case in question, there was no insolvency.[419]

It is not, however, an invariable rule that a set-off is denied under the inherent jurisdiction **2.112** in a bankruptcy where the bankruptcy set-off section does not apply.[420] Consider the South

---

[414] See para. 2.108 above.

[415] Compare *Knight v Knight* [1925] 1 Ch 835 (appeal costs).

[416] See ch. 12 below.

[417] *Doe v Darnton* (1802) 3 East 149, 102 ER 554. See also *Loughnan v O'Sullivan* [1922] 1 IR 103 (affirmed [1922] 1 IR 160), in which A had become bankrupt.

[418] *Mitchell v Oldfield* (1791) 4 TR 123, 100 ER 929.

[419] See para. 2.107 above.

[420] In *Alliance Bank of London & Liverpool Ltd v Holford* (1864) 16 CB(NS) 460, 143 ER 1207 cross-judgments arising out of the same transaction were set off in a bankruptcy. The bankruptcy set-off section (Bankruptcy Act 1849, s. 171 – see para. 6.41 below) was not mentioned in the judgments, but the cross-claims the subject of the judgments (other than a damages claim for dishonour of a cheque) would appear to have come within the terms of the section. See also *J. Earle Hermann Ltd v Municipality of North Sydney* (1914) 31 WN (NSW) 166 (cross-orders for costs in the same suit set off in a liquidation).

Australian decision in *Gertig v Davies*.[421] Davies had obtained an award of damages against Gertig for personal injury, but as a result of a payment into court costs were awarded to Gertig in an amount in excess of the damages. Gertig applied for an order that the costs be set off against the damages. Before an order was made on that application, Davies became bankrupt. It was accepted that the costs order was provable in the bankruptcy, but pursuant to the Bankruptcy Act 1966 (Cth), s. 116(2)(g) the damages award for personal injury did not vest in Davies's trustee in bankruptcy. This reflects a principle that also applies in English bankruptcy law, by which certain causes of action personal to a bankrupt do not vest in his trustee.[422] Because the damages award did not vest in Davies's trustee, the bankruptcy set-off section did not apply to the award and the costs order.[423] Nevertheless, the Full Court of the South Australian Supreme Court considered that they could be set off under the court's inherent jurisdiction. This was justified on the ground that the protection accorded to a bankrupt in relation to a personal cause of action only applies as against the trustee in bankruptcy. The asset is not protected in any other way.[424] Further, while the decision in favour of a set-off had the effect of securing a better outcome for Gertig than would be obtained by other creditors, this was not at the expense of the other creditors, who had no right of access to the asset represented by the damages award.[425] On the contrary, other creditors benefited from the set-off in that Gertig would not be proving in competition with them to the extent of the set-off.

2.113   Accepting that a set-off was available in principle, the question then arose in *Gertig v Davies* as to whether the set-off was constrained by s. 58(3) of the Australian Bankruptcy Act. Section 58(3) substantially corresponds with s. 285(3) of the English Insolvency Act 1986. It has two limbs. In the first place, s. 58(3)(a) prohibits a creditor of a bankrupt from enforcing a remedy against the person or property of the bankrupt in respect of a provable debt. Doyle CJ in the leading judgment concluded that, in the circumstances in issue in *Gertig v Davies*, where the damages award and the costs order arose out of the same proceeding, a set-off would not constitute the enforcement of a remedy against the property of Davies, but would merely be a step in the process of determining whether an enforceable judgment would be entered in favour of Davies, and, if so, for what amount.[426] The second limb, in s. 58(3)(b), prohibits the commencement of a legal proceeding against a bankrupt in respect of a provable debt without the leave of the court. Doyle CJ accepted that this could extend to a distinct step in an existing action, such as an application for costs. But in

---

[421] (2003) 85 SASR 226.

[422] *Heath v Tang* [1993] 1 WLR 1421, 1423. Compare *Cork v Rawlins* [2001] Ch 792.

[423] See para. 7.31 below.

[424] (2003) 85 SASR 226 at [19], [48] and [49].

[425] (2003) 85 SASR 226 at [20].

[426] (2003) 85 SASR 226 at [37]–[39], [50]. See also the explanation of *Gertig v Davies* in *Piccone v Suncorp Metway Insurance Ltd* (2005) 148 FCR 437 at [27]. In the *Piccone* case, the defendant in an action for personal injuries brought by a bankrupt pleaded a debt provable in the bankruptcy as a set-off under general law principles (as opposed to the bankruptcy set-off section – see para. 6.32 below). The Full Federal Court held that pleading the set-off was not contrary to s. 58(3)(a), commenting (at [29]) that, to the extent that a set-off would go in reduction of the bankrupt's claim, no question of enforcement would arise upon which s. 58(3)(a) could operate.

Gertig v Davies, the application for costs had been made *before* the bankruptcy, and so it was not within s. 58(3)(b). However, the Australian provision goes further than its English counterpart,[427] in that it applies not only to the commencement of a proceeding but also to the taking of a 'fresh step' in a proceeding after a bankruptcy. It was accepted that a 'fresh step' could be constituted by an application for an order for a set-off. Once again, the application for a set-off in that case was made before the bankruptcy, but Doyle CJ suggested that the 'fresh step' extended also to the hearing of the application after the bankruptcy and to the making of the decision on the application.[428] Since this occurred after the bankruptcy, it was held that it was necessary to obtain the leave of the court under s. 58(3)(b).

Solicitor's lien

A solicitor who conducts a case to trial is said to have a 'lien' over the proceeds of a judgment   **2.114** obtained by his or her client for the solicitor's costs in relation to the action. If the judgment were subject to a set-off, the fund available to satisfy the lien would be reduced to the extent of the set-off, to the evident disadvantage of the solicitor.

English and Australian courts have adopted different views as to the nature of the lien. In   **2.115** England it is said that a solicitor's lien is simply a right in the solicitor to ask for the court's intervention for his or her protection when, having obtained judgment for the client, there is a probability that the solicitor will be deprived of his or her costs.[429] In Australia, on the other hand, a solicitor's lien is regarded as more than a mere personal equity, and it is said that the assistance of the court is invoked, not to create rights, but to enforce them. The solicitor is regarded as having equitable rights analogous to an equitable assignment[430] of, or a charge[431] on, the fruits of the judgment or order produced by his or her efforts, which rights arise when the judgment or order is obtained.[432]

At one time the various common law courts adopted different attitudes to the treatment of   **2.116** a solicitor's lien in an application to set off judgments.[433] The Court of King's Bench held that the set-off was subject to the lien, so that the lien had to be satisfied before the set-off

---

[427] Insolvency Act 1986, s. 285(3)(b).

[428] (2003) 85 SASR 226 at [63]–[64]. Mullighan J agreed with Doyle CJ. Besanko J dissented on this point.

[429] *Halvanon Insurance Co Ltd v Central Reinsurance Corp* [1988] 3 All ER 857, 862; *Fairfold Properties Ltd v Exmouth Docks Co Ltd* [1993] Ch 196, 200–1; *Halsbury's Laws of England* (5th edn, 2009) vol. 66 ('Legal Professions'), 233–4, para. 1006.

[430] *Ex p Patience; Makinson v The Minister* (1940) 40 SR(NSW) 96, 100; *Worrell v Power & Power* (1993) 46 FCR 214, 224.

[431] *Philippa Power & Associates v Primrose Couper Cronin Rudkin* [1997] 2 Qd R 266, 273; *Carew Counsel Pty Ltd v French* (2002) 4 VR 172 at [33].

[432] *Worrell v Power & Power* (1993) 46 FCR 214 (preference claim against solicitors who transferred the proceeds of a costs order from their trust account to their general account in satisfaction of the client's liability for costs); *Akki Pty Ltd v Martin Hall Pty Ltd* (1994) 35 NSWLR 470, 474; *Philippa Power & Associates v Primrose Couper Cronin Rudkin* [1997] 2 Qd R 266; *Carew Counsel Pty Ltd v French* (2002) 4 VR 172 at [33]; *Michell Sillar McPhee (a firm) v First Industries Corp* [2006] WASCA 24 at [22].

[433] *Reid v Cupper* [1915] 2 KB 147, 155–6 (Pickford LJ); *R (on the Application of Burkett) v London Borough of Hammersmith and Fulham* [2004] EWCA Civ 1342 at [39]; *Akki Pty Ltd v Martin Hall Pty Ltd* (1994) 35 NSWLR 470, 480.

could take effect,[434] unless, it would seem, the orders arose in the same suit.[435] The Common Pleas, on the other hand, said that the lien should be disregarded, on the basis that the solicitor should look in the first instance to the personal security of his or her client for payment.[436] In so far as the Court of Exchequer was concerned, it has been said that it would exercise its discretion according to the circumstances.[437]

2.117 The position was also complicated by rules of court. In 1832, a rule was made for the purpose of unifying the practice of the courts.[438] It provided that: 'No set-off of damages or costs between parties shall be allowed to the prejudice of the attorney's lien for costs in the particular suit against which the set-off is sought,' subject to an exception in the case of interlocutory costs in the same suit.[439] The rule gave supremacy to the solicitor's lien. However, that principle was reversed by later rules of court in 1883.[440] Unlike the earlier rule, Ord. LXV, r. 14 of the 1883 rules was permissive, rather than prohibitory, in nature. It provided that: 'A set-off for damages or costs between parties may be allowed notwithstanding the solicitor's lien for costs in the particular cause or matter in which the set-off is sought.'[441]

2.118 Order LXV, r. 14 conferred a discretion on the court to set off damages or costs notwithstanding a solicitor's lien. The question of the scope of the rule came before the courts on a number of occasions.[442] On the one hand, there was authority for the proposition that the

---

[434] *Mitchell v Oldfield* (1791) 4 TR 123, 100 ER 929; *Randle v Fuller* (1795) 6 TR 456, 101 ER 646; *Mercer v Graves* (1872) LR 7 QB 499, 503. In *Mercer v Graves* a set-off in fact was allowed, but that was because of a peculiar circumstance, that the plaintiff was required to bring an action in England in order to enforce the judgment that he had obtained in Ireland. The lien that the plaintiff's solicitor had over the judgment for his costs was not such as to give rise to a relationship of trustee and beneficiary as between the plaintiff and the solicitor, and therefore there was no equitable ground for disallowing the set-off that otherwise was available to the defendant under the Statutes of Set-off in the plaintiff's action.

[435] *Howell v Harding* (1807) 8 East 362, 103 ER 382; *R v Burke* (1824) 7 LJOSKB 330. Compare *Aspinall v Stamp* (1824) 3 B & C 108, 107 ER 674. It appears that the Court of Chancery exercised its discretion in the same way as the King's Bench. See *Reid v Cupper* [1915] 2 KB 147, 156 (Pickford LJ), *Wright v Mudie* (1823) 1 Sim & St 266, 267–8, 57 ER 107, 108 and *Throckmorton v Crowley* (1866) LR 3 Eq 196, 199 (referring to *Collett v Preston* (1852) 15 Beav 458, 51 ER 615).

[436] *Hall v Ody* (1799) 2 Bos & Pul 28, 126 ER 1136; *Bridges v Smyth* (1831) 8 Bing 29, 131 ER 311; Babington, *The Law of Set-off and Mutual Credit* (1827), 111. Compare *Thompson v Parish* (1859) 5 CB (NS) 685, 695–6, 141 ER 276, 280.

[437] *Reid v Cupper* [1915] 2 KB 147, 156 (Pickford LJ).

[438] Reg Gen Hilary Term, 2 Will 4, r. 93. The rule was reproduced in rules made in 1853. See Reg Gen Hilary Term, 1853, r. 63 and *Reid v Cupper* [1915] 2 KB 147, 150. For a discussion of those rules, and of Ord. LXV, r. 14 in the 1883 rules referred to below, see *Edwards v Hope* (1885) 14 QBD 922; *Reid v Cupper*; *Re A Debtor, No. 21 of 1950 (No. 2)* [1951] 1 Ch 612, 619–20; *R (on the Application of Burkett) v London Borough of Hammersmith and Fulham* [2004] EWCA Civ 1342 at [38]–[41].

[439] The terms of the rule are set out in the judgment of Buckley LJ in *Reid v Cupper* [1915] 2 KB 147, 150.

[440] See *Reid v Cupper* [1915] 2 KB 147, 150, 154. In 1875 the Rules of the Supreme Court (Costs), r. 19 permitted a set-off of costs, but that rule referred only to the powers of the taxing master. See *Reid v Cupper* at 151, referring to *Barker & Co v Hemming* (1880) 5 QBD 609 (the terms of the rule are set out at 610), and *Pringle v Gloag* (1879) 10 Ch D 676. In Australia, see *Watkins Ltd v Calcaria Pty Ltd* (1985) 78 FLR 417, 429; *Wentworth v Wentworth* (NSW SC, Young J, 12 December 1994, BC9403409 at 9).

[441] The terms of Ord. LXV, r. 14 are reproduced in Buckley LJ's judgment in *Reid v Cupper* [1915] 2 KB 147, 150.

[442] Some of the cases are referred to in *R (on the Application of Burkett) v London Borough of Hammersmith and Fulham* [2004] EWCA Civ 1342 at [38].

rule permitted a set-off of damages in different actions.[443] On the other, it was held in the case of costs that the discretion conferred by the rule only applied where the orders for costs were in the same action or proceeding.[444] As a matter of substance the distinction is difficult to justify,[445] but the courts overcame the restrictive operation of the Ord. LXV, r. 14 in relation to costs by also accepting that the repeal of the prohibition in the earlier rules against set-off to the prejudice of an attorney's lien had the effect of reviving the court's inherent jurisdiction as to set-off.[446] Therefore, where costs were incurred in different actions, the court had a discretion to set them off under its inherent jurisdiction, notwithstanding a solicitor's lien, even though the set-off was not within the terms of r. 14.[447] In relation to costs in the same proceedings, the discretion is now set out in s. 51 of the Senior Courts Act 1981.[448]

The view of English courts now is that a set-off of judgments should not be refused on **2.119** account of a solicitor's lien if as between the parties themselves a set-off would be fair and just, and if no fraud or imposition has been practised upon the solicitor by collusion between the parties.[449]

The point was made earlier that Australian and English courts have a different view as to **2.120** the nature of a solicitor's lien, the prevailing view in Australia being that the lien confers rights analogous to an equitable assignment of or a charge on the fruits of the judgment obtained by the efforts of the solicitor.[450] Given this approach, it could perhaps be said that in Australia the question of competition between a solicitor's lien and a set-off should be determined on the basis of the principles which govern assignments,[451] so that the lien should not be defeated by a cross-judgment obtained after notice of the lien. However, in *Akki Pty Ltd v Martin Hall Pty Ltd*[452] Windeyer J in the New South Wales Supreme Court rejected the proposition that the Australian view of the lien would give a solicitor a better claim to payment of a judgment than the client would have had if there were no lien,[453] commenting that the court retains a discretion allowing it to control the extent of the

---

[443] *Goodfellow v Gray* [1899] 2 QB 498; *Reid v Cupper* [1915] 2 KB 147, 155; *R (on the Application of Burkett) v London Borough of Hammersmith and Fulham* [2004] EWCA Civ 1342 at [40].

[444] *David v Rees* [1904] 2 KB 435.

[445] See Pickford LJ's comments in *Reid v Cupper* [1915] 2 KB 147, 155.

[446] *Reid v Cupper* [1915] 2 KB 147, following *Edwards v Hope* (1885) 14 QBD 922. See also *Elphick v MMI General Insurance Ltd* [2002] QCA 347 at [7] (and later proceedings *Elphick v Elliott* [2003] 1 Qd R 362) in relation to rules of court in Queensland.

[447] *Reid v Cupper* [1915] 2 KB 147. See also *Bank of New South Wales v Preston* (1894) 20 VLR 1, 3; *Ryan v South Sydney Junior Rugby League Club Ltd* [1975] 2 NSWLR 660, 664.

[448] *R (on the Application of Burkett) v London Borough of Hammersmith and Fulham* [2004] EWCA Civ 1342 at [38] and [41] (referring to the Supreme Court Act 1981).

[449] *Puddephatt v Leith (No. 2)* [1916] 2 Ch 168; *Currie v The Law Society* [1977] 1 QB 990, 999. See also *Re A Debtor, No. 21 of 1950 (No. 2)* [1951] 1 Ch 612; *R (on the Application of Burkett) v London Borough of Hammersmith and Fulham* [2004] EWCA Civ 1342 (esp. at [39]–[42]); *Revenue and Customs Commissioners v Xicom Ltd* [2008] EWHC 1945 (Ch) at [17]. Compare *Knight v Knight* [1925] 1 Ch 835 (charging order in favour of solicitor).

[450] See para. 2.115 above.

[451] See paras 2.108–2.110 above.

[452] (1994) 35 NSWLR 470, 482–3.

[453] See also *Pong Property Development Pty Ltd v Paradise Constructors Pty Ltd* [2005] VSC 241 at [26].

solicitor's lien or to place limitations on the manner in which the solicitor may exercise it.[454] This is consistent with other authority in Australia, which accords with the English practice of favouring set-off over the solicitor's lien.[455]

Legal aid

2.121 In *Lockley v National Blood Transfusion Service*,[456] the Court of Appeal held that the question of set-off when one party to litigation was legally aided under the Legal Aid Act 1988 was no different from, and no more extensive than, the availability of set-off to or against parties who were not legally aided.[457] The Legal Aid Act 1988 was repealed in 2000 and replaced by the Access to Justice Act 1999, but the Court of Appeal has confirmed that the same principle applies under the new statutory regime.[458]

2.122 A set-off was denied in the context of legal aid in *Brookes v Harris*,[459] but the circumstances were exceptional. The plaintiff obtained judgment against the defendant for £130,000, and issued a writ of *fieri facias*. Pursuant to the writ, the sheriff entered into possession of a collection of music records, tapes and compact discs belonging to the defendant. The defendant, who was legally aided, successfully argued that the collection constituted tools of his trade, as a presenter of music programs, as a consequence of which the execution was unlawful.[460] The plaintiff accordingly was ordered to pay his costs. The plaintiff then sought to have the costs set off against the unsatisfied judgment. Ferris J held that a set-off was inappropriate in the circumstances. The defendant had sought to preserve his property from an illegal execution, and for that he required legal aid. Pursuant to the Legal Aid Act 1988, s. 16(6), however, the Legal Aid Board had a charge on the collection, as property preserved in the proceedings, as security for the payment of a contribution in respect of the

---

[454] Windeyer J suggested (at (1994) 35 NSWLR 470, 483) that the solicitor's rights under the lien may affect persons other than the client in cases where those persons may benefit from the efforts of the solicitor, but that there was no reason to extend that reasoning to cases where the actions of the solicitor are detrimental to a person against whom the lien is asserted (such as the judgment debtor).

[455] *J. Earle Hermann Ltd v Municipality of North Sydney* (1914) 31 WN (NSW) 166; *Butcher v Colonial Wholesale Meat Co Ltd* (1920) 38 WN(NSW) 24; *Miller & Co Machinery Pty Ltd v Bear* [1934] VLR 85; *Ryan v South Sydney Junior Rugby League Club Ltd* [1975] 2 NSWLR 660; *Wentworth v Wentworth* (NSW SC, Young J, 12 December 1994, BC9403409 at 11), (decision affirmed NSW CA, 21 February 1996, BC9600213); *Cade Pty Ltd v Thomson Simmons (No. 2)* [2000] SASC 369 (compromise and set-off of costs orders entered into in good faith); *Konstandopoulos v Giammaria* [2004] NSWSC 1010; *Pong Property Development Pty Ltd v Paradise Constructors Pty Ltd* [2005] VSC 241 at [26]. See also *Griffiths v Boral Resources (Qld) Pty Ltd (No. 2)* (2006) 157 FCR 112, which concerned a lawyer who had acted *pro bono* and who was seeking payment of fees from a costs order under Ord. 80, r. 9(2) FCR, as opposed to a solicitor's lien. In Queensland, UCPR 734(2) provides that cross-costs may be set off even though a solicitor for a party has a lien for costs of the proceeding. Compare *New South Wales v Hamod* [2009] NSWSC 1042, in which an order had been made that interlocutory costs be paid 'forthwith'.

[456] [1992] 1 WLR 492. See also *Klein v Jeffcoat* [1996] EWCA Civ 686; *Gorman v Carter* [1998] EWCA Civ 1038; *Arab Monetary Fund v Hashim* [1997] EWCA Civ 1298; *Shine v English Churches Housing Group* [2004] EWCA Civ 434 at [137].

[457] [1992] 1 WLR 492, 496. In Australia, see *Griffiths v Boral Resources (Qld) Pty Ltd (No. 2)* (2006) 157 FCR 112 in relation to a lawyer who had acted *pro bono* and who sought payment of fees under FCR Ord. 80, r. 9(2) from a costs order made in favour of the assisted litigant.

[458] *R (on the Application of Burkett) v London Borough of Hammersmith and Fulham* [2004] EWCA Civ 1342. See also *Hill v Bailey* [2003] EWHC 2835 (Ch).

[459] [1995] 1 WLR 918.

[460] Pursuant to the former Supreme Court Act 1981, s. 138(3A).

cost of the legal aid. Therefore, unless the plaintiff paid the costs ordered against him, the Legal Aid Board would have had the right to enforce a charge over the very property which was saved from the illegal execution. In his Lordship's opinion, it would not have been a just result if, having been guilty of unjustified conduct which led to the statutory charge being brought into existence, the plaintiff were to be allowed a set-off which would have prevented the amount secured by the charge being satisfied otherwise than by realization of the property in question.

I. Common Law Abatement

(1) General principle

It used to be the practice of the common law courts in an action for the agreed price of **2.123** goods sold with a warranty, or of work to be performed according to a contract, to allow the plaintiff to recover the stipulated sum and to require the defendant to bring a separate action for damages for any breach of warranty or contract by the plaintiff.[461] Compliance with the warranty, or proper performance of every portion of the work contracted for, was not regarded as a condition precedent to payment of the stipulated price.[462] However, in the latter part of the eighteenth century and the early part of the nineteenth century, the courts began to develop a different practice, by which the defendant in these cases was permitted to show that the goods by reason of non-compliance with the warranty, or the work in consequence of the improper performance of the contract, was diminished in value or was of no value.[463] This was not in the nature of raising the cross-demand as a set-off,[464] because at common law the only right of set-off available was under the Statutes of Set-off, and the Statutes required liquidated cross-demands in the form of mutual debts. Rather, the defendant was permitted to defend him or herself[465] by showing how much less the subject-matter of the contract was worth by reason of the breach, and to obtain an abatement of the price accordingly.[466] The revised practice received the imprimatur of the Court

---

[461] See e.g. *Broom v Davis* (1794) 7 East 480n, 103 ER 186.

[462] The ensuing discussion concerns an action for an agreed price. If the claimant is suing for a *quantum meruit* rather than for a specific agreed sum, he or she must prove what the work was worth, and it is open to the defendant in such a case to show that the work in fact was not worth as much as the claimant claims. See *Basten v Butter* (1806) 7 East 479, 103 ER 185; *Farnsworth v Garrard* (1807) 1 Camp 38, 170 ER 867; *Riverside Motors Pty Ltd v Abrahams* [1945] VLR 45.

[463] *King v Boston* (1789) 7 East 481n, 103 ER 186; *Germaine v Burton* (1821) 3 Stark 32, 171 ER 757 (sale by sample); *Poulton v Lattimore* (1829) 9 B & C 259, 109 ER 96; *Street v Blay* (1831) 2 B & Ad 456, 109 ER 1212; *Thornton v Place* (1832) 1 M & Rob 218, 174 ER 74 (plaintiff only entitled to the agreed price of work minus the sum necessary for the defendant to expend to complete the work according to the specifications); *Allen v Cameron* (1833) 1 C & M 832, 149 ER 635 (breach of obligation to tend trees the subject of a sale); *Cousins v Paddon* (1835) 2 C M & R 547, 150 ER 234; *Dicken v Neale* (1836) 1 M & W 556, 150 ER 556.

[464] *Bright v Rogers* [1917] 1 KB 917; *Hanak v Green* [1958] 2 QB 9, 17, 23; *Henriksens Rederi A/S v THZ Rolimpex (The Brede)* [1974] 1 QB 233, 252, 260; *United Dominions Corporation Ltd v Jaybe Homes Pty Ltd* [1978] Qd R 111, 115–16; *R v McKay, ex p Cassaniti* [1993] 2 Qd R 95. See also *A Cameron Ltd v John Mowlem & Co plc* (1990) 52 BLR 24, 33. Compare *BICC Plc v Burndy Corporation* [1985] 1 Ch 232, 246. Abatement is distinct from equitable set-off. See para. 2.134 below.

[465] The order as to costs should follow accordingly. See e.g. *Lowe v Holme* (1883) 10 QBD 286, though compare *Chell Engineering Ltd v Unit Tool and Engineering Co, Ltd* [1950] 1 All ER 378.

[466] *Mondel v Steel* (1841) 8 M & W 858, 870–2, 151 ER 1288, 1293–4 (Parke B).

of Exchequer[467] in the leading case of *Mondel v Steel*,[468] and it is now firmly established.[469] Indeed, in the case of a sale of goods the right has been enshrined in the sale of goods legislation.[470] On the other hand, it is tightly confined, being restricted to contracts for the sale of goods and for work and labour.[471] It is unlikely, for example, that it would be extended to a contract for the sale of shares with a warranty.[472]

2.124   The principle of abatement applies to building contracts,[473] including shipbuilding contracts.[474] At one time it was thought that the defence is not available in building cases in which the price is to be paid by instalment on certificate,[475] though that view is no longer current.[476] On the other hand, Parke B emphasized in *Mondel v Steel*[477] that the principle does not apply to all contracts for work and labour.[478] It does not apply, for example, to a contract of carriage,[479] including carriage by sea.[480] Further, Parke B accepted that it did not extend to an attorney, unless no benefit whatever was derived from the work.[481] Consistent with that view, the Court of Appeal in *Hutchinson v Harris*[482] doubted that

---

[467] Parke B, Alderson B, Gurney B and Rolfe B.

[468] (1841) 8 M & W 858, 151 ER 1288.

[469] In addition to the cases cited below, see *Parson v Sexton* (1847) 4 CB 899, 136 ER 763; *Dawson v Collis* (1851) 10 CB 523, 138 ER 208 and *Towerson v The Aspatria Agricultural Co-Operative Society Ltd* (1872) 27 LT 276 (sale by sample); *Webber v Aarons* [1972] 2 NSWLR 95. There cannot be both an award of damages for defective work and an abatement of the price, since it would result in payment twice over. See *Hutchinson v Harris* (1978) 10 BLR 19.

[470] Sale of Goods Act 1979, s. 53(1)(a).

[471] *Gilbert-Ash (Northern) Ltd v Modern Engineering (Bristol) Ltd* [1974] AC 689, 717 (Lord Diplock); *Aries Tanker Corporation v Total Transport Ltd* [1977] 1 WLR 185, 190; *Sim v Rotherham Metropolitan BC* [1987] 1 Ch 216, 258–9; *Mellowes Archital Ltd v Bell Projects Ltd* (1997) 87 BLR 26, 37.

[472] The issue was referred to, but not decided, in *Intag Microelectronics Pty Ltd v AWA Ltd* (1995) 18 ACSR 284, 287.

[473] See e.g. *Gilbert-Ash (Northern) Ltd v Modern Engineering (Bristol) Ltd* [1974] AC 689; *Acsim (Southern) Ltd v Danish Contracting & Development Co Ltd* (1989) 47 BLR 55. An employer who has wrongfully repudiated a building contract is not precluded from relying on abatement for defective work. See *Slater v C A Duquemin Ltd* (1992) 29 Con LR 24.

[474] *Mondel v Steel* (1841) 8 M & W 858, 151 ER 1288.

[475] *Dawnays Ltd v F G Minter Ltd* [1971] 1 WLR 1205.

[476] *Gilbert-Ash (Northern) Ltd v Modern Engineering (Bristol) Ltd* [1974] AC 689. See para. 5.50 below.

[477] (1841) 8 M & W 858, 871, 151 ER 1288, 1293.

[478] *Quaere* whether the common law defence of abatement ever extended to a claim for wages under a contract of employment. In *Sagar v H Ridehalgh and Son Ltd* [1931] 1 Ch 310, 326 Lord Hanworth MR accepted that it did, although Scott J left the question open in *Sim v Rotherham Metropolitan BC* [1987] 1 Ch 216, 255–9, commenting (at 257) that Lord Hanworth's remarks were *obiter* and seemed inconsistent with the restrictive comments about the nature of the defence made by Lord Diplock in *Gilbert-Ash (Northern) Ltd v Modern Engineering (Bristol) Ltd* [1974] AC 689, 717. For set-off in relation to contracts of employment, see paras 5.64–5.66 below.

[479] *Aries Tanker Corporation v Total Transport Ltd* [1977] 1 WLR 185, 190.

[480] *Mondel v Steel* (1841) 8 M & W 858, 871, 151 ER 1288, 1293 (freight); *Aries Tanker Corporation v Total Transport Ltd* [1977] 1 WLR 185. Nor is the defence available to defeat a claim for hire under a time charter of a ship. See *Century Textiles and Industry Ltd v Tomoe Shipping Co (Singapore) Pte Ltd (The Aditya Vaibhav)* [1991] 1 Lloyd's Rep 573, 575.

[481] (1841) 8 M & W 858, 871, 151 ER 1288, 1293, referring to *Templer v M'Lachlan* (1806) 2 Bos & Pul (NR) 136, 127 ER 576.

[482] (1978) 10 BLR 19, 31–2 (Stephenson LJ, with whom Waller and Cumming-Bruce LJJ agreed).

abatement extends to fees for professional services,[483] in that case for an architect.[484] This view has also been expressed in relation to a consulting engineer.[485] On the other hand, a cross-claim for professional negligence and breach of duty in such a case may give rise to an equitable set-off.[486]

If a bill of exchange is given as payment for the purchase of goods or for the performance of work, the bill must be honoured irrespective of any breach of contract by the seller which amounts only to a partial failure of consideration.[487] Similarly, the defence of abatement does not apply where the price of goods was paid by means of a loan from the seller secured by a mortgage, so that the sellor's action is for repayment of the loan rather than for payment of the price.[488] **2.125**

It was held in *Mondel v Steel* that the defendant in an action for the agreed price of work and labour, or of goods sold and delivered, is only entitled to an abatement to the extent that, at the time of delivery, the value of the subject-matter of the contract[489] has been reduced as a result of the breach of warranty or contract.[490] All claims beyond that, for example on **2.126**

---

[483] See also *Multiplex Constructions (UK) Ltd v Cleveland Bridge UK Ltd* [2006] EWHC 1341 (TCC) at [652] and [657] (defective design work). Compare *Foster Wheeler Group Engineering Ltd v Chevron UK Ltd* [1996] EWHC QB 381 at [296]–[324]. The contract in that case was for a variety of services, mainly but not exclusively of an engineering nature. Judge Humphrey Lloyd QC held on the facts that the contract was for work and labour rather than for professional services, so that the defence of abatement applied. In *Hutchinson v Harris* (1978) 10 BLR 19, 31 Stephenson LJ noted the decision in *Hoenig v Isaacs* [1952] 2 All ER 176, in which the Court of Appeal allowed an abatement in relation to a contract with an interior decorator and designer of furniture. However, the complaint in that case related to some articles of furniture which the designer supplied and which were said to be faulty and defective. In Victoria, the question whether abatement extends to fees for professional services was noted, but not decided, in *Hyder Consulting (Victoria) Pty Ltd v Transfield Pty Ltd* (2000) 17 BCL 129, 134. It has been suggested that abatement nevertheless may apply in this context as regards work not done. See *Keating on Building Contracts* (8th edn, 2006), 665. In relation to a claim for costs by a solicitor, see *Cachia v Isaacs* [1985] 3 NSWLR 366, 371, 376–7.

[484] One of the complaints against the architect was that she had incorrectly certified work as having been completed by a builder, and the plaintiff therefore sought to abate the architect's fees to the extent of the cost to remedy the work. However, Stephenson LJ pointed out (at (1978) 10 BLR 19, 31–2) that the subject-matter of the architect's contract was not the same as that of the builder. The fact that work that the architect certified had not been done by the builder did not necessarily mean that the architect had not done the equivalent amount of her own work.

[485] *Cathery v Lithodomos Ltd* (1987) 41 BLR 76, 82. In Victoria, the question of the application of the principle of abatement has been left open in the context of a design engineer (*Hyder Consulting (Victoria) Pty Ltd v Transfield Pty Ltd* (2000) 17 BCL 129 at [24]), and in relation to a contract for the provision of contract management consulting services. See *Leighton Contractors Pty Ltd v East Gippsland Catchment Management Authority* (2000) 17 BCL 35 at [25]. On the other hand, in *Dames & Moore Pty Ltd v Jovista Pty Ltd* (1998) 14 BCL 421 Master Sanderson in the Western Australian Supreme Court accepted, in a summary judgment application, that abatement may apply to a contract to design the materials and equipment for a conveying and crushing system.

[486] *Cathery v Lithodomos Ltd* (1987) 41 BLR 76, 82. See also *Cathery* in relation to security for costs in such a case.

[487] See paras 5.25–5.31 below.

[488] *Bow, McLachlan & Co, Ltd v Ship 'Camosun'* [1909] AC 597, 610–13. See para. 4.128 below.

[489] In the case of a sale of goods, the defence of abatement is only available when the claimant's action is for the price of the same goods in which the defect occurred. See *W. Pope & Co Pty Ltd v Edward Souery & Co Pty Ltd* [1983] WAR 117 and *Bayview Quarries Pty Ltd v Castley Development Pty Ltd* [1963] VR 445 in relation to equitable set-off.

[490] In addition to the cases cited below, see *Bow, McLachlan & Co, Ltd v Ship 'Camosun'* [1909] AC 597, 605; *Henriksens Rederi A/S v THZ Rolimpex (The Brede)* [1974] 1 QB 233, 248; *Hotel Services Ltd v Hilton*

account of a subsequent necessity for more extensive repairs,[491] or for damages for delay,[492] or for misrepresentation not amounting to a breach of warranty,[493] or damage caused to anything other than that which a contractor has constructed,[494] or incidental claims in respect of overheads and insurance,[495] will not result in an abatement under the common law principle. Two points should be noted in relation to this limitation. The first is that, following the expansion in recent times of the defence of equitable set-off,[496] a damages claim which could not form the subject of an abatement might now give rise to a defence under the equitable principle.[497] The second is that, in the case of a sale of goods, s. 53(1)(a) of the Sale of Goods Act 1979 may have taken the matter further than the common law position. Section 53(1)(a) provides that a damages claim for breach of warranty by a seller may be set up in diminution or extinction of the price. One of the warranties set out in the Act is that the buyer will enjoy quiet possession of the goods.[498] In Australia the High Court has held that this encompasses a subsequent interference with the goods by the seller and, further, that this breach could be set up in diminution of the price pursuant to the New South Wales equivalent of s. 53(1)(a).[499] Yet, this could hardly be regarded as evidencing a reduction in the value of the goods as they were delivered. The notion that this breach of warranty may come within the ambit of s. 53(1)(a) is difficult to reconcile with the view that s. 53(1)(a) is a codification of the principle laid down in *Mondel v Steel*.[500]

2.127 The measure of the abatement is the reduction in the value of the goods or the works caused by the breach.[501] In the case of a contract for the sale of goods, this, *prima facie*,

---

International Hotels (UK) Ltd [2000] BLR 235, 239 (referring to *Mellowes Archital Ltd v Bell Projects Ltd* (1997) 87 BLR 26).

[491] As in *Mondel v Steel* (1841) 8 M & W 858, 151 ER 1288. See also *Davis v Hedges* (1871) LR 6 QB 687, 691; *R v McKay, ex p Cassaniti* [1993] 2 Qd R 95, 100.

[492] See *Oastler v Pound* (1863) 7 LT 852; *Henriksens Rederi A/S v THZ Rolimpex (The Brede)* [1974] 1 QB 233, 248; *Mellowes Archital Ltd v Bell Projects Ltd* (1997) 87 BLR 26. This is also implicit in *Hermcrest plc v G Percy Trentham Ltd* (1991) 53 BLR 104 (esp. at 112–13). Compare Windeyer J in *Healing (Sales) Pty Ltd v Inglis Electrix Pty Ltd* (1968) 121 CLR 584, 618.

[493] *Intag Microelectronics Pty Ltd v AWA Ltd* (1995) 18 ACSR 284, 287. Similarly, a claim for damages for breach of the Trade Practices Act 1974 (Cth), not amounting to a breach of contract, will not give rise to a defence of abatement. See *Intag v AWA* at 287.

[494] *Multiplex Constructions (UK) Ltd v Cleveland Bridge UK Ltd* [2006] EWHC 1341 (TCC) at [652].

[495] *Multiplex Constructions (UK) Ltd v Cleveland Bridge UK Ltd* [2006] EWHC 1341 (TCC) at [655].

[496] See ch. 4 below.

[497] *R v McKay, ex p Cassaniti* [1993] 2 Qd R 95, 100; *Henriksens Rederi A/S v THZ Rolimpex (The Brede)* [1974] 1 QB 233, 248. Thus, a cross-demand for damages for delay may be employed in a set-off. See e.g. *Young v Kitchin* (1878) 3 Ex D 127; *Mitchell v Purnell Motors Pty Ltd* [1961] NSWR 165; *Galambos & Son Pty Ltd v McIntyre* (1974) 5 ACTR 10; *Henriksens Rederi v Rolimpex* at 248.

[498] Sale of Goods Act 1979, s. 12(2).

[499] *Healing (Sales) Pty Ltd v Inglis Electrix Pty Ltd* (1968) 121 CLR 584. Indeed, Barwick CJ and Menzies J suggested in their joint judgment (at 595) that the equivalent of s. 53(1)(a) allowed a buyer to set up any breach of warranty against the price.

[500] *Multiplex Constructions (UK) Ltd v Cleveland Bridge UK Ltd* [2006] EWHC 1341 (TCC) at [646] (referring to *Gilbert-Ash (Northern) Ltd v Modern Engineering (Bristol) Ltd* [1974] AC 689, 717); *Benjamin's Sale of Goods* (7th edn, 2006), 1067–8. See also the minority view of Windeyer J in *Healing v Inglis* (1968) 121 CLR 584, 617–18.

[501] *Henriksens Rederi A/S v THZ Rolimpex (The Brede)* [1974] 1 QB 233, 247–8; *Mellowes Archital Ltd v Bell Projects Ltd* (1997) 87 BLR 26, 37, 39; *Multiplex Constructions (UK) Ltd v Cleveland Bridge UK Ltd* [2006] EWHC 1341 (TCC) at [652].

is the difference between the value of the goods at the time of delivery and the value they would have had if they had complied with the warranty.[502] In the case of a contract for work and labour, in some cases the measure of abatement may be determined by comparing the current market value of the thing which has been constructed with the market value which it ought to have had,[503] but usually it would be the cost of remedial work required to correct defects in the work.[504]

The defendant in an action for the agreed price of goods or of work and labour is not bound **2.128** to set up the claim for breach of warranty or for failure to perform the work properly as a defence in that action. He or she may choose to pay the price and bring a separate action for his or her damages.[505] In the case of a contract for the sale of goods, this principle is reflected in s. 53(1)(b) of the Sale of Goods Act 1979. Alternatively, the purchaser of the goods or services may sue for damages *before* paying the price. In such a case, there is no principle of abatement to which the seller may have recourse as a means of reducing the damages award. The seller is not entitled to an 'abatement' under the common law principle from his or her liability for damages to the extent of the unpaid price.[506]

(2) Substantive or procedural?

A question in respect of which conflicting views have been expressed is whether common **2.129** law abatement is a procedural or a substantive defence. Historically, it seems that the justification for its introduction was to avoid circuity of action,[507] which is consistent with a procedural defence. This indeed would appear to be the prevailing view in Australia, where it has been referred to, in that country's highest court, as a 'procedural concession' which 'the law has come to concede for the sake of convenience'.[508] In England, however, the defence has been described as substantive.[509]

---

[502] See the Sale of Goods Act 1979, s. 53(3).

[503] *Multiplex Constructions (UK) Ltd v Cleveland Bridge UK Ltd* [2006] EWHC 1341 (TCC) at [652].

[504] *Hoenig v Isaacs* [1952] 2 All ER 176, 180, 181; *Thornton v Place* (1832) 1 M & Rob 218, 174 ER 74; *H Dakin & Co Ltd v Lee* [1916] 1 KB 566, 572–3, 576, 581–2; *Multiplex Constructions (UK) Ltd v Cleveland Bridge UK Ltd* [2006] EWHC 1341 (TCC) at [654] (but compare at [652]). See also *Argento v Cooba Developments Pty Ltd* (1987) 13 FCR 579, 584, 589, *Barnett v Peter Cox Group Ltd* (1995) 45 Con LR 131, and the commentary by the editors of the *Building Law Reports* on *C A Duquemin Ltd v Raymond Slater* (1993) 65 BLR 124, 126–7 (criticizing the judgment of Judge John Newey QC in that case).

[505] *Davis v Hedges* (1871) LR 6 QB 687 (disapproving of Lord Ellenborough in *Fisher v Samuda* (1808) 1 Camp 190, 191, 170 ER 925); *Healing (Sales) Pty Ltd v Inglis Electrix Pty Ltd* (1968) 121 CLR 584; *Henriksens Rederi A/S v THZ Rolimpex (The Brede)* [1974] 1 QB 233, 248; *Sidney Raper Pty Ltd v Commonwealth Trading Bank of Australia* [1975] 2 NSWLR 227, 238. See also *Rigge v Burbidge* (1846) 15 M & W 598, 153 ER 988.

[506] *Healing (Sales) Pty Ltd v Inglis Electrix Pty Ltd* (1968) 121 CLR 584.

[507] *Street v Blay* (1831) 2 B & Ad 456, 462–3, 109 ER 1212, 1214; *Allen v Cameron* (1833) 1 C & M 832, 840, 149 ER 635, 639; *Mondel v Steel* (1841) 8 M & W 858, 869–70, 151 ER 1288, 1293; *Davis v Hedges* (1871) LR 6 QB 687, 691; *Bow, McLachlan & Co, Ltd v Ship 'Camosun'* [1909] AC 597, 611, 613; *Healing (Sales) Pty Ltd v Inglis Electrix Pty Ltd* (1968) 121 CLR 584, 614–15.

[508] See Kitto J in *Healing (Sales) Pty Ltd v Inglis Electrix Pty Ltd* (1968) 121 CLR 584, 601. The tenor of the judgment of Windeyer J suggests that he agreed with this view. See also *Cellulose Products Pty Ltd v Truda* (1970) 92 WN (NSW) 561, 570. Compare *Newman v Cook* [1963] VR 659.

[509] See e.g. *Gilbert-Ash (Northern) Ltd v Modern Engineering (Bristol) Ltd* [1974] AC 689, 717; *Aectra Refining and Marketing Inc v Exmar NV* [1994] 1 WLR 1634, 1650.

2.130   In *Aectra Refining and Marketing Inc v Exmar NV*,[510] Hoffmann LJ (as he then was) equated
abatement with the substantive defence of equitable set-off, and in contradistinction to the
procedural defence provided by the Statutes of Set-off.[511] Equitable set-off is said to be a
substantive defence because, unlike the Statutes, it does not require a judgment of a court
in order for it to have effect. It may be set up by a debtor, not merely as a means of preventing a creditor from obtaining judgment, but as an immediate answer to liability. When
circumstances exist which support an equitable set-off, it is unconscionable for a creditor
to assert that moneys are due to it from the debtor to the extent of the debtor's cross-
demand, and the creditor cannot take any action against the debtor which is predicated
upon the debtor having failed to pay. A court of equity can protect the debtor's position by
means of an injunction and a declaration.[512] On the other hand, it is unclear how the substantive quality arises at common law in relation to the defence of abatement, or what is
meant by saying that the common law defence is substantive. The notion that abatement
is substantive would not mean that a debt for the price does not arise to the extent of the
reduction in value caused by the breach, as perhaps may be suggested by statements to the
effect that abatement at common law reduces or diminishes or extinguishes the claim.[513] If
that indeed were the case, it would be difficult to see how separate claims could be regarded
as subsisting at common law so as to entitle the purchaser to elect to pay the full price and
to sue separately for the damages.[514] Nor does the purchaser bring about an extinction or
diminution in the debt simply by electing to rely on the defence.[515]

2.131   The substantive view may be based on the notion that the availability of the defence is
determined as at the date of delivery of the goods or completion of the work. In other
words, the value of the goods delivered or of the work performed as at that date is reduced
because of the breach of contract, and the nature of the defence is such that the purchaser,
if he or she so chooses, can defend him or herself in a subsequent action for the price by
showing the true value of what in fact was received as at that date. But if this were the justification for ascribing a substantive operation to the defence, one would have thought that
it would continue to apply if the damages claim subsequently ceased to exist as a result of
the expiration of a limitation period which has the effect of taking away, not only the remedy, but also the right itself. That eventuality would not affect the proposition that the
value of the goods at the time of delivery, or the value of the work that was actually performed, was of diminished value. Yet, Lord Wilberforce in *Aries Tanker Corporation v Total*

[510]   [1994] 1 WLR 1634, 1649–50.
[511]   See paras 4.29–4.57 below in relation to equitable set-off, and paras 2.34–2.52 above in relation to the
Statutes of Set-off.
[512]   See para. 4.30 below.
[513]   See e.g. *Dole Dried Fruit and Nut Co v Trustin Kerwood Ltd* [1990] 2 Lloyd's Rep 309, 311 (Lloyd LJ);
Aectra Refining and Marketing Inc v Exmar NV [1994] 1 WLR 1634, 1650 (Hoffmann LJ).
[514]   See para. 2.128 above, and *Healing (Sales) Pty Ltd v Inglis Electrix Pty Ltd* (1968) 121 CLR 584, 601.
[515]   *Healing (Sales) Pty Ltd v Inglis Electrix Pty Ltd* (1968) 121 CLR 584, 602–3 (Kitto J). See also para.
4.32 below (referring to *Aries Tanker Corporation v Total Transport Ltd* [1977] 1 WLR 185, 188) in relation to
equitable set-off. Compare Robert Goff J in *Impex Transport Aktieselskabet v AG Thames Holdings Ltd* [1981]
2 Lloyd's Rep 566, 570 ('plead by way of defence that the debt is extinguished, on the principle in *Mondel v
Steel*').

Transport Ltd,[516] said that a claim which has ceased to exist cannot be introduced into legal proceedings as a defence, and his Lordship would seem to have had in mind common law abatement as well as equitable set-off. Certainly this was assumed by Mustill LJ in his discussion of the *Aries Tanker* case in the Court of Appeal in *Bank of Boston Connecticut v European Grain and Shipping Ltd*.[517]

Whatever the explanation of the substantive view, one situation in which the procedural **2.132** and the substantive theories would produce different results is where the damages claim remains in existence although unenforceable, as, for example, where the expiration of a limitation period merely affects the remedy. If abatement were simply a procedural defence designed to avoid circuity of action, there would be no reason for allowing a defence in the situation where the claim for breach of warranty in any event could not be enforced.[518] This may be the position in Australia, where the defence has been described as a 'procedural concession'.[519] In England, however, both Lord Denning and Roskill LJ in *Henriksens Rederi A/S v THZ Rolimpex (The Brede)*[520] considered that the defence of abatement is not defeated by the expiration of a limitation period, a view which was shared by the Canadian Federal Court of Appeal in *The Didymi*.[521]

The question whether abatement is a procedural or a substantive defence in most cases **2.133** would be of little practical consequence. Following the expansion and development of equitable set-off,[522] the equitable defence to a considerable extent now overlaps the common law defence of abatement, and the tendency in recent cases in which the plaintiff was suing for the price of work done or of goods sold and delivered has been to consider both equitable set-off and common law abatement when the defendant sets up a defence that the plaintiff had breached the contract sued upon.[523] Indeed, Lord Salmon remarked in *Aries Tanker Corporation v Total Transport Ltd*[524] that: 'Whether [the defence] stems from the development of the common law in the last century or from equitable defences or equitable set-off, as it is sometimes called, or from both, seems to me to be only of academic interest since the passing of the Judicature Act 1873 made equitable defences available in common law courts.'[525] Consequently, if in a particular case the question arises whether the defence

---

[516] [1977] 1 WLR 185, 188.

[517] [1989] 1 AC 1056, 1071.

[518] See the discussion by Roskill LJ in *Henriksens Rederi A/S v THZ Rolimpex (The Brede)* [1974] 1 QB 233, 259, referring to Kitto J in *Healing (Sales) Pty Ltd v Inglis Electrix Pty Ltd* (1968) 121 CLR 584, 601.

[519] See para. 2.129 above. In *Buttrose v Versi* (NSW SC, 14 May 1992, BC9201877), Young J, after noting that the defence was based upon circuity of action, said that if the defendants in that case could not sue for the damages they had suffered they could not abate the loss against the price, though that was in the context of a loss in respect of which there was no cause of action, as opposed to a right to sue which was unenforceable. Compare *Sidney Raper Pty Ltd v Commonwealth Trading Bank of Australia* [1975] 2 NSWLR 227, 238, in which Moffitt P said that a defence of abatement can be used outside a time limitation period.

[520] [1974] 1 QB 233, 248, 260.

[521] *Atlantic Lines & Navigation Co Inc v The Ship 'Didymi' (The Didymi)* [1988] 1 Lloyd's Rep 97, 102.

[522] See para. 4.05 below.

[523] See e.g. *Gilbert-Ash (Northern) Ltd v Modern Engineering (Bristol) Ltd* [1974] AC 689. See also *Compania Sud Americana de Vapores v Shipmair BV (The Teno)* [1977] 2 Lloyd's Rep 289, 297, and the judgment of Hudson J in *Newman v Cook* [1963] VR 659.

[524] [1977] 1 WLR 185, 194.

[525] See also *Federal Commerce & Navigation Co Ltd v Molena Alpha Inc* [1978] 1 QB 927, 974; *Sim v Rotherham Metropolitan BC* [1987] 1 Ch 216, 257, 259.

raised is procedural or substantive, the court may decide that it is substantive by reference to principles of equitable set-off without the need to have recourse to abatement.[526]

(3) Abatement is distinct from equitable set-off

2.134 But while in the majority of cases Lord Salmon's comment no doubt would be correct, the courts nevertheless have emphasized that abatement and equitable set-off are distinct,[527] and there may be circumstances in which abatement is available but not equitable set-off.[528] Thus, the contract between the parties to an action may have excluded the right of the defendant to assert a set-off, but not have affected the right to rely on the common law defence of abatement.[529] Further, abatement is a common law defence available as of right.[530] It is not subject to discretionary factors relevant to equitable set-off.[531] There may also be cases where the party being sued has not suffered a loss as a result of defective performance, for example where A entered into a contract for the renovation of premises which were not owned by him but by a family company, B Co, which bore the cost of remedial work. If A is sued for the price, he or she may not have suffered any loss so as to give rise to a cross-claim available by way of set-off. On the other hand, A should still be able to defend the action for payment on the ground that the work was of less value because of the defects.[532]

---

[526] Compare *Newman v Cook* [1963] VR 659, in which Hudson J considered that equitable set-off but not common law abatement provided a substantive defence to which the purchaser could have recourse in order to defeat the claim to exercise a power of sale. The other judges, Herring CJ and Dean J, decided the case by reference to the common law defence.

[527] *Gilbert-Ash (Northern) Ltd v Modern Engineering (Bristol) Ltd* [1974] AC 689, 717; *Mellowes Archital Ltd v Bell Projects Ltd* (1997) 87 BLR 26 (see in particular at 38–9), *Edlington Properties Ltd v J H Fenner & Co Ltd* [2006] 1 WLR 1583 at [72].

[528] Compare the view of Scott J in *Sim v Rotherham Metropolitan BC* [1987] 1 Ch 216, 259 that, if the circumstances of the case do not warrant equitable set-off, they would not establish an abatement.

[529] As in *Acsim (Southern) Ltd v Danish Contracting and Development Co Ltd* (1989) 47 BLR 59. See also *Mellowes Archital Ltd v Bell Projects Ltd* (1997) 87 BLR 26.

[530] *Gilbert-Ash (Northern) Ltd v Modern Engineering (Bristol) Ltd* [1974] AC 689, 717.

[531] See paras 4.58–4.62 below.

[532] As in *C A Duquemin Ltd v Raymond Slater* [1993] 65 BLR 124 (see esp. at 130).

3

SET-OFF BETWEEN SOLVENT PARTIES: EQUITABLE SET-OFF

A. Introduction

Prior to the Judicature Acts, equitable set-offs generally were enforced by means of an injunction to restrain the plaintiff at law from either proceeding with the action or enforcing a judgment against the defendant until he or she had given credit to the defendant for the amount of a cross-demand.[1] This could also include an order for delivery up of documents.[2] Since the Judicature Acts, the defendant has been permitted to plead the set-off directly as a defence in the claimant's action.[3] **3.01**

(1) Money claims

As in the case of other forms of set-off, equitable set-off is concerned with monetary demands.[4] A person cannot retain an asset by way of equitable set-off against a money claim. **3.02**

---

[1] Hobhouse LJ described the practice in *Schiffahrtsgesellschaft Detlev von Appen GmbH v Voest Alpine Intertrading GmbH* [1997] 2 Lloyd's Rep 279, 286.

[2] See e.g. *Ex p Hanson* (1811) 18 Ves Jun 232, 34 ER 305.

[3] See now the Senior Courts Act 1981, s 49, and CPR r 16.6. The Supreme Court of Judicature Act 1873, s 24(5) abolished the common injunction as a means of restraining a cause or proceeding pending in the High Court or before the Court of Appeal. Therefore, courts of equity no longer have power to grant injunctions against common law courts. See *T. C. Trustees Ltd v J. S. Darwen (Successors) Ltd* [1969] 2 QB 295, 302. However, an injunction may still be available if the action against the defendant is brought in another jurisdiction which does not recognize the defendant's equitable set-off. See *Schiffahrtsgesellschaft Detlev Von Appen GmbH v Voest Alpine Intertrading GmbH* [1997] 2 Lloyd's Rep 279, 286.

[4] *Tony Lee Motors Ltd v M. S. McDonald & Son (1974) Ltd* [1981] 2 NZLR 281, 288; *Hamilton Ice Arena Ltd v Perry Developments Ltd* [2002] 1 NZLR 309, 311. See also *Air New Zealand Ltd v Wellington International Airport Ltd* [2008] 3 NZLR 87, and generally ch. 9 below. The statement in Meagher, Gummow and Lehane's *Equity Doctrines and Remedies* (4th edn, 2002), 1064 [37–065], that an equitable set-off can be pleaded in defence to a non-money claim, in particular as a defence to a claim for specific performance, is unobjectionable if understood to mean that a court of equity can take into account the availability of a right of set-off when determining whether to grant equitable relief consequent upon non-payment of a debt.

As Lord Hoffmann observed in *Smith v Bridgend County BC*,[5] if it were otherwise, every creditor in effect would have a lien over any property of the debtor that happened to be in the creditor's possession.

B. The Forms of Equitable Set-off

(1) Implied agreement

3.03 An equitable set-off can take a number of forms. There are some early cases in which debts were set off in equity based upon an implied agreement that a set-off should occur,[6] and indeed Sir Joseph Jekyll once said that: 'the least evidence of an agreement for a [set-off] will do,' and that 'equity will take hold of a very slight thing to do both parties right'.[7] In *Wallis v Bastard*,[8] a mortgagor's estate sold the mortgaged property to the mortgagee on terms that interest was to be paid on the outstanding balance of the purchase money. The mortgagee entered into possession and remained in possession for a period of eleven years without any demand being made for the outstanding purchase money. In a subsequent suit for specific performance of the sale contract, it was held that an agreement was to be inferred that the mortgage debt was to be set off against the purchase price, so that to that extent neither the mortgagor's estate nor the mortgagee was liable to the other for interest in relation to the intervening period. There was no written or oral agreement for a set-off; it was simply inferred from the circumstance that no claim had been made for interest for a number of years. Lord Cranworth in his judgment commented that set-off 'is an arrangement which this Court will be very ready to assist...', and that the parties 'must be understood, like reasonable persons, to have adopted an arrangement perfectly obvious and in conformity with what ought to have been done'.[9]

3.04 More recently, the principle was recognized in New Zealand in the context of a cheque swapping arrangement between two parties for a monthly settlement of their mutual dealings. Pursuant to the arrangement, either party could refuse to provide a cheque in respect of its indebtedness if it was not at the same time provided with a cheque in respect of what it was owed. Hammond J commented that, even if this did not amount to a contract *strictu sensu*, it nevertheless was an arrangement that equity would recognize.[10]

See paras 2.58–2.62 above. *Logan v Director of Housing* (2004) 13 Tas SR 324 at [18] is susceptible to a similar comment.

[5] [2002] 1 AC 336 at [36].

[6] *Downam v Matthews* (1721) Prec Ch 580, 24 ER 260; *Hawkins v Freeman* 2 Eq Ca Abr 10, 22 ER 8; *Jeffs v Wood* (1723) 2 P Wms 128, 24 ER 668; *Wallis v Bastard* (1853) 4 De G M & G 251, 43 ER 503. See also *Whitaker v Rush* (1761) Amb 407, 408, 27 ER 272, 273 (Sir Thomas Clarke MR referring to 'presumptive evidence of an agreement or intention that one should be set off against the other'), and the discussion in *Commercial Factors Ltd v Maxwell Printing Ltd* [1994] 1 NZLR 724, 738–40.

[7] *Jeffs v Wood* (1723) 2 P Wms 128, 130, 24 ER 668, 669.

[8] (1853) 4 De G M & G 250, 43 ER 503.

[9] (1853) 4 De G M & G 250, 257, 43 ER 503, 506.

[10] *Commercial Factors Ltd v Maxwell Printing Ltd* [1994] 1 NZLR 724, 740. In *Southern Textile Converters Pty Ltd v Stehar Knitting Mills Pty Ltd* [1979] 1 NSWLR 692, 698, Sheppard J (at first instance) observed that an agreement for a set-off could arise by implication from a course of dealing.

(2) Equitable proprietary estoppel

Another instance has arisen in the context of equitable proprietary estoppel. If A as a result **3.05** of the expenditure of money in respect of B's land is entitled to an equitable charge or lien on the land, but A also happens to be personally indebted to B, B may set off the debt owing to him or her against the sum secured by the charge, so that the amount that must be paid by B in order to take the land free of the charge is the amount secured on the land less the debt.[11] The set-off does not apply, however, in the converse situation, in which B is suing for payment of the debt. In that circumstance, A cannot set off the amount for which he or she has a charge on the land.[12]

In *Unity Joint Stock Mutual Banking Association v King*,[13] A (in the example) had granted **3.06** security over his interest in the land to a purchaser for value without notice before A became indebted to B, as a result of B having made a payment under a guarantee given in respect of A's liabilities. Lord Romilly held that the set-off did not arise until after the purchaser had obtained its interest, and therefore the purchaser took free of the set-off, notwithstanding that B gave the guarantee before the grant of the security.

(3) Acting by analogy with the Statutes

Equity may act by analogy with the legal right of set-off conferred by the Statutes of Set-off **3.07** when liquidated cross-demands are mutual having regard to equitable rights.[14] This may arise because one of the debts itself is a matter of equitable jurisdiction[15] (other than for payment of a trust fund, a claim for which generally cannot be met by a set-off under the Statutes[16]). Alternatively, it may arise because a common law debt is held on trust or has been the subject of an equitable assignment, so that the requirement of mutuality is satisfied only by reference to the equitable titles.[17] If special circumstances render it unjust that a set-off should occur, a court of equity in the exercise of its discretion nevertheless may refuse to allow a set-off by analogy with the Statutes.[18] On the other hand, when there are mutual liquidated cross-demands having regard to equitable rights, it is not necessary for

---

[11] *Unity Joint Stock Mutual Banking Association v King* (1858) 25 Beav 72, 79–80, 53 ER 563, 566, and see also *Baillie v Edwards* (1848) 2 HLC 74, 9 ER 1020, in which it had been agreed that advances made on account of the estate would give rise to a right of repayment only from the estate itself. *Baillie v Edwards* is discussed in paras 4.79, 4.90 and 6.30 below.

[12] Lord Lyndhurst expressed this view during argument in *Baillie v Edwards* (1848) 2 HLC 74, 81, 9 ER 1020, 1023.

[13] (1858) 25 Beav 72, 79–80, 53 ER 563, 566.

[14] See also para. 11.18 below in relation to mutuality.

[15] *Kostka v Addison* [1986] 1 Qd R 416. Thus, the amount which a defaulting trustee is bound to pay to make good a breach of trust has been described as an equitable debt. See *Webb v Stenton* (1883) 11 QBD 518, 530; *Wickstead v Browne* (1992) 30 NSWLR 1, 14.

[16] See ch. 10 below. On the other hand, when a person has a right to participate in a trust fund and also has an obligation to contribute to it, the rule in *Cherry v Boultbee* (1839) 4 My & Cr 442, 41 ER 171 may apply. See ch. 14 below.

[17] See e.g. *Clark v Cort* (1840) Cr & Ph 154, 41 ER 449; *Cochrane v Green* (1860) 9 CB(NS) 448, 142 ER 176; *Thornton v Maynard* (1875) LR 10 CP 695; *Manley & Sons Ltd v Berkett* [1912] 2 KB 329, 333; *High v Bengal Brass Co* (1921) 21 SR (NSW) 232, 238; *Tony Lee Motors Ltd v M S MacDonald & Son* (1974) Ltd [1981] 2 NZLR 281.

[18] See Spry, *Equitable Remedies* (8th edn, 2010), 175.

the defendant to show some additional equity in order to give rise to a set-off. Suggestions to the contrary[19] cannot be supported.[20]

3.08   The right of set-off available pursuant to the Statutes is procedural in its operation.[21] It provides a defence to an action for payment, and the debts remain separate and distinct until there is judgment for a set-off. Further, as Lord Eldon once remarked, the construction of the Statutes is the same in equity as at law, unless there is a natural equity going beyond the Statutes.[22] A natural equity would arise if the cross-demands are sufficiently closely connected to give rise to the substantive form of equitable set-off discussed in the next chapter. Ordinarily, however, the Statutes receive the same construction in equity. This proposition brings into question the decision of Street J in the New South Wales Supreme Court in *Stewart v Latec Investments Ltd*.[23] A company had executed a trust deed in order to regulate the issue of debenture stock. The trust deed was in a common form, by which the trustee appointed under the deed was constituted the creditor of the company in respect of the issued stock, while each individual stockholder was the beneficial owner of his or her stock. In the event of a transfer of stock, the deed provided that, upon registration of the transfer, the transferee should be recognized as entitled to the stock free from any equity, set-off, or counterclaim possessed by the company against the transferor. The court was asked to determine a question of law, whether the company was bound to register a transferee as the owner of stock when the transferor was indebted to the company on an independent transaction. The perceived difficulty for the transferee was that the trust deed only stipulated that a transferee took free from equities after registration had been effected, and so it was held that the company could assert a set-off against the transferee before then in order to prevent registration.[24] When the company received the formal transfer, it credited the principal and interest payable in respect of the debenture stock against the transferor's indebtedness. Street J said that this book-keeping entry itself amounted to a valid redemption of the debenture.[25] Consistent with that view, *Stewart v Latec Investments* has been referred to as showing a species of equitable set-off having a substantive operation independently of any court order.[26]

3.09   The decision in *Stewart v Latec Investments* is difficult to justify. There was no question of the demands being sufficiently closely connected to give rise to a substantive equitable set-off of the kind considered in chapter 4.[27] Further, because of the interposition of the trustee, there was not mutuality at law as between the company and the transferor for

---

[19] *Middleton v Pollock, ex p Nugee* (1875) LR 20 Eq 29, 36–7, and see *Welton v Harnett* (1886) 7 NSWR 74; *Goode on Legal Problems of Credit and Security* (4th edn (ed. Gullifer), 2008), 308.

[20] *Tony Lee Motors Ltd v M. S. MacDonald (1974) Ltd* [1981] 2 NZLR 281, 287–8.

[21] See paras 2.34–2.52 above.

[22] *Ex p Stephens* (1805) 11 Ves Jun 24, 27, 32 ER 996, 997.

[23] [1968] 1 NSWR 432.

[24] See e.g. *Re Richard Smith & Co Ltd* [1901] 1 IR 73.

[25] Street J commented (at [1968] 1 NSWR 432, 437) that: 'when Latec Investments Ltd purported, on 13 July 1962, to credit the principal and interest payable in respect of the debenture stock against Mr Stewart's indebtedness to it this amounted to a valid redemption of the debenture.'

[26] See Gummow and von Doussa JJ in the Federal Court of Australia in *McIntyre v Perkes* (1990) 22 FCR 260, 270.

[27] See ch. 4 below.

the purpose of the Statutes of Set-off. There was on the other hand mutuality in equity, so that equity would have acted by analogy with the Statutes. But the Statutes should have received the same construction as at law, given that there does not appear to have been a natural equity taking the case beyond the Statutes. The right of set-off therefore should have been regarded as merely procedural, in the sense that it merely provided a defence to an action for payment, and it should not have permitted the company to bring about a set-off itself by making an entry to that effect in its books. Street J relied in his judgment on the earlier decision of Buckley J in *Re Palmer's Decoration & Furniture Co*,[28] which concerned a similar trust deed. The cases are distinguishable, however. In *Palmer* the transferor's title was defective,[29] in that he had obtained the debentures from the company by misrepresentation, and it was held that the transferee took subject to this defect in title. While the question in issue was whether the transferee was entitled to be paid, Buckley J also said that the defect of title would have provided a ground for the company to refuse to register the transfer. The nature of the equity in that case should be compared to the equity which arises under the Statutes of Set-off. This provides a procedural defence to an action but does not give rise to a defect in the title to the debt in question. The tenor of Buckley J's judgment admittedly suggests that the principle in that case was thought to apply to equities generally,[30] but the particular nature of the defence of set-off under the Statutes was not considered.[31]

(4) Substantive equitable set-off

There is another form of equitable set-off which is both broader and narrower than the **3.10** Statutes of Set-off. It is broader in that it is not confined to the case of mutual debts, but can arise when one or both of the demands is for damages. On the other hand it is narrower, in that there must be a connection between the demands. In contrast, the Statutes do not require any such connection. This form of equitable set-off has another characteristic which has come into prominence in recent years, and which distinguishes it from the Statutes, and that is that it operates substantively, as opposed to providing merely a procedural defence. The substantive equitable defence is considered in the next chapter.

---

[28] [1904] 2 Ch 743.

[29] Buckley J expressed it ([1904] 2 Ch 743, 751) in terms that: 'by reason of the company's equity the title is not clear.'

[30] See also *Palmer's Company Precedents* (16th edn, 1952), Pt 3 ('Debentures'), 18, 235, 236.

[31] *Re Goy & Co Ltd* [1900] 2 Ch 149, which Buckley J discussed in his judgment in *Palmer's Decoration* [1904] 2 Ch 743, 749–51, was concerned with the rule in *Cherry v Boultbee* (1839) 4 My & Cr 442, 41 ER 171 (see para. 14.77 below) rather than set-off under the Statutes.

4

SUBSTANTIVE EQUITABLE SET-OFF

4.01 There is a substantive[1] form of equitable set-off which is not confined to mutual debts,[2] and which has attracted considerable attention in recent years. It is the most elusive, but at the same time the most important, of the various forms of equitable set-off.

A. The Traditional Formulation

4.02 The seminal authority on this form of equitable set-off is Lord Cottenham's judgment in *Rawson v Samuel*.[3] The Lord Chancellor said that the mere existence of cross-demands is not sufficient to give rise to a set-off. Rather, he said that the applicant for relief must show some good equitable ground for being protected against the demand of the plaintiff at law, such that the plaintiff's title to his or her demand is impeached.[4] In *Rawson v Samuel*, the plaintiff at law was suing for damages for breach of contract.[5] The defendant at law (the plaintiff in equity) sought an account of transactions under the contract, and an injunction to restrain the plaintiff at law from executing any judgment obtained at law until he had given credit for any balance that may be found to be due to the defendant on the account. Lord Cottenham said that: 'The object and subject matters are . . . totally distinct', and that 'the fact that the agreement was the origin of both does not form any bond of union for the purpose of supporting an injunction.'[6] The result was that the absence of a sufficient equity prevented a set-off despite the fact that both demands had their origin in the same contract.

4.03 The traditional basis of this form of equitable set-off is that the plaintiff's title to his or her demand is impeached. The concept of impeachment has not been precisely defined.[7] In general terms, what it requires, in the absence of some other equitable ground for being protected such as fraud,[8] is that there be a sufficiently close connection between the

---

[1] See paras 4.29–4.57 below.

[2] In a number of cases in Australia it was suggested that an unliquidated demand cannot be employed in a set-off. See e.g. *McDonnell & East Ltd v McGregor* (1936) 56 CLR 50, 62; *Classic Ceramic Importers Pty Ltd v Ceramica Antiga SA* (1994) 13 ACSR 263, 269. However, that suggestion is clearly incorrect in so far as it relates to equitable set-off. See e.g. *Beasley v Darcy* (1800) 2 Sch & Lef 403n (in which the Lord Chancellor ordered that the defendant's cross-claim for damages be assessed by a jury); *Galambos & Son Pty Ltd v McIntyre* (1974) 5 ACTR 10 (in which the cases are discussed); *United Dominions Corporation Ltd v Jaybe Homes Pty Ltd* [1978] Qd R 111; *British Anzani (Felixstowe) Ltd v International Marine Management (UK) Ltd* [1980] 1 QB 137, 145–6; *Zeekap (No. 47) Pty Ltd v Anitam Pty Ltd* (1989) 14 Tas R 206 at [12].

[3] (1841) Cr & Ph 161, 41 ER 451.

[4] (1841) Cr & Ph 161, 178–80, 41 ER 451, 458–9. See also *Hanak v Green* [1958] 2 QB 9, 18–19; *Smith v Bridgend County BC* [2002] 1 AC 336 at [36] ('some equitable reason for protection'). In *Ex p Branwhite, re The West of England and South Wales District Bank* (1879) 40 LT 652, 654, Fry J commented that equitable set-off 'only arises when there are certain equitable circumstances which give a right to the person who sets them up against his antagonist.' In 1761, Sir Thomas Clarke MR said in *Whitaker v Rush* (1761) Amb 407, 408, 27 ER 272 that equity required that there should be a connection between the demands.

[5] An equitable set-off may be pleaded as a defence to an action for damages. See e.g. *Hanak v Green* [1958] 2 QB 9; *Filross Securities Ltd v Midgeley* [1998] 3 EGLR 43; *Bim Kemi AB v Blackburn Chemicals Ltd* [2001] 2 Lloyd's Rep 93 at [21]–[23].

[6] (1841) Cr & Ph 161, 178, 41 ER 451, 458.

[7] *Altarama Ltd v Camp* (1981) 5 ACLR 513, 519.

[8] See *Ex p Stephens* (1805) 11 Ves Jun 24, 32 ER 996; *Vulliamy v Noble* (1817) 3 Mer 593, 36 ER 228 (explained in paras 4.71–4.76 below); *Walker v Department of Social Security* (1995) 56 FCR 354, 370; *Western Bulk Carriers K/S v Li Hai Maritime Inc (The Li Hai)* [2005] 2 Lloyd's Rep 389 at [41].

demands. In its traditional sense, this was not simply a question whether the demands arose out of the same transaction,[9] although the principle has been expressed in those terms, including in the House of Lords.[10] It involves a consideration of the circumstances of the particular case, and indeed a close connection may not suffice to impeach the title if there are other discretionary factors which militate against equitable relief.[11] The closeness of the connection that courts of equity traditionally required has been expressed in various terms, for example that the cross-demand must go to the very root of the plaintiff's claim,[12] or that it must call in question, impugn, disparage or impede the title to the claim,[13] or that there must be some equitable ground for protection such as inseparability,[14] or, as the New Zealand Court of Appeal expressed it, that the link between the demands must be such that the two in effect are interdependent.[15] It is the nature of the cross-claim relative to the claim, rather than the amount of the damages recoverable or the severity of the breach, that matters.[16] The fact that the claimant is insolvent by itself does not give rise to an equity sufficient to support an equitable set-off.[17] Further, *Rawson v Samuel* illustrates that it is not sufficient that the demands arose out of the same contract.[18] Nor is the claimant's demand necessarily regarded as impeached because the cross-claim is in some way related to the transaction which gave rise to the claim,[19] or because the claim and the cross-claim turn on similar findings of fact.[20] If, on the other hand, cross-demands arise out of separate transactions, they usually would not be sufficiently closely connected so as to justify an equitable set-off.[21]

In *Rawson v Samuel*, Lord Cottenham referred to a number of cases which illustrate the impeachment principle. In *Beasley v Darcy*,[22] a tenant was allowed to set off against   **4.04**

---

⁹ See para. 4.14 below.

¹⁰ *Bank of Boston Connecticut v European Grain and Shipping Ltd* [1989] 1 AC 1056, 1102–3, 1110–11. See para. 4.13 below.

¹¹ See paras 4.58–4.62 below.

¹² *British Anzani (Felixstowe) Ltd v International Marine Management (UK) Ltd* [1980] 1 QB 137, 145; *Walker v Department of Social Security* (1995) 56 FCR 354, 363.

¹³ *MEK Nominees Pty Ltd v Billboard Entertainments Pty Ltd* (1993) V Conv R 54–468 at 65,466 (Vic SC, Tadgell J).

¹⁴ *Tooth v Brisbane City Council* (1928) 41 CLR 212, 224 (Isaacs J).

¹⁵ *Grant v NZMC Ltd* [1989] 1 NZLR 8, 13. See also *Hoverd Industries Ltd v Supercool Refrigeration and Air Conditioning (1991) Ltd* [1995] 3 NZLR 577, 586; *Hamilton Ice Arena Ltd v Perry Developments Ltd* [2002] NZLR 309, 312.

¹⁶ *Sim v Rotherham Metropolitan BC* [1987] 1 Ch 216, 262.

¹⁷ *Rawson v Samuel* (1841) Cr & Ph 161, 175, 41 ER 451, 457. Compare *Clarkson v Smith and Goldberg* [1926] 1 DLR 509, 511.

¹⁸ See in particular (1841) Cr & Ph 161, 178, 41 ER 451, 458 (Lord Cottenham), and also *Best v Hill* (1872) LR 8 CP 10; *Re K L Tractors Ltd* [1954] VLR 505, 507–8; *Banco Central SA v Lingoss & Falce Ltd (The Raven)* [1980] 2 Lloyd's Rep 266, 272; *Covino v Bandag Manufacturing Pty Ltd* [1983] 1 NSWLR 237, 238 (claim for the price of goods supplied and cross-claim for damages for breach of warranty as regards territorial monopoly not set off); *Westwind Air Charter Pty Ltd v Hawker De Havilland Ltd* (1990) 3 WAR 71.

¹⁹ *Hanak v Green* [1958] 2 QB 9, 23.

²⁰ *Bim Kemi AB v Blackburn Chemicals Ltd* [2001] 2 Lloyd's Rep 93 at [19].

²¹ *Re Convere Pty Ltd* [1976] VR 345, 349. See also *Abignano v Wenkart* (1998) 9 BPR 16,765, 16,773. See also *Saitta Pty Ltd v Commissioner of Taxation* (2002) 125 FCR 388 at [22]–[23] (claim by the Commissioner of Taxation in Australia for payment of tax and a cross-claim for damages against the Health Insurance Commission).

²² (1800) 2 Sch & Lef 403n. See the discussion of the case in *British Anzani (Felixstowe) Ltd v International Marine Management (UK) Ltd* [1980] 1 QB 137, 149–51.

his liability for rent a damages claim that he had against the landlord for damage suffered as a result of timber on the demised land being cut down and carried away. Lord Cottenham said that the equity against the landlord was that he should not recover possession of the farm for non-payment of rent when he owed to the tenant a sum for damage to that same farm, although on other occasions it has been suggested that the decision in *Beasley* may be justified on the ground that the produce of the farm may have been lessened as a result of the landlord's conduct, which in turn may have affected the tenant's ability to pay the rent.[23] In *Piggott v Williams*[24] a solicitor filed a bill for foreclosure of an estate pledged as security for costs. The relief sought by the solicitor was denied to him because of a set-off held to be available to the client.[25] The cross-claim was based upon an allegation of negligence, and it was argued that the costs claimed would not have been incurred were it not for the negligence. This was a case in which the plaintiff's own breach of duty brought about, or at least contributed to the existence of, the defendant's liability to him.[26] Reference was also made to *Lord Cawdor v Lewis*.[27] In that case a claim for compensation for improvements effected to another's land was set off against a cross-claim for *mesne* profits, in circumstances where the party claiming title to the land had stood by and watched the other spend money on the improvements without giving the other notice of his title. On the other hand, Lord Cottenham was critical of the decision in *Williams v Davies*.[28] The plaintiff had obtained judgment at law against the defendant upon some promissory notes, and the defendant had obtained judgment at law against the plaintiff for damages for wrongful distress. The plaintiff applied to the Court of King's Bench to set off the judgments pursuant to the court's inherent jurisdiction.[29] The application was refused, and so the plaintiff sought an injunction in equity. This succeeded before Sir Lancelot Shadwell, who said that it was right that the judgments should be set off. It is unclear, however, why equitable relief should have been available when a remedy had been refused at law, and Lord Cottenham

---

[23] *O'Mahony v Dickson* (1805) 2 Sch & Lef 400, 412 (Lord Redesdale); *Stimson v Hall* (1857) 1 H & N 831, 835–6, 156 ER 1436, 1438 (Bramwell B).

[24] (1821) 6 Madd 95, 56 ER 1027.

[25] In relation to claims for costs by solicitors, see *Cachia v Isaacs* (1985) 3 NSWLR 366, 371, 376–7.

[26] See also *Popular Homes Ltd v Circuit Developments Ltd* [1979] 2 NZLR 642, 659–60; *Long Leys Co Pty Ltd v Silkdale Pty Ltd* (1991) 5 BPR 11,512, 11,519; *James v Commonwealth Bank of Australia* (1992) 37 FCR 445, 459; *Walker v Department of Social Security* (1995) 56 FCR 354, 363; *Ling v Commonwealth* (1996) 68 FCR 180, 191; *Forsyth v Gibbs* [2009] 1 Qd R 403 at [11]. Similarly, in an action by an employer under a building contract against the contractor arising out of a delay in completion, a cross-claim available to the contractor against the employer for hindering or preventing the contractor's performance may give rise to an equitable set-off. See *Hanak v Green* [1958] 2 QB 9; *Rosehaugh Stanhope (Broadgate Phase 6) Plc v Redpath Dorman Long Ltd* (1990) 50 BLR 75; *Beaufort House Development Ltd v Zimmcor (International) Inc* (1990) 50 BLR 91. In some such cases a defence of circuity of action may be available. See e.g. *Post Office v Hampshire County Council* [1980] 1 QB 124. This defence is limited, however. It only applies in a situation in which, if the claimant recovered against the defendant, the defendant would recover exactly the same sum, or if damages, exactly the same measure of damages, against the plaintiff. See *Aktieselskabet Ocean v B Harding and Sons Ltd* [1928] 2 KB 371, 385; *McCamley v Harris* (1998) NSW Conv R 55–827 at 56,479.

[27] (1835) 1 Y & C Ex 427, 160 ER 174. Compare *Tai Te Whetu v Scandlyn* [1952] NZLR 30.

[28] (1829) 2 Sim 461, 57 ER 860.

[29] See paras 2.98–2.122 above.

doubted in *Rawson v Samuel* whether there was a sufficient equity to support an equitable set-off.[30]

The rigour with which the impeachment test originally was applied has weakened over **4.05** time, so that in some more recent cases it is difficult to see what the basis for the set-off was apart from the fact that both demands arose out of the same contract or transaction. This would appear to be a consequence of the view that has been expressed,[31] that the courts should not be astute to restrict the right of set-off, but rather should develop it as a discouragement to litigation. In particular, two Court of Appeal decisions have been referred to as illustrating a departure from the principle originally applied by Lord Cottenham.[32] The defendant in *Morgan & Son, Ltd v S Martin Johnson & Co, Ltd*[33] had delivered a number of vehicles to the plaintiff for the purpose of storage. The plaintiff subsequently claimed a sum for storage charges, and applied for summary judgment. The defendant resisted the application on the basis of an alleged damages claim for non-delivery of one of the vehicles. The Court of Appeal held that the facts set out in the defendant's affidavit supported a claim to an equitable set-off, and that accordingly the defendant should be granted unconditional leave to defend. That conclusion could hardly be questioned if the set-off had been confined to the charges for storing the particular vehicle which was the subject of the cross-action. The equity in favour of a set-off in such a case would have been that the plaintiff should not be permitted to sue for the cost of storing a vehicle when the plaintiff had failed to account for it.[34] In relation to the part of the storage charges which related to the other vehicles, however, it is not clear what the connection was other than that all the vehicles seem to have been stored under the one contract. The decision nevertheless has been referred to subsequently with evident approval,[35] and indeed there are other cases which support the availability of a set-off in analogous circumstances.[36] The second case, *Hanak v Green*,[37] concerned a building contract. The plaintiff sued the defendant builder for breach of contract for failing to complete or properly complete certain items of work.

---

[30] (1841) Cr & Ph 161, 178, 41 ER 451, 458. See also *Stimson v Hall* (1857) I H & N 831, 836, 156 ER 1436, 1438; *Aboussafy v Abacus Cities Ltd* (1981) 124 DLR 3d 150, 160; *J C Scott Constructions v Mermaid Waters Tavern Pty Ltd (No. 1)* [1983] 2 Qd R 243.

[31] *Hanak v Green* [1958] 2 QB 9, 29 (Sellers LJ). But see paras 5.163–5.177 below.

[32] See Spry, 'Equitable Set-offs' (1969) 43 *Australian Law Journal* 265, 269–70; *Meagher, Gummow and Lehane's Equity Doctrines and Remedies* (4th edn, 2002), 1061 [37–050].

[33] [1949] 1 KB 107 (Tucker and Cohen LJJ).

[34] In this respect the case would have been analogous to *Beasley v Darcy* (1800) 2 Sch & Lef 403n, referred to above. See also *Re Wallace Smith & Co Ltd* [1992] BCLC 970, 984 (claim by an agent for the purchase price of Treasury bills purchased as agent and cross-claim against the agent for failure to deliver the bills).

[35] See e.g. *Hale v Victoria Plumbing Co Ltd* [1966] 2 QB 746, 751 (CA); *Federal Commerce & Navigation Co Ltd v Molena Alpha Inc* [1978] 1 QB 927, 975 (Lord Denning); *Newman v Cook* [1963] VR 659, 674.

[36] See *Kaps Transport Ltd v McGregor Telephone & Power Construction Co Ltd* (1970) 73 WWR 549 (in which the set-off claimed in respect of the damage to the appellant's equipment does not appear to have been confined to the claim for the price of the trucking services relating to the particular contract for the carriage of that equipment); *John Dee Group Ltd v WMH (21) Ltd* [1997] BCC 518, 531 (referring to *Business Computers Ltd v Anglo-African Leasing Ltd* [1977] 1 WLR 578, 585); *Parsons v Sovereign Bank of Canada* [1913] AC 160 (see para. 4.105 below) (in which the contracts appear to have been separate). See also *Marubeni Corp v Sea Containers Ltd* Queen's Bench Division, Waller J, 17 May 1995, in which it seems to have been accepted that a set-off would have been available against the claim for the price by reason of defects in other containers delivered under the same contract, were it not for the clause which was held to have excluded set-offs.

[37] [1958] 2 QB 9 (Hodson, Morris and Sellers LJJ).

The defendant counterclaimed or claimed by way of set-off: (1) on a *quantum meruit* in respect of extra work done outside the contract; (2) on the ground that loss was caused by the plaintiff's refusal to admit the defendant's workmen; and (3) for trespass to the defendant's tools. It may be accepted that the second of those items exhibited a good equitable ground sufficient to impeach the plaintiff's title to her demand, assuming that her refusal to admit the defendant's workmen was one of the reasons why the defendant had not completed the work. In that circumstance, the plaintiff's own conduct may have contributed to the existence of the defendant's liability to her.[38] A similar comment may be made in respect of the third item.[39] On the other hand, it is not clear what connection the first item had with the plaintiff's claim, in the sense considered by Lord Cottenham. The Court of Appeal, however, held that it could be set off in equity. *Hanak v Green* has since become a leading case in the area, and Morris LJ's judgment in particular has been described as authoritative[40] and a masterly account of the subject.[41]

4.06   In the course of his judgment in *Rawson v Samuel*, Lord Cottenham commented:[42]

> It was said that the subjects of the suit in this Court, and of the action at law, arise out of the same contract; but the one is for an account of transactions under the contract, and the other for damages for the breach of it. The object and subject-matters are, therefore, totally distinct; and the fact that the agreement was the origin of both does not form any bond of union for the purpose of supporting an injunction.

This should not be taken to mean that a claim for a sum of money payable under a contract cannot be met by a set-off in respect of a damages claim for breach of the contract.[43] Indeed, situations of that kind are a prime source of equitable set-offs.[44] Lord Cottenham's statement should be understood in the context of the case before him. It concerned an agreement by which the defendant was to consign goods to some mercantile houses in which one of the plaintiffs had an interest for the purpose of sale. Part of the agreement was that, upon each shipment of goods, the defendant should be at liberty to draw bills of exchange upon

---

[38] As in *Piggott v Williams* (1821) 6 Madd 95, 56 ER 1027.

[39] The status of the third item was not considered by Hodson and Morris LJJ, the first and second items when added together being sufficient to overtop the plaintiff's claim. However, Sellers LJ thought that it could be marshalled as a set-off.

[40] *BICC Plc v Burndy Corporation* [1985] 1 Ch 232, 247 (Dillon LJ).

[41] Lord Diplock in *Gilbert-Ash (Northern) Ltd v Modern Engineering (Bristol) Ltd* [1974] AC 689, 717, and see also *Compania Sud Americana de Vapores v Shipmair BV (The Teno)* [1977] 2 Lloyd's Rep 289, 297; *British Anzani (Felixstowe) Ltd v International Marine Management (UK) Ltd* [1980] 1 QB 137, 144; *Dole Dried Fruit and Nut Co v Trustin Kerwood Ltd* [1990] 2 Lloyd's Rep 309, 310; *Geldof Metaalconstructie NV v Simon Carves Ltd* [2010] EWCA Civ 667 at [22].

[42] (1841) Cr & Ph 161, 178, 41 ER 451, 458.

[43] *AWA Ltd v Exicom Australia Pty Ltd* (1990) 19 NSWLR 705, 713–14.

[44] For example, in the case of a time charter of a ship there is ample authority for the proposition that a claim for hire may be met by a damages claim for breach of contract which deprives the charterer of the full use of the vessel. See *Compania Sud Americana de Vapores v Shipmair BV (The Teno)* [1977] 2 Lloyd's Rep 289, 297; *Federal Commerce & Navigation Co Ltd v Molena Alpha Inc* [1978] 1 QB 927, 976. Similarly, a damages claim for breach of a building contract may be set off against a claim for moneys otherwise due under the contract. See e.g. *Young v Kitchin* (1878) 3 Ex D 127; *Government of Newfoundland v Newfoundland Railway Co* (1888) 13 App Cas 199. A claim for payment of fees charged for the performance of services may be impeached by a cross claim for negligence in the performance of the services. See *Re Kostezky* (1996) 67 FCR 101, 106.

the plaintiffs for the amount of his charges and disbursements in respect of the shipments. After the agreement had run for some time, the plaintiffs refused to accept bills in accordance with the agreement in respect of certain shipments that had been made, whereupon the defendant sued at common law for damages. The plaintiffs sought an injunction restraining execution on any judgment that may be obtained at law. Their bill sought an account of all the dealings and transactions between the parties under the agreement, and an order setting off against their damages liability the amount which, upon taking the accounts, should be found due from the defendant to the plaintiffs. The subject-matters of the claims were considered to be distinct, and Lord Cottenham was concerned to emphasize that the fact that they arose out of the same agreement was not sufficient to give rise to an equitable set-off.

This explanation of *Rawson v Samuel* appears not to have been appreciated in *Best v Hill*.[45]   **4.07**
The defendant had consigned goods to the plaintiffs for sale, the agreement between them being that the plaintiffs should make advances to the defendant against the goods, and that the plaintiffs should sell the goods and obtain payment from the proceeds for the advances and their expenses and commission. The plaintiffs sued for money lent and paid and commission in respect of the goods. The defendant pleaded as a defence on equitable grounds a cross-claim for damages for negligence in the care of part of the goods and for negligence in the management of the sale. The allegation was that the plaintiffs were guilty of such negligence and improper conduct in the care of the goods and the conduct of the sale that the goods fetched less than they ought to, such that the amount recovered was insufficient to satisfy the advances, expenses and commission. The Court of Common Pleas held that the plea was bad. One reason given was that the proceedings to ascertain the amount of damages would have involved considerable delay. But in addition Bovill CJ held, on the authority of *Rawson v Samuel*, that an equitable set-off was not available because: 'although these cross claims in one sense are connected . . . this does not appear to be sufficient, according to the doctrine of equity in relation to set-off; one claim arises out of the performance of the contract, the other out of its breach.'[46] As a general proposition for denying an equitable set-off, this is difficult to support. One would have thought that, apart from the discretionary consideration concerning delay in the assessment of the damages, the cross-claims were sufficiently connected to give rise to an equitable set-off. This would seem to have been the case notwithstanding that the Court of Exchequer in *Atterbury v Jarvie*[47] previously had denied a defence on equitable grounds in similar circumstances. The advances, commission and expenses the subject of the plaintiffs' claim in *Best v Hill* were intended to be satisfied out of the proceeds of sale. The substance of the cross-claim against the plaintiffs was that, as a result of their own negligence and misconduct, the amount received from the sale was insufficient to satisfy the debts. The cross-claim would appear to have impeached the title of the plaintiffs to sue. As counsel unsuccessfully argued in *Best v Hill*, it was similar to *Beasley v Darcy*.[48] In that case the landlord's claim for rent was

---

[45] (1872) LR 8 CP 10.
[46] (1872) LR 8 CP 10, 15.
[47] (1857) 2 H & N 114, 157 ER 47.
[48] (1800) 2 Sch & Lef 403n.

impeached by a cross-claim against him for damage done in cutting timber on the demised land, because this reduced the produce of the farm and therefore affected the tenant's ability to pay the rent.

B. New Approaches

4.08   In recent years the courts have sought to re-define the basis upon which an equitable set-off may arise, which has had the effect of expanding the scope of the defence.

4.09   In *Henriksens Rederi A/S v THZ Rolimpex (The Brede)*,[49] Lord Denning cited *Morgan v Johnson* and *Hanak v Green*[50] as authorities for the proposition that equitable set-off 'is available whenever the cross-claim arises out of the same transaction as the claim; or out of a transaction that is closely related to the claim'.[51] There was no mention of an additional requirement of some equitable ground sufficient to impeach the plaintiff's title to his or her demand, and to this extent his statement of the law would appear to represent a broader basis for the defence than that originally contemplated by Lord Cottenham. Thus, Lord Denning accepted that 'with any breach by the plaintiff of the self-same contract, the defendant can in equity set up his loss in diminution or extinction of the contract price',[52] whereas Lord Cottenham emphasized in *Rawson v Samuel*[53] that the fact that the one contract was the origin of both demands is not sufficient to found an equitable set-off.[54] However, the traditional approach was reiterated in *Aries Tanker Corporation v Total Transport Ltd*.[55] The House of Lords in that case affirmed the principle that freight owing under a voyage charter must be paid without deduction.[56] Accordingly, the charterers could not deduct a sum for short delivery of cargo. But even apart from that principle, Lord Simon of Glaisdale said that an equitable set-off would not have been available on the facts. He said that, in order to succeed, the equity of the bill would have had to impeach the title to the legal demand, and the title to a claim for freight is not impeached by short delivery unless it amounts to a repudiation of the contract of carriage.[57] Similarly, Lord Wilberforce referred to *Rawson v Samuel* as setting out the relevant principle, and the courts on other occasions since then have emphasized impeachment of title as the foundation of equitable set-off.[58]

---

[49] [1974] 1 QB 233.

[50] See para. 4.05 above.

[51] [1974] 1 QB 233, 248. See also *Box v Midland Bank Ltd* [1981] 1 Lloyd's Rep 434, 437, where Lord Denning allowed an equitable set-off on the basis that the 'claim and counterclaim arose out of a whole series of transactions in regard to the obtaining of the loan'.

[52] [1974] 1 QB 233, 249.

[53] (1841) Cr & Ph 161, 175, 41 ER 451, 457.

[54] See para. 4.91 below.

[55] [1977] 1 WLR 185.

[56] See paras 5.02–5.24 below.

[57] However, the fact that the shipowner may have repudiated the charterparty does not preclude the operation of the principle that freight which has been earned must be paid without deduction. See *Bank of Boston Connecticut v European Grain and Shipping Ltd* [1989] 1 AC 1056, and para. 5.04 below.

[58] See e.g. *British Anzani (Felixstowe) Ltd v International Marine Management (UK) Ltd* [1980] 1 QB 137, 145 (referred to in *Sim v Rotherham Metropolitan BC* [1987] 1 Ch 216, 261); *BICC Plc v Burndy Corporation* [1985] Ch 232, 258, 259; *Atlantic Lines & Navigation Co Inc v The Ship 'Didymi' (The Didymi)* [1988]

After *Aries Tanker*, there were some important observations on equitable set-off in the **4.10**
Court of Appeal in *Federal Commerce & Navigation Co Ltd v Molena Alpha Inc*,[59] particularly by Lord Denning. In contrast with his earlier judgment in *Henriksens Rederi v Rolimpex*,
Lord Denning acknowledged that there must be some equitable ground sufficient to
impeach the plaintiff's demand.[60] In doing so, however, he rejected the notion that the
categories of equitable grounds should be ascertained by examining the practice of the
courts in matters of set-off prior to the Judicature Acts.[61] Instead, he said that the relevant
question is: 'what should we do now so as to ensure fair dealing between the parties?'[62] He
then went on to explain the circumstances that would give rise to an equitable set-off
today:

> [I]t is not every cross-claim which can be deducted. It is only cross-claims that arise out of the
> same transaction or are closely connected with it. And it is only cross-claims which go directly
> to impeach the plaintiff's demands, that is, so closely connected with his demands that it
> would be manifestly unjust to allow him to enforce payment without taking into account the
> cross-claim.[63]

Parker J had expressed the principle earlier, in similar terms, in *The Teno*,[64] and it has since
been widely adopted.[65]

On Lord Denning's approach, two things must be established in order for equitable set-off **4.11**
to apply: first, the cross-claim must arise out of the same transaction as the claim or be
closely connected with it; and, second, the relationship between the respective claims must
be such that it would be manifestly unjust to allow one claim to be enforced without regard

1 Lloyd's Rep 97 (Canadian Federal Court of Appeal); *Exmar BV v National Iranian Tanker Co (The Trade
Fortitude)* [1992] 1 Lloyd's Rep 169, 172; *Aectra Refining and Marketing Inc v Exmar NV* [1994] 1 WLR
1634, 1649; *Mortgage Corporation v Ubah* (1996) 73 P & CR 500, 508; *Courage Ltd v Crehan* [1999] 2 EGLR
145, 155–6; *Western Bulk Carriers K/S v Li Hai Maritime Inc (The Li Hai)* [2005] 2 Lloyd's Rep 389 at [41].
See also *Edlington Properties Ltd v J H Fenner & Co Ltd* [2006] 1 WLR 1583 at [20], [21] and [37] (CA).

[59] [1978] 1 QB 927.
[60] [1978] 1 QB 927, 974.
[61] See also *British Anzani (Felixstowe) Ltd v International Marine Management (UK) Ltd* [1980] 1 QB 137,
155.
[62] [1978] 1 QB 927, 974. In *A B Contractors Ltd v Flaherty Brothers Ltd* (1978) 16 BLR 8, 11 Cumming-
Bruce LJ considered whether the dealings were so connected 'as to make it fair and sensible' that a set-off
occur. See also Stephenson LJ at 14.
[63] [1978] 1 QB 927, 974–5. Similarly, Goff LJ commented in *Federal Commerce v Molena* (at 981): 'The
circumstances must be such as to make it unfair for the creditor to be paid his claim without allowing that
of the debtor if and so far as well founded and thus to raise an equity against the creditor or, as it has been
expressed, impeach his title to be paid.'
[64] *Compania Sud Americana de Vapores v Shipmair BV (The Teno)* [1977] 2 Lloyd's Rep 289, 297.
[65] See e.g. *British Anzani (Felixstowe) Ltd v International Marine Management (UK) Ltd* [1980] 1 QB 137,
145; *SL Sethia Liners Ltd v Naviagro Maritime Corporation (The Kostas Melas)* [1981] 1 Lloyd's Rep 18, 25;
Dole Dried Fruit and Nut Co v Trustin Kerwood Ltd [1990] 2 Lloyd's Rep 309, 311; *Esso Petroleum Co Ltd v
Milton* [1997] 1 WLR 938, 950; *Peninsular and Oriental Steam Navigation Co v Youell* [1997] 2 Lloyd's Rep
136, 144; *Courage Ltd v Crehan* [1999] 2 EGLR 145, 155; *Muscat v Smith* [2003] 1 WLR 2853, 2863; *R (on the
Application of Burkett) v London Borough of Hammersmith and Fulham* [2004] EWCA Civ 1342 at [45]; *Geldof
Metaalconstructie NV v Simon Carves Ltd* [2010] EWCA Civ 667/[43] (point (vi)). In *National Westminster
Bank Plc v Skelton* [1993] 1 WLR 72, 76 Slade LJ said that, in deciding whether to allow a set-off, 'the court will
be much influenced by what it regards as the essential requirements of justice.' In *Federal Commerce v Molena*
[1978] 1 QB 927, 987 Goff LJ described Parker J's analysis in *The Teno* as 'impeccable'. See also *BICC v Burndy
Corporation* [1985] Ch 232, 250; *Sim v Rotherham Metropolitan BC* [1987] Ch 216, 261–2.

to the other.[66] In relation to the prevention of manifest injustice, or fairness, there is nothing new in that element. In truth, it has always been the concept underlying equitable set-off.[67] The relevant inquiry is, what are the circumstances in which equity regards it as unjust or unfair that one claim should be enforced without reference to another, and traditionally this has been expressed in terms that, in the absence of some other equitable ground for being protected,[68] the claims must be connected such that the title to sue is impeached. It is apparent from Lord Denning's reference to impeachment that his formulation was not intended to replace the impeachment test as such,[69] but rather to define it in terms which may be more familiar to the courts today. There is one situation in which he was careful not to extend the ambit of the defence. He said that, 'as at present advised', he would limit the right of a time charterer to make deductions from hire to cases where the shipowner has wrongfully deprived the charterer of the use of the vessel or has prejudiced the charterer in the use of it. He said that he would not extend it to other breaches or defaults of the shipowner, such as damage to cargo arising from the negligence of the crew.[70] This is consistent with the traditional approach, because depriving a charterer of the use of the ship or prejudicing the charterer's use is the very type of circumstance that would impeach a claim for hire.[71] It suggests a narrower view than that expressed in his earlier judgment in *Henriksens Rederi v Rolimpex*, that an equitable set-off is available whenever cross-claims arise out of the same transaction. But, leaving that aside, the definition of impeachment in terms of fairness, or the prevention of manifest injustice, would tend to expand the scope of the defence, a proposition that may be illustrated by *Dole Dried Fruit & Nut Co v Trustin Kerwood Ltd*,[72] in which the Court of Appeal allowed an equitable set-off on the basis of Lord Denning's formulation in circumstances that would not appear to have satisfied the traditional test.[73]

4.12 The difficulty with a formulation expressed in terms of 'justice' or 'fairness' is that those concepts are inherently subjective, often depending on from whose perspective the matter is looked at. As Professor Birks observed, words such as 'fair' and 'just' and 'unconscionable' are

---

[66] *Esso Petroleum Co Ltd v Milton* [1997] 1 WLR 938, 950 (Simon Brown LJ); *Star Rider Ltd v Inntrepreneur Pub Co* [1998] 1 EGLR 53, 56.

[67] *Peninsular and Oriental Steam Navigation Co v Youell* [1997] 2 Lloyd's Rep 136, 144. As Drummond J observed in *Walker v Department of Social Security* (1995) 56 FCR 354, 365, the prevention of unconscionable conduct is the core justification for equitable intervention.

[68] For example, fraud. See *Vulliamy v Noble* (1817) 3 Mer 593, 36 ER 228 (explained in paras 4.71–4.76 below); *Ex p Stephens* (1805) 11 Ves Jun 24, 32 ER 996; *Walker v Department of Social Security* (1995) 56 FCR 354, 370.

[69] Similarly, Parker J in *Compania Sud Americana de Vapores v Shipmair BV (The Teno)* [1977] 2 Lloyd's Rep 289, 297 acknowledged that the cross-claim must be such as to impeach the plaintiff's title, but then went on to express the principle in terms whether it was manifestly unjust to allow the claimant to recover without taking into account the cross-claim.

[70] [1978] 1 QB 927, 976. Goff LJ (at 981) expressed a similar view. See also *Aliakmon Maritime Corporation v Trans Ocean Continental Shipping Ltd (The Aliakmon Progress)* [1978] 2 Lloyd's Rep 499, 501.

[71] See also *Leon Corporation v Atlantic Lines and Navigation Co Ltd (The Leon)* [1985] 2 Lloyd's Rep 470, 475; *Exmar BV v National Iranian Tanker Co (The Trade Fortitude)* [1992] 1 Lloyd's Rep 169, 172.

[72] [1990] 2 Lloyd's Rep 309.

[73] See paras 4.107–4.109 below. A Similar comment may be made in relation to *Geldof Metaalconstructie NV v Simon Carves Ltd* [2010] EWCA Civ 667. See paras 4.17–4.18 below.

so unspecific that they simply conceal a private and intuitive evaluation.[74] This subjectivity is reflected in Thorpe LJ's comment in *Esso Petroleum Co Ltd v Milton*,[75] that: 'claims to equitable set-off ultimately depend upon the judge's assessment of the result that justice requires'. On the other hand, Hobhouse J, in *The Leon*,[76] rejected the notion that the test is simply one of fairness. He said:

> [E]quitable principles derive from a sense of what justice and fairness demand ... But this does not mean that equitable set-off has been reduced to an exercise of discretion. Since the merging of equity and law, equitable set-off gives rise to a legal defence. This defence does not vary according to the length of the Lord Chancellor's, or arbitrator's, foot. The defence has to be granted or refused by an application of legal principle.

He went on to emphasize that the relevant principle is identified in Lord Cottenham's judgment in *Rawson v Samuel*.

After the *Federal Commerce* case, the House of Lords considered the question of equitable **4.13** set-off in *Bank of Boston Connecticut v European Grain and Shipping Ltd*.[77] Lord Brandon of Oakbrook, who delivered the judgment of the Law Lords, said that the concept of impeachment is not a familiar one today. Instead, he approved a formulation that the Privy Council had expressed in *Government of Newfoundland v Newfoundland Railway Co*,[78] that an equitable set-off may occur if there is a cross-claim 'flowing out of and inseparably connected with the dealings and transactions which also give rise' to the claim.[79] As a consequence, it has been suggested that the impeachment of title test should no longer be used.[80]

Lord Brandon did not regard that formulation as a departure from the impeachment test **4.14** set out in *Rawson v Samuel*. On the contrary, he affirmed that, in the determination today of whether a particular cross-claim can give rise to an equitable set-off, it is still necessary to see whether it is of such a character that it would have led a court of equity before the Judicature Acts to prohibit by injunction the enforcement of the plaintiff's claim.[81] This seems a rejection of the approach advocated by Lord Denning in the *Federal Commerce* case, that we should no longer ask ourselves what the courts of equity would have done before the Judicature Acts, but rather we should ask what should be done now so as to ensure fair dealing between the parties.[82] Nevertheless, it has been said in later cases that the

---

[74] Birks, 'Equity in the Modern Law: An Exercise in Taxonomy' (1996) 26 *University of Western Australia Law Review* 1, 16–17.

[75] [1997] 1 WLR 938, 953.

[76] *Leon Corporation v Atlantic Lines and Navigation Co Inc (The Leon)* [1985] 2 Lloyd's Rep 470, 474. See also *Benford Ltd v Lopecan SL* [2004] 2 Lloyd's Rep 618 at [13]; *Edlington Properties Ltd v J H Fenner & Co Ltd* [2006] 1 WLR 1583 at [44]–[46] (CA); *Zeecap (No. 47) Pty Ltd v Anitam Pty Ltd* (1989) 14 Tas R 206 at [26].

[77] [1989] 1 AC 1056.

[78] (1888) 13 App Cas 199.

[79] See, in particular, the judgment at [1989] 1 AC 1056, 1102–3, 1110–11. See also *Kaps Transport Ltd v McGregor Telephone & Power Construction Co Ltd* (1970) 73 WWR 549.

[80] *Geldof Metaalconstructie NV v Simon Carves Ltd* [2010] EWCA Civ 667 at [43] (point (i)).

[81] [1989] 1 AC 1056, 1101.

[82] [1978] 1 QB 927, 974.

authority of the *Federal Commerce* case has not been diminished by *Bank of Boston*,[83] and that the test enunciated by Lord Brandon was 'broadly similar' to and 'essentially the same as' that in *Federal Commerce v Molena*.[84] Lord Brandon went on to say that the test approved by the House of Lords was a 'different version' of the impeachment test,[85] while Lloyd LJ later characterized it is 'the same test in different language'.[86] That view is debatable, however. The notion that an equitable set-off may arise whenever the cross-claim is inseparably connected with the transaction founding the plaintiff's claim would not appear to reflect the concept of impeachment as it was originally developed. Thus, it is difficult to see how the *Bank of Boston* approach would ever operate to deny an equitable set-off when the same transaction is the source of both demands. While there have indeed been statements suggesting that that may suffice for an equitable set-off,[87] the courts on other occasions have emphasized in the context of the impeachment test that it is not sufficient that the cross-demands arose out of the same transaction.[88] As Bramwell B once expressed the principle: 'where there is a transaction between two parties, and cross claims originate from it, a court of equity will *in some cases* interfere to prevent the one party from enforcing his claim without allowing the claim of the other.'[89]

4.15 Whatever the position in that regard, the Court of Appeal[90] reached the correct decision in *Guinness Plc v Saunders*.[91] The second defendant, through a company controlled by him, received payment from the plaintiff for services performed. The second defendant was also

---

[83] *Dole Dried Fruit and Nut Co v Trustin Kerwood Ltd* [1990] 2 Lloyd's Rep 309, 311 (Lloyd LJ).

[84] See Potter LJ in *Peninsular and Oriental Steam Navigation Co v Youell* [1997] 2 Lloyd's Rep 136, 144, and again in *Bim Kemi AB v Blackburn Chemicals Ltd* [2001] 2 Lloyd's Rep 93 at [27].

[85] [1989] 1 AC 1056, 1102.

[86] *Dole Dried Fruit and Nut Co v Trustin Kerwood Ltd* [1990] 2 Lloyd's Rep 309, 310. According to Rix LJ, Lord Brandon was concerned 'to replace the impeachment test by something which was easier to understand and apply in the modern world': *Geldof Metaalconstructie NV v Simon Carves Ltd* [2010] EWCA Civ 667 at 31.

[87] See e.g. *Hale v Victoria Plumbing Co Ltd* [1966] 2 QB 746, 751 (CA).

[88] *Leon Corporation v Atlantic Lines and Navigation Co Inc (The Leon)* [1985] 2 Lloyd's Rep 470, 474; *Century Textiles and Industry Ltd v Tomoe Shipping Co (Singapore) Pte Ltd (The Aditya Vaibhav)* [1991] 2 Lloyd's Rep 573 (esp. at 574); *Western Bulk Carriers K/S v Li Hai Maritime Inc (The Li Hai)* [2005] 2 Lloyd's Rep 389 at [41]; *Clambake Pty Ltd v Tipperary Projects Pty Ltd (No. 3)* [2009] WASC 52 at [167]; *Halsbury's Laws of England* (5th edn, 2009) vol. 11 ('Civil Procedure'), 515 para. 662. In the Court of Appeal in the *Bank of Boston* case [1989] 1 AC 1056, 1075, Mustill LJ said in relation to equitable set-off that: 'the fact that the origin of the demands lay in the same transaction was plainly not enough.' In Australia, see *Re K L Tractors Ltd* [1954] VLR 505, 508; *Davkot Pty Ltd v Custom Credit Corporation Ltd* (NSW SC, Wood J, 28th March 1991, BC8801896); *Griffiths v Commonwealth Bank of Australia* (1994) 123 ALR 111, 124 (in which Lee J held that a claim against a bank in tort for interference in the customer's contractual relations with a second bank was not impeached by the first bank's claim for repayment of a loan advanced to the customer, notwithstanding that Lee J agreed (at 124) that the bank's claim was part of the transaction which lead to its conduct the subject of the claim against it); *Walker v Department of Social Security* (1995) 56 FCR 354, 364 (referring to *James v Commonwealth Bank of Australia* (1992) 37 FCR 445). See also Spry, 'Equitable Set-offs' (1969) 43 *Australian Law Journal* 265, 268, referred to in *Popular Homes Ltd v Circuit Developments Ltd* [1979] 2 NZLR 642, 659 and *Parry v Grace* [1981] 2 NZLR 273, 276, 277.

[89] *Stimson v Hall* (1857) 1 H & N 831, 835, 156 ER 1436, 1438 (emphasis added).

[90] Fox and Glidewell LJJ, and Sir Frederick Lawton.

[91] [1988] 1 WLR 863, affirmed on different grounds, without reference to the set-off point, at [1990] 2 AC 663. See also *Zemco Ltd v Jerrom-Pugh* [1993] BCC 275; *Neptune (Vehicle Washing Equipment) Ltd v Fitzgerald* [1996] Ch 274, 278; *Lehman Brothers International (Europe) v CRC Credit Fund Ltd* [2009] EWHC 3228 (Ch) at [325]–[335].

a director of the plaintiff, and it was held that the payment was received in breach of his fiduciary duty to the plaintiff and that he held it as constructive trustee. He argued that he nevertheless had a valid defence based upon a cross-claim for *quantum meruit* in respect of the services. However, the cross-claim did not impeach the trust, the plaintiff's claim being for the return of its money improperly received by the second defendant. Accordingly, an equitable set-off was not available. Indeed, the allowance of an equitable set-off would have had the effect of putting the second defendant in the same position that he would have been in had the payment not been impugned in equity.[92]

Similarly, the Court of Appeal was correct in rejecting an argument for a set-off in *Peninsular and Oriental Steam Navigation Co v Youell*.[93] Underwriters had paid P & O in respect of various claims made on a policy of liability insurance for the year 1992/1993, but alleged that they had been induced to do so by fraud or mistake. They sought to plead their claim for repayment as a defence to an action brought by P & O on a separate policy in respect of a similar claim for the year 1991/1992. But as Potter LJ pointed out in delivering the judgment of the court,[94] different insurance contracts were in issue relating to different years.[95] The fact that they may have been part of an overall insurance programme was not a sufficient connection to support an equitable set-off.[96]   **4.16**

After the *Peninsular and Oriental* case, Potter LJ again reviewed the authorities on equitable set-off in *Bim Kemi AB v Blackburn Chemicals Ltd*.[97] In the first place, he adopted the test approved by the House of Lords in the *Bank of Boston* case, in terms whether the cross-claim flows out of and is inseparably connected with the dealings and transactions which gave rise to the claim. He said that this emphasizes that the degree of closeness required for an equitable set-off is that of 'inseparable connection'.[98] But the availability of a set-off does not rest solely upon the determination of that issue. He said that, in addition, it is appropriate in every case to give separate consideration to the question of manifest injustice. He pointed out that, in *Federal Commerce v Molena*,[99] the question whether it would be manifestly unjust to allow a set-off was presented as the criterion by which to judge the closeness of the connection. The issue of closeness has since been determined by the House   **4.17**

---

[92] Compare *Smith v Bridgend County BC* [2002] 1 AC 336 at [36].

[93] [1997] 2 Lloyd's Rep 136.

[94] Nourse, Potter and Mummery LJJ.

[95] Compare para. 4.63 below in relation to overpayments under the same contract.

[96] A claim under a policy of indemnity insurance is a claim for unliquidated damages, and therefore a set-off would not have been available under the Statutes of Set-off. See para. 2.26 above.

[97] [2001] 2 Lloyd's Rep 93 (Jonathan Parker LJ and Sedley J agreeing with Potter LJ). Potter LJ referred to *Bim Kemi* in his later judgment in *ISS Machinery Services Ltd v Aeolian Shipping SA (The Aeolian)* [2001] 2 Lloyd's Rep 641 at [20] (claim for the price of spare parts required to repair machinery and cross-claim for damages for breach of a term as to the quality of the machinery in the contract for the sale of the machinery, where the delivery of spare parts was only necessary because of the defect in the machinery). See also *Benford Ltd v Lopecan SL* [2004] 2 Lloyd's Rep 618 (breach of an overriding distribution agreement). In *S & D Property Investments Ltd v Nisbet* [2009] EWHC 1726 (Ch), the claimant sued for payment of a debt. The defendant cross-claimed for damages for harassment by an officer of the defendant in attempting to recover payment. McNicol J held (at [123]–[124]), by reference to *Bim Kemi*, that the cross-claim gave rise to an equitable set-off since it was inseparably connected with the claim and it was manifestly unfair to allow the claimant to enforce the claim without giving allowance for the cross-claim. *Sed quaere*.

[98] [2001] 2 Lloyd's Rep 93 at [29].

[99] *Sub nom The Nanfri*. See para. 4.10 above.

of Lords in *Bank of Boston* without reference to manifest injustice, although if the *Bank of Boston* test is satisfied, Potter LJ said that it would be difficult to envisage in what circumstances it would be other than just to allow a set-off. Nevertheless, he suggested that it is still appropriate to give separate consideration to the question of manifest injustice, and to whether there are factors or circumstances which militate against the justice or fairness of recognizing a set-off.[100] The requirement of manifest injustice was affirmed in *Geldof Metaalconstructie NV v Simon Carves Ltd.*[101] On this occasion the Court of Appeal favoured Lord Denning's formulation in *Federal Commerce v Molena*, though freed of any reference to the concept of impeachment. *Bim Kemi* is more in accord with the approach adopted in *Bank of Boston*.

4.18   The claimant in *Bim Kemi* was suing the defendant for damages for repudiation of an exclusive distribution agreement alleged to have been made in 1994, by which the claimant was to have the exclusive right to sell the defendant's product for three years. By way of defence, the defendant asserted a set-off. It alleged that the claimant had breached a technology trademark and licensing agreement entered into in 1984, pursuant to which the defendant granted the claimant a licence to use the defendant's technology to process a chemical concentrate made by the defendant and to sell the product. The defence included an allegation that the claimant had promoted a competing product made by its subsidiary at the expense of the defendant's product. The cross-claims concerned separate contracts made ten years apart, and the contracts related to different products, but the Court of Appeal considered that the claims were sufficiently connected to satisfy the *Bank of Boston* test. The parties in this case had a single trading relationship, and it has been said that a single relationship does not suffice to support an equitable set-off.[102] Potter LJ nevertheless considered that the principle stated in *Bank of Boston* is apt to cover a case where there are claims and cross-claims for damages in respect of different but closely connected contracts arising out of a longstanding trading relationship which was terminated. He went on to comment that this circumstance would not *per se* establish the requisite connection, but in an appropriate case it may well be manifestly unjust to allow one claim to be enforced without taking into account the other. In the present case, Potter LJ accepted that both agreements contemplated a continuing expansion and exploitation of the market for the defendant's products in Scandinavia, and the 1994 agreement supplemented rather than replaced the 1984 agreement. In those circumstances, the claimant's conduct in promoting its subsidiary's product at the expense of the defendant's product was considered to be in breach of obligations contained in both agreements, which he said gave rise to the 'close and inseparable connection' necessary for an equitable set-off.[103] Further, there were no competing factors which militated against the justice and fairness of recognizing a set-off. In the *Geldof* case, a circumstance relied on as supporting the view that two contracts were inseparable was the claimant's conduct in demanding payment of invoices under both contracts as a condition of continuing to perform under one of them. It would seem odd,

---

[100] [2001] 2 Lloyd's Rep 93 at [38] and [39].
[101] [2001] EWCA Civ 667 at [43].
[102] *Esso Petroleum Co Ltd v Milton* [1997] 1 WLR 938, 951. But see paras 4.106–4.109 below.
[103] [2001] 2 Lloyd's Rep 93 at [37]. See also the *Geldof* case [2010] EWCA Civ 667 at [44]–[47].

however, that the conduct of one of the parties in the course of a dispute could result in the contracts becoming inseparable for the purpose of a substantive equitable set-off.

C. Equitable Set-off in Australia

In Australia the courts[104] generally have continued to emphasize impeachment of title as **4.19** the basis of equitable set-off,[105] and have tended to be more conservative on questions of equitable set-off than their English counterparts.

In *Hill v Ziymack*,[106] the plaintiff at law had obtained judgment for damages for conversion **4.20** against the defendant, and the High Court held that the plaintiff's title to issue execution was not impeached by a cross-claim for an account between the parties of sums paid by the defendant on behalf of the plaintiff in satisfaction of a number of promissory notes given in payment of the property the subject of the conversion claim. A claim for a set-off also failed in *Bayview Quarries Pty Ltd v Castley Development Pty Ltd*.[107] The plaintiff was suing for the price of goods delivered to the defendant pursuant to an arrangement involving a running account between the parties. Sholl J held that a cross-claim for damages arising out of defects in other earlier deliveries did not constitute a sufficient reason in equity to protect the defendant from the plaintiff's demand, even though, because of payments made pursuant to the running account, the defendant had already paid for the defective goods.[108] The *Bayview Quarries* case should be contrasted with *Zeekap (No. 47) Pty Ltd v Anitam Pty Ltd*.[109] A contract provided for the purchase of a business, at a price of $1,320,000 which was paid in full, and for the purchase of stock at a valuation to be

---

[104] The Federal Court of Australia is a court of equity (see the Federal Court of Australia Act 1976 (Cth), s. 5(2), and *Scarel Pty Ltd v City Loan & Credit Corporation Pty Ltd* (1988) 17 FCR 344, 349), and as such it should have jurisdiction in relation to equitable set-off in respect of matters that are otherwise within its jurisdiction. Compare *Intag Microelectronics Pty Ltd v AWA Ltd* (1995) 18 ACSR 284, 287. This has been assumed in a number of cases. See e.g. *Westpac Banking Corporation v Eltran* (1987) 14 FCR 541; *Tomlinson v Cut Price Deli Pty Ltd* (1992) 38 FCR 490; *James v Commonwealth Bank of Australia* (1992) 37 FCR 445; *Griffiths v Commonwealth Bank* (1994) 123 ALR 111, 124; *Walker v Department of Social Security* (1995) 56 FCR 354, 368, 375. The New South Wales District Court can give effect to equitable defences to matters within its jurisdiction. See *Bitannia Pty Ltd v Parkline Constructions Pty Ltd* (2006) 67 NSWLR 9 at [10].

[105] In addition to the cases referred to below, see *Stephenson Nominees Pty Ltd v Official Receiver* (1987) 16 FCR 536, 558 (claim by agent against the principal impeached by the agent's liability to account to the principal for misapplied funds); *Signature Resorts Pty Ltd v DHD Constructions Pty Ltd* (1995) 18 ACSR 627, 635 (claim for costs payable in a winding up not impeached by a cross-claim for damages for breach of contract); *Re Kostezky* (1996) 67 FCR 101, 106; *Jackson v Crosby (No. 2)* (1979) 21 SASR 280, 297–8 (plaintiff's claim for damages under Lord Cairns' Act taken instead of a half interest in a property not impeached by a claim for reimbursement of moneys paid by the defendant to discharge the plaintiff from bankruptcy).

[106] (1908) 7 CLR 352.

[107] [1963] VR 445.

[108] See also *W. Pope & Co Pty Ltd v Edward Souery & Co Pty Ltd* [1983] WAR 117. Compare *Edward Ward & Co v McDougall* [1972] VR 433, which involved a claim by share brokers for the balance due on moneys paid to the defendant's use as the purchase price of shares or as stamp duty, and for brokerage charged on work done in buying and selling shares, and a cross-claim for damages for negligence or breach of contract in respect of the purchase of some of the shares and the sale of others. Gowans J said that there was a real case in law to be investigated as to whether this gave rise to a defence. Compare also *British American Tobacco Services Ltd v Kanakis* [2001] NSWSC 48.

[109] (1989) 14 Tas R 206.

conducted. The purchaser had a cross-claim for breach of warranty which was material to the valuation of the business but which did not directly relate to the value of the stock. Since the amount ascribed to the business had been paid in full, the breach of warranty cross-claim could not be set off against the obligation to pay that amount. Nevertheless, it was held that there was a sufficient relationship between the obligation to pay the stock valuation and the cross-claim so as to permit a set-off. The purchase of the stock and the purchase of the business were part of the same agreement, and the plaintiff's claim in substance was for part of the aggregate purchase price.

4.21 In a case such as *Bayview Quarries*, in which there are various contracts for the sale of goods, in principle the result should be the same when the contracts are subject to an overriding master agreement which governs their trading relationship, and which sets out the terms applicable to all the contracts. The contracts are still separate transactions. There is, however, authority in Victoria which suggests that damages payable for breach of one contract in that circumstance can be set off in equity against the price payable under another contract.[110]

4.22 The case law concerning equitable set-off was the subject of an extensive review by Woodward J in *Galambos & Son Pty Ltd v McIntyre*.[111] The case involved an action for payment of the balance due on a building contract. It was held that cross-claims possessed by the defendant against the plaintiff relating to non-performance of the contract or defective work, requiring remedial work or directly reducing the value of the work done, constituted matters of pure defence sufficient to defeat the plaintiff's claim. Further, his Honour said that a claim for damages for loss of enjoyment of the premises was so closely connected with the plaintiff's claim that it would have been appropriate, as a matter of equity, to set it off, had it been so pleaded and had it been necessary to do so.[112] Woodward J considered generally the situation in which there is a claim for money under a contract and a cross-claim for damages for breach of the same contract. These cross-claims may be set off *provided* that the equity of the case requires that this should be so. This was said to depend upon how closely the respective claims are related, particularly as to time and subject-matter, and also upon the general conduct of the respective parties.[113] But when cross-claims arise out of the same contract and are closely related to each other, he suggested that a set-off should normally be allowed.[114]

---

[110] *Auspac Trade International Pty Ltd v Victorian Dairy Industry Authority* (Vic SC, Byrne J, 30 June 1993, BC9300782 at 67–70). On appeal, the Appeal Division of the Victorian Supreme Court (Southwell, Nathan and O'Bryan JJ) expressed approval of his Honour's observations on set-off. See *Auspac Trade International Pty Ltd v Victorian Dairy Industry Authority* (22 February 1994, BC9406099 at 39). Compare that view with *Century Textiles and Industry Ltd v Tomoe Shipping Co (Singapore) Pte Ltd (The Aditya Vaibhav)* [1991] 1 Lloyd's Rep 573, for which see para. 4.121 below. Compare also paras 4.106–4.109 below in relation to the repudiation of an overriding agreement which governs the trading relationship between the parties to it.

[111] (1974) 5 ACTR 10.

[112] In fact it was not necessary, because the defendant's cross-claims for non-performance of the contract and for defective work were sufficient to overtop the plaintiff's claim.

[113] (1974) 5 ACTR 10, 26.

[114] (1974) 5 ACTR 10, 22.

Since *Galambos*, a set-off has been denied in a case in which the plaintiff was suing **4.23**
for money due under a mortgage of land given by the defendant to the plaintiff, and the
defendant asserted a cross-claim against the plaintiff for breach of an alleged agreement
by the plaintiff to lend other moneys to the defendant on the security of other lands
purchased by the defendant from the plaintiff.[115] On another occasion it was held that a
purchaser of land and a dwelling-house could not set off against the price a damages claim
that the purchaser had against the vendor for failure to assign a policy of insurance which
indemnified the insured against loss of and damage to the dwelling and its contents.[116]
In Western Australia, a vendor of land claimed possession of the land from the purchaser,
as a result of the purchaser's failure to pay the purchase price on the settlement date. The
purchaser asserted that the vendor held moneys on trust for it, and that it was entitled to
complete the contract by tendering a reduced amount after setting off the amount of
the trust moneys. However, Kennedy J (with whom Malcolm CJ and Murray J agreed)
held that the tendering of the reduced amount could not be justified on the basis of
an equitable set-off, since the moneys said to be held on trust were unconnected with the
contract of sale out of which the vendor's claim arose.[117]

On the other hand, when a plaintiff applied for summary judgment on a claim for payment **4.24**
of his charges for the performance of earth-moving works, the Queensland Supreme Court
said that there was at least an arguable case that an equitable set-off could arise in relation to
a cross-claim for sums incurred by the defendant in repairing the plaintiff's machinery, so
that the plaintiff could perform the work contracted for.[118] Moreover, Moffitt P, in *Sidney
Raper Pty Ltd v Commonwealth Trading Bank of Australia*,[119] as an alternative ground for his
decision, held that a customer of a bank could not sue on a bank cheque issued to him by the
bank without giving credit for a dishonoured cheque deposited by him with the bank, and
which he had used in order to obtain the issue of the bank cheque.[120] Similarly, an impeachment of title would arise when a vendor of property is suing for the price, and the purchaser
has a cross-claim for damages for breach of a warranty in the contract of sale which directly

---

[115] *United Dominions Corporation Ltd v Jaybe Homes Pty Ltd* [1978] Qd R 111.

[116] *Eagle Star Nominees Ltd v Merril* [1982] VR 557.

[117] *Hazcor Pty Ltd v Kirwanon Pty Ltd* (1995) 12 WAR 62. Indeed, it appears that the entitlement to some
of the trust moneys was assigned to the purchaser by a third party a month after the settlement date.

[118] *Phillips v Mineral Resources Developments Pty Ltd* [1983] 2 Qd R 138. In *Gilsan v Optus (No. 3)* [2005]
NSWSC 518 (see esp. at [41]–[44], [56]–[58]) the services giving rise to the defendant's *quantum meruit*
cross-claim enabled the plaintiff to carry on its business, or at least facilitated the plaintiff in doing so, and it
was through carrying on the business that way that the plaintiff became entitled to the payments the subject
of its claim against the defendant. McDougall J's 'tentative view' (at [42], referring to para. 462 of an earlier
judgment) was that the circumstances established the availability of equitable set-off, though (at [44]) he
declined to determine the question since the parties had agreed that equitable set-off applied.

[119] [1975] 2 NSWLR 227.

[120] In fact, the customer had paid the bank cheque to a company, and the company was the party suing on
the cheque. However, the company held the cheque as trustee for the customer, and so a set-off in equity was
still available to the bank.

affects the value of the property sold.[121] In this situation, if the property in question consists of goods, a common law defence of abatement in any event may be available.[122]

4.25 In a claim for the price of goods sold, a set-off was thought not to be available based upon a cross-claim arising out of a breach by the vendor of a promise under a franchise agreement to grant a territorial monopoly to the purchaser, notwithstanding that the claims had their respective origins in the same agreement.[123] But if the breach of the territorial monopoly has the consequence that the expenditure incurred in purchasing the goods the subject of the claim has been wasted, more recent authority in England suggests that a set-off may be available in equity.[124]

4.26 There have been instances in which Australian judges have adopted tests similar to Lord Denning's formulation in *Federal Commerce v Molena*.[125] In New South Wales, Clarke J commented in *Tooth & Co Ltd v Smith*[126] that: 'no general rule can be laid down except by stating that [an equitable] set-off will arise when there exist circumstances which make it unjust or inequitable that a plaintiff should be permitted to proceed with his claim.'[127] Wood J later remarked that, as presently advised, he could not see any fault with that test.[128] Subsequently, Giles J in *AWA Ltd v Exicom Australia Pty Ltd*,[129] after referring to those cases, said that the 'ultimate question' is whether it would be 'unjust or inequitable' that the plaintiff should be permitted to proceed with his claim, an approach that has been referred to with approval in later cases.[130] In other cases, however, the courts have emphasized the traditional formulation.[131] The impeachment test has been affirmed in

---

[121] *Altarama Ltd v Camp* (1980) 5 ACLR 513, 519–20. Compare the situation in which the purchaser's indebtedness for the price is satisfied by a loan from the vendor secured by a mortgage or other security, and the vendor is suing for repayment of the loan. See para. 4.129 below.

[122] See paras 2.123–2.134 above.

[123] *Covino v Bandag Manufacturing Pty Ltd* [1983] 1 NSWLR 237 (see esp. Hutley JA at 238).

[124] *Benford Ltd v Lopecan SL* [2004] 2 Lloyd's Rep 618.

[125] [1978] 1 QB 927, 975. See para. 4.10 above.

[126] New South Wales Supreme Court, 5 September 1984.

[127] See also *Sydmar Pty Ltd v Statewise Developments Pty Ltd* (1987) 73 ALR 289, 295.

[128] *Tooth & Co Ltd v Rosier* (NSW SC, 7 June 1985, BC8500768). Wood J repeated this view in *Davkot v Custom Credit Corporation Ltd* (NSW SC, 28 March 1991). See also *Sydmar Pty Ltd v Statewise Developments Pty Ltd* (1987) 73 ALR 289, 295.

[129] (1990) 19 NSWLR 705, 712.

[130] *Australian Mutual Provident Society v Specialist Funding Consultants Pty Ltd* (1991) 24 NSWLR 326, 328–9; *Lambert Pty Ltd v Papadatos Pty Ltd* (1991) 5 ACSR 468, 470–1; *Westmex Operations Pty Ltd (in liq) v Westmex Ltd (in liq)* (1992) 8 ACSR 146, 153 (affirmed (1993) 12 ACLC 106). See also *Signature Resorts Pty Ltd v DHD Constructions Pty Ltd* (1995) 18 ACSR 627, 634; *Opal Maritime Agencies Pty Ltd v Baltic Shipping Co* (1998) 158 ALR 416, 423; *Primus Telecommunications Pty Ltd v Kooee Communications Pty Ltd* [2007] NSWSC 374 at [10]–[12]. In Victoria, see *Auspac Trade International Pty Ltd v Victorian Dairy Industry Authority* (Vic SC, Byrne J, 30 June 1993, BC9300782) (appeal allowed in part *Auspac Trade International Pty Ltd v Victorian Dairy Industry Authority* Vic SC Appeal Div, 22 February 1994, BC9406099).

[131] In addition to the cases referred to below, see *General Credits (Finance) Pty Ltd v Stoyakovich* [1975] Qd R 352, 355; *Hill Corcoran Constructions Pty Ltd v Navarro* (Qld CA, 6 March 2002, BC9202488) (referred to in *Clairview Developments Pty Ltd v Law Mortgages Gold Coast Pty Ltd* [2007] 2 Qd R 501 at [24]); *Jackson v Crosby (No. 2)* (1978) 21 SASR 280, 297–8 (South Australia). In *Zeecap (No. 47) Pty Ltd v Anitam Pty Ltd* (1989) 14 Tas R 206 at [26] Crawford J emphasized that it is not simply a question of what the court would regard as fair or just.

Queensland.[132] In Victoria,[133] Tadgell J said that a dilution of the requirement of impeachment has not occurred in the Victorian Supreme Court, and this would also appear to be the case in Western Australia.[134] In particular, Kennedy J (with whom Malcolm CJ and Murray J agreed) said in *Hazcor Pty Ltd v Kirwanon Pty Ltd*[135] that he was, 'quite unable to accept . . . that the test is no more than whether the set-off is reasonable in the interests of justice and fair dealing'. In the Federal Court,[136] the impeachment test was affirmed by Gummow J in *James v Commonwealth Bank of Australia*,[137] by Lee J in *Griffiths v Commonwealth Bank of Australia*,[138] and by Cooper J (with whom Spender J agreed) in *Walker v Department of Social Security*,[139] though Gummow J in *James* nevertheless emphasized that the requirement of impeachment has not been narrowly construed.[140] In *James*, a receiver claimed an indemnity from his appointing banks in respect of certain debts and liabilities that he had incurred. The banks in their cross-claim alleged that the debts and liabilities were the result of the personal neglect or default of the receiver, and that this gave rise to a cross-claim for damages which could be set off against their indemnity obligation. While for other reasons it was not necessary to decide the point, Gummow J nevertheless said that the cross-claim would have impeached the receiver's demand, since his demand owed its existence to, or at least it was contributed to by, his own breach of duty to the banks.

In a similar vein, the New South Wales Court of Appeal in *Lord v Direct Acceptance* **4.27** *Corporation Ltd*[141] accepted that it is still an indispensable requirement of equitable

---

[132] *Forsyth v Gibbs* [2009] 1 Qd R 403 at [10].

[133] *MEK Nominees Pty Ltd v Billboard Entertainments Pty Ltd* (1993) V Conv R 54–468 at 65,466. See also *Eagle Star Nominees Ltd v Merril* [1982] VR 557, 561; *Indrisie v General Credits Ltd* [1985] VR 251, 254; *Doherty v Murphy* [1996] 2 VR 553, 565; *Mirvac Hotels Pty Ltd v 333 Collins Street Pty Ltd* (Vic SC, Byrne J, 20 December 1994, BC9401396 at 12); *Cathedral Place Pty Ltd v Hyatt of Australia Ltd* [2003] VSC 385 at [39].

[134] *Westwind Air Charter Pty Ltd v Hawker De Havilland Ltd* (1990) 3 WAR 71; *Geraldton Building Co Pty Ltd v Christmas Island Resort Pty Ltd* (1992) 11 WAR 40. See also *W. Pope & Co Pty Ltd v Edward Souery & Co Pty Ltd* [1983] WAR 117, 122; *Hazcor Ltd v Kirwanon Pty Ltd* (1995) 12 WAR 62, 67–8; *Young v National Australia Bank Ltd* (2004) 29 WAR 505 at [34]; *Clambake Pty Ltd v Tipperary Projects Pty Ltd (No. 3)* [2009] WASC 52 at [158].

[135] (1995) 12 WAR 62, 68.

[136] In addition to the cases referred to below, see *Westpac Banking Corporation v Eltran Pty Ltd* (1987) 14 FCR 541, 547–8; *Cunningham v National Australia Bank Ltd* (1987) 15 FCR 495. In *Saitta Pty Ltd v Commissioner of Taxation* (2002) 125 FCR 388 at [22]–[23] Finklestein J held that a claim by the Commonwealth for payment of tax and a cross-claim for damages against the Health Insurance Commission did not admit of set-off.

[137] (1992) 37 FCR 445.

[138] (1994) 123 ALR 111, 124.

[139] (1995) 56 FCR 354, 375. Compare the discussion by Drummond J in his dissenting judgment at 363–70.

[140] (1992) 37 FCR 445, 458.

[141] (1993) 32 NSWLR 362 (Kirby P, Meagher and Sheller JJA). See also *Covino v Bandag Manufacturing Pty Ltd* [1983] 1 NSWLR 237, 238; *Horrobin v Australia and New Zealand Banking Group Ltd* (1996) 40 NSWLR 89, 100; *Bitannia Pty Ltd v Parkline Constructions Pty Ltd* (2006) 67 NSWLR 9 at [88]; *Equititrust Ltd v Franks* (2009) 258 ALR 388 at [61]. At first instance, see *Signature Resorts Pty Ltd v DHD Constructions Pty Ltd* (1995) 18 ACSR 627, 635; *Perpetual Trustees (WA) Ltd v Equus Corp Pty Ltd* (NSW SC, Young J, 5 March 1998, BC9800921 at 12); *Abignano v Wenkart* (1998) 9 BPR 16,765, 16,773 (different transactions); *Metal Manufacturers Ltd v Hall* (2002) 41 ACSR 466, 471; *Australian Beverage Distributors Pty Ltd v Evans & Tate Premium Wines Pty Ltd* (2006) 58 ACSR 22 at [65] (claim for a debt for goods sold and delivered not impeached by a costs order against the plaintiff resulting from an unsuccessful attempt by the plaintiff to prove that the debtor was insolvent); *Gilsan v Optus (No. 3)* [2005] NSWSC 518 at [44].

set-off in that state that the set-off 'impeach' the title of the plaintiff. Subsequently, a differently constituted Court of Appeal in New South Wales considered equitable set-off in *Roadshow Entertainment Pty Ltd v (ACN 053 006 269)*.[142] The *Roadshow Entertainment* case concerned a receivership, which relevantly was governed by the same principles applicable in the case of an equitable assignment of a debt.[143] On the one hand, the Court of Appeal reiterated the impeachment principle for equitable set-off.[144] On the other, the Court also adopted the principle approved by the Privy Council in *Government of Newfoundland v Newfoundland Railway Company*,[145] and more recently by the House of Lords in the *Bank of Boston* case,[146] in relation to equitable assignments, that an unliquidated cross-demand available to the debtor against the assignor may be set off against the assignee if it flows out of and is inseparably connected with the dealings and transactions which also gave rise to the assigned debt.[147] In light of that formulation, the Court of Appeal in the *Roadshow Entertainment* case accepted that a cross-claim for unliquidated damages arising out of the contract which gave rise to the assigned debt can be the subject of a set-off,[148] even though it is generally said in the context of the traditional impeachment test that it is not sufficient for equitable set-off that the cross-claims arose out of the same contract.[149] However, the Court of Appeal's acceptance of the *Government of Newfoundland* formulation appears not to have been on the basis that it set out the circumstances in which an equitable set-off is available as between a debtor and a creditor.[150] Rather, its acceptance seems to have been in the context of a view which has found favour in Australia, that an assignee cannot recover moneys owing under the contract without being met by a counterclaim for breach by the assignor of the same contract, whether or not the breach would have given rise to an equitable set-off as between the original parties.[151] The proposition inherent in that analysis, that an assignee may take subject to a counterclaim available to the debtor that would not have given rise to a defence of set-off as against the assignor, was rejected by the House of Lords in the *Bank of Boston* case,[152] and it is suggested that it is incorrect.[153]

---

[142] (1997) 42 NSWLR 462.

[143] (1997) 42 NSWLR 462, 483. See generally paras 17.99–17.120 below. Note, however, paras 17.102–17.104 below in relation to the Personal Property Securities Act 2009 (Cth).

[144] (1997) 42 NSWLR 462, 481.

[145] (1888) 13 App Cas 199.

[146] [1989] 1 AC 1056, 1102–3, 1110.

[147] See para. 4.13 above.

[148] (1997) 42 NSWLR 462, 482. See also *McDonnell & East Ltd v McGregor* (1936) 56 CLR 50, 60. That view is nevertheless curious, because the Privy Council in the *Government of Newfoundland* case (1888) 13 App Cas 199, 212 itself acknowledged that: 'There is no universal rule that claims arising out of the same contract may be set against each other in all circumstances.'

[149] See para. 4.91 below.

[150] Compare *Lord v Direct Acceptance Corporation Ltd* (1993) 32 NSWLR 362, 367.

[151] See Gummow J in *James v Commonwealth Bank of Australia* (1992) 37 FCR 445, 461–2, referring to Dixon J in *McDonnell & East Ltd v McGregor* (1936) 56 CLR 50, 59–60 and Spry, 'Equitable Set-offs' (1969) 43 *Australian Law Journal* 265, 268–70, and the *Roadshow Entertainment* case (1997) 42 NSWLR 462, 482.

[152] [1989] 1 AC 1056, 1105–6, 1109–11, approving of the analysis of Hobhouse J at first instance [1987] 1 Lloyd's Rep 239, 254–7.

[153] See paras 17.06–17.09 below, and also Derham, 'Recent Issues in Relation to Set-off' (1994) 68 *Australian Law Journal* 331, 334–7.

Notwithstanding the breadth of Giles J's language in *AWA v Exicom*,[154] the circumstances **4.28** in issue in that case lent themselves to an equitable set-off on both the traditional and the more recent formulations. AWA had sold a business to the defendant, and was suing for moneys due under the contract by way of adjustments consequent upon the transfer of the business. The adjustments arose out of orders which had been accepted and contracts which had been undertaken prior to completion but which were incomplete as at the date of completion. The defendant claimed damages for breach of warranty which went to the value of the business. Giles J held that this gave rise to an equitable set-off, on the basis that it would have been unjust or inequitable to permit AWA to proceed with its claim without giving credit for them. The same result would have been achieved applying the formulation approved by the House of Lords in the *Bank of Boston* case, because the cross-claim was inseparably connected with the transaction which gave rise to the claim.[155] Further, the impeachment test would appear to have been satisfied. If the claim had been for the price itself, the cross-claim undoubtedly would have given rise to an equitable set-off under the traditional formulation. Instead, the claim related to adjustments to take into account incomplete contracts. Nevertheless, as Giles J noted, it affected what the defendant as the purchaser had to pay, and in such a case it should not make any difference that the adjustments were treated separately in the contract rather than being built into the price.

D. The Substantive Nature of Equitable Set-off

The defence of set-off derived from the Statutes of Set-off is commonly described as a pro- **4.29** cedural defence.[156] By this it is meant that separate and distinct debts remain in existence until judgment for a set-off, and, moreover, the defence has no effect until judgment. Prior to judgment the rights consequent upon being a creditor still attach, as do the obligations and liabilities consequent upon being a debtor. A similar analysis should apply when equity acts by analogy with the Statutes.[157] However, a characteristic of the form of equitable set-off which arises in the case of closely connected cross-claims is that it operates as a true, or substantive, defence.[158] It may be invoked independently of any order of the court or

---

[154] (1990) 19 NSWLR 705. See para. 4.26 above.

[155] See Giles J at (1990) 19 NSWLR 705, 707.

[156] See paras 2.34–2.52 above.

[157] Compare *Stewart v Latec Investments Ltd* [1968] 1 NSWR 432. See para. 3.08 above.

[158] In addition to the cases referred to below, see *Newman v Cook* [1963] VR 659, 674–5; *AWA Ltd v Exicom Australia Pty Ltd* (1990) 19 NSWLR 705, 711; *Long Leys Co Pty Ltd v Silkdale Pty Ltd* (1991) 5 BPR 11,512, 11,520 ('equitable set-off . . . operates to absolve the appellant in whole or in part from liability'); *Fuller v Happy Shopper Markets Ltd* [2001] 1 WLR 1681 at [22]; *Safeway Stores Ltd v Interserve Project Services Ltd* [2005] EWHC 3085 (TCC) at [52]–[53] ('has no liability'); *Pacific Rim Investments Pte Ltd v Lam Seng Tiong* [1995] 3 SLR 1 (Singapore CA); *Golf Australia Holdings Ltd v Buxton Construction Pty Ltd* [2007] VSCA 200 at [23] ('Unlike equitable set-off . . . legal set-off admits the debt which is due . . .'). Compare the judgments of Cairns and Roskill LJJ in *Henriksens Rederi A/S v THZ Rolimpex (The Brede)* [1974] 1 QB 233, and *Re K L Tractors Ltd* [1954] VLR 505, 507 (although O'Bryan J relied upon some observations by Byrne J in *Re Hiram Maxim Lamp Company* [1903] 1 Ch 70 which were concerned with the Statutes of Set-off). Since the prevailing view is that the defence is substantive, it has been suggested that it is better described as an equitable defence rather than a set-off. See *Henriksens Rederi v Rolimpex* at 248; *Sidney Raper Pty Ltd v Commonwealth Trading Bank of Australia* [1975] 2 NSWLR 227, 236, 238. See also *Altarama Ltd v Camp* (1980) 5 ACLR 513, 519.

of arbitrators.[159] It may be set up by a person indebted to another, not merely as a means of preventing that other person from obtaining judgment, but as an immediate answer to his or her liability to pay the debt otherwise due.[160] While it is only in comparatively recent times that the substantive nature of this defence has come into prominence,[161] it is consistent with the tenor of Lord Cottenham's judgment in *Rawson v Samuel*.[162] The Lord Chancellor referred to earlier cases in which an equitable set-off had been allowed as cases in which 'the equity of the bill impeached the title to the legal demand'. It was not merely the right to obtain judgment on the demand that was impeached, but the title to the demand itself.

(1) What is meant by 'substantive'?

4.30 Notwithstanding various judicial statements which on their face may suggest the contrary,[163] the view that the defence is substantive does not mean that it operates as an automatic extinguishment of cross-demands. The availability of an equitable set-off operates in equity to impeach the title to a demand.[164] It affects the conscience of a creditor, so as to impugn the creditor's right to assert that any moneys are owing by the debtor to the extent of the debtor's cross-claim. At law the cross-demands remain in existence and retain their separate identities[165] until extinguished by judgment or agreement.[166] But as far as equity is concerned, it is unconscionable for the creditor, even before judgment, to assert that moneys are due to it from the debtor, or to proceed on the basis that the debtor has defaulted in payment, if and to the extent that circumstances exist which support an equitable set-off.[167] In this sense, it operates in equity as a complete or a partial defeasance of the plaintiff's

---

[159] *SL Sethia Liners Ltd v Naviagro Maritime Corporation (The Kostas Melas)* [1981] 1 Lloyd's Rep 18, 26 (Robert Goff J).

[160] *Federal Commerce & Navigation Co Ltd v Molena Alpha Inc* [1978] 1 QB 927, 982 (Goff LJ); *Clambake Pty Ltd v Tipperary Projects Pty Ltd (No. 3)* [2009] WASC 52 at [152].

[161] As Cumming-Bruce LJ remarked in *Federal Commerce v Molena* [1978] 1 QB 927, 997: 'it is probably true to say that it was only Morris LJ's judgment in *Hanak v Green* [1958] 2 QB 9 that brought clearly to the attention of the legal profession and the commercial world the possibilities of equitable set-off as a defence.'

[162] (1841) Cr & Ph 161, 179, 41 ER 451, 458. See paras 4.02–4.03 above.

[163] See e.g. *Hanak v Green* [1958] 2 QB 9, 29; *Covino v Bandag Manufacturing Pty Ltd* [1983] 1 NSWLR 237, 238; *AWA Ltd v Exicom Australia Pty Ltd* (1990) 19 NSWLR 705, 710–11; *Barclays Bank plc v Gruffydd* Court of Appeal, 30 October 1992 *per* Scott LJ ('A set-off, whether legal or equitable, available to the principal debtor extinguishes, or reduces pro tanto, the amount of the creditor's claim'); *Aectra Refining and Manufacturing Inc v Exmar NV* [1994] 1 WLR 1681, 1650; *Lockley v National Blood Transfusion Service* [1992] 1 WLR 492, 495; *TSB Bank plc v Platts* [1998] 2 BCLC 1, 9; *Benford Ltd v Lopecan SL* [2004] 2 Lloyd's Rep 618 at [10]; *R (on the Application of Burkett) v London Borough of Hammersmith and Fulham* [2004] EWCA Civ 1342 at [45].

[164] *Rawson v Samuel* (1841) Cr & Ph 161, 179, 41 ER 451, 458.

[165] In Australia, see *National Australia Bank Ltd v Market Holdings Pty Ltd* (2000) 35 ACSR 572 at [33].

[166] Before the Judicature Acts, the permanency of an equitable set-off was achieved by way of a perpetual injunction.

[167] This view has been accepted in Australia. See *Re Kleiss, ex p Kleiss v Capt'n Snooze Pty Ltd* (1996) 61 FCR 436, 440–1; *Roadshow Entertainment Pty Ltd v (ACN 053 006 269) Pty Ltd* (1997) 42 NSWLR 462, 481 (CA); *IRM Pacific Pty Ltd v Nudgegrove Pty Ltd* [2008] QSC 195 at [11]. See also *Re Sgambellone; Ex p Jaques* (1994) 53 FCR 275, 280 and *Gilsan v Optus (No. 3)* [2005] NSWSC 518 at [52]–[55] (but note the discussion of the case at para. 5.94 below). In Canada, see *Saskatchewan Wheat Pool v Feduk* [2004] 2 WWR 69 at [54] (fn 53)–[55] (Saskatchewan CA).

claim.[168] A court of equity can protect the debtor's position by means of an injunction,[169] and the debtor's right may be the subject of a declaration.[170] This explains how equitable set-off can operate substantively without working an automatic discharge.[171] Judicial statements to the effect that equitable set-off operates to absolve a debtor from liability,[172] or that it has the consequence that the debtor has no liability,[173] describe the effect of the set-off in equity when circumstances are such as to support a set-off.[174]

The notion that the claimant's claim is not extinguished prior to judgment for a set-off is reflected in one of the grounds for the decision of the House of Lords in *Aries Tanker Corporation v Total Transport Ltd*.[175] Charterers of a vessel were being sued for payment of freight, and argued as a defence that they had an equitable set-off arising from a damages claim that they had against the owners for short delivery. The defence failed, for two reasons. The first was on the basis of a long-standing principle, that a damages claim in respect of cargo cannot be asserted by way of deduction from freight.[176] But as an alternative ground,

4.31

---

[168] *Aectra Refining and Manufacturing Inc v Exmar NV* [1994] 1 WLR 1634, 1649; *Fuller v Happy Shopper Markets Ltd* [2001] 1 WLR 1681 at [22] and [25]; *Young v National Australia Bank Ltd* (2004) 29 WAR 505 at [32] ('in equity there is no sum due'); *Prekons Insaat Sanayi AS v Rowlands Castle Contracting Group Ltd* [2007] 1 Lloyd's Rep 98 at [11].

[169] As in *Eller v Grovecrest Investments Ltd* [1995] QB 272 (CA) (injunction to restrain a landlord from levying distress).

[170] See *Sim v Rotherham Metropolitan BC* [1987] 1 Ch 216 (discussed at para. 4.34 below) and, in New South Wales, *P Rowe Graphics Pty Ltd v Scanagraphix Pty Ltd* NSW SC, Young J, 6 September 1988. In Australia, see also *Lean v Tumut River Orchard Management Ltd* [2003] FCA 269. In the case of a periodic payment obligation, the declaration may relate to future payments. See *Sim v Rotherham* (para. 4.34 below), and see also *Philip Collins Ltd v Davis* [2000] 3 All ER 808 (esp. at 830–2) (royalties).

[171] See e.g. the discussion of *Beasley v Darcy* (1800) 2 Sch & Lef 403n in *O'Mahoney v Dickson* (1805) 2 Sch & Lef 400, 408, 412, where it was acknowledged that the rent had been due in *Beasley*. In *Westpac Banking Corporation v Eltran Pty Ltd* (1987) 14 FCR 541, 549 Fox and Burchett JJ in their joint judgment said that: 'Equity permits certain privileged cross-claims to put on the armour of a set-off, but they do not therefore lose the character of cross-claims. They operate to extinguish the debt, not by ceasing to be cross-claims, but by virtue of being cross-claims which possess additional features.' Compare, however, *Stehar Knitting Mills Pty Ltd v Southern Textile Converters Pty Ltd* [1980] 2 NSWLR 514, 518.

[172] *Long Leys Co Pty Ltd v Silkdale Pty Ltd* (1991) 5 BPR 11,512, 11,520 (NSW CA).

[173] *Safeway Stores Ltd v Interserve Project Services Ltd* [2005] EWHC 3085 (TCC) at [53]. See also *Phoenix Commercial Enterprises v City of Canada Bay Council* [2009] NSWSC 17 at [94] ('the plaintiff's liability for rent would be treated as having been reduced') (appeal dismissed on other grounds: [2010] NSWCA 64).

[174] The above analysis of equitable set-off is doubted in *Goode on Legal Problems of Credit and Security* (4th edn (ed. Gullifer), 2008), 313 n 224. In particular, it is suggested that the analysis does not sit very happily with *Safeway Stores Ltd v Interserve Project Services Ltd* [2005] EWHC 3085 (TCC) or *Burton v Mellham* [2006] 1 WLR 2820 (HL). In the *Safeway* case at [53], Ramsey J referred to an equitable set-off available to Interserve as having the effect that Interserve had 'no liability' to Chelverton. But, as suggested above, that description does not derogate from the proposed analysis. It describes the effect of the set-off in equity. In the *Safeway* case, *quaere* why it was necessary in any event to have recourse to equitable set-off. Chelverton was in liquidation, in which case a set-off *prima facie* would have occurred automatically on the date of the liquidation under the Insolvency Rules 1986, r. 4.90. See paras 6.05–6.08 and para. 6.123 below. In relation to *Burton v Mellham*, that case was concerned with a question of construction of tax legislation, the House of Lords concluding that the word 'payment' should not be construed as requiring the 'absurd formality' of a solemn exchange of cheques. See [2006] 1 WLR 2820 at [27]. The discussion of Lord Wilberforce in *Aries Tanker Corporation v Total Transport Ltd* [1977] 1 WLR 185, 188 (see para. 4.32 below) presents a problem for the alternative analysis proposed in *Goode* at 310–13. See *Goode* at 311.

[175] [1977] 1 WLR 185.

[176] See paras 5.02–5.22 below.

which the House of Lords later described as the primary ground for the decision,[177] the point was made that the time bar set out in art. III, r. 6 of the Hague Rules for the enforcement of the charterer's damages claim had expired, with the result that the charterer's claim had ceased to exist as distinct from being merely unenforceable. Lord Wilberforce in the leading judgment said that a claim which had ceased to exist could not be introduced into legal proceedings as a set-off.[178] That was so notwithstanding that the charterers had asserted their claim within the limitation period by deducting the amount of the claim from the freight. Their problem was that they had not taken the extra step of commencing a suit during the period so as to preserve the claim. Therefore, any formerly existing right of equitable set-off that they otherwise may have had was lost. A necessary consequence of that view is that a set-off had not already taken effect as an automatic extinction of the liabilities.

4.32 Philip Wood has presented a different analysis of the substantive nature of the defence.[179] Essentially, his analysis has two aspects. The first is that an equitable set-off (or, as he terms it, a transaction set-off) is a 'self-help' remedy, by which it is meant that it entitles the debtor to 'exercise' or 'declare' the set-off so as to bring about a discharge or payment of the cross-demands.[180] The second is that, if the debtor does not exercise the right in this manner, he or she may rely on the set-off as a defence in judicial proceedings, in which case the judgment for a set-off has a 'retroactive' effect to the date that the debtor's cross-claim accrued.[181] Taking the second point first, it is not necessary to have recourse to an artificial notion of retroactivity of the judgment. The substantive nature of the defence in the period before the demands have been extinguished by judgment or by agreement is adequately explained on the basis outlined above. In so far as the concept of 'self-help' is concerned, the *Aries Tanker* case (above) is authority for the proposition that a right to an equitable set-off does not entitle a debtor to act unilaterally so as to bring about a discharge of the cross-demands by setting them against each other.[182] The charterers in that case had deducted the amount of their claim from the freight payable and tendered the balance before the expiration of the

---

[177] *Bank of Boston Connecticut v European Grain and Shipping Ltd* [1989] 1 AC 1056, 1103. See also Mustill LJ in the Court of Appeal, at 1071.

[178] Compare Lord Denning's reference to the *Aries Tanker* case in *Federal Commerce & Navigation Co Ltd v Molena Alpha Inc* [1978] 1 QB 927, 973–4, which is difficult to follow.

[179] See generally Wood, *English and International Set-off* (1989), 111–12.

[180] Wood, *English and International Set-off* (1989), 112, para. 4–25, 663 para. 11–24 (in the context of foreign currency claims), 784 para. 14–56, 894 para. 16–125, and 895 para. 16–128. See also McCracken, *The Banker's Remedy of Set-off* (3rd edn, 2010), 167–8, 185–6; *Goode on Legal Problems of Credit and Security* (4th edn (ed. Gullifer), 2008), 310–13. In *BICC v Burndy Corporation* [1985] 1 Ch 232, 254–5 Kerr LJ suggested that Burndy could have acted unilaterally to bring about a set-off so as to extinguish BICC's claim. However, the case concerned legal set-off under the Statutes of Set-off (see Dillon LJ at 247 and Kerr LJ at 256 and 259), and presumably the comment was intended to apply in that context. It would not be correct in that context, however. See para. 2.38 above.

[181] Wood, *English and International Set-off* (1989), 112, cross-referring to para. 2–192 *et seq.*

[182] See also *Mellham Ltd v Burton* [2003] STC 441 at [12] (referred to on appeal *Burton v Mellham Ltd* [2006] 1 WLR 2820 at [17]) and *Healing (Sales) Pty Ltd v Inglis Electrix Pty Ltd* (1968) 121 CLR 584, 602–3 in relation to the common law defence of abatement (though compare paras 2.129–2.133 above). In *Pacific Rim Investments Pte Ltd v Lam Seng Tiong* [1995] 3 SLR 1, 8–9 the Singapore Court of Appeal's statement of the consequences of characterizing equitable set-off as substantive made no mention of a right to effect a discharge of the cross-claims at law.

limitation period. The owners, on the other hand, made it clear that they did not accept the validity of the deduction.[183] Lord Wilberforce (in a judgment with which Viscount Dilhorne, Lord Simon of Glaisdale and Lord Edmund-Davies agreed[184]) rejected the argument that the charterer's action brought about a set-off. He said: 'The deduction of $30,000, unaccepted by the respondents, conferred no legal rights, and could not alter the legal position.'[185] That statement was made in the context of the primary ground for the decision in the *Aries Tanker* case, that a claim that had ceased to exist could not be relied on by way of set-off. The fact that the charterers had asserted their claim within the limitation period and purported to make a deduction did not affect his Lordship's view. Even if it were possible to have a set-off against a claim for freight, the unilateral deduction and the assertion of a right to make it were regarded as insufficient to bring about a cancellation of the cross-demands. That view is consistent with an earlier comment by Megarry J in *Samuel Keller (Holdings) Ltd v Martins Bank Ltd*.[186] In response to an argument that a mortgagor's indebtedness to the mortgagee had been reduced as a result of the appropriation to it by the mortgagor of a damages claim available against the mortgagee, Megarry J said that: 'the concept that the appropriation of an unliquidated claim to a mortgage debt by the mortgagor will effect a discharge nisi of that debt seems both novel and awkward.'[187]

Equitable set-off has admittedly been referred to in a number of cases as a self-help remedy.[188] That expression is unobjectionable if it is used in the sense that a debtor is entitled to withhold payment of the debt to the extent of an equitable set-off. This accords with the view that, while circumstances exist which support an equitable set-off, it is unconscionable for the creditor to regard the debtor as being indebted. It does not require a conclusion that the debtor's equitable right is such as to entitle him or her to act unilaterally to extinguish the cross-demands at law. **4.33**

Sim v Rotherham Metropolitan BC[189] is susceptible to a similar explanation. A local authority made a deduction from a teacher's salary because of a breach of contract by the teacher in failing to comply with a request to perform certain duties. The teacher issued a writ **4.34**

---

183 See [1977] 1 WLR 185, 187 (Lord Wilberforce).
184 See also Lord Salmon [1977] 1 WLR 185, 196.
185 [1977] 1 WLR 185, 188.
186 [1971] 1 WLR 43.
187 [1971] 1 WLR 43, 47. In the Court of Appeal Russell LJ (at 51) agreed with that view. See also *Inglis v Commonwealth Trading Bank* (1972) 126 CLR 161, 165; *Mobil Oil Co Ltd v Rawlinson* (1981) 43 P & CR 221, 226; *Ashley Guarantee plc v Zacaria* [1993] 1 WLR 62, 69, 70; *Clairview Developments Pty Ltd v Law Mortgages Gold Coast Pty Ltd* [2007] 2 Qd R 501 at [8]. While Megarry J in *Samuel Keller* did not mention equitable set-off, the judgment of Russell LJ in the Court of Appeal suggests that he recognized that the cross-claim in that case would have been available by way of defence to an action for payment of the mortgage debt, and his approval of Megarry J's comment should be considered with that in mind. See the reference (at 49) to unconditional leave to defend, and also (at 49 and 51) to the earlier Court of Appeal decision in *Morgan & Son Ltd v S Martin Johnson & Co Ltd* [1949] 1 KB, 107, which was concerned with equitable set-off.
188 *SL Sethia Liners Ltd v Naviagro Maritime Corporation (The Kostas Melas)* [1981] 1 Lloyd's Rep 18, 26; *Fuller v Happy Shopper Markets Ltd* [2001] 1 WLR 1681 at [22]; *Bluestorm Ltd v Portvale Holdings Ltd* [2004] 2 EGLR 38 at [19]; *Mellham Ltd v Burton* [2003] STC 441 at [11]–[12] (where the notion that a 'self-help set-off' can expunge a claim was doubted, which doubt was noted on appeal: *Burton v Mellham Ltd* [2006] 1 WLR 2820 at [17]); *Altonwood Ltd v Crystal Palace FC (2000) Ltd* [2005] EWHC 292 (Ch) at [32]. See also *Connaught Restaurants Ltd v Indoor Leisure Ltd* [1994] 1 WLR 501, 506.
189 [1987] 1 Ch 216.

claiming payment of the amount of the deduction, and also seeking a declaration that the local authority was not entitled to make a deduction from her salary. It was argued that, even if the teacher were in breach of contract, the only remedy of the local authority was to bring a separate action. Scott J rejected that view. He held that the teacher's failure to act constituted a breach, and that the resulting damages cross-claim gave rise to an equitable set-off which justified the deduction. The local authority had counterclaimed for various declarations, including that it was entitled to make the deduction,[190] and Scott J at the end of his judgment indicated that he was prepared to make the declarations sought by the local authority, subject to hearing counsel as to their form.[191] A declaration to the effect that the local authority was entitled to make a deduction may suggest that the local authority could act unilaterally to extinguish the cross-claims to the extent of the set-off. However, that proposition was not suggested in the judgment. Scott J said that the cross-claim impeached the plaintiff's claim for salary, so that she could not recover her salary without taking into account the loss to the local authority.[192] The declaration was simply a recognition that it was unjust for the plaintiff to regard the local authority as being indebted to the extent of the deduction, and that as a matter of equity the local authority was entitled to tender the reduced amount.

(2) Some possible problems

4.35 The debtor in most cases would be adequately protected by this view of the substantive nature of equitable set-off. In relation to limitation periods, the point is made below that the debtor would not be adversely affected by the expiration of the usual form of limitation period, which merely renders the cross-claim unenforceable by action. The debtor may, however, be at risk in a case such as *Aries Tanker*,[193] where the debtor's cross-claim has a shorter limitation period than the creditor's claim and the effect of the expiration of the period is to *extinguish* the cross-claim. In such a case the debtor would be well-advised to commence a suit so as to preserve the position, unless representations by the creditor would give rise to an estoppel so as to preclude him or her from relying on the time bar in any event. In substance, this was the view of Lord Wilberforce in the *Aries Tanker* case.[194]

4.36 A similar difficulty may arise when an equitable set-off is available to a debtor, and the creditor assigns the debt to a third party. The third party assignee should take subject to the set-off in accordance with normal principles.[195] Consider, however, that the assignor becomes bankrupt. Because of the assignment the debt would no longer be an asset of the estate, and accordingly a set-off would not be available under the insolvency set-off section.[196] Normally, this would not concern the debtor if he or she could still assert an equitable set-off against the assignee. But what if the assignee does not proceed against the debtor until after the assignor's discharge from bankruptcy? In that circumstance,

---

[190] For the declarations sought by the local authority, see the report of *Sim v Rotherham* at [1986] 3 All ER 387, 389.

[191] [1987] 1 Ch 216, 263.

[192] [1987] 1 Ch 216, 261–2.

[193] See para. 4.31 above.

[194] [1977] 1 WLR 185, 189.

[195] See para. 17.32 below.

[196] See para. 11.16 below.

Wood would appear to be correct in his view that the set-off would be lost.[197] The discharge should have the effect of releasing the assignor from liability to the debtor,[198] in which case the *Aries Tanker* case[199] suggests that the debtor would no longer have a right of set-off available against the assignor which he or she could assert against the assignee. This problem is not confined to equitable set-off. It may also apply in relation to the principle in *Cherry v Boultbee*,[200] as well as set-off under the Statutes of Set-off.[201] It is justifiable in the case of set-off under the Statutes, which in any event is only a procedural defence,[202] but equitable set-off is substantive. At least in the *Aries Tanker* case the charterers could have preserved their position by commencing a suit within the limitation period. However, that mechanism would not be available when an assignor has become bankrupt. The debtor's position would be ameliorated if he or she could apply before the discharge for a declaration[203] and a permanent injunction to restrain an action by the assignee on the assigned debt, but this is unsupported by authority. Moreover, an injunction operates *in personam*, and the debtor would require protection against the possibility of a further assignment by the assignee.

Wood has also expressed a concern in relation to the situation in which a trustee, in his or her capacity as such, enters into a transaction with a third party pursuant to which the trustee incurs a debt, though a cross-claim for damages is available against the third party which is sufficiently closely connected to give rise to an equitable set-off.[204] While the trustee is personally liable for the debt and the damages claim is an asset of the estate held on trust for the beneficiaries, the apparent lack of mutuality would not suffice to deny an equitable set-off.[205] The situation posited by Wood is that the set-off is not 'declared' before the bankruptcy of the trustee or the third party. The concern is that the damages claim and the debt in such a case would have retained their separate identities, and accordingly they may not be available for a set-off under the insolvency set-off section because of lack of mutuality. However, this should not present a problem if equitable set-off is analysed in the manner suggested above. If the cross-demands are sufficiently closely connected, the third party's title to the debt would be impeached such that it would be unconscionable for the third party to regard the trustee as a debtor, and this should continue to be the case during

4.37

---

[197] Wood, *English and International Set-off* (1989), 894–5.

[198] Insolvency Act 1986, s. 281. Discharge from bankruptcy extinguishes the bankrupt's debts. See *Wight v Eckhardt Marine GmbH* [2004] 1 AC 147 at [27]. *Law Society v Shah* [2009] Ch 223 at [31]–[38] suggests otherwise, but see paras 14.20–14.22 below.

[199] [1977] 1 WLR 185. See para. 4.31 above.

[200] See para. 14.22 below.

[201] See para. 17.40 below.

[202] See paras 2.34–2.52 above.

[203] See e.g. *Sim v Rotherham Metropolitan BC* [1987] 1 Ch 216 (para. 4.34 above), and in Australia *P Rowe Graphics Pty Ltd v Scanagraphix Pty Ltd* NSW SC, Young J, 6 September 1988. On the other hand, Young J doubted that a similar declaration would be available in the case of a procedural defence such as that conferred by the Statutes of Set-off. In that situation, the defendant would be required to wait until he or she is sued before the set-off could be given effect. See also the discussion of *Parker v Jackson* [1936] 2 All ER 281 in paras 2.40–2.45 above.

[204] Wood, *English and International Set-off* (1989), 784.

[205] *Murphy v Zamonex Pty Ltd* (1993) 31 NSWLR 439, referred to with approval in *Penwith District Council v V P Developments Ltd* [2005] 2 BCLC 607 at [20]–[23]. See para. 4.82 below. In relation to mutuality generally, see paras 11.01 and 11.13–11.20 below.

the third party's bankruptcy or liquidation.[206] Further, while the leave of the court is required for the commencement of proceedings against a bankrupt or a company after a winding-up order has been made against it,[207] leave should be available when an injunction is sought to restrain the taking of action which is inconsistent with the substantive nature of the defence of equitable set-off. A similar result should follow in the converse situation in which the third party incurs a debt to the trustee but at the same time has a cross-claim available as an equitable set-off, and the trustee becomes insolvent. The third party should still retain his or her equitable set-off.[208]

(3) Is the set-off confined to litigation?[209]

4.38 In *Mellham Ltd v Burton*,[210] Buxton LJ referred to what he called 'equitable set-off properly so-called', which he described as a defence or counterclaim that can be introduced into legal proceedings after action brought. Buxton LJ expanded on that view in *Muscat v Smith*.[211] He said that this category of set-off is 'restricted to the introduction of a defence to legal proceedings after action brought',[212] and that it operates only as 'an incident of litigation'.[213] He described it as merely 'a sub-species of counterclaim', albeit that it is a special and privileged type of cross-claim in that it does not simply provide a sum to be balanced off against the plaintiff's claim once established. Rather, he said that it operates in the litigation to extinguish the claim and prevent its original establishment.[214] He has also suggested that a 'self-help' set-off, in the sense of a right to make a deduction from a debt otherwise payable,[215] may be available in equity, but he referred to this as a different category, or species, or form, of set-off to that which arises when a cross-claim is pleaded as a defence to an action for payment.[216] This 'self-help' form of set-off was said to be 'of uncertain reach and content'.[217]

4.39 Three comments may be made in relation to those points.

4.40 The first is that any suggestion that equitable set-off is to be confined to the case of a defence to legal proceedings would have little merit.

---

[206] There is authority which suggests that equitable set-off cannot apply in bankruptcy or company liquidation, but it is suggested that that view is wrong. See para. 6.25–6.32 below.

[207] Insolvency Act 1986, s. 130(2) for company liquidation, and for bankruptcy s. 285(3).

[208] Compare Wood, *English and International Set-off* (1989), 1055.

[209] Some of the material in this section first appeared in an article published in the *Law Quarterly Review*, titled 'Equitable Set-off: A Critique of *Muscat v Smith*' (2006) 122 LQR 469. It is reproduced with the permission of the editor of the *Law Quarterly Review*.

[210] [2003] STC 441 at [10].

[211] [2003] 1 WLR 2853.

[212] [2003] 1 WLR 2853 at [37].

[213] [2003] 1 WLR 2853 at [44].

[214] [2003] 1 WLR 2853 at [44].

[215] See para. 4.32 above.

[216] *Mellham Ltd v Burton* [2003] STC 441 at [10]–[13]; *Bluestorm Ltd v Portvale Holdings Ltd* [2004] EGLR 38 at [19]. See also *Muscat v Smith* [2003] 1 WLR 2853 at [37] and [44], where Buxton LJ emphasized that he was concerned in that case with set-off as a defence to legal proceedings.

[217] *Bluestorm Ltd v Portvale Holdings Ltd* [2004] EGLR 38 at [19] (Buxton LJ).

Prior to the Judicature Acts, equitable set-offs generally were enforced by means of a common injunction to restrain the plaintiff at law from proceeding with an action or enforcing a judgment against the defendant until he or she had given credit to the defendant for the amount of a cross-demand.[218] The procedure changed with the enactment of the Judicature Acts, which permitted the defendant to plead the set-off directly as a defence in the plaintiff's action.[219] The Supreme Court of Judicature Act 1873 went further, and abolished the common injunction as a means of restraining a cause or proceeding pending in the High Court or before the Court of Appeal.[220] But since the emergence in recent years of the substantive quality of equitable set-off,[221] there is no reason why an injunction should not be available in other situations to restrain conduct which is contrary to the availability of the set-off. It would be entirely consistent with the former practice. For example, if a shipowner were to threaten to withdraw the vessel from a time charterer for non-payment of hire, but the charterer has an equitable set-off which impeaches the claim to hire,[222] the charterer should be entitled to seek an injunction restraining the owner from employing the vessel in a manner inconsistent with the time charter,[223] or a declaration that the charterer is entitled in equity to a set-off against the hire. The charterer should not be restricted to the introduction of a defence to any legal proceedings that may be brought by the shipowner. **4.41**

Consider in that regard *Baillie v Edwards*.[224] The question of a set-off in equity in that case arose in the context of an application by the holder of a life interest in an estate to redeem the estate free of a charge, on the basis that the debt the subject of the charge should be set off against a personal debt owing by the chargee to the tenant for life. The set-off did not arise by way of a defence to legal proceedings, or to restrain the prosecution of a common law action. It was the person claiming the set-off who instituted the suit in equity in which the set-off was given effect.[225] **4.42**

The second comment is that, in so far as it may have been thought[226] that 'self-help' set-off was based upon a notion that it permits a debtor to unilaterally expunge a claim and that observations by Lord Wilberforce in *Aries Tanker Corporation v Total Transport Ltd*[227] caused difficulty for that contention, no such difficulty arises on the analysis of the substantive nature of the set-off set out above. This analysis is not based upon a right to bring about a discharge of cross-demands at law, but rather upon an impeachment in equity of a creditor's right to take action against a debtor while circumstances subsist which support an equitable set-off. **4.43**

---

[218] See para. 3.01 above.
[219] In England, see now the Senior Courts Act 1981, s. 49, and CPR r. 16.6. In New South Wales, see the Supreme Court Act 1970, s. 59.
[220] Supreme Court of Judicature Act 1873, s. 24(5). In New South Wales, there is a similar provision in the Supreme Court Act 1970, s. 61.
[221] See para. 4.29 above.
[222] See para. 4.46 below in relation to this situation.
[223] See generally *Lauritzencool AB v Lady Navigation Inc* [2005] 1 WLR 3686 (CA).
[224] (1848) 2 HLC 74, 9 ER 1020. See para. 4.79 below.
[225] See the report of the proceedings at first instance *Baillie v Innes* (1845) 14 LJ Ch 341, 341–2.
[226] See *Mellham Ltd v Burton* [2003] STC 441 at [12].
[227] [1977] 1 WLR 185, 188. See para. 4.32 above.

4.44 Thirdly, the cases which illustrate the substantive effect of equitable set-off in a context other than as a defence to an action for payment in truth do not represent a separate category or species or form of set-off. It is the same set-off, albeit arising in different circumstances. Goff LJ correctly described the position in *Federal Commerce & Navigation Co Ltd v Molena Alpha Inc*:[228]

> Fourthly, in my judgment, this defence by its nature is such that it must be open to the charterer to set it up before ascertainment, not merely as a means of preventing the owner obtaining judgment or, at any rate, execution, but also as an immediate answer to his liability to pay hire otherwise due.

(4) Right to take action consequent upon default[229]

4.45 The characterization of the defence as substantive can have important consequences.[230] For example, a contract may entitle one party to take a particular course of action if the other party defaults in making a payment pursuant to the contract. If the other party indeed fails to pay but has available a substantive defence of equitable set-off, the first party could not treat that other party as having defaulted,[231] and accordingly could not take the action which is available upon default.[232]

---

[228] [1978] 1 QB 927, 982. See also *Eller v Grovecrest Investments Ltd* [1995] QB 272, 280 in relation to distress for rent.

[229] In addition to the cases referred to below, see paras 5.73–5.74 below in relation to forfeiture for non-payment of rent and distress for rent.

[230] Compare *Porter v McDonald* [1984] WAR 271 in relation to an application to remove a caveat under the Transfer of Land Act 1893 (WA) on the basis of an equitable set-off impeaching the debt owed by the caveator.

[231] In addition to the cases referred to below, see *Roadshow Entertainment Pty Ltd v (ACN 053 006 269) Pty Ltd* (1997) 42 NSWLR 462, 481. *Quaere* whether indeed it was correct to say that Roadshow was entitled, by virtue of equitable set-off, to withhold the payment due by it on 31 October 1993, given that the repudiation by CEL/Vision that led to the rescission did not occur until late November or early December when the receiver sold the business. While the New South Wales Court of Appeal accepted that there had been an anticipatory breach of contract by CEL/Vision by early October (see at 480–1), in order to be able to sue for damages for anticipatory breach there must have been an acceptance of the repudiation and thus a termination. See *Ogle v Comboyuro Investments Pty Ltd* (1976) 136 CLR 444, 450; *Johnstone v Milling* (1886) 16 QBD 460, 467. But termination did not occur until 6 December. The *Roadshow Entertainment* case should be compared to *Sloan Stanley Estate Trustees v Barribal* [1994] 2 EGLR 8, in which the Court of Appeal held that an equitable set-off was not available in respect of a cross-demand that was still contingent. Indeed, the awarding of interest to CEL/Vision in the *Roadshow Entertainment* case (see at 490) seems inconsistent with the view that Roadshow was entitled to withhold payment on the basis of an equitable set-off. See para. 4.56 below in relation to interest.

[232] See Lord Denning in *Federal Commerce & Navigation Co Ltd v Molena Alpha Inc* [1978] 1 QB 927, 974, referred to with approval by Dillon LJ in *BICC Plc v Burndy Corporation* [1985] 1 Ch 232, 248–9. In *Ashley Guarantee Plc v Zacaria* [1993] 1 WLR 62, 68, Nourse LJ agreed with counsel's submission that, if an equitable set-off was available in that case, the company would not have defaulted in any of its obligations. When a contract entitles one party to terminate the contract in the event of a failure by the other party to pay any sums payable by it to the first party, it has been held in Victoria that there will not have been a failure by the second party to pay sums payable to the first party if the second party has an equitable set-off. See *Auspac Trade International Pty Ltd v Victorian Dairy Industry Authority* (Vic SC, Byrne J, 30 June 1993, BC9300782 at 67–71). Byrne J's observations on set-off were affirmed on appeal: see *Auspac Trade International Pty Ltd v Victorian Dairy Industry Authority* (Vic SC Appeal Div, 22 February 1994, BC9406099 at 38 and 39). See also *Pacific Rim Investments Pte Ltd v Lam Seng Tiong* [1993] 3 SLR 1 (Singapore CA).

Consider a time charter of a ship. In *Federal Commerce & Navigation Co Ltd v Molena Alpha* **4.46**
Inc,[233] Lord Denning MR and Goff LJ[234] accepted that a charterer of a vessel on a time
charter has a right of equitable set-off entitling it to make a deduction[235] from the hire
otherwise stipulated in the charter if the owner through its neglect or default has deprived
the charterer of the use of the vessel, or has otherwise hindered or prejudiced the charterer's
use, for example through a breach of a speed warranty.[236] The right arises on the due date
for payment, and it does not merely provide a defence to an action at law for the payment
of hire.[237] A charterer possessed of the right, and who pays less than the sum stipulated in
the contract, is not considered to be in breach of contract. Therefore, when the time charter
contains the usual provision whereby the owner can withdraw the vessel in the event of
non-payment of hire, their Lordships accepted that the charterer can tender a reduced
amount in consequence of the cross-demand without bringing into existence the right of
withdrawal.[238] If the owner does not accept the tender, it acts at its peril. It will be liable in
damages if it withdraws the vessel. If, on the other hand, the defence were procedural rather
than substantive, the owner would have been entitled to withdraw the vessel because, until
there had been a judgment for a set-off, the charterer would be regarded as having defaulted
in payment. A similar analysis may apply when a landlord asserts a right to re-take possession of the premises because of the tenant's failure to pay rent.[239] If an equitable set-off
is available, the tenant may say that there was no such failure upon which the landlord
can rely.[240] Similarly, when a debt is payable by instalments, and the contract provides that,
in the event of a default in payment of one instalment the creditor may accelerate the
debt so that the full amount is presently payable, there would not be a default for the purpose of the right to accelerate if the debtor is entitled to an equitable set-off in relation to

---

[233] [1978] 1 QB 927, affirmed on other grounds [1979] AC 757.

[234] Cumming-Bruce LJ dissenting on the question whether there may be a set-off against hire.

[235] While the right in question was described as a right of deduction, the courts on other occasions have
been reluctant to accept that 'deduction' describes equitable set-off. See e.g. *Connaught Restaurants Ltd v
Indoor Leisure Ltd* [1994] 1 WLR 501, and generally paras 5.101–5.106 below.

[236] See [1978] 1 QB 927, 976 (Lord Denning MR), 981 (Goff LJ). Set-off in the context of charterparties
is considered in paras 5.02–5.24 below.

[237] See also *Compania Sud Americana de Vapores v Shipmair BV (The Teno)* [1977] 2 Lloyd's Rep 289, 294
(explaining *Steelwood Carriers Inc v Evimeria Compania Naviera SA (The Agios Giorgis)* [1976] 2 Lloyd's Rep
192); *Santiren Shipping Ltd v Unimarine SA (The Chrysovalandou-Dyo)* [1981] 1 Lloyd's Rep 159; *SL Sethia
Liners Ltd v Naviagro Maritime Corporation (The Kostas Melas)* [1981] 1 Lloyd's Rep 18, 26–7.

[238] See [1978] 1 QB 927, 974 (Lord Denning), 982 (Goff LJ). A similar analysis may apply when a shipowner claims to exercise a lien in the event of non-payment of hire. See *Santiren Shipping Ltd v Unimarine SA
(The Chrysovalandou-Dyo)* [1981] 1 Lloyd's Rep 159.

[239] See also para. 5.74 below in relation to a landlord's right to levy distress for non-payment of rent.

[240] *Federal Commerce & Navigation Co Ltd v Molena Alpha Inc* [1978] 1 QB 927, 974; *Televantos v
McCulloch* [1991] 1 EGLR 123; *Tomlinson v Cut Price Deli Ltd* (1992) 38 FCR 490, 494–5; *MEK Nominees
Pty Ltd v Billboard Entertainments Pty Ltd* (1993) V Conv R 54–468. See also *British Anzani (Felixstowe)
Ltd v International Marine Management (UK) Ltd* [1980] 1 QB 137; *BICC Plc v Burndy Corporation* [1985]
1 Ch 232, 249; *Connaught Restaurants Ltd v Indoor Leisure Ltd* [1994] 1 WLR 501; *Liangis Investments Pty Ltd
v Daplyn Pty Ltd* (1994) 117 FLR 28, 36. For analogous situations in Australia, see *Novamaze Pty Ltd v Cut
Price Deli Pty Ltd* (1995) 128 ALR 540, 544 (franchisor's contractual right to re-take possession consequent
upon default by the franchisee), and *Parraville Pty Ltd v Madden Woods Pty Ltd* (Vic SC, Coldrey J, 2 April
1997, BC9701118) (vendor's right to possession following default in payment by the purchaser). Compare
Hazcor Pty Ltd v Kirwanon Pty Ltd (1995) 12 WAR 62 and *Star Rider Ltd v Inntrepreneur Pub Co* [1998]
1 EGLR 53, in which a defence of equitable set-off was not made out. Note that different principles may apply
in relation to a claim for possession by a mortgagee. See paras 4.131–4.148 below.

the instalment which is otherwise due.[241] It has also been suggested (without deciding) that a retention of title clause in a contract for the sale of goods might not work if the purchaser has a cross-claim available by way of equitable set-off which exceeds the price (in that case, arising from a breach of an exclusive territory agreement).[242]

4.47   In a case in Australia,[243] a bank provided a foreign currency facility to a customer on terms that, if the Australian dollar equivalent of the moneys from time to time 'owing to the bank' exceeded a certain amount, the bank could call for further security. The Full Court of the Federal Court[244] said that there was a serious question to be tried as to whether a cross-claim by the customer relating to the grant and management of the foreign currency facility gave rise to an equitable set-off, so as to call in question whether the amount 'owing to the bank' exceeded the stipulated level, and therefore to impeach the bank's right to call for further security. A lease may give an option to the tenant to renew the lease for a further term if the tenant has complied with its obligations under the lease, including in the payment of rent. In a case in Queensland, the tenants admittedly had not tendered the rent stipulated in the lease. But since they had an equitable set-off, it was held that they had not breached the payment obligation and accordingly they were entitled to exercise the option.[245] This was the converse of the other instances referred to above, in that the 'debtors' had to show that they were not in default before they could exercise a right (i.e. renew the lease), rather than that a right of a creditor to take a particular course of action depended upon whether the debtor had defaulted, but the principle nevertheless is the same.

(5) Action taken by a creditor before a set-off has been asserted

4.48   A question has been raised as to the effect of action taken by a creditor consequent upon a default by a debtor, for example termination of an agreement, in circumstances where the debtor, who was entitled to an equitable set-off, had not asserted the set-off prior to the taking of the action.[246] The point was discussed in the context of an assumption that an equitable set-off properly asserted operates to extinguish the cross-claims. The question was whether, if a set-off is not asserted until after action taken by the creditor, the assertion of the set-off would operate retrospectively to reduce the claims, with the consequence that the creditor's action would have been ineffective. The view formed was that the set-off only takes effect from the time it is asserted.

4.49   The premise that equitable set-off permits a debtor to effect a discharge of cross-claims at law is contrary to authority.[247] It is also suggested that there is nothing retrospective about

---

[241] This was assumed in *Marubeni Corp v Sea Containers Ltd* Queen's Bench Division, Waller J, 17 May 1995, although it was held that the contract excluded the right to rely on an equitable set-off. *Quaere* whether the position would be different under the Statutes of Set-off. See the discussion of *Shipton v Casson* (1826) 5 B & C 378, 108 ER 141 in para. 2.57 above.

[242] *Benford Ltd v Lopecan SL* [2004] 2 Lloyd's Rep 618 at [18] (Morison J).

[243] *Westpac Banking Corporation v Eltran Pty Ltd* (1987) 14 FCR 541.

[244] Fox and Burchett JJ, Northrop J dissenting.

[245] *Knockholt Pty Ltd v Graff* [1975] Qd R 88.

[246] *Goode on Legal Problems of Credit and Security* (4th edn (ed. Gullifer), 2008), 310–13.

[247] *Aries Tanker Corporation v Total Transport Ltd* [1977] 1 WLR 185, 188. See para. 4.32 above.

the operation of the set-off.[248] It operates in equity by way of impeachment of a creditor's right at any particular point in time to regard the debtor as having defaulted in payment. *Prima facie*, it should not be critical whether the set-off is asserted before or after the creditor takes action. On the other hand, equitable set-off is a discretionary remedy and, depending on the circumstances, a debtor may be precluded by his or her conduct from relying upon the set-off.[249] Questions of estoppel and waiver could also arise.

(6) Estimating the value of the cross-claim

Since the cross-demand in these cases usually is for an unliquidated sum, a person asserting a right to an equitable set-off may have to make an estimate of the value of his or her damages claim when the time arrives for payment of the sum stipulated in the contract. For example, a charterer of a vessel may not be in a position to calculate with precision the value of a cross-demand available to it against the owner for breach of a speed warranty when the next payment of hire becomes due. Goff LJ, in the *Federal Commerce* case,[250] suggested that the charterer acts at its peril if it pays less than the amount otherwise required by the contract. If the charterer is wrong, the owner would be justified in withdrawing the vessel for non-payment of hire. Lord Denning, on the other hand, considered that the charterer would not be in default if it has quantified the loss by a reasonable assessment made in good faith,[251] and this approach has since been favoured in other cases.[252]

4.50

(7) Statute of limitation

The substantive nature of the defence of equitable set-off may assume importance in the case of a statute of limitation. The usual form of statute of limitation preserves the existence of the right but takes away the remedy of enforcing the right by action at law.[253] Since the Statutes of Set-off merely perform a procedural function, a defence of set-off under the Statutes may only be based upon a debt that is enforceable by action. Therefore, a debt owing by the claimant which is unenforceable as a result of the expiration of a limitation period would not give rise to a defence under the Statutes.[254] Equitable set-off, on the other hand, is a substantive defence which does not require an order of the court for its enforcement.[255] As a consequence, it is not sufficient to deny an equitable set-off that the cross

4.51

---

[248] See para. 4.32 above.

[249] See paras 4.58–4.62 below.

[250] [1978] 1 QB 927, 982.

[251] [1978] 1 QB 927, 975.

[252] *SL Sethia Liners Ltd v Naviagro Maritime Corporation (The Kostas Melas)* [1981] 1 Lloyd's Rep 18, 26–7; *Santiren Shipping Ltd v Unimarine SA (The Chrysovalandou-Dyo)* [1981] 1 Lloyd's Rep 159, 163–4. See also *Gilbert-Ash (Northern) Ltd v Modern Engineering (Bristol) Ltd* [1989] AC 689, 712 in the context of building contracts ('amounts bona fide claimed'), and *Modern Trading Co Ltd v Swale Building and Construction Ltd* (1990) 24 Con LR 59. Compare *Steelwood Carriers Inc v Evimeria Compania Naviera SA (The Agios Giorgis)* [1976] 2 Lloyd's Rep 192.

[253] For example, the Limitation Act 1980, ss. 2 and 5, which deal respectively with claims in tort and contract, each stipulate that: 'An action . . . shall not be brought' after the expiration of six years from the date on which the cause of action accrued. Compare ss. 3 and 17, which extinguish title to chattels and land.

[254] See para. 2.47 above.

[255] *SL Sethia Liners Ltd v Naviagro Maritime Corporation (The Kostas Melas)* [1981] 1 Lloyd's Rep 18, 26.

demand upon which it is based is no longer enforceable by action[256] because of the expiration of a limitation period.[257] Indeed, that approach has been adopted in circumstances where an action brought on the cross-demand previously had been struck out for want of prosecution.[258]

4.52   Subsections 35(1) and (2) of the Limitation Act 1980 deem a claim by way of set-off or counterclaim to be a separate action and to have been commenced on the same date as the original action. There is substantial authority for the proposition that this refers only to set-off under the Statutes of Set-off, and does not preclude a time-barred cross-claim from being the subject of an equitable set-off.[259] As Hobhouse J observed at first instance in *Westdeutsche*

---

[256] Compare *J & S Holdings Pty Ltd v NRMA Insurance Ltd* (1982) 41 ALR 539, 554, but in that case there was no right of recovery as opposed to a right which was not enforceable by action. See para. 4.53 below. Since equitable set-off does not require that the cross-claim be enforceable by action, there would seem to be no reason why a statutory right to a money benefit which is enforceable only by a public law remedy should not be able to be the subject of an equitable set-off, although this ultimately would depend on the terms of the relevant legislation. See *Walker v Department of Social Security* (1995) 56 FCR 354, 367–8 (Drummond J, dissenting). The circumstance that a debt has ceased to be enforceable by action does not mean that it is no longer due and payable. See *Helou v P D Mulligan Pty Ltd* (2003) 57 NSWLR 74, but compare *National Australia Bank Ltd v Idoport Pty Ltd* [2007] NSWSC 1349 at [68] and [71].

[257] See Lord Denning in *Henriksens Rederi A/S v THZ Rolimpex (The Brede)* [1974] 1 QB 233, 245–6, 249 (though compare Cairns and Roskill LJJ at 254 and 264), and again in *Federal Commerce v Molena* [1978] 1 QB 927, 973–4. See also *Re McGreavy* [1950] 1 Ch 150, 158 (referring to set-off generally, but compare above in relation to the Statutes of Set-off); *Sidney Raper Pty Ltd v Commonwealth Trading Bank of Australia* [1975] 2 NSWLR 227, 236–40 (Moffitt P, though compare Glass JA at 255–6, which is difficult to follow); *AMP v Specialist Funding Consultants Pty Ltd* (1991) 24 NSWLR 326, 331–2; *Westdeutsche Landesbank v Islington BC* [1994] 4 All ER 890, 944–5 (Hobhouse J); *Pacific Rim Investments Pte Ltd v Lam Seng Tiong* [1995] 3 SLR 1, 9 (Singapore CA); *Philip Collins Ltd v Davis* [2000] 3 All ER 808, 831; *Concrete Constructions Group v Litevale Pty Ltd (No. 2)* [2003] NSWSC 411 at [74]; *Young v National Australia Bank Ltd* (2004) 29 WAR 505 at [32] (note that the discussion in that case at [35]–[48] in relation to the construction of the Limitation Act 1935 (WA), s. 46 would not be relevant to causes of action accrued since the enactment of the Limitation Act 2005 (WA), s. 81, which excludes from the operation of that section a counterclaim solely by way of defence); *Almario v Allianz Australia Workers Compensation (NSW) Insurance Ltd* (2005) 62 NSWLR 148 at [28]; *Taylor Aston Ltd v Aon Ltd* [2005] EWHC 1684 (Comm) at [77] and [81]. There is also support for this proposition in the judgment of Lord Salmon in *Aries Tanker Corporation v Total Transport Ltd* [1977] 1 WLR 185, 196–7 (on the assumption that English law permitted deductions from freight by way of equitable set-off). For the contrary view, see *NV Bureau Wijsmuller v The Owners of the MV Tojo Maru (The Tojo Maru)* [1970] P 21, 48; *Renner v Racz* (1971) 22 DLR (3d) 443. On the same principle, a possessory lien may be exercised in respect of a statute-barred debt, because the right to exercise the lien is not dependent upon an action at law. See e.g. *Spears v Hartly* (1800) 3 Esp 81, 170 ER 545; *Higgins v Scott* (1831) 2 B & Ad 413, 109 ER 1196; *Australia and New Zealand Banking Group Ltd v Douglas Morris Investments Pty Ltd* [1992] 1 Qd R 478, 497. See also the discussion of unenforceable claims in the context of the rule in *Cherry v Boultbee* (1839) 4 My & Cr 442, 41 ER 171 in paras 14.17–14.22 below, and generally, as to the exercise of rights by a creditor in relation to a time-barred debt which do not require recourse to the courts, *Commonwealth v Mewett* (1997) 191 CLR 471, 535. Compare *Strachan v Marriott* [1995] 3 NZLR 272, 291–2 in relation to the Property Law Act 1952 (NZ), s. 92(6). In Australia, compare also the case of a time-barred cross-claim for misleading or deceptive conduct contrary to the Trade Practices Act 1974 (Cth), s. 52. See para. 4.118 below.

[258] *Filross Securities Ltd v Midgeley* [1998] 3 EGLR 43.

[259] See Lord Denning MR in *Henriksens Rederi A/S v THZ Rolimpex (The Brede)* [1974] 1 QB 233, 246 (though compare Cairns and Roskill LJJ at 254 and 264), and Hobhouse J at first instance in *Westdeutsche Landesbank v Islington BC* [1994] 4 All ER 890, 943–6, whose views were followed by the Court of Appeal in *Filross Securities Ltd v Midgeley* [1998] 3 EGLR 43 and by Jonathan Parker J in *Philip Collins Ltd v Davis* [2000] 3 All ER 808, 831. See also *Cheltenham BC v Laird* [2009] EWHC 1253 (QB) at [459]. Compare art. 32(4) of the Convention on the Contract for the International Carriage of Goods by Road (CMR), which stipulates that: 'A right of action which has become barred by lapse of time may not be exercised by way of counter claim or set-off.' *Impex Transport Aktieselskabet v A G Thames Holdings Ltd* [1981] 2 Lloyd's

Landesbank Girozentrale v Islington LBC,[260] what is contemplated by the legislation is something which can be expressed as a 'claim', not something which has a mere status as a defence. Equitable set-off is in the latter category. Speaking of that form of set-off, he said:[261]

> If a plaintiff, in equity, is not entitled to assert his cause of action without at the same time giving credit to the defendant for the relevant matters, no question of any claim being made by a defendant against the plaintiff arises and the sole question is what is the proper claim that the plaintiff should make against the defendant.

Unlike set-off under the Statutes, equitable set-off is a substantive defence which does not require an order of the court for its enforcement.[262] Its essence is not the prosecution of a cross-claim in a proceeding against the plaintiff, but the impugning of the plaintiff's right to sue. It is a true defence, and not a 'claim' for the purpose of s. 35.

When questions of equitable set-off arise in relation to time bars, the conclusion that the availability of the defence survives the expiration of a limitation period governing a cross-claim assumes that the statute of limitation in question merely takes away the remedy without affecting the existence of the underlying right. If, however, the right itself is extinguished,[263] the circumstances necessary to support an equitable set-off would no longer exist, and the time-barred cross-claim would not provide a defence. *Aries Tanker Corporation v Total Transport Ltd*[264] illustrates that proposition.   **4.53**

In New South Wales, the Limitation Act 1969, s. 63 provides for the extinguishment of a claim on the expiration of the applicable limitation period.[265] Notwithstanding the extinguishment, Mason P opined, in *Concrete Constructions Group v Litevale Pty Ltd (No. 2)*,[266] that a claim which is time-barred under the Act can give rise to an equitable defence of set-off. That opinion is difficult to reconcile with the *Aries Tanker* case, which was not referred to.   **4.54**

(8) Arbitration and foreign jurisdiction clauses

The distinction between a substantive and a procedural defence may be important when a cross-demand asserted as a set-off is subject to an arbitration clause or a foreign jurisdiction clause to which the court would give effect. In an application by a claimant for summary judgment, leave to defend will not be granted when a procedural defence of set-off is asserted under the Statutes of Set-off, if the court in the claimant's action would refuse to   **4.55**

Rep 566 supports the view that this encompasses equitable set-off, but it was held subsequently in *R H & D International Ltd v IAS Animal Air Services Ltd* [1984] 1 WLR 573 that freight payable under a contract for the carriage of goods by road cannot be reduced by equitable set-off in any event. See para. 5.06 below. In Western Australia, a different view was expressed in *Young v National Australia Bank Ltd* (2004) 29 WAR 505 at [35]–[36] in relation to the Limitation Act 1935 (WA), s. 46, but that would not apply to the Limitation Act 2005 (WA), s. 81, which excludes from the operation of the section a counterclaim solely by way of defence.

[260] [1994] 4 All ER 890, 943–4.
[261] [1994] 4 All ER 890, 945.
[262] See paras 4.29–4.30 above.
[263] See e.g. art. III, r. 6 of the Hague Rules, which was in issue in *Aries Tanker Corporation v Total Transport Ltd* [1977] 1 WLR 185. See also *Macquarie International Investments Ltd v Glencore UK Ltd* [2009] EWHC 2267 (Comm) at [242]–[243] in relation to a contractual time bar.
[264] [1977] 1 WLR 185. See para. 4.31 above.
[265] Note, however, the effect of s. 68A.
[266] [2003] NSWSC 411 at [74].

try the merits of the cross-claim because of the arbitration or foreign jurisdiction clause applicable to the cross-claim. There is no such difficulty, however, when a substantive defence of equitable set-off is in issue which impugns the claimant's title to sue.[267]

(9) Interest

4.56 Consider the case of an interest-bearing debt. If the debtor has a valid claim for an equitable set-off, the principal sum upon which interest is payable is reduced to the extent of the value of the cross-demand during the period while circumstances exist which support an equitable set-off.[268] This is indicative of a substantive defence, as opposed to the form of procedural defence available under the Statutes of Set-off.

(10) Winding-up petition

4.57 If an equitable set-off is available to a debtor in an amount exceeding the debt, the creditor may be restrained from presenting a winding-up petition because of failure to pay, given that the set-off provides a substantive defence to the debtor.[269]

E. Discretion

4.58 In order for a court of equity to provide relief by way of set-off, the person claiming relief must demonstrate some equitable ground for being protected from the other party's demand.[270] As a corollary, an equitable set-off may be denied, notwithstanding that cross-claims are otherwise sufficiently closely connected, if there are present factors or circumstances which militate against the justice or fairness of a set-off.[271] Thus, the conduct of the parties may be relevant to the question of the availability of equitable relief by way of set-off.[272] The courts have given little guidance as to the circumstances in which this

---

[267] *Aectra Refining and Marketing Inc v Exmar NV* [1994] 1 WLR 1634, 1649–50; *Glencore Grain Ltd v Agros Trading Co* [1999] 2 Lloyd's Rep 410, 416–17; *Bim Kemi AB v Blackburn Chemicals Ltd* [2001] 2 Lloyd's Rep 93 at [9]; *Prekons Insaat Sanayi AS v Rowlands Castle Contracting Group Ltd* [2007] 1 Lloyd's Rep 98 at [11].

[268] *Connaught Restaurants Ltd v Indoor Leisure Ltd* [1994] 1 WLR 501; *Newman v Cook* [1963] VR 659 (particularly the judgment of Hudson J at 676–7). See also *Barnett v Peter Cox Group Ltd* (1995) 45 Con LR 131. The sentence in the text was quoted in *Clambake Pty Ltd v Tipperary Projects Pty Ltd (No. 3)* [2009] WASC 52 at [152]. In *Wallis v Bastard* (1853) 4 De G M & G 251, 43 ER 503 the court found an implied agreement for a set-off so that interest was only payable on the balance. In relation to interest where one of the claims is in a foreign currency, see paras 5.93–5.94 below. Compare *Axel Johnson Petroleum AB v MG Mineral Group AG* [1992] 1 WLR 270, 275 with respect to a counterclaim. Compare also the order made in *Roadshow Entertainment Pty Ltd v (ACN 053 006 289) Pty Ltd* (1997) 42 NSWLR 462, 490 in relation to interest under the Supreme Court Act (NSW). Equitable set-off would not affect interest which accrued before the cross-claim arose. See the *Clambake* case at [154].

[269] *McDonald's Restaurants Ltd v Urbandivide Co Ltd* [1994] 1 BCLC 306; *Penwith District Council v V P Developments Ltd* [2005] 2 BCLC 607 (application to strike out or stay a petition). See also *Re Wallace Smith & Co Ltd* [1992] BCLC 970. Compare *TSB Bank plc v Platts* [1998] 2 BCLC 1, 8–12.

[270] *Hanak v Green* [1958] 2 QB 9, 18–19. See para. 4.02 above.

[271] *Bim Kemi AB v Blackburn Chemicals Ltd* [2001] 2 Lloyd's Rep 93 at [39]. In Australia, see the dissenting judgment of Drummond J in *Walker v Department of Social Security* (1995) 56 FCR 354, 365–7.

[272] In addition to *Bluestorm Ltd v Portvale Holdings Ltd* [2004] EGLR 38 (below), see *Galambos & Son Pty Ltd v McIntyre* (1974) 5 ACTR 10, 26; *Sydmar Pty Ltd v Statewise Developments Pty Ltd* (1987) 73 ALR 289, 296; *AMP v Specialist Funding Consultants Pty Ltd* (1991) 24 NSWLR 326, 329; *AWA Ltd v Exicom Australia*

concept may apply. In Australia, an equitable set-off seems to have been denied in one case, notwithstanding the closeness of the claims, because the cross-claimant had failed to investigate, quantify or press its cross-claim.[273] However, mere delay in prosecuting a cross-claim should not disentitle a defendant from relying on it as a set-off. The whole point of a right of set-off is that it entitles a person possessed of the right to wait until he or she is sued and then rely on the cross-claim as a defence.[274]

In *Bluestorm Ltd v Portvale Holdings Ltd*,[275] the defendant was denied an equitable set-off **4.59** because of its conduct. The case concerned a block of flats in a poor state of repair. The freehold was owned by a company, PVL. PVL was a subsidiary of another company, PHL, which had acquired leasehold interests in a substantial number of the flats. Some of the other tenants obtained judgment against PVL for breaches of the landlord's repairing covenant. PVL was dissolved, and Bluestorm, a company controlled by the tenants who were unconnected with PHL, acquired the freehold. Bluestorm commenced proceedings against PHL claiming arrears of rent and service charges. PHL counterclaimed for damages for breach of the repairing covenant, and sought to set off that damages claim against its liability for the arrears. In reply, Bluestorm contended that, if it was liable for breach of the repairing covenant, it was entitled to set off against that liability a claim for special damage caused by PHL's failure to pay the money. The Court of Appeal held that the set-off relied on by PHL was equitable in origin, and that in the circumstances PHL should be denied equitable relief by way of set-off. Its claim was in respect of the dilapidated state of the building, but that state originally was due to the neglect of PHL's subsidiary, PVL. Moreover, PHL had refused to pay service charges, as a result of which other tenants had also refused to contribute. This, in turn, deprived Bluestorm of funds to effect repairs. PHL's own conduct, therefore, was a substantial cause of Bluestorm's breaches of the repair covenant the subject of PHL's cross-claim. On the other hand, PHL was liable to Bluestorm for any special damage suffered by Bluestorm consequent upon PHL's failure to pay.[276] The damage suffered by Bluestorm included its own liability to PHL, and it was held that Bluestorm could set off its damages claim for that loss against its liability to PHL, so as to extinguish it. The net effect was that PHL remained liable for the unpaid money.

If a charge granted by a company is void as against an administrator or a liquidator for non- **4.60** registration under the companies legislation,[277] and the chargee is liable for damages for

---

Pty Ltd (1990) 19 NSWLR 705, 712; *Walker v Department of Social Security* (1995) 56 FCR 354, 365; *Radin v Vekic* (NSW SC, Young J, 6 June 1997, BC9702448 at 12) ('laches or other conduct'). See also *Blacksheep Productions Pty Ltd v Waks* [2008] NSWSC 488 at [24]–[25]. In *Televantos v McCulloch* [1991] EGLR 123, it was argued that the defendant should be precluded from asserting an equitable set-off because of her conduct, but it was held that the conduct in question was not sufficient to have that effect. See also *IRM Pacific Pty Ltd v Nudgegrove Pty Ltd* [2008] QSC 195 at [20]–[24].

[273] *APM Wood Products Pty Ltd v Kimberley Homes Pty Ltd* NSW SC, Cole J, 17 February 1989, referred to in *AWA Ltd v Exicom Australia Pty Ltd* (1990) 19 NSWLR 705, 712. See also *Australian Beverage Distributors Pty Ltd v Evans & Tate Premium Wines Pty Ltd* (2006) 58 ACSR 22 at [64].

[274] *Muscat v Smith* [2003] 1 WLR 2853 at [6]–[7].

[275] [2004] EGLR 38.

[276] The Court of Appeal accepted ([2004] EGLR 38 at [27]), by reference to *Wadsworth v Lydall* [1981] 1 WLR 598, that special damage could be caused by a failure to pay money.

[277] See the Companies Act 2006, s. 860.

conversion as a result of a wrongful dealing with the property the subject of the void charge, the chargee cannot set off against its damages liability its claim against the company arising out of the transaction which gave rise to the charge.[278] This is because a set-off would allow the chargee to exercise the very right which it could have exercised if the charge had been registered. Parliament has said that the charge is void if it is not registered, and in that circumstance equity will not intervene to protect the chargee from its failure to comply with the statute. Further, a creditor holding an asset belonging to the debtor, but without the benefit of a lien or other security, could not claim to retain the asset by way of a set-off against the debt,[279] in which case the creditor should not be able to improve his or her security in equity by wrongfully converting the property and attempting to set off the resulting damages liability.[280]

4.61 An equitable set-off may be denied if the quantum of the cross-claim is highly speculative,[281] or if the cross-claim depends upon the outcome of the taking of a long and complicated account,[282] or if the determination of the cross-claim would otherwise involve considerable delay such that the claimant would not be adequately compensated for being kept from his or her money for this period,[283] although in that circumstance interest may be an adequate remedy if it turns out that some or all of the claimant's claim is not reduced by a set-off.[284] Alternatively, terms may be imposed as a condition of equitable relief.[285] Thus, a defendant may be given leave to defend, or a claimant may be restrained from exercising a right consequent upon non-payment, only on condition that the defendant pays all or part of the claimant's claim into court, or provides some other acceptable form of security pending the determination of the cross-claim.[286] This has arisen particularly in the context of mortgages, where a mortgagor has sought to restrain the mortgagee from exercising his or her security rights consequent upon default on the basis of an alleged equitable set-off.[287]

---

[278] *Smith v Bridgend County BC* [2002] 1 AC 336 at [36] (Lord Hoffmann), [76] (Lord Scott of Foscote).

[279] See para. 3.02 above.

[280] [2002] 1 AC 336 at [36].

[281] *Star Rider Ltd v Inntreprenneur Pub Co* [1983] 1 EGLR 53, 56. See also *Abignano v Wenkart* (1998) 9 BPR 16,765, 16,774. On the other hand, it is not necessary that the damages should have been fully quantified or properly formulated. See *Benford Ltd v Lopecan SL* [2004] 2 Lloyd's Rep 618 at [17].

[282] *Rawson v Samuel* (1841) Cr & Ph 161, 41 ER 451, and see also *General Credits (Finance) Pty Ltd v Stoyakovich* [1975] Qd R 352. In *Re Interesting Developments Pty Ltd* [2009] VSC 12 the question whether the respondents had a cross-claim depended on the outcome of other litigation involving other parties. In the circumstances, it was not considered to be just that the applicant be delayed in the receipt of moneys due to it.

[283] *Best v Hill* (1872) LR 8 CP 10, 15; *Roadshow Entertainment Pty Ltd v (ACN 053 006 269) Pty Ltd* (1997) 42 NSWLR 462, 489. See also *Rawson v Samuel* (1841) Cr & Ph 161, 179, 41 ER 451, 458; *Abignano v Wenkart* (1998) 9 BPR 16,765, 16,774.

[284] *Best v Hill* (1872) LR 8 CP 10, 15; *Roadshow Entertainment Pty Ltd v (ACN 053 006 269) Pty Ltd* (1997) 42 NSWLR 462, 489.

[285] *Roadshow Entertainment Pty Ltd v (ACN 053 006 269) Pty Ltd* (1997) 42 NSWLR 462, 489.

[286] In addition to the mortgage cases referred to below, see *General Credits (Finance) Pty Ltd v Stoyakovich* [1975] Qd R 352; *Tomlinson v Cut Price Deli Pty Ltd* (1992) 38 FCR 490. See also *Atterbury v Jarvie* (1857) 2 H & N 114, 121, 157 ER 47, 50 (Bramwell B), and *Gale v Luttrell* (1826) 1 Y & J 180, 195, 148 ER 636, 642 (Alexander CB).

[287] See paras 4.136–4.148 below.

If the claims are otherwise sufficiently closely connected, it is not necessary that the defend-   **4.62**
ant should have commenced proceedings against the claimant on the cross-claim.[288]
Furthermore, in contrast to the position under the Statutes of Set-off,[289] a defendant will
not be precluded from raising a cross-claim as a defence by way of equitable set-off merely
because the parties had agreed that the cross-claim should be the subject of arbitration, or
that it should be determined by the courts of a foreign jurisdiction.[290] Therefore, in an
application by the claimant for summary judgment, the defendant in such a case may
be granted leave to defend. Indeed, in the case of the usual arbitration agreement which
provides for all 'disputes' to be referred to arbitration, the availability of an equitable set-off
would mean that the claimant's claim is also in dispute, so that both the claim and the cross-
claim may be referred.[291] This is a consequence of the substantive nature of the defence.[292]

F. Liquidated Cross-Claims

Equitable set-offs commonly arise when there is a claim for a contract debt on one side of   **4.63**
the account and on the other a claim for damages in either contract or tort which, in the
traditional formulation, impeaches the title to the debt.[293] Usually, the damages claim is
asserted as a defence to an action to enforce the debt, but the defence similarly may be available in the converse situation in which a debt[294] is raised as a defence to an action for damages.[295] Furthermore, equitable set-off is not confined to cases involving a debt and a
damages claim, but in an appropriate case may apply when both demands are liquidated.[296]

---

[288] *McDonald's Restaurants Ltd v Urbandivide Co Ltd* [1994] 1 BCLC 306.

[289] See para. 2.51 above.

[290] *Aectra Refining and Marketing Inc v Exmar NV* [1994] 1 WLR 1634, 1649, referring to *Gilbert-Ash (Northern) Ltd v Modern Engineering (Bristol) Ltd* [1974] AC 689 (esp. at 720, 726). See also *Glencore Grain Ltd v Agros Trading Co* [1999] 2 Lloyd's Rep 410, 416–17.

[291] *Federal Commerce & Navigation Co Ltd v Molena Alpha Inc* [1978] 1 QB 927, 974, and see para. 1.08 above.

[292] See paras 4.29–4.57 above.

[293] However, both claims may be for unliquidated damages, as in *Bim Kemi AB v Blackburn Chemicals Ltd* [2001] 2 Lloyd's Rep 93.

[294] Subject to the terms of the relevant legislation, this should include a statutory right to a money benefit which is enforceable by a public law remedy as opposed to an action at law for payment. See the dissenting judgment of Drummond J in *Walker v Department of Social Security* (1995) 56 FCR 354, 367–8, and compare para. 2.14 above in relation to the Statutes of Set-off.

[295] *Filross Securities Ltd v Midgeley* [1983] 3 EGLR 43. In *Cullinane v British 'Rema' Manufacturing Co Ltd* [1953] 2 All ER 1257, 1271, Sir Raymond Evershed MR was prepared to assume (without deciding) that a set-off was available in this situation. See also *Hanak v Green* [1958] 2 QB 9 (cross-claim based on *quantum meruit* set off in an action for damages); *Safeway Stores Ltd v Interserve Project Services Ltd* [2005] EWHC 3085 (TCC) at [38] and [52] (where the form of set-off considered was equitable set-off notwithstanding that Chelverton was in liquidation: see paras 6.05–6.08 below). Compare *McCreagh v Judd* [1923] WN 174 (DC), and also *Rawson v Samuel* (1841) Cr & Ph 161, 41 ER 451 (in which the claims were insufficiently connected to give rise to an equitable set-off). Compare also para. 2.128 above in relation to the common law defence of abatement.

[296] See e.g. *Coba Industries Ltd v Millie's Holdings (Canada) Ltd* [1985] 6 WWR 14; *Telford v Holt* (1987) 41 DLR (4th) 385; *Roadshow Entertainment Pty Ltd v (ACN 053 006 269) Pty Ltd* (1997) 42 NSWLR 462; *Taylor Aston Ltd v Aon Ltd* [2005] EWHC 1684 (Comm) (commission payable by the defendant to the claim-ant and cross-claim by the defendant for advances of commission); *Primus Telecommunications Pty Ltd v Kooee Communications Pty Ltd* [2007] NSWSC 374. The liquidated cross-demand need not be payable when the plaintiff commences proceedings. See *Roadshow Entertainment* at 489. See also *Gilsan v Optus (No. 3)* [2005]

If there are mutual debts, a set-off would be available under the Statutes of Set-off.[297] But that form of set-off essentially is a procedural defence to an action for payment.[298] It differs in nature from an equitable set-off, which is a substantive defence.[299] For example, a substantive defence may preclude a creditor from taking action permitted by the contract upon non-payment in circumstances where a mere procedural defence to payment would not have that effect.[300] The fact that there are mutual debts which would give rise to a procedural defence under the Statutes of Set-off[301] does not mean that a substantive defence of equitable set-off is not also available if the debts are sufficiently closely connected.[302] Thus, in an action involving a tenant who had failed to pay rent, Lightman J held that a cross-claim by the tenant for repayment of earlier overpayments of rent gave rise to an equitable set-off, so as to deny the landlord the right to levy distress for unpaid rent[303] (though there is authority in Australia which is difficult to reconcile with that view[304]). Similarly, it has been held that an overpayment of royalties may be the subject of an equitable set-off against future royalties.[305]

NSWSC 518 at [39]–[62] (*quantum meruit* claim and liquidated cross-claims). It does not suffice, however, that cross-debts arose out of the same contract. See *Phoenix Commercial Enterprises v City of Canada Bay Council* [2009] NSWSC 17 at [92] (appeal dismissed on other grounds: [2010] NSWCA 64), and para. 4.91 below. See also *Penwith District Council v V P Developments Ltd* [2005] 2 BCLC 607 at [20]–[26] (contract debt claims and costs awarded against the creditor in relation to various arbitration proceedings, *sed quaere* to the extent that the costs related to different arbitrations).

[297] See ch. 2.

[298] See paras 2.34–2.52 above.

[299] See paras 4.29–4.57 above.

[300] See paras 4.45–4.47 above. See *Phoenix Commercial Enterprises v City of Canada Bay Council* [2009] NSWSC 17 at [92] (the Civil Procedure Act 2005 (NSW), s. 21 being a re-enactment of the Statutes of Set-off in New South Wales: see para. 2.66 above).

[301] See para. 2.34–2.52 above.

[302] *Fuller v Happy Shopper Markets Ltd* [2001] 1 WLR 1681 at [26]. The circumstance that both debts accrue interest under the contract, but at different rates, would tend against the view that they give rise to a substantive defence of equitable set-off. See *Phoenix Commercial Enterprises v City of Canada Bay Council* [2009] NSWSC 17 at [91] (appeal dismissed on other grounds: [2010] NSWCA 64).

[303] *Fuller v Happy Shopper Markets Ltd* [2001] 1 WLR 1681. See also *Phoenix Commercial Enterprises v City of Canada Bay Council* [2009] NSWSC 17 at [86], [93] and [95]; *Clambake Pty Ltd v Tipperary Projects Pty Ltd (No. 3)* [2009] WASC 52 at [168]; *Etablissement Esefka Anstalt v Central Bank of Nigeria* [1979] 1 Lloyd's Rep 445 (payments under a letter of credit: see para. 4.114 below). Compare *Ory & Ory v Betamore Pty Ltd* (1993) 60 SASR 393 (where the unpaid rent was claimed by a mortgagee in possession as opposed to the landlord/mortgagor who was the recipient of the overpayment: see paras 17.72–17.95 below); *Peninsular and Oriental Steam Navigation Co v Youell* [1997] 2 Lloyd's Rep 136 (in which different contracts were in issue: see para. 4.16 above); *Walker v Department of Social Security* (1995) 56 FCR 354 (overpayment of sickness benefit: see para. 4.114 below); *Unchained Growth III Plc v Granby Village (Manchester) Management Co Ltd* [2000] 1 WLR 739 (overpayment of service charge to a management company, where set-off had been excluded by agreement); *Altonwood Ltd v Crystal Palace FC (2000) Ltd* [2005] EWHC 292 (Ch) at [31]–[34] (in which an overpayment of turnover rent was not permitted to be set off against an obligation to pay basic rent, in circumstances where the lease provided that basic rent was to be paid without deduction or set-off).

[304] *Ex p Alcock, re McConnell* (1955) 55 SR (NSW) 259, 262, referred to in *Reid v Hipkiss* (2001) 10 BPR 19,305 at [14].

[305] *Philip Collins Ltd v Davis* [2000] 3 All ER 808 (esp. at 830–2). See also *Joinery Plus Ltd v Laing Ltd* [2003] BLR 184 at [98]–[101] in relation to total failure of consideration, although *quaere* whether an equitable set-off should have been available to the *payee* in that case. In relation to an overpayment of a performance bonus, see *Jones v Commerzbank AG* [2003] EWCA Civ 1663, although the nature of the set-off was not analysed.

An equitable set-off may arise when the debt owing to a creditor is the source from which **4.64** a debt owing by the creditor to the debtor is to be satisfied.[306] In *Ralston v South Greta Colliery Co*,[307] A had leased a coal mine to B, the consideration for which included the payment of a royalty by B in respect of the coal won. In consideration of work and labour done by C, A agreed to pay C a part of the royalty that A received from time to time, and C then assigned this right to B. When A sued B for payment of the royalty, the New South Wales Supreme Court held that B had a set-off to the extent of the portion of the royalty that had been assigned back to him.[308] This was not a case of mutual debts under the Statutes of Set-off, because until A actually received payment there was no debt owing to B. The set-off was regarded instead as an equitable set-off. Sir William Cullen CJ said that there was 'a good equity in the defendant to restrain the prosecution of so much of the demand as the plaintiff has parted with and which has come back into the hands of the original debtor.'[309]

(1) Contingent debts, and debts not yet payable

A set-off under the Statutes of Set-off is not available in respect of a debt that is not yet **4.65** payable,[310] and it has been suggested that set-off in equity is subject to a similar restriction.[311] This should be the case when equity acts by analogy with the Statutes of Set-off,[312] but it should not represent an inflexible principle when the peculiarly equitable form of set-off arising from a close connection is in issue. Rather, the fact that the debt is not yet payable should constitute a factor to be taken into consideration in the exercise of the

---

[306] See also the analogous circumstances in issue in *Safa Ltd v Banque du Caire* [2000] 2 Lloyd's Rep 600, 609, where the bank paying the beneficiary under the letter of credit would have been entitled to immediate reimbursement. See paras 5.46–5.48 below. *Quaere* whether this could also have been explained on the basis of circuity of action. See para. 4.04n above. The *Safa* case was referred to without adverse comment in *Burton v Mellham Ltd* [2006] 1 WLR 2820 at [27].

[307] (1912) 13 SR (NSW) 6, distinguished in *Mellham Ltd v Burton* [2003] STC 441 at [13] and *Victoria Place Pty Ltd v Hyatt of Australia Ltd* [2003] VSC 385 at [40]–[41].

[308] The defence in *Ralston v South Greta Colliery* was based upon set-off (see the discussion at (1912) 13 SR (NSW) 6, 15–16), as opposed to circuity of action (see para 4.04n above). In the circumstances, a defence of circuity of action would appear not to have been available. In the first place, it is said that the defence only applies when the cross-claim arises *directly* between the parties to the proceeding in which it is used as a defence. See *Aktieselskabet Ocean v B Harding and Sons Ltd* [1928] 2 KB 371, 384–5 (Scrutton LJ) and *Co-operative Retail Services Ltd v Taylor Young Partnership* [2000] BLR 461, 474–5, although compare *Schenker & Co (Aust) Pty Ltd v Maplas Equipment and Services Pty Ltd* [1990] VR 834, 849. In *Ralston*, on the other hand, there was an intervening assignment. Moreover, the defence only applies in circumstances where, if the claimant recovered against the defendant, the defendant could recover exactly the same sum from the claimant. See *Aktieselskabet Ocean* at 385; *McCamley v Harris* (1998) NSW Conv R 55–827 at 56,479. For that reason, a covenant not to sue may be pleaded as a defence to an action brought in breach of the covenant. See *Thompson v Australian Capital Television Pty Ltd* (1996) 186 CLR 574, 609. In the *Ralston* case, however, only part of the amount payable by B to A was assigned.

[309] (1912) 13 SR (NSW) 6, 16.

[310] See para. 2.29 above.

[311] *Manzanilla Ltd v Corton Property and Investments Ltd* [1996] EWCA Civ 942 at [42].

[312] See para. 3.07 above.

court's discretion.[313] In particular, equitable relief may not be available if the cross-demand is not payable for a long time, or terms may be imposed as a condition of relief.[314]

4.66 It would be more difficult to justify an equitable set-off in the case of a debt which is merely contingent,[315] because in such a case there is not an existing debt until the contingency occurs. There may nevertheless be cases where in the circumstances a set-off would be appropriate. An example is *Ralston v South Greta Colliery Co*[316] (above), in which B's claim against A on the assigned debt was contingent upon B having first paid the royalty to A. On the other hand, an equitable set-off should not be available when a debtor has merely a contingent right of reimbursement from the creditor, in circumstances where the right only arises upon payment by the debtor to a third party, and at the time when the question of set-off falls to be determined the debtor has not made the payment. Until such time as the debtor takes the step of paying the third party so as to crystallize his or her right of reimbursement from the creditor, the circumstances ordinarily would not be such as to render it unconscionable for the creditor to regard the debtor as being indebted. This situation arose in *Sloan Stanley Estate Trustees v Barribal*.[317] A tenant of a farm was liable under the Land Drainage Act 1976 to pay a drainage rate, but was entitled to recover the amount paid from the landlord. The tenant argued that he was entitled to an equitable set-off against rent even before he had paid the rate, so that he could not be evicted for non-payment of rent.[318] The Court of Appeal held that a set-off was not available until the tenant himself had paid.

G. Mutuality[319]

(1) Is mutuality always necessary?

4.67 Set-off under the Statutes of Set-off and in insolvency set-off requires mutuality.[320] Essentially this means that the demands must be between the same parties and be held in the same right or interest,[321] or, as the House of Lords recently expressed it, that each party should be debtor and creditor in the same capacity.[322]

---

[313] See *Roadshow Entertainment Pty Ltd v (ACN 053 006 269) Pty Ltd* (1997) 42 NSWLR 462, 489, and paras 4.58–4.62 above in relation to discretion.

[314] *Roadshow Entertainment Pty Ltd v (ACN 053 006 269) Pty Ltd* (1997) 42 NSWLR 462, 489.

[315] *Manzanilla Ltd v Corton Property and Investments Ltd* [1996] EWCA Civ 942 at [42].

[316] (1912) 13 SR (NSW) 6. See also *Safa Ltd v Banque du Caire* [2000] 2 Lloyd's Rep 600, 609, referred to in *Burton v Mellham Ltd* [2006] 1 WLR 2820 at [27].

[317] [1994] 2 EGLR 8.

[318] This would have been a consequence of the substantive nature of equitable set-off. See paras 4.45–4.47 above and para. 5.73 below.

[319] Some of the material in this section first appeared in an article published in the *Law Quarterly Review*, titled 'Equitable Set-off: A Critique of *Muscat v Smith*' (2006) 122 LQR 469. It is reproduced with the permission of the editor of the *Law Quarterly Review*.

[320] See ch. 11 below.

[321] *Peel v Fitzgerald* [1982] Qd R 544, 547; *Halsbury's Laws of England* (5th edn, 2009) vol. 11 ('Civil Procedure'), 510, para. 653 n 2.

[322] *Secretary of State for Trade and Industry v Frid* [2004] 2 AC 506 at [26].

Ordinarily, it would not be just or equitable that cross-demands be set off in equity unless **4.68** there is mutuality. In its simplest form, mutuality means that A can sue B and B can sue A. If the situation instead is that A can sue B and B can sue C, it would not usually be just that the demands be set off because this would mean that A's asset (the claim against B) would be used to pay C's liability. This would include a case where A and C are related entities. In equity, their relationship would not justify the use of A's claim to pay C's debt through a set-off.[323] It also includes the situation in which A is a manager appointed under the Landlord and Tenant Act 1987, s. 24(1) in relation to leased premises, the manager having functions as a court-appointed official and acting in a capacity independent of the landlord, and the tenant (B) has cross-claims against the landlord (C).[324] Nevertheless, the test for equitable set-off traditionally has not been formulated in terms of a requirement of mutuality.[325] Consistent with the inherent flexibility of equitable remedies, if in an exceptional case a set-off would be appropriate in all the circumstances notwithstanding that the claims in issue are not mutual, as a matter of principle there would seem to be no compelling reason why a court of equity should not have a discretion to permit a set-off despite the absence of mutuality, subject to compliance with the rule of practice of the Court of Chancery that all persons materially interested in the subject of a suit generally should be made parties to the suit.[326]

In Australia, the courts have emphasized that mutuality is not an indispensable require- **4.69** ment of equitable set-off.[327] This was also recognized by the Canadian Supreme Court in *Telford v Holt*,[328] the Supreme Court referring with approval to an earlier statement by the

---

[323] *Fuller v Happy Shopper Markets Ltd* [2001] 1 WLR 1681 at [11] (HSM being a wholly owned subsidiary of N & P). See also *Hamilton Ice Arena Ltd v Perry Developments Ltd* [2002] 1 NZLR 309 (claim against company and cross-claim by shareholders) and *Savory Holdings Ltd v Royal Oak Mall Ltd* [1992] 1 NZLR 12, 14 (assuming, as appears to have been the case (see e.g. the reference at 16 to the 'change of name') that the plaintiffs were related entitles). Compare *Kendray v Hassall* [2001] NTSC 40.

[324] *Maunder Taylor v Blaquiere* [2003] 1 WLR 379.

[325] Hence, the 'dearth of specific statements supporting the proposition that a cross-claim must be a claim against the original claimant . . .', to which Buxton LJ referred in *Muscat v Smith* [2003] 1 WLR 2853 at [45].

[326] *Daniell's Chancery Practice* (8th edn, 1914) vol. 1, 147; *John Alexander's Clubs Pty Ltd v White City Tennis Club Ltd* (2010) 266 ALR 462 at [139]. In *Murphy v Zamonex Pty Ltd* (1993) 31 NSWLR 439 (see para. 4.82 below) the former trustee (Burns Philp) was not a party to the action (see at 462), but it was in liquidation and had no interest in the action.

[327] *West Street Properties Pty Ltd v Jamison* [1974] 2 NSWLR 435, 441–2; *Sidney Raper Pty Ltd v Commonwealth Bank of Australia* [1975] 2 NSWLR 227, 255; *Westmex Operations Pty Ltd (in liq) v Westmex Ltd (in liq)* (1992) 8 ACSR 146, 153 (affirmed (1993) 12 ACLC 106); *Murphy v Zamonex Pty Ltd* (1993) 31 NSWLR 439, 464 (see para. 4.82 below); *Walker v Department of Social Security* (1995) 56 FCR 354, 367; *Kendray v Hassall* [2001] NTSC 40 at [32]; *Maertin v Klaus Maertin Pty Ltd* (2006) 57 ACSR 714 at [27]; *Australian Finance Direct Ltd v Director of Consumer Affairs Victoria* (2006) 16 VR 131 at [128]; *Concrete Equipment Australia (Trading) Pty Ltd v Bonfiglioli Transmission (Aust) Pty Ltd* [2010] NSWSC 393 at [24]. In *Forsyth v Gibbs* [2009] 1 Qd R 403 at [16] Keane JA (McMurdo P agreeing) referred to lack of mutuality as 'one indication, among other more powerful indications' that there was an insufficient connection between the claims to support an equitable set-off. Compare *Hypec Electronic v Registrar-General (No. 3)* [2008] NSWSC 167 at [13].

[328] (1987) 41 DLR (4th) 385, 394. See also *Canada Trustco Mortgage Co v Sugarman* (1999) 179 DLR (4th) 548 at [18]; *Keith G Collins Ltd v McKenzie* (2005) 252 DLR (4th) 717 at [28]; *Pierce v Canada Trustco Mortgage Co* (2005) 254 DLR (4th) 79 at [39]; *Reilly v Insurance Corp of British Columbia* 2007 BCCA 261 at [41]–[43] (British Columbia CA); *Caisse populaire Desjardins de l'Est de Drummond v Canada* (2009) 309 DLR (4th) 323 at [20] (SC).

British Columbia Court of Appeal that set-off in equity 'can apply where mutuality is lost or never existed'.[329] Nevertheless, recent judgments in England suggest that mutuality is necessary.[330] In *Muscat v Smith*,[331] Buxton LJ, in a judgment with which Sedley and Ward LJJ expressed agreement,[332] said that equitable set-off does not apply where the defendant has a claim against someone other than the claimant, and that the cross-claims must lie between the same parties.[333] That view has since been repeated in the Court of Appeal.[334] An 'exception' has been recognized in the form of the principle that an assignee takes subject to equities,[335] which principle is considered later.[336] But apart from that, this view imports the concept of mutuality as a requirement of equitable set-off.[337]

4.70 Ordinarily, the justice of the case would require mutuality. But the problem with expressing it in rigid terms is that there have been cases where equity has permitted a set-off despite the absence of mutuality. Those cases were not referred to in the Court of Appeal judgments. In truth, mutuality has not been regarded as a strict requirement of equitable set-off.

4.71 Equitable set-off was permitted in circumstances where cross-claims were not mutual in an early case involving fraud. In *Vulliamy v Noble*[338] a firm of bankers had made various loans to the first plaintiff ('BV'), as security for which BV transferred some stock into the name of one of the partners of the firm (Noble). BV repaid some of the loans, though an amount of £2,750 remained outstanding. On 5 April 1809, BV gave a promissory note for that amount to the firm, expressed in terms: 'I promise to pay to the order of Messrs Devaynes, Dawes, and Co the sum of £2,750, with lawful interest, for value received, they transferring

---

[329] *CIBC v Tuckerr Industries Inc* (1983) 149 DLR (3d) 172, 175. See also *Coopers & Lybrand Ltd v Lumberland Building Materials Ltd* (1983) 150 DLR (3d) 411, 416.

[330] Compare *Freeman v Lomas* (1851) 9 Hare 109, 113–14, 68 ER 435, 437 ('except under special circumstances'). Comapre also *Re Kaupthing Singer and Friedlander Ltd* [2009] 2 Lloyd's Rep 154 at [9], where Sir Andrew Morritt C explained the unavailability of an equitable set-off in that case on the basis of lack of a sufficient connection as opposed to lack of mutuality.

[331] [2003] 1 WLR 2853 at [42]–[45].

[332] [2003] 1 WLR 2853 at [31], [56]–[57].

[333] Similarly, Mocatta J in *First National Bank of Chicago v The West of England Shipowners Mutual Protection and Indemnity Association (Luxembourg) (The Evelpidis Era)* [1981] 1 Lloyd's Rep 54, 67 accepted a submission by counsel that an equitable set-off where different parties are involved in the respective claims is 'a creature unknown to the law'.

[334] *R (on the Application of Burkett) v London Borough of Hammersmith and Fulham* [2004] EWCA Civ 1342 at [57]–[58]; *Edlington Properties Ltd v J H Fenner & Co Ltd* [2006] 1 WLR 1583 at [20]. The comment in *Maunder Taylor v Blaquiere* [2003] 1 WLR 379 at [42], to the effect that set-off was not possible in that case because there was no mutuality, should be considered by reference to the circumstances there in issue, in particular that the justice of the case did not support an equitable set-off. See at [43] and [50].

[335] *Muscat v Smith* [2003] 1 WLR 2853 at [50]; *R (on the Application of Burkett) v London Borough of Hammersmith and Fulham* [2004] EWCA Civ 1342 at [58].

[336] See ch. 17 below.

[337] See *Maunder Taylor v Blaquiere* [2003] 1 WLR 379 at [42], and the reference in *R (on the Application of Burkett) v London Borough of Hammersmith and Fulham* [2004] EWCA Civ 1342 at [57] to 'lack of mutuality under the rules as understood in *Hanak v Green*', *Hanak v Green* [1958] 2 QB 9 being a leading authority on equitable set-off.

[338] (1817) 3 Mer 593, 36 ER 228. See also *Ex p Stephens* (1805) 11 Ves Jun 24, 32 ER 996 in relation to a joint and several debt (see paras 12.11–12.13 below), though note the explanation of that case in *Re Bank of Credit and Commerce International SA (No. 8)* [1996] Ch 245, 265–70, which explanation is criticized in paras 12.29–12.39 below.

to me, or my order, [the stock], which they hold as a collateral security.' On 2 May 1809, BV and his son (the second plaintiff) borrowed a sum of £3,000 from the firm, for which they gave a joint promissory note. On 2 May 1810, BV repaid the sum of £2,750 borrowed on his own account, whereupon his promissory note was returned to him. However, the stock given as security was not transferred back to him. The firm later became bankrupt, whereupon BV demanded the return of the security. It transpired that the firm had fraudulently sold most of the stock and applied the proceeds to the firm's use. BV accordingly had a personal claim against the firm for the amount received and dissipated. At the same time, he and his son were jointly indebted to the firm. A joint debt and a separate claim ordinarily are not regarded as mutual,[339] but Lord Eldon LC permitted BV to set off the claims notwithstanding the absence of mutuality.[340]

An alternative interpretation of *Vulliamy v Noble* has been proposed. In *Middleton v Pollock, ex p Knight and Raymond*,[341] Sir George Jessel MR sought to explain *Vulliamy v Noble* on the basis that the stock was retained by the bank under an agreement that it should constitute security for the joint debt. The summary of the plaintiffs' bill set out in the report of *Vulliamy v Noble* records that the plaintiffs alleged that, when BV repaid his personal borrowings: **4.72**

> the stock ought to have been re-transferred; but the same being considered by the banking-house to remain in Noble's name as a collateral security for the money advanced to both Plaintiffs on their joint notes, and the Plaintiff Vulliamy, the father, having a high opinion of the honour and solvency of the house, he (the said Plaintiff) did not require a re-transfer.

In their answer, Noble and the assignees in bankruptcy said that the stock was not re-transferred 'because the Plaintiff had always remained indebted to the house during that time'. Sir George Jessel concluded that both parties had agreed that the stock was kept as security for payment of the joint note, and that BV accordingly had a right in equity to insist that the proceeds of the security be applied in reduction of joint debt. He therefore said that *Vulliamy v Noble* was not an authority on set-off, properly so-called. Rather, it was a case in which the proceeds were to be regarded as having been applied in payment of the secured debt. However, an examination of the report of *Vulliamy v Noble* does not support that analysis. The case in truth concerned equitable set-off.

Notwithstanding the pleading in the plaintiffs' bill and the answer of Noble and the assignees in bankruptcy, the question whether the stock stood as security for the joint debt was in issue in the case. The estate of one of the defendants, Devaynes, was separately represented. Devaynes had been a partner in the firm. He died on 29 November 1809, which was after the sale of the stock but before BV repaid his personal debt and received back his promissory note on 2 May 1810. Counsel for Devaynes' representatives argued that the stock did not stand as security for the general balance but only as security for particular advances, and that BV's rights in relation to the joint note rested on equitable set-off notwithstanding the   **4.73**

---

[339] *Re Pennington and Owen Ltd* [1925] 1 Ch 825. See para. 12.02 below.
[340] See the discussion of *Vulliamy v Noble* at para. 12.11 below.
[341] (1875) LR 20 Eq 515, 521–3. See also *Goode on Legal Problems of Credit and Security* (4th edn (ed. Gullifer), 2008), 309 n 207.

joint liability.[342] That is to say, the stock was not security for the joint note. This was in support of an argument that BV's failure to call for a re-transfer of the security in May 1810 should be considered as a repudiation of all claim on Devaynes' estate. The basis of that argument was that Devaynes' estate should not be chargeable for a loss occasioned solely by a want of common prudence on the part of BV.[343] That argument depended upon BV being entitled to call for a re-transfer of the security in May 1810, which he could not have done if the stock stood as security for the joint note.

4.74   In support of his explanation of *Vulliamy v Noble*, Sir George Jessel referred to an exchange during argument in that case.[344] Lord Eldon commented that there was a difficulty as to the joint note of BV and his son, and queried what evidence there was of an agreement that the stock was to be held as security for the joint loan. The report records the following reply from counsel for the plaintiffs:

> That evidence is to be found in the nature, and in the continuance, of the transaction. And when all circumstances are taken together, and coupled with the fact, that no re-transfer was called for, and the books being attended to, in which both Vulliamys, the father and son, are credited, and the accounts made up according to this course of dealing and mutual understanding between the parties, it is impossible not to infer an intention that the stock of Vulliamy should remain a security for all the notes, both his own separate notes, and the joint note of himself and his son.

Thus, there was no direct evidence of an agreement. It was said that an agreement was to be inferred. But notwithstanding that the point was in issue, the report does not record Lord Eldon as having accepted that there was such an agreement. On the contrary, it is evident that Lord Eldon did not accept it. He noted that BV had 'signed papers' stating the particular purposes for which the stock was specifically pledged, and commented that this 'cannot but be taken against him'.[345] This, presumably, was a reference to the promissory note of 5 April 1809 signed by BV, which recorded that the stock was security for his separate debt of £2,750. Lord Eldon also dismissed the defendant's answer to the bill, to the effect that the stock would have been re-transferred if the whole of the debt to the firm had been paid, as amounting to 'nothing'.[346] Moreover, the suggestion that the stock was security for the joint loan is not reflected in the reason adduced by Lord Eldon for rejecting the argument of Devaynes' estate that Devaynes was not liable given BV's failure to call for a re-transfer of the stock in May 1810.[347] If it was the case that the stock remained as security for the joint debt, the argument could have been dismissed simply on the ground that BV was not entitled to call for a re-transfer. But that was not the basis upon which the argument was rejected. Rather, Lord Eldon said that, at the time of his death, Devaynes, along with the other partners, knew that the firm no longer held the stock, and that nothing could be taken from the circumstance that BV had failed to call for a re-transfer.

---

[342] (1817) 3 Mer 593, 605–6, 36 ER 228, 233.
[343] (1817) 3 Mer 593, 607–11, 36 ER 228, 234–5.
[344] (1817) 3 Mer 593, 612–13, 36 ER 228, 235–6.
[345] (1817) 3 Mer 593, 617, 36 ER 228, 237.
[346] (1817) 3 Mer 593, 609, 617, 36 ER 228, 234, 237.
[347] See the discussion at (1817) 3 Mer 593, 619–20, 36 ER 228, 238.

In his judgment, Lord Eldon treated the issue as one of set-off. He said that at law a joint **4.75** debt cannot be set off against a separate debt, but went on to say that: 'there is no doubt that, under particular circumstances, a joint debt may be set off against a separate debt, in equity.'[348] He proceeded to justify a set-off in that case on the basis of the defendants' concealed fraud.[349]

Vulliamy v Noble is authority for the proposition that equitable set-off does not always **4.76** require strict mutuality. Other cases support that proposition.

Consider *Ex p Hanson*.[350] Assignees in bankruptcy brought an action at law against two **4.77** joint debtors on a bond. One of the joint debtors had only joined in the bond as a surety. The other joint debtor, who was the principal debtor (Hanson), had a separate claim against the bankrupts. Since a joint debt and a separate claim are not mutual,[351] Hanson's separate claim could not be relied on as a set-off in the assignee's action. Hanson therefore presented a petition in equity praying that he be allowed to set off his separate claim against the joint debt. Lord Eldon held in favour of a set-off.[352] He said that the joint debt was nothing more than a security for Hanson's separate debt, and upon 'equitable considerations' a creditor who has a joint security for a separate debt cannot resort to that security without allowing for the claim of the principal debtor.[353]

Ex p Hanson was followed by the Ontario Supreme Court Appellate Division in *Clarkson v* **4.78** *Smith and Goldberg*.[354] A partnership owed a debt to a bank. As security, one of the partners charged his separate deposit to the bank. The bank went into liquidation, and the liquidator sued the partnership for payment of the debt, refusing to give credit for the deposit. The court noted that a right of set-off does not ordinarily exist between a debt due by a firm and an amount due separately to a partner. In the present case, however, judgment on the partnership debt could have been levied against the firm assets or against those of each partner singly. Since the partner who provided the deposit could have been required to pay the whole debt out of his personal assets, it was considered unjust that he should be denied the right to have his deposit applied against the firm's debt for which it was security.[355] Accordingly, a set-off was permitted in equity.

Another example is *Baillie v Edwards*,[356] a decision of the House of Lords in 1848. Baillie **4.79** had a life interest in an estate. One Innes had made advances in respect of the estate to the

---

[348] (1817) 3 Mer 593, 618, 36 ER 228, 237–8.
[349] See para. 12.11 below.
[350] (1811) 18 Ves Jen 232, 34 ER 305.
[351] See para. 12.02 below.
[352] See also Lord Erskine in earlier proceedings: *Ex p Hanson* (1806) 12 Ves Jun 346, 33 ER 131.
[353] The case proceeded on the basis that the subject of the set-off was a joint debt and a separate debt. The joint debt was security for a loan made separately to Hanson. The modern theory of insolvency set-off is that the set-off takes effect automatically upon the occurrence of a bankruptcy or liquidation. See paras 6.119–6.146 below. On that basis, *Ex p Hanson* could now be explained on the ground that Hanson's separate claim was set off automatically upon the occurrence of the bankruptcy against his debt for the underlying loan, and to that extent the security was released.
[354] [1926] 1 DLR 509. See also para. 12.42 below.
[355] See also the discussion at paras 16.83–16.88 below.
[356] (1848) 2 HLC 74, 9 ER 1020. I am indebted to Mr Berg's discussion of *Baillie v Edwards* in his article, 'Liquidation Set-off: The Mutuality Principle and Security over Bank Balances' [1996] LMCLQ 176.

extent of some £8,000, on terms that Baillie should not be personally liable for them but that Innes would look only to the estate for repayment. Innes accordingly had a charge or lien on the estate for that amount, but no personal claim against Baillie. In addition, Innes was separately indebted to Baillie in the amount of £11,884. Baillie instituted a suit in equity against Innes, seeking redemption of the estate. Innes became bankrupt, whereupon his assignees in bankruptcy were joined as defendants. The House of Lords held that Baillie was entitled to have Innes's claim against the estate for £8,000 paid and satisfied by the application of a sufficient part of the £11,884 due from Innes to Baillie,[357] and on that basis Baillie was entitled to have the estate restored to him. The question was regarded as one of set-off,[358] but it is evident that there was no mutuality. While Innes was indebted to Baillie personally, Innes's claim was against the estate, not against Baillie. Indeed, Lord Lyndhurst earlier had emphasized lack of mutuality as a reason for disallowing a set-off,[359] his Lordship's decision to that effect being the subject of a successful appeal to the House of Lords in this proceeding. Counsel for Baillie, Mr Bethell,[360] justified Baillie's right on the ground that it was in the nature of an equitable set-off.[361] He argued that Baillie was entitled to say that, although he was not personally liable in respect of Innes' charges against the estate, he could require that the charges be paid out of the moneys that Innes owed him.[362] *Baillie v Edwards* therefore is an example of a set-off in equity where there was no mutuality.

4.80   *Hamp v Jones*[363] concerned a landlord (Hamp) who levied distress for unpaid rent upon goods of the tenant, the landlord acting through a bailiff. The tenant subsequently obtained judgment against both Hamp and the bailiff for damages because of irregularities in the distress and sale of the goods. Hamp, on the other hand, had a claim against the tenant for arrears of rent. Sir Lancelot Shadwell VC accepted that there was no set-off at law because the tenant had a demand against Hamp and the bailiff jointly, whereas the tenant was liable only to Hamp for the rent. In other words, there was a lack of mutuality.[364] However, Hamp had agreed to indemnify the bailiff on the judgment, so that Hamp was the party who would bear the ultimate burden of the judgment. The Vice Chancellor regarded this as a reason for the interference of the Court of Chancery, with the consequence that the judgment was set off against the claim for rent. One may query the justification given for the set-off, but it illustrates that mutuality is not always required for a set-off in equity.

4.81   That proposition is also suggested by *dicta* in the Court of Appeal in *Sovereign Life Assurance Company v Dodd*.[365] The defendant (Dodd) took out some policies of life insurance with the plaintiff. The plaintiff advanced some loans to the defendant, and as security took an assignment of the policies by way of mortgage. The plaintiff subsequently went into

---

[357]   See the terms of the order at (1848) 2 HLC 74, 86–7, 9 ER 1020, 1025.

[358]   See (1848) 2 HLC 74, 81, 84, 9 ER 1020, 1023, 1024.

[359]   'I think there was no mutual credit between the parties. Mr Baillie, the plaintiff, trusts Mr Innes – gives credit to Mr Innes; but Mr Innes on his side gives no credit whatever to Mr Baillie; he looked to the estate, and the estate only; and, as there was no mutuality of debt, there is not, also, any mutuality of credit, according to my opinion and my view of the case.' See *Baillie v Innes* (1845) 14 LJ Ch 341, 343.

[360]   Possibly Richard Bethell, later Lord Westbury LC.

[361]   (1848) 2 HLC 74, 79, 9 ER 1020, 1022.

[362]   See Bethell's argument at (1848) 2 HLC 74, 78–9, 9 ER 1020, 1022.

[363]   (1840) 9 LJ Ch 258.

[364]   See para. 12.02 below. This was the substance of counsel's submission against the set-off.

[365]   [1892] 2 QB 573, affirming [1892] 1 QB 405.

liquidation. The liquidator brought an action against the defendant for repayment of the loans, whereupon the defendant sought to set off the amount owing on the policies. It was held that the defendant was entitled to the set-off. One of the arguments adduced by the liquidator against the set-off was that the policies had been assigned to the company as security for the loans.[366] Though not expressly formulated in terms of mutuality, the essence of the argument was that there was no mutuality for the purpose of the insolvency set-off section[367] given the assignment.[368] Because the defendant's claim on the policies had been assigned to the plaintiff, it was not a case in which the plaintiff had a claim against the defendant for repayment of the loans and the defendant had a cross-claim. The Court of Appeal rejected the argument. Bowen LJ said that, even if the assignment otherwise would have prevented a set-off, there was in any event a good set-off in equity.[369] Kay LJ adopted a similar view. He said that the argument founded upon the assignment of the policies could be discounted, 'for there will be a set-off in equity in cases where, but for some such circumstance as this assignment, there would have been a legal set-off'.[370] He went on to comment that the defendant 'probably' had a set-off wholly independent of the insolvency set-off section, but if he had not there were mutual dealings between the company and the assured. The point, however, is that both Bowen LJ and Kay LJ considered that, if there was not mutuality because of the assignment, there could still be a set-off in equity.

Consider also the case of a trustee of a trading trust who enters into a contract with a third **4.82** party. The third party may be indebted to the trustee under the contract, but at the same time the third party may have a cross-claim against the trustee arising from the trustee's conduct in relation to the transaction, such that the demands ordinarily would be regarded as sufficiently closely connected to give rise to an equitable set-off. In this case there would be mutuality by reference to legal titles, but *prima facie* not by reference to equitable titles. The trustee holds the debt on trust for the beneficiaries, but the trustee is personally liable for the claim against it. Nevertheless, Giles J in the New South Wales Supreme Court in *Murphy v Zamonex Pty Ltd*,[371] accepted that a set-off was available to the third party in this circumstance, commenting that: 'equitable principles admit of set-off even in the absence of mutuality, if the circumstances are otherwise such as to attract the intervention of a court of equity . . .'[372] In the case of a trustee, there is an argument that the trustee's right of indemnity from the trust assets, together with the trustee's lien on the assets, could provide a basis for establishing mutuality.[373] But Giles J refused to go into the question whether the trustee in that case was entitled to an indemnity, or whether the right to an indemnity may have been lost because of breaches of trust. His Honour made it clear that his decision was

---

[366] See the argument at first instance [1892] 1 QB 405, 408, and Kay LJ's summary of the argument in the Court of Appeal [1892] 2 QB 573, 584.

[367] See paras 11.13–11.17 below. The applicable provision was the Bankruptcy Act 1883, s. 38.

[368] See paras 16.83–16.88 below.

[369] [1892] 2 QB 573, 582.

[370] [1892] 2 QB 573, 585.

[371] (1993) 31 NSWLR 439. See also *Doherty v Murphy* [1996] 2 VR 553. *Murphy v Zamonex* was referred to with approval in *Penwith District Council v V P Developments Ltd* [2005] 2 BCLC 607 at [20]–[23] (Laddie J).

[372] (1993) 31 NSWLR 439, 464.

[373] See paras 17.122–17.127 below, and *Murphy v Zamonex* (1993) 31 NSWLR 439, 463–4.

not founded upon the trustee's indemnity, and that it was an instance in which the circumstances justified an equitable set-off regardless of the question of mutuality.

4.83   There is, then, substantial authority for the proposition that in some circumstances a set-off may be available in equity where there is no mutuality, which is consistent with judicial opinions in Australia and Canada.[374] In so far as recent statements in the Court of Appeal may suggest that mutuality is a requirement of equitable set-off,[375] those statements were made without reference to authorities suggesting that it is not always necessary and they should be regarded as having inaccurately stated the position. In particular, it is suggested that an equitable set-off was appropriate in the circumstances in issue in *Muscat v Smith*,[376] notwithstanding the absence of mutuality in that case. This aspect of the case is considered later.[377]

(2) Misrepresentation inducing a contract with a third party

4.84   Consider that A is induced to enter into a contract with C as a result of misrepresentations by B, such that A becomes indebted to C under the contract but has a damages claim against B. In the absence of special circumstances which would justify equitable intervention, those facts would not give rise to an equitable set-off. But if C subsequently should assign A's indebtedness under the contract to B, an equitable set-off may become available to A at that point, based on B's initial misrepresentations inducing the contract, so as to impeach B's right to enforce the assigned debt against A.[378]

(3) Guarantees and related parties

4.85   In the situation in which A has a claim against B and A is liable to C, if A becomes insolvent, and B and C are related, it may well be to the advantage of B and C that there should be a set-off. However, the fact that one of the parties to a dealing has become insolvent on its own does not give rise to an equity sufficient to support an equitable set-off. Lord Cottenham emphasized this point in *Rawson v Samuel*.[379] If a set-off is to occur, the facts should support an equitable set-off irrespective of A's insolvency.

4.86   The decision of Brownie J in the New South Wales Supreme Court in *Bank of New Zealand v Harry M Miller & Co Ltd*[380] should be considered in light of that proposition. A lender entered into a loan agreement with the defendant debtor, as security for which a number of guarantees were obtained. Pursuant to a deed of guarantee, the guarantors promised to deposit their surplus funds with the lender on interest bearing deposits, and the lender was authorized on the happening of an event of default to appropriate the money so deposited

---

[374] See para. 4.69 above.
[375] See para. 4.69 above.
[376] [2003] 1 WLR 2853.
[377] See paras 17.69 (setting out the basic principle in relation to the 'taking subject to equities' doctrine) and 17.72–17.89 below.
[378] *Horrobin v Australia & New Zealand Banking Group Ltd* (1996) 40 NSWLR 89, 100, and see also *Ling v Commonwealth* (1996) 68 FCR 180, 190–1.
[379] (1841) Cr & Ph 161, 175, 41 ER 451, 457.
[380] (1992) 26 NSWLR 48.

in reduction of the debtor's debt arising from the loan. Subsequently, the lender assigned both the debt and the benefit of the guarantees to the plaintiff. However, the deposits made by the guarantors remained with the lender. The amount paid by the plaintiff assignee for the assignment was the sum calculated as the principal debt then outstanding together with accrued interest, and no deduction was made for the deposits. The lender went into liquidation and, after that, the assignee brought this action against the debtor claiming the amount outstanding and interest. The debtor asserted as a defence an entitlement to an equitable set-off in respect of the amounts deposited with the lender by the guarantors. Brownie J held that the defence was available. He analysed the situation in two parts. First, he considered the position that would have applied if the deposits had been made by the debtor itself rather than by the guarantors. In that circumstance, if the lender had sued the debtor, his Honour said that there would have been available to the debtor a substantive defence by way of equitable set-off to the extent of the deposits made, since the cross-claim in respect of the deposits raised an equity which impeached, or was essentially bound up with or went to the root of, the lender's title to the claim against the debtor, and it flowed out of and was inseparably connected with the dealing and the transactions which gave rise to the lender's claim. Further, his Honour said that an assignee would have taken subject to this equity available against the lender/assignor.[381] In fact, the guarantors rather than the debtor had made the deposits, and his Honour then considered whether this made any difference to the result. He concluded that it did not. Admittedly, there was a lack of mutuality, since the lender had a claim against the debtor but was subject to a cross-claim from the guarantors in respect of the deposits. His Honour noted, however, that mutuality is not an essential requirement of an equitable set-off. The important point was that the lender had agreed to advance the money to the debtor upon terms which included the taking of the guarantee and the guarantors agreeing to deposit and keep deposited their surplus funds, with a right in the lender upon the happening of an event of default to appropriate those funds towards satisfaction of the debt owing by the debtor. The deposits were said to be inseparably connected with the obligations arising out of the loan agreement. Accordingly, Brownie J concluded that an equitable set-off was available to the debtor and the guarantors in respect of the deposits,[382] notwithstanding the lack of mutuality,[383] and the assignee took subject to this equity.

Was it appropriate to allow an equitable set-off in *Harry M Miller* when different parties **4.87** were involved in the claims, notwithstanding that the claims arose out of and were inseparably connected with the same transaction? In *Lord v Direct Acceptance Corporation Ltd*,[384] the New South Wales Court of Appeal expressed 'considerable doubt' as to the correctness

---

[381] See paras 17.32–17.38 below.

[382] Brownie J acknowledged ((1992) 26 NSWLR 48, 56) that some adjustment may have had to be made as between the debtor and the guarantors, but he said that the question did not arise for decision in the proceedings before him.

[383] Because of the assignment, and the consequent lack of mutuality, the insolvency set-off section did not apply, and for this reason the case is distinguishable from *M S Fashions Ltd v Bank of Credit and Commerce International* [1993] Ch 425. See para. 12.24 below.

[384] (1993) 32 NSWLR 362.

of Brownie J's decision.[385] The substance of the agreement in *Harry M Miller* was that the debtor was primarily liable to discharge the debt, though the lender could apply the deposits in satisfaction of the debt if default occurred. The lender was authorized to apply the deposits, but it was not required to do so. It had a discretion in that regard. If it did not do so, the deposits would be repaid to the guarantors if and when the principal debt was repaid. On the other hand, the effect of allowing an equitable set-off to the principal debtor in relation to the deposits was to override the agreement between the parties, by requiring the application of the deposits against the debt and making the guarantors primarily liable to the extent of their deposits. As Sheller JA noted in delivering the Court of Appeal's judgment, there was no equity in that result.[386] The English Court of Appeal expressed a similar sentiment in *Re Bank of Credit and Commerce International SA (No. 8)*[387] in the context of insolvency set-off, commenting that to allow the principal debtor to compel the creditor to look to the surety rather than to his own personal liability (or vice versa) would invert the ordinary rule of priorities between the creditor, the surety and the principal debtor.[388] As it turned out, because of the insolvency of the lender and the assignment of the loan, a set-off would have benefited the guarantors in *Harry M Miller*, since the guarantors and the debtor were closely associated, and it was not in their interests that the debtor should be liable to pay the principal debt in full and that the guarantors be confined to a dividend in respect of their deposits. Nevertheless, the mere fact of insolvency is not a sufficient justification for allowing an equitable set-off.[389] If the intention was that the guarantors should be primarily liable to the extent of their deposits, that should have been made clear in the agreement.

(4) A deposit as security, where the depositor is not personally liable

4.88 The facts in issue in *Lord v Direct Acceptance* were similar to those in *Harry M Miller*, though the case differed in that the person providing the deposit as security for the loan to the borrower had not assumed a personal liability, whether as guarantor or by agreeing to be jointly and severally liable. Direct Acceptance lent money to Bonnie Breck Pty Ltd secured by a guarantee given by the appellant. In addition, another company associated with the appellant, Me and Angus Pty Ltd, placed a sum on deposit with Direct Acceptance, on terms that it could not be withdrawn until the principal debt was repaid in full, and Direct Acceptance was authorized in its discretion to set off and appropriate the deposit in total or partial satisfaction of the principal debt. Me and Angus, however, was not personally liable for the debt, Direct Acceptance's rights as against that company being confined to the deposit. When Bonnie Breck defaulted in repayment of the loan Direct Acceptance sued the appellant on the guarantee, whereupon the appellant asserted that the deposit should be set off against the debt so as to reduce his liability as guarantor. The impetus for this was that Direct Acceptance was in liquidation so that, if the deposit was not applied

---

[385] (1993) 32 NSWLR 362, 371.

[386] See the discussion at (1993) 32 NSWLR 362, 369.

[387] [1996] Ch 245, 256. See para. 4.89 below.

[388] In the context of insolvency set-off, compare the situation in which the surety contracted on the basis of being a principal debtor. See *M S Fashions Ltd v Bank of Credit and Commerce International* [1993] Ch 425, for which see paras 12.24–12.28 below.

[389] *Rawson v Samuel* (1841) Cr & Ph 161, 175, 41 ER 451, 457.

against the loan, the appellant would be liable for the full amount of the debt under the guarantee, and Me and Angus would be confined to a proof in the liquidation in respect of the deposit. The New South Wales Court of Appeal held that there was no set-off. In the first place, there was nothing in the terms of the contract governing the deposit which required Direct Acceptance to apply the deposit in reduction of the debt. On the contrary, the deposit was expressed not to be repayable until the loan was repaid, and the right to set off the deposit was given to Direct Acceptance 'in its absolute discretion'. Nor did the insolvency set-off section apply, since the demands were not mutual.[390] While Me and Angus was a creditor of Direct Acceptance in relation to the deposit, it was not liable to Direct Acceptance, so that it was not a case of cross-demands which could be set against each other to produce a balance.[391] Moreover, for the reason noted above in relation to the *Harry M Miller* case, it was not an appropriate case for an equitable set-off. In delivering the court's judgment, Sheller JA said that he had difficulty in discerning a basis for saying that Direct Acceptance's title to demand payment from the appellant guarantor was impeached because of a debt owing by Direct Acceptance to a third party representing moneys deposited to secure repayment of the principal debt, when the agreement stated that Direct Acceptance was not required to repay the deposit unless and until the principal debt was paid in full.[392] To allow a set-off would have overridden the terms on which the moneys were deposited and make the depositor primarily liable to discharge the debt.[393] In support of an equitable set-off the appellant relied on the *Harry M Miller* case, but Sheller JA doubted the correctness of that decision.[394] In any event, *Harry M Miller* was distinguishable because, unlike the depositors in that case, the depositor in *Lord v Direct Acceptance* had not assumed a personal liability for the debt which could be the subject of a set-off against the deposit.[395]

In England, circumstances similar to those in *Lord v Direct Acceptance* arose for consideration in *Re Bank of Credit and Commerce International SA (No. 8)*.[396] A bank lent money to a customer secured by a third party deposit which was charged with repayment of the loan, though without the third party having provided a guarantee or other personal covenant as to repayment. The bank subsequently went into liquidation. The liquidator declined to apply the deposit against the loan, preferring to proceed against the customer and to confine the depositor to a proof in the liquidation. The House of Lords held that there was a lack of mutuality which prevented a set-off under the insolvency set-off section.[397] Equitable set-off was not in issue before their Lordships, but it was considered by the Court of Appeal, which rejected an argument that an equitable set-off was available in that case in circumstances that were outside the scope of the insolvency set-off section.[398]

4.89

---

[390] See ch. 11 below.
[391] (1993) 32 NSWLR 362, 373.
[392] (1993) 32 NSWLR 362, 367–8.
[393] (1993) 32 NSWLR 362, 369, 371.
[394] (1993) 32 NSWLR 362, 371.
[395] (1993) 32 NSWLR 362, 369.
[396] [1998] AC 214, affirming [1996] Ch 245 (Court of Appeal).
[397] See also *Lord v Direct Acceptance* (1993) 32 NSWLR 362 (above), and para. 12.41 below.
[398] [1996] Ch 245, 265–70. Compare *Clarkson v Smith and Goldberg* [1926] 1 DLR 509. See para. 12.42 below.

The better view is that equitable set-off is not confined by the insolvency section, and that in an appropriate case an equitable set-off may be available in bankruptcy or company liquidation in circumstances where the statutory right does not apply.[399] Nevertheless, consistent with the earlier reasoning of the New South Wales Court of Appeal in *Lord v Direct Acceptance Corporation* (above), the decision in *BCCI (No. 8)* not to allow an equitable set-off would seem correct.

4.90 In a case such as *BCCI (No. 8)*, it has been suggested that it may be possible to support an equitable set-off on the basis of the decision of the House of Lords in 1848 in *Baillie v Edwards*.[400] The case was considered earlier.[401] Based on that decision, it has been suggested that the depositor in *BCCI (No. 8)*, although not personally liable for the borrower's debt, may have been entitled to require BCCI's liquidators to satisfy the debt out of the sum which BCCI owed to the depositor, and to assign to him their claim against the borrower. However, *Baillie v Edwards* would not appear to justify that result. In the first place, *Baillie v Edwards* was concerned with the redemption of an estate and the determination of the amount required to be paid in order to take the estate free of an equitable lien. The point in issue in *BCCI (No. 8)*, on the other hand, was not the redemption of the deposit charged in favour of the bank, but whether the deposit should be applied in a particular way. Further, pursuant to the agreement governing the deposit in *BCCI (No. 8)*, the depositor had limited its rights in relation to the deposit by charging it in favour of the bank. The bank was not obliged to release the deposit until the principal debt was paid in full, and it was empowered, but not obliged, to apply the deposit in reduction of the debt. In contrast, Baillie's rights in relation to the money owing to him by Innes were not limited.

H. Different Contracts

4.91 Lord Cottenham emphasized in *Rawson v Samuel*[402] that it is not sufficient for an equitable set-off that both demands arose out of the same contract. Under more modern formulations of the principle governing equitable set-off approved by English courts,[403] cross-claims arising out of the same contract ordinarily would give rise to a set-off. Nevertheless, it is still the case that there is no universal rule that claims arising out of the same contract may be set against each other in all circumstances.[404]

---

[399] There is nevertheless authority to the contrary. See paras 6.25–6.32 below.

[400] (1848) 2 HLC 74, 9 ER 1020. See Berg, 'Liquidation Set-off: The Mutuality Principle and Security over Bank Balances' [1996] LMCLQ 176.

[401] See para. 4.79 above.

[402] (1841) Cr & Ph 161, 178, 41 ER 451, 458.

[403] See paras 4.08–4.18 above.

[404] *Government of Newfoundland v Newfoundland Railway Co* (1888) 13 App Cos 199, 212, referred to with evident approval in *Bank of Boston Connecticut v European Grain and Shipping Ltd* [1989] 1 AC 1056, 1102. See also *Atlantic Lines & Navigation Co Inc v The Ship 'Didymi' (The Didymi)* [1988] 1 Lloyd's Rep 97; *Grant v NZMC Ltd* [1989] 1 NZLR 8, 13. This principle has been emphasized in Australia. See *Covino v Bandag Manufacturing Pty Ltd* [1983] 1 NSWLR 237, 238; *AWA Ltd v Exicom Australia Pty Ltd* (1990) 19 NSWLR 705, 712; *Lambert Pty Ltd v Papadatos Pty Ltd* (1991) 5 ACSR 468, 470; *Westwind Air Charter Pty Ltd v Hawker De Havilland Ltd* (1990) 3 WAR 71; *Cade Pty Ltd v Thomson Simmons* (1998) 71 SASR 571, 594; *Cathedral Place Pty Ltd v Hyatt of Australia Ltd* [2003] VSC 385 at [39]; *Queensland University of Technology v Project Constructions (Aust) Pty Ltd* [2003] 1 Qd R 259 at [21] ('Depending on the closeness

The converse proposition equally holds true, that it is not an essential requirement **4.92** of an equitable set-off that the claim and the cross-claim should have originated in the same contract,[405] notwithstanding occasional statements that appear to suggest the contrary.[406] A crucial question, according to the formulation approved by the House of Lords in the *Bank of Boston* case,[407] is whether the cross-claim is inseparably connected with the transaction that gave rise to the claim, or, alternatively, in the traditional formulation, whether the claims are so closely connected that the title of the claimant to prosecute his or her demand is impeached. While the fact that the claim and the cross-claim each arose under different contracts is a factor to be considered in relation to the question whether there is a sufficient connection, it is not conclusive. Consider *The Angelic Grace*.[408] The owners of a vessel had let the vessel under three consecutive charterparties to the same charterers. When the vessel was re-delivered after the expiration

---

of their connection . . .'). Compare however *Westacott v Bevan* [1891] 1 QB 774, 780; *Parsons v Sovereign Bank of Canada* [1913] AC 160, 166 (PC); *R M Douglas Construction Ltd v Bass Leisure Ltd* (1990) 53 BLR 119, 133; *Metal Manufacturers Ltd v Hall* (2002) 41 ACSR 466 at [13]; *Altonwood Ltd v Crystal Palace FC (2000) Ltd* [2005] EWHC 292 (Ch) at [32]; *Edlington Properties Ltd v J H Fenner & Co Ltd* [2006] 1 WLR 1583 at [4]; *Secret Hotels 2 Ltd v E A Traveller Ltd* [2010] EWHC 1023 (Ch) at [42]. Compare also *Roadshow Entertainment Pty Ltd v (ACN 053 006 269) Pty Ltd* (1997) 42 NSWLR 462, 482, although the comment regarding an assignee taking subject to unliquidated cross-claims arising out of the same contract should be considered in the context of a proposition that has found favour in Australia, that an assignee may take subject to a counterclaim available to the debtor against the assignor which arises out of the same contract as the assigned debt, whether or not it would have given rise to an equitable set-off as between the assignor and the debtor. See the discussion of *Roadshow Entertainment* in para. 4.27 above.

[405] *Galambos & Son Pty Ltd v McIntyre* (1974) 5 ACTR 10, 26; *Japan Line Ltd v Aggeliki Charis Compania SA (The Angelic Grace)* [1980] 1 Lloyd's Rep 288; *British Anzani (Felixstowe) Ltd v International Marine Management (UK) Ltd* [1980] 1 QB 137; *Banco Central SA v Lingoss & Falce Ltd (The Raven)* [1980] 2 Lloyd's Rep 266, 272; *Coba Industries Ltd v Millie's Holdings (Canada) Ltd* [1985] 6 WWR 14; *Grant v NZMC Ltd* [1989] 1 NZLR 8; *National Westminster Bank plc v Skelton* [1993] 1 WLR 72, 76; *Bim Kemi AB v Blackburn Chemicals Ltd* [2001] 2 Lloyd's Rep 93 at [29] and [30]; *Saskatchewan Wheat Pool v Feduk* [2004] 2 WWR 69 at [81] and [87] (Saskatchewan CA); *Benford Ltd v Lopecan SL* [2004] 2 Lloyd's Rep 618 at [16]; *Geldof Metaalconstructie NV v Simon Carves Ltd* [2010] EWCA Civ 667. See also *Melville v Grapelodge Developments Ltd* (1978) 39 P & C R 179; *Hill Corcoran Constructions Pty Ltd v Navarro* (Qld CA, 6 March 1992, BC9202488) (claim for repayment of loan advanced by builder to employer to assist employer in the construction of home units, which loan was to be repaid from the sale proceeds of the units, and cross-claim against builder under the building contract for defects). In *Hanak v Green* [1958] 2 QB 9, 31 Sellers LJ considered that a set-off could proceed where the cross-claim was 'closely associated with and incidental to the contract'. In *Telford v Holt* (1987) 41 DLR (4th) 385, 401 the Canadian Supreme Court said that the debts in that case could only be set off if they arose out of the same contract or closely related contracts. Compare Art 19(3) of the UNCITRAL Arbitration Rules, which provides that the respondent in an arbitration may raise a set-off only if it is founded on a claim arising out of the same contract as that on which the claimant's claim is based. See *Econet Satellite Services Ltd v VEE Networks Ltd* [2006] 2 Lloyd's Rep 423, disapproving of *Ronly Holdings Ltd v JSC Zestafoni G Nikoladze Ferroalloy Plant* [2004] BLR 323 at [33].

[406] See e.g. *Provident Finance Corporation Pty Ltd v Hammond* [1978] VR 312, 321.

[407] [1989] 1 AC 1056. See para. 4.13 above.

[408] *Japan Line Ltd v Aggeliki Charis Compania SA (The Angelic Grace)* [1980] 1 Lloyd's Rep 288. See also *Parsons v Sovereign Bank of Canada* [1913] AC 160 (see para. 4.105 below); *Kaps Transport Ltd v McGregor Telephone & Power Construction Co Ltd* (1970) 73 WWR 549 (in which the set-off claimed in respect of the damage to the appellant's equipment does not appear to have been confined to the claim for the price of the trucking services relating to the particular contract for the carriage of that equipment); *John Dee Group Ltd v WMH (21) Ltd* [1997] BCC 518, 531 (referring to *Business Computers Ltd v Anglo-African Leasing Ltd* [1977] 1 WLR 578, 585); *Bim Kemi AB v Blackburn Chemicals Ltd* [2001] 2 Lloyd's Rep 93 (see paras 4.17–4.18 above), and paras 4.106–4.109 below in relation to repudiation of an overriding agreement.

of the third charter it contained a large quantity of bunkers for which the owners were liable to reimburse the charterers. However, the owners had a cross-claim for stevedore damage occurring during the currency of both the second and the third charterparties for which the charterers were liable under the terms of the charterparties. Lord Denning and Waller LJ considered that the claim and cross-claim under the charters were so closely connected that it would be a case for equitable set-off. The three charterparties in this case involved the same vessel being chartered to the same charterers over a continuous period. In effect they were all a part of the same transaction. The decision illustrates the difference between the modern and the traditional approaches to equitable set-off. While the cross-claim for stevedore damage could be said to have been inseparably connected with the same transaction which gave rise to the claim, it is not easy to see how one claim could be said to be impeached by the other within Lord Cottenham's traditional formulation in *Rawson v Samuel*.[409] Nevertheless, the principle that in appropriate circumstances claims under separate contracts can give rise to an equitable set-off would seem to be correct.

4.93 If, on the other hand, separate contracts in truth each involve separate transactions, a set-off generally should not be allowed.[410] This brings into question *Bankes v Jarvis*.[411] The plaintiff's son bought a veterinary surgeon's practice from the defendant. The defendant was lessee of a house used in connection with the practice, and at the time of the sale he assigned the lease to the plaintiff's son, who covenanted to pay the rent and perform the covenants in the lease and also to indemnify the defendant against all claims arising thereunder. Some six years later the plaintiff's son left the country, having given the plaintiff authority to sell the practice. The plaintiff then sold it back to the defendant. When the plaintiff sued for the balance of the purchase price the defendant sought to set off a cross-claim for damages against the plaintiff's son for breach of the covenant to indemnify against claims arising under the lease. It was held that, if the son instead had been the party suing, the defendant would have been entitled to the set-off, and that the plaintiff suing as a trustee accordingly should also be subject to this defence.[412] Morris LJ later commented in *Hanak v Green*[413] that this 'conclusion seems to me to be clearly correct and obviously fair', and the decision was referred to with approval in *Geldof v Metaalconstructie NV v Simon Carves Ltd*.[413a]

---

[409] Stone J in the Canadian Federal Court of Appeal in *Atlantic Lines & Navigation Co Inc v The Ship 'Didymi' (The Didymi)* [1988] 1 Lloyd's Rep 97, 105 appears not to have been entirely comfortable with the view that *The Angelic Grace* was an appropriate case for an equitable set-off.

[410] See in this regard *Minshull v Oakes* (1858) 2 H & N 793, 157 ER 327; *Indrisie v General Credits Ltd* [1985] VR 251, 254 (distinguished in *Hill Corcoran Constructions Pty Ltd v Navarro* (Qld CA, 6 March 1992, BC9202488)); *Peninsular and Oriental Steam Navigation Co v Youell* [1997] 2 Lloyd's Rep 136. See also the fact situation considered by Isaacs J in *Tooth v Brisbane City Council* (1928) 41 CLR 212, 223–4. A claim for an indemnity under a policy of insurance and a cross-claim for premiums due on other policies covering other subject-matters are not sufficiently connected for an equitable set-off. See *E Pellas & Co v Neptune Marine Insurance Co* (1879) 5 CPD 34, and also *Baker v Adam* (1910) 15 Com Cas 227.

[411] [1903] 1 KB 549.

[412] Wills J in his judgment ([1903] 1 KB 549, 552) said that he had some difficulty in seeing how the plaintiff even had standing to sue in this case, though he declined to express a decided opinion on the point.

[413] [1958] 2 QB 9, 24.

[413a] [2010] EWCA Civ 667 at [23].

Nevertheless, the transactions appear to have been separate and distinct, and it is not at all clear what the justification for a set-off was.[414]

(1) Overriding agreements

The issue of equitable set-off in relation to claims arising under different contracts has **4.94** arisen in circumstances where the parties' dealings are the subject of an overriding agreement such as a distribution, agency or licensing agreement.[415]

There have been cases where A sued B for the price of goods supplied by A to B for the **4.95** purpose of on-sale by B, and B had a cross-claim against A for repudiation of an agency or licensing agreement. The question of set-off in this context is considered later.[416]

Alternatively, the cross-claim against A may be for damages for breach of a territorial **4.96** monopoly conferred on B in the overriding agreement. In *Covino v Bandag Manufacturing Pty Ltd*,[417] Hutley JA in the New South Wales Court of Appeal considered that breach of a territorial monopoly did not impeach a liability to pay the price of goods sold and delivered.[418] In contrast, Morison J in *Benford Ltd v Lopecan SL*[419] accepted, in a summary judgment application, that it was strongly arguable that the breach gave rise to a defence of set-off. It was pleaded in that case that, by reason of the breach of the territorial monopoly, the distributor had incurred wasted expense.[420] This included that the distributor was unable to sell the goods the subject of the claim and had lost the revenues on those goods, so that purchase of the goods represented wasted expense. That allegation, if established, would have sufficed to establish an impeachment of title. However, the view that there was an arguable set-off appears not to have been confined to the cross-claim for that particular expense. Other wasted expenditure was alleged, for example expenses in relation to the premises, overheads, spare parts and the cost of hiring and training its workforce, as well as lost profits on other sales. It appears to have been accepted that the cross-claim for those losses could also rise to an arguable set-off against the claim for the price of goods sold and delivered.[421] The justification given for the set-off was that: 'the sale contract was under the umbrella of the distribution agreement and the claims and cross claims are closely connected in a commercial sense.'[422] This accords with the broad approach now adopted by

---

[414] Channell J in *Bankes v Jarvis* [1903] 1 KB 549, 553 said that: 'the Judicature Act, and more especially the rules, distinctly put an unliquidated claim on the same footing as a liquidated claim for the purpose of set-off.' This is clearly incorrect (see *McDonnell & East Ltd v McCregor* (1936) 56 CLR 50, 61–2; *Galambos & Son Pty Ltd v McIntyre* (1974) 5 ACTR 10, 19), and it detracts from the weight that otherwise would be accorded to his Lordship's judgment.

[415] In addition to the cases referred to below, see *Bim Kemi AB v Blackburn Chemicals Ltd* [2001] 2 Lloyd's Rep 93, for which see paras 4.17–4.18 above.

[416] See paras 4.106–4.109 below.

[417] [1983] 1 NSWLR 237.

[418] [1983] 1 NSWLR 237, 238. See also Glass JA at 241.

[419] [2004] 2 Lloyds Rep 618.

[420] [2004] 2 Lloyds Rep 618 at [8].

[421] See [2004] Lloyds Rep 618 at [17], but compare at [12].

[422] [2004] Lloyds Rep 618 at [17], referring to *Bim Kemi AB v Blackburn Chemicals Ltd* [2001] 2 Lloyd's Rep 93 at [36], for which see paras 4.17–4.18 above.

English courts in relation to questions of equitable set-off, and it should be contrasted with the narrower Australian approach illustrated by the *Covino* case.

I. Creditor's Conduct Affecting Debtor's Ability to Pay

4.97 It is sometimes asserted that a creditor's own conduct is the cause of the debtor's inability to pay, and that the resulting cross-claim against the creditor accordingly should be set off against the debt.

4.98 An early instance is *Beasley v Darcy*.[423] A landlord brought an action for ejectment against the tenant for non-payment of rent. The tenant, however, had a claim for damages against the landlord for cutting down timber on the demised land. The House of Lords affirmed a decree granting relief from forfeiture to the tenant, on paying what was due for rent after deducting the damages. The set-off in this case has been explained on the ground that the landlord's trespass resulted in a loss of the produce of the land to the tenant, thereby rendering the land of less value and affecting the tenant's ability to get rent out of it.[424]

4.99 It does not suffice for an equitable set-off that the creditor's conduct affected in some general way the debtor's profitability and hence the debtor's ability to pay the debt.[425] There must be a connection between the demands. In *Beasley v Darcy*, it may be inferred that the rent was set on the basis that the land in question was income producing, so that the rent was to come out of the land. On that basis, there was a clear connection between the claim for rent and the cross-claim in respect of the landlord's actions which reduced the tenant's ability to pay rent. There was also a sufficient connection in *Popular Homes Ltd v Circuit Developments Ltd*.[426] The plaintiff, a building contractor, bought some land from the defendant with the intention of building some town houses on it, the unpaid price being secured by a mortgage in favour of the defendant. As part of the consideration for the purchase, the defendant also agreed to provide development finance so as to enable the plaintiff to complete the construction. The defendant defaulted in its obligation to provide the finance, as a result of which the plaintiff was unable to complete the project and to repay the mortgage debt. Barker J in the New Zealand Supreme Court held that the plaintiff's resulting damages claim could be set off against the debt. The cross-claims were based on the same contract and, moreover, the defendant's default was a direct cause of the plaintiff's inability to repay. A similar situation arose in *Doherty v Murphy*.[427] A financier agreed to

---

[423] (1800) 2 Sch & Lef 403n. See the discussion of the case in *British Anzani (Felixstowe) Ltd v International Marine Management (UK) Ltd* [1980] 1 QB 137, 149–51.

[424] See Lord Redesdale in *O'Mahony v Dickson* (1805) 2 Sch & Lef 400, 412–13, and Bramwell B in *Stimson v Hall* (1857) 1 H & N 831, 835–6, 156 ER 1436, 1438.

[425] *Hill Corcoran Constructions Pty Ltd v Navarro* (Qld CA, 6 March 1992, BC9202488) (referring to *Indrisie v General Credits Ltd* [1985] VR 251); *Forsyth v Gibbs* [2009] 1 Qd R 403 at [15]. See also *Hamilton Ice Arena Ltd v Perry Developments Ltd* [2002] 1 NZLR 309, 318, 319; *Van Leeuwen v Bank of Western Australia Ltd* [2001] FCA 1826 at [14].

[426] [1979] 2 NZLR 642. See also *Hill Corcoran Constructions Pty Ltd v Navarro* (Qld CA, 6 March 1992, BC9202488).

[427] [1996] 2 VR 553. See also *Murphy v Zamonex Pty Ltd* (1993) 31 NSWLR 439 (in which the cross-claim was based upon a false representation that certified claims would be paid).

provide finance for the purpose of a property development. However, the financier was unable to make all the required payments, as a result of which work ceased on the project. The borrower was unable to sell any part of the uncompleted development, and was unable to repay the amount outstanding to the financier.[428] In a summary judgment application, the Appeal Division of the Supreme Court of Victoria held that the circumstances showed an arguable defence of equitable set-off.

Those cases should be compared to *United Dominions Corporation Ltd v Jaybe Homes Pty Ltd*.[429] A vendor of land had agreed to provide finance to the purchaser to enable the purchaser to erect houses on the land for the purpose of sale. When the vendor defaulted in its obligation to provide the finance, Andrews J in the Queensland Supreme Court held that the resulting damages claim did not provide the purchaser with a defence to the vendor's claim for payment of the price. The agreement to provide finance was entered into after the agreement for the sale and purchase of the land, and in truth it was a separate transaction.[430]   **4.100**

The circumstances in issue in *Cunningham v National Australia Bank Ltd*,[431] similarly,   **4.101** were insufficient to support an equitable set-off. Customers of a bank requested the bank to obtain a credit check on a company with whom they were proposing to do business. The bank obtained a favourable report and advised the customers, who entered into a contract with the company. Shortly after making the contract, the customers borrowed from the bank in order to acquire plant for the purpose of carrying out the contract. Subsequently, the company failed, as a result of which the customers lost the benefit of the contract and were unable to repay the bank. They argued that they had a claim in damages against the bank for negligence and for misleading or deceptive conduct[432] in relation to the credit check, which should be set off against the outstanding loan. Jenkinson J in the Federal Court of Australia disagreed. It was not sufficient that the customers, to the knowledge of the bank, intended to discharge the loan with funds expected to be obtained from carrying out the contract. The subject of the loan had not been raised between the customer and the bank before the customers entered into the contract with the company, and it was not alleged that the bank's conduct induced the making of the contract of loan. The bank's title to sue on the loan therefore was not impeached by the cross-claim.

A debtor's inability to pay the debt may be due simply to the creditor's insolvency, in   **4.102** that the creditor is unable to pay an amount that it in turn owes to the debtor on a cross-claim. Insolvency, without more, however, is not sufficient to give rise to an equitable set-off.[433]

---

[428] See [1996] 2 VR 553, 559–60.

[429] [1978] Qd R 111.

[430] Similarly, in *Indrisie v General Credits Ltd* [1985] VR 251, 253–4, the principal debtor's cross-claim for damages for breach of the agreement to lend money was regarded as a separate transaction from that upon which the principal debtor was liable.

[431] (1987) 15 FCR 495.

[432] Contrary to the Trade Practices Act 1974 (Cth), s. 52.

[433] *Rawson v Samuel* (1841) Cr & Ph 161, 175, 41 ER 451, 457.

J. Repudiation of a Contract

4.103   If a person suing for payment of a sum due under a contract has repudiated the contract, the resulting liability for damages ordinarily can be set off in equity against the claim for payment. This occurred in *Government of Newfoundland v Newfoundland Railway Company,*[434] where a contract for the construction of a railway line was repudiated by the contractor before completion, and the contractor's claim for payment in respect of the completed part was met by a cross-claim for damages arising from the repudiation.

(1) Contracts requiring periodic performance

4.104   This may also apply in the situation in which a single contract requires performance on a periodic basis. A damages claim arising from a repudiation of the contract may give rise to an equitable set-off against a claim for payments due under the contract.

4.105   In *Parsons v Sovereign Bank of Canada,*[435] a company which operated a paper mill had entered into various contracts with the appellant. Each contract was for the periodic supply of quantities of paper, and each extended over a considerable period. During the currency of the contracts, receivers were appointed by the court to the company. After the appointment, the appellant continued to send orders for paper pursuant to the contracts, which the receivers duly accepted and satisfied. Subsequently, the receivers notified the appellant that they would not execute any more orders under the existing contracts, thereby repudiating the contracts. The appellant was then sued for the price of paper delivered to it. The Privy Council[436] held that the amount sued for was due under the old contracts with the company, rather than under new contracts made with the receivers. Further, the company was responsible for the repudiation, and so the appellant was permitted to set off its damages resulting from the breach of the contracts. The set-off was allowed, notwithstanding that the orders in respect of which payment was sought had been carried out, by the delivery of paper to the appellant. The judgment is open to criticism in that the set-off appears to have been considered on an aggregate basis, as opposed to in relation to each contract separately.[437] Nevertheless, the authority of *Parsons* has not been questioned.[438]

---

[434] (1888) 13 App Cas 199. See also *Queensland University of Technology v Project Constructions (Aust) Pty Ltd* [2003] 1 Qd R 259 at [24] (termination of contract), referred to in *Aquatec-Maxcon Pty Ltd v Minson Nacap Pty Ltd* (2004) 8 VR 16 at [50]–[56].

[435] [1913] AC 160. Compare *Maunder Taylor v Blaquiere* [2003] 1 WLR 379 (manager appointed under the Landlord and Tenant Act 1987, s. 24(1)).

[436] Viscount Haldane, Lord MacNaghten, Lord Atkinson and Lord Shaw of Dunfermline.

[437] But see para. 4.05 above.

[438] The *Parsons* case was followed and applied by the New South Wales Court of Appeal in the context of a repudiation in *Roadshow Entertainment Pty Ltd v (ACN 053 006 269) Pty Ltd* (1997) 42 NSWLR 462, 483–4. The judgment is difficult to follow, *sed quaere* whether this was a case of a true equitable set-off, or alternatively an example of a proposition that has been put forward in Australia, that an assignee (including a secured creditor under a crystallized floating charge) takes subject to a counterclaim available to the debtor against the assignor which arises out of the same contract as the assigned debt, whether or not it would have given rise to an equitable set-off as between the assignor and the debtor. See the discussion of *Roadshow Entertainment* in para. 4.27 above. *Parsons* was similarly concerned with an assignment, the receivers having assigned the amounts due from the appellant to the Sovereign Bank of Canada. It was not suggested, however, that the assignment affected the availability of the set-off.

(2) Repudiation of an overriding agreement

The *Parsons* case concerned a number of contracts, each for the periodic supply of goods, **4.106**
and the Privy Council in allowing a set-off emphasized the fact that the debts for the price
and the damages claims for repudiation related to the original contracts. Alternatively,
separate contracts may be entered into in the course of a trading relationship, but each
contract is subject to an overriding agreement between the parties, for example a distribution, agency or licensing agreement. If the overriding agreement is repudiated, can the
resulting damages claim be set off against a debt for the price of goods sold pursuant to the
separate contracts? The question of set-off in this context has been the subject of two Court
of Appeal decisions which are not easy to reconcile.

In *Dole Dried Fruit & Nut Co v Trustin Kerwood Ltd*,[439] the plaintiffs had appointed the **4.107**
defendants as their exclusive agent for importing the plaintiffs' goods into and distributing
the goods in England. Subsequently, the plaintiffs purported to terminate the agency agreement without notice, and proceeded to sue the defendants for the price of goods sold and
delivered under a series of sale contracts. The defendants sought to set off their damages
claim against the plaintiffs arising from the repudiation of the agency agreement. Lloyd LJ
(with whom Beldam LJ concurred) said that the whole purpose and intent of the agency
agreement was that the parties should enter into contracts for the purchase and sale of the
plaintiff's goods, and therefore the sale contracts were concluded in fulfilment of the agency
agreement. In those circumstances he was of the view, applying Lord Denning's formulation of the test for equitable set-off in *Federal Commerce v Molena*,[440] that the claims were
sufficiently closely connected to make it unjust to allow the plaintiffs to claim the price of
goods sold and delivered without taking into account the cross-claim.

The *Dole Dried Fruit* case should be compared to the later decision of the Court of Appeal **4.108**
in *Esso Petroleum Co Ltd v Milton*.[441] Esso was suing for the price of nine deliveries of petrol
made to the defendant, who occupied and managed two petrol service stations under
a licence agreement with Esso. Under the licence agreement, Esso agreed to sell to the
defendant, and the defendant agreed to buy from Esso, his entire requirements for petrol.
The sales took place in fulfilment of the licence agreement, and in that sense the licence
agreement was similar to the agency agreement in the *Dole Dried Fruit* case. However,
a differently constituted Court of Appeal[442] in *Esso v Milton* held that an equitable set-off
was not available to the defendant in respect of a cross-claim for damages for loss of future
profit (and for other future losses) as a result of an alleged repudiation by Esso of the licence
agreement, the reason being that that there was an insufficient connection between the
cross-demands. Simon Brown LJ, with whom Sir John Balcombe agreed on this point,
commented:[443]

> At the point when those deliveries were made, there was no cross-claim at all in existence and
> no loss yet suffered by the defendant. No case has been cited to us in which payment of a debt

---

[439] [1990] 2 Lloyd's Rep 309.
[440] [1978] 1 QB 927, 9745. See para. 4.10 above.
[441] [1997] 1 WLR 938.
[442] Simon Brown and Thorpe LJJ, and Sir John Balcombe.
[443] [1997] 1 WLR 938, 951.

> presently due has been required to await the resolution of a cross-claim for future losses. There mere fact that both claim and counterclaim arise out of a single trading relationship between the parties is in my judgment wholly insufficient to supply the close link necessary to support an equitable set-off.

The fact that no loss had been suffered at the date of delivery should not have been a sufficient reason to preclude an equitable set-off.[444] Rather, the comment should be considered in the context that there was no connection between the claims other than that they arose out of a single trading relationship, which was thought to be insufficient to found an equitable set-off.

4.109 The similarity between the *Dole Dried Fruit* case and *Esso v Milton* is evident, and in both cases reference was made to Lord Denning's judgment in *Federal Commerce v Molena*. The results were different, however. In *Esso v Milton* the losses sought to be set off were future losses, whereas in *Dole Dried Fruit* the report refers simply to a damages claim arising from the repudiation of the agency agreement. It may be assumed, however, that the damages for repudiation would have included future loss. In concluding that the claims in *Esso v Milton* were insufficiently connected, Simon Brown LJ also emphasized that the deliveries of petrol were to be converted immediately into cash through forecourt sales, so that, as he said, even less reason existed for the defendant to postpone the discharge of his debt until after the cross-claim was litigated.[445] That point may not have had the same cogency in the *Dole Dried Fruit* case. Nevertheless, the tenor of Simon Brown LJ's judgment suggests a more rigorous approach to the question of set-off than that evident in the earlier decision. While there was a connection between the demands in the *Dole Dried Fruit* case, in the sense described by Lloyd LJ,[446] that connection, as the Court of Appeal later observed in *Peninsular and Oriental Steam Navigation Co v Youell*,[447] would not appear to have been such as to give rise to an impeachment of the plaintiff's title to sue. More recently, however, the *Dole Dried Fruit* case was referred to with evident approval in *Bim Kemi AB v Blackburn Chemicals Ltd*,[448] the Court of Appeal in that case recognizing an equitable set-off in circumstances where the connection between the demands was described as 'less close' than that in *Dole Dried Fruit*.[449] Potter LJ, in delivering the judgment of the court in *Bim Kemi*, commented that the formulation approved by the House of Lords in the *Bank of Boston* case[450] 'is apt to cover a situation where there are claims and cross-claims for damages in respect of different but closely connected contracts arising out of a long-standing trading relationship which is terminated'.[451] He went on to comment that this situation would not

---

[444] But compare *Young v National Australia Bank Ltd* (2004) 29 WAR 505 at [34].

[445] [1997] 1 WLR 938, 951–2. Also considered relevant (at 951) were the payment was to be by way of direct debit (see para. 5.49 below, Simon Brown LJ dissenting on that point), and that the contract provided that the defendant could not withhold payment of any amount properly due to Esso, though of itself this did not exclude equitable set-off. See para. 5.118 below.

[446] See above.

[447] [1997] 2 Lloyd's Rep 136, 144 (Potter LJ, with whom Mummery and Nourse LJJ agreed).

[448] [2001] 2 Lloyd's Rep 93 (Potter, Sedley and Jonathan Parker LJJ). See paras 4.17–4.18 above. See also *Benford Ltd v Lopecan SL* [2004] 2 Lloyd's Rep 618; *Geldof Metaalconstructie NV v Simon Carves Ltd* [2010] EWCA Civ 667 at [34]–[37].

[449] [2001] 2 Lloyd's Rep 93 at [37].

[450] See para. 4.13 above.

[451] [2001] 2 Lloyd's Rep 93 at [30].

per se establish the requisite connection for an equitable set-off, but where it applies he said that in an appropriate case it may be manifestly unjust to allow one claim to be enforced without taking account of the other.

K. Misrepresentation, Fraud, and Misleading or Deceptive Conduct

(1) Misrepresentation inducing a contract

A question in respect of which there are conflicting views is whether a claim in tort for dam- **4.110** ages for fraudulent misrepresentation inducing a contract may be brought into account in an action for payment of a sum of money owing under the contract. Typically, this may arise where the vendor of a business is suing for the price and the purchaser has a cross-claim for damages for fraud inducing the contract.

It has been held in the context of assignments of debts that an assignee does not take subject **4.111** to a cross-claim for fraud inducing the contract under which the debt arose, the reason being, it is said, that it is not a claim arising under the contract, or for breach of the contract, but is a claim *dehors* the contract.[452] Since an assignee takes subject to rights of set-off available to the debtor against the assignor, but not mere counterclaims,[453] those cases may suggest that the damages claim similarly would not give rise to an equitable set-off in an action between the original parties. There are two difficulties with that view, however.[454] The first is that it is contrary to the principle applied in bankruptcy, that a claim for damages for misrepresentation inducing a contract entered into with the bankrupt representor[455] is not a mere personal tort but rather it arises out of the bilateral relationship of contract between the bankrupt and the claimant.[456] Therefore, even before the insolvency legislation was amended in 1986 to allow claims in tort to be proved in a bankruptcy, it could be employed in a set-off.[457] The second is that, in any event, it is not a prerequisite to an equitable set-off that the demands should have arisen under the same contract.[458] The better view is that a cross-claim available to a purchaser against the vendor for fraud inducing the purchaser to enter into the contract is capable of being set off in an action brought by

---

[452] *Stoddart v Union Trust, Ltd* [1912] 1 KB 181; *Cummings v Johnson* (1913) 4 WWR 543; *Provident Finance Corporation Pty Ltd v Hammond* [1978] VR 312. See also *Birchal v Birch, Crisp & Co* [1913] 2 Ch 375, 379.

[453] A different view has been expressed in Australia. See para. 17.06 below.

[454] In *Banco Santander SA v Bayfern Ltd* [2001] 1 All ER (Comm) 776, Waller LJ (at 780) noted that *Stoddart v Union Trust* [1912] 1 KB 181 has been criticized.

[455] Contrast the situation in which the representation induced the claimant to make a contract with a third party. See *Coventry v Charter Pacific Corporation Ltd* (2005) 227 CLR 234 at [5], [45]–[50], [59]–[62].

[456] *Coventry v Charter Pacific Corporation Ltd* (2005) 227 CLR 234 at [48] and [50].

[457] *Jack v Kipping* (1882) 9 QBD 113; *Tilley v Bowman, Ltd* [1910] 1 KB 745. In New South Wales, McLelland CJ in Eq in *Re NIAA Corporation Ltd (in liq)* (NSW SC, 2 December 1994, BC9403369) questioned whether the claim in *Jack v Kipping* indeed was provable, and whether the insolvency set-off section therefore applied. Rather, he suggested that the set-off may have been an equitable set-off. Subsequently, Charles JA in the Victorian Court of Appeal referred to that view in terms suggesting approval in *Aliferis v Kyriacou* (2000) 1 VR 447 at [48]. However, the High Court of Australia in *Gye v McIntyre* (1991) 171 CLR 609, 630–1, and again in *Coventry v Charter Pacific Corporation Ltd* (2005) 227 CLR 234 at [38]–[50], accepted *Jack v Kipping* as an authority on insolvency set-off. For the current position in bankruptcy and company liquidation in relation to claims in tort, see paras 8.53–8.61 below.

[458] See para. 4.92 above.

the vendor for the price. While this view has been rejected in New Zealand,[459] there is support for it in Australia.[460] To adopt the test approved by the House of Lords in the *Bank of Boston* case,[461] the cross-claim for damages would be inseparably connected with the transaction that gave rise to the claim.[462] The traditional impeachment test espoused by Lord Cottenham in *Rawson v Samuel* would also appear to be satisfied. If the fraud induced the purchaser to enter into the contract, the purchaser in the absence of fraud presumably would not have contracted, in which case he or she would not have breached any contractual obligation to the vendor to tender a sum of money as payment of a purchase price. In other words, the vendor's own conduct contributed to the existence of the purchaser's liability, so as to impeach the vendor's title to his or her demand.[463] The argument for a set-off would be even stronger if the statements giving rise to the fraud also constitute a term of the contract.[464] Furthermore, for a set-off to occur, it would not be necessary that the person who induced the contract was a party to it, if the benefit of the contract has since been transferred to that person.[465]

4.112 A party may have been induced to enter into a contract by a false representation made other than fraudulently, but the same principle should apply. A resulting damages claim should be able to be employed in a set-off against a claim on the contract,[466] the important point being that the party would not have entered into the contract but for the false representation. This should also apply where a false representation can be construed as a contractual promise, including where it is contained in a collateral contract.[467] It should be the fact of the inducement, not the nature of the misrepresentation, that gives rise to the set-off.

---

[459] *Wilsons (NZ) Portland Cement Ltd v Gatx-Fuller Australasia Pty Ltd (No. 2)* [1985] 2 NZLR 33 (in particular at 37–8).

[460] *Petersville Ltd v Rosgrae Distributors Pty Ltd* (1975) 11 SASR 433; *Altarama Ltd v Camp* (1980) 5 ACLR 513, 519–20; *AMP v Specialist Funding Consultants Pty Ltd* (1991) 24 NSWLR 326; *Tomlinson v Cut Price Deli Pty Ltd* (1992) 38 FCR 490, 494; *Re Kleiss, ex p Kleiss v Capt'n Snooze Pty Ltd* (1996) 61 FCR 436, 441. See also para. 4.116–4.118 below in relation to the Trade Practices Act 1974 (Cth), s. 52. Compare *Provident Finance Corporation Pty Ltd v Hammond* [1978] VR 312, 318.

[461] [1989] 1 AC 1056. See para. 4.13 above.

[462] See *Altarama Ltd v Camp* (1980) 5 ACLR 513, 519–20.

[463] See *Piggott v Williams* (1821) 6 Madd 95, 56 ER 1027, and para. 4.04 above.

[464] As in *Sun Candies Pty Ltd v Polites* [1939] VLR 132.

[465] *Horrobin v Australia & New Zealand Banking Group Ltd* (1996) 40 NSWLR 89, 100.

[466] See *Aquaflite Ltd v Jaymar International Freight Consultants Ltd* [1980] 1 Lloyd's Rep 36; *Petersville Ltd v Rosgrae Distributors Pty Ltd* (1975) 11 SASR 433; *Box v Midland Bank Ltd* [1981] 1 Lloyd's Rep 434 (customer of a bank induced to draw on an overdraft as a result of negligent advice by a manager of the bank that further facilities would be made available); *IRM Pacific Pty Ltd v Nudgegrove Pty Ltd* [2008] QSC 195 (negligent misrepresentation). At common law an action for damages generally did not lie for an innocent misrepresentation which was not a term of the contract, but see the Misrepresentation Act 1967, s. 2(2) which gives the court a discretion to award damages in lieu of rescission of the contract. See *Chitty on Contracts* (30th edn, 2008) vol. 1, 553–9.

[467] *Grant v NZMC Ltd* [1989] 1 NZLR 8. See also *British Anzani (Felixstowe) Ltd v International Marine Management (UK) Ltd* [1980] 1 QB 137.

(2) Fraudulent claim on a contract

The discussion in the preceding section concerned fraud inducing a contract. It should be **4.113** compared to *Etablissement Esefka International Anstalt v Central Bank of Nigeria*,[468] in which the question related to an alleged fraudulent claim on a contract. The plaintiff made a claim on letters of credit issued by the defendant in respect of demurrage. Prior to the action the plaintiff had been paid various sums of money on the same letters of credit in respect of demurrage when there was evidence to suggest that the shipments in question had never taken place. As a result, the defendant appeared to have a cross-claim to recover this as money paid under a mistake of fact. In an application for a Mareva injunction, Lord Denning said that all the claims on the letter of credit should be considered as part of the one transaction, and that the cross-claim was so closely connected with the instant claim that it could well be a case for an equitable set-off. [469]

Etablissement Esefka should be compared to *Walker v Department of Social Security*,[470] **4.114** a decision of the Federal Court of Australia. The Department had paid the appellant a sum by way of sickness benefits as a result of various fraudulent claims made by him. Subsequently, he made a further claim for benefits, to which he was entitled. The Department said that the appellant's entitlement should be applied to meet the overpayment. The Full Court of the Federal Court[471] held that this was not justified on the basis of equitable set-off, since the Department was unable to point to an equity of the type necessary to sustain the defence.[472] The *Etablissement Esefka* case was not referred to, but the cases differed in that, in *Walker*, the claims were not derived from a single transaction or contract with the Department, but were separate.

In any event, the question whether the circumstances in the *Etablissement Esefka* case **4.115** gave rise to an equitable set-off may well have been unnecessary. The cross-claims would appear to have constituted mutual debts giving rise to a defence of set-off under the Statutes of Set-off,[473] in which case it would not have been necessary to show any connection between them.

---

[468] [1979] 1 Lloyd's Rep 445. See also *Black King Shipping Corporation v Massie (The Litsion Pride)* [1985] 1 Lloyd's Rep 437, 518–19.

[469] See also para. 4.63 above. Compare *Attorney-General v McLeod* (1893) 14 NSWLR 121, in which a plea of cross-action, pursuant to the Common Law Procedure Act 1857 (NSW), for breach of contract in an action for damages for fraud was held to be bad, on the ground that the cause of action could not be said to have arisen out of the same subject-matter as the plaintiff's claim.

[470] (1995) 56 FCR 354.

[471] Cooper and Spender JJ, Drummond J dissenting.

[472] (1995) 56 FCR 354, 375. Moreover, there was no set-off under the Statutes of Set-off, since the appellant's entitlement was not a debt for the purpose of the Statutes. See at 373–4, and para. 2.14 above. Drummond J dissented. He regarded the appellant's conduct in procuring the earlier payments by fraud as sufficient, when added to the connection that both lots of claims involved the disbursement of moneys from the consolidated revenue, as to make it unjust to allow recovery without bringing into account his liability.

[473] See paras 2.14–2.20 above. Certainly a sum specified in a shipping contract as being payable by way of demurrage is regarded as constituting liquidated damages (see *President of India v Lips Maritime Corporation* [1988] 1 AC 395), so that a claim for demurrage may be the subject of a set-off under the Statutes. See *Axel Johnson Petroleum AB v MG Mineral Group AG* [1992] 1 WLR 270.

(3) Misleading or deceptive conduct in Australia

4.116 In Australia, the Trade Practices Act 1974 (Cth), s. 52 provides that a corporation must not, in trade or commerce, engage in conduct that is misleading or deceptive or likely to mislead or deceive. The question has arisen whether a claim arising as a result of a contravention of s. 52 is capable of being employed defensively as an equitable set-off.[474]

4.117 In *Bank of New Zealand v Spedley Securities Ltd*,[475] the New South Wales Court of Appeal held that conduct which was prohibited by s. 52 could not be relied on as a defence in proceedings to establish a constructive trust. Mahoney JA, with whom Hope JA agreed, decided the case on the basis that the allegation of misleading or deceptive conduct did not constitute a defence to the particular claim made in that case.[476] Kirby P, however, proceeded on a broader basis. He endorsed earlier authority to the effect that s. 52 on its own does not give rise to a duty which is enforceable at law.[477] Rather, it prescribes a 'norm of conduct' which 'should not be interpreted according to established principles of liability under the general law and which, since it may be offended by acts both honest and reasonable . . . is morally neutral'.[478] If the 'norm of conduct' specified in s. 52 is not complied with, sanctions are provided elsewhere in the Act. In particular, s. 82 provides that a person who suffers loss by the conduct of another person which contravenes s. 52 may recover the amount of the loss 'by action against that other person'. Section 82, it has been said, is a provision which creates both right and remedy.[479] In the *Spedley Securities* case a claim for relief under s. 82 had not been made.[480] It was simply argued that conduct which contravened s. 52 gave rise to a defence. But even where a remedy is sought under s. 82, Kirby P suggested that the words of s. 82, in so far as they contemplate an action, are not apt to support a defence.[481]

4.118 The favoured view, however, is that misleading or deceptive conduct in contravention of s. 52 can give rise to a defence in an appropriate case, including a defence by way of equitable set-off where the breach of s. 52 gives rise to a claim for damages under s. 82 or s. 87.[482]

---

[474] Compare *Westco Motors (Distributors) Pty Ltd v Palmer* [1979] 2 NSWLR 93. The claim in that case related to the price payable for goods sold and delivered, and the cross-claim was for damages under the Trade Practices Act consequent upon allegations of restraint of trade, misuse of market power and resale price maintenance. Sheppard J (at 98–9) considered that the claims were insufficiently connected to give rise to an equitable set-off.

[475] (1992) 27 NSWLR 91.

[476] (1992) 27 NSWLR 91, 106 (Mahoney JA), Hope A-JA.

[477] See e.g. *State of Western Australia v Wardley Australia Ltd* (1991) 30 FCR 245, 256–7, referring to *Tobacco Institute of Australia Ltd v Australian Federation of Consumer Organisations Inc* (1988) 19 FCR 469. See also Toohey J on appeal in the High Court in *Wardley* (1992) 175 CLR 514, 551.

[478] *Commonwealth Bank of Australia v Mehta* (1991) 23 NSWLR 84, 88 *per* Samuels JA.

[479] *State of Western Australia v Wardley Australia Ltd* (1991) 30 FCR 245, 257.

[480] This was emphasized by Cole J at first instance. See *Spedley Securities Ltd v Bank of New Zealand* (1991) 13 ATPR 41–143 at 53,066.

[481] (1992) 27 NSWLR 91, 99.

[482] See *Bitannia Pty Ltd v Parkline Constructions Pty Ltd* (2006) 67 NSWLR 9 at [11], [83]–[104], reference being made (at [11] and [102]) to the terms of s. 87. In the *Spedley Securities* case Hope A-JA (at (1992) 27 NSWLR 91, 109) commented that: 's 52 of the Trade Practices Act cannot be pleaded by way of defence, absent a claim for relief under s. 82 or s. 87 of the Act . . .' See also Cole J at first instance (1991) 13 ATPR 41–143 at 53,066.

This accords with a number of cases in which it was assumed that an equitable set-off may be based upon a damages cross-claim for breach of s. 52.[483] But because the set-off depends upon the availability of a claim for relief under the Act, it has been said that it does not apply where the remedy under the Act is barred because of the expiration of the statutory limitation period in s. 82(2) or s. 87(1CA) of the Act.[484] This is a consequence of s. 82 (and, it may be said, s. 87) creating both right and remedy.[485] It should be contrasted with the usual principle applicable to equitable set-off, that the expiration of a limitation period in relation to a cross-claim does not preclude reliance on the cross-claim as an equitable set-off in the situation where the legislation affects the remedy and not the right.[486] Further, the relationship between the claims must be sufficiently close to give rise to an equitable set-off. Where a claim is made for payment of a contract debt, a cross-claim based on a contravention of s. 52 ordinarily would not be regarded as impeaching the plaintiff's title to sue if the representation giving rise to the s. 52 claim did not induce the contract being sued upon.[487]

L. Limitation on Liability

It may be that the liability of one of the parties is limited by contract or statute to a certain amount. In such a case the principle ordinarily would be that the liability should first be limited and a set-off may then take place against this limited sum, rather than that the two demands are first set against each other at their full face value with the limitation rule then being applied to the balance.[488] This approach should be compared to the rule applied in admiralty law in the event of a collision at sea, that a balance should be struck before the limit is applied.[489]

4.119

---

[483] *Tomlinson v Cut Price Deli Pty Ltd* (1992) 38 FCR 490; *Murphy v Zamonex Pty Ltd* (1993) 31 NSWLR 439 (see in particular at 463); *Walker v Department of Social Security* (1995) 56 FCR 354, 367; *Doherty v Murphy* [1996] 2 VR 553, 565; *Re Kleiss, ex p Kleiss v Capt'n Snooze Pty Ltd* (1996) 61 FCR 436. See also *Westpac Banking Corporation v Eltran Pty Ltd* (1987) 14 FCR 541 (and subsequent proceedings: *Eltran Pty Ltd v Westpac Banking Corporation* (1988) 32 FCR 195, 204); *Glass & Co Pty Ltd v Soonhock* (1996) 18 ATPR 41–453 (esp. at 41,567); *John Shearer Ltd v Gehl Co* (1995) 60 FCR 136, 142; *Lean v Tumut River Orchard Management Ltd* [2003] FCA 269 at [60]–[61] (where it was accepted that the availability of equitable set-off was reasonably arguable); *IRM Pacific Pty Ltd v Nudgegrove Pty Ltd* [2008] QSC 195.

[484] See Cole J at first instance in *Spedley Securities Ltd v Bank of New Zealand* (1991) 13 ATPR 41–143 at 53,066 and Kirby P on appeal (1992) 27 NSWLR 91, 99–100 (not following *AMP v Specialist Funding Consultants Pty Ltd* (1991) 24 NSWLR 326). See also the qualification in terms of the limitation period in *Bitannia Pty Ltd v Parkline Constructions Pty Ltd* (2006) 67 NSWLR 9 at [102].

[485] See para. 4.117 above.

[486] See paras 4.51–4.54 above.

[487] *Cunningham v National Australia Bank Ltd* (1987) 15 FCR 495; *Clambake Pty Ltd v Tipperary Projects Pty Ltd (No. 3)* [2009] WASC 52 at [164]–[165]. See also *Williams v Calivil Park Holstein Pty Ltd* [2009] NSWSC 389 at [28]–[29], [37]–[38].

[488] *NV Bureau Wijsmuller v The Owners of the MV Tojo Maru (The Tojo Maru)* [1970] P 21, 48, 67–8, 75.

[489] For a discussion on the practice of the courts in these cases, see *Stoomvaart Maatschappy Nederland v Peninsular and Oriental Steam Navigation Co (The Khedive)* (1882) 7 App Cas 795. As Lord Selborne noted (at 806–7), the admiralty rule operates independently of any principle of set-off.

M. Periodic Payments

4.120 A contract may impose an obligation on one party to make periodic payments to another,[490] for example a tenant's obligation to pay rent to the landlord under a periodic tenancy,[491] or a time charterer's obligation to pay hire to the owner of the vessel. The question may arise whether a set-off based upon a damages claim for breach of contract should be confined to the payment obligation that relates to the particular period in which the breach occurred, or whether the damages claim may be employed in a set-off against payment obligations that accrue in respect of other periods.

4.121 In *Government of Newfoundland v Newfoundland Railway Co*[492] the Privy Council held that a claim for damages against a contractor for failure to complete a railway line could be set off against the contractor's entitlement to an annual subsidy for each five mile section of the track that had been completed. In this case the failure to complete went to the value of what previously had been performed. In the context of a time charter of a ship, on the other hand, there is authority for the view that, if the shipowner breached the contract during one or more periods, but in subsequent periods the contract was properly performed, the charterer cannot set off the damages claim against the obligation to pay the hire applicable to those later periods.[493] In *The Aditya Vaibhav*[494] charterers alleged that, in breach of the charter, the owners failed to perform their hold-cleaning obligations,[495] which resulted in the vessel being delayed at port for about fourteen days. The charterers suffered consequential loss and expense as a result of the vessel not being available for service, which they deducted in part from the hire due during the fourteen-day period. They then submitted that they could set off the remainder of the damages claim against subsequent payments of hire. Saville J held that the damages claim did not impeach the owners' entitlement to hire for periods during which they had actually performed the services contracted for, so that a set-off was not available in respect of the remainder of the damages. This accords with Parker J's explanation in *The Teno*[496] of the rationale for allowing an equitable set-off against a claim for hire under a time charter, that 'it would be grossly unjust to allow an owner to recover hire in respect of a period during which he had,

---

[490] Compare *Peninsular and Oriental Steam Navigation Co v Youell* [1997] 2 Lloyd's Rep 136 (see para. 4.16 above), in which there were different contracts relating to different periods.

[491] See Waite, 'Disrepair and Set-off of Damages Against Rent: The Implications of British Anzani' [1983] *The Conveyancer* 373, 381–2.

[492] (1888) 13 App Cas 199.

[493] Compare *Japan Line Ltd v Aggeliki Charis Compania Maritima SA (The Angelic Grace)* [1980] 1 Lloyd's Rep 288, which concerned successive charters.

[494] *Century Textiles and Industry Ltd v Tomoe Shipping Co (Singapore) Pte Ltd (The Aditya Vaibhav)* [1991] 1 Lloyd's Rep 573.

[495] At the subsequent trial the charterers failed to prove this allegation. See *Century Textiles and Industry Ltd v Tomoe Shipping Co (Singapore) Pte Ltd (The Aditya Vaibhav)* [1993] 1 Lloyd's Rep 63.

[496] *Compania Sud Americana de Vapores v Shipmair BV (The Teno)* [1977] 2 Lloyd's Rep 289, 296. See also *Atlantic Lines & Navigation Co Inc v The Ship 'Didymi' (The Didymi)* [1988] 1 Lloyd's Rep 97, 110 (Canadian Federal Court of Appeal). This is also consistent with Lord Denning's comments in *Federal Commerce & Navigation Co Ltd v Molena Alpha Inc* [1978] 1 QB 927, 975, 976 in relation to the charterer being deprived of part of the consideration for which hire had been paid in advance.

in breach of contract, failed to provide that for which the hire was payable'. Nevertheless, it seems an unduly strict approach. The charterparty is a single contract, and the choice of periods of hire to an extent is arbitrary. Yet the shorter the period, the more limited the scope for a set-off.

A time charter usually provides for payment of hire in advance at the commencement of **4.122** each period. If, during the period, there is a breach of contract which has the effect of depriving the payer of part of the consideration for which the advance payment was made, it would be too late for a set-off to occur against the pre-paid consideration for that period. Instead, a set-off may occur against the amount due in respect of the next period, even though the contract may have been performed properly during that period.[497]

The Aditya Vaibhav concerned a time charter of a ship and, if it is followed, it may be **4.123** restricted to that context. It has been said that it does not apply to rent payable periodically under a lease. In *Courage Ltd v Crehan*[498] it was argued that, if a tenant in an action for payment of rent has a cross-claim in damages against the landlord, the cross-claim will only give rise to a set-off if it arises in respect of the same period as that for which the claim for rent was made. The Court of Appeal, while acknowledging the decision in *The Aditya Vaibhav* in relation to a time charter, nevertheless rejected the suggestion that any such temporal limitation should be introduced in the case of a lease of land.[499] *Melville v Grapelodge Developments Ltd*[500] is consistent with that view. A prospective tenant went into occupation of the premises, at the outset rent free. Protracted negotiations then took place concerning the condition of the premises. It was agreed that, if the tenant signed a lease, the landlord would carry out repairs as soon as possible. The first quarter's rent became due a few days later. When the landlord failed to carry out the repairs, Neill J held that the tenant could set off the resulting damages claim against unpaid rent, including the first quarter's rent, even though there was no determination that the landlord was in breach of the repair obligation by failing to have the repairs completed during the first quarter.[501] However, there is authority to the contrary in Western Australia. In *Clambake Pty Ltd v Tipperary Projects Pty Ltd (No. 3)*,[502] Heenan J considered that a claim for rent referable to a period *before* the occurrence of circumstances giving rise to a cross-claim against the landlord was not impeached by the cross-claim,[503] although his Honour accepted that the cross-claim could well have constituted a set-off against claims for future rent. This illustrates the

---

[497] *Federal Commerce & Navigation Co Ltd v Molena Alpha Inc* [1978] 1 QB 927, 975–6.

[498] [1999] 2 EGLR 145.

[499] See the discussion at [1999] 2 EGLR 145, 156.

[500] (1978) 39 P & CR 179.

[501] The first quarter commenced on 25 March 1977. Neill J was prepared to accept (at (1979) 39 P & CR 179, 185–6) that the landlord was obliged to *commence* the work by 21 June, but that would not have required completion by the end of the quarter, on 25 June. Nor was there a specific finding, or indeed an assumption made, that work did not commence by 21 June, which suggests that it was not regarded as significant to the question of set-off. There was simply a concession for the purpose of the case (at 184) that 'no sufficient repairs' were carried out in fulfilment of the repair obligation.

[502] [2009] WASC 52 at [163].

[503] Contrast *The Aditya Vaibhav* (above), where set-off was sought against subsequent hire.

stricter approach in relation to equitable set-off generally adopted in Australia, where the courts have continued to emphasize the impeachment test.[504]

4.124   If a breach of contract constituted a repudiation of the contract, which was accepted so as to result in the termination of the contract, the resulting damages claim ordinarily could be set off against sums previously due to the repudiating party under the contract,[505] including in relation to prior periods.

N. Mortgages

(1) The scope of equitable set-off

4.125   The right to an equitable set-off against a mortgage debt has been recognized in a number of circumstances,[506] including where the mortgagee is liable to the mortgagor for failing to renew insurance on the mortgaged property,[507] where the mortgagee's title to sue for the debt is impeached as a result of a sale of the mortgaged property at an undervalue,[508] where the mortgagee breached its duty to take reasonable steps to obtain the best price upon a sale of the mortgaged property by failing to preserve the property when in possession of it,[509] and where the mortgagee is liable in damages to the mortgagor for breach of contract in not providing further finance to the mortgagor for the purpose of a development on the mortgaged land, with the result that the mortgagor was unable to complete the development and consequently to repay the debt.[510]

---

[504] See paras 4.19 and 4.26–4.27 above.

[505] *Parsons v Sovereign Bank of Canada* [1913] AC 160. See paras 4.103–4.105 above.

[506] The discussion in *Clairview Developments Pty Ltd v Law Mortgages Gold Coast Pty Ltd* [2007] 2 Qd R 501, while in some places expressed in general terms suggesting that an unliquidated claim cannot be set off against a mortgage debt, should be considered in the context that the mortgagor in substance was seeking to restrain the sub-mortgagee from exercising a power of sale, for which special considerations apply. See below.

[507] *Campbell v Canadian Co-operative Investment Co* (1906) 16 Man LR 464.

[508] *General Credits (Finance) Pty Ltd v Stoyakovich* [1975] Qd R 352, 355 (leave to defend granted subject to conditions); *TSB Bank plc v Platts* [1998] 2 BCLC 1, 9–10; *GE Capital Australia v Davis* (2002) 11 BPR 20,529, [2002] NSWSC 1146 at [82]. See also *Harrison v Australian and New Zealand Banking Group Ltd* (Vic CA, 15 May 1996, BC9602140) (equitable set-off by a guarantor based on a remedy in damages available to the guarantor against a mortgagee under the Property Law Act 1994 (Qld), s. 85 for failure to take reasonable care in selling the mortgaged property). This may be expressed more accurately as a claim that an account be taken in equity of the amount due under the mortgage. See *GE Capital v Davis* at [82]; *Artistic Builders Pty Ltd v Elliot & Tuthill (Mortgages) Pty Ltd* (2002) 10 BPR 19,565, [2002] NSWSC 16 at [118]–[121]; *Barclays Bank Plc v Kingston* [2006] 2 Lloyd's Rep 59 at [30]. Compare *Continental Illinois National Bank & Trust Co of Chicago v Papanicolaou (The Fedora)* [1986] 2 Lloyd's Rep 441 and *Skipskreditforeningen v Emperor Navigation* [1998] 1 Lloyd's Rep 66 (ship mortgages) in which the contracts excluded set-offs.

[509] *National Australia Bank Ltd v Jenkins* (1999) V ConvR 54–601 at 67,217 (appeal dismissed (1999) V Conv R 54–602). See also *Imperial Bank of Canada v G M Annable Co* [1925] 1 DLR 946.

[510] *Popular Homes Ltd v Circuit Developments Ltd* [1979] 2 NZLR 642. See also *Doherty v Murphy* [1996] 2 VR 553 (in particular, the explanation given for the default at 560); *Murphy v Zamonex Pty Ltd* (1993) 31 NSWLR 439 (in which the cross-claim was based upon a false representation that certified claims would be paid). Compare *United Dominions Corporation Ltd v Jaybe Homes Pty Ltd* [1978] Qd R 111, in which the agreement to provide finance was not part of the same transaction as the debt sued upon.

(2) Mortgage to secure the unpaid price of property sold

Alternatively, the issue may arise in the context of a contract for the sale of property which **4.126** stipulates for a mortgage (or other form of security) back to the vendor to secure payment of the unpaid balance of the purchase price. A purchaser being sued for the price generally could set off in that action a cross-claim for damages for breach of warranty in the contract of sale directly affecting the value of the property, and the right to a set-off should not be lost simply because the debt is secured by a mortgage.[511] Further, as a matter of principle it should not matter that the action for payment is brought on a covenant to pay contained in the mortgage, rather than upon the original contract. While the damages cross-claim in this situation would arise under a different contract to that pursuant to which the action is brought for payment, it is not essential for equitable set-off that the cross-claims should have their source in the same contract.[512] The mortgage is part of the same transaction as the contract of sale.[513] Its purpose is to secure payment of the price, and if the purchaser would have had a set-off in an action brought against him or her on the contract of sale the amount outstanding secured by the mortgage similarly should be regarded as reduced *pro tanto*.[514] This is consistent with the substantive nature of this form of set-off.[515]

In Victoria, Lush J reached a different conclusion in *Provident Finance Corporation Pty Ltd* **4.127** *v Hammond*.[516] The purchaser of a business had agreed to pay the unpaid balance of the price in a number of instalments, and signed a bill of sale for the outstanding amount. The vendor then assigned the bill of sale to the plaintiff. When the plaintiff sued on the bill for payment, it was held that the purchaser could not set off a damages claim available against the vendor for breach of warranty and for fraudulent misrepresentation inducing the contract.[517] The basis of any set-off would have been the principle that an assignee takes subject to equities, which include rights of set-off available to the debtor against the assignor.[518] Lush J justified the conclusion that there was no set-off on the ground that a debtor may not set up against an assignee a claim for damages under a contract other than that assigned.[519] But equitable set-off does not require a single contract as the source of the cross-demands, and if the claims are otherwise sufficiently closely connected to give rise to a set-off as between the assignor and the debtor, the set-off ordinarily should be available as against the assignee.[520] Lush J also sought to explain the result on another ground.[521] He said that one of the objects of the contract of sale in providing for the execution of a bill of sale was to give the debt and security aspects of the contract a separate existence. That had

---

[511] *Altarama Ltd v Camp* (1980) ACLR 513; *Newman v Cook* [1963] VR 659 (in particular, the judgment of Hudson J in relation to equitable set-off). Compare *Indrisie v General Credits Ltd* [1985] VR 251, 254.

[512] See para. 4.92 above.

[513] *Altarama Ltd v Camp* (1980) 5 ACLR 513, 520. See also *Popular Homes Ltd v Circuit Developments Ltd* [1979] 2 NZLR 642, 658.

[514] See the discussion in *Newman v Cook* [1963] VR 659.

[515] See para. 4.29–4.57 above.

[516] [1978] VR 312.

[517] See para. 4.110–4.112 above.

[518] See ch. 17 below.

[519] [1978] VR 312, 321.

[520] See para. 17.32 below.

[521] [1978] VR 312, 321.

as a consequence that a separate document was brought into existence, in the form of the bill of sale, which in the ordinary course of business was transferable. From that he inferred that the rights embodied in the bill of sale were not intended to be 'intertwined' with the various other rights and obligations in the contract of sale. That inference is doubtful, however. Often it would simply be as a matter of convenience, and prevailing commercial practice, that separate documents are used.

(3) Payment of the price by way of a loan from the vendor

4.128 Sometimes a different arrangement is adopted. Instead of the mortgage securing the unpaid price, the price is satisfied by means of a loan from the vendor, and it is the repayment of this loan which is secured by a mortgage. In such a case, the Privy Council in *Bow, McLachlan & Co, Ltd v Ship 'Camosun'*[522] considered that a damages claim for breach of warranty will not provide the purchaser with a defence to an action to enforce the mortgage debt, either on the basis of equitable set-off or the common law defence of abatement,[523] since the sale and the loan secured by the mortgage are separate contracts.[524] Their Lordships' view on this point was *obiter*,[525] but it has nevertheless been regarded as correct by Australian courts.[526] The loan, and the security for it, is considered to be a separate transaction from the sale.[527]

4.129 A comment in the judgment of the Court of Appeal in *Samuel Keller (Holdings) Ltd v Martins Bank Ltd*[528] suggests the contrary view. A purchaser bought all the issued shares in a company, the vendor providing a loan to the purchaser to pay part of the price, with the loan being secured by a mortgage over certain property. The vendor sued for payment, whereupon the purchaser was granted unconditional leave to defend on the basis of a counterclaim for unliquidated damages for breach of warranties and conditions in the sale of shares agreement. The case then proceeded on another issue,[529] but Russell LJ, in delivering the judgment of the Court of Appeal, commented in passing that the grant of unconditional leave to defend seemed to have been in accordance with *Morgan & Son Ltd v S Martin Johnson & Co Ltd*,[530] which at the time was a leading authority on equitable set-off. The Court of Appeal therefore seems to have been of the opinion that the cross-claim for damages provided an arguable defence of equitable set-off to the action for payment, notwithstanding that the case was one involving a loan to pay the price.[531]

---

[522] [1909] AC 597.

[523] See paras 2.123–2.134 above.

[524] [1909] AC 597, 612–13.

[525] The case was decided on the ground that the Exchequer Court of Canada in Admiralty was not possessed of a general common law jurisdiction to enforce the damages cross-claim.

[526] *Newman v Cook* [1963] VR 659, 675–6; *Altarama Ltd v Camp* (1980) 5 ACLR 510, 520.

[527] Compare *Altarama Ltd v Camp* (1980) 5 ACLR 513, 520.

[528] [1971] 1 WLR 43.

[529] See para. 4.138 below.

[530] [1949] 1 KB 107.

[531] In *Parry v Grace* [1981] 2 NZLR 273, 278–9, *Samuel Keller* was discussed in terms suggesting that the Court of Appeal was of the view that the facts did not give rise to an equitable set-off. However, the passage in *Samuel Keller* (at [1971] 1 WLR 43, 51) to which reference was made was concerned with a different issue, as to whether the mortgagee could be kept out of its rights as mortgagee on the basis of a cross-claim available to the mortgagor. See paras 4.130–4.148 below.

The point was not the subject of detailed discussion, however, and the *Bow, MacLachlan* case was not referred to. The effect of the arrangement in these cases is to separate the payment obligation from the sale, and on that basis the view of the Privy Council is to be preferred.

(4) Enforcing rights under the mortgage

The position is more complex when the mortgagee is not suing for the debt, but rather is **4.130** seeking to enforce his or her rights as mortgagee. In considering this issue, a distinction may be drawn between a claim by a legal mortgagee for possession of the mortgaged premises, and the exercise of other rights by a mortgagee which depend upon default, for example the exercise of a power of sale.

(5) Claim for possession, where possession does not depend on default

In the absence of a contractual or a statutory provision to the contrary, the right of a legal **4.131** mortgagee in England to possession of the premises is independent of any question of default.[532] He 'may go into possession before the ink is dry on the mortgage unless there is something in the contract, express or by implication, whereby he has contracted himself out of that right'.[533] This is a consequence of the mortgagee's legal estate.[534]

In *Birmingham Citizens Permanent Building Society v Caunt*,[535] Russell J said that the court **4.132** has no jurisdiction to decline to order possession in favour of the mortgagee unless the mortgagor pays the full principal, interest and costs secured by the mortgage,[536] the 'sole exception' being that the application may be adjourned for a short time to afford to the mortgagor a chance of paying off the mortgagee in full. He emphasized, however, that the application should not be adjourned if there is no reasonable prospect of payment occurring.[537] Consistent with that strict approach, the courts have held that a mortgagee should not be denied possession of the premises on the ground that the mortgagor has a counterclaim against the mortgagee for an amount in excess of the mortgage debt,[538] and this has also been held to apply when there is a cross-claim which would give rise to an equitable set-off in an action to enforce the debt.[539] Nor does it make any difference that

---

[532] This is also the case in Australia in relation to an old title mortgage of land. See *Ex p Jackson, re Australasian Catholic Assurance Co Ltd* (1941) 41 SR (NSW) 285, 289. It should be compared to a mortgage under the Torrens system, where the mortgagor is entitled to possession until default. See Sykes and Walker, *The Law of Securities* (5th edn, 1993), 248.

[533] *Four-Maids Ltd v Dudley Marshall (Properties) Ltd* [1957] 1 Ch 317, 320 *per* Harman J.

[534] The same principle applies where a legal mortgage of land is created by a charge by deed expressed to be by way of legal mortgage. See the Law of Property Act 1925, s. 87(1), and *Four-Maids Ltd v Dudley Marshall (Properties) Ltd* [1957] 1 Ch 317, 320. See also para. 17.75 below in relation to the Land Registration Act 2002.

[535] [1962] 1 Ch 883.

[536] [1962] 1 Ch 883, 891.

[537] [1962] 1 Ch 883, 912.

[538] *Mobil Oil Co Ltd v Rawlinson* (1981) 43 P & C R 221, 226; *Citibank Trust Ltd v Ayivor* [1987] 1 WLR 1157.

[539] *Mobil Oil Co Ltd v Rawlinson* (1981) 43 P & C R 221; *National Westminster Bank plc v Skelton* [1993] 1 WLR 72 (esp. at 78); *Ashley Guarantee plc v Zacaria* [1993] 1 WLR 62, 66–7, 70. See also *TSB Bank plc v Platts* [1998] BCLC 1, 10.

the mortgagor is willing to pay into court the difference between the amount owing under the mortgage and the estimate of the sum sought to be set off.[540] An equitable set-off is a substantive defence, in that it is unconscionable for a creditor against whom the defence may be asserted to regard the debtor as being in default to the extent of the set-off while circumstances exist which support an equitable set-off.[541] Nevertheless, until the debt is paid, including by judgment for a set-off, so that the mortgagor is entitled to redemption, the principle by which the mortgagee as the party with the legal estate has the right to possession still applies.[542]

4.133   Slade LJ re-affirmed the general principle in *National Westminster Bank plc v Skelton*,[543] but he left open the question whether it would apply where the mortgagor 'establishes that he has a claim to a quantified sum by way of equitable set-off'.[544] He said that: 'Possibly such a claim might have the effect of actually discharging the mortgage debt.'[545] An equitable set-off does not operate as an automatic extinction of cross-demands, although because of the substantive nature of the defence its effect in equity is similar to a discharge to the extent of the set-off.[546] In any event, given that the availability of an equitable set-off is not dependent upon whether the cross-demand is liquidated or unliquidated, it is difficult to see why a cross-claim for a 'quantified sum' should be treated differently from a damages cross-claim available by way of equitable set-off, if it can be established that the damages payable would exceed the mortgage debt.[547]

4.134   The view that a mortgagee is entitled to possession notwithstanding that an action to enforce the mortgage debt could be met by an equitable set-off also applies when the

---

[540] *Mobil Oil Co Ltd v Rawlinson* (1981) 43 P & C R 221. Indeed, Nourse J said (at 227) that payment of the full amount secured into court will not suffice to prevent the mortgagee obtaining possession. Payment must be made to the mortgagee.

[541] See para. 4.30 above.

[542] Compare *National Westminster Bank Plc v Gaskin* [1998] EWCA Civ 1449, though the terms of the mortgage are not set out in the judgment, in particular as to whether the mortgagee's right to possession was limited to the case of default. See para. 4.136–4.148 below.

[543] [1993] 1 WLR 72.

[544] [1993] 1 WLR 72, 78. Nourse LJ noted this reservation in *Ashley Guarantee plc v Zacaria* [1993] 1 WLR 62, 66, as did Gleeson CJ in *Murphy v Abi-Saab* (1995) 37 NSWLR 280, 289. See also *Clairview Developments Pty Ltd v Mortgages Gold Coast Pty Ltd* [2007] 2 Qd R 501 at [42], referring to a 'legal' right of set-off in the case of mutual debts.

[545] [1993] 1 WLR 72, 78. It appears that the principal debtor in *Skelton* was in liquidation (see [1993] 1 WLR 72, 78, 80), in which case *quaere* why there was not an automatic set-off under the insolvency set-off section upon the occurrence of the liquidation (see paras 6.119–6.146 below) so as to discharge the principal debt to the extent of the set-off at that date.

[546] See para. 4.30 above. The point was noted, but not discussed, in *Ashley Guarantee plc v Zacaria* [1993] 1 WLR 62, 66.

[547] Ralph Gibson LJ in *Ashley Guarantee plc v Zacaria* [1993] 1 WLR 62, 70–1, while not doubting Slade LJ's judgment in *National Westminster v Skelton*, nevertheless commented, in the context of a mortgage given by a surety, that: 'it is to me an arresting concept that a mortgagor, who is a guarantor of the debt of the principal debtor . . . could be required to give possession of his home despite the existence of unliquidated claims which are admitted or shown to be likely to succeed, in an amount which would either exceed the sum due from the principal debtor or be such as, when established, to enable the principal debtor or the mortgagor to pay in full. It might possibly, in a particular case, be that an implied term could be held to have arisen which would exclude the immediate right to possession, but it is obvious that there are difficulties against such an implication in most ordinary cases.'

mortgage was given by a third party as surety for the debt secured by the mortgage,[548] and, *a fortiori*, when the third party had agreed that the mortgage should apply as if the third party was primarily liable for the debt.[549]

The Administration of Justice Act 1970, s. 36[550] may provide some relief to a mortgagor **4.135** faced with an application by the mortgagee for possession when the mortgaged property is a dwelling-house. Pursuant to s. 36, where in such a case it appears to the court that the mortgagor is likely to be able within a reasonable period to pay any sums due under the mortgage or to remedy any other default, the court may adjourn the proceedings or postpone the date for delivery of possession for such period as it thinks reasonable. In *Citibank Trust Ltd v Ayivor*,[551] Mervyn Davies J suggested that, in determining whether the mortgagor is likely to be able to pay the sums due within a reasonable time, it may be an inadmissible consideration to take into account that the mortgagor may succeed on a cross-claim, since this might nullify or circumvent the general rule that the existence of a cross-claim does not prevent the mortgagee from taking possession. Indeed, it has been said that, for s. 36 to apply, the court must be able to fix a period ending with some specified or ascertainable date during which it is likely that payment will be made,[552] and it may be difficult to do this when reliance is placed on the fruits of an unlitigated cross-claim as the source of the repayment. Notwithstanding that view, in *Ashley Guarantee plc v Zacaria*[553] Ralph Gibson LJ noted the possibility that a stay under s. 36 pending trial of the cross-claim may be appropriate if the existence and the prospects of success of the cross-claim could, in all the circumstances, be regarded as enabling the sum due to be paid within a reasonable period, and Woolf LJ also countenanced that possibility in his judgment.[554]

(6) Remedies dependent upon default

Alternatively, the remedy sought to be exercised by the mortgagee may depend upon the **4.136** occurrence of a default, for example the exercise of a power of sale, or a claim to possession of the premises in circumstances where either the mortgage limits the mortgagee's right to possession to the occurrence of a default by the mortgagor[555] or, as in Australia in relation to land under the Torrens system, where this is the position that applies in any event.[556]

---

[548] *Ashley Guarantee plc v Zacaria* [1993] 1 WLR 62, 69. In *Ashley Guarantee*, however, the mortgagee's right to possession was expressed in the mortgage instrument to depend upon 'default' by the principal debtor. See para. 4.142 below.

[549] *National Westminster Bank plc v Skelton* [1993] 1 WLR 72 (esp. at 79–80). In *Ashley Guarantee plc v Zacaria* [1993] 1 WLR 62, 69 Nourse LJ said that he could: 'see no distinction in principle between a case where the mortgagor is the principal debtor of the mortgagee and one where he is only a guarantor. In each case the mortgagee has, as an incident of his estate in the land, a right to possession of the mortgaged property.'

[550] As amended by the Administration of Justice Act 1973, s. 8.

[551] [1987] 1 WLR 1157, 1163–4.

[552] *Royal Trust Co of Canada v Markham* [1975] 1 WLR 1416; *Bristol & West Building Society v Ellis and Ellis* (1996) 73 P & CR 158.

[553] [1993] 1 WLR 62, 71.

[554] [1993] 1 WLR 62, 71.

[555] The courts will not readily imply such a restriction in a mortgage. See *National Westminster Bank plc v Skelton* [1993] 1 WLR 72, 77.

[556] Sykes and Walker, *The Law of Securities* (5th edn, 1993), 248.

Restraining the exercise of a power of sale

4.137 In the case of a power of sale, it is commonly said that a mortgagee (which includes a sub-mortgagee and a transferee of a mortgage[557]) will not generally be restrained by interlocutory injunction[558] from exercising the power unless the amount which the mortgagee claims is due is paid into court, or some other compensatory form of security is provided.[559] The basis of the principle is said to be the precept that he who seeks equity must do equity.[560] The rule is subject to a number of exceptions,[561] but in Australia, Walsh J, sitting as a single judge in the High Court, held in *Inglis v Commonwealth Trading Bank of Australia*[562] that it applies in the situation in which a mortgagor has an unlitigated cross-claim which, if established, would exceed the debt secured by the mortgage. The mortgagee will not be restrained from exercising a power of sale on the basis of the cross-claim in the absence of a payment into court or the provision of some other form of security such as a banker's bond. The decision to that effect was subsequently affirmed on appeal to the Full Court of the High Court.[563] Neither the judgment of Walsh J nor that of Barwick CJ on appeal referred specifically to the question whether the cross-claim in issue in that case gave rise to an equitable set-off. Indeed, set-off was not mentioned in the judgments,[564] and nor did Walsh J suggest that there was any connection between the circumstances out of which the mortgagor's claim for damages arose and the circumstances surrounding the grant of the mortgage.[565] On the other hand, Walsh J referred to some well-known authorities on

---

[557] *Clairview Developments Pty Ltd v Law Mortgages Gold Coast Pty Ltd* [2007] 2 Qd R 501 (see in particular at [38]). Compare *Popular Homes Ltd v Circuit Developments Ltd* [1979] 2 NZLR 642 (sub-mortgage), referred to in *Clairview Developments* at [41]–[42], [53].

[558] In Australia, this would be similar to lodging a caveat under the applicable Torrens legislation. See *Clairview Developments Pty Ltd v Law Mortgages Gold Coast Pty Ltd* [2007] 2 Qd R 501 at [52] (and see also [38]).

[559] *Fisher and Lightwood's Law of Mortgage* (12th edn, 2006), 646, para. 30.36; Cousins, *The Law of Mortgages* (2nd edn, 2001), 303, para. 16–79; *Warner v Jacob* (1882) 20 Ch D 220, 224; *Hill v Kirkwood* (1880) 28 WR 358; *Inglis v Commonwealth Trading Bank of Australia* (1972) 126 CLR 161, 164; *Murphy v Abi-Saab* (1975) 37 NSWLR 280, 289; Bryson, 'Restraining sales by mortgagees and a curial myth' (1993) 11 *Australian Bar Review* 1. Compare *Rottenberg v Monjack* [1993] BCLC 374. It has been said that the requirement to pay into court applies only in the case of interlocutory injunctions, and not to claims for final relief. See *ANZ Banking Group Ltd v Comer* (1993) 5 BPR 11,748, 11,753 (Young J, NSW Supreme Court), referring to *Hill v Kirkwood* (1880) 28 WR 358, 359–60 and *Harvey v McWatters* (1948) 49 SR (NSW) 173, 177; *Brutan Investments Pty Ltd v Underwriting and Insurance Ltd* (1980) 39 ACTR 47, 55; *Mediservices International Pty Ltd v Stocks & Realty (Security Finance) Pty Ltd* [1982] 1 NSWLR 516, 525; *Clairview Developments Pty Ltd v Law Mortgages Gold Coast Pty Ltd* [2007] 2 Qd R 501 at [53]; *Fisher and Lightwood*, *op. cit.* 646, n. 13. In New Zealand, the principle appears not to have been applied in *Popular Homes Ltd v Circuit Developments Ltd* [1979] 2 NZLR 642 (see in particular at 649).

[560] *Town & Country Sport Resorts (Holdings) Pty Ltd v Partnership Pacific Ltd* (1988) 20 FCR 540, 545. *Clarke v Japan Machines (Australia) Pty Ltd (No. 2)* [1984] 1 Qd R 421, 422; *Clairview Developments Pty Ltd v Law Mortgages Gold Coast Pty Ltd* [2007] 2 Qd R 501 at [50].

[561] See generally *Fisher and Lightwood's Law of Mortgage* (12th edn, 2006), 646, para. 30.36, and in Australia Bryson, 'Restraining sales by mortgagees and a curial myth' (1993) 11 *Australian Bar Review* 1.

[562] (1972) 126 CLR 161.

[563] (1972) 126 CLR 161, 168 (Barwick CJ, Menzies and Gibbs JJ).

[564] Set-off is referred to in the headnote, however.

[565] This point has been made in later cases. See *Cunningham v National Australia Bank Ltd* (1987) 15 FCR 495, 499; *Eltran Pty Ltd v Westpac Banking Corporation* (1988) 32 FCR 195, 203.

equitable set-off,[566] and Australian courts on a number of occasions have accepted that the principle applies in that situation.[567]

Walsh J in the *Inglis* case was influenced particularly by the decision of Megarry J, and that **4.138** of the Court of Appeal on appeal, in *Samuel Keller v Martins Bank*.[568] In the *Samuel Keller* case, a second mortgagee held a surplus from the proceeds of sale of the mortgaged property after satisfying the debt due to it. A third mortgagee sought to have the balance paid to it. However, the mortgagor said that it had a damages claim against the third mortgagee exceeding the mortgage debt and that, until this could be litigated, the surplus should be paid into court. The judgment of the Court of Appeal was delivered by Russell LJ.[569] He seems to have accepted that the cross-claim would have provided grounds for a set-off in an action for payment of the mortgage debt,[570] but he nevertheless held that the proceeds should be paid to the third mortgagee rather than into court. The *Inglis* and *Samuel Keller* cases differed in that, unlike the exercise of the power of sale by the mortgagee in *Inglis*, the third mortgagee's right to the surplus in *Samuel Keller* was not dependent upon default.[571] Nor was the *Samuel Keller* case concerned with an interlocutory injunction. On the other hand, Russell LJ noted a concession from counsel, which his Lordship also apparently accepted, that the court would not prevent a mortgagee from exercising a power of sale when the mortgage was created as a result of the same contract that gave rise to an unliquidated cross-claim.[572] The way in which that proposition was expressed would not necessarily extend to equitable set-off, since it is neither necessary nor sufficient for an equitable set-off that the claims originated in the same contract.[573] Nevertheless, it should be considered in the context of his Lordship's evident view that the circumstances in issue would have

---

[566] *Rawson v Samuel* (1841) Cr & Ph 161, 41 ER 451 and *Morgan & Son Ltd v S Martin Johnson & Co Ltd* [1949] 1 KB 107.

[567] *Altarama Ltd v Camp* (1980) 5 ACLR 513, 518; *Murphy v Abi-Saab* (1995) 37 NSWLR 280, 289. See also *Glandore Pty Ltd v Elders Finance and Investment Co Ltd* (1984) 4 FCR 130, 133, 135; *Graham v Commonwealth Bank of Australia* (1988) 10 ATPR 40–908 at 49,757; *Nicholas John Holdings Pty Ltd v ANZ Banking Group Ltd* [1992] 2 VR 715, 728; *Latrobe Capital and Mortgage Corp Ltd v Mt Eliza Mews Pty Ltd* [2001] VSC 464; *Kennedy v General Credits Ltd* (1982) 2 BPR 9456, 9464 (though in that case the set-off was characterized as procedural and not substantive); *Radin v Vekic* (NSW SC, Young J, 6 June 1997, BC9702448 at 10); *Clairview Developments Pty Ltd v Law Mortgages Gold Coast Pty Ltd* [2007] 2 Qd R 501 (caveat). In *Murphy v Abi-Saab* the New South Wales Court of Appeal referred to *National Westminster Bank plc v Skelton* [1993] 1 WLR 72 as supporting that proposition. *Skelton*, however, turned on a different principle, that a mortgagee in England is entitled by virtue of his or her legal estate to go into possession, whether or not there has been default, unless the mortgagee has contracted him or herself out of that right. See para. 4.131 above. In New Zealand, see *Parry v Grace* [1981] 2 NZLR 273, 278, 280, in which Thorp J, without deciding the point, seemed inclined to accept that an unlitigated cross-claim which, if successful, would give rise to an equitable set-off would not be a sufficient ground for restraining the mortgagee in the absence of payment into court.

[568] [1971] 1 WLR 43.

[569] Edmund Davies and Cross LJJ concurring.

[570] See the reference in Russell LJ's judgment ([1971] 1 WLR 43, 49) to unconditional leave to defend, and also (at 49 and 51) to the earlier Court of Appeal decision in *Morgan & Son Ltd v S Martin Johnson & Co Ltd* [1949] 1 KB 107, which was concerned with equitable set-off.

[571] The mortgagee's claim in *Samuel Keller* has been equated with a claim for possession of the mortgaged property (for which see above). See *TSB Bank plc v Platts* [1998] 2 BCLC 1, 10. A mortgagee who has a surplus after the exercise of a power of sale holds the surplus subject to a constructive trust in favour of a subsequent mortgagee. See *Banner v Berridge* (1881) 18 Ch D 254.

[572] [1971] 1 WLR 43, 50–1.

[573] See paras 4.91–4.92 above.

provided an arguable basis for an equitable set-off, sufficient for unconditional leave to defend, in an action for payment.[574] To that extent, the judgment in the *Samuel Keller* case also suggests that a mortgagee will not be restrained from exercising a power of sale because of an equitable set-off that would have been available to the mortgagor in an action for payment of the mortgage debt.

4.139 There are, however, other cases in Australia where it has been suggested that injunctive relief could be granted to a mortgagor free of the condition that the amount secured be paid into court if the mortgagor's cross-claim is sufficiently connected with the mortgage so as to give rise to an equitable set-off.[575] The suggestion is not easy to reconcile with the *Inglis* case. Nevertheless, there is much to commend that view,[576] at least where the cross-claim raised by way of equitable set-off exceeds the mortgage debt[577] and the strength of the cross-claim and the availability of a set-off are sufficiently clear.[578] It reflects what has been described as a 'lack of enthusiasm' for the rule applied in *Inglis*,[579] and 'judicial uneasiness' as to its operation.[580] A power of sale ordinarily is expressed to be exercisable in the event of a 'default' in payment. A 'default' in this context should be taken as referring to a failure to pay in circumstances where there is a legal obligation to do so.[581] An equitable set-off does not operate as an automatic cancellation of cross-demands,[582] and in the situation posited there will have been a failure by the mortgagor to pay. On the other hand, because of the equitable set-off the mortgagor is not required to pay, and because of the

---

[574] See above.

[575] *Cunningham v National Australia Bank Ltd* (1987) 15 FCR 495, 500–1, referred to with approval in *Eltran Pty Ltd v Westpac Banking Corporation* (1988) 32 FCR 195, 204. See also *Australian Natives' Association Friendly Society v Peball Pty Ltd* (1993) V Conv R 54–482 at 65,612–13; *Rawcliffe v Custom Credit Corporation* (1994) 16 ATPR 41–292 at 41,923; *Swift v Westpac Banking Corporation* (1995) 17 ATPR 41–401 at 40,431. Note also, and compare, *Ridgecape Holdings Pty Ltd v Cobb* [2006] WASC 33. The statements in question mainly were made in the context of claims under the Trade Practices Act 1974 (Cth), and they may have had in contemplation an application for an injunction under s. 80 of that Act. It has been said of the injunctive power under the Trade Practices Act that it is not necessarily confined by principles observed in courts of equity in their traditional jurisdiction, and that the court may grant interlocutory or final injunctive relief under the Act that does not correspond with what would follow from the application of the traditional rules. See *Town & Country Sport Resorts (Holdings) Pty Ltd v Partnership Pacific Ltd* (1988) 20 FCR 540, 545 *per* Davies, Gummow and Lee JJ, and see also *ANZ Banking Group Ltd v Comer* (1993) 5 BPR 11,748, 11,753, NSW SC, *per* Young J. However, the views expressed were not in their terms confined to the statutory injunction.

[576] See also paras 4.141–4.142 below in relation to foreclosure and possession. In *Nicholas John Holdings Pty Ltd v ANZ Banking Group Ltd* [1992] 2 VR 715, 728 Hedigan J contemplated the possibility that a cross-claim available by way of equitable set-off could be relevant in determining the amount that might be required to be brought into court, depending on the strength of the evidence and the estimation of the possible damages, and also that the availability of an equitable set-off could be capable of forming one of the matters to be taken into account in weighing the balance of convenience for the purpose of an application for an interlocutory injunction. Nevertheless, he went on to say that 'an examination of the cases does not justify an easy departure from the *Inglis* principle'.

[577] Compare *Atkinson v Hastings Deering (Queensland) Pty Ltd* (1985) 6 FCR 331, 333.

[578] It would be necessary to show that the cross-claim is clearly arguable. See *Town & Country Sport Resorts (Holdings) Pty Ltd v Partnership Pacific Ltd* (1988) 20 FCR 540, 545; *Swift v Westpac Banking Corporation* (1995) 17 ATPR 41–401 at 40,431.

[579] *Atkinson v Hastings Deering (Queensland) Pty Ltd* (1985) 6 FCR 331, 333.

[580] *Angelatos v National Australia Bank* (1994) 51 FCR 574, 581.

[581] *The Oxford English Dictionary* defines 'default', *inter alia*, as a 'failure to perform some legal requirement or obligation'.

[582] See para. 4.30 above.

substantive nature of the defence[583] the mortgagee is not permitted in equity to treat the mortgagor as having failed to pay. The mortgagee, therefore, should not be permitted to assert that there has been default in payment, so as to be able to rely on the condition for the exercise of the power. It has been suggested that the 'payment in' rule does not apply where the matter in dispute relates to whether the power of sale has arisen at all,[584] so that the mortgagee in that situation may be restrained by injunction from exercising the power without the mortgagor being required to bring the money into court.[585] There is a cogent argument that a similar principle should apply in the situation in which the mortgagee's right to sell is impeached by a clearly arguable equitable set-off.

In any event, where a mortgagor has a cross-claim over-topping the mortgage debt, the mortgagee would not be permitted to exercise a power of sale if the cross-claim has been liquidated and an equitable set-off in respect of it has been established by the court. This occurred in Victoria, in *Newman v Cook*.[586] In that case, a vendor's application for a declaration that he was entitled to exercise a power of sale pursuant to a mortgage given as security for the unpaid part of the purchase price took the form of a counterclaim in the purchaser's action for damages for breach of contract. The court[587] was in a position to declare that the damages claim should be brought into an account with the price on the basis of common law abatement,[588] and also, according to Hudson J, by way of equitable set-off, so that to that extent the price was paid. **4.140**

Restraining other remedies dependent upon default

The payment rule is often expressed generally, in terms not confined to the exercise of a power of sale, but rather in terms that a mortgagee will not be restrained by interlocutory injunction from exercising his or her rights under the mortgage instrument unless the amount owing is paid into court.[589] Indeed, the point has been made that the requirement **4.141**

---

[583] See paras 4.29–4.57 above.

[584] *Fisher and Lightwood's Law of Mortgage* (12th edn, 2006), 646, para. 30.36; *Allfox Building Pty Ltd v Bank of Melbourne Ltd* (1992) NSW ConvR 55–634 at 59,627. See also *Halsbury's Laws of England* (4th edn, 2005) vol. 32, 334, para. 658. This includes a failure to give a proper statutory notice as a pre-condition to the exercise of a power of sale. See *Mediservices International Pty Ltd v Stocks & Realty (Security Finance) Pty Ltd* [1982] 1 NSWLR 516; *Atkinson v Hastings Deering (Queensland) Ltd* (1985) 6 FCR 331; *National Australia Bank Ltd v Zollo* (1992) 59 SASR 76. See also *Rawcliffe v Custom Credit Corporation Ltd* (1994) 16 ATPR 41–492 (challenge to the validity of the mortgage).

[585] In Australia the principle has been expressed in terms that, where the matter in dispute is whether the power of sale has arisen at all, the terms as to payment into court may be moulded so as to require payment in of so much only as will suffice to give adequate protection to the mortgagee, depending on what the justice of the case requires. See *Harvey v McWatters* (1948) 49 SR (NSW) 173; *Glandore Pty Ltd v Elders Finance and Investment Co Ltd* (1984) 4 FCR 130 (in which there was an allegation of misleading or deceptive conduct against the mortgagee contrary to the Trade Practices Act 1974 (Cth), s. 52, and the relief sought included an order varying the terms of the loan agreement); *Nicholas John Holdings Pty Ltd v ANZ Banking Group Ltd* [1992] 2 VR 715, 728–9. Compare *Mainbanner Pty Ltd v Dadincroft Pty Ltd* (1988) ATPR 40–896.

[586] [1963] VR 659. See also *Clairview Developments Pty Ltd v Law Mortgages Gold Coast Pty Ltd* [2007] 2 Qd R 501 at [41]–[42], [53] (referring to *Popular Homes Ltd v Circuit Developments Ltd* [1979] 2 NZLR 642).

[587] Herring CJ, Dean and Hudson JJ.

[588] See para. 2.123–2.134 above.

[589] See e.g. *Inglis v Commonwealth Trading Bank* (1971) 126 CLR 161, 164 (Walsh J), 169 (Barwick CJ); *Glandore Pty Ltd v Elders Finance and Investment Co Ltd* (1984) 4 FCR 130, 133; *Murphy v Abi-Saab* (1995) 37 NSWLR 280, 289.

imposed by the courts in relation to an attempt to restrain the exercise of a power of sale seems merely to have continued earlier practices adopted where mortgagors sought to restrain the exercise of other remedies of mortgagees, such as the enforcement of bonds and covenants or an action for foreclosure.[590] Thus, the payment in rule has been invoked in the context of an attempt to stay a foreclosure action.[591] On the other hand, it is the practice to give a mortgagor a period of time after the foreclosure order nisi (usually six months) in which to pay the debt before the order is made absolute. That period may then be enlarged, or the foreclosure may be re-opened.[592] Consistent with that indulgence to mortgagors, there is authority for the view that an equitable set-off may be pleaded as a defence to an action for foreclosure.[593] In *Piggott v Williams*,[594] a decision of Sir John Leach VC in 1821, a solicitor failed in an application for an order for foreclosure of an estate pledged as security for costs, because of an allegation by the client that the costs claimed would not have been incurred were it not for the solicitor's own negligence. The Vice Chancellor said that, taking the matter alleged to be true, the client had a clear title to restrain the solicitor from proceeding to enforce his security and leaving the client's demand for damages unsatisfied. In the *Inglis* case in Australia,[595] Walsh J sought to explain *Piggott v Williams* on the ground that the client's allegation in that case went to the question whether the debt which the security was intended to secure had ever been incurred at all. It is true that the client's cross-bill alleged that nothing was due to the solicitor. Nevertheless, Sir John Leach referred to the client's 'demand for damages', and commented that the facts alleged, if true, disclosed 'a clear case of equitable set-off'.[596] He said that the course which the cause would probably take would be to retain the solicitor's bill until an action for damages were tried. The Vice Chancellor in truth proceeded on the basis that the allegations, if true, showed cross-demands operating by way of equitable set-off. More recently, the British Columbia Court of Appeal in *Coba Industries Ltd v Millie's Holdings (Canada) Ltd*[597] refused foreclosure on the basis of an equitable set-off available to the mortgagor.

---

[590] See Bryson, 'Restraining sales by mortgagees and a curial myth' (1993) 11 *Australian Bar Review* 1, 11–12, referring to Faucett J in *Bank of New South Wales v Tyson* (1871) 11 SCR (NSW) (Eq) 1, 20 *et seq*.

[591] *Paynter v Carew* (1854) Kay App 36, 39, 69 ER 331, 333; *Bank of New South Wales v Tyson* (1871) 11 SCR (NSW) (Eq) 1, 20–2. For examples of payments into court in foreclosure actions, see *Jones v Tinney* (1845) Kay App 45, 69 ER 336 and *Challie v Gwynne* (1846) Kay App 46, 69 ER 337. See also the order made by Wigram VC in *Dodd v Lydall* (1842) 1 Hare 333, 66 ER 1060. The set-off in issue in *Dodd v Lydall* appears to have been an equitable set-off based upon equity acting by analogy with the Statutes. See generally, as to that form of set-off, para. 3.07 above.

[592] See *Fisher and Lightwood's Law of Mortgage* (12th edn, 2006), 698–702, 712–14.

[593] In addition to the cases discussed below, see *Dodd v Lydall* (1841) 1 Hare 333, 66 ER 1060. Wigram VC in that case was prepared to make a decree of foreclosure notwithstanding a cross-claim by the mortgagor for an account of amounts due from the mortgagee in his capacity as one of the trustees of a trust in which the mortgagor was beneficially interested. In doing so he emphasized that the mortgage and the trust accounts had no original or necessary connection with each other, but the tenor of his judgment suggests that, if that had not been the case, and if there had not been an issue in relation to acquiescence, he would not have made the decree. However, the Vice Chancellor said that he would suspend the decree until the trust account could be taken if the amount of the mortgage debt was paid into court.

[594] (1821) 6 Madd 95, 56 ER 1027.

[595] (1972) 126 CLR 161, 167.

[596] (1821) 6 Madd 95, 56 ER 1027.

[597] [1985] 6 WWR 14.

In cases of foreclosure, where it is the practice in any event to give the mortgagor time to pay, there is not the same urgency that may exist in relation to the exercise of a power of sale, in circumstances where a delay in selling may adversely affect the price obtainable for the property in the short term. For that reason, it is suggested that the courts should favour the approach adopted in *Piggott v Williams* and the *Coba Industries* case, notwithstanding Walsh J's comments in the *Inglis* case.

Action for possession, where possession depends upon default

The preceding discussion related to the position in equity. In Australia, where a mortgagee's right to possession of land under the Torrens system depends on default,[598] there is support for the proposition that the equitable requirement to pay money into court in an application for an interlocutory injunction to restrain a mortgagee from exercising rights under the mortgage does not apply where a mortgagor instead is seeking to defend a common law action for possession of the mortgaged land because of a dispute as to the amount of the debt,[599] though it has also been said that the judge in such a case has a discretion to require payment.[600] Similarly, in England, comments in the Court of Appeal in *Ashley Guarantee plc v Zacaria*[601] suggest that an equitable set-off exceeding the mortgage debt may provide a defence to an action for possession in circumstances where possession depends upon default, without the imposition of a requirement of payment into court.[602] The plaintiff in that case had lent money to a company, repayment of which was secured by a mortgage given by the defendant. The mortgage contained a provision to the effect that the plaintiff could exercise its rights and remedies over the mortgaged property only in the event of default by the company. The plaintiff sought possession of the property consequent upon a default in repayment of the loan. The defendant argued that the company had a cross-claim against the plaintiff which gave it a right of equitable set-off, and that, because of the set-off, the company had not defaulted in any of its obligations to the plaintiff. Accordingly, it was said that the plaintiff was not entitled to possession under the mortgage. The argument failed because, as Nourse LJ pointed out, the cross-claim did not come anywhere near the amount of the company's debt to the plaintiff.[603] But if it had

4.142

---

[598] *Fisher and Lightwood's Law of Mortgage* (2nd Aust edn, 2005), 442 *et seq*. Compare the case of an old title mortgage, in which the mortgagee is entitled to possession by virtue of the legal estate, and irrespective of default, unless the contract provides otherwise. See *Ex p Jackson. Re Australasian Catholic Assurance Co Ltd* (1941) 41 SR (NSW) 285, 289, and para. 4.131 above.

[599] *Murphy v Abi-Saab* (1995) 37 NSWLR 280, 289 (NSW CA) and *Fisher and Lightwood's Law of Mortgage* (2nd Aust edn, 2005), [19.22], each referring to *ANZ Banking Group Ltd v Comer* (1993) 5 BPR 11,748, 11,753–4 (Young J, NSW SC). See also *Long Leys Co Pty Ltd v Silkdale Pty Ltd* (1991) 5 BPR 11,512, 11,519–20, where the New South Wales Court of Appeal countenanced that equitable set-off may provide a defence. Compare *Indrisie v General Credits* (1984) 5 FCR 582, in which an injunction was sought to restrain a mortgagee from executing a judgment obtained for possession, as opposed to the mortgagor defending a common law action for possession. In that circumstance, the 'payment in' rule was regarded as applicable. See at 587–8. Similarly, the 'payment in' rule may apply where an injunction is sought prevent the mortgagee remaining in possession. See *Harvey v McWatters* (1948) 49 SR (NSW) 173, 177, referring to *Hill v Kirkwood* (1880) 28 WR 358.

[600] *Murphy v Abi-Saab* (1995) 37 NSWLR 280, 289 (NSW CA), but compare *Fisher and Lightwood's Law of Mortgage* (2nd Aust edn, 2005), [19.22].

[601] [1993] 1 WLR 62.

[602] See also *National Westminster Bank Plc v Gaskin* [1998] EWCA Civ 1449.

[603] See also *Murphy v Abi-Saab* (1995) 37 NSWLR 280, 290.

exceeded the debt, he indicated that he would have been prepared to accept the argument.[604] Similarly, Woolf LJ suggested that possession would have been refused if a set-off had been available for a sum greater than the mortgage debt.[605] Neither of their Lordships indicated that this would have been subject to payment in.[606]

4.143   When a mortgagor is asserting an equitable defence of set-off, it would be difficult from a historical perspective to justify a distinction between, on the one hand, an application to a court of equity for an injunction to restrain a mortgagee from exercising rights under the mortgage instrument, and on the other a defence to a common law action for possession, given that, before the Judicature Acts, the mortgagor's equitable set-off in any event would have been given effect by means of an injunction to restrain the common law proceeding.[607] Having said that, the approach suggested by the *dicta* in the *Ashley Guarantee* case would seem correct,[608] based on the construction of the contract. The mortgagee in *Ashley Guarantee* was only entitled to possession in the event of a default. In that circumstance, the point made above in relation to a power of sale should apply equally here.[609] An entitlement to an equitable set-off equal to or exceeding the debt should preclude the mortgagee from asserting that there has been a 'default', in the sense of a failure to pay a sum where there was a legal obligation to do so, so that the mortgagee should not be able to assert that the contractual condition circumscribing the mortgagee's right to possession has been satisfied.

4.144   Similarly, in Australia a mortgagee of land under the Torrens system is only entitled to go into possession upon 'default' in payment by the mortgagor.[610] If the mortgagor has an equitable set-off exceeding the debt, the mortgagee should not be in a position to assert that there has been a default in payment, so as to establish the element necessary to support the mortgagee's statutory claim for possession in a possession action.[611]

---

[604] [1993] 1 WLR 62, 68. Compare, however, Nourse LJ's comments at 69. *Quaere* whether the cross-claim must be admitted or be shown to be likely to succeed. See Ralph Gibson LJ at 70.

[605] [1993] 1 WLR 62, 71.

[606] In Australia, Professor O'Donovan has suggested (*Company Receivers and Administrators* (looseleaf) vol. 1, APX3.210) that the 'payment in' rule in any event may not apply if the mortgagee has caused damage to the secured property before going into possession, so that the mortgagor's ability to service the secured debt is impaired. This suggestion is based on *Beasley v Darcy* (1800) 2 Sch & Lef 403n, which concerned possession as between landlord and tenant. See para. 4.04 above.

[607] See para. 3.01 above. Before the Judicature Acts, the payment principle applied when an injunction was sought to restrain ejectment proceedings by a mortgagee. See *Booth v Booth* (1742) 2 Atk 343, 26 ER 609.

[608] In Australia, compare *Radin v Vekic* (NSW SC, Young J, 6 June 1997, BC9702448 at 11–12).

[609] See para. 4.139 above.

[610] See e.g. the Transfer of Land Act 1958, s. 78(1), and the Real Property Act 1900 (NSW), s. 60.

[611] *Fisher and Lightwood's Law of Mortgage* (2nd Aust edn, 2005), [19.24], and see also the qualification to the statement of principle by Tadgell J in *MEK Nominees Pty Ltd v Billboard Entertainments Pty Ltd* (1993) V ConvR 54–468 at 65,469, in terms of a statute which cuts down the mortgagee's right to possession. In the case of a Torrens mortgage, the mortgagee's right to possession is indeed cut down by statute, by the imposition of a requirement of showing default by the mortgagor. Compare the comments of Sheller JA in *Horrobin v Australia & New Zealand Banking Group Ltd* (1996) 40 NSWLR 89, 100, which were of a general nature and not specifically directed to the case of a Torrens mortgage. His Honour referred to *National Westminster Bank plc v Skelton* [1993] 1 WLR 72, 78, which concerned a mortgage in England where the mortgagee was entitled to possession by virtue of its legal estate without the necessity of showing default. The court nevertheless may have a discretion to require payment in. See *Murphy v Abi-Saab* (1995) 37 NSWLR 280, 289, though compare *Fisher and Lightwood's Law of Mortgage* (2nd Aust edn, 2005), [19.22].

In any event, if the mortgagor has an arguable cross-claim against the mortgagee for fraud- **4.145**
ulent misrepresentation, in circumstances where it is said that the giving of the mortgage
itself was induced by fraud, the mortgagee will not be entitled to summary judgment to
recover possession, and the 'payment in' rule will not apply.[612]

In the *Ashley Guarantee* case, the defendant was a surety for the debts of the company, and **4.146**
the right to possession under the mortgage was contingent upon default by the company.
Nourse and Woolf LJJ were of the view that, if the company's cross-claim against the plaintiff had exceeded the debt secured by the mortgage, and that cross-claim was available to
the company by way of equitable set-off, the defendant would have had a defence to the
claim for possession pursuant to the mortgage.[613] That view should be compared to *Indrisie
v General Credits Ltd*,[614] in which the Supreme Court of Victoria considered that, even if
the principal debtor's cross-claim in that case gave rise to an equitable set-off,[615] it would
not have assisted the surety in resisting the creditor's claim for possession of the property
mortgaged by the surety.[616] In the *Indrisie* case, however, the court seems to have proceeded
on the incorrect assumption that the surety in these cases is seeking to employ the principal's claim in a set-off against the surety's own liability under the guarantee, rather than that
the surety is asserting that the principal has a defence as against the creditor, and that the
surety is also entitled to rely on that defence as against the creditor.[617] For that reason, the
views of Nourse and Woolf LJJ should be preferred.[618]

(7) Statutes of Set-off

The above discussion concerned equitable set-off. A question attracting different consider- **4.147**
ations is whether the court on the application of a mortgagor will order that an independent cross-debt owing to the mortgagor be set off against the mortgage debt under the
Statutes of Set-off, so as to allow the mortgagor to redeem.[619] This was considered earlier in
the context of a discussion of *Parker v Jackson*.[620]

---

[612] *Horrobin v Australia & New Zealand Banking Group Ltd* (1996) 40 NSWLR 89 (in particular the judgment of Sheller JA at 100). Compare *Radin v Commonwealth Bank of Australia* (Federal Court of Australia,
Lindgren J, 25 May 1998, BC9802429), in which the bank's alleged fraud did not relate to the giving of the
mortgage.

[613] See para. 4.142 above.

[614] [1985] VR 251, 254.

[615] In fact, the Supreme Court in the *Indrisie* case was of the view that the circumstances did not give rise
to an equitable set-off. See [1985] VR 251, 253–4.

[616] Under the Transfer of Land Act 1958 (Vic), s. 78, a mortgagee is only entitled to possession in the event
of default.

[617] See para. 18.22 below.

[618] The High Court refused special leave to appeal from the decision in the *Indrisie* case (see [1985] VR
251, 254), but the reason for the refusal is not clear.

[619] Set-off of mutual debts under the Statutes of Set-off should not be relevant to the 'payment in' rule,
which applies when it is sought to restrain the exercise of a power of sale on the basis of an unlitigated cross-
claim. See para. 4.137 above. This is because that form of set-off merely provides a procedural defence to
an action for payment of a debt. See paras 2.34–2.52 above. Compare *Clairview Developments Pty Ltd v
Mortgages Gold Coast Pty Ltd* [2007] 2 Qd R 501 at [42], which is not altogether clear.

[620] [1936] 2 All ER 281. See paras 2.40–2.45 above.

(8) Rent payable to a mortgagee in possession

4.148 The question sometimes arises as to whether a mortgagee in possession who is entitled to rent payable by a tenant takes subject to an equitable set-off that otherwise would have been available to the tenant as against the mortgagor. This issue is considered later.[621]

---

[621] See paras 17.72–17.95 below.

5

SET-OFF BETWEEN SOLVENT PARTIES:
VARIOUS ASPECTS

5.01 This chapter considers various aspects of set-off between solvent parties.

A. Charterparties and Bills of Lading

(1) Equitable set-off and abatement – freight under a voyage charter or bill of lading

5.02 Questions of set-off in the context of charterparties have been the subject of particular attention in recent years.[1] In that regard the courts have drawn a distinction between, on the one hand, freight payable under a voyage charter or bill of lading, and on the other hire payable under a time charter or a charter by demise.[2] In the former case, equitable set-off generally is not available, whereas it may apply in the latter.

5.03 There is a general common law principle whereby the defendant in an action for payment of the price of goods sold with a warranty, or of work to be performed according to a contract, can deduct the amount of any damage sustained by the defendant by reason of a breach of warranty or contract. This is not by way of set-off, but rather it is a means by which the defendant can defend him- or herself by showing how much less the subject-matter of the contract is worth as a result of the claimant's breach. This principle, known as abatement, or the rule in *Mondel v Steel*,[3] was considered earlier.[4] However, the right to abate does not apply to every contract for work and labour. It was established early in the nineteenth century[5] that, in the case of a contract for the carriage of goods by sea, a bill of

---

[1] See Rose, 'Deductions from freight and hire under English law' [1982] *Lloyd's Maritime and Commercial Law Quarterly* 33. In *Japan Line Ltd v Aggeliki Charis Compania Maritime SA (The Angelic Grace)* [1980] 1 Lloyd's Rep 288 the Court of Appeal (Lord Denning MR and Waller LJ) held that a shipowner's liability to reimburse charterers for a quantity of bunkers remaining on the vessel at the expiration of the charter could be set off against the owner's cross-claim for stevedore damage. In *Exmar BV v National Iranian Tanker Co (The Trade Fortitude)* [1992] 1 Lloyd's Rep 169, arbitrators had decided that a charterer's cross-claim in respect of cargo shortages could be set off against the owner's claim for demurrage. Judge Diamond QC in the Commercial Court (at 178–9) found it unnecessary to decide if the arbitrators were correct on this point. On the traditional impeachment test the claims would seem to be insufficiently connected to give rise to an equitable set-off, but a set-off could perhaps be supported on the broader formulations which have found favour in recent years. See paras 4.08–4.18 above.

[2] For a discussion of the difference between the modern form of time charter and a charter by demise, see *Sea and Land Securities Ltd v William Dickinson and Company Ltd* [1942] 2 KB 65, 69 (McKinnon LJ).

[3] (1841) 8 M & W 858, 151 ER 1288.

[4] See paras 2.123–2.134 above.

[5] *Bornmann v Tooke* (1808) 1 Camp 376, 170 ER 991; *Sheels v Davies* (1814) 4 Camp 119, 171 ER 39, subsequent proceedings *sub nom Shields v Davis* (1815) 6 Taunt 65, 128 ER 957.

lading holder or a voyage charterer cannot make a deduction from the freight payable[6] except to the extent specifically allowed by the contract.[7] As a consequence of this exception,[8] a defence of abatement has failed in cases involving damage done to the goods being shipped,[9] short delivery[10] and delay.[11]

It is unclear whether the rule against deductions from freight was originally thought to extend to the equitable defence of set-off as well as the common law defence. In *Stimson v Hall*[12] a lighterman brought an action against the owner of goods for freight owing for the conveyance of the goods. The goods owner alleged that other goods had been lost as a result of the negligence of the lighterman,[13] and said that his cross-claim for damages for the loss of those goods gave rise to an equitable defence to the claim. While the Court of Exchequer rejected this contention on the ground that the facts failed to disclose a natural equity sufficient to ground a set-off, there is nothing in the judgments or in the arguments of counsel to suggest that an equitable set-off was considered to be unavailable in any event against a claim for freight. However, the courts have since accepted that equitable set-off is subject to the same restriction as for common law abatement with respect to the payment of freight.[14] The restriction is not confined to cases of loss of or damage to goods

5.04

---

[6] In addition to the cases cited below, see *Mondel v Steel* (1841) 8 M & W 858, 871, 151 ER 1288, 1293; *Kish v Charles Taylor, Sons & Co* [1912] AC 604, 616; *St John Shipping Corporation v Joseph Rank Ltd* [1957] 1 QB 267, 291.

[7] As e.g. in *Lakeport Navigation Co Panama SA v Anonima Petroli Italiana SpA (The Olympic Brilliance)* [1982] 2 Lloyd's Rep 205.

[8] Strictly, the rule prohibiting deductions from freight is an application of the rule which was generally in force before the common law courts developed the defence of abatement. See *Aries Tanker Corporation v Total Transport Ltd* [1977] 1 WLR 185, 192–3. Nevertheless, to the extent that the allowance of an abatement in a contract for work and labour has now become the general rule, the freight rule may be regarded as the exception.

[9] *Davidson v Gwynne* (1810) 12 East 381, 104 ER 149; *Sheels v Davies* (1814) 4 Camp 119, 171 ER 39; *Garrett v Melhuish* (1858) 33 LTOS 25; *Dakin v Oxley* (1864) 15 CB(NS) 646, 143 ER 938; *Hoenig v Isaacs* [1952] 2 All ER 176, 178; *Henriksens Rederi A/S v THZ Rolimpex (The Brede)* [1974] 1 QB 233. Compare *Bellamy v Russell* (1681) 2 Show KB 167, 89 ER 865, in which a merchant was permitted to retain the freight otherwise payable under a charterparty as compensation for damage caused to the goods by the fault of the master. This was not based upon a defence of abatement or set-off, but rather upon a custom of merchants which permitted a deduction.

[10] *Aries Tanker Corporation v Total Transport Ltd* [1977] 1 WLR 185 (in which freight was to be calculated according to the *intaken* quantity of cargo rather than the quantity delivered, for which see *Dakin v Oxley* (1864) 15 CB(NS) 646, 664–5, 143 ER 938, 946). See also *Blanchet v Powell's Llantivit Collieries Co Ltd* (1874) LR 9 Ex 74. *A fortiori* there may not be a deduction in respect of the value of missing goods against the freight due upon other goods actually delivered. See *Meyer v Dresser* (1864) 16 CB(NS) 646, 143 ER 1280.

[11] *A/S Gunnstein & Co v K/S Jensen, Krebs and Nielsen (The Alfa Nord)* [1977] 2 Lloyd's Rep 434. See also *Bornmann v Tooke* (1808) 1 Camp 376, 170 ER 991; *R H & D International Ltd v IAS Animal Air Services Ltd* [1984] 1 WLR 573.

[12] (1857) 1 H & N 831, 156 ER 1436, 5 WR 367.

[13] The plaintiff's claim for freight was not in respect of the goods alleged to have been lost. This appears more clearly from the report of the case at 5 WR 367. Watson B commented (at 368) that he was uncertain how equity would have dealt with the matter in a case in which there was a demand for freight and the goods in respect of which the freight was claimed were damaged by the shipowner or carrier.

[14] *Cleobulos Shipping Co Ltd v Intertanker Ltd (The Cleon)* [1983] 1 Lloyd's Rep 586; *Elena Shipping Ltd v Aidenfield Ltd (The Elena)* [1986] 1 Lloyd's Rep 425; *Bank of Boston Connecticut v European Grain and Shipping Ltd* [1989] 1 AC 1056; *Protank Shipping Inc v Total Transport Corporation (The Protank Orinoco)* [1997] 2 Lloyd's Rep 42, 44. See also *Henriksens Rederi A/S v THZ Rolimpex (The Brede)* [1974] 1 QB 233; *Aries Tanker Corporation v Total Transport Ltd* [1977] 1 WLR 185, 193, 195; *Compania Sud Americana de*

or delay,[15] but applies to any damages claim available to the charterer or bill of lading holder.[16] In *Bank of Boston Connecticut v European Grain and Shipping Ltd*,[17] the House of Lords confirmed that the restriction extends to the situation in which the voyage was never completed as a result of the shipowner's wrongful repudiation of the charterparty, in circumstances where the right to freight had accrued under the charterparty before it was terminated by acceptance of the repudiation.[18] Moreover, it applies equally to advance freight and to freight payable on delivery of the goods at the port of discharge.[19] It has also been held to extend to a claim for additional freight, in circumstances where additional freight became payable because of the owner's own breach of contract.[20]

5.05 The principle precluding deductions is not limited to the situation in which a shipowner is suing a voyage charterer or a bill of lading holder for freight. An agent who collects freight on behalf of the shipowner or charterer must account for the freight without deduction or set-off.[21] Similarly, a freight forwarder who arranges carriage as agent for a goods owner, and who pays the cost of carriage on behalf of the owner, is entitled to be reimbursed without a set-off in respect of an allegation of breach of duty as agent.[22] The principle is also relevant when the right to freight has been assigned. The assignee is entitled to the freight undiminished by an equitable set-off.[23]

Vapores v Shipmair BV (The Teno) [1977] 2 Lloyd's Rep 289, 293; *A/S Gunnstein & Co K/S v Jensen, Krebs and Nielsen (The Alfa Nord)* [1977] 2 Lloyd's Rep 434; *Nova (Jersey) Knit Ltd v Kammgarn Spinnerei GmbH* [1977] 1 WLR 713, 721. Compare Stephenson LJ in *James & Co Scheepvaart en Handelmij BV v Chinecrest Ltd* [1979] 1 Lloyd's Rep 126, 129 ('unless you can find an equity sufficient to override that longstanding rule of common law').

[15] Compare *Contigroup Companies Inc v Glencore AG* [2005] 1 Lloyd's Rep 241 in which the action was for the price of goods sold.

[16] Thus, Roskill LJ in *A/S Gunnstein & Co K/S v Jensen, Krebs and Nielsen (The Alfa Nord)* [1977] 2 Lloyd's Rep 434, 436 referred to: 'the well-established principle that there is no right of set-off for claims for damages for breach of charter, whether for loss of or damage to goods or for alleged failure to prosecute a voyage with reasonable dispatch or otherwise, against a claim for freight.' See also *Exmar BV v National Iranian Tanker Co (The Trade Fortitude)* [1992] 1 Lloyd's Rep 169, 177 ('no deductions are possible').

[17] [1989] 1 AC 1056.

[18] Compare Lord Simon of Glaisdale in *Aries Tanker Corporation v Total Transport Ltd* [1977] 1 WLR 185, 193, whose comments were explained in the *Bank of Boston* case [1989] 1 AC 1056, 1104–5. In *Bank of Boston* the bills of lading were signed on 14 July 1982, the charterparty provided that the freight was deemed to be earned on the signing of the bills of lading, and the chargerparty was terminated as a result of acceptance of the owner's repudiation on 22 July. Since the right to freight had accrued before acceptance of the repudiation, it was unaffected by the termination. See [1989] 1 AC 1056, 1098–9. On the other hand, there may be a total failure of consideration which prevents freight becoming payable. See the *Bank of Boston* case at 1105, and *Britannia Distribution Co Ltd v Factor Pace Ltd* [1998] 2 Lloyd's Rep 420, 423.

[19] *Bank of Boston Connecticut v European Grain and Shipping Ltd* [1989] 1 AC 1056, 1100.

[20] *Cleobulos Shipping Co Ltd v Intertanker Ltd (The Cleon)* [1983] 1 Lloyd's Rep 586. However, the rule does not apply to diversion expenses. See *Re Bayoil SA* [1999] 1 WLR 147, 149–50.

[21] *James & Co Scheepvaart en Handelmij BV v Chinecrest Ltd* [1979] 1 Lloyd's Rep 126; *Opal Maritime Agencies Pty Ltd v Baltic Shipping Co* (1998) 158 ALR 416. *Aliter* if there is an agreement for a set-off. See *Opal Maritime Agencies Pty Ltd v 'Skulptor Konenkov'* (2000) 98 FCR 519, 562 *et seq*. The decision in *Samuel v West Hartlepool Steam Navigation Co* (1906) 11 Com Cas 115, (1907) 12 Com Cas 203, in so far as it allowed a set-off of the damages claim, seems contrary to this principle and is difficult to support. See *Colonial Bank v European Grain & Shipping Ltd (The Dominique)* [1987] 1 Lloyd's Rep 239, 256–7, where Hobhouse J nevertheless left open the question whether the decision could stand together with the *Chinecrest* case (above). Compare also *Wehner v Dene Steam Shipping Co* [1905] 2 KB 92, for which see para. 5.23 below.

[22] *Britannia Distribution Co Ltd v Factor Pace Ltd* [1998] 2 Lloyd's Rep 420.

[23] *Bank of Boston Connecticut v European Grain and Shipping Ltd* [1989] 1 AC 1056; *Britannia Distribution Co Ltd v Factor Pace Ltd* [1998] 2 Lloyd's Rep 420, 423.

Nor is the principle confined to shipping. Contracts for the carriage of goods by road **5.06** pursuant to the Convention on the Contract for the International Carriage of Goods by Road (CMR) are subject to the rule,[24] even though Articles 32 and 36 of the Schedule to the Convention seem to contemplate that set-offs are possible. Further, it has been held, albeit with reluctance, that the principle is equally applicable to a domestic contract for carriage by land.[25] It would probably also apply to a contract for carriage of goods by air.[26]

In the *Bank of Boston* case,[27] the House of Lords warned that the rules of procedure should **5.07** not be used to bring about a result contrary to the principle. Lord Brandon of Oakbrook, who delivered their Lordships' judgment, rejected an argument that the court could try both the claim and the counterclaim and then make an order pursuant to the former Ord. 15, r. 2(4) RSC. The rule provided that: 'Where a defendant establishes a counterclaim against the claim of a plaintiff and there is a balance in favour of one of the parties, the court may give judgment for the balance . . .' He said that to utilize the rule for that purpose would constitute a wrong exercise of the court's discretion. Similarly, a cross-claim available to a charterer ordinarily does not constitute a ground for staying execution on a judgment obtained against the charterer for payment of freight.[28]

While freight must be paid without deduction in respect of a damages cross-claim, Judge **5.08** Diamond QC in the Commercial Court suggested that, in the case of an arbitration, when an arbitrator is called upon to exercise his or her discretion to make an interim award in respect of freight, he or she may make it a condition of the issue of the interim award that the owner provide reasonable security for the charterer's cross-claim. He also suggested that there 'may perhaps' be exceptional cases where an arbitrator in the exercise of his or her discretion may find a valid reason for refusing to issue an interim award in respect of a claim for freight, but he conceded that those cases would be rare.[29]

On the other hand, the freight rule does not apply when a shipowner has presented a **5.09** petition to wind up a company for non-payment of freight and the company has a genuine and serious cross-claim against the petitioner. If the amount of the cross-claim exceeds the debt to the shipowner, the court may dismiss or stay the petition unless there are

---

[24] *R H & D International Ltd v IAS Animal Air Services Ltd* [1984] 1 WLR 573, following six unreported cases to the same effect. See also *Britannia Distribution Co Ltd v Factor Pace Ltd* [1998] 2 Lloyd's Rep 420. Compare *Impex Transport Aktieselskabet v AG Thames Holdings Ltd* [1981] 2 Lloyd's Rep 566, in which Robert Goff J seemed to assume that a set-off is possible in contracts for the carriage of goods by road, though in the particular case it was denied on other grounds.

[25] *United Carriers Ltd v Heritage Food Group (UK) Ltd* [1996] 1 WLR 371 (May J).

[26] This seems to have been accepted in *Britannia Distribution Co Ltd v Factor Pace Ltd* [1998] 2 Lloyd's Rep 420, 422.

[27] [1989] 1 AC 1056, 1109.

[28] *Cleobulos Shipping Co Ltd v Intertanker Ltd (The Cleon)* [1983] 1 Lloyd's Rep 586; *Colonial Bank v European Grain & Shipping Ltd (The Dominique)* [1987] 1 Lloyd's Rep 239, 257–8. See also *Sherborne v Sifkin* (1811) 3 Taunt 525, 128 ER 208, in which the court refused to order that the freight be paid into court to be applied towards payment of any damages that may be awarded for damage to cargo. Compare *Halsbury's Laws of England* (5th edn, 2009) vol. 11 ('Civil Procedure'), 506, para. 645. In *James & Co Scheepvaarten en Hendelmij BV v Chinecrest Ltd* [1979] 1 Lloyd's Rep 126, a stay was granted on condition that the amount of the freight be paid into court, but in that case there was an unresolved issue as to the terms of the contract.

[29] *Exmar BV v National Iranian Tanker Co (The Trade Fortitude)* [1992] 1 Lloyd's Rep 169, 177.

special circumstances which make it inappropriate for the petition to be dismissed or stayed.[30]

(2) Equitable set-off – hire under a time charter

5.10 Different considerations apply to hire payable under a time charter.[31] Admittedly, it was assumed in *Russell v Pellegrini*,[32] after a concession by counsel to that effect, that a cross-claim for damages for breach of an implied warranty of seaworthiness could not be set off against a claim for hire,[33] while more recently Donaldson J applied the freight rule in that context in two unreported decisions on interlocutory applications,[34] and later in *Seven Seas Transportation Ltd v Atlantic Shipping Co SA*.[35] Subsequently, however, Parker J in *The Teno*[36] followed an unreported decision of Ackner J to the contrary,[37] and held that the rule by which freight must be paid without deduction does not extend to hire. Parker J's judgment received the approval of the Court of Appeal in *Federal Commerce & Navigation Co Ltd v Molena Alpha Inc*,[38] and the principle has since become accepted.[39] It applies in the case of a charter by demise (sometimes called a bareboat charter),[40] as well as when a time charter is expressed to be for the period of a particular voyage,[41] so that in substance it resembles a voyage charter.[42]

---

[30] *Re Bayoil SA* [1999] 1 WLR 147. See also para. 5.33 below in relation to cheques and bills of exchange. Notwithstanding the reference to inability to litigate in the *Bayoil* case, the better view is that delay in litigating the cross-claim is not fatal. See *Hurst v Bennett* [2001] 2 BCLC 290 at [9] and [19] and *Montgomery v Wanda Modes Ltd* [2002] 1 BCLC 289, 297–9, each referring to *Re A Debtor (No. 87 of 1999)*, Times Law Reports, 14 February 2000.

[31] For the position in relation to interim awards in arbitrations, see *Exmar BV v National Iranian Tanker Co (The Trade Fortitude)* [1992] 1 Lloyd's Rep 169, 177.

[32] (1856) 26 LJQB 75, 6 El & Bl 1020, 119 ER 1144.

[33] See also, and compare, *Daunt v Lazard* (1858) 27 LJ Ex 399. For a discussion of these cases, see *Compania Sud Americana de Vapores v Shipmair BV (The Teno)* [1977] 2 Lloyd's Rep 289, 295.

[34] Parker J referred to the decisions in *Compania Sud Americana de Vapores v Shipmair BV (The Teno)* [1977] 2 Lloyd's Rep 289, 293.

[35] [1975] 2 Lloyd's Rep 188. See also *Steelwood Carriers Inc v Evimeria Compania Naviera SA (The Agios Giorgis)* [1976] 2 Lloyd's Rep 192, 201.

[36] *Compania Sud Americana de Vapores v Shipmair BV (The Teno)* [1977] 2 Lloyd's Rep 289.

[37] *Naxos Shipping Corporation v Thegra Shipping Co NV (The Corfu Island)* (1973). Parker J also referred to a number of statements in other cases as constituting authorities in support of the proposition that there may be a set-off against hire. See *Sea and Land Securities Ltd v William Dickinson and Co Ltd* [1942] 1 KB 286, 298; *Halcyon Steamship Co Ltd v Continental Grain Supply* (1943) 75 Ll L Rep 80, 84; *Nippon Yusen Kaisha v Acme Shipping Corporation (The Charalambos N Pateras)* [1971] 2 Lloyd's Rep 42, 48. For a discussion of these cases, see Rose, 'Deductions from freight and hire under English law' [1982] *Lloyd's Maritime and Commercial Law Quarterly* 33, 43–8.

[38] [1978] 1 QB 927, the result of which was affirmed by the House of Lords [1979] AC 757 on other grounds.

[39] In addition to the cases cited below, see *SL Sethia Liners Ltd v Naviagro Maritime Corporation (The Kostas Melas)* [1981] 1 Lloyd's Rep 18.

[40] See *Banco Central SA v Lingoss & Falce Ltd (The Raven)* [1980] 2 Lloyd's Rep 266 (esp. at 273). For the difference between the modern form of time charter and a charter by demise, see *Sea and Land Securities Ltd v William Dickinson and Co Ltd* [1942] 2 KB 65, 69 (McKinnon LJ).

[41] *SL Sethia Liners Ltd v Naviagro Maritime Corporation (The Kostas Melas)* [1981] 1 Lloyd's Rep 18; *Santiren Shipping Ltd v Unimarine SA (The Chrysovalandou Dyo)* [1981] 1 Lloyd's Rep 159.

[42] See the discussion in *Carver's Carriage by Sea* (13th edn, 1982) vol. 1, 472–4.

This right to an equitable set-off against a claim for hire is not confined to cases in which **5.11** there has been a total withdrawal of the vessel for a specified time.[43] A set-off against hire may take place when the master has wrongfully refused to load a full cargo,[44] and when a speed warranty has been breached.[45] An equitable set-off may also be available when the shipowner has failed to perform its hold-cleaning obligations resulting in a delay to the vessel at port,[46] and when the vessel had to proceed to another port to discharge the cargo because of contamination which was caused by the owners' breach of the charterparty.[47] A time charterparty may contain a stipulation to the effect that the owner must provide and pay for all provisions and wages, insurance, and deck and engine-room stores. If the owner fails to make those payments and the charterer, in order to ensure the vessel's availability and use, instead expends the money, the charterer's damages claim against the owner for breach of the clause may be employed in a set-off against hire.[48]

It is not every cross-claim that can be set off. In *Federal Commerce v Molena*,[49] Lord Denning **5.12** suggested that the right of deduction should be limited to cases where the owner through its neglect or default has either deprived the charterer of the use of the vessel or has hindered or prejudiced the charterer's use.[50] For example, both he and Lord Goff in that case said that a deduction would not be available when the cross-claim arises merely from damage to cargo. Similarly, a charterer may not set off the estimated value of bunkers remaining on re-delivery of the vessel, unless the charterparty specifically sanctions a deduction.[51] The principle is illustrated by *The Leon*.[52] Charterers alleged three breaches by the owners: (1) that the master had failed to keep full and accurate logs of the fuel consumption; (2) that the master had procured that invoices which did not represent the fuel actually taken on board should be sent to and paid for by the charterers; and (3) that the owners had breached their duty as bailees of the bunkers to use them during the charterparty in

---

[43] *Compania Sud Americana de Vapores v Shipmair BV (The Teno)* [1977] 2 Lloyd's Rep 289, 297.

[44] *Compania Sud Americana de Vapores v Shipmair BV (The Teno)* [1977] 2 Lloyd's Rep 289, 297.

[45] *Naxos Shipping Corporation v Thegra Shipping Co SA (The Corfu Island)* Ackner J, 10 April 1974 (referred to in *Federal Commerce & Navigation Co Ltd v Molena Alpha Inc* [1978] 1 QB 927, 974, 976). See also *Marbienes Compania Naviera SA v Ferrostal AG (The Democritos)* [1975] 1 Lloyd's Rep 386, 402; *Federal Commerce & Navigation Co Ltd v Molena Alpha Inc*; *Santiren Shipping Ltd v Unimarine SA (The Chrysovalandou-Dyo)* [1981] 1 Lloyd's Rep 159.

[46] Compare *Century Textiles and Industry Ltd v Tomoe Shipping Co (Singapore) Pte Ltd (The Aditya Vaibhav)* [1991] 1 Lloyd's Rep 573.

[47] *Stargos SpA v Petredec Ltd (The Sargasso)* [1994] 1 Lloyd's Rep 412, 426–7.

[48] *Banco Central SA v Lingoss & Falce Ltd (The Raven)* [1980] 2 Lloyd's Rep 266, 273.

[49] [1978] 1 QB 927, 976, following Parker J in *Compania Sud Americana de Vapores v Shipmair BV (The Teno)* [1977] 2 Lloyd's Rep 289, 297. See also *Atlantic Lines & Navigation Co Inc v The Ship 'Didymi' (The Didymi)* [1988] 1 Lloyd's Rep 97, 104 (Canadian Federal Court of Appeal).

[50] [1978] 1 QB 927, 976 (Lord Denning), 981 (Goff LJ).

[51] *Tropwind AG v Jade Enterprises Ltd (The Tropwind)* [1981] 1 Lloyd's Rep 45, 48. Compare *Aurora Borealis Compania Armadora SA v Marine Midland Bank NA (The Maistros)* [1984] 1 Lloyd's Rep 646, in which there was an agreement for a set-off.

[52] *Leon Corporation v Atlantic Lines and Navigation Co Inc (The Leon)* [1985] 2 Lloyd's Rep 470. See also *Western Bulk Carriers K/S v Li Hai Maritime Inc (The Li Hai)* [2005] 2 Lloyd's Rep 389 at [39]–[46]. It was held in that case that a breach by shipowners which had the consequence that the vessel had less fuel oil on board than it otherwise would have had, in circumstances where the vessel's trading was in no way impeded, did not give rise to a set-off. The loss arising from the breach consisted only of a US$500 cancellation fee, as opposed to a loss of earnings. See at [46].

accordance with the charterer's orders. It was held that none of the breaches affected the use of the vessel, and that consequently they did not give rise to a set-off against hire. Hobhouse J emphasized, however, that there was nothing to show 'overriding fraud' on the part of the owners. If there had been, he suggested that the result may have been different.[53]

5.13   Lord Denning's later judgment in *The Aliakmon Progress*[54] suggested a narrower scope to the set-off than that described in *Federal Commerce v Molena*. A vessel the subject of a time charter sustained damage while attempting to berth at a port in Iceland. Temporary repairs were effected there, and the vessel then sailed to Antwerp where permanent repairs were undertaken. Owing to the resulting delay the vessel lost an anticipated cargo at Antwerp and had to wait some thirty-nine days for a new cargo. Lord Denning, with whom Geoffrey Lane LJ agreed, doubted that the loss sustained by the charterers constituted a ground for equitable set-off. He cited *Federal Commerce v Molena* as authority for the proposition that equitable set-off is only available against a claim for hire 'where the charterers have been deprived of the use of the ship by the fault of the owner'.[55] He said that, in the case before him, the charterers did in fact have the use of the ship but could not get a cargo. There was no mention of whether a set-off may arise when the shipowner merely prejudiced the charterer in the use of the vessel, and there was no discussion of whether in the instant case there had been any such prejudice. Subsequently, however, the courts have reiterated that prejudice in the use of the vessel not amounting to total deprivation may ground a set-off.[56]

5.14   Counsel in *The Leon*[57] attacked the proposition that equitable set-off in the context of time charters should be limited to cases in which the charterer has been deprived of or prejudiced in the use of the vessel. Rather, it was suggested that the allowance or otherwise of a set-off should be determined by reference to whether it would be unfair in the particular case to allow the owner to sue for hire without giving credit for the cross-demand. However, Hobhouse J declined to depart from the statements of the ambit of the set-off by Lord Denning and Goff LJ in *Federal Commerce v Molena*, and emphasized that the relevant principle is set out in Lord Cottenham's judgment in *Rawson v Samuel*,[58] that the equity of the bill must impeach the title to the legal demand.[59] In the case of a time charter, hire is paid for the right to use the vessel for a specified period of time, irrespective of whether the charterer chooses to use it for carrying cargo or instead lays it up out of use. The hire is required to be paid in advance, and failure to make punctual payment gives the owner the right to withdraw the vessel. In those circumstances, Hobhouse J said that it is not a coincidence that, in cases where the right to an equitable set-off was upheld, the cross-claim

---

[53] [1985] 2 Lloyd's Rep 470, 476.

[54] *Aliakmon Maritime Corporation v Trans Ocean Continental Shipping Ltd (The Aliakmon Progress)* [1978] 2 Lloyd's Rep 499.

[55] [1978] 2 Lloyd's Rep 499, 501.

[56] *Banco Central SA v Lingoss & Falce Ltd (The Raven)* [1980] 2 Lloyd's Rep 266, 273; *Leon Corporation v Atlantic Lines and Navigation Co Inc (The Leon)* [1985] 2 Lloyd's Rep 470, 475.

[57] *Leon Corporation v Atlantic Lines and Navigation Co Inc (The Leon)* [1985] 2 Lloyd's Rep 470.

[58] (1841) Cr & Ph 161, 41 ER 451.

[59] See also *Western Bulk Carriers K/S v Li Hai Maritime Inc (The Li Hai)* [2005] 2 Lloyd's Rep 389 at [41].

involved something which could be identified as depriving the charterer of the use of the vessel or which prejudiced or hindered that use, because, in the context of a time charter contract and a claim for time charter hire, it is that type of cross-claim which has the requisite effect of impeaching the plaintiff's demand.[60]

In a case where hire is payable periodically under a time charter, the charterer may have **5.15** been prejudiced in the use of the vessel only in certain defined periods. In other periods the vessel may in fact have been made available in accordance with the contract. If the charterer's damages claim in such a case exceeds the amount of hire owing for the periods during which the use of the vessel was prejudiced, the charterer may wish to set off the excess against payments of hire relating to other periods. The question whether this is permissible was considered earlier.[61]

(3) The justification for the freight rule

Given that there is this distinction between freight and hire as regards equitable set-off, **5.16** the question arises whether there is any justification for it. It has been suggested that the original justification for the freight rule may have been based upon cash flow considerations, in that the master would require the freight to be paid in full at the end of the voyage in order to pay off the crew, and to refit and victual the ship. Communications in those days were slow, and the master could not wait a long time for funds to be remitted.[62] Yet, in the context of building contracts, the courts have said that cash flow considerations are not a sufficient reason for denying a set-off.[63] Lord Wilberforce, on the other hand, doubted whether the freight rule indeed is anything other than an arbitrary rule, 'in the sense that no very clear justification for it has ever been stated and perhaps also in the sense that the law might just, or almost, as well have settled for a rule to the opposite effect'.[64] Despite this, he concluded that the rule is too well established to be departed from now.[65] There are, nevertheless, *dicta* to the effect that it should not be extended,[66] and the attitude of the

---

[60] [1985] 2 Lloyd's Rep 470, 475.

[61] See paras 4.120–4.124 above.

[62] See Goff LJ in *Federal Commerce & Navigation Co Ltd v Molena Alpha Inc* [1978] 1 QB 927, 983. See also *Henriksens Rederi A/S v THZ Rolimpex (The Brede)* [1974] 1 QB 233, 263. Thus, Willes J commented in *Meyer v Dresser* (1864) 16 CB(NS) 646, 663, 143 ER 1280, 1287 that it would have been inconvenient for a vessel to be delayed while disputes as to the amount of freight were being settled. See also *Dakin v Oxley* (1864) 15 CB(NS) 646, 667, 143 ER 938, 946–7 (Willes J).

[63] *Gilbert-Ash (Northern) Ltd v Modern Engineering (Bristol) Ltd* [1974] AC 689, 707, 718; *Mottram Consultants Ltd v Bernard Sunley & Sons Ltd* [1975] 2 Lloyd's Rep 197, 214. See the discussion of building contracts in para. 5.50 below. See also *Federal Commerce & Navigation Co Ltd v Molena Alpha Inc* [1978] 1 QB 927, 983, 986.

[64] *Aries Tanker Corporation v Total Transport Ltd* [1977] 1 WLR 185, 190. Similarly, Lord Simon of Glaisdale said (at 193) that 'there is no question of high legal policy involved at all'. See also *Dole Dried Fruit and Nut Co v Trustin Kerwood Ltd* [1990] 2 Lloyd's Rep 309, 310. Compare Lord Salmon in the *Aries Tanker* case (at 195), who suggested that the incidence of insurance cover in respect of freight may be based upon the rule. See also, with respect to insurance, *Henriksens Rederi A/S v THZ Rolimpex (The Brede)* [1974] 1 QB 233, 244, 263.

[65] Similarly, Lord Brandon in the House of Lords in the *Bank of Boston* case [1989] 1 AC 1056, 1100 accepted that, whatever its merits or demerits, the rule is not open to challenge.

[66] *Seven Seas Transportation Ltd v Atlantic Shipping Co SA* [1975] 2 Lloyd's Rep 188, 191; *Federal Commerce & Navigation Co Ltd v Molena Alpha Inc* [1978] 1 QB 927, 982. Notwithstanding those *dicta*, the freight rule has been extended to contracts for the carriage of goods by road. See para. 5.06 above.

courts has been that voyage and time charters are sufficiently dissimilar in their operation to justify the application in the case of hire of the general rule permitting deductions, rather than having resort to the exception precluding deductions found in the freight rule. Thus, Lord Denning, in justifying the distinction, noted that freight is the sum payable for the carriage of goods from one place to another, while hire is paid for the right to use the vessel for a specified period of time irrespective of whether or not the charterer chooses to use it for carrying cargo.[67] But even this as a basis for treating them differently becomes blurred when a time charter is for the period of a particular trip.[68]

(4) The Statutes of Set-off

5.17 A question in respect of which conflicting opinions have been expressed is whether the principle which precludes a defence of equitable set-off against a claim for freight also extends to the defence provided by the Statutes of Set-off in the case of mutual debts.[69]

5.18 The cases favour the view that the freight rule does not apply in this context.[70] In *Wilson v Gabriel*,[71] the defendant in an action for payment of freight pleaded set-off as a defence, based upon an unconnected debt owing by the plaintiff. The plaintiff replied, on equitable grounds,[72] that when the freight was in the course of being earned he had assigned it for value to a third party, and that the plaintiff brought this action as trustee for the third party. The Court of Queen's Bench held that this did not to constitute an answer to the plea, the defendant not having had notice of the assignment before the mutual debts arose.[73] Cockburn CJ[74] and Blackburn J each accepted that the defendant was entitled to a set-off at law against the liability for freight, and that it was not affected by the assignment. Since this was after the courts had adopted the principle that the common law defence of abatement does not extend to freight,[75] it is evident that the statutory defence was thought to be subject to different considerations. The contrary view, however, was accepted in *The Khian*

---

[67] *Federal Commerce & Navigation Co Ltd v Molena Alpha Inc* [1978] 1 QB 927, 973.

[68] See e.g. *SL Sethia Liners Ltd v Naviagro Maritime Corporation (The Kostas Melas)* [1981] 1 Lloyd's Rep 18 and *Santiren Shipping Ltd v Unimarine SA (The Chrysovalandou-Dyo)* [1981] 1 Lloyd's Rep 159, and generally the discussion in *Carver's Carriage by Sea* (13th edn, 1982) vol. 1, 472–4. Note, however, Steyn J's justification of the distinction in *Itex Itagrani Export SA v Care Shipping Corporation (The Cebu) (No. 2)* [1990] 2 Lloyd's Rep 316, 320.

[69] There is no reason why a set-off under the Statutes should not be available against a claim for hire under a time charter, given that it is susceptible to an equitable set-off. This was assumed to be the case in *Aectra Refining and Marketing Inc v Exmar NV* [1994] 1 WLR 1634.

[70] See also *Jones v Moore* (1841) 4 Y & C Ex 351, 160 ER 1041. Compare *Isberg v Bowden* (1853) 8 Ex 852, 155 ER 1599, though in that case the action for freight was brought by the master rather than by the owner of the vessel. It was held that a debt owing by the owner could not be set off, but this was on the basis of a perceived lack of mutuality. There is nothing in the judgments, or indeed in the arguments of counsel, to suggest that it was thought that an action for freight was not susceptible in any event to a defence of set-off under the Statutes.

[71] (1863) 4 B & S 243, 122 ER 450.

[72] *Wilson v Gabriel* was decided at common law before the Judicature Acts fused the courts of law and equity, but the Common Law Procedure Act 1854, ss. 83–6 allowed equitable defences to be pleaded in the common law courts.

[73] (1863) 4 B & S 243, 248, 122 ER 450, 452–3 (Blackburn J). See para. 17.13 below.

[74] With whom Wightman J concurred.

[75] *Sheels v Davies* (1814) 4 Camp 119, 171 ER 39; *Mondel v Steel* (1841) 8 M & W 858, 871, 151 ER 1288, 1293.

Captain (No. 2).[76] Hirst J held in that case that set-off under the Statutes is subject to the freight rule, and suggested that *Wilson v Gabriel* was impliedly overruled by the House of Lords in *Aries Tanker Corporation v Total Transport Ltd.*[77] The issue in the *Aries Tanker* case, however, was whether a damages claim in respect of cargo could be applied in reduction of a liability for freight either on the basis of equitable set-off or common law abatement. The House of Lords held that those defences did not apply. The statutory defence of set-off was not in issue, and nor was it considered. Subsequently, Hobhouse J at first instance in the *Bank of Boston* case[78] disagreed with Hirst J. He accepted that a freight debt and another debt can be set off under the Statutes, and that *Wilson v Gabriel* was not overruled by *Aries Tanker.*

Apart from *The Khian Captain*, it is difficult to find authority for the proposition that the **5.19** Statutes do not apply in this context.[79] Two cases which have been said to support that view[80] are explicable on other grounds.

In *Weguellin v Cellier*,[81] consignees of cargo had accepted six-month bills of exchange at **5.20** the request of the shipowner. The shipowner assigned the freight payable by way of security to the respondents, who then brought the present action seeking a declaration that they were entitled to be paid the freight. However, the consignees, having honoured the bills, had a claim against the shipowner, and argued that this gave rise to a set-off against the liability for freight and that the respondents as assignees took subject to the set-off. It is apparent that any right of set-off would have arisen under the Statutes, based upon mutual debts, given that the demands would not have been sufficiently closely connected to give rise to an equitable set-off. While Lord Chelmsford held that there was no such set-off which would defeat the respondent's right to the freight, this was not because of a general principle that a claim for freight is not susceptible to a defence of set-off under the Statutes. In the first place, as counsel for the respondents argued, the bills did not mature until after the consignees received notice of the assignment, so that at the date of notice there was no accrued debt owing by the shipowner. An assignee does not take subject to a cross-debt which arises after notice, albeit as a result of a prior contract.[82] But even apart from that, the Statutes of Set-off only provided a procedural defence to an action for payment of a debt; until a judgment for a set-off is obtained, separate and distinct debts

---

[76] *Freedom Maritime Corporation v International Bulk Carriers SA (The Khian Captain) (No. 2)* [1986] 1 Lloyd's Rep 429.

[77] [1977] 1 WLR 185.

[78] *Sub nom Colonial Bank v European Grain & Shipping Ltd (The Dominique)* [1987] 1 Lloyd's Rep 239, 250–1.

[79] In *Opal Maritime Agencies Pty Ltd v Baltic Shipping Co* (1998) 158 ALR 416, the cross-claim of the agent which had collected freight was for liquidated amounts, in the form of fees and disbursements. Tamberlin J in the Federal Court of Australia held that the non-deduction rule applied, so that the agent had to account for the freight without a set-off. In coming to that conclusion his Honour considered only cases concerned with equitable set-off. The possible application of the Statutes of Set-off was not countenanced. However, the case was decided in New South Wales at a time when set-off under the Statutes of Set-off had been abolished in that state. Compare now the Civil Procedure Act 2005 (NSW), s. 21. See paras 2.64–2.80 above.

[80] Wood, *English and International Set-off* (1989), 707.

[81] (1873) LR 6 HL 286, 42 LJ Ch 758.

[82] *Watson v Mid Wales Railway Co* (1867) LR 2 CP 593. See para. 17.15 below.

remain in existence.[83] In *Weguellin v Cellier*, when the goods arrived at the port of discharge the respondents put a stop on them. They had a lien and, as Lord Chelmsford pointed out, the consignees could not have obtained the cargo without payment of the freight, and the master of the ship would have been bound to insist upon payment before delivery.[84] Because of the procedural nature of the defence of set-off, the consignees could not have acted uni-laterally to bring about a set-off so as to obtain the release of goods the subject of the lien. The circumstances in *Weguellin v Cellier* were different, in that the consignees after some correspondence had paid the amount of the freight to the dock company holding the goods so as to obtain their release, and the respondents then filed a bill seeking a declaration that the freight in the hands of the dock company should be applied towards payment of what was due to them by the shipowner.[85] But it was still not a case of set-off under the Statutes, because it was not an action against the consignees for payment.

5.21   The second case, *Tanner v Phillips*,[86] similarly may be explained on other grounds. The plaintiff was mortgagee of a ship, and as further security held a mortgage of freight. The ship was chartered to the defendant. The charterparty provided that the defendant could make advances not exceeding £150 to the master as agent for the mortgagor/owner on account of freight, though other advances in excess of that amount were made. Before the cargo was unloaded and freight became due, the mortgagee took possession of the ship. When the freight later became payable the mortgagee sued the defendant for payment, and it was held that the defendant could not set off the excess advances. This was so notwith-standing that the advances were made before the defendant had notice of the mortgage, whereas ordinarily, if there are mutual debts in existence before notice of an assignment, the assignee takes subject to a right of set-off under the Statutes.[87] However, the mortgagee's entitlement to freight in *Tanner v Phillips* was not based upon an assignment of a debt. Rather, the mortgagee claimed payment of freight as mortgagee in possession. The mort-gagee became entitled in his own right to freight which the ship was in the course of earning. As Lord Cairns pointed out in *Keith v Burrows*,[88] the right of a mortgagee in pos-session to freight in the course of being earned does not arise by virtue of any contract or antecedent right, but rather it is payable to the mortgagee once he or she goes into posses-sion because the mortgagee is then regarded as the master or owner of the ship.[89] The

---

[83]   See paras 2.34–2.39 above.

[84]   Compare *Campbell v Thompson* (1816) 1 Stark 490, 171 ER 539, in which it was accepted that an assignee of freight was not entitled to refuse to allow delivery of the cargo unless freight was paid without deduction, though Dr Lushington doubted the authority of that case in *The Salacia* (1862) Lush 578, 167 ER 263.

[85]   This appears more clearly from the report at (1873) 42 LJ Ch 758, 760.

[86]   (1872) 42 LJ Ch 125.

[87]   See paras 17.13–17.15 below.

[88]   (1877) 2 App Cas 636, 646. See also *Kerswill v Bishop* (1832) 2 C & J 529, 149 ER 224; *Japp v Campbell* (1888) 57 LJQB 79; *Wilson v Wilson* (1872) LR 14 Eq 32 (mortgagee's right to freight has priority over an earlier assignment of freight of which the mortgagee did not have notice).

[89]   In the same way, when there is a sale of a ship the right to freight in the course of being earned passes to the purchaser. See e.g. *Morrison v Parsons* (1810) 2 Taunt 407, 127 ER 1136. As Lord Ellenborough observed in *Case v Davidson* (1816) 5 M & S 79, 82, 105 ER 980, 981: 'freight follows, as an incident, the property in the ship.'

mortgagee's right depends on property, not on contract.[90] *Tanner v Phillips* was not, there-fore, a case in which there were mutual debts between the mortgagor and the charterer which would have given rise to a set-off available against the mortgagee, were it not for a supposed principle that there may not be a set-off under the Statutes against a claim for freight. Rather, mutuality for the purpose of the Statutes was lacking in that, on the one hand, the charterer had a claim against the mortgagor for the excess advances and, on the other, the mortgagee in his own right was entitled to the freight from the charterer.[91]

The better view is that the freight rule, which precludes an equitable set-off or a common law defence of abatement against a claim for freight, does not extend to the Statutes of Set-off. In the case of the Statutes, the defence is statutory in origin, and the Statutes specifically allowed a set-off in the case of mutual debts. While the Statutes themselves have been repealed, the repealing legislation preserved the right of set-off conferred by the Statutes.[92] The proper approach in the case of a statutory-based defence is to interpret the legislation,[93] and there is nothing in the language of the Statutes to suggest that there is an exception in the case of an action for freight.   **5.22**

(5) Bill of lading freight when the vessel is chartered

When a ship has been chartered, and the master signs bills of lading with third party shippers for the carriage of goods, the question whether the shipowner or the charterer is entitled to the bill of lading freight depends upon whether the master signed as agent for the shipowner or the charterer. If the charter is by demise the contract will be with the charterer, but in other cases the question will depend upon the documents and circum-stances of the particular case.[94] When the contract is with the shipowner, the shipowner can sue the shipper for freight. If the charterer has nevertheless appointed an agent to collect the freight, and the shipowner gives notice to the agent before the freight has been received requiring the freight to be paid to it rather than the charterer, the shipowner can sue the agent for the freight as money had and received.[95] Any expenses incurred by the agent in carrying out the charterer's instructions cannot be set off by the agent,[96] since mutuality for the purpose of the Statutes of Set-off is lacking. If, on the other hand, the owner as the contracting party is paid the bill of lading freight, the owner is only entitled to retain an amount equal to the hire or freight then unpaid under the charterparty. The surplus must be paid to the charterer. Channell J decided this in *Wehner v Dene Steam Shipping Co.*[97] The reason is not that the owner is liable to the charterer for the bill of lading freight received   **5.23**

---

[90] *Rusden v Pope* (1868) LR 3 Ex 269, 276–7.
[91] See para. 17.96 below.
[92] See para. 2.06 above.
[93] Consistent with Lightman J's comments in *Fuller v Happy Shopper Markets Ltd* [2001] 1 WLR 1681 at [23] in relation to the character of the defence provided by the Statutes.
[94] *Samuel v West Hartlepool Steam Navigation Co* (1906) 11 Com Cas 115, 125–6.
[95] *Molthes Rederi Aktieselskabet v Ellerman's Wilson Line Ltd* [1927] 1 KB 710, 715–16. Greer J left open the question whether the agent similarly could be sued in respect of freight received before notice from the shipowner.
[96] *Molthes Rederi v Ellerman's Wilson Line* [1927] 1 KB 710.
[97] [1905] 2 KB 92.

and the charterer is liable for hire or freight under the charterparty, and that these obligations are set off.[98] It is not a case of cross-demands at all. Rather, the owner had contracted
by the charterparty that it would be satisfied with the payment of the freight or hire specified in the charterparty for the use of the ship, and accordingly if the owner receives the
bill of lading freight it is part of their contract that it will account for any surplus to
the charterer.[99]

5.24 When the contract is with the charterer rather than the shipowner, the shipowner may have
reserved a lien on sub-freights, entitling the shipowner to require payment to it of the bill
of lading freight that is otherwise due to the charterer.[100] The lien can be exercised only
before the freight has been paid to the charterer or the charterer's agent.[101] Moreover, it can
be exercised only in respect of sums due to the shipowner at the time that the demand for
payment is made pursuant to the lien.[102] The lien does not confer a proprietary interest in
the freight. It is merely a personal right to intercept freight before it is paid. It is analogous
to a right of stoppage *in transitu*.[103] The lien therefore would be subject to a right of set-off
available to the shipper against the charterer, including under the Statutes in the case of
mutual debts, since the set-off would have the effect that nothing would be paid to the
extent of the set-off which could be intercepted.

B. Negotiable Instruments, Letters of Credit and Direct Debits

(1) Negotiable instruments – equitable set-off

5.25 An unliquidated cross-demand generally cannot be employed as an equitable set-off in an
action to enforce payment of a bill of exchange or other negotiable instrument.[104] The House
of Lords affirmed the principle in *Nova (Jersey) Knit Ltd v Kammgarn Spinnerei GmbH*,[105]

---

[98] Compare Wood, *English and International Set-off* (1989), 705, 978–9.

[99] *Wehner v Dene Steam Shipping Co* [1905] 2 KB 92, 99, explained in *Molthes Rederi v Ellerman's Wilson Line* [1927] 1 KB 710. See also *Tradigrain SA v King Diamond Shipping SA (The Spiros C)* [2000] 2 Lloyd's Rep 319, 328; *Carver's Carriage by Sea* (13th edn, 1982) vol. 2, 1225–6, para. 1744.

[100] See generally *Carver's Carriage by Sea* (13th edn, 1982) vol. 2, 1395, para. 2013.

[101] *Tagart, Beaton & Co v Fisher & Sons* [1903] 1 KB 391.

[102] *Wehner v Dene Steam Shipping Co* [1905] 2 KB 92.

[103] *Agnew v Commissioner of Inland Revenue* [2001] 2 AC 710 at [39]–[41].

[104] This includes a cheque. See *Finch Motors Ltd v Quin* [1980] 2 NZLR 513, 516.

[105] [1977] 1 WLR 713. See also *Morgan v Richardson* (1806) 7 East 482n, 170 ER 868; *Tye v Gwynne* (1810) 2 Camp 346, 170 ER 1179; *Solomon v Turner* (1815) 1 Stark 51, 171 ER 398; *Day v Nix* (1824) 2 LJOSCP 133; *Obbard v Betham* (1830) M & M 483, 173 ER 1232; *Glennie v Imri* (1839) 3 Y & C Ex 436, 160 ER 773; *Trickey v Larne* (1840) 6 M & W 278, 151 ER 414; *Sully v Frean* (1854) 10 Ex 535, 156 ER 551; *Warwick v Nairn* (1855) 10 Ex 762, 156 ER 648; *Jackson v Murphy* (1886) 4 TLR 92n; *Bow, McLachlan & Co Ltd v Ship 'Camosun'* [1909] AC 597, 612; *James Lamont & Co Ld v Hyland Ld* [1950] 1 KB 585; *Montecchi v Shimco (UK) Ltd* [1979] 1 WLR 1180, 1183; *Montebianco Industrie Tessili SpA v Carlyle Mills (London) Ltd* [1981] 1 Lloyd's Rep 509; *Case Poclain Corporation Ltd v Jones* [1986] ECC 569. Compare the uncertainty of the Court of Appeal in *Oscar Harris, Son & Co v Vallarman & Co* [1940] 1 All ER 185, and the decision in *Court v Sheen* (1891) 7 TLR 556 (the report of which is criticized in *James Lamont v Hyland* at 592). Compare also the statement by Thesiger LJ in *Anglo-Italian Bank v Wells* (1878) 38 LT 197, 201, though note the more cautious approach of Jessel MR at 199. The view of the Master of the Rolls was preferred in *James Lamont v Hyland* at 592–3. The principle continues to apply under the Civil Procedure Rules 1998. See *Safa Ltd v Banque du Caire* [2000] 2 Lloyd's Rep 600, 605, 606, 610, and also *Balfour Beatty Civil Engineering v Technical & General Guarantee Co Ltd* (1999) 68 Con LR 180, 190 in relation to fraud. In Canada, the

and it is also accepted in Australia[106] and New Zealand.[107] The principle applies whether the parties are immediate or remote,[108] and whether the cross-demand arose out of the transaction in respect of which the instrument was given or, *a fortiori*, in any other way.[109]

The principle typically is invoked when a cheque is given as payment for the price of goods sold, and the vendor has breached a term in the contract which amounts to a partial failure of consideration[110] so as to give rise to a claim against him or her for unliquidated damages. The breach does not provide the purchaser with a defence to an action by the vendor for payment of the cheque. This is sometimes explained on the ground that the cheque is a separate contract from the contract of sale, although it is not an essential requirement of an equitable set-off that the claim and the cross-claim should have originated in the same contract.[111] The cheque has also been described as constituting a separate transaction from the sale,[112] and indeed in the case of letters of credit in sale transactions this principle has been expressly incorporated in the Uniform Customs and Practice for Documentary

5.26

Nova (Jersey) Knit case was distinguished by the Supreme Court in *Williams & Glyn's Bank Ltd v Belkin Packaging Ltd* (1983) 147 DLR (3d) 577 in circumstances where promissory notes were delivered subject to conditions.

[106] *Eversure Textiles Manufacturing Co Ltd v Webb* [1978] Qd R 347; *K D Morris & Sons Ltd v Bank of Queensland* (1980) 30 ALR 321, 350; *Rigg v Commonwealth Bank of Australia* (1989) 97 FLR 261, 267–268. See also the discussion in, and compare, *John Shearer Ltd v Gehl Co* (1995) 60 FCR 136 (application to set aside a statutory demand, for which see para. 5.33 below). In Victoria the principle was held to apply when the claim on the bill was brought pursuant to the summary procedure set out in the Instruments Act 1958 (Vic). See *Mobil Oil Australia Ltd v Caulfield Tyre Service Pty Ltd* [1984] VR 440. Compare *Graham v Seagoe* [1964] 2 Lloyd's Rep 564, in which an action on promissory notes given in connection with the sale of a boat was stayed while disputes as to the condition of the boat were referred to arbitration. However, the court concerned itself only with the construction of the particular arbitration clause, and no mention was made of the principle under discussion. Compare also Moffitt P and Glass JA in *Sidney Raper Pty Ltd v Commonwealth Trading Bank* [1975] 2 NSWLR 227, 238–9, 255, who seemed to accept that a claim on a bank cheque could be the subject of an equitable set-off. This aspect of their judgment is unlikely to be followed, though a set-off may have been available in any event in that case on the basis of equity acting by analogy with the Statutes of Set-off. See the discussion of the Statutes in paras 5.35–5.42 below. In New South Wales, the Common Law Procedure Act 1899, s. 79 formerly provided that matters which were the subject of a cross-action between the parties could by leave of a judge be pleaded by way of set-off. The courts accepted that s. 79 permitted a damages claim to be pleaded by way of set-off against a claim on a promissory note if the demands arose out of the same transaction. See e.g. *Karbowsky v Redaelli* (1914) 31 WN(NSW) 80; *Richardson v Hill* (1922) 22 SR(NSW) 326. The requirement that the demands should have originated in the same transaction followed from a requirement that the courts held was inherent in s. 79 and applied generally. See e.g. *Assets & General Finance Co v Crick* (1911) 28 WN(NSW) 91; *Austral Bronze Co Ltd v Sleigh* (1916) 34 WN(NSW) 143. For a discussion of s. 79, see Russell, 'Defences by way of set-off, counterclaim and cross action' (1928) 2 *Australian Law Journal* 80. Section 79 was repealed by the Supreme Court Act 1970, and so those cases would no longer apply.

[107] *Finch Motors Ltd v Quin* [1980] 2 NZLR 513; *International Ore & Fertilizer Corporation v East Coast Fertilizer Co Ltd* [1987] 1 NZLR 9. *Union Bank of Australia v Williams* (1892) 11 NZLR 65 would no longer appear to be good law.

[108] For remote parties, see e.g. *All Trades Distributors Ltd v Agencies Kaufman Ltd* (1969) 113 Sol Jo 995, 996; *Brown, Shipley & Co Ltd v Alicia Hosiery Ltd* [1966] 1 Lloyd's Rep 668.

[109] *Cebora SNC v SIP (Industrial Products) Ltd* [1976] 1 Lloyd's Rep 271, 278–9; *Buying Systems (Aust) Pty Ltd v Tien Mah Litho Printing Co Ltd* (1986) 5 NSWLR 317, 328.

[110] Compare total failure of consideration. See para. 5.31 below.

[111] See para. 4.92 above.

[112] *Eversure Textiles Manufacturing Co Ltd v Webb* [1978] Qd R 347, 348–9. Compare *Montecchi v Shimco (UK) Ltd* [1979] 1 WLR 1180, 1183.

Credits.[113] But the most commonly accepted explanation is that the rule precluding a defence of equitable set-off is based upon a policy consideration, that a cheque or bill of exchange given as payment is considered to be equivalent to cash, albeit with payment deferred, and if an unliquidated cross-demand could provide a defence to an action on the instrument there would be a substantial inroad upon this commercial principle.[114]

Stay of execution

5.27 Stays of execution are subject to a similar restriction. A defendant in an application for summary judgment who asserts a counterclaim not amounting to a set-off ordinarily would not be granted leave to defend. On the other hand, the court in its discretion may order a stay of execution[115] on the claimant's judgment until the defendant's cross-action has been tried,[116] so that if the defendant succeeds in the cross-action execution would only issue for the balance of the two claims. However, a different practice applies when the claimant's claim is on a cheque or bill of exchange. The fact that the defendant in an action to enforce payment of a cheque asserts a counterclaim for unliquidated damages is not usually regarded as a ground for staying execution.[117] This is not an inflexible principle, however, because it is said that the court may grant a stay if there are exceptional circumstances.[118] But while the existence of this exception is generally recognized, the courts have been reluctant to recognize 'exceptional circumstances' which may detract from the principle that cheques and bills of exchange should be treated as cash.[119] Indeed, in

---

[113] Article 3(a) of the Uniform Customs and Practice provides that: 'Credits, by their nature, are separate transactions from the sales or other contract(s) on which they may be based . . .' See paras 5.43–5.48 below in relation to letters of credit.

[114] *Nova (Jersey) Knit Ltd v Kammgarn Spinnerei GmbH* [1977] 1 WLR 713, 721 (Lord Wilberforce), 722 (Viscount Dilhorne). See also *Jackson v Murphy* (1887) 4 TLR 92; *Fielding & Platt Ltd v Najjar* [1969] 1 WLR 357, 361; *Montecchi v Shimco (UK) Ltd* [1979] 1 WLR 1180, 1183.

[115] Formerly, pursuant to RSC Ord. 14, r. 3(2). See now CPR rr. 3.1(3) and 24.6, and para. 5.1 of the Practice Direction supplementing CPR Part 24. See generally *Civil Procedure* (2010) vol. 1, paras 24.2.6 and 24.6.3.

[116] See e.g. *Mottram Consultants Ltd v Bernard Sunley & Sons Ltd* [1975] 2 Lloyd's Rep 197, 214, and para. 1.05 above.

[117] *Brown, Shipley & Co Ltd v Alicia Hosiery Ltd* [1966] 1 Lloyd's Rep 668; *Cebora SNC v SIP (Industrial Products) Ltd* [1976] 1 Lloyd's Rep 271; *Walek & Co K G v Seafield Gentex Ltd* [1978] IR 167; *Montecchi v Shimco (UK) Ltd* [1979] 1 WLR 1180, 1183; *Montebianco Industrie Tessili SpA v Carlyle Mills (London) Ltd* [1981] 1 Lloyd's Rep 509. In Queensland, compare *Hoe and Bickley v Baulch* [1951] QWN 14.

[118] *Brown, Shipley & Co Ltd v Alicia Hosiery Ltd* [1966] 1 Lloyd's Rep 668, 669; *Mottram Consultants Ltd v Bernard Sunley & Sons Ltd* [1975] 2 Lloyd's Rep 197, 214; *Eversure Textiles Manufacturing Co Ltd v Webb* [1978] Qd R 347, 350–1; *Continental Illinois National Bank and Trust Co of Chicago v Papanicolaou (The Fedora)* [1986] 2 Lloyd's Rep 441, 445; *Thoni GmbH v RTP Equipment Ltd* [1979] 2 Lloyd's Rep 282, 284, 285; *Case Poclain Corporation Ltd v Jones* [1986] ECC 569, 573; *Safa Ltd v Banque du Caire* [2000] 2 Lloyd's Rep 600, 605. See also *Begley Industries Ltd v Cramp* [1977] 2 NZLR 207, 213, *John Shearer Ltd v Gehl Co* (1995) 60 FCR 136, 141, and Lord Salmon in his dissenting judgment in *Nova (Jersey) Knit Ltd v Kammgarn Spinnerei GmbH* [1977] 1 WLR 713, 726. Any such discretion should be available whether or not the counterclaim arises directly out of the transaction in respect of which the bills were given. See *Cebora SNC v SIP (Industrial Products) Ltd* [1976] 1 Lloyd's Rep 271, 275 (referring to *James Lamont v Hyland* [1950] 1 KB 585).

[119] In *Cebora SNC v SIP (Industrial Products) Ltd* [1976] 1 Lloyd's Rep 271, 279, Sir Eric Sachs warned that: 'the Courts should be really careful not to whittle away the rule of practice by introducing unnecessary exceptions to it under the influence of sympathy-evoking stories, and should have due regard to the maxim that hard cases can make bad law. Indeed, in these days of increasing international interdependence and increasing need to foster liquidity of resources, the rule may be said to be of special import to the business

Nova (Jersey) Knit Ltd v Kammgarn Spinnerei GmbH[120] Viscount Dilhorne said that it would 'seldom, if ever'[121] be right to allow a cross-claim to operate as a bar to execution, while Lord Russell of Killowen said that an unliquidated cross-demand is not available as a counterclaim in an action on a bill of exchange without referring to an exception of 'exceptional circumstances' in relation to a stay.[122] Certainly it is not sufficient for a stay that there is a counterclaim which is likely to succeed,[123] or that the claim on the cheque and the cross-action for unliquidated damages are part of the same transaction.[124]

A stay was ordered in *Barclays Bank Ltd v Aschaffenburger Zellstoffwerke AG.*[125] A German **5.28** acceptor of bills of exchange had a cross-claim against the English drawer that was the subject of an arbitration to be held in Copenhagen. Judgment was given against the acceptor on the bills, but the Court of Appeal stayed execution until the result of the arbitration was known.[126] The reason for the stay is not altogether clear, although it appears from the judgment of Harman LJ[127] that the German acceptor had argued that there may have been some difficulty in obtaining payment if it succeeded. The case received a mixed reception when the Court of Appeal later considered it in *Cebora SNC v SIP (Industrial Products) Ltd.*[128] Buckley LJ said that it should be regarded as turning on its own particular facts. Stephenson LJ was more positive. He said that he was 'not surprised'[129] that a stay was granted in the circumstances of the case. Sir Eric Sachs, on the other hand, was critical of the decision. He noted that the report of the case, 'perhaps wisely',[130] had not been included in the Law Reports or the All England Reports, and suggested that it was out of line with other authorities. Notwithstanding that criticism, a first instance judge ordered a stay in similar circumstances in *Montecchi v Shimco (UK) Ltd.*[131] The plaintiff was an Italian businessman who had sold some goods to the defendant English company. The goods

---

community. Pleas to leave in Court large sums to deteriorate in value while official referee scale proceedings are fought out may well to that community seem rather divorced from business realities, and should perhaps be examined with considerable caution.'

[120] [1977] 1 WLR 713.

[121] [1977] 1 WLR 713, 722.

[122] [1977] 1 WLR 713, 732. See also *Associated Bulk Carriers Ltd v Koch Shipping Inc (The Fuohsan Maru)* [1978] 1 Lloyd's Rep 24, 28; *Exmar BV v National Iranian Tanker Co (The Trade Fortitude)* [1992] 1 Lloyd's Rep 169, 177.

[123] *Cebora SNC v SIP (Industrial Products) Ltd* [1976] 1 Lloyd's Rep 271, 277; *Continental Illinois National Bank and Trust Co of Chicago v Papanicolaou (The Fedora)* [1986] 2 Lloyd's Rep 441, 445.

[124] *Walek & Co K G v Seafield Gentex Ltd* [1978] IR 167.

[125] [1967] 1 Lloyd's Rep 387. In *Eversure Textiles Manufacturing Co Ltd v Webb* [1978] Qd R 347, 350–1, Connolly J contemplated that, if a bill of exchange constituted the consideration for the purchase of goods which were acquired by the defendant for resale to third parties, the defendant 'might at least have an argument' in support of a stay if the plaintiff had acted in some manner which made it difficult for the defendant to sell the goods. Nevertheless, he went on to comment that it was 'extremely doubtful' whether in principle this should lead to a stay.

[126] The drawer had indorsed the bills to the plaintiff bank. When the plaintiff sued on the bills the acceptor sought leave to defend, alleging that it had a set-off and cross-claim against the drawer which it could assert against the plaintiff because the plaintiff was either an agent for collection on behalf of the drawer or alternatively it was a trustee for the drawer.

[127] [1967] 1 Lloyd's Rep 387, 389.

[128] [1976] 1 Lloyd's Rep 271.

[129] [1976] 1 Lloyd's Rep 271, 278.

[130] [1976] 1 Lloyd's Rep 271, 279.

[131] [1979] 1 WLR 1180.

were paid for by bill of exchange drawn by the defendant. The defendant alleged that the goods were defective, and refused to honour the bill. The plaintiff then sought, and obtained, summary judgment for the amount of the bill, though execution was stayed until after the hearing of the counterclaim on condition that the defendant pay the amount of the judgment into a joint account or into court. In addition, the judge granted a Mareva injunction restraining the plaintiff from dealing in any way with or disposing of the proceeds of the judgment. Subsequently, however, the Court of Appeal upheld an appeal by the plaintiff against the order, principally on the ground that a Mareva injunction was inappropriate because there was no evidence that the plaintiff would attempt to avoid enforcement of a judgment obtained against him on the cross-action. In delivering the judgment of the court,[132] Bridge LJ emphasized that it is not sufficient for a stay that the plaintiff suing on the bill, and against whom there is a cross-claim for damages, is foreign.[133] This would particularly be the case if the claimant has a substantial business in its own country.[134] On the other hand, Bridge LJ said that he should not be taken as saying that in no circumstances whatever could an injunction be granted to restrain a plaintiff from dealing with the fruits of a judgment in a case such as that before him.

5.29   The size of the paid up capital of a foreign company is regarded as of little significance,[135] while Sir Eric Sachs in *Cebora SNC v SIP (Industrial Products) Ltd*[136] rejected a submission that it is material to inquire into the virtues or defects of legal procedures in the country of a foreign plaintiff to which recourse may be necessary to enforce any judgment obtained on a cross-action. It has been suggested that a stay may be granted if there are 'real grounds' for supposing that the foreign plaintiff would not be likely to meet the counterclaim.[137] If Sir Eric Sachs was correct in the *Cebora* case in saying that it is not relevant to inquire into defects of the legal procedures of the plaintiff's country, it is difficult to see what could give rise to 'real grounds' for supposing that the counterclaim would not be met other than issues relating to the solvency of the claimant. But that circumstance should be just as relevant in the case of an English plaintiff. In *Continental Illinois National Bank and Trust Co of Chicago v Papanicolaou (The Fedora)*,[138] Parker LJ suggested, in the context of a guarantee given in circumstances such that it was the equivalent of a letter of credit, to which principles similar to those applicable to bills of exchange apply,[139] that it 'might be' that a stay would be granted if there was a counterclaim which was likely to succeed, coupled with cogent evidence that the holder of the guarantee, if paid, would be unable to meet a judgment on the counterclaim. Even in those circumstances, however, it is

---

[132]   Bridge, Geoffrey Lane and Roskill LJJ.

[133]   See also *Cebora SNC v SIP (Industrial Products) Ltd* [1976] 1 Lloyd's Rep 271, followed and applied in *Walek & Co KG v Seafield Gentex Ltd* [1978] IR 167.

[134]   *Cebora SNC v SIP (Industrial Products) Ltd* [1976] 1 Lloyd's Rep 271, 280.

[135]   *Cebora SNC v SIP (Industrial Products) Ltd* [1976] 1 Lloyd's Rep 271, 277.

[136]   [1976] 1 Lloyd's Rep 271, 279.

[137]   See Stephenson LJ in *Montebianco Industrie Tessile SpA v Carlyle Mills (London) Ltd* [1981] 1 Lloyd's Rep 509, 512, referring to *Cebora SNC v SIP (Industrial Products) Ltd* [1976] 1 Lloyd's Rep 271 ('In that case also comment was made on the need to have real grounds for supposing that the Italian company would not be likely to meet any counterclaim that was made').

[138]   [1986] 2 Lloyd's Rep 441, 445.

[139]   See para. 5.43 below.

suggested that the courts would be reluctant to grant a stay. Thus, it has been held that it is not sufficient for a stay that the claimant on the cheque is a company in administration.[140]

Can 'exceptional circumstances' affect the entitlement to judgment?

The concept of exceptional circumstances is usually referred to in the context of a stay of execution, but there is authority suggesting that it might also be relevant in relation to the primary question, whether the holder of the instrument is entitled to judgment.[141] In *Barclays Bank v Aschaffenburger*,[142] Lord Denning said that, while the holder of a bill of exchange ordinarily is entitled to judgment notwithstanding a cross-claim for damages available against him or her, there may be exceptions to the rule,[143] and similarly Salmon LJ indicated that the rule is not invariable.[144] It is noticeable, however, that a stay of execution was granted to the defendant in that case, as opposed to a judgment recognizing that there was a defence to the extent of the cross-claim. Subsequently, in *Brown, Shipley & Co Ltd v Alicia Hosiery Ltd*,[145] Lord Denning once again expressed the principle in terms that 'in the ordinary way' judgment should be given upon a bill notwithstanding a cross-claim, although the discussion later in his judgment concerned the possibility that the court in its discretion may grant a stay of execution, and indeed the availability of a stay was the issue in the case. In *Saga of Bond Street Ltd v Avalon Promotions Ltd*,[146] the defendant against whom judgment had been given on a bill succeeded in an application to set aside the judgment because of a breach of contract by the plaintiff. In later cases, however, the courts have sought to distinguish the case (albeit unsatisfactorily).[147] In view of the *Nova (Jersey) Knit* case,[148] it is doubtful if it would now be followed.[149]

5.30

Circumstances which may provide a defence

The preceding discussion concerned the situation in which the unliquidated cross-demand either is unrelated to the transaction for which the bill of exchange or cheque constituted consideration or, if it arose out of the same transaction as the instrument, it merely gives rise to a case of partial failure of consideration. On the other hand, an acceptor of a bill of

5.31

---

[140] *Isovel Contracts Ltd v ABB Building Technologies Ltd* [2002] 1 BCLC 390.

[141] In addition to the cases referred to below, see *Newman v Lever* (1887) 4 TLR 91, 92; *Safa Ltd v Banque du Caire* [2000] 2 Lloyd's Rep 600, 606. In *Finch Motors Ltd v Quin* [1980] 2 NZLR 513, 516 it is unclear whether the reference to 'exceptional circumstances' was in the context of a stay of execution or leave to defend on the basis of a set-off. A similar comment may be made in respect of *John Shearer Ltd v Gehl Co* (1995) 60 FCR 136, 141.

[142] [1967] 1 Lloyd's Rep 387.

[143] [1967] 1 Lloyd's Rep 387, 388.

[144] [1967] 1 Lloyd's Rep 387, 391.

[145] [1966] 1 Lloyd's Rep 668, 669.

[146] [1972] 2 QB 325.

[147] See *Cebora SNC v SIP (Industrial Products) Ltd* [1976] 1 Lloyd's Rep 271, 279, in which Sir Eric Sachs said of the *Saga of Bond Street* case that it 'was a case extremely close to a total failure of consideration' (for which see below), and *Eversure Textiles Manufacturing Ltd v Webb* [1978] Qd R 347, 349.

[148] See para. 5.25 above.

[149] In *Anglo-Italian Bank v Wells* (1878) 38 LT 197, 199, Jessel MR said that he could not imagine a case which would justify allowing an equitable set-off against a claim on promissory notes. See also *Isovel Contracts Ltd v ABB Building Technologies Ltd* [2002] 1 BCLC 390, 398.

exchange has a defence to a claim brought against him or her by the drawer if his or her acceptance was procured by fraud, invalidity, or for a consideration which has totally failed.[150] Therefore, if there has been a total failure of the consideration for which the bill was given,[151] the acceptor has a defence.[152] Similarly, fraud in relation to the transaction in respect of which the bill constituted payment or security may provide a defence to an action on the bill by the drawer,[153] while it has been held in Australia that the principle under discussion does not apply where the cross-claim is to have the bill set aside or treated as a nullity pursuant to the Trade Practices Act 1974 (Cth), s. 87.[154] In addition, in Australia the Full Court of the Federal Court has suggested that the rule might not apply where the bill was obtained as a result of conduct that was misleading or deceptive in breach of s. 52 of the Trade Practices Act.[155]

Debt on a negotiable instrument pleaded as a defence

5.32 The principle precluding an equitable set-off against a claim on a cheque or similar instrument should not apply in the converse situation in which the holder is seeking to employ the debt on the instrument in a set-off. In *Williams v Davies*[156] Sir Lancelot Shadwell permitted a person who had obtained judgment on some promissory notes to set off the judgment against a damages liability to the maker of the notes. While the case has been criticized on the ground that the cross-demands were not sufficiently closely connected to give rise to an equitable set-off,[157] it nevertheless suggests that a claim on a negotiable instrument may be employed defensively in a set-off.

---

[150] See *Churchill & Sim v Goddard* [1937] 1 KB 92, 109; *Nova (Jersey) Knit Ltd v Kammgarn Spinnerei GmbH* [1977] 1 WLR 713, 721, 722, 726.

[151] Compare *Fielding & Platt Ltd v Najjar* [1969] 1 WLR 357. *Quaere* if it is sufficient if it is a case 'extremely close to a total failure of consideration'. See Sir Eric Sachs in *Cebora SNC v SIP (Industrial Products) Ltd* [1976] 1 Lloyd's Rep 271, 279 (distinguishing the *Saga of Bond Street* case [1972] 2 QB 325).

[152] *Obbard v Betham* (1830) M & M 483, 485, 173 ER 1232; *Glennie v Imri* (1839) 3 Y & C Ex 436, 443, 160 ER 773, 776; *Trickey v Larne* (1840) 6 M & W 278, 280, 151 ER 414, 415; *Bow, McLachlan & Co Ltd v Ship 'Camosun'* [1909] AC 597, 612; *James Lamont & Co Ltd v Hyland Ltd* [1950] 1 KB 585, 592; *Cebora SNC v SIP (Industrial Products) Ltd* [1976] 1 Lloyd's Rep 271, 279; *Nova (Jersey) Knit Ltd v Kammgarn Spinnerei GmbH* [1977] 1 WLR 713, 732–3; *Finch Motors Ltd v Quin* [1980] 2 NZLR 513; *Montebianco Industrie Tessili SpA v Carlyle Mills (London) Ltd* [1981] 1 Lloyd's Rep 509, 511; *International Ore & Fertilizer Corporation v East Coast Fertilizer Co Ltd* [1987] 1 NZLR 9. In *All Trades Distributors Ltd v Agencies Kaufman Ltd* (1969) 113 Sol Jo 995 there was a thin, but at least arguable, case of total failure of consideration. Conditional leave to defend was granted, the condition being that the money due on the bill be brought into court.

[153] *Brown v Trynor* (1980) 109 DLR (3d) 312. See also *Ledger v Ewer* (1794) Peake 283, 170 ER 157; *Fleming v Simpson* (1806) 1 Camp 40n, 170 ER 868; *Solomon v Turner* (1815) 1 Stark 51, 171 ER 398; *Glennie v Imri* (1839) 3 Y & C Ex 436, 443, 160 ER 773, 776; *John Shearer Ltd v Gehl Co* (1995) 60 FCR 136, 142; *Solo Industries UK Ltd v Canara Bank* [2001] 1 WLR 1800 at [38]. See also *Ex p Stephens* (1805) 11 Ves Jun 24, 32 ER 996 in which the set-off was an equitable set-off. Fraud also may be raised against a remote party who is not a holder in due course. See the Bills of Exchange Act 1882, ss. 29(2) and 38.

[154] *Ferro Corporation (Aust) Pty Ltd v International Pools Aust Pty Ltd* (1993) 30 NSWLR 539; *John Shearer Ltd v Gehl Co* (1995) 60 FCR 136, 142. This should also be the case where relief is sought under the Contracts Review Act 1980 (NSW) to strike down a bill of exchange or otherwise to fashion appropriate relief. See the *Ferro Corporation* case at 541.

[155] *John Shearer Ltd v Gehl Co* (1995) 60 FCR 136, 142.

[156] (1829) 2 Sim 461, 57 ER 860.

[157] *Rawson v Samuel* (1841) Cr & Ph 161, 178, 179, 41 ER 451, 458. See para. 4.04 above.

(2) Setting aside a statutory demand

5.33 Further, the existence of a cross-demand may provide a ground for setting aside a statutory demand served under the Insolvency Act 1986, s. 268 as a prelude to a bankruptcy petition based upon non-payment of a cheque. Pursuant to the Insolvency Rules 1986, r. 6.5(4)(a), the court may grant an application for an order setting aside a statutory demand if the debtor appears to have a 'counterclaim, set-off or cross demand' which equals or exceeds the amount of the debt. 'Cross-demand' has a wider meaning than the technical terms 'set-off' and 'counterclaim'.[158] The fact that the damages cross-claim would not have given rise to a defence to a claim on the cheque, and would not have constituted grounds for a stay of execution on a judgment on the cheque, does not mean that it is not a cross-demand for the purpose of r. 6.5(4)(a).[159] A similar principle applies in the case of a petition to wind up a company for failure to pay a cheque or other instrument. If the company has a genuine and serious cross-claim in an amount which exceeds the debt to the petitioner, the petition may be dismissed or stayed unless there are special circumstances which make it inappropriate to do so.[160]

(3) Insolvency set-off

5.34 Similarly, a claim on a cheque or other instrument may be the subject of a mandatory set-off under the insolvency legislation in the event of a bankruptcy or a liquidation of the party liable on the instrument, provided that the other requirements of the insolvency set-off section are satisfied.[161]

(4) Negotiable instruments – Statutes of Set-off

5.35 While it is now settled that an equitable set-off based upon a cross-claim for damages is not available (save possibly in exceptional circumstances) as a defence to an action on a bill of exchange or other negotiable instrument, conflicting views have been expressed in relation to the availability of a set-off under the Statutes of Set-off in the case of mutual debts.

5.36 It is sometimes suggested that the principle which precludes an equitable set-off in respect of an unliquidated cross-demand also applies to the Statutes, so that generally the drawer of a cheque or the acceptor of a bill being sued for payment cannot raise as a defence an independent debt owing by the holder. There is one situation in which it is recognized that

---

[158] *Re A Bankruptcy Notice* [1934] 1 Ch 431, 438; *John Shearer Ltd v Gehl Co* (1995) 60 FCR 136, 142.

[159] *Hofer v Strawson* [1999] 2 BCLC 336. In Australia, see *John Shearer Ltd v Gehl Co* (1995) 60 FCR 136, distinguishing *Buying Systems (Aust) Pty Ltd v Tien Mah Litho Printing Co (Pte) Ltd* (1986) 5 NSWLR 317. See also *Equuscorp Pty Ltd v Perpetual Trustees WA Ltd* (1997) 24 ACSR 194, 203 in relation to a letter of credit (appeal dismissed (1997) 25 ACSR 675).

[160] *Hofer v Strawson* [1999] 2 BCLC 336, 341–2, referring to *Re Bayoil SA* [1999] 1 WLR 147. *Quaere* whether delay in litigating the cross-claim affects the position. See para. 5.09n above. In Australia, see *John Shearer Ltd v Gehl Co* (1995) 60 FCR 136.

[161] *Willment Brothers Ltd v North West Thames Regional Health Authority* (1984) 26 BLR 51; *Isovel Contracts Ltd v ABB Building Technologies Ltd* [2002] 1 BCLC 390, 398. See also *John Shearer Ltd v Gehl Co* (1995) 60 FCR 136, 143. In the *Isovel* case a stay of execution was refused on the basis of a cross-claim where a company in administration had obtained judgment on a dishonoured cheque. Since that case, however, set-off under the Insolvency Rules has been extended to companies in administration. See para. 6.10 below.

a set-off may arise under the Statutes, and that is when a cheque or other instrument is given as payment for goods sold or services performed and there is a liquidated cross-demand arising from a partial failure of consideration.[162] That situation is referred to below.[163] But if the cross-debt is not connected in that way, it has been suggested that it cannot be set off.[164] This view is said to be supported by a comment by Sir Eric Sachs in *Cebora SNC v SIP (Industrial Products) Ltd*,[165] which has been referred to by the courts on other occasions with evident approval.[166] Sir Eric Sachs said that the courts will refuse to regard as a defence to a claim on a bill of exchange 'any set off, *legal or equitable*, or any counterclaim, whether arising on the particular transaction upon which the bill of exchange came into existence, or, a fortiori, arising in any other way'.[167] There are four points to note in relation to this comment. The first is that, in so far as it extended to legal set-offs, it was *obiter*. The second is that the reference to 'legal' set-off may have had in contemplation the common law cases which have held that the principle of abatement[168] does not apply when the price had been paid by way of bill of exchange, as opposed to the form of set-off conferred by the Statutes of Set-off in the case of mutual debts.[169] The third is that the decision of the House of Lords in *Nova (Jersey) Knit Ltd v Kammgarn Spinnerei GmbH*[170] does not require the conclusion that the Statutes have a limited operation in the case of bills of exchange. The *Nova (Jersey) Knit* case concerned equitable set-off, not the statutory defence.[171] The fourth point is that, if Sir Eric Sachs did intend to refer to the Statutes, it is not an accurate statement of the traditionally accepted position. The right of set-off in the

---

[162] *Agra & Masterman's Bank v Leighton* (1866) LR 2 Ex 56, 65; *Nova (Jersey) Knit Ltd v Kammgarn Spinnerei GmbH* [1977] 1 WLR 713, 720, 732–3; *Safa Ltd v Banque du Caire* [2000] 2 Lloyd's Rep 600, 605; *Isovel Contracts Ltd v ABB Building Technologies Ltd* [2002] 1 BCLC 390, 396–8. See also *Eversure Textiles Manufacturers Co Ltd v Webb* [1978] Qd R 347, 349.

[163] See para. 5.41 below.

[164] See e.g. Wood, *English and International Set-off* (1989), 700–1. In addition to *Cebora SNC v SIP (Industrial Products) Ltd* [1976] 1 Lloyd's Rep 271, 278 (see below), Wood has referred to the cross-claim for commissions in *Eversure Textiles Manufacturing Co Ltd v Webb* [1978] Qd R 347. However, Connolly J commented in that case (at 348) that the claims for commission were not clearly raised against the plaintiff.

[165] [1976] 1 Lloyd's Rep 271.

[166] *Begley Industries Ltd v Cramp* [1977] 2 NZLR 207, 212–13; *Buying Systems (Aust) Pty Ltd v Tien Mah Litho Printing Co Ltd* (1986) 5 NSWLR 317, 327–8; *Re Julius Harper Ltd* [1983] NZLR 215, 224; *Finch Motors Ltd v Quin* [1980] 2 NZLR 513, 516. See also *Halsbury's Laws of England* (5th edn, 2008) vol. 49 ('Financial Services and Institutions'), 814, para. 1599. In *Power Curber International Ltd v National Bank of Kuwait* [1981] 1 WLR 1233, 1241, Lord Denning MR said that: 'No set-off or counterclaim is allowed to detract from' the principle that a bill is equivalent to cash, though this comment was made in the context of a bill given for the price of goods, and his Lordship may have had in mind a damages claim arising out of the underlying contract.

[167] [1976] 1 Lloyd's Rep 271, 278 (emphasis added).

[168] See paras 2.123–2.134 above.

[169] E.g. in *Bank of Boston Connecticut v European Grain & Shipping Ltd* [1989] 1 AC 1056, 1105 Lord Brandon would appear to have used the expression 'legal set-off' in the sense of a claim for an abatement (though in the context of freight payable under a charterparty).

[170] [1977] 1 WLR 713.

[171] Lord Wilberforce commented in *Nova (Jersey) Knit* [1977] 1 WLR 713, 720 that: 'As between the immediate parties, a partial failure of consideration may be relied upon as a pro tanto defence, but only when the amount involved is ascertained and liquidated.' However, the emphasis was on confining the set-off to the case of liquidated debts, in other words set-off under the Statutes, rather than to immediate parties where there was a partial failure of consideration. The case concerned bills of exchange given as payment for goods where the parties to the action were immediate parties to the bills, and the *dictum* should be considered in that context. The same point may be made in relation to Lord Russell of Killowen's comments at 732–3.

case of mutual debts was not developed as an equitable or a common law doctrine, but rather it is statutory in origin. In the case of a defence conferred by statute the proper approach is to examine the words of the relevant legislation,[172] and the Statutes of Set-off simply stipulated that a set-off could occur in the case of mutual debts. There is nothing in them to suggest that they were not intended to apply when the plaintiff is suing on a cheque or other instrument.

At least since the latter half of the eighteenth century the courts have recognized that an **5.37** independent cross-debt may be set off under the Statutes against a claim on a negotiable instrument.[173] In *Baskerville v Brown*[174] Lord Mansfield accepted that Baskerville could have pleaded the debt owing to him as a defence in Brown's action against him on the promissory note, and Lord Kenyon allowed a set-off in a similar situation in *Lechmere v Hawkins*.[175] In 1812 the Court of King's Bench in *Wake v Tinkler*[176] did not dispute that a set-off under the Statutes was available in principle against a claim on a promissory note, although a set-off was denied on another ground. The availability of a set-off is also supported by the line of cases which developed in the middle of the nineteenth century dealing with overdue bills and promissory notes.[177] The cases established the proposition that, when the indorsee of an overdue bill sues the acceptor, the indorsee does not take subject to a set-off under the Statutes in respect of an unconnected cross-debt owing to the acceptor by an earlier holder.[178] Nevertheless, it was assumed that a set-off would have been available if instead the earlier holder had sued. For example, in *Burrough v Moss*[179] the defendant gave a promissory note to a married woman. According to the then applicable law, this entitled her husband (one Fearn) to treat it as his own property. Fearn himself was indebted to the defendant on an unrelated matter. After the note became due, Fearn indorsed it to the plaintiff. When the plaintiff sued the defendant on the note, the defendant sought to set off Fearn's indebtedness to him. It was held that a set-off was not available against the plaintiff as indorsee. On the other hand, Bayley J considered that one of the consequences of Fearn treating the note as his own 'would be, to let in by way of set-off to any claim by him, any debts due from him',[180] and he said that: 'As to the other sum of

---

[172] Consistent with Lightman J's comment in *Fuller v Happy Shopper Markets Ltd* [2001] 1 WLR 1681 at [23] in relation to the procedural nature of the defence under the Statutes of Set-off.

[173] In addition to the cases cited below, see *L D Nathan & Co Ltd v Vista Travel Ltd* [1973] 1 NZLR 233, which may have been correctly decided on the basis of a set-off under the Statutes, though compare *Finch Motors Ltd v Quin* [1980] 2 NZLR 513, 516 and *International Ore & Fertilizer Corporation v East Coast Fertilizer Co Ltd* [1987] 1 NZLR 9, 15. This also may explain *Murphy v Glass* (1869) LR 2 PC 408, where the cross-claim had been the subject of an award by an arbitrator.

[174] (1761) 2 Burr 1229, 97 ER 804.

[175] (1798) 2 Esp 626, 170 ER 477. See also *Ord v Ruspini* (1797) 2 Esp 569, 170 ER 458.

[176] (1812) 16 East 36, 104 ER 1002.

[177] The relevant cases are *Burrough v Moss* (1830) 10 B & C 558, 109 ER 558; *Stein v Yglesias* (1834) 1 Cr M & R 565, 149 ER 1205; *Whitehead v Walker* (1842) 10 M & W 696, 152 ER 652; *Oulds v Harrison* (1854) 10 Ex 572, 156 ER 566; *Re Overend Gurney. Ex p Swan* (1868) LR 6 Eq 344.

[178] See paras 17.69–17.71 below. Compare *Holmes v Kidd* (1858) 3 H & N 891, 157 ER 729, in which there was an agreement for a set-off which constituted an equity attaching to the bill, as opposed to merely a personal equity.

[179] (1830) 10 B & C 558, 109 ER 558.

[180] (1830) 10 B & C 558, 562, 109 ER 558, 559.

28*l* due from Fearn alone . . . it might have been set off had Fearn sued on the note.'[181] That also accords with views expressed by counsel for both parties during argument. *Oulds v Harrison*[182] was a similar case. In the course of giving the judgment of the Court of Exchequer, Parke B asked:[183]

> [W]hat is the effect of an indorsement of an overdue bill under the circumstances mentioned in the plea? These though inaccurately stated, we think, amount to an averment, that both the indorser and indorsee, knowing that *there was a debt due to the defendant, which would be set off if the action should be brought by the indorser against the defendant*, in order to defeat that set-off, and fraudulently, so far as that was a fraud but no further, agreed that the bill should be indorsed, and it was therefore indorsed, without value, to the plaintiff.

It was held that the circumstances referred to did not prevent the application of the principle that an indorsee of an overdue note takes free from rights of set-off available against the indorser. Parke B nevertheless recognized that, if the indorser instead had been the party suing on the bill, he could have been met by a set-off under the Statutes in respect of the debt that he owed to the acceptor. Nor is there anything in the report to suggest that the indorser's debt to the acceptor was connected with the transaction in respect of which the bill was given. These cases were decided after some of the early cases which had established that a claim on a bill of exchange given as payment of the price of goods sold and delivered cannot be met by a defence based upon a cross-claim for damages for a defect in the goods,[184] and it may be assumed that the judges were aware of those earlier cases.

5.38 There are instances in Victoria in which the courts have held that a debt arising otherwise than as a result of a partial failure of consideration could be set off under the Statutes against a claim on a negotiable instrument. One such case is *Ingleton v Coates*,[185] a decision of Madden CJ, in which the debt sought to be set off originated in a loan made to the person to whom the promissory note being sued upon had been indorsed, the debt on the loan having been assigned to the maker of the promissory note. In *Mobil Oil Australia Ltd v Caulfield Tyre Service Pty Ltd*[186] Young CJ, having quoted the passage from the judgment of Sir Eric Sachs in the *Cebora* case referred to above, suggested that the decision in *Ingleton v Coates* to allow the maker leave to defend may need to be reconsidered,[187] though the better view is that it was correct. Two other Victorian cases support that view. The first is *Nisbet v Cox*,[188] which concerned a set of bills. The report only takes the form of a short note, but it appears to have accepted that a set-off under the Statutes was available once the last bill became due. The report simply states that a debt was alleged to be due from the plaintiff to the defendant acceptor. The nature of the debt is not mentioned, and presumably it was

---

[181] (1830) 10 B & C 558, 562, 109 ER 558, 560.
[182] (1854) 10 Ex 572, 156 ER 566.
[183] (1854) 10 Ex 572, 579, 156 ER 566, 569 (emphasis added).
[184] See e.g. *Morgan v Richardson* 1 Camp 40n, 170 ER 868; *Tye v Gwynne* (1810) 2 Camp 346, 170 ER 1179; *Day v Nix* (1824) 2 LJOSCP 133; *Obbard v Betham* (1830) M & M 483, 173 ER 1232; *Glennie v Imri* (1839) 2 Y & C Ex 436, 160 ER 773.
[185] (1896) 2 ALR 154.
[186] [1984] VR 440.
[187] [1984] VR 440, 443.
[188] (1873) 4 AJR 115.

not regarded as significant. The second case is *Woodroffe v Moss*.[189] The defendant in an action brought against him on a cheque pleaded by way of defence that the plaintiffs had been his agents for the sale of some goods, and in breach of their duty as agents themselves purchased the goods and sold them on their own account at enhanced prices without accounting for the difference in price. The Full Court of the Victorian Supreme Court held that this could be pleaded as a defence of set-off. It has been suggested that the case turned on the circumstance that it involved delinquency by a fiduciary.[190] However, that point was not emphasized in argument or in any of the judgments. The whole discussion centred on whether the claim against the plaintiff was liquidated. It was held that it was. Therefore, a set-off was allowed under the Statutes.

Further, in *Hongkong and Shanghai Banking Corporation v Kloeckner & Co AG*[191] Hirst J   **5.39**
accepted as 'well settled' a general statement by counsel to the effect that a set-off is permissible against a claim on a bill of exchange when the cross-claim is liquidated though not when it is unliquidated.[192]

The case of freight payable to a shipowner provides an analogy.[193] The position in relation   **5.40**
to freight is similar to that applicable to bills of exchange, in that neither equitable set-off nor the common law defence of abatement may be asserted in answer to a claim for freight. But there is also authority in that context for the proposition that the principle which precludes those defences does not affect the application of the Statutes of Set-off when the case involves mutual debts.[194]

Nevertheless, recent comments in the Court of Appeal support the more restrictive view.   **5.41**
In *Safa Ltd v Banque du Caire*[195] Waller LJ, in a judgment with which Lady Justice Hale and Lord Justice Schiemann agreed, said in the context of bills of exchange that set-off is '*only* available between immediate parties in relation to liquidated sums'.[196] This was not expressly limited to the case of a partial failure of consideration,[197] although the discussion earlier in the judgment[198] suggests that he also had in mind that limitation. Thus, Mance LJ, in delivering the judgment of the Court of Appeal[199] in *Solo Industries UK Ltd v Canara Bank*,[200] later referred to Waller LJ in *Safa* as having cited: 'the principles governing bills of

---

[189] [1915] VLR 237.

[190] Wood, *English and International Set-off* (1989), 700.

[191] [1990] 2 QB 514.

[192] [1990] 2 QB 514, 524. The *Kloeckner* case concerned a letter of credit, which is regarded as similar to a bill of exchange. See below. The beneficiary sought summary judgment against the bank on the letter. The bank asserted a set-off in respect of a liquidated sum owing to it by the beneficiary. Hirst J allowed the set-off. While he emphasized that it was a 'striking feature' that the debt to the bank arose out of the same transaction as the letter, he went on to say (at 526) that this was an *additional* circumstance for allowing a set-off. The Statutes of Set-off themselves do not require that the cross-debts should be connected in any way, and the better view is that the set-off in *Kloeckner* was not dependent upon the connection to which Hirst J referred.

[193] See paras 5.02–5.24 above.

[194] See paras 5.17–5.22 above.

[195] [2000] 2 Lloyd's Rep 600.

[196] [2000] 2 Lloyd's Rep 600, 606 (emphasis added).

[197] See para. 5.36 above.

[198] [2000] 2 Lloyd's Rep 600, 605.

[199] Potter and Mance LJJ, and Sir Martin Nourse.

[200] [2001] 1 WLR 1800 at [22].

exchange, according to which set-off is not admissible, other than between immediate parties in cases of partial failure of consideration when the amount involved is both ascertained and liquidated . . .' However, the justification for restricting the defence to immediate parties and to cases of partial failure of consideration remains unclear. When a bill of exchange is issued by reference to an underlying transaction,[201] and there has been a partial failure of consideration where the amount involved is liquidated and ascertained,[202] the case is one of mutual debts, and therefore the Statutes of Set-off *prima facie* apply. But the Statutes do not require any connection between the debts the subject of the set-off,[203] and so the connection or otherwise between the debt sought to be set off and the transaction that gave rise to the instrument should not be relevant to the question whether the Statutes apply. For the same reason, it should not matter whether the parties are immediate or remote. The comments in the *Safa* and *Solo Industries* cases were *obiter*, and the point was not subjected to detailed analysis. In view of the earlier authorities suggesting that the defence is not so restricted, and in view of the language of the Statutes of Set-off themselves, those comments should not be regarded as having settled the issue.

(5) Statutes of Set-off – set-off against a subsequent holder

5.42 If, as suggested, a set-off under the Statutes of Set-off may be asserted against a claim on a bill of exchange or other negotiable instrument, the further question may arise whether a subsequent holder of a bill takes subject to a right of set-off that would have been available against the prior holder under the Statutes if the prior holder had sued on the bill. If the subsequent holder is a holder in due course, he or she takes free from personal defences between prior parties, which include rights of set-off. This is a longstanding principle which has been codified in the Bills of Exchange Act 1882, s. 38(2). On the other hand, s. 38(2) does not state what happens when the subsequent holder is not a holder in due course, and opinions differ amongst text-writers as to whether a subsequent holder in such a case is bound by rights of set-off between prior parties.[204] The issue is dealt with later.[205] The better view is that the subsequent holder is not bound, even if he or she is a mere holder who has not given value.

(6) Letters of credit

5.43 Letters of credit are generally treated in a similar manner to cheques and bills of exchange. An irrevocable letter of credit is regarded in mercantile practice as being the equivalent of

---

[201] See *Safa Ltd v Banque du Caire* [2000] 2 Lloyd's Rep 600, 605.

[202] See para. 5.36 above.

[203] See para. 2.14 above.

[204] For the view that a subsequent holder who is not a holder in due course takes subject to rights of set-off available between prior parties, see Wood *English and International Set-off* (1989), 901, and Goode, *Commercial Law* (3rd edn, 2004), 515–16. See also *Paget's Law of Banking* (13th edn, 2007) [22.21] pp. 569–70. For the contrary (and preferred) view, see Crawford and Falconbridge, *Banking and Bills of Exchange* (8th edn, 1986) vol. 2, 1524 *et seq.* and *Chitty on Contracts* (30th edn, 2008) vol. 2, 320–1, para. 34–095. See also *Chalmers and Guest on Bills of Exchange, Cheques and Promissory Notes* (17th edn, 2009), 255–6, para. 4–027 in relation to a holder for value. *Byles on Bills of Exchange and Cheques* (28th edn, 2007) 234 also appears to support this view in relation to set-off of unconnected cross-debts under the Statutes of Set-off.

[205] See paras 17.69–17.71 below.

cash in hand.[206] In the absence of fraud, it must be paid regardless of any cross-claim available to the person at whose request the letter was issued against the holder, even if the cross-claim arose out of the transaction on which the letter was based.[207] This is also the case for performance bonds and bank guarantees when they are given in circumstances such that they are equivalent to letters of credit.[208]

A transaction involving a letter of credit typically differs from a transaction in which a **5.44** cheque or bill of exchange is given. A cheque or a bill is often given as payment for the price of goods or services. In that situation the person liable on the instrument is commonly a party to the transaction which gave rise to the instrument. A letter of credit also may be given in order to effect payment to the seller of goods, but it would be rare for the issuer of the letter of credit, typically a bank, to be involved in the underlying transaction. But what if, in a rare case, the bank is involved in the transaction?

In *Power Curber International Ltd v National Bank of Kuwait SAK*,[209] goods had been **5.45** sold on terms that they were to be paid for by letter of credit issued by the defendant bank in favour of the seller. In the course of his judgment Lord Denning commented that: 'A letter of credit is like a bill of exchange given for the price of goods. It ranks as cash and must be honoured. No set-off or counterclaim is allowed to detract from it . . .'[210] Later, Hirst J, in *Hongkong and Shanghai Banking Corporation v Kloeckner & Co AG*,[211] said of that statement that it must be interpreted as meaning a set-off or counterclaim by the buyer against the seller, and not one by the bank against the seller, the latter situation not being under consideration in the *Power Curber* case. In the *Kloeckner* case a bank had issued a standby letter of credit in relation to transactions in which the bank itself was involved. The transactions involved back-to-back sales, and the beneficiary of the letter of credit in turn had given a payment undertaking to the bank. One of the questions was whether the bank could set off its claim on the payment undertaking against its liability on the letter of credit. Hirst J said that the case before him had two striking features. The first was that the bank's claim arose out of the banking transactions which gave rise to the letter of credit, and the second was that the set-off in issue was a 'liquidated set-off'. In those circumstances, he concluded that the case in favour of a set-off was overwhelming.

---

[206] *Intraco Ltd v Notis Shipping Corporation (The Bhoja Trader)* [1981] 2 Lloyd's Rep 256, 257; *Power Curber International Ltd v National Bank of Kuwait SAK* [1981] 1 WLR 1233, 1241, 1243; *Solo Industries UK Ltd v Canara Bank* [2001] 1 WLR 1800 at [31].

[207] *Power Curber International Ltd v National Bank of Kuwait SAK* [1981] 1 WLR 1233, 1241, 1243; *Hongkong and Shanghai Banking Corporation v Kloeckner & Co AG* [1990] 2 QB 514, 521–2; *Safa Ltd v Banque du Caire* [2000] 2 Lloyd's Rep 600, 605.

[208] *Intraco Ltd v Notis Shipping Corporation (The Bhoja Trader)* [1981] 2 Lloyd's Rep 256; *Balfour Beatty Civil Engineering v Technical & General Guarantee Co Ltd* (1999) 68 Con LR 180, 189. See also *Continental Illinois National Bank and Trust Co of Chicago v Papanicolaou (The Fedora)* [1986] 2 Lloyd's Rep 441, 445; *Sim v Rotherdam Metropolitan BC* [1987] 1 Ch 216, 259; *Solo Industries UK Ltd v Canara Bank* [2001] 1 WLR 1800 (performance bond).

[209] [1981] 1 WLR 1233.

[210] [1981] 1 WLR 1233, 1241.

[211] [1990] 2 QB 514, 525–6.

5.46   Subsequently, the issue received the attention of the Court of Appeal in *Safa Ltd v Banque du Caire*.[212] A bank had given a letter of credit to an insurance broker, the purpose of the letter of credit being to cover the premium payable to an insurance company which was to provide a financial insurance guarantee to the bank in relation to a facility to be provided by the bank to a third party. The broker made a claim on the letter of credit which the bank alleged was fraudulent. After a review of the authorities, including the *Kloeckner* case, Waller LJ formulated a number of propositions:[213]

1. The principle that letters of credit must be treated as cash is an important one, and must be maintained.

2. It is however unusual for a bank which has opened a letter of credit to be involved in the related transaction to the extent this bank was.

3. When a bank is involved in the related transaction it may be unjust for that bank to be forced to pay on a summary judgment where it has a real prospect of succeeding by reference to a claim on the underlying transaction, and particularly if that claim is a liquidated claim, the Court should not give summary judgment either because a set-off has a reasonable prospect of success or because there is a compelling reason to have a trial of the letter of credit issue.

4. If a bank can establish a claim with a real prospect of success, either that the demand was fraudulent even if it had no clear evidence of fraud at the time of demand, or that there was a misrepresentation by the beneficiary directed at persuading the bank to enter into the letter of credit, it may also be unjust to enter summary judgment against the bank either because the bank has a reasonable prospect of succeeding in a defence of set-off or because there is a compelling reason for a trial of the letter of credit issue.

In his third proposition, dealing with the situation in which the bank is involved in the underlying transaction, Waller LJ referred to a case in which the bank's claim is liquidated. But he seems to have regarded that factor as an additional reason for refusing summary judgment to the beneficiary of the letter of credit, as opposed to constituting a necessary element. He said that a set-off may be available, and the court should not therefore give summary judgment, if the bank has a claim on the underlying transaction which has a real prospect of success,[214] and he continued that this *particularly* should be the case if the bank's claim is liquidated. This leaves open the possibility that the bank's claim in some cases may be unliquidated, though presumably subject to a requirement that the cross-claims must be sufficiently connected to give rise to an equitable set-off. Later, Mance LJ, in *Solo Industries UK Ltd v Canara Bank*,[215] after referring to the propositions in *Safa*, commented that he agreed that: 'special considerations arise in circumstances such as those in the *Safa* case itself, where the beneficiary and bank are both intimately involved in a wider underlying transaction.' In the *Safa* case, Waller LJ said that if the bank in that case paid under the letter of credit it would have been entitled in the circumstances to immediate reimbursement by the broker. The claim would be for a liquidated

---

[212]   [2000] 2 Lloyd's Rep 600, referred to without adverse comment *Burton v Mellham Ltd* [2006] 1 WLR 2820 at [27].

[213]   [2000] 2 Lloyd's Rep 600, 608. Lady Justice Hale and Lord Justice Schiemann agreed with Waller LJ's judgment.

[214]   CPR r. 24.2.

[215]   [2001] 1 WLR 1800 at [27]–[28].

sum, and he said that the connection between the claims would be such that a set-off would be allowed if the bank's claim were established.[216] Any such set-off would not have been based on the Statutes of Set-off. For the Statutes to apply, there must be mutual debts. However, the bank's right to reimbursement would only have crystallized into a debt after the bank had paid under the letter of credit. But at that point there would no longer have been a debt owing by the bank. There would not therefore have been mutual debts, so that the set-off could not have been based on the Statutes. It could only have been an equitable set-off arising from the closeness of the connection of the claims, and equity has never regarded the distinction been liquidated and unliquidated claims as critical to the question whether the equitable defence should apply.

This view would give rise to a problem, however. If a bank which has issued a letter of credit **5.47** is entitled to assert a set-off when it has a claim against the beneficiary arising out of the underlying transaction in respect of which the letter of credit was given, so as to justify refusing summary judgment to the beneficiary of the letter, and if that may apply also when the bank's claim is unliquidated, the letter of credit cases would depart from the principle applicable in the case of cheques and bills of exchange. In the case of a cheque or a bill of exchange given as payment of the price of goods sold or services performed, it is established that the fact that the drawer of the cheque or the acceptor of the bill may have a damages claim against the other party arising out of the underlying transaction is not sufficient to give rise to a set-off.[217] The generality of the third proposition in the *Safa* case, therefore, may require reconsideration. In the *Safa* case, there were allegations of fraud. Fraud was the subject of the fourth proposition put forward by Waller LJ, but, as Mance LJ later remarked, this appears to have been an independent point and it is not clear that the case was decided by reference to it.[218] In order to preserve the analogy with bills of exchange,[219] the *Safa* case should be regarded as turning on its peculiar facts, in particular the allegation of fraud. Furthermore, in so far as the third proposition is to be regarded as an independent principle, it should be confined to liquidated claims, so as to accommodate set-off under the Statutes of Set-off. This reflects the circumstances in issue in the *Kloeckner* case, though in the case of the Statutes it is not clear why the availability of the defence should be limited to a claim arising out of the underlying transaction.[220]

In his fourth point in the *Safa* case, Waller LJ referred to a fraudulent claim on a letter of **5.48** credit and to a situation in which there was misrepresentation inducing the bank to enter into the letter of credit. In both cases he suggested that it would suffice in a summary judgment application for the bank to establish a claim with a real prospect of success.

---

[216] See also the analogous circumstances in *Ralston v South Greta Colliery Co* (1912) 13 SR (NSW) 6, for which see para. 4.64 above. Waller LJ referred to the defence as a set-off, but another possibility in the circumstances may have been a defence of circuity of action, as discussed in *Aktieselskabet Ocean v B Harding and Sons Ltd* [1928] 2 KB 371, 384–5 and *Co–operative Retail Services Ltd v Taylor Young Partnership* [2000] BLR 461, 474–5. See para. 4.64n above.
[217] See para. 5.25 above.
[218] *Solo Industries UK Ltd v Canara Bank* [2001] 1 WLR 1800 at [28]. Waller LJ in the *Safa* case seems to have referred to fraud as an alternative ground for the decision in that case. See [2000] 2 Lloyd's Rep 600, 609–10.
[219] See *Solo Industries UK Ltd v Canara Bank* [2001] 1 WLR 1800 at [38].
[220] See paras 5.35–5.42 above in relation to the Statutes of Set-off.

Subsequently, the Court of Appeal in *Solo Industries UK Ltd v Canara Bank*[221] declined to accept that view. Mance LJ, in delivering the judgment of the Court, drew a distinction between fraud going to the validity of the instrument itself and a fraudulent demand under the instrument. In the former case he said that the bank may be granted leave to defend in a summary judgment application if it can show that it has a real prospect of successfully defending the claim.[222] A higher standard applies, however, in the case of a fraudulent demand. If the bank paid under a fraudulent demand, it would have a cause of action against the beneficiary for fraudulent misrepresentation.[223] That cause of action may provide a defence to the bank, but in order to justify leave to defend the fraud must be established, or clear. It is not sufficient that the defence has a real prospect of success. Short of established fraud, a bank would not normally be allowed to raise an alleged impropriety affecting the demand as a defence.

(7) Direct debit

5.49 In *Esso Petroleum Co Ltd v Milton*,[224] the Court of Appeal held that the principle applicable to cheques extends also to a direct debit arrangement. The case concerned a purchaser of goods who had authorized payment by way of a direct debit to his bank account, but cancelled the bank's mandate to debit the account after the goods were delivered. The majority (Thorpe LJ and Sir John Balcombe, Simon Brown LJ dissenting on this point) considered that the vendor was entitled to summary judgment for the amount otherwise admitted to be due, and the purchaser was not granted leave to defend on the basis of an unliquidated damages cross-claim. This conclusion was justified by reference to a perception that in modern commercial practice a direct debit is treated in the same way as payment by cheque and, as such, as being the equivalent of cash.[225] There is nevertheless much force in Professor Tettenborn's criticism of the decision,[226] which expands on the dissenting judgment of Simon Brown LJ on this issue.[227] A direct debit arrangement in truth differs in an important respect from payment by cheque or bill of exchange. When a cheque is given as payment for goods or services supplied, the vendor does not sue on the underlying contract for the price, but on the cheque. On the other hand, when a direct debit arrangement is cancelled, the vendor's action is for the price pursuant to the original contract. Unlike a cheque, a direct debit arrangement does not confer any rights upon the vendor which are independent of the original contract. Subsequently, a differently constituted Court of Appeal in *Courage Ltd v Crehan*[228] followed the *Milton* case in the context of a commercial lease. In giving the court's judgment, Morritt LJ said that he was bound by the *Milton* case, and he declined to express a view on the merits of the decision.[229]

---

[221] [2001] 1 WLR 1800.
[222] CPR r. 24.2.
[223] *Balfour Beatty Civil Engineering v Technical & General Guarantee Co Ltd* (1999) 68 Con LR 180, 189.
[224] [1997] 1 WLR 938. Compare *Star Rider Ltd v Inntreprenneur Ltd* [1998] 1 EGLR 53, 55–6.
[225] See Sir John Balcombe at [1997] 1 WLR 938, 954, and Thorpe LJ at 952–3.
[226] Tettenborn, Note (1997) 113 LQR 374. See also *Paget's Law of Banking* (13th edn, 2007), 405–6.
[227] [1997] 1 WLR 938, 947–8.
[228] [1999] 2 EGLR 145 (Morritt, Schiemann and Mance LJJ). See also *Gibbs Mew Plc v Gemmell* [1999] 1 EGLR 43, 50 (Peter Gibson, Schiemann and Mantell LJJ).
[229] [1999] EGLR 145, 157.

C. Building and Construction Contracts

(1) General principle

A cross-claim for damages for delay,[230] or bad workmanship, or failure to complete is capable in principle[231] of being employed in a set-off against an amount due for work performed under a building contract.[232] At one time it was thought that a set-off was not available in cases in which the price was to be paid by instalment on the certificate of an architect or engineer, or some other such person. In a series of cases, commencing in 1971 with the Court of Appeal decision in *Dawnays Ltd v F. G. Minter Ltd*,[233] it was held that a certificate issued in respect of the work done to date by a contractor or a subcontractor under a building contract was to be regarded as equivalent to cash, and therefore the debt due under the certificate had to be paid save only for deductions permitted by the contract. A claim on the certificate by the contractor against the employer, or by a subcontractor against the contractor, could not be met by a set-off or a counterclaim in respect of an unliquidated cross-demand. Nor would the existence of the unliquidated cross-demand provide a ground for a stay of an action on the certificate pending arbitration. Provisions in the contract permitting certain deductions or set-offs were interpreted as referring only to liquidated ascertained sums which were established or admitted as being due.[234] Unliquidated cross-demands had to be prosecuted separately. The impetus for these decisions was cash flow. It was said that, if the contractor or subcontractor failed to receive the money stipulated in the certificate, it might not be in a position to complete the contract works. The contracts in question, therefore, were construed so as to give effect to the presumed intention of the

5.50

---

[230] In the context of a contract for the sale of goods, see *Contigroup Companies Inc v Glencore AG* [2005] 1 Lloyd's Rep 241.

[231] Subject to the Housing Grants, Construction and Regeneration Act 1996, s. 111 (see below) and to any contracting out of rights of set-off (see paras 5.122–5.132 below).

[232] For examples of cases concerned with delay, see *Young v Kitchin* (1878) 3 Ex D 127; *Mitchell v Purnell Motors Pty Ltd* [1961] NSWLR 165; *Rapid Building Group Ltd v Ealing Family Housing Association Ltd* (1984) 29 BLR 5; *Archital Luxfer Ltd v A J Dunning & Sons (Weyhill) Ltd* (1987) 47 BLR 1; *M. L. Paynter Ltd v Ben Candy Investments Ltd* [1987] 1 NZLR 257. See also *Galambos & Sons Pty Ltd v McIntyre* (1974) 5 ACTR 10; *R. M. Douglas Construction Ltd v Bass Leisure Ltd* (1990) 53 BLR 119. In an action by an employer arising out of a delay in completion, a cross-claim available to the contractor against the employer for hindering or preventing the contractor's performance of the contract may give rise to an equitable set-off. See *Rosehaugh Stanhope (Broadgate Phase 6) Plc v Redpath Dorman Long Ltd* (1990) 50 BLR 75; *Beaufort House Development Ltd v Zimmcor (International) Inc* (1990) 50 BLR 91. See also *Hanak v Green* [1958] 2 QB 9. For cases concerned with bad workmanship, see e.g. *Mitchell v Purnell Motors Pty Ltd*; *Galambos & Son Pty Ltd v McIntyre*; *Acsim (Southern) Ltd v Danish Contracting and Development Co Ltd* (1989) 47 BLR 55 (equitable set-off restricted by contract). See also *Lowe v Holme* (1883) 10 QBD 286; *Hanak v Green*. In relation to failure to complete, see *Queensland University of Technology v Project Constructions (Aust) Pty Ltd* [2003] 1 Qd R 259 at [21].

[233] [1971] 1 WLR 1205. See also *Frederick Mark Ltd v Schield* [1972] 1 Lloyd's Rep 9; *GKN Foundations Ltd v Wandsworth London Borough Council* [1972] 1 Lloyd's Rep 528; *John Thompson Horseley Bridge Ltd v Wellingborough Steel & Construction Co Ltd* (1972) 1 BLR 69; *Token Construction Co Ltd v Naviewland Properties Ltd* (1972) 2 BLR 1; *Carter Horseley (Engineers) Ltd and John Thompson Horseley Bridge Ltd v Dawnays Ltd* (1972) 2 BLR 8.

[234] See e.g. *Algrey Contractors Ltd v Tenth Moat Housing Society Ltd* [1973] 1 Lloyd's Rep 369 (liquidated damages clause).

parties that cash flow should be preserved.[235] However, *Dawnays v Minter* and the cases following it were the subject of trenchant criticism by one commentator,[236] and it was overruled some two years later by the House of Lords in *Gilbert-Ash (Northern) Ltd v Modern Engineering (Bristol) Ltd.*[237] The House of Lords held that there is no presumption in building cases in which the price is to be paid by instalment on certificate that the parties intend that the ordinary defences of set-off and abatement[238] should not apply. The perceived desirability of facilitating cash flow was not considered to be something unique to the building industry, and it was not regarded as a sufficient justification for ousting those rights.[239]

(2) Housing Grants, Construction and Regeneration Act 1996

5.51 The right to assert a defence of set-off or abatement in this context is now subject to Part II of the Housing Grants, Construction and Regeneration Act 1996.

5.52 Part II of the Act deals with payment and adjudication under a 'construction contract'.[240] It has a number of aspects. In cases where it is agreed that the duration of the contract is to be 45 days or more, s. 109 establishes a general entitlement to payment by instalments, stage payments or other periodic payments for work done under the contract. In the event of a dispute arising under a construction contract, s. 108 provides for adjudication. The decision of the adjudicator is to be binding until the dispute is finally determined by legal

---

[235] Curiously, the courts also denied a right of deduction when the claim for payment was on the final certificate or the contract works in any even were completed, even though the case would not have been one in which the funds were required in order to finance the completion of the contract works. See *GKN Foundations Ltd v Wandsworth LBC* [1972] 1 Lloyd's Rep 528; *Token Construction Co Ltd v Naviewland Properties Ltd* (1972) 2 BLR 1; *Carter Horseley (Engineers) Ltd v Dawnays Ltd* (1972) 2 BLR 8. See the discussion of these cases in Wallace, 'Set Back to Set-off' (1973) 89 LQR 36, 54–6, 58–9, 59–60.

[236] Wallace, 'Set Back to Set-off' (1973) 89 LQR 36.

[237] [1974] AC 689, discussed in Wallace, 'Set Fair for Set-off' (1974) 90 LQR 21. See also *Mottram Consultants Ltd v Bernard Sunley & Sons Ltd* [1975] 2 Lloyd's Rep 197 and *M. L. Paynter Ltd v Ben Candy Investments Ltd* [1987] 1 NZLR 257. *Gilbert-Ash* has been followed in Scotland. See *Redpath Dorman Long Ltd v Cummins Engine Co Ltd* [1981] SC 370. See also, in Ireland, *P J Hegarty & Sons Ltd v Royal Liver Friendly Society* [1985] IR 524. In New Zealand, compare *Savory Holdings Ltd v Royal Oak Mall Ltd* [1992] 1 NZLR 12, 27, where Smellie J said that the particular circumstances of that case distinguished it from the *Gilbert-Ash* case, so as to disentitle the employer from relying on an equitable set-off in order to defeat a claim for summary judgment. The circumstances were that the moneys had been certified as owing almost a year before, further substantial sums were likely to be certified in due course, and the amount certified was merely 'provisional' and there was an ample margin for adjustment. The New Zealand Court of Appeal referred to Smellie J's judgment with evident approval in *Hempseed v Durham Developments Ltd* [1998] 3 NZLR 265, 269.

[238] See paras 2.123–2.134 above.

[239] See Viscount Dilhorne and Lord Diplock [1974] AC 689, 707, 718. See also *Mottram Consultants Ltd v Bernard Sunley & Sons Ltd* [1975] 2 Lloyd's Rep 197, 214; *Compania Sud Americana de Vapores v Shipmair BV (The Teno)* [1977] 2 Lloyd's Rep 289, 293–4; *Federal Commerce & Navigation Co Ltd v Molena Alpha Inc* [1978] 1 QB 927, 983, 986.

[240] Defined in s. 104. There are exclusions from the operation of the legislation in ss. 105(2) and 106 (contract with a residential occupier). *Steve Domsalla v Kenneth Dyason* [2007] BLR 348 concerned a contract with a residential occupier, so that the legislation did not apply. The provisions of the Act had been incorporated into the contract, but the question was raised whether the Unfair Terms in Consumer Contracts Regulations 1999 (S.I. 1999 No. 2083) ('UTCCR') applied. Judge Thornton QC held (following (at [92]) *Bryen & Langley Ltd v Boston* [2005] BLR 508 (CA)) that the adjudication provisions contained in the contract were not unfair for the purpose of the UCTTR but that, in the unusual circumstances of the case (see at [95]), the withholding notice clause was unfair.

proceedings, arbitration or agreement. Pursuant to s. 110, the contract is required to provide a mechanism for determining what payments are due under the contract, and also for the giving of a notice specifying the amount of the payment made or proposed to be made and the basis on which that amount was calculated.[241] Section 111 is of considerable importance. It precludes a party to a construction contract from withholding payment after the final date for payment of a sum due under the contract unless that party has given an effective notice of intention to withhold payment pursuant to the Act.[242] If a timeous notice is not given under s. 111, summary judgment may be sought for the amount due.[243] The purpose of the legislation has been said to be to introduce a speedy mechanism for settling disputes in construction contracts on a provisional interim basis and requiring the decisions of adjudicators to be enforced pending the final determination of disputes.[244]

Section 111 has been held to extend to an asserted right to withhold payment on account **5.53** of equitable set-off[245] or abatement,[246] where the sum claimed is otherwise payable in accordance with the terms of the contract.[247] On one view, this might be thought a surprising conclusion. For s. 111(1) to apply there must be a 'sum due', whereas if an equitable set-off is available there is nothing due, so far as equity is concerned, to the extent of the set-off.[248] Similarly, nothing is due when there is a defence of abatement. Nevertheless, the adoption of that analysis to a considerable extent would denude the provision of effect, and the courts are likely to adhere to the view that s. 111 may apply when defences of equitable set-off and abatement are in issue.[249] The intention is that valid adjudicators' decisions are to be enforced without set-off.[250] Set-offs should be raised in the adjudication, where the adjudicator may allow or disallow them, as opposed to the losing party raising set-offs in the enforcement proceedings.

---

[241] The purpose of s. 110(2) has been said to be something of a puzzle, since serving a notice under the subsection seems to have no consequences other than that it may stand as a notice under s. 111 (below). See *Melville Dundas Ltd v George Wimpey UK Ltd* [2007] 1 WLR 1136 at [16] (Lord Hoffmann).

[242] However, s. 111 does not entitle the court to refuse to grant a stay under the Arbitration Act 1996, s. 9 if a stay would otherwise be granted. See *Collins (Contractors) Ltd v Baltic Quay Management (1994) Ltd* [2005] BLR 63.

[243] The amount may have been the subject of an adjudication. See e.g. *Solland International Ltd v Daraydan Holdings Ltd* [2002] EWHC 220 (TCC) (esp. at [30]–[32]); *Wimbledon Construction Company 2000 Ltd v Vago* [2005] BLR 374 (esp. at [26]; *Bouygues (UK) Ltd v Dahl-Jensen (UK) Ltd* [2000] BLR 522 at [29]. For an example of summary judgment where there was no adjudication, see *Rupert Morgan Building Services (LLC) Ltd v Jervis* [2004] 1 WLR 1867.

[244] *Macob Civil Engineering Ltd v Morrison Construction Ltd* [1999] BLR 93, 97 (Dyson J).

[245] *VHE Construction Plc v RBSTB Trust Co Ltd* [2000] BLR 187 at [36] and [66]; *Northern Developments (Cumbria) Ltd v J & J Nichol* [2000] BLR 158 at [29]–[31]; *Solland International Ltd v Daraydan Holdings Ltd* [2002] EWHC 220 (TCC); *Levolux AT Ltd v Ferson Contractors Ltd* [2002] BLR 341 at [41].

[246] *Whiteways Contractors (Sussex) Ltd v Impresa Castelli Construction UK Ltd* (2000) 75 Con LR 92 at [32].

[247] Compare *Melville Dundas Ltd v George Wimpey UK Ltd* [2007] 1 WLR 1136, where the contractor's employment was terminated under the contract consequent upon the appointment to it of administrative receivers, but see *Pierce Design International Ltd v Mark Johnston* [2007] BLR 381.

[248] See para. 4.30 above.

[249] Consistent with the reasoning in *Balfour Beatty Construction Northern Ltd v Modus Corovest (Blackpool) Ltd* [2008] EWHC 3029 (TCC) at [68], [71] and [72]. See also *Keating on Construction Contracts* (8th edn, 2006), 623 [17–055].

[250] *Rok Building Ltd v Celtic Composting Systems Ltd* [2009] EWHC 2664 (TCC) at [17].

5.54 On the other hand, it is only a withholding from a sum which is due 'under the contract' which attracts the requirement of a notice under s. 111. This requires an identification of the amount payable under the terms of the contract. In considering this point, the courts have drawn a distinction between, on the one hand, a case where the circumstance which makes a sum due under the contract is the fact of the work having been done, and, on the other, the situation in which the contract provides that the amount payable is the amount certified by an architect or other such person. In the former case, the amount due under the contract is the value of the work done. A dispute about whether the work in respect of which the claim was made had been done, or about whether it was properly measured or valued, goes to the initial question whether the sum claimed indeed is due under the contract, and a withholding notice is unnecessary in respect of that dispute.[251] But where the contract requires payment of an amount certified, it is not the actual work done which defines the sum payable but the amount in the certificate. Any withholding from that amount must be the subject of a notice under s. 111.[252]

5.55 As Jacob LJ observed in *Rupert Morgan Building Services (LLC) Ltd v Jervis*,[253] s. 111 is a provision about cash flow. It does not purport to make a payment certificate conclusive, and it does not preclude a person who has paid from subsequently showing that he or she has overpaid. If the overpayment was made on an interim certificate, the matter can be put right in subsequent certificates. Otherwise, it can be raised by way of adjudication[254] or, if necessary, arbitration or legal proceedings.[255] However, as Jacob LJ also observed in the *Rupert Morgan* case,[256] the statutory procedure has the disadvantage that a person who has overpaid a claimant is at risk of the claimant's insolvency. The claimant may not be able to repay the amount of an overpayment made pursuant to a certificate at a later date. Notwithstanding that risk, if a claimant who has obtained an adjudication in its favour is insolvent, the fact of the insolvency is not regarded as a sufficient ground for refusing an application for summary judgment for the amount of the adjudication,[257] though (depending on the circumstances) it could provide a ground for a stay of enforcement of the judgment pending trial of the counterclaim.[258] A stay might be refused, however, if the claimant was in the same or a similar financial position when the contract was

---

[251] *SL Timber Systems Ltd v Carillion Construction Ltd* [2001] BLR 516 (explained in *Rupert Morgan Building Services (LLC) Ltd v Jervis* [2004] 1 WLR 1867 at [13]); *Whiteways Contractors (Sussex) Ltd v Impresa Castelli Construction UK Ltd* (2000) 75 Con LR 92 at [32].

[252] *Rupert Morgan Building Services (LLC) Ltd v Jervis* [2004] 1 WLR 1867. See also *Collins (Contractors) Ltd v Baltic Quay Management (1994) Ltd* [2005] BLR 63 at [50]–[52]; *Melville Dundas Ltd v George Wimpey Ltd* [2006] BLR 164 at [15]–[19], [30] (appeal allowed on other grounds: *Melville Dundas Ltd v George Wimpey UK Ltd* [2007] 1 WLR 1136).

[253] [2004] 1 WLR 1867 at [11]–[14]. See also *Melville Dundas Ltd v George Wimpey Ltd* [2006] BLR 164 at [30] and on appeal *Melville Dundas Ltd v George Wimpey UK Ltd* [2007] 1 WLR 1136 at [11].

[254] Pursuant to the Housing Grants, Construction and Regeneration Act 1996, s. 108.

[255] *Rupert Morgan Building Services (LLC) Ltd v Jervis* [2004] 1 WLR 1867 at [14].

[256] [2004] 1 WLR 1867 at [15].

[257] *SL Timber Systems Ltd v Carillion Construction Ltd* [2001] BLR 516.

[258] *Rainford House Ltd v Cadogan Ltd* [2001] BLR 416 (administrative receivership) (the stay in that case was made conditional upon the defendant paying the amount of the adjudicator's decision plus interest into court); *JPA Design and Build Ltd v Sentosa (UK) Ltd* [2009] EWHC 2312 (TCC) at [29], [35]–[39]. Compare *Read General Building Ltd v Dartmoor Properties Ltd* [2009] BLR 225 (CVA).

entered into,[259] or if the claimant's financial position is due, either wholly or in significant part, to the defendant's failure to pay the sum awarded by the adjudicator.[260]

The position is different if the claimant who succeeded in the adjudication is bankrupt or is in liquidation.[261] In either of those cases, the cross-claims between the parties will be the subject of an automatic set-off pursuant to the mutual credit provision in the insolvency legislation.[262] Under the insolvency set-off provision, an account is deemed to have been taken upon the occurrence of the bankruptcy or the liquidation so that, as between the insolvent and the other party, there is only a single claim for the balance. In those circumstances, Chadwick LJ in *Bouygues (UK) Ltd v Dahl-Jensen (UK) Ltd*[263] considered that summary judgment should not be given on a claim arising out of an adjudication which is merely provisional.[264]   **5.56**

In a number of cases the question has arisen whether a claim for liquidated and ascertained damages under a contract can be set off against sums due pursuant to an adjudicator's decision. In *Balfour Beatty Construction v Serco Ltd*[265] Jackson J (as he then was) derived the following principles from the authorities: **5.57**

(a) Where it follows logically from an adjudicator's decision that the employer is entitled to recover a specific sum by way of liquidated and ascertained damages, then the employer may set off that sum against monies payable to the contractor pursuant to the adjudicator's decision, provided that the employer has given proper notice (in so far as required).

---

[259] See the commentary to the report of *Rainford House Ltd v Cadogan Ltd* [2001] BLR 416 at 417–18, and *Wimbledon Construction Co 2000 Ltd v Vago* [2005] BLR 374 at [26]. See also *SG South Ltd v King's Head Cirencester LLP* [2009] EWHC 2645 (TCC) at [41], where the claimant was not incorporated when work began.

[260] *Wimbledon Construction Co 2000 Ltd v Vago* [2005] BLR 374 at [26] and [40]; *Read General Building Ltd v Dartmoor Properties Ltd* [2009] BLR 225; *SG South Ltd v King's Head Cirencester LLP* [2009] EWHC 2645 (TCC) at [41].

[261] Or if the claimant is a company in administration and the administrator, being authorized to make a distribution, has given notice to creditors that he proposes to make it. See the Insolvency Rules 1986, r. 2.85, and para. 6.124 below. See also *Melville Dundas Ltd v George Wimpey UK Ltd* [2007] 1 WLR 1136, in which the contract permitted the employer to determine the employment of the contractor if an administrative receiver was appointed to the contractor and to retain funds by way of security for cross-claims. Note also para. 5.61 below in relation to corresponding legislation in New South Wales.

[262] See paras 6.119–6.146 below. For bankruptcy, the relevant provision is the Insolvency Act 1986, s. 323. For company liquidation, see the Insolvency Rules 1986, r. 4.90.

[263] [2000] BLR 522. See also *Melville Dundas Ltd v George Wimpey UK Ltd* [2007] 1 WLR 1136 at [13], [32] and [78].

[264] Buxton and Peter Gibson LJJ agreeing. However, since the point had not been taken before the first instance judge or on appeal, and counsel for the appellant had not embraced it with any enthusiasm when it was drawn to his attention by the Court of Appeal, Chadwick LJ refused to set aside the order for summary judgment made by the first instance judge and instead ordered a stay of execution. In *Enterprise Managed Services Ltd v Tony McFadden Utilities Ltd* [2010] BLR 89 Coulson J held that a claim to a net balance under the Insolvency Rules 1986, r. 4.90 could not be referred to adjudication, *inter alia* on the ground that an adjudication is provisional whereas r. 4.90 envisages a single and final process for ascertaining the balance.

[265] [2004] EWHC 3336 (TCC) at [53]. See also *Balfour Beatty Construction Northern Ltd v Modus Corovest (Blackpool) Ltd* [2008] EWHC 3029 (TCC) at [84]–[89] (referring to the cases); *JPA Design and Build Ltd v Sentosa (UK) Ltd* [2009] EWHC 2312 (TCC) at [22]–[26]; *Avoncroft Construction Ltd v Sharba Homes (CN) Ltd* [2008] EWHC 933 (TCC) at [8]–[13]; *R J Knapman Ltd v Richards* [2006] EWHC 2518 (TCC) at [17] and [19]. Compare *Hart v Smith* [2009] EWHC 2223 (TCC).

(b) Where the entitlement to liquidated and ascertained damages has not been determined either expressly or impliedly by the adjudicator's decision, then the question whether the employer is entitled to set off liquidated and ascertained damages against sums awarded by the adjudicator will depend upon the terms of the contract and the circumstances of the case.

The allowance of a set-off in this situation has been described as a 'particular exception'[266] which does not give a wider power to set off sums generally against an adjudicator's decision.[267]

(3) 'Security of payment' legislation in Australia

5.58   In New South Wales, the Building and Construction Industry Security of Payment Act 1999 serves a similar function to the Housing Industry, Construction and Regeneration Act. Similar (but not identical) legislation exists in other Australian jurisdictions.[268] The discussion below relates to the New South Wales Act, which was the first such legislation in Australia.

5.59   Briefly, the scheme of the New South Wales legislation is as follows. Section 8 provides that a person who has undertaken to carry out construction work under a construction contract is entitled to progress payments. Pursuant to s. 13, a person who is entitled to a progress payment (the 'claimant') may serve a payment claim on the person liable to make the payment (the 'respondent'). The respondent may reply to the claim by providing a payment schedule to the claimant which sets out reasons for withholding payment. If the respondent does not provide a payment schedule to the claimant, the respondent becomes liable to pay the claimed amount.[269] In proceedings by the claimant to recover the claimed amount, s. 15(4)(b) provides that the respondent is not entitled: (i) to bring any cross-claim against the claimant; or (ii) to raise any defence in relation to matters arising under the construction contract. Alternatively, if the respondent serves a payment schedule in

---

[266]   The exception in (a) would apply *a fortiori* where the entitlement has been decided by an adjudicator. See *JPA Design and Build Ltd v Sentosa (UK) Ltd* [2009] EWHC 2312 (TCC) at [22]–[27]. The losing party in an adjudication must comply with the decision and cannot withhold payment on the ground of an anticipated recovery in a future adjudication based on different issues, unless possibly they are effectively simultaneous adjudications. See *YCMS Ltd v Grabiner* [2009] EWHC 127 (TCC) at [51] and [63]–[64], referring to *Interserve Industrial Services Ltd v Cleveland Bridge UK Ltd* [2006] EWHC 741 (TCC) at [43]. See also *Hillview Industrial Developments (UK) Ltd v Botes Building Ltd* [2006] EWHC 1365 (TCC). Compare *Workspace Management Ltd v YJL London Ltd* [2009] BLR 497 (interim costs order made by an arbitrator in favour of a claimant set off against a sum which an adjudicator had decided was due from the claimant to the defendant consequent upon an overpayment by the defendant, both debts relating to the same contract and the same underlying dispute). As to the court's jurisdiction to set off judgments and orders, see paras 2.98–2.122 above.

[267]   *Ledwood Mechanical Engineering Ltd v Whessoe Oil and Gas Ltd* [2008] BLR 198 at [37].

[268]   Building and Construction Industry Security of Payment Act 2002 (Vic); Building and Construction Industry Payments Act 2004 (Qld); Construction Contracts (Security of Payments) Act 2004 (NT); Construction Contracts Act 2004 (WA); Building and Construction Industry (Security of Payment) Act 2009 (ACT); Building and Construction Industry Security of Payment Act 2009 (SA); Building and Construction Industry Security of Payment Act 2009 (Tas). See generally Jacobs, *Security of Payment in the Australian Building and Construction Industry* (3rd edn, 2010).

[269]   Building and Construction Industry Security of Payment Act 1999 (NSW), s. 14.

response to the payment claim which provides for a lesser amount than the amount indicated in the payment claim, the claimant may apply for adjudication under s. 17.[270] If the respondent fails to pay the adjudicated amount, the claimant may obtain an adjudication certificate which may be filed as a judgment debt in a court of competent jurisdiction.[271] The respondent may apply to have the judgment set aside. In those proceedings, however, s. 25(4) provides that the respondent is not entitled to challenge the adjudicator's determination. Moreover, the respondent is subject to constraints similar to those set out in s. 15(4)(b) (above), in that the respondent cannot bring any cross-claim against the claimant or raise any defence in relation to matters arising under the construction contract.[272] Section 32 emphasizes the provisional nature of the procedure under the Act. It provides that the procedure does not affect any right that a party to a construction contract may have under the contract or may have apart from the Act in respect of anything done or omitted to be done under the contract.

A curious aspect of s. 15(4)(b) (above) is that, while the prohibition in relation to cross-claims is absolute, the prohibition in relation to raising a defence is limited to matters arising under the construction contract.[273] This would pick up an equitable defence of set-off arising from defects or delay. But defences which are not in relation to matters arising under the contract are not precluded. In *Bitannia Pty Ltd v Parkline Constructions Pty Ltd*,[274] the New South Wales Court of Appeal accepted that s. 15(4)(b) did not preclude a defence based upon misleading or deceptive conduct contrary to the Trade Practices Act 1974 (Cth), s. 52, in circumstances where an essential element of the claimant's entitlement to judgment (the failure of the respondent to provide a payment schedule) had been brought about by the claimant's misleading conduct. The defence was not prohibited by s. 15(4)(b)(ii) because it did not arise 'under the construction contract', and nor was it in relation to a matter arising under the contract.[275] Hodgson JA justified the defence in that case on the availability of an injunction under the Trade Practices Act,[276] but both he and Basten JA accepted that a defence of equitable set-off could apply where damages are sought under the Trade Practices Act, ss. 82 or 87.[277]

5.60

---

[270] *Quaere* if an adjudicator can recognize an equitable set-off, as opposed to a statutory right (e.g. under the Sale of Goods Act 1923 (NSW), s. 54(1)(a)) to set up a breach by the other party in diminution or extinction of the price. See *Perform (NSW) Pty Ltd v MEV-AUS Pty Ltd* [2009] NSWCA 157 at [136]–[141] (but compare Giles JA at [99]). In relation to the statutory right, see paras 2.123 and 2.126 above.

[271] Building and Construction Industry Security of Payment Act 1999 (NSW), s. 25.

[272] Building and Construction Industry Security of Payment Act 1999 (NSW), s. 25(4)(a).

[273] See *Bitannia Pty Ltd v Parkline Constructions Pty Ltd* [2006] NSWCA 238 at [78].

[274] (2006) 67 NSWLR 9.

[275] See Basten JA (2006) 67 NSWLR 9 at [78], [79] and [96], with whom Hodgson and Tobias JJA agreed at [12] and [17].

[276] (2006) 67 NSWLR 9 at [10].

[277] (2006) 67 NSWLR 9 at [11] (Hodgson JA), [83]–[104] (Basten JA). If the court was wrong and there was no right to proceed by way of defence, so that the respondent had to proceed by way of cross-claim, Basten J suggested that the state Act would have been inconsistent with the Trade Practices Act (Cth) and to that extent it would have been inoperative because of s. 109 of the Constitution. See at [105]–[119]. Hodgson and Tobias JJA did not decide this point.

5.61 Similar to the view adopted in England in the *Bouygues* case,[278] courts in New South Wales have said that the Building and Construction Industry Security of Payment Act 1999 (NSW) does not preclude a set-off in the liquidation of a contractor pursuant to the Corporations Act 1981 (Cth), s. 553C (or under a deed of company arrangement executed by the contractor which incorporates s. 553C).[279] In particular, Young CJ in Eq held in *Brodyn Pty Ltd v Dasein Constructions Pty Ltd*[280] that s. 25 of the New South Wales Act did not preclude a set-off where an adjudication certificate had been filed as a judgment debt. This view would seem correct. As a result of the operation of s. 553C, a set-off will have occurred automatically at the date of the liquidation (or the date of the deed),[281] so that to the extent of the set-off the amount owing to the contractor under the contract will have been paid.[282] Later cases support this view.[283]

(4) Excluding or limiting equitable set-off and abatement by contract

5.62 In building and construction contracts, a cross-claim for damages for defective workmanship can give rise not only to a set-off in equity but also to the common law defence of abatement.[284] Therefore, if in a particular case s. 111 of the Housing Grants, Construction and Regeneration Act 1996 (above) does not apply,[285] and it is intended that the contract sum is to be paid in full without any deduction for cross-claims arising out of defects, or that a defined procedure should be followed before any such deduction is permitted, care must be taken to negative or limit both defences. In *Acsim (Southern) Ltd v Danish Contracting and Development Co Ltd*[286] the contract provided that Danish Contracting ('Dancon') could set off against any moneys otherwise due to Acsim as contractor the amount of any cross-claim which Dancon had for loss suffered as a result of a breach by Acsim, but only if the cross-claim was quantified and notified to Acsim within a specified time limit. The contract went on to provide that this fully set out the rights of the parties in respect of set-off. The Court of Appeal considered that the contract was effective to prevent

---

[278] [2000] BLR 522. See para. 5.56 above. As Lord Hoffmann observed in *Melville Dundas Ltd v George Wimpey UK Ltd* [2007] 1 WLR 1136 at [11]: 'Upon insolvency, liability to make an interim payment therefore becomes a matter which relates not to cash flow but to the substantive rights of the employer on the one hand and the contractor's secured or unsecured creditors on the other.'

[279] *Brodyn Pty Ltd v Dasein Constructions Pty Ltd* [2004] NSWSC 1230 at [76]–[93]; *Veolia Water Solutions v Kruger Engineering (No. 3)* [2007] NSWSC 459; *Reed Constructions Australia Ltd v DM Fabrications Pty Ltd* (2007) 25 ACLC 1463 at [35]–[38].

[280] [2004] NSWSC 1230 at [76]–[93].

[281] See paras 6.119–6.146 below (in relation to Australia, see paras 6.142–6.146 below).

[282] The set-off would reduce or extinguish the contract price, but it would also reduce or extinguish the judgment debt arising out of the certificate for the progress payment (which debt would not exceed the contract price). Consequently, there would be no need to set aside the judgment. See *Veolia Water Solutions v Kruger Engineering (No. 3)* [2007] NSWSC 459 at [24]–[25].

[283] *Veolia Water Solutions v Kruger Engineering (No. 3)* [2007] NSWSC 459; *Reed Constructions Australia Ltd v DM Fabrications Pty Ltd* (2007) 25 ACLC 1463 at [27], [35]–[38].

[284] See para. 2.123–2.134 above.

[285] See ss. 104(4), 105(2) and 106 of the Act. In New South Wales, see the exclusions from the definition of 'construction work' in the Building and Construction Industry Security of Payment Act 1999 (NSW), s. 5(2). See para. 5.58 above.

[286] (1989) 47 BLR 55. See also, and compare, *Mellowes Archital Ltd v Bell Projects Ltd* (1997) 87 BLR 26 (damages for delay not within the common law principle of abatement).

a cross-claim for damages for bad workmanship that was quantified outside the required period from being employed as an equitable set-off. On the other hand, there were not sufficiently clear and express words to exclude the common law defence of abatement.[287] Pursuant to the common law principle, the subject of the cross-claim was not being raised as a set-off as such. Rather, Dancon was defending itself by showing that, by reason of Acsim's breaches of contract, the value of the work done was less than the sum claimed. That defence was not affected by the contract.

The question whether the parties have agreed to exclude the defences is one of interpreta- **5.63** tion of the contract, and in that regard it is often said that the intention to exclude must be evidenced by clear express words, or at least there must be a clear implication in the contract that they are not to apply. Contracting out of set-off is considered in greater detail later.[288]

D. Contracts of Employment

(1) Failure to work

An employee may have refused or failed to work in accordance with the contract of employ- **5.64** ment for part of a period in respect of which a claim for wages is made. The analysis in such a case is not that the employee has a *prima facie* entitlement to wages for that period but subject to a set-off available to the employer, to the extent of a proportion of the wages equal to the proportion of the period during which the employee failed to work.[289] Rather, the employee fails at the first hurdle, in that the employee is not entitled to wages to the extent that he or she was not ready and willing to perform the services required by the contract.[290]

(2) Claim for damages

Alternatively, an employer may have suffered loss as a result of the actions of an employee **5.65** which give rise to a claim in damages against the employee. There is authority supporting the availability of an equitable set-off in that circumstance,[291] although it has been said that the principles upon which an equitable set-off can be effective in a claim for wages are

---

[287] Compare *Skipskredittforeningen v Emperor Navigation* [1998] 1 Lloyd's Rep 66, 78–9 (Mance J).
[288] See paras 5.95–5.141 below.
[289] Compare *Sim v Rotherham Metropolitan BC* [1987] 1 Ch 216.
[290] *Miles v Wakefield Metropolitan DC* [1987] 1 AC 539; *Wiluszynski v Tower Hamlets LBC* [1989] ICR 493. In Australia, see *Coal & Allied Mining Services Pty Ltd v MacPherson* [2010] FCAFC 83 at [38]–[39], [115]. However, as Lord Oliver of Aylmerton noted in the *Miles* case (at 571), this would be subject to an implied term exonerating the employee from inability to perform in certain circumstances, e.g. illness.
[291] *Sim v Rotherham Metropolitan BC* [1987] 1 Ch 216, and see also *Sagar v H Ridehalgh and Son Ltd* [1931] 1 Ch 310; *New Centurion Trust v Welch* [1990] ICR 383. In *Miles v Wakefield Metropolitan DC* [1987] 1 AC 539, 570 Lord Oliver of Aylmerton left open the possibility of a set-off in this situation. Compare *Cooper v The Isle of Wight College* [2007] EWHC 2831 (QB) in which the employer had not counterclaimed for damages for breach of contract. An employee sued by his or her employer for money had and received may set off a claim for arrears of wages under the Statutes of Set-off. See *East Anglian Railway Co v Lythgoe* (1851) 10 CB 726, 138 ER 287.

extremely limited, and that it would depend upon a careful analysis of the nature of the breach relative to the nature of the employee's contractual claim.[292] The Employment Rights Act 1996, s. 13 prohibits an employer from making a 'deduction' from wages except in certain defined circumstances,[293] but on one view this would not preclude an equitable set-off. Equitable set-off is a substantive defence.[294] If the defence is available, it would not be a case of the employer making a deduction from wages to which the employee was entitled. Rather, the set-off would render it unconscionable for the employee to regard the employer as being liable to pay wages to the extent of the cross-claim,[295] so as to impugn the employee's right to claim wages. In other contexts, a stipulation in a contract that a payment is to be made 'without any deduction' has been held not to be effective to exclude an equitable set-off.[296] Nevertheless, this would be contrary to the evident legislative intent in enacting a provision such as s. 13, and in Australia it has been doubted whether an equitable set-off is available against a claim for wages in the face of a statute to that effect.[297]

(3) Insolvency set-off

5.66 In any event, if the employer becomes bankrupt or goes into liquidation,[298] cross-demands between the employer and the employee, including a cross-demand in relation to wages, *prima facie* would come within the ambit of the insolvency set-off section.[299] The prevailing view of insolvency set-off is that it is automatic and self-executing,[300] and, provided that the requirements of the section are satisfied, a set-off should occur at the date of the bankruptcy or liquidation by force of law.[301] It would not be a case of the employer making a deduction from wages.

---

[292] *New Centurion Trust v Welch* [1990] ICR 383, 386 (EAT).

[293] The prohibition extends to an attempt by an employer to set off a sum which is otherwise recoverable by the employer from the employee as a mistaken payment. See *In re A Company (No. 005174 of 1999)* [2000] 1 WLR 502. In New South Wales, compare the Industrial Relations Act 1996, ss. 118 and 120, which restrict deductions from remuneration (s 118) and set-offs in any proceedings by an employee against the employer to recover remuneration (s 120). However, the restrictions are limited to defined circumstances involving the supply of goods or services to the employee. See *Rodenstock v Leahy* [2002] NSWSC 957 at [40].

[294] See paras 4.29–4.57 above.

[295] See para. 4.30 above.

[296] See paras 5.101–5.106 below.

[297] Macken, O'Grady, Sappideen and Warburton, *The Law of Employment* (5th edn, 2002), 294–5; *Conti Sheffield Real Estate v Brailey* (1992) 48 IR 1, 7 (WA Industrial Relations Commission).

[298] Or, in England, if the employer is a company in administration where the administrator, being authorized to make a distribution, has given notice that he proposes to make it. See the Insolvency Rules 1986, r. 2.85, and para. 6.124 below.

[299] For bankruptcy see the Insolvency Act 1986, s. 323, and for company liquidation the Insolvency Rules 1986, r. 4.90. See generally paras 6.01–6.19 below.

[300] See paras 6.119–6.146 below.

[301] *Secretary of State for Employment v Wilson* [1996] IRLR 330 (Employment Appeal Tribunal). Similarly, a cross-demand available to an employer against an employee should be able to provide a ground for setting aside a statutory demand served on the employer for non-payment of wages as a prelude to a bankruptcy petition. In Australia, see *Lighting Sciences Australasia Pty Ltd v Southgate* (1997) 15 ACLC 632 (statutory demand served on company); *Kwik & Swift Co Pty Ltd v Shawyer* [2002] WASC 14; *Rodenstock v Leahy* [2002] NSWSC 957 at [41]–[43].

E. Landlord and Tenant

(1) Equitable set-off

At one time it was thought that special considerations applied to a landlord's claim for rent, **5.67**
in that a tenant could not raise an unliquidated cross-claim against the landlord, for example for breach of an obligation to repair, as a defence to an action by the landlord against the
tenant for payment of arrears of rent.[302] Whether indeed that view ever had a solid foundation in equity may be doubted. Thus, in *Beasley v Darcy*[303] a landlord had served the tenant
with an ejectment for non-payment of rent and duly recovered possession, but the tenant
obtained an injunction restoring him to possession on the basis of a cross-claim in damages
against the landlord for damage suffered as a result of timber on the demised land being cut
down and carried away.[304] But whatever the position formerly was, a tenant's liability to pay
rent is now regarded as being no different in kind to other forms of indebtedness as regards
set-off, so that an equitable set-off may proceed if the tenant's cross-demand is sufficiently
closely connected with his or her liability to pay rent.[305] The principle was confirmed
in *British Anzani (Felixstowe) Ltd v International Marine Management (UK) Ltd.*[306]
The plaintiff had a leasehold interest in a plot of land. It agreed with the defendant that it
would construct a warehouse on part of the land, after which it would grant an underlease

---

[302] *Hart v Rogers* [1916] 1 KB 646; *Fong v Cilli* (1968) 11 FLR 495; *Galambos & Son Pty Ltd v McIntyre*
(1974) 5 ACTR 10, 24–5; *Chatfield v Elmstone Resthouse Ltd* [1975] 2 NZLR 269; *Knockholt Pty Ltd v Graff*
[1975] Qd R 88, 91; *Reid v Hipkiss* (2001) 10 BPR 19,305 at [14]–[16]; *Halsbury's Laws of England* (3rd edn,
1960) vol. 34, 406–7, para. 705. See also the reference to rent in *Bim Kemi AB v Blackburn Chemicals Ltd*
[2001] 2 Lloyd's Rep 93 at [38] (referred to in *Geldof Metaalconstructie NV v Simon Carves Ltd* [2010] EWCA
Civ 667 at [43] point (iii)), and *A. B. Contractors Ltd v Flaherty Brothers Ltd* (1978) 16 BLR 8, 12 in relation
to a stay of execution. In *Taylor v Webb* [1937] 2 KB 283, du Parcq J held that the landlord in that case was
not absolved from his obligation to repair because of the tenant's non-payment of rent. Scrutton J in *Hart v
Rogers* was influenced by *Surplice v Farnsworth* (1844) 7 Man & G 576, 135 ER 232, but in truth questions of
equitable set-off were not considered in that case. Compare *IRM Pacific Pty Ltd v Nudgegrove Pty Ltd* [2008]
QSC 195 at [13] in relation to a chattel lease.
[303] (1800) 2 Sch & Lef 403n, explained in *Rawson v Samuel* (1841) Cr & Ph 161, 179, 41 ER 451,
458–9.
[304] See also *O'Connor v Spaight* (1804) 1 Sch & Lef 305 (explained in *Rawson v Samuel* (1841) Cr & Ph
161, 179, 41 ER 451, 459 and *South Eastern Railway Co v Brogden* (1850) 3 Mac & G 8, 24–5, 42 ER 163,
170), in which Lord Redesdale granted an injunction to restrain an action for ejectment so that an account
could be taken of the various dealings between the landlord and the tenant, the justification for equitable relief
being that the account was too complicated to be taken at law. Compare *O'Mahony v Dickson* (1805) 2 Sch &
Lef 400.
[305] In addition to the cases referred to below, see *Melville v Grapelodge Developments Ltd* (1978) 39 P &
CR 179; *BICC Plc v Burndy Corporation* [1985] 1 Ch 232, 249; *Lambert Pty Ltd v Papadatos Pty Ltd* (1991)
5 ACSR 468, 471; *Gibb Australia Pty Ltd v Cremor Pty Ltd* (1992) 108 FLR 129; *MEK Nominees Pty Ltd v
Billboard Entertainments Pty Ltd* (1993) V Conv R 54–468; *Televantos v McCulloch* [1991] 1 EGLR 123;
Connaught Restaurants Ltd v Indoor Leisure Ltd [1994] 1 WLR 501; *Liangis Investments Pty Ltd v Daplyn
Pty Ltd* (1994) 117 FLR 28, 36. See also *Filross Securities Ltd v Midgeley* [1998] 3 EGLR 43 (service charge
payable as additional rent). In *Coba Industries Ltd v Millie's Holdings (Canada) Ltd* [1985] 6 WWR 14 a cross-
claim for damages for repudiating a lease was held to give rise to an equitable set-off. In relation to a chattel
lease, see *IRM Pacific Pty Ltd v Nudgegrove Pty Ltd* [2008] QSC 195 and *ACG Acquisition XX LLC v Olympic
Airlines SA* [2010] EWHC 923 (Comm) at [52] (aircraft lease).
[306] [1980] 1 QB 137. In Australia, see *Bennett v Excelsior Land, Investment and Building Co Ltd* (1893) 14
NSWR (Eq) 179, 185.

to the defendant. Under the terms of the agreement, the plaintiff was obliged to make good any defects which appeared in the floor of the warehouse. The building was completed and a sub-lease entered into. The plaintiff subsequently sued the defendant for arrears of rent, whereupon the defendant raised as a defence a cross-demand against the plaintiff for breach of the agreement to repair defects in the floor. Forbes J held that there was a sufficiently close connection between the demands to give rise to an equitable set-off, notwithstanding that the cross-demand did not arise out of the lease itself, but rather pursuant to the original agreement.[307]

5.68 Equitable set-off against rent has been recognized in the case of a breach of a covenant to repair or other similar undertaking[308] and a breach of a covenant for quiet enjoyment.[309] It has been suggested that the set-off is available in the case of any cross-claim arising out of the provisions of the lease and the operation of the lease.[310] Under modern formulations of the principle governing the availability of equitable set-off, a cross-claim arising out of the same contract as the claim would ordinarily give rise to an equitable set-off, but it is still the case that there is no universal principle that cross-claims arising out of the same contract

---

[307] See also *Melville v Grapelodge Developments Ltd* (1978) 39 P & CR 179 (covenant to repair contained in a separate letter); *Grant v NZMC Ltd* [1989] 1 NZLR 8 (collateral contract); *Edlington Properties Ltd v J. H. Fenner & Co Ltd* [2006] 1 WLR 1583 at [4] (breach of building obligations under an agreement for a lease); *Lotteryking Ltd v AMEC Properties Ltd* [1995] 2 EGLR 13 (criticized on another ground in the *Edlington Properties* case at [55]–[60]). Compare *Hamilton Ice Arena Ltd v Perry Developments Ltd* [2002] 1 NZLR 309, in which the demands were insufficiently connected, and *Blacksheep Productions Pty Ltd v Waks* [2008] NSWSC 488 at [23] (tenant agreed to pay rent in a deed of settlement consequent upon a mediation, and a cross-claim by the tenant pursuant to a lease entered into after the settlement).

[308] In addition to the *British Anzani* case, see *Melville v Grapelodge Developments Ltd* (1978) 39 P & CR 179; *Filross Securities Ltd v Midgeley* [1998] 3 EGLR 43; *Muscat v Smith* [2003] 1 WLR 2853; *Edlington Properties Ltd v J. H. Fenner & Co Ltd* [2006] 1 WLR 1583 at [4] (breach of a building obligation); *Batshita International (Pte) Ltd v Lim Eng Hock Peter* [1997] 1 SLR 241 (Sing CA). In Australia, see *Knockholt Pty Ltd v Graff* [1975] Qd R 88 (explained in Weir, 'A tenant's right of set-off' (1994) 68 *Australian Law Journal* 857, 863–5); *Re Partnership Pacific Securities Ltd* [1994] 1 Qd R 410, 421–4 (breach of covenant relating to refurbishment of the premises); *Mirvac Hotels Pty Ltd v 333 Collins St. Pty Ltd* (Vic SC, Byrne J, 20 December 1994, BC9401396); *Carrathool Hotel Pty Ltd v Scutti* [2005] NSWSC 401 at [61]. In *Sloan Stanley Estate Trustees v Barribal* [1994] 2 EGLR 8, Balcombe LJ (at 11) was prepared to accept that a tenant's right to be reimbursed by the landlord for a rate paid under the Land Drainage Act 1976 could be the subject of an equitable set-off against rent. See also the formulation adopted in *Hamilton Ice Arena Ltd v Perry Developments Ltd* [2002] 1 NZLR 309, 318–19.

[309] *Connaught Restaurants Ltd v Indoor Leisure Ltd* [1994] 1 WLR 501 (see at 504) (flooding); *MEK Nominees Pty Ltd v Billboard Entertainments Pty Ltd* (1993) V Conv R 54–468; *Liangis Investments Pty Ltd v Daplyn Pty Ltd* (1994) 117 FLR 28, 36; *Filross Securities Ltd v Midgeley* [1998] 3 EGLR 43; *John Smith & Co (Edinburgh) Ltd v Hill* [2010] EWHC 1016 (Ch) at [24]–[25]; *Saratoga Integration Pty Ltd v Canjs Pty Ltd* (2010) 78 ACSR 600 at [39] (breach of covenant for quiet enjoyment and claim for wrongful detention of tenant's chattels). See also *Khan v Islington LBC* [1999] EWCA Civ 1546, in which a tenant's entitlement to a home loss payment under the Land Compensation Act 1973 consequent upon an order for possession made against the tenant was set off in equity against arrears of rent.

[310] *Altonwood Ltd v Crystal Palace FC (2000) Ltd* [2005] EWHC 292 (Ch) at [32]. See also the reference in *Edlington Properties Ltd v J. H. Fenner & Co Ltd* [2006] 1 WLR 1583 at [4] (CA) to a breach of the provisions of the lease. A cross-claim against a landlord in negligence or for breach of statutory duty in relation to a fire which damaged the leased premises should be capable of giving rise to an equitable set-off against future rent since it affects the future operation of the lease. See *Clambake Pty Ltd v Tipperary Projects Pty Ltd (No. 3)* [2009] WASC 52 at [161]–[163]. At [160], Heenan J said that a cross-claim in nuisance in relation to such a fire would not impeach a claim for rent, *sed quaere*. In any event, Heenan J considered (at [163]–[169]) that a set-off was not available against unpaid rent for periods *before* the fire, though there is authority suggesting the contrary. See para. 4.123 above.

may be set against one another in all circumstances.[311] It should not therefore suffice that the cross-claim arises out of the provisions of the lease. The point is illustrated by the New South Wales decision in *Phoenix Commercial Enterprises v City of Canada Bay Council*.[312] A local council had leased land to the plaintiff to be used for the purpose of erecting advertising structures. The leases contained a provision to the effect that, if the council approved the erection of a general advertising structure on other land within the council's local government area, it would be liable to pay an amount by way of compensation to the plaintiff fixed by reference to the rental. Subsequently, the council approved the erection of other advertising structures, thereby triggering the operation of the provision. The claim for rent and the cross-claim for compensation both arose out of the leases, but it was held that the circumstances did not give rise to an equitable set-off against the rent. The council's liability to pay compensation was not a consequence of a breach of the lease (there being no promise or undertaking by the council not to approve other advertising structures), and the physical enjoyment or use of the demised land for which the rent was payable was unaffected. Moreover, the lease provided for interest on both the amount payable by the council and on unpaid rent, but at different rates. This suggested that the claims were separate.[313]

In the *Phoenix Commercial Enterprises* case, the court emphasized the lack of any effect on the use and physical enjoyment of the demised premises. Earlier, Blackburne J considered a suggested limitation on the scope of the set-off in similar terms in *Star Rider Ltd v Inntreprenneur Pub Co*.[314] Counsel had submitted that equitable set-off against a landlord's claim for outstanding rent is confined to a claim which relates to the quality of occupation of the demised premises. Blackburne J said that he was unwilling to attempt a definition of what must be established in order to give rise to an equitable set-off against unpaid rent, but that he would ordinarily expect the cross-claim to be of that nature. This is similar to the position that has been said to apply in the case of a time charter of a ship, that equitable set-off is confined to cases where the shipowner has wrongly deprived the charterer of the use of the ship or has prejudiced the charterer in the use of it.[315] Subsequently, however, the Court of Appeal in *Courage Ltd v Crehan*[316] rejected the proposition that equitable set-off against rent is limited to claims affecting the tenant's physical use or occupation of the premises, Morritt LJ (who gave the judgment of the court) commenting that, while the connection referred to is likely to be sufficient, it should not in all cases be necessary.[317] For example, if (as in that case) the lease required the tenant to carry on a particular business with the landlord, he could see no reason why cross-claims arising out of the conduct of the business should not be set off against rent. In support of a broader view, Morritt LJ referred to the decision of the New Zealand Court of Appeal in *Grant v NZMC Ltd*.[318] In that case

5.69

---

[311] See para. 4.91 above.
[312] [2009] NSWSC 17 (White J) (appeal dismissed on other grounds: [2010] NSWCA 64).
[313] [2009] NSWSC 17 at [91].
[314] [1998] 1 EGLR 53, 56.
[315] *Federal Commerce & Navigation Co Ltd v Molena Alpha Inc* [1978] 1 QB 927, 976 (Lord Denning). See paras 5.12–5.13 above.
[316] [1999] 2 EGLR 145 I (Morritt, Schiemann and Mance LJJ).
[317] [1999] 2 EGLR 145, 156.
[318] [1989] 1 NZLR 8.

an equitable set-off was allowed against rent in circumstances where tenants were induced to enter into the lease by a collateral contract with the lessor pursuant to which the lessor agreed to refer business to the tenants, and the lessor breached that agreement. The point is also illustrated by the later decision of the Court of Appeal in *Fuller v Happy Shopper Markets Ltd*,[319] where a tenant liable for unpaid rent was allowed an equitable set-off in respect of a claim for earlier overpayments of rent under the lease.[320] On the other hand, a set-off was denied in *Courage Ltd v Crehan*.[321] The tenant of a public house was sued for arrears of rent. The lease contained a 'beer tie'[322] that was alleged to have infringed (the former) art. 85 of the EC Treaty. The Court of Appeal considered that the connection between the claim for rent and any claim in damages that may have resulted from the breach[323] was tenuous and not such as to support a set-off. Of particular significance was the circumstance that art. 85 did not avoid one tie in isolation from other similar ties. The avoidance of one tie arose from the combined effect of that and other similar ties in foreclosing the market to outsiders, and the other ties which were necessary to avoid the tie in the present case had no connection with the tenant's obligation to pay rent. Further, the invalidity of the tie did not affect the validity of the lease or the covenant to pay rent. Therefore the right of the landlord to the rent was not impeached by the cross-claim.

5.70 The *Star Rider* case concerned a similar fact situation to that in issue in *Courage Ltd v Crehan*. In similarly denying a set-off, Blackburne J commented that, at most, the tie affected the extent to which the plaintiff was able to derive profit from the use of the premises. This suggests that a cross-claim based upon conduct which merely affected the profit that the tenant could derive from the premises does not suffice for an equitable set-off.[324] However, a general proposition expressed in those terms would not represent the law. The situations referred to by the Court of Appeal in *Courage Ltd v Crehan*[325] in which it was accepted that a set-off may arise, being the circumstances in issue in *Grant v NZMC Ltd*[326] and the case

---

[319] [2001] 1 WLR 1681. See also para. 4.63 above.

[320] Compare *Ory & Ory v Betamore Pty Ltd* (1993) 60 SASR 393, where the unpaid rent was claimed by a mortgagee in possession, as opposed to the landlord/mortgagor who was the recipient of the overpayment. See paras 17.72–17.95 below.

[321] See also *Star Rider Ltd v Inntreprenneur Pub Co* [1998] 1 EGLR 53; *Gibbs Mew Plc v Gemmell* [1999] 1 EGLR 43, 50.

[322] Pursuant to the tie, the tenant had to purchase all or most of its beer for sale in the premises from the landlord or a brewer nominated by the landlord at prices prescribed by the supplier.

[323] The question whether damages could be claimed where there was a breach of art. 85 was the subject of a reference to the European Court of Justice, which held that an individual could in principle claim damages for loss caused to him or her by a contract which was contrary to the article. See *Courage Ltd v Crehan* [2002] QB 507.

[324] Compare *Phoenix Commercial Enterprises v City of Canada Bay Council* [2009] NSWSC 17, discussed at para. 5.68 above. The purpose of the provision for payment of compensation by the council was to provide exclusivity for the plaintiff's advertising structures in the local government area, apparently on the basis (see at [64]) that this enhanced their value to the plaintiff. White J in his judgment noted (at [90]) that the erection of other advertising structures meant that the plaintiff could not offer exclusive advertising signage to a licensee, but considered that this did not suffice to support a set-off. However, the plaintiff already had a fixed licence agreement in place with another party (Boyer) for use of its advertising structures, so that the council's conduct in approving other structures (as opposed to the council's conduct in determining the leases for non-payment of rent) would not appear to have affected the plaintiff's profitability.

[325] See para. 5.69 above.

[326] [1989] 1 NZLR 8.

of a lease which required the tenant to carry on a particular business with the landlord and a cross-claim had arisen out of the conduct of the business, illustrate the point. In addition, there is early authority which suggests that a set-off may be available if the landlord's conduct affected the tenant's ability to get rent from the land, which is a function of profitability. In *Beasley v Darcy*[327] a landlord brought an action against the tenant for ejectment for non-payment of rent. The tenant applied for relief from forfeiture, based upon a cross-claim against the landlord for damages occasioned by cutting down and carrying away timber on the demised land. The House of Lords affirmed a decree by the Lord Chancellor of Ireland[328] granting the tenant relief from forfeiture on condition that he paid what was due for rent after deducting the damages. This was a case in which there was physical damage to the land. Nevertheless, the point that has been emphasized in later discussions of the case is the effect of the conduct on the tenant's ability to pay rent from the land. In *O'Mahony v Dickson*[329] Lord Redesdale said that the money that was due to the tenant in *Beasley v Darcy* 'ought, in point of conscience, under the circumstances, to have been paid by the landlord, in order to enable the tenant to pay his rent; the nature of the demand for damages, *supposing a loss by the tenant of the produce of the land*, arising from the act of the landlord'.[330] Similarly, Bramwell B in *Stimson v Hall*,[331] justified the decision on the ground that the landlord 'had committed a trespass on the land which rendered it of less value, and prevented the tenant, to a certain extent, from getting the rent out of it'.

Where rent is payable periodically, the question may arise whether a cross-claim against the landlord which arises in one period may be set off against rent due for another period. The question of set-off in relation to periodic payments was considered earlier.[332] **5.71**

The discussion above relates to equitable set-off of unliquidated cross-demands. If the tenant's cross-demand is for a liquidated sum, a set-off against a claim for rent may proceed on the basis of mutual debts under the Statutes of Set-off[333] as a defence to an action for payment. **5.72**

(2) Forfeiture for non-payment of rent

Equitable set-off and the right of set-off conferred by the Statutes of Set-off differ in a fundamental respect. Equitable set-off is a substantive defence which may be set up by a person as an immediate answer to liability.[334] The Statutes, on the other hand, only provided a procedural defence, in the sense that prior to judgment for a set-off the rights and **5.73**

---

[327] (1800) 2 Sch & Lef 403n. The case is discussed in *British Anzani (Felixstowe) Ltd v International Marine Management (UK) Ltd* [1980] 1 QB 137, 149–51.

[328] Lord Clare.

[329] (1805) 2 Sch & Lef 400.

[330] (1805) 2 Sch & Lef 400, 412–13 (emphasis added).

[331] (1857) 1 H & N 831, 835–6, 156 ER 1436, 1438.

[332] See paras 4.120–4.124 above.

[333] *Gower v Hunt* (1734) Barnes 290, 291, 94 ER 920; *Brown v Holyoak* (1734), referred to in *Hutchison v Sturges* (1741) Willes 261, 263, 125 ER 1163, 1164; *Cleghorn v Durrant* (1858) 31 LTOS 235. See also *Hamp v Jones* (1840) 9 LJ Ch 258 (cross-demand for rent set off against a judgment obtained by the tenant against the landlord and another). Compare *Samways v Eldsley* (1676) 2 Mod 73, 86 ER 949, which was decided before the enactment of the Statutes of Set-off. See generally ch. 2 above.

[334] See paras 4.29–4.57 above.

obligations consequent upon being a creditor or a debtor still attach.[335] This distinction may be important in the context of forfeiture and re-entry for non-payment of rent. Because of the substantive nature of equitable set-off, a landlord is not permitted to proceed on the basis that the tenant has defaulted in payment of rent to the extent that the tenant has available that form of set-off. As a result, the landlord would not be justified in claiming forfeiture, and the tenant would have a defence to an action for possession.[336] However, given that the defence under the Statutes is merely procedural, a landlord should be entitled to assert that a tenant relying on this defence nevertheless has defaulted in payment of rent, and therefore under the contract the landlord has a ground for forfeiting the lease. The question then should be whether the court in its discretion would grant relief from forfeiture.[337]

(3) Distress

5.74 Traditionally, a right of set-off under the Statutes of Set-off has not been regarded as a ground sufficient to protect a tenant against a landlord levying distress for rent.[338] The Statutes only provided a procedural defence to an action at law,[339] whereas distress is a form of self-help remedy to which a landlord is entitled without recourse to legal process. On the other hand, equitable set-off is a substantive defence which may be set up independently of an order of the court,[340] in the sense that the circumstances render it unconscionable for a creditor to proceed on the basis that the debtor has defaulted in payment to the extent of the set-off.[341] Therefore, when a tenant is possessed of a cross-claim that gives rise to an equitable set-off, the landlord should not be permitted to assert that the tenant is in arrears in payment of rent so as to entitle the landlord to distrain for non-payment. Consistent with that view, the Court of Appeal in *Eller v Grovecrest Investments Ltd*[342] granted an

---

[335] See paras 2.34–2.52 above.

[336] See e.g. *Televantos v McCulloch* [1991] 1 EGLR 123 and *Beasley v Darcy* (1800) 2 Sch & Lef 403n. See also *British Anzani (Felixstowe) Ltd v International Marine Management (UK) Ltd* [1980] 1 QB 137, where the question whether the circumstances gave rise to an equitable set-off was determined as a separate issue, and *Eagle Star Nominees Ltd v Merril* [1982] VR 557, 560–1, which concerned a claim for possession of land by an unpaid vendor. Compare *Logan v Director of Housing* (2004) 13 Tas SR 324 at [18], where the substantive nature of equitable set-off was not considered, and the doubt expressed in *Lambert Pty Ltd v Papadatos Pty Ltd* (1991) 5 ACSR 468, 471. Alternatively, an equitable set-off may provide grounds for an interlocutory injunction to restrain re-entry by a landlord. See e.g. *Meade v Sansom Nominees Pty Ltd* [2001] WASC 124.

[337] See the Senior Courts Act 1981, s. 38(1), and *Belgravia Insurance Co Ltd v Meah* [1964] 1 QB 436, 443. Compare *BICC Plc v Burndy Corporation* [1985] 1 Ch 232, which concerned an action for specific performance of an agreement to transfer property. See paras 2.58–2.62 above.

[338] *Absolon v Knight* (1743) Barnes 450, 94 ER 998; *Townrow v Benson* (1818) 3 Madd 203, 56 ER 484. See also *Sapsford v Fletcher* (1792) 4 TR 511, 512–13, 514, 100 ER 1147, 1148, 1149; *Andrew v Hancock* (1819) 1 Brod & B 37, 43, 46, 47, 129 ER 637, 639–41; *Willson v Davenport* (1833) 5 Car & P 531, 172 ER 1085; *Pratt v Keith* (1864) 33 LJ Ch 528; *British Anzani (Felixstowe) Ltd v International Marine Management (UK) Ltd* [1980] 1 QB 137, 149. Distress for rent has been abolished in some jurisdictions. See e.g. the Conveyancing Act 1919 (NSW), s. 177A, and Sykes and Walker, *The Law of Securities* (5th edn, 1993), 285–8.

[339] See paras 2.34–2.39 above.

[340] See *SL Sethia Liners Ltd v Naviagro Maritime Corporation (The Kostas Melas)* [1981] 1 Lloyd's Rep 18, 26.

[341] See para. 4.30 above.

[342] [1995] QB 272. See also *Fuller v Happy Shopper Markets Ltd* [2001] 1 WLR 1681. Compare *Halsbury's Laws of England* (4th edn reissue, 2006) vol. 27(1), 273 para. 266, and the earlier comments of Neill LJ (one of the judges in the Court of Appeal in *Eller*) in *Connaught Restaurants Ltd v Indoor Leisure Ltd* [1994] 1 WLR 501, 511. Note also *Townrow v Benson* (1818) 3 Madd 203, 56 ER 484, in which Sir John Leach said that a court of equity would follow the law in relation to the principle that a set-off does not defeat

injunction to a tenant to restrain the landlord from proceeding against the tenant's goods because of an equitable set-off. However, the substantive nature of the defence was not referred to, and there are indications that the court would have been sympathetic to the view that the availability of a procedural defence of set-off under the Statutes should have the same effect. Thus, Hoffmann LJ[343] said that: 'It is contrary to principle that a landlord should be able to recover more by distress than he can by action',[344] which would appear to be equally applicable when a tenant has a defence under the Statutes to an action for payment of rent. Hoffmann LJ concluded his judgment by commenting that 'this court is free to hold that set-off is available against a claim to levy distress',[345] without drawing a distinction between the various forms of set-off. However, in his later judgment in *Aectra Refining and Marketing Inc v Exmar NV*,[346] Hoffmann LJ appeared to distinguish between equitable set-off and set-off under the Statutes in this context, so as, apparently, to re-assert the traditional position in relation to the Statutes. More recently, Lightman J affirmed that view in *Fuller v Happy Shopper Markets Ltd*.[347]

(4) Payment in satisfaction of an obligation of the landlord

Whatever the position in relation to a landlord's right to levy distress where the tenant is entitled to a set-off under the Statutes, it is necessary to distinguish the cases which have held that, where a sub-tenant is compelled by the superior landlord to pay a sum owing by the sub-tenant's immediate landlord for unpaid rent or other like charges, to the extent of the payment the immediate landlord cannot levy distress for unpaid rent.[348] The principle applies where the sub-tenant's payment was such as to give rise to a right of action against the immediate landlord for money paid to his use,[349] but the sub-tenant's right nevertheless is not characterized as a set-off.[350] When a sub-tenant is compelled to make a payment to the superior landlord which ought to have been made by the immediate landlord, the sub-tenant is considered as having been authorized by the immediate landlord to apply rent which is either due or accruing due to the immediate landlord in this manner.[351] Accordingly, the basis upon which the sub-tenant impugns a subsequent attempt by the immediate landlord to distrain for unpaid rent is that the rent alleged to be outstanding in fact has been paid.[352]

5.75

---

an entitlement to levy distress, though that was in the context of whether equity would grant an injunction to restrain the landlord from levying distress on the basis of a set-off under the Statutes, as opposed to whether the substantive form of equitable set-off under discussion is subject to the same principle.

[343] Waite LJ agreed with Hoffmann LJ's judgment.
[344] [1995] QB 272, 278. See also Neill LJ at 280.
[345] [1995] QB 272, 278.
[346] [1994] 1 WLR 1634, 1650.
[347] [2001] 1 WLR 1681.
[348] See e.g. *Sapsford v Fletcher* (1792) 4 TR 511, 100 ER 1147; *Carter v Carter* (1829) 5 Bing 406, 130 ER 1118.
[349] *Graham v Allsopp* (1848) 3 Ex 186, 198, 199, 154 ER 809, 814–15.
[350] Compare Wood, *English and International Set-off* (1989), 130.
[351] *Graham v Allsopp* (1848) 3 Ex 186, 198, 154 ER 809, 814; *Jones v Morris* (1849) 3 Ex 742, 746–7, 154 ER 1044, 1046–7.
[352] *Sapsford v Fletcher* (1792) 4 TR 511, 100 ER 1147; *Graham v Allsopp* (1848) 3 Ex 186, 198, 154 ER 809, 814; *Jones v Morris* (1849) 3 Ex 742, 154 ER 1044.

5.76 The principle is not confined to sub-tenancies. It applies generally to payments made to encumbrancers having a title paramount to that of the landlord.[353] Thus, it has been held to apply when a tenant paid sums owing by his or her landlord to a mortgagee or to a rent-chargee with power to distrain.[354] Indeed, in a passage which Millett LJ later quoted with approval in *Mortgage Corporation Ltd v Ubah*,[355] Forbes J, in the *British Anzani* case,[356] expressed the principle broadly in terms of a payment by the tenant 'in respect of some obligation of the landlord connected with the land demised'. To a like effect, Millett LJ, in the *Mortgage Corporation* case,[357] spoke in terms of 'expenditure which it was the landlord's legal obligation to defray', referring by way of example to the payment of insurance. Further, while the principle has been expressed in terms of a payment made under compulsion,[358] in that same passage Forbes J referred instead to a payment made at the 'request' of the landlord. This is consistent with the explanation of the principle when expressed in terms of compulsion, that a landlord is presumed to have authorized the tenant to apply rent in satisfaction of paramount claims on the land.[359] In the early case of *Taylor v Beal*,[360] to which Forbes J referred, the report states that part of the rent in issue was paid by the tenant to a rentchargee 'by the commandment of the lessor', and this was held to provide a defence to an action by the lessor for payment of rent.

(5) Recoupment

5.77 A principle which is analogous to, but which nevertheless is distinct from, set-off may apply where leased premises have fallen into disrepair and responsibility for the repairs is on the landlord.[361] In such a case, the tenant may expend money in executing the repairs and recoup him or herself from future payments of rent or from arrears of rent.[362] This is not bound up with technical rules of set-off, but rather it is an ancient common law right of recoupment which entitles the tenant to treat the amount expended on repairs as payment

---

[353] *Graham v Allsopp* (1848) 3 Ex 186, 198, 154 ER 809, 814; *Jones v Morris* (1849) 3 Ex 742, 746–7, 154 ER 1044, 1046–7.

[354] *Taylor v Zamira* (1816) 6 Taunt 524, 128 ER 1138 (rentcharge); *Johnson v Jones* (1839) 9 Ad & E 809, 112 ER 1421 (mortgage). See also *Taylor v Beal* (1591) Cro Eliz 222, 223, 78 ER 478, 479 (rentcharge), *Doe v Hare* (1833) 2 C & M 145, 149 ER 709 (claim for mesne profits). Compare *Boodle v Cambell* (1844) 7 Man & G 386, 135 ER 161.

[355] (1996) 73 P & CR 500, 507.

[356] [1980] 1 QB 137, 147.

[357] (1996) 73 P & CR 500, 507–8.

[358] *Graham v Allsopp* (1848) 3 Ex 186, 198, 154 ER 809, 814; *Jones v Morris* (1849) 3 Ex 742, 746–7, 154 ER 1044, 1046–7.

[359] See para. 5.75 above.

[360] (1591) Cro Eliz 222, 78 ER 478.

[361] The landlord must be under an obligation to repair. See *Batiste v Lenin* (2002) 11 BPR 20,403, [2002] NSWCA 316 at [47]–[49] and *Waters v Weigall* (1795) 2 Anst 575, 145 ER 971 (below). The cases have concerned breach of a landlord's covenant to repair, but compare the broader statement of the principle in *Muscat v Smith* [2003] 1 WLR 2853 at [9] in terms of money expended by a tenant on discharging the landlord's covenants.

[362] See generally Rank, 'Repairs in lieu of rent' (1976) 40 Conv (NS) 196; Waite, 'Repairs and deduction from rent' [1981] *The Conveyancer* 199. The money must be expended. A tenant is not justified in withholding rent in an effort to compel the landlord to address his or her grievances. See *Camden Nominees Ltd v Forcey* [1940] 1 Ch 352. *Quaere* whether recoupment is confined to rent, or whether it may extend to other moneys payable to a landlord, such as an obligation to pay outgoings. See *Batiste v Lenin* (2002) 10 BPR 19,441, [2002] NSWSC 233 at [102].

of rent.[363] As early as 1591, Gawdy J in *Taylor v Beal*[364] is reported to have said[365] that: 'the law giveth this liberty to the lessee to expend the rent in reparations, for he shall be otherwise at great mischief, for the house may fall upon his head before it be repaired; and therefore the law alloweth him to repair it, and recoupe the rent.'[366] There is surprisingly little case law on this right, but its existence appears to have been accepted in 1795 in *Waters v Weigall*.[367] The tenant in that case had covenanted to keep the premises in repair 'accidents by fire and tempest excepted'. The house was damaged by tempest and, being in want of emergency repairs, the tenant repaired it himself in order to prevent further mischief.[368] The landlord refused to allow the tenant to deduct the cost of repairs from the rent, and brought an action for payment of rent. The tenant then filed a bill in the equity side of the Exchequer, seeking relief in the form of a right to retain the amount of the repairs out of the rent. It appears from the report of the argument in support of the bill that the tenant proceeded in equity because there was no express covenant in the lease that the landlord was liable to repair in the case that happened, and it was thought that consequently the tenant did not have a cross-claim at law against the landlord.[369] For that reason, MacDonald CB held that the tenant similarly was not entitled to relief in equity. Nevertheless, it seems clear that in the opinion of the Chief Baron a right of recoupment would have been available if the landlord had been bound to repair in consequence of the accident that happened.[370]

The next reported occasion on which it appears that English courts were called upon to **5.78** consider the right of recoupment was in 1971, in *Lee-Parker v Izzet*.[371] Goff J in that case

---

[363] *Connaught Restaurants Ltd v Indoor Leisure Ltd* [1994] 1 WLR 501, 507 (Waite LJ), 511 (Neill LJ), referring to *Lee-Parker v Izzet* [1971] 1 WLR 1688, 1693 (Goff J); *Muscat v Smith* [2003] 1 WLR 2853 at [9] ('operate as a partial or a complete discharge') *Carrathool Hotel Pty Ltd v Scutti* [2005] NSWSC 401 at [62]; *Edlington Properties Ltd v J. H. Fenner & Co Ltd* [2006] 1 WLR 1583 at [53]–[54]. See also para. 17.93 below.

[364] (1591) Cro Eliz 222, 78 ER 478.

[365] Citing three cases from the Year Books, for which see Waite, 'Repairs and deduction from rent' [1981] *The Conveyancer* 199, 200–1.

[366] Clench J apparently agreed with the proposition that the tenant 'might well expend the rent in reparations', though he found against the tenant on a point of pleading. Fenner J, on the other hand, considered that the tenant had to bring a separate action.

[367] (1795) 2 Anst 575, 145 ER 971.

[368] It appears from the report of the subsequent proceedings at law in *Weigall v Waters* (1795) 6 TR 488, 101 ER 663 that: 'a violent tempest arose and threw down with great force and violence a stack of chimneys belonging to the house on the roof of the house . . . and damaged the house so much that it would soon have become uninhabitable, if he [the tenant] had not immediately repaired it.'

[369] See the subsequent proceedings at law in *Weigall v Waters* (1795) 6 TR 488, 101 ER 663.

[370] MacDonald CB referred in his judgment ((1795) 2 Anst 575, 576, 145 ER 971) to a right of 'set-off' against the demand for rent. However, the claim of the tenant appears to have been that he should be allowed to recoup or 'retain' his expenses from the rent otherwise payable to the landlord, rather than that a cross-demand constituted a defence to the landlord's demand for rent. The question appears to have been one concerning recoupment, or payment, rather than set-off.

[371] [1971] 1 WLR 1688. See also *British Anzani (Felixstowe) Ltd v International Marine Management (UK) Ltd* [1980] 1 QB 137, 146–9; *Muscat v Smith* [2003] 1 WLR 2853 at [9]. In Australia, see *Knockholt Pty Ltd v Graff* [1975] Qd R 88 and *Batiste v Lenin* (2002) 11 BPR 20,403, [2002] NSWCA 316 at [47]–[49]. The common law right of recoupment did not apply in the *British Anzani* case given that the tenants had not expended any money on repairs. However, they were entitled to an equitable set-off against the obligation to pay rent because of a cross-demand against the landlord for breach of the repair obligation. See also *Melville v Grapelodge Developments Ltd* (1978) 39 P & CR 179.

granted a declaration to tenants to the effect that, in so far as repairs carried out by the tenants were within the express or implied repairing covenants of the landlord, including those imported by s. 32(1) of the Housing Act 1961,[372] they were entitled to deduct[373] the proper cost from future payments of rent, and, moreover, to the extent of such proper costs they were not liable to be sued for the rent. Further, if a tenant with a right of recoupment has, to the extent of the sum expended, a defence to a claim for rent, the availability of the right should also provide an answer to a claim to distrain,[374] on the ground that the rent has been paid.[375] Subsequently, Megarry VC held in *Asco Developments Ltd v Gordon*[376] that a right of recoupment is available not only against future rent but also against arrears of rent.

5.79 A landlord must have information as to the existence of a defect in the premises, such as would put a reasonable man upon inquiry as to whether works of repair were needed, before an obligation arises to carry out the works.[377] The landlord's obligation is to effect the repairs within a reasonable time of receiving notice.[378] Consistent with that proposition, it has been said that the landlord must have notice of want of repair before the right of recoupment can be exercised.[379] This may give rise to difficulty in a situation in which the damage is such that emergency repairs are necessary in order to prevent the premises sustaining further damage. There is much to be said for the view that, in cases of emergency, the tenant should be able to effect repairs and recoup the expense from rent despite the absence of prior notice to the landlord.[380]

5.80 Forbes J in *British Anzani (Felixstowe) Ltd v International Marine Management (UK) Ltd*[381] suggested a limitation on the right of recoupment, that it must not be based upon a sum which is regarded as unliquidated damages. By this he meant that it must be in respect of a sum certain which has actually been paid, and of which, in addition, the quantum has either been acknowledged by the landlord or in some other way it can no longer be disputed by him. But, notwithstanding that Forbes J's suggestion has since been referred to with approval,[382] the better view is that there is no such limitation, and that, as long as the

---

[372] See now the Landlord and Tenant Act 1985, s. 11.

[373] In truth, 'deduct' seems an inaccurate description of the right. See para. 5.105 below.

[374] Distress for rent has been abolished in some jurisdictions. See e.g. the Conveyancing Act 1919 (NSW), s. 177A.

[375] There have been suggestions to this effect. See *Connaught Restaurants Ltd v Indoor Leisure Ltd* [1994] 1 WLR 501, 511; *Lee-Parker v Izzet* [1971] 1 WLR 1688, 1692–3. See also para. 17.93 below.

[376] (1978) 248 EG 683.

[377] *O'Brien v Robinson* [1973] AC 912, 928–30; *Gration v C. Gillan Investments Pty Ltd* [2005] 2 Qd R 267.

[378] *Chatfield v Elmstone Resthouse Ltd* [1975] 2 NZLR 269; *Andrews v Brewer* [1997] EWCA Civ 1029.

[379] *Lee-Parker v Izzet* [1971] 1 WLR 1688, 1693; *British Anzani (Felixstowe) Ltd v International Marine Management (UK) Ltd* [1980] 1 QB 137, 147–8; *Mortgage Corporation Ltd v Ubah* (1996) 73 P & CR 500, 507 (referring to the *British Anzani* case); *Andrews v Brewer* [1997] EWCA Civ 1029.

[380] Waite, 'Repairs and deduction from rent' [1981] *The Conveyancer* 199, 203–4, and see also the headnote to *Waters v Weigall* (1795) 2 Anst 575, 145 ER 971. Waite also suggested that, if the landlord has disappeared so that notice of disrepair is not possible, a tenant effecting repairs should not be deprived of a right of recoupment in respect of the expenditure incurred.

[381] [1980] 1 QB 137, 148.

[382] *Mortgage Corporation Ltd v Ubah* (1996) 73 P & CR 500, 507, and see also *Edlington Properties Ltd v J. H. Fenner & Co Ltd* [2006] 1 WLR 1583 at [53].

expenditure was properly incurred by the tenant,[383] it makes no difference that the quantum is disputed by the landlord.[384] Forbes J based the suggested limitation upon the judgment of Lord Kenyon CJ in *Weigall v Waters*.[385] *Weigall v Waters* was decided at common law, and was in respect of the same situation considered in the earlier proceedings in equity referred to above in *Waters v Weigall*. The landlord was suing for rent, and the tenant sought to set off his expenditure incurred in effecting the repairs. Lord Kenyon held against a set-off, *inter alia* on the ground that, if the landlord indeed was liable to repair the premises, the defendant's cross-demand would have had to be assessed by a jury and consequently it was for unliquidated damages. However, it is important to note that the only defence pleaded by the defendant was set-off, and a prerequisite to a set-off in an action at law under the Statutes of Set-off was mutual debts.[386] The defendant had not pleaded the alternative defence that he was entitled to recoup his expenditure from rent, and that this recoupment constituted payment of the rent.

F. Specific Performance

The question may arise whether a right of set-off constitutes a defence to an action for specific performance of a contract. In *Phipps v Child*,[387] the plaintiff and the defendant agreed that the defendant would purchase the plaintiff's interest in a colliery. The defendant failed to complete the purchase in accordance with the contract, whereupon the plaintiff sought an order for specific performance. The defendant argued that, as a result of dealings between the parties, the plaintiff was liable to him for a sum of money which should be set off against the purchase money. Sir Richard Kindersley VC rejected the defence, commenting: 'There may be a right in the Defendant to bring an action against the Plaintiff. But, if there is such a right, that is not a reason for non-performance of the contract.'[388] However, the decision, and the Vice Chancellor's comment, should be considered in the context that the monetary cross-demands in issue appear not to have been such as would have given rise to a set-off in an action for the price.[389]

5.81

This question of the availability of set-off as a defence to an action for specific performance came before the Court of Appeal in *BICC Plc v Burndy Corporation*.[390] The plaintiff and the defendant had traded together for a number of years in a joint enterprise. They decided to dissolve the relationship, and accordingly entered into a number of agreements.

5.82

---

[383] *Lee-Parker v Izzet* [1971] 1 WLR 1688, 1693; *Connaught Restaurants Ltd v Indoor Leisure Ltd* [1994] 1 WLR 501, 511.

[384] See Waite, 'Repairs and deduction from rent' [1981] *The Conveyancer* 199, 205–7, citing *Mason v Kerver* (1387) YB Barr, 11 Ri 2 f 242.

[385] (1795) 6 TR 488, 101 ER 663.

[386] See para. 2.14 above.

[387] (1857) 3 Drewry 709, 61 ER 1074.

[388] (1857) 3 Drewry 709, 715, 61 ER 1074, 1076.

[389] See also Spry, *Equitable Remedies* (8th edn, 2010), 177, and also *BICC Plc v Burndy Corporation* [1985] 1 Ch 232, 250, 257. The defendant's cross-demand appears to have been for an unliquidated sum, in which case a set-off would not have been available under the Statutes of Set-off. Moreover, there does not appear to have been a sufficient connection between the cross-demands to support an equitable set-off.

[390] [1985] 1 Ch 232.

One agreement provided for the continued sale of goods by the defendant to the plaintiff. According to a second agreement, the plaintiff was responsible for the processing and maintenance of the joint rights, and the defendant had to reimburse the plaintiff for half of any expenses thereby incurred. This second agreement further provided that, if either of the parties failed to fulfil its obligations under the agreement, the party not in default could require the party in default to assign to it the defaulter's interest in the joint rights. The plaintiff incurred expenses in relation to a number of joint rights and duly invoiced the defendant for half of that sum. When the defendant failed to make reimbursement within the stipulated time, the plaintiff claimed that it was entitled to an assignment of the defendant's interests in the joint rights pursuant to the second agreement, and brought an action seeking specific performance of the agreement. As a defence, the defendant argued that it had a right to set off against the sums owing by it the sums due to it from the plaintiff under the first agreement for the sale of goods. The form of set-off considered to be in issue was the right to set off mutual debts under the Statutes of Set-off.[391] It was not regarded as a case of equitable set-off. Dillon LJ, with whom Ackner LJ concurred, considered that statutory and equitable set-off both constitute a good defence to a claim for specific performance. That view would seem to be correct with respect to equitable set-off.[392] Equitable set-off is a substantive defence which may be invoked independently of an order of the court.[393] If a person has a money obligation under a contract but also has a cross-demand which is sufficiently closely connected to give rise to an equitable set-off, the other party to the contract could not in good conscience assert that moneys are due to it from the first person to the extent of the value of the cross-demand, in which case that other party should not be entitled to an order for specific performance when the right to the equitable relief sought depends upon a recognition of the existence of that very debt. However, this explanation would not extend to the Statutes of Set-off.[394] Unlike equitable set-off, the defence provided by the Statutes is procedural, in that the set-off depends for its effect upon a judgment. Prior to judgment for a set-off each of the parties is still indebted to the other, and the rights consequent upon being a creditor still attach, as do the obligations and liabilities consequent upon being a debtor.[395]

5.83 The third member of the Court of Appeal, Kerr LJ, similarly refused to grant specific performance, though he adopted a different approach. In his Lordship's opinion the existence of a right of set-off, whether legal or equitable, does not *per se* provide a defence to a claim for specific performance, though it does constitute a factor relevant to the exercise of the court's discretion in determining whether to grant the relief sought. The problem with this view, in so far as it applies to substantive equitable set-off, is that, if indeed the cross-demands are such that an equitable set-off would be available, it is difficult to see how

---

[391] See [1985] 1 Ch 232, 245, 249, 259.

[392] Longmore LJ's comments in *Saudi Arabian Monetary Agency v Dresdner Bank AG* [2005] 1 Lloyd's Rep 12 at [35] in relation to a cross-claim as a defence to an action for specific performance should not be considered as having had in contemplation the substantive form of equitable set-off.

[393] *SL Sethia Liners Ltd v Naviagro Maritime Corporation (The Kostas Melas)* [1981] 1 Lloyd's Rep 18, 26. See paras 4.29–4.30 above.

[394] Compare Dillon LJ at [1985] 1 Ch 232, 251.

[395] See paras 2.34–2.39 above.

a court could ever grant an order for specific performance without detracting from the substantive nature of the defence. On the other hand, there is much to commend Kerr LJ's analysis in relation to the availability of a statutory right of set-off upon an application for an order for specific performance. The better view is that it constitutes a factor which, along with other relevant circumstances, the court should take into consideration in the exercise of its discretion. Other cases support this approach.[396] In the case before him, Kerr LJ noted that the conduct of the plaintiff throughout the negotiations between the parties had been inconsistent with the applicability of the agreement for an assignment, which it suddenly sought to impose without any warning.[397] This factor, when combined with the defendant's claim for a set-off under the Statutes, led Kerr LJ to conclude that an order for specific performance was inappropriate.

In *BICC v Burndy*, set-off was raised as a defence to an application for an order for specific performance. Alternatively, the applicant for the order could assert a set-off. This could arise where the applicant's obligation under the contract is to pay money. In order to obtain specific performance the applicant must show that he or she is ready and willing to perform his or her own obligations under the contract, but because of an equitable set-off the applicant may assert that he or she need only tender a reduced amount, after taking into account the set-off, in order to satisfy that requirement. This issue is considered below.[398]   **5.84**

Consider that a vendor has entered into a contract to sell land to a purchaser, who happens   **5.85** to be separately indebted to the vendor, but the vendor becomes bankrupt before conveyance. In *Re Taylor, ex p Norvell*,[399] the Court of Appeal[400] held that the purchaser in such a case is entitled to specific performance of the contract on terms that the purchase price should be reduced to the extent of a set-off available to the purchaser pursuant to the set-off section in the insolvency legislation.[401] Buckley LJ in his judgment[402] noted that title had been accepted before the bankruptcy, so that, when the bankruptcy occurred, there was nothing to be done but for the purchaser to pay the money and the vendor to execute the conveyance. However, the preferred view was expressed by Cozens-Hardy MR,[403] that it was not material when title was accepted as long as a good title had in fact been made. A similar result should follow when the vendor is not bankrupt or in liquidation, so that the insolvency set-off section does not apply, but the purchaser has a cross-action which is available as an equitable set-off.[404]

---

[396] *Handley Page Ltd v Commissioners of Customs and Excise and Rockwell Machine Tool Company Ltd* [1970] 2 Lloyd's Rep 459 (in particular at 466); *Saudi Arabian Monetary Agency v Dresdner Bank AG* [2005] 1 Lloyd's Rep 12 at [35]. The *Saudi Arabian Monetary Agency* case concerned equitable set-off arising by analogy with the Statutes of Set-off where debts are mutual having regard to equitable rights. See para. 11.23 below. That form of equitable set-off is not substantive but has the same procedural operation as the Statutes. See paras 3.07–3.09 above.

[397] [1985] 1 Ch 232, 253.

[398] See para. 5.86 below.

[399] [1910] 1 KB 562.

[400] Cozens-Hardy MR and Buckley LJ, Fletcher Moulton LJ dissenting.

[401] See ch. 6 below.

[402] [1910] 1 KB 562, 580.

[403] [1910] 1 KB 562, 572.

[404] Compare *King v Poggioli* (1923) 32 CLR 222 (esp. Starke J at 248), in which equitable set-off was not considered. See *Eagle Star Nominees Ltd v Merril* [1982] VR 557, 560.

G. Set-off as a Sword

(1) Equitable set-off

5.86 It is sometimes said that set-off is a shield, not a sword,[405] an aphorism that, in Australia, has been said to have the same meaning in this context as it has in the case of equitable estoppel. In other words, it is capable of being used offensively, but whether or not it can be used offensively it is also capable of being pleaded as a ground for absolution, as a shield.[406] When a substantive defence of equitable set-off is in issue,[407] the set-off should be capable in an appropriate case of being used offensively. For example, an applicant for a decree of specific performance must show that he or she is ready and willing to perform his or her own essential obligations under the contract. If this involves the payment of money, the applicant should be entitled to assert that the liability in question is reduced because of an equitable set-off available against the defendant.[408] In that regard, in contracts for the sale of land where there is a deficiency in the quantity or quality of the estate agreed to be transferred, for example, because the vendor does not have title to part of the land,[409] or because the vendor's title is different to that which he or she represented,[410] or because the property deteriorated as a result of the vendor's neglect between the date of the contract and the date the purchaser obtained possession,[411] the purchaser may obtain an abatement in the price by way of compensation for the deficiency. Further, there is authority for the proposition that a purchaser seeking specific performance need only prove a readiness and a willingness to tender the contract price less the amount of the abatement.[412] This right to an abatement

---

[405] See e.g. *Commercial Factors Ltd v Maxwell Printing Ltd* [1994] 1 NZLR 724, 735 and, in the context of the Statutes of Set-off, *Stooke v Taylor* (1880) 5 QBD 569, 575 and *Galambos & Son Pty Ltd v McIntyre* (1974) 5 ACTR 10, 18. In Australia, set-off has been described as a 'defensive equity'. See *Giumelli v Giumelli* (1999) 196 CLR 101, 113, referring to Deane J in *The Commonwealth v Verwayen* (1990) 170 CLR 394, 435.

[406] *Meagher, Gummow and Lehane's Equity Doctrines and Remedies* (4th edn, 2002), 1047.

[407] See paras 4.29–4.57 above.

[408] This may require a reasonable, good faith quantification of the cross-claim. See para. 4.50 above.

[409] See e.g. *Western v Russell* (1814) 3 V & B 187, 35 ER 450; *Jones v Evans* (1848) 17 LJ Ch 469; *Hooper v Smart* (1874) LR 18 Eq 683.

[410] See e.g. *Mortlock v Buller* (1804) 10 Ves Jun 292, 315–16, 32 ER 857, 866; *Nelthorpe v Holgate* (1844) 1 Coll 203, 63 ER 384; *Barnes v Wood* (1869) LR 8 Eq 424.

[411] *Phillips v Silvester* (1872) LR 8 Ch App 173, and see also *Clarke v Ramuz* [1891] 2 QB 456, 461–2. It has been suggested in New South Wales that this covers also questions of interest for delay and costs of ensuring vacant possession as promised by the vendor. See *Goodger v Ayre* (1988) 88 FLR 188, 190 (Young J).

[412] *King v Poggioli* (1923) 32 CLR 222. Compare Harpum, 'Specific performance with compensation as a purchaser's remedy – a study in contract and equity' [1981] *Cambridge Law Journal* 47, 69, where the view is expressed that a purchaser seeking specific performance musts be in a position to tender the whole purchase price and not merely the purchase price less the amount of an abatement. See also Jones and Goodhart, *Specific Performance* (2nd edn, 1996), 298. It is suggested in that article that support for the view that the purchaser need only tender the reduced amount is confined to the dissenting judgment of Higgins J in *King v Poggioli* at 241–3. However, the authority of the case in relation to that proposition is not so confined. Essentially, the point of difference between the dissenting judgment of Higgins J and the opinions of the majority (Knox CJ and Starke J) related to whether the purchaser's claim in that case (for breach of an agreement to give possession by a certain day) was such as to give rise to an abatement. Higgins J (at 238–9) considered that the circumstances indeed showed a deficiency in the subject-matter of the contract for the purpose of an abatement, whereas Starke J (at 246 and 249), with whom Knox CJ agreed (at 236–7), considered that the claim did not give rise to a diminution or deterioration in the property purchased. But where there is a right to an abatement

was developed independently of the principles of set-off. It does not apply where there is a breach of contract by the vendor which does not have the effect of lessening the value of the property as such.[413] However, in the cases in which that proposition was accepted, the possible application of equitable set-off was not considered. If the circumstances are such as to give rise to an equitable set-off, the vendor's title to the claim for the price is impeached in equity to the extent of the set-off, such that the vendor to that extent is not permitted in equity to assert that any moneys are owing by the debtor.[414] Given this substantive operation, it is suggested that a purchaser entitled to an equitable set-off should be in a similar position in an application for specific performance as a purchaser entitled to an abatement in the purchase money, in that the purchaser should only be required to show that he or she is ready and willing to pay the price as reduced by the set-off.[415]

(2) Statutes of Set-off

It is more difficult to see how the availability of a right of set-off under the Statutes of Set-off could be used offensively. The nature of this defence is such that it has a procedural operation,[416] in the sense that the Statutes only authorized a set-off if it is pleaded as a defence to an action for payment of a debt. Until such time as judgment for a set-off is obtained, each of the parties has the rights and obligations of creditor and debtor in relation to the cross-debts. Therefore, if in the example referred to the applicant seeking specific performance merely tendered the balance after deducting a separate debt owing to him or her by the defendant, the applicant would not have shown that he or she was ready and willing to perform the applicant's own obligation.

H. Foreign Currencies

It may be that one or both of the claims in a proposed set-off is in a foreign currency. The **5.88** question of how a set-off should proceed is considered, first, in the context of the Statutes of Set-off, and then in relation to equitable set-off.

(1) Statutes of Set-off

Until comparatively recently it was a settled principle of English law that, when a foreign **5.89** currency obligation was enforced in an English court, any judgment for the plaintiff had to be in sterling measured at the rate of exchange prevailing at the date when the obligation became due and payable.[417] However, in 1975 the House of Lords held in

---

based upon a diminution or deterioration in the value of the property, the judgment of Starke J (at 248–50) suggests that he accepted that the purchaser need only be ready and willing to tender the reduced amount.

[413] *King v Poggioli* (1923) 32 CLR 222; *Rutherford v Acton-Adams* [1915] AC 866, 870; *Batey v Gifford* (1997) 42 NSWLR 710, 718; *Re Mujaj* [1998] 2 Qd R 152.

[414] See para. 4.30 above.

[415] Consistent with Tadgell J's discussion in *Eagle Star Nominees Ltd v Merril* [1982] VR 557, 560–1 in the context of an unpaid vendor's claim for possession of land.

[416] See paras 2.34–2.39 above.

[417] *Re United Railways of Havana and Regla Warehouses Ltd* [1961] AC 1007.

Miliangos v George Frank (Textiles) Ltd[418] that this restriction no longer applies. An English court may give judgment for a sum of money expressed in a foreign currency and, if the defendant fails to tender payment in that currency, execution may issue for the sterling equivalent. Conversion for this purpose theoretically should take place at the rate prevailing at the date of actual payment.[419] But, as Lord Fraser of Tullybelton pointed out,[420] theory must yield to practical necessity to the extent that, if the judgment has to be enforced in England, it must be converted before enforcement.[421] Accordingly, the date of conversion was said to be the date that the court authorizes enforcement of the judgment in sterling.[422]

5.90 The effect of this development upon set-off under the Statutes of Set-off has yet to be determined. The Law Commission, in its report on *Private International Law Foreign Money Liabilities*,[423] suggested that a right of set-off should not be available in an action when different currencies are involved. Each party should obtain judgment for the amount of his or her claim expressed in the appropriate currency, though, as a qualification, it suggested that neither judgment should be enforceable without the other judgment being taken into account. The problem with this proposal is that it may have the effect of making the parties to mutual debts vulnerable to an assignment or other intervening third party interest. If one of the claims is assigned, the debtor on that claim would not have a right of set-off available as a defence to an action brought by the assignor which could be asserted against the assignee.[424] The recommendation that the judgments themselves should be capable of being set off at the date of enforcement would not assist in this situation, since an assignee only takes subject to prior equities, or defences. A right of set-off that only accrues upon the enforcement of a judgment could not be classed as a defence. Nor, on one view, would it be a *prior* equity. An alternative, and the preferable, approach is to convert the foreign currency into sterling at the rate prevailing at the date of judgment for a set-off. If both demands are in foreign currencies, the currency of the lesser debt should be converted into the currency of the greater debt at the date of judgment, and a set-off should then be effected.[425] This is consistent with the *Miliangos* principle, since the set-off effectively constitutes payment and, to the extent of the set-off, conversion accordingly takes place at the time of payment. Once the balance is struck in this manner, if the currency of the balance is not sterling and payment is not forthcoming in that currency, it should be converted into sterling at the date that leave is given to enforce the judgment, in accordance with the *Miliangos* case.

---

[418] [1976] AC 443. See also the earlier Court of Appeal decision in *Schorsch Meier GmbH v Hennin* [1975] 1 QB 416.

[419] Alternatively, it has been said in Victoria that, where the plaintiff so elects, it is open to the court to give judgment converted into domestic currency at the date of judgment, with interest to be calculated at the rate applicable in the country of the foreign currency. See *Vlasons Shipping, Inc v Neuchatel Swiss General Insurance Co Ltd (No. 2)* [1998] VSC 135 (Byrne J).

[420] [1976] AC 443, 501.

[421] Compare *Carnegie v Giessen* [2005] 1 WLR 2510.

[422] [1976] AC 443, 468–9 (Lord Wilberforce), 497–8 (Lord Cross), 501 (Lord Edmund-Davies), 501 (Lord Fraser).

[423] *Report on Private International Law Foreign Money Liabilities* (Cmnd 9064, 1983), 32–5.

[424] See paras 17.06–17.10 below.

[425] See Brandon J at first instance in *The Despina R* [1978] 1 QB 396, 414–15 in the context of a 'both to blame' collision under Admiralty law, and also *The Transoceanica Francesca* [1987] 2 Lloyd's Rep 155.

(2) Equitable set-off

Equitable set-off differs from set-off under the Statutes of Set-off in that it provides a sub- **5.91**
stantive rather than a procedural defence.[426] This does not mean that it operates as an
automatic extinction of cross-demands prior to judgment for a set-off. Rather, the notion
that the defence is substantive is a consequence of the closeness of the connection between
the cross-claims, and its effect is to render it unconscionable for the creditor to assert that
moneys are due to it from the debtor to the extent of the debtor's cross-claim while the
circumstances exist which support the set-off. Therefore, where a contract permits a creditor
to take a particular course of action if the debtor defaults in payment, for example a shipowner's right to withdraw the vessel in the event of non-payment of hire, or a landlord's
right to terminate the lease in the event that rent is not paid, the creditor would not be
permitted to take that course of action if the debtor has an equitable set-off overtopping the
claim.[427]

There is little authority on the question of foreign currency claims in the context of **5.92**
equitable set-off,[428] but the following is consistent with the true nature of the defence.
When an equitable set-off is pleaded as a defence to an action and one or both of the claims
is in a foreign currency, the principle should be the same as that suggested above for the
Statutes of Set-off, in that conversion should take place by reference to the exchange rate
applicable at the date of judgment for a set-off. However, the creditor's conscience is affected
even before judgment, so that to the extent of the defence the creditor is not permitted to
proceed on the basis that the debtor has defaulted in payment. In the determination at any
point in time prior to judgment whether the debtor has defaulted, and whether the creditor
can take action on the basis that a default has occurred, regard should be had to the exchange
rate at that time.[429]

What if foreign currency cross-claims are interest bearing? The analysis in that circum- **5.93**
stance should be as follows. Conversion of the principal amounts (and accrued interest)
should take place at the date of judgment for a set-off. Interest, on the other hand, ordinarily would accrue on the daily balance. When a creditor has an interest bearing debt the
subject of an equitable set-off, the sum upon which interest accrues is reduced to the extent
of the cross-claim while circumstances exist which support the set-off.[430] Therefore, when
foreign currency cross-claims are interest bearing, *prima facie* there should be a notional
conversion and set-off of the principal amounts on each day during the relevant period,
and interest should be calculated each day on the notional daily balance at the rate applicable to the currency of the greater of the claims on that day.

---

[426] See paras 4.29–4.34 above.
[427] See paras 4.45–4.47 above.
[428] But see *Gilsan v Optus (No. 3)* [2005] NSWSC 518 below. In relation to interest where there is no
foreign currency involved, see para. 4.56 above.
[429] Compare Wood, *English and International Set-off* (1989), 663, para. 11–24, 664–5, para. 11–28, and
665, para. 11–29. However, Wood has adopted a different analysis of the substantive nature of equitable
set-off (see para. 4.32 above), and his view of foreign currency conversions should be considered with that
in mind.
[430] See para. 4.56 above.

5.94   However, a different procedure was adopted in New South Wales in a case concerned with a statutory power to include interest in the sum for which judgment was given, calculated from the time when the cause of action arose. In *Gilsan v Optus (No. 3)*,[431] the plaintiff had foreign currency claims against the defendant, and the defendant had a cross-claim in Australian dollars against the plaintiff. It was accepted that equitable set-off applied, and one of the questions in issue was the calculation of interest for the purpose the court's statutory power to award interest on judgments. The defendant had provided services to the plaintiff which facilitated the business conducted by the plaintiff, and by carrying on its business the plaintiff became entitled to receive payments from the defendant.[432] The defendant supplied the services to the plaintiff month by month, and the defendant was obliged to pay the plaintiff, in respect of the business generated by the plaintiff by use of those services, month by month.[433] McDougall J considered that a monthly set-off should occur, with the requisite currency conversion taking place as at the end of the month. Interest was to accrue on the monthly balance in favour of the party to whom the balance was owing at the rate applicable to the currency of the balance.[434]

I. Contracting Out of Set-off

(1) Equitable set-off and common law abatement

General principle

5.95   It may be important for cash flow reasons that a party should receive payment in full under a contract so that, if the other party has a cross-claim which otherwise would give rise to an equitable set-off or a common law defence of abatement, that other party should not be entitled to rely upon it as a justification for tendering a reduced amount, but should be required to seek his or her remedy in separate proceedings. There is no ground of public policy which would preclude parties to a contract from agreeing to exclude defences of equitable set-off and abatement,[435] including in relation to a cross-claim based on fraud.[436]

5.96   Different views have been expressed as to the approach to be adopted in the interpretation of a contract which, it is asserted, operates to exclude or restrict defences of set-off and

---

[431] [2005] NSWSC 518 at [39]–[62]. In relation to interest, see also earlier proceedings: *Gilsan v Optus (No. 2)* [2005] NSWSC 38 at [64]–[67]. The relevant statutory power was the Supreme Court Act 1970 (NSW), s. 94.

[432] [2005] NSWSC 518 at [43].

[433] See in particular [2005] NSWSC 518 at [45].

[434] See in particular [2005] NSWSC 518 at [56]–[59].

[435] *Coca-Cola Financial Corporation v Finsat International Ltd* [1998] QB 43; *Morrison Knudsen Corporation of Australia Ltd v Australian National Railways Commission* (1996) 22 ACSR 262, 267; *Society of Lloyd's v Fraser* [1999] Lloyd's Rep IR 156, 171; *James v Bank of Western Australia* (2004) 51 ACSR 325 at [16]; *GE Capital Australia v Davis* (2002) 11 BPR 20,529, [2002] NSWSC 1146 at [96]–[98]. In New Zealand, see *Liapis v Vasey* (1989) 4 NZCLC 64,959. See also *Melville Dundas Ltd v Hotel Corporation of Edinburgh Ltd* [2006] BLR 474 (Scottish law). The Court of Appeal in *Coca-Cola v Finsat* (at 52) rejected an argument that contracting out of set-off rights is contrary to the Supreme Court Act 1981, s. 49(2) (now the Senior Courts Act 1981), which preserves the power of the Court of Appeal and the High Court to stay any proceedings.

[436] *Society of Lloyd's v Leighs* [1997] 6 Re LR 289; *WRM Group Ltd v Wood* [1997] EWCA Civ 2802.

abatement. On the one hand, Lord Diplock in *Gilbert-Ash (Northern) Ltd v Modern Engineering (Bristol) Ltd*[437] said that there is a presumption that the defences are not excluded, and that clear words are required to rebut the presumption:

> It is, of course, open to parties to a contract for sale of goods or for work and labour or for both to exclude by express agreement a remedy for its breach which would otherwise arise by operation of law or such remedy may be excluded by usage binding upon the parties . . . But in construing such a contract one starts with the presumption that neither party intends to abandon any remedies for its breach arising by operation of law, and clear express words must be used in order to rebut this presumption.[438]

Lord Morris, on the other hand, considered that the question depends simply and solely upon the interpretation of the contract,[439] an approach that was reflected in the judgment of Lord Cross of Chelsea (with whom Lord Hodson and Lord Wilberforce agreed) a year later, in *Mottram Consultants Ltd v Bernard Sunley & Sons Ltd*,[440] Lord Cross said that: 'one should approach each case without any "parti pris" in favour or against the existence of a right of set-off . . .' While there is support for that view,[441] the tendency in subsequent cases has been to refer to Lord Diplock's judgment as setting out the relevant principle. In other words, it is said that there is a presumption that the parties to a contract do not intend to give up rights of set-off and abatement otherwise available at law in the event of a breach by the other,[442] and if they intend to exclude those rights they must use clear words.[443]

---

[437] [1974] AC 689.

[438] [1974] AC 689, 717. Later in his judgment Lord Diplock commented (at 718): 'So when one is concerned with a building contract one starts with the presumption that each party is to be entitled to all those remedies for its breach as would arise by operation of law, including the remedy of setting up a breach of warranty in diminution or extinction of the price of material supplied or work executed under the contract. To rebut that presumption one must be able to find in the contract clear unequivocal words in which the parties have expressed their agreement that this remedy shall not be available in respect of breaches of that particular contract.' As to the presumption generally, see *Waterways Authority of NSW v Coal & Allied (Operations) Pty Ltd* [2007] NSWCA 276 at [217]–[238].

[439] [1974] AC 689, 702. See also Lord Reid at 699.

[440] [1975] 2 Lloyd's Rep 197, 205.

[441] In Australia, see *Triden Contractors Pty Ltd v Belvista Pty Ltd* (1986) 3 BCL 203, 215; *Algons Engineering Pty Ltd v Abigroup Contractors Pty Ltd* (1997) 14 BCL 215, 222 (referring to *Gilbert-Ash*); *Daewoo Australia Pty Ltd v Porter Crane Imports Pty Ltd* [2000] QSC 050 (BC200000992) at [17]. *Quaere* whether in fact this differs from Lord Diplock's approach. See *Totsa Total Oil Trading SA v Bharat Petroleum Corp Ltd* [2005] EWHC 1641 (Comm) at [27].

[442] *Federal Commerce & Navigation Co Ltd v Molena Alpha Inc* [1978] 1 QB 927, 988; *BICC Plc v Burndy Corporation* [1985] 1 Ch 232, 248; *Acsim (Southern) Ltd v Danish Contracting & Development Co Ltd* (1989) 47 BLR 55, 69–70; *Rosehaugh Stanhope (Broadgate Phase 6) Plc v Redpath Dorman Long Ltd* (1990) 50 BLR 75, 84; *Connaught Restaurants Ltd v Indoor Leisure Ltd* [1994] 1 WLR 501, 505; *Re Partnership Pacific Securities Ltd* [1994] 1 Qd R 410, 424–5; *Marubeni Corp v Sea Containers Ltd* Queen's Bench Division, Waller J, 17 May 1995; *Melbourne Glass Pty Ltd v Coby Constructions Pty Ltd* (1997) 14 BCL 409, 415 (Gillard J, Victorian Supreme Court). See also *Morrison Knudsen Corporation of Australia Ltd v Australian National Railways Commission* (1996) 22 ACSR 262, 267–8; *Esso Petroleum Co Ltd v Milton* [1997] 1 WLR 938, 948; *Beaufort Development (NI) Ltd v Gilbert-Ash NI Ltd* [1999] 1 AC 266, 279, 286–7; *Parsons Plastics (Research and Development) Ltd v Purac Ltd* [2002] EWCA Civ 459 at [12]. However, this should not involve twisting the words so as to achieve that result. See *GE Capital Australia v Davis* (2002) 11 BPR 20,529, [2002] NSWSC 1146 at [94]. Compare Lloyd LJ in *NEI Thompson Ltd v Wimpey Construction UK Ltd* (1987) 39 BLR 70, 73, who expressed the principle in terms of a '*prima facie*' entitlement to an equitable set-off or a common law defence of abatement.

[443] In addition to the cases referred to above in relation to the presumption, see *Compania Sud Americana de Vapores v Shipmair BV (The Teno)* [1977] 2 Lloyd's Rep 289, 293; *Redpath Dorman Long Ltd v Cummins*

Clauses which refer expressly to set-off have been held to be effective to exclude the defence,[444] but it is not necessary that the word 'set-off' be specifically used if it is otherwise clear from the language that the defence is intended to be excluded.[445]

5.97 There was no such clear implication in *BOC Group plc v Centeon LLC*,[446] and the Court of Appeal therefore held that the contract did not exclude set-offs. Evans LJ, with whose judgment Brooke LJ agreed, framed the relevant question in terms of whether the clause in

---

Engine Co Ltd [1981] SC 370, 374 (Scotland); *Wilson's (NZ) Portland Cement Ltd v Gatx-Fuller Australasia Pty Ltd (No. 2)* [1985] 2 NZLR 33, 39; *C M Pillings & Co Ltd v Kent Investments Ltd* (1985) 30 BLR 80, 92–3; *Construction Services Civil Pty Ltd v J. & N. Allen Enterprises Pty Ltd* (1985) 1 BCL 363, 367–8 (White J, South Australian Supreme Court); *Nile Co for the Export of Agricultural Crops v H. & J. M. Bennett (Commodities) Ltd* [1986] 1 Lloyd's Rep 555, 588; *John Dee Group Ltd v WMH (21) Ltd* [1997] BCC 518, 521, 527 (decision affirmed [1998] BCC 972); *WRM Group Ltd v Wood* [1997] EWCA Civ 2802 at [9] ('clear and unambiguous language'); *Liberty Mutual Insurance Co (UK) Ltd v HSBC Bank Plc* [2002] EWCA Civ 691 at [56]; *Edlington Properties Ltd v J. H. Fenner & Co Ltd* [2006] 1 WLR 1583 at [68] and [74] ('clear and specific words'); *Braspetro Oil Services Co v FPSO Construction Co Inc* [2005] EWHC 1316 (Comm) at [231]; *Altonwood Ltd v Crystal Palace FC (2000) Ltd* [2005] EWHC 292 (Ch) at [32].

[444] See e.g. *Continental Illinois National Bank & Trust Co of Chicago v Papanicolaou* [1986] 2 Lloyd's Rep 441 ('All payments . . . shall be made without set-off or counterclaim and without deductions or withholdings whatsoever'); *Star Rider Ltd v Inntrepnenneur Pub Co* [1998] 1 EGLR 53, 55 ('without deduction or set-off whatsoever'); *Coca-Cola Financial Corporation v Finsat International Ltd* [1998] QB 43 ('free and clear of any right of set-off or counterclaim or any withholding or deduction whatsoever'); *Daewoo Australia Pty Ltd v Porter Crane Imports Pty Ltd* [2000] QSC 050 ('free of any set-off or counterclaim and without deduction or withholding'); *Altonwood Ltd v Crystal Palace FC (2000) Ltd* [2005] EWHC 292 (Ch) at [32] ('without deduction or set-off'); *Unchained Growth III Plc v Granby Village (Manchester) Management Co Ltd* [2000] 1 WLR 739 ('without any deduction (whether by way of set-off lien charge or otherwise) whatsoever'); *Clambake Pty Ltd v Tipperary Projects Pty Ltd (No. 3)* [2009] WASC 52 at [52] and [173] ('without deduction or set-off'). See also, in the context of the Statutes of Set-off, *Hongkong & Shanghai Banking Corporation v Kloeckner & Co AG* [1990] 2 QB 514 ('irrevocably undertake to make payment in full . . . without any discount, deduction, offset, or counterclaim whatsoever on the due date'). Compare *Esso Petroleum Co Ltd v Milton* [1997] 1 WLR 938. The clause in that case stated that: 'The Licensee agrees that he will not for any reasons withhold payment of any amount properly due to Esso . . .' Sir John Balcombe commented (at 954) that in his opinion the clause in its terms would have been sufficient to exclude an equitable set-off, were it not for the Unfair Contract Terms Act 1977 (see paras 5.114–5.120 below). Simon Brown LJ, on the other hand, (at 949) considered, on balance, that it was not sufficiently clear to exclude the defence, apparently for the reason given by counsel, that the use of the words 'properly due' begged the very question in issue. This seems the preferred view. On that point, see also para. 5.99 below in relation to an obligation to pay 'all sums immediately when due, without deduction or set-off'.

[445] *Gilbert-Ash* [1974] AC 689, 723 ('clear implication') (Lord Salmon); *Grant v NZMC Ltd* [1989] 1 NZLR 8, 13; *Connaught Restaurants Ltd v Indoor Leisure Ltd* [1994] 1 WLR 501, 505 ('by implication from the language of the contract'); *Sonat Offshore SA v Amerada Hess Development Ltd* (1987) 39 BLR 1, 22 ('express term or necessary intention'); *T & N Ltd v Royal & Sun Alliance Plc* [2003] EWHC 1016 (Ch) at [491]–[498] (implication); *Edlington Properties Ltd v J. H. Fenner & Co Ltd* [2006] 1 WLR 1583 at [75] ('clear indication'). See also *Marubeni Corp v Sea Containers Ltd* Queen's Bench Division, Waller J, 17 May 1995 (discussed in para. 5.103 below); *Melville Dundas Ltd v Hotel Corporation of Edinburgh Ltd* [2006] BLR 474 (Scottish law); *Port of Tilbury (London) Ltd v Stora Enso Transport & Distribution Ltd* [2009] 1 Lloyd's Rep 391 (construing the contract as a whole). In *Nile Co for the Export of Agricultural Crops v H. & J. M. Bennett (Commodities) Ltd* [1986] 1 Lloyd's Rep 555 a contract of sale provided that, if the consignment arrived in bad condition, the purchaser had to advise the seller immediately so that the seller could send a representative to inspect the goods, and in addition the purchaser had to provide its own survey report to the seller. The purchaser could then 'deduct the landed value of the damaged goods from the FOB amount drawn by the [seller] and only the balance will then be payable against the documents'. Evans J held (at 588–9) that the purchaser's failure to comply with the procedure did not preclude the purchaser from later claiming damages for damage to the goods, but it did preclude the purchaser from relying upon its claim by way of defence to its liability for the price.

[446] [1999] 1 All ER (Comm) 970.

that case provided 'with sufficient clarity' that the purchaser was to pay the price regardless of any cross-claim that it may have had, and he emphasized that the court should take account of all the surrounding circumstances.[447] He regarded this as consistent with the approach advocated by Lord Hoffmann in relation to the interpretation of contractual documents in *Investors Compensation Scheme Ltd v West Bromwich Building Society*.[448] *BOC v Centeon* concerned the sale of a research and development company, Delta Biotechnology Ltd. The sale agreement provided for the payment of the price by way of instalments, and the present action was for payment of one of the instalments. The purchaser asserted a set-off in respect of cross-claims for damages for breach of the agreement and misrepresentation, but the vendor responded that set-off was precluded by the terms of clause 2.7 of the agreement. The clause provided that the purchaser's payment obligation was:

> absolute and unconditional and *shall not be affected by* any transfer of any of the equity interest in Delta, the transfer of any or all of Delta's assets or business, the dissolution of Delta, the termination of the business of Delta (or any part thereof), the success or failure of any research projects undertaken by Delta, the future commercialization or otherwise of any products, Delta's future business prospects or technological or technical successes *or by any other matter whatsoever*.[449]

The vendor sought to justify its argument that set-off was excluded by reference to the inclusion of 'whatsoever', which, it said, is a word of the widest possible import.[450] The difficulty with the argument was that the other matters listed were all concerned with the subsequent fate of Delta and its project, and the general words that followed the list were capable of referring to other factors concerned with the future progress of the venture. The word 'whatsoever', therefore, was ambivalent. Moreover, the parties were legally represented during the negotiation of the contract, and so they were aware of their legal rights. In that context the question was, what words might they have used to make their meaning clear if they had intended to exclude set-off? Evans LJ regarded the absence of words such as 'deduction', 'withholding' or 'payment in full' as an 'eloquent silence'[451] in that regard. In the circumstances, he considered that the clause did not provide with sufficient clarity that the right to invoke the defence was excluded.

Evans LJ in *BOC v Centeon* discussed the issue without recourse to the label 'presumption', and indeed he exhibited a degree of hesitancy in adopting that term.[452] However, the relevant passage in Lord Diplock's judgment in *Gilbert-Ash* has since been cited with evident approval in the House of Lords,[453] and 'presumption' would seem to be accepted as an accurate description of the approach to be adopted in these cases.

5.98

---

[447] [1999] 1 All ER (Comm) 970, 979–80.

[448] [1998] 1 WLR 896, 912–13.

[449] Emphasis added.

[450] Referring to *Smith v New South Wales Switchgear Co Ltd* [1978] 1 WLR 165, 178 (Lord Keith of Kinkel). See also the cases to which Rix J referred at first instance in *BOC Group plc v Centeon LLC* [1999] 1 All ER (Comm) 53, 61–2.

[451] [1999] 1 All ER (Comm) 970, 980.

[452] After referring to Lord Diplock's judgment in *Gilbert-Ash*, Evans LJ continued with the comment: 'Whether there is such a presumption or not . . .'. See [1999] 1 All ER (Comm) 970, 979.

[453] *Beaufort Developments (NI) Ltd v Gilbert-Ash NI Ltd* [1999] 1 AC 266, 279 (Lord Hoffmann), 286–7 (Lord Hope of Craighead); *Stocznia Gdanska SA v Latvian Shipping Co* [1998] 1 WLR 574, 585 (Lord Goff of Chieveley). In Australia, see *Concut Pty Ltd v Worrell* (2000) 75 ALJR 312, 317.

5.99 One should distinguish a provision to the effect that one party must pay 'all sums immediately when due, without deduction or set-off'. The better view is that a contract in those terms would be ineffective to preclude an equitable set-off in relation to a damages cross-claim which is inseparably connected with a debt the subject of the plaintiff's claim, because the substantive nature of the set-off[454] would mean that the plaintiff could not assert that the debt is 'due' for the purpose of the clause.[455] That reasoning would not apply, however, in relation to set-off under the Statutes of Set-off. The statutory form of set-off has a procedural operation in that, prior to judgment for a set-off, the rights consequent upon being a creditor still attach, as do the obligations and liabilities consequent upon being a debtor.[456] The availability of the set-off would not mean that the debt to the plaintiff is not due, in which case the clause should be effective to preclude reliance on that form of set-off.

5.100 If a contract provides that a debt is payable without set-off, contractual interest on the debt ordinarily should also be payable without set-off.[457]

Payment 'without deduction'

5.101 Contracts often provide that payment is to be made 'without deduction', which invites the question whether those words are apt to exclude a defence of equitable set-off. The issue came before the Court of Appeal in *Connaught Restaurants Ltd v Indoor Leisure Ltd*.[458] In dispute was a lease which provided that rent was to be paid 'without any deduction'. The word 'deduction' is sometimes used by the courts to describe the result which follows when a right of set-off is exercised,[459] and indeed Lord Salmon, in the *Gilbert-Ash* case,[460] rejected the view that it does not describe the process of set-off in the case of a contract for the sale of goods where the purchaser sets up a cross-claim for damages under the contract in extinction of the purchase price. In the *Connaught Restaurants* case, however, Waite LJ considered that the term was ambiguous. He said that 'deduction' may be used in its strict sense to describe the ordinary process of subtraction, in other words the action of taking

---

[454] See para. 4.29–4.57 above.

[455] This was the view of Mr Geoffrey Brice QC, sitting as a deputy High Court judge in *Schenkers Ltd v Overland Shoes Ltd* [1998] 1 Lloyd's Rep 498, 502–3 (decision affirmed by the Court of Appeal at 504 *et seq.* without reference to this point). In *Esso Petroleum Co Ltd v Milton* [1997] 1 WLR 938, 949 Simon Brown LJ considered, on balance, that an agreement not to withhold payment of any sum 'properly due' was insufficiently clear to exclude equitable set-off, though compare Balcombe LJ at 954. In *Electricity Supply Nominees Ltd v IAF Group Ltd* [1993] 1 WLR 1059 Mr Adrian Hamilton QC, sitting as a deputy High Court judge, considered that a clause which obliged a tenant 'to pay the rent and all other sums payable under this lease . . . without any deduction or set-off whatsoever' precluded a defence of equitable set-off, though the question whether an amount indeed was payable in view of the equitable set-off should have raised a similar issue. The question of construction of the contract was not addressed in detail in the judgment, the point in issue being the construction of the Unfair Contract Terms Act 1977. See para. 5.115 below. Compare para. 5.96 above in relation to clauses which specifically refer to set-off but without being qualified by an expression such as 'due'.

[456] See paras 2.34–2.39 above.

[457] *Clambake Pty Ltd v Tipperary Projects Pty Ltd (No. 3)* [2009] WASC 52 at [180].

[458] [1994] 1 WLR 501, referred to in *Esso Petroleum Co v Milton* [1997] 1 WLR 938, 948.

[459] See e.g. *Hanak v Green* [1958] 2 QB 9, 26; *Gilbert-Ash (Northern) Ltd v Modern Engineering (Bristol) Ltd* [1974] AC 689, 726; *Federal Commerce & Navigation Co Ltd v Molena Alpha Inc* [1978] 1 QB 927, 974, 975; *SL Sethia Liners Ltd v Naviagro Maritime Corporation (The Kostas Melas)* [1981] 1 Lloyd's Rep 18, 26.

[460] [1974] AC 689, 726.

something away. The process of subtraction may encompass contractual or statutory deductions, where the contract or the statute authorizes a subtraction from rent.[461] Alternatively, 'deduction' may be used in a broader sense, to describe the result which follows when one claim is set against another and a balance is struck. Because clear words are needed to exclude the remedy of equitable set-off, he considered that the word 'deduction' in the lease before him was insufficiently clear to achieve that result. In a short judgment Neill LJ agreed with Waite LJ's reasons, and Simon Brown LJ agreed with both judgments. The decision subsequently was followed by a differently constituted Court of Appeal in *Edlington Properties Ltd v J. H. Fenner & Co Ltd*.[462]

The Court of Appeal in the *Connaught Restaurants* case followed an earlier decision of the New Zealand Court of Appeal[463] in which it was held that 'deduction' does not in its natural sense embrace a set-off. This view has been adopted in Australia,[464] although there is also support there for the contrary view,[465] and in Singapore.[466] It is also consistent with the view expressed in relation to a stipulation in a time charter of a ship that hire was to be paid 'without discount',[467] and similarly a stipulation that payment is to be made 'without abatement' has been said to be insufficiently precise to exclude set-off.[468]   **5.102**

While Waite LJ considered that the expression 'without any deduction' in the case before him was insufficient to exclude equitable set-off, he nevertheless contemplated that there   **5.103**

---

[461] Various statutory provisions which empowered a tenant to make deductions from rent were noted at [1994] 1 WLR 501, 509, 511.

[462] [2006] 1 WLR 1583 at [66]–[75]. See also Waite, 'Disrepair and set-off of damages against rent' [1983] *The Conveyancer* 373, 389; *Altonwood Ltd v Crystal Palace FC (2000) Ltd* [2005] EWHC 292 (Ch) at [32]. Waite LJ declined to follow *Famous Army Stores v Meehan* [1993] EGLR 73, in which Steyn J adopted a contrary view. Compare *Sheridan Millenium Ltd v Odyssey Property Co* [2004] NI 117 in which the clause also referred to set-off.

[463] *Grant v NZMC Ltd* [1989] 1 NZLR 8.

[464] *Re Partnership Pacific Securities Ltd* [1994] 1 Qd R 410, not following *Citibank Pty Ltd v Simon Fredericks Pty Ltd* [1993] 2 VR 168, 175, and see also *Batiste v Lenin* (2002) 11 BPR 20,403, [2002] NSWCA 316 at [49] in relation to a tenant's right of recoupment. See para. 5.105 below. *Partnership Pacific* was referred to without adverse comment in *Morrison Knudsen Corporation of Australia Ltd v Australian National Railways Commission* (1996) 22 ACSR 262, 267–8. See also *Saratoga Integration Pty Ltd v Canjs Pty Ltd* (2010) 78 ACSR 600 at [40].

[465] In addition to *Citibank v Simon Fredericks* [1993] 2 VR 168, 175 (see para. 5.102n above), see *Batiste v Lenin* (2002) 10 BPR 19,441, [2002] NSWSC 233 at [94]–[105] (Bryson J, at first instance); *Webster v Barning Holdings Pty Ltd* [2001] WASC 11 at [29]; *R. & J. Lyons Family Settlement Pty Ltd v 155 Macquarrie St Pty Ltd* (2008) 13 BPR 25, 161, [2008] NSWSC 310 at [73]. See also, in the context of guarantees, *Langford Concrete Pty Ltd v Finlay* [1978] 1 NSWLR 14, 17; *Australia and New Zealand Banking Group Ltd v Harvey* (1994) 16 ATPR 46–132 at p. 53,643; *Commonwealth Development Bank v Windermere Pastoral Co Pty Ltd* [1999] NSWSC 518 at [52]–[57]. Bryson J in *Batiste v Lenin* did not refer to the *Connaught Restaurants* case or *Re Partnership Pacific Securities* (see para. 5.102n above), while *Debonair Nominees Pty Ltd v J & K Berry Nominees Pty Ltd* (2000) 77 SASR 261, to which Bryson J did refer, did not canvas equitable set-off. Further, Sheller JA on appeal in *Batiste v Lenin* (2002) 11 BPR 20,403, [2002] NSWCA 316 at [49] commented that he was not persuaded by Bryson J's view in the context of a tenant's right of recoupment. See para. 5.105 below. The question was left open in *Carrathool Hotel Pty Ltd v Scutti* [2005] NSWSC 401 at [62]–[65], and it was referred to, but not decided, in *Heggies Bulkhaul Ltd v Global Minerals Australia Pty Ltd* (2003) 59 NSWLR 312 at [195]–[199], *Australian Receivables Ltd v Tekitu Pty Ltd* [2008] NSWSC 433 at [23] and *Sandbank Holdings Pty Ltd v Durkan* [2010] WASCA 122 at [35]–[36].

[466] *Batshita International (Pte) Ltd v Lim Eng Hock Peter* [1997] 1 SLR 241 (CA).

[467] *Compania Sud Americana de Vapores v Shipmair BV (The Teno)* [1977] 2 Lloyd's Rep 289.

[468] *Edlington Properties Ltd v J. H. Fenner & Co Ltd* [2006] 1 WLR 1583 at [72]–[73].

may be instances where the context suggests by implication that the words were intended to have that effect.[469] An illustration is *Marubeni Corp v Sea Containers Ltd*.[470] It concerned a sale of containers by Marubeni to Sea Containers. The contract provided for payment of the price by instalments on the nominated due dates 'without any deductions or with-holdings whatsoever'. There were defects in some of the containers, and Sea Containers sought to 'deduct' by way of equitable set-off from an instalment of the price an amount corresponding to the damages flowing from the defects. Waller J accepted that neither 'deduction' nor 'withholding' is a term of art, and they could not be described as clear words. The question was one of construction in the context of the contract as a whole, and looking at the contract as a whole he held that the purported 'deduction' in respect of an equitable set-off was precluded by the exclusion of deductions and withholdings. In the first place, he said that the court has to find some meaning for the words and, in contrast to the *Connaught Restaurants* case, it was difficult in this case to see to what else they could apply. Moreover, the price was to be paid over a substantial period of nine years after delivery. Marubeni, therefore, in substance was providing finance, and it was likely that a finance party would insist that instalments should be paid without deducting for a cross-claim arising from a breach of warranty. In that respect he considered that the context was different from a building contract or a lease or a charter of a ship. Furthermore, the contract provided for a bank guarantee to secure payment of some of the instalments. If a claim were made against the bank on the guarantee, Sea Containers could not have exercised a right of set-off, and it would produce consistency in the contract if the same position were held to apply in relation to other instalments not secured by a bank guarantee.

5.104 In *BOC v Centeon*,[471] Evans LJ referred to 'payment in full without deduction or with-holding of any sort' as being familiar words in the context of agreements which purport to exclude rights of set-off. If 'deduction' or 'withholding' is insufficiently precise to exclude set-off, the addition of 'of any sort' would hardly add the necessary clarity.[472] It may also be queried whether 'payment in full' would overcome the perceived difficulty. It begs the question as to what constitutes 'payment in full', in circumstances where there is an equitable defence of set-off which renders it unconscionable for the creditor to assert that moneys are due from the debtor to the extent of the set-off.[473] Evans LJ emphasized, however, that there is not necessarily a magic formula, and where the parties do not expressly refer to set-off one should have regard to the surrounding circumstances of the case.[474]

---

[469] [1994] 1 WLR 501, 510.

[470] Queen's Bench Division, Waller J, 17 May 1995, referred to in *BOC Group plc v Centeon LLC* [1999] 1 All ER (Comm) 970, 978 and *Edlington Properties Ltd v J. H. Fenner & Co Ltd* [2006] 1 WLR 1583 at [71]. See also *Valeo Materiaux de Frictions v VTL Automotive Ltd* [2005] EWHC 1855 (TCC) at [54]–[58] where, in the circumstances, the expression 'without any deductions whatsoever' could not have been referring to a process of subtraction and it was held to extend to set-off.

[471] [1999] 1 All ER (Comm) 970, 980.

[472] As Waite LJ remarked in *Connaught Restaurants Ltd v Indoor Leisure Ltd* [1994] 1 WLR 501, 510: 'Added words of exception or qualification are relevant to the construction of [a phrase such as 'without any deduction'], but they too are subject to the general requirement of clarity and will only be effective to displace the lessee's right of equitable set-off if their effect is to create a clear context for exclusion.'

[473] See para. 4.30 above.

[474] [1999] 1 All ER (Comm) 970, 979–80.

A stipulation in a lease that rent is to be paid without deduction ordinarily should not **5.105** extend to the right of recoupment considered by Goff J in *Lee-Parker v Izzet*.[475] This right of recoupment may apply where leased premises have fallen into disrepair, and the tenant expends money in executing the repairs in circumstances where responsibility for the repairs is on the landlord. The tenant in such a case may recoup the cost from future payments of rent or from arrears of rent. Goff J admittedly referred in his order to the right of the tenant to 'deduct' the cost of repairs from future payments of rent,[476] though that expression may have been used for the sake of brevity.[477] The exercise of the right does not involve a deduction from rent otherwise due, but rather the tenant is entitled to treat the amount expended on repairs as a payment of rent.[478] Accordingly, a stipulation for payment 'without deduction' should not be relevant.[479]

On the other hand, in *Totsa Total Oil Trading SA v Bharat Petroleum Corp Ltd*[480] Clarke J **5.106** considered that the common law defence of abatement to an action for the price of goods sold and delivered or of work performed[481] involves a 'deduction' from the price.[482] The *Totsa Oil* case concerned a contract for the sale of oil on FOB terms. The contract provided that payment was to be made against the seller's invoice 'without discount, deduction, set-off or counterclaim'. This was held to preclude a deduction from the price for short delivery.[483]

The effect of specifying some deductions

Because of the need for clear words to exclude equitable set-off, the fact that a **5.107** contract makes provision for certain specified deductions from contract payments is not regarded as sufficient to give rise to an implication that a right of set-off in respect of other sums is excluded,[484] though there is authority in Australia which suggests

---

[475] [1971] 1 WLR 1688. See paras 5.77–5.80 above.

[476] [1971] 1 WLR 1688, 1695.

[477] *Connaught Restaurants Ltd v Indoor Leisure Ltd* [1994] 1 WLR 501, 507 (Waite LJ).

[478] *Connaught Restaurants Ltd v Indoor Leisure Ltd* [1994] 1 WLR 501, 507 (Waite LJ), 511 (Neill LJ). See para. 17.93 below.

[479] *Connaught Restaurants Ltd v Indoor Leisure Ltd* [1994] 1 WLR 501, 507 (disapproving of the contrary opinion expressed by the New Zealand Court of Appeal in *Grant v NZMC Ltd* [1989] 1 NZLR 8, 13), and *Batiste v Lenin* (2002) 11 BPR 20,403, [2002] NSWCA 316 at [34] and [49] (Sheller JA disapproving of Bryson J's contrary view at first instance (2002) 10 BPR 19,441, [2002] NSWSC 233 at [102]–[105]). See also Waite, 'Repairs and deduction from rent' [1981] *The Conveyancer* 199, 210–11. Compare however *Becklay Pty Ltd v A.R.J. Freights Pty Ltd* [2003] NSWSC 155 at [25] and *R. & J. Lyons Family Settlement Pty Ltd v 155 Macquarrie St Pty Ltd* (2008) 13 BPR 25, 161, [2008] NSWSC 310 at [72]–[73].

[480] [2005] EWHC 1641 (Comm).

[481] See paras 2.123–2.134 above.

[482] See [2005] EWHC 1641 (Comm) at [20] and [31].

[483] See also *Society of Lloyd's v Leighs* [1997] 6 Re LR 289, 298 (CA), where the Court of Appeal considered that the words 'or other deduction on any account whatsoever' would probably be wide enough to encompass a 'pure' defence, including, it would seem, by way of abatement. This view is consistent with Lord Salmon's observations in relation to the word 'deduct' in *Gilbert-Ash (Northern) Ltd v Modern Engineering (Bristol) Ltd* [1974] AC 689, 725–6.

[484] *Compania Sud Americana de Vapores v Shipmair BV (The Teno)* [1977] 2 Lloyd's Rep 289, 292–3; *Federal Commerce & Navigation Co Ltd v Molena Alpha Inc* [1978] 1 QB 927, 988; *Acsim (Southern) Ltd v Danish Contracting and Development Co Ltd* (1989) 47 BLR 55, 69–70. See also *Redpath Dorman Long Ltd v Cummins Engine Co Ltd* [1981] SC 370 (Scotland); *Ellis Tylin Ltd v Co-operative Retail Services Ltd* [1999] BLR 205, 220–1; *Pacific Rim Investments Pte Ltd v Lam Seng Tiong* [1995] 3 SLR 1, 15 (Singapore CA) (where

the contrary.[485] The contract may go further, however, and stipulate that payments are to be made 'less only' a list of specified deductions.

5.108   In *Mottram Consultants Ltd v Bernard Sunley & Sons Ltd*,[486] a building contract provided that the employer was to pay the amount specified in an architect's certificate 'less only' retention money and any sum previously paid. The printed form which the parties used originally provided for a third item, being any amount which the employer was entitled to deduct from or set off against any money due to the contractor by virtue of any breach of the contract by the contractor. However, the third item had been deleted. Lord Cross (with whom Lord Hodson and Lord Wilberforce agreed) said that: 'When the parties use a printed form and delete parts of it one can, in my opinion, pay regard to what has been deleted as part of the surrounding circumstances in the light of which one must construe what they have chosen to leave in.'[487] He said that the fact that the parties had deleted the third item showed that they had turned their minds to the question of deductions under the common law principle of abatement, and had decided that no such deductions should be allowed.[488] That reasoning would apply equally to equitable set-off.[489]

5.109   *Mottram v Sunley* was complicated by the deletion. That factor was not present in relation to the clause in a standard RIBA building contract[490] considered earlier in *Gilbert-Ash*.[491] The clause appeared in the main contract, between the employer and the contractor, though it dealt with the contractor's obligation to pay the sub-contractor. It provided that the contractor had to pay the sub-contractor the amount stated in a certificate less only a list of a specified deductions. Lord Diplock said that this did not seem to him to be strong enough to amount to an undertaking by the contractor to the employer that the contractor

---

the circumstance that a contract made provision for a contractual set-off at or after completion of construction did not exclude equitable set-off against contract payments prior to completion).

[485]   *Melbourne Glass Pty Ltd v Coby Construction Pty Ltd* (1997) 14 BCL 409, 417; *Novawest Contracting Pty Ltd v Taras Nominees Pty Ltd* [1998] VSC 205 at [103] and [104]. See also *Re Concrete Constructions Group Pty Ltd* [1997] 1 Qd R 6, 13. But there are also Australian cases which support the English approach. See *Hyder Consulting (Victoria) Pty Ltd v Transfield Pty Ltd* (2000) 17 BCL 129 (a provision in a contract to the effect that a debt due under the agreement may be deducted from any moneys payable by the creditor to the debtor would not preclude defences of set-off or abatement in respect of other claims against the debtor) and *Leighton Contractors Pty Ltd v East Gippsland Catchment Management Authority* (2000) 17 BCL 35 at [21]–[24] (contractual set-off right in relation to quantified amounts did not preclude an equitable set-off in relation to an unquantified claim).

[486]   [1975] 2 Lloyd's Rep 197.

[487]   [1975] 2 Lloyd's Rep 197, 209.

[488]   In Australia, see also *Melbourne Glass Pty Ltd v Coby Constructions Pty Ltd* (1997) 14 BCL 409, 413, referring to *Codelfa Construction Pty Ltd v State Rail Authority of NSW* (1982) 149 CLR 337, 352–3. Lord Cross's comment on abatement was *obiter*. The case concerned overpayments said to have been made by the employer, which the employer sought to deduct from subsequent payments sought by the contractor, including on the basis of a cross-claim against the contractor for negligence and breach of an implied term in paying out sums which had not been incurred in accordance with the contract.

[489]   This is suggested by Lord Cross's discussion at [1975] 2 Lloyd's Rep 197, 209–210. See also Lord Morris (at 204) and Lord Salmon (at 212–13) in their dissenting judgments, who both indicated that they were prepared to assume that the condition precluded a set-off, though neither expressed a concluded view on the subject. Moreover, Lord Salmon, in deciding that leave to defend should be granted, went on to refer (at 214, and see also at 212) to authorities on equitable set-off.

[490]   Clause 27(b) of the RIBA Local Authorities (with Quantities) 1963 edition.

[491]   [1974] AC 689, 721.

would not rely on a common law defence of abatement in an action by a sub-contractor for payment. He considered that it was directed simply at calculating the amount of the instalment due to the sub-contractor, and not to defences available to the contractor if sued by the sub-contractor for payment.[492] While those comments were expressed in the context of a defence of abatement, the view that Lord Diplock also expressed in his judgment, that clear words are required in order to rebut the presumption that neither party to a contract intends to abandon any remedies for its breach arising by operation of law, suggests that he would have regarded the provision similarly as being ineffective to preclude a defence of equitable set-off.[493] As Mr Duncan Wallace commented in a note on *Mottram v Sunley*:

> the right of set-off is so fundamental, and the potential injustices and anomalies of departing from it so great, that the mere use of the words 'less only' when referring to certain inevitable deductions required by the scheme of the contract (prior payment, retention money, and so on) should not be construed as intending to apply to and exclude other contingent situations which might justify a deduction under the general principles of law relating to defence, set-off, or counterclaim.[494]

With respect, there is much to commend that view.

Stay of execution

If there is an effective agreement excluding equitable set-off, this would not only preclude the defendant from being able to defend a claim for payment on the basis of a cross-claim, but in addition in a summary judgment application the court ordinarily would regard it as inappropriate to order a stay of execution pending adjudication on the cross-claim.[495] As the Court of Appeal noted in *Continental Illinois National Bank & Trust Co of Chicago v Papanicolaou*[496] when it allowed an appeal against an order granting a stay in this situation, the contrary conclusion would negate the very purpose of inserting a provision excluding rights of set-off, the purpose being to prevent a situation arising in which the creditor is

5.110

---

[492] Lord Salmon (at [1974] AC 689, 726) agreed with Lord Diplock's analysis of clause 27. See also Viscount Dilhorne in *Gilbert-Ash* at 709, referring to the provisions of the main contract relating to payment by the contractor to a sub-contractor (for which see 707–8).

[493] See in that regard Viscount Dilhorne at [1974] AC 689, 709.

[494] Note (1975) 91 LQR 471, 474–5.

[495] In addition to *Continental Illinois* (below), see *Mottram Consultants Ltd v Bernard Sunley & Sons Ltd* [1975] 2 Lloyd's Rep 197, 210 (in which the contract was interpreted as having excluded the defence of abatement); *BWP (Architectural) Ltd v Beaver Building Systems Ltd* (1988) 42 BLR 86; *Skipskredittforeningen v Emperor Navigation* [1998] 1 Lloyd's Rep 66, 79; *Coca-Cola Financial Corporation v Finsat International Ltd* [1998] QB 43, 53; *Sheridan Millenium Ltd v Odyssey Property Co* [2004] NI 117 at [15]; *Braspetro Oil Services Co v FPSO Construction Inc* [2005] EWHC 1316 (Comm) at [231]; *Barclays Bank plc v Kufner* [2008] EWHC 2319 (Comm) at [36]; *Remblance v Octagon Assets Ltd* [2009] EWCA Civ 581 at [66]. See also *John Dee Group Ltd v WMH (21) Ltd* [1988] BCC 972, 976 (in which it was regarded as relevant that the plaintiff had charged its assets, including the claim against the defendant, to a third party). In Australia, see *L. U. Simon Builders Pty Ltd v H. D. Fowles* [1992] 2 VR 189, 196; *John Holland Construction and Engineering Pty Ltd v Majorca Projects Pty Ltd* (Vic SC, 27 July 1995, BC9503852). Compare *Stewart Gill Ltd v Horatio Myer & Co Ltd* [1992] 1 QB 600, 604, where Lord Donaldson of Lymington MR contemplated that a stay of execution could be ordered, and *Hegarty & Sons Ltd v Royal Liver Friendly Society* [1985] IR 524, 531, in which Murphy J indicated that, if he had reached the conclusion in that case that the right of set-off had been excluded, he would have stayed execution.

[496] [1986] 2 Lloyd's Rep 441.

kept waiting for payment. Admittedly, the contract in that case specifically stated that the debt should be paid without counterclaim as well as set-off, but Parker LJ's analysis suggests that the same result would have followed if the contract had only excluded set-off. The court nevertheless has a discretion to grant a stay, and his Lordship postulated that a stay may be granted in exceptional circumstances notwithstanding the exclusion.[497] In that regard he said that it would not be enough that the defendant has a counterclaim which is likely to succeed, though he contemplated that it might suffice if there is such a counterclaim coupled with cogent evidence that the plaintiff would, if paid, be unable to meet a judgment on the counterclaim.[498] But in the absence of special circumstances, execution on a judgment should not be stayed pending determination of a cross-claim if the contract has excluded defences of set-off.

Negligence claims

5.111 The Court of Appeal in the *Continental Illinois* case also noted that a clause which purports to exclude rights of set-off is not subject to the same rule of construction applicable to exclusion of liability clauses in relation to claims for negligence.[499] In order to be effective to exclude liability for negligence it is usually necessary that the clause should refer specifically to negligence, or (possibly) use a sufficiently wide term such as 'whatsoever'.[500] However, it is not necessary that similar terminology be employed in order to exclude an equitable set-off based upon a cross-claim for negligence. The clauses serve different functions. An exclusion clause purports to exclude liability altogether, whereas a clause excluding set-off does not touch liability. The debtor can still prosecute the cross-claim to judgment, but in a separate action.

Arbitration clauses

5.112 While conceding that comments by Lord Salmon in the *Gilbert-Ash* case[501] were against his view, Wood has suggested that a party to a contract might perhaps be taken to have agreed to exclude equitable set-off in relation to a disputed cross-claim if he or she has agreed to submit disputes to arbitration, and no arbitration has been held.[502] Whether this is the case would depend upon the terms of the particular arbitration clause, but the usual clause providing for disputes to be referred to arbitration ordinarily should not require the debtor to pay in full if a cross-demand available as an equitable set-off has not been arbitrated.

---

[497] See also *ACG Acquisition XX LLC v Olympic Airlines SA* [2010] EWHC 923 (Comm) at [55], and RSC Ord. 47, r. 1(a) ('special circumstances').

[498] [1986] 2 Lloyd's Rep 441, 445.

[499] [1986] 2 Lloyd's Rep 441, 443–4. In *Society of Lloyd's v Leighs* [1997] 6 Re LR 289, 297 the Court of Appeal was 'far from persuaded' that a clause excluding rights of set-off should be treated as an exceptions clause. See also *WRM Group Ltd v Wood* [1997] EWCA Civ 2802 at [10]; *Sinochem International Oil (London) Co Ltd v Mobil Sales and Supply Corp* [2000] 1 All ER (Comm) 474, 483.

[500] See *Continental Illinois National Bank & Trust Co of Chicago v Papanicolaou* [1986] 2 Lloyd's Rep 441, 444, and generally Treitel, *The Law of Contract* (12th edn, 2007), 259 [7–033].

[501] [1974] AC 689, 726. See also Lord Diplock at 720, and *Aectra Refining and Marketing Inc v Exmar NV* [1994] 1 WLR 1634, 1649 (Hoffmann LJ).

[502] Wood, *English and International Set-off* (1989), 691. The authority principally relied on by Wood, *Cuddy v Cameron* (1911) 1 WWR 35, was concerned with a contractual right of deduction rather than equitable set-off, and in any event it was ultimately reversed on appeal by the Privy Council in *Cameron v Cuddy* [1914] AC 651.

Indeed, the availability of an equitable set-off would mean that the debt is also in dispute, so that both the debt and the cross-claim should be referred.[503] This is a consequence of the substantive nature of the defence.[504]

Conclusive evidence certificate

A contract may provide that a certificate from an authorized officer of one of the parties as to the amount owing to that party by the other shall be conclusive evidence of the amount owing. Conclusive evidence clauses are not contrary to public policy, and the courts will give effect to them in the absence of some factor such as fraud.[505] On the other hand, subject to the specific terms of the agreement, a conclusive evidence certificate ordinarily should not have the effect of precluding recourse to an equitable set-off,[506] which admits the existence of the debt at law, in the sense that an equitable set-off does not operate as an automatic extinction of cross-demands, but renders it unconscionable in equity for the creditor to treat the debtor as being indebted.[507]

5.113

(2) Unfair Contract Terms Act 1977

The Unfair Contract Terms Act 1977 prohibits in certain situations contract terms which exclude or restrict liability in relation to a claim for negligence or breach of contract, except, in some cases, in so far as the term satisfies a requirement of reasonableness. In particular, the prohibition may apply, subject to the reasonableness requirement, in the situation in which one party's written standard terms of business are used.[508] The reference to excluding or restricting liability is expressed in s. 13(1)(b) to encompass also excluding or restricting any right or remedy in respect of the liability. In *Stewart Gill Ltd v Horatio Myer & Co Ltd*,[509] the Court of Appeal held that this extended to a term in a standard contract which purported to exclude a right to raise a cross-claim for negligence or breach of contract by way of set-off.[510]

5.114

The Act contains an exemption, in para. 1(b) of Sch. 1, in the case of a contract so far as it relates to the creation or transfer of an interest in land. In *Electricity Supply Nominees Ltd v*

5.115

---

[503] See e.g. *Federal Commerce & Navigation Co Ltd v Molena Alpha Inc* [1978] 1 QB 927, 974, and para. 1.08 above.

[504] See paras 4.29–4.57 above.

[505] *Dobbs v National Bank of Australasia Ltd* (1935) 53 CLR 643; *Bache & Co (London) Ltd v Banque Vernes et Commerciale de Paris SA* [1973] 2 Lloyd's Rep 437.

[506] *Long Leys Co Pty Ltd v Silkdale Pty Ltd* (1991) 5 BPR 11,512, 11,520 (NSW CA); *Shomat Pty Ltd v Rubinstein* (1995) 124 FLR 284, 290 (Young J, NSW SC); *State Bank of New South Wales v Chia* (2000) 50 NSWLR 587 at [261].

[507] See para. 4.30 above.

[508] See s. 3(1).

[509] [1992] 1 QB 600.

[510] See also *Moriarty v Various Customers of BA Peters plc* [2008] EWHC 2205 (Ch) at [61] in relation to the Unfair Terms in Consumer Contracts Regulations 1999 (S.I. 1999 No. 2083). In the *Stewart Gill* case Lord Donaldson of Lymington MR also referred to s. 13(1)(c), to the effect that excluding or restricting liability includes also excluding or restricting rules of procedure. His Lordship said (at [1992] 1 QB 600, 606) that a clause which excludes or restricts set-off operates to exclude or restrict the procedural rules as to set-off, and on that ground also the clause is within the scope of the Act. The point may be made that set-off, even under the Statutes of Set-off, is not wholly procedural. See paras 2.53–2.62 above. But to the extent that it does have procedural aspects, s. 13(1)(c) would appear to apply.

IAF Group Ltd[511] Mr Hamilton QC, sitting as a deputy High Court judge, held that a term in a lease, by which rent was to be paid 'without any deduction or set-off whatsoever', was an integral part of the creation of the lease, and therefore it was a provision which related to the creation of an interest in land for the purpose of the exemption. The decision has since been followed,[512] and indeed it has been extended to the case of an obligation in a standard form of lease to pay a service fee to a management company charged with responsibility for the maintenance and management of the demised property.[513]

5.116 The test for determining reasonableness is laid down in s. 11(1) of the Act. The term in question must have been a fair and reasonable one to be included in the contract having regard to the circumstances which were, or ought reasonably to have been, known to or in the contemplation of the parties when the contract was made. In relation to contracts covered by ss. 6 and 7 of the Act, which deal with sales and hire purchase and miscellaneous contracts under which goods pass, s. 11(2) goes on to provide that, for the purpose of determining whether a term in the contract satisfies the requirement of reasonableness, regard is to be had in particular to the various matters set out in Sch. 2. The guidelines in Sch. 2 are also regarded as relevant to the determination of 'reasonableness' in other contexts.[514]

5.117 Section 11(1) stipulates that reasonableness is to be determined by reference to the circumstances when the contract was made. The parties therefore must be able to judge at that time whether a term is reasonable. Moreover, the Court of Appeal in the *Stewart Gill* case emphasized that the term as a whole must be looked at, and not merely the part of it upon which reliance is sought to be placed when the issue ultimately arises.[515] In issue in the *Stewart Gill* case was the following clause:

> The customer shall not be entitled to withhold payment of any amount due to the company under the contract by reason of any payment credit set off counterclaim allegation of incorrect or defective goods or for any other reason whatsoever which the customer may allege excuses him from performing his obligations hereunder.

Lord Donaldson of Lymington MR and Stuart-Smith LJ[516] considered that it was unreasonable that the defendant should not be entitled to withhold payment to the plaintiff of any amount due under the contract by reason of a 'credit' owing by the plaintiff to the defendant, or a 'payment' made by the defendant to the plaintiff, which Lord Donaldson interpreted as having in contemplation an overpayment under another contract.[517] Stuart-Smith LJ noted that the concluding words of the clause were unlimited, and would extend to a defence based on fraud. The clause as a whole therefore was unreasonable, notwithstanding that it was not sought to rely on those particular aspects of it in this case, but simply on the exclusion in relation to set-offs.

---

[511] [1993] 1 WLR 1059.

[512] *Star Rider Ltd v Inntreprenneur Pub Co* [1998] 1 EGLR 53 (licence fee payable under an agreement to grant a lease); *Unchained Growth III Plc v Granby Village (Manchester) Management Co Ltd* [2000] 1 WLR 739 (CA).

[513] *Unchained Growth III Plc v Granby Village (Manchester) Management Co Ltd* [2000] 1 WLR 739.

[514] *Stewart Gill Ltd v Horatio Myer & Co Ltd* [1992] 1 QB 600, 608; *Schenkers Ltd v Overland Shoes Ltd* [1998] 1 Lloyd's Rep 498, 505.

[515] [1992] 1 QB 600, 606–7, 608–9. See also *Skipskredittforeningen v Emperor Navigation* [1998] 1 Lloyd's Rep 66, 75; *Schenkers Ltd v Overland Shoes Ltd* [1998] 1 Lloyd's Rep 498, 506.

[516] Balcombe LJ agreeing with both judgments.

[517] [1992] 1 QB 600, 606.

The clause in issue in *Esso Petroleum Co Ltd v Milton*,[518] similarly, was thought to be unrea-   **5.118**
sonably wide for the purpose of the Unfair Contract Terms Act.[519] The clause was in
a licence agreement between Esso (as licensor) and a person who occupied and managed a
service station the subject of the licence. The clause provided: 'The licensee agrees that he
will not for any reasons withhold payment of any amount properly due to Esso under this
licence whatsoever . . .' The objectionable aspect of this, in the opinion of Simon Brown
LJ,[520] was that it would have precluded deductions for credits which could have been
due and owing from Esso to the licensee, in circumstances where the licence agreement
contemplated that credits could accrue in favour of the licensee.

Notwithstanding the rigorous attitude to the question of reasonableness suggested by those   **5.119**
cases, Mance J adopted a commercially sensible approach to the issue in *Skipskredittforeningen
v Emperor Navigation*.[521] In the *Stewart Gill* case the Court of Appeal said that reasonableness is to be determined by reference to the clause as a whole, and not simply in relation to
the point currently in issue. Mance J warned nevertheless that the courts 'should not be too
ready to focus on remote possibilities or to accept arguments that a clause fails the test by
reference to relatively uncommon or unlikely situations'.[522] In particular, he noted that the
clause before the Court of Appeal in the *Stewart Gill* case contained express provisions
which were so wide and obviously unacceptable as to invite overall rejection of the clause.
That was not the case, however, in the *Emperor Navigation* case. The plaintiff had advanced
a loan to the defendant. The loan agreement provided, *inter alia*, that:

> All payments to be made by or on behalf of the Borrowers pursuant to this Agreement . . .
> shall be made (a) without set-off, counterclaim or condition whatsoever and (b) free and clear
> of, and without deduction for or on account of, any present or future Taxes . . .

Mance J considered that the clause was not unreasonable in the context of the loan agreement; on the contrary it was 'generally familiar, sensible and understandable'.[523] While on
its face it would have precluded a set-off in respect of a cross-claim for fraud, he said that
the possibility of fraud by the lender is unlikely to have played any significant part in either
party's thinking when they entered into the loan agreement. The practical reality was that
the parties could not be taken as having envisaged it as likely that there would be a call to
invoke the clause in relation to fraud. The clause was not, therefore, unreasonable when the
loan agreement was entered into.

A clause precluding set-offs was also held to be reasonable in *Schenkers Ltd v Overland*   **5.120**
Shoes Ltd.[524] The plaintiffs were freight forwarders who were seeking to recover the cost
of freight and ancillary charges in relation to the importation of goods for the defendants.

---

[518] [1997] 1 WLR 938.
[519] See also *Fastframe Ltd v Lohinski* Court of Appeal, 3 March 1993, discussed in Adams, '"No deduction
or set-off" clauses' (1994) 57 MLR 960.
[520] [1997] 1 WLR 938, 949, and see also Sir John Balcombe at 954.
[521] [1998] 1 Lloyd's Rep 66. See also *WRM Group Ltd v Wood* [1997] EWCA Civ 2802 at [26]; *Barclays
Bank plc v Kufner* [2008] EWHC 2319 (Comm) at [35].
[522] [1998] 1 Lloyd's Rep 66, 75–6. See also *Bacardi-Martini Beverages Ltd v Thomas Hardy Packaging Ltd*
[2002] 2 All ER (Comm) 335 at [26].
[523] [1998] 1 Lloyd's Rep 66, 76.
[524] [1998] 1 Lloyd's Rep 498.

The defendants asserted that they had a cross-claim against the plaintiffs for failure to reclaim VAT on goods that had come through Portugal, and that this could be set off against the plaintiffs' claim. The plaintiffs were members of the British International Freight Association ('BIFA'), and their contract with the defendant incorporated the BIFA standard trading conditions, which required the customer to pay all sums immediately when due, 'without deduction or deferment on account of any claim, counterclaim or set-off'. The Court of Appeal rejected the defendants' argument that the clause was unreasonable for the purpose of the Unfair Contract Terms Act. The clause was in common use and was well known in the trade. It was in standard conditions which had been adopted following comprehensive discussions with various interested and representative bodies, and it was thought to represent a general view as to what was reasonable in the trade concerned. There was no significant inequality of bargaining power between the parties, and in that circumstance the custom of the trade was an important factor. Another factor, which in itself nevertheless was said not to be conclusive, was that the plaintiffs would incur substantial disbursements in the course of their business on behalf of customers. The point was also made that the clause did not purport to exclude or limit the plaintiffs' contractual liability, but aimed to achieve the 'different and lesser objective' of making it necessary for the defendant to sue the plaintiffs separately for breach of contract.[525]

(3) Misrepresentation Act 1967

5.121 The Misrepresentation Act 1967, s. 3 in substance provides that, if a contract contains a term which would exclude or restrict any liability for misrepresentation to which a party may be subject, or any remedy available to another party to the contract by reason of that misrepresentation, the term is of no effect except in so far as it satisfies the requirement of reasonableness as stated in s. 11(1) of the Unfair Contracts Terms Act 1977. A clause in a contract which excludes a set-off in respect of a cross-claim for damages for misrepresentation is regarded as a term which excludes a remedy available 'by reason of such misrepresentation', and as such it is of no effect unless it satisfies the same test of reasonableness applicable in the case of the Unfair Contract Terms Act.[526]

(4) Building and construction contracts[527]

5.122 Building and construction contracts have been a prime source of litigation in relation to attempts to exclude defences of set-off and abatement.[528] Typically, the issue arose when a certificate was presented by an architect or an engineer requiring a progress payment by

---

[525] [1998] 1 Lloyd's Rep 498, 507 (Pill LJ), and see also Thorpe LJ at 508.

[526] *Skipskredittforeningen v Emperor Navigation* [1998] 1 Lloyd's Rep 66; *WRM Group Ltd v Wood* [1997] EWCA Civ 2802. Mance J in *Skipskredittforeningen v Emperor Navigation* declined to follow *Society of Lloyd's v Wilkinson (No. 2)* (1997) 6 Re LR 214, in which Colman J expressed the contrary view, Mance J noting (at [1998] 1 Lloyd's Rep 66, 74–5) that the decision in the *Stewart Gill* case was not cited to Colman J in this connection. After Mance J's judgment, the Court of Appeal on appeal affirmed the decision of Colman J, though the Misrepresentation Act point does not appear to have been argued before their Lordships. See *Society of Lloyd's v Leighs* [1997] 6 Re LR 289.

[527] See also paras 5.50–5.63 above.

[528] As *Keating on Construction Contracts* (8th edn, 2006), 666 [18–056] observes, the Housing Grants, Construction and Regeneration Act 1996, s. 11 in effect is a statutory exclusion of the right of set-off if a withholding notice has not been served. See para. 5.52 above.

the employer to the contractor, or by the contractor to a sub-contractor, and the employer or the contractor refused to pay because of allegations of bad workmanship or delay. Summary judgment was then sought for the amount of the certificate. The question was whether leave to defend should be given on the basis of the cross-claim, or whether the contract excluded defences of set-off and abatement with the consequence that the amount of the certificate had to be paid and the cross-claim litigated or arbitrated later. The determination of that question often was important for cash flow.[529]

In *Gilbert-Ash (Northern) Ltd v Modern Engineering (Bristol) Ltd*,[530] the House of Lords **5.123** rejected the proposition that the Court of Appeal had developed in cases such as *Dawnays Ltd v F. G. Minter Ltd*,[531] that a certificate issued under a building contract is to be regarded as equivalent to cash, and that therefore the debt due under the certificate has to be paid save only for deductions permitted by the contract. On the other hand, the parties could choose to exclude defences of equitable set-off and common law abatement. In the *Gilbert-Ash* case,[532] Lord Diplock said that there is a presumption that the parties to a contract do not intend to give up remedies for its breach that otherwise would arise by operation of law. This applies to rights of set-off and abatement. In order to rebut the presumption, there must be clear words, or at least a clear implication, to that effect.[533] Following the *Gilbert-Ash* case, various attempts were made by draftsmen of standard-form contracts to exclude or restrict rights of set-off and abatement in relation to interim certificates. It is not proposed to consider these in detail. They are referred to in specialist texts on building contracts.[534] The point has been made,[535] however, that, when the constraints of the express wording permitted, English courts have not been slow to re-affirm the *Gilbert-Ash* principle. *Acsim (Southern) Ltd v Danish Contracting & Development Co Ltd*[536] illustrates that proposition. A building contract included a term to the effect that Danish Contracting ('Dancon') could set off against any moneys otherwise due to Acsim as contractor the amount of any claim for loss, provided the claim had been quantified and notified to Acsim within a specified period. The contract went on to provide that this fully set out the rights of the parties in respect of set-off. While the Court of Appeal held that the contract was effective to prevent a cross-claim for damages for bad workmanship that was quantified outside the period from being employed as an equitable set-off, there were not sufficiently clear words to exclude the common law defence of abatement.[537] The subject of the cross-claim was not being raised as a set-off as such. Rather, Dancon was defending itself by showing that, by

---

[529] The Privy Council has described cash flow as 'the life blood of a business'. See *Agnew v Commissioner of Inland Revenue* [2001] 2 AC 710 at [7]. See also *Modern Engineering (Bristol) Ltd v Gilbert-Ash (Northern) Ltd* (1973) 71 LGR 162, 167 (CA) in relation to the construction industry.

[530] [1974] AC 689.

[531] [1971] 1 WLR 1205. See para. 5.50 above.

[532] *Gilbert-Ash (Northern) Ltd v Modern Engineering (Bristol) Ltd* [1974] AC 689, 717.

[533] See Lord Salmon in *Gilbert-Ash (Northern) Ltd v Modern Engineering (Bristol) Ltd* [1974] AC 689, 723.

[534] See e.g. *Hudson's Building and Engineering Contracts* (11th edn, 1995) vol. 1, 856–60, and the cases referred to in *Keating on Construction Contracts* (8th edn, 2006), 666–7 [18–056].

[535] *Hudson's Building and Engineering Contracts* (11th edn, 1995) vol. 1, 858.

[536] (1989) 47 BLR 55.

[537] (1989) 47 BLR 55, 72. See also, and compare, *Mellowes Archital Ltd v Bell Projects Ltd* (1997) 87 BLR 26 (damages for delay not within the common law principle of abatement). Compare also, in a different context, *Skipskredittforeningen v Emperor Navigation* [1998] 1 Lloyd's Rep 66, 78–9.

reason of Acsim's breaches of contract, the value of the work was less than the sum claimed.[538] This defence was not prohibited by the contract.

Australia

5.124 Australian courts have generally shown a greater preparedness than those in England to interpret building and construction contracts as excluding defences of set-off and abatement in relation to interim or progress certificates.[539] While the cases were not all concerned with the same form of contract, a number of factors have been emphasized as indicating an intention that interim or progress certificates were to be paid without deductions for cross-claims.[540] Of particular significance have been the terms of the payment clause. For example, clause 42.1 of Australian General Conditions of Contract AS 2124-1992 provided that the employer 'shall pay . . . an amount not less than the amount shown in the certificate as due to the contractor . . .'. The obligation was expressed in terms of paying the amount shown in the certificate, as opposed to the amount due to the contractor. Considered in conjunction with other relevant factors mentioned below, it was interpreted as requiring payment of the amount shown in the certificate without a deduction for liquidated damages payable by the contractor for delay.[541] The same interpretation has been adopted in other cases in Australia where the payment clause was expressed in similar terms.[542]

5.125 Other aspects of construction contracts have been referred to as supporting that view. In one case, it was regarded as persuasive that the clause dealing with payment of progress certificates made no provision for the situation in which the proprietor disputed the whole or part of the certificate, whereas it was expressly dealt with in relation to the final certificate in that the obligation to pay only extended to the amount that was not in dispute.[543] Similarly, it has been said to be relevant that the contract provides a scheme for making

---

[538] See para. 2.123 above.

[539] In addition to the cases referred to below, see *John Holland Construction and Engineering Pty Ltd v Majorca Projects Pty Ltd* (Vic SC, Hansen J, 27 July 1995, BC9503852). See also in New Zealand *Hempseed v Durham Developments Ltd* [1998] 3 NZLR 265, 269. For cases in which an intention to exclude defences of set-off and abatement was not found, see *Construction Services Civil Pty Ltd v J. & N. Allen Enterprises Pty Ltd* (1985) 1 BCL 363; *Melbourne Glass Pty Ltd v Coby Constructions Pty Ltd* (1997) 14 BCL 409; *Dames & Moore Pty Ltd v Jovista Pty Ltd* (1998) 14 BCL 421; *Fifty Sixth Taljan Pty Ltd v Dattilo Holdings Pty Ltd* [2007] VSC 226.

[540] In *Melbourne Glass Pty Ltd v Coby Constructions Pty Ltd* (1997) 14 BCL 409, 417, Gillard J said that two substantial factors which have influenced the courts in Australia to exclude the defence of set-off in building contracts are, first, the presence of a detailed scheme allowing for deductions, and, second, a dispute resolution procedure which obliges the works to continue even though the parties have commenced some form of litigation. See below.

[541] *Re Concrete Constructions Group Pty Ltd* [1997] 1 Qd R 6; *Novawest Contracting Pty Ltd v Taras Nominees Pty Ltd* [1998] VSC 205.

[542] *Algons Engineering Pty Ltd v Abigroup Contractors Pty Ltd* (1997) 14 BCL 215; *L. U. Simon Builders Pty Ltd v H. D. Fowles* [1992] 2 VR 189; *Sabemo Pty Ltd v de Groot* (1991) 8 BCL 132. Compare *Dames & Moore Pty Ltd v Jovista Pty Ltd* [1998] WASC 157. Compare also *Queensland University of Technology v Project Constructions (Aust) Pty Ltd* [2003] 1 Qd R 259 at [24] and *Aquatec-Maxcon Pty Ltd v Minson Nacap Pty Ltd* (2004) 8 VR 16 at [50]–[60] in relation to the situation in which the contract has been terminated.

[543] *L. U. Simon Builders Pty Ltd v H. D. Fowles* [1992] 2 VR 189, 192–3. See also *Sabemo Pty Ltd v de Groot* (1991) 8 BCL 132, 143. On that view, the contract had the effect of deferring the right to a set-off until the final claim for payment under the contract. See *Algons Engineering Pty Ltd v Abigroup Contractors Pty Ltd* (1997) 14 BCL 215, 230, 231.

deductions in respect of defects and for delay.[544] In the case of defects, the contract in issue provided that the employer could employ others to rectify defects if the contractor failed to do so, and the employer could then recover the cost from moneys payable to the contractor. In the case of delay, the contract enabled the employer to deduct liquidated damages from progress certificates issued after practical completion. Courts in Australia have also had regard to a clause entitling the contractor to suspend or terminate the contract in the event of a failure to pay by the proprietor. It has been said that it would be curious if the proprietor could refuse to pay because of a cross-claim when the contractor is entitled to terminate in the event of non-payment.[545] In that regard the point has been made that the contractor would not know whether it could act where the proprietor is raising a cross-claim until a decision was made on the dispute. Until that occurred, it would not be possible to determine whether the proprietor had 'failed to pay', and the power given to the contractor in practice would be rendered worthless.[546] Reference has also been made to arbitration clauses. The presence of an arbitration clause in relation to disputes on its own should not suffice to exclude defences of set-off and abatement.[547] Nevertheless, it has been suggested that the clause may indicate an intention to that effect if the clause requires disputes to be referred to arbitration, and also requires the contractor to continue to perform and execute the works pending resolution of the dispute. It has been said that, unless the contractor continues to receive progress payments, it may not be able to execute the works, and that the entitlement to progress payments should be regarded as the *quid pro quo* for the obligation to continue working while the parties are in dispute.[548]

In relation to Australian General Conditions of Contract AS 2124-1992 (to which reference was made above), while the payment clause was expressed in terms of the amount shown in the certificate, it was nevertheless the case that the amount shown was intended to be the amount 'due' to the contractor,[549] and when a substantive defence of equitable set-off is available courts of equity proceed on the basis that nothing is due to the creditor

5.126

---

[544] See *L. U. Simon Builders Pty Ltd v H. D. Fowles* [1992] 2 VR 189, 194–6. See also *Main Roads Construction Pty Ltd v Samary Enterprises Pty Ltd* [2005] VSC 388 (esp. at [21] and [40]–[47]); *Gunns Ltd v Gregson Property Development Pty Ltd* [2005] TASSC 115.

[545] *Triden Contractors Pty Ltd v Belvista Pty Ltd* (1986) 3 BCL 203, 215–16. On the other hand, this was not regarded as significant in *Construction Services Civil Pty Ltd v J. & N. Allen Enterprises Pty Ltd* (1985) 1 BCL 363, 369.

[546] *L. U. Simon Builders Pty Ltd v H. D. Fowles* [1992] 2 VR 189, 193, referring to *Sabemo Pty Ltd v de Groot* (1991) 8 BCL 132, 143.

[547] See para. 5.112 above.

[548] *L. U. Simon Builders Pty Ltd v H. D. Fowles* [1992] 2 VR 189, 193. See also *Sabemo Pty Ltd v de Groot* (1991) 8 BCL 132, 143; *Algons Engineering Pty Ltd v Abigroup Contractors Pty Ltd* (1997) 14 BCL 215, 220, 224; *Melbourne Glass Pty Ltd v Coby Constructions Pty Ltd* (1997) 14 BCL 409, 417; *Novawest Contracting Pty Ltd v Taras Nominees Pty Ltd* [1998] VSC 205 at [96]. In *G. Hawkins & Sons Pty Ltd v Cable Belt (Australia) Pty Ltd* (1984) 2 BCL 246 an employer's claims against a contractor for delay and bad workmanship were the subject of an arbitration, which was proceeding. The contract provided that any payment due to the contractor was not to be withheld on account of arbitration proceedings unless authorized by the contractor or required by the arbitrator. Rogers J in the New South Wales Supreme Court held that the employer was required to pay retention moneys due to the contractor, and that the clause precluded any right to withhold payment on the basis of equitable set-off.

[549] Thus, clause 42.1 of AS 2124–1992 required the contractor to: 'deliver to the Superintendent claims for payment supported by evidence of the amount due to the Contractor . . .'

to the extent of the set-off.[550] It is unlikely that an English court, applying the presumption to which Lord Diplock referred in the *Gilbert-Ash* case,[551] would have regarded a clause in those terms as sufficiently clear to show that the parties intended to exclude their ordinary rights of set-off and abatement. Thus, it was doubted in *Hudson's Building and Engineering Contracts* whether some of the Australian cases in truth were consistent with the *Gilbert-Ash* case,[552] and the point may be made that some of the reasons given by Australian courts for denying a set-off do not seem persuasive in the light of the views expressed in the House of Lords in that case.

5.127 In the *Gilbert-Ash* case, the main contract between the employer and the contractor was in the form issued by the RIBA for Local Authorities 1963 Edition (December 1967 issue).[553] Viscount Dilhorne said that there was no ground for inferring that the contract excluded reliance by the employer on its common law and equitable rights of set-off if sued,[554] and that was also the view of Lord Salmon.[555] Lord Diplock expressed a similar opinion in relation to the common law defence of abatement.[556] One of the features of the RIBA contract was that it entitled the contractor to terminate the contract in the event that the employer failed to pay the amount due on a certificate.[557] In Australia a clause in those terms has been regarded as a factor indicating that defences of equitable set-off and abatement have been excluded in relation to progress certificates,[558] whereas it did not affect the views expressed in the *Gilbert-Ash* case that the defences applied in that case.[559] A similar issue has arisen in the context of a time charter of a ship. The charterparty usually gives the owner the right to determine the charter in the event of non-payment of hire, and it has been said that the power of determination is not sufficient to exclude equitable set-off in favour of the charterer in relation to breaches of the charterparty by the owner.[560] If the charterer asserts a cross-claim which, if established, would give rise to an equitable set-off, the owner would act at its peril if it nevertheless determined the charterparty for non-payment. If it should

---

[550] See para. 4.30 above.

[551] See para. 5.96 above.

[552] *Hudson's Building and Engineering Contracts* (11th edn, 1995) vol. 1, 730 n. 23, 856 and 860–1, referring to *Triden Contractors Pty Ltd v Belvista Pty Ltd* (1986) 3 BCL 203, *Sabemo Pty Ltd v de Groot* (1991) 8 BCL 132 and *L. U. Simon Builders Ltd v H. D. Fowles* [1992] 2 VR 189. But see *Hudson's Building and Engineering Contracts* (11th edn, First Supplement, 2003), 147 in relation to other cases.

[553] See [1974] AC 689, 696. The contract immediately in issue was a contract between the contractor and a sub-contractor, but the contract between those parties incorporated the parts of the main contract that were applicable to the works.

[554] [1974] AC 689, 707, 709–10. The sub-contract in fact gave an express right of deduction, but Viscount Dilhorne (at 712) said that, even if that had not been the case, it similarly would not have excluded common law and equitable rights of set-off.

[555] [1974] AC 689, 726–7.

[556] [1974] AC 689, 720.

[557] See clause 26(1), the terms of which are set out in Keating, *Law and Practice of Building Contracts* (3rd edn, 1969), 370. The form set out in Keating is the July 1968 revision, as opposed to the December 1967 issue which was the subject of *Gilbert-Ash*, though the differences between the two forms are not material. See the history of the amendments to the 1963 edition in Keating, *op. cit.* 295–6.

[558] See para. 5.125 above.

[559] See in particular Viscount Dilhorne at [1974] AC 689, 709, who was influenced by the presence of other clauses which conferred express rights of deduction in certain specified circumstances.

[560] *Federal Commerce & Navigation Co Ltd v Molena Alpha Inc* [1978] 1 QB 927, 981, 988–9 (Goff LJ).

turn out that the deduction was justified, the owner's purported determination would constitute a repudiation.[561]

Another factor emphasized in Australia is the presence of a clause permitting the employer **5.128** to deduct liquidated damages for delay from progress certificates issued after practical completion.[562] However, the RIBA contract the subject of consideration in the *Gilbert-Ash* case contained a similar provision,[563] so that it would seem that in *Gilbert-Ash* the presence of that clause was not regarded as having militated against the employer's right to set up defences of set-off and abatement against the contractor in relation to a cross-claim for delay.

Furthermore, the fact that the contract gives a remedy in relation to defects, in that the **5.129** employer may employ someone else to rectify defects if the contractor has failed to do so and to deduct the cost from progress payments,[564] seems insufficient to give rise to a clear implication that the contract excludes reliance by the employer on equitable and common law rights of set-off and abatement in other circumstances.[565]

Reliance has also been placed on a provision to the effect that an interim payment was not **5.130** to prejudice the right of either party to dispute whether the amount paid was properly due and payable, and that payment was not evidence of the value of the work or an admission that the work had been executed satisfactorily, but was to be a payment on account only.[566] However, the sub-contract in the *Gilbert-Ash* case had a similar clause,[567] and in any event it simply reflects the effect which has been ascribed to interim certificates.[568]

The presence of an express clause in the contract allowing the principal to make certain **5.131** deductions has also been regarded as a factor suggesting that other rights of set-off and abatement have been excluded.[569] It is difficult, however, to reconcile that proposition with the view adopted by English courts, that the fact that a contract makes provision for certain specified deductions does not give rise to an implication that a right of set-off in respect of other sums has been excluded.[570]

---

[561] *Federal Commerce & Navigation Co Ltd v Molena Alpha Inc* [1978] 1 QB 927, 981. The cases favour the view that the charterer will not be in default in making a deduction from hire payments if the amount of the loss has been quantified by a reasonable assessment made in good faith. See para. 4.50 above.

[562] See para. 5.125 above.

[563] See clause 22, the terms of which are set out in Keating, *Law and Practice of Building Contracts* (3rd edn, 1969), 352.

[564] This has been regarded as a relevant factor in Australia. See para. 5.125 above.

[565] See also Viscount Dilhorne in *Gilbert-Ash (Northern) Ltd v Modern Engineering (Bristol) Ltd* [1974] AC 689, 707, 710 in relation to clauses 2(1) and 6 of the RIBA contract, and also Lord Diplock at 719.

[566] *Novawest Contracting Pty Ltd v Taras Nominees Pty Ltd* [1998] VSC 205 at [96]–[99]. See also *Algons Engineering Pty Ltd v Abigroup Contractors Pty Ltd* (1997) 14 BCL 215, 219, 227; *Leighton Contractors Pty Ltd v East Gippsland Catchment Management Authority* (2000) 17 BCL 35 at [11].

[567] See clause 14 of the sub-contract, the terms of which are set out at [1974] AC 689, 697. While the sub-contract expressly conferred a right of deduction, Viscount Dilhorne (at 712) commented that, even in the absence of that provision, the sub-contract would not have excluded the contractor's common law and equitable rights of set-off.

[568] See *Hudson's Building and Engineering Contracts* (11th edn, 1995) vol. 1, 849–51, and *Re Concrete Constructions Group Pty Ltd* [1997] 1 Qd R 6, 12.

[569] *Melbourne Glass Pty Ltd v Coby Constructions Pty Ltd* (1997) 14 BCL 409, 417; *Novawest Contracting Pty Ltd v Taras Nominees Pty Ltd* [1998] VSC 205 at [101]–[103]. See also *Re Concrete Constructions Group Pty Ltd* [1997] 1 Qd R 6, 13.

[570] See para. 5.107 above.

5.132 Australian courts have also emphasized the presence of an arbitration clause which requires disputes to be referred to arbitration, and which also requires the contractor to continue to execute the works pending resolution of the dispute. The point has been made in relation to a clause in that form that, if the contractor is not paid, it may not be able to complete the works, so that the entitlement to progress payments should be regarded as the *quid pro quo* for the obligation to continue.[571] One may query the significance of the stipulation that the contractor must continue with the work. The stipulation that the work must continue simply reflects the position that would apply if defences of equitable set-off and abatement were available against a claim on a progress certificate. If in a summary judgment application by a contractor for payment of the amount certified the court was satisfied that there was a *bona fide* cross-claim which, if established, would give rise to a set-off or an abatement, the contractor would not obtain immediate payment to the extent of the cross-claim. Furthermore, the contractor would have to continue work unless it was prepared to take the risk that the cross-claim would not be made out. If the contractor ceased work and the cross-claim ultimately was established, its conduct would have constituted a breach of the contract.[572] The stipulation adds certainty to the question of what happens in the event of a dispute. It is debatable, however, whether it gives rise to a clear implication that the parties had intended to exclude defences of set-off and abatement in relation to progress certificates, for the purpose of rebutting the presumption referred to in the *Gilbert-Ash* case.[573]

(5) Statutes of Set-off

5.133 The House of Lords has held that the set-off section in the insolvency legislation[574] is mandatory in its operation, so that it is not possible to contract out of its terms.[575] This was justified on two grounds. The first is the mandatory language used in the section, which provides that an account 'shall be taken' in the stated circumstances. The second is based upon a perceived policy consideration,[576] that the insolvency set-off section relates to a matter in which the public have an interest. According to this view, the section was not enacted for the benefit of a particular person or persons, but rather it is a part of a code of procedure dealing with the administration of the estate of a bankrupt or a company in liquidation. Neither of those grounds apply, however, to the right of set-off conferred by the Statutes of Set-off. In the first place, the Statutes provided that mutual debts 'may', as opposed to 'shall', be set off.[577] Moreover, the occurrence of a set-off under the Statutes

---

[571] See para. 5.125 above.

[572] See the discussion in *Federal Commerce & Navigation Co Ltd v Molena Alpha Inc* [1978] 1 QB 927, 975, and also para. 4.50 above.

[573] See para. 5.96 above.

[574] Insolvency Act 1986, s. 323 (bankruptcy). For company liquidation, see the Insolvency Rules 1986, r. 4.90, and for administration see r. 2.85. See generally ch. 6.

[575] *National Westminster Bank Ltd v Halesowen Presswork & Assemblies Ltd* [1972] AC 785. See para. 6.111 below.

[576] See Lord Simon of Glaisdale in *National Westminster Bank Ltd v Halesowen Presswork & Assemblies Ltd* [1972] AC 785, 808–9, and Vinelott J in *Re Maxwell Communications Corp plc (No. 2)* [1993] 1 WLR 1402, 1411. For a criticism of this view, see paras 6.111–6.112 below.

[577] See (1729) 2 Geo II, c. 22, s. 13, and (1735) 8 Geo II, c. 24, s. 5.

would not appear to be a matter in which the public have an interest. Rather, the right was introduced by the Statutes for the benefit of defendants.[578] Consistent with that view, a defendant is not obliged to raise a cross-debt as a defence under the Statutes,[579] but may bring separate proceedings in respect of it, though in such a case he or she could be penalised in relation to costs.[580] *Prima facie*, then, the maxim 'quilibet potest renunciare juri pro se introducto'[581] should apply, so that it should be possible to renounce the right to invoke the defence. There is nevertheless early authority to the contrary.[582] In *Lechmere v Hawkins*,[583] the defendant had promised to repay money borrowed from the plaintiff without taking any notice of a debt due to him from the plaintiff, and without setting one demand against the other. Lord Kenyon said that this was an honorary obligation only, and that the defendant could not be compelled to abide by it when the Statutes themselves conferred upon him the right to set one demand against the other. That decision was subsequently followed by Lord Erskine in *Taylor v Okey*.[584] There are also cases in which a purchaser of goods was allowed a set-off in an action for the price even though the purchaser had agreed to pay in ready money,[585] an agreement which would appear to be inconsistent with payment by way of set-off.[586] However, this is no longer the prevailing view.[587] In *Hongkong & Shanghai Banking Corporation v Kloeckner & Co AG*,[588] Hirst J held that a person can contract out of the right of set-off, a view which was shared by Dillon LJ in *BICC Plc v Burndy Corporation*[589] and which was affirmed by the Court of Appeal in *Coca-Cola Financial Corporation v Finsat International Ltd*.[590] Sir Andrew Morritt C also accepted that view in *Re Kaupthing Singer and Friedlander Ltd*.[591] The New South Wales

---

[578] *Davis v Hedges* (1871) LR 6 QB 687, 690.

[579] See e.g. *Green v Law* (1805) 2 Smith KB 668; *Laing v Chatham* (1808) 1 Camp 252, 170 ER 947; *Jenner v Morris* (1861) 3 De G F & J 45, 54, 45 ER 795, 798; *Davis v Hedges* (1871) LR 6 QB 687, 690. In *Coca-Cola Financial Corporation v Finsat International Ltd* [1998] QB 43, 52 Neill LJ noted that, under the Statutes of Set-off, there was no obligation for a solvent debtor to exercise his or her right of set-off.

[580] See *Green v Law* (1805) 2 Smith KB 668.

[581] Anyone may, at his pleasure, renounce the benefit of a stipulation or other right introduced entirely in his own favour. See *Broom's Legal Maxims* (10th edn, 1939), 477.

[582] The cases are discussed by Farrar, 'Contracting out of set-off' (1970) 120 *New Law Journal* 771. Professor Farrar rightly pointed out that *Skyring v Greenwood* (1825) 4 B & C 281, 107 ER 1064 was a case in which the debt itself, as opposed to a right of set-off, had been waived. *Quaere* whether this would explain *Baker v Langhorn* (1816) 6 Taunt 519, 128 ER 1136, in which the broker was claiming payment of a loss as agent for the insured rather than for himself, though in any event the case was concerned with bankruptcy set-off as opposed to the Statutes of Set-off.

[583] (1798) 2 Esp 626, 170 ER 477.

[584] (1806) 13 Ves Jun 180, 33 ER 263.

[585] *Eland v Karr* (1801) 1 East 375, 102 ER 145; *Cornforth v Rivett* (1814) 2 M & S 510, 105 ER 471. See also *M'Gillivray v Simson* (1826) 5 LJOSKB 53.

[586] *Brandao v Barnett* (1846) 12 Cl & Fin 787, 808, 8 ER 1622, 1630 (Lord Campbell).

[587] In addition to the cases referred to below, see *Hoverd Industries Ltd v Supercool Refrigeration and Air Conditioning (1991) Ltd* [1995] 3 NZLR 577, 588, in which there was a clear implication that set-off was to be excluded. See para. 5.135 below. In Victoria, contracting out is permitted in relation to SCR r. 13.14. See *John Holland Construction & Engineering Pty Ltd v Majorca Projects Pty Ltd* (Vic SC, Hansen J, 27 July 1995, BC9503852 at 12), and generally as to the position in Victoria paras 2.83–2.86 above.

[588] [1990] 2 QB 514.

[589] [1985] 1 Ch 232, 248.

[590] [1998] QB 43.

[591] [2009] 2 Lloyd's Rep 154.

Supreme Court came to the same conclusion in *Stephen v Doyle*,[592] and it is also supported by cases in which the courts have given effect to a term of a contract between a debtor and a creditor by which the debtor agreed that he or she would not invoke against an assignee of the debt any right of set-off otherwise available to the debtor against the creditor/assignor.[593] The circumstance that one of the parties has become insolvent and either gone into administration[594] or receivership does not reduce or minimize the effect of an exclusion of rights of set-off under the Statutes.[595]

Clear words

5.134　In the context of equitable set-off and common law abatement, the courts have said that there is a presumption that neither party to a contract intends to abandon any remedies for its breach arising by operation of law, and that accordingly there must be clear words to exclude a set-off or a defence of abatement.[596] In *BICC Plc v Burndy Corporation*,[597] Dillon LJ commented that this applies 'equally, if not *a fortiori*', to set-off under the Statutes.[598]

5.135　As in the case of equitable set-off, it should not be necessary that the agreement refers specifically to set-off in order to exclude the defence. The defence may be excluded if there is a clear implication to that effect.[599] In a case in New Zealand, B owed a debt to A, and A had issued redeemable preference shares to C, B and C being related companies, and the parties had agreed that B was not required to make repayments of the debt unless there was simultaneously a redemption by A of a corresponding amount of preference shares. The New Zealand Court of Appeal considered that the agreement showed a clear intention to tie repayments of the debt by B to payments by A for redemption of shares, so as to preclude a set-off of B's debt against a separate debt owing by A to B.[600]

Waiver

5.136　Given that it is possible to contract out of this statutory right of set-off, in an appropriate case the right may be held to have been waived.[601]

---

[592] (1882) 3 NSWR (Eq) 1. See also *Morrison Knudsen Corporation of Australia Ltd v Australian National Railways Commission* (1996) 22 ACSR 262, 267 (Federal Court of Australia, Mansfield J).

[593] See e.g. *Re Blakely Ordnance Co, ex p New Zealand Banking Corporation* (1867) LR 3 Ch App 154 and *Re Goy & Co Ltd. Farmer v Goy & Co Ltd* [1900] 2 Ch 149, 154, and generally para. 17.45 below.

[594] Note, however, the Insolvency Rules 1986, r. 2.85 in the situation where the administrator, being authorized to make a distribution to creditors, has given notice under r. 2.95 that he proposes to make it. See para. 6.10 below.

[595] *Re Kaupthing Singer and Friedlander Ltd* [2009] 2 Lloyd's Rep 154.

[596] See para. 5.96 above.

[597] [1985] 1 Ch 232, 248.

[598] In New South Wales, *quaere* whether this would apply to set-off under the Civil Procedure Act 2005, s. 21 (for which see paras 2.64–2.73 above). Subsection (3) provides that parties may agree that debts may not be set off against each other, without reference to any presumption in relation to intent.

[599] See para. 5.96 above.

[600] *Hoverd Industries Ltd v Supercool Refrigeration and Air Conditioning (1991) Ltd* [1995] 3 NZLR 577, 586, 588.

[601] See *Baker v Langhorn* (1816) 6 Taunt 519, 128 ER 1136. Compare *Moore v Jervis* (1845) 2 Coll 60, 63 ER 637. *Skyring v Greenwood* (1825) 4 B & C 281, 107 ER 1064 was a case in which the debt itself, as opposed to a right of set-off, was waived. See Farrar, 'Contracting out of set-off' (1970) 120 *New Law Journal* 771, 772.

(6) Second ranking security, and subordination

A creditor may have agreed that security given for the debt is to be second ranking after **5.137** security given by the debtor to another creditor. Ordinarily, this would not be regarded as an agreement by the first creditor not to set off the debt owing to him or her until the prior ranking secured creditor has been paid. The agreement goes to the ranking of the security, not to the payment of the debts.[602] It should be contrasted with an agreement by a creditor to subordinate the debt in point of payment to another creditor's debt. In such a case the first creditor may not employ the subordinated debt in a set-off under the Statutes.[603] This may be justified on the basis of an implied agreement to that effect arising from the subordination,[604] though it should also follow from the principle that set-off under the Statutes requires that both debts be due and payable.[605] Until the other creditor's debt has been paid, the subordinated debt is not payable.

(7) Agreement not to assign

An agreement by a creditor not to assign the debt to a third party ordinarily would not be **5.138** interpreted as precluding the creditor from employing the debt in a set-off. *Gathercole v Smith*[606] may seem contrary to that view. A statute which provided that a pension payable to a retired incumbent of a benefice was not transferable was interpreted as also precluding a set-off against it. However, the decision should be regarded as turning on the object of the legislation, to provide for the maintenance of retired clergy. The object would have been defeated if the pension were to be reduced or extinguished by a set-off.

(8) Estoppel, and credit notes

When a contract provides for payments under it to be made without set-off, the fact that **5.139** the parties in the past have settled their debts by tendering a net amount on its own should not suffice to give rise to an estoppel so as to preclude reliance by the creditor on the clause. Often it would simply mean that, while the parties appeared to be solvent and their relationship was continuing on a satisfactory basis, there was no point in each of them tendering a separate payment. In the absence of an agreement or a clearly expressed understanding that this was intended to alter their contractual rights, it should not preclude the creditor from insisting on its strict legal rights in the future.[607] Further, when a creditor has issued a credit note to the debtor pursuant to a contract which contains a clause precluding set-offs, it would be a question of construction as to whether the credit note was intended to operate by way of a set-off against future contract payments. It may simply be an acknowledgment of indebtedness by the creditor which, in accordance with the contract, cannot be utilized by the debtor in a set-off.[608]

---

[602] *Edward Nelson & Co Ltd v Faber & Co* [1903] 2 KB 367, 377.

[603] *H Wilkins & Elkington Ltd v Milton* (1916) 32 TLR 618. In relation to set-off in bankruptcy and company liquidation, see paras 6.114–6.116 below.

[604] See Wood, *English and International Set-off* (1989), 690.

[605] See para. 2.29 above.

[606] (1881) 17 Ch D 1 (and see further proceedings at (1881) 7 QBD 626).

[607] *John Dee Group Ltd v WMH (21) Ltd* [1997] BCC 518, 525–6 (decision affirmed [1998] BCC 972).

[608] *John Dee Group Ltd v WMH (21) Ltd* [1998] BCC 972.

(9) Payment in advance

5.140 Consider the case of a payment in advance under a contract. The payment may operate as a prepayment of a debt, in which case the question of set-off would not arise in relation to the debt the subject of the prepayment, or alternatively it may constitute a security for future debts generally, in which case the question whether the debtor (as opposed to the creditor) can bring it into account in an action for payment of one such debt would depend on the terms of the contract.[609]

(10) Company under administration

5.141 In Australia, Mansfield J in the Federal Court, when faced with a clause which clearly and unambiguously excluded rights of set-off, declined to interpret it so as to permit a set-off when an administrator was appointed to the plaintiff pursuant to Part 5.3A of the Corporations Law,[610] notwithstanding that the statutory moratorium consequent upon the appointment[611] meant that the plaintiff under administration was entitled to payment of the debts owing to it though it could not be sued for the debts which it owed.[612] The same view has been adopted in England in relation to a company in administration.[613]

J. Failure to Assert a Cross-claim as a Defence

(1) Introduction

5.142 Consider that A is suing B for payment of a debt or other money sum and B has a cross-claim against A which is available as a defence by way of set-off, but B does not rely on it as a defence. In that circumstance, if A obtains judgment on the claim, can B enforce the cross-claim in a later action against A?

5.143 In *Henderson v Henderson*,[614] Sir James Wigram VC formulated the relevant principle in the following terms:

> [W]here a given matter becomes the subject of litigation in, and of adjudication by, a Court of competent jurisdiction, the Court requires the parties to that litigation to bring forward their whole case, and will not (except under special circumstances) permit the same parties to open the same subject of litigation in respect of matter which might have been brought forward as part of the subject in contest, but which was not brought forward, only because

---

[609] *John Dee Group Ltd v WMH (21) Ltd* [1998] BCC 972, 975–6 (CA), affirming [1997] BCC 518.

[610] Now the Corporations Act 2001 (Cth).

[611] Corporations Law, s. 440D.

[612] *Morrison Knudsen Corporation of Australia Ltd v Australian National Railways Commission* (1996) 22 ACSR 262.

[613] *Re Kaupthing Singer and Friedlander Ltd* [2009] 2 Lloyd's Rep 154. Note, however, the Insolvency Rules 1986, r. 2.85 in the situation where the administrator, being authorized to make a distribution to creditors, has given notice under r. 2.95 that he proposes to make it. A set-off under r. 2.85 would be mandatory and automatic. See paras 6.10, 6.111 and 6.124 below.

[614] (1843) 3 Hare 100, 115, 67 ER 313, 319. This has since been affirmed by the courts on numerous occasions. See e.g. *Hoystead v Commissioner of Taxation* [1926] AC 155, 170 (PC); *Yat Tung Investment Co Ltd v Dao Heng Bank Ltd* [1975] AC 581, 590 (PC); *Brisbane City Council v Attorney-General* [1979] AC 411, 425 (PC); *Port of Melbourne Authority v Anshun Pty Ltd* (1981) 147 CLR 589 (HCA).

they have, from negligence, inadvertence, or even accident, omitted part of their case. The plea of *res judicata* applies, except in special cases, not only to points upon which the Court was actually required by the parties to form an opinion and pronounce a judgment, but to every point which properly belonged to the subject of litigation, and which the parties, exercising reasonable diligence, might have brought forward at the time.

The principle has been described variously as an extended doctrine of *res judicata*,[615] or as *res judicata* in its wider sense,[616] or as an estoppel.[617] It is based on abuse of process.[618]

The scope of the doctrine has been expressed in various terms. In *Greenhalgh v Mallard*[619] **5.144** Somervell LJ said that it 'covers issues or facts which are so clearly part of the subject-matter of the [original] litigation and so clearly could have been raised that it would be an abuse of the process of the court to allow a new proceeding to be started in respect of them'. Subsequently, the Privy Council in *Yat Tung Investment Co Ltd v Dao Heng Bank Ltd*,[620] adopted a wider formulation, commenting that it would be 'an abuse of process to raise in subsequent proceedings matters which could and therefore should have been litigated in earlier proceedings'. In other words, if the matter *could* have been raised in earlier proceedings, it *should* have been, and failure to do so may result in the doctrine being invoked where there is an attempt to raise the matter in later proceedings. On the hand, while Wigram VC in *Henderson v Henderson* said that 'negligence, inadvertence, or even accident' would not justify the failure to bring forward the matter in the earlier litigation, he also recognized that it may be excused in special circumstances. For example, it has been said that it would be a special circumstance if the party seeking to litigate the matter at a later date was unaware, and could not reasonably have been expected to be aware, of the circumstances attending that matter at the time of the earlier litigation.[621]

The House of Lords considered the issue in *Johnson v Gore Wood & Co*,[622] and in doing so **5.145** signalled a flexible approach to the application of the principle. Lord Bingham of Cornhill[623]

---

[615] Spencer Bower and Handley, *Res Judicata* (4th edn, 2009), 305, para. 26.01.

[616] *Brisbane City Council v Attorney-General* [1979] AC 411, 425.

[617] See e.g. *Port of Melbourne Authority v Anshun* (1981) 147 CLR 589, 602, 604.

[618] *Brisbane City Council v Attorney-General* [1979] AC 411, 425; *Barrow v Bankside Agency Ltd* [1996] 1 WLR 257, 263; *Johnson v Gore Wood & Co* [2002] 2 AC 1. In Australia, Gibbs CJ and Mason and Aickin JJ in their joint judgment in *Port of Melbourne Authority v Anshun Pty Ltd* (1981) 147 CLR 589, 602 nevertheless said that 'the abuse of process test is not one of great utility', and proceeded to formulate a principle based on unreasonableness. See para. 5.146 below.

[619] [1947] 2 All ER 255, 257, referred to in *Johnson v Gore Wood & Co* [2002] 2 AC 1, 23. Similarly, Colman J said in *Stocznia Gdanska SA v Latvian Shipping Co* [1997] 2 Lloyd's Rep 228, 239 that: 'One must therefore look to the subject-matter of the new proceedings and compare it with that of the original proceedings. If the issues raised in the later proceedings ought properly to have been raised in the earlier proceedings because they arose from the same subject-matter, the Court will treat the subsequent attempt to raise the issues as an abuse of process, unless there are special circumstances.'

[620] [1975] AC 581, 590. See also *Republic of India v India Steamship Co* [1993] AC 410, 417.

[621] *Yat Tung Investment Co Ltd v Dao Heng Bank Ltd* [1975] AC 581, 590; *Ling v Commonwealth* (1996) 68 FCR 180, 195 (where, however, it was suggested that this is a situation in which the rule would not apply at all, as opposed to a special circumstance requiring the non-application of the rule). See also *Arnold v National Westminster Bank Plc* [1991] 2 AC 93 (change in the interpretation of the law); *C (A Minor) v Hackney LBC* [1996] 1 WLR 789, 792.

[622] [2002] 2 AC 1. See also *Gairy v Attorney General of Grenada* [2002] 1 AC 167 at [26] and [27] (PC).

[623] [2002] 2 AC 1, 31. Lord Goff of Chieveley, Lord Cooke of Thorndon and Lord Hutton agreed with Lord Bingham's judgment on this point.

rejected the *Yat Tung* approach, commenting that it would be wrong to hold that, because a matter could have been raised in earlier proceedings, it should have been, so as to render the raising of it in later proceedings necessarily abusive.[624] He criticized that approach as too dogmatic, and said that the question calls for:

> a broad, merits-based judgment which takes account of the public and private interests involved and also takes account of all the facts of the case, focusing attention on the crucial question whether, in all the circumstances, a party is misusing or abusing the process of the court by seeking to raise before it the issue which could have been raised before. As one cannot comprehensively list all possible forms of abuse, so one cannot formulate any hard and fast rule to determine whether, on given facts, abuse is to be found or not.

Lord Bingham went on to reject the approach that hitherto had been adopted, of asking whether the conduct is an abuse and then, if it is, asking whether the abuse is excused or justified by special circumstances. Rather, he suggested that the question should be framed simply in terms whether in all the circumstances the party's conduct is an abuse. In that regard, he said that there would rarely be a finding of abuse unless the later proceeding involves what the court regards as unjust harassment of a party.

(2) Australia

5.146 The *Yat Tung* formulation has also been criticized in Australia. In a joint judgment in the High Court in *Port of Melbourne Authority v Anshun Pty Ltd*,[625] Gibbs CJ, Mason and Aickin JJ said that in the *Yat Tung* case the adoption of the *Henderson v Henderson* principle 'was taken too far'.[626] Instead, they proposed a test based on reasonableness. In other words, was the matter now sought to be raised so relevant to the subject-matter of the former proceeding that it is reasonable to expect that it would have been raised in that proceeding?

> In this situation we would prefer to say that there will be no estoppel unless it appears that the matter relied upon as a defence in the second action was so relevant to the subject matter of the first action that it would have been unreasonable not to rely on it. Generally speaking, it would be unreasonable not to plead a defence if, having regard to the nature of the plaintiff's claim, and its subject matter it would be expected that the defendant would raise the defence and thereby enable the relevant issues to be determined in the one proceeding.[627]

(3) Statutes of Set-off

5.147 Consider the case of a creditor (A) who failed to assert the debt being sued upon as a defence under the Statutes of Set-off[628] in an earlier action brought against him or her by the debtor (B) for payment of another debt.

---

[624] See also Lord Millett at [2002] 2 AC 1, 59–60.

[625] (1981) 147 CLR 589.

[626] (1981) 147 CLR 589, 601–2. See also *Champerslife Pty Ltd v Manojlovski* [2010] NSWCA 33 at [4] and [89].

[627] (1981) 147 CLR 587, 602. It has been questioned whether the notion of relevance indeed is helpful when the issue concerns a failure to advance a claim which might have been raised in an earlier proceeding, as opposed to a defence. See *Gibbs v Kinna* [1999] 2 VR 19, 27, referring to *Boles v Esanda Finance Corporation Ltd* (1989) 18 NSWLR 666, 674.

[628] See ch. 2 above.

The Statutes do not require that there be any connection between the debts. They may be **5.148** totally unconnected, both as to their subject-matter and the circumstances relating to their creation. According to the formulation approved in the *Yat Tung* case, the absence of a connection would not matter. The cross-debt 'could and therefore should' have been litigated in the original proceeding as a defence, a view that is also consistent with statements suggesting that all defences should be brought forward.[629] The *Yat Tung* formulation is no longer current, however.[630] If the debts exhibit no commonality of issues or facts, and they relate to different subject-matters, enforcing the debt in a later action should not constitute unjust harassment of the debtor, in which case it should not be an abuse of process to enforce it separately.[631] Similarly, in Australia it should not be regarded as unreasonable in those circumstances to sue for it separately, for the purpose of the test set out in the *Anshun* case. This indeed reflects the position that has been adopted in the cases. The courts have said that a defendant is not obliged to raise a cross-debt as a defence under the Statutes but is entitled to bring separate proceedings in respect of it,[632] though the defendant may be penalized in relation to costs if he or she adopts that course of action.[633]

Separate judgments on the debts would not result in conflicting or contradictory judg- **5.149** ments, so that the concern expressed in that regard in other contexts[634] would not apply. A set-off under the Statutes does not occur until judgment for a set-off. Prior to judgment the debts retain their separate identities.[635] Therefore, the fact that A may obtain judgment on a debt owing to him or her by B, who as claimant in an earlier action had obtained judgment against A for payment of an unrelated debt, would not contradict A's earlier judgment. There may be contradictory judgments if the judgment in the first action

---

[629] See e.g. *Ord v Ord* [1923] 2 KB 432, 439, 443; *Ling v Commonwealth* (1996) 68 FCR 180, 182.
[630] See above.
[631] *Johnson v Gore Wood & Co* [2002] 2 AC 1, 31.
[632] *Green v Law* (1805) 2 Smith KB 668; *Jenner v Morris* (1861) 3 De G F & J 45, 53–4, 45 ER 795, 798 (Lord Campbell); *Davis v Hedges* (1871) LR 6 QB 687, 690; *Bank of Ireland v Martin* [1937] IR 189, 206. See also *Laing v Chatham* (1808) 1 Camp 252, 170 ER 947 and *Baskerville v Brown* (1761) 2 Burr 1229, 97 ER 804. In *Coca-Cola Financial Corporation v Finsat International Ltd* [1998] QB 43, 52 Neill LJ (with whose judgment Morritt and Hutchison LJJ agreed) noted that, under the Statutes of Set-off, there was no obligation for a solvent debtor to exercise his or her right of set-off. Thus, in *Port of Melbourne Authority v Anshun* (1981) 147 CLR 589 it was not sufficient that the indemnity gave rise to a defence. Rather, the High Court emphasized (at 604) the additional elements that the indemnity was closely connected with the subject-matter of the first action, and that, if it could be the subject of separate proceedings, it would give rise to a conflicting judgment. Compare Hobhouse LJ in *Escudier v Lloyd's Bank Plc* [1996] EWCA Civ 1131 at [3], who left open the question of the application of the *Henderson v Henderson* estoppel in the case of legal set-off.
[633] This was contemplated in *Green v Law* (1805) 2 Smith KB 668.
[634] *Caird v Moss* (1886) 33 Ch D 22, 35–6; *Re Konigsberg* [1949] Ch 348, 360–1; *Port of Melbourne Authority v Anshun Pty Ltd* (1981) 147 CLR 589, 596, 603–4; *Republic of India v India Steamship Co Ltd (The Indian Grace)* [1992] 1 Lloyd's Rep 124, 133 (Leggatt LJ, referred to in subsequent proceedings [1996] 2 Lloyd's Rep 12, 24). Thus, a factor that influenced the Australian High Court in the *Anshun* case to apply *Henderson v Henderson* was that the indemnity which the Authority sought to litigate in the later action would have impugned Ashun's entitlement to contribution that was the subject of the order in the first action. Accordingly, there could have been contradictory judgments if the second action proceeded. See the discussion at (1981) 147 CLR 589, 596 and 603–4. Further, while the Authority claimed contribution on one basis in the first action, in the second action it was seeking indemnity from the same person on a different basis. See *Triantafillidis v National Australia Bank* (1995) V Conv R 54–536 at p. 66,371.
[635] See para. 2.35 above.

determined that there was no set-off,[636] or if it was for the taking of an account which in its terms would have extended to the debt sought to be agitated in the second action,[637] but in the ordinary case, where the judgment in the first action related simply to payment of a debt, and this is also the effect of the judgment sought in the second action in relation to an unrelated cross-debt, there would not be any element of contradiction. Nor, if the debt to A had been pleaded in the original action, would it have obviated the necessity to inquire into and establish B's claim in that action.[638]

(4) Common law abatement

5.150　At common law, a defendant being sued for the price of goods sold with a warranty, or of work to be performed according to a contract, can plead in that action by way of defence circumstances which constitute a breach of the warranty or of the contract, and which show a diminution in the value of the subject-matter of the contract.[639] This is not in the way of pleading a cross-claim as a set-off. Rather, the defendant is permitted to defend him or herself by showing how much less the subject of the contract was worth by reason of the breach, and to obtain an abatement of the price accordingly.[640]

5.151　There is longstanding authority for the view that the purchaser need not rely on the circumstances giving rise to the breach as a defence to an action for the price, but that those circumstances instead can form the basis of a later action. Indeed, in the case of a sale of goods this is reflected in s. 53 of the Sale of Goods Act 1979. The principle was established in *Davis v Hedges*,[641] a decision of the Court of Queen's Bench handed down some twenty-eight years after *Henderson v Henderson*, though without reference to that case. In issue was a claim for damages for the improper performance of work agreed to be done by the defendant for the plaintiff. The defendant argued that he had previously sued for the price and had recovered the whole amount, and that, not having complained of the defective performance on that occasion, the plaintiff was precluded from bringing this action. The defence was rejected, Hannen and Blackburn JJ declining to follow an opinion earlier expressed by Lord Ellenborough in *Fisher v Samuda*,[642] that the defence should be made out in the original action.

---

[636] *Johnson v Durant* (1831) 2 B & Ad 925, 109 ER 1386. If the first action resulted in a judgment for a set-off, a later action obviously could not be brought on the cross-claim. See *Hennell v Fairlamb* (1800) 3 Esp 104, 170 ER 554. Lord Kenyon held in *Hennell v Fairlamb* that, to the extent that the cross-claim exceeded the amount of the plaintiff's claim in the first action, and therefore of the set-off, the surplus could be sued for separately. However, that was before the Judicature Acts introduced a right of counterclaim. It is likely that *Henderson v Henderson* would now preclude a second action where the surplus was not (but could have been) the subject of a counterclaim in the first action.

[637] See *Henderson v Henderson* (1843) 3 Hare 100, 67 ER 313 (explained in Handley, 'Anshun today' (1997) 71 *Australian Law Journal* 934, 936–7, and Spencer Bower and Handley, *Res Judicata* (4th edn, 2009), 306, para. 26.03), and *Public Trustee v Kenward* [1967] 1 WLR 1062.

[638] Compare *Port of Melbourne Authority v Anshun Pty Ltd* (1981) 147 CLR 589, 604.

[639] See paras 2.123–2.134 above.

[640] *Mondel v Steel* (1841) 8 M & W 858, 871–2, 151 ER 1288, 1293–4.

[641] (1871) LR 6 QB 687, 25 LT 155.

[642] (1808) 1 Camp 190, 191, 170 ER 925.

In *Davis v Hedges*, the action for the price was settled without having proceeded to judg-   **5.152**
ment, whereas Wigram VC in his statement of the principle in *Henderson v Henderson*
referred to the earlier action as having been the subject of an adjudication by a court of
competent jurisdiction.[643] The House of Lords has now accepted, however, that the fact
that the first action was settled prior to judgment does not preclude the application of the
Henderson v Henderson principle,[644] and in any event this aspect of *Davis v Hedges* has not
been emphasized in subsequent discussions of the case. *Davis v Hedges* has been accepted as
authority for a general proposition that a purchaser of goods or of work and labour is not
obliged to set up as a defence a cross-claim relating to a breach of warranty or contract
which diminishes the value of the subject-matter of the contract, but can pay the agreed
price and bring a separate action.[645] It has not been suggested that a different principle may
apply when an action for the price proceeded to judgment without the defence having been
pleaded. Indeed, the contrary has been stated.[646] Moreover, *Davis v Hedges* has continued
to be accepted notwithstanding that the main reason given by Hannen J for not following
the contrary view expressed earlier by Lord Ellenborough in *Fisher v Samuda*[647] has ceased
to be relevant after the Judicature Acts.[648] Hannen J said[649] that the effect of Lord
Ellenborough's opinion would be that part of the damages recoverable by the buyer of
goods or of work and labour, to the extent that they represented a depreciation in the value
of the subject-matter of the contract, could be pleaded as a defence to an action for the

---

[643] (1843) 3 Hare 100, 115, 67 ER 313, 319. See also *Dallal v Bank Mellat* [1986] 1 QB 441, 454–5
(Hobhouse J). This applies to *res judicata* generally. See *Thoday v Thoday* [1964] P 181, 197–8.

[644] *Johnson v Gore Wood & Co* [2002] 2 AC 1, 32–3, 59. Compare *Hoppe v Titman* [1996] 1 WLR 841
(referring to *A Martin French v Kingswood Hill Ltd* [1961] 1 QB 96); *Rigge v Burbidge* (1846) 15 M & W 598,
153 ER 988; *McIver Transport Pty Ltd v Byrne* (Qld SC, Atkinson J, 20 Nov 1998, BC9806577 at [13]) (referring, *inter alia*, to *Atsas v Gertsch* (NSW SC, Hodgson CJ in Eq, 28 July 1998, BC9803443 at 18)). *Aliter* if the
settlement proceeded on the basis of an underlying assumption that a further proceeding could be brought.
See *Johnson v Gore Wood & Co* at 33–4 and *McIver Transport Pty Ltd v Byrne* (express reservation of rights).

[645] *Caird v Moss* (1886) 33 Ch D 22, 34 (Cotton LJ), 35 (Lindley LJ); *Healing (Sales) Pty Ltd v Inglis
Electrix Pty Ltd* (1968) 121 CLR 584, 593, 601, 615, *Henriksens Rederi A/S v THZ Rolimpex (The Brede)*
[1974] 1 QB 233, 248; *Langford Concrete Pty Ltd v Finlay* [1978] 1 NSWLR 14, 18; *Port of Melbourne
Authority v Anshun Pty Ltd* (1981) 147 CLR 589, 600; *Bellowes Archital Ltd v Bell Projects Ltd* (1997) 87 BLR
31, 35; *McIver Transport Pty Ltd v Byrne* (Qld SC, Atkinson J, 20 Nov 1998, BC9806577 at [19]); Spencer
Bower and Handley, *Res Judicata* (4th edn, 2009), 112 para. 8.16, 319 para. 26.17; *Benjamin's Sale of Goods*
(7th edn, 2006), 1068. See also *Champerslife Pty Ltd v Manojlovski* [2010] NSWCA 33 at [97]. In a case where
the breach of warranty was set up as a defence to the seller's action for the price, the Sale of Goods Act 1979,
s. 53(4) provides that the purchaser is not prevented by that circumstance from maintaining an action for the
same breach of warranty if he or she has suffered 'further damage'. *Quaere* if 'further damage' refers to damage which was not taken into account in assessing the reduction in the price, or if it merely refers to damage
which the purchase could not have set up in the first action such as fresh damage suffered after the first action
was disposed of. See Benjamin *loc. cit.* The latter view is consistent with the *Henderson v Henderson* principle
and is to be preferred. See *Halsbury's Laws of England* (4th edn, 2005 reissue) vol. 41, 227 para. 308 and also
Benjamin *loc. cit.*, but compare *AFA Electronics Pty Ltd v Strathfield Group Wholesale Pty Ltd* [2001] VSC 289
at [87].

[646] See Lindley LJ in *Caird v Moss* (1886) 33 Ch D 22, 35 (who seems to have assumed that the plaintiff
in *Davis v Hedges* had obtained a judgment in the first action); Spencer Bower and Handley, *Res Judicata*
(4th edn, 2009), 112 para. 8.16, 319 para. 26.17; *Benjamin's Sale of Goods* (7th edn, 2006), 1068.

[647] (1808) 1 Camp 190, 191, 170 ER 925. See above.

[648] See *Port of Melbourne Authority v Anshun Pty Ltd* (1981) 147 CLR 589, 601.

[649] (1871) LR 6 QB 687, 691.

price, but that other consequential damages recoverable by the buyer could not,[650] thereby complicating and increasing litigation. Since the Judicature Acts, however, it has been possible to include a claim for consequential damages by way of a counterclaim in the plaintiff's action, and in any event a claim for consequential damages could be the subject of a separate defence of equitable set-off in the action.

(5) Equitable set-off

5.153 Alternatively, the question may concern the availability of an equitable set-off, in circumstances where a debtor suffered judgment on the debt and later seeks to enforce an unliquidated damages claim against the creditor which could have provided a defence in equity to the action on the debt if it had been so asserted. Equitable set-off differs from set-off under the Statutes in that the cross-claims generally must be connected. The traditional formulation is that the defendant's cross-claim must be sufficiently closely connected with the plaintiff's claim such that the plaintiff's title to sue is impeached.[651]

5.154 When it is sought to litigate in a later action a cross-claim that would have given rise to a defence of equitable set-off if pleaded in an earlier action to enforce a debt, a judgment on the cross-claim in the later action would not contradict the earlier judgment for payment of the debt.[652] Equitable set-off, unlike set-off under the Statutes of Set-off, admittedly is regarded as a substantive defence. But this does not mean that it takes effect as an automatic extinction of the cross-demands to the extent of the set-off. If that were the case, judgment in a later action on the cross-claim would contradict the earlier judgment. Rather, the substantive nature of the defence means that, prior to judgment for a set-off, the unpaid creditor's conscience is affected in equity such that he or she is not entitled to assert that moneys are due from the debtor to the extent of the cross-demand, notwithstanding that at law the cross-claims continue to subsist.[653] If the question of unconscionability in equity has not been raised, the simple fact of separate judgments on the common law claims should not show any inconsistency.[654]

---

[650] The defence of abatement only applies to the extent that the value of the goods or the work and labour the subject of the contract has been reduced as a result of the breach of warranty or contract. Other claims for consequential damage are not within the principle. See para. 2.126 above.

[651] See para. 4.02 above.

[652] *Aliter* if the present claimant earlier had failed to establish the claim when he or she unsuccessfully asserted it as an equitable set-off in a summary judgment application brought against him or her by the present defendant. See *Escudier v Lloyd's Bank Plc* [1996] EWCA Civ 1131.

[653] See para. 4.30 above.

[654] See *Murphy v Abi-Saab* (1995) 37 NSWLR 280, 290–1. In *Triantafillidis v National Australia Bank* (1995) V Conv R 54–536 at p 66,370, the later damages claim against the mortgagee for negligence, fraud and misleading or deceptive conduct in relation to the mortgage transaction was not regarded as inconsistent with the earlier judgment for possession in favour of the mortgagee, where the judgment for possession was founded upon default in the mortgage payments. There may, however, be cases where the circumstances would show conflicting judgments. An example mentioned by Handley JA of the New South Wales Court of Appeal (writing extra-judicially) is where the first judgment in favour of the creditor involved the taking of an account, for example for the balance due under the mortgage. The account would be regarded as covering all debit and credit items that could have been brought forward, and a subsequent action on a cross-claim that would have been admissible as an item in that account accordingly would be inconsistent with the earlier judgment. See Handley, 'Anshun today' (1997) 71 *Australian Law Journal* 934, 937–8, and the discussion of the *Yat Tung* case in Spencer Bower and Handley, *Res Judicata* (4th edn, 2009), 307–8 para. 26.05.

The question is whether it would nevertheless be an abuse of process for the purpose of the **5.155** *Henderson v Henderson* principle to bring a separate action on the cross-claim, rather than raising it as a defence in earlier proceedings. In *Escudier v Lloyd's Bank Plc*,[655] Hobhouse LJ, with whom Peter Gibson LJ agreed, accepted that a defendant who is sued in debt is not under any obligation to raise an equitable set-off,[656] and Simon Brown LJ expressed a similar opinion in relation to the circumstances in issue in that case.[657] Views to a similar effect have been expressed on other occasions.[658] Indeed, the contrary view would sit uncomfortably with the position that the courts to date have accepted in relation to the common law defence of abatement,[659] and it would be difficult to offer a rational explanation for treating the common law and the equitable defences differently.

The position in Australia is more complex. There is authority in that country which sug- **5.156** gests that the *Henderson v Henderson* principle may apply in the case of closely connected cross-claims, on the basis of the principle as formulated by the High Court in *Port of Melbourne Authority v Anshun*,[660] and there is also support for that view in Canada.[661]

In the *Anshun* case,[662] Gibbs CJ, Mason and Aickin JJ warned that: 'To require that the **5.157** defendant always raise his cross-claim or set-off at the first available time could cause great inconvenience.' Subsequently, in *Tanning Research Laboratories Inc v O'Brien*,[663] Brennan and Dawson JJ said that a plaintiff could not be precluded from taking proceedings in respect of a cause of action merely because he or she could have counterclaimed on that cause of action in an earlier proceeding brought by the opposite party, except in a case where the relief claimed in the second proceeding is inconsistent with the judgment in the first. That view was qualified, however, by the Full Court of the Federal Court in *Bryant v Commonwealth Bank of Australia*,[664] their Honours suggesting that, in making that comment in the *Tanning Research Laboratories* case, Brennan and Dawson JJ may have had in mind a situation, such as that before them in that case, where the cross-claim depended on facts remote from those in the principal claim. In that circumstance, there is no policy justification for forcing a defendant to litigate his or her own claim as a cross-claim rather than as a principal claim in a separate action. But where a defendant's cross-claim is intimately connected with the plaintiff's claim, in the sense that each arises substantially out of the same matters of fact, the Full Court in the *Bryant* case considered that the claims should

---

[655] [1996] EWCA Civ 1131.
[656] [1996] EWCA Civ 1131 at [3].
[657] [1996] EWCA Civ 1131 at [56].
[658] *Mullen v Conoco Ltd* [1998] QB 382, 397; *Specialist Group International Ltd v Deakin* [2001] EWCA Civ 777 at [14]–[15] and [25]. Compare *Ron Jones (Burton-on-Trent) Ltd v Hall* [1998] EWHC Tech 328 (arbitration).
[659] See paras 5.150–5.152 above.
[660] See para. 5.146 above.
[661] *420093 BC Ltd v Bank of Montreal* (1995) 128 DLR (4th) 488 (Alberta Court of Appeal).
[662] (1981) 147 CLR 589, 600.
[663] (1990) 169 CLR 332, 346.
[664] (1995) 57 FCR 287, 297–8 (Beaumont, Wilcox and Moore JJ). Compare also *Yat Tung Investment Co Ltd v Dao Heng Bank Ltd* [1975] AC 581, 589 in relation to the possibility of a counterclaim (though note the explanation for the case offered by Handley, 'Anshun today' (1997) 71 *Australian Law Journal* 934, 937), and also compare Buckley J's qualified comment in *Public Trustee v Kenward* [1967] 1 WLR 1062, 1067 in relation to a 'counterclaim . . . relating to some quite different cause of action . . .').

be litigated at the one time,[665] so as to minimize costs and avoid the possibility of inconsistent judgments.[666]

5.158 Subsequently, Wilcox J, who was one of the judges in *Bryant v Commonwealth Bank*, offered a refinement on the views expressed in that case. He pointed out in *Ling v Commonwealth*[667] that some cross-claims overlap the facts of the principal claim but also involve additional facts. In such a case, a question of degree arises. He emphasized that it would be wrong to say that the principle in *Henderson v Henderson* is excluded where there are additional facts. But where the additional facts are substantial, he suggested that it may be appropriate to accept the reasonableness of separate proceedings. Further, separate proceedings might be reasonable if the defendant was not in a position to know the existence or extent of any breach of contract or warranty by the plaintiff when the plaintiff commenced the action.[668]

5.159 In relation to the common law defence of abatement, Hannen J, in *Davis v Hedges*,[669] noted that the extent to which the breach of warranty or contract may afford a defence may be uncertain at the date that the plaintiff issues a writ for payment of the price, and it may take some time to ascertain to what amount the value of the subject-matter of the contract is diminished by the plaintiff's default. This is a valid consideration[670] which should apply equally to equitable set-off. It may provide a justification in Australia for not pleading a damages cross-claim by way of a defence of set-off in the original action.

(6) Default judgments

5.160 The Privy Council in *Kok Hoong v Leong Cheong Kwen Mines Ltd*,[671] said that 'it would be wrong to apply the full vigour' of the principle in *Henderson v Henderson* where the

---

[665] In Australia, see also *Ling v Commonwealth* (1996) 68 FCR 180 (though in the circumstances of that case it was held that it was not unreasonable to commence separate proceedings); *Atsas v Gertsch* (NSW SC, Hodgson CJ in Eq, 28 July 1998, BC9803443 at 17–18); *Ryan v Hanson* (2000) 49 NSWLR 184, 194–5; *Emanuel Management Pty Ltd v Foster's Brewing Group Ltd* (2003) 178 FLR 1 at [1085]–[1103]. In the New South Wales Court of Appeal in *O'Brien v Tanning Research Laboratories Inc* (1988) 14 NSWLR 601, 613, Kirby P referred to 'a cross or counter-claim which was so relevant to the subject matter of the litigation that it would have been unreasonable not to plead it'. Compare *Pertsinidis v Australian Central Credit Union* (2001) 80 SASR 76; *Leisure Boating Club (Roseville) Inc v Q-Corp Marine Pty Ltd* (2003) 127 FCR 55.

[666] In the *Bryant* case, the Commonwealth Bank had obtained judgment against the appellant on a claim for payment of an amount owing under guarantees and for possession of premises mortgaged to the bank, and the appellant sought in the present action to sue the bank on representations alleged to have been made by the bank and upon which he relied in executing the guarantees, as well as for breaches of various duties by the bank in relation to the obtaining of the guarantees and the mortgages. Since the matters sought to be raised by the appellant in the claim against the bank were all matters connected with the claims formerly prosecuted by the bank against the appellant, the principle in *Henderson v Henderson* was held to apply.

[667] (1996) 68 FCR 180, 183. See also Handley, 'Anshun today' (1997) 71 *Australian Law Journal* 934, 940 ('there cannot be any general proposition that all related cross actions and set-offs which could have been pleaded, but were not, will be barred').

[668] *McIver Transport Pty Ltd v Byrne* (Qld SC, Atkinson J, 20 Nov 1998, BC9806577 at [18]).

[669] (1871) LR 6 QB 687, 690–1.

[670] *Port of Melbourne Authority v Anshun Pty Ltd* (1981) 147 CLR 589, 600–1.

[671] [1964] AC 993, 1011. See also *Arnold v National Westminster Bank Plc* [1991] 2 AC 93, 107.

judgment was a default judgment, so that it was not contested.[672] A default judgment gives rise to an estoppel only for what must 'necessarily and with complete precision' have been determined by the judgment.[673] Ordinarily, this should not preclude an action on a cross-claim which is not inconsistent with the earlier judgment.[674]

(7) Dismissal of cross-claim for want of prosecution

The dismissal of a defendant's cross-claim for want of prosecution does not preclude the defendant from employing it defensively as a set-off against the claimant's claim. The dismissal would nevertheless affect the defendant if the cross-claim exceeds the claimant's claim, since the defendant would not be able to recover the excess by way of a counterclaim.[675]   **5.161**

(8) Discontinuance

A similar principle should apply when an action is discontinued without the imposition of a condition preventing the subject-matter from again being litigated. A person who discontinued proceedings in those circumstances should not be precluded from later employing the claim in a set-off.[676]   **5.162**

K. Criticisms of the State of the Law of Set-off

Before insolvency, a set-off may occur at law under the Statutes of Set-off when there are mutual liquidated debts, even if they are unconnected, and a set-off may occur in equity in relation to claims which are sufficiently connected, even if they are unliquidated, but there may not be a set-off of cross-claims if one or both is unliquidated and they are unconnected. This has been described as unsatisfactory and lacking logic and sense.[677] Yet, on other occasions, the courts have commented adversely on suggestions that it should be possible for a cross-claim for libel to be set off against a claim for the price of goods sold and delivered,[678] or that, if A sues B for damages for breaking his leg, B should be able to set up as a defence a claim against A as the acceptor of a bill of exchange.[679] Is it really the case, then, that the law of set-off is in an unsatisfactory state?   **5.163**

---

[672] Compare summary judgment, which is a final judgment on the merits. See *Vehicles and Supplies Ltd v Financial Institutions Services Ltd* [2005] UKPC 24 at [22].

[673] *Kok Hoong v Leong Cheong Kwen Mines Ltd* [1964] AC 993, 1012 (referring to Lord Maugham in *New Brunswick Railway Co v British and French Trust Corporation Ltd* [1939] AC 1, 21); *Carl Zeiss Stiftung v Rayner & Keeler Ltd* [1967] AC 853, 946 (Lord Upjohn); *Mullen v Conoco Ltd* [1998] QB 382, 389. Compare *Triantafillidis v National Australia Bank* (1995) V Conv R 54–536 at p 66,371.

[674] See *Mullen v Conoco Ltd* [1998] QB 382, and also *Atsas v Gertsch* (NSW SC, Hodgson CJ in Eq, 28 July 1998, BC9803443 at 17–18).

[675] *Owen v Pugh* [1995] 3 All ER 345, 351–2.

[676] This would follow from *Running Pygmy Productions Pty Ltd v AMP General Insurance Co Ltd* [2001] NSWSC 431 at [33]–[36]. Compare *Pertsinidis v Australian Central Credit Union Ltd* (2001) 80 SASR 76.

[677] *Axel Johnson Petroleum AB v MG Mineral Group AG* [1992] 1 WLR 270, 274 (Leggatt LJ), 275–6 (Staughton LJ). See also *B Hargreaves Ltd v Action 2000 Ltd* [1993] BCLC 1111, 1116 (Nolan LJ).

[678] *Stooke v Taylor* (1880) 5 QBD 569, 591–2 (Manisty J).

[679] *Pellas v Neptune Marine Insurance Co* (1879) 5 CPD 34, 41 (Bramwell LJ, with whom Brett and Cotton LJJ agreed), referred to in *McDonnell & East Ltd v McGregor* (1936) 56 CLR 50, 59 (Dixon J).

5.164   Consider set-off under the Statutes of Set-off. For this form of set-off, there must be a debt on each side of the account.[680] In such a case, the net position often would have been apparent to the claimant, and he or she therefore should have taken it into account in considering whether to sue.[681] It would difficult to question the availability of a defence in that circumstance. The same cannot be said when one or both of the claims is unliquidated. However, when the defendant's unliquidated cross-claim is closely connected with the plaintiff's claim, so that, in the language of Lord Cottenham in *Rawson v Samuel*,[682] the plaintiff's title to sue is impeached, the justice of a set-off is also apparent. The outstanding question is whether the defence should be extended to include an unconnected damages claim. In considering this question, it should be appreciated that an expansion in the scope of the defence could have important consequences.

5.165   In the first place, it could adversely affect the rights and interests of third parties. For example, an assignee of a debt takes subject to any defences, including rights of set-off, available to the debtor against the assignor before the debtor had notice of the assignment.[683] An expansion in the scope of the defence of set-off accordingly could reduce the value of the assigned debt in the hands of the assignee, even though the assignee may have provided full consideration for the assignment and may not have been aware at the time of the assignment of the existence of an unrelated damages cross-claim against the assignor.

5.166   Third parties in other contexts could also be affected. Thus, a secured creditor may have a fixed charge over a debt owing to the chargor but the chargor itself is liable to the debtor.[684] The creditor would take subject to a defence of set-off available to the debtor against the chargor before the debtor had notice of the security,[685] but under the law as it now stands the creditor would not be bound by an unrelated damages cross-claim that would not constitute a defence as between the chargor and the debtor. The issue could also arise in the context of subrogation,[686] for example in the case of a subrogated insurer, where the insurer is subrogated to its insured's claim against a third party, but the third party has a cross-claim against the insured. A subrogated insurer takes subject to defences available to the third party against the insured,[687] which should include defences of set-off. Similarly, the issue

---

[680]   See para. 2.14 above.

[681]   *Stooke v Taylor* (1880) 5 QBD 569, 576, 586; *Hanak v Green* [1958] 2 QB 9, 23; *BICC plc v Burndy Corporation* [1985] 1 Ch 232, 248, 249.

[682]   (1841) Cr & Ph 161.

[683]   See ch. 17 below. In Australia it has been suggested that an assignee of a debt may take subject to an unliquidated cross-demand available to the debtor against the assignor, notwithstanding that it would not have given rise to a defence as between those parties, if it arose out of the same contract as the assigned debt. See paras 17.06–17.09 below. The point is that it is not sufficient for an equitable set-off that the cross-demands arose out of the same contract. See para. 4.91 above. The proposition inherent in the Australian view, that an assignee could take subject to a cross-demand that is not available as a set-off against an assignor, was rejected by the House of Lords in *Bank of Boston Connecticut v European Grain and Shipping Ltd* [1989] 1 AC 1056, 1105–6, 1109–11, and the better view is that it is incorrect.

[684]   See paras 17.99–17.118 below.

[685]   Compare the position in relation to equitable set-off. See para. 17.32 below.

[686]   See paras 17.151–17.157 below.

[687]   *Sydney Turf Club v Crowley* [1971] 1 NSWLR 724, 734 *per* Mason JA ('When an insurer is subrogated to the rights of the insured against a third party . . . . . [the action] is brought in the name of the insured and it is subject to all the defences which would be available if the action had been brought by the insured for his own benefit'), and see Derham, *Subrogation in Insurance Law* (1985), 122–3.

would be relevant to a judgment creditor who is seeking to attach a debt owing by a third party to the judgment debtor by way of a third party debt order (formerly, a garnishee order). The judgment creditor would take subject to any defence of set-off available to the third party against the judgment debtor before service of the interim order.[688] An analogous principle applies when an undisclosed principal sues for payment of a debt arising on a contract entered into by the agent. The principal may be met by a defence of set-off that arose before the debtor had notice of the agency.[689]

Secondly, set-off affects cash flow,[690] and an extension in the ambit of the defence could adversely affect a business which is sensitive to cash flow. Indeed, the Privy Council has referred to cash flow as 'the life blood of business',[691] and, in a shipping case, Robert Goff J described it as 'a matter of considerable, sometimes crucial, importance'.[692] The problem is that, if a debtor being sued for a debt has an arguable defence, the creditor ordinarily would not be able to obtain prompt payment through the summary judgment procedure.[693]   **5.167**

Consider, for example, that A has completed work for B, and it is not disputed that the work was completed in accordance with the contract, so that A is otherwise entitled to payment from B. However, B alleges that A was negligent in relation to other work that is not connected with the present claim for payment, or B asserts some other damages claim against A that is unrelated to A's claim, for example for defamation. If the defence of set-off were expanded to include unconnected damages cross-claims, and B has a real prospect of succeeding on the cross-claim,[694] the availability of a defence to B ordinarily would preclude A from being able to obtain summary judgment for payment of the otherwise admitted debt.[695] A could be kept out of its money, with the result that it may not be able to pay suppliers, or pay wages, or service bank loans, until the determination of what may be a protracted and an uncertain action for damages. But in the interim, suppliers could deny A credit or employees could leave because they have not been paid, or A could default under its bank facilities, which in turn could result in the failure of the business.   **5.168**

Indeed, a claimant could be denied summary judgment even though it has insurance covering it for liability on an unrelated damages cross-claim asserted against it. The defendant   **5.169**

---

[688] See *Bishop v Woinarski* (1875) 1 VLR (L) 31; *Tapp v Jones* (1875) LR 10 QB 591, 593. See generally paras 17.136–17.145 below.

[689] See e.g. *Turner v Thomas* (1871) LR 6 CP 610, 613 *per* Willes J ('Where the factor sells in his own name to a third party who buys without notice that he is dealing with an agent, the latter . . . may set up against the concealed principal any defence which he may have against the factor'), and generally paras 13.79–13.99 below.

[690] *Stein v Blake* [1996] AC 243, 251.

[691] *Agnew v Commissioner of Inland Revenue* [2001] 2 AC 710 at [7].

[692] *SL Sethia Liners Ltd v Naviagro Maritime Corporation (The Kostas Melas)* [1981] 1 Lloyd's Rep 18, 26. See also *Modern Engineering (Bristol) Ltd v Gilbert-Ash (Northern) Ltd* (1973) 71 LGR 162, 167 (CA) in relation to the construction industry.

[693] CPR Part 24.

[694] Under CPR r. 24.2(a)(ii) the court may give summary judgment against a defendant if it considers that the defendant has no real prospect of successfully defending the claim.

[695] Andrews, 'The proper limits of set-off' [1992] *Cambridge Law Journal* 239. This should also apply under the new Civil Procedure Rules 1998. See para. 1.05 above.

could sit back until the determination of the damages cross-claim, and use it in order to resist the claimant's demand for payment, even though the defendant is assured of payment in any event because of the claimant's insurance cover, and notwithstanding that the claimant requires cash flow to support its business.

5.170 This discussion is subject to three qualifications.

5.171 The first is that, if a cross-claim does not amount to a defence, the court in giving summary judgment on the claim has a discretion to order a stay on enforcement pending trial of the counterclaim.[696] An order to that effect would still deny the claimant cash flow from the judgment. In a particular case, however, the court may regard a stay as inappropriate. Under former rules of court, the question whether enforcement of a judgment should be stayed depended on such factors as whether the counterclaim arose out of a separate and distinct transaction or whether there was a connection between the claims, the strength of the counterclaim and the ability of the plaintiff to satisfy any judgment on the counter-claim.[697] The court could also take into account the needs of the parties for cash.[698] In *A. B. Contractors Ltd v Flaherty Brothers Ltd*[699] a sub-contractor obtained judgment for payment of an amount owing for work completed at one site, and the contractor sought a stay of execution pending trial of a counterclaim for damages arising out of a separate and distinct contract at a different site. The Court of Appeal[700] held that the circumstances did not justify a stay. Cumming-Bruce LJ delivered the leading judgment. He posed the question in terms whether it was 'fair and reasonable to keep the plaintiffs out of their money on a judgment which they have obtained . . .'.[701] In the circumstances, where there was no connection between the contracts, he said that it was not just and equitable for the plaintiffs to be kept out of their money. It has been suggested that, under the new Civil Procedure Rules 1998, the courts may be prepared to grant summary judgment and a delay on enforcement more frequently than hitherto.[702] However, the factors to which the courts formerly had regard should still be relevant to the determination of whether a stay should be granted.

5.172 The second qualification is that B (in the example) would be entitled to leave to defend if it is owed an unrelated debt, because the case would then be one of mutual debts giving rise to a defence of set-off under the Statutes of Set-off. Often, however, an action for payment of a debt is more straightforward than a damages claim, so that the period during which A would be kept out of its money while the cross-debt is determined would not be as significant. Moreover, when both demands are for liquidated debts, it can be said that the existence and amount of the set-off should have been apparent to the claimant, who should

---

[696] See CPR rr. 3.1(3) and 24.6, and para. 5.1 of the Practice Direction supplementing CPR Part 24. See generally *Civil Procedure* (2010) vol. 1, paras 24.2.6 and 24.6.3.

[697] See para. 1.05 above.

[698] *Aectra Refining and Manufacturing Inc v Exmar NV* [1994] 1 WLR 1634, 1652.

[699] (1978) 16 BLR 8. See also *Anglian Building Products Ltd v W & C French (Construction) Ltd* (1972) 16 BLR 1.

[700] Stephenson, Geoffrey Lane and Cumming-Bruce LJJ

[701] (1978) 16 BLR 8, 12. Geoffrey Lane and Stephenson LJJ agreed with Cumming-Bruce LJ's judgment.

[702] *Civil Procedure* (2010) vol. 1, para. 24.2.6.

have given credit for it in his action.[703] That consideration would not apply with the same force when one or both of the demands requires an assessment of damages.

The third qualification is that, if B's damages cross-claim arises from defects in the work the subject of A's claim for payment, B would ordinarily be entitled to an equitable set-off, or alternatively a defence under the common law principle of abatement.[704] But in that circumstance there would be nothing inequitable in B withholding payment pending the determination of the damages claim, since it goes to the question of the true value of the work performed for which payment is sought. It is in the situation in which an *unrelated* cross-claim for damages could be used to keep a person out of his or her money that an extended defence could operate harshly. **5.173**

Because of these considerations, it is suggested that it is undesirable to extend the defence of set-off to encompass unrelated damages cross-claims.[705] But this does not mean that there is no scope for reform. **5.174**

There have been occasions where the question whether a cross-claim gives rise to a set-off or a counterclaim has resulted in time-consuming debate in the courts for no purpose other than for the determination of costs. A defendant is generally in a better position in relation to costs if he or she has a defence of set-off than in the case of a mere counterclaim. A successful defence ordinarily results in an order for costs in favour of the defendant, whereas in the event of a successful claim and counterclaim the defendant ordinarily is entitled to a costs order in relation to the counterclaim but will have to pay the claimant's costs in relation to the claim.[706] Costs are within the court's discretion, and the circumstances of a particular case may warrant a different order, but this represents the *prima facie* position. It would seem an unproductive use of the courts time to determine whether a cross-claim gives rise to a set-off or a counterclaim simply for the purpose of deciding costs. This sentiment is reflected in a comment by Morris LJ in *Hanak v Green*:[707] **5.175**

> So it has come about that we have heard a learned debate, rich in academic interest, but, save so far as costs are affected, barren of practical consequence, on the subject as to whether certain claims could be proudly marshalled as set-off or could only be modestly deployed as counterclaim.

An extension in the ambit of the defence to include unconnected damages cross-claims would remedy this perceived problem. But it could have other results that are not as easy to justify. In particular, it would affect the interests of third parties, for example assignees for value, and it would affect legitimate business requirements for cash flow. With that in mind, there is another way of dealing with the issue, and that is by way of the order for costs. Where a defendant in an action for payment of a debt or damages succeeds in establishing a cross-claim for a debt or damages, in appropriate cases costs could be awarded as **5.176**

---

[703] See para. 5.164 above.
[704] See para. 2.123–2.134 above.
[705] This was also the view of the New South Wales Law Reform Commission in its report on '*Set-off*', No 94, February 2000, paras 4.10–4.13, 5.10–5.12.
[706] See para. 1.06 above.
[707] [1958] 2 QB 9, 16.

if the defendant had succeeded in defending the claim to the extent of the cross-claim, whether or not that was the case. The advantage of this approach is that it would not affect third parties, whose position would still depend on whether the cross-claim gave rise to a defence in fact, but at the same time it would avoid arid debates as to the distinction between set-off and counterclaim where the only consequence is in relation to costs. Under the new CPR 44.3 the principle that 'costs follow the event' is still the general rule, but the rule also emphasizes that the court can make a different order.[708]

5.177   In *Axel Johnson Petroleum AB v M G Mineral Group AG*[709] Leggatt and Staughton LJJ questioned the utility of the distinction between set-off and counterclaim in the context of summary judgment. In other words, should the question whether a defendant can resist an application for summary judgment on the basis of a cross-claim depend on the technical question whether the defendant has a defence of set-off or a counterclaim? In truth, though, the case for reform in this area is not compelling. The point was made above that the notion that any monetary cross-claim can be utilized by way of defence, and that therefore it should be sufficient to defeat an application for summary judgment on a claim for payment of an admitted debt to the extent of the cross-claim, could operate harshly where cash flow is essential for the ongoing operation of a business. As mentioned above also, a defendant with a cross-claim not amounting to a defence is not without a remedy, because the court in giving judgment for the claimant on the claim can order a stay of execution pending trial of the counterclaim. Whether the court will order a stay is a matter of discretion. The degree of connection between the claim and counterclaim, the strength of the counterclaim, and the ability of the claimant to satisfy any judgment on the counterclaim are considerations that the court will take into account in the exercise of its discretion.[710] In cases where there is no set-off, Staughton LJ commented, in the *Axel Johnson* case,[711] that the grant of a stay pending the trial of a counterclaim 'has generally been sufficient to safeguard the defendant's cashflow when justice requires that result, and not if the defendant does not deserve indulgence'. He therefore concluded that: 'perhaps, we can continue to tolerate the law as it stands.'

---

[708] See the discussion of CPR 44.3 in *AEI Rediffusion Music Ltd v Phonographic Performance Ltd* [1999] 1 WLR 1507, 1522–3.
[709] [1992] 1 WLR 270.
[710] See para. 5.171 above.
[711] [1992] 1 WLR 270, 276.

6

SET-OFF IN BANKRUPTCY AND
COMPANY LIQUIDATION

A. Set-off in Bankruptcy

6.01 The principal source of rights of set-off in the event of a bankruptcy is the Insolvency Act 1986, s. 323,[1] which provides:

> (1) This section applies where before the commencement of the bankruptcy there have been mutual credits, mutual debts or other mutual dealings between the bankrupt and any creditor of the bankrupt proving or claiming to prove for a bankruptcy debt.
>
> (2) An account shall be taken of what is due from each party to the other in respect of the mutual dealings and the sums due from one party shall be set off against the sums due from the other.
>
> (3) Sums due from the bankrupt to another party shall not be included in the account taken under subsection (2) if that other party had notice at the time they became due that a bankruptcy petition relating to the bankrupt was pending.
>
> (4) Only the balance (if any) of the account taken under subsection (2) is provable as a bankruptcy debt or, as the case may be, to be paid to the trustee as part of the bankrupt's estate.

In company liquidation, the relevant provision is set out in the Insolvency Rules 1986, r. 4.90,[2] and in administration r. 2.85.[3] Set-off in bankruptcy and company liquidation (and, in England, administration) are referred to collectively in this book as 'insolvency set-off'.

6.02 The availability of set-off may be crucial in circumstances where a bankrupt and a creditor have had prior mutual dealings giving rise to cross-demands. In the absence of a set-off, the creditor would be obliged to pay the full amount of his or her debt to the trustee in bankruptcy, and would be confined to proving with the other creditors in the bankruptcy for the amount owing on the cross-claim against the bankrupt. If, however, the requirements of the insolvency set-off section (or, as it is sometimes called, the mutual credit provision) are satisfied, only the balance remaining after deducting one claim from the other is payable.

---

[1] The corresponding provision in Australia is the Bankruptcy Act 1966 (Cth), s. 86. In relation to the bankruptcy of an underwriting member of a Lloyd's syndicate, note para. 6.174 below.

[2] See para. 6.06 below. In Australia, see the Corporations Act 2001 (Cth), s. 553C.

[3] See para. 6.10 below. There is no equivalent provision in the Australian Corporations Act 2001 (Cth).

Therefore, if the bankrupt's claim against the creditor exceeds the creditor's cross-claim against the bankrupt, the creditor in effect obtains payment in full for the cross-claim in the form of a deduction from his or her liability and is only required to pay the balance to the trustee. Alternatively, if the creditor's claim is the greater,[4] the creditor receives payment in full to the extent of the creditor's liability to the bankrupt and need only prove for the balance.

Notwithstanding the reference in s. 323(1) to a 'creditor of the bankrupt proving or claiming to prove for a bankruptcy debt', it is not necessary that the creditor should have lodged, or attempted to lodge, a proof in the bankruptcy as a prerequisite to invoking the section. Thus, the set-off may be given effect as a defence to an action brought by a trustee in bankruptcy or a liquidator rather than in the context of a proof in the insolvency.[5] Indeed, it is now accepted that the insolvency set-off section takes effect automatically upon the occurrence of a bankruptcy or a liquidation,[6] so that, to the extent of a set-off, nothing would remain that could be proved. In *Stein v Blake*,[7] Lord Hoffmann said that the words in sub-s. (1) should be construed to mean a 'creditor of the bankrupt who (apart from s. 323) would have been entitled to prove for a bankruptcy debt'.[8]

6.03

The mutual credit provision may apply in the event of a bankruptcy or a company liquidation, including when an insolvent partnership is wound up in accordance with the Insolvent Partnerships Order 1994.[9] It also may apply in the winding up of a limited liability partnership incorporated under the Limited Liability Partnerships Act 2000.[10] It is not expressed to apply, however, to an individual voluntary arrangement under Part VIII of the Insolvency Act,[11] or to an arrangement under the Deeds of Arrangements Act 1914 unless it has been expressly incorporated into the deed itself.[12]

6.04

---

[4] The insolvency set-off section operates regardless of whether the result of a set-off would give a balance in favour of or against the bankrupt. See *Coventry v Charter Pacific Corporation Ltd* (2005) 227 CLR 234 at [57].

[5] *Mersey Steel & Iron Co v Naylor, Benzon & Co* (1882) 9 QBD 648 (affirmed (1884) 9 App Cas 434); *Gye v McIntyre* (1991) 171 CLR 609, 622; *Stein v Blake* [1996] AC 243, 255; *Coventry v Charter Pacific Corporation Ltd* (2005) 227 CLR 234 at [57]; *Mine & Quarry Equipment International Ltd v McIntosh* (2005) 54 ACSR 1 at [6]. If a cross-claim raised by way of defence to an action by a trustee in bankruptcy or a company in liquidation is perceived to be weak, summary judgment may be given in favour of the trustee or the company subject (in appropriate cases) to conditions which may protect the position of the defendant pending determination of the cross-claim. See *Swissport (UK) Ltd v Aer Lingus Ltd* [2007] EWHC 1089 (Ch).

[6] See paras 6.119–6.146 below.

[7] [1996] AC 243.

[8] [1996] AC 243, 253. See also *Re Bank of Credit and Commerce International SA (No. 8)* [1998] AC 214, 228. In Australia, a similar meaning has been ascribed to the expression 'a person claiming to prove a debt in the bankruptcy' in the Bankruptcy Act 1966 (Cth), s. 86, and also to the expression 'a person who wants to have a debt or claim admitted against the company' in the Corporations Act 2001 (Cth), s. 553C in the case of company liquidation. See *Gye v McIntyre* (1991) 171 CLR 609, 621; *G. M. & A. M. Pearce and Co Pty Ltd v RGM Australia Pty Ltd* [1998] 4 VR 888, 890, 896–9. See also *Handberg v Smarter Way (Aust) Pty Ltd* (2002) 20 ACLC 856, 868.

[9] S.I. 1994 No. 2421. See also para. 12.05 below. In Australia, a partnership, association or other body that consists of more than five members may be wound up under the Corporations Act 2001 (Cth) as a Part 5.7 body, in which case the set-off section (s 553C) applies. See s. 583.

[10] See the Limited Liability Partnerships Regulations 2001, regs 5 and 10 (S.I. 2001 No. 1090).

[11] See paras 6.17–6.19 below.

[12] See *Re E. J. Casse, ex p G. H. Robinson v The Trustee* [1937] 1 Ch 405; *Re Rissik* [1936] 1 Ch 68. See also *Baker v Lloyd's Bank, Ltd* [1920] 2 KB 322, but compare *Baker v Adam* (1910) 15 Com Cas 227. Compare also the concession made by counsel in *Re Fenton, ex p Fenton Textile Association, Ltd* [1931] 1 Ch 85, 97.

B. Companies

(1) Company liquidation

6.05   Prior to the enactment of the Supreme Court of Judicature Act 1875, the insolvency set-off section in the bankruptcy legislation did not apply to company liquidation. There were instances of set-offs being enforced in liquidations,[13] but the set-offs in those cases were founded upon the right of set-off conferred by the Statutes of Set-off in the case of mutual debts,[14] as opposed to the bankruptcy section. In a number of respects, however, the courts appear to have departed from orthodoxy in allowing a set-off.[15] The Statutes only operated as a procedural defence to an action at law to obtain payment of a debt.[16] *Prima facie* they should not have justified a set-off in the context of a proof lodged in a liquidation.[17] Nevertheless, a set-off was allowed in that context.[18] Moreover, the application of the Statutes when the set-off was asserted as a defence to an action brought by the liquidator in a court ordered winding up[19] or a winding up subject to the supervision of the court[20] is not free from difficulty. The debt sought to be set off should have been recoverable by action against the company.[21] But after a winding-up order, or an order directing that a voluntary winding up should continue but subject to the court's supervision, an action could not have been brought against the company without the leave of the court.[22]

6.06   The Supreme Court of Judicature Act 1875, s. 10, incorporated the rules of bankruptcy 'as to debts and liabilities provable' into the law of company liquidation whenever the assets

---

[13] See e.g. *Re Agra and Masterman's Bank. Anderson's Case* (1866) LR 3 Eq 337; *Re South Blackpool Hotel Co, ex p James* (1869) LR 8 Eq 225 (though *quaere* if this was a case of equitable set-off arising from closely connected cross-claims); *Brighton Arcase Co Ltd v Dowling* (1868) LR 3 CP 175; *Re China Steamship Co, ex p Mackenzie* (1869) LR 7 Eq 240; *Re Progress Assurance Co, ex p Bates* (1870) 22 LT 430, 39 LJ Ch 496. In *Smith, Fleming, & Co's Case* (1866) LR 1 Ch App 538, a set-off was denied on the ground that the company's cross-debt was not due and payable (see para. 2.29 above), but the judgment of Sir George Turner (with whom Knight Bruce LJ concurred) suggests that, were it not for that circumstance, a set-off would have been available.

[14] *Brighton Arcade Co, Ltd v Dowling* (1868) LR 3 CP 175, 182, 184; *Sankey Brook Coal Co, Ltd v Marsh* (1871) LR 6 Ex 185, 187, 189; *Ex p Price, re Lankester* (1875) LR 10 Ch App 648, 650.

[15] See *FCT v Linter Textiles Australia Ltd* (2005) 220 CLR 592 at [40].

[16] See paras 2.34–2.39 above.

[17] *Ex p Price* (1875) LR 10 Ch App 648, 650; *Re Daintrey* [1900] 1 QB 546, 547–548.

[18] *Re South Blackpool Hotel Co, ex p James* (1869) LR 8 Eq 225 (though this case may be explicable on the basis of an equitable set-off arising from closely connected cross-claims: see ch. 4 above). See also *Re China Steamship Co, ex p MacKenzie* (1869) LR 7 Eq 240 (set-off against an assignee), and para. 17.42 below.

[19] As in *Re Agra and Masterman's Bank (Anderson's Case)* (1866) LR 3 Eq 337.

[20] As in *Re Progress Assurance Co, ex p Bates* (1870) 22 LT 430, 39 LJ Ch 496.

[21] See para. 2.46 above.

[22] Companies Act 1862, ss. 87 (winding-up order), 148 and 151 (voluntary winding up subject to supervision). See now the Insolvency Act 1986, s. 130(2). Thus, there were suggestions in *Brighton Arcade Co, Ltd v Dowling* (1868) LR 3 CP 175, 183–4 and *Sankey Brook Coal Co Ltd v Marsh* (1871) LR 6 Ex 185, 189 that the set-off only applied in a voluntary winding up because, unlike in a court ordered winding up (see s. 87) or a voluntary winding up subject to the supervision of the court (see ss. 148 and 151), there was no restriction in the Companies Act 1862 on actions against a company the subject of a voluntary winding up. But set-offs were recognized in those other situations. See *Re Agra and Masterman's Bank. Anderson's Case* (1866) LR 3 Eq 337 (court order); *Re Progress Assurance Co, ex p Bates* (1870) 22 LT 430, 39 LJ Ch 496 (subject to supervision); *Re China Steamship Co, ex p MacKenzie* (1869) LR 7 Eq 240 (subject to supervision).

of the company were insufficient for the payment of its debts and liabilities and the costs of the winding up, and it was confirmed by the House of Lords in 1884 that the incorporation included the set-off section.[23] The relevant provision is now set out in the Insolvency Rules 1986, r. 4.90.[24] When it was first made, r. 4.90 was similar in form to the corresponding bankruptcy section (the Insolvency Act 1986, s. 323), albeit with a number of changes which reflected the distinction between bankruptcy and company liquidation. In 2005, however, r. 4.90 was recast in order to address various issues that had arisen in relation to the construction of the rule.[25] Rule 4.90 now provides:

(1) This Rule applies where, before the company goes into liquidation there have been mutual credits, mutual debts or other mutual dealings between the company and any creditor of the company proving or claiming to prove for a debt in the liquidation.

(2) The reference in paragraph (1) to mutual credits, mutual debts or other mutual dealings does not include –
  (a) any debt arising out of an obligation incurred at a time when the creditor had notice that –
    (i) a meeting of creditors had been summoned under section 98; or
    (ii) a petition for the winding up of the company was pending;
  (b) any debt arising out of an obligation where –
    (i) the liquidation was immediately preceded by an administration; and
    (ii) at the time the obligation was incurred the creditor had notice that an application for an administration order was pending or a person had given notice of intention to appoint an administrator;
  (c) any debt arising out of an obligation incurred during an administration which immediately preceded the liquidation; or
  (d) any debt which has been acquired by a creditor by assignment or otherwise, pursuant to an agreement between the creditor and any other party where that agreement was entered into –
    (i) after the company went into liquidation;
    (ii) at a time when the creditor had notice that a meeting of creditors had been summoned under section 98;
    (iii) at a time when the creditor had notice that a winding-up petition was pending;
    (iv) where the liquidation was immediately preceded by an administration, at a time when the creditor had notice that an application for an administration order was pending or a person had given notice of intention to appoint an administrator; or
    (v) during an administration which immediately preceded the liquidation.

(3) An account shall be taken of what is due from each party to the other in respect of the mutual dealings, and the sums due from one party shall be set off against the sums due from the other.

---

[23] *Mersey Steel and Iron Co v Naylor, Benzon & Co* (1884) 9 App Cas 434, 437–8. See *also Re Bank of Credit and Commerce International SA (No. 8)* [1996] Ch 245, 256 (CA); *Re One. Tel Ltd* (2002) 43 ACSR 305 at [25].

[24] Made pursuant to the Insolvency Act 1986, s. 411. See *Bouygues (UK) Ltd v Dahl-Jensen (UK) Ltd* [2000] BLR 522 at [31] (referring to s. 411(2) and Sch. 8, para. 12).

[25] Insolvency (Amendment) Rules 2005 (S.I. 2005 No. 527). Rule 4.90 had been amended earlier by the Insolvency (Amendment) Rules 2003 (S.I. 2003 No. 1730). The new form of r. 4.90 does not apply to a company which entered into administration or went into liquidation before 1 April 2005. See the Insolvency (Amendment) Rules 2005, r. 3. Note that some peculiar rules may apply in the liquidation of an insurance company or of an underwriting member of a Lloyd's syndicate. See paras 6.79 and 6.174 below.

(4) A sum shall be regarded as being due to or from the company for the purposes of paragraph (3) whether –
  (a) it is payable at present or in the future;
  (b) the obligation by virtue of which it is payable is certain or contingent; or
  (c) its amount is fixed or liquidated, or is capable of being ascertained by fixed rules or as a matter of opinion.

(5) Rule 4.86 shall also apply for the purposes of this Rule to any obligation to or from the company which, by reason of its being subject to any contingency or for any other reason, does not bear a certain value.

(6) Rules 4.91 to 4.93 shall apply for the purposes of this Rule in relation to any sums due to the company which –
  (a) are payable in a currency other than sterling;
  (b) are of a periodical nature; or
  (c) bear interest.

(7) Rule 11.13 shall apply for the purposes of this Rule to any sum due to or from the company which is payable in the future.

(8) Only the balance (if any) of the account owed to the creditor is provable in the liquidation. Alternatively the balance (if any) owed to the company shall be paid to the liquidator as part of the assets except where all or part of the balance results from a contingent or prospective debt owed by the creditor and in such a case the balance (or that part of it which results from the contingent or prospective debt) shall be paid if and when that debt becomes due and payable.

(9) In this Rule 'obligation' means an obligation however arising, whether by virtue of an agreement, rule of law or otherwise.

6.07 In Australia, the company liquidation set-off provision is set out in the Corporations Act 2001 (Cth), s. 553C.

6.08 Formerly, the company liquidation set-off provision was considered to be applicable to any company in liquidation unless and until it was shown that the company's assets were sufficient to pay all the company's debts in full, together with the costs of the winding up.[26] This is no longer the position in England. Rule 4.90 can apply in any company liquidation, compulsory or voluntary, irrespective of the solvency or otherwise of the company.[27] It should be contrasted with the corresponding Australian provision, the Corporations Act 2001 (Cth), s. 553C,[28] which is expressed to apply only to insolvent companies.[29]

---

[26] *Fryer v Ewart* [1902] AC 187, 192; *Re Pink. Elvin v Nightingale* [1927] 1 Ch 237, 241; *Re Rolls-Royce Co Ltd* [1974] 1 WLR 1584, 1590. See also *Re Fine Industrial Commodities Ltd* [1956] 1 Ch 256. It was held in *Re Canada Cycle and Motor Agency (Queensland) Ltd* [1931] St R Qd 281 (and see also *Page v Commonwealth Life Assurance Society Ltd* (1935) 36 SR (NSW) 85, 89) that this applied also to voluntary liquidation, but compare *Gerard v Worth of Paris Ltd* [1936] 2 All ER 95 in relation to a members' voluntary winding up.

[27] In relation to a members' voluntary winding up, see the Insolvency Rules 1986, r. 4.1(1)(c), and *Rayden v Edwardo Ltd* [2008] EWHC 2689 (Comm) at [10] and [23]. In relation to a creditors' voluntary winding up and a winding up by the court, see r. 4.1(2).

[28] In *Re Parker* (1997) 80 FCR 1, 7 Mansfield J said of s. 553C that it: 'amounts to an adoption of the concepts underlying s. 86 of the Bankruptcy Act in terms more appropriate to corporations.' See also *G. M. & A. M. Pearce and Co Pty Ltd v RGM Australia Pty Ltd* [1998] 4 VR 888, 899; *Chadmar Enterprises Pty Ltd v IGA Distribution Pty Ltd* (2006) 160 ACTR 29 at [10].

[29] A company is insolvent if it is unable to pay all its debts as and when they become due and payable. See the Corporations Act 2001 (Cth), s. 95A. Section 553C also applies in the winding up of a 'Part 5.7 body' under the Corporations Act 2001 (Cth). See s. 583. A Part 5.7 body is defined in s. 9 as including various

Leave to proceed not necessary

Set-off in company liquidation provides a defence to an action brought by the liquidator **6.09** for payment of a sum due to the company.[30] Because it is a defence to the action, it is not necessary to obtain leave to proceed against the company[31] in order to assert the set-off.[32] Leave is necessary, however, if the cross-claim against the company exceeds the debt due to the company and it is sought to pursue the balance by way of a counterclaim.[33]

(2) Administration

Prior to 2003, the Insolvency Rules conferred no right of set-off in the case of a company **6.10** subject to an administration order as opposed to a liquidation.[34] Rights of set-off in administration were determined instead by reference to the forms of set-off available as between solvent parties.[35] The position changed in 2003 when the Insolvency Rules were amended by the substitution of a new Part 2.[36] This included a new r. 2.85, which permitted set-offs in circumstances where an administrator, being authorized to make a distribution,[37] gave notice to creditors of his intention to do so under r. 2.95. In 2005, r. 2.85 was recast in a form similar to the new r. 4.90 (above).[38]

The notice to creditors under r. 2.95 must state whether the distribution is to preferential **6.11** creditors or preferential creditors and unsecured creditors.[39] A set-off under r. 2.85 is only available to a creditor to whom a distribution would be made in accordance with the notice, were it not for a set-off. This follows from r. 2.85(2), which defines 'mutual dealings' in terms of mutual credits, mutual debts or other mutual dealings between the company 'and any creditor of the company proving or claiming to prove for a debt in the administration'. It is also consistent with r. 2.85(8), which provides that the balance of the account owed to the creditor is provable in the administration.

---

entities such as a foreign company, and a partnership, association or other body that consists of more than five members.

[30] See para. 6.03 above.

[31] Pursuant to the Insolvency Act 1986, s. 130(2). In Australia, see the Corporations Act 2001 (Cth), s. 471B.

[32] *Mersey Steel & Iron Co v Naylor, Benzon & Co* (1882) 9 QBD 648 (decision affirmed (1884) 9 App Cas 434). See also *Langley Constructions (Brixham) Ltd v Wells* [1969] 1 WLR 503 (esp. at 513); *Mine & Quarry Equipment International Ltd v McIntosh* (2005) 54 ACSR 1 at [4]–[5].

[33] *Langley Constructions (Brixham) Ltd v Wells* [1969] 1 WLR 503; *Mine & Quarry Equipment International Ltd v McIntosh* (2005) 54 ACSR 1 at [4]–[5].

[34] *Isovel Contracts Ltd v ABB Building Technologies Ltd* [2002] 1 BCLC 390.

[35] See below. Administration does not affect the legal or beneficial title to the company's property and accordingly does not affect mutuality.

[36] Insolvency (Amendment) Rules 2003 (S.I. 2003 No. 1730). Pursuant to r. 5, the new Part 2 did not apply to administrations where the petition for the administration order was presented before 15 September 2003.

[37] An administrator requires the permission of the court to make a distribution to a creditor who is neither secured nor preferential. See the Insolvency Act 1986, Sch. B1 para. 65(3).

[38] Insolvency (Amendment) Rules 2005 (S.I. 2005 No. 527). Pursuant to r. 3, the new provision applies to companies which entered administration on or after 1 April 2005. In relation to an underwriting member of Lloyd's, the application of r. 2.85 is qualified by r. 22 of the Insurers (Reorganisation and Winding Up) (Lloyd's) Regulations 2005 (S.I. 2005 No. 1998). See para. 6.174 below.

[39] Insolvency Rules 1986, r. 2.95(2)(b).

6.12 In Australia, the insolvency set-off section does not apply when an administrator is appointed to a company under Part 5.3A of the Corporations Act 2001 (Cth).[40] The position is different in the case of a deed of company arrangement entered into pursuant to Div. 10 of Part 5.3A of the Corporations Act. Section 553C of the Act, which permits set-off in the case of company liquidation, is incorporated by Sch. 8A, cl. 8 of the Corporations Regulations into a deed of company arrangement unless the deed provides otherwise.[41] If cl. 8 of the Schedule is excluded, the deed otherwise may expressly incorporate the set-off provision.[42] Failure to incorporate set-off into a deed could provide grounds to have it set aside.[43]

6.13 Under the English Insolvency Rules, if an administrator has not been authorized to make a distribution to creditors[44] or, being authorized, the administrator has not given notice that he or she proposes to make a distribution pursuant to r. 2.95, the set-off conferred by r. 2.85 does not apply in the administration. Other forms of set-off may be available, however. While a company is in administration, no legal process (including legal proceedings) may be instituted or continued against the company except with the consent of the administrator or the permission of the court.[45] This statutory moratorium should not

---

[40] *Morrison Knudsen Corporation of Australia Ltd v Australian National Railways Commission* (1996) 22 ACSR 262, 266, 268.

[41] Corporations Act 2001 (Cth), s. 444A(5), and the Corporations Regulations 2001, reg. 5.3A.06. For the application of s. 553C in the case of a deed of company arrangement, see *G. M. & A. M. Pearce and Co Pty Ltd v RGM Australia Pty Ltd* [1998] 4 VR 888; *Handberg v Smarter Way (Aust) Pty Ltd* (2002) 190 ALR 130 at [25]; *Arcfab Pty Ltd v Boral Ltd* (2002) 43 ACSR 573; *Brodyn Pty Ltd v Dasein Constructions Pty Ltd* [2004] NSWSC 1230; *Veolia Water Solutions v Kruger Engineering (No. 3)* [2007] NSWSC 459; *Reed Constructions Australia Ltd v DM Fabrications Pty Ltd* (2007) 25 ACLC 1463 at [35]–[38]. See also *Winterton Constructions Pty Ltd v M. A. Coleman Joinery Co Pty Ltd* (1996) 20 ACSR 671; *Meehan v Stockmans Australian Café (Holdings) Pty Ltd* (1996) 22 ACSR 123. It seems to have been assumed in *Winterton Constructions* (at 674–6) that set-off under the deed had a procedural operation, in that it depended upon the creditor's claim being dealt with under the deed, whereas it is now accepted that insolvency set-off operates automatically. See paras 6.119–6.146 below, and *Pearce v RGM Australia* (above). Any surplus in favour of the company after the set-off may be recovered by the company after termination of the deed, notwithstanding that any net claim against the company would have been extinguished by the deed. See *Arcfab Pty Ltd v Boral Ltd* (above). If s. 553C is not incorporated into a deed, creditors who are also debtors would not have the benefit of a set-off unless set-off is dealt with in other provisions of the deed (see below), or a right of set-off is available under the Statutes of Set-off or by way of equitable set-off. In the case of the Statutes of Set-off, however, the statutory moratorium on proceedings against the company by a person bound by the deed save with the leave of the court (see s. 444E) would appear to preclude a set-off as a defence to an action to enforce payment of a debt owing to the company unless leave has been obtained. See paras 2.46–2.50 above. Compare *Helou v P D Mulligan Pty Ltd* (2003) 57 NSWLR 74, which concerned the construction of a guarantee given for the debts of a company that executed a deed of company arrangement.

[42] *Metal Manufacturers Ltd v Hall* (2002) 41 ACSR 466. In *Central Data Networks Pty Ltd v Global Diagnostics Ltd* (1998) 84 FCR 304, 320–1 Sch. 8A, cl. 8 had been excluded, and the deed did not otherwise contain an express set-off provision, but French J nevertheless countenanced that entitlements under the deed could be calculated having regard to any off-setting debt. The justification for this was not explained.

[43] See the Corporations Act 2001 (Cth), s. 445D(1)(f), and *Re Opes Prime Stockbroking Ltd* (2008) 171 FCR 473 at [16]. Compare *Central Data Networks Pty Ltd v Global Diagnostics Ltd* (1998) 84 FCR 304, 320–1.

[44] See the Insolvency Act 1986, Sch. B1 para. 65(3).

[45] Insolvency Act 1986, Sch. B1 para. 43(6). See also Sch. B1 para. 44(5), in the situation where an administration application has been made in respect of a company and the application has not yet been granted or dismissed or the application has been granted but the administration order has not yet taken effect, and the Insolvency Act, s. 252(2), in the situation in which an interim order has been made under Part VIII in relation

prevent a creditor from relying on a substantive defence of equitable set-off,[46] or preclude a bank from asserting a combination of accounts.[47] Nor should it prevent a creditor from exercising a contractual right of set-off[48] before notice is given under r. 2.95.[49] None of these involve the institution or continuation of a legal process.[50] On the other hand, the Insolvency Act also prohibits any steps being taken to enforce a security over the company's property.[51] Whether this would extend to the exercise of a contractual right of set-off would depend on whether the agreement takes effect as a charge. This issue is considered later.[52]

Different considerations apply to the procedural defence of set-off available under the Statutes of Set-off. It is a requirement of this form of set-off that the debt sought to be   **6.14**

---

to an individual voluntary arrangement. A similar moratorium applies in Australia when a company is the subject of an administration order and in the case of a deed of company arrangement. See the Corporations Act 2001 (Cth), ss. 440D and 440F in relation to administration and, for deeds of company arrangement, s. 444E(3).

[46] For the substantive nature of equitable set-off, see paras 4.29–4.57 above.

[47] See ch. 15 below.

[48] *Re Electro Magnetic (S) Ltd v Development Bank of Singapore Ltd* [1994] 1 SLR 734, distinguishing (at 740) *Stehar Knitting Mills Pty Ltd v Southern Textile Converters Pty Ltd* [1980] 2 NSWLR 514 on the basis of the form of set-off in issue. In the *Stehar* case, a company had entered into a scheme of arrangement which precluded a creditor from commencing or continuing an action or proceeding against the company. It was held that, because of the scheme, a claim to recover a sum of money could not be raised by way of defence to an action by the company for payment of a debt, Hutley JA commenting (at [35]) that this would involve commencing a proceeding against the company contrary to the scheme. The form of set-off in issue arose under a rule of court which was said to have replaced the Statutes of Set-off in New South Wales. See para. 2.64 above. The decision is explicable on the basis that a set-off under the Statutes of Set-off (and under the rule of court that replaced them) is only available in the case of a cross-debt that is enforceable by action. See below, and para. 2.46 above. There should be no such requirement in the case of a self-help remedy such as a contractual right of set-off. See *National Australia Bank Ltd v Idoport Pty Ltd* [2007] NSWSC 1349 at [85] and [86]. In the *Idoport* case, Young CJ in Eq held (see at [67]–[73], referring to *Re Moss, ex p Hallet* [1905] 2 KB 307, 314) that a cross-claim that was not presently enforceable by action was not due and payable for the purpose of a contractual set-off clause. However, that proposition is doubtful. See *Jowitt v Callaghan* (1938) 38 SR(NSW) 512, 521–2 (CA); *Quainoo v NZ Breweries Ltd* [1991] 1 NZLR 161 (CA).

[49] In relation to the position after notice, see para. 16.23 below.

[50] See the discussion of 'proceedings' and 'legal process' in *Re Olympia & York Canary Wharf Ltd* [1993] BCLC 453, referring *inter alia* to *Bristol Airport Plc v Powdrill* [1990] Ch 744, 765. In Australia, the Corporations Act 2001 (Cth), s. 437D may apply where a person enters into, on behalf of a company under administration, a transaction or dealing affecting property of the company. The transaction is void unless the administrator or the court consented to it. This does not affect the exercise of a contractual right of set-off by a creditor of the company since the creditor in exercising the right does not do so on behalf of the company. See *Cinema Plus Ltd v ANZ Banking Group Ltd* (2000) 49 NSWLR 513 and, in a different context, *Osborne Computer Corporation Pty Ltd v Airroad Distribution Pty Ltd* (1995) 17 ACSR 614.

[51] Insolvency Act 1986, Sch. B1 para. 43(2). See also the interim moratorium in Sch. B1 para. 44. In Australia there is a similar provision in s. 440B of the Corporations Act 2001 (Cth), and see also s. 444F(2) in relation to the situation in which it has been proposed that the company execute a deed of company arrangement or the company has executed the deed. There is, however, an exception in Australia in relation to security which is over all or substantially all of the company's property. See s. 441A.

[52] See paras 16.93–16.107 below. In Australia, an administrator is entitled to be indemnified out of the company's property for debts for which the administrator is liable and for his or her remuneration, and as security for the right of indemnity the administrator has a lien on the company's property. See the Corporations Act 2001 (Cth), ss. 443D and 443F. In *Cinema Plus Ltd v ANZ Banking Group Ltd* (2000) 49 NSWLR 513, the New South Wales Court of Appeal held that, where the company has a bank account in credit, a contractual right of set-off held by the bank is not affected by the administration, although the exercise of the right is subject to the administrator's right to be indemnified out of the account in respect of debts and remuneration incurred before the set-off is effected. See paras 16.68–16.71 below.

set off be enforceable by action,[53] and that requirement would not be satisfied in relation to a debt owing by a company the subject of an administration order unless the consent of the administrator or the leave of the court has been obtained. Therefore, if r. 2.85 does not apply, it would appear that the debt would not be able to be employed defensively in a set-off under the Statutes in the absence of consent or leave.[54]

6.15   In the case of a contractual right of set-off, if the administrator of a company in administration gives notice of intention to make a distribution under r. 2.95, so that the set-off regime in r. 2.85 becomes operative, the contractual right of set-off would no longer apply and any set-off rights would be determined instead by r. 2.85. This is because of the '*British Eagle*' principle,[55] which is considered later.[56]

(3) Bank insolvency and bank administration under the Banking Act 2009

6.16   There is special provision for set-off in the case of a bank insolvency[57] and a bank administration[58] under Parts 2 and 3 respectively of the Banking Act 2009. In the case of a bank administration, r. 2.85 of the Insolvency Rules[59] applies with some minor modifications.[60] In the case of a bank insolvency, the applicable set-off provision is set out in r. 72 of the Bank Insolvency (England and Wales) Rules 2009.[61] This is similar in terms to r. 4.90 of the Insolvency Rules 1986, which applies generally in company liquidation.[62] However, they differ in two respects. The first relates to the scope of the qualification to the operation of the set-off rule, to which reference is made later.[63] The second concerns the situation in which compensation is payable to an eligible depositor in respect of protected deposits under the Financial Services Compensation Scheme. The effect of r. 73 of the 2009 rules is that, to the extent that the bank's debt to the eligible depositor is covered by compensation, it is to be excluded from any set-off between the bank and the depositor.

---

[53]   See paras 2.46–2.50 above.

[54]   See *Stehar Knitting Mills Pty Ltd v Southern Textile Converters Pty Ltd* [1980] 2 NSWLR 514 (NSW CA). The *Stehar* case concerned a scheme of arrangement between a company and its unsecured creditors which provided, *inter alia*, that no creditor could commence or continue an action or proceeding against the company. The set-off in issue was pursuant to a rule of court which was said to have replaced the Statutes of Set-off. See para. 2.64 above. For the contrary view, see Wood, *English and International Set-off* (1989), 277. Compare also *Morrison Knudsen Corporation of Australia Ltd v Australian National Railways Commission* (1996) 22 ACSR 262, in which Mansfield J decided the case on the basis that rights of set-off had been excluded by agreement, and *Helou v P D Mulligan Pty Ltd* (2003) 57 NSWLR 74, which concerned the construction of a guarantee given for the debts of a company that executed a deed of company arrangement.

[55]   Named after *British Eagle International Air Lines Ltd v Compagnie Nationale Air France* [1975] 1 WLR 758.

[56]   See paras 16.21–16.26 below.

[57]   Defined in the Banking Act 2009, s. 94 in terms of the appointment of a person as the bank liquidator of a bank.

[58]   See the Banking Act 2009, s. 136.

[59]   See paras 6.10 and 6.11 above.

[60]   Bank Administration (England and Wales) Rules 2009 (S.I. 2009 No. 357), rr. 58 and 61. The modifications are set out in r. 60. See also the Banking Act 2009 (Parts 2 and 3 Consequential Amendments) Order 2009 (S.I. 2009 No. 317), art 3(4)(d).

[61]   S.I. 2009 No. 356. See also the Banking Act 2009 (Parts 2 and 3 Consequential Amendments) Order 2009 (S.I. 2009 No. 317), art 3(4)(d).

[62]   See para. 6.06 above.

[63]   See para. 6.80 below.

(4) Company voluntary arrangement and individual voluntary arrangement

Consider the case of a company voluntary arrangement ('CVA') under Part I of the **6.17** Insolvency Act 1986 pursuant to which various assets (including claims) are held by the supervisor for the benefit of CVA creditors. This creates a trust of the assets in favour of the creditors.[64]

The insolvency set-off section is not expressed to apply to a CVA. Unless the section is **6.18** otherwise incorporated into the arrangement, any set-offs (in the absence of a contractual right of set-off) would depend upon the Statutes of Set-off and equitable set-off. If cross-claims were in existence before the trust arose, the CVA creditors as trust beneficiaries may take subject to a prior right of set-off available to the debtor against the company, on the basis that they take subject to equities.[65] Consider, however, that the claim against the company was incurred after the trust was established. *Prima facie* there would be a lack of mutuality for the purpose of the Statutes of Set-off,[66] since the claim against the debtor would be held on trust for the CVA creditors but the debtor's cross-claim would be against the company itself. Nevertheless, if the company has a right of indemnity from the trust assets in respect of the liability,[67] and a consequent lien over those assets, the lien may suffice to establish mutuality for the purpose of a set-off.[68] Alternatively, the cross-claims may be sufficiently closely connected to give rise to an equitable set-off.[69]

Similar principles may apply in the case of an individual voluntary arrangement under **6.19** Part VIII of the Insolvency Act 1986, where a similar trust may arise.[70]

C. The Rationale for Insolvency Set-off

The right of set-off in insolvency has received almost universal approbation in English **6.20** law. Its operation has been steadily enlarged since 1705,[71] and the courts have said that it should be supported and given the widest possible scope.[72] It is designed to ameliorate a perceived injustice, that a person should have to pay the full amount of his or her liability to a bankrupt and at the same time be confined to receiving a dividend on a cross-claim

---

[64] *Re N T Gallagher & Son Pty Ltd* [2002] 1 WLR 2380; *Wellburn v Dibb Lupton Broomhead* [2002] EWCA Civ 1601 at [14] and [20].

[65] See para. 17.128 below.

[66] See paras 11.18–11.20 below. For mutuality in relation to equitable set-off, see paras 4.67–4.90 above.

[67] The trust assets would include the claim against the debtor.

[68] See para. 17.125 below, and *Penwith District Council v V P Developments Ltd* [2005] 2 BCLC 607 at [17]–[19].

[69] *Penwith District Council v V P Developments Ltd* [2005] 2 BCLC 607 at [20]–[26]. See also paras 4.82 and 17.122 below.

[70] *Wellburn v Dibb Lupton Broomhead* [2002] EWCA Civ 1601 at [11]–[22].

[71] See paras 6.38–6.44 below.

[72] *Peat v Jones & Co* (1881) 8 QBD 147, 150 (Cotton LJ); *Mersey Steel and Iron Co v Naylor, Benzon, & Co* (1882) 9 QBD 648, 660–661; *Eberle's Hotels and Restaurant Company, Ltd v E Jonas & Brothers* (1887) 18 QBD 459, 465; *Day & Dent Constructions Pty Ltd v North Australian Properties Pty Ltd* (1982) 150 CLR 85, 108; *Gye v McIntyre* (1991) 171 CLR 609, 619; *Coventry v Charter Pacific Corporation Ltd* (2005) 227 CLR 234 at [56]. Compare Chambré J's warning in *Ouchterlony v Easterby* (1813) 4 Taunt 888, 893, 128 ER 582, 583, that: 'we ought to be particularly cautious how we admit these things to be mutual credits; for it may lead, if abused, to great mischief.'

against the bankrupt.[73] But it should also be borne in mind that the effect of a set-off is to prefer one creditor over the general body of creditors,[74] and that consequently it operates against the policy favouring equal treatment of creditors. That being the case, it is perhaps surprising that the rationale for the existence of the right has not been questioned to any great extent, and that Lord Mansfield's aphorism: 'Natural equity says, that cross demands should compensate each other, by deducting the less sum from the greater',[75] has been accepted almost without reservation. While admittedly it may seem harsh that a creditor of the bankrupt should only receive a dividend for what the bankrupt owes him or her and at the same time be required to pay the full value of what he or she owes to the bankrupt, other creditors are similarly disadvantaged by being confined to a rateable dividend for the debts owing to them. It is debatable whether the justice in favour of setting off cross-demands is always so great that the assets available for distribution amongst the general body of creditors should be depleted in favour of a single creditor with a set-off entitlement, with the consequent reduction in the dividend payable generally. Consider, for example, that A has accepted a bill of exchange drawn in favour of C. A also happens to be a creditor of B. If B becomes bankrupt, the result would be that A would only be entitled to a dividend for the amount owing by B, and at the same time would be liable to pay the full amount of the bill to C. Assume, however, that, unknown to A, C had negotiated the bill to B before the bankruptcy. There would then be a situation of mutual credit between A and B which may result in a set-off in favour of A. As far as A is concerned, however, the negotiation of the bill to B was entirely fortuitous, and yet it may have the result of improving his or her overall position by effectively enabling A to obtain the full value of the claim against B to the extent of the set-off rather than merely a dividend. In that circumstance, it hardly seems just that A should be favoured with a set-off at the expense of the other creditors. In *Forster v Wilson*[76] Parke B commented that the object of the mutual credit provision is 'to do substantial justice between the parties'.[77] But, as Marks J observed in the Victorian Supreme Court, justice must extend also to the unsecured creditors.[78]

6.21 There is an alternative justification for the right of set-off, and that is that it enhances the provision of credit and generally acts as a stimulus to trade and commerce. If an enterprise

---

[73] *National Westminster Bank Ltd v Halesowen Presswork & Assemblies Ltd* [1972] AC 785, 813; *Day & Dent Constructions Pty Ltd v North Australian Properties Pty Ltd* (1982) 150 CLR 85, 95, 107; *Gye v McIntyre* (1991) 171 CLR 609, 618–19. The Statutes of Set-off serve a different purpose. See *Coventry v Charter Pacific Corporation Ltd* (2005) 227 CLR 234 at [30]–[31], and para. 2.04 above.

[74] *Re Bank of Credit and Commerce International SA (No. 8)* [1996] Ch 245, 256 (CA).

[75] *Green v Farmer* (1768) 4 Burr 2214, 2220, 98 ER 154, 157. The justice or equity of set-off has been referred to on other occasions. See e.g. *Ex p Flint* (1818) 1 Swans 30, 34, 36 ER 285, 287; *Forster v Wilson* (1843) 12 M & W 191, 203–4, 152 ER 1165, 1171.

[76] (1843) 12 M & W 191, 203–4, 152 ER 1165, 1171.

[77] This has been repeated on numerous occasions. See e.g. *Ex p Cleland, re Davies* (1867) LR 2 Ch App 808, 813; *Re City Life Assurance Co, Ltd (Stephenson's Case)* [1926] 1 Ch 191, 216; *Re D H Curtis (Builders) Ltd* [1978] 1 Ch 162, 173; *Re Cushla Ltd* [1979] 3 All ER 415, 421; *Re Unit 2 Windows Ltd* [1985] 1 WLR 1383, 1387; *Gye v McIntyre* (1990) 171 CLR 609, 618; *Stein v Blake* [1994] Ch 16, 22 (CA); *G. M. & A. M. Pearce and Co Pty Ltd v RGM Australia Pty Ltd* [1998] 4 VR 888, 900; *Gertig v Davies* (2003) 85 SASR 226 at [22]; *Coventry v Charter Pacific Corporation Ltd* (2005) 227 CLR 234 at [31]; *Foots v Southern Cross Mine Management Pty Ltd* (2007) 234 CLR 52 at [123].

[78] *Lloyds Bank NZA Ltd v National Safety Council* [1993] 2 VR 506, 513.

wishes to raise cash, or does not wish to pay for goods or services immediately, but is otherwise reasonably sound, the possibility of a set-off in an insolvency may encourage other parties to deal with it, or to deal in negotiable securities upon which the enterprise is liable. In other words, the possibility of a set-off may be perceived as a form of security,[79] and while it is not a security in the strict sense of the word, it may give a degree of confidence to parties dealing with each other.[80] Nevertheless, in any particular case it could only be said that there may have been reliance on the security offered by a set-off if the party claiming the benefit of the set-off was aware, at the time of transacting the later of the two dealings upon which the set-off is sought to be based, of the possibility of there being cross-demands. Unless this were so, the possibility of a set-off would not have influenced his or her decision to deal with the bankrupt, in which case it is questionable whether indeed there is any justification for preferring that party over the other creditors by means of a set-off. It is difficult, then, to see why a set-off should be allowed in the situation posited above, where the bankrupt's right to sue the creditor came into existence as a result of a transaction with a third party, of which the creditor was unaware, after the creditor had entered into the dealing which gave rise to his or her own claim against the bankrupt. The conferral of a set-off effectively would constitute a windfall in comparison to what the creditor otherwise would have expected to be the overall financial position.

D. The Statutes of Set-off, Equitable Set-off and Counterclaim in Bankruptcy and Liquidation

(1) Counterclaim

Counterclaim, when used in contradistinction to set-off, has no application after the occurrence of a bankruptcy or the commencement of a liquidation.[81] A debtor of the bankrupt who has a claim against the bankrupt's estate is remitted to a proof in respect of the claim unless he or she has a right of set-off.

6.22

(2) Statutes of Set-off

Similarly, the Insolvency Act 1986 and the Insolvency Rules made pursuant to it provide the sole *statutory* right of set-off[82] available as a defence to an action brought by a bankrupt's trustee or the liquidator of a company for payment of a sum owing to the bankrupt or

6.23

---

[79] Thus, Vaughan Williams J in *Re Washington Diamond Mining Co* [1893] 3 Ch 95, 104 referred to 'the security, by way of set-off'. In *Stein v Blake* [1996] AC 243, 251, Lord Hoffmann commented that bankruptcy set-off enables a creditor 'to use his indebtedness to the bankrupt as a form of security'. See also *Melville Dundas Ltd v George Wimpey UK Ltd* [2007] 1 WLR 1136 at [13] ('the security arises . . . from the law of bankruptcy set-off') (Lord Hoffmann); *Re Opes Prime Stockbroking Ltd* (2008) 171 FCR 473 at [9].

[80] Indeed, in the United States Supreme Court Lamar J warned that in some situations the abolition of set-off could: 'interfere with the course of business as to produce evils of serious and far reaching consequence.' See *Studley v Boylston National Bank of Boston* (1913) 229 US 523, 529.

[81] *Peat v Jones & Co* (1881) 8 QBD 147, 150. See also, in the context of company liquidation, *Government Security Investment Co v Dempsey* (1880) 50 LJQB 199; *Langley Constructions (Brixham) Ltd v Wells* [1969] 1 WLR 503.

[82] Compare equitable set-off, below.

the company.[83] The Statutes of Set-off (including where equity would otherwise act by analogy with the Statutes[84]) would not apply in that context. This has not always been the accepted view. In the eighteenth century, defendants in actions at law instituted by assignees in bankruptcy for the recovery of a debt commonly would base their argument for a set-off upon both the Statutes of Set-off and the bankruptcy section.[85] The Statutes of Set-off were said to apply on the ground that 'the assignees are the bankrupt'.[86] According to Professor Christian,[87] it was only after 1786, when Buller J in *Grove v Dubois*[88] confirmed that the bankruptcy section provided a defence to such an action, that pleaders began to rely solely on the bankruptcy provision. However, that early view as to the relevance of the Statutes would not be followed today. For example, if a person against whom a bankruptcy petition was pending (A) incurred a debt to another person (B) who was already indebted to A, B would not have the benefit of a set-off in the bankruptcy under the Insolvency Act, s. 323 if, at the time that sums became due to him or her, B had notice that the petition was pending.[89] Nor could that result be avoided by pleading a set-off under the Statutes of Set-off and arguing that A's trustee in bankruptcy took subject to the equity.

6.24 This is not to suggest that that the right to set off mutual debts under the Statutes of Set-off has no application to bankruptcies and company liquidations. When it is said that an assignee of a debt takes subject to rights of set-off available to the debtor against the assignor,[90] it is meant rights of set-off which could have provided a defence to an action brought against the debtor by a solvent assignor, including pursuant to the Statutes. If the assignor has become bankrupt or is a company in liquidation, the debtor cannot have recourse to the wider right of set-off provided by the insolvency legislation.[91]

(3) Equitable Set-off

6.25 It has been suggested that insolvency set-off also displaces equitable set-off.[92] In *Re Daintrey*,[93] Bigham J commented that the law regulating the adjustment of cross-claims between a bankrupt and his creditor is to be found 'exclusively' in the bankruptcy

---

[83] See *Day & Dent Constructions Pty Ltd v North Australian Properties Pty Ltd* (1981) 34 ALR 595, 599, 601 (Federal Court of Australia); *Re Daintrey* [1900] 1 QB 546, 548, 567. See also *McIntyre v Perkes* (1990) 22 FCR 260, 271. Compare the comments of Lord Esher MR in *Sovereign Life Assurance Co v Dodd* [1892] 2 QB 573, 577–8.

[84] See para. 3.07 above.

[85] See e.g. *Ridout v Brough* (1774) 1 Cowp 133, 98 ER 1006.

[86] *Ridout v Brough* (1774) 1 Cowp 133, 135, 98 ER 1006, 1008. See also *Freeman v Lomas* (1851) 9 Hare 109, 115, 68 ER 435, 438; *McIntyre v Perkes* (1990) 22 FCR 260, 271.

[87] Christian, *Bankrupt Law* (2nd edn, 1818) vol. 1, 504–5.

[88] (1786) 1 TR 112, 99 ER 1002.

[89] See the Insolvency Act, s. 323(3), and generally paras 6.66–6.99 below.

[90] See ch. 17 below.

[91] See e.g. *Re Asphaltic Wood Pavement Co. Lee & Chapman's Case* (1885) 30 Ch D 216, 225, and para. 17.39 below.

[92] In addition to the cases referred to below, see Goode, *Principles of Corporate Insolvency Law* (3rd edn, 2005), 221.

[93] [1900] 1 QB 546, 567.

set-off section. Further, the Court of Appeal in *Brown v Cork*[94] accepted without demur the proposition that 'there is, in bankruptcy at any rate, no equity outside the [set-off] section'. Opinions to a similar effect have been expressed in Australia and New Zealand.[95] More recently, the Court of Appeal, in *Re Bank of Credit and Commerce International SA (No. 8)*,[96] rejected an argument that an equitable set-off was available in that case in circumstances that were outside the operation of the insolvency set-off section, and concluded that two cases[97] said to support the existence of an equitable right of set-off in bankruptcy that was wider than the statutory right in fact were not authority for that proposition.[98] However, the discussion was confined to an examination of the two cases in question, and moreover the conclusion seems correct that the circumstances in issue in *BCCI (No. 8)* were not such as to support an equitable set-off.[99] The better view, notwithstanding those opinions, is that equitable set-off may still apply after insolvency.

As a matter of principle, bankruptcy or liquidation should not preclude the application of **6.26** the equitable doctrine.[100] The traditional ground for an equitable set-off is impeachment of title.[101] If a debtor's title to sue was impeached before bankruptcy, so should the title of the debtor's trustee in bankruptcy, given that the trustee steps into the shoes of the debtor and takes the debtor's property subject to all clogs and fetters affecting it in the hands of the debtor.[102] Similar reasoning should apply in company liquidation.[103] If a company's title

---

[94] [1985] BCLC 363, 376, referring to *Re A Debtor (No. 66 of 1955)* [1956] 1 WLR 1226, 1236 (Lord Evershed MR).

[95] *Day & Dent Constructions Pty Ltd v North Australian Properties Pty Ltd* (1981) 34 ALR 595, 599, 601, 636–7 (Federal Court); *Paganini v The Official Assignee* (NZ Court of Appeal, CA308/98, 22 March 1999 at [10]) ('no claim for set off can be made outside the legislation'). *Ansett Australia Ltd v Travel Software Solutions Pty Ltd* (2007) 65 ACSR 47 at [94], while expressed generally, was directed primarily at contractual set-off. See paras 16.21–16.26 below.

[96] [1996] Ch 245, 269–70 (Rose, Saville and Millett LJJ).

[97] *Ex p Stephens* (1805) 11 Ves Jun 24, 32 ER 996 and *Jones v Mossop* (1844) 3 Hare 568, 67 ER 506.

[98] In relation to *Ex p Stephens* (1805) 11 Ves Jun 24, 32 ER 996, Lord Eldon's judgment (at 27) (and see also *Ex p Blagden* (1815) 19 Ves Jun 465, 467, 34 ER 589, 589–90) indeed suggests that he was of the view that there may be a set-off in equity where it is not available under the statute relating to mutual credit. The Court of Appeal in *Re BCCI (No. 8)* [1996] Ch 245, 266, 269 considered that *Ex p Stephens* is 'no authority for the existence of any equitable right of set-off in bankruptcy wider than the statutory right'. However, the statement in Lord Eldon's judgment in *Ex p Stephens* (at 27) to which the Court of Appeal referred in *BCCI (No. 8)* (at 266), that 'as to mutual debt and credit, equity must make the same construction as the law . . .', should be read subject to the qualification by Lord Eldon that preceded it, that '*where the court does not find a natural equity, going beyond the statute* the construction of the law is the same in equity as at law . . .' (emphasis added). Lord Eldon went on to comment (at 27) that: 'the contract was entered into by Miss Stephens in ignorance; and, if not, I should make the same construction . . .' In other words, if Miss Stephens had not entered into the contract in ignorance of her right, equity would have given the 'same construction', which referred to the statute relating to mutual debt and credit. But since she had entered into the contract in ignorance of her right, equity was not bound by the construction otherwise applicable to the statute. See the explanation of *Ex p Stephens* in paras 12.30–12.39 below.

[99] See paras 4.89–4.90 above.

[100] Compare *Provincial Bill Posting Co v Low Moor Iron Co* [1909] 2 KB 344, in which a counterclaim, or a set-off of judgments (see paras 2.98–2.122 above), was in issue, as opposed to an equitable set-off of cross-demands.

[101] See para. 4.02 above.

[102] See Jenkins LJ in *Bradley-Hole v Cusen* [1953] 1 QB 300, 306.

[103] See generally Goode, *Principles of Corporate Insolvency Law* (3rd edn, 2005), 72–3 and *Attorney-General v McMillan & Lockwood* [1991] 1 NZLR 53, 65. Professor Goode nevertheless regards the pre-liquidation

to sue was impeached before liquidation, it should continue to be impeached during liquidation. Normally there would be little scope for equitable set-off in insolvency. If cross-demands would give rise to an equitable set-off, usually they would also come within the terms of the insolvency set-off section, with the consequence that the demands would be automatically set off under the section upon the occurrence of the bankruptcy or the liquidation.[104] But if in a particular case the insolvency set-off section would not apply, an equitable set-off should not be affected by the insolvency.

6.27   Consider, for example, that X entered into a contract with Y after notice that a petition for winding up Y was pending. X incurred a debt to Y under the contract, but Y reached the contract and as a consequence X has a cross-claim in damages against Y. A set-off would not be available to X in a subsequent liquidation of Y pursuant to the Insolvency Rules 1986, r. 4.90, since X had notice of a pending petition when the contract was entered into.[105] But it would be unjust to deny an equitable set-off otherwise available given the closeness of the connection between the cross-claims. Further, notwithstanding recent judicial statements suggesting the contrary, there may be situations in which equitable set-off is available notwithstanding a lack of mutuality.[106] This is in contrast with insolvency set-off, which requires strict mutuality. If in a particular case an equitable set-off is available notwithstanding the absence of mutuality, the right to rely on it should not be lost on the ground that the person against whom it is asserted has become bankrupt or gone into liquidation.[107] If the title to sue was impeached before insolvency, it is difficult to see why the commencement of a formal insolvency administration should affect that position. Certainly the insolvency set-off section itself says nothing about exclusivity.

6.28   Equitable set-off has been allowed in bankruptcy where fraud was involved, notwithstanding an absence of mutuality.[108] Further, in *Ex p Hanson*,[109] a set-off was permitted in

---

right of set-off as an exception to the general principle that a liquidator takes subject to equities. See Goode, *op. cit.* 73 and 221.

[104] See paras 6.119–6.146 below.

[105] See r. 4.90(2)(a)(ii). The 'debt' referred to in r. 4.90(2)(a) may be on either side of the account. See para. 6.77 below.

[106] See paras 4.67–4.83 above.

[107] In addition to the cases referred to below, see *Clarkson v Smith and Goldberg* [1926] 1 DLR 509 (see para. 12.42 below), and also the note to the report of *Jeffs v Wood* (1723) 2 P Wms 128, 130, 24 ER 668, 669. The proposition is also consistent with Lord Loughborough's judgment in *Ex p Quintin* (1796) 3 Ves Jun 248, 30 ER 994. *Quintin* effectively was overruled by Lord Eldon on *Ex p Twogood* (1805) 11 Ves Jun 517, 32 ER 1189, not on the ground that a set-off was not available in equity in circumstances going beyond the bankruptcy set-off section, but rather because of the consequences of allowing a set-off in the circumstances in issue. See para. 12.20 below. Compare *Day & Dent Constructions Pty Ltd v North Australian Properties Pty Ltd* (1981) 34 ALR 595, 636–7 (Federal Court of Australia), and also *McIntyre v Perkes* (1990) 22 FCR 260, 271, wherein Gummow and von Doussa JJ left the question open.

[108] *Vulliamy v Noble* (1817) 3 Mer 593, 36 ER 228 (Lord Eldon). See also *Ex p Stephens* (1805) 11 Ves Jun 24, 27, 32 ER 996, 997, which is explained in paras 12.35–12.39 below. In *Middleton v Pollock, ex p Knight and Raymond* (1875) LR 20 Eq 515, 521–3 Sir George Jessel MR advanced the theory that *Vulliamy v Noble* was not concerned with a question of set-off and sought to explain the decision on another ground. It is suggested that *Vulliamy v Noble* is not explicable on the basis suggested by the Master of the Rolls and that in truth it concerned equitable set-off. See paras 4.71–4.76 above.

[109] (1811) 18 Ves Jun 232, 34 ER 305, affirming (1806) 12 Ves Jun 346, 33 ER 131. In *Addis v Knight* (1817) 2 Mer 117, 121, 35 ER 885, 887 Sir William Grant said of *Ex p Hanson* and *Ex p Stephens* (1805)

a bankruptcy in circumstances where a surety had been made jointly liable with the principal debtor. Since the joint liability was no more than a form of security for the principal debtor's debt, Lord Eldon said that upon equitable considerations the principal debtor should be allowed to set off the debt in the creditor's bankruptcy against a separate debt owing to him by the creditor, even though the demands were not mutual.[110]

It was assumed in *Sovereign Life Assurance Co v Dodd*,[111] that equitable set-off could apply **6.29** in company liquidation. An insured had assigned a policy of insurance back to the insurance company as security for loans made by the company. Subsequently, the company went into liquidation. The company by its liquidator sued to recover the loans, whereupon the defendant sought to set off a claim that he had on the policy. The liquidator argued that, because the insured had assigned the policy back to the company, the insured could not employ the claim on the policy in a set-off in the liquidation.[112] However, Bowen LJ in the Court of Appeal accepted that, even if the assignment otherwise would have prevented a set-off, there was in any event a set-off in equity,[113] and Kay LJ also suggested that that was probably the case.[114]

Consider also the situation in which A as a result of the expenditure of money in respect **6.30** of B's land is entitled to an equitable charge or lien on the land, but A happens also to be personally indebted to B. In that circumstance, there is authority for the proposition that B may set off the debt owing to him or her against the sum secured on the land, so that the amount that B must pay in order to take the land free of the charge is the amount secured less the separate debt owing to B.[115] In *Baillie v Edwards*,[116] this occurred in circumstances where A was bankrupt, even though there was a lack of mutuality. While A was indebted to B, A's claim was not against B but rather it was against the land. Indeed, Lord Lyndhurst earlier had emphasized lack of mutuality as a reason for disallowing a set-off,[117] his Lordship's decision to that effect being the subject of a successful appeal to the House of Lords in this proceeding. Bethell[118] in his argument in favour of the set-off in the House of Lords acknowledged that it could not be supported on the strict legal principles of

---

11 Ves Jun 24, 32 ER 996 that they 'establish that, under certain circumstances, there may be a set-off in Equity when there can be none at Law'.

[110] Lord Eldon's later comments in *Ex p Blagden* (1815) 19 Ves Jun 465, 467, 34 ER 589, 589–90 also suggest that set-off in equity was not thought to be limited by the statute relating to mutual credit.

[111] [1892] 2 QB 573, affirming [1892] 1 QB 405.

[112] See the argument at first instance [1892] 1 QB 405, 408, and the discussion of charge-backs and mutuality in paras 16.83–16.88 below.

[113] [1892] 2 QB 573, 582.

[114] [1892] 2 QB 573, 585–6. See also para. 16.87 below.

[115] *Baillie v Edwards* (1848) 2 HLC 74, 9 ER 1020; *Unity Joint Stock Mutual Banking Association v King* (1858) 25 Beav 72, 79–80, 53 ER 563, 566. See also paras 3.05 and 4.89–4.90 above.

[116] (1848) 2 HLC 74, 9 ER 1020. I acknowledge my debt to Alan Berg's discussion of *Baillie v Edwards* in his article, 'Liquidation set-off: the mutuality principle and security over bank balances' [1996] LMCLQ 176, 177–8.

[117] *Baillie v Innes* (1845) 14 LJ Ch 341, 343.

[118] Presumably Richard Bethell, later Lord Westbury LC. See Berg, 'Liquidation set-off: the mutuality principle and security over bank balances' [1996] LMCLQ 176, 178, n. 16, and also Holdsworth, *A History of English Law* (1966) vol. 16, 70 *et seq.*

set-off in respect of mutual debts and demands, but instead described it as being in the nature of an equitable set-off.[119]

6.31   In Australia there is substantial authority supporting the continued application of equitable set-off after bankruptcy or liquidation. In New South Wales, Young J, in *Re Trivan Pty Ltd*,[120] considered that the equitable doctrine of set-off is not completely displaced by the insolvency set-off section, and, in *Westmex Operations Pty Ltd v Westmex Ltd*,[121] the New South Wales Court of Appeal contemplated that there could have been a set-off in the liquidations in that case either on the basis of equitable set-off or pursuant to the insolvency section.[122] Reference also may be made to *Murphy v Zamonex Pty Ltd*,[123] a decision of Giles J in the New South Wales Supreme Court. In that case one of the parties to a contract had contracted as the trustee of a unit trust. A debt was owing to the trustee under the contract but the debtor had a cross-claim for damages against the trustee for misleading conduct in relation to the contract.[124] The trustee went into liquidation and a new trustee was appointed.[125] The new trustee sued to recover the debt for the benefit of the unit holders beneficially interested in the trust property. It was accepted that the new trustee was in no better position than the original trustee, in that it took subject to equities.[126] Giles J held that the debtor could set off the damages cross-claim. The set-off was not under the insolvency set-off section consequent upon the liquidation of the original trustee, since there was a lack of mutuality. The claim was brought for the benefit of the trust beneficiaries whereas the cross-claim was against the trustee personally. Rather, the set-off was an equitable set-off. The lack of mutuality did not preclude that form of set-off.[127] A similar situation has arisen in the context of an equitable assignment of a debt, where the assignor had gone into liquidation and the debtor had a closely connected

---

[119]   (1848) 2 HLC 74, 79, 9 ER 1020, 1022.

[120]   (1996) 134 FLR 368, 373.

[121]   (1994) 12 ACLC 106.

[122]   Similarly, the New South Wales Court of Appeal in *Lord v Direct Acceptance Corporation Ltd* (1993) 32 NSWLR 362 considered the possibility of equitable set-off as well as insolvency set-off in the liquidation of Direct Acceptance, but held that the facts in issue supported neither form of set-off. See also *Signature Resorts Pty Ltd v DHD Constructions Pty Ltd* (1995) 18 ACSR 627, 634–5. In relation to a deed of company arrangement, see *Metal Manufacturers Ltd v Hall* (2002) 41 ACSR 466. In *Re NIAA Corporation Ltd (in liq)* (NSW SC, 2 December 1994, BC9403369), McLelland CJ in Eq questioned whether *Jack v Kipping* (1882) 9 QBD 113 was correct in so far as it held that a claim for damages for misrepresentation inducing a contract was provable in the representor's bankruptcy and therefore could be the subject of a set-off under the insolvency set-off section. See para. 8.54 below. Rather, he suggested that the decision should properly be treated as illustrating the availability of equitable set-off (see paras 4.110–4.112 above). In *Aliferis v Kyriacou* (2000) 1 VR 447 at [48], Charles JA referred to McLelland CJ in Eq's comments without criticism. Subsequently, the Australian High Court in *Coventry v Charter Pacific Corporation Ltd* (2005) 227 CLR 234 at [38]–[50] (and see also *Gye v McIntyre* (1991) 171 CLR 609, 630–1) accepted *Jack v Kipping* as an authority on insolvency set-off. Nevertheless, McLelland CJ in Eq's comments pre-suppose that equitable set-off may be available in bankruptcy in circumstances where the insolvency set-off section does not apply.

[123]   (1993) 31 NSWLR 439. See also *Doherty v Murphy* [1996] 2 VR 553. *Murphy v Zamonex* was referred to with approval by Laddie J in *Penwith District Council v V P Developments Ltd* [2005] 2 BCLC 607.

[124]   Contrary to the Trade Practices Act 1974 (Cth), s. 52.

[125]   See (1993) 31 NSWLR 439, 442, 462.

[126]   See (1993) 31 NSWLR 439, 462–3, 468.

[127]   See the discussion at (1993) 31 NSWLR 439, 463–5, 467.

cross-claim against the assignor. The fact of the assignment meant that there was no mutuality for the purpose of a set-off under the insolvency set-off section in the liquidation, but the assignee nevertheless took subject to an equitable set-off available to the debtor against the assignor on the basis of the principle that an assignee takes subject to equities.[128]

In *Murphy v Zamonex*, the beneficial owners of the claim (the unit holders) were not insolvent. The insolvency set-off section only applies in the administration of an insolvent estate.[129] It has no application outside of such administration. When a claim is enforced outside the insolvency administration, there is no reason why other forms of set-off should not be available. That point is illustrated also by the decision of the Full Court of the South Australian Supreme Court in *Gertig v Davies*.[130] A bankrupt prior to the bankruptcy had obtained judgment in a claim for damages for personal injuries, but had costs awarded against him. The personal injuries claim did not vest in the trustee in bankruptcy,[131] with the consequence that it could not be the subject of a set-off under the bankruptcy set-off section.[132] Nevertheless, the Full Court accepted that the judgments could be set off under the court's inherent jurisdiction to set off judgments and orders.[133] Subsequently, the Full Federal Court in *Piccone v Suncorp Metway Insurance Ltd*[134] accepted the principle that the defendant in a personal injuries action brought by a bankrupt can plead a provable debt by way of set-off in accordance with general law principles, as opposed to the bankruptcy set-off section.[135] In fact, the circumstances of that case would not appear to have supported a set-off,[136] but the fundamental proposition was not queried.

6.32

---

[128] *Popular Homes Ltd v Circuit Development Ltd* [1979] 2 NZLR 642, and see also *Lean v Tumut River Orchard Management Ltd* [2003] FCA 269. See further para. 17.32 below.

[129] See para. 7.31 below, and *Piccone v Suncorp Metway Insurance Ltd* (2005) 148 FCR 437 at [12].

[130] (2003) 85 SASR 226.

[131] Bankruptcy Act 1966 (Cth), s. 116(2)(g). A similar principle applies in English bankruptcy law. See para. 7.31 below.

[132] See para. 7.31 below.

[133] See paras 2.112–2.113 above.

[134] (2005) 148 FCR 437.

[135] See in particular (2005) 148 FCR 437 at [12] and [14]. The issue in the *Piccone* case was whether the pleading of the set-off was contrary to the Bankruptcy Act 1966 (Cth), s. 58(3)(a), which substantially corresponds with the Insolvency Act 1986, s. 285(3)(a). The Full Federal Court held that, to the extent that the set-off went in reduction of the bankrupt's claim, no question of enforcement would arise upon which s. 58(3)(a) could operate. On the other hand, the court recognized (at [27]) that s. 58(3)(a) could operate to bar enforcement of any excess of the amount recovered on the claim pleaded by way of set-off over and above the amount of the bankrupt's claim. The court was not asked to determine whether pleading the set-off required the leave of the court under s. 58(3)(b) (which substantially corresponds with the Insolvency Act 1986, s. 285(3)(b)), but nevertheless commented (at [14]) that it would be odd if a bankrupt was at liberty to pursue a claim against a defendant but that the defendant could not raise a relevant defence without the leave of the court. See also, in relation to s. 58(3), the discussion of *Gertig v Davies* (2003) 85 SASR 226 at para. 2.113 above.

[136] There was no (or no sufficient) connection between the cross-claims for the purpose of an equitable set-off. The Full Court suggested ((2005) 148 FCR 437 at [29]) that r. 173 of the Uniform Civil Procedure Rules 1999 (Qld) seemed to allow any claim to be raised by way of set-off, but the better view is that the rule has no such effect. See paras 2.81–2.82 above.

E. Early Development, and the Influence of Equity

6.33 The insolvency set-off section has a long ancestry which can be traced back to legislation enacted during the reign of Queen Anne.[137] But even before then accounts between merchants used to be balanced when one became bankrupt, and indeed the judgment of Flemming CJ in *Powel v Stuff and Timewell*[138] suggests that the practice had been adopted as early as 1612. The case involved an application of s. 13 of the statute (1603) 1 Jac, c. 15, which empowered the commissioners appointed in a bankruptcy to assign to a creditor of the bankrupt a debt owing to the bankrupt by a third party. The creditor could then institute proceedings in his or her own name to recover the debt.[139] The present case concerned such an action. The Chief Justice in the course of his judgment is reported as having commented that, 'if the plaintiff had been in debt, in as great a sum as the bankrupt was indebted unto him, and yet his debt assigned, this assignment had not been good'.[140]

6.34 By 1675, the right to a balanced account in bankruptcy appears to have been accepted. In that year North CJ is reported as having said:[141]

> If there are accounts between two merchants, and one of them become bankrupt, the course is not to make the other, who perhaps upon stating the accounts is found indebted to the bankrupt, to pay the whole that originally was entrusted to him, and to put him for the recovery of what the bankrupt owes him, into the same condition with the rest of the creditors; but to make him pay that only which appears due to the bankrupt on the foot of the account; otherwise it will be for accounts betwixt them after the time of the other's becoming bankrupt, if any such were.

Similarly, in 1689 reference was made in *Chapman v Derby*[142] to an earlier judgment of Sir Matthew Hale CJ, in which the Chief Justice is said to have commented to the effect that, where there were dealings on account, a man should not be charged with the account on the credit side and be put to come in as a creditor for the debt owing to himself, but should only answer to the bankrupt's estate for the balance of the account.

---

[137] (1705) 4 & 5 Anne, c. 17, s. 11.

[138] (1612) 2 Bulst 26, 80 ER 930.

[139] It appears that the commissioners acting pursuant to this provision would sometimes assign the debts to creditors as payment of their dividends, although the usual practice was to make an assignment to one or more creditors who would then recover the debts as trustees for the creditors as a whole. See Goodinge, *The Law Against Bankrupts* (2nd edn, 1701), 147–8, and also Christian, *Bankrupt Law* (2nd edn, 1818) vol. 1, 469–70, 499–500. It was not until 1706 that s. 4 of the statute 5 & 6 Anne, c. 22 empowered the creditors of the bankrupt to choose the assignees to whom the commissioners were required to assign all the bankrupt's estate and effects. These assignees were obliged by s. 33 of (1732) 5 Geo II, c. 30 to make a distribution to the creditors, and to account to the commissioners for their receipts and for their payments concerning the bankrupt's estate. A further modification occurred in 1831, when a number of official assignees were appointed from the ranks of merchants, brokers, accountants, and traders. An official assignee had to be one of the assignees of the bankrupt's estates and effects in every bankruptcy. See (1831) 1 & 2 Will IV, c. 56, s. 22. Eventually, the office of assignee was replaced by that of trustee by the Bankruptcy Act 1869.

[140] (1612) 2 Bulst 26, 80 ER 930.

[141] *Anon* (1675) 1 Mod 215, 86 ER 837.

[142] (1689) 2 Vern 117, 23 ER 684.

(1) Competing explanations

There are two competing explanations as to how the right to a balanced account in bankruptcy developed before the enactment of the first mutual credit provision in 1705.[143] The first is that it may have originated as a principle of equity. This appears to have been the view of Lord Eldon,[144] of Fletcher Moulton LJ,[145] and possibly also of Sir George Turner.[146] Professor Christian,[147] on the other hand, argued that it had a statutory basis. The law of bankruptcy in force during the seventeenth century was set out primarily in an Elizabethan statute, (1570) 13 Eliz, c. 7. The commissioners in bankruptcy were required by s. 2 of the Act to pay 'to every of the said creditors a portion, rate and rate like, according to the quantity of his or their debts'. Christian suggested that quantity of the creditor's debt was taken to mean any balance due to the creditor.[148] The early cases referred to above support that explanation, and it should be preferred over the view that a right of set-off in bankruptcy was developed in equity.[149]

6.35

A significant point is that both North and Hale were common law judges. This by itself is not conclusive, because they may have been enunciating a principle that had been adopted by the commissioners as a result of the influence of the Chancellor. However, there are two arguments which detract from that explanation. The first is the apparent lack of Chancery cases reported from this period in which a right of set-off was enforced in a bankruptcy.[150] It is true that, towards the end of the seventeenth century, equity was beginning to enforce set-offs in actions at law by restraining the plaintiff at law from proceeding with his or

6.36

---

[143] See also *Gye v Davies* (1995) 37 NSWLR 421, 425.

[144] *Ex p Stephens* (1805) 11 Ves Jun 24, 27, 32 ER 996, 997. See also *Bacon's Abridgement of the Law* (7th edn, 1832) vol. 1, 652; Houlden and Morawetz, *Bankruptcy Law of Canada* (1960), 160.

[145] *Lister v Hooson* [1908] 1 KB 174, 178.

[146] See *Freeman v Lomas* (1851) 9 Hare 109, 112–13, 68 ER 435, 436–7. It is unclear, however, whether Sir George Turner was referring to bankruptcy set-off.

[147] See Christian, *Bankrupt Law* (2nd edn, 1818) vol. 1, 499–500. Christian was the first Downing Professor of the Laws of England at Cambridge, but according to Holdsworth he was not well regarded by his contemporaries. Indeed, Holdsworth tells us that it had been said of Christian upon his death that he died in 'the full vigour of his incapacity'. See Holdsworth, *A History of English Law* (1952) vol. 13, 480–1. Whether Christian deserved that harsh judgment is debatable. For example Maddock, in his *Principles and Practice of the High Court of Chancery* (3rd edn, 1837) vol. 2, 786n described Christian's *Bankrupt Law* as 'a work, profound, original and useful. No book so strikingly exhibits the fallibility of judges'. For a discussion of Christian's contribution to the law, see Hoffheimer, 'The common law of Edward Christian' [1994] *Cambridge Law Journal* 140.

[148] Therefore, when the commissioners, acting pursuant to (1603) 1 Jac 1, c. 15, s. 13, assigned the debts owing to the bankrupt to one creditor as trustee for the creditors as a whole, the accounts between the bankrupt and his creditors would already have been balanced. See Christian, *Bankrupt Law* (2nd edn, 1818) vol. 1, 499–500.

[149] See also *Gye v Davies* (1995) 37 NSWLR 421, 425.

[150] Compare *Peters v Soame* (1701) 2 Vern 428, 23 ER 874. In that case the Lord Keeper, Sir Nathan Wright, said that the assignee of a debt should take subject to a right of set-off that the debtor could have asserted in an action brought against him by the assignor, who had become bankrupt. However, the bankruptcy appears to have been incidental to the main question of the effect of an assignment, which was within the exclusive jurisdiction of equity. It seems that the fact of the assignor's bankruptcy prevented the assignee from bringing an action at law against the debtor in the assignor's name (compare subsequently *Winch v Keeley* (1787) 1 TR 619, 99 ER 1284), and so the assignee had to bring this bill in equity in order to obtain payment.

her claim unless he or she gave credit for the defendant's cross-demand.[151] Those cases, however, were not concerned with bankruptcies, and indeed there is evidence to suggest that equity was encouraged to advance its jurisdiction in this area because of the fact that such a practice already existed in bankruptcy.[152]

6.37   There is a second reason for doubting that the Chancellor may have originated the early practice of balancing accounts. This arises from an examination of the development of the Chancellor's jurisdiction in matters of bankruptcy. In particular, it brings into question the assertion made by Fletcher Moulton LJ in *Lister v Hooson*,[153] that 'the jurisdiction in bankruptcy was from the first an equitable jurisdiction'. What he meant by that statement is unclear. The jurisdiction and power of the commissioners over the person and property of the bankrupt arose by force of an Act of Parliament, and presumably his Lordship meant that the exercise of those powers was controlled and influenced by the Chancellor. In fact, this is not an accurate description of what appears to have happened. Section 2 of the statute 13 Eliz, c. 7 empowered the Lord Chancellor to commission 'wise and honest discreet persons' in each case to conduct bankruptcy proceedings. This was the only power conferred on the Chancellor by the statute, and initially it seems to have represented the extent of the Chancellor's involvement in bankruptcy. Cooper explained in 1828[154] that, while the Chancellor would act to prevent unfair dealing or abuse of power by the commissioners he had appointed,[155] he did not exercise an extensive jurisdiction in matters of bankruptcy in the early years of the operation of the legislation. The common law courts from early times had reserved the right to review a finding by the commissioners that a person was bankrupt.[156] Moreover, when the Elizabethan bankruptcy legislation was first enacted, commissioners acting in bankruptcy proceedings often applied to the common law judges, rather than to the Chancellor, for advice as to how they should exercise the extensive powers conferred upon them.[157] It was

---

[151] See para. 3.01 above.

[152] In *Arnold v Richardson* (1699) 1 Eq Ca Abr 8, 21 ER 833 the Master of the Rolls, Sir John Trevor, ordered that the plaintiff in an action at law should reduce his claim to the extent that he was indebted to the defendant, commenting that if the plaintiff at law had been bankrupt, the commissioners would have allowed a discount. Indeed, it is noticeable that, when the court in *Chapman v Derby* (1689) 2 Vern 117, 23 ER 684 was considering whether to sanction a set-off, it saw fit to refer to a judgment of Hale, a common law judge, for the proposition that accounts may be balanced in bankruptcy.

[153] [1908] 1 KB 174, 178.

[154] *Cooper's Parliamentary Proceedings* (1828), 242–5. Holdsworth referred extensively to this section of Cooper's book. See Holdsworth, *A History of English Law* (7th edn, 1956) vol. 1, 470–3.

[155] See e.g. *Wood v Hayes* (1606–7) Tothill 62, 21 ER 125.

[156] See *Dr Bonham's Case* (1609) 8 Co Rep 113b, 121a, 77 ER 646, 657, in which Coke CJ said that the commissioner's decision was traversable in an action for false imprisonment. It seems from *Bacon's Abridgement of the Law* (7th edn, 1832) vol. 1, 526–7 that the common law courts continued as the proper forum for determining questions relating to the construction of the bankruptcy legislation, so that if a bankruptcy was denied, the Chancellor usually ordered the issue to be tried in a court of law.

[157] See *Cooper's Parliamentary Proceedings* (1828), 246, and also Yale, *Lord Nottingham's Chancery Cases* vol. 1, 73 *Selden Society* (1957), p.cxv. Neither of those writers has cited any instances in which this happened, although four cases are mentioned in Christian, *Bankrupt Law* (2nd edn, 1818) vol. 2, 8–10. In *Anon* (1583) Cro Eliz 13, 78 ER 279 the Common Pleas was asked to determine whether a person who had kept his house in order to avoid arrest had committed an act of bankruptcy. In *Osborne and Bradshaw v Churchman* (1606) Cro Jac 127, 79 ER 111, the King's Bench ruled that a surety who paid the debt was a creditor of the principal debtor within the terms of the bankruptcy legislation. In the first volume of Brownlow and Goldsborough's

only in 1676[158] that the Chancellor was prepared for the first time to review a decision made by the commissioners, in that case whether a creditor ought to be admitted to proof.[159] It appears from the report of the decision that Lord Nottingham's initial reaction was not to interfere, but to 'leave it to the Course the Statute hath provided'.[160] Ultimately, however, he changed his mind and ordered that the creditor's debt should be admitted.[161] Thus it was only in the last quarter of the seventeenth century that it can be said that the Chancellor began to exercise any great influence over bankruptcy law,[162] and indeed it was not until Lord Hardwicke's time that the jurisdiction flourished.[163] The Chancellor does not appear to have been active in matters of bankruptcy when North and Hale mentioned

---

report of cases in the Common Pleas, there is a reference at p. 47 (123 ER 656) to a case decided in 1612, in which: 'The Court was moved, to know whether the wife of a bankrupt can be examined by the commissioners upon the Statute of Bankrupt; and they were of the opinion she could not be examined.' Finally, the Common Pleas was asked upon motion in *Ruggles Case* (1619) Hutton 37, 123 ER 1084 to advise on the procedure to be adopted in distributing the estate of the bankrupt.

[158] See *Anon* (1676) 1 Chan Cas 275, 22 ER 798.

[159] See Yale, *Lord Nottingham's Chancery Cases* vol. 1, 73 *Selden Society* (1957), cxv–cxvi. It seems that, as the influence of the Chancellor over bankruptcy law developed, this remained the most extensive part of his jurisdiction, i.e. deciding whether to order the commissioners to admit the proof of a debt which they had rejected, or to expunge the proof of a debt which they had admitted. See Christian, *Bankrupt Law* (2nd edn, 1818) vol. 2, 11. Yale has pointed out that there were earlier instances in which decrees had been made by the Chancellor in matters concerning bankruptcy. However, the issue of bankruptcy in those cases arose as an incident to a question involving an established area of equitable jurisdiction, for example a bill for an account and for redemption of a mortgage, or a bill for discovery. See Yale, *op. cit.*, cxvi–cxx.

[160] (1676) 1 Chan Cas 275, 22 ER 798.

[161] There is a passage in the fourth part of Coke's *Institutes* which suggests that little recourse was had to the Chancellor in matters of bankruptcy during the earlier part of the seventeenth century. Coke commented that the commissioners 'are subject to the action of the party grieved, for he hath no other remedy'. Presumably he meant by this an action at law, while the only authority of the Chancellor mentioned was the power to grant the commission. See *Coke's Institutes* (1648), 277.

[162] See Holdsworth, *A History of English Law* (2nd edn, 1937) vol. 8, 241–3. The Chancellor decided a number of issues in the next few decades, particularly in relation to the bankruptcy of partnerships, the distribution of the bankrupt's estate, and the effect of a bankruptcy upon equitable interests.

[163] See Yale, *Lord Nottingham's Chancery Cases* vol. 1, 73 *Selden Society* (1957), cxv. The bankruptcy legislation of the first two decades of the eighteenth century conferred a number of discreet powers upon the Chancellor. Included amongst them was the power to remove the assignees if petitioned by creditors and to make such order as he thought just and reasonable, for example that a new assignment be made (see 1718) 5 Geo 1, c. 24, s. 23), while s. 25 of that Act allowed the Chancellor in some cases to supersede the commission. See also the statutes (1705) 4 & 5 Anne, c. 17; (1706) 5 & 6 Anne, c. 22, and (1718) 5 Geo 1, c. 24. However, the legislation did not confer a general jurisdiction in the Chancellor over matters in bankruptcy. Lord Eldon thought that the bankruptcy legislation was framed with the general authority of the Chancellor in mind, and that, if the legislation was silent as to the means of giving effect to its provisions, the Chancellor had a general jurisdiction to act to attain the objects of the commission. See *Anon* (1808) 14 Ves Jun 449, 451, 33 ER 593 and also Henley, *A Digest of the Bankrupt Law* (3rd edn, 1832), 451–2. Professor Christian expressed a different view. He argued that the Chancellor's authority in matters over which he had not been given express jurisdiction was recommendatory only, but was enforceable by means of his control over the appointment of commissioners. The power and authority of the commissioners was conferred by an Act of Parliament, and for that reason Christian said that they were not bound to obey the Chancellor. They depended upon him, however, for their appointment as commissioners, and failure to follow his directions could have resulted in the Chancellor renewing the commission under (1732) 5 Geo II, c. 30, s. 45 with other more compliant persons being appointed. See Christian, *Bankrupt Law* (2nd edn, 1818) vol. 2, 6–24. In any event, there is probably some truth in Cooper's assertion that equity usurped jurisdiction in this area, possibly because of the immense fees and the control of patronage that went with it. See *Cooper's Parliamentary Proceedings* (1828), 251–2.

the right to a balanced account,[164] and it is unlikely that the Chancellor was influential in its development.

F. The Development of the Set-off Section

6.38 A set-off section was first incorporated into the bankruptcy legislation in 1705.[165] Section 11 of the statute (1705) 4 & 5 Anne, c. 17[166] provided:

> Where there shall appear to the commissioners or the major part of them that there hath been mutual credit given between such person or persons against whom such commission shall issue forth and any person or persons who shall be debtor or debtors to such person or persons and due proof thereof made and that the accounts are open and unbalanced that then it shall be lawful for the commissioners in the said commission named or the major part of them or the assignee or assignees of such commission to adjust the said account and to take the balance due in full discharge thereof and the person debtor to such bankrupt shall not be compelled or obliged to pay more than shall appear to be due on such balance.

This section has formed the foundation of the modern right of set-off in bankruptcy, although subsequent amendments have considerably enlarged the scope of its operation. The language of the provision was simplified in 1718,[167] and in 1732[168] the ambit of the right was expressed in terms of mutual credit and mutual debts, rather than simply mutual credit.[169]

6.39 It was a feature of the early legislation that there could only be a set-off if the mutual debts or mutual credit existed 'at any time such person became bankrupt',[170] by which was meant when an act of bankruptcy was committed.[171] In 1806 the legislation was amended so as to

---

[164] North CJ made his statement in 1675, while the judgment of Lord Hale referred to in *Chapman v Derby* could not have been delivered later than 1676, when he retired as Chief Justice of the King's Bench.

[165] Contrary to Sir George Jessel MR's assertion in *Peat v Jones & Co* (1881) 8 QBD 147, 149, that the enactment as to 'mutual credits' first appeared in (1732) 5 Geo II, c. 30.

[166] It was not until 1797 that the mutual credit provision in the bankruptcy legislation was made permanent. Until then, it was to be found in a number of temporary statutes, the operation of each of which was continued, with occasional amendment, by a subsequent enactment. The 1705 Act was to remain in force for only three years (see s. 17), although it was continued *in toto* by (1708) 7 Anne, c. 25, and then by (1716) 3 Geo I, c. 12.

[167] See (1718) 5 Geo 1, c. 24, which was continued by (1724) II Geo I, c. 29, and by (1726) 13 Geo I, c. 27. The words 'assignee or assignees' were omitted from the 1718 legislation, so that apparently only the commissioners were empowered to balance the accounts. However, those words were reintroduced in 1732.

[168] See 5 Geo II, c. 30, s. 28.

[169] Apart from this, there were only minor differences between the language of the 1718 and the 1732 set-off sections, although the latter did bring assignees back within the scope of the right. The Act of 1732 was only to remain in force for a period of three years (see s. 49), but its operation was continued by the following statutes: (1736) 9 Geo II, c. 18; (1743) 16 Geo II, c. 27; (1751) 24 Geo II, c. 57; (1758) 31 Geo II, c. 35; (1763) 4 Geo III, c. 36; (1772) 12 Geo III, c. 47; (1776) 16 Geo III, c. 54; (1781) 21 Geo III, c. 29; (1786) 26 Geo III, c. 80; (1788) 28 Geo III, c. 24, and by (1794) 34 Geo III, c. 57. It was made perpetual in 1797 by 37 Geo III, c. 124.

[170] See s. 28 of (1732) 5 Geo II, c. 30. This notion first appeared in the statute (1718) 5 Geo I, c. 24, which required that there should have been 'mutual credit given by the bankrupt and any other person at any time before the person against whom such commission is or shall be awarded became bankrupt'.

[171] See *Bamford v Burrell* (1799) 2 Bos & Pul 1, 126 ER 1120. Acts of bankruptcy were a series of defined acts the commission of any one of which constituted a statutory recognition of insolvency. A person must have committed an act of bankruptcy before he or she could be made bankrupt. The concept of the act of bankruptcy has been abolished in the Insolvency Act 1986, the sole ground for bankruptcy proceedings now being inability to pay debts.

offer some protection in the event that the person giving credit to the bankrupt was not aware of the commission of an act of bankruptcy.[172] Subject to two qualifications, s. 3 of the statute (1806) 46 Geo III, c. 135 allowed one debt or demand to be set against another notwithstanding that a prior act of bankruptcy had been committed by the bankrupt before credit was given to or a debt contracted by the bankrupt. The qualifications were that the section only applied when the credit was given to the bankrupt at least two calendar months before the date of the commission,[173] and the person claiming the set-off must not have had notice of an act of bankruptcy committed by the bankrupt at the time of giving credit or notice that he or she was insolvent or had stopped payment.

In 1825 the various statutes which until then had set out the law of bankruptcy were **6.40** repealed and replaced by a consolidating statute 6 Geo IV, c. 16.[174] The new mutual credit provision was set out in s. 50 of the Act, and it contained a number of amendments to the pre-existing law. In particular, there was a further liberalization of the right to a set-off in the event of credit being given to, or a debt contracted by, the bankrupt after the commission of a secret act of bankruptcy. The proviso in (1806) 46 Geo III, c. 135, s. 3, that the credit must have been given at least two calendar months before the date of the commission in bankruptcy, was deleted,[175] while the scope of the second proviso was narrowed so that only notice of a prior act of bankruptcy at the time that credit was given to the bankrupt would operate to prevent a set-off. Notice of the fact that the bankrupt was insolvent or had stopped payment was no longer sufficient. The legislation also provided that every debt or demand made provable by the Act could be the subject of a set-off against the bankrupt's estate. The idea that all provable debts could be the subject of a set-off was not new.[176] However, the insertion of this principle into the 1825 mutual credit provision ensured that contingent debts could be set off, since it was only as a result of s. 56 of (1825) 6 Geo IV, c. 16 that contingent debts became provable.

The terms of the 1825 set-off section remained essentially unaltered when the law of **6.41** bankruptcy once again was consolidated in 1849,[177] the only difference being that the creation in 1831 of a separate Court of Bankruptcy with jurisdiction over all matters in bankruptcy[178] meant that the court, rather than the commissioners, was to control the balancing of the accounts.

When another consolidation took place in 1869,[179] the ambit of the right of set-off was **6.42** extended from mutual credit and mutual debts to cover also mutual dealings. The proviso relating to notice of an act of bankruptcy was also amended. Whereas it had been

---

[172] See e.g. *Dickson v Cass* (1830) 1 B & Ad 343, 358–9, 109 ER 814, 820 (Parke J).

[173] The date of the commission was the date upon which it was sealed and issued by the Chancellor. See Christian, *Bankrupt Law* (2nd edn, 1818) vol. 1, 457–9.

[174] In fact an earlier bankruptcy consolidation Act (5 Geo IV, c. 98) had been enacted the previous year, but it was repealed by 6 Geo IV, c. 16 the day after it was due to take effect.

[175] Therefore, the account could be taken down to the issuing of the commission, rather than two months before. See Babington, *The Law of Set-off and Mutual Credit* (1827), 118, and also Henley, *A Digest of the Bankrupt Law* (3rd edn, 1832), 187.

[176] See e.g. Christian, *Bankrupt Law* (2nd edn, 1818) vol. 1, 509.

[177] See the Bankrupt Law Consolidation Act 1849, s. 171.

[178] See (1831) 1 & 2 Will IV, c. 56.

[179] See the Bankruptcy Act, 1869, s. 39.

a prerequisite to the operation of the previous sections that the person claiming the benefit of the set-off should not have given credit to the bankrupt after notice of an act of bankruptcy, the new section stipulated that the notice had to be of an act of bankruptcy that was available against the bankrupt for adjudication. This referred to s. 6 of the Act, and required that the act of bankruptcy must have occurred within six months of the presentation of the petition.[180] In addition, the legislation no longer specifically provided that every debt or demand which was provable against the estate of the bankrupt could also be the subject of a set-off, although this omission was of little consequence because the courts in any event continued to emphasize that point.[181]

6.43 The 1869 mutual credit provision was, with one exception, virtually identical to the set-off section in the 1914 legislation. The 1869 Act stipulated that the mutual dealings had to be between a 'bankrupt and any other person proving or claiming to prove a debt under his bankruptcy'. However, in the Bankruptcy Act 1883, s. 38,[182] which was similar to the Bankruptcy Act 1914, s. 31, the language was altered so that the mutual dealings had to be 'between a debtor against whom a receiving order shall be made under this Act, and any other person proving or claiming to prove a debt under such receiving order'. The concept of the receiving order was introduced in the 1883 Act[183] as a step between the presentation of the petition and the adjudication of bankruptcy. It served to stay all actions against the debtor, and to vest the possession and control of the debtor's property in an official receiver,[184] while the creditors considered whether any proposals for a composition or scheme of arrangement should be accepted, or whether it was expedient for the debtor to be adjudged bankrupt.

6.44 The concept of the receiving order was discarded in the Insolvency Act 1986. Reference to it was therefore deleted from the set-off section (s. 323), which is drafted in terms of sanctioning a set-off in the event of 'mutual dealings between the bankrupt and any creditor of the bankrupt proving or claiming to prove for a bankruptcy debt'. It has been said of the current section that it was recast in a simpler and more modern form than its predecessor, but that it was not intended to alter the substantive scope or effect of the earlier section.[185]

G. The Relevant Date for Determining Rights of Set-off

(1) Bankruptcy, company liquidation and administration

6.45 The right of set-off essentially is an aspect of the rules regulating the proof of debts,[186] and ever since the incorporation of a right of set-off into the bankruptcy legislation it has

---

[180] Compare the Bankruptcy Act 1914, *s.* 4(1)(c), which specified a three-month period.

[181] See paras 7.24–7.26 below.

[182] The Bankruptcy Act 1883 repealed the Bankruptcy Act 1869, and amended and consolidated the law of bankruptcy.

[183] Bankruptcy Act 1883, ss. 5–14, and also the Bankruptcy Act 1914, s. 7.

[184] See the Bankruptcy Act 1914, s. 7.

[185] *Re Bank of Credit and Commerce International SA (No. 8)* [1996] Ch 245, 256 (CA).

[186] See *Mersey Steel and Iron Co Ltd v Naylor, Benzon, & Co* (1884) 9 App Cas 434, 437–8; *Re Northside Properties Pty Ltd and the Companies Act* [1971] 2 NSWLR 320, 323; *Re Bank of Credit and Commerce International SA (No. 8)* [1996] Ch 245, 256 (CA); *Re One. Tel Ltd* (2002) 43 ACSR 305 at [25].

generally been the case that the date which defined the accounts to be balanced was the same as that which determined what claims could be proved in the bankruptcy.[187] The Insolvency Act 1986 conforms with that approach in bankruptcy, since the 'commencement of the bankruptcy' is expressed to constitute the relevant date in both cases.[188] This refers to the day of the bankruptcy order,[189] as opposed to the date of the petition.[190]

The significance of the relevant date is that claims which arise after that date and which are **6.46** not derived from a prior dealing between the parties to the proposed set-off cannot be employed in a set-off.[191] However, claims which arise before that date may also be excluded from set-off by operation of the qualification to the set-off section.[192] The scope of the qualifications to the various insolvency set-off provisions is considered later.[193]

Company liquidation

In company liquidation, the provable debts are determined by reference to when the **6.47** company goes into liquidation or, if the winding up was immediately preceded by an administration, when the company entered administration.[194] A company goes into liquidation if it passes a resolution for a voluntary winding up, or if an order is made for its winding up by the court at a time when it has not already gone into liquidation by passing such a resolution.[195] In relation to set-off, the Insolvency Rules 1986, r. 4.90(1) provides

---

[187] Before the amendment of the 1732 Act in 1806 (see para. 6.39 above), the date of the act of bankruptcy applied to both proof and set-off. See e.g. *Bamford v Burrell* (1799) 2 Bos & Pul 1, 7, 126 ER 1120, 1123–4 for proof of debts, and *Collins v Jones* (1830) 10 B & C 777, 780, 109 ER 638, 639 for set-off. Under the 1825 consolidation, the date of the issuing of the commission, and after 1831 of the fiat, was applied in both instances. See s. 47 of (1825) 6 Geo IV, c. 16 for the proof of debts, and for set-off *Collins v Jones* at 780–1, 639. However, the dates did not always coincide when Parliament acted in 1806 to ameliorate the harsh consequences under the 1732 Act of a secret act of bankruptcy. Section 2 of the statute (1806) 46 Geo III, c. 135 allowed debts contracted before the issuing of the commission to be proved if the creditor did not have notice of a prior act of bankruptcy, while for set-off s. 3 only provided relief when credit was given to the bankrupt at least two calendar months before the issuing of the commission. It is difficult to ascertain the position under the 1849 and 1869 Acts. Section 165 of the Bankrupt Law Consolidation Act 1849 allowed a creditor to prove any debt or demand contracted before the filing of the petition, and similarly it was accepted in Doria and Macrae *The Law and Practice of Bankruptcy* (1863) vol. 2, 804–5 that this date applied to set-off. On the other hand, in *Astley v Gurney* (1869) LR 4 CP 714 the report only refers to the date of the adjudication, not the date of the petition, and the former may have been regarded as the relevant date for the purpose of set-off. The Bankruptcy Act 1869, s. 31 differed from its 1849 predecessor in relation to the proof of debts, in that it allowed claims to which the bankrupt was subject at the date of the adjudication order to be proved, although in 1874 Doria had not changed his opinion that the existence of a right of set-off should be ascertained as at the date of the petition. See Doria, *The Law and Practice of Bankruptcy* (1874), 679. The 1883 and 1914 Acts both conformed with the general rule, since in each case the date of the receiving order determined questions relating to both proof and set-off. See *Re Daintrey, ex p Mant* [1900] 1 QB 546.

[188] See s. 323 for set-off and, for proof, the definition of 'bankrupt debt' in s. 382.

[189] See the Insolvency Act 1986, s. 278.

[190] See also, with respect to proof of debts, the Insolvency Rules 1986, rr. 6.98(1)(b), 6.111–6.114.

[191] See paras 6.63–6.65 below.

[192] In bankruptcy, the Insolvency Act 1986, s. 323(3).

[193] See paras 6.66–6.99 below.

[194] See the Insolvency Rules 1986, r. 13.12 (together with r. 12.3), and r. 4.75(1)(b).

[195] See the Insolvency Act 1986, s. 247(2). Pursuant to s. 247(3), the reference to a resolution for voluntary winding up includes a resolution deemed to occur by virtue of an order made following conversion of a voluntary arrangement or administration into winding up under Article 37 of the Council Regulation (EC) No. 1346/2000. Section 247(2) should be distinguished from s. 129 dealing with the commencement of the

that the rule applies when there are mutual credits, mutual debts or other mutual dealings 'before the company goes into liquidation'. But where the liquidation was immediately preceded by an administration, the reference to mutual credits, mutual debts or other mutual dealings in r. 4.90(1) does not include any debt arising out of an obligation incurred during the administration.[196]

6.48   The positions in relation to set-off in bankruptcy and company liquidation differ in a curious respect. In bankruptcy, the dividing line is expressed in terms of a particular day, being the day of the bankruptcy order. In company liquidation, on the other hand, the *prima facie* reference point for set-off is when the company 'goes into liquidation',[197] which seems to contemplate a particular time within the day.[198]

Administration

6.49   As a consequence of amendments made to the Insolvency Rules in 2003 and 2005,[199] set-off may apply in the case of a company in administration if the administrator, being authorized to make a distribution, has given notice of his intention to do so under r. 2.95. Rule 2.85(3) provides that an account is to be taken as at the date of the notice under r. 2.95. On the other hand, the debts provable in the administration are determined by reference to the date that the company went into administration,[200] and r. 2.85(2)(a) provides that 'mutual credits, mutual debts or other mutual dealings' for the purpose of a set-off does not include any debt arising out of an obligation incurred after the company entered administration.[201] This indicates that the relevant date, in the sense of the date which determines what claims may be included in a set-off, generally is the date that the company entered administration. Rule 2.85(3) is directed at a different question, being the date of the taking of the account.[202]

6.50   The general effect of this scheme is that, if an administrator gives notice of intention to make a distribution under r. 2.95, the date for determining what claims can be included in a set-off is back-dated to the commencement of the administration. The resulting

---

winding up. While s. 247(2) is not specifically expressed to apply to the Insolvency Rules, r. 4.90, its application in that context would be consistent with the approach which the courts generally have adopted in the past. See *Re Fenton* [1931] 1 Ch 85, 105; *Barclays Bank Ltd v TOSG Trust Fund Ltd* [1984] BCLC 1, 25; *Re Charge Card Services Ltd* [1987] 1 Ch 150, 177; *MS Fashions Ltd v Bank of Credit and Commerce International SA* [1993] Ch 425, 446. Compare *Re City Equitable Fire Insurance Co Ltd* [1930] 2 Ch 293, 310 and *Re Dynamics Corporation of America* [1976] 1 WLR 757, 769, which supported the date of the petition rather than the date of the winding-up order.

[196]   Rule 4.90(2)(c). For the meaning of 'debt' in that context, see para. 6.78 below.

[197]   Insolvency Rules 1986, r. 4.90(1).

[198]   However, in relation to proof of debts compare the Insolvency Rules 1986, rr. 4.91, 4.92, 4.93 and 13.12, which refer to the *date* on which the company goes into liquidation.

[199]   Insolvency Rules 1986, r. 2.85. See para. 6.10 above.

[200]   Or, if the company was in liquidation when it entered administration, the date on which it went into liquidation. See r. 2.72(3)(b)(ii) and r. 13.12(5) (in relation to r. 13.12). See also r. 2.86 (conversion of foreign currency claims), r. 2.87 (payments of a periodic nature), r. 2.88 (interest) and r. 2.89 (debt payable at a future time). See generally, with respect to the proof of debts in administration, r. 12.3.

[201]   But if the administration was immediately preceded by a winding up, any debt arising out of an obligation incurred during the winding up is excluded from the set-off. See r. 2.85(2)(d). As to the meaning of 'debt' in that context, see para. 6.83 (and the note thereto) below.

[202]   See para. 6.124 below.

uncertainty as to the position in relation to set-offs in the period after a company has entered administration but before the administrator has determined to give notice of intention to make a distribution can give rise to practical difficulties for persons dealing with a company in administration.[203] If a debt arising out of an obligation incurred after a company entered administration is not available for set-off under r. 2.85 where a notice subsequently is given under r. 2.95,[204] it is unlikely that a contractual right of set-off would be effective to remedy the situation. In that regard, the exercise of a contractual right in relation to post-administration debts before the administrator has given notice should not be objectionable. But once a notice is given, a subsequent exercise of the contractual right is unlikely to be effective to the extent that it goes beyond the statutory right of set-off conferred by r. 2.85.[205]

(2) Australia – bankruptcy

In Australia, the date of the bankruptcy determines the availability of both rights of proof and rights of set-off in bankruptcy.[206]   **6.51**

(3) Australia – company liquidation, administration and deeds of company arrangement

In company liquidation,[207] the provable debts are determined by reference to the 'relevant   **6.52** date',[208] which is defined in the Corporations Act 2001 (Cth), s. 9 as the day that the winding up is taken because of Div. 1A of Part 5.6 of the Act to have begun.[209] This in turn refers to the day of the winding-up order or the day on which a resolution was passed for a winding up, but if the company immediately before the winding up was under administration or was subject to a deed of company arrangement, it is the day on which the administration began.[210] The date is modified in relation to proof of debts by ss. 553(1A) and 553(1B) of the Corporations Act, to accommodate the situation in which the circumstances giving rise to a claim against the company occurred at a time when the company was under a deed of company arrangement, and the company was under the deed

---

[203] For discussions of the point, see Turing, 'Setting off down a new road' (2004) 19 *Journal of International Banking and Financial Law* 349 and Bewick, Hertz, Marshall and Tett, 'Administration set-off: a commentary on the paper of the FMLC Working Group' (2008) 23 *Journal of International Banking and Financial Law* 287. An administrator who incurs liabilities on behalf of the company before giving a notice under r. 2.95 has a charge on the company's property pursuant to para. 99 of Sch. B1 to the Insolvency Act 1986, but that may not be an adequate substitute for a right of set-off to a creditor dealing with the company post administration. See Lightman and Moss, *The Law of Administrators and Receivers of Companies* (4th edn, 2007), 552–3 [20–044].

[204] Rule 2.85(2)(a).

[205] See paras 16.21–16.23 below.

[206] See, for proof of debts, the Bankruptcy Act 1966 (Cth), s. 82(1) and, for set-off, *Gye v McIntyre* (1991) 171 CLR 609, 619–20. When a debtor is made bankrupt on a creditor's petition, the date of the bankruptcy is the date of the sequestration order. See the definition of 'the date of the bankruptcy' in s. 5, and *Hiley v The Peoples Prudential Assurance Co Ltd* (1938) 60 CLR 468, 487; *Gye v McIntyre* at 619–20.

[207] The insolvency set-off section also may be incorporated into a deed of company arrangement. See para. 6.12 above.

[208] See the Corporations Act 2001 (Cth), s. 553(1).

[209] See s. 9.

[210] Corporations Act 2001 (Cth), ss. 513A–513C.

immediately before the resolution or the court order for a winding up. In that case, the claim is admissible to proof against the company and, for the purpose of applying the sections in Div. 6 of Part 5.6 of the Act (dealing with proof and ranking of claims), the relevant date for the claim is the date on which the deed terminates.

6.53 The concept of the 'relevant date' is not specifically incorporated into s. 553C of the Corporations Act dealing with mutual credit and set-off. Traditionally, the question whether there are mutual debts, mutual credits or other mutual dealings between a company in liquidation and a creditor so as to qualify for a set-off has been said to be determined by reference to the date of the liquidation.[211] In a voluntary liquidation this has been taken as referring to the date of the resolution, while in a court-ordered winding up the weight of authority has favoured the view that it means the date of the order.[212] However, the authorities in question pre-dated the inclusion in the Corporations legislation of both the definition of the 'relevant date' and the concept of administration of companies. In *Re Parker*,[213] Mansfield J held that the determination of set-off entitlements should also take place by reference to the 'relevant date', so that when, as in that case, liquidation follows immediately after an administration, the date for determining whether there are mutual credits, mutual debts or other mutual dealings is the day on which the administration began.[214]

6.54 Three points may be made in relation to the situation in which there was a prior administration. In the first place, if a debt incurred *by* a company while under administration is not provable in a subsequent liquidation, the debt similarly could not be employed in a set-off, since the set-off section requires that the creditor's claim be provable. Therefore, at least to that extent, the concept of 'the relevant date' must apply to set-off. Second, in relation to the claim on the other side of the account, being a claim accruing to the company while under administration, the same result often would follow whether the determinative date is the day the administration began or the date of the winding-up order.[215] This is because of the qualification to the insolvency set-off section in s. 553C(2) of the Corporations Act, which provides that a creditor is not entitled to claim a set-off if at the time of giving credit to or receiving credit from the company the creditor had notice of the fact that the company was insolvent.[216] The board of a company may resolve to appoint an administrator if in the opinion of the directors the company is insolvent or it is likely to become insolvent at some future time.[217] It is not necessary that the company be insolvent at the time of the

---

[211] *Day & Dent Constructions Pty Ltd v North Australian Properties Pty Ltd* (1982) 150 CLR 85, 98.

[212] See Street J in *Re Northside Properties Pty Ltd and the Companies Act* [1971] 2 NSWLR 320, 323 (decision affirmed [1972] 2 NSWLR 573), whose view was accepted by Mason J in *Day and Dent Constructions Pty Ltd v North Australian Properties Pty Ltd* (1982) 150 CLR 85, 98–9 (Stephen J concurring at 96). Compare the opinions of Barwick CJ and Taylor J in *Motor Terms Co Pty Ltd v Liberty Insurance Ltd* (1967) 116 CLR 177, that one should look to the date of the presentation of the petition in order to ascertain the rights of the creditors.

[213] (1997) 80 FCR 1.

[214] See, in particular, at (1997) 80 FCR 1, 15–16.

[215] Or, as the case may be, the resolution for a winding up.

[216] See generally para. 6.87 below.

[217] Corporations Act 2001 (Cth), s. 436A(1).

appointment,[218] and so bare knowledge of the appointment by itself would not seem to constitute notice of the fact that the company was insolvent.[219] However, other circumstances combined with the appointment may provide notice of present insolvency,[220] in which case any debt that the creditor subsequently incurred to the company could not be set off in a subsequent liquidation whether the date for determining set-offs is the date of the liquidation or the date of the administration. The third point is that a creditor often would not be disadvantaged by being unable to prove a debt incurred by the company after an administrator has been appointed,[221] and therefore being denied a set-off in respect of it. This is because an administrator is personally liable for debts incurred in the exercise of his or her functions and powers for services rendered, or for goods bought or property hired, leased, used or occupied.[222] In those circumstances, the creditor can sue the administrator personally. Moreover, expenses properly incurred by an administrator in preserving, realizing or getting in property of the company or in carrying on the company's business have priority of payment in a liquidation.[223] If the creditor would be paid in full in any event, he or she would not need a set-off. For those reasons, the question whether the availability of a set-off is determined by reference to the date that the administration began, or the date of the winding-up order or the resolution for a voluntary winding up, often would not be significant.

The question was important, however, in *Re Parker*.[224] The creditors of a company under administration resolved that it be wound up. The company had a holding company, and it was alleged that there were cross-debts between them. The holding company had given a floating charge over all its assets to a secured creditor, which assets included debts owing to the holding company. Because of the charge, nothing would be available for the holding company's unsecured creditors. The charge crystallized after the commencement of the subsidiary's administration and before the resolution for its winding up. Mansfield J was asked to determine whether, in those circumstances, there could be a set-off in the subsidiary's liquidation. One of the issues was the date for determining rights of set-off. If the date was the date of the winding up, the crystallized charge would have had the effect of destroying mutuality as between the subsidiary and the holding company in relation

6.55

---

[218] See, in a different context, *Re AFG Insurances Ltd* (2002) 20 ACLC 1588, 1590.

[219] See *JLF Bakeries Pty Ltd v Baker's Delight Holdings Ltd* (2007) 64 ACSR 633 at [32] (administration 'might not itself be conclusive evidence of notice of insolvency') *per* White J. Compare the Australian Law Reform Commission Report No 45, *General Insolvency Inquiry* (1988) ('the Harmer Report'), which recommended (in para. 819) that a person should not have a right of set-off if at the time of a transaction occurring within six months of the winding up the person had reason to suspect that the company was unable to pay its debts. That recommendation is not reflected in the more stringent requirement in s. 553C(2), that the person must have had notice of the fact that the company was insolvent. As to notice of a deed of company arrangement, see para. 6.56n below.

[220] E.g. insolvency may be disclosed in the report provided to creditors pursuant to the Corporations Act, s. 439A(4).

[221] When performing a function or exercising a power as administrator of a company the administrator acts as the company's agent. See the Corporations Act 2001 (Cth), s. 437B.

[222] Corporations Act 2001 (Cth), s. 443A.

[223] Corporations Act 2001 (Cth), s. 556(1).

[224] (1997) 80 FCR 1.

to the debts.[225] The secured creditor, therefore, would have obtained the benefit of the holding company's claim against the subsidiary without reduction for a set-off.[226] However, Mansfield J held that the appropriate date was the same as that fixed for determining what debts were provable in the winding up, being the date that the administration began. He accepted that there were mutual debts for the purpose of the insolvency set-off section at that date,[227] and therefore the secured creditor took subject to the prior set-off entitlement.[228]

6.56 The approach adopted in *Re Parker* would become complicated in the situation in which an administration is followed by a deed of company arrangement before the company goes into liquidation. The day on which the administration began is still defined as the relevant date,[229] but special provision is made in s. 553(1A) for the situation in which the circumstances giving rise to a debt or claim against the company occurred while the company was under the deed. The debt may be proved in the liquidation, and s. 553(1B) provides that, for the purpose of applying the other sections of Div. 6 of Part 5.6 dealing with proof and ranking of claims, the relevant date for that debt is the date on which the deed terminates. If a debt is provable under s. 553(1A), it would ordinarily be regarded as capable of being included in a set-off,[230] so that the view expressed in *Re Parker* would have to be qualified

---

[225] See para. 11.51 below.

[226] The holding company's liability to the subsidiary was founded upon an allegation of insolvent trading pursuant to the Corporations Act 2001 (Cth), s. 588W. Since the liability had not vested at the date of crystallization of the charge, it was not a case of existing mutual debts at the date of crystallization giving rise to a defence of set-off under the Statutes of Set-off to which the secured creditor as an equitable assignee took subject. See paras 17.15 and 17.106 below.

[227] See the discussion at (1997) 80 FCR 1, 11–12. The view that a claim against a holding company under s. 588W of the Corporations Act 2001 (Cth) for compensation for loss resulting from insolvent trading can be the subject of a set-off is criticized in paras 13.20–13.29 below.

[228] Mansfield J commented ((1997) 80 FCR 1, 15–16) that, as a result of the decision, crystallization of a security after the appointment of an administrator would not remove from the assets of the company available to the unsecured creditors who are eligible to prove in the winding up as at the date of the administrator's appointment any assets of the company as at that date. He said that there is, therefore, preserved: 'a contemporaneity between the date to determine the assets available in the winding up, not vulnerable to change even through the processes of s. 553C of the Law, and the date to determine those eligible to participate in the distribution of those assets.' However, when an administrator is appointed to a company, the assets available in a subsequent winding up may not be the same as those at the date of the administration, particularly if the company continues to trade. Moreover, there may be changes after the date of the appointment of an administrator in the identity of those eligible to participate in the distribution of the assets. See e.g. the Corporations Act, s. 553(1A) (debt incurred by a company while under a deed of company arrangement which immediately preceded the winding up), and the various circumstances referred to in *Re Jay-O-Bees Pty Ltd* (2004) 50 ACSR 565 at [90]–[92] (Campbell J). See also *Wight v Eckhardt Marine GmbH* [2004] 1 AC 147.

[229] Corporations Act 2001 (Cth), ss. 513A(d) and 513B(c).

[230] See (and compare) paras 7.24–7.26 below. This is subject to s. 553C(2) of the Corporations Act 2001 (Cth), which provides that a person is not entitled to claim the benefit of a set-off in a company's liquidation if at the time of giving credit to or receiving credit from the company the person had notice of the fact that the company was insolvent. See generally paras 6.87–6.89 below. However, when an insolvent company enters into a deed of company arrangement, the terms of the deed would ordinarily be such that the company is no longer insolvent, in that, if it complies with the deed, it could pay its debts as and when they fall due. The deed would ordinarily permit the creditors to terminate it and resolve to wind the company up if the administrator determines that it is no longer practicable or desirable to continue to carry on the company's business. See the Corporations Regulations, Sch. 8A, cl. 3 of which applies to a deed of company arrangement unless it has been excluded (see the Corporations Act, s. 444A(5), and the Corporations Regulations, reg. 5.3A.06).

to accommodate a set-off in relation to debts coming within the ambit of s. 553(1A). In such a case, there could be two relevant dates for determining rights of set-off. Once a company goes into administration, the day on which the administration began would constitute a relevant date for the purpose of a subsequent liquidation. But if the administration was followed by a deed of company arrangement before the liquidation, the date on which the deed terminated would constitute a second relevant date for debts of the company arising out of circumstances occurring while the company was under the deed. In either case, however, a debt of the company which arose out of circumstances that occurred while the company was under administration and before the deed would not be provable, in which case it could not be set off under s. 553C.[231]

But how would this work for the claim on the other side of the account which it is sought **6.57** to include in a set-off, being the company's claim against the creditor? If the company's claim arose before the day on which the administration began, and the administration was followed by a deed of company arrangement before the liquidation, the claim should be capable of being included in a set-off against a provable debt whether that provable debt relates to the first or the second relevant date.[232] Further, if the company's claim against the creditor arose while the company was under the deed, it should be capable of being included in a set-off against a provable debt arising in that period.[233] But what about a claim which accrued to the company before the deed, while the company was under administration? Once a debt of the company which arises out of circumstances occurring during the period of a deed becomes provable under s. 553(1A), so that pursuant to s. 553(1B) the relevant date for that debt is the date that the deed terminates, there is nothing in s. 553C to suggest that a set-off in respect of that debt should be limited to cross-debts which similarly accrued to the company during that period. A person dealing with a company during the period of the administration may have notice of insolvency so as to preclude a set-off under s. 553C(2),[234] but apart from that there is nothing in s. 553C which would exclude a set-off in relation to a claim which accrued to the company before the deed and while it was under administration. A limitation to that effect would not follow from the concept of mutuality, because mutuality does not require that there should be a temporal or other connection between the claims the subject of a set-off.[235] As the High Court observed in *Gye v McIntyre*,[236] the word 'mutual' conveys the notion of reciprocity rather than of correspondence. If, then, *Re Parker* is followed, and if administration is followed by a deed of company arrangement before liquidation, it may be that a claim possessed by the company that arose out of circumstances occurring before the deed and while the company was

---

But, depending on the terms of the deed, the fact that a person dealing with a company is aware that the company has executed a deed of company arrangement may not have the consequence in a subsequent liquidation that the person had notice at the time of the dealing that the company was insolvent. As to notice of the appointment of an administrator, see para. 6.54 above.

[231] See para. 7.24 below.

[232] This assumes that the deed incorporated the insolvency set-off section. See para. 6.12 above.

[233] This is subject to set-off not being excluded under s. 553C(2) of the Corporations Act 2001 (Cth) because of notice of insolvency. But see para. 6.56n above.

[234] See para. 6.54 above.

[235] See para. 11.01 below.

[236] (1991) 171 CLR 609, 623.

under administration would be treated differently for the purpose of set-off to a claim *against* the company which arose out of circumstances occurring in the same period.[237] Moreover, while it was held in *Re Parker* that a floating charge held by a third party over the company's assets which crystallized during the period of the administration is subject to a set-off determined as at the date the administration began, the crystallized charge should nevertheless preclude a set-off in relation to a provable debt that was incurred while the company was under the deed. This is because crystallization would destroy mutuality for the purpose of a set-off determined as at the date that the deed terminated,[238] the date of termination being the relevant date for that particular debt.[239]

6.58   The *Re Parker* approach would be artificial in the common situation in which an administrator carries on the company's business during the administration,[240] the object of administration being to maximize the chances of the company, or as much of its business as possible, continuing in existence.[241] Consider, for example, the case of a company which has a credit balance on a current account with its bank on the day that an administrator is appointed.[242] At the same time, the company has a contingent liability to indemnify the bank, for example in relation to letters of credit which the bank has issued at its request. Subsequently, the company goes into liquidation, and the bank is called upon to honour the letters of credit. The bank has a provable debt in the liquidation for its right of indemnity from the company, the amount of which is to be valued as at the day of the appointment of the administrator.[243] On that day there were mutual dealings between the bank and the company, which could be the subject of a set-off.[244] But what if during the administration the administrator drew on the current account in the course of carrying on the company's business? The drawings would have reduced the credit balance, but a set-off entitlement determined as at the date of the administrator's appointment would not take them into account. Alternatively, the administrator after his appointment may have closed the account, and transferred the credit funds to an account with another bank. It would make little sense in that situation to talk of determining the set-off rights of the first bank in the liquidation as at the date that the administration began. The point is that the account remained an operating bank account notwithstanding the administration, and the company through the administrator[245] was entitled to deal with the funds on deposit.

6.59   Further difficulties arise from the nature of insolvency set-off. The prevailing view is that a set-off under the insolvency set-off section occurs automatically. It does not require the procedural step of taking an account in the liquidation.[246] The question of the automatic

---

237   See para. 6.56 above.
238   See para. 11.50 below.
239   Corporations Act 2001 (Cth), s. 553(1B).
240   Pursuant to the Corporations Act 2001 (Cth), s. 437A(1)(b).
241   Corporations Act 2001 (Cth), s. 435A.
242   As in *Cinema Plus Ltd v Australia and New Zealand Banking Group Ltd* (2000) 49 NSWLR 513.
243   Corporations Act 2001 (Cth), s. 554A.
244   The bank's contingent claim for an indemnity could be the subject of a set-off. See paras 8.10–8.34 below.
245   See the Corporations Act 2001 (Cth), s. 437D.
246   See paras 6.119–6.146 below.

nature of insolvency set-off was not specifically addressed in *Re Parker*. However, the decision suggests that the set-off in that case was regarded as having occurred at the date of commencement of the administration, as opposed to the date of the liquidation. In other words, it was not simply a matter of looking at the date of commencement of the administration in order to determine which claims could be included in a set-off, which set-off occurred as at the liquidation date. In *Re Parker*, a floating charge over the holding company's assets crystallized after the appointment of administrators to the subsidiary and before the subsidiary's winding up, and Mansfield J held that the chargee took subject to a set-off under s. 553C determined as at the date of commencement of the administration. Section 553C provides that, 'an account is to be taken of what is due from the one party to the other in respect of those mutual dealings', and 'the sum due from the one party is to be set off against any sum due from the other party'. The 'one party' and 'the other' are the parties to the set-off, and the use of the present tense ('is due') suggests that there should be mutuality when the set-off occurs.[247] If it was thought in *Re Parker* that a set-off, if available, would have taken place on the date of the liquidation, there should not in fact have been a set-off in that case. Mutuality in insolvency set-off is determined by reference to equitable interests,[248] but crystallization of the charge before liquidation would have had the consequence that there was no mutuality in equity when the liquidation occurred.[249] In equity, the subsidiary's debt was due to the secured creditor rather than to the holding company. Therefore, the decision to allow a set-off would appear to have been on the basis that a set-off was thought of as having occurred before crystallization, at the date of the administration, when there was mutuality. It would be a curious notion, however, if a set-off in a liquidation were regarded as having taken place retrospectively at the date of commencement of a prior administration, when the company's business was still operating and it continued to operate during the period of the administration. Consider, for example, the situation posited above, where a company's current account with its bank had a credit balance when an administrator was appointed, and the company and the bank had entered into a dealing before the administration, for example the issue by the bank of a letter of credit at the request of the company, which later gave rise to a claim by the bank against the company. If a set-off in a subsequent liquidation were thought of as having occurred at the date the administration began, where would that leave drawings on the account after the commencement of the administration, including where the administrator transferred the funds to another account?[250] Looking at the matter retrospectively, the conclusion would be that, to the extent of the bank's claim against the company, the current account was not in credit when the administrator was appointed because the account was the subject of an automatic set-off occurring as at that date. If there was no credit balance, the administrator should not have been entitled to draw on the account.

---

[247] In adopting the automatic theory in *Stein v Blake* [1996] AC 243, the House of Lords (at 255–6) rejected the application of a notion of 'taking subject to equities' in the context of insolvency set-off.

[248] See paras 11.13–11.17 below.

[249] See para. 11.50 below.

[250] See para. 6.58 above.

6.60   Moreover, if the set-off were taken to have occurred retrospectively on the date of the administrator's appointment, the administrator could be adversely affected in relation to his or her lien on the company's assets. An administrator is personally liable for certain debts incurred in the performance of his or her functions or powers.[251] On the other hand, the administrator is entitled to be indemnified out of the company's property for debts for which he or she is liable and also for remuneration,[252] the right of indemnity being secured by a lien on the company's property.[253] An administrator may look upon a credit balance on the company's bank account as an asset against which he or she is entitled to exercise the right of indemnity, and on the faith of that assumption may incur debts for which he or she is personally liable.[254] But if the company goes into liquidation while the debts are still outstanding, and the bank has a claim against the company, for example in relation to letters of credit issued at the request of the company before the administration which the bank was later called upon to honour, the application of the automatic theory of insolvency set-off as at the date of commencement of the administration would mean that, because of the liquidation, the company's asset in the form of the credit balance will have disappeared in a set-off occurring retrospectively when the administration began. The administrator would therefore be personally liable for the debts without a valuable right of indemnity from the credit funds. If, on the other hand, set-offs were regarded as occurring at the date of the liquidation, albeit that the provable debt necessary for the set-off is determined as at the commencement of the administration,[255] the administrator's lien on the account in credit would destroy mutuality in the liquidation in relation to the account and the company's liability to the bank. To the extent of the lien there would not be a set-off,[256] and the administrator, therefore, would not be prevented by the liquidation from exercising the lien against the account.

6.61   But notwithstanding those difficulties, the evident view in *Re Parker* as to the operation of the insolvency set-off section has since been followed.[257] It is also consistent with views expressed in the Victorian Court of Appeal in *G. M. & A. M. Pearce and Co Pty Ltd v RGM Australia Pty Ltd*,[258] in the context of a deed of company arrangement that was not followed by a liquidation. The deed in that case incorporated the insolvency set-off section applicable in company liquidation.[259] In accordance with s. 444A(4)(i) of the Corporations Law,[260] the deed specified that the admissible claims under the deed were those which arose on or before the date of the appointment of the administrator to the company. The Court of Appeal held that a set-off occurred automatically under the deed,[261] so that it was not

---

[251] Corporations Act 2001 (Cth), s. 443A.

[252] Corporations Act 2001 (Cth), s. 443D.

[253] Corporations Act 2001 (Cth), s. 443F.

[254] See e.g. *Cinema Plus Ltd v Australia and New Zealand Banking Group Ltd* (2000) 49 NSWLR 513.

[255] See para. 6.54 above.

[256] See paras 11.37–11.51 below.

[257] *JLF Bakeries Pty Ltd v Baker's Delight Holdings Ltd* (2007) 64 ACSR 633 at [17] (White J). See also *Silberman v One. Tel Ltd* (2001) 20 ACLC 93 at [23].

[258] [1998] 4 VR 888.

[259] See para. 6.12 above.

[260] See now the Corporations Act 2001 (Cth), s. 444A(4)(i).

[261] Any surplus in favour of the company after the set-off may be recovered by the company after termination of the deed, notwithstanding that any net claim against the company would have been extinguished by the deed. See *Arcfab Pty Ltd v Boral Ltd* (2002) 43 ACSR 573.

necessary for a debtor to the company who also had a claim against the company to make a claim under the deed in order to obtain a set-off. The date that the set-off occurred, accepting an automatic operation, was not in issue. While there are judicial statements which might be said to favour the date of the deed as the date for the occurrence of set-offs,[262] it was assumed in the *Pearce* case that the set-off would have taken place when the administration began.[263] This has also been suggested in other cases.[264] At least in the case of a deed of company arrangement, the Corporations Act does not require that the insolvency set-off section be incorporated into the deed,[265] so that the parties may have some control over its operation.[266] However, this is not so in a company liquidation, given that the section is mandatory in a liquidation and cannot be contracted out of.[267]

In the circumstances in issue in *Re Parker*, an alternative view is that the date for determin-   **6.62**
ing the availability of a set-off should remain the date of the liquidation, given that the concept of 'the relevant date' has not been specifically incorporated into s. 553C. On the other hand, there still has to be a provable debt, and the determination whether there is a provable debt would take place by reference to 'the relevant date', including as modified by s. 553(1B) when the company was under a deed of company arrangement before the liquidation. This alternative view would have the consequence that the company's claim against the creditor and the provable debt owing by the company would be treated differently for the purpose of a set-off, but that may also happen in some circumstances on the *Re Parker* approach.[268] It would also mean that the date for determining set-offs and the date for determining the provable debts would not coincide, which would represent a departure from the approach generally adopted in the past.[269] There would still neverthe-less be a connection because of the requirement that there be a provable debt, and in any

---

[262] *Metal Manufacturers Ltd v Hall* (2002) 41 ACSR 466 at [9] (Gzell J) ('upon the execution of the deed'); *Arcfab Pty Ltd v Boral Ltd* (2002) 43 ACSR 573 at [20], [32] and [35] (Austin J) ('upon commencement of the deed'); *Reed Constructions Australia Ltd v DM Fabrications Pty Ltd* (2007) 25 ACLC 1463 at [35] (30 May 2007 being the date of the deed of company arrangement).

[263] See Callaway JA at [1998] 4 VR 888, 891 (23 May 1994 being the date that the directors resolved to appoint an administrator), with which view Batt JA at 900 appears to have agreed. See also Ormiston JA at 889. This view is consistent with cl. 7(d) of the prescribed provisions in Sch. 8A of the Corporations Regulations.

[264] *Handberg v Smarter Way (Aust) Pty Ltd* (2002) 190 ALR 130 at [30], [39] and [55]; *Ansett Australia Ltd v Travel Software Solutions Pty Ltd* (2007) 65 ACSR 47 at [63] (12 September 2001 being the date of the appointment of the administrators: see at [33]). See also *JLF Bakeries Pty Ltd v Baker's Delight Holdings Ltd* (2007) 64 ACSR 633 at [17].

[265] *G. M. & A. M. Pearce and Co Pty Ltd v RGM Australia Pty Ltd* [1998] 4 VR 888, 891 (Callaway JA). The insolvency set-off section (s. 553C) applies if the deed does not exclude the prescribed provisions in Sch. 8A of the Corporations Regulations. See the Corporations Act 2001 (Cth), s. 444A(5), and cl. 8 of Sch. 8A. Compare *Central Data Networks Pty Ltd v Global Diagnostics Ltd* (1998) 84 FCR 304, 320–1.

[266] This is subject to the question whether the omission of the insolvency set-off section from the deed may provide grounds for setting it aside, as being unfairly prejudicial to or unfairly discriminatory against one of more creditors. See the Corporations Act 2001 (Cth), s. 445D(1)(f), and *Re Opes Prime Stockbroking Ltd* (2008) 171 FCR 473 at [16]. Compare *Central Data Networks Pty Ltd v Global Diagnostics Ltd* (1998) 84 FCR 304, 320–1.

[267] See para. 6.111–6.112 below.

[268] See paras 6.56 and 6.57 above.

[269] See para. 6.45 above.

event it has not always been the case in the past that the dates coincided.[270] This view would avoid the difficulties that may follow consequent upon the *Re Parker* approach.

(4) Claims accruing subsequent to the relevant date

6.63 Once a particular date is fixed for determining the existence of a set-off, the acquisition of a right or a liability after that date which is not the result of a prior dealing[271] will not result in a set-off.[272] Thus, a sale of goods by a liquidator in the course of winding up the company will not entitle the purchaser to employ his or her liability for the price in a set-off against a provable debt owing to the purchaser by the company.[273] An amount paid by a director of a company after the commencement of the company's liquidation in order to settle an action that had been commenced against both the director and the company similarly has been held not to be available as a set-off in the liquidation,[274] and a set-off cannot be based upon an assignment of the benefit of a proof of debt lodged by someone else.[275] On the same principle, save for an exception relating to a temporary suspension of mutuality,[276] a set-off cannot be based upon an assignment of a debt or a dealing with a negotiable instrument that took place after the relevant date.[277] A debt or a negotiable instrument

---

[270] This was the position when Parliament intervened in 1806 to ameliorate the harsh consequences of a secret act of bankruptcy under the early Bankruptcy Act (1732) 5 Geo II, c. 30. Section 2 of the statute (1806) 46 Geo III, c. 135 allowed debts contracted before the issuing of the commission to be proved if the creditor did not have notice of a prior act of bankruptcy, but s. 3 only provided relief in the case of set-off when credit was given to the bankrupt at least two calendar months before the issuing of the commission. See paras 6.39 and 6.45n above.

[271] See ch. 7 below.

[272] In addition to the cases referred to below, see *Glennie v Edmunds* (1813) 4 Taunt 775, 128 ER 536; *Re Henley, Thurgood, & Co* (1863) 11 WR 1021; *Sankey Brook Coal Co, Ltd v Marsh* (1871) LR 6 Ex 185; *Re The United Ports and General Insurance Co, ex p The Etna Insurance Co* (1877) 46 LJ Ch 403; *Re Milan Tramways Co, ex p Theys* (1884) 24 Ch D 587; *Re Gunson (A Bankrupt), ex p Official Receiver* [1966] NZLR 187; *Ansett Australia Ltd v Travel Software Solutions Pty Ltd* (2007) 65 ACSR 47 (declaration of a dividend in favour of a shareholder after the shareholder had executed a deed of company arrangement under the Australian Corporations Act; compare para. 8.05 below in relation to a dividend declared by a solvent company in liquidation). In relation to a costs order against a company in liquidation, see *Re Bank of Hindustan, China and Japan, ex p Smith* (1872) LR 3 Ch App 125; *Fused Electrics Pty Ltd v Donald* [1995] 2 Qd R 7. See also *Re Buchanan Enterprises Pty Ltd* (1982) 7 ACLR 407 (no equitable set-off); *Hague v Nam Tai Electronics Inc* [2006] 2 BCLC 194 at [8] (PC) (amendment of company's articles of association after the liquidation of a shareholder for the purpose of redeeming the shares and setting off the redemption price against a debt owing by the shareholder). Given the inclusion of the mutual dealings head in the set-off section in 1869, *quaere* whether *Graham v Allsopp* (1848) 3 Ex 186, 154 ER 809 would now be followed in relation to the claim for a set-off against the rent due before the immediate landlord's bankruptcy. This is because the payment by the lessee to the superior landlord after the bankruptcy as a result of the distress levied pursuant to the lease which had not been taken up by the assignees in bankruptcy nevertheless arose out of a prior dealing, in the form of the lease.

[273] *Hiley v The Peoples Prudential Assurance Co Ltd* (1938) 60 CLR 468, 496; *Re Kidsgrove Steel, Iron, and Coal Co* (1894) 38 Sol Jo 252; *JLF Bakeries Pty Ltd v Baker's Delight Holdings Ltd* (2007) 64 ACSR 633 at [24]. See also *Re Henley, Thurgood & Co* (1863) 11 WR 1021. *Quaere* if this would apply if assets are purchased from a company in liquidation pursuant to a prior option. See paras 13.59–13.63 below.

[274] *Re Buchanan Enterprises Pty Ltd* (1982) 7 ACLR 407.

[275] *Re Gill, ex p Official Receiver* (1964) 6 FLR 273, 276.

[276] See para. 6.105 below.

[277] *Marsh v Chambers* (1749) 2 Str 1234, 93 ER 1152; *Dickson v Evans* (1794) 6 TR 57, 101 ER 433; *Sempill v The Oriental Bank* (1868) 7 SCR (NSW) 68; *Middleton v Pollock, ex p Nugee* (1875) LR 20 Eq 29 (assignment of debt); *Re Gillespie, ex p Reid & Sons* (1885) 14 QBD 963. See also *McColl's Wholesale Pty Ltd v State Bank of NSW* [1984] 3 NSWLR 365, 381.

admittedly may be proved even though it may have been acquired from another party after the cut-off date for determining rights of proof.[278] However, the proof in that case should not be lodged by the subsequent holder, but rather by the holder at the relevant date as trustee for the latter.[279] The subsequent holder would take subject to any set-off that may have been available as between the bankrupt and the holder at that date.[280]

Receipt of money by an agent after the principal's bankruptcy

If a person appointed as an agent receives the principal's money after the principal has become bankrupt, the person could not ordinarily employ his or her liability to account in a set-off. The bankruptcy would have terminated the agency, and no claim of mutual credit or mutual dealings based upon its expected continuance could be supported.[281] This is in addition to any difficulty that may arise from the possibility that the agent may have received the moneys impressed with a trust.[282]   **6.64**

Unaware of the bankruptcy

It has been suggested that a claim arising after the relevant date, and not related to a dealing entered into before that date, may be employed in a set-off if the fact of the bankruptcy was unknown to the other party.[283] The only instance in which this has occurred is *Billon v Hyde*,[284] but the facts in issue were exceptional. The case concerned the old doctrine of relation back, and an attempt by Lord Hardwicke to use set-off as a means of bringing about a result consistent with a statute[285] which had been enacted in order to ameliorate the harshness of the doctrine, but which had not come into force when the dealings before him occurred. In *Kinder v Butterworth*,[286] claims entered into after the relevant date in ignorance of the bankruptcy were not allowed to be set-off,[287] and moreover the contrary conclusion would seem to conflict with judicial opinions to the effect that the question whether there is a set-off cannot be varied by transactions entered into subsequent to the relevant date.[288]   **6.65**

H. Qualification to the Set-off Section

In both individual and corporate insolvency, the availability of a set-off under the insolvency set-off section is qualified. Insolvency set-off constitutes an exception to the *pari passu* principle, in that a creditor with an entitlement to a set-off receives payment in full   **6.66**

---

[278] *Ex p Deey* (1796) 2 Cox 423, 30 ER 196; *Ex p Atkins, re Atkins* (1820) Buck 479; *Ex p Rogers, re Bowles* (1820) Buck 490.

[279] *Ex p Dickenson, Re Gibson* (1832) 2 Deac & Ch 520.

[280] *Ex p Deey* (1796) 2 Cox 423, 424, 30 ER 196. This would follow from the automatic nature of insolvency set-off. See paras 6.119–6.146 below.

[281] *Elgood v Harris* [1896] 2 QB 491, 495. In Australia, compare *Re Clune* (1988) 14 ACLR 261, 267–8.

[282] See ch. 10 below.

[283] *Re Gill, ex p Official Receiver* (1964) 6 FLR 273, 276. See also *Re Clements* (1931) 7 ABC 255, 268.

[284] (1749) 1 Ves Sen 326, 27 ER 1061.

[285] (1746) 19 Geo II, c. 32.

[286] (1826) 6 B & C 42, 108 ER 369.

[287] Compare the headnote to *Re Gillespie, ex p Reid & Sons* (1885) 14 QBD 963, although Cave J in his judgment seems to have been referring to notice of an act of bankruptcy.

[288] See *Dickson v Evans* (1794) 6 TR 57, 59, 101 ER 433, 434; *Re Milan Tramways Co, ex p Theys* (1884) 25 Ch D 587, 591; *Savage v Thompson* (1903) 29 VLR 436, 440.

for his or her claim against the insolvent rather than being confined to a dividend along with other creditors. The effect of a set-off, therefore, is to prefer one creditor over the general body of creditors. The purpose of the qualification is to protect the assets of a person who is or is approaching insolvency against manipulation of set-offs in a subsequent bankruptcy or liquidation to the detriment of creditors generally.[289] For example, a person who buys a debt at a discount is entitled to base a claim for a set-off upon the full face value of the debt.[290] Therefore, in the absence of a qualification to the insolvency set-off section, a creditor who otherwise might only receive a small dividend could sell the debt at a discount to a person who himself is indebted to the insolvent party, and who could obtain the full value of the assigned debt by means of a set-off in the ensuing bankruptcy.[291]

(1) Onus

6.67 The qualification in most cases is expressed in terms of notice of a circumstance or an event by a creditor. The onus in that situation should be on the person denying the occurrence of a set-off (ordinarily the trustee in bankruptcy or the liquidator) to establish the requisite notice.[292]

(2) What constitutes notice?

6.68 There is little authority on what constitutes notice for the purpose of the insolvency set-off section. Before the current Insolvency Act 1986, the qualification to the bankruptcy set-off section was expressed in terms of notice of an act of bankruptcy.[293] That concept also

---

[289] As in *Law v James* [1972] 2 NSWLR 573 and *Re Eros Films Ltd* [1963] 1 Ch 565. For statements of the purpose of the qualification, see *Central Brake Service (Sydney) Pty Ltd v Central Brake Service (Newcastle) Pty Ltd* (1992) 27 NSWLR 406, 413; *Gye v McIntyre* (1991) 171 CLR 609, 619; *Trans Otway Ltd v Shepherd* [2006] 2 NZLR 289 at [17]; *JLF Bakeries Pty Ltd v Baker's Delight Holdings Ltd* (2007) 64 ACSR 633 at [41].

[290] *Stonehouse v Read* (1825) 3 B & C 669, 107 ER 881. Similarly, in the absence of fraud in the inception or preparation of a bill of exchange, a discounter is entitled to prove for its face value. See *Re Gomersall* (1875) 1 Ch D. 137, 146–7.

[291] See *Gye v McIntyre* (1991) 171 CLR 609, 619.

[292] In Australia, see *Thomas v Hatzipetros* (1997) 24 ACSR 286, 290 and *Jetaway Logistics Pty Ltd v DCT* (2008) 68 ACSR 226 at [18]–[29] (reversed on other grounds (2009) 76 ACSR 404). In *Thomas v Hatzipetros* it was held that the onus was not on the liquidator, but the facts were exceptional. The case concerned the question whether a disposition of property, in the form of a cheque, made by a company in favour of a bank after the commencement of proceedings to wind the company up was void pursuant to the Corporations Law, s. 468. The bank and a director of the company argued that the court should make an order validating the disposition pursuant to s. 468, on the ground that the bank in any event would have been entitled to a set-off in the liquidation so that the company was no worse off by the disposition. In a situation where the bank and the director were seeking an order from the court validating a disposition of property, they had the onus of proving the circumstances which would justify the order, which in that case was the availability of a set-off to the bank. This included proof that the bank would not have been disentitled from set-off by reason of the qualification to the set-off section. Those circumstances should be contrasted with the *Jetaway* case, in which the liquidators contended that the transaction in question constituted an unfair preference, which carried with it the proposition that a set-off would not have been available to the Commissioner. See para. 13.10 below. The liquidators, therefore, were asserting that the qualification applied to preclude a set-off, and so they had the onus of proof. Compare the Companies Act 1993 (NZ), s. 310(2), which places the onus on the person claiming the benefit of the set-off to prove that he or she did not have reason to suspect that the company was unable to pay its debts. See *Trans Otway Ltd v Shephard* [2006] 2 NZLR 289 at [18]–[19].

[293] Bankruptcy Act 1914, s. 31. The reference to notice of an act of bankruptcy in the bankruptcy set-off section can be traced back to the statute (1806) 46 Geo III, c. 135, s. 3. In that Act, however, the provision

appeared in other provisions in the bankruptcy legislation which provided protection against the avoidance of transactions, for example execution on judgments or pursuant to the doctrine of 'relation back' of the trustee's title to the date of the act of bankruptcy.[294] Acts of bankruptcy have been discarded in the Insolvency Act 1986. But the concept of notice in the current bankruptcy set-off section should have the same meaning as in earlier bankruptcy legislation, and in relation to earlier legislation there is no reason to think that the concept of notice of an act of bankruptcy for the purpose of denying a set-off had a different meaning to that ascribed to the expression in relation to other provisions in the legislation. Further, the set-off section in company liquidation is derived from the bankruptcy set-off section,[295] and notice should have the same meaning in that context as in bankruptcy.

In other contexts, notice of an act of bankruptcy was said to mean knowledge of the act or wilfully abstaining from acquiring knowledge.[296] But it was also accepted that a person may be proved to have had notice by proof that the person knew facts which were sufficient to inform him or her that an act of bankruptcy had been committed, whether or not the person drew the natural inference from the facts.[297] On the other hand, *Evans v Hallam*[298] suggested that there had to be knowledge of circumstances which themselves indicated that there had been an act of bankruptcy, as opposed to putting a person on inquiry. Thus, Cockburn CJ said: 'It is not notice of an act of bankruptcy to say something to him which might possibly put him to further inquiry; it is not notice to tell him something which, if he were to inquire further, would shew him that an act of bankruptcy did exist.'[299] In that same case Blackburn J expressed the principle in terms that: 'The matter to be ascertained in these cases is, whether sufficient information was given of those facts which amount to an act of bankruptcy, so as to make it reasonable for the execution creditor to hesitate in enforcing his judgment.'[300]

6.69

---

was not cast in terms of denying a set-off when there was notice of an act of bankruptcy. Rather, it provided protection against loss of a set-off in circumstances where the set-off section otherwise denied a set-off in relation to debts and credits which arose after an act of bankruptcy. See para. 6.39 above.

[294] See e.g. the Bankruptcy Act 1914, ss. 37, 40 and 45. The doctrine of relation back no longer applies under the Insolvency Act 1986.

[295] Prior to the current liquidation set-off provision (the Insolvency Rules 1986, r. 4.90), the set-off provision applicable in company liquidation was the bankruptcy section. See e.g. the Companies Act 1948, s. 317, which incorporated into company liquidation the principles of bankruptcy as to debts provable, a concept which included set-off. See para. 6.06 above. In Australia, that was also the effect of the Corporations Law, s. 553(2), prior to the repeal of that section by the Corporate Law Reform Act 1992 (Cth) and the introduction of s. 553C.

[296] *Bird v Bass* (1843) 6 Man & G 143, 134 ER 841.

[297] *Ex p Snowball, re Douglas* (1872) LR 7 Ch App 534. In *Herbert's Trustee v Higgins* [1926] 1 Ch 794, 800 Lawrence J framed the question in terms whether the defendant had 'established that he had no knowledge or notice of any facts which would reasonably lead an ordinary man of business to conclude that an act of bankruptcy had been committed.'

[298] (1871) LR 6 QB 71. See also *Herbert's Trustee v Higgins* [1926] 1 Ch 794.

[299] (1871) LR 6 QB 713, 716.

[300] (1871) LR 6 QB 713, 717. The notice should have caused hesitation because it was of the occurrence of an act of bankruptcy, which may or may not have resulted in a bankruptcy. There was no mention of further inquiry. Compare *Re Boocock* [1916] 1 KB 816, 820.

6.70 Notice for the purpose of the insolvency set-off section should import similar principles. Thus, it was said in Australia that notice of an act of bankruptcy for the purpose of the qualification in the set-off section meant: 'such knowledge of the act and of its attendant circumstances conditions and consequences as are necessary to make it an act of bankruptcy.'[301] That statement is consistent with the principles set out above.

6.71 The precise terms of the qualification differ in bankruptcy and corporate insolvency. There are also differences between the English and the Australian provisions.

(3) Bankruptcy

6.72 In bankruptcy, the Insolvency Act 1986, s. 323(3) provides that: 'Sums due from the bankrupt to another party shall not be included in the account . . . if that other party had notice at the time they became due that a bankruptcy petition relating to the bankrupt was pending.'[302] A petition is pending if the petition has been presented but as yet a bankruptcy order has not been made consequent upon it.[303]

6.73 Curiously, s. 323(3) only applies in relation to sums due *from* the bankrupt. It does not preclude a set-off in relation to sums due on the other side of the account, being a debt incurred in favour of the bankrupt after notice that a bankruptcy petition was pending. It should be contrasted with the qualifications in the Australian insolvency set-off sections, which extend to claims on both sides of the account.[304] Generally, this also now applies in company liquidation and administration in England.[305]

(4) Company liquidation

6.74 The qualification in company liquidation (being the Insolvency Rules 1986, r. 4.90(2)) is more comprehensive than that in bankruptcy. In summary,[306] it precludes a set-off in respect of the following:

(a) any debt arising out of an obligation incurred at a time when the creditor had notice that a meeting of creditors had been summoned under the Insolvency Act 1986, section 98 or that a petition for the winding up of the company was pending;

(b) where the liquidation was immediately preceded by an administration, any debt arising out of an obligation incurred at a time when the creditor had notice that an application for an administration order was pending or that a person had given notice of intention to appoint an administrator;

(c) where the liquidation was immediately preceded by an administration, any debt arising out of an obligation incurred during the administration;

---

[301] *Re Hardman* (1932) 4 ABC 207, 212 *per* Lukin J, referred to in *Central Brake Service (Sydney) Pty Ltd v Central Brake Service (Newcastle) Pty Ltd* (1992) 27 NSWLR 406, 412 (NSW CA). The analysis of the Victorian Court of Appeal in *Jetaway Logistics Pty Ltd v DCT* (2009) 76 ACSR 404 in relation to the Australian company liquidation set-off provision (see para. 6.89 below) is consistent with this view.

[302] In the case of an assignment, 'due' in s. 323(3) should refer to the time that the sum became due to the assignee. See para. 6.97 below.

[303] See e.g. the Insolvency Act 1986, s. 285.

[304] See paras 6.85 (bankruptcy) and 6.87 (company liquidation) below.

[305] See paras 6.77 (liquidation) and 6.83 (administration) below.

[306] See para. 6.06 above.

(d) any debt which was acquired by a creditor by assignment or otherwise, where the agreement pursuant to which the creditor acquired the debt was entered into:

   (i) after the company went into liquidation;

   (ii) at a time when the creditor had notice that a meeting of creditors had been summoned under the Insolvency Act 1986, section 98;

   (iii) at a time when the creditor had notice that a winding-up petition was pending;

   (iv) where the liquidation was immediately preceded by an administration, at a time when the creditor had notice that an application for an administration order was pending or that a person had given notice of intention to appoint an administrator; or

   (v) during an administration that immediately preceded the liquidation.

In (a), (b) and (c) of the qualification (above), the question is to be determined by reference **6.75** to the circumstances at the time when an obligation was incurred which gave rise to a debt, as opposed to when the debt itself arose. In relation to (c), it suffices that the obligation was incurred during an administration. There is no requirement of notice of the administration. Similarly, there is no requirement of notice in (d)(i) (assignment after the company went into liquidation) and (d)(v) (assignment after the company entered an administration that immediately preceded the liquidation).

In relation to (a), (d)(ii) and (d)(iii), a petition is filed in a court-ordered winding up and **6.76** a s. 98 meeting takes place in a creditors' voluntary winding up. A creditors' voluntary winding up should be distinguished from a members' voluntary winding up. Briefly, a voluntary winding up may proceed as a members' voluntary winding up if the directors made a statutory declaration within the five-week period immediately preceding the date of the passing of the resolution for winding up to the effect that in their opinion the company would be able to pay its debts in full together with interest.[307] A creditor's voluntary winding up is a voluntary winding up in which the directors failed to make such a declaration. The qualifications in (a) and (d)(ii) apply in the case of a creditors', but not a members', voluntary winding up.

Prior to the amendments to the Insolvency Rules in 2005,[308] the qualification to the set-off **6.77** in r. 4.90, in the former sub-r. (3), was expressed in terms of excluding a set-off in relation to sums due *from* the company to the creditor.[309] Claims on the other side of the account, being sums due *to* the company, were not within the terms of the qualification. However, there is no such limitation in r. 4.90(2)(a), (b) and (c). The debt referred to can be on either side of the account.

On its face, each of the exclusions from set-off in r. 4.90(2)(a), (b) and (c) is confined **6.78** to a 'debt' arising out of an obligation, as opposed to a damages claim for breach of

---

[307] See the Insolvency Act 1986, ss. 89 and 90.

[308] See para. 6.06 above.

[309] Including when r. 4.90 was amended by r. 7 of the Insolvency (Amendment) Rules 2003 (S.I. 2003 No. 1730) prior to the current form of the rule. This is still the position in bankruptcy. See paras 6.72–6.73 above.

the obligation. Rule 13.12 defines a 'debt' in terms which include a liability for damages. However, that definition does not apply if the context otherwise requires.[310] If it was intended to apply to r. 4.90(2) one would have thought that it would have extended to both sides of the account, but the definition in r. 13.12 is confined to a debt or liability to which the company is subject, being a provable debt. It does not extend to a debt or liability owed *to* the company. If r. 4.90(2)(a), (b) and (c) are intended to exclude from set-off a damages claim for breach of an obligation in the stated circumstances, as opposed to a debt (properly so-called) arising from the obligation, they are not well drafted.

6.79 Special provision is made in the Financial Services and Markets Act 2000 (Administration Orders Relating to Insurers) Order 2002[311] for the case of an insurance company[312] in liquidation in the situation where it had been subject to a prior administration order. In that circumstance, art. 5 provides that sums due from the insurer to another party are not to be included in a set-off under r. 4.90 of the Insolvency Rules if, at the time they became due, an administration application had been made under para. 12 of Sch. B1, a notice of appointment had been filed under para. 18 of Sch. B1, or a notice of intention to appoint had been filed under para. 27 of Sch. B1, in each case in relation to that insurer. They are not expressed to depend upon notice of the relevant event. It is unclear why special provisions were thought to be necessary for insurance companies.

6.80 Special provisions also apply in the case of a bank insolvency under the Banking Act 2009.[313] The scope of the right of set-off in that situation is set out in r. 72 of the Bank Insolvency (England and Wales) Rules 2009,[314] which is in similar terms to r. 4.90. However, the qualifications differ.[315] Rule 72 precludes a set-off in respect of a debt arising out of an obligation incurred at a time when the creditor had notice that an application for a bank insolvency order in respect of the bank was pending, and a debt acquired by a creditor pursuant to an agreement where the agreement was entered into at a time when the creditor had notice of the application. On the other hand, there is no equivalent in r. 72 of r. 4.90(2) (b), (c) or (d)(iv) relating to a prior administration.

(5) Administration

6.81 In the case of a company in administration, set-off may apply under the Insolvency Rules 1986, r. 2.85 if the administrator, being authorized to make a distribution, has given notice

[310] Rule 13.1.

[311] S.I. 2002 No. 1242, amended by the Financial Services and Markets Act 2000 (Administration Orders Relating to Insurers) (Amendment) Order 2003 (S.I. 2003 No. 2134). Pursuant to art. 3(3) of the Enterprise Act 2002 (Commencement No 4 and Transitional Provisions and Savings) Order 2003 (S.I. 2003 No. 2093), the law relating administration under Part II of the Insolvency Act 1986, without the amendments and repeals made by the provisions of the Enterprise Act 2002 mentioned in art. 3(2) of the Order, continue to apply in so far as is necessary to give effect to the Financial Services and Markets Act 2000 (Administration Orders relating to Insurers) Order 2002.

[312] As defined in the Financial Services and Markets Act 2000 (Insolvency) (Definition of 'Insurer') Order 2001 (S.I. 2001 No. 2634).

[313] See para. 6.16 above.

[314] S.I. 2009 No. 356.

[315] Compare r. 4.90(2) with r. 72(1).

of his intention to do so under r. 2.95.[316] The availability of the set-off is qualified by r. 2.85(2), which is in a format similar to r. 4.90(2) in relation to liquidation but amended to take into account that administration rather than liquidation is in issue. In summary, r. 2.85(2) precludes a set-off in relation to the following debts:

(a) any debt arising out of an obligation incurred after the company entered administration;

(b) any debt arising out of an obligation incurred at a time when the creditor had notice that an application for an administration order was pending or that any person had given notice of intention to appoint an administrator;

(c) where the administration was immediately preceded by a winding up, any debt arising out of an obligation incurred at a time when the creditor had notice that a meeting of creditors had been summoned under the Insolvency Act 1986, section 98 or that a petition for the winding up of the company was pending;

(d) where the administration was immediately preceded by a winding up, any debt arising out of an obligation incurred during the winding up;

(e) any debt which was acquired by a creditor by assignment or otherwise, where the agreement pursuant to which the creditor acquired the debt was entered into:

  (i) after the company entered administration;

  (ii) at a time when the creditor had notice that an application for an administration order was pending;

  (iii) at a time when the creditor had notice that a person had given notice of intention to appoint an administrator;

  (iv) where the administration was immediately preceded by a winding up, at a time when the creditor had notice that a meeting of creditors had been summoned under the Insolvency Act 1986, section 98 or that a winding-up petition was pending; or

  (v) during a winding up that immediately preceded the administration.

6.82 Similar to the position in liquidation,[317] there is no requirement of notice in (a) (debt arising out of an obligation incurred after the company entered administration),[318] (d) (debt arising out of an obligation incurred during a winding up that immediately preceded the administration), (e)(i) (assignment after the company entered administration) and (e)(v) (assignment during a winding up that immediately preceded the administration).

6.83 The exclusions from set-off in (a), (b), (c) and (d) extend to debts on both sides of the account, and not simply to debts owing by the company.[319]

(6) Australia – bankruptcy

6.84 In Australia, the Bankruptcy Act 1966 (Cth), s. 86(2) provides that a person cannot claim the benefit of a set-off if, at the time of giving credit to the person who has become

---

[316] See para. 6.10 above.

[317] See para. 6.74 above.

[318] On the other hand, a debt incurred after the company entered administration may have priority as an expense of the administration in accordance with the Insolvency Rules 1986, rr. 2.67 and 2.68(3)(c), and the Insolvency Act 1986, Sch. B1 para. 99(3). See generally Lightman and Moss, *The Law of Administrators and Receivers of Companies* (4th edn, 2007), 134–45.

[319] See also para. 6.77 above in relation to company liquidation. Compare para. 6.73 above in relation to bankruptcy. As to whether 'debt' includes a liability in damages for breach of an obligation, as opposed to a debt (properly so-called) arising out of the obligation, see para. 6.78 above. In that regard, the definition of 'debt' in r. 13.12 referred to in para. 6.78 also applies when a company is in administration. See r. 13.12(5).

bankrupt or at the time of receiving credit from that person, he or she had notice of an available act of bankruptcy committed by that person.[320] An available act of bankruptcy is an act of bankruptcy committed within six months of the presentation of the petition,[321] while notice of the act has been said to mean such knowledge of the act and its attendant circumstances, conditions and consequences as are necessary to make it an act of bankruptcy.[322]

6.85 Unlike the English bankruptcy section,[323] s. 86(2) applies to debts incurred on both sides of the account after a person has the requisite notice.[324]

6.86 The circumstance which attracts the operation of s. 86(2) is notice of the relevant event at the time of giving or receiving credit.[325] The better view is that the concept of giving credit does not extend to a damages claim, although there is support for the contrary view.[326]

(7) Australia – company liquidation

6.87 In company liquidation in Australia, the qualification is expressed simply in terms of notice of insolvency.[327] Pursuant to the Corporations Act 2001 (Cth), s. 553C(2), a person is not entitled to claim the benefit of a set-off if, at the time of giving credit to the company or at the time of receiving credit from the company,[328] the person had notice of the fact that the company was insolvent. Insolvency is defined in s. 95A in terms of inability to pay debts as and when they become due and payable.

6.88 Section 553C(2) should be contrasted with s. 588FG, which was introduced into the Corporations Law at the same time as s. 553C.[329] Section 588FG provides a defence to a claim to set aside a transaction in a liquidation as an unfair preference, an uncommercial transaction or an unfair loan, if the person the subject of the application 'had no reasonable grounds for suspecting that the company was insolvent'. Section 553C(2) should also be

---

[320] For the meaning of 'credit', see paras 7.02–7.06 below. In the case of an assignment, the 'time of giving credit' for the purpose of s. 86(2) is the time when the assignment became effective. See para. 6.99 below.

[321] See the Bankruptcy Act 1966 (Cth), ss. 5 and 44(1)(c).

[322] *Re Hardman* (1932) 4 ABC 207, 212, referred to in *Central Brake Service (Sydney) Pty Ltd v Central Brake Service (Newcastle) Pty Ltd* (1992) 27 NSWLR 406, 412 (NSW CA).

[323] See paras 6.72–6.73 above.

[324] See also para. 6.87 below in relation to company liquidation.

[325] For the time that credit is given or received, see para. 6.93 below. The same concept applies in company liquidation. See para. 6.87 below.

[326] See paras 7.02–7.06 below, questioning (at para. 7.06) a suggestion in the judgment of the High Court in *Gye v McIntyre* (1991) 171 CLR 609, 624–5 that a damages claim for fraudulent misrepresentation may come within the term 'mutual credits'.

[327] This accords with the recommendation of the Cork Committee in England, that the qualification should be framed in terms of notice of inability to pay debts. See the *Cork Committee Report on Insolvency Law and Practice* (Cmnd 8558, 1982), 127, 307. Prior to the Corporate Law Reform Act 1992 (Cth), the bankruptcy set-off section, in s. 86 of the Bankruptcy Act 1966 (Cth), was incorporated into the winding-up provisions in the corporations legislation, including the qualification expressed in terms of notice of an available act of bankruptcy. Acts of bankruptcy do not apply in company liquidation. For the application of the qualification in that context, see *Law v James* [1972] 2 NSWLR 573. After the 1992 Act, set-off in company liquidation ceased to be governed by the bankruptcy section.

[328] See para. 6.93 below in relation to when credit is given or received.

[329] See the Corporate Law Reform Act 1992 (Cth), ss. 92 and 111.

contrasted with the earlier recommendation of the Australian Law Reform Commission in its report (the 'Harmer Report') on insolvency law,[330] that a person should not have a right of set-off in a liquidation if at the time of the relevant transaction the person had reason to suspect that the company was unable to pay its debts. That recommendation (and the similar language in s. 588FG) is not reflected in the more confined terms of 553C(2), which requires 'notice of the fact that the company was insolvent'.

The question of what constitutes notice for the purpose of s. 553C(2) was considered by the Victorian Court of Appeal in *Jetaway Logistics Pty Ltd v DCT*.[331] The following points were made in the judgment: **6.89**

1. The notice referred to is actual notice, as opposed to constructive notice.
2. The liquidator has to establish that the creditor had notice of facts that would have indicated to a reasonable person the fact that the company was insolvent. This requires more than reasonable grounds for suspecting insolvency.
3. The notice must be of the fact that the company is insolvent. This does not refer to the matters set out in the Corporations Act 2001 (Cth), s. 459C(2) which may found a presumption of insolvency for the purpose of an application to wind up a company.
4. A person will have notice of the fact that that a company is insolvent if the person has notice of facts which disclose that the company lacks the ability to pay its debts as and when they fall due.[332] It is unnecessary to show that the person actually formed the view that the company lacked that ability.
5. Since 'grounds for suspecting insolvency' does not suffice, it is not enough that insolvency is a possible inference from the known facts.[333]

This analysis produces a result similar to that formerly applied by the courts in relation to the concept of notice of an act of bankruptcy.[334]

(8) The identity of the party asserting the set-off

In England, the qualifications to the insolvency set-off provisions draw no distinction between which of the parties is asserting the set-off. They should be contrasted with the Australian provisions, which are drafted in terms that, '[a] person is not entitled under this section to claim the benefit of a set-off' if at the time of giving credit to the bankrupt or the company, or at the time of receiving credit, 'he or she' (in the case of bankruptcy) or 'the person' (in company liquidation) had the requisite notice. These provisions assume **6.90**

---

[330] Australian Law Reform Commission, Report No 45, *General Insolvency Inquiry* (1988), para. 819.

[331] (2009) 76 ACSR 404 at [16]–[22].

[332] Corporations Act 2001 (Cth), s. 95A.

[333] The court left open the question whether the fact of insolvency must be the only reasonable inference open, but doubted whether a creditor could be said to have had notice of the fact of insolvency if another inference, consistent with solvency, was also reasonably open on the known facts. See (2009) 76 ACSR 404 at [22]. Thus, bare knowledge of the appointment of an administrator to a company under Part 5.3A of the Corporations Act by itself would not seem to constitute notice of the fact that the company is insolvent, since the ground for the appointment could be the directors' belief that the company is likely to become insolvent at some future time as opposed to present insolvency. See the Corporations Act 2001 (Cth), s. 436A, and para. 6.54 above. In relation to notice of a deed of company arrangement, see para. 6.56n above.

[334] See paras 6.68–6.70 above.

that the creditor of the bankrupt or the company is the party 'claiming' a set-off, which usually is the case. The creditor wants a set-off so that he or she would not be confined to receiving a dividend in the bankruptcy or the liquidation, and at the same time be obliged to pay the full value of the cross-claim against him or her. But what if in an exceptional case, such as occurred in *Re Parker*,[335] the trustee in bankruptcy or the liquidator is the party arguing for a set-off, and the creditor is opposing it? On the face of the Australian legislation, the creditor's notice of an act of bankruptcy or of insolvency would not preclude a set-off, because the creditor is not claiming the benefit of a set-off.[336] The difficulty with that analysis is the prevailing view as to the nature of insolvency set-off, that it takes effect automatically by force of the operation of section.[337] It seems contrary to that view that the question whether there is a set-off should depend upon which of the parties is claiming it. But notwithstanding that objection, it is suggested that the words used in the qualification in the Australian sections should be given their ordinary meaning. The evident purpose of the qualification is to prevent a creditor being able to manipulate set-offs so as to defeat the requirement of a *pari passu* distribution in the event of a subsequent bankruptcy or liquidation, by obtaining the full value of a provable debt by way of a set-off rather then being confined to a dividend.[338] But if the creditor is not claiming a set-off, that would not be an issue. As a matter of policy there is no reason why the qualification should be invoked to prevent a set-off, based upon the creditor's notice, when the set-off is sought, not by that party, but by the trustee in bankruptcy or the liquidator.

(9) The meaning of 'due' (England), and the time of giving credit (Australia)

6.91 Under the English bankruptcy section, a critical question is the meaning of 'due'. Section 323(3) provides that sums due from the bankrupt to another party cannot be included in a set-off if that other party had notice at the time they 'became due' that a bankruptcy petition was pending. If 'due' were interpreted as meaning 'due and payable', the qualification in many cases would operate to deny a set-off in respect of a debt which was contracted by the debtor well before insolvency but which only became payable after the presentation of the petition. That result would have little merit and, in order to avoid it, it is suggested that the courts would readily interpret 'due' in this context as encompassing a debt which is owing whether or not it is presently payable. If at the time that the liability was incurred the creditor did not have notice of a bankruptcy petition, it should not matter that a petition is presented before the due date for payment.

6.92 But that approach would not provide a solution in the situation in which a person incurred a contingent liability while solvent and the contingency occurred and the liability vested

---

[335] (1997) 80 FCR 1. A creditor lodged a proof of debt in the liquidation of a company in circumstances where the liquidator asserted a cross-claim against the creditor. The problem was that the creditor had charged all its assets in favour of a bank, so that the creditor had no assets with which to satisfy the cross-claim. Therefore, the liquidator was the party asserting a set-off, so as to prevent a situation arising in which a dividend would have to be paid on the provable debt and at the same time nothing would be recoverable by the company in liquidation in respect of the cross-claim.

[336] See Duns, Note (1998) 6 *Insolvency Law Journal* 4, 5. The question of notice was referred to only in passing in *Re Parker* (1997) 80 FCR 1, 8.

[337] See paras 6.119–6.146 below.

[338] See para. 6.66 above.

after presentation of a petition against the person. Until the liability vested nothing was owing so that, even if 'due' were interpreted as meaning 'owing' rather than merely 'payable', the liability in question could not be set off. Yet it is difficult to see why a set-off would be objectionable in that situation.

The reference to sums becoming due in s. 323(3) should be taken as referring to the time **6.93** that a transaction was entered into out of which a liability subsequently arose, as opposed to the time when the liability vested pursuant to the transaction.[339] As long as the creditor did not have notice at the time of entering into the transaction, any liability of the debtor that arises subsequently should not be precluded from being employed in a set-off merely on the ground that a bankruptcy petition was presented before the liability vested. In essence this appears to have been the position under earlier bankruptcy legislation, where the qualification was drafted in terms whether the creditor had notice of an available act of bankruptcy at the time that credit was given to the debtor,[340] and it would remain the position in Australia, where the set-off section in both bankruptcy and company liquidation is still drafted in terms of notice at the time of giving or receiving credit.[341] Thus, when it was held in the nineteenth century that an accommodation acceptor or indorser of a bill of exchange could employ his or her claim for an indemnity in a set-off in the drawer's bankruptcy, the pleadings were framed in terms that the acceptor or indorser gave credit for the purpose of the qualification when he or she accepted or indorsed the bill, as opposed to when the claim for an indemnity subsequently vested by payment.[342] More recently, in New South Wales,[343] a creditor of a company purchased goods from the company after the commencement of the company's liquidation but pursuant to a prior contract, and in determining whether the resulting liability to the company[344] could be employed in a set-off Hodgson J considered that the qualification to the set-off section should be applied

---

[339] Consistent with *Secretary of State for Trade and Industry v Frid* [2004] 2 AC 506 at [9] and [17]. This was the view of Sir John Jarvis QC, sitting as a deputy judge in the Chancery Division, in *Ashurst v Coe* (1999) Times Law Reports, 25 March. Compare *Re A Company (No. 1641 of 2003)* [2004] 1 BCLC 210, in which Judge Norris QC (sitting as a judge of the High Court) accepted that arrears of holiday pay and payments in lieu of notice arising out of termination of employment with a company became 'due' for the purpose of the qualification to the set-off provision when the employee was wrongfully dismissed (being the date of the petition for the winding up of the company or when the winding-up order was made), as opposed to when the contract of employment was entered into. This was in the context of the equivalent provision in company liquidation (the Insolvency Rules, r. 4.90(3)), which has since been amended. See para. 6.95 below.

[340] See e.g. the Bankruptcy Act 1914, s. 31.

[341] See the Bankruptcy Act 1966 (Cth), s. 86(2) (see para. 6.84 above) and the Corporations Act 2001 (Cth), s. 553C(2) (see para. 6.87 above). In addition to the cases referred to below, see *Tooth & Co Ltd v Rosier* (NSW SC, Wood J, 7 June 1985, BC 8500768 at 22) ('The relevant date is . . . the date on which is carried through the transaction or dealing which leads to the creation of a credit against the debtor, or of the debt owing to it'); *Commissioner of Taxation v Dexcam Australia Pty Ltd* (2003) 129 FCR 582 at [28] (contingent tax debt); *Hall v Poolman* (2007) 65 ACSR 123 at [429].

[342] *Hulme v Muggleston* (1837) 3 M & W 30, 150 ER 1043; *Russell v Bell* (1841) 8 M & W 277, 151 ER 1042; *Bittleston v Timmis* (1845) 1 CB 389, 135 ER 591. The set-off section in issue in those cases was s. 50 of (1825) 6 Geo IV, c. 16, which provided that the creditor claiming the benefit of a set-off must not have had 'when such credit was given, notice of an act of bankruptcy by such bankrupt committed'.

[343] *Shirlaw v Lewis* (1993) 10 ACSR 288, 295–6.

[344] Hodgson J held that the sale constituted a void disposition pursuant to the Corporations Law, s. 468, so that it was not a question of setting off the price. He nevertheless considered the issue of set-off on the assumption that the creditor was liable on the basis of unjust enrichment, or possibly in conversion.

on the basis that credit was given when the contract was entered into, as opposed to when the sale occurred. To a similar effect, White J in the New South Wales Supreme Court held in relation to an option to purchase fittings and equipment that credit was given for the price when the agreement conferring the option was entered into, as opposed to when the option was exercised or the debt for the price became payable.[345] In Victoria Hayne J held, in the case of a licence fee payable periodically, that credit was given when the transaction was entered into which gave rise to the fee, rather than on each occasion when an instalment of the licence fee became payable.[346]

6.94 This suggested interpretation of 'due' in s. 323(3) may be criticized on the ground that 'due' normally is not regarded as including an amount that is only contingently due.[347] Moreover, it would have the consequence that a different meaning would be ascribed to 'due' in s. 323(3) than in s. 323(2). Subsection (2) provides that an account is to be taken of what is 'due' from each party to the other. In the case of a debt owing by a bankrupt which is still contingent, this should extend to an estimation made by the trustee in bankruptcy pursuant to the Insolvency Act 1986, s. 322.[348] However, when a bankrupt is a contingent creditor, the claim, while it remains contingent, is not 'due' for the purpose of a set-off.[349] There is a presumption that when a word is repeated in the same section it has the same meaning, but it has been emphasized that this is only a presumption,[350] and that it yields to the requirements of the context.[351] In the present case, unless the word 'due' where it appears in the qualification is interpreted in the manner suggested, a contingent liability of a bankrupt often would not be able to be employed in a set-off where the contingency occurred after the petition, even though it is now accepted that a debt which was still contingent at the date of the bankruptcy is capable of being the subject of a set-off.[352] Indeed, the bankruptcy legislation of 1825 and 1849 in each case stipulated that a proof could be lodged in respect of a debt which was still contingent at the time of the bankruptcy,[353] and it also specifically provided that all provable debts could be set off.[354] As Sir George Jessel MR once remarked, the whole tendency of the history of the bankruptcy legislation has been to extend the principle upon which the right of set-off is based,[355] and it would be strange if in this context it has been narrowed by the use of the word 'due' in s. 323(3). The courts have emphasized that the right of set-off should be given the widest possible

---

[345] *JLF Bakeries Pty Ltd v Baker's Delight Holdings Ltd* (2007) 64 ACSR 633.

[346] *Old Style Confections Pty Ltd v Microbyte Investments Pty Ltd* [1995] 2 VR 457, 464. The provision in issue was the Corporations Law, s. 553C(2).

[347] *Ex p Kemp, re Fastnedge* (1874) LR 9 Ch App 383; *Merritt Cairns Constructions Pty Ltd v Wulguru Heights Pty Ltd* [1995] 2 Qd R 521, 526.

[348] See para. 8.34 below.

[349] See para. 8.35 below. A different principle now applies in company liquidation in England under the Insolvency Rules. See para. 8.35 below.

[350] *Littlewoods Mail Order Stores Ltd v Inland Revenue Commissioners* [1963] AC 135, 159 (Lord Reid).

[351] *Madras Electricity Supply Corp Ltd v Boarland (Inspector of Taxes)* [1955] AC 667, 685.

[352] See paras 8.19–8.23 below.

[353] See (1825) 6 Geo IV, c. 16, s. 56, and the Bankrupt Law Consolidation Act 1849, s. 177.

[354] See (1825) 6 Geo IV, c. 16, s. 50, and the Bankrupt Law Consolidation Act 1849, s. 171.

[355] *Peat v Jones & Co* (1881) 8 QBD 147, 149. See also *Re Fenton, ex p Fenton Textile Association Ltd* [1931] 1 Ch 85, 107 (Lord Hanworth MR).

scope,[356] which suggests that they would incline to an interpretation of 'due' in s. 323(3) that would not restrict the availability of the right in the absence of a compelling policy reason for doing so. Nevertheless, the uncertainty surrounding the meaning of s. 323(3) is unsatisfactory, and it would be appropriate for the position to be clarified.

The problem which arises in bankruptcy in England in relation to the meaning of 'due' is **6.95** no longer relevant in corporate insolvency. As a result of amendments to the Insolvency Rules 1986, r. 4.90 in 2005,[357] the qualification in company liquidation is now expressed in terms of the incurring of an obligation as opposed to a sum being due. A similar formulation is used in r. 2.85 in relation to administration. Nor is this a problem in Australia, where the qualification in both bankruptcy and company liquidation is expressed in terms of notice at the time of giving or receiving of credit.[358]

In Australia, it has been doubted whether the Commissioner of Taxation gives or receives **6.96** credit in assessing a tax liability for the purpose of the qualification in s. 553C(2) of the Corporations Act.[359]

(10) Assignment of a debt

Consider that a debt is assigned before the bankruptcy of the debtor. Under the English **6.97** bankruptcy set-off section, the qualification to the set-off in the Insolvency Act 1986, s. 323(3) is expressed in terms that a sum due from the bankrupt to another party is not to be included in a set-off if that other party had the requisite notice at the time that the sums became 'due'.[360] This should refer to the time that sums became due to the person asserting the right to the set-off, that is, the assignee.[361] Therefore, if the assignee did not have the requisite notice at the time that sums first became due on the assigned debt to the assignor, but the assignee did have notice at the time of the assignment itself, he or she should not be entitled to employ the debt in a set-off.

The relevant set-off provisions applicable in company liquidation[362] and administration[363] **6.98** now deal expressly with the operation of the qualification in relation to assignments. Each provides that, where a debt of the company has been acquired by assignment or otherwise, the qualification is to be applied by reference to the time of the agreement for the assignment,

---

[356] *Eberle's Hotels and Restaurant Co Ltd v E Jonas & Brothers* (1887) 18 QBD 459, 465; *Day & Dent Constructions Pty Ltd v North Australian Properties Pty Ltd* (1982) 150 CLR 85, 108; *Gye v McIntyre* (1991) 171 CLR 609, 619; *Central Brake Service (Sydney) Pty Ltd v Central Brake Service (Newcastle) Pty Ltd* (1992) 27 NSWLR 406, 411; *Coventry v Charter Pacific Corporation Ltd* (2005) 227 CLR 234 at [56]. See also *Peat v Jones & Co* (1881) 8 QBD 147, 150 (Cotton LJ); *Mersey Steel and Iron Co v Naylor, Benzon, & Co* (1882) 9 QBD 648, 660–1.
[357] See para. 6.06 above.
[358] See paras 6.84 and 6.87 above.
[359] *Commissioner of Taxation v Dexcam Australia Pty Ltd* (2003) 129 FCR 582 at [28] (Ryan and Dowsett JJ) (referring to the equivalent provision in the Corporations Law).
[360] See para. 6.72 above.
[361] Shea, 'Further reflections on statutory set-off' (1987) 3 *Journal of International Banking Law* 183, 184.
[362] Insolvency Rules 1986, r. 4.90(2)(d). See para. 6.74 above.
[363] See para. 2.85(2)(e). See para. 6.81 above.

rather than, for example, the time when the debt became due or the time when the assignment itself occurred pursuant to the agreement.[364]

6.99 In Australia, the qualification in both bankruptcy and company liquidation is expressed in terms of the giving and receiving of credit.[365] In the case of an assignment of a debt, credit is given by the assignee to the insolvent at the time of the assignment.[366]

I. Assignment of a Debt as a Preference

6.100 In bankruptcy, the qualification to the set-off section, in the Insolvency Act 1986, s. 323(3), only applies after notice of a pending petition.[367] It would therefore seem that a person who takes an assignment of a debt after notice that the debtor cannot pay his or her debts but before notice of a pending petition would not be precluded by the qualification from employing the debt in a set-off, even though in the absence of a set-off a repayment of the debt may have been voidable as a preference. *Watts v Christie*[368] suggests that a set-off may not be available in this situation, but there are difficulties with Lord Langdale's judgment in the case.

6.101 In *Watts v Christie*, a partnership consisting of A and B was indebted to a firm of bankers, while the bank was separately indebted to A on an account in credit. After the partners became aware that the bank was insolvent, they entered into an agreement by which A purported to assign the credit account to the partnership. The assignment was an equitable assignment since the ability to assign at law did not arise until later, with the enactment of the Judicature Acts.[369] The partners gave notice of the assignment to the banking firm, and directed that the balance on the account be applied in reduction of the partners' joint debt. The direction was not complied with, however, and the banking firm became bankrupt. Their assignees in bankruptcy sued the partners on their joint debt, whereupon the partners filed a bill for an injunction to restrain the action on the ground that the joint debt should be set off against the assigned debt. If, instead, A had withdrawn the credit balance in order to pay off the partnership debt, the payment to A would have constituted a preference, since A had notice that the bank was insolvent. The purpose of the assignment evidently was to avoid that result, by bringing about a situation in which the partners' joint liability could be set off against a joint asset in the form of the credit account assigned to them.[370] Under the bankruptcy legislation then in force, the qualification to the set-off

---

[364] See Lightman and Moss, *The Law of Administrators and Receivers of Companies* (4th edn, 2007), 549 [20–040].

[365] See paras 6.84 (bankruptcy) and 6.87 (company liquidation) above.

[366] *Southern Cross Construction Ltd (In Liq) v Southern Cross Club Ltd* [1973] 1 NZLR 708, and see also *Citizens Investments Pty Ltd v Murphy* (1994) 14 ACSR 575, 579.

[367] See para. 6.72 above.

[368] (1849) 11 Beav 546, 50 ER 928.

[369] See para. 17.04 below.

[370] In the absence of an effective assignment a set-off would not have been available, since A's separate demand and the partners' joint liability would not have been mutual for the purpose of the set-off section. See para. 12.02 below.

section was drafted in terms of notice of an act of bankruptcy[371] whereas, while the assignment in *Watts v Christie* occurred after notice of insolvency, an act of bankruptcy as yet had not taken place. The qualification, therefore, was not applicable. Despite this, it was held that a set-off was not available. Lord Langdale in his judgment concentrated on the direction to the bank to apply A's credit balance in reduction of the joint debt.[372] Since this occurred after notice of insolvency, he said that an application of the credit balance in accordance with the direction would have constituted a preference. It is unclear, however, why the case was decided in terms of the direction as opposed to the assignment itself. It is now recognized that a direction to pay, or indeed notice to the debtor, is not a necessary requirement of an equitable assignment.[373] Notice may be desirable for the purpose of preserving the assignee's priority in accordance with the rule in *Dearle v Hall*[374] (when the rule applies[375]) and to ensure that the debtor cannot discharge the debt by payment to the assignor.[376] But the failure to give notice does not mean that the assignment itself is ineffective. If in a case such as *Watts v Christie* there has been a valid assignment, whether legal or equitable, it would be difficult, on the language of the current set-off section, to see why the fact that a payment by the debtor at the time of the assignment would have constituted a preference should affect the argument for a set-off.

It has been suggested that an assignment in that circumstance could nevertheless constitute **6.102** a preference if the insolvent debtor was involved in the assignment with a preferential motive,[377] for example where the debtor consented to the assignment pursuant to a provision in the contract which required the debtor's consent.[378] Whether the giving of consent is a preference would depend on the circumstances. The preference section is expressed to apply where a person does something or suffers something to be done in favour of a creditor,[379] by which is meant someone who, but for the payment or other transaction being impugned, would share in the distribution of the assets.[380] Further, the person must have been influenced by a desire to improve the position of the creditor.[381] In the assignment under discussion there are two parties to consider, the assignor and the assignee. If the

---

[371] See (1825) 6 Geo IV, c. 16, s. 50.

[372] This accords with the argument of counsel for the partners, which was presented in terms that the direction to transfer operated as an equitable transfer of the separate debt to the partners. See (1849) 11 Beav 546, 548, 50 ER 928, 929.

[373] *Re Patrick; Bills v Tatham* [1891] 1 Ch 82.

[374] (1828) 3 Russ 1, 38 ER 475.

[375] See *Goode on Legal Problems of Credit and Security* (4th edn (ed. Gullifer), 2008), 177–8 [5–08]. In Australia, compare the position under the Personal Property Securities Act 2009 (Cth).

[376] Compare *Brice v Bannister* (1878) 3 QBD 569. In Australia, see the Personal Property Securities Act 2009 (Cth), s. 80(7) and (8).

[377] Compare in Australia where motive, or intention, is irrelevant to the question whether a transaction is voidable as a preference. See the Bankruptcy Act 1966 (Cth), s. 122 and the Corporations Act 2001 (Cth), s. 588FA.

[378] Wood, *English and International Set-off* (1989), 358, 371–2. The courts will give effect to a stipulation in a contract that the benefit of the contact is not assignable save with the consent of the other party. See *Linden Gardens Trust Ltd v Lenesta Sludge Disposals Ltd* [1994] 1 AC 85. In Australia, compare the Personal Property Securities Act 2009 (Cth), s. 81.

[379] See the Insolvency Act 1986, ss. 239(4)(a) and 340(3)(a).

[380] *Re Paine, ex p Read* [1897] 1 QB 122, 123–4, and see generally the discussion in *Re Blackpool Motor Car Co, Ltd* [1901] 1 Ch 77.

[381] See the Insolvency Act 1986, ss. 239(5) and 340(4).

debtor in consenting to the assignment was influenced by a desire to improve the position of the assignor, for example because the consideration for the assignment was greater than what the assignor otherwise would have received in the bankruptcy or liquidation, the giving of the consent may be a preference. But if the debtor was influenced only by a desire to benefit the assignee, for example because the consideration payable by the assignee for the debt was less than the benefit that would accrue to him or her by being able to set off the full value of the assigned debt against the liability to the debtor, it is doubtful whether the debtor's consent would be a preference. The assignee is not a person who, apart from the transaction in question, would have shared in the administration of the estate. Before the assignment the assignee was a debtor, not a creditor.

6.103   *Watts v Christie* should be contrasted with *Re Land Development Association. Kent's Case.*[382] A shareholder who held partly paid shares in a company, and who therefore had a contingent liability to contribute the unpaid amount, took an assignment of a debt owing by the company to a third party. The company resolved that the seal of the company be affixed to the assignment.[383] The shareholder on the same day wrote to the directors requesting them to transfer from the amount due on the debt a sum sufficient to pay up his shares, and the directors that same day passed a resolution to that effect. The arrangement was struck down as giving the shareholder a preference in the company's subsequent liquidation. The critical point was that one of the debts was for an amount unpaid on shares, and therefore it could not have been employed in a set-off in the liquidation.[384] Were it not for the directors' action in applying the debt against the unpaid capital, the shareholder would have been obliged to pay the unpaid capital and would only have received a dividend in the liquidation on the assigned debt. It is apparent then that the arrangement with the company prior to its liquidation resulted in the shareholder receiving a preference.[385] The preference was not the assignment, however, or the company's consent to it, but rather the company's act in setting off the debt against the liability for unpaid capital. The event constituting the preference, therefore, took effect in favour of a person who at the time was a creditor. On the other hand, where the issue is whether the giving of consent required for an assignment can constitute a preference in relation to the assignee, the giving of the consent, in so far as the assignee is concerned, would not have the effect of preferring an existing creditor because, even if consent is a prerequisite to the validity of the assignment, the assignee was not a creditor before the consent was given.

6.104   While this appears to be the effect of the preference and set-off sections, it is not a felicitous result. The Cork Committee in its report on the reform of insolvency law in 1982 recommended that the qualification to the bankruptcy set-off section be framed in terms of notice of inability to pay debts.[386] Adoption of this recommendation would have the consequence that there would not be a set-off in a case such as *Watts v Christie*.

---

[382] (1888) 39 Ch D 259, referred to in Wood, *English and International Set-off* (1989), 371–2.
[383] *Quaere* what the significance of this was, although it appears from the judgment of Fry LJ ((1888) 39 Ch D 259, 267) that it may have been done in order to fix the amount of one of the instalments of the debt.
[384] See paras 8.64–8.79 below.
[385] See also *Re Washington Diamond Mining Co* [1893] 3 Ch 95, and para. 13.10 below.
[386] Cork Committee Report on Insolvency Law and Practice (Cmnd 8558, 1982), 127, 307.

J. Temporary Suspension of Mutual Credit

For the insolvency set-off section to apply there must have been mutual credits, mutual **6.105**
debts or other mutual dealings 'before' the commencement of the bankruptcy or the
liquidation.[387] Therefore, some time before the bankruptcy or the liquidation there must
have been mutuality. It is not necessary, however, that mutuality be present on the date
of the bankruptcy or the liquidation, if it is merely in suspense at that time.[388] In *Bolland v
Nash*,[389] a creditor of some debtors had accepted a bill of exchange, and the bill, having
come into the hands of the debtors, was indorsed by them before their bankruptcy to a
third person. After the debtors' bankruptcy, the creditor dishonoured the bill, and the bill
was returned to the bankrupts as indorsers. It was held that the creditor could set off his
liability on the bill against the debt owing to him by the bankrupts. This was so notwithstanding that at the date of the bankruptcy the bill was in the hands of the third party, so
that at that date there was not mutual credit as between the creditor and the bankrupts.
Conversely, in *Collins v Jones*[390] it was the bankrupt acceptor who dishonoured the bill, and
a debtor of the bankrupt who had indorsed it prior to the bankruptcy was forced to take it
up again as indorser after the bankruptcy. Once again, it was held that the debtor could set
off the claim on the bill against the debt that he owed to the bankrupt acceptor, despite the
absence of mutual credit between the parties when the bankruptcy occurred. A similar situation may arise when a creditor assigns the debt by way of security to a third party. If the
security is redeemed after the bankruptcy of either the creditor or the debtor, so that the
debt comes back to the creditor, the debt can be the subject of a set-off as between them.[391]
The important point in these cases is that the debt was taken up again after the insolvency
as a result of a prior obligation[392] or a prior right of redemption. Unless this limitation is
imposed, a debtor of the bankrupt would be able to buy up at a discount any liabilities

---

[387] Insolvency Act 1986, s. 323(1), and for company liquidation the Insolvency Rules 1986, r. 4.90(1).
This is also the effect of the Australian legislation, which applies where there 'have been' mutual credits,
mutual debts or other mutual dealings. See the Bankruptcy Act 1966 (Cth), s. 86(1) and the Corporations
Act 2001 (Cth), s. 553C(1). See also *Bolland v Nash* (1828) 8 B & C 105, 109, 108 ER 982, 984 and *Collins
v Jones* (1830) 10 B & C 777, 781, 109 ER 638, 639–40.

[388] This is also the case for the proof of debts. See e.g. *Joseph v Orme* (1806) 2 Bos & Pul (NR) 180, 127
ER 593, where the indorser had been obliged to take up the bill again after the acceptor's bankruptcy, but
compare *Ex p Isbester* (1810) 1 Rose 20.

[389] (1828) 8 B & C 105, 108 ER 982. Selwyn LJ in *Re Anglo-Greek Steam Navigation and Trading Co*
(1869) LR 4 Ch App 174 followed *Bolland v Nash* as an alternative ground for his decision. See also *Ex p
Banes, re the Royal British Bank* (1857) 28 LTOS 296.

[390] (1830) 10 B & C 777, 109 ER 638. See also *Ex p Hastie and Hutchinson, re Alexander and Co* (1850)
1 Fonbl 59, 14 LTOS 402; *McKinnon v Armstrong Brothers & Co* (1877) 2 App Cas 531; *Hiley v The Peoples
Prudential Assurance Co Ltd* (1938) 60 CLR 468, 501. A similar principle may apply in the context of receivership. See *Handley Page Ltd v Commissioners of Customs and Excise and Rockwell Machine Tool Co Ltd* [1970]
2 Lloyd's Rep 459.

[391] See *Hiley v The Peoples Prudential Assurance Co Ltd* (1938) 60 CLR 468, where the debt in question was
redeemed as part of a compromise rather than by payment to the assignee of the secured amount. *Re City Life
Assurance Co Ltd. Stephenson's Case* [1926] 1 Ch 191, 214 was distinguished on the ground that the mortgages
in that case had not been redeemed.

[392] See *Collins v Jones* (1830) 10 B & C 777, 782, 109 ER 638, 640, and also Robson, *Law of Bankruptcy*
(7th edn, 1894), 367. Compare *Ex p Isbester* (1810) 1 Rose 20 in the context of proof of debts.

of the bankrupt that had passed through his or her hands, and yet be able to obtain the full value of those liabilities by means of a set-off.[393] This would be unfair to the general body of creditors, and the courts have emphasized that the buying up of liabilities in order to obtain rights of set-off should not be encouraged.[394]

6.106   The essence of a set-off on this ground is that there was merely a temporary suspension of mutual credit. If there never was mutuality prior to the relevant date, the person upon acquiring the debt could not employ it in a set-off. This may be the case, for example, when a third party had contracted with a creditor to take an assignment of the debt upon the occurrence of an event which occurred after the relevant date for determining rights of set-off in the debtor's bankruptcy. Even though the debt was acquired pursuant to a pre-existing obligation, there never was mutuality as between the third party and the debtor prior to the relevant date so as to entitle the third party to employ the debt in a set-off in the debtor's bankruptcy.

6.107   Consider that a creditor before its liquidation had assigned the debt by way of security to a third party, and the liquidator redeemed the security after the liquidation. In addition, the creditor is separately indebted to the debtor. If the creditor incurred the debt to the debtor before the assignment, there will have been mutuality of debts before the liquidation, and the case will be one of suspension of mutuality so as to permit a set-off on that ground. But if the creditor became indebted to the debtor *after* the assignment, there never will have been mutuality in relation to the debts. Mutuality in insolvency set-off is determined by reference to equitable interests.[395] The debtor in this situation is the beneficial owner of the cross-claim against the creditor, but at the time when the creditor became liable to the debtor on the cross-claim, the debtor's debt had already been assigned to the third party. That assignment would have prevented mutuality in equity arising before the liquidation in relation to the debts.[396] However, the absence of prior mutuality in equity in relation to the debts should not preclude a set-off if the creditor's debt to the debtor, though accruing after the assignment, arose out of a dealing between the parties before the assignment.

---

[393] In the absence of fraud in the inception or preparation of a bill of exchange, a discounter is entitled to prove for its full value. See *Re Gomersall* (1875) 1 Ch D 137, 146–7 (Baggallay JA). In *Stonehouse v Read* (1825) 3 B & C 669, 107 ER 881, an accommodation acceptor of various bills had entered into a composition with the holders of the bills, so that the bills were delivered up to him upon payment of a sum less than their full face value. Since the composition had been effected solely for the relief of the acceptor, and not for the drawer, the acceptor was entitled to a set-off in the drawer's bankruptcy to the extent of the full face value of the bills.

[394] *Re Moseley Green Coal and Coke Co Ltd. Barrett's Case (No. 2)* (1865) 4 De G J & S 756, 760, 46 ER 1116, 1118; *Day & Dent Constructions Pty Ltd v North Australian Properties Pty Ltd* (1982) 150 CLR 85, 95. In the *Moseley Green* case, the surety obtained the debtor's promissory note by way of an assignment from his sister after the debtor's liquidation, the sister having paid the creditor and obtained a transfer of the note from the creditor. Lord Westbury considered that the prior contract of suretyship gave such retrospective operation to the surety's possession of the note as to justify the surety employing it in a set-off in the liquidation. See paras 8.28 and 13.62 below.

[395] See paras 11.13–11.17 below.

[396] See para. 11.13 below, and *Re City Life Assurance Co. Stephenson's Case* [1926] 1 Ch 191, 214, as explained by Dixon J in *Hiley v Peoples Prudential Assurance Co Ltd* (1938) 60 CLR 468, 501–5, and see also Rich J at 488.

There would then have been prior mutual dealings before the liquidation for the purpose of a set-off.

K. The Necessity for Cross-Demands

Set-off in bankruptcy and company liquidation depends upon the existence of cross-demands between the parties to the proposed set-off. Consider, for example, that a bank has made a loan to a customer on the security of a deposit provided by a third party. If the third party has not assumed a personal liability in respect of the customer's debt, whether on the basis of a joint or a joint and several liability or as a guarantor, the case would not be one of mutual cross-demands between the bank and the third party. Nor, if the bank has gone into liquidation, could the bank's claim against the customer be set off against the bank's liability to the third party on the deposit, because the requirement of mutuality would be lacking.[397] Since set-off would not apply, the liquidator in such a case could sue the customer on the loan and confine the third party to a proof in the liquidation in respect of the deposit,[398] subject, however, to any contractual limitation on the third party's right to recover all or part of the deposit until repayment of the loan in full.[399]

6.108

L. Enforceable Demands

A creditor may not prove in a bankruptcy or a company liquidation for a debt which, though existing, is unenforceable, for example because of the expiration of a limitation period.[400] Further, because the insolvency set-off section only applies when the creditor has a provable debt,[401] this unenforceable debt similarly could not be the subject of a set-off.[402] Consider, however, that it is a debt on the other side of the account, being a debt owing by the creditor to the bankrupt or to the company, which is unenforceable. *Prima facie* there is nothing in the language of the insolvency set-off section which suggests that the debt may not be set off. While the debt may not be enforceable, it is still an existing debt. If the person liable on the debt in turn has a provable claim against the bankrupt or the company, it may be said that there are mutual debts which, according to the set-off section, must be set against each other. The creditor would regard this as unfair, however. In the absence of a set-off, the creditor would have been entitled to receive a dividend on the provable debt, and at the same time he could not have been sued on his or her unenforceable liability. The effect of setting off the unenforceable liability against the provable debt would be to deprive the creditor of the dividend that he or she otherwise would have received. The courts, therefore, may incline against that result on the ground that the purpose of the set-off

6.109

---

[397] See para. 12.41 below.

[398] *Lord v Direct Acceptance Corporation Ltd* (1993) 32 NSWLR 362; *Re Bank of Credit and Commerce International SA (No. 8)* [1998] AC 214.

[399] See the discussion in *Re Bank of Credit and Commerce International SA (No. 8)* [1996] Ch 245, 262–3 (CA).

[400] *Ex p Dewdney* (1809) 15 Ves Jun 479, 33 ER 836.

[401] See the Insolvency Act, s. 323(1), and the Insolvency Rules, r. 4.90(1).

[402] *Pott v Clegg* (1847) 16 M & W 321, 153 ER 1212.

section is to do substantial justice between the parties,[403] and a set-off in that situation would hardly be just.[404]

6.110 The prevailing view of the operation of the insolvency set-off section is that it is self-executing and takes effect automatically on the date of the bankruptcy or the liquidation.[405] The cross-demands are set against each other and to the extent of the set-off they are extinguished as at that date. This should have the consequence that the question whether a limitation period has expired for the purpose of ascertaining set-off entitlements should also be determined by reference to that date.[406]

M. Insolvency Set-off is Mandatory

(1) Contracting out of insolvency set-off

6.111 In *National Westminster Bank Ltd v Halesowen Presswork & Assemblies Ltd*,[407] the House of Lords[408] held that the set-off section in the insolvency legislation is mandatory in its oper-ation, so that the parties to mutual dealings cannot contract out of its terms.[409] Their Lordships have since re-affirmed that view,[410] and it has also been followed in Australia[411] and New Zealand.[412] If it is not possible to contract out of the terms of the set-off section, it should not be possible to waive its operation,[413] and nor could a creditor be estopped by his or her conduct from asserting a set-off.[414] Nevertheless, while Lord Kilbrandon in

---

[403] *Forster v Wilson* (1843) 12 M & W 191, 203–4, 152 ER 1165, 1171.

[404] In New South Wales, the corresponding passage in the second edition of this book was quoted by Sheller JA in *Centurian Constructions Pty Ltd v Beca Developments Pty Ltd* [1999] NSWCA 457 at [27]. In Australia, compare *Maniotis v Valimi Pty Ltd* (2002) 4 VR 386 in relation to the setting aside of a statutory demand served on a company on the basis of an 'offsetting claim' pursuant to the Corporations Act 2001 (Cth), s. 459H, where a proceeding to enforce the offsetting claim had been temporarily stayed.

[405] See paras 6.119–6.146 below. In relation to the situation where set-off applies in the administration of a company (pursuant to the Insolvency Rules 1986, r. 2.85: see para. 6.10 above), see para. 6.124 below.

[406] Compare *Centurian Constructions Pty Ltd v Beca Developments Pty Ltd* [1999] NSWCA 457. Given that Beca was wound up in April 1992, which was within the limitation period for Centurian's claim, it should not have mattered that the limitation period for Centurian's claim had expired when Beca commenced proceedings.

[407] [1972] AC 785.

[408] Viscount Dilhorne, Lord Simon of Glaisdale and Lord Kilbrandon, Lord Cross of Chelsea dissenting.

[409] In Ireland, compare Breslin, 'Set-off under Irish law' (1997) 18 *Company Lawyer* 198, 200. For a criti-cism of the mandatory principle, see Berg, 'Contracting out of set-off in a winding up' [1996] LMCLQ 49. If an administrator, being authorized to make a distribution, has given a notice under the Insolvency Rules 1986, r. 2.95, it is likely that the set-off available under r. 2.85 (see para. 6.10 above) would be held to be mandatory.

[410] *Stein v Blake* [1996] AC 243, 254, 255; *Secretary of State for Trade and Industry v Frid* [2004] 2 AC 506 at [6]. See also *Re ILG Travel Ltd* [1995] 2 BCLC 128, 160; *Rayden v Edwardo Ltd* [2008] EWHC 2689 (Comm) at [10].

[411] *Re Paddington Town Hall Centre Ltd* (1979) 41 FLR 239. In *Gye v McIntyre* (1991) 171 CLR 609, 622 the High Court described this as 'the traditional and better view'.

[412] *Rendell v Doors and Doors Ltd* [1975] 2 NZLR 191.

[413] *Re Cushla Ltd* [1979] 3 All ER 415, 423; *Rennie v Ramath Investments No 6 Pty Ltd* [2002] NSWSC 672 at [43].

[414] *Re Paddington Town Hall Centre Ltd* (1979) 41 FLR 239; *Rennie v Ramath Investments No 6 Pty Ltd* [2002] NSWSC 672 at [5]. Compare *Hunter v The Official Assignee of Bispham* (1898) 17 NZLR 175.

the *Halesowen* case agreed with the view that the terms of the set-off section are mandatory, he expressed reservation about the desirability of preserving the rule.[415] Subsequently, the Cork Committee reiterated his Lordship's call for legislative intervention in this area, and recommended that the *Halesowen* case be reversed.[416] As a result of the decision in that case, whenever a company which is indebted to a bank attempts to realize its assets for the benefit of its creditors generally, or to arrange a moratorium, if properly advised it should open a new account with a different bank in order to ensure that future credits do not solely benefit the first bank in the event of the company's winding up in the form of a set-off against the debt. It would not be sufficient for the first bank to agree not to assert a set-off. In the opinion of the Cork Committee, this is an unnecessary and an undesirable complication. It is difficult to see any convincing reason why a creditor who otherwise would be benefited by a set-off should not be permitted to renounce that benefit, with a consequent increase in the value of the assets available for distribution generally, and it is unfortunate that the Cork proposal was not adopted in the Insolvency Act.

In the *Halesowen* case, Lord Simon of Glaisdale [417] justified the decision on two grounds. The first is the mandatory nature of the language of the set-off section. The section provides that an account 'shall' be taken, and that the sums due on each side of the account 'shall' be set-off.[418] But, in addition, he supported the decision on the basis of a policy consideration, that the set-off section appears in a part of the insolvency legislation which lays down a procedure for a proper and orderly administration of a bankrupt's estate and this is a matter in which the commercial community has an interest. In truth, it is not clear why the setting off of cross-demands should be regarded as necessary for a proper and orderly administration of the estate. In *Re Maxwell Communications Corp plc (No. 2)*,[419] Vinelott J suggested a reason. He postulated that, if a creditor could waive a set-off, he or she might then prove in the bankruptcy and leave it to the trustee to recover the debt due to the estate in proceedings that might be protracted and expensive, and which might not result in the recovery of the full amount of the debt. Vinelott J said that, in the meantime, the distribution of the insolvent estate might be held up, and a question might arise whether the creditor would be entitled to a dividend while proceedings to recover the debt due from him or her were on foot. In truth, this should not a significant problem. If, indeed, it were possible to contract out of the set-off, and a creditor did so, the rule in *Cherry v Boultbee* [420] should apply so that, when the creditor later sought to participate in the fund represented by the

6.112

---

[415] His Lordship said (at [1972] AC 785, 824) that: 'such a rule . . . may be expected to form a serious embarrassment to those wishing to adopt the beneficial course of agreeing to moratoria for the assistance of a business in financial difficulties.'

[416] *Cork Committee Report*, 305–6. If this recommendation were adopted, any agreement would have to be such that it was intended to survive bankruptcy or winding up proceedings. Compare *Victoria Products Ltd v Tosh and Co Ltd* (1940) 165 LT 78; *Ex p Fletcher, re Vaughan* (1877) 6 Ch D 350; *National Westminster Bank Ltd v Halesowen Presswork & Assemblies Ltd* [1972] AC 785.

[417] [1972] AC 785, 808–9. See also Viscount Dilhorne at 805, and Lord Kilbrandon at 824.

[418] Compare the New Zealand legislation considered in *Rendell v Doors and Doors Ltd* [1975] 2 NZLR 191, which provided that a debt 'may' be set off, although Chilwell J nevertheless followed *Halesowen* and held that the section is mandatory.

[419] [1993] 1 WLR 1402, 1411. See also *Stotter v Ararimu Holdings Ltd* [1994] 2 NZLR 655, 660.

[420] (1839) 4 My & Cr 442, 41 ER 171. See ch. 14 below.

insolvent's estate by claiming a dividend, the creditor would be told that he or she already had an asset of the estate, in the form of his or her own indebtedness, which should be appropriated as satisfaction of the right to the dividend.[421] Vinelott J was concerned that the trustee in bankruptcy or the liquidator may have to undertake protracted and expensive litigation. If the purpose of the litigation was to establish the creditor's liability, in circumstances where the creditor was denying that he or she was liable and at the same time was claiming a dividend on the bankrupt's or the company's liability, the litigation presumably would have to be undertaken in any event before a set-off could be accepted. Apart from that, the application of *Cherry v Boultbee* should obviate the concern. The adoption of a rule that a creditor can renounce the benefit of a set-off that otherwise may be available to him or her in the insolvency of the debtor would have the effect of increasing the estate available for distribution to the unsecured creditors, and it is difficult to see what policy ground there is which would override this benefit.

(2) Agreement not to prove

6.113 While it appears settled that the parties to mutual dealings cannot contract out of the insolvency set-off section, a creditor may agree not to prove for his or her debt in the debtor's bankruptcy or liquidation. In such a case there would not be a creditor proving or claiming to prove for a debt, so that the prerequisite to the operation of the set-off section to that effect in s. 323(1) of the Insolvency Act and in r. 4.90(1) of the Insolvency Rules would not be satisfied.[422] By this method a creditor can renounce a right of set-off, but at a cost. The creditor gives up not only the set-off but also the right to a dividend on the debt owing to him or her.

(3) Subordinated debt

6.114 It is a basic principle of insolvency law that the debts of a bankrupt or a company in liquidation (other than preferential and secured debts) must be paid *pari passu*.[423] However, that principle does not render debt subordination ineffective. Pursuant to a subordination agreement, a creditor agrees that the debt is to be subordinated, or postponed, to debts owing to one or more other (unsubordinated) creditors, so that the subordinated creditor is not to be paid anything until the unsubordinated creditors have been paid in full. One method of achieving subordination in substance is for a creditor to agree to hold the debt or its proceeds on trust for other creditors,[424] or to assign the benefit of the debt to those

---

[421] Williams J in *Fused Electrics Pty Ltd v Donald* [1995] 2 Qd R 7 doubted that *Cherry v Boultbee* applies in the context of a company liquidation, but the cases suggest otherwise. See para. 14.07 below.

[422] *Kitchen's Trustee v Madders* [1950] 1 Ch 134, and see also *Re Bank of Credit and Commerce International SA (No. 8)* [1996] Ch 245, 256 (CA). An agreement not to prove is enforceable. See *Re SSSL Realisations (2002) Ltd* [2006] Ch 610.

[423] See the Insolvency Act 1986, s. 107 for voluntary winding up. The same principle applies in a winding up by the court. See the Insolvency Rules, r. 4.181 and *Webb v Smith* (1872) LR 5 HL 711, 735. For bankruptcy, see the Insolvency Act, s. 328(3)

[424] The distinction between a trust of a debt and a trust of the proceeds of a debt when received may be important in relation to set-off. In the former case a declaration of trust by the subordinated creditor would mean that mutuality would be lacking between the subordinated debt and a separate debt owing by the subordinated creditor to the debtor. See paras 11.13–11.17 below. If, however, the trust only attaches to the proceeds of the debt once received, the subordinated creditor would still have the equitable title to the debt

creditors, so that they obtain the benefit of the debt in question.[425] However, in *Re Maxwell Communications Corp plc (No. 2)*,[426] Vinelott J held that a simple contractual subordination, without a trust or an assignment, is also effective in the insolvency of the debtor. Courts in Australia have expressed similar views,[427] and indeed in Australia subordination now has statutory support in certain defined circumstances pursuant to the Corporations Act 2001 (Cth), s. 563C.[428] Subordination has also been upheld in New Zealand.[429] Contractual subordination has been said[430] not to infringe the requirement of a *pari passu* distribution because it does not lessen the rights of creditors who are not a party to it.

Accepting the validity of contractual subordination, it is apparent that the effect of the subordination would be defeated if the subordinated creditor could set off the subordinated debt against a separate cross-debt owing to the debtor in the latter's bankruptcy or liquidation. There is no authority directly on point,[431] but the better view is that the **6.115**

---

itself, so that there should be mutuality in relation to that debt and the subordinated creditor's separate debt to the debtor for the purpose of a set-off. The discussion in paras 17.66–17.67 below in relation to an assignment merely of the proceeds of a debt is equally relevant here. As Lord Templeman remarked in *Barclays Bank Ltd v TOSG Trust Fund Ltd* [1984] 1 AC 626, 674 (although in another context), equity does not overlook the distinction between a debt and a dividend on a debt. Before bankruptcy or liquidation, the question of a set-off under the Statutes of Set-off may depend, not only on whether the subordination agreement has given rise to a trust of the debt, but also whether the debt is enforceable at the time. See *Atlantic Acceptance Corporation Ltd v Burns & Dutton Construction (1962) Ltd* (1970) 14 DLR (3d) 175.

[425] See *Re Maxwell Communications Corp plc (No. 2)* [1993] 1 WLR 1402, 1404–5, 1416, referring to *Re British and Commonwealth Holdings plc (No. 3)* [1992] 1 WLR 672.

[426] [1993] 1 WLR 1402. See also *Cheah v Equiticorp Finance Group Ltd* [1992] 1 AC 472, 477 (PC); *Re Pinecord Ltd* [1995] 2 BCLC 57, 61–2 (where the effectiveness of subordination was assumed); *Stotter v Equiticorp Australia Ltd* [2002] 2 NZLR 686 at [41]; *Re SSSL Realisations (2002) Ltd* [2006] Ch 610 at [55]–[67] (CA).

[427] *Horne v Chester and Fein Property Developments Pty Ltd* [1987] VR 913; *Re NIAA Corp Ltd* (1993) 33 NSWLR 344; *United States Trust Co of New York v Australia and New Zealand Banking Group Ltd* (1995) 37 NSWLR 131. Compare *TBGL Enterprises Ltd v Belcap Enterprises Pty Ltd* (1995) 14 ACLC 205.

[428] The Corporations Act 2001 (Cth), s. 563C(1) provides that nothing in Div. 6 of Part 5.6 of the Act, dealing with proof and ranking of claims, renders a debt subordination by a company unlawful or unenforceable, except so far as it would disadvantage a creditor who was not a party to, or otherwise concerned in, the debt subordination. Debt subordination is defined in sub-s. (2) for the purpose of that provision, in terms of an agreement or declaration by a creditor of a company to the effect that, in specified circumstances, a specified debt that the company owes the creditor, or a specified part of the debt, will not be repaid until other specified debts that the company owes are repaid to a specified extent.

[429] *Stotter v Ararimu Holdings Ltd* [1994] 2 NZLR 655, referring to the Companies Act 1993 (NZ), s. 313(3).

[430] See the discussion in *Horne v Chester and Fein Property Developments Pty Ltd* [1987] VR 913 (Vic SC, Southwell J).

[431] The Partnership Act 1890, s. 3 provides that, if a person lends money in return for a share of profits in a business, and the borrower becomes bankrupt, the lender shall not be entitled to 'recover' anything in respect of the loan until the claims of the other creditors of the borrower have been satisfied. In *Ex p Sheil, re Longeran* (1877) 4 Ch D 789, 791 James LJ suggested during argument that a similar provision in the Partnership Law Amendment Act 1865 would not have prevented the lender from setting off his claim on the loan against a separate indebtedness to the borrower. That suggestion turned, however, on the meaning of 'recover' in the legislation. A set-off was thought not to be prohibited because it does not involve any form of recovery. Accordingly, James LJ's comment is not an authority against the view expressed in the text in relation to set-off against subordinated debt generally. In *Atlantic Acceptance Corporation Ltd v Burns & Dutton Construction (1962) Ltd* (1970) 14 DLR (3d) 175 it was held that a subordinated debt could not be set off, but that case concerned a claim for a set-off under the Statutes of Set-off where the debtor was not in liquidation. The debt

subordinated debt would not be the subject of a set-off.[432] This may be justified on either of two grounds. The first is that a subordination agreement may be said to import an agreement by the subordinated creditor not to prove for the debt in the debtor's liquidation until the debts of the unsubordinated creditors have been paid in full. The agreement not to prove should preclude a set-off.[433] Thus, Vinelott J in *Re Maxwell Communications*,[434] while not expressly equating subordination with a waiver by a creditor of his or her right to prove save to the extent of any surplus assets remaining after other unsecured creditors have been paid, nevertheless had recourse to that concept as support for the validity of subordination. Alternatively, the agreement to postpone may be regarded as having the consequence that, until the unsubordinated creditors have been paid in full, nothing is to be regarded as due to the subordinated creditor for the purpose of the administration of the insolvent estate, including by way of dividend.[435] The set-off section provides that 'the sums due from one party shall be set off against the sums due from the other'.[436] If there is nothing due, there is nothing that can be set off.

6.116   The Insolvency Act 1986, s. 74(2)(f) provides that a sum due to a member of a company in his character of a member,[437] by way of dividends profits or otherwise, is not deemed to be a debt of the company payable to that member in a case of competition between himself and external creditors, although it may be taken into account for the purpose of the final adjustment of the rights of contributories among themselves. The section effects a statutory subordination, so that the sum due should not be able to be employed by the member in a set-off against a separate liability owing to the company where this would operate to

---

could not be the subject of a set-off under the Statutes because according to its terms it was unenforceable at that time. See para. 2.46 above.

[432] Compare the form of subordination (commonly called turnover subordination) which takes effect by the imposition of a trust upon any proceeds of the subordinated debt received by the subordinated creditor. See paras 17.66–17.67 below in relation to an assignment merely of the proceeds of a debt, which should apply equally to a trust of the proceeds.

[433] See para. 6.113 above.

[434] [1993] 1 WLR 1402, 1411–12.

[435] Compare the discussion in *Gore-Browne on Companies* (45th edn, looseleaf, Update 71) vol. 2, §27[15] 27–42. Contractual subordination is sometimes explained on the basis that the subordinated debt is subject to a contingency, the contingency being that the unsubordinated debts have been paid in full. Accordingly, if the debtor's assets are insufficient to pay the unsubordinated creditors' claims in full, the value of the subordinated debt would be nil for the purpose of proof. See e.g. in Australia *United States Trust Co of New York v Australia & New Zealand Banking Group Ltd* (1993) 11 ACLC 707, 711; *Re NIAA Corp Ltd* (1993) 33 NSWLR 344, 358. However, Vinelott J in *Re Maxwell Communications* [1993] 1 WLR 1402, 1418 doubted that a subordinated debt is accurately described as a contingent liability. The contingent theory does not adequately reflect the intended effect of subordination in all cases. Consider that the value of the debtor's assets exceeds the amount of the unsubordinated debts, but is less than the aggregate of the subordinated and the unsubordinated debts. According to the contingent theory, the trustee in bankruptcy or the liquidator would be required to value the subordinated debt. In the situation posited, the subordinated debt would have a value, because there are assets available to pay part of it after satisfying the unsubordinated debts. The difficulty is that, once a value is put upon the subordinated debt, that value under normal principles would be provable and would rank *pari passu* with the unsubordinated debts, which would be contrary to the intended effect of the subordination. Nevertheless, this should not matter, because the value of the subordinated creditor's claim should be such that the unsubordinated creditors in any event would be paid in full.

[436] See the Insolvency Act 1986, s. 323(2), and for companies the Insolvency Rules 1986, r. 4.90(3).

[437] For a discussion of that expression, see *Soden v British & Commonwealth Holdings Plc* [1998] AC 298. See also Hogan, 'Set-off, members' rights and winding up' (1998) 19 *Company Lawyer* 16.

the detriment of the external creditors. In Australia a similar provision appears in s. 563A of the Corporations Act 2001 (Cth),[438] according to which payment of a debt owed by a company to a member in that capacity is to be 'postponed' to other creditors.[439]

(4) Ancillary liquidation

A foreign company in liquidation in the country of its incorporation may also be the sub-   **6.117**
ject of an ancillary winding up in England. In that situation, Sir Richard Scott VC in *Re Bank of Credit and Commerce International SA (No. 10)*[440] held that the set-off conferred by r. 4.90 of the Insolvency Rules 1986, being a substantive rule of English law,[441] must under English law be given effect in the English winding up. He considered that the court does not have a discretion to disapply it, notwithstanding that the law of the principal liquidation in that case did not recognize a similar set-off. This reflects the mandatory nature of the set-off.[442] Nevertheless, the approach adopted in *Re BCCI (No. 10)* has been criticized. In *Re HIH Casualty and General Insurance Ltd*[443] Lord Hoffmann considered that the court has jurisdiction at common law to disapply insolvency set-off in an ancillary liquidation, and said that the question instead is one of discretion. In determining whether to exercise the discretion, he said that much would depend on the degree of connection that the mutual debts have with England.[444] Lord Walker of Gestingthorpe agreed with Lord Hoffmann's judgment. However, Lord Scott of Foscote, who delivered the judgment in *Re BCCI (No. 10)*, affirmed his earlier opinion, and Lord Neuberger of Abbotsbury agreed with Lord Scott. The fifth member of the House, Lord Phillips of Worth Matravers, expressed no opinion on the correctness or otherwise of *Re BCCI (No. 10)*. The House of Lords was therefore evenly divided on the issue. It is suggested, with respect, that the

---

[438] See *Sons of Gwalia Ltd v Margaretic* (2007) 231 CLR 160.

[439] See also the Corporations Act 2001 (Cth), s. 553A, which provides that a debt due by a company to a person in the person's capacity as a member, whether by way of dividends, profits or otherwise, is not admissible to proof unless the person has paid all amounts for which the person is liable as a member.

[440] [1997] Ch 213. See Smart, 'International insolvency: banks and set-off' (1999) 1 *Journal of International Banking and Financial Law* 10.

[441] [1997] Ch 213, 246, referring to *Stein v Blake* [1996] AC 243. See also *Re A Company (No. 1641 of 2003)* [2004] 1 BCLC 210 at [17]. Compare *Macfarlane v Norris* (1862) 2 B & S 783, 792, 121 ER 1263,1266.

[442] See para. 6.111 below. It also accords with the position under the European Union Regulation on Insolvency (General Regulation (EC) 1346/2000 of 29 May 2000 on insolvency proceedings), which came into force on 31 May 2002. See art. 47. Pursuant to art. 4(2)(d) of the Regulation, the law of the state within whose territory insolvency proceedings are opened determines the conditions under which set-offs may be invoked. See Lightman and Moss, *The Law of Administrators and Receivers of Companies* (4th edn, 2007), 854–6, and generally ch. 33 of that text. In addition, art. 6 provides that the opening of insolvency proceedings does not affect the right of a creditor to demand a set-off against a claim by the debtor if a set-off is permitted under the law of the insolvent debtor's claim. Lightman and Moss makes the point (at 856) that, if a company is being wound up in another member state, and the insolvent company's claim against a creditor is governed by English law, it is doubtful whether art. 6 would have the effect of permitting a set-off under the Insolvency Rules 1986, r. 4.90, because for r. 4.90 to apply there must be a liquidation under English law. Article 6 would seem to contemplate instead rights of set-off before insolvency, in other words pursuant to the Statutes of Set-off and in accordance with the principles applicable to equitable set-off.

[443] [2008] 1 WLR 852.

[444] [2008] 1 WLR 852 at [17] and [25]. On this basis, Lord Hoffmann (at [17]) accepted that *Re BCCI (No. 10)* was correctly decided on the facts in issue, given that the debts to be set off appeared to be governed entirely by English law and were closely connected with England.

approach of Lord Scott is to be preferred. As his Lordship remarked,[445] English courts have a statutory obligation to apply the English statutory scheme in an English winding up, and in that circumstance it is difficult to see how they can have an inherent jurisdiction not to apply a substantive provision in that scheme. Indeed, it is now accepted that set-off occurs automatically upon the occurrence of a liquidation,[446] and it is unclear how the courts would have power to unwind a set-off that had already occurred under the Insolvency legislation.

6.118   The common law position has been modified by the Insolvency Act 1986, s. 426. Section 426(4) requires English courts having jurisdiction in relation to insolvency law to assist the courts having the corresponding jurisdiction in any other part of the United Kingdom or 'any relevant country or territory'.[447] Pursuant to sub-s. (5), if a request is made to an English court by a court in a relevant country or territory, the English court is given a discretion to apply, in relation to any matters specified in the request, the insolvency law which is applicable by the court making the request. The discretion may be exercised notwithstanding that some creditors may be worse off under the foreign law, with no countervailing advantages sufficient to counteract such prejudice.[448] In particular, if the law of a relevant country has different rules in relation to set-off, it would appear that an English court, acting in accordance with a request under s. 426, could disapply the English set-off provision and apply the foreign law.

N. The Nature of Insolvency Set-off

(1) Automatic or procedural?

6.119   A fundamental issue in relation to the insolvency set-off section is whether it operates automatically upon the occurrence of a bankruptcy or a liquidation[449] so as to bring about an extinguishment of the claims at that date to the extent of the set-off, or whether the section is procedural in its operation, in the sense that it requires the taking of an account during the insolvency administration and, until that occurs, the demands retain their separate identities. In that regard, the commencement of the bankruptcy or, as the case may be, the time when the company goes into liquidation, generally is the point for determining what mutual debts, credits and dealings can be brought into an account.[450] But it does not necessarily follow that this is also the time when the demands are set against each other to produce a balance.

---

[445] [2008] 1 WLR 852 at [59]. See also Lord Neuberger at [67]–[69], [72]–[77].

[446] See paras 6.119–6.146 below.

[447] Defined in s. 426(11) as any of the Channel Islands or the Isle of Man, or any country or territory designated for the purpose of s. 426 by the Secretary of State by order made by statutory instrument.

[448] *Re HIH Casualty and General Insurance Ltd* [2008] 1 WLR 852 (contrary to the view of the Court of Appeal in that case that this was a critical factor: see *Re HIH Casualty and General Insurance Ltd* [2007] 1 All ER 177 at [51]–[56], [71]). In exercising the discretion under s. 462, Lord Hoffmann at [30]–[36] considered that English courts should, so far as is consistent with justice and UK public policy, cooperate with the courts in the country of the principal liquidation to ensure that all the company's assets are distributed to its creditors under a single system of distribution. See also Lord Phillips at [42]–[43], Lord Scott at [62] and Lord Neuberger at [79]–[81].

[449] See also para. 6.124 below in relation to company administration.

[450] *Ellis & Company's Trustee v Dixon-Johnson* [1924] 1 Ch 342, 356. See paras 6.45–6.62 above.

A key provision in the insolvency set-off section in both bankruptcy and company liquid- **6.120**
ation[451] is the stipulation that: 'An account shall be taken of what is due from each party to
the other in respect of the mutual dealings and the sums due from one party shall be set off
against the sums due from the other.' This might be thought to support a procedural operation, given that it appears to require the taking of an account of amounts which are due at
the date of the account. An account could be taken in a bankruptcy either by the trustee in
bankruptcy or by the court in proceedings before it. This interpretation would not mean
that the trustee would have a discretion as to whether a set-off should occur,[452] and nor
would it be inconsistent with the view that set-off in insolvency cannot be contracted out
of,[453] particularly given that Lord Simon of Glaisdale, who as one of the majority in
the *Halesowen* case[454] held that contracting out is not possible, nevertheless regarded the
section as prescribing a course of procedure.[455] In other words, he said that it lays down a
'code of procedure'[456] which must be followed regardless of any agreement to the contrary.[457] The procedural view is consistent with views expressed in a long line of cases,[458]
and in 1993 it was approved by the Court of Appeal in *Stein v Blake*.[459]

---

[451] Insolvency Act 1986, s. 323(2) (bankruptcy) and, for company liquidation, the Insolvency Rules, r. 4.90(3). Rule 2.85(3), dealing with administration, is in similar terms.

[452] A creditor could request the trustee to take an account and, if the trustee refused, or the creditor was otherwise dissatisfied with the result, the creditor could ask the court to review the decision under the Insolvency Act 1986, s. 303. See *Stein v Blake* [1994] Ch 16, 29 (CA).

[453] See para. 6.111 above.

[454] [1972] AC 785.

[455] [1972] AC 785, 808. This is also consistent with Lord Simon's reference (at 808) to 'the imposition of a duty on a public officer'. The officer that he had in mind presumably was a trustee in bankruptcy, with the duty being the taking of an account. The comment would hardly have been apt if a set-off was thought to occur automatically. Viscount Dilhorne referred (at 305) to the set-off section as 'prescribing the course to be followed in the administration of the bankrupt's property'.

[456] [1972] AC 785, 809.

[457] Similarly, while Hallett J in *Victoria Products Ltd v Tosh & Co* (1940) 165 LT 78, 80 agreed that the set-off section cannot be contracted out of, he nevertheless described it in terms of laying down a 'process'.

[458] In *Sovereign Life Assurance Co v Dodd* [1892] 2 QB 573, Lord Esher MR appears to have considered (see esp. at 578) that the cross-demands in issue in that case were still subsisting at the date of the liquidator's action, which accords with his earlier *dictum* (as Brett J) in *New Quebrada Co, Ltd v Carr* (1869) LR 4 CP 651, 653–4, that the set-off section does not extinguish mutual debts. In a similar vein, Rich J in the Australian High Court in *Hiley v The Peoples Prudential Assurance Co Ltd* (1938) 60 CLR 468, 487 referred with evident approval to Bigham J's description of the operation of the set-off section in *Re Daintrey* [1900] 1 QB 546, 568 in terms that: 'the account which the section of the Act directed should be taken is to be taken when the claim on the one side or the other is presented.' This suggests that an account is required to be taken in respect of subsisting cross-demands. See also Romer LJ at 574 ('It is quite sufficient if the account can be taken when the set-off arises'). Wright J in that case noted (at 552) that Lord Selborne in *Ex p Barnett, re Deveze* (1874) LR 9 Ch App 293, 295 seemed to have considered that a set-off took effect at the time that the creditor came in to prove. Lord Selborne was a member of the House of Lords in *Mersey Steel and Iron Co v Naylor, Benzon & Co* (1874) 9 App Cas 434 when it affirmed an order made by the Court of Appeal ((1882) 9 QBD 648, 672) in an action brought by a liquidator for payment of a debt, to the effect that 'the defendants are entitled to set-off against the 1713*l admitted to be due* to the plaintiffs such damages as they the defendants may have sustained' (emphasis added). This contemplated that there was still an amount due to the plaintiffs at the time of the action, notwithstanding the availability of a set-off, and that it was the order of the court itself which brought about the set-off. See also Lord Selborne in *Re Milan Tramways Co, ex p Theys* (1884) 25 Ch D 587, 591. On another occasion Kay LJ referred to a 'right of set-off after the bankruptcy'. See *Re Washington Diamond Mining Co* [1893] 3 Ch 95, 113. More recently, see *Re Bank of Credit and Commerce International SA (No. 8)* [1995] Ch 46, 63–4 (Rattee J); *Day & Dent Constructions Pty Ltd v North Australian Properties Pty Ltd* (1982) 150 CLR 85, 109 (Murphy J); *McIntyre v Perkes* (1990) 22 FCR 260, 270 (Gummow and von Doussa JJ); *Re Capel, ex p Marac Finance Australia Ltd v Capel* (1994) 48 FCR 195.

[459] [1994] Ch 16.

6.121   It is difficult, on the other hand, to find clear support for the automatic extinguishment theory before 1984,[460] when it was adopted by Neill J in *Farley v Housing and Commercial Developments Ltd.*[461] After that judgment, however, it gained rapid favour. It received the approval of the High Court of Australia in *Gye v McIntyre*,[462] and it was accepted by Hoffmann LJ in the Chancery Division, as well as by the Court of Appeal on appeal, in *MS Fashions Ltd v Bank of Credit and Commerce International SA.*[463] The *MS Fashions* case concerned a bank which had provided an advance to a customer secured by both a guarantee and a cash deposit by the guarantor. The bank went into liquidation. The liquidator, instead of claiming against the guarantor, made a demand on the debtor, and said that the guarantor should be confined to a proof in the liquidation in respect of the deposit. The Court of Appeal held that there was a set-off as between the guarantor and the bank which had the effect of automatically satisfying the guarantor's liablity to the bank, and since the guarantor had paid the debt by means of the set-off the customer could no longer be sued.[464] Following the conflicting decisions by differently constituted Courts of Appeal in the *MS Fashions* case and *Stein v Blake*, the issue came before the House of Lords by way of an appeal in *Stein v Blake*.[465] Their Lordships[466] unanimously held that the automatic extinguishment theory provides the correct analysis of the operation of the insolvency set-off section, and rejected the argument that the section has a procedural operation. Subsequently, the House of Lords re-affirmed that view in *Re Bank of Credit and Commerce International SA (No. 8)*,[467] and it is now firmly established.[468]

6.122   The issue in *Stein v Blake* was whether a trustee in bankruptcy could assign a debt owing to the bankrupt in circumstances where the debtor had a cross-claim available for a set-off. The Court of Appeal held that the debt could be assigned. The set-off section was regarded as being procedural in its operation, so that it did not of itself extinguish the mutual debts. For the debts to be extinguished an account had to be taken,[469] either by the trustee in bankruptcy or by the court. Since this had not occurred at the date of the assignment, it was

---

[460] An exception is Wright J's comment in passing in *Watkins v Lindsay and Co* (1898) 67 LJQB 362, 364, that set-off in bankruptcy is automatic. In *Ex p Barnett, re Deveze* (1874) LR 9 Ch App 293, 297 Mellish LJ said in relation to the insolvency set-off section that: 'I doubt whether it does not affect it even before either party comes in to prove; but, at any rate, when the party does come in to prove, the statute sets the one debt against the other, and that is equivalent to payment.'

[461] (1984) 26 BLR 66.

[462] (1991) 171 CLR 609, 622 ('The section is self-executing in the sense that its operation is automatic and not dependent upon "the option of either party" . . .').

[463] [1993] Ch 425.

[464] Why was a set-off available as between the guarantor and the bank? See the discussion of the case in paras 12.24–12.25 below.

[465] [1996] AC 243.

[466] Lord Keith of Kinkel, Lord Ackner, Lord Lloyd of Berwick, Lord Nicholls of Birkenhead and Lord Hoffmann.

[467] [1998] AC 214, 223.

[468] See e.g. *Manson v Smith* [1997] 2 BCLC 161, 164 (Millett LJ); *Re Bank of Credit and Commerce International SA (No. 10)* [1997] Ch 213, 226, 236 (Sir Richard Scott VC); *Craig v Humberclyde Industrial Finance Group Ltd* [1999] 1 WLR 129; *Bank of Credit and Commerce International (Overseas) Ltd v Habib Bank Ltd* [1999] 1 WLR 42; *Bouygues (UK) Ltd v Dahl-Jensen (UK) Ltd* [2000] BLR 522, 528 (CA). In Australia, see paras 6.142–6.146 below.

[469] See Staughton LJ at [1994] Ch 16, 29.

held that the separate debts retained their separate identities and therefore they could be assigned. This did not mean that the defendant lost the benefit of the set-off otherwise available in the bankruptcy. Because the assignment occurred after the bankruptcy, the assignee would still have taken subject to the defendant's right of set-off under the insolvency legislation on the basis of the principle that an assignee takes subject to equities.[470] However, that analysis was rejected on appeal.[471] The judgment of the House of Lords was delivered by Lord Hoffmann, who also had delivered the judgment in the Chancery Division in the *MS Fashions* case. His view on the point had not changed. He said that insolvency set-off 'is self-executing and takes effect on the bankruptcy date'.[472] Its operation does not depend upon any procedural step, but rather it 'results, as of the bankruptcy date, in only a net balance being owing',[473] so that at that date the cross-claims cease to exist as separate choses in action. Accordingly, it was not possible for a trustee in bankruptcy to assign the debt owing to the bankrupt to the extent that it had already been extinguished by a set-off.[474]

Company liquidation

That analysis is equally applicable in company liquidation, with set-offs taking place automatically on the date of the liquidation.[475]   **6.123**

Administration

The Insolvency Rules 1986, r. 2.85 permits set-off in the case of a company which has entered administration in circumstances where the administrator, being authorized to   **6.124**

---

[470] See ch. 17 below.

[471] [1996] AC 243, following *Farley v Housing and Commercial Developments Ltd* (1984) 26 BLR 66 (company liquidation). In particular, the House of Lords rejected (at 255–6) the application of the notion of 'taking subject to equities' in this context.

[472] [1996] AC 243, 256. In *Re Bank of Credit and Commerce International SA (No. 8)* [1996] Ch 245, 255 the Court of Appeal (Rose, Saville and Millett LJ) described insolvency set-off as: 'mandatory, automatic and immediate on the bankruptcy or liquidation taking place.' On appeal in the House of Lords in that case ([1998] AC 214, 223) Lord Hoffmann commented: 'When the conditions of [r 4.90 of the Insolvency Rules 1986] are satisfied, a set-off is treated as having taken place automatically on the bankruptcy date.'

[473] [1996] AC 243, 255.

[474] See also *Craig v Humberclyde Industrial Finance Group Ltd* [1999] 1 WLR 129 and *Enterprise Managed Services Ltd v Tony McFadden Utilities Ltd* [2010] BLR 89, and paras 6.144–6.146 below (Australia). The House of Lords in *Stein v Blake* went on to hold that the trustee nevertheless could assign any claim for the net balance owing to the estate after taking into account the set-off, and that as a matter of construction the assignment of the claim in that case carried the right to the balance after deducting the cross-claim. See [1996] AC 243, 258–9. In *Citicorp Australia Ltd v Official Trustee in Bankruptcy* (1996) 71 FCR 550, 567–8 the Full Court of the Federal Court rejected an argument that there could be no assignment where it was not possible on the evidence available to the trustee or the court to conclude that the net balance after any set-off was in favour of the bankrupt. Rather, the merits and the quantum of the claim and cross-claim could be litigated, and that litigation would determine whether there was a balance one way or the other.

[475] *Re Bank of Credit and Commerce International SA (No. 10)* [1997] Ch 213, 226, 236; *Re Bank of Credit and Commerce International SA (No. 8)* [1998] AC 214, 222–3 (and see also in the Court of Appeal [1996] Ch 245, 255); *Bank of Credit and Commerce International (Overseas) Ltd v Habib Bank Ltd* [1999] 1 WLR 42, 51, 52. See also *Bouygues (UK) Ltd v Dahl-Jensen (UK) Ltd* [2000] BLR 522, 528 ('the date of the insolvency order').

make a distribution, has given notice of his intention to do so under r. 2.95.[476] Rule 2.85(3) corresponds with r. 4.90(3) in company liquidation.[477] It provides:

> An account shall be taken as at the date of the notice referred to in paragraph (1) of what is due from each party to the other in respect of the mutual dealings and the sums due from one party shall be set off against the sums due from the other.

The use of the present tense in r. 2.85(3) ('is due') suggests that the cross-claims retain their separate identities until the date of the notice referred to in paragraph (1) of r. 2.85 (being a notice under r. 2.95). Consequently, set-offs would be taken to have occurred automatically on that date rather than the date that the company entered administration.[478]

(2) Advantages and disadvantages of the automatic theory

6.125 The notion of an automatic cancellation of cross-demands on the date of a bankruptcy may be inconvenient in some circumstances. Consider that a trustee in bankruptcy is proposing to assign a debt owing to the bankrupt. Neither the trustee nor the bankrupt may be aware that the debtor has a cross-claim extinguishing the debt, for example where the debtor before the bankruptcy had taken an assignment of a debt owing by the bankrupt to a third party. Under the automatic theory the debtor need not do anything. There would not be any incentive for him or her to notify the trustee of the set-off, or indeed to respond to inquiries, since a set-off would have occurred automatically. It may not be until some time later, when the debt assigned by the trustee matures and the assignee seeks payment, that the set-off comes to light. If, on the other hand, the set-off were procedural in its operation, it is more likely that the debtor would have informed the trustee of the set-off entitlement, in which case the trustee could have tempered his dealings with the proposed assignee accordingly. In other respects, however, the notion of an automatic cancellation of cross-demands at the date of the bankruptcy or liquidation would simplify the position in an insolvency administration. For example, when an interest-bearing debt is owing to a bankrupt or a company in liquidation, it prevents an argument that interest continues to run until the account is taken.[479] Furthermore, when a trustee in bankruptcy assigns a debt owing to the bankrupt, and the debtor has a cross-claim available as a set-off, the set-off would have occurred automatically and the assignee would be bound by it. It would not be necessary for the debtor to insist that the trustee take an account, so as to prevent a situation arising whereby the assignee could take free of the set-off if the bankrupt is discharged from bankruptcy, and as a result is released from his or her liability to the debtor, before a set-off has occurred.[480] From this perspective, *Stein v Blake* is a welcome development. Nevertheless, the automatic theory raises a number of questions.

---

[476] See para. 6.10 above. There is no similar provision in the Australian Corporations Act 2001 (Cth) in relation to administration.

[477] See para. 6.120 above.

[478] See also Lightman and Moss, *The Law of Administrators and Receivers of Companies* (4th edn, 2007), 533 [20–020], 547 [20–038].

[479] See paras 6.156–6.161 below.

[480] See *Farley v Housing and Commercial Developments Ltd* (1984) 26 BLR 66. In Australia, compare *Re Capel, ex p Marac Finance Australia Ltd v Capel* (1994) 48 FCR 195. See paras 6.144–6.146 below. Compare also *Edmonds Judd v Official Assignee* [1999] NZCA 283, in which it was assumed that the discharge

(3) Pleading set-off as a defence to an action by a trustee in bankruptcy

A trustee in bankruptcy may sue for a debt owing to the estate, and the defendant may **6.126** plead as a defence a set-off under the insolvency legislation.[481] In *Stein v Blake*, Lord Hoffmann said that this does not mean that separate claims exist until the court has decided the issue. Rather, he considered that the litigation is merely part of a process of retrospective calculation, from which it will appear that from the date of the bankruptcy the only chose in action that continued to exist was a claim for the balance.[482] However, this is not the way that the issue appears to have been regarded historically. From early days, the defendant in an action brought by assignees in bankruptcy who wished to defend the action on the basis of a set-off would not deny that he or she was liable to the bankrupt because of a set-off that had occurred at the date of the bankruptcy. Rather, the defendant would plead that the bankrupt 'was, *and still is*, indebted to the defendant'.[483] A similar form of pleading is to be found in successive editions of Bullen and Leake.[484] This suggests that the cross-claims were regarded as still retaining their separate identities at the date of the action, which of course was after the bankruptcy. Indeed, when the Court of Appeal in 1881[485] confirmed that insolvency set-off could be relied on as a defence to an action at law brought by a trustee in bankruptcy for payment of a debt owing to the bankrupt,[486] Sir George Jessel explained this on the ground that, while the bankruptcy legislation contemplated a set-off occurring in the Bankruptcy Court, the common law courts considered that it was within 'the equity of the statute' that it should also provide a defence to a trustee's action.[487] But if the bankruptcy legislation were regarded as bringing about an automatic extinguishment of cross-demands upon the occurrence of a bankruptcy, it would hardly have been necessary for the common law courts to have recourse to that concept.

---

from bankruptcy affected the creditor's right to assert the set-off. The creditor had received a dividend, but see para. 6.165 below.

[481] See para. 6.03 above.

[482] [1996] AC 243, 255. Compare Bigham J in *Re Daintrey* [1900] 1 QB 546, 568, who equated the stipulation in the 1883 bankruptcy set-off section (Bankruptcy Act 1883, s. 38), that there should be a person 'proving or claiming to prove a debt under such receiving order', with the notion that there should be a person 'having a right to prove a debt in the bankruptcy proceedings initiated by the receiving order'. See also para. 6.03 above.

[483] See e.g. *Hulme v Muggleston* (1837) 3 M & W 30, 31, 150 ER 1043, 1044; *Russell v Bell* (1841) 8 M & W 277, 278, 151 ER 1042, 1043; *Bittleston v Timmis* (1845) 1 CB 389, 391, 135 ER 591, 592. See also *West v Baker* (1875) 1 Ex D 44, 45. In *Gibson v Bell* (1835) 1 Bing NC 743, 131 ER 1303 the defendant pleaded (at 746, 1305) that: 'the said sum of money still remained unpaid and unsatisfied to the Defendant.'

[484] In the second edition of Bullen and Leake, *Precedents of Pleading* in 1863, the plea was set out (at 580) in terms that a debt owing by the bankrupt: 'at the commencement of this suit was and still is due to the defendant.' The substance of the plea was repeated in subsequent editions, save for the 13th edition in 1990 where (at 1420–1) the pleading was in terms that: 'there is due from the plaintiff to the defendant the sum of £–. The defendant is entitled to set off such sum against the plaintiff's claim under section 323 of the Insolvency Act 1986.' A pleading for insolvency set-off was omitted from the 14th, 15th and 16th editions in 2001, 2004 and 2008 respectively.

[485] *Peat v Jones & Co* (1881) 8 QBD 147.

[486] In the case of company liquidation, see e.g. *Mersey Steel and Iron Co v Naylor, Benzon & Co* (1884) 9 App Cas 434.

[487] (1881) 8 QBD 147, 149. See also *Mersey Steel and Iron Co v Naylor, Benzon & Co* (1882) 9 QBD 648, 664; *McIntyre v Perkes* (1990) 22 FCR 260, 270–1 (Federal Court of Australia). For a discussion of the concept of the equity of a statute, see *Nelson v Nelson* (1995) 184 CLR 538, 552–4.

6.127 Therefore, when considering nineteenth-century cases, it must be appreciated that insolvency set-off at the time was not thought of as operating automatically at the date of the bankruptcy. Attempts to explain those cases by reference to the automatic theory would be founded upon a false premise.[488]

(4) Contingent debts and claims: the use of hindsight

6.128 The insolvency set-off section stipulates that 'the sums due from one party shall be set off against the sums due from the other'.[489] There must be a sum 'due' on each side of the account when the set-off occurs which, on the automatic theory of the set-off, is the date of the bankruptcy or the liquidation.[490] The requirement of a sum due would be satisfied in relation to a claim which has accrued and which is presently payable at that date. It would also be satisfied in relation to a debt which is presently existing but which is expressed not to be payable until a future date. It would be appropriate in that regard to interpret 'due' as including 'owing, although not payable until some future date'.[491] It may also be accepted that 'due' would encompass a liability which has accrued but which remains to be quantified.[492] The position is more difficult, however, in the case of a debt or liability which is still contingent at that date of the bankruptcy. 'Due' is not usually interpreted as extending to contingent debts.[493] Nevertheless, the fact that a debt or liability is contingent does not suffice to exclude it from the operation of the set-off section.

6.129 Consider that the subject of a set-off is a contingent debt owing *by* a bankrupt (or a company in liquidation). The fact that the liability is contingent at the date of the bankruptcy is not inconsistent with the automatic theory. Debts must be proved according to their value as at the date of the bankruptcy. If a liability of the bankrupt is contingent, the trustee must estimate its value as at that date, and that value may be proved in the bankruptcy.[494] This provable valuation may be treated as the amount due for the purpose of the set-off section.[495] In the case of company liquidation, the availability of set-off in relation to

---

[488] The Court of Appeal failed to appreciate this in *Re Bank of Credit and Commerce International SA (No. 8)* [1996] Ch 245, 265–9 when it attempted to reconcile Lord Eldon's decision in *Ex p Stephens* (1805) 11 Ves Jun 24, 32 ER 996 with the automatic theory. This led the Court of Appeal to suggest that discharge of a surety by way of set-off may not discharge the principal debtor. See paras 12.29–12.39 below.

[489] Insolvency Act 1986, s. 323(2) (bankruptcy), and Insolvency Rules 1986, rr. 2.85(3) (company in administration) and 4.90(3) (company liquidation).

[490] In the case of a company which has entered administration, set-offs under the Insolvency Rules, r. 2.85 would appear to occur on the date of the administrator's notice to creditors under r. 2.95 that he proposes to make a distribution. See para. 6.124 above.

[491] *Clyne v Deputy Commissioner of Taxation* (1981) 150 CLR 1, 8. In relation to company liquidation, see the Insolvency Rules 1986, r. 4.90(4).

[492] See e.g. *Gye v McIntyre* (1991) 171 CLR 609. See also Malins VC in *Booth v Hutchinson* (1872) LR 15 Eq 30, 34 in the context of the judgment for damages for £50 given after the deed of assignment in relation to the prior breach. In company liquidation, this is reflected in r. 4.90(4) ('whether . . . its amount is fixed or ascertained, or is capable of being ascertained by fixed rules or as a matter of opinion').

[493] *Ex p Kemp, re Fastnedge* (1874) LR 9 Ch App 383; *Merritt Cairns Constructions Pty Ltd v Wulguru Heights Pty Ltd* [1995] 2 Qd R 521, 526.

[494] See the Insolvency Act 1986, s. 322. For company liquidation see the Insolvency Rules 1986, r. 4.86 and for administration r. 2.81.

[495] See paras 8.19–8.34 below. Compare *Ex p Price, re Lankester* (1875) LR 10 Ch App 648, 650–1, the decision in which was criticized, and not followed, in *Re City Life Assurance Co Ltd. Grandfield's Case* [1926] 1 Ch 191. Moreover, the valuation of the policy holder's claim in *Ex p Price* occurred in the liquidation of

contingent debts is confirmed by the Insolvency Rules 1986, r. 4.90(4), which provides that a sum is to be regarded as being due to or from a company where the obligation by virtue of which it is payable is contingent. This is a consequence of amendments made to the Insolvency Rules in 2005.[496]

Alternatively, the contingent debt may be on the other side of the account, in other words the insolvent is possessed of a contingent claim. In so far as the automatic theory is concerned, this no longer presents a problem in company liquidation in England, given that r. 4.90(4) (above), which provides that a contingent debt is to be regarded as due for the purpose of a set-off, is expressed to apply to both sides of the account, and the liquidator's obligation in r. 4.86 to value contingent debts is extended, for the purpose of set-off, to debts owing to the company.[497] However, in bankruptcy the position remains that there is no mechanism in the Insolvency Act for a trustee or the court to value the bankrupt's contingent claims. If the contingency occurs after the bankruptcy, the claim ordinarily should be capable of being employed in a set-off.[498] But given that there is no power in the insolvency legislation to put a value on the contingent claim as at the date of the bankruptcy, *prima facie* it seems difficult to say that anything was 'due' in respect of it as at that date. The same comment may be made in Australia in both bankruptcy and company liquidation, the liquidation set-off section in that country[499] not having been amended in terms similar to r. 4.90 in England. **6.130**

One thing that is clear is that it would not simply be a matter of interpreting 'due' in the insolvency set-off section as extending to contingent debts. If 'due' had that extended meaning, a contingent debt owing to a bankrupt where the contingency had not occurred could be included in a set-off, but it is accepted that a contingent debt possessed by a bankrupt cannot be the subject of a set-off until the contingency has occurred and the claim vested.[500] How, then, do contingent debts owing to the insolvent fit in with the automatic theory of insolvency set-off in bankruptcy in both England and Australia, and in company liquidation in Australia? **6.131**

Hindsight and estimation

In *Stein v Blake*,[501] Lord Hoffmann sought to explain set-off with respect to contingent debts by reference to two 'techniques': **6.132**

> How does the law deal with the conundrum of having to set off, as of the bankruptcy date, 'sums due' which may not yet be due or which may become owing upon contingencies which have not yet occurred? It employs two techniques. The first is to take into account everything which has actually happened between the bankruptcy date and the moment when it becomes necessary to ascertain what, on that date, was the state of account between the creditor and

---

the company whereas the question of set-off arose in the policy holder's bankruptcy, the rules of set-off in bankruptcy not having been extended to company liquidation until later. See para. 6.05 above.

[496] See para. 6.06 above. In relation to administration, see r. 2.85(4), and para. 6.10 above.
[497] Rule 4.90(5). In relation to administration, see r. 2.85(5).
[498] See paras 8.35–8.46 below.
[499] Corporations Act 2001 (Cth), 553C.
[500] See para. 8.35 below.
[501] [1996] AC 243, 252.

the bankrupt. If by that time the contingency has occurred and the claim has been quantified, then that is the amount which is treated as having been due at the bankruptcy date . . .

But the winding up of the estate of a bankrupt or an insolvent company cannot always wait until all possible contingencies have happened and all the actual or potential liabilities which existed at the bankruptcy date have been quantified. Therefore the law adopts a second technique, which is to make an estimation of the value of the claim.

Later he said that: '"due" merely means treated as having been owing at the bankruptcy date with the benefit of the hindsight and, if necessary, estimation prescribed by the bankruptcy law.'[502]

The difficulty with hindsight as an explanation in bankruptcy

6.133   While the application of the hindsight principle is not open to question in the case of a contingent liability of a bankrupt, the same cannot be said where the issue concerns a *claim* of a bankrupt[503] that was contingent at the relevant date,[504] given that in bankruptcy[505] the power of estimation does not apply in that context.[506] In that regard, it should be appreciated the first technique of hindsight is not independent of the second technique of estimation.

6.134   Consider the application of the techniques when a bankrupt's contingent *liability* is in issue. In such a case, a subsequent occurrence of the contingency may be taken into account for the purpose of proof and of set-off. This is not because the happening of the contingency is regarded as accelerated so as to fix the amount of the liability on the basis of the contingency having occurred at the date of the bankruptcy.[507] The hindsight principle does not deem a state of affairs to have existed at the bankruptcy date that in fact did not exist.[508]

---

[502] [1996] AC 243, 256. Similarly, the Court of Appeal in *Re Bank of Credit and Commerce International SA (No. 8)* [1996] Ch 245, 269 commented that: 'it is now settled that the set-off operates automatically upon the date of bankruptcy, and that the hindsight principle enables debts to be treated as owing or not on that date with the benefit of hindsight . . .'

[503] As opposed to a company in liquidation, since the amendments to the Insolvency Rules, r. 4.90 in 2005. See paras 6.06 and 6.129–6.130 above.

[504] The ensuing discussion is also relevant to Lord Hoffmann's earlier discussion of contingent claims in the *MS Fashions* case [1993] Ch 425, 435. His Lordship there referred to *Re Daintrey, ex p Mant* [1900] 1 QB 546 as an illustration of the hindsight principle applied to a contingent claim in favour of the insolvent. See the explanation of *Re Daintrey* at para. 8.37 below. However, the judgments in that case do not suggest that the set-off was regarded as having taken place automatically before the occurrence of the contingency, on the date of the receiving order. On the contrary, statements in the case suggest a procedural operation for the set-off section. See para. 6.120n above.

[505] And in company liquidation in Australia. See para. 6.130 above.

[506] See para. 6.130 above. *Sovereign Life Assurance Co v Dodd* [1892] 2 QB 573, to which Lord Hoffmann referred in *Stein v Blake* [1996] AC 243, 252, concerned a contingent liability of a company in liquidation, rather than a contingent claim of the company. The full matured value of the policies was allowed to be set off, because that was the provable value. In other words, this was an aspect of the second technique of estimation, which in bankruptcy only applies to a contingent liability owing by the bankrupt, and not to a contingent claim.

[507] *Ellis & Company's Trustee v Dixon-Johnson* [1924] 1 Ch 342, 356–7 (P O Lawrence J). This has since been regarded as a correct statement of the principle. See *Re Dynamics Corporation of America* [1976] 1 WLR 757, 768 (Oliver J); *Re Hurren* [1983] 1 WLR 183, 189 (Walton J).

[508] Thus, statements to the effect that the distribution of the assets of the insolvent is treated as notionally taking place on the date of the bankruptcy or liquidation (see e.g. *Re Bank of Credit and Commerce International SA (No. 8)* [1996] Ch 245, 269) have been said not to represent a rigid rule. See *Wight v Eckhardt*

That accords with the ordinary meaning of 'hindsight', that one sees what has happened after the event.[509] Rather, the insolvency legislation has provided in the case of a contingent liability that a sum is to be regarded as due for the purpose of the administration of the bankruptcy, in the form of the value which the trustee must put on a it.[510] This has been interpreted as requiring a valuation as at the date of the bankruptcy,[511] and in taking into account a subsequent occurrence of the contingency the trustee is merely using all the available evidence to ascertain what, with hindsight, was *as a matter of fact* the true value of the liability as at that date.[512] The position is entirely different, however, when a bankrupt's *claim* was still subject to a contingency when the bankruptcy occurred. In such a case there is no question of a valuation as at the date of the bankruptcy, because there is no machinery in the insolvency legislation for a trustee or the court to put a value on a bankrupt's claim as at that date.[513] If there is no basis for valuing it as at the date of the bankruptcy, then, unlike a contingent liability of the bankrupt, there is no apparent justification for saying that there was an amount then 'due' for the purpose of the administration of the bankrupt's estate. The bankruptcy set-off section provides that: 'the sums due from one party shall be set off against the sums due from the other.' The fundamental point is that it only contemplates a set-off occurring against a sum which is then due,[514] and on the ordinary meaning of 'due'[515] it would be difficult to assert that a sum was due to the bankrupt at the date of the bankruptcy for the purpose of an automatic set-off occurring at that date if the claim in question was still subject to a contingency.

For example, there have been cases in which property was deposited with a person with authority to sell, and the sale did not occur until after the depositor's bankruptcy,[516] or a policy of insurance was deposited by an insured with a broker with authority to collect the insurance money in the event of a loss, and the loss occurred and the proceeds were received after the insured had become bankrupt.[517] In each case it was held that the claim brought by **6.135**

Marine GmbH [2004] 1 AC 147 at [29]. Equally, it is not a rigid rule that the identities of those entitled to participate in the insolvent estate are fixed at the insolvency date. See *Wight v Eckhardt Marine* (above), and compare *Stotter v Equiticorp Australia Ltd* [2002] 2 NZLR 686 at [39] and [66].

[509] 'Hindsight' is defined in *The Oxford English Dictionary* (2nd edn, 1989) vol. VII, 244 as: 'Seeing what has happened, and what ought to have been done, after the event; perception gained by looking backward . . .'

[510] In company liquidation see the Insolvency Rules 1986, r. 4.86, and in administration see r. 2.81.

[511] *Ellis & Company's Trustee v Dixon-Johnson* [1924] 1 Ch 342, 356–7 (date of the receiving order under the Bankruptcy Act 1914); *Re Dynamics Corporation of America* [1976] 1 WLR 757, 767 (winding up).

[512] *Ellis & Company's Trustee v Dixon-Johnson* [1924] 1 Ch 342, 356–7; *Re Dynamics Corporation of America* [1976] 1 WLR 757, 767–8; *Re Hurren* [1983] 1 WLR 183, 189; *Wight v Eckhardt Marine GmbH* [2004] 1 AC 147 at [32]. See also *Transit Casualty Co v Policyholders Protection Board* [1992] 2 Lloyd's Rep 358, 359, 361.

[513] *Re Daintrey* [1900] 1 QB 546, 557, 565, 573. Compare the position in company liquidation and administration. See para. 6.130 above.

[514] The question, according to Lawrence LJ in *Re Fenton* [1931] 1 Ch 85, 113, is whether 'there was any sum due . . . when the right to set off was claimed . . .'.

[515] See paras 6.128 and 6.131 above.

[516] *Palmer v Day & Sons* [1895] 2 QB 618; *French v Fenn* (1783) 3 Dougl 257, 99 ER 642. See also *Astley v Gurney* (1869) LR 4 CP 714.

[517] *Olive v Smith* (1813) 5 Taunt 56, 128 ER 607. See also *Parker v Carter* (1788), unreported but noted in Cooke, *The Bankrupt Laws* (8th edn, 1823) vol. 1, 578.

the assignees or the trustee in bankruptcy of the depositor could be the subject of a set-off. But until the sale occurred, or the insurance proceeds were received in respect of the loss occurring after the bankruptcy, there was no sum which could be described as 'due' to the bankrupt. Moreover, since the question concerned a contingent claim possessed by a bankrupt, as opposed to a contingent liability, there was no question of the contingent claim being valued as at the date of the bankruptcy for the purpose of the administration of the estate.[518] In truth, until the relevant event occurred, there was nothing due.[519] Consider also *Lee & Chapman's Case*.[520] A company had contracted with the Commissioners of Sewers to pave a street. The company went into liquidation before completion of the works, but the liquidator subsequently completed them and claimed the price. The Court of Appeal held that the Commissioners were entitled to a set-off under the Bankruptcy Act 1869 in respect of a damages claim that they had against the company. Once again, however, it would be difficult to argue that the price was due to the company at the date of the liquidation, given that the works had not then been completed. Indeed, Brett MR referred in his judgment to: 'a right of set-off as between the company in liquidation and these Commissioners accruing *after* the winding-up.'[521]

6.136 Admittedly, the set-off section in issue in some of those cases did not specifically provide that the debts to be set off had to be 'due'.[522] The section was not drafted in this manner until the 1869 Act, which was similar to the current bankruptcy provision. It has never been suggested, however, that the 1869 Act had the effect of narrowing the scope of insolvency set-off, which would have been the consequence if those early cases were not good law after that Act.[523] On the contrary, as Sir George Jessel MR remarked in the context of a discussion of the 1869 Act, the whole tendency of the history of the insolvency legislation has been to extend the principle upon which the right of set-off is founded.[524]

---

[518] The right to obtain a valuation of a contingent debt and to prove in respect of that amount was introduced by the statute (1825) 6 Geo IV, c. 16, s. 56.

[519] To a like effect, in *Graham v Russell* (1816) 5 M & s. 498, 105 ER 1133 an underwriter was allowed to set off his liability on a policy to the insured in the insured's bankruptcy, even though the loss occurred after the bankruptcy. See also *Booth v Hutchinson* (1872) LR 15 Eq 30, 35 in relation to rent accruing to a landlord after he had executed a deed of assignment.

[520] (1885) 30 Ch D 216.

[521] (1885) 30 Ch D 216, 222 (emphasis added).

[522] Prior to the 1869 Act the set-off section in force was s. 171 of the Bankrupt Law Consolidation Act 1849, which provided that, where there was mutual credit between a bankrupt and another person, 'the court shall state the account between them, and one debt or demand may be set against another . . . .'. The set-off section in the previous 1825 Act (6 Geo IV, c. 16, s. 50) was expressed in similar terms, although referring to the commissioners rather than the court. The House of Lords in *Stein v Blake* [1996] AC 243, 257 noted the reference to 'may' in the 1849 Act, and suggested that, because of this, the self-executing nature of the set-off may not have been as fully apparent then as it is today. On the contrary, one would have thought that the stipulation that 'the court shall state the account' indicates a procedural operation.

[523] Nor, apparently, did text-writers at the time attach any great consequence to the change in the wording of the section. Thus, Robson in his *Treatise on the Law of Bankruptcy* (3rd edn, 1876), 330 commented in relation to the 1869 Act that, apart from the expansion in the scope of the set-off section by the introduction of mutual dealings as forming a ground of set-off, and some other 'verbal variations' from the old clause, the principles and practice relating to set-off did not appear to have been substantially altered by the new provision, and a similar view was expressed in the first edition of *Williams on Bankruptcy*, being Williams and Williams, *The New Law and Practice in Bankruptcy* (1870), 51.

[524] *Peat v Jones & Co* (1881) 8 QBD 147, 149. See also Brett LJ (at 149–50) (referring to Malins VC in *Booth v Hutchinson* (1872) LR 15 Eq 30, 35 with respect to the addition of 'mutual dealings' to the set-off

The problem comes even more sharply into focus if one considers the cases concerning **6.137** a temporary suspension of mutual credit,[525] such as *Bolland v Nash*.[526] In *Bolland v Nash*, a bill of exchange had been accepted by a creditor of some debtors and, having come into the hands of the debtors, it was indorsed by them before their bankruptcy to a third party. After the debtors' bankruptcy the bill was dishonoured by the creditor and then returned to the bankrupts as indorsers. It was held that the creditor could set off a debt owing to him by the bankrupts against his liability to them on the bill, the important point being that the bankrupts were required to take up the bill again as a result of a prior obligation. Yet at the date of the bankruptcy the bill was held by the third party, and so it is difficult to see how it could be said that a set-off occurred at that date.[527] Consider also the decision of the High Court of Australia in *Hiley v The Peoples Prudential Assurance Co Ltd*.[528] A mortgagee before its liquidation assigned the mortgage to a third party as security for moneys owing. After the liquidation, the mortgage was transferred back to the mortgagee. When the mortgagee's liquidator brought proceedings to enforce the mortgage debt, it was held that the mortgagor could set off a cross-demand that he had against the mortgagee. The justification for the set-off was that the mortgage had been assigned by the mortgagee by way of security, so that the mortgagee had an equity of redemption, and the mortgagee got back the claim by virtue of this right subsisting at the commencement of the winding up. By itself the equity of redemption was not regarded as sufficient to give rise to a set-off, at least to the extent of the amount of the debt in respect of which the mortgage had been assigned by way of security.[529] If the mortgage had not been transferred back, a set-off would not have occurred to the extent of that amount.[530] But, once again, the view that a set-off occurred at the date of the liquidation would not be easy to explain in this context, given that the mortgage at that date was held by a third party.

'Hindsight' has become a fiction

The ordinary meaning of 'hindsight', in terms of seeing what has happened after the **6.138** event,[531] accurately describes the process when a contingent debt owing *by* a bankrupt is valued as at the bankruptcy date for the purpose of proof and set-off. Subsequent events may be looked at, including a subsequent occurrence of the contingency, in order to ascertain what was the true value of the contingent debt as at the date of the bankruptcy. That process does not involve deeming an event to have occurred that did not occur. In *Stein v Blake*, however, the concept of 'hindsight' appears to have taken on a broader meaning, so

---

section); *Sovereign Life Assurance Co v Dodd* [1892] 2 QB 573, 582; *Secretary of State for Trade and Industry v Frid* [2004] 2 AC 506 at [22]; Williams and Williams, *The New Law and Practice in Bankruptcy* (1870), 51.

[525] See para. 6.105 above.
[526] (1828) 8 B & C 105, 108 ER 982.
[527] In *Re Anglo-Greek Steam Navigation and Trading Co* (1869) LR 4 Ch App 174 Selwyn LJ followed *Bolland v Nash* as an alternative ground for his decision. See also *Ex p Banes, re the Royal British Bank* (1857) 28 LTOS 296.
[528] (1938) 60 CLR 468.
[529] Compare *Re Asphaltic Wood Pavement Co. Lee & Chapman's Case* (1885) 30 Ch D 216, explained in *Hiley* (1938) 60 CLR 468, 497–9 (Dixon J). See paras 11.39–11.41 below.
[530] See *Re City Life Assurance Co. Stephenson's Case* [1926] 1 Ch 191, 214, explained in *Hiley* (1938) 60 CLR 468, 501–5 (Dixon J), and see Rich J at 488.
[531] See *The Oxford English Dictionary* (2nd edn, 1989) vol. VII, 244, and para. 6.134 above.

as to assume the characteristics of a fiction.[532] Thus, the House of Lords said in that case that 'due' in the bankruptcy set-off section means: *'treated as having been owing* at the bankruptcy date with the benefit of the hindsight and, if necessary, estimation prescribed by the bankruptcy law.'[533] The Court of Appeal expressed a similar view in *Re Bank of Credit and Commerce International SA (No. 8)*,[534] commenting that 'the hindsight principle enables debts to be treated as owing or not on [the date of bankruptcy] with the benefit of hindsight . . .'. Those statements, on their face, would extend not only to a contingent debt owing by a bankrupt but also to a contingent debt on the other side of the account, being a contingent debt owing *to* a bankrupt, where the contingency occurs after the bankruptcy so as *then* to become due and accordingly susceptible to a set-off.[535] They suggest that the debt nevertheless may be treated as having been due at the earlier bankruptcy date, notwithstanding that the contingency had not then occurred, and notwithstanding the absence of a mechanism for valuing such a debt as at that date for the purpose of the administration of the estate. Further, in order to reconcile cases such as *Bolland v Nash* and *Hiley v Peoples Prudential Assurance* (above) with the views expressed in *Stein v Blake*, presumably it would have to be said that the hindsight principle may extend also to deeming a debt to have been owing to a party at the date of the bankruptcy or liquidation, when in truth at that date it was owing to someone else.

(5) *BCCI v Habib Bank* criticized

6.139 The hindsight principle was applied in a questionable manner in *Bank of Credit and Commerce International (Overseas) Ltd v Habib Bank Ltd*.[536] The liquidator of BCCI had obtained a default judgment against Habib Bank for payment of some debts owing to BCCI. Habib Bank sought to set aside the default judgment on a number of grounds, including that BCCI was indebted to it with the consequence that a set-off was available in the liquidation. The liquidator responded that BCCI's debts to Habib Bank had been assumed by other third party banks after the liquidation, and had been paid by those banks. Applying the automatic theory, however, that should not have affected the position as between BCCI and Habib Bank. When the third party banks assumed the debts a set-off would already have taken place, on the date of the liquidation. The set-off would have extinguished the cross-demands as at that date, so that to that extent BCCI would no longer have been indebted to Habib Bank. Accordingly, nothing would have remained which could have been the subject of a later assumption of liability. Park J nevertheless held that the payments by the third party banks precluded a set-off, on the basis of the hindsight principle.[537] He acknowledged that Lord Hoffmann had referred to the hindsight principle

---

[532] Contrary to the view that has been expressed, that the spirit of the times does not favour the preservation or creation of legal fictions. See Gummow J in *Pyrenees Shire Council v Day* (1998) 192 CLR 330, 387, and again in *Scott v Davis* (2000) 204 CLR 333 at [128].

[533] [1996] AC 243, 256 (emphasis added).

[534] [1996] Ch 245, 269.

[535] See paras 8.35–8.46 below.

[536] [1999] 1 WLR 42, 50–3.

[537] Habib Bank had submitted proofs for the debts said to be owing to it, which the liquidator had rejected. Park J said that Habib Bank should have applied to the court to reverse the liquidator's decision, and its failure to do so precluded it from asserting the debts by way of a set-off. It is suggested, however, that the failure to take that course of action should not have precluded a set-off. See para. 6.166 below.

in *Stein v Blake* in the context of contingent debts, where a debt did not exist at the date of the liquidation but arose subsequently, whereas he said that the situation in *BCCI v Habib Bank* was the converse of that, in that the debts owing to Habib Bank had existed at the commencement of the liquidation but did not exist when it became necessary to ascertain the state of the account. Nevertheless, in his Lordship's opinion the principle must be the same: 'just as the law takes account of the arising of debts in the intervening period, so it must take account of the disappearance of debts in the intervening period.'[538] To illustrate the issue, he referred to a situation in which Habib Bank owed 150 units of value to BCCI at the date of the liquidation, and BCCI owed 100 to Habib Bank. In that context, Park J continued:[539]

> It follows that in my example of cross-debts of 150 and 100, if one of those debts is in some way eliminated after the commencement of the liquidation, the automatic set-off, under rule 4.90, though done at the liquidation date, leaves out of account the debt which is eliminated. So if the debt of 100 which BCCI(O) owed to Habib Bank was paid to Habib Bank in full by a third party . . . the set-off is of 150 owed by Habib Bank to BCCI(O) against nil owed by BCCI(O) to Habib Bank.

The difficulty with this analysis is the notion that the third party banks paid BCCI's debts **6.140** to Habib Bank. In truth they did not, because a set-off had already occurred on the date of the liquidation and set-off is equivalent to payment.[540] BCCI's debts, therefore, had already been extinguished before the third party banks purported to assume liability, and so it could not be said that they had paid the debts. It is true that the Court of Appeal in *Re Bank of Credit and Commerce International SA (No. 8)*[541] canvassed the possibility that, in a three-party situation, discharge by set-off may not be equivalent to discharge by payment. That was in the context of suretyship. The court acknowledged that a payment by the surety to the creditor would discharge the principal debtor, and a set-off under the insolvency set-off section as between the creditor and the surety would discharge the surety. However, their Lordships suggested that a set-off as between the creditor and the surety may not discharge the debtor. As a consequence, it was suggested that the creditor may be able to sue the principal debtor, notwithstanding a set-off as between the creditor and the surety, and if the creditor recovered from the principal debtor it could then be said with hindsight that nothing was owing by the surety to the creditor and, also with hindsight, that there was no set-off as between them. That suggestion is criticized later.[542] But leaving aside that criticism, the Court of Appeal nevertheless accepted that a discharge of the principal debtor by a set-off as between the creditor and the principal debtor is not subject to the same principle.

---

[538] [1999] 1 WLR 42, 52. In Australia, compare *New Cap Reinsurance Corporation v Faraday Underwriting Ltd* (2003) 47 ACSR 306 at [29] where Windeyer J suggested that the hindsight principle is relevant only to the valuation of contingent debts.

[539] [1999] 1 WLR 42, 52.

[540] *Ex p Barnett, re Deveze* (1874) LR 9 Ch App 293, 297; *Inland Revenue Commissioners v John Dow Stuart Ltd* [1950] AC 149, 164; *Re Loteka Pty Ltd* [1990] 1 Qd R 322, 324; *MS Fashions Ltd v Bank of Credit and Commerce International SA* [1993] Ch 425, 439 (Hoffmann LJ), 448 (CA). The House of Lords in *Re Bank of Credit and Commerce International SA (No. 8)* [1998] AC 214, 225 referred in a discussion of set-off to 'payment or deemed payment'. See also *Gye v Davies* (1995) 37 NSWLR 421, 431–2 ('moneys deemed paid by them in consequence of the set-off').

[541] [1996] Ch 245, 265–9 (Rose, Saville and Millett LJJ) (decision affirmed [1998] AC 214 (HL)).

[542] See paras 12.29–12.39 below.

The set-off in that circumstance would discharge the surety.[543] In *BCCI v Habib Bank* Habib Bank was a principal debtor and, even if one were to accept the view floated by the Court of Appeal in *BCCI (No. 8)*, a set-off as between BCCI and Habib Bank should have been equivalent to a discharge by payment as between those parties. The basis upon which the third party banks assumed liability was not made clear in the judgment, but it may have been by way of a novation as opposed to the assumption of a suretyship obligation as such.[544] Nevertheless, the set-off should have been an effective discharge as against them also.

6.141 If then BCCI's debts to Habib Bank had been discharged by a set-off, where did that leave the third party banks? This would depend upon the nature of their obligations, but they may have paid under a mistake. They assumed that they were liable to pay Habib Bank, whereas the debts in question had ceased to exist. Since the payments by the third party banks in truth did not discharge the debts which were owing by BCCI, it is difficult to see how the hindsight principle could have any application in the liquidation of BCCI. Park J expressed a concern that, if a set-off were recognized, Habib Bank in effect would have obtained an undue profit. In the situation posited, the net position of Habib Bank at the date of the liquidation was minus 50, whereas he said that, if a set-off were allowed, Habib Bank's net position would not have been minus 50 but plus 50; it would have received 100 from the third party banks but would have owed only 50 to BCCI. But that ignores the possibility that the third party banks may have been entitled to recover the payments made to Habib Bank as mistaken payments. If that occurred, Habib Bank's net position would have been the same as at the date of the liquidation (i.e. minus 50). The effect of the judgment was that BCCI, which should have borne the burden of any set-off arising in its liquidation, shifted that burden on to the third party banks, by denying them the opportunity of recovering the sums that they had paid to Habib Bank where there was no obligation to do so.

(6) Australia

6.142 The difficulties noted above in relation to the automatic theory would also be relevant to Australia. Indeed, in Australia there is an additional problem. The qualification to the insolvency set-off section[545] is drafted differently to that in England. For example, in the context of company liquidation, s. 553C(2) of the Corporations Act 2001 (Cth) provides:

> A person is not entitled under this section to claim the benefit of a set-off if, at the time of giving credit to the company, or at the time of receiving credit from the company, the person had notice of the fact that the company was insolvent.

This suggests that a set-off is something that is *claimed*, which is inconsistent with the notion of an automatic cancellation. Further, the terms of the qualification seem inapt to deny a set-off in a situation where the creditor had the requisite notice but in the particular case the

---

[543] [1996] Ch 245, 268, referring to *Ex p Hanson* (1806) 12 Ves Jun 346, 33 ER 131.

[544] Thus, reference is made in the judgment ([1999] 1 WLR 42, 50) to Habib Bank itself having assumed liability for the debts of BCCI's Pakistan branch under a statutory scheme and a novation agreement.

[545] See the Bankruptcy Act 1966 (Cth), s. 86(2), and the Corporations Act 2001 (Cth), s. 553C(2). See generally paras 6.66–6.99 above.

set-off is sought, not by the creditor, but by the trustee in bankruptcy or liquidator.[546] Once again, the notion that the occurrence of a set-off may depend upon which party is claiming it seems inconsistent with the automatic theory. Nevertheless, as in England, the automatic theory now appears established in Australia.[547]

Prior to *Stein v Blake*, the High Court of Australia had considered the nature of insolvency set-off in *Gye v McIntyre*[548] in the context of a composition[549] under the Bankruptcy Act 1966 (Cth).[550] In doing so, it made some observations[551] which support the automatic theory. That was so, notwithstanding an earlier decision of the High Court which sits uncomfortably with that theory.[552] The High Court observed in *Gye v McIntyre*:[553] **6.143**

> Section 86[554] is a statutory directive ('shall be set off') which operates as at the time the bankruptcy takes effect. It produces a balance upon the basis of which the bankruptcy administration can proceed. Only that balance can be claimed in the bankruptcy or recovered by the trustee. If its operation is to produce a nil balance, its effect will be that there is nothing at all

---

[546] As in *Re Parker* (1997) 80 FCR 1. See para. 6.90 above.

[547] In addition to the cases referred to below, see *Lord v Direct Acceptance Corporation* (1993) 32 NSWLR 362, 372 (NSW CA); *Gye v Davies* (1995) 37 NSWLR 421, 428 *per* Powell JA ('for the purposes of s. 86 of the [Bankruptcy] Act, the set-off . . . was to be made as at the dates of their respectively entering into a composition with their creditors . . .'); *Barton v Atlantic 3 Financial (Australia) Pty Ltd* (2004) 212 ALR 348 (set-off occurring at the date of the winding-up order not affected by a stay of the winding up); *Mine & Quarry Equipment International Ltd v McIntosh* (2004) 51 ACSR 339 at [9] (appeal dismissed (2005) 54 ACSR 1); *Krishell Pty Ltd v Nilant* (2006) 32 WAR 540 at [72], [111]–[121]; *Pitt-Owen v Lenin* (2006) 24 ACLC 964; *Independent Civil Contractors Pty Ltd v JGE Earthmoving Pty Ltd* [2007] NSWSC 132 at [17]; *JLF Bakeries Pty Ltd v Baker's Delight Holdings Ltd* (2007) 64 ACSR 633 at [17].

[548] (1991) 171 CLR 609.

[549] In the case of a composition an automatic set-off would occur at the date of the composition. See *Gye v Davies* (1995) 37 NSWLR 421, 428.

[550] It has been said that the word 'creditor' is used in various senses throughout the Bankruptcy Act, and that it takes its colour from the particular context. See *Staples v Milner* (1998) 83 FCR 203, 209, referring to *Pyramid Building Society v Terry* (1997) 189 CLR 176, 192. But certainly where a bankrupt submits a proposal for a composition to his or her creditors under the Bankruptcy Act, it has been held that a determination by the trustee under s. 64ZA as to whether a person is a creditor so as to be entitled to vote is to be made after considering any set-off under s. 86. In making that determination it is the trustee's duty to make a judgment about the prospects of a cross-claim. See *Re Dingle; Westpac Banking Corporation v Worrell* (1993) 47 FCR 478.

[551] The High Court's observations as to the automatic nature of insolvency set-off have been said to be part of the ratio decidendi. See *G. M. & A. M. Pearce and Co Pty Ltd v RGM Australia Pty Ltd* [1998] 4 VR 888, 896. At least in relation to the composition of Mr Perkes this would appear to be correct, since the application to the Federal Court for a declaration in relation to the set-off was made after the trustee issued his certificate that Mr Perkes had carried out the terms of his composition (see the dates set out in the judgment of Gummow and von Doussa JJ in the Federal Court in *McIntyre v Perkes* (1990) 22 FCR 260, 265–6), and there was no procedural step before then which would have brought about a set-off.

[552] *Hiley v The Peoples Prudential Assurance Co Ltd* (1938) 60 CLR 468. See para. 6.137 above.

[553] (1991) 171 CLR 609, 622. See also *Lord v Direct Acceptance Corporation Ltd* (1993) 32 NSWLR 362, 372 (NSW Court of Appeal); *Citicorp Australia Ltd v Official Trustee* (1996) 71 FCR 550, 567; *G. M. & A. M. Pearce and Co Pty Ltd v RGM Australia Pty Ltd* [1998] 4 VR 888 (deed of company arrangement); *Wily v Rothschild Australia Ltd* (1999) 47 NSWLR 555, 565–6. Compare Gummow and von Doussa JJ in the Federal Court in *McIntyre v Perkes* (1990) 22 FCR 260, 270. Compare also *Day v Dent Constructions Pty Ltd v North Australian Properties Pty Ltd* (1982) 150 CLR 85, 109, in which Murphy J appeared to distinguish between the date of the winding up and the time when the account was taken. Similarly, some comments by Mason J in that case (at 107) appear to support the procedural view, but it is suggested that little weight should now be attached to those comments in this context given that his Honour, as Chief Justice, was a member of the High Court in *Gye v McIntyre*.

[554] The Bankruptcy Act 1966 (Cth), s. 86 is the set-off section applicable to bankruptcies in Australia.

which can be claimed in the bankruptcy or recovered in proceedings by the trustee. The section is self-executing in the sense that its operation is automatic and not dependent upon 'the option of either party' . . .

6.144 Subsequently, Drummond J, in *Re Capel; Ex p Marac Finance Australia Ltd v Capel*,[555] suggested an interpretation of that passage which constitutes a half-way position between the procedural view and the automatic extinguishment theory later favoured by the House of Lords in *Stein v Blake*. *Re Capel* concerned an assignment of a claim by a trustee in bankruptcy back to the bankrupt in circumstances where the debtor on the claim had a provable debt against the bankrupt which had not been proved, and where an account otherwise had not been taken in the bankruptcy. Drummond J followed the analysis of the Court of Appeal in *Stein v Blake*,[556] his judgment being delivered after that of the Court of Appeal and before the subsequent appeal to the House of Lords in *Stein v Blake*, and held that the insolvency set-off section did not prevent the assignment. In relation to *Gye v McIntyre*, he expressed the view that the High Court in that case was not saying that the insolvency set-off section operates automatically at the date of the bankruptcy or liquidation to extinguish the cross-demands. Rather, all that the High Court meant was that 'the account, whenever taken, is to be taken by reference to the position obtaining at that date', and that, independently of whether an account has ever been taken, the rights of the parties to the cross-claims:

> are to be taken to be the right to recover or to prove for the balance (if any) that would exist if the two claims were set-off against each other at the date of the sequestration order. That is not at all the same as saying that the various claims are extinguished by the operation of the section on the day the sequestration order is made.[557]

However, this does not seem to be what the High Court meant. In *Citicorp Australia Ltd v Official Trustee in Bankruptcy*,[558] the Full Court of the Federal Court[559] said of the decision of the House of Lords in *Stein v Blake* that it applied the reasoning of the High Court in *Gye v McIntyre*, and that the reasoning of the House of Lords should be followed. Similarly, the Victorian Court of Appeal in *G. M. & A. M. Pearce and Co Pty Ltd v RGM Australia Pty Ltd*,[560] in applying *Gye v McIntyre*, accepted the automatic nature of insolvency set-off in the context of a deed of company arrangement,[561] so that it was immaterial to the question

---

[555] (1994) 48 FCR 195. See also *Re Turner, Ex p Mulley* (Federal Court of Australia, Northrop J, 22 June 1995, BC9507910).
[556] [1994] Ch 16. See para. 6.122 above.
[557] (1994) 48 FCR 195, 206–7.
[558] (1996) 71 FCR 550, 567.
[559] Foster, von Doussa and Sundberg JJ.
[560] [1998] 4 VR 888.
[561] See also *Metal Manufacturers Ltd v Hall* (2002) 41 ACSR 466; *Handberg v Smarter Way (Aust) Pty Ltd* (2002) 190 ALR 130; *Arcfab Pty Ltd v Boral Ltd* (2002) 43 ACSR 573; *Brodyn Pty Ltd v Dasein Constructions Pty Ltd* [2004] NSWSC 1230 at [93] and [98]; *Reed Constructions Australia Ltd v DM Fabrications Pty Ltd* (2007) 25 ACLC 1463 at [35]–[38]; *Ansett Australia Ltd v Travel Software Solutions Pty Ltd* (2007) 65 ACSR 47 at [63]. The deed of company arrangement in the *Pearce* case did not exclude the prescribed provisions in Sch. 8A of the Corporations Regulations, including cl. 8 which incorporated the insolvency set-off section in s. 553C of the Corporations Law (now the Corporations Act 2001 (Cth)), and so the set-off section was incorporated into the deed. See the Corporations Act 2001 (Cth), s. 444A(5), and para. 6.12 above.

of set-off in that case that the creditor had failed to make a claim under the deed before it terminated.[562]

One of the decisions considered by Drummond J in *Re Capel* was *Martin v Lewis*.[563] A debt **6.145** which was owing to a bankrupt, and which had vested in the trustee in bankruptcy, was assigned back to the bankrupt after he had obtained his discharge.[564] The debtor had a cross-claim against the bankrupt, but a proof of debt had not been lodged in the bankruptcy, and neither had an account otherwise been taken in the bankruptcy. The effect of a discharge from bankruptcy is to release the bankrupt from all bankruptcy debts.[565] Notwithstanding that an account had not been taken in the bankruptcy, the Queensland Supreme Court[566] held that the assignee took subject to a set-off in respect of the cross-claim. While the circumstances in issue in *Re Capel* were similar, the cases differed. Whereas in *Martin v Lewis* the assignment occurred after the bankrupt's discharge from bankruptcy, in *Re Capel* it occurred before discharge, although the question of the efficacy of the assignment did not arise until later. Drummond J doubted the correctness of *Martin v Lewis*. Since the cause of action in that case was assigned after the bankrupt's discharge, he found it difficult to see how the creditor could retain the right to set off the amount owing to him when the bankrupt had been released from liability.[567] In *Re Capel*, on the other hand, where the assignment occurred before the discharge, Drummond J accepted that the creditor could still assert a set-off against the assignee notwithstanding the later discharge, on the basis that the assignee took subject to the prior equity constituted by the right of set-off otherwise available to the debtor in the bankruptcy.[568] He considered that the essence of the equity to which the assignee took subject was that the account, whenever it was taken, was to be taken by reference to the position obtaining at the date of the bankruptcy, and that this also applied when the account was taken outside the bankruptcy administration in the context of a claim by the assignee.[569] Because the assignment occurred before the discharge, the debt when assigned had the equity 'attached'[570] to it, and in a later accounting

---

In *Metal Manufacturers Ltd v Hall* (above) Sch. 8A was excluded but it was accepted that s. 553C was otherwise incorporated into the deed.

[562] Compare the *ex tempore* judgment of Young J in the New South Wales Supreme Court in *Winterton Constructions Pty Ltd v M A Coleman Joinery Co Pty Ltd* (1996) 20 ACSR 671, 674–7, in which it seems to have been assumed that set-off pursuant to the deed was procedural. After termination of the deed, any surplus in favour of the company after the set-off may be recovered by the company notwithstanding that any net claim against the company would have been extinguished by the deed. See *Arcfab Pty Ltd v Boral Ltd* (2002) 43 ACSR 573.

[563] Full Court of the Queensland Supreme Court, 7 June 1985.

[564] This was possible because the right of action remained vested in the trustee notwithstanding the discharge. See *Piwinski v Corporate Trustees of the Diocese of Armidale* [1977] 1 NSWLR 266.

[565] See the Insolvency Act 1986, s. 281 and, in Australia, the Bankruptcy Act 1966 (Cth), s. 153. In *Law Society v Shah* [2009] Ch 223 at [31]–[38] Floyd J considered that s. 281 of the English Act extinguishes only the remedy of enforcement as against the bankrupt and that the underlying cause of action remains, but see paras 14.20–14.22 below.

[566] Andrews ACJ, Kelly and Shepherdson JJ.

[567] See the discussion at (1994) 48 FCR 195, 205.

[568] This may have been what French J had in mind in *Re Nguyen* (1992) 35 FCR 320, 327. In *Stein v Blake* [1996] AC 243, 255–6 the House of Lords rejected the application of the 'taking subject to equities' doctrine in this context. See also *Citicorp Australia Ltd v Official Trustee in Bankruptcy* (1996) 71 FCR 550, 567.

[569] See the discussion at (1994) 48 FCR 195, 206–7.

[570] (1994) 48 FCR 195, 203.

reference would have to be made to the position at the time of the bankruptcy when the bankrupt was still liable to the creditor.

6.146   Subsequently, Northrop J, in *Re Turner, ex p Mulley*,[571] expressed approval of Drummond J's analysis in *Re Capel*. Nevertheless, given the later acceptance of the automatic theory of insolvency set-off,[572] it is unlikely that Drummond J's analysis would now be adopted. *Martin v Lewis* is consistent with the automatic theory and its application in *Stein v Blake*,[573] and it should be followed.

O. Foreign Currencies

6.147   Consider that one or both of the cross-demands between an insolvent and a creditor is in a foreign currency.[574]

(1) Proof of debts

6.148   For the purpose of proving a debt in a bankruptcy, the Insolvency Rules provide that a foreign currency claim is to be converted into sterling at the official exchange rate[575] prevailing at the date of the bankruptcy order.[576] In company liquidation, conversion takes place by reference to the official exchange rate prevailing at the date when the company went into liquidation or, if the liquidation was immediately preceded by an administration, on the date that the company entered administration.[577] In the case of a company which is in administration, where the administrator, being authorized to make a distribution, has given notice pursuant to r. 2.95 that he proposes to make it,[578] foreign currency claims are converted into sterling for the purpose of proof at the official exchange rate prevailing on

---

[571]   Federal Court of Australia, 22 June 1995, BC9507910.

[572]   See para. 6.144 above. See also the New South Wales Court of Appeal in *Lord v Direct Acceptance Corporation* (1993) 32 NSWLR 362, 372.

[573]   [1996] AC 243. See para. 6.122 above. See also *Citicorp Australia Ltd v Official Trustee in Bankruptcy* (1996) 71 FCR 550, 567; *Barton v Atlantic 3 Financial (Australia) Pty Ltd* (2004) 212 ALR 348 (stay of the winding up held not to affect the set-off); *Krishell Pty Ltd v Nilant* (2006) 32 WAR 540 at [45], [111]–[121]; *Pitt-Owen v Lenin* (2006) 24 ACLC 964; *Equititrust Ltd v Franks* (2009) 258 ALR 388 at [79]–[80] (assignment after a deed of company arrangement which incorporated the insolvency set-off section).

[574]   The following discussion assumes that the obligation in question is a money obligation. See paras 9.11–9.20 below.

[575]   Defined in r. 6.111(2).

[576]   Insolvency Rules 1986, r. 6.111. For the position prior to the Insolvency Rules, see *Re Dynamics Corporation of America* [1976] 1 WLR 757; *Re Lines Bros Ltd* [1983] 1 Ch 1; *Re Amalgamated Investment and Property Co Ltd* [1985] 1 Ch 349, 364. In Australia see *Re Griffiths* (2004) 139 FCR 185 (*prima facie* rule). Compare *Re Pearce* (1933) 6 ABC 126 (conversion at the date when the debt became payable), which was decided before *Miliangos v George Frank (Textiles) Ltd* [1976] AC 443 (discussed below).

[577]   Insolvency Rules 1986, r. 4.91. The reference to administration applies to companies that entered administration or went into liquidation on or after 1 April 2005. See the Insolvency (Amendment) Rules 2005, r. 3 (S.I. 2005 No. 527). A company goes into liquidation if it passes a resolution for voluntary winding up, or an order for its winding up is made by the court at a time when it has not already gone into liquidation by passing such a resolution. See the Insolvency Act 1986, s. 247(2). In relation to company liquidation in Australia, see the Corporations Act 2001 (Cth), s. 554C.

[578]   See paras 6.10 and 6.11 above.

the date when the company entered administration or, if the administration was immediately preceded by a winding up, on the date that the company went into liquidation.[579]

The conversion takes place by reference to the date of the bankruptcy or liquidation, or the date when the company went into administration, as opposed to the date of payment of the dividend. This is consistent with the principle that has been said to govern the valuation of contingent debts for the purpose of proof. The general principle is that the claims of creditors are valued as at the date of the bankruptcy or the winding up.[580] Admittedly later events may be looked at, but only in the sense that they may provide evidence of the true value that the debt in fact had at the relevant date. In the case of a foreign currency claim, however, there is no need to look at later events. The exchange rate current at the commencement of the bankruptcy or the liquidation provides a clear measure for ascertaining its value as at that date.[581] Conversion at the date of the bankruptcy or the liquidation is also consistent with the decision of the House of Lords in *Miliangos v George Frank (Textiles) Ltd*,[582] that in an action to enforce a foreign currency debt an English court can give judgment expressed in the foreign currency, with the debt being converted into sterling for the purpose of enforcement of the judgment at the exchange rate prevailing on the date that the claimant is given leave to enforce. Since bankruptcy and company liquidation provide a process of collective enforcement, the Court of Appeal, in *Re Lines Bros Ltd*,[583] considered that it is in accordance with the *Miliangos* case to convert currencies for the purpose of proof by reference to the rate prevailing at the commencement of that process.[584]

6.149

(2) Set-off

The preceding discussion set out the position with respect to proof of debts. In relation to set-off in bankruptcy, the House of Lords, in *Stein v Blake*[585] held that the set-off occurs automatically upon the occurrence of the bankruptcy.[586] The discharge of the cross-demands by way of a set-off does not depend upon the procedural step of taking an account. The conversion of a foreign currency claim on either side of the account, therefore, should take place by reference to the date of the bankruptcy,[587] since according to the automatic theory that date is the date of payment. This accords with the date upon which foreign

6.150

---

[579] Insolvency Rules 1986, r. 2.86.

[580] *Wight v Eckhardt Marine GmbH* [2004] 1 AC 147 at [23]. See also the cases referred to in *Re Lines Bros Ltd* [1983] 1 Ch 1, 17–19.

[581] *Re Dynamics Corporation of America* [1976] 1 WLR 757, 767–8. See also *Re Lines Bros Ltd* [1983] 1 Ch 1, 19–20.

[582] [1976] AC 443.

[583] [1983] 1 Ch 1 (in particular, see Lawton LJ at 12–13 and Brightman LJ at 20).

[584] In *Miliangos* [1976] AC 443, 498, Lord Wilberforce and Lord Cross of Chelsea suggested that, in the case of a liquidation, conversion should take place at the date when the creditor's claim is admitted by the liquidator. The statements in question, however, were *obiter*, and the Court of Appeal in *Re Lines Bros* said that the date of the liquidation in fact is more in accordance with the principle actually applied by the House of Lords in *Miliangos*. The approach adopted in *Re Lines Bros* was referred to with evident approval in *Wight v Eckhardt Marine GmbH* [2004] 1 AC 147 at [23] and [24].

[585] [1996] AC 243.

[586] See paras 6.119–6.146 above.

[587] *Stein v Blake* [1996] AC 243, 252.

currency claims are to be converted into sterling for the purpose of proof.[588] A similar approach should apply in bankruptcy in Australia, with the consequence that foreign currency conversions on both sides of the account for the purpose of set-off should occur by reference to the exchange rates prevailing on the date of the bankruptcy,[589] being also the date of set-off.

6.151   In company liquidation in Australia, conversion for the purpose of proof takes place by reference to the 'relevant date',[590] which term is defined in s. 9 in terms of Div. 1A of Part 5.6 of the Corporations Act. The 'relevant date' determines generally what debts are provable in a liquidation,[591] and there is also authority which suggests that it is the date when a set-off would be regarded as having occurred in accordance with the automatic theory.[592] On that basis, currency conversions for both sides of the account should take place by reference to that date.

6.152   The position is more complicated under the English legislation in relation to a company in liquidation and where the question of set-off arises in an administration pursuant to r. 2.85.[593]

6.153   In company liquidation, set-offs occur automatically on the date of the liquidation,[594] but this does not precisely reflect the date for conversion of foreign currency claims for the purpose of a set-off. Rule 4.91 provides that, for the purpose of proving a debt incurred or payable in a currency other than sterling, the amount of the debt is to be converted into sterling at the official exchange rate prevailing on the date when the company went into liquidation, or if the liquidation was immediately preceded by an administration, on the date that the company entered administration. Moreover, r. 4.90(6) has the effect of importing the same principle for the purpose of set-off in relation to a foreign currency claim on the other side of the account, being a foreign currency claim owed to the company. The dates for the occurrence of a set-off and for converting foreign currency claims for the purpose of the set-off coincide when the liquidation was not immediately preceded by an administration. But when the liquidation was immediately preceded by an administration, currency conversions for claims on both sides of the account occur by reference to the exchange rates prevailing on a date which differs from the date of the set-off, being the date on which the company entered administration rather than the date of the liquidation.

6.154   A similar point may be made in relation to a set-off pursuant to r. 2.85 when a company has entered administration. In that situation, it would appear that set-offs occur on the date that the administrator gave notice under r. 2.95 that he or she proposed to make a distribution to creditors.[595] On the other hand, for the purpose of proving a foreign currency debt in the administration, r. 2.86 requires that the debt be converted into sterling at the prevailing

---

[588] Insolvency Rules 1986, r. 4.91 (company liquidation) and r. 6.111 (bankruptcy). See para. 6.148 above.
[589] See para. 6.51 above.
[590] Corporations Act 2001 (Cth), s. 554C.
[591] Corporations Act 2001 (Cth), s. 553, but see ss. 553(1A), 553(1B) and 553(2).
[592] See paras 6.52–6.62 above.
[593] See para. 6.10 above.
[594] See para. 6.123 above.
[595] See the Insolvency Rules 1986, r. 2.85(3) and para. 6.124 above.

official exchange rate on the date that the company entered administration or, if the administration was immediately preceded by a winding up, on the date that the company went into liquidation. Pursuant to r. 2.85(6), the same principle applies, for the purpose of a set-off, to any foreign currency claim on the other side of the account.[596] Once again, the dates for the occurrence of a set-off and for converting foreign currency debts for the purpose of the set-off appear to differ.

(3) Insolvent's foreign currency cross-claim exceeds the creditor's provable debt

If a foreign currency cross-claim possessed by a bankrupt or by a company in liquidation **6.155** or administration overtops the creditor's provable debt, the remainder of the cross-claim not extinguished by the set-off may be converted at a different rate to that applied for the set-off. The trustee in bankruptcy, or the company through its liquidator or administrator, may sue for payment of the surplus, and once judgment is obtained against the creditor the currency conversion should take place in accordance with the *Miliangos* case at the exchange rate applicable when leave to enforce is given.

P. Interest

When an insolvency occurs, and there are cross-demands the subject of a set-off under the **6.156** insolvency set-off section, interest (to the extent that it would otherwise accrue for the purpose of the insolvency[597]) could hardly accrue on a claim on either side of the account after, and to the extent that, the claim has been extinguished in a set-off. The date of the set-off, therefore, should be the latest possible date for the accrual of interest on cross-claims the subject of a set-off.

For the purpose of proof debts in a bankruptcy, interest ceases to accrue at the commence- **6.157** ment of the bankruptcy.[598] This is also the date for the occurrence of automatic set-offs in a bankruptcy,[599] and that date should also apply in relation to an interest bearing claim on the other side of the account to the extent that it has been extinguished in a set-off.

In company liquidation, r. 4.93 deals with interest on provable debts, both in relation to **6.158** when interest can be claimed and, in some situations, the rate of interest. It provides for interest in some circumstances where it was not previously reserved or agreed.[600] Under the rule, when liquidation was not immediately preceded by an administration, interest (when available) may accrue on a debt for the purpose of proof until the time when the company

---

[596] Thus, the same valuation principle applies on both sides of the account. See *Re Kaupthing Singer & Friedlander Ltd* [2009] EWHC 2308 (Ch) at [20].

[597] For bankruptcy, see the Insolvency Rules 1986, r. 6.113, for company liquidation see r. 4.93 and for administration see r. 2.88.

[598] Insolvency Act 1986, s. 322(2) and the Insolvency Rules 1986, r. 6.113. A bankruptcy commences on the date of the order. See s. 278.

[599] See paras 6.119–6.122 above. In *Ex p Prescot* (1753) 1 Atk 230, 26 ER 147 interest appears to have been allowed on the bankrupt's claim the subject of a set-off for the period between the bankruptcy and the taking of the account, but that could no longer stand following the decision of the House of Lords in *Stein v Blake* [1996] AC 243 that the set-off takes effect automatically upon the occurrence of the bankruptcy.

[600] Rule 4.93(2).

went into liquidation. In relation to the claim on the other side of the account, r. 4.90(6) provides that r. 4.93 applies for the purpose of a set-off under r. 4.90 'in relation to any sums due to the company which . . . bear interest'. This suggests that those sums must be interest bearing in their own right, that is, apart from the operation of r. 4.93. In any event, r. 4.90(6) has the effect that interest on sums due to the company similarly accrues until the date of the liquidation, which accords with the date upon which set-offs automatically occur in a liquidation.[601] The position differs, however, when a liquidation was immediately preceded by an administration.[602] Set-offs would still occur at the date of the liquidation. However, r. 4.93 provides that interest does not accrue for the period after the company went into administration, and because of r. 4.90(6) this date should also apply in relation to interest on sums due to the company.

6.159   The date of the occurrence of set-offs and the date for the accrual of interest do not coincide for the purpose of set-off in company administration under r. 2.85, that is, when the administrator, being authorized to make a distribution to creditors, has given notice that he or she proposes to make it. In such a case, it would appear that set-offs occur on the date of the notice.[603] On the other hand, r. 2.88, which is in similar terms to r. 4.93, provides for the accrual of interest for the purpose of proof up to the date when the company entered administration (or, if administration was immediately preceded by a winding up, up to the date when the company went into liquidation),[604] and because of r. 2.85(6), which is in similar terms to r. 4.90(6) (above), that date also applies for the purpose of set-off to interest on sums due to the company.[605] After the occurrence of the set-off, interest should continue to accrue on any balance due to the company in accordance with the terms of the contract, including for the period between the date that the company entered administration and the date of the notice.[606] The position in liquidation should be similar in that regard.

6.160   Rule 2.88 has additional provisions dealing with the situation where there are surplus assets after paying debts proved in the administration.[607] It provides (in para. (7)) that any such surplus is to be applied in paying interest on those claims in respect of the periods during which they have been outstanding since the company entered administration (or, if the administration was immediately preceded by a winding up, the date on which the company went into liquidation). In the event of a set-off, the set-off would not occur until the date of the notice under r. 2.95. Until that date, the company's debt the subject of the set-off would have retained its identity as a debt owing by the company and in that sense it

---

[601] See para. 6.123 above.

[602] See the definition of 'the relevant date' in r. 4.93(A1).

[603] See r. 2.85(3), and para. 6.124 above.

[604] See the definition of 'the relevant date' in r. 2.88(A1).

[605] *Re Kaupthing Singer & Friedlander Ltd* [2009] EWHC 2308 (Ch) at [24], referred to on appeal [2010] EWCA Civ 518 at [14].

[606] *Re Kaupthing Singer & Friedlander Ltd* [2009] EWHC 2308 (Ch) at [28], referred to on appeal [2010] EWCA Civ 518 at [15]–[16]. As Norris J observed, the creditor would have to be credited with any interest that he or she paid after the date that the company entered administration on so much of the debt due to the company as was extinguished in the set-off.

[607] In relation to company liquidation, see the Insolvency Act 1986, s. 189.

would have remained outstanding. Therefore, if there is a surplus, the creditor arguably would have a claim to payment of interest on the debt from the surplus for the period between the date that the company entered administration and the date of the notice. The point has yet to be determined, however.

In bankruptcy in Australia, interest for the purpose of set-off should cease to run on claims **6.161** on both sides of the account at the date of the bankruptcy, this being the date for determining what claims can included in a set-off[608] and also the date of the occurrence of the set-off.[609] In company liquidation, the corresponding date would appear to be the 'relevant date',[610] which is defined in the Corporations Act 2001 (Cth), s. 9 as the day on which the winding up is taken because of Div. 1A of Part 5.6 of the Act to have begun. This accords with s. 554, which provides that the amount of a debt or claim of a company, including a debt or claim that includes interest, is to be computed for the purposes of the winding up as at the relevant date.[611]

Q. Set-off as a Void Disposition of Property

The Insolvency Act 1986, s. 127 provides that a disposition of a company's property after **6.162** the commencement of a court-ordered winding up is void unless the court otherwise orders. In *Barclays Bank Ltd v TOSG Trust Fund Ltd*,[612] Nourse J said that, where there is a conflict between the then equivalent of s. 127[613] and the insolvency set-off section, s. 127, must prevail. That view cannot be supported. Section 127 refers to a disposition after the commencement of the winding up, which in a winding up by the court which is not preceded by a resolution for a winding up is the time of the presentation of the petition.[614] But it would always be the case in that situation that a set-off would occur later, when the order is made for a winding up.[615] An automatic set-off under the insolvency set-off section is not readily susceptible to characterization as a disposition of property.[616] But even if it were, in order for the set-off section to operate effectively in a compulsory winding up it must prevail over s. 127.

---

[608] See para. 6.51 above.
[609] See paras 6.119–6.122 above.
[610] However, there are difficulties in using that date in relation to set-off. See paras 6.52–6.62 above.
[611] Interest may be paid in respect of the period after the relevant date but only after all other debts and claims in the winding up have been satisfied (other than debts owed to members of the company as members of the company). See s. 563B.
[612] [1984] BCLC 1, 25–6.
[613] Companies Act 1948, s. 227.
[614] Insolvency Act 1986, s. 129(2).
[615] See para. 6.47 above, and para. 6.123 above in relation to the automatic nature of insolvency set-off.
[616] In the context of a contractual right of set-off, Otton J in *Re K (Restraint Order)* [1990] 2 QB 298, 305 considered that the exercise of the right was not a 'disposing of' assets for the purpose of the Drug Trafficking Offences Act 1986, and see also *Re Loteka Pty Ltd* [1990] 1 Qd R 322, 324. But there is authority which suggests otherwise. See *Couve v J Pierre Couve Ltd* (1933) 49 CLR 486, 494, and also Goode, *Principles of Corporate Insolvency Law* (3rd edn, 2005), 494.

R. Mistake as to Set-off

(1) Payment to the insolvent's estate without asserting a set-off

6.163 It may be that a person possessed of a cross-claim against a bankrupt paid a sum of money to the trustee in bankruptcy in satisfaction of a liability owing to the bankrupt, in the mistaken belief that a set-off was not available.[617] Ordinarily the payment should be recoverable, whether the mistake was one of fact or of law.[618] In the case of bankruptcy, the assets of the bankrupt vest in the trustee for division amongst the bankrupt's creditors.[619] Unlike the bankrupt, the trustee is not insolvent, and so the mistaken payment should be recoverable in full from the trustee in an action for money had and received.[620] On the other hand, the assets of a company in liquidation ordinarily do not pass to the liquidator[621] who, it has been said, is principally and really an agent of the company who occupies a position which is fiduciary in some respects, and is bound by the statutory duties imposed on him by the insolvency legislation.[622] The money will have vested instead in the insolvent company. In order to recover it in full from the insolvent company, the payer's right to it ordinarily should be proprietary in nature. In *Chase Manhattan Bank NA v Israel-British Bank (London) Ltd*,[623] Goulding J held that: 'a person who pays money to another under a factual mistake retains an equitable property in it and the conscience of that other is subjected to a fiduciary duty to respect his proprietary right.' Subsequently, Lord Browne-Wilkinson in *Westdeutsche Landesbank Girozentrale v Islington LBC*[624] doubted the breadth of that proposition. He considered that a trust could only arise after the recipient became aware of the mistake, because it would only be at that time that the recipient's conscience would be affected. If in the circumstances there is a subsisting trust, the mistaken payment should be recoverable *in toto*. In *Re Cushla Ltd*,[625] a payment was made to a company in liquidation in circumstances where the payer did not realize that it had a right of set-off. Vinelott J held that the payer was entitled to recover the money and that a set-off should proceed, although the question of a trust was not considered.

---

[617] In relation to the rule in *Cherry v Boultbee* (1839) 4 My & Cr 442, 41 ER 171, see para. 14.96 below.

[618] The principle formerly applied, that a payment made under a mistake of law is not recoverable, no longer represents the law. See *Kleinwort Benson Ltd v Lincoln City Council* [1999] 2 AC 349. In Australia, see *David Securities Pty Ltd v Commonwealth Bank of Australia* (1992) 175 CLR 353.

[619] See the Insolvency Act 1986, s. 306, and in Australia the Bankruptcy Act 1966 (Cth), s. 58.

[620] As in *Bize v Dickason* (1786) 1 TR 285, 99 ER 1097. See also *Edmeads v Newman* (1823) 1 B & C 418, 107 ER 155; *Booth v Hutchinson* (1872) LR 15 Eq 30.

[621] Note, however, the Insolvency Act 1986, s. 145, and in Australia the Corporations Act 2001 (Cth), s. 474(2), each of which enables the court, on the application of the liquidator, to direct that the property of the company is to vest in the liquidator.

[622] *Thomas Franklin & Sons Ltd v Cameron* (1935) 36 SR (NSW) 286, 296 (Davidson J, NSW SC); *Re Timberland Ltd* (1979) 4 ACLR 259, 285 (Marks J, Vic SC). See also *Ayerst v C & K (Constructions) Ltd* [1976] AC 167, 176–7.

[623] [1981] 1 Ch 105, 119. The *Chase Manhattan* case has been both criticised and applauded. Compare Tettenborn, 'Remedies for the recovery of money paid by mistake' [1980] CLJ 272 with Jones, 'Comment' [1980] CLJ 275.

[624] [1996] AC 669, 714–15. Compare Millett, 'Restitution and constructive trusts' (1998) 114 LQR 399, 412–13.

[625] [1979] 3 All ER 415.

But even if there is no trust, the rule in *Ex p James*[626] may provide relief. The essence of **6.164**
that rule is that trustees in bankruptcy are officers of the court, and as such may be ordered
by the court not to rely on their strict legal rights when to do so would be regarded as
dishonourable. It allows recovery of payments made under a mistake of fact or of law,[627]
including the law of set-off.[628] A liquidator in a compulsory winding up is an officer of the
court,[629] and on two occasions[630] recourse has been had to the rule as a means of ordering
the return of a sum of money mistakenly paid to a liquidator in a compulsory winding up
in satisfaction of a liability to the company. As a result, a set-off based upon that liability
could proceed against an independent indebtedness of the company to the payer. A liquidator in a voluntary winding up, however, is not an officer of the court, and it has been held
that the *Ex p James* principle accordingly does not apply in that context.[631]

(2) Creditor proves without asserting a set-off

Another possibility is that a creditor, in ignorance of the availability of a set-off, lodges a **6.165**
proof in the debtor's bankruptcy in respect of the debt. On its own this should not preclude
the creditor from subsequently asserting a set-off. The proof can be amended to reflect the
set-off.[632] But what if the creditor, before asserting the set-off, is paid a dividend? It may be
said in such a case that the debt has been paid, so that there is nothing 'due' to the creditor
within the meaning of the set-off section, and that therefore the creditor has lost the right
of set-off. There is some support for that view in the judgment of Knight Bruce VC in *Ex p
Staddon, re Wise*.[633] In that case the Vice Chancellor, in allowing a set-off, said that he
would disregard a proof of debt made by the creditor since the creditor had not received a
dividend or obtained any benefit from the proof. However, under the automatic theory of
insolvency set-off approved by the House of Lords in *Stein v Blake*,[634] the analysis now
would be that a set-off took place automatically at the date of the bankruptcy, in which case
the subsequent receipt of a dividend should not affect the position. Consistent with that
view, Hoffmann LJ (as he then was) in *MS Fashions v Bank of Credit and Commerce
International SA*[635] suggested that the receipt of a dividend would not preclude the creditor

---

[626] *Ex p James, re Condon* (1874) LR 9 Ch App 609.
[627] *Re Tyler, ex p The Official Receiver* [1907] 1 KB 865; *R v Tower Hamlets LBC* [1988] AC 858, 874–6.
[628] See *Re Paddington Town Hall Centre Ltd* (1979) 41 FLR 239.
[629] See e.g. *Re Associated Dominions Assurance Society Pty Ltd* (1962) 109 CLR 516.
[630] *Re Cushla Ltd* [1979] 3 All ER 415; *Re Paddington Town Hall Centre Ltd* (1979) 41 FLR 239.
[631] *Re David A Hamilton and Co Ltd* [1928] NZLR 419; *Re T H Knitwear (Wholesale) Ltd* [1988] Ch 275
(overruling *Re Temple Fire and Accident Assurance Co*, noted at (1910) 129 LT Jo 115). See also *Clutha Ltd
v Millar (No. 5)* (2002) 43 ACSR 295; *Shannon v JMA Accounting* [2005] QSC 240 at [20]. On the other
hand, in *Re Autolook Pty Ltd* (1983) 8 ACLR 419, 421 Needham J in the New South Wales Supreme Court
considered that the rule in *Ex p James* applies to any liquidator, whether an officer of the court or not, and in
Downs Distributing Co Pty Ltd v Associated Blue Star Stores Pty Ltd (1948) 76 CLR 463 the Australian High
Court considered the rule in the context of a voluntary liquidation but held that it did not apply for other
reasons.
[632] *Re Parker* (1997) 80 FCR 1, 9; *Mine & Quarry Equipment International Ltd v McIntosh* (2005)
54 ACSR 1.
[633] (1843) 3 Mont D & De G 256, 12 LJ Bcy 39.
[634] [1996] AC 243. See paras 6.119–6.146 above.
[635] [1993] Ch 425, 435.

from relying on the full claim as a set-off, although credit would have to be given for the dividend received.[636]

(3) Rejection of the creditor's proof

6.166   Alternatively, the creditor may have lodged a proof of debt but the proof was rejected by the trustee in bankruptcy or liquidator. Can the creditor then assert a set-off based upon the debt? The issue arose in *Bank of Credit and Commerce International (Overseas) Ltd v Habib Bank Ltd*.[637] Habib Bank had lodged a proof of debt in the liquidation of BCCI. The liquidator rejected the proof, on the ground that the debt had been paid by a third party after the winding up commenced. BCCI's liquidator later sued Habib Bank for payment of a debt owing by Habib Bank to BCCI, and obtained default judgment. Habib Bank then sought to set aside the judgment, *inter alia* on the ground that it had a set-off based on the debt the subject of the rejected proof. Park J held that, because of the rejection of the proof, and Habib Bank's failure to apply to the court for the liquidator's decision to be reversed,[638] Habib Bank was precluded from relying on the debt as a set-off. He said that, if a person who claims to be a creditor has his or her proof rejected but does not exercise the right to apply to the court, he or she could not have a second bite at the cherry by submitting a second proof in respect of the same debt, and equally the person should not be permitted to have a second attempt at recovery of the alleged debt by way of a set-off.[639] This reasoning should not be followed. A set-off would have had the effect that the debt allegedly owing to Habib Bank had been extinguished automatically to the extent of the set-off at the date of the liquidation.[640] If that was case, it could not thereafter have been the subject of a proof, in which case one may ask why Habib Bank should have been prejudiced by its failure to apply to the court to have the liquidator's rejection of the proof reversed. The assertion of a set-off would not have provided a ground for reversing the decision to reject the proof; on the contrary, it was entirely consistent with that rejection.[641] The decision is open to objection on another ground. The proof was rejected, not because the liquidator was of the view that the debt had never existed, or that it had been paid prior to the liquidation, but rather because it was paid by a third party after the commencement

---

[636] Compare the situation in which a trustee in bankruptcy estimates a contingent debt, but after a later occurrence of the contingency it is apparent that the estimate was below the true value. The creditor may prove for the balance, but not so as to disturb prior dividends. See *Ellis and Company's Trustee v Dixon-Johnson* [1924] 1 Ch 342, 357 and para. 8.10 below. Compare also *Khan v Permayer* [2001] BPIR 95 in relation to a secured creditor who voted in favour of an individual voluntary arrangement and received payments under the arrangement as an unsecured creditor.

[637] [1999] 1 WLR 42.

[638] Pursuant to the Insolvency Rules 1986, r. 4.83.

[639] [1995] 1 WLR 42, 49–50.

[640] See paras 6.119–6.146 above.

[641] Park J found support for that view in *Brandon v McHenry* [1891] 1 QB 538, but the case is distinguishable. A trustee in bankruptcy rejected a proof of debt, and the person lodging the proof did not appeal against the rejection. Subsequently, the bankruptcy was annulled, and the person then sought to sue the former bankrupt for payment of the alleged debt. The Court of Appeal held that the action was barred by the rejection of the proof. The decision was based, however, on the terms of the Bankruptcy Act 1869, s. 81, which provided that, where a bankruptcy was annulled, all acts done by the trustee nevertheless remained valid. See now the Insolvency Act 1986, s. 282(4), and in Australia the Bankruptcy Act 1966 (Cth), s. 154(1). A rejection of a proof was regarded as an act done by the trustee within the meaning of the section. Therefore, the rejection remained valid after the annulment, and precluded a subsequent action on the debt. There was no similar provision operating in *BCCI v Habib Bank*.

of the liquidation. However, that should not have affected an automatic set-off occurring at the date of the liquidation as between BCCI and Habib Bank. Rather, the question should have been whether the third party payer was entitled to recover the payment made to Habib Bank on the ground that the payment was made under a mistake.[642]

(4) Mistake as to the valuation of a contingent debt in a set-off

A set-off may be based upon a valuation of a contingent debt owing by the insolvent or, in a **6.167** company liquidation or administration under the English Insolvency Rules, a contingent claim of the insolvent.[643] With the benefit of hindsight,[644] it may become apparent that the valuation was incorrect so that the account has to be adjusted. If the consequence of the adjustment is that the creditor has a provable debt, being the balance of the account in his or her favour, for a greater amount than originally thought, the creditor may amend his or her proof or lodge a fresh proof for the balance. If there are insufficient assets in the estate to pay a *pari passu* dividend on the balance, prior dividends will not be disturbed.[645] Alternatively, it may transpire that the creditor has a greater set-off entitlement than previously thought. If this has the consequence that the creditor has proved for a greater balance in his or her favour than that to which, with the benefit of hindsight, he or she was entitled, credit would have to be given for the additional dividend.[646]

S. Multiple Claims, and Preferential Debts

(1) General principle

The insolvency legislation accords preferential status to certain classes of debts. In the event **6.168** of a bankruptcy or a company liquidation, those debts, or at least in some cases a part of them, are paid in priority to other debts of the bankrupt or the company.[647] If the preferred creditor is possessed of a second, separate claim against the bankrupt or the company, or the amount of the claim in question is greater than the amount for which preferential status is accorded, the question may arise whether a set-off should take effect in the first instance against the preferred debt, or the preferred part of the debt, or whether it should operate first against the debt or the part of it which is not preferred, or in any other way. The creditor would be better off if the set-off occurred first against the non-preferred debt, because the preferred debt still in existence after the set-off would have priority in the bankruptcy or the liquidation, whereas the creditor could not claim priority if the set-off instead extinguished the debt which otherwise would have been preferred.

---

[642] See the discussion of *BCCI v Habib Bank* in paras 6.139–6.141 above.
[643] Pursuant to the Insolvency Rules 1986, r. 4.90(5) (company liquidation) or r. 2.85(5) (administration).
[644] *Stein v Blake* [1996] AC 243, 252–3. See para. 6.132 above.
[645] *Ellis and Company's Trustee v Dixon-Johnson* [1924] 1 Ch 342, 357, referred to in *Re Hurren* [1983] 1 WLR 183, 189.
[646] *MS Fashions v Bank of Credit and Commerce International SA* [1993] Ch 425, 435.
[647] See the Insolvency Act 1986, ss. 175, 176(3), 328 and 386 (referring to Sch. 6). In the case of a company in administration where set-off applies (see para. 6.10 above), see the Insolvency Act 1986, Sch. B1 para. 73(1)(b) and Sch. 6.

6.169   An early authority on point is *Ex p Boyle, re Shepherd*, a decision of Lord Eldon which appears not to have been reported but which is noted in Cooke's *Bankrupt Laws*.[648] The case concerned some promissory notes drawn by Lord Cork at the request of the bankrupt, the bankrupt having agreed to indemnify Lord Cork in respect of payments made pursuant to them. Lord Cork paid one of the notes before the bankruptcy and two of them afterwards. In addition, Lord Cork was separately indebted to the bankrupt. Under the bankruptcy legislation then in force, Lord Cork could only have proved in the bankruptcy for the payment made before the bankruptcy, but it was considered that his right to an indemnity for the subsequent payments, although not provable, could still be the subject of a set-off.[649] It would have been better for Lord Cork if his liability to the bankrupt could be set off against the claim for an indemnity which was not provable, because he would still have had a right to receive a dividend on the provable claim, and this indeed was the effect of the order made by Lord Eldon.

6.170   Lord Eldon's approach favoured the creditor. However, Buckley J adopted the opposite approach in *Re E J Morel (1934) Ltd*.[650] In his view, the insolvency set-off provision should be applied on the basis that the debt which would otherwise be preferential in a company liquidation should be the first claim brought into an account. His Lordship said that the result of a set-off is to give a creditor payment in full of his or her claim to the extent of the set-off, and in that way he or she is better off than creditors who merely have to rely on their right to prove and receive a dividend. Accordingly, if the creditor obtains payment in full by means of a set-off, it was 'reasonable' that that payment should be treated as being in respect of the debt which otherwise would rank first in priority.

6.171   Walton J subsequently considered the issue in *Re Unit 2 Windows Ltd*.[651] While there was no discussion of Lord Eldon's decision in *Ex p Boyle*, Walton J did consider *Re Morel*, but he was not persuaded by Buckley J's analysis. As his Lordship remarked, 'reasonableness' often depends on the point of view of the person considering it. He proposed a third approach. He said that the maxim that equality is equity should apply, and accordingly he held that the set-off in that case should occur rateably as between the preferential and the non-preferential parts of the indebtedness of the company in liquidation.[652] This has been followed in Australia,[653] and it would now appear to represent the law.

---

[648] Cooke, *The Bankrupt Laws* (8th edn, 1823) vol. 1, 571–2.

[649] Compare paras 7.24–7.26 (see in particular para. 7.25) below.

[650] [1962] 1 Ch 21.

[651] [1985] 1 WLR 1383.

[652] See also *Re South Blackpool Hotel Co* (1869) LR 8 Eq 225 in relation to debentures which ranked equally (although this case was decided before the bankruptcy set-off section was extended to company liquidation: see para. 6.05 above). In Scotland compare *Turner, Petitioner* [1993] BCC 299. Similarly, if a creditor receives a dividend upon a debt partly secured by a guarantee, the dividend should be applied rateably to the whole debt, and the creditor cannot appropriate it to the excess of the debt above the sum guaranteed unless the guarantee provides otherwise. See *Raikes v Todd* (1838) 8 Ad & E 846, 112 ER 1058, and *Rowlatt on Principal and Surety* (5th edn, 1999), 99, para. 4–83. A rateable allocation of set-offs was adopted in *Secretary of State for Trade and Industry v Frid* [2004] 2 AC 506 without any adverse judicial comment.

[653] *Central Brakes Service (Newcastle) Pty Ltd v Central Brakes Service (Sydney) Pty Ltd (in liq)* (1989) 7 ACLC 1199, 1202 (although the question was left open on appeal: *Central Brake Service (Sydney) Pty Ltd v Central Brake Service (Newcastle) Pty Ltd* (1992) 27 NSWLR 406, 411); *New Cap Reinsurance Corp v Faraday Underwriting Ltd* (2003) 47 ACSR 306 at [65].

A similar analysis should apply when a creditor has two (or more) claims against an **6.172** insolvent, neither of which is preferential, and the creditor is separately indebted to the insolvent. The set-off should take effect rateably as between the claims.

However, the rateable approach would not appear to apply in relation to preferential debts **6.173** when a receiver is appointed to a company under a crystallized floating charge.[654] Further, it is not relevant when a creditor of an insolvent has two debts owing to him or her, one secured and the other unsecured. The creditor is entitled to rely on the security in respect of the secured debt and not have it dealt with in the insolvency, in which case that debt would not be susceptible to a set-off under the insolvency legislation. If the insolvent has a cross-claim, the set-off would take place against the unsecured debt.[655]

(2) Lloyd's syndicates

The *Unit 2 Windows* approach is not reflected in reg. 22 of the Insurers (Reorganisation and **6.174** Winding Up) (Lloyd's) Regulations 2005.[656] Regulation 22 applies in the situation in which an underwriting member[657] of Lloyd's (termed a 'debtor') is bankrupt or is a company in administration or liquidation.[658] It provides that, where there have been mutual credits, mutual debts or other mutual dealings between the debtor in the course of his business as a member of a particular syndicate ('syndicate A') and a creditor, an account is to be taken[659] of what is due from the debtor to the creditor, and from the creditor to the debtor, in respect of business transacted by the debtor as a member of that syndicate only. Therefore, if the debtor is a member of more than one syndicate and is liable to the creditor in relation to each of the syndicates, a cross-claim possessed by the debtor against the creditor in relation to one of the syndicates (syndicate A) would only be available for set-off in relation to the dealings with that syndicate. The cross-claim would not be applied rateably as between each of the debtor's syndicates. Further, if the debtor's cross-claim exceeds the debt owing in relation to that syndicate, there is no provision for utilizing the surplus in a set-off against a debt owing by the debtor in relation to another syndicate. It is unclear why this is the case.

A similar principle applies where the creditor is also an underwriting member of Lloyd's **6.175** (whether or not a member of syndicate A). In such a case, where there have been mutual credits, mutual debts or other mutual dealings between the debtor as a member of syndicate A and the creditor in the course of the creditor's business as a member of syndicate A or of another syndicate of which he or she is a member, a separate account is to be taken in relation to each syndicate of which the creditor is a member of what is due from the debtor to the creditor, and from the creditor to the debtor, in respect only of business transacted between the debtor as a member of syndicate A and the creditor as a member of the syndicate in question.

---

[654] See paras 17.116–17.118 below.

[655] *Re Norman Holding Co Ltd* [1991] 1 WLR 10. See below.

[656] S.I. 2005 No. 1998 (amended by the Insurers (Reorganisation and Winding Up) (Amendment) Regulations 2007 (S.I. 2007 No. 851)).

[657] This includes a former member. See reg. 22(6)(a).

[658] Unless an order under reg. 13(3) is in effect in relation to the member. See reg. 22(1)(b).

[659] Pursuant to s. 323 of the Insolvency Act 1986 (bankruptcy) or, in the case of a company, r. 2.85 or r. 4.90 of the Insolvency Rules 1986 (administration and liquidation). See reg. 22(2). In relation to administration, see paras 6.10 and 6.11 above.

T. Secured Debts

6.176 In *Ex p Barnett, re Deveze*,[660] Lord Selborne LC said of the bankruptcy set-off section that: 'the fact that nothing is said about security or lien one way or the other in the section seems to me only to shew that the existence of security is not to affect its operation.' Similarly, in the Australian High Court, in *Hiley v Peoples Prudential Assurance Co Ltd*,[661] Dixon J commented that: 'secured debts or liabilities are no less the subject of set-off than unsecured debts as mutual debts, credits or dealings. To the extent that the secured debt is answered by set-off the security is freed . . .'. More recently, Dillon LJ, in delivering the judgment of the Court of Appeal in *MS Fashions Ltd v Bank of Credit and Commerce International*,[662] said that: 'If there are indeed mutual credits or mutual debts or mutual dealings between a company, or a bankrupt, and a creditor, then the set-off applies, notwithstanding that one or other of the debts or credits may be secured.' The difficulty with these statements is that they draw no distinction between, on the one hand, a secured debt owing by a bankrupt or a company in liquidation (or administration[663]), and on the other a secured debt owing to the bankrupt or the company. On the contrary, they suggest that the same result should follow in either case. In truth those scenarios should attract different analyses.

(1) Security provided by the insolvent

6.177 As those statements indicate, the fact that a creditor of a bankrupt or an insolvent company has security for the debt owing to him or her[664] on its own does not preclude the operation of the set-off section.[665] A secured creditor has a choice. The creditor can value the security and prove for the difference between the amount of the debt and the value, or surrender the security and prove for the whole debt, or enforce the security and prove for the balance remaining of the debt.[666] In any of those situations, the provable debt should be able to be the subject of a set-off.[667]

---

[660] (1874) LR 9 Ch App 293, 295–6.

[661] (1938) 60 CLR 468, 498. See also *A E Goodwin Ltd v A G Healing Ltd* (1979) 7 ACLR 481, 488. Dixon J referred to *Ex p Barnett, re Deveze* (1874) LR 9 Ch App 293 and *Ex p Law, re Kennedy* (1846) De Gex 378 as support for the proposition. *Ex p Barnett* was a case in which the bankrupt was the secured creditor (see para. 6.179 below), while in *Ex p Law* the petitioner submitted to the jurisdiction of the bankruptcy court by applying to the Commissioner to value the annuity for the purpose of a set-off.

[662] [1993] Ch 425, 446.

[663] Where the insolvency set-off provision in the Insolvency Rules 1986, r. 2.85 applies. See para. 6.10 above.

[664] Including security provided by a third party. See *McKinnon v Armstrong Brothers & Co* (1877) 2 App Cas 531.

[665] This also applies in the case of set-off under the Statutes of Set-off. See *Lechmere v Hawkins* (1798) 2 Esp 626, 170 ER 477.

[666] In bankruptcy, see the Insolvency Rules 1986, rr. 6.98(1)(e) and 6.109 (together with rr. 6.115–6.119), in company liquidation see rr. 4.75(1)(e) and 4.88 (together with rr. 4.95–4.99), and in the case of a company which has entered administration see rr. 2.72(3)(b)(vii) and 2.83 (together with rr. 2.90–2.94). In Australia, see the Corporations Act 1981 (Cth), s. 554E (company liquidation) and the Bankruptcy Act 1966 (Cth), s. 90 (bankruptcy).

[667] See the discussion in *Re Norman Holding Co Ltd* [1991] 1 WLR 10. In *Clark v Cort* (1840) Cr & Ph 154, 41 ER 449 a set-off was allowed in equity to the extent of the difference between the value of the bankrupt's indebtedness and the proceeds of realization of a security for that debt. See also *Stewart v Scottish Widows and Life Assurance Society Plc* [2005] EWHC 1831 (QB) at [187] (debt proved in the liquidation).

Consider, however, that the creditor chooses to rely on the security[668] for all or part of the debt and, to that extent, not to prove in the insolvency. For the insolvency set-off section to apply there must be a creditor 'proving or claiming to prove',[669] but in the situation posited, in which the creditor has chosen to rely on the security, he or she is not 'proving or claiming to prove'. The insolvency set-off section, therefore, should not apply. Mervyn Davies J accepted an argument to this effect in *Re Norman Holding Co Ltd*,[670] and it is consistent with Rose LJ's comment in delivering the judgment of the Court of Appeal in *Re Bank of Credit and Commerce International SA (No. 8)*[671] that: 'Set-off ought not to prejudice the right of a secured creditor to enforce his securities in any order he chooses and at a time of his choice.' There may be both a secured and an unsecured debt owing to the creditor. In that circumstance, Mervyn Davies J held in *Re Norman Holding* that the creditor is entitled to rely on the security in respect of the secured debt and to utilize the unsecured debt in a set-off. [672]

6.178

(2) Security held by the insolvent

Alternatively, it may be that a bankrupt or a company in liquidation (or administration[673]) is a secured creditor. In that situation, if the bankrupt or the company is separately indebted to the debtor on the secured debt, the debtor would be 'proving or claiming to prove' for the separate debt,[674] in which case there is no reason why the insolvency set-off section should not apply. The cases indeed support that view.[675] To the extent of the set-off, the security would be freed.

6.179

---

[668] This does not include a guarantee. See *Stewart v Scottish Widows and Life Assurance Society Plc* [2005] EWHC 1831 (QB) at [187].

[669] See the Insolvency Act 1986, s. 323(1) (bankruptcy) and the Insolvency Rules 1986, r. 4.90(1) (company liquidation). Where set-off applies in the administration of a company (see para. 6.10 above), see r. 2.85(2). In Australia, the Bankruptcy Act 1966 (Cth), s. 86 refers to a creditor 'claiming to prove', while in company liquidation the Corporations Act 2001 (Cth), s. 553C requires that there should be a person who 'wants to have a debt or claim admitted against the company'.

[670] [1991] 1 WLR 10, 14–15. See also *Brown v Cork* [1985] BCLC 363, 370–1, where the Court of Appeal seemed to accept the respondent's argument to this effect. The decision in *Re Norman Holding* is not affected by the adoption of the automatic theory of insolvency set-off (see paras 6.119–6.146 above) by the House of Lords in *Stein v Blake* [1996] AC 243. See *Stewart v Scottish Widows and Life Assurance Society Plc* [2005] EWHC 1831 (QB) at [182]–[186]. Compare Powell J in *McColl's Wholesale Pty Ltd v State Bank of NSW* [1984] 3 NSWLR 365, 380, who considered that the requirement that debts be set off means that a secured creditor may only enforce his or her rights under the security to the extent of the balance of the cross-debts.

[671] [1996] Ch 245, 256.

[672] This is consistent with the principle that a secured creditor is entitled to apply the security in discharge of whatever secured liability of the debtor he or she may think fit. See *Re William Hall (Contractors) Ltd* [1967] 1 WLR 948. The debtor in that case was in liquidation, and Plowman J held that the creditor could appropriate the proceeds first in discharge of a non-preferential claim, leaving the creditor free to prove for the whole of the preferential part of the claim.

[673] Where the Insolvency Rules 1986, r. 2.85 applies. See para. 6.10 above.

[674] It is not necessary that a proof be lodged, however. See para. 6.03 above.

[675] *Lord Lanesborough v Jones* (1716) 1 P Wms 325, 24 ER 409; *Ex p Barnett, re Deveze* (1874) LR 9 Ch App 293; *Hiley v Peoples Prudential Assurance Co Ltd* (1938) 60 CLR 468; *Re ILG Travel Ltd* [1995] 2 BCLC 128, 158–60. Compare *Clarke v Fell* (1833) 4 B & Ad 404, 110 ER 507, which is explained in *Ex p Barnett* at 296.

(3) Payment to the secured creditor

6.180 When a negotiable instrument is lodged as security for an advance, the trustee in bankruptcy of the debtor on the instrument is entitled to recover the instrument after tendering the amount of the advance, and the creditor is not entitled to retain it for a set-off against another debt owing to him or her by the debtor.[676]

(4) Surplus proceeds, after realizing the security

6.181 After a security is realized the proceeds may be more than sufficient to satisfy the secured moneys. The question whether the creditor may set off his or her obligation to account for the surplus proceeds against a separate unsecured debt owing by the debtor is discussed below.[677]

(5) A debt as property the subject of a security

6.182 A debt itself may be property the subject of a security. This situation is considered later in the context of mutuality.[678]

---

[676] *Key v Flint* (1817) 8 Taunt 21, 129 ER 289, petition in equity dismissed *Ex p Flint* (1818) 1 Swans 30, 36 ER 285. See also *Trustee of the Property of Ellis and Co v Dixon-Johnson* [1925] AC 489.
[677] See paras 10.36–10.46 below.
[678] See paras 11.37–11.51 below.

7

DEBTS, CREDITS, AND DEALINGS

A. The Meaning of Debts, Credits, and Dealings

The insolvency set-off section applies when there are mutual credits, mutual debts or other **7.01** mutual dealings. It was not always in this form. The original set-off section in 1705[1] referred only to mutual credit, and in 1732 it was expressed in terms of mutual credit and mutual debts.[2] It was not until 1869 that 'mutual dealings' was added.[3]

(1) Debts and credits

The courts interpreted 'mutual debts' as referring to debts that were both in existence and **7.02** presently payable before the bankruptcy.[4] It is apparent that 'mutual credits' would include mutual debts, in the sense that, in the case of a presently payable debt, credit is given to the debtor for payment. But the concept is broader than that.

An early authority is *Rose v Hart*.[5] The question in issue was whether a fuller with whom **7.03** cloths had been deposited by a bankrupt prior to the bankruptcy could retain them as a set-off against a debt owing by the bankrupt. Gibbs CJ said that mutual credit meant: 'such credits only as must in their nature terminate in debts, as where a debt is due from one party, and credit given by him on the other for a sum of money payable at a future day, and

---

[1] (1705) 4 & 5 Anne, c. 17, s. 11. See para. 6.38 above.

[2] (1732) 5 Geo II, c. 30, s. 28.

[3] Bankruptcy Act 1869, s. 39. See para. 6.42 above.

[4] *Ex p Prescot* (1753) 1 Atk 230, 26 ER 147, and see also *Young v Bank of Bengal* (1836) 1 Moore 150, 164–5, 12 ER 771, 777. Compare the definition of 'debt' in the Insolvency Rules 1986, r. 13.12 in relation to a company in liquidation or administration, and for bankruptcy the definition of 'bankruptcy debt' in the Insolvency Act 1986, s. 382.

[5] (1818) 8 Taunt 499, 129 ER 477.

which will then become a debt, or where there is a debt on one side, and a delivery of property with directions to turn it into money on the other; in such case the credit given by the delivery of the property must in its nature terminate in a debt . . .'[6] Since the cloths in that case had not been deposited with authority to turn them into money, there was not mutual credit for the purpose of the set-off section.

7.04 According to the formulation in *Rose v Hart*, mutual credit extends only to credits which must in their nature end in a debt. In later cases, however, this requirement was relaxed,[7] so that it came to be regarded as sufficient if a transaction was such that it would naturally or in the ordinary course of business end in a debt,[8] or if it would probably result in a debt,[9] or if a debt was the likely result[10] or a natural outcome.[11] A transaction would naturally end in a debt if it would do so without the intervention of a new and independent transaction.[12] Therefore, where rights are vested in a person[13] before a bankruptcy which would naturally (in that sense), and which ultimately do, result in a debt, the vesting of the rights is regarded as constituting the giving of credit, so that the resulting debt may be included in a set-off notwithstanding that it may not arise until after the bankruptcy. In *Secretary of State for Trade and Industry v Frid*[14] the House of Lords recognized that those rights may also arise out of a statutory obligation which was contingent at the insolvency date and which fell due for payment and was paid after that date, as opposed to arising out of a consensual contract. Lord Hoffmann, in a speech with which the other Law Lords agreed,[15] said that it makes no difference whether the debts arise voluntarily or by compulsion.[16] This relaxation in the requirements for mutual debts and credits is consistent with the courts' expressed policy of construing the set-off section liberally.[17]

---

[6] (1818) 8 Taunt 499, 506, 129 ER 477, 480. See also *Gibson v Bell* (1835) 1 Bing (NC) 743, 754, 131 ER 1303, 1308; *Clarke v Fell* (1833) 4 B & Ad 404, 409, 110 ER 507, 509; *Young v Bank of Bengal* (1836) 1 Moore 150, 168–9, 12 ER 771, 779 (PC); *Groom v West* (1838) 8 Ad & E 758, 772–3, 112 ER 1025, 1030.

[7] Compare *Young v Bank of Bengal* (1836) 1 Moore 150, 168–9, 12 ER 771, 779.

[8] *Day & Dent Constructions Pty Ltd v North Australian Properties Pty Ltd* (1982) 150 CLR 85, 95 (Gibbs CJ), 103–4 (Mason J), referring to *Naoroji v The Chartered Bank of India* (1868) LR 3 CP 444, 451. See also *Palmer v Day & Sons* [1895] 2 QB 618, 621; *Re Mid-Kent Fruit Factory* [1896] 1 Ch 567, 569; *Wreckair Pty Ltd v Emerson* [1992] 1 Qd R 700, 707–8; *Smith's Leading Cases* (12th edn, 1915) vol. 2, 281.

[9] *Sovereign Life Assurance Co v Dodd* [1892] 1 QB 405, 411–12.

[10] *Easum v Cato* (1822) 5 B & Ald 861, 867, 106 ER 1406, 1408.

[11] *Re Daintrey* [1900] 1 QB 546, 568 ('the natural outcome of previous transactions'); *Re Parker* (1997) 80 FCR 1, 12.

[12] See *Hiley v The Peoples Prudential Assurance Co Ltd* (1938) 60 CLR 468, 487 (Rich J), 499 (Dixon J); *Re Collinson; Smith v Sinnathamby* (1978) 33 FLR 39, 41–2.

[13] In *Hiley v Peoples Prudential Assurance Co Ltd* (1938) 60 CLR 468, 487, 499 Rich and Dixon JJ spoke in terms of prior 'rights'. Compare the formulation in *Gye v McIntyre* (1991) 171 CLR 609, 623, 626 in relation to 'dealings'.

[14] [2004] 2 AC 506. See para. 8.12 below. See also *Deputy Commissioner of Taxation v Dexcam Australia Pty Ltd* (2003) 129 FCR 582 at [28] (contingent tax debt).

[15] Lord Nicholls of Birkenhead, Lord Hope of Craighead, Lord Phillips of Worth Matravers and Lord Brown of Eaton-under-Heywood.

[16] [2004] 2 AC 506 at [19].

[17] *Eberle's Hotels and Restaurant Co, Ltd v E Jonas & Brothers* (1887) 18 QBD 459, 465; *Day & Dent Constructions Pty Ltd v North Australian Properties Pty Ltd* (1982) 150 CLR 85, 108; *Gye v McIntyre* (1991) 171 CLR 609, 619; *Re Kolb* (1994) 51 FCR 31, 34; *Re Parker* (1997) 80 FCR 1, 8; *Coventry v Charter Pacific Corporation Ltd* (2005) 227 CLR 234 at [56].

In 1861 the range of provable debts was expanded, the principal change being the inclusion   **7.05**
of a right of proof in respect of damages claims for breach of contract.[18] In addition, the
Bankruptcy Act 1869 contained a general right of proof in respect of debts and liabilities to
which the bankrupt became subject after the bankruptcy by reason of an obligation incurred
before the bankruptcy.[19] This was broader than the situation which had applied under the
Bankrupt Law Consolidation Act 1849, by which only certain types of contingent liabilities were provable.[20] A set-off section that referred only to mutual debts and mutual credit
would not have been adequate to bring about an expansion in the scope of the insolvency
set-off section that corresponded to these changes, since mutual debts and mutual credit
encompassed only debts which were in existence and presently payable before the bankruptcy, and debts which came into existence subsequent to the bankruptcy but which were
a natural result of a prior transaction. A damages claim is not a debt, and it does not come
within those concepts.[21] As Lord Russell of Killowen CJ remarked in relation to the giving
of credit:[22] 'the credits must be such as either must terminate in debts or have a natural
tendency to terminate in debts, and must not be such as terminate in claims differing in
nature from debts.' Thus, it had been held in 1830, in *Rose v Sims*,[23] that a damages claim
for breach of contract was not within the ambit of the bankruptcy set-off section. It appears
that 'mutual dealings' was added to the set-off section in the 1869 Act in order to accommodate this increase in the range of provable debts,[24] a view which is consistent with judicial observations equating the scope of the set-off section in that Act with the ambit of the
proof of debt provision.[25] It is also consistent with Brett LJ's comment in *Peat v Jones &
Co*,[26] that: 'mutual dealings was added to get rid of any questions which might arise whether
a transaction would end in a debt or not.' This contemplates damages claims for breach of

---

[18] See the Bankruptcy Act 1861, ss. 149–54. Damages claims for breach of contract were dealt with
in s. 153.

[19] Bankruptcy Act 1869, s. 31.

[20] See the Bankrupt Law Consolidation Act 1849, ss. 174–8. For example, s. 177 conferred a right of proof
in respect of contingent *debts*. While s. 178 also conferred a right of proof in respect of contingent *liabilities*,
this was confined to traders.

[21] *Rose v Sims* (1830) 1 B & Ad 521, 109 ER 881; *Palmer v Day & Sons* [1895] 2 QB 618, 621. See also
Harrop v Fisher (1861) 10 CB(NS) 196, 204, 142 ER 426, 429. In *Gibson v Bell* (1835) 1 Bing (NC) 743,
131 ER 1303 and *Groom v West* (1838) 8 Ad & E 758, 112 ER 1025 the claim was framed in damages, and a
set-off was allowed. In each case, however, the transaction was regarded as one which of necessity would end in
a debt, and that in truth was the substance of the claim, notwithstanding the form of the pleading. Compare
Makeham v Crow (1864) 15 CB(NS) 847, 143 ER 1018, in which an unliquidated damages claim arising out
of a contract of sale was set off in an action by the vendor's assignees in bankruptcy for the price. However, the
purchaser presented alternative arguments for a set-off. It was based not only upon the scope of the proof of
debt provision in the 1861 Act, but also equitable set-off. The report is silent as to which of these was regarded
as the justification for the decision. Certainly, in cases decided after the 1869 Act, set-off of unliquidated damages was justified on the basis of mutual dealings as opposed to mutual credit. See below.

[22] *Palmer v Day & Sons* [1895] 2 QB 618, 621.

[23] (1830) 1 B & Ad 521, 109 ER 881.

[24] In *Turner v Thomas* (1871) LR 6 CP 610, 613–14 Willes J discussed the 'very large extension of the law
of set-off' in the 1869 Act by reference to the proof of debt provision. Malins VC in *Booth v Hutchinson* (1872)
LR 15 Eq 30, 35 commented that the addition of the words 'mutual dealings' was 'intended to give a more
extended right of set-off than previously existed . . .'. See also *Gye v McIntyre* (1991) 171 CLR 609, 623.

[25] See e.g. *Re Asphaltic Wood Pavement Co. Lee & Chapman's Case* (1885) 30 Ch D 216, 222 (Brett MR),
224 (Cotton LJ).

[26] (1881) 8 QBD 147, 149, referring to *Booth v Hutchinson* (1872) LR 15 Eq 30, 35.

contract, which the courts quickly settled came within the scope of the mutual dealings head in the 1869 set-off section so as to be available for set-off on that ground.[27]

7.06 There are passages in Lord Hoffmann's judgment in *Secretary of State for Trade and Industry v Frid*[28] which may suggest that the expression 'mutual debts' (as opposed to mutual dealings) extends to damages claims.[29] However, it would be difficult to reconcile that view with the historical development of the bankruptcy set-off section,[30] and the statements in question may have been intended merely as support for more general propositions.[31] Nevertheless, the High Court of Australia in *Gye v McIntyre*,[32] suggested that it was 'strongly arguable' that a damages claim for fraudulent misrepresentation may come within the ambit of the expression 'mutual credits'. The point was not decided, since the High Court accepted that the claims in issue in any event were in respect of mutual dealings. Normally, it would not matter whether a damages claim is characterized as a credit or a claim arising out of a dealing. That would be particularly so if it is the case that the insolvency set-off section always requires claims arising out of dealings, a point which is considered below.[33] But the point may be significant in Australia, because the qualification to the set-off section in both bankruptcy and company liquidation[34] is drafted in terms of having the requisite notice at the time of giving or receiving *credit*, as opposed to entry into a dealing which may

---

[27] See e.g. *Booth v Hutchinson* (1872) LR 15 Eq 30 (esp. at 35); *Peat v Jones & Co* (1881) 8 QBD 147 (esp. at 149 and 150); *Re Asphaltic Wood Pavement Co. Lee & Chapman's Case* (1885) 30 Ch D 216 (esp. at 224). See also *Mersey Steel & Iron Co v Naylor, Benzon, & Co* (1884) 9 App Cas 434. In relation to *Makeham v Crow* (1864) 15 CB(NS) 847, 143 ER 1018, to which Sir Richard Malins VC referred in *Booth v Hutchinson* at 34–5, see para. 7.05n above.

[28] [2004] 2 AC 506.

[29] At [2004] 2 AC 506 at [9] Lord Hoffmann commented: 'The principle has typically been applied to claims for breach of contract where the contract was made before the insolvency date but the breach occurred afterwards . . .' At [7] (and see also at [22]), Lord Hoffmann had indicated that he was considering first whether mutual debts existed, which may suggest that in that passage he was referring to that concept. Further, at [19] Lord Hoffmann said: 'The term mutual debts does not in itself require anything more than commensurable cross-obligations between the same people in the same capacity. How those debts arose – whether by contract, statute *or tort*, voluntarily or by compulsion – is not material' (emphasis added).

[30] See above. The Insolvency Rules 1986, r. 13.12 defines 'debt' in terms which include a liability in damages. However, the definition extends only to a debt or liability to which the company is subject. It does not extend to a claim on the other side of the account. Rule 13.12 does not apply if the context otherwise requires (see r. 13.1), and it is suggested that the context would require otherwise in the set-off provision given the compendious expression 'mutual credits, mutual debts or other mutual dealings', which encompasses both sides of the account. In bankruptcy, the corresponding definition is of 'bankruptcy debt' rather than 'debt' (Insolvency Act 1986, s. 382), so that the point in any event could not be made in bankruptcy.

[31] At [2004] 2 AC 506 at [9], Lord Hoffmann referred to the case of a breach of contract occurring after the insolvency date as support for, and as being consistent with, the general proposition that it is not necessary that a debt should have been due and payable before the insolvency date in order that it may be included in a set-off. In *Re Asphaltic Wood Pavement Co. Lee & Chapman's Case* (1885) 30 Ch D 216, to which Lord Hoffmann referred, Lord Cotton (at 224) explained the set-off in that case on the basis of mutual dealings. In relation to Lord Hoffmann's comments at [19], it would appear that the reference to 'tort' was made by way of illustrating the fundamental point that it is immaterial, for the purpose of the expression 'mutual debts', how the debts arose, as opposed to suggesting that all claims in tort are debts for the purpose of the insolvency set-off section.

[32] (1991) 171 CLR 609, 625.

[33] See paras 7.12–7.22 below.

[34] Bankruptcy Act 1966 (Cth), s. 86(2), and for company liquidation the Corporations Act 2001 (Cth), s. 553C(2).

give rise to a damages claim.[35] The suggestion in *Gye v McIntyre* was made in the context of a discussion of a comment by Byles J in *Naoroji v Chartered Bank of India*,[36] that mutual credit encompasses reciprocal demands which must (or would) naturally terminate in a debt. In *Gye v McIntyre* the claim in issue had been liquidated by judgment after the relevant date for determining rights of set-off, and the High Court may have had in mind that a damages claim would naturally terminate in a judgment debt. However, in relation to the question whether credit has been given, as opposed to whether a set-off may be based upon a claim arising out of a prior dealing, the relevant inquiry is whether the claim would naturally end in a debt, as opposed to whether it does end in debt, and the courts have never considered that the fact that a damages claim may end in a judgment debt as sufficient to bring it within the concept of giving credit. If that view had prevailed, there would not have been any necessity for the courts after 1869 to have recourse to the concept of mutual dealings in order to allow a damages claim for breach of contract to be set off in a bankruptcy. Thus, in *Peat v Jones & Co*,[37] Cotton LJ said that the damages claim for breach of contract in that case would not have come within the earlier mutual credit clauses, but it did come within the mutual dealing head in the 1869 Act.[38] More recently, it was said in the Victorian Supreme Court in relation to a provable claim for damages that it could 'surely not be characterized as the bankrupt "giving credit"'.[39]

(2) Dealings

The Australian High Court in *Gye v McIntyre*[40] noted that the expression 'or *other* mutual dealings'[41] in the insolvency set-off section gives rise to a linguistic problem, in that 'credits' and 'debts' ordinarily represent the outcome of dealings rather than the dealings themselves, whereas dealings do not of themselves, as distinct from their outcome, represent claims susceptible to a set-off. Therefore, the set-off section speaks of set-off 'in respect of' mutual dealings. **7.07**

The concept of 'dealings' has never been precisely defined. In *Gye v McIntyre*,[42] the High Court of Australia described it as a term of 'very wide scope' and said that it is used 'in a non-technical sense' in the insolvency set-off section. It does not matter that other parties may have been involved in the dealings, that either the creditor or the bankrupt may have been involved in the dealings in more than one capacity, or that those dealings also give rise to different claims between other parties or between the same parties in different beneficial **7.08**

---

[35] See also paras 6.84–6.87 above. Compare the qualifications applicable under the English insolvency set-off sections. See paras 6.72–6.73 (bankruptcy) and 6.74–6.83 (company liquidation and administration) above.

[36] (1868) LR 3 CP 444, 451.

[37] (1881) 8 QBD 147, 150.

[38] See also *Booth v Hutchinson* (1872) LR 15 Eq 30, 33, 35; *Re Asphaltic Wood Pavement Co. Lee & Chapman's Case* (1885) 30 Ch D 216, 224 (referring to 'mutual dealings'); *Brodyn Pty Ltd v Dassein Constructions Pty Ltd* [2004] NSWSC 1230 at [77].

[39] *Lloyds Bank NZA Ltd v National Safety Council of Australia Victorian Division* [1993] 2 VR 506, 521 (J D Phillips J, with whose reasons Fullagar J agreed).

[40] (1991) 171 CLR 609, 623. See also *Secretary of State for Trade and Industry v Frid* [2004] 2 AC 506 at [22]–[24].

[41] Emphasis added by the High Court.

[42] (1991) 171 CLR 609, 625.

interests.[43] The High Court observed that 'dealings' has been construed as referring to matters having a commercial or business flavour.[44] However, it embraces far more than a legally binding contract or 'deal'.[45] Their Honours said:

> Even if it is correct to construe 'dealings' in [the set-off section] as confined to a commercial or business setting, it covers the communings, the negotiations, verbal and by correspondence, and other matters which occur or exist in that setting. Whatever may be the outer limits of the word 'dealings' in [the set-off section], it encompasses, as a matter of ordinary language, commercial transactions and the negotiations leading up to them.[46]

In that case, a fraudulent misrepresentation was made in the course of negotiations leading up to a contract for the purchase of property and a loan. The representation was not a term of the contract, but the High Court considered that the misrepresentation claim nevertheless was in respect of a dealing for the purpose of the set-off section. That was so notwithstanding that the resulting purchase contract[47] was not entered into with the person who had made the misrepresentation, but with a company associated with her.[48]

7.09 Subsequently the House of Lords considered the meaning of 'dealings' in *Secretary of State for Trade and Industry v Frid*.[49] Consistent with the view that it is a term of very wide scope, Lord Hoffmann said that it is to be construed in an 'extended sense'. It is not confined to consensual arrangements. It can include a statutory obligation, in that case by a company in liquidation to the Secretary of State for Trade and Industry as a result of the Secretary of State having made payments after the liquidation to employees of the company pursuant to the Employment Rights Act 1996, which resulted in a transfer to the Secretary of State of the employees' rights against the company.[50] The Secretary of State in effect was a guarantor of the employees' entitlements, albeit that the guarantee existed by statute rather than through a consensual contract.

7.10 Lord Hoffmann also accepted[51] that the commission of a tort can constitute a dealing. This would include the tortious claim in issue in *Gye v McIntyre* (above). But the commission of a tort is not always a dealing.[52] Thus, Lord Esher MR observed in *Eberle's Hotels and Restaurant Co Ltd v E Jonas & Brothers*[53] that if 'one man assaults another or injures him through negligence, that gives rise to a claim, but is not a dealing . . .'. Claims of that nature

---

[43] *Gye v McIntyre* (1991) 171 CLR 609, 625–6.

[44] (1991) 171 CLR 609, 625. See also *Re Kolb* (1994) 51 FCR 31, 34. In *Eberle's Hotels and Restaurant Co Ltd v E Jonas & Brothers* (1887) 18 QBD 459, 465 Lord Esher MR said that he was: 'disposed to think that whatever comes within the description of an ordinary business transaction would be a dealing within the section.'

[45] (1991) 171 CLR 609, 625.

[46] (1991) 171 CLR 609, 625. See also *Coventry v Charter Pacific Corporation Ltd* (2005) 227 CLR 234 at [58] ('the mutual dealings which may give rise to a set-off include commercial transactions and the negotiations leading up to them').

[47] As opposed to the loan, which was obtained from the representor.

[48] Note, however, *Coventry v Charter Pacific Corporation Ltd* (2005) 227 CLR 234. See paras 8.58–8.61 below.

[49] [2004] 2 AC 506 at [24].

[50] Employment Rights Act 1996, ss. 161(1) and 167.

[51] [2004] 2 AC 506 at [24].

[52] See paras 8.53–8.54 below.

[53] (1887) 18 QBD 459, 465, referred to in *Gye v McIntyre* (1991) 171 CLR 609, 625.

do not have a commercial or business flavour.[54] Similarly, a misappropriation of assets or a theft of money or a conversion of property is not a dealing.[55]

(3) Non-contract claims

There are to be found judicial statements which suggest that the set-off section is limited to **7.11** claims that arise out of contract,[56] but that view was rejected by Brightman J in *Re D H Curtis (Builders) Ltd*[57] and it can no longer be supported. The purpose of insolvency set-off, he said, is to do substantial justice between a bankrupt and the bankrupt's creditors.[58] On that basis, he concluded that: 'one would expect to find that any mutual demands capable of being proved in bankruptcy can be the subject-matter of set-off whether or not arising out of contract.'[59] In the *D H Curtis* case, the Crown (through the Inland Revenue and the Department of Health and Social Security) had a claim for unpaid taxes against a company in liquidation, and at the same time the Crown (through the Customs and Excise Commissioners) was indebted to the company for the repayment of excess input tax. It was held that the debts could be set off in the liquidation, even though they were statutory rather than contractual in origin. This has been accepted and applied in subsequent cases,[60] including by the House of Lords.[61] The suggested limitation was also rejected by the High Court of Australia in *Gye v McIntyre*[62] when it held that a claim in tort for damages for fraudulent misrepresentation could be the subject of a set-off.

B. The Necessity for a Dealing

The insolvency set-off section may apply where there are 'mutual credits, mutual debts **7.12** or other mutual dealings' between the creditor and the bankrupt or the company (as the case may be). The insertion of 'other' before 'mutual dealings' appears to qualify both mutual credits and mutual debts, suggesting that they should also have arisen out of a dealing between the parties to the proposed set-off. There are difficulties with that view, however.

---

[54] *Gye v McIntyre* (1991) 171 CLR 609, 625.
[55] *Manson v Smith* [1997] 2 BCLC 161, 164; *Smith v Bridgend County BC* [2002] 1 AC 336 at [35]; *Re Leeholme Stud Pty Ltd* [1965] NSWR 1649.
[56] *Palmer v Day & Sons* [1895] 2 QB 618, 621; *Re Mid-Kent Fruit Factory* [1896] 1 Ch 567, 571; *Re Canada Cycle & Motor Agency (Queensland) Ltd* [1931] St R Qd 281; *Re Hurburgh* [1959] Tas SR 25, 46.
[57] [1978] 1 Ch 162.
[58] [1978] 1 Ch 162, 173, referring to *Forster v Wilson* (1843) 12 M & W 191, 203–4, 152 ER 1165, 1171, *Ex p Cleland, re Davies* (1867) LR 2 Ch App 808, 812–813, and *Re City Life Assurance Co* [1926] Ch 191, 216.
[59] [1978] 1 Ch 162, 173. See paras 7.24–7.26 below in relation to the suggestion that all provable demands can be the subject of a set-off.
[60] *Re Cushla Ltd* [1979] 3 All ER 415; *Re Unit 2 Windows Ltd* [1985] 1 WLR 1383; *Re Kolb* (1994) 51 FCR 31; *Re Parker* (1997) 80 FCR 1, 10 (referring to statutory debts). See also *Deputy Commissioner of Taxation v Dexcam Australia Pty Ltd* (2003) 129 FCR 582 at [28] (tax credits and tax liabilities).
[61] *Secretary of State for Trade and Industry v Frid* [2004] 2 AC 506.
[62] (1991) 171 CLR 609.

7.13   The current form of set-off section first appeared in the Bankruptcy Act 1869, s. 39. Prior to that enactment, the section extended only to mutual credit and mutual debts.[63] In determining whether the case was one of mutual credit or mutual debts, it was not necessary that the parties should have dealt directly with each other. This is apparent from *Hankey v Smith*,[64] decided in the Court of King's Bench in 1789. Lord Kenyon and Buller J held in that case that the indebtedness of a bankrupt acceptor upon a bill of exchange could be brought into an account by the holder, even though the bankrupt was unaware that the bill had been indorsed to the holder.[65] The acceptor and the holder had not dealt with each other and yet a set-off was allowed, Buller J commenting that, in order to constitute mutual credit, it is not necessary that the parties should have meant to trust each other in the transaction in question.[66] If a bill of exchange is sent out into the world, he said that credit is given to the acceptor by every person who takes the bill. A similar result occurred in *Forster v Wilson*[67] in the context of bearer promissory notes, and the same point may be made in relation to the situation in which one of the parties to the proposed set-off gained a right to sue the other only as a result of an assignment to him or her of the other's indebtedness.[68] When the set-off section was recast in 1869 in terms of mutual credits, mutual debts or other mutual dealings, it was not suggested that this had the effect of narrowing the scope of mutual credits and mutual debts, so that henceforth they should be considered as encompassing only debts and credits arising out of dealings between the parties to the set-off. On the contrary, Malins VC commented in 1872 that the addition of the words 'mutual dealings' was 'intended to give a more extended right of set-off than previously existed . . .'.[69] Further, as Sir George Jessel MR remarked in the context of the 1869 Act,[70] the whole tendency of the history of the insolvency legislation has been to extend the principle upon which the right of set-off is founded. Given the position that formerly applied, this suggests that it is not necessary for a set-off that the claims should have arisen out of a dealing between the parties to the proposed set-off if the claims constitute debts or the giving of credit,[71] despite the word 'other' before 'mutual dealings'. In other words, the section

---

[63] See para. 6.42 above.

[64] (1789) 3 TR 507n, 100 ER 703.

[65] See also *Collins v Jones* (1830) 10 B & C 777, 109 ER 638; *Ex p Hastie and Hutchinson, Re Alexander and Co* (1850) 14 LTOS 402; *Re Morris and M'Murray* (1874) 5 AJR 157, affd at 185 (Victoria) (in which the relevant legislation was expressed in terms of mutual credits, mutual debts or other mutual dealings, and Molesworth J accepted that there was no dealing between the parties).

[66] There have nevertheless been occasions when mutual credit has been equated with trust. See *Baillie v Innes* (1845) 14 LJ Ch 341, 343 (Lord Lyndhurst); *Knox v Cockburn* (1862) 1 QSCR 80, 83 (equitable set-off).

[67] (1843) 12 M & W 191, 152 ER 1165.

[68] *Clark v Cort* (1840) Cr & Ph 154, 41 ER 449; *Mathieson's Trustee v Burrup, Mathieson and Co* [1927] 1 Ch 562; *Southern Cross Construction Ltd v Southern Cross Club Ltd* [1973] 1 NZLR 708; *Kon Strukt Pty Ltd v Storage Developments Pty Ltd* (1989) 96 FLR 43. Compare *Re Eros Films Ltd* [1963] 1 Ch 565 and *Law v James* [1972] 2 NSWLR 573, in which the assignment occurred after the company law equivalent of notice of an act of bankruptcy.

[69] *Booth v Hutchinson* (1872) LR 15 Eq 30, 35. See also *Gye v McIntyre* (1991) 171 CLR 609, 623.

[70] *Peat v Jones & Co* (1881) 8 QBD 147, 149, referred to in *Secretary of State for Trade and Industry v Frid* [2004] 2 AC 506 at [22].

[71] This proposition was accepted in *Re Parker* (1997) 80 FCR 1, 10. It is consistent with Brightman J's explanation in *Re D H Curtis* [1978] Ch 162, 172 of the comment of Lord Russell in *Palmer v Day & Sons* [1895] 2 QB 618, 621 regarding the necessity for the claims to arise out of contract, given that an unliquidated

should be interpreted as referring to an account of sums due in respect of cross-demands each of which constitutes a debt, a credit or the outcome of a prior dealing. The view that a dealing is not necessary in the case of mutual debts and credits *prima facie* finds support in the authorities which have established that a tax liability to the Crown can be the subject of a set-off.[72]

But the adoption of that interpretation of the insolvency set-off section would also **7.14** have problems. It is contrary to a number of judicial statements, for example Lawrence LJ's comment in *Re Fenton, ex p The Fenton Textile Association, Ltd,*[73] that 'the account which has to be taken . . . is an account of what is due from the one party to the other in respect of the mutual dealings', and Winn LJ's observation in *Rolls Razor Ltd v Cox,*[74] that the proper construction of the set-off section 'involves placing emphasis primarily upon the concept of mutual dealings and consequentially regarding the debts and credits referred to as such mutual debts and mutual credits as arise from mutual dealings'. Moreover, it is difficult to reconcile with the stipulation in the insolvency set-off section that an account is to be taken of what is due from each party to the other 'in respect of the mutual dealings'.[75] This suggests that the set-off section only applies to claims which arose out of a dealing.[76]

That proposition was accepted by the House of Lords in *Secretary of State for Trade and* **7.15** *Industry v Frid.*[77] After noting that the word 'other', in the expression 'mutual credits, mutual debts or other mutual dealings', suggests that mutual credits and mutual debts must be qualified by a requirement that the credits or debts can 'in some sense' be described as mutual dealings,[78] Lord Hoffmann observed:[79]

> All that is necessary therefore is that there should have been 'dealings' (in an extended sense which includes the commission of a tort or the imposition of a statutory obligation) which give rise to commensurable cross-claims.

---

claim could only come within the set-off section on the basis that it is the outcome of a dealing (see para. 7.05 above). See also Pincus J in the Federal Court of Australia in *McIntyre v Perkes* (1990) 22 FCR 260, 262, referring to the earlier judgment of Hill J in that case at (1989) 89 ALR 460, 470–1.

[72] See para. 7.11 above. But see the 'extended' meaning of 'dealings' referred to in *Secretary of State for Trade and Industry v Frid* [2004] 2 AC 506 at [24] and [25], discussed below.

[73] [1931] 1 Ch 85, 113.

[74] [1967] 1 QB 552, 574. See also the discussion in *Gye v McIntyre* (1991) 171 CLR 609, 623.

[75] See the Insolvency Act 1986, s. 323(2) (bankruptcy), and the Insolvency Rules 1986, rr. 4.90(3) (liquidation) and 2.85(3) (administration). In Australia, see the Bankruptcy Act 1966 (Cth), s. 86(1)(a) and the Corporations Act 2001 (Cth), s. 553C(1)(a).

[76] In interpreting the bankruptcy legislation, the Australian High Court has: 'affirmed the primacy of the statutory text, freed from . . . anachronistic. nineteenth century judicial accretions.' See *Foots v Southern Cross Mine Management Pty Ltd* (2007) 234 CLR 52 at [62].

[77] [2004] 2 AC 506. It is also suggested by the comment of Gleeson CJ, Gummow, Hayne and Callinan JJ in their joint judgment in the Australian High Court in *Coventry v Charter Pacific Corporation Ltd* (2005) 227 CLR 234 at [34] that 'the set-off provisions . . . are engaged where there have been *mutual dealings* between the bankrupt and another person *proving or claiming to prove a debt* in the bankruptcy' (emphasis as in the report).

[78] [2004] 2 AC 506 at [22].

[79] [2004] 2 AC 506 at [24]. Lord Nicholls of Birkenhead, Lord Hope of Craighead, Lord Phillips of Worth Matravers and Lord Brown of Eaton-under-Heywood agreed with Lord Hoffmann's judgment.

'Dealings' are 'necessary'. Lord Hoffmann said that the term is used in an 'extended sense' in the set-off section, but he gave little indication as to what precisely it means other than that it may include the commission of a tort and the imposition of a statutory obligation. A statutory obligation, for example an obligation to pay tax to a revenue authority,[80] would not be a 'dealing' in the ordinary sense of that word, and on other occasions it has been said that a tort may not be a dealing.[81]

7.16 While Lord Hoffmann affirmed the primacy of the concept of dealings in that extended sense, the question arises as to the relationship between that concept and the requirement of mutuality.

7.17 Lord Hoffmann prefaced his remarks in relation to 'dealings' by referring to the 'linguistic problem' noted by the High Court of Australia in *Gye v McIntyre*,[82] that 'credits' and 'debts' ordinarily represent the outcome of dealings rather than the dealings themselves, whereas dealings do not of themselves, as distinct from their outcome, represent claims susceptible to a set-off. In considering that point, Lord Hoffmann adopted an observation in *Gye v McIntyre*[83] that:

> [T]he requirement of mutuality in respect of 'other . . . dealings', as distinct from 'credits' or 'debts' susceptible of immediate set-off, is directed not so much to the relationship between the dealings as such but to the relationship between the claims which have arisen from them.

This suggests that dealings must give rise to mutual cross-claims but the concept of mutuality does not apply to the dealings themselves.[84] That distinction formed the basis of a criticism by Lord Hoffmann of an earlier suggestion by Millett J (as he then was) in *Re Charge Card Services Ltd*,[85] that debts the subject of a set-off must be 'exclusively referrable' to a contract or other transaction between the parties to the set-off. That view was expressed in the context of an attempt by Millett J to explain the much-criticized decision of the Court of Appeal in *Re A Debtor (No 66 of 1955)*.[86] In that case, a set-off was denied to a principal debtor in the bankruptcy of a surety against the surety's claim for an indemnity from the principal debtor, in circumstances where the surety's trustee in bankruptcy had paid the creditor after the bankruptcy. The point in relation to Millett J's suggestion was that the principal debtor's indemnity obligation was not referable to a transaction between the debtor and the surety, but rather to the guarantee which the surety had given to the creditor and to which the principal debtor was not a party. As Lord Hoffmann observed,[87] Millett J's

---

[80] See *Re D H Curtis (Builders) Ltd* [1978] 1 Ch 162, and para. 7.11 above. The decision in *Re D H Curtis* was accepted as correct in *Secretary of State v Frid* [2004] 2 AC 506 at [18] and [25], and there is no doubt that Lord Hoffmann regarded that case as illustrating the extended meaning of 'dealings'.

[81] See paras 8.53–8.54 below.

[82] (1991) 171 CLR 609, 623. See para. 7.07 above.

[83] *Gye v McIntyre* (1991) 171 CLR 609, 623.

[84] Compare Phillimore J's reference in *Re Taylor. Ex p Norvell* [1910] 1 KB 562, 568 to an 'obligation [which] arises out of mutual dealings between the debtor and a creditor', and Romer LJ's reference in *Re Fenton* [1931] 1 Ch 85, 117 to 'mutuality of dealings'.

[85] [1987] 1 Ch 150, 189–90. See paras 8.24–8.26 above.

[86] [1956] 1 WLR 1226. See paras 8.20–8.23, 8.42–8.43 above.

[87] [2004] 2 AC 506 at [25].

explanation implied that the insolvency set-off section requires mutual transactions. In rejecting the attempt to explain *Re A Debtor (No. 66 of 1955)* on that basis, Lord Hoffmann said:

> [T]here is nothing in the term 'mutual debts' which requires that both debts must be, as Millett J put it, 'exclusively referable' to a contract or other 'transaction' between the parties to the set-off. It is true that if it were not for the historical background, one might have been able to argue that such a notion was implied by the words 'mutual dealings'. But once one accepts that the debts need not arise from consensual transactions at all, but can arise from statutory obligations as in *In re D H Curtis (Builders) Ltd* [1978] Ch 162 or torts as in *Gye v McIntyre* 171 CLR 609, such a requirement of mutuality in the transactions giving rise to the cross-claims becomes untenable.[88]

The notion that mutuality is directed at the claims resulting from dealings, as opposed to the dealings themselves, is consistent with the fundamental principle that mutuality in insolvency set-off is determined by reference to equitable interests.[89] Consider the case of a contract entered into with a trustee for the benefit of a third party beneficiary. A trustee contracts as a principal, not as an agent.[90] The beneficiary is not a party to the contract, but if the other contracting party becomes insolvent the availability of a set-off in the insolvency against a claim accruing to the trustee under the contract is determined by reference to the position of the beneficiary, as the person entitled in equity to the benefit of the claim, not that of the trustee.

7.18

If there is no requirement of mutuality in the transactions which give rise to the cross-claims, there would be grounds for reconciling the pre-1869 cases referred to above,[91] such as *Hankey v Smith*[92] and *Forster v Wilson*,[93] with the view that insolvency set-off requires commensurable cross-claims that arose out of dealings. In *Hankey v Smith* the holder of the bill of exchange obtained the bill through an indorsement of the bill to him. The bankrupt had accepted the bill, but he was not a party to the indorsement. However, the circumstance that the acceptor was not a party to the latter transaction would not be fatal to a set-off.[94] It could still be said that there were dealings which gave rise to mutual cross-claims.

7.19

There are nevertheless problems with the adoption of that approach in Australia.[95] Comments in the judgment of the High Court in *Gye v McIntyre* suggest that dealings

7.20

---

[88] [2004] 2 AC 506 at [25].

[89] See paras 11.13–11.17 below.

[90] *Lewin on Trusts* (18th edn, 2008), 13 §1–17; *Construction Engineering (Aust) Pty Ltd v Hexyl Pty Ltd* (1985) 155 CLR 541, 546.

[91] See para. 7.13 above.

[92] (1789) 3 TR 507n, 100 ER 703.

[93] (1843) 12 M & W 191, 152 ER 1165.

[94] In the same way, consistent with the House of Lords' criticism of the reasoning in *Re A Debtor (No. 66 of 1955)* (above) in *Secretary of State v Frid* [2004] 2 AC [14]–[17] as well as other authorities, a surety who has paid the creditor may employ the debtor's obligation to indemnify the surety in a set-off in the debtor's bankruptcy notwithstanding that the debtor was not a party to the guarantee. See paras 8.27–8.28 below.

[95] In addition to the following, Dixon J in *Hiley v The Peoples Prudential Assurance Co Ltd* (1938) 60 CLR 468, 496 commented that it is 'enough' for a set-off that: 'at the commencement of the winding up mutual

the subject of a set-off should have involved both the bankrupt and the creditor. Their Honours said:

> There will, for the purposes of s. 86, be mutual dealings at the date of the sequestration order if there existed at that date 'dealings' which involved the bankrupt and the other party and which were capable of giving rise to, and subsequently did give rise to, 'mutual' claims between them . . .[96]

And:

> The critical matters for the purposes of s. 86 are that there had been dealings in which the creditor and the bankrupt were both involved and that those dealings gave rise to mutual claims between them in the relevant sense.[97]

7.21 The later discussion by Gleeson CJ, Gummow, Hayne and Callinan JJ in their joint judgment in the Australian High Court in *Coventry v Charter Pacific Corporation Ltd*[98] also suggests that view. The point in issue was whether a damages claim for misleading or deceptive conduct under the Corporations Law, ss. 995(2) and 1005 was provable in the bankruptcy of the representor pursuant to the Bankruptcy Act 1966 (Cth), s. 82. In the course of their judgment, their Honours considered some old English cases concerning the analogous situation of a fraudulent misrepresentation which had induced a contract. In that context, there was authority for the proposition that, if the misrepresentation induced a contract with the representor (a 'bilateral' case), the damages claim against the representor for misrepresentation could be the subject of a set-off between the representor and the person misled in the representor's bankruptcy.[99] If, on the other hand, the misrepresentation induced the person misled to contract with a third party as opposed to with the representor (a 'tripartite' case), *Re Giles, ex p Stone*[100] was authority for the proposition that the resulting damages claim was not provable in the representor's bankruptcy. This was on the basis that the damages claim in that circumstance was regarded as having arisen otherwise than by reason of a contract, promise or breach of trust, so that the exception in those terms in the description of 'debts provable' in the Bankruptcy Act 1883, s. 37 applied so as to preclude a proof.[101] If a claim against a bankrupt is not provable in the bankruptcy, it cannot be included in a set-off.[102] Therefore, had *Re Giles* been a set-off case, a set-off would have been denied on that ground. But the High Court also suggested that in such a case there would have been lacking the necessary mutual dealing between the representor and the person misled to support a set-off between them in the representor's bankruptcy, on the basis that a damages claim in a tripartite transaction (where the representation induced a contract

---

dealings exist which involve rights and obligations whether absolute or contingent of such a nature that afterwards in the events that happen they mature or develop into pecuniary demands capable of set-off.' This suggests that mutuality was thought to apply to the dealings.

[96] (1991) 171 CLR 609, 623.
[97] (1991) 171 CLR 609, 626.
[98] (2005) 227 CLR 234. See also the discussion of the case at paras 8.58–8.61 below.
[99] *Jack v Kipping* (1882) 9 QBD 113.
[100] (1889) 61 LT (NS) 82.
[101] Section 37 provided that demands in the nature of unliquidated damages arising otherwise than by reason of contract, promise or breach of trust were not provable in bankruptcy. The Bankruptcy Act 1966 (Cth), s. 82(2), being the provision in issue in *Coventry v Charter Pacific*, is in similar terms.
[102] See para. 7.24 below.

with a third party) does not arise from a mutual dealing between them.[103] This is consistent with the suggestion in *Gye v McIntyre* that the parties to the set-off must have been involved in the dealings which give rise to the mutual claims the subject of the proposed set-off.

That view would be difficult to reconcile with cases such as *Hankey v Smith*,[104] notwith- **7.22**
standing the wide meaning that has been ascribed to 'dealings'.[105] An alternative (and the preferred) view is that a dealing between the insolvent and the creditor is not necessary when the subject of the set-off is a mutual debt or credit.[106] This would avoid that problem, and moreover it is consistent with the historical development of the bankruptcy set-off section. But for the reasons given above it also is not free of difficulty.[107]

C. Different Dealings and Contracts

In *Peat v Jones & Co*,[108] Jessel MR said that: 'a contract of sale and purchase is in its nature **7.23**
mutual, imposing reciprocal obligations on the vendor and purchaser. Any claim arising out of the mutual dealings could be set off.'[109] Reciprocal obligations under a contract ordinarily would be mutual,[110] but when it is sought to base a set-off upon a damages claim for breach of contract the concept of mutual dealings does not require that the cross-de-mand should have arisen out of the same contract.[111] Further, when a claim by one party is for a debt, or is based upon the giving of credit, or is a damages claim arising from a dealing, it is not necessary that the cross-claim should be of the same nature. The important point is that the claims are commensurable, in the sense that they are money claims which are capable of being brought into an account.[112]

D. The Insolvent's Liability

For the insolvency set-off section to apply in bankruptcy there must be mutual credits, **7.24**
mutual debts or other mutual dealings between the bankrupt and: 'any creditor of the bankrupt proving or claiming to prove for a bankruptcy debt.'[113] The set-off provision in

---

[103] (2005) 227 CLR 234 at [49] and [50]. The discussion at [49] was expressed equivocally, in terms that there 'may have been' lacking a mutual dealing, but compare the discussion at [50] and [59]–[61]. See also [39], where their Honours referred to 'the reciprocity involved in a mutual dealing'.

[104] See para. 7.13 above.

[105] See paras 7.08–7.10 above.

[106] See para. 7.13 above.

[107] See paras 7.14–7.15 above.

[108] (1881) 8 QBD 147.

[109] (1881) 8 QBD 147, 149. See also *Jack v Kipping* (1882) 9 QBD 113, 116.

[110] Unless, for example, the benefit of the contract is held on trust for someone else.

[111] *McIntyre v Perkes* (1990) 22 FCR 260, 263 (Pincus J, referring to *Hiley v The Peoples Prudential Assurance Co Ltd* (1938) 60 CLR 468), and see also 'Set-off in case of mutual dealings' (1882) 26 Sol Jo 575.

[112] In *Re D H Curtis (Builders) Ltd* [1978] 1 Ch 162, 171 Brightman J commented: 'In my view the word "mutual" in this context connotes that comparable acts or events are to be found on both sides. The type of acts or events seem to me to be immaterial provided that they are comparable, i.e. commensurable.' 'Commensurable' means that the claims are for money. See ch. 10 below.

[113] Insolvency Act 1986, s. 323(1).

the case of an insolvent company is expressed in similar terms.[114] The requirement that there should be a person proving or claiming to prove for a debt in the bankruptcy has as a corollary that the creditor's claim against the bankrupt must be capable of proof.[115] In addition, however, the courts have often indicated that the converse proposition also applies, that the fact that a claim may be proved means that it should also be capable of being employed in a set-off.[116] This proposition would appear to be based on the notion that insolvency set-off is an aspect of the rules relating to proof of debts.[117] But while that converse proposition may be accepted at a general level, there is a difficulty with the view that it constitutes an invariable principle, and that is that there is nothing in the language of the set-off section which expressly supports it.[118] The section states that the creditor must be proving or claiming to prove a debt, but it does not say that it is sufficient that the claim is provable. In deciding whether a claim may be employed in a set-off, the primary question should always be whether the cross-demands are such as to come within the language of the section. In other words, there must be mutual credits, mutual debts or other mutual dealings.

7.25 The connection between proof and set-off has not always been emphasized by the courts. For example, in 1791 it was held in *Smith v Hodson*[119] that an accommodation acceptor paying after the bankruptcy of the drawer could employ his claim for an indemnity in a set-off, even though prior to 1809 an acceptor paying under those circumstances did not have a right of proof.[120] *Smith v Hodson* concerned the 1732 set-off section, which applied only in the case of mutual debts and mutual credit. The section did not refer to any connection

---

[114] Insolvency Rules 1986, rr. 2.85(2) (administration) and 4.90(1) (liquidation).

[115] *Secretary of State for Trade and Industry v Frid* [2004] 2 AC 506 at [13]. Compare the situation in which a creditor with an otherwise provable debt had agreed not to prove. See *Kitchen's Trustee v Madders* [1950] 1 Ch 134, and para. 6.113 above. It has been suggested in Australia that the set-off provisions were used to extend the reach of debts provable in bankruptcy. See *Coventry v Charter Pacific Corporation Ltd* (2005) 227 CLR 234 at [34].

[116] *Graham v Russell* (1816) 5 M & S 498, 501, 105 ER 1133, 1134; *Re Asphaltic Wood Pavement Co. Lee & Chapman's Case* (1885) 30 Ch D 216, 222, 224; *Palmer v Day & Sons* [1895] 2 QB 618, 621; *Re Taylor, ex p Norvell* [1910] 1 KB 562, 580; *Paddy v Clutton* [1920] 2 Ch 554, 567; *Ellis and Company's Trustee v Dixon-Johnson* [1924] 1 Ch 342, 357; *Re City Life Assurance Co Ltd. Grandfield's Case* [1926] 1 Ch 191, 210–11, 212; *Re Fenton* [1931] 1 Ch 85, 113; *Hiley v The Peoples Prudential Assurance Co, Ltd* (1938) 60 CLR 468, 490; *Re Bank of Credit and Commerce International SA (No 8)* [1996] Ch 245, 256 (CA). See also *Peat v Jones & Co* (1881) 8 QBD 147, 150; *Sovereign Life Assurance Co v Dodd* [1892] 1 QB 405, 412; *Re D H Curtis (Builders) Ltd* [1978] 1 Ch 162, 173–4; *Re Cushla Ltd* [1979] 3 All ER 415, 420; *Willment Brothers Ltd v North West Thames Regional Health Authority* (1984) 26 BLR 51, 59; *Re Charge Card Services Ltd* [1987] 1 Ch 150, 179, 181, 187.

[117] *Mersey Steel and Iron Co Ltd v Naylor, Benzon, & Co* (1884) 9 App Cas 434, 437–8; *Re Northside Properties Pty Ltd and the Companies Act* [1971] 2 NSWLR 320, 323; *Re Bank of Credit and Commerce International SA (No 8)* [1996] Ch 245, 256 (CA); *Re One. Tel Ltd* (2002) 43 ACSR 305 at [25].

[118] The qualification to the set-off section could preclude a set-off in respect of an otherwise provable debt. See paras 6.66–6.99 above.

[119] (1791) 4 TR 211, 100 ER 979. See also *Ex p Boyle, re Shepherd*, unreported, but noted in Cooke, *The Bankrupt Laws* (8th edn, 1823) vol. 1, 571, and *Ex p Wagstaff* (1806) 13 Ves Jun 65, 33 ER 219.

[120] *Chilton v Whiffin* (1768) 3 Wils KB 13, 95 ER 906; *Young v Hockley* (1772) 3 Wils KB 346, 95 ER 1092; *Snaith v Gale* (1797) 7 TR 364, 101 ER 1023. The statute (1809) 49 Geo III, c. 121, s. 8 introduced a right of proof in favour of a surety who paid after the bankruptcy of the debtor. Though at common law an accommodation acceptor was not regarded as a surety (see *Fentum v Pocock* (1813) 5 Taunt 192, 128 ER 660, but compare the position in equity, for which see *Coles Myer Finance Ltd v Commissioner of Taxation* (1993) 176 CLR 640, 657, 683–4), it was considered nevertheless that the statute applied to accommodation

---

between set-off and provable debts, so that on its face there was nothing objectionable in the decision in *Smith v Hodson*. In 1825 new legislation (6 Geo IV, c. 16) came into force. While the set-off section (s 50) was still confined to mutual credit and mutual debts, it contained an express statutory recognition of the principle that all provable debts could be set off.[121] A provision to that effect also appeared in the set-off section in the bankruptcy legislation of 1849.[122] Neither of those sections, however, addressed the question of the susceptibility to a set-off of demands that were not in the nature of provable debts. Sometimes, when the courts held that a claim against a bankrupt could not be employed in a set-off pursuant to the 1825 or the 1849 set-off section, the justification was that the claim was not provable, although this was not always the case. There are instances in which the courts instead had regard to the definition of mutual credit adopted in *Rose v Hart*[123] as a reason for rejecting an argument for a set-off. For example, in *Abbott v Hicks*[124] it was held that a contingent liability of the bankrupt could not be the subject of a set-off, the court emphasizing that the liability was not provable.[125] That case should be contrasted with *Rose v Sims*,[126] in which a person indebted to a bankrupt sought to set off a claim that he had against the bankrupt for damages for breach of contract. Prior to 1861 damages claims were not provable in a bankruptcy.[127] It was held in *Rose v Sims* that the cross-demand could not be employed in a set-off, not because it was not provable, but on the basis of the principle that mutual credit was confined to transactions that would end in debts, and a damages claim is not a debt.[128]

The stipulation in the 1825 and the 1849 set-off sections, that all provable debts could be **7.26** set off, was omitted from the 1869 and the subsequent sections, although the courts continued to emphasize the principle. The continued emphasis of the principle, however, should be considered in the context of the changes to the proof of debt and the set-off sections that occurred in 1861 and 1869. In 1861, damages claims for breach of contract became provable. A claim for damages is not a debt and nor does it constitute the giving of credit.[129] If, therefore, it was intended that such claims should be able to be included in

---

acceptors. See Cooke, *The Bankrupt Laws* (8th edn, 1823) vol. 1, 175, referring to *Ex p Yonge* (1814) 3 V & B 31, 39–40, 35 ER 391, 394.

[121] The section provided that: 'every Debt or Demand hereby made proveable against the Estate of the Bankrupt, may also be set off in manner aforesaid.'

[122] Bankrupt Law Consolidation Act 1849, s. 171.

[123] (1818) 8 Taunt 499, 506, 129 ER 477, 480. See para. 7.03 above.

[124] (1839) 5 Bing (NC) 578, 132 ER 1222.

[125] See in particular the judgments of Coltman and Erskine JJ. Thus, *Abbott v Hicks* was cited in *Smith's Leading Cases* (2nd edn, 1842) vol. 2, 182 as authority for the proposition that a demand that was not provable under the fiat could not be set off. While s. 56 of the statute (1825) 6 Geo IV, c. 16 allowed a right of proof in respect of contingent debts, the contingent liability in *Abbott v Hicks* was not within the ambit of that section.

[126] (1830) 1 B & Ad 521, 109 ER 881.

[127] See the Bankruptcy Act 1861, s. 153.

[128] While *Rose v Hart* was not mentioned in the judgments, it was referred to in a note to the report, and it is evident that the decision in *Rose v Sims* was based upon that case. Even though a claim may have been framed as a claim for damages, if in truth it was liquidated, so that the amount could be ascertained without the intervention of a jury, it could be proved in a bankruptcy, and similarly it could be the subject of a set-off. See, as to proof, *Utterson v Vernon* (1790) 3 TR 539, 100 ER 721 and, as to set-off, *Gibson v Bell* (1835) 1 Bing (NC) 743, 131 ER 1303 and *Groom v West* (1838) 8 Ad & E 758, 112 ER 1025.

[129] See paras 7.05 and 7.06 above.

a set-off, it would not have been satisfactory to rely on a general statement that all provable debts could be set off if at the same time the scope of the set-off section was confined to mutual debts and mutual credit. In the 1869 Act, the reference in the earlier legislation to provable debts being able to be set off was omitted from the set-off section, and instead the scope of the section was expanded to include mutual dealings. Subsequent judicial statements to the effect that a provable debt can be included in a set-off may well have been a correct summary of the position that applied after 1869, and that continued to apply in relation to the 1883 and the 1914 Bankruptcy Acts, in light of the scope of the right of proof in those Acts. It should not, however, be regarded as a fixed principle that applies regardless of the language of the set-off section and of any changes to the right of proof. In truth, as Mason J remarked in the High Court of Australia,[130] the fact that a claim against a bankrupt is provable should only provide indirect assistance in considering whether it can be set off. The set-off section requires that the claim against the bankrupt must be capable of proof, but this is expressed as a necessary, rather than a sufficient, condition for a set-off. Thus, in *Bank of Credit and Commerce International SA v Al-Saud*[131] Neill LJ commented that, while it is true that a debt which is not eligible for proof is not eligible for set-off, this does not mean that all debts which are eligible for proof are eligible for set-off. The primary question should always be whether there are mutual credits, mutual debts or other mutual dealings.[132] In that regard, the Insolvency Act 1986 further increased the range of provable debts, by allowing a proof in respect of a damages claim in tort,[133] but without any corresponding change to the set-off section. The position accordingly would appear to be that, if a claim in tort arose out of a prior dealing between the parties, it should be able to be included in a set-off.[134] But if the claim in question did not arise out of a dealing, it is difficult to see what basis there is for including it in a set-off, notwithstanding that it is provable, since it is not a debt and nor does it come within the concept of giving credit.[135]

E. The Insolvent's Claim

(1) The insolvent's claim and provability

7.27   Consider the claim on the other side of the account, being the bankrupt's or the company's claim against the creditor. In *Graham v Russell*,[136] Lord Ellenborough said that: 'in taking an account between parties, the question, whether any particular item shall be introduced

---

[130] *Day & Dent Constructions Pty Ltd v North Australian Properties Pty Ltd* (1982) 150 CLR 85, 108.

[131] [1997] 1 BCLC 457, 466.

[132] As Lord Hoffmann expressed the principle in *Stein v Blake* [1996] AC 243, 251, insolvency set-off: 'applies to any claim arising out of mutual credits or other mutual dealings before the bankruptcy for which a creditor would be entitled to prove as a "bankruptcy debt".'

[133] See the Insolvency Act 1986, s. 322, 'bankruptcy debt' being defined in s. 382 as including liabilities in tort. For company liquidation, see the Insolvency Rules 1986, r. 13.12. In Australia, a liability in tort is still not provable in a bankruptcy (see the Bankruptcy Act 1966 (Cth), s. 82(2)), although it may now be proved in a company liquidation. See the Corporations Act 2001 (Cth), s. 553(1).

[134] See *Gye v McIntyre* (1991) 171 CLR 609 (fraudulent misrepresentation) and *Secretary of State for Trade and Industry v Frid* [2004] 2 AC 506 at [24], and paras 7.08–7.10 above.

[135] See paras 8.53–8.61 below.

[136] (1816) 5 M & S 498, 502, 105 ER 1133, 1135.

into it, must depend upon the nature and character of the item itself, and not upon the side of the account at which it is to be placed.' The case concerned a statute[137] which allowed an insured under a policy of insurance to prove a claim on the policy in the bankruptcy of the underwriter, even though the loss may not have occurred until after the bankruptcy.[138] *Graham v Russell* differed from the situation contemplated by the statute in that it was the insured rather than the underwriter who was bankrupt, and the underwriter wanted to set off a liability that had accrued on the policy after the insured's bankruptcy against a prior debt of the insured for premiums. Because the bankrupt's claim against the underwriter would have been provable in the underwriter's bankruptcy, and could have been the subject of a set-off, if the underwriter instead had been the bankrupt party, Lord Ellenborough in delivering the judgment of the Exchequer Chamber held that the underwriter could employ his liability on the claim in a set-off when the question arose in the context of the bankruptcy of the insured. The proposition which is the converse of that approach is that, if the bankrupt's claim against the creditor is such that it could not have been proved if the creditor instead had been bankrupt, it similarly should not be capable of being employed in a set-off in the present bankruptcy, irrespective of whether it arises out of a dealing between the parties.

In Australia, the High Court rejected that converse proposition in *Gye v McIntyre*,[139] as did **7.28** Gummow and von Doussa JJ in the Federal Court in that case.[140] The High Court reached its conclusion without considering *Graham v Russell*. However, *Graham v Russell* was considered in the Federal Court, Gummow and von Doussa JJ distinguishing it on the ground that it was concerned only with facilitating, not restricting, the right of set-off. It is true that, in *Graham v Russell*, Lord Ellenborough looked at whether the bankrupt's claim would have been provable if the creditor had been bankrupt as a means of allowing a set-off. It is nevertheless correct to say that the rationale underlying Lord Ellenborough's judgment was that the question whether an item can be included in a set-off should depend upon the nature and character of the item itself, and not upon the side of the account at which it is to be placed.[141] Recourse was had to that notion in *Graham v Russell* in order to allow a set-off. But given that, since 1869, it has been a requirement of the set-off section that the creditor's claim against the bankrupt be provable,[141a] the rationale upon which the decision in *Graham v Russell* was based suggests that the bankrupt's claim should also now be in the nature of a provable debt. *Graham v Russell* suggests that it is the nature of the claim that matters, not the side of the account on which it appears. There are other cases which support that view. In *Young v Bank of Bengal*,[142] debtors defaulted after the date of their bankruptcy in payment of a secured debt. The creditor realised the security and, after

---

[137] (1746) 19 Geo II, c. 32, s. 2.
[138] Prior to 1825 (see s. 56 of 6 Geo IV, c. 16) contingent debts as a general rule could be neither proved nor set off in a bankruptcy.
[139] (1991) 171 CLR 609, 628–9. See also *Coventry v Charter Pacific Corporation Ltd* (2005) 227 CLR 234 at [54]–[55] and [106].
[140] (1990) 22 FCR 260, 273–4. Compare the earlier judgment of Hill J at (1989) 89 ALR 460, 471, 472.
[141] (1816) 5 M & S 498, 502, 105 ER 1133, 1135.
[141a] See paras 6.42–6.43 above.
[142] (1836) 1 Moore 150, 12 ER 771.

satisfying the secured debt, held a surplus. The creditor then sought to apply the surplus in reduction of a separate unsecured debt of the bankrupts. One of the reasons that the Privy Council gave for holding against a set-off was that the creditor's contingent liability to account for any surplus would not have been a provable debt under the then current legislation if the creditor instead had been made bankrupt before selling the security.[143] In other words, provability was used to restrict the right of set-off in the context of the bankrupt's claim. This was also the approach adopted by Maule J, with whom Cresswell and Williams JJ concurred, in *Bell v Carey*.[144] The bankrupt in that case had a claim in damages against a creditor. Maule J said that the claim could not be the subject of a set-off because, under the bankruptcy legislation in force at the time: 'you could not say that the damages, great or small, would be a demand provable under a fiat.'[145] Reference also may be made to *Booth v Hutchinson*.[146] In that case, Malins VC, in deciding that a claim for rent which accrued to a landlord after the landlord had executed a deed of assignment could be the subject of a set-off,[147] relied on the definition of 'liability' in the Bankruptcy Act 1869, s. 31 in relation to the right of proof.[148] Those cases, which suggest that the availability of a set-off in relation to a bankrupt's claim is limited by the scope of the proof of debt provision, were not referred to in *Gye v McIntyre*. More recently, Rose LJ, in delivering the judgment of the Court of Appeal[149] in *Re Bank of Credit and Commerce International SA (No 8)*,[150] also accepted that view. He said that 'a claim is not capable of set-off unless it is admissible to proof,' and that:

> This is true of both sides of the account. The right to set off a particular claim depends on the nature and character of the claim itself and not upon the side of the account on which it is to be placed: *Graham v Russell* (1816) 5 M & S 498, 501.[151]

7.29 On appeal, however, the House of Lords doubted that proposition,[152] referring to *Gye v McIntyre*. The view expressed in *Gye v McIntyre* would seem to be correct. The question is one of construction of the insolvency set-off section, and there is nothing in the section to suggest that the bankrupt's claim against the creditor should be in the nature of a provable debt.

7.30 *Gye v McIntyre* concerned two debtors who had entered into compositions with their creditors, one of whom was liable to the debtors in tort for damages for fraudulent misrepresentation.[153] The misrepresentations arose in the course of negotiations for the

---

[143] See the discussion at (1836) 1 Moore 150, 166–7, 12 ER 771, 778. This view is also consistent with Brightman J's comment in *Re D H Curtis (Builders) Ltd* [1978] Ch 162, 173, that a natural assumption would be that the set-off section is intended to cover the same subject-matter as the section dealing with proof of debt.

[144] (1849) 8 CB 887, 137 ER 757.

[145] (1849) 8 CB 887, 894, 137 ER 757, 760. See also the comments of Cresswell J during argument at 892, 759.

[146] (1872) LR 15 Eq 30 (esp. at 35).

[147] The case concerned a deed of assignment rather than a bankruptcy, but it was considered that it was subject to the same principle as for a bankruptcy.

[148] The decision is nevertheless unsatisfactory, because the Vice Chancellor failed to consider the question of mutuality which may arise in lease cases as a result of the vesting of the property in the trustee. See paras 13.64–13.68 below.

[149] Rose, Saville and Millett LJJ.

[150] [1996] Ch 245.

[151] [1996] Ch 245, 256.

[152] *Re Bank of Credit and Commerce International SA (No 8)* [1998] AC 214, 228.

[153] The Bankruptcy Act 1966 (Cth), s. 243 provides that the set-off section (s. 86) is to apply to compositions.

purchase of a hotel by the debtors from a company associated with the creditor. The misrepresentations did not arise out of a contract between the debtors and the creditor, the parties to the contract instead being the debtors and the company. They did arise, however, in the course of the negotiations between the debtors and the creditor leading up to the contract. The High Court said that the concept of 'dealing' in the set-off section includes contractual negotiations. It is not confined to the resulting contract. Accordingly, the claim in this case did arise out of a dealing and could be set off. The claim in question was a claim in tort. Unlike the Insolvency Act in England, the proof of debt provision in the Australian Bankruptcy Act 1966 (Cth) does not extend to tortious demands.[154] Nevertheless, the High Court said that there was nothing in the language of the set-off section which required that the bankrupt's claim (or, as in that case, the claim of the debtors subject to the compositions) should be in the nature of a provable debt.[155]

(2) The bankrupt's claim must vest in the trustee

On the other hand, the High Court in *Gye v McIntyre* indicated that the availability of **7.31** a set-off in relation to the bankrupt's claim is not unqualified. In order to come within the set-off section, the bankrupt's claim must be a presently payable debt at the date of the bankruptcy, or the result of giving credit, or it must be the outcome of a prior dealing between the parties. In addition, however, the High Court suggested, though without expressing a concluded view, that the claim should be such that it would vest in a trustee in bankruptcy,[156] an opinion earlier expressed by Wood.[157] This would exclude, for example, claims for damages for personal injury or wrong done to the bankrupt.[158] The requirement was thought to follow from the stipulation in the set-off section that the balance of the

---

[154] See the Bankruptcy Act 1966 (Cth), s. 82(2). This is no longer the case, however, in company liquidation. See the Corporations Act 2001 (Cth), s. 553.

[155] (1991) 171 CLR 609, 628–9.

[156] (1991) 171 CLR 609, 626–7. It was unnecessary for the High Court in *Gye v McIntyre* to express a concluded view on this point since the claim for fraudulent misrepresentation against Mrs McIntyre would, if a sequestration order had been made at the time of the composition, have vested in the trustee in bankruptcy. See (1991) 171 CLR 609, 627. *Gye v McIntyre* concerned compositions entered into by two debtors under Part X of the Bankruptcy Act 1966 (Cth), rather than bankruptcy. The claim possessed by each of the debtors had not been included in the composition, but the High Court considered that it would be unjust if a statutory majority of creditors, by excluding a claim of the debtor against a particular creditor from the property vesting in the trustee of the composition, could deprive that creditor of the benefit of a set-off to which he or she would have been entitled if a bankruptcy had occurred. See (1991) 171 CLR 609, 627–8. The important point for a set-off was that the claim would have vested in a trustee in bankruptcy, if the case had involved a bankruptcy. A set-off therefore was allowed.

[157] Wood, *English and International Set-off* (1989), 315–16.

[158] See e.g. *Beckham v Drake* (1849) 2 HLC 579, 604, 621, 9 ER 1213, 1222, 1228; *Ex p Vine, re Wilson* (1878) 8 Ch D 364; *Wilson v United Counties Bank, Ltd* [1920] AC 102; *Heath v Tang* [1993] 1 WLR 1421, 1423. Compare *Cork v Rawlins* [2001] Ch 792 (sums payable under assurance policies). When a bankrupt has a cause of action in negligence, which includes a head of damage relating to property and another head of damage relating to personal injury, there is but one cause of action, and since it relates to property it vests in the trustee. On the other hand, the right to recover the damages which are personal, and any damages recovered, are held by the trustee on constructive trust for the bankrupt. See *Ord v Upton* [2000] Ch 352 (esp. at 369–70). Because the constructive trust relates not only to the damages recovered but also to the right to recover them, that part of the claim should not be the subject of a set-off in the bankruptcy. In Australia, the Bankruptcy Act 1966 (Cth), s. 116(2)(g) specifically exempts any right of the bankrupt to recover damages or compensation for personal injury or wrong done to the bankrupt from the property which is divisible among the creditors.

account should be provable in the bankruptcy, or, as the case may be, payable to the trustee in bankruptcy. If the balance is payable to the trustee, the section could only apply if the bankrupt's claim has vested in the trustee. This seems correct.[159] It should also apply in England, where tortious demands are now provable. A damages claim in tort should not be able to be employed in a set-off unless it arose out of a dealing between the parties to the proposed set-off.[160] Normally, the claims in tort which do not pass to the trustee, for example a damages claim for personal injury, are unlikely to arise out of a dealing. But if in an exceptional case the claim is derived from a dealing, the fact that it does not vest in the trustee should mean that it cannot be set off under the insolvency set-off section.[161]

7.32 However, in cases where the bankrupt's claim does not vest in the trustee, other forms of set-off may be available, for example a set-off of judgments or orders pursuant to the court's inherent jurisdiction[162] or equitable set-off,[163] depending on the circumstances.

(3) Assignment of a debt

7.33 A similar principle applies in the case of an assignment of a debt. If a creditor assigns the debt to a third party, and the creditor later becomes bankrupt, the assigned debt does not vest in the trustee in bankruptcy as part of the insolvent's estate,[164] and the debtor, therefore, cannot invoke the insolvency set-off section as a defence to an action for payment.[165]

---

[159] See also *De Mattos v Saunders* (1872) LR 7 CP 570, 582; *Gertig v Davies* (2003) 85 SASR 226 at [21]; *Piccone v Suncorp Metway Insurance Ltd* (2005) 148 FCR 437 at [12].

[160] See paras 8.53–8.54 below.

[161] Compare *Gertig v Davies* (2005) 85 SASR 226 and *Piccone v Suncorp Metway Insurance Ltd* (2005) 148 FCR 457 in relation to other forms of set-off. See para. 6.32 above.

[162] See paras 2.112–2.113 above.

[163] See paras 6.25–6.32 above.

[164] See the Insolvency Act 1986, ss. 283(3) and 306.

[165] *De Mattos v Saunders* (1872) LR 7 CP 570; *Re Asphaltic Wood Pavement Co. Lee & Chapman's Case* (1885) 30 Ch D 216, 225; *Popular Homes Ltd v Circuit Developments Ltd* [1979] 2 NZLR 642, 657. See also *Turner v Thomas* (1871) LR 6 CP 610, 615, and generally paras 11.16 and 17.39 below.

8

CLAIMS SUSCEPTIBLE TO INSOLVENCY SET-OFF

8.01 In the preceding chapter some general observations were made on the meaning of mutual credit and mutual dealings. The purpose of this chapter is to consider the application of the insolvency set-off section to various categories of claims.

A. Presently Existing Debts

(1) Presently payable or payable in the future

Presently payable

8.02 A debt which is both presently existing and payable at the relevant date for determining rights of set-off in an insolvency[1] may be the subject of a set-off. This includes a debt in equity,[2] other than an equitable debt in the form of an obligation to account for a trust fund.[3]

Payable at a future date

8.03 Subject to a possible discount for early payment,[4] a debt on either side of the account which is in existence at the relevant date, although not payable until a future date, may be the subject of a set-off.[5] In some early cases doubts were expressed as to whether this was strictly a debt for the purpose of the expression 'mutual debts', but in any event it was held to constitute the giving of credit so as to be available for set-off on that ground.[6]

(2) Unquantified or unascertained debts

8.04 A set-off is also available in respect of a debt which, although existing, was unquantified at the relevant date,[7] for example where the amount depended upon a valuation by a valuer,[8] or where an arithmetical calculation had to be undertaken,[9] or where an award of costs had been made before the relevant date but it was not taxed until after that date.[10]

---

[1] See paras 6.45–6.65 above.

[2] *Ryall v Rowles* (1750) 1 Ves Sen 348, 376, 27 ER 1074, 1090.

[3] See ch. 10 below.

[4] See paras 8.06–8.08 below.

[5] See e.g. *Ex p Prescot* (1753) 1 Atk 230, 26 ER 147 (debt owing to the bankrupt); *Atkinson v Elliott* (1797) 7 TR 378, 101 ER 1030 (debt owing by the bankrupt); *Rolls Razor Ltd v Cox* [1967] 1 QB 552, 569, 576.

[6] *Ex p Prescot* (1753) 1 Atk 230, 26 ER 147; *Atkinson v Elliott* (1797) 7 TR 378, 381, 101 ER 1030, 1031. See also *Hankey v Smith* (1789) 3 TR 507n, 100 ER 703; *Re Morris and M'Murray* (1874) 5 AJR 157 (affirmed at 185).

[7] See *Re Daintrey, ex p Mant* [1900] 1 QB 546 (although compare the interpretation put upon that case in *Day & Dent Constructions Pty Ltd v North Australian Properties Pty Ltd* (1982) 150 CLR 85, 92, 94, 103 and in *Re Charge Card Services Ltd* [1987] 1 Ch 150, 182–3, 188); *Handberg v Smarter Way (Aust) Pty Ltd* (2002) 190 ALR 130 at [56].

[8] *Ex p Hope, re Hanson* (1858) 3 De G & J 92, 44 ER 1203. See also *Re Rushforth, ex p J R Holmes and Sons* (1906) 95 LT 807.

[9] *Greater Britain Insurance Corporation Ltd v C T Bowring & Co (Insurance) Ltd* (1926) 24 Ll L Rep 7, 9.

[10] *Shand v M J Atkinson Ltd* [1966] NZLR 551; *Re Collinson; Smith v Sinnathamby* (1977) 33 FLR 39; *Gertig v Davies* (2003) 85 SASR 226 at [21] (the amount of the costs had not been determined: see at [39]). See also *Foots v Southern Cross Mine Management Pty Ltd* (2007) 234 CLR 52 at [67] (HCA) with respect to proof of debts. Compare *Ex p Rhodes* (1809) 15 Ves Jun 539, 33 ER 858. Compare also para. 8.11 below in relation to a costs order made after the relevant date in respect of proceedings commenced before that date.

In *Re The West Australian Lighterage, Stevedoring and Transport Co Ltd*,[11] a shareholder in a   **8.05**
company who was indebted to the company became bankrupt. Prior to the bankruptcy the
company had gone into voluntary liquidation. Its assets were more than sufficient to pay
its liabilities, although the extent of the surplus had not as yet been ascertained. When the
liquidator subsequently declared a dividend in favour of shareholders, the Western
Australian Supreme Court held that the company could set off in the bankruptcy the shareholder's dividend entitlement against the shareholder's debt to it, the point being that,
because the company went into voluntary liquidation before the bankruptcy under circumstances where there would be a surplus, the bankrupt at the date of the bankruptcy had
a claim for a share of the surplus which could be the subject of a set-off, notwithstanding
that the amount of the claim had not been ascertained at that date.

(3) Discount for early payment

When a creditor proves in a bankruptcy or a liquidation for a debt the due date for payment   **8.06**
of which has not yet occurred, r. 11.13 of the Insolvency Rules 1986 provides that, for 'the
purpose of dividend (and no other purpose)', the amount of the creditor's admitted proof
is to be discounted according to a formula to take into account that payment is to be
received early. On its face, r. 11.13 would not apply to the extent that the debt is to be
employed in a set-off, because to that extent there is no dividend payable. But while this
would appear to be the position in bankruptcy, it is not so in company liquidation. Rule
4.90(7) provides that r. 11.13 applies, for the purpose of a set-off under r. 4.90, to any sum
due to or from the company which is payable in the future.[12] Therefore, a debt on either
side of the account payable in the future is to be discounted for the purpose of a set-off in a
liquidation according to the formula in r. 11.13. In the case of a company in administration
where set-off applies,[13] rr. 2.85(7) and 2.105 operate to a similar effect.

In both liquidation and administration, the discount applies under the Insolvency Rules to   **8.07**
a debt (on either side of the account) which was not due for payment at the date of the
declaration of dividend. A debt payable before that date is included in a set-off at full value.[14]
But where the discount does apply, it is applied as from the date of the liquidation,[15] or
the date that the company entered administration,[16] in accordance with the terms of the

---

[11] (1903) 5 WAR 132, discussed in *Ansett Australia Ltd v Travel Software Solutions Pty Ltd* (2007) 65 ACSR
47 at [78]–[80]. The *Ansett* case concerned the declaration of a dividend after a shareholder had executed a
deed of company arrangement under the Corporations Act 2001 (Cth), which incorporated the insolvency
set-off section. Since the debt consequent upon the declaration arose after the execution of the deed, it could
not be the subject of a set-off in the insolvency. See para. 6.63 above. The *West Australian Lighterage* case was
distinguished (at [78] and [79]) on the ground that the shareholder in that case had an existing right to share
in the surplus (albeit that it was unquantified) when the bankruptcy occurred.
[12] A debt is 'future' for the purpose of the rule if it was not due for payment at the relevant time. See
Re Kaupthing Singer and Friedlander Ltd [2009] EWHC 2308 (Ch) at [16], referred to on appeal [2010]
EWCA Civ 518 at [13].
[13] See para. 6.10 above.
[14] *Re Kaupthing Singer & Friedlander Ltd* [2009] EWHC 2308 (Ch) at [16] (administration), referred to
on appeal [2010] EWCA Civ 518 at [13].
[15] When the winding up was not immediately preceded by an administration.
[16] When the administration was not immediately preceded by a winding up.

applicable formula.[17] In the case of an interest-bearing debt payable after the declaration of a dividend, 'X' in the formula[18] includes interest only to the extent that interest is included in the set-off.[19] Interest beyond that, to the contractual payment date of the debt, is not included.[20] Further, the incorporation of the discounting mechanism is expressed in the set-off rules in administration and liquidation as being for the purpose of the relevant rule,[21] and it applies no further than is necessary for that purpose. Therefore, if future debts are discounted to a present value for the purpose of a set-off, and a balance remains due to the company for payment on the contractual date[22] (being a date after the declaration of dividend), the amount payable is the equivalent undiscounted amount of the balance.[23]

8.08 In company liquidation in Australia, the Corporations Act 2001 (Cth), s. 554B provides for the discounting of a debt payable in the future 'that is admissible to proof', the amount of the discount to be worked out in accordance with the regulations. The reduction is not expressed to occur solely for the purpose of payment of a dividend, but for the purpose of calculating the debt that may be proved. Insolvency set-off is regarded as an aspect of the rules relating to the proof of debts,[24] which may suggest that a reduction in the amount of a debt which is admissible to proof would have a corresponding effect on the value of the debt for the purpose of a set-off. That would not appear to be the case, however. Regulation 5.6.44 of the Corporations Regulations 2001, which sets out the discount rate, provides that the amount payable is to be reduced by 8 per cent per annum calculated from the declaration of the dividend to the time when the debt would have become payable according to the terms on which it was contracted. But there is no dividend declared on a debt to the extent that the debt is extinguished in a set-off, which suggests that the provision does not apply in that context. The position differs from that in England, where the discounting procedure in expressly incorporated into the company set-off rules. In any event, s. 554B only provides for a reduction in the case of the company's debt to the creditor. If the debt is payable by the creditor to the company, there is no basis for reducing the amount of the debt to compensate for early payment by means of a set-off.[25]

(4) Capitalized interest

8.09 A presently existing debt payable at a future date should be distinguished from the case of a deposit made on terms that interest is to be capitalized so that, upon maturity, the value of the deposit will have increased. If prior to the maturity the depositor becomes bankrupt, and the depositee has a cross-demand against the depositor available by way of set-off, the

---

[17] See *Re Kaupthing Singer & Friedlander Ltd* [2009] EWHC 2308 (Ch) at [30] (administration).

[18] Insolvency Rules 1986, r. 2.105(2)(a) and r. 11.13(2)(a).

[19] See paras 6.158–6.160 above.

[20] *Re Kaupthing Singer & Friedlander Ltd* [2009] EWHC 2308 (Ch) at [29]–[39], referred to on appeal [2010] EWCA Civ 518 at [17].

[21] Insolvency Rules 1986, r. 2.85(7) (administration) and r. 4.90(7) (liquidation).

[22] In accordance with the Insolvency Rules 1986, r. 2.85(8) (administration) and r. 4.90(8) (liquidation).

[23] *Re Kaupthing Singer & Friedlander Ltd* [2010] EWCA Civ 518.

[24] *Mersey Steel and Iron Co v Naylor, Benzon & Co* (1884) 9 App Cas 434, 437–8; *Re Northside Properties Pty Ltd* [1971] 2 NSWLR 320, 323; *Re Bank of Credit and Commerce International SA (No. 8)* [1996] Ch 245, 256; *Re One. Tel Ltd* (2002) 43 ACSR 305 at [25].

[25] See e.g. *Ex p Prescot* (1753) 1 Atk 230, 26 ER 147.

automatic theory of insolvency set-off[26] dictates that the debt representing the deposit would have been extinguished on the date of the bankruptcy as a result of a set-off occurring on that date. To the extent that the debt has ceased to exist, interest should cease to accrue on it. Therefore, for the purpose of the set-off, the amount of the debt should be the initial deposit together with accrued interest as at the bankruptcy date,[27] as opposed to the value that the debt would have had if interest had continued to be capitalized until the agreed maturity date.

B. Contingent Debt Owing by the Insolvent

The insolvency set-off section requires that there be a creditor proving or claiming to prove for a debt in the insolvency. It is therefore a requirement of a set-off that the claim against the bankrupt or the company be provable.[28] When a person who becomes bankrupt or goes into liquidation has a contingent debt pursuant to a prior contract,[29] the fact of the bankruptcy or the liquidation will sometimes[30] constitute a repudiation of the contract which, if accepted, would give rise to a vested liability in damages.[31] The damages claim could be proved and it could be the subject of a set-off.[32] If, however, the case is not one involving an accepted repudiation, the insolvency legislation requires the trustee or the liquidator to estimate the value of a contingent debt[33] as at the date of the bankruptcy or the liquidation,[34] and a proof may be lodged for that amount. If the contingency subsequently occurs the full amount of the debt may be proved notwithstanding an earlier estimation, and if a proof has already been lodged based upon the estimation the proof may be adjusted, but not so as to disturb prior dividends.[35] The reason that a subsequent occurrence of the contingency is taken into account is not that the bankruptcy or the liquidation is deemed to have accelerated the contingency, so as to fix the value of the claim on the basis of the contingency having occurred on the date of the bankruptcy or the liquidation. Rather, it is because the

8.10

---

[26] See paras 6.119–6.146 above.

[27] See para. 6.157 above.

[28] See para. 7.24 above.

[29] For the meaning of a contingent debt, see *Glenister v Rowe* [2000] Ch 76. In Australia, see *Community Development Pty Ltd v Engwirda Construction Co* (1969) 120 CLR 455, 459; *Ansett Australia Ltd v Travel Software Solutions Pty Ltd* (2007) 65 ACSR 47 at [69]–[72]. Note that, in the case of a primary obligation, as opposed to a secondary obligation such as a guarantee, a provision for a demand in writing is not regarded as creating a contingency. See *MS Fashions Ltd v Bank of Credit and Commerce International SA* [1993] Ch 425, 435–6, referring to *Re J Brown's Estate* [1893] 2 Ch 300.

[30] But not always. See para. 9.05 below.

[31] *Re Northern Counties of England Fire Insurance Co. Macfarlane's Claim* (1880) 17 Ch D 337, 341; *Baker v Lloyd's Bank Ltd* [1920] 2 KB 322, 326.

[32] See para. 8.51 below.

[33] See the Insolvency Act 1986, s. 322 for bankruptcy. In the case of a company, see the Insolvency Rules 1986, rr. 2.81 (administration) and 4.86 (liquidation).

[34] *Ellis and Company's Trustee v Dixon-Johnson* [1924] 1 Ch 342, 356–7 (date of the receiving order under the Bankruptcy Act 1914); *Re Dynamics Corporation of America* [1976] 1 WLR 757, 767 (winding up).

[35] *Ellis and Company's Trustee v Dixon-Johnson* [1924] 1 Ch 342, 357. See the Insolvency Rules 1986, rr. 2.82(1) (administration) and 4.86(1) (liquidation). Compare the situation in which a creditor receives a dividend on a debt in ignorance of the availability of a set-off. See para. 6.165 above.

fact of the occurrence of the contingency is the best evidence of the true value of the claim as at that date.[36]

(1) Costs order after insolvency

8.11 A costs order made against a debtor after the debtor's bankruptcy or liquidation in relation to proceedings commenced before the bankruptcy or the liquidation is not regarded as having been a contingent liability at the insolvency date, for the purpose of being able to lodge a proof of debt in respect of it in the insolvency.[37] If it is not provable, it cannot be included in a set-off.[38] Similarly, a costs order on the other side of the account, being a costs order made in favour of a bankrupt or a company in liquidation in relation to proceedings commenced before the insolvency, should not be able to be included in a set-off.[39] An order for costs is discretionary and does not arise from an obligation incurred before the insolvency.[40]

(2) Statutory contingent debt

8.12 Contingent debts susceptible to a set-off may include a statutory obligation which was contingent at the insolvency date. That proposition was confirmed by the House of Lords in *Secretary of State for Trade and Industry v Frid*.[41] The case concerned the Employment Rights Act 1996. Pursuant to s. 166, if an employee claimed that the employer was liable to make redundancy or other stipulated payments to him or her, and either the employee had taken all reasonable steps to recover payment and the employer had refused or failed to pay or the employer was insolvent and had not paid, the employee could apply to the Secretary of State for payment. Section 167 provided that, upon payment by the Secretary of State to the employee, all rights and remedies of the employee against the employer were transferred to and vested in the Secretary of State. The employer in that case was a company that had gone into liquidation. After the liquidation, the Secretary of State made payments to employees of the company in accordance with s. 166 and thereby became subrogated, by way of statutory assignment, to the employees' rights against the company. As a consequence, the Crown (through the Secretary of State) had a provable claim in the liquidation for the sums paid. On the other hand, the company had a claim against the Crown in respect of a VAT credit. The question was whether the company's claim against the Crown, or the Crown's provable debt in the liquidation, should be determined on the basis that the

---

[36] *Ellis and Company's Trustee v Dixon-Johnson* [1924] 1 Ch 342, 356–7; *Re Dynamics Corporation of America* [1976] 1 WLR 757, 767–8; *Re Hurren* [1983] 1 WLR 183, 189. See also *Transit Casualty Co v Policyholders Protection Board* [1992] 2 Lloyd's Rep 358, 359, 361.

[37] *Glenister v Rowe* [2000] Ch 76; *Foots v Southern Cross Mine Management Pty Ltd* (2007) 234 CLR 52 (HCA) (judgment given before bankruptcy but costs not ordered until after bankruptcy).

[38] See para. 7.24 above.

[39] Compare *Chadmar Enterprises Pty Ltd v IGA Distribution Pty Ltd* (2006) 160 ACTR 29.

[40] *Glenister v Rowe* [2000] Ch 76, 84; *Foots v Southern Cross Mine Management Pty Ltd* (2007) 234 CLR 52 at [35] and [36] (HCA). See para. 6.63 above.

[41] [2004] 2 AC 506. See also *Deputy Commissioner of Taxation v Dexcam Australia Pty Ltd* (2003) 129 FCR 582 at [28] (contingent tax debt); *Re T. & N. Ltd* [2006] 1 WLR 1728 at [56]–[59].

VAT credit had to be set off against the Crown's subrogated claim.[42] Earlier authority had recognized that statutory debts could be the subject of a set-off in a liquidation,[43] but in this case the statutory obligation to reimburse the Secretary of State was contingent at the date of the liquidation. Lord Hoffmann in the leading judgment regarded the Secretary of State's position as analogous to that of a guarantor. He said that, if the Secretary of State had agreed by contract before the insolvency date to guarantee the company's liability for the debts referred to in s. 166, the contract of guarantee would have created a contingent liability which was capable of set-off when the employees were afterwards paid,[44] and that it made no difference that the contingent liability existed by virtue of statute rather than contract.[45]

(3) The rule against double proof

The meaning of the rule

While contingent debts generally are provable, this is subject to the rule against double proof. The rule essentially provides that there can only be one dividend in respect of what in substance is the same debt, even though various claims for a dividend may be based upon different contracts.[46] The rule can apply in a number of situations,[47] but often finds its expression in the context of guarantees. **8.13**

A guarantor who has guaranteed the whole of the debt owing to a creditor, and who pays the creditor in accordance with the guarantee, is entitled to be indemnified by the debtor. Prior to payment to the creditor, the guarantor's right of indemnity is subject to a contingency. If the debtor is bankrupt, and the guarantor pays the creditor after the bankruptcy but before the creditor has lodged a proof in the bankruptcy, the guarantor may prove in respect of the claim for an indemnity notwithstanding that at the date of the bankruptcy it was still contingent.[48] Different considerations apply if the guarantor has not paid the creditor and the creditor has either proved in the debtor's bankruptcy or, if the creditor has not proved, he or she is entitled to do so.[49] The guarantor in those circumstances has a contingent claim for an indemnity which *prima facie* would appear to be provable in the debtor's bankruptcy, on the basis of a valuation of the claim by the trustee in bankruptcy. But if the creditor has proved or is entitled to prove in the bankruptcy, and in addition the guarantor were allowed to prove for his or her contingent claim, the debtor's estate could be subjected to two proofs in respect of what essentially is the same debt. The creditor is the **8.14**

---

[42] The fact that different government departments were involved did not preclude a set-off. See paras 13.120–13.121 below.

[43] See para. 7.11 above.

[44] See paras 8.27–2.28 below.

[45] See [2004] 2 AC 506 at [17]–[19].

[46] *Re Oriental Commercial Bank, ex p European Bank* (1871) LR 7 Ch App 99, 103–4. See generally *Barclays Bank v TOSG Trust Fund Ltd* [1984] 1 AC 626; *WA v Bond Corporation Holdings Ltd* (1992) 8 ACSR 352, 364 *et seq.*

[47] See e.g. *Deering v Bank of Ireland* (1886) 12 App Cas 20; *The Liverpool (No. 2)* [1960] 3 WLR 597.

[48] *Re Fenton, ex p Fenton Textile Association Ltd* [1931] 1 Ch 85, 118.

[49] See e.g. *Re Fenton* [1931] 1 Ch 85, in which not all the creditors had proved in the principal debtor's liquidation and the rule against double proof was held to apply.

party who is out of pocket, and so the creditor's right of proof should be preferred. Therefore, in order to prevent the possibility of a double proof against the debtor's estate, the guarantor is not permitted to prove for his or her contingent claim.[50] The same principle applies if the guarantor makes a payment to the creditor after the creditor has a lodged a proof, including a payment in the form of a dividend in the guarantor's own bankruptcy. Indeed, the principle is still applicable if the creditor, having proved in the debtor's bankruptcy and received a dividend, is paid the full amount which remains outstanding by the guarantor. Because the creditor has proved in the debtor's bankruptcy, the debtor's estate cannot be subjected to a second proof from the guarantor for the same debt.[51] On the other hand, if the guarantor's payment is such that the creditor is paid in full, the guarantor is entitled to be subrogated to the benefit of the creditor's proof in the bankruptcy as regards future dividends to the extent required to indemnify him or her for the payment to the creditor.[52] It has been suggested that the guarantor is only entitled to be subrogated to the rights of the creditor if the guarantor has paid the full amount of the debt,[53] but in Australia the courts have adopted the preferred view that the right of subrogation arises when the creditor is paid in full, whether or not entirely by the guarantor.[54]

Guarantee limited to a stated amount

8.15 The guarantee may be limited to a stated amount. If that amount is less than the debt owing to the creditor, and the guarantor pays the full amount for which he or she is liable under the guarantee, the question whether the rule against double proof applies depends upon whether the guarantee is of the whole of the debt but with a limitation on liability to a certain amount, or whether the guarantee is of only part of the debt.[55] In the former case, a proof by the guarantor would be in respect of the same debt owing by the debtor to the

---

[50] *Re Fenton* [1931] 1 Ch 85 (esp at 107, 114, 118–19) (not following *Re Herepath & Delmar* (1890) 7 Morr 129, 190); *Staples v Milner* (1996) 83 FCR 203, 211. It was held in *Re Paine, ex p Read* [1897] 1 QB 122, and again in *Re Blackpool Motor Car Co Ltd* [1901] 1 Ch 77, that a surety before payment to the creditor is a 'creditor' of the bankrupt for the purpose of the preference provision. In *Re Fenton* both Lord Hanworth MR (at 106) and Romer LJ (at 118–20) agreed that those cases were correctly decided, but said that the issue determined was separate from the question whether the surety should be entitled to prove in the bankruptcy. See also *The Liverpool (No. 2)* [1960] 3 WLR 597, 606; *Re Bruce David Realty Pty Ltd* [1969] VR 240, 243; *Re Glen Express Ltd* Ch D, Neuberger J, 15 Oct 1999; *Secretary of State for Trade and Industry v Frid* [2004] 2 AC 506 at [13]; *Re SSSL Realisations (2002) Ltd* [2006] Ch 610 at [14] and [94].

[51] *Re Oriental Commercial Bank* (1871) LR 7 Ch App 99; *Re Fenton* [1931] 1 Ch 85, 115.

[52] *Re Whitehouse. Whitehouse v Edwards* (1887) 37 Ch D 683, 694–5; *Re Fenton* [1931] 1 Ch 85, 118; *Westpac Banking Corporation v Gollin & Co Ltd* [1988] VR 397, 403; *Western Australia v Bond Corporation Holdings Ltd (No. 2)* (1992) 37 FCR 150, 163.

[53] See e.g. *Re Fenton* [1931] 1 Ch 85, 115; *Ex p Brett, re Howe* (1871) LR 6 Ch App 838, 841; *Ex p Turquand, re Fothergill* (1876) 3 Ch D 445, 450. See also *Re Polly Peck International plc* [1996] 2 All ER 433, 442; *Re SSSL Realisations (2002) Ltd* [2006] Ch 610 at [93]. Compare *Gedye v Matson* (1858) 25 Beav 310, 312, 53 ER 655, 656 (Sir John Romilly MR).

[54] *A. E. Goodwin Ltd v A. G. Healing Ltd* (1979) 7 ACLR 481; *McColl's Wholesale Pty Ltd v State Bank of NSW* [1984] 3 NSWLR 365, 378; *Raffle v AGC (Advances) Ltd* (1989) ASC 55–933 (Young J, NSW SC); *Bayley v Gibsons Ltd* (1993) 1 Tas R 385; *Macedone v Collins* (1996) 7 BPR 15,127, 15,142; *Austin v Royal* (1999) 47 NSWLR 27, 32. See also *Equity Trustees Executors & Agency Co Ltd v New Zealand Loan & Mercantile Agency Co Ltd* [1940] VLR 201; *Westpac Banking Corporation v Gollin & Co Ltd* [1988] VR 397, 402.

[55] See generally the discussion in *Barclay's Bank Ltd v TOSG Trust Fund Ltd* [1984] 1 AC 626, 643–4.

creditor, so that the rule would apply.[56] Nor would the guarantor be subrogated to a part of the creditor's proof before the creditor has been paid in full.[57] If, however, the guarantee is merely in respect of part of the debt, and the guarantor has paid the creditor that part in accordance with the guarantee before the creditor has proved, the guarantor may prove in the debtor's bankruptcy for an indemnity in relation to that part and the creditor may prove for the unpaid part.[58] If the creditor has already proved for the whole debt, the guarantor upon payment of the part guaranteed becomes subrogated to the proof to the extent of that part.[59] When a guarantee in truth relates only to a part of a debt, that part as between the creditor and the guarantor is treated as a separate debt.[60]

Guarantee of the whole debt, where there is part payment

When a guarantee is of the whole debt, the creditor is entitled to prove for the full amount of the debt in the debtor's bankruptcy or liquidation despite having received a payment from a guarantor, if a part of the debt remains unpaid.[61] This principle has been recognized in circumstances where the guarantor paid the creditor before the principal debtor's bankruptcy or liquidation,[62] when the guarantor paid the creditor after the principal debtor's bankruptcy or liquidation but before the creditor's proof,[63] and when the payment

8.16

---

[56] *Re Fenton* [1931] 1 Ch 85, 115.

[57] This is consistent with the discussion in *Re Sass* [1896] 2 QB 12, 15, and see also *Westpac Banking Corporation v Gollin & Co Ltd* [1988] VR 397, 405–6.

[58] *Re Sass* [1896] 2 QB 12, 15; *Seabird Corporation Ltd v Sherlock* (1990) 2 ACSR 111, 116.

[59] *Re Sass* [1896] 2 QB 12, 15; *Westpac Banking Corporation v Gollin & Co Ltd* [1988] VR 397, 405.

[60] See *Re Sass* [1896] 2 QB 12, 15.

[61] *Re Sass* [1896] 2 QB 12, 14–15; *Ulster Bank Ltd v Lambe* [1966] NI 161; *Westpac Banking Corporation v Gollin & Co Ltd* [1988] VR 397, 401, 403; *Seabird Corporation Ltd v Sherlock* (1990) 2 ACSR 111, 115–16 (guarantee of the whole of the debt but with a limit on the liability); *Farrow Finance Co Ltd v ANZ Executors and Trustee Co Ltd* [1998] 1 VR 50, 76. If the aggregate amount received by the creditor from both sources exceeds the debt, the excess must be held by the creditor in trust for the guarantor. See *Westpac v Gollin* at 403, 409–10; *Midland Montague Australia Ltd v Harkness* (1994) 35 NSWLR 150, 166.

[62] *Westpac Banking Corporation v Gollin & Co Ltd* [1988] VR 397. In New Zealand, Fisher J declined to follow *Westpac v Gollin* in *Stotter v Equiticorp Australia Ltd* [2002] 2 NZLR 686 on the ground that payment by a guarantor to a creditor before the principal debtor's liquidation reduces the guaranteed debt. However, that statement does not accurately reflect the position. See *Sheahan v Carrier Air Conditioning Pty Ltd* (1997) 189 CLR 407, 430–1 and *Crantrave Ltd v Lloyds Bank Plc* [2000] QB 917, 923–4. Moreover, as Tadgell J pointed out in *Westpac v Gollin* at 409–10, the contrary view would mean that the unsecured debtors of the principal debtor would obtain a windfall. The creditor, having received part payment of the debt from the guarantor, could not prove for the full debt, and nor could the guarantor prove before the creditor has been fully paid because of the principle that a guarantor who has given a whole moneys guarantee cannot prove in competition with the creditor. However, the position would appear to be different if the principal debtor is solvent. In that situation, there is authority for the proposition that payment by a guarantor operates to extinguish the principal debt. See *MS Fashions Ltd v Bank of Credit and Commerce International SA* [1993] Ch 425 (in particular, at 439 & 448); *Milverton Group Ltd v Warner World Ltd* [1995] 2 EGLR 28; *Romain v Scuba TV Ltd* [1997] QB 887, 892; *Lumley General Insurance Ltd v Oceanfast Marine Pty Ltd* [2001] NSWCA 479 at [32] (but see [32] and [166]–[167] in relation to an insolvent principal debtor). Compare, however, *Ulster Bank Ltd v Lambe* [1966] NI 161. See also *Re Bank of Credit and Commerce International SA (No. 8)* [1996] Ch 245, 268 (though referring to the position in the insolvency of the creditor as opposed to the principal debtor).

[63] *Re Sass* [1896] 2 QB 12. See also *Re Houlder* [1929] 1 Ch 205, 214–15; *Farrow Finance Co Ltd v ANZ Executors and Trustee Co Ltd* [1998] 1 VR 50, 71; *Barclays Bank Ltd v TOSG Trust Fund Ltd* [1984] 1 All ER 628, 641.

was made after the creditor's proof.[64] There is an exception, however, in the case of bills of exchange. The position of the drawer and a prior indorser of a bill as regards the holder is similar to that of a guarantor, but it is nevertheless accepted that the holder in proving in the bankruptcy of the acceptor must give credit for anything that he or she received from the drawer or the indorser before the proof.[65] In such a case Wood's view would appear to be correct, that the rule against double proof would not apply so as to prevent a proof by the drawer or the indorser.[66]

Contribution between guarantors

8.17 The rule against double proof is also important in the context of rights of contribution between guarantors. When there is more than one guarantor of the same debt, a guarantor who has paid more than his or her share is entitled to contribution from a co-guarantor.[67] Consider that the co-guarantor has become bankrupt. Prior to making payment to the creditor, the paying guarantor has a contingent right to contribution from the co-guarantor, but since the creditor has a provable debt in the co-guarantor's bankruptcy the paying guarantor could not prove for the contingent claim. Further, if the paying guarantor pays more than his or her just share, but the creditor nevertheless has not been paid in full so that the creditor remains entitled to prove in the co-guarantor's bankruptcy, the rule against double proof would still operate to prevent a proof by the paying guarantor. This would also be the case if the paying guarantor pays more than his or her share after the creditor has lodged a proof in the co-guarantor's bankruptcy. On the other hand, once the creditor has been paid in full, the paying guarantor is entitled to be subrogated to the creditor's proof and to receive the dividends until that guarantor has received an amount sufficient to satisfy his or her claim for contribution.[68]

Set-off

8.18 If the rule against double proof operates to deny a contingent creditor a right of proof, the contingent creditor similarly could not employ the claim in a set-off, since the set-off section stipulates that there should be a creditor proving or claiming to prove for a debt.[69] In *Re Fenton, ex p Fenton Textile Association Ltd*[70] a debtor had gone into liquidation, and a guarantor of the debt had executed two deeds of arrangement. The creditor had lodged

---

[64] *Re Rees* (1881) 17 Ch D 98; *Midland Montagu Australia Ltd v Harkness* (1994) 35 NSWLR 150, 159.

[65] The holder, however, is not obliged to reduce the proof in respect of anything paid to him or her after lodging the proof. See generally *Re Houlder* [1929] 1 Ch 205, 212. This principle is confined to negotiable instruments. See *Re Blackburne* (1892) 9 Morr 249, 252, and also the discussion in *Westpac Banking Corporation v Gollin & Co Ltd* [1988] VR 397, 407–8. If, on the other hand, the acceptor is not bankrupt or in liquidation, and the holder is suing the acceptor in an action at law on the bill, the holder need not reduce his or her claim to the extent of a part payment received from the drawer or a prior indorser, although to the extent of that part payment the holder sues as trustee for the drawer or the prior indorser, as the case may be. See *Thornton v Maynard* (1875) LR 10 CP 695.

[66] Wood, *English and International Set-off* (1989), 611.

[67] See e.g. *Craythorne v Swinburne* (1807) 14 Ves Jun 160, 33 ER 482.

[68] *Ex p Stokes* (1848) De Gex 618; *Re Parker. Morgan v Hill* [1894] 3 Ch 400.

[69] See para. 7.24 above.

[70] [1931] 1 Ch 85. See also *Western Australia v Bond Corporation Holdings Ltd (No. 2)* (1992) 37 FCR 150, 163; *Re Glen Express Ltd* Ch D, Neuberger J, 15 Oct 1999; *Secretary of State for Trade and Industry v Frid* [2004] 2 AC 506 at [13]; *Re SSSL Realisations (2002) Ltd* [2006] Ch 610 at [14].

a proof under the deeds in respect of the guaranteed amount but had not been paid anything, by either the debtor or the guarantor. Because of the rule against double proof, the guarantor did not have a debt which was provable in the debtor's liquidation,[71] and the Court of Appeal held that the trustee of the guarantor's estate under the deeds similarly was not permitted to employ the guarantor's contingent claim for an indemnity in a set-off.[72]

(4) Set-off where there is no double proof issue

The 'in principle' position

Consider that the rule against double proof does not apply, so that a contingent debt arising **8.19** out of a prior agreement is provable. A prime example is the case of a guarantor who pays the creditor in full after the debtor's bankruptcy or liquidation but before the creditor had lodged a proof.[73] The debt in principle should be able to be employed in a set-off on the basis that it is a natural result of a prior transaction so as to come within the concept of giving credit.[74] This assumes that the qualification to the set-off section[75] is not a bar to a set-off in respect of contingent debts. The operation of the qualification ordinarily should not be a problem in company administration and liquidation under the Insolvency Rules 1986, given that the qualification is expressed in terms of the incurring of the obligation as opposed to when a debt arises under it.[76] The position should be similar in bankruptcy. The Insolvency Act 1986, s. 323(3) provides that sums due from a bankrupt shall not be included in an account if the creditor had notice at the time they became 'due' that a bankruptcy petition was pending.[77] In the case of a contingent debt, this should be determined by reference to the creditor's knowledge at the time that a contract was entered into out of which a debt subsequently arose, as opposed to the time that a liability vested upon the occurrence of the contingency.[78] Accepting that a debt owing by a bankrupt or a company in liquidation that was contingent at the relevant date in principle can be the subject of a set-off,[79] the contrary conclusion would mean that the operation of the qualification could significantly curtail the availability of a set-off in the case of contingent debts.

The cases

There is nevertheless authority suggesting that a debt which is contingent at the relevant **8.20** date cannot be the subject of a set-off. *Re A Debtor (No. 66 of 1955), ex p The Debtor v The Trustee of the Property of Waite (A Bankrupt)*[80] concerned a bankrupt surety. After the bankruptcy the surety's trustee in bankruptcy paid the creditor in full in order to obtain the release of security given by the surety to the creditor. The trustee then sought to recover this amount from the debtor. When the debtor failed to pay, the trustee issued a bankruptcy

---

[71] See para. 8.14 above.
[72] A set-off was not available in either insolvency. See para. 11.05n below.
[73] *Re Fenton* [1931] 1 Ch 85, 118.
[74] See paras 7.02–7.06 above and 8.27 below.
[75] See paras 6.66–6.99 above.
[76] Insolvency Rules 1986, rr. 2.85(2) (administration) and 4.90(2) (winding up).
[77] For the position in Australia, see paras 6.84–6.86 (bankruptcy) and 6.87 (winding up) above.
[78] See paras 6.91–6.95 above.
[79] See below.
[80] [1956] 1 WLR 1226.

notice against him. The debtor argued in response that, because of a separate debt owing to him by the surety, he had a right of set-off in the surety's bankruptcy against his indemnity obligation, and that after a set-off the amount for which he was indebted would have been less than the amount required for a bankruptcy notice. The Court of Appeal rejected the argument on the ground that a claim which is merely contingent at the relevant date, and consequently not 'due', cannot be employed in a set-off. In that case the surety, rather than the principal debtor, was the bankrupt party. It was not a case in which a bankrupt had a contingent liability at the relevant date. The bankrupt had a contingent claim, and *Re A Debtor (No. 66 of 1955)* is referred to later in that context.[81] Nevertheless, the Court of Appeal appeared to base its decision to deny a set-off on a general proposition, that both demands must be 'due' at the relevant date so that, irrespective of whether the principal debtor or the surety is the bankrupt party, a surety's right to an indemnity will not give rise to a set-off as between those parties if the right was still contingent at the relevant date.[82]

8.21 The Court of Appeal distinguished an earlier decision of that court in *Re Daintrey*,[83] on the ground that that case was not concerned with a contingent debt but rather with a debt which was due at the relevant date but remained to be quantified.[84] A business had been sold on terms that the price was to be calculated as a proportion of the profits made over a three-year period. The vendor became bankrupt before any profits had been earned. At the end of the three-year period, when the price was calculated in accordance with the agreed formula, it was held that the purchaser could set off his resulting liability against a separate debt owing to him by the vendor. However, the Court of Appeal in *Re A Debtor* would appear to have proceeded on an incorrect characterization of *Re Daintrey*. No profits had been earned at the date of the bankruptcy, so that the debt was contingent at that date upon profits subsequently being earned.[85] On that basis, *Re Daintrey* was a case in which a contingent debt was the subject of a set-off.

---

[81] See paras 8.42–8.43 below.

[82] See Lord Evershed MR and Hodson LJ at [1956] 1 WLR 1226, 1230, 1237. In later cases *Re A Debtor (No. 66 of 1955)* has been regarded as authority for that proposition. See *Carreras Rothmans Ltd v Freeman Mathews Treasure Ltd* [1985] 1 Ch 207; *Re Hawkins, dec'd* (Walton J, 2 February 1978); *Re Charge Card Services Ltd* [1987] 1 Ch 150, 188–90. See also *Re Bruce David Realty Pty Ltd* [1969] VR 240, 243 (in which Adam J accepted that a surety must have paid the creditor before the principal debtor's bankruptcy in order to have a set-off in the bankruptcy), and *Brown v Cork* [1985] BCLC 363, 368, 376 (CA). In Canada, see *Re Mitchell, Houghton Ltd* (1970) 14 CBR (NS) 301.

[83] [1900] 1 QB 546. The Court of Appeal in *Re A Debtor (No. 66 of 1955)* also relied on *dicta* in *Re Fenton* [1931] 1 Ch 85, although, as Gibbs CJ commented in *Day & Dent Constructions Pty Ltd v North Australian Properties Pty Ltd* (1982) 150 CLR 85, 94, the *dicta* in question appear to be ambiguous, if not conflicting. Indeed, Mason J (at 102) said that, according to his reading of the judgments, the surety would have been entitled to a set-off in *Re Fenton* if he had paid the debt.

[84] This view has been expressed on other occasions. See e.g. *Re National Benefit Assurance Co Ltd* [1924] 2 Ch 339, 343 (Eve J); *Carreras Rothmans Ltd v Freeman Mathews Treasure Ltd* [1985] 1 Ch 207, 230 (Peter Gibson J).

[85] See Millett J in *Re Charge Card Services Ltd* [1987] 1 Ch 150, 182–3, and the cases to which he refers. As Millett J noted, this was the view of Gibbs CJ and Mason J in the High Court of Australia in *Day & Dent Constructions Pty Ltd v North Australian Properties Pty Ltd* (1982) 150 CLR 85, 92, 94, 103. Compare Lindley MR in the Court of Appeal in *Re Daintrey* [1900] 1 QB 546, 572.

Subsequently, the Court of Appeal in *Brown v Cork*[86] referred to *Re A Debtor (No. 66 of*   **8.22**
1955) with approval in the context of a contingent claim possessed by a company in liquidation.[87] Nevertheless, in so far as *Re A Debtor (No. 66 of 1955)* suggests a general proposition that a surety under a pre-insolvency guarantee is not entitled to a set-off unless he or
she actually paid the debt before the insolvency date, it can no longer be supported.[88] In
Secretary of State for Trade and Industry v Frid,[89] the House of Lords said that the case was
wrong in so far as it suggested that proposition, and accepted that a contingent liability (in
that case, arising under statute), where that liability existed before the insolvency date and
was paid afterwards, can be the subject of a set-off.[90] This would also be the position in
Australia, following criticism of *Re A Debtor (No. 66 of 1955)* by the High Court in *Day &
Dent Constructions Pty Ltd v North Australian Properties Pty Ltd*.[91] The suggestion is also
inconsistent with Dixon J's often-quoted statement in the Australian High Court in *Hiley
v The People's Prudential Assurance Co Ltd*[92] that:

> It is enough that at the commencement of the winding up mutual dealings exist which involve
> rights and obligations whether absolute or contingent of such a nature that afterwards in the
> events that happen they mature or develop into pecuniary demands capable of set-off.

There are other cases in which English courts have recognized that a contingent debt can   **8.23**
be included in a set-off.[93] For example, the holder of a bill of exchange has been permitted
to set off his or her claim against the drawer or an indorser of the bill in the drawer's or the
indorser's bankruptcy, even though dishonour by the acceptor only occurred after the
bankruptcy.[94] Similarly, it has been held that an accommodation acceptor or indorser of a
bill could set off his or her claim for an indemnity in the drawer's bankruptcy notwithstanding that the bill was paid after the bankruptcy.[95] In *Graham v Russell*,[96] Lord Ellenborough,

---

[86] [1985] BCLC 363, 368, 376.

[87] See para. 8.42 below.

[88] It has been suggested nevertheless that *Re A Debtor (No. 66 of 1955)* may have been correctly decided
on the ground that the payment was made by the surety's trustee in bankruptcy out of assets that had vested
in him for the benefit of creditors. See paras 13.41 and 13.56 below, referring to *Secretary of State for Trade
and Industry v Frid* [2004] 2 AC 506 at [15]–[16] (Lord Hoffmann) and *Day & Dent Constructions Pty Ltd
v North Australian Properties Pty Ltd* (1982) 150 CLR 85, 94 (Gibbs CJ). See generally the discussion of *Ince
Hall Rolling Mills Co Ltd v The Douglas Forge Co* (1882) 8 QBD 179 in paras 13.37–13.57 below.

[89] [2004] 2 AC 506 at [14]–[16].

[90] It was assumed in *Stein v Blake* [1996] AC 243, 252 that a contingent debt can be set off in bankruptcy,
and see also Hoffmann LJ (as he then was) in the Chancery Division in *MS Fashions Ltd v Bank of Credit and
Commerce International SA* [1993] Ch 425, 435.

[91] (1982) 150 CLR 85, 94, 106.

[92] (1938) 60 CLR 468, 496–7.

[93] In addition to the cases referred to below, see the authorities referred to in para. 8.28 below and also
Re Taylor, ex p Norvell [1910] 1 KB 562, 568; *Baker v Lloyd's Bank Ltd* [1920] 2 KB 322; *Hiley v The Peoples
Prudential Assurance Co Ltd* (1938) 60 CLR 468, 491, 497; *Re Northside Properties Pty Ltd* [1971] 2 NSWLR
320, 324. In *Willment Brothers Ltd v North West Thames Regional Health Authority* (1984) 26 BLR 51, Ackner
and O'Connor LJJ said that, even if the creditor's claim against the company in liquidation was merely contingent at the date of the liquidation, it could still be employed in a set-off, although no mention was made of
the earlier decision in *Re A Debtor*.

[94] *Arbouin v Tritton* (1816) Holt 408, 171 ER 287; *Alsager v Currie* (1844) 12 M & W 751, 152 ER 1402.

[95] *Smith v Hodson* (1791) 4 TR 211, 100 ER 979; *Ex p Boyle, re Shepherd*, unreported but noted in Cooke,
The Bankrupt Laws (8th edn, 1823) vol. 1, 571; *Ex p Wagstaff* (1806) 13 Ves Jun 65, 33 ER 219; *Hulme v
Muggleston* (1837) 3 M & W 30, 150 ER 1043; *Russell v Bell* (1841) 8 M & W 277, 151 ER 1042; *Bittleston v
Timmis* (1845) 1 CB 389, 135 ER 591.

[96] (1816) 5 M & S 498, 105 ER 1133.

in delivering the judgment of the Exchequer Chamber, accepted that an insured could set off the underwriter's liability on a loss which occurred after the underwriter's bankruptcy, despite the contingent nature of the liability at the relevant date. It has also been held that the holder of a policy of life insurance who was indebted to the insurance company could set off the value of the policy in the winding up of the company, even though the policy had not matured at the relevant date for determining rights of set-off in the liquidation either by payment of the requisite number of premiums or by death.[97] In *Lee & Chapman's Case*,[98] a damages claim for breach of contract against a company, where the breach occurred after the liquidation, was the subject of a set-off.[99]

Must the debt be exclusively referable to a prior agreement?

8.24 In *Re Charge Card Services Ltd*,[100] Millett J (as he then was) sought to explain the decision in *Re A Debtor (No. 66 of 1955)*.[101] The *Charge Card Services* case concerned a company which operated a charge card scheme. The company assigned its receivables to a factor, the agreement providing that, if the company went into liquidation, the factor could require it to re-purchase the debts at face value. One of the issues in dispute was whether, if a notice of re-purchase was given after the liquidation, the factor could set off the company's resulting liability to pay the price against a debt owing by the factor to the company. The company's liability to pay the price was contingent at the date of the liquidation, a notice of re-purchase not having then been given, and accordingly it was argued that *Re A Debtor (No. 66 of 1955)* was authority against a set-off in this situation. However, Millett J held that a contingent claim can be employed in a set-off provided that it is exclusively referable to a prior agreement between the parties to the proposed set-off.[102] In the case of a principal debtor's obligation to indemnify the surety, the obligation is not exclusively referable to a contract between the principal debtor and the surety. Rather, it is referable to the contract of guarantee to which the principal often is not a party. On the other hand, since the contingent liability in issue in *Re Charge Card Services* was exclusively referable to a contract between the parties to the proposed set-off, Millett J concluded that *Re A Debtor (No. 66 of 1955)* did not constitute authority against a set-off in the case before him.

8.25 The source of Millett J's analysis appears to have been a comment by Lord Evershed MR in *Re A Debtor (No. 66 of 1955)*,[103] in which the Master of the Rolls distinguished the case before him from *Re Daintrey*[104] on the ground that in *Re Daintrey* the amount of the debt

---

[97] *Re City Life Assurance Co Ltd. Grandfield's Case* [1926] 1 Ch 191 (not following *Ex p Price, re Lankester* (1875) LR 10 Ch App 648 and *Paddy v Clutton* [1920] 2 Ch 554). See also *Sovereign Life Assurance Co v Dodd* [1892] 2 QB 573, in which the insured paid the final premium after the petition and before the winding-up order, although the date of the petition seems to have been regarded as the relevant date. Compare *Re National Benefit Assurance Co Ltd* [1924] 2 Ch 339 (and see also *Hiley v The Peoples Prudential Assurance Co Ltd* (1938) 60 CLR 468, 493), in which the winding up was treated as a repudiation by the company.

[98] *Re Asphaltic Wood Pavement Co. Lee & Chapman's Case* (1885) 30 Ch D 216.

[99] See also para. 8.52 below.

[100] [1987] 1 Ch 150.

[101] [1956] 1 WLR 1226.

[102] See the discussion at [1987] 1 Ch 150, 189–90.

[103] [1956] 1 WLR 1226, 1230. Millett J referred to this passage in *Re Charge Card Services* [1987] 1 Ch 150, 188–9.

[104] [1900] 1 QB 546.

in question was exclusively referable to an obligation to pay the price incurred prior to the relevant date. However, that comment was in the context of Lord Evershed's characterization of *Re Daintrey* as a case in which there was a prior debt which merely remained to be quantified after the relevant date, as opposed to a subsequently arising debt.[105] A quantification of a debt would require that the quantum be exclusively referable to the debt. The position is different when the question is whether a contingent debt can be included in a set-off. Subsequently, the House of Lords in *Secretary of State for Trade and Industry v Frid*[106] rejected the notion that there is anything in the term 'mutual debts' (or, it may also be accepted, in the term 'mutual credits') which requires that both debts must be 'exclusively referrable' to a contract or other transaction between the parties to the set-off. As Lord Hoffmann observed,[107] debts the subject of a set-off need not arise from consensual transactions but can arise, for example, from statutory obligations.[108] Once it is accepted that debts need not be based upon consensual transactions, he said that a requirement of mutuality in the transactions giving rise to the cross-claims becomes untenable.[109]

For example, an acceptor of a bill of exchange may not have been aware at the time of his or her bankruptcy that the bill had been endorsed to the holder. While in such a case the bankrupt and the holder had not dealt with each other in relation to the bill, and nor was the indebtedness of the acceptor to the holder 'exclusively referable' to an agreement between them, it was held in *Hankey v Smith*[110] that the holder could employ the claim on the bill in a set-off in the bankruptcy, on the ground that credit nevertheless had been given by the holder. Moreover, the 1825 and 1849 Bankruptcy Acts each specifically provided that all debts provable against the estate could be set off, and the legislation in each case allowed a right of proof to a person who was a surety at the time of the bankruptcy of the principal debtor, if the surety paid the debt.[111] The contingent debt was allowed to be set off on the ground that credit was given at the date of the debtor's bankruptcy. In other words, there was a prior transaction which would naturally, or in the ordinary course of business, end in a debt.[112] The question whether the principal debtor's indemnity obligation to the surety was exclusively referable to a contract between them was not an issue.

Surety paying after the debtor's bankruptcy

Consider the case of a surety who pays the creditor after the debtor's bankruptcy. If the rule against double proof does not apply, the surety's claim for an indemnity should be able to be employed in a set-off in the bankruptcy, on the ground that the debt was a natural result of a prior transaction and therefore it constituted the giving of credit.[113] It is not necessary

8.26

8.27

---

[105] See para. 8.21 above.
[106] [2004] 2 AC 506 at [25].
[107] [2004] 2 AC 506 at [25].
[108] See paras 7.04 and 7.11 above.
[109] See paras 7.12–7.22 above in relation to the necessity for a dealing.
[110] (1789) 3 TR 507n, 100 ER 703.
[111] See (1825) 6 Geo IV, c. 16, ss. 50 and 52, and the Bankrupt Law Consolidation Act 1849, ss. 171 and 173.
[112] See para. 7.04 above.
[113] See para. 7.04 above. This was the ground upon which the High Court of Australia upheld the surety's claim for a set-off in *Day & Dent Constructions Pty Ltd v North Australian Properties Pty Ltd* (1982) 150 CLR 85.

that the claim for an indemnity should have arisen from a mutual transaction between the surety and the debtor.[114]

8.28 The availability of a set-off in this situation now has the support of both the High Court of Australia[115] and the House of Lords.[116] In so far as *Re A Debtor (No. 66 of 1955)*[117] stood as authority to the contrary, it is no longer good law.[118] Other cases support the availability of a set-off in this situation.[119] In *Hiley v The Peoples Prudential Assurance Co Ltd*,[120] Starke J indicated that that a surety paying the creditor after the debtor's bankruptcy could employ his or her claim for an indemnity in a set-off. This is consistent with a suggestion by Wigram VC in *Jones v Mossop*[121] that, if the person who in that case was the principal debtor on some promissory notes in respect of which the plaintiff was surety had been made bankrupt, the plaintiff subsequently paying the notes would have had a right of set-off. It is also supported by *Re The Moseley Green Coal and Coke Co Ltd. Barrett's Case (No. 2)*.[122] *Barrett's Case* was distinguished in *Re A Debtor (No. 66 of 1955)* on the ground that the surety's claim against the principal debtor was based on a promissory note given as security to the creditor, but it is difficult to see why this should justify a different result, given that a surety's right to securities held by the creditor is just as much a consequence of the payment to the creditor as is the right to an indemnity.[123] *Barrett's Case* is directly on point.[124]

---

[114] *Secretary of State for Trade and Industry v Frid* [2004] 2 AC 506 at [25], and see paras 7.12–7.22 and 8.24–8.26 above. In any event, the surety's claim usually would arise out of a dealing or transaction with the debtor, being the giving of the guarantee at the request (express or implied) of the principal debtor. Where a surety acted officiously in giving the guarantee, it was held in *Owen v Tate* [1976] 1 QB 402 that the surety is not entitled to an indemnity from the principal debtor, in which case the surety would not have a provable debt which could be set off. *Quaere* whether *Owen v Tate* would be followed. See Birks, *An Introduction to the Law of Restitution* (1989), 311–12, and Goff and Jones, *The Law of Restitution* (7th edn, 2007), 138–9 (where it is suggested that subrogation may apply).

[115] *Day & Dent Constructions Pty Ltd v North Australian Properties Pty Ltd* (1982) 150 CLR 85.

[116] *Secretary of State for Trade and Industry v Frid* [2004] 2 AC 506 at [14]–[17].

[117] [1956] 1 WLR 1226.

[118] See para. 8.22 above.

[119] In addition to the cases referred to below, see *Re Last, ex p Butterell* (1994) 124 ALR 219. See also *Stein v Blake* [1996] AC 243, 256, where the House of Lords referred to *Day & Dent Constructions Pty Ltd v North Australian Properties Pty Ltd* (1982) 150 CLR 85 without suggesting that it was wrongly decided.

[120] (1938) 60 CLR 468, 491. See also Latham CJ at 483 and Dixon J at 500–1, referring to *Re The Moseley Green Coal and Coke Co Ltd. Barrett's Case (No. 2)* (1865) 4 De G J & S 756, 46 ER 1116, 34 LJ Bcy 41, discussed below.

[121] (1844) 3 Hare 568, 571, 67 ER 506, 508.

[122] (1865) 4 De G J & S 756, 46 ER 1116, 12 LT 193, 34 LJ Bcy 41.

[123] Two points should be noted in relation to *Barrett's Case*. The first is that the set-off was against a liability to the company in liquidation for an unpaid call on shares. While it is now accepted that a set-off is not available in such a case (see paras 8.64–8.79 below), the applicable legislation when *Barrett* was decided specifically allowed a set-off to a contributory in respect of any sums due to him from the company on an independent contract or dealing. See the Joint Stock Companies Amendment Act 1858, s. 17. The second point is that the set-off section in the bankruptcy legislation had not been incorporated at that time into the joint stock companies legislation, although it was nevertheless accepted that the right of set-off allowed to a contributory should be governed by the same principles. See the comments of Lord Cranworth in subsequent proceedings at (1865) 4 De G J & S 756, 762, 46 ER 1116, 1119.

[124] See *Day & Dent Constructions Pty Ltd v North Australian Properties Pty Ltd* (1982) 150 CLR 85, 94, 106 and *Secretary of State for Trade and Industry v Frid* [2004] 2 AC 506 at [12]. Nevertheless, Lord Hoffmann queried in *Secretary of State v Frid* (at [12]) whether the surety's payment to his sister could properly be characterized as a payment under the guarantee.

(5) Subrogation, where the creditor had proved before the surety's payment

The creditor may have proved for the debt in the debtor's bankruptcy before payment in **8.29** full by the surety. In that circumstance, the rule against double proof would preclude the guarantor from lodging a second proof.[125] It has been suggested that, where the guarantor is denied the right to lodge a separate proof in the debtor's bankruptcy after payment in full to the creditor, the guarantor similarly could not set off his or her claim for an indemnity against a liability to the debtor.[126] If that were the law it would be unsatisfactory, but the better view is that a set-off may be available to the guarantor. The set-off section admittedly stipulates that there should be a person proving or claiming to prove for a bankruptcy debt.[127] The guarantor does not have a provable debt in his or her own right. That much is clear.[128] Nevertheless, upon payment in full to the creditor the guarantor is entitled to be subrogated to the creditor's proof in the bankruptcy.[129] The court of bankruptcy is a court of equitable jurisdiction[130] and, although the proof is still nominally the creditor's, it should be possible to go behind the proof and proceed on the basis that in equity it has become the proof of the guarantor. As far as equity is concerned, the position should be the same as if the surety had acquired a right to prove in his or her own name upon payment to the creditor. The important point is that the guarantor's entitlement to the benefit of the proof is referrable to rights vested in the guarantor prior to the bankruptcy, consequent upon the execution of the guarantee, and does not involve any new and independent transaction.[131] That analysis may not apply, however, if the creditor receives payment in full from a number of sureties, so that there is more than one surety subrogated to the proof.[132] The surety's right of subrogation has been described as a class right,[133] in which case there may not be mutuality as between the proof to which the sureties are subrogated and a separate debt owing by one of the sureties to the principal debtor.[134]

Acquisition of an interest after bankruptcy or liquidation

In the case of a single surety, the circumstance that the surety only acquires an interest **8.30** in the creditor's proof by way of subrogation after the principal debtor's bankruptcy or liquidation should not preclude a set-off. This would follow from the decision of the House of Lords in *Secretary of State for Trade and Industry v Frid*,[135] in which the Secretary

---

[125] See para. 8.18 above.

[126] Wood, *English and International Set-off* (1989), 303, 608.

[127] See the Insolvency Act, s. 323(1). In company liquidation see the Insolvency Rules 1986, r. 4.90(1) and in administration see r. 2.85(2).

[128] *Re Whitehouse. Whitehouse v Edwards* (1887) 37 Ch D 683, 694–5.

[129] *Re Whitehouse* (1887) 37 Ch D 683, 694–5; *Re Fenton* [1931] 1 Ch 85, 118; *Westpac Banking Corporation v Gollin & Co Ltd* [1988] VR 397, 403.

[130] *Mathieson's Trustee v Burrup, Mathieson & Co* [1927] 1 Ch 562, 569.

[131] *Hiley v The Peoples Prudential Assurance Co Ltd* (1938) 60 CLR 468, 487 (Rich J), 499 (Dixon J).

[132] This assumes that it is sufficient for subrogation that the creditor has been paid in full, whether or not entirely by the surety. See para. 8.14 above.

[133] *A. E. Goodwin Ltd v A. G. Healing Ltd* (1979) 7 ACLR 481, 489; *Rowlatt on Principal and Surety* (5th edn, 1999), 157; Andews and Millett, *Law of Guarantees* (5th edn, 2008), 456–7; O'Donovan and Phillips, *Modern Contract of Guarantee* (looseleaf), [12.2450].

[134] See paras 12.02–12.07 below.

[135] [2004] 2 AC 506. See para. 8.12 above.

of State, as a statutory guarantor, paid the employees after the employer's liquidation and thereby became subrogated to the employees' rights and remedies against the employer.

8.31 There is nevertheless authority in New South Wales which suggests the contrary. In *MPS Constructions Pty Ltd v Rural Bank of New South Wales*[136] a building contractor had entered into a contract with a local council for the construction of a building. The contract provided for the establishment of a retention fund, by the deposit into a bank account of a percentage of the progress payments due to the contractor. The account was required to be in the joint names of the council and the contractor, and it was to be held by them on trust for the council subject to the discharge by the contractor of its obligations. Before final completion the contractor went into liquidation. The liquidator decided to complete the contract, which would have had the effect of releasing the retention moneys. The bank then asserted that it was entitled to set off the account against a separate debt owing to it by the contractor. One of the reasons given by Helsham CJ in Eq for not allowing the set-off was that, at the commencement of the liquidation, the account was held on trust for the council, so that there was a lack of mutuality.[137] The contractor's interest in the account at that time was still contingent on completion of construction. But the fact that the contractor was not then the beneficial owner of the debt should not have been sufficient to prevent a set-off. The contractor gave credit to the bank before the liquidation,[138] by entering into a transaction with the bank (along with the council) which would naturally or in the ordinary course of business, and without the interposition of any new and independent transaction,[139] end in a debt owing by the bank to the contractor as the sole beneficial owner. This should have provided a basis for a set-off. The acquisition of the sole beneficial interest in this situation would not have involved a new and independent transaction, because it was the contemplated end to the transaction which gave rise to the deposit. Further, the better view is that the circumstance that the liquidator may have used the company's resources to complete the contract for the benefit of creditors was not a sufficient reason for denying a set-off.[140] Nevertheless, in the circumstances in issue, the *MPS Constructions* case may have been correctly decided. It involved a contingent claim possessed by a company in liquidation, as opposed to a contingent liability. When an insolvent's contingent claim is in issue, the position in Australia is that the contingency must have occurred before an account can be taken,[141] whereas in the *MPS Constructions* case it appears that the liquidator had not yet obtained the final certificate discharging the council's interest in the account.

---

[136] (1980) 4 ACLR 835.

[137] (1980) 4 ACLR 835, 845.

[138] See para. 7.02–7.06 above.

[139] *Hiley v The Peoples Prudential Assurance Co Ltd* (1938) 60 CLR 468, 487 (Rich J), 499 (Dixon J).

[140] See e.g. *Re Asphaltic Wood Pavement Co. Lee & Chapman's Case* (1885) 30 Ch D 216, and generally the discussion of *Ince Hall Rolling Mills Co Ltd v The Douglas Forge Co* (1882) 8 QBD 179 in paras 13.37–13.57 below. The contrary argument may be stronger in bankruptcy than in company liquidation. See paras 13.41–13.42 and 13.56 below.

[141] See paras 8.35–8.46 below.

Surety's set-off where the creditor had received a dividend

The creditor may have been paid a dividend in the debtor's bankruptcy before the guaran- **8.32**
tor paid the balance of the debt. It has been suggested that a guarantor is only entitled to be
subrogated to the rights of the creditor if the guarantor has paid the full amount of the
debt,[142] but there is much to commend the view, which has been adopted in Australia,[143]
that the right of subrogation arises when the creditor is paid in full, whether or not entirely
by the guarantor. Assuming that this latter view is followed, so that the guarantor has a right
of subrogation, the fact of the dividend received by the creditor from the debtor's estate
means that the guarantor will be subrogated to a debt the face amount of which is greater
than the amount that he or she in fact has paid to the creditor, and which forms the basis of
the claim for an indemnity. The guarantor should nevertheless still be entitled to receive
future dividends on the full amount of the debt. A similar issue has arisen in the context of
contribution between guarantors. Consider that there are two guarantors of a debt, one of
whom has become bankrupt, and the creditor has proved for the full amount of the debt in
the bankruptcy. Subsequently, the creditor is paid in full, including as a result of a payment
from the solvent guarantor which is more than that guarantor's *pro rata* share. The solvent
guarantor is entitled to be subrogated to the creditor's proof in the co-guarantor's bankruptcy, and to be paid dividends until he or she has received an amount sufficient to satisfy
the claim for contribution.[144] The right of subrogation extends in this case to the full
amount of the debt for which the creditor proved, and not just to a part equal to the claim
for contribution itself, although the guarantor could not recover by way of dividend more
than his or her contribution entitlement. A similar analysis should apply when a guarantor
is subrogated to the creditor's proof in the debtor's bankruptcy.

But how would that concept work if the guarantor wishes to use the creditor's proof to **8.33**
which the guarantor is subrogated in a set-off? In the first place, credit should be given in
the set-off for any dividend already paid to the creditor.[145] Unless that occurs, the bankrupt
debtor's estate will have paid twice in respect of the debt, once in the form of a dividend to
the creditor and a second time through a set-off. Further, while the right of subrogation
extends to the full amount proved by the creditor, the guarantor would not be entitled to
receive by way of dividend more than his or her actual entitlement. Similarly, if the guarantor wishes to utilize the proof to which he or she is subrogated in a set-off against a separate
debt owed to the bankrupt debtor, or to a bankrupt co-guarantor, the guarantor should not
be entitled to do so for an amount in excess of his or her entitlement.

[142] *Re Fenton* [1931] 1 Ch 85, 115 (Lawrence LJ); *Ex p Brett, re Howe* (1871) LR 6 Ch App 838, 841
(Mellish LJ); *Ex p Turquand, re Fothergill* (1876) 3 Ch D 445, 450 (James LJ). Compare *Gedye v Matson*
(1858) 25 Beav 310, 312, 53 ER 655, 656 (Sir John Romilly MR).

[143] *A. E. Goodwin Ltd v A. G. Healing Ltd* (1979) 7 ACLR 481; *McColl's Wholesale Pty Ltd v State Bank
of New South Wales* [1984] 3 NSWLR 365, 378; *Raffle v AGC (Advances) Ltd* (1989) ASC 55–933 (Young
J, NSW SC); *Bayley v Gibsons Ltd* (1993) 1 Tas R 385; *Macedone v Collins* (1996) 7 BPR 15,127, 15,142;
Austin v Royal (1999) 47 NSWLR 27, 32. See also *Westpac Banking Corporation v Gollin & Co Ltd* [1988] VR
397, 402.

[144] *Ex p Stokes* (1848) De Gex 618; *Re Parker; Morgan v Hill* [1894] 3 Ch 400.

[145] See, in a different context, *MS Fashions Ltd v Bank of Credit and Commerce International SA* [1993]
Ch 425, 435 (Hoffmann LJ, Chancery Division).

(6) Must the contingency have occurred?

8.34 In the case of a contingent debt owing by an insolvent, the debt may be proved in the insolvency before the contingency has occurred based upon an estimate of its value made by the trustee in bankruptcy or the liquidator. Similarly, it should not be necessary for a set-off that the contingency should have occurred.[146] The test as to whether credit has been given requires a characterization of the nature of the transaction that was entered into. In other words, is the transaction of the kind that would naturally or in the ordinary course of business end in a debt?[147] There must also be a sum 'due' for a set-off, but an estimate of the contingent debt for the purpose of proof[148] should suffice to satisfy that requirement.[149] The estimated value may be regarded as the sum 'due' from the bankrupt for the purpose of the set-off section. In company liquidation in England, amendments to the Insolvency Rules in 2005[150] confirmed that a contingent debt may be set off based upon an estimate of its value made by the liquidator.[151]

C. Contingent Debt Owing to the Insolvent

(1) Set-off, when the debt is still contingent

8.35 Alternatively, a person may be contingently indebted *to* an insolvent at the date of the insolvent's bankruptcy or liquidation. Traditionally, the insolvency legislation only empowered a trustee in bankruptcy or a liquidator to estimate the value of a contingent debt owing by the insolvent. The power did not extend to a contingent debt on the other side of the account. Therefore, while the debt to the bankrupt or the insolvent company remained contingent,[152] the fact that nothing was 'due' in respect of it, whether by way of an estimate of its value or otherwise, meant that it could not be brought into account in a set-off.[153]

---

[146] Compare Millett J's comment in *Re Charge Card Services Ltd* [1987] 1 Ch 150, 183, that: 'In every case the claim to set off requires that any contingency to which the liability was still subject at the date of the receiving order has since occurred.' On other occasions it has been said that 'it is enough' for a set-off of a contingent debt that it has matured into a pecuniary demand. See *Hiley v The Peoples Prudential Assurance Co Ltd* (1938) 60 CLR 468, 497 (Dixon J); *Day & Dent Constructions Pty Ltd v North Australian Properties Pty Ltd* (1982) 150 CLR 85, 95 (Gibbs CJ); *Gye v Davies* (1995) 37 NSWLR 421, 428 (Powell JA). See also *Day & Dent Constructions* at 109 (Murphy J). The comment in *Secretary of State for Trade and Industry v Frid* [2004] 2 AC 506 at [17], that the guarantor's claim for reimbursement 'became capable of set-off when the employees were afterwards paid', should be considered in the context of the rule against double proof. See paras 8.13–8.18 above.

[147] See para. 7.04 above.

[148] In bankruptcy, see the Insolvency Act 1986, s. 322.

[149] *Re Daintrey* [1900] 1 QB 546, 557 (Wright J); *MS Fashions Ltd v Bank of Credit and Commerce International SA* [1993] Ch 425, 435 (Hoffmann LJ, Chancery Division).

[150] Insolvency (Amendment) Rules 2005 (S.I. 2005 No. 527). See para. 6.06 above.

[151] Insolvency Rules 1986, r. 4.90(4)(b) and (5), referring to r. 4.86. In administration, see r. 2.85(4)(b) and (5), referring to r. 2.86.

[152] Note that, in the case of a primary obligation to pay, as opposed to a secondary obligation such as that of a guarantor, a provision in the contract for a demand in writing upon the debtor is not regarded as creating a contingency. See *MS Fashions Ltd v Bank of Credit and Commerce International SA* [1993] Ch 425, 435–6, referring to *Re J Brown's Estate* [1893] 2 Ch 300.

[153] *Re Daintrey* [1900] 1 QB 546, 557, 565; *MS Fashions Ltd v Bank of Credit and Commerce International SA* [1993] 1 Ch 425, 435 (Hoffmann LJ). See also *Re Bank of Credit and Commerce International SA (No. 8)*

This is still the case in relation to bankruptcy in England, and in bankruptcy and company liquidation in Australia. However, the position is now different in company liquidation and administration in England consequent upon amendments to the Insolvency Rules in 2005.[154] The Rules now provide that a sum is to be regarded as being due to (as well as from) the company when the obligation in question is contingent, and for the purpose of set-off the power to estimate the value of a contingent debt has been extended to contingent obligations owing to the company.[155] The estimated value is only relevant for that purpose. Any balance owed to the company after the set-off is payable to the liquidator if and when the debt becomes due and payable.[156]

(2) Set-off, after the contingency has occurred

In relation to bankruptcy in England, and bankruptcy and company liquidation in Australia,[157] the inability to include a contingent debt in a set-off only continues while the debt remains contingent. If the contingency occurs after the bankruptcy (or, in Australia, the liquidation), there would then be a sum 'due' to the insolvent which should be able to be the subject of a set-off, given that the debt would have resulted from a prior dealing.[158] This principle is reflected in a number of cases.

8.36

In *Re Daintrey*,[159] a business was sold on terms that the price was to be calculated as a proportion of the profits earned over a three-year period. The vendor became bankrupt before the expiration of the period and before any profits had been made. After the end of the three-year period, when the price was calculated in accordance with the agreed formula, the Court of Appeal held that the purchaser could set off his liability for the price against

8.37

[1998] AC 214, 224 (the depositor's liability to the bank in liquidation remained contingent after the liquidation because a demand had not been made), and *MPS Constructions Pty Ltd v Bank of New South Wales* (1980) 4 ACLR 835 (see para. 8.31 above). Compare *Re Taylor, ex p Norvell* [1910] 1 KB 562, 568 (Phillimore J), aspects of which seem contrary to this view.

[154] See para. 6.06 above.
[155] Insolvency Rules 1986, r. 4.90(4)(b) and (5), referring to r. 4.86. In administration, see r. 2.85(4)(b) and (5), referring to r. 2.86.
[156] See the Insolvency Rules 1986, r. 4.90(8). In administration, see r. 2.85(8).
[157] See para. 8.35 above.
[158] In addition to the cases discussed below, see *Wreckair Pty Ltd v Emerson* [1992] 1 Qd R 700; *Re Taylor, ex p Norvell* [1910] 1 KB 562, 568 (Phillimore J); *MS Fashions Ltd v Bank of Credit and Commerce International SA* [1993] Ch 425, 435 (Hoffmann LJ, Chancery Division); *Stein v Blake* [1996] 1 AC 243, 252–3; *JLF Bakeries Pty Ltd v Baker's Delight Holdings Ltd* (2007) 64 ACSR 633 (exercise of an option to purchase after liquidation, for which see paras 13.59–13.63 below). See also the cases concerned with a temporary suspension of mutuality in paras 6.105–6.107 above. In *Ex p Hope, re Hanson* (1858) 3 De G & J 92, 44 ER 1203 the bankrupts' claim for improvements appears to have been contingent at the date of the bankruptcy on the lease being determined. When a determination subsequently occurred, a set-off was allowed in respect of the claim. In *Thornton v Maynard* (1872) LR 10 CP 695 the bankrupt drawer's estate first obtained the claim against the acceptor after the bankruptcy, when the dividend was paid to the plaintiff indorsee. But since this arose out of the prior obligation incurred as drawer, a set-off was allowed. See also *Re Inglis, ex p The Trustee* (1932) 5 ABC 255. A contract for the sale of wheat was entered into on terms that the purchaser could elect to pay cash or deliver wheat of equal quality. The wheat was delivered before the vendor's bankruptcy, but it was not until later that the purchaser elected to pay cash. It was held that the resulting debt could be the subject of a set-off. Compare *MPS Constructions Pty Ltd v Rural Bank of NSW* (1980) 4 ACLR 835, for which see para. 8.31 above.
[159] [1900] 1 QB 546.

a separate debt owing to him by the vendor. *Re Daintrey* is sometimes characterized as a case in which there was a presently existing debt at the relevant date for determining rights of set-off which only remained to be quantified,[160] but in truth it is an example of a contingent debt.[161] No profits had been earned as at the relevant date, so that any debt to the bankrupt was contingent upon profits subsequently being earned.

8.38　There are other examples. In *Palmer v Day & Sons*,[162] a person before his bankruptcy had delivered some pictures to auctioneers for the purpose of sale. The sale occurred after the bankruptcy, and it was held that the auctioneers could employ their liability to account for the proceeds of sale in a set-off. *Palmer v Day & Sons* is an example of a set-off based upon the principle enunciated by Gibbs CJ in *Rose v Hart*.[163] According to that principle, where property has been deposited with a person with directions or authority to turn it into money, the depository may set off the obligation to account for the proceeds against a separate debt owing to him or her by the depositor. In a number of cases this has been held to apply even though the proceeds were received after the depositor's bankruptcy.[164] While these *Rose v Hart* cases may be criticized on the ground that the proceeds of sale may have been impressed with a trust, in which case *prima facie* they should not have been susceptible to a set-off,[165] they were nevertheless instances in which a set-off occurred against a sum that first became due to a bankrupt after the bankruptcy as a result of a prior dealing.

8.39　*Graham v Russell*[166] provides an early illustration of the set-off. It concerned a statute[167] which allowed an insured to prove a claim on a policy in the underwriter's bankruptcy when the loss occurred after the bankruptcy.[168] Since the insured's claim in that situation could have been proved, Lord Ellenborough said that it could have grounded a set-off, and if the insured's claim on the policy could have been set off if the underwriter had been bankrupt, he concluded that the underwriter similarly should be able to set off his liability on the policy when the insured instead was bankrupt, even though the loss occurred after the insured's bankruptcy.[169] Another example is *Lee & Chapman's Case*.[170] A contractor

---

[160] *Re National Benefit Assurance Co Ltd* [1924] 2 Ch 339, 343; *Re A Debtor (No. 66 of 1955)* [1956] 1 WLR 1226, 1230, 1238; *Carreras Rothmans Ltd v Freeman Mathews Treasure Ltd* [1985] 1 Ch 207, 230.

[161] *Re Taylor, ex p Norvell* [1910] 1 KB 562, 580–1; *Re Fenton* [1931] 1 Ch 85, 113; *Re Charge Card Services Ltd* [1987] 1 Ch 150, 182–3; *Day & Dent Constructions Pty Ltd v North Australian Properties Pty Ltd* (1982) 150 CLR 85, 92, 94, 103; *MS Fashions Ltd v Bank of Credit and Commerce International SA* [1993] Ch 425, 435.

[162] [1895] 2 QB 618.

[163] (1818) 8 Taunt 499, 506, 129 ER 477, 480. See paras 10.14–10.35 below.

[164] In addition to *Palmer v Day & Sons*, see *French v Fenn* (1783) 3 Dougl 257, 99 ER 642; *Olive v Smith* (1813) 5 Taunt 56, 128 ER 607; *Astley v Gurney* (1869) LR 4 CP 714.

[165] See paras 10.18–10.20 below.

[166] (1816) 5 M & S 498, 105 ER 1133.

[167] (1746) 19 Geo II, c. 32, s. 2.

[168] *Graham v Russell* was decided before 1825, when the bankruptcy legislation was amended to allow contingent debts to be set off. The set-off section in the 1825 Act (6 Geo IV, c. 16, s. 50) stipulated that 'every debt or demand hereby made provable against the estate of the bankrupt, may also be set-off in the manner aforesaid against such estate', and the 1825 bankruptcy legislation was the first to provide for proof in respect of contingent debts. See s. 56.

[169] The court declined to follow *Glennie v Edmunds* (1813) 4 Taunt 775, 128 ER 536. Compare also *Ex p Blagden* (1815) 19 Ves Jun 465, 34 ER 589.

[170] *Re Asphaltic Wood Pavement Co. Lee & Chapman's Case* (1885) 30 Ch D 216.

under a construction contract went into liquidation. The liquidator subsequently completed the work, whereupon the price became payable to the company. The Court of Appeal held that the debt for the price could be the subject of a set-off. Further, Dixon J seems to have had in mind both sides of the account when he said in *Hiley v The Peoples Prudential Assurance Co Ltd*[171] that: 'It is enough that at the commencement of the winding up mutual dealings exist which involve rights and obligations whether absolute or contingent of such a nature that afterwards in the events that happen they mature or develop into pecuniary demands capable of set-off.'

In Victoria, Hayne J held that a claim for post liquidation licence fees, which existed only as a contingent claim at the date of the payee's liquidation, could be included in a set-off in the liquidation.[172] Similarly, in *Booth v Hutchinson*,[173] Malins VC accepted that rent accruing to a bankrupt landlord[174] after the bankruptcy could be the subject of a set-off. The judgment is unsatisfactory because the Vice Chancellor failed to consider issues of mutuality which arise in lease cases as a result of the vesting of the property in the trustee.[175] It nevertheless indicates an acceptance of the view that a debt arising in favour of a bankrupt after the bankruptcy but pursuant to a prior contract can be included in an account in the bankruptcy. **8.40**

The set-off section admittedly provides that an account is to be taken of what is due from each party 'to the other',[176] and in the case of a bankruptcy a debt arising after the bankruptcy pursuant to a prior contract is a debt due to the trustee rather than to the bankrupt, given that the property of the bankrupt vests in the trustee.[177] Therefore, at no time could it be said that there is, or has been, a sum due to the bankrupt personally. But that circumstance by itself should not suffice to preclude a set-off in the situations under consideration.[178] When a debt arises in this manner as a result of a prior contract between the bankrupt and a creditor, 'to the other' should be interpreted as including 'to the trustee', on the basis that the trustee takes subject to the prior equity resulting from mutual credits, mutual debts or other mutual dealings. The whole thrust of the set-off section is to look at the position at the date of the bankruptcy, and if prior to that date there were mutual credits or mutual dealings one would expect that cross-claims resulting from the credits and dealings ordinarily would be set off. *Re Daintrey*, *Booth v Hutchinson* and *Palmer v Day & Sons* all suggest this view. In any event, there should not be the same difficulty in that regard in company liquidation, since the assets of a company after its liquidation ordinarily do not **8.41**

---

[171] (1938) 60 CLR 468, 497.

[172] *Old Style Confections Pty Ltd v Microbyte Investments Pty Ltd* [1995] 2 VR 457.

[173] (1872) LR 15 Eq 30, 35.

[174] In fact, the landlord had executed a deed of assignment of his estate upon trust for his creditors, but the deed provided that all questions should be decided according to bankruptcy law.

[175] See paras 13.64–13.68 below.

[176] Insolvency Act 1986, s. 323(2). In Australia, see the Bankruptcy Act 1966 (Cth), s. 86(1)(a) and, in company liquidation, the Corporations Act 2001 (Cth), s. 553C(1)(a).

[177] Insolvency Act 1986, s. 306.

[178] Being bankruptcy in England, and bankruptcy and company liquidation in Australia. See para. 8.36 above. Compare para. 8.35 above in relation to company liquidation and administration in England.

vest in the liquidator.[179] Any debt arising in favour of the company after the liquidation would still be a debt due to the company. The House of Lords has held that a company in liquidation is divested of the beneficial title to its assets,[180] which includes debts owing to the company, but it is still not possible to identify another person to whom it can be said that the debt is due.[181] In Australia, liquidation is not regarded as depriving the company of the beneficial title to its assets,[182] so that this point would be even less likely to be regarded as an issue there.

8.42   *Re A Debtor (No. 66 of 1955)*[183] is authority against the availability of a set-off in this situation. The Court of Appeal held in that case that a bankrupt surety's claim for an indemnity from the principal debtor could not be the subject of a set-off in the bankruptcy, since the payment by the surety's estate to the creditor occurred after the bankruptcy, and therefore at that date there was nothing due by way of indemnity from the debtor for the purpose of the set-off section. In other words, it was regarded as essential that an amount be due at the date of the bankruptcy, even though the resulting debt had its source in a prior obligation. *Re A Debtor* is difficult to reconcile with earlier authority,[184] and the reasoning of the Court of Appeal was criticized by the House of Lords in *Secretary of State for Trade and Industry v Frid*.[185] It should no longer be followed.[186]

8.43   In *Secretary of State v Frid*,[187] the House of Lords left open the question whether *Re A Debtor* nevertheless may have been correctly decided in the particular circumstances in issue, on the ground that the payment to the creditor which gave rise to the claim for an indemnity had been made out of assets which had vested in the trustee for the benefit of creditors, and which were no longer the surety's assets. This aspect of the reasoning is considered later.[188]

---

[179] *Re Oriental Inland Steam Co* (1874) LR 9 Ch App 557, 560. Note, however, that the Insolvency Act 1986, s. 145 empowers the court on the application of a liquidator to direct that all or part of the company's property shall vest in the liquidator.

[180] *Ayerst v C. & K. Construction Ltd* [1976] AC 167. See also *Wight v Eckhardt Marine GmbH* [2004] 1 AC 147 at [22] (PC).

[181] *Ayerst v C. & K. Construction Ltd* [1976] AC 167, 178–9.

[182] *Franklin's Selfserve Pty Ltd v Federal Commissioner of Taxation* (1970) 125 CLR 52; *FCT v Linter Textiles Australia Ltd* (2005) 220 CLR 592.

[183] [1956] 1 WLR 1226.

[184] See above.

[185] [2004] 2 AC 506 at [15]–[16].

[186] See also para. 8.28 above in relation to a contingent debt owing *by* an insolvent. This is consistent with the House of Lords' earlier apparent acceptance in *Stein v Blake* [1996] 1 AC 243, 252–3 of the proposition that set-off in bankruptcy can extend to debts on both sides of the account which were contingent at the bankruptcy date. In Australia, Gibbs CJ in *Day & Dent Constructions Pty Ltd v North Australian Properties Pty Ltd* (1982) 150 CLR 85, 94 left open the question whether *Re A Debtor (No. 66 of 1955)* was correct, on the ground that the payment was made by the trustee to enable him to obtain the bankrupt's property (see also para. 8.43 below), but Mason J (at 106) said that it was anomalous and should not be followed. Prior to *Secretary of State v Frid* and *Stein v Blake*, the Court of Appeal had followed *Re A Debtor* in *Brown v Cork* [1985] BCLC 363. See also in Australia *A. E. Goodwin Ltd v A. G. Healing Ltd* (1979) 7 ACLR 481 and *Westmex Operations Pty Ltd v Westmex Ltd* (1994) 12 ACLC 106, 110 (guarantee provided to the NCSC pursuant to a Class Order in order to obtain exemption from filing individual company accounts).

[187] [2004] 2 AC 506 at [15]–[16]. See also *Day & Dent Constructions Pty Ltd v North Australian Properties Pty Ltd* (1982) 150 CLR 85, 94 (Gibbs CJ).

[188] See paras 13.39–13.56 below.

Likelihood of the contingency occurring

It has been suggested[189] that the question whether a contingent debt owing to an insolvent **8.44** can be the subject of a set-off if the contingency subsequently occurs may depend upon whether it could be said at the insolvency date that the claim was likely to mature into an actual liquidated debt during the course of the insolvency proceedings. That view appears to be based upon a commonly accepted definition of mutual credit.[190] However, since the expansion of the set-off section in 1869[191] to include mutual dealings, it should suffice if the debt arose out of a prior dealing between the parties to the proposed set-off without the intervention of any new and independent transaction.[192] It should not be necessary in such a case to show likelihood. In any event, there would be no such difficulty in company liquidation and administration in England.[193]

Proof in the contingent creditor's insolvency before the contingency occurs

Consider that, before the contingency occurred, the person contingently liable had proved **8.45** in the bankruptcy or liquidation of the contingent creditor in respect of a debt separately owing to him or her, and had received a dividend. If after the occurrence of the contingency the creditor's insolvency representative sues for payment of the resulting debt, the better view was expressed by Hoffmann LJ in the Chancery Division in *MS Fashions Ltd v Bank of Credit and Commerce International SA*,[194] that the person may still rely on the provable debt in a set-off, notwithstanding the payment of the dividend, though credit must be given for the dividend.

Contract for the sale of property or for the performance of work

When a trustee in bankruptcy or a liquidator completes a prior contract for the sale of **8.46** property or for the performance of work so as to earn the price, the purchaser's resulting debt would have been contingent at the relevant date for determining set-offs. It has been suggested that a lack of mutuality may be an objection to employing the debt in a set-off. The question of the availability of a set-off in such cases is considered later.[195]

D. Insolvent Corporate Group

It is common for the members of a group of companies to provide guarantees supported by **8.47** fixed and floating charges to a major creditor, usually a bank, in order to secure the indebtedness of one or more group members to the creditor. In addition, the group members may be indebted to each other on trading accounts or other inter-company debts. In the event of the collapse of the group and the liquidation of the companies the creditor would realise its securities. If the creditor is not paid in full, the rule against double proof would operate

---

[189] Wood, *English and International Set-off* (1989), 592.
[190] See para. 7.04 above.
[191] Bankruptcy Act 1869, s. 39.
[192] See *Hiley v The Peoples Prudential Assurance Co Ltd* (1938) 60 CLR 468, 487 (Rich J), 499 (Dixon J).
[193] See para. 8.35 above.
[194] [1993] Ch 425, 435.
[195] See paras 13.35–13.57 below.

to deny rights of contribution to group members that have paid more than their share of the debt as against underpaying members. Similarly, rights of subrogation would not be available.[196] Alternatively, the creditor may be paid in full and may hold a surplus from the securities. The question would then arise as to how the surplus is to be dealt with. In particular, the issue may be complicated where some of the members whose assets were used to pay a greater proportion of the debt, and who therefore would be entitled to contribution from underpaying members, are indebted on inter-company accounts to the underpaying members.

8.48 The circumstances of each case would require consideration, but the problem is illustrated by *Brown v Cork*.[197] The members of a group of companies executed a joint and several cross-guarantee, whereby each guaranteed to a bank the liability of each of the other companies to the bank. In addition, the cross-guarantee was supported by fixed and floating charges granted by each company which covered the whole of the company's assets. The group got into difficulties, and the bank appointed a receiver pursuant to the securities. The receiver realised the companies' assets secured to the bank, and after paying the bank he held a surplus. One of the companies had gone into liquidation before the bank was paid, and the other companies went into liquidation after payment to the bank. The question arose as to how the surplus was to be applied. The Court of Appeal held that the surplus should be distributed amongst the companies in proportions, on the basis that each company (so far as the money realised from its charge permitted) would have discharged its own indebtedness to the bank, and also an equal share of the deficiency attributable to the indebtedness to the bank of those companies which were unable to discharge their own indebtedness in full.[198] Oliver LJ, who delivered the judgment of the court, rejected an alternative suggestion, that a separate account should be prepared for each company showing the amounts due to and from it by way of contribution to or from its co-sureties, and in making the calculation there should be set off against contribution liabilities any sums due from one company to another on their inter-company trading accounts.

8.49 The issue with which the Court of Appeal was concerned was whether a set-off was available. Two reasons appear in the judgment as to why it was not. The company that went into liquidation before payment in full to the bank had paid more than its share. Oliver LJ said[199] in relation to that company that there was no set-off because the liability of the underpaying companies for contribution under the cross-guarantee arose after the liquidation, and a set-off in that circumstance was precluded by the earlier decision of the Court of Appeal in *Re A Debtor (No. 66 of 1955)*.[200] This aspect of that case was

---

[196] See paras 8.13–8.18 above.

[197] [1985] BCLC 363 (Oliver, Parker and Balcombe LJJ). In Australia, see also *A. E. Goodwin Ltd v A. G. Healing Ltd* (1979) 7 ACLR 481, and *Westmex Operations Pty Ltd v Westmex Ltd* (1994) 12 ACLC 106, 110 (guarantee provided by a group of companies to the National Companies and Securities Commission pursuant to a class order in order to obtain exemption from filing individual company accounts).

[198] See Lightman and Moss, *The Law of Receivers and Administrators of Companies* (3rd edn, 2000), 315.

[199] [1985] BCLC 363, 368 (and see also at 376).

[200] [1956] 1 WLR 1226.

criticized earlier.[201] It is suggested that the fact that the debt arose after the liquidation should not have precluded a set-off in circumstances where it arose out of a prior dealing between the parties in the form of the cross-guarantee. However, Oliver LJ noted another, more general, argument put forward by the respondent, which he seemed to accept.[202] Each of the companies which had paid more than its share had a right of contribution from the others, and for the purpose of obtaining contribution it was entitled to be subrogated to the securities provided to the bank by the other companies. The subrogation entitlement extended also to the surplus in the receiver's hands.[203] To that extent the indebtedness of each of the companies to the other for contribution was a secured indebtedness. Because of the security there was no question of an overpaying surety having to prove in the liquidation of an underpaying surety, in which case a set-off under the insolvency set-off section would not have occurred in the liquidation. The overpaying surety was entitled to rely on its security and to call on the receiver to hand over the moneys in his hands to the extent of the charge. In addition, Oliver LJ rejected an argument that the proviso to s. 5 of the Mercantile Law Amendment Act 1856, to the effect that a surety is entitled to recover from a co-surety no more than the 'just proportion' to which the co-surety is liable, itself required a set-off in respect of other debts as between the parties.

The difficulty with the second argument is that it only considered the effect of the liquidation of an underpaying surety. In that liquidation, an overpaying surety was a secured creditor. As such it was entitled to elect not to prove but to rely on its security, in which case the better view is that, in that liquidation, the insolvency set-off section did not apply.[204] But the overpaying sureties themselves were in liquidation, so that *prima facie* the question of set-off in the liquidation of an overpaying surety also had to be considered.[205] Unlike in the case of a secured creditor of a company in liquidation, when a company in liquidation itself holds security for a debt, there is no question of an election. If the debtor on the secured debt is also owed a debt by the company in liquidation, an automatic set-off[206] may occur in that liquidation in relation to the debts, in which case, to the extent of the set-off, the security would be released.[207] Furthermore, for the reason given above it should not have mattered, in the case of one of the overpaying sureties, that it went into liquidation before the debt arose. It is suggested, therefore, that there should have been a set-off in *Brown v Cork*.[208]

8.50

---

[201] See para. 8.42 above.

[202] [1985] BCLC 363, 369–71, and see also at 374 (referring to the first instance judge) and 376 (approving of the respondent's submissions).

[203] See also *Bayley v Gibsons Ltd* (1993) 1 Tas R 385, 387–8, 390.

[204] See paras 6.177–6.178 above.

[205] *Re SSSL Realisations (2002) Ltd* [2006] Ch 610 at [90] is against this view. See the criticism of that aspect of the judgment in that case at paras 11.03–11.11 below.

[206] See paras 6.119–6.146 above.

[207] See para. 6.179 above.

[208] In *A. E. Goodwin Ltd v A. G. Healing Ltd* (1979) 7 ACLR 481, 491 Powell J similarly concluded that an overpaying surety's claim for contribution from an underpaying surety could not be the subject of a set-off in respect of an inter-company debt, in circumstances where it appears that both companies were in liquidation. Powell J justified that conclusion on a different ground, that subrogation was a class right which enured to the benefit of all the sureties, and therefore there was a lack of mutuality for the purpose of a set-off. See also para. 8.29 above. However, while the view that subrogation operated as a class right would have been relevant to

E. Damages Claims

(1) Breach of contract

8.51   Prior to 1869, the set-off section in the bankruptcy legislation was confined to mutual credit and mutual debts. The concept of giving credit itself related to debts, in that it encompassed a debt arising out of a transaction entered into before the relevant date for determining rights of set-off where it could be said that the transaction was of the type that would naturally, or in the ordinary course of business, end in a debt.[209] Accordingly, a claim for damages for breach of contract was regarded as not being within the ambit of the set-off section.[210] Nor would the amendment of the bankruptcy legislation in 1861, by which damages claims for breach of contract became provable,[211] have sufficed to remedy that situation. After the amendment, the point nevertheless remained that, as long as the set-off section was cast only in terms of mutual debts and mutual credits, it did not contemplate a set-off in relation to a damages claim.[212] In 1869, however, the set-off section was expanded to include mutual dealings.[213] This, in conjunction with the 1861 amendment to the proof of debt provision, had the effect of allowing a damages claim for breach of a contract entered into before the bankruptcy to be included in a set-off, since in such a case the claim arose out of a prior dealing between the parties to the set-off.[214]

8.52   In *Carreras Rothmans Ltd v Freeman Mathews Treasure Ltd*,[215] Peter Gibson J held that a claim for damages for breach of a prior contract could only be employed in a set-off if the

---

the question of subrogation to the creditor's securities, it should not have impacted on the personal liability of an underpaying surety to pay contribution to an overpaying surety, for the purpose of a set-off in the overpaying surety's liquidation. Thus, in *Brown v Cork* [1985] BCLC 363, 369, the Court of Appeal seems to have accepted that the claims for contribution in that case could have been the subject of a set-off, were it not for the points that it made (see above) to the effect that the indebtedness for contribution was a secured indebtedness and, in relation to one of the companies, that the debt arose after its liquidation.

[209] See paras 7.04–7.05 above.

[210] *Rose v Sims* (1830) 1 B & Ad 521, 109 ER 881.

[211] Bankruptcy Act 1861, s. 153.

[212] See para. 7.05 above. Compare *Makeham v Crow* (1864) 15 CB(NS) 847, 143 ER 1018, in which an unliquidated damages claim arising out of a contract of sale was set off in an action by the vendor's assignees in bankruptcy for payment of the price. However, the purchaser presented alternative arguments for a set-off. A set-off was claimed, not only under the bankruptcy legislation based upon the scope of the proof of debt provision in the 1861 Act, but also on equitable set-off. The report is silent as to which of these was regarded as the justification for the decision. Certainly, in cases decided after the Bankruptcy Act 1869, which introduced 'mutual dealings' into the insolvency set-off section, set-off of unliquidated damages claims was justified on that ground. Thus, in *Booth v Hutchinson* (1872) LR 15 Eq 30, 32 Malins VC said that he would probably have concluded that the damages claim in that case could not have been set off under the old law. He said (at 34) that there was no mutual debt, and there was hardly a mutual credit, but that there was certainly a mutual dealing.

[213] Bankruptcy Act 1869, s. 39.

[214] See e.g. *Booth v Hutchinson* (1872) LR 15 Eq 30; *Peat v Jones & Co* (1881) 8 QBD 147; *Mersey Steel & Iron Co v Naylor, Benzon, & Co* (1884) 9 App Cas 434; *Re Asphaltic Wood Pavement Co. Lee & Chapman's Case* (1885) 30 Ch D 216; *Palmer v Day & Sons* [1895] 2 QB 618, 621. See also *Baker v Lloyd's Bank Ltd* [1920] 2 KB 322, in which Roche J treated the declaration of insolvency as a repudiation, although there is no indication as to whether the repudiation in fact was accepted.

[215] [1985] 1 Ch 207. See also *Re Opes Prime Stockbroking Ltd* (2008) 171 FCR 473 at [17]. Indeed, that case appears to suggest that insolvency set-off is confined to debts as opposed to damages claims.

breach occurred on or before the relevant date for determining rights of set-off. This proposition was said to be supported by *Re A Debtor (No. 66 of 1955)*,[216] but that case has been criticized.[217] The *Carreras Rothmans* case is contrary to *Re Asphaltic Wood Pavement Co. Lee & Chapman's Case*,[218] in which a set-off was allowed notwithstanding that the breach of contract occurred after the winding up of the company,[219] as well as the decision of Roche J in *Telsen Electric Co Ltd v J J Eastick & Sons*[220] in relation to the alternative finding that the breach occurred when the liquidator refused to accept the return of the goods. This aspect of the *Carreras Rothmans* case should not be regarded as good law, which indeed was the view of Millett J in *Re Charge Card Services Ltd*.[221]

(2) Tort

The necessity for a dealing

It used to be the case that a claim in tort which remained unliquidated at the date of the bankruptcy or liquidation was not provable,[222] and similarly it could not be employed in a set-off.[223] The position changed in England in 1986, when the Insolvency Act introduced a right of proof in respect of an unliquidated claim in tort,[224] and this has since been adopted in Australia in the context of company liquidation.[225] But this should not have the consequence that a tortious claim which is still unliquidated at the relevant date

8.53

---

[216] [1956] 1 WLR 1226.

[217] See paras 8.28 and 8.42 above. Note, however, the possible explanation of *Re A Debtor* referred to in para. 8.43 above.

[218] (1885) 30 Ch D 216.

[219] This aspect of *Lee & Chapman's Case* was accepted as correct in *Secretary of State for Trade and Industry v Frid* [2004] 2 AC 506 at [9]. See also *Re Charge Card Services Ltd* [1987] 1 Ch 150, 180–1; *Striker Resources NL v Australian Goldfields NL* [2006] WASC 153 at [329]. In relation to proof of debts, see *Re National Express Group Australia (Swanston Trams) Pty Ltd* (2004) 50 ACSR 434 at [8]–[14].

[220] [1936] 3 All ER 266.

[221] [1987] 1 Ch 150, 178, 190.

[222] See the former Bankruptcy Act 1914, s. 30(1), which provided that demands in the nature of unliquidated damages arising otherwise than by reason of a contract, promise or breach of trust were not provable in the bankruptcy. Compare *Re Berkeley Securities (Property) Ltd* [1980] 1 WLR 1589 in relation to a claim in tort that had been liquidated by judgment after winding up but before the claimant lodged a proof in the winding up. However, the development in that case was short-lived. See *Re Islington Metal and Plating Works Ltd* [1984] 1 WLR 14, and *Re Autolook Pty Ltd* (1983) 2 ACLC 30.

[223] *Aliter* if judgment had been obtained and the claim liquidated before the relevant date. See *Re D. H. Curtis (Builders) Ltd* [1978] 1 Ch 162, 172, and, with respect to proof, *Page v Commonwealth Life Assurance Society Ltd* (1935) 36 SR (NSW) 85, 90, *Re Berkeley Securities (Property) Ltd* [1980] 1 WLR 1589, 1606 and *Re Autolook Pty Ltd* (1983) 2 ACLC 30. An award of costs made in the tort action, being a mere addition or appurtenance to the damages, was said to follow the same rule. See *Re Newman, ex p Brooke* (1876) 3 Ch D 494, 497 (but compare *Foots v Southern Cross Mine Management Pty Ltd* (2007) 234 CLR 52 at [48], [57] and [65] (HCA)).

[224] See s. 322, 'bankruptcy debt' being defined in s. 382 as including tortious liabilities. For company liquidation, see the Insolvency Rules 1986, r. 13.12. It was held in *Re T. & N. Ltd* [2006] 1 WLR 1728 that a future damages claim in tort, where the tortfeasor had committed the relevant act or omission that would give rise to liability before its liquidation but compensable loss had not yet been suffered at the date of the liquidation, was not provable in the liquidation. The effect of that decision in liquidation was reversed by the inclusion of r. 13.12(2)(b) in the Insolvency Rules (see the Insolvency (Amendment) Rules 2002 (S.I. 2006 No. 1272)), but compare the Insolvency Act 1986, s. 382(2) in bankruptcy.

[225] See the Corporations Act 2001 (Cth), s. 553(1). The old position still applies in bankruptcy, however. See the Bankruptcy Act 1966 (Cth), s. 82(2).

for determining rights of set-off[226] can always be employed in a set-off. In order for the insolvency set-off section to apply there must be mutual credits, mutual debts or other mutual dealings. A damages claim is not a debt, unless it has been liquidated by judgment prior to the relevant date.[227] In relation to the giving of credit, that concept has traditionally been confined to a transaction which would naturally end in a debt, as opposed to a damages claim.[228] Moreover, a damages claim in tort might not result from a dealing between the parties.[229] As Lord Esher MR once remarked:[230] 'There are, no doubt, matters which give rise to claims, but are not dealings within the section. If one man assaults another or injures him through negligence, that gives rise to a claim, but is not a dealing . . .' Similarly, it has been said that a misappropriation of assets or a theft of money or a conversion of property is not a dealing for the purpose of the set-off section.[231] If a claim in tort is not the result of a dealing, it would not come within the language of the set-off section.

8.54 This is not to suggest that a tortious claim can never arise out of a dealing. One situation that was recognized before the 1986 Insolvency legislation is the case of a claim for damages for misrepresentation inducing a contract entered into with the representor.[232] The claim, though based upon tort, was considered to be provable[233] on the ground that it was not simply a personal tort but rather it arose by reason of the contract between the parties.[234] Similarly, it could be employed in a set-off, the justification being that it arose out of a dealing between those parties.[235] But if a claim in tort did not arise out of a dealing, it would

---

[226] See paras 6.45–6.65 above.

[227] This is implicit in Brightman J's comment in *Re D. H. Curtis (Builders) Ltd* [1978] 1 Ch 162, 172.

[228] *Rose v Sims* (1830) 1 B & Ad 521, 109 ER 881; *Palmer v Day & Sons* [1895] 2 QB 618, 621. See paras 7.04 and 7.05 above. Note, however, para. 7.06 above.

[229] See para. 7.10 above. But note *Secretary of State for Trade and Industry v Frid* [2004] 2 AC 506 at [24].

[230] *Eberle's Hotels and Restaurant Co Ltd v E. Jonas & Brothers* (1887) 18 QBD 459, 465.

[231] *Manson v Smith* [1997] 2 BCLC 161, 164; *Smith v Bridgend County BC* [2002] 1 AC 336 at [35]; *Re Leeholme Stud Pty Ltd* [1965] NSWR 1649. Compare *Shirlaw v Lewis* (1993) 10 ACSR 288. Hodgson J in that case (at 295–6) considered that, if there had been a liability in conversion, in the particular circumstances in issue it would have arisen out of a prior dealing between the parties, and he contemplated the possibility that it could have been included in a set-off.

[232] Compare the situation where the misrepresentation induces a contract with a third party. See paras 8.57–8.61 below.

[233] See *Jack v Kipping* (1882) 9 QBD 113, 117, and also the discussion in *Gye v McIntyre* (1991) 171 CLR 609, 631.

[234] *Jack v Kipping* (1882) 9 QBD 113, 117; *Palmer v Day & Sons* [1895] 2 QB 618, 622; *Tilley v Bowman Ltd* [1910] 1 KB 745, 753. See e.g. the Bankruptcy Act 1869, s. 31, and the discussion of the development of that provision in *Coventry v Charter Pacific Corporation Ltd* (2005) 227 CLR 234 at [23]–[27].

[235] *Jack v Kipping* (1882) 9 QBD 113 (explained in *Coventry v Charter Pacific Corporation Ltd* (2005) 227 CLR 234 at [38]–[50]); *Re Mid-Kent Fruit Factory* [1896] 1 Ch 567, 571–2; *Tilley v Bowman Ltd* [1910] 1 KB 745. Compare *Kitchen's Trustee v Madders* [1950] 1 Ch 134, in which there was an undertaking not to prove the damages claim in the bankruptcy. The allowance of a set-off in *Jack v Kipping* has been said to give rise to difficulty. See *Tilley v Bowman Ltd* at 752, and note also *Provident Finance Corporation Pty Ltd v Hammond* [1978] VR 312, 318. It is not easy to reconcile with the principle which has been applied in the case of an assignment of a debt, that an assignee does not take subject to a cross-claim for damages for fraud inducing the contract out of which the assigned debt arose, on the ground that the damages claim is not a claim arising under the contract itself. See *Stoddart v Union Trust Ltd* [1912] 1 KB 181. *Quaere* whether *Stoddart v Union Trust* was correctly decided. See para. 17.37 below. In Australia, it has been questioned whether the claim for fraudulent misrepresentation inducing a contract in *Jack v Kipping* in fact was provable, and therefore whether the insolvency set-off section indeed applied to it. Rather, it has been suggested that the case should be treated as illustrating the availability of equitable set-off. See *Re NIAA Corporation Ltd (in liq)* (NSW SC, McLelland

not be within the ambit of the set-off section. It should not suffice that the claim is provable. While it is true to say that set-off is an aspect of the rules relating to proof of debts,[236] this notion does not import an absolute principle that all provable debts are capable of being set off.[237] Rather, the principle is as Lord Hoffmann expressed it in *Stein v Blake*,[238] that: 'Bankruptcy set-off . . . applies to any claim arising out of mutual credits or other mutual dealings before the bankruptcy for which a creditor would be entitled to prove.'

Bankrupt's claim must vest in the trustee

The Insolvency Act, s. 323 provides that only the balance of the account taken under the section is provable in the bankruptcy or, as the case may be, is to be paid to the trustee in bankruptcy. As a corollary, the High Court of Australia, in *Gye v McIntyre*,[239] said that the bankrupt's claim against the creditor must be such that it would vest in a trustee in bankruptcy.[240] This would exclude claims for damages for personal injury or wrong done to the bankrupt.[241] Normally, claims of that nature are unlikely to arise out of a dealing so that in any event they should not be able to be employed in a set-off.[242] But even if in an exceptional case the claim is derived from a dealing, the fact that it does not vest in the trustee should mean that it cannot be set off. **8.55**

Australia

In Australia, damages claims in tort are now provable in company liquidation,[243] but it remains the case that they are not provable in bankruptcy.[244] This is a consequence of the Bankruptcy Act 1966 (Cth), s. 82(2),[245] which provides that a demand in the nature of **8.56**

CJ in Eq, 2 December 1994, BC9403369), referred to in *Aliferis v Kyriacou* (2000) 1 VR 447 at [48] (Charles JA). However, *Jack v Kipping* has been regarded by the Australian High Court as an authority on insolvency set-off. See *Gye v McIntyre* (1991) 171 CLR 609, 630–1 and *Coventry v Charter Pacific Corporation Ltd* (2005) 227 CLR 234 at [38]–[50].

[236] *Mersey Steel and Iron Co v Naylor, Benzon & Co* (1884) 9 App Cas 434, 437–8; *Re Northside Properties Pty Ltd and the Companies Act* [1971] 2 NSWLR 320, 323; *Re One.Tel Ltd* (2002) 43 ACSR 305 at [25]; *Re Bank of Credit and Commerce International SA (No. 8)* [1996] Ch 245, 256.

[237] See paras 7.24–7.26 above.

[238] [1996] 1 AC 243, 251 (emphasis added).

[239] (1991) 171 CLR 609, 626–7. See paras 7.31–7.32 above.

[240] Wood earlier had expressed this view in *English and International Set-off* (1989), 315–16.

[241] See e.g. *Beckham v Drake* (1849) 2 HLC 579, 604, 621, 9 ER 1213, 1222, 1228; *Ex p Vine, re Wilson* (1878) 8 Ch D 364; *Wilson v United Counties Bank Ltd* [1920] AC 102; *Heath v Tang* [1993] 1 WLR 1421, 1423. When a bankrupt has a cause of action in negligence, which includes a head of damage relating to property and another head of damage relating to personal injury, there is but one cause of action, and since it relates to property it vests in the trustee. On the other hand, the right to recover the damages which are personal, and any damages recovered, are held by the trustee on constructive trust for the bankrupt. See *Ord v Upton* [2000] 1 All ER 193 (esp at 206). Because the constructive trust relates not only to the damages recovered but also to the right to recover them, that part of the claim should not be the subject of a set-off in the bankruptcy. In Australia, the Bankruptcy Act 1966 (Cth), s. 116(2)(g) specifically exempts any right of the bankrupt to recover damages or compensation for personal injury or wrong done to the bankrupt from the property which is divisible among the creditors.

[242] See para. 8.53 above.

[243] Corporations Act 2001 (Cth), s. 553(1).

[244] Bankruptcy Act 1966 (Cth), s. 82(2).

[245] The origin of s. 82 is discussed in *Coventry v Charter Pacific Corporation Ltd* (2005) 227 CLR 234 at [22]–[29].

unliquidated damages arising otherwise than by reason of a contract, promise or breach of trust is not provable. Because a claim in tort against a bankrupt is not provable, it cannot be included in a set-off.[246] On the other hand, while the set-off section requires that the claim against the bankrupt be provable, there is no such principle that the bankrupt's claim against the creditor must be in the nature of a provable debt.[247] Therefore, an unliquidated damages claim in tort available to a bankrupt against a creditor should be able to be included in a set-off if it arose out of a dealing, even though it would not have been provable in the creditor's bankruptcy if the creditor instead had been the bankrupt party.

8.57 Consider the case of a claim against a bankrupt for damages for misrepresentation inducing a contract. The claim, although in tort, is provable in the bankruptcy of the representor where the contract was entered into with the representor. This is justified on the basis that the claim arose by reason of a contract between the parties, so that the exclusion from proof in s. 82(2) does not apply.[248] But where the misrepresentation induced the claimant to enter into a contract with a third party, for example a company associated with the representor, that explanation is not available. As a bare damages claim in tort, the exclusion from proof in s. 82 would operate to deny the claimant a right of proof in the representor's bankruptcy.[249] Similar principles apply in the case of a claim for damages for misleading or deceptive conduct contrary to the various statutory provisions in Australia which proscribe that form of conduct.[250]

Misrepresentation inducing a contract with a third party

8.58 Consider the particular case of a damages claim for misrepresentation inducing a contract where the claimant was induced to contract with a third party, as opposed to with the representor.

8.59 In Australia, an analogous situation came before the High Court in *Coventry v Charter Pacific Corporation Ltd*.[251] The case concerned legislation[252] which prohibited misleading or deceptive conduct in relation to a dealing in securities. The misleading conduct in that case had induced the claimant to contract with third parties. The representor had become bankrupt, and the question was whether the claimant's consequent damages claim against the representor[253] was provable in the bankruptcy. The High Court[254] accepted that the claim would have been provable if the representation had induced the claimant to contract with the representor (termed a 'bilateral' case),[255] but held[256] that it was not provable in

---

[246] See para. 7.24 above.
[247] *Gye v McIntyre* (1991) 170 CLR 609. See paras 7.27–7.30 above.
[248] See para. 8.56 above.
[249] *Re Giles, ex p Stone* (1889) 61 LT 82, discussed with approval in *Coventry v Charter Pacific Corporation Ltd* (2005) 227 CLR 234 at [5], [45]–[62] and [71].
[250] *Coventry v Charter Pacific Corporation Ltd* (2005) 227 CLR 234 (misleading or deceptive conduct claim pursuant to the Corporations Law, ss. 995(2) and 1005). See also e.g. the Fair Trading Act 1987 (NSW), s. 42.
[251] (2005) 227 CLR 234.
[252] Corporations Law, s. 995.
[253] Pursuant to the Corporations Law, s. 1005.
[254] Gleeson CJ, Gummow, Hayne and Callinan JJ, Kirby J dissenting.
[255] On the authority of *Jack v Kipping* (1882) 9 QBD 113.
[256] Following *Re Giles, ex p Stone* (1889) 61 LT 82.

a case (a 'tripartite' case) where the contract was with a third party. This was justified on the ground that, since there was no contract with the bankrupt, the claim was for unliquidated damages arising otherwise than by reason of a contract, promise or breach of trust for the purpose of the exclusion from proof in s. 82(2) of the Australian Bankruptcy Act.[257] In addition, the majority in their joint judgment suggested that, in a tripartite (as opposed to a bilateral) case, the damages claim does not arise from a mutual dealing.[258] If a damages claim does not arise from a dealing, it cannot be the subject of a set-off between the claimant and the representor.[259]

The proposition, that under the Australian bankruptcy legislation a damages claim against **8.60** the representor in a tripartite situation is not provable in the representor's bankruptcy, has the consequence in Australia that the claim cannot be the subject of a set-off. This is because of the express requirement in the bankruptcy set-off section that the claim against the bankrupt be provable in the bankruptcy.[260] But the further proposition suggested by the High Court, that there is no dealing in a tripartite case, would prevent a set-off in other situations where a misrepresentation induces a contract with a third party. Thus, unlike in a bankruptcy in Australia, the claimant's damages claim against the representor would be provable in bankruptcy and company liquidation in England[261] and in Australia where the representor is a company in liquidation. But if a damages claim does not arise from a dealing, a set-off would not be available notwithstanding that it may be provable.[262] It would also mean that there could be no set-off where the claimant rather than the representor is bankrupt. The point in relation to that proposition is that, unlike an insolvent's liability, it is not necessary that a claim possessed by an insolvent be in the nature of a provable debt in order that it can be included in a set-off.[263] Nevertheless, the absence of a dealing would preclude a set-off.

In *Coventry v Charter Pacific*, the emphasis in the discussion of set-off was on the identity **8.61** of the person with whom the contract was entered into. However, it is unclear why pre-contractual negotiations during which representations were made themselves should not be characterized as a mutual dealing between the person to whom the representations were made and the representor.[264] On that basis, the question whether the ultimate contract was entered into with the representor or a third party should not be critical to whether the person's claim against the representor can be included in a set-off between them.

---

[257] See paras 8.56 and 8.57 above.
[258] Thus, the majority commented (227 CLR 234 at [50]) that: 'a claim which comes from a tripartite transaction, in which the bankrupt's misrepresentation induced the claimant to make a contract with a third party, does not arise from a mutual dealing and it arises otherwise than by reason of a contract or promise.' See also at [49] and [59]–[61]. Similar reasoning was applied in *Hoop & Javelin Holdings Ltd v BT Projects Pty Ltd (No. 3)* [2010] FCA 191 in relation to liability for involvement in a contravention of the Trade Practices Act within the meaning of s. 75B(1).
[259] See paras 8.53 and 8.54 above.
[260] Bankruptcy Act 1966 (Cth), s. 86(1), referring to 'a person proving or claiming to prove a debt in the bankruptcy'. See also para. 7.24 above.
[261] See para. 8.53 above.
[262] See para. 8.53 above. Provable claims ordinarily are capable of set-off. See para. 7.24 above.
[263] See paras 7.27–7.30 above.
[264] See *Gye v McIntyre* (1991) 171 CLR 609, 625.

F. Breach of Trust

8.62 The introduction in 1861 of a right of proof in respect of claims for unliquidated damages only applied to damages arising by reason of a contract or promise.[265] This was extended in the Bankruptcy Act 1883, s. 37 to damages for breach of trust. However, the liability of a trustee who disposed of trust property in breach of trust traditionally has been regarded in equity as being in the nature of an obligation to restore the property or to pay compensation, and as creating an equitable debt or liability in the nature of a debt, as opposed to being for unliquidated damages.[266] Therefore, even before the amendment to the proof of debt section in 1883, the equitable debt could be proved in a bankruptcy.[267]

8.63 When a beneficiary is bankrupt, there is an issue as to whether the trustee should be permitted to profit from his or her own breach of trust by employing the liability for breach of trust in a set-off in the bankruptcy. This is considered later.[268]

G. Calls on Shares

(1) Introduction

8.64 Section 17 of the Joint Stock Companies Amendment Act 1858 provided that, in fixing the amount payable by a contributory in the event of the winding up of a joint stock company, a set-off could occur between the amount of the call made upon him and any sum due to him on an independent contract or dealing with the company. It applied not only to companies in which contributories had unlimited liability, but also to companies where the liability was limited pursuant to the Joint Stock Companies Act 1856.[269] In the Companies Act 1862, however, the right to a set-off was restricted. Section 101 was drafted in terms similar to the current Insolvency Act 1986, s. 149, in that it only provided for a set-off against a call where the company was an unlimited company and, in addition, the call had been made before the winding up.[270]

---

[265] Bankruptcy Act 1861, s. 153.

[266] *Ex p Adamson, re Collie* (1878) 8 Ch D 807, 819; *Wickstead v Browne* (1992) 30 NSWLR 1, 14–15; *Coventry v Charter Pacific Corporation Ltd* (2005) 227 CLR 234 at [47]. See also *Target Holdings Ltd v Redferns* [1996] AC 421, 434. Compare *Space Investments Ltd v Canadian Imperial Bank of Commerce Trust Co (Bahamas) Ltd* [1986] 1 WLR 1072, 1074.

[267] *Ex p Westcott, re White* (1874) LR 9 Ch App 626; *Emma Silver Mining Co v Grant* (1880) 17 Ch D 122. See also Williams, *The Law and Practice in Bankruptcy* (2nd edn, 1876), 161.

[268] See para. 8.88 below.

[269] See e.g. *Garnet and Mosely Gold Mining Co of America Ltd v Sutton* (1862) 3 B & S 321, 122 ER 121. This would explain Dixon J's query in *Hiley v The Peoples Prudential Assurance Co Ltd* (1938) 60 CLR 468, 500 in relation to *Re The Moseley Green Coal and Coke Co Ltd. Barrett's Case (No. 2)* (1865) 4 De G J & S 756, 46 ER 1116 (the application of s. 17 of the 1858 Act in that case is more readily apparent from the reports in 12 LT 193 and 34 LJ Bcy 41).

[270] Any money due to the contributory as a member of the company in respect of any dividend or profit was excluded from the set-off. See now the Insolvency Act 1986, s. 149(2)(a). The restriction in s. 101, in terms that it only applied to a call made before the winding up, followed from the exclusion in s. 101 in relation to any moneys which the person was liable to contribute by virtue of a call made by the court pursuant to the Act. This referred to a call made by the court after the making of a winding-up order pursuant to s. 102 of the Act. See *Re Breech-Loading Armoury Co (Calisher's Case)* (1868) LR 5 Eq 214, 217. See now the Insolvency Act 1986, ss. 149(1) and 150. In Australia see the Corporations Act 2001 (Cth), s. 483(2) and (3).

In *Grissell's Case*,[271] it was held in the context of the 1862 Act, and it has since become an established principle, that, when a limited liability company is being wound up, a shareholder who is also a creditor of the company cannot set off the company's debt[272] against the shareholder's liability for unpaid calls.[273] Nor may the shareholder set off the dividend payable on the debt against the call. Indeed, given that there is no right of set-off, the rule in *Cherry v Boultbee*[274] dictates that the call, being an obligation to contribute to the fund represented by the company's assets, must be paid in full before the shareholder is entitled to participate in the fund by receiving a dividend along with the other creditors on the company's debt.[275] Despite early authority to the contrary,[276] it is now settled that the rule extends to voluntary liquidations.[277] Moreover, it makes no difference that the call may have been made before the winding up,[278] or that the call is being enforced in a common law action brought by the liquidator in the name of the company rather than in a proceeding in the winding up,[279] or that the company's unpaid capital has been charged or assigned to a third party.[280] Further, an agreement for a set-off between the company and

---

[271] *Re Overend, Gurney, and Co (Grissell's Case)* (1866) LR 1 Ch App 528. It was said in *Grissell's Case* (at 534 *per* Lord Chelmsford LC) that the question depended entirely upon the construction of the Companies Act 1862. The case was decided before the insolvency set-off section in the bankruptcy legislation was extended to company liquidation. See paras 6.05 and 6.06 above. The subsequent introduction of the rules of bankruptcy into the law of company liquidation has not affected the principle enunciated in *Grissell's Case*. See *Re General Works Co. Gill's Case* (1879) 12 Ch D 755; *Re North Queensland Brick and Pottery Co Ltd (MacBrair's Case)* [1902] St R Qd 286.

[272] The same principle applies where the company is liable in damages. See *Government Security Investment Co v Dempsey* (1880) 50 LJQB 199; *Re Pyramid Building Society* (1992) 8 ACSR 33, 48, 50.

[273] Compare *Re The London and Scottish Bank; Logan's Case* (1870) 21 LT 742. A counterclaim will similarly not succeed. See *Government Security Investment Co v Dempsey* (1880) 50 LJQB 199.

[274] (1839) 4 My & Cr 442, 41 ER 171. See ch. 14 below.

[275] *Re Overend, Gurney, and Co (Grissell's Case)* (1866) LR 1 Ch App 528, 536; *Re China Steamship Co, ex p MacKenzie* (1869) LR 7 Eq 240, 244; *Ramsay v Jacobs* (1987) 12 ACLR 595, 597; *Re Pyramid Building Society* (1992) 8 ACSR 33, 48. Note also the effect of s. 74(2)(f) of the Insolvency Act 1986, that a sum due to a member of a company, payable to that member in his character of a member (by way of dividends, profits or otherwise), is not deemed to be a debt of the company payable to that member in competition with other creditors, but any such sum may be taken into account for the purpose of the final adjustment of the rights of the contributories among themselves. In Australia, see the Corporations Act 2001 (Cth), s. 563A, and also s. 553A, which provides that a debt owed by a company to a person in the person's capacity as a member of the company is not admissible to proof unless the person has paid all amounts that he or she is liable to pay as a member of the company.

[276] *Brighton Arcade Co Ltd v Dowling* (1868) LR 3 CP 175. See also *Groom v Rathbone* (1879) 41 LT 591.

[277] *Re International Life Assurance Society (Gibbs and West's Case)* (1870) LR 10 Eq 312, 330; *Re Paraguassu Steam Tramroad Co (Black & Co's Case)* (1872) LR 8 Ch App 254, 262–3; *Re Whitehouse & Co* (1878) 9 Ch D 595; *Hoby and Co Ltd v Birch* (1890) 62 LT 404; *Re Pyle Works* (1890) 44 Ch D 534, 585–6; *Ramsay v Jacobs* (1987) 12 ACLR 595.

[278] *Re Breech-Loading Armoury Co (Calisher's Case)* (1868) LR 5 Eq 214; *Re Stranton Iron and Steel Co (Barnett's Case)* (1875) LR 19 Eq 449; *Re Whitehouse and Co* (1878) 9 Ch D 595; *Re Auriferous Properties Ltd* [1898] 1 Ch 691, 696; *Re Hiram Maxim Lamp Company* [1903] 1 Ch 70; *Re John Dillon Ltd (in liq), ex p Jefferies* [1960] WAR 30.

[279] *Re Whitehouse & Co* (1878) 9 Ch D 595, 604–5; *Alliance Film Corporation Ltd v Knoles* (1927) 43 TLR 678. For the form of proceeding in a winding up to enforce payment of a call, see *Palmer's Company Law* (looseleaf, 1993) vol. 3, para. 15.404.

[280] See *Re International Life Assurance Society (Gibbs and West's Case)* (1870) LR 10 Eq 312, 327 (in which the calls had been charged); *Bank of Australasia v Zohrab* (1891) 10 NZLR 310; *Re John Dillon, ex p Jefferies* [1960] WAR 30. See also *Re Matheson Bros & Co Ltd, ex p Matheson* (1884) NZLR 3 SC 323, 324 in the context of an assignment of calls by a liquidator after the commencement of the winding up. While an

the shareholder will not be effective to exclude the rule if the set-off has not been effected pursuant to the agreement before the liquidation,[281] even though the shareholder may have been induced to take the shares on the faith of the agreement.[282] If a set-off against a call has taken place before the company's liquidation, it nevertheless may be avoided by the liquidator if the circumstances were such as to give rise to a voidable preference.[283]

(2) Rationale

8.65 Sir George Jessel sought to explain the denial of a set-off on the basis of lack of mutuality.[284] He said that, once a winding up commences, a liability to contribute unpaid capital no longer takes the form of a debt owing to the company, but rather it constitutes a liability to contribute to the assets of the company enforceable by the liquidator, and there is a lack of mutuality between that liability and an indebtedness of the company.[285] This theory has been criticized on the ground that a call in a winding up does in fact give rise to a debt due to the company.[286] The fact that the call may be made by the liquidator does not mean that it is a liability owed to the liquidator.[287] Nor should the fact that the court's power to make a call in a compulsory winding up[288] is exercised by the liquidator as an officer of the court[289] have the consequence that the call is not a debt due to the company. In that regard,

---

assignee of calls takes free from any debt owing by the company to the contributory, the contributory may bring into account an indebtedness of the assignee. See *Matheson* at 324.

[281] *Re Law Car and General Insurance Corporation* [1912] 1 Ch 405; *Harding and Co Ltd v Hamilton* [1929] NZLR 338. Compare *Re Blakely Ordnance Co (Blakely's Case)* (1867) 17 LT 307. *Contra* if the set-off is effected before liquidation. See e.g. *Re Harmony and Montague Tin and Copper Mining Co (Spargo's Case)* (1873) LR 8 Ch App 407; *Re Jones, Lloyd & Co Ltd* (1889) 41 Ch D 159 (which is explained in *Harding v Hamilton*); *Re The Switchback Railway and Outdoor Amusement Co Ltd, ex p Mount* (1890) 16 VLR 339, 341; *Re New Zealand Pine Co Ltd, ex p The Official Liquidator: Guthrie's Case* (1898) 17 NZLR 257; *Randall v The Liquidator of the Santa Claus Gold Mining Co Ltd* (1906) 8 WALR 36; *Re Pinecord Ltd* [1995] 2 BCLC 57, 61. See also *Ramsay v Jacobs* (1987) 12 ACLR 595, 597–8 (payment in advance). Compare *Official Assignee of Romco Corporation Ltd v Walker* [1995] 1 NZLR 652 (see esp. at 658) in relation to an agreement at the time of subscription that shares are to be paid otherwise than in cash.

[282] *Re Paraguassu Steam Tramroad Co (Black & Co's Case)* (1872) LR 8 Ch App 254.

[283] *Re Land Development Association. Kent's Case* (1888) 39 Ch D 259; *Re Washington Diamond Mining Co* [1893] 3 Ch 95; *Re Atlas Engineering Co (Davy's Case)* (1889) 10 LR (NSW) Eq 179, 6 WN (NSW) 64; *Mitchell v Booth* [1928] SASR 367.

[284] *Re Whitehouse & Co* (1878) 9 Ch D 595.

[285] See also *Ex p Branwhite* (1879) 40 LT 652; *Monkwearmouth Flour Mill Co Ltd v Lightfoot* (1897) 13 TLR 327; *Re GEB, A Debtor* [1903] 2 KB 340, 346, 352. Lord Selborne's reference in *Re Paraguassu Steam Tramroad Co (Black & Co's Case)* (1872) LR 8 Ch App 254, 262 to the liquidator receiving the calls 'as a statutory trustee for the equal and rateable payment of all the creditors' may suggest lack of mutuality. See also the discussion of that case in *FCT v Linter Textiles Australia Ltd* (2005) 220 CLR 592 at [40]–[42]. However, *Black & Co's Case*, like *Grissell's Case* (1866) LR 1 Ch App 528, was decided before the insolvency set-off section in the bankruptcy legislation was extended to company liquidation. See paras 6.05 and 6.06 above. In *Grissell's Case* Lord Chelmsford LC (at 534) said that the question depended entirely on the construction of the Companies Act 1862, and Lord Selborne's comment in *Black & Co's Case* is perhaps better understood as supporting an alternative explanation for denying a set-off, based upon the construction of the insolvency legislation. See para. 8.66 below.

[286] See *Re Pyle Works* (1890) 44 Ch D 534, 575 (Cotton LJ), 585–6 (Lindley LJ). See also *Re A Debtor (No. 41 of 1951)* [1952] 1 Ch 192 in the context of a voluntary winding up.

[287] Compare Wood, *English and International Set-off* (1989), 729.

[288] Insolvency Act 1986, s. 150.

[289] See the Insolvency Act 1986, s. 160 and the Insolvency Rules 1986, r. 4.202.

the liability to contribute unpaid capital differs from the obligation to repay a preference, against which there similarly cannot be a set-off.[290] In the case of unpaid capital, the shareholder had a liability to contribute the capital before the winding up, albeit that the liability was contingent upon a call being made.[291] A preferential payment, on the other hand, is voidable only by order of the court on the application of the liquidator.[292] The lack of mutuality theory is difficult to reconcile with *Re China Steamship Co, ex p MacKenzie.*[293] *Ex p MacKenzie* concerned a shareholder who, after the commencement of the company's liquidation, assigned to a third party a debt owing to him by the company. It was held that the assignee took subject to a right in the company[294] to set off a call subsequently made on the assignor's shares against the debt. An assignee takes subject to equities, including rights of set-off, available to the debtor against the assignor.[295] But if lack of mutuality were the reason that a shareholder after the commencement of the winding up is denied a set-off against a call, there should not have been an equity available to the company against the assignor (shareholder) in *Ex p MacKenzie* to which the assignee was subject.

An alternative explanation is that the insolvency legislation itself forbids a set-off. The legislation, when taken as a whole, contemplates that the proceeds of a call are to be used with the other assets of the company in the *pari passu* payment of the company's debts,[296] and it would be contrary to that principle to allow a set-off against the call.[297] But perhaps the simplest explanation is that the change to the legislation which occurred in 1862, by which the right of set-off that was formerly available to a contributory against a call was confined to unlimited companies where the call had been made before the winding up,[298] gave rise to an implication that in the case of a limited company Parliament intended that the call should be paid without set-off,[299] and this principle has since become entrenched. **8.66**

(3) Set-off asserted by the company rather than by the contributory

While the principle applied in *Grissell's Case* operates to prevent the creditor from asserting a set-off against a call, *Ex p MacKenzie*,[300] shows that there is no such objection when the **8.67**

---

[290] See paras 13.07–13.16 below.

[291] Compare *Palmer's Company Law* (looseleaf, 1998) vol. 1, para. 6.202 in relation to public companies.

[292] Insolvency Act 1986, s. 239. In Australia, see the Corporations Act 2001 (Cth), s. 588FF(1) in the context of company liquidation.

[293] (1869) LR 7 Eq 240.

[294] See below.

[295] See ch. 17 below.

[296] See, in particular, the Insolvency Act 1986, s. 74(1), and in Australia the Corporations Act 2001 (Cth), s. 515.

[297] *Re Overend, Gurney and Co (Grissell's Case)* (1866) LR 1 Ch App 528, 535–6; *Re Paraguassu Steam Tramroad Co (Black & Co's Case)* (1872) LR 8 Ch App 254, 262, 265; *Re Auriferous Properties Ltd* [1898] 1 Ch 691, 696; *Re Patrick Corporation Ltd and the Companies Act* (1980) ACLC 40–643 at 34,272. See also *Re Duckworth* (1867) LR 2 Ch App 578, 579–80.

[298] See para. 8.64 above.

[299] See *Re Breech-Loading Armoury Co (Calisher's Case)* (1868) LR 5 Eq 214, 217, although compare *Re Stranton Iron and Steel Co (Barnett's Case)* (1875) LR 19 Eq 449, 452.

[300] *Re China Steamship Co, ex p MacKenzie* (1869) LR 7 Eq 240.

set-off is asserted by the company. In *Ex p MacKenzie* a shareholder after the commencement of the company's liquidation assigned to a third party a debt owing to him by
the company, and Lord Romilly MR held that the assignee took subject to a right in the
company to set off a subsequent call against the debt.

8.68   The set-off in issue in *Ex p MacKenzie* presumably would have been based upon the Statutes
of Set-off, given that, at the time the case was decided, the bankruptcy set-off section had
not been incorporated into the law of company liquidation.[301] The question arises whether
a liquidator could now assert against an assignee the wider right of set-off available under
the insolvency legislation. A potential difficulty is the view that has gained general acceptance by the courts, that the insolvency set-off section is self-executing and operates automatically on the occurrence of a liquidation.[302] It would hardly be consistent with that
analysis to hold that the section can be invoked by one party but not the other. The question may be academic, however. When a debt is assigned after the commencement of a
liquidation, any proof in respect of it should be lodged in the name of the assignor as the
creditor at the relevant date for determining the provable debts.[303] The assignee is not considered to be in any better position than the assignor.[304] The liquidator in *Ex p MacKenzie*
undoubtedly would have been entitled to invoke *Grissell's Case* against the assignor, and
similarly he should have been entitled to assert the same equity against the assignee. In fact,
it was the liquidator in *Ex p MacKenzie* who sought the set-off, and it was the assignee who
relied on *Grissell's Case* in an attempt to prevent a set-off occurring. It seems to have been
assumed that, in the absence of a set-off, the assignee would have been entitled to receive a
dividend on the assigned debt and the liquidator would have had to look to the assignor for
payment of the call. A set-off therefore was perceived to be a means by which the company
in effect could obtain payment to the extent that its liability on the assigned debt was
thereby extinguished. Yet it would have been more valuable for the liquidator to assert
Grissell's Case against the assignee, since the liquidator in that circumstance would have
been entitled[305] to decline to pay anything to the assignee by way of dividend until the call
had been satisfied in full.[306] This course of action, for some reason that is not apparent, was
not adopted.

(4) Assignment

8.69   In the case of an assignment of a debt, the assignee does not take subject to a set-off
in respect of a debt owing by the assignor to the debtor that only came into existence
after the debtor received notice of the assignment, even if the assignor's debt was the

---

[301] The incorporation first occurred with the enactment of the Supreme Court of Judicature Act 1875,
s. 10. See paras 6.05 and 6.06 above. The set-off in *Ex p MacKenzie* occurred in the context of a claim to
prove in the liquidation, but the Statutes of Set-off strictly should not have applied in that context. See para.
17.42 below.
[302] See paras 6.119–6.146 above.
[303] *Ex p Dickenson, re Gibson* (1832) 2 Deac & Ch 520.
[304] *Re Wickham* (1917) 34 TLR 158. See also *Ex p Deey* (1796) 2 Cox 423, 30 ER 196.
[305] In accordance with the rule in *Cherry v Boultbee* (1839) 4 My & Cr 442, 41 ER 171. See ch. 14
below.
[306] *Re Overend, Gurney and Co (Grissell's Case)* (1866) LR 1 Ch App 528, 536. See para. 8.64 above.

result of a contract entered into before notice.[307] The assignee does take subject, however, to a debt that arose before notice, whether or not the debt was presently payable at that date.[308] The order of events in *Ex p MacKenzie* was: (1) commencement of the winding up; (2) assignment, and notice of assignment given to the company; and (3) call made in the winding up. Normally, a shareholder before a call would be regarded as having only a contingent liability to contribute unpaid capital.[309] But this must be considered in the context of s. 80 of the Insolvency Act 1986,[310] which stipulates that the liability of a contributory in a winding up[311] creates a debt accruing due from him or her at the time when the contributory's liability commenced but payable when the call is made. Even though the call in *Ex p MacKenzie* was made after notice of the assignment, the effect of the then equivalent of s. 80[312] was that the liability to contribute was deemed to have had reference back so as to give rise to an existing debt (payable *in futuro*) before notice.[313] Sir John Romilly said that the debt had reference back to the time when the winding up began.[314] It was on that ground that Stirling J in *Christie v Taunton, Delmard, Lane and Co*[315] held that, when the assignment of the company's debt instead had taken place before the winding up, the assignee did not take subject to a right in the company to set off the assignor's liability for calls made after the winding up. The debt for calls in that case was not considered to have had reference back to the time before notice of the assignment. There is an alternative interpretation of s. 80, however, and that is that the debt is deemed to have been created when the contributory first took out the shares.[316] If that view were applied, it would be difficult to see why, as a matter of principle, the existence or otherwise of a right in the company to set off the calls against the assignee's claim on the assigned debt should depend on whether the assignment took place before or after the commencement of the winding up. But whatever the position is in that regard, if both the call and the assignment took place before the winding up, and notice of the assignment was not given until after the call, the assignee will take subject to the company's pre-existing right of set-off.[317]

---

[307] *Watson v Mid Wales Railway Co* (1867) LR 2 CP 593. See para. 17.15 below.

[308] *Re Pinto Leite and Nephews, ex p Visconde des Olivaes* [1929] 1 Ch 221. See para. 17.14 below.

[309] Compare *Palmer's Company Law* (looseleaf, 1998) vol. 1, para. 6.202 with respect to public companies.

[310] In Australia, see the Corporations Act 2001 (Cth), s. 527.

[311] See the meaning of 'contributory' in the Insolvency Act 1986, s. 79.

[312] Companies Act 1862, s. 75.

[313] For another instance in which a reversion back of a title resulted in a set-off, see *Bailey v Johnson* (1872) LR 7 Ex 263 in the context of an annulment of a bankruptcy. See para. 11.15 below.

[314] See also Pennington, *Company Law* (7th edn, 1995), 610–11.

[315] [1893] 2 Ch 175, following a *dictum* of Lord Romilly in *Re China Steamship Co, ex p MacKenzie* (1869) LR 7 Eq 240, 244. See also *Re The McKay Harvesting Machinery Co* (1894) 20 VLR 153; *Re Matheson Bros & Co* (1884) NZLR 3 SC 323, 325.

[316] See *Buckley on the Companies Acts* (14th edn, 1981) vol. 1, 507 (in relation to the Companies Act 1948, s. 214), referring to *Ex p Canwell, re Vaughan* (1864) 4 De G J & S 539, 46 ER 1028, *Williams v Harding* (1866) LR 1 HL 9, and *Re West of England Bank, ex p Hatcher* (1879) 12 Ch D 284. In *Re Northern Assam Tea Co, ex p Universal Life Assurance Co* (1870) LR 10 Eq 458, 463 Lord Romilly agreed with counsel's argument to that effect.

[317] *Christie v Taunton, Delmard, Lane and Co* [1993] 2 Ch 175. Notwithstanding the winding up, when there is a prior assignment set-off under the Statutes of Set-off is in issue. See para. 17.42 below.

(5) Solvent company

8.70 The prohibition against setting off a call against a debt only applies in a winding up. When a company is a going concern, a set-off may take effect under the Statutes of Set-off.[318] It may be that a set-off is pleaded as a defence to an action brought by a company for payment of a call while the company is a going concern, but before judgment the company commences to be wound up. Since a set-off under the Statutes does not take place until a judgment for a set-off is given, the demands will not have been extinguished at the commencement of the winding up, and so the ordinary rule that a set-off may not proceed in a liquidation will apply.[319]

(6) Bankrupt contributory

8.71 *Grissell's Case* does not apply when the contributory is bankrupt. In *Re Duckworth*,[320] the Court of Appeal held that, when the liquidator of a company lodges a proof in the bankruptcy of a contributory in respect of a call, the contributory's trustee may bring into account a debt owing by the company to the contributory.[321] Lord Cairns in his judgment considered that this was consistent with the power conferred upon the liquidator by the Companies Act 1862 to prove in the bankruptcy of a contributory for any 'balance' against his estate.[322] The current English provision similarly is drafted in terms of a liquidator proving for a 'balance',[323] although this is no longer the case in Australia.[324] But the more immediate justification for the set-off in *Re Duckworth* was that, while the companies legislation may have prohibited a set-off in the company's liquidation,[325] it did not have the effect of overriding the statutory right of set-off otherwise available in the bankruptcy under the bankruptcy legislation.[326] This explains why a set-off may proceed when the question arises in the context of a proof lodged by the bankrupt's trustee

---

[318] *Re Stranton Iron and Steel Co (Barnett's Case)* (1875) LR 19 Eq 449, 451. See also *Re White Star Line Ltd* [1938] 1 Ch 458, 470 (Clauson J).

[319] *Re Hiram Maxim Lamp Co* [1903] 1 Ch 70; *Re A Shadler Ltd (McPhillamy's Case)* (1904) 4 SR (NSW) 619 (verdict by consent for a set-off obtained after the liquidation held to be ineffective); *Re John Dillon Ltd, ex p Jefferies* [1960] WAR 30.

[320] (1867) LR 2 Ch App 578. See also *Ex p Cooper, re A Trust Deed* (1867) 15 LT 637; *Re Anglo-Greek Steam Navigation and Trading Co (Carralli & Haggard's Claim)* (1869) LR 4 Ch App 174; *Re Universal Banking Corporation, ex p Strang* (1870) LR 5 Ch App 492 (but see the criticism of that case below); *Re GEB, A Debtor* [1903] 2 KB 340, 352; *Re Bailey, deceased: Duchess Mill Ltd v Bailey* (1932) 76 Sol Jo 560, 561; *Re Patrick Corporation Ltd and the Companies Act* (1980) ACLC 40–643 at 34,272 (NSW SC). The estimated amount claimable from a bankrupt in respect of future calls by a solvent company may be brought into an account in the bankruptcy. See *Re Anderson* [1924] NZLR 1163.

[321] However, because the set-off only arises after the contributory has become bankrupt, a petition presented by the liquidator of a company for the bankruptcy of a contributory based upon the non-payment of calls may not be impugned because of a set-off that would become available in the bankruptcy on the basis of a debt owing by the company to the contributory. See *Re John Sloss, ex p Robison Bros, Campbell & Sloss Ltd* (1893) 19 VLR 710; *Re GEB, A Debtor* [1903] 2 KB 340.

[322] Companies Act 1862, s. 95.

[323] See the Insolvency Act 1986, s. 167, and also s. 165 with respect to voluntary liquidations, in each case referring to Pt III of Sch. 4.

[324] See the Corporations Act 2001 (Cth), s. 477(2)(e).

[325] See para. 8.66 above.

[326] See *Re Duckworth* (1867) LR 2 Ch App 578, 580–1.

in the winding up,[327] as opposed to the case of a liquidator proving for the 'balance' in the contributory's bankruptcy. Nevertheless, it should still be necessary to show that a set-off is available in the bankruptcy according to the principles generally applicable to bankruptcy set-off. On that basis, it is difficult to understand the decision of Giffard LJ in *Re Universal Banking Corporation, ex p Strang*.[328] A shareholder assigned a debt owing to him by the company to a third party after an order was made to wind up the company. Subsequently, the shareholder executed a deed of composition, which incorporated the principles of bankruptcy. It was held that the shareholder's liability for a call made in the winding up could be set off against the assigned debt. However, the assignment occurred before the composition, so that at the date of the composition the position was that the company's debt was owing to the assignee while the shareholder was the party liable for the call. There was therefore no mutuality at that date, which should have prevented a set-off under the bankruptcy set-off section.[329] Nor would a set-off have been available in the company's liquidation on the basis of *Ex p MacKenzie*,[330] since the company (through the liquidator) was not the party asserting a set-off.

The *Universal Banking* case should be compared to *Re Matheson Bros & Co*,[331] a decision of **8.72** Williams J in the New Zealand Supreme Court. In *Re Matheson*, the benefit of a call made by a liquidator, as opposed to a debt owing by the company to the contributory, was assigned before the contributory's bankruptcy, and Williams J held (correctly, it is submitted) that lack of mutuality prevented a set-off in the bankruptcy against the company's debt. It could not be said in a case such as *Re Matheson* that an assignee of calls takes subject to a prior right of set-off available to the contributory in the liquidation, since the effect of *Grissell's Case* is that there would not have been any such right. But if the assignee of the call happens to be indebted to the contributory, a set-off should be available in the contributory's bankruptcy against the assigned call. The assignee would be claiming payment of the call personally, rather than for the company, and there would not be any reason in such a case for applying *Grissell's Case*.[332]

The ambit of the set-off where the contributory is bankrupt is sometimes framed in **8.73** terms of a contributory who becomes bankrupt after the commencement of the winding up.[333] It is not clear why the availability of the set-off should be so limited, particularly if the debt resulting from a call has relation back to the date of the acquisition of the shares rather than the date of the winding up.[334] In any event, it is apparent from *Re Duckworth* that it is not an objection to a set-off that the call is made after the commencement of the bankruptcy.

---

[327] *Re Anglo-Greek Steam Navigation and Trading Co (Carralli & Haggard's Claim)* (1869) LR 4 Ch App 174. Compare *Re The Oxford and Canterbury Hall Co Ltd, ex p Morton* (1869) 38 LJ Ch 390.
[328] (1870) LR 5 Ch App 492.
[329] See e.g. *De Mattos v Saunders* (1872) LR 7 CP 570.
[330] *Re China Steamship Co, ex p MacKenzie* (1869) LR 7 Eq 240. See para. 8.67 above.
[331] (1884) NZLR 3 SC 323.
[332] *Re Matheson Bros & Co* (1884) NZLR 3 SC 323, 324.
[333] See e.g. *McPherson's Law of Company Liquidation* (5th edn (looseleaf), 2006), [10.1100].
[334] See para. 8.69 above.

(7) Contributory is a company in liquidation

8.74 In *Re Auriferous Properties Ltd*[335] Wright J held that a set-off is not available when the contributory is a company that has gone into liquidation, as opposed to a bankrupt.[336] Rather *Grissell's Case* applied, so that the contributory company had to pay the call in full before receiving a dividend on the debt.[337] It seems difficult to justify this distinction between an incorporated contributory and a contributory who is a natural person, since the right of set-off conferred by the insolvency legislation in a contributory's insolvency applies equally in both cases.

(8) Costs and expenses of the winding up

8.75 The preceding discussion concerned the right to set off a debt incurred by the company before its liquidation. The costs and expenses of the winding up, including debts or liabilities incurred by the company or the liquidator in the course of carrying on the company's business after the commencement of the winding up, stand on a different footing. These debts have priority in the liquidation, and are payable in full.[338] Alternatively, the creditor may employ the debt in a set-off, including against a liability to pay a call on shares.[339]

(9) Unlimited companies

8.76 The Insolvency Act 1986, s. 149[340] empowers the court, at any time after the making of a winding up order, to make an order on a contributory to pay any moneys due from him or her to the company, exclusive of any sum payable by the contributory by virtue of a call made in pursuance of the Insolvency Act.[341] The only sum which could be payable by virtue of a call made in pursuance of the Act is a call made in the winding up,[342] so that the effect is to exclude those calls. It does not, however, exclude a call made by the directors before the winding up which remains unpaid.[343] Section 149(2) goes on to provide that,

---

[335] [1898] 1 Ch 691.

[336] Wright J in *Re Auriferous Properties* expressed doubt as to the correctness of *Re Duckworth* (see para. 8.71 above), but he said that it had stood for too long to be interfered with. It was held in *Re West Hartlepool Iron Co Ltd (Gunn's Case)* (1878) 38 LT 139 that the exception in *Re Duckworth* does not apply when the estate of a deceased person is being administered in bankruptcy, but that result may be explained on the basis that the death (in March 1875) occurred before the rules of bankruptcy, including the bankruptcy set-off section, were incorporated into the administration of a deceased estate, by the Supreme Court of Judicature Act 1875, s. 10. See para. 13.133 below. Compare also *Re Bailey, deceased, Duchess Mill Ltd v Bailey* (1932) 76 Sol Jo 560, 561 (company under a scheme sanctioned by the court).

[337] *Re Auriferous Properties Ltd (No. 2)* [1898] 2 Ch 428.

[338] See e.g. *Re International Marine Hydropathic Co* (1884) 28 Ch D 470.

[339] *Re London and Colonial Co, ex p Clark* (1869) LR 7 Eq 550. Compare *Re General Exchange Bank* (1867) LR 4 Eq 138 with respect to the costs of the petition, although the set-off in that case was sought by the liquidator rather than the contributory.

[340] In Australia, see the Corporations Act 2001 (Cth), s. 483(2).

[341] Section 149 also excludes a call made pursuant to the Companies Act 1985, although that exclusion would now have little practical significance.

[342] See the Insolvency Act 1986, s. 150, and also the Insolvency Rules, r. 4.202. For voluntary liquidation, see s. 165(4).

[343] *Re Whitehouse & Co* (1878) 9 Ch D 595, 601.

if the company is an unlimited company, the court, in making the order, may allow[344] the contributory to set off any sum due to him or her on an independent dealing or contract with the company.[345] Thus, the effect of s. 149 is to allow to a contributory in an unlimited company a set-off in respect of a prior unpaid call made by the directors.

There is competing authority as to whether *Grissell's Case* extends to unlimited companies **8.77** so as to prevent a set-off against a call made *after* the winding up. Malins VC in *Gibbs and West's Case*,[346] following a *dictum* of Lord Chelmsford in *Grissell's Case*,[347] held in favour of a set-off, although the judgment is not satisfactory because the Vice Chancellor assumed, mistakenly, that the then equivalent of s. 149[348] in fact extended to this situation. Fry J, on the other hand, held that a set-off was not available in *Ex p Branwhite*.[349] The relevant question is whether Parliament, by specifically allowing a set-off in relation to calls made before the winding up of an unlimited company, evinced an intention that calls made after the winding up could not be the subject of a set-off. On that basis, Fry J's conclusion in *Ex p Branwhite* is to be preferred.

(10) All creditors have been paid in full

The Insolvency Act 1986, s. 149(3)[350] provides that, when all the creditors of a company, **8.78** whether it is limited or unlimited, have been paid in full, any money due on any account whatever to a contributory may be allowed to him or her by way of set-off against any subsequent call. Lord Romilly once said[351] that it is difficult to put an intelligible construction upon this provision because, if all the creditors have been paid in full, *prima facie* there would not appear to be any scope for a set-off. It has been suggested,[352] however, that it may refer to a sum due to a member in his or her character of member by way of dividend or profit, on the ground that this is not considered to be a debt of the company.[353]

(11) Debt for equity swap

In Australia the courts have held that a debt for equity swap entered into between an insolv- **8.79** ent company not in liquidation and creditors of the company, by which the creditors are issued with fully paid shares on terms that the allotment is paid for by setting off debts equal

---

[344] The court has a discretion in the matter. See *Re Norwich Equitable Fire Assurance Co; Brasnett's Case* (1885) 53 LT 569, in which the shareholder's claim against the company required further investigation.
[345] This does not include any money due to the contributory as a member of the company in respect of any dividend or profit. See s. 149(2)(a).
[346] *Re International Life Assurance Society (Gibbs and West's Case)* (1870) LR 10 Eq 312.
[347] (1866) LR 1 Ch App 528, 536. *Grissell's Case* itself was concerned with a call made after the winding up. See also *Re Paraguassu Steam Tramroad Co (Black & Co's Case)* (1872) LR 8 Ch App 254, 265.
[348] See the Companies Act 1862, s. 101.
[349] *Ex p Branwhite, re The West of England and South Wales District Bank* (1879) 40 LT 652.
[350] In Australia, see the Corporations Act 2001 (Cth), s. 483(2).
[351] *Re Breech-Loading Armoury Co (Calisher's Case)* (1868) LR 5 Eq 214, 217.
[352] *Buckley on the Companies Act* (14th edn, 1981) vol. 1, 628, cited with approval in *Re Compania de Electricidad de la Provincia de Buenos Aires Ltd* [1980] 1 Ch 146, 172.
[353] See the Insolvency Act 1986, s. 74(2)(f). In Australia, see the Corporations Act 2001 (Cth), s. 563A, which postpones debts due to a person in his or her capacity as a member of a company, whether by way of dividends, profits or otherwise, to other debts of the company, and also s. 553A, which restricts the right of proof where the company is liable to a member in that person's capacity as member.

to the nominal value of the shares, does not amount to an issue of shares at a discount, provided that the debts were genuinely created in the course of the company's business and are immediately payable.[354] In such circumstances it is not to the point that the company otherwise had insufficient assets to pay its debts in full, since the value of the debts the subject of the set-off is still considered to be the face value of the legally and immediately enforceable obligations that they represent.

H. Basing a Claim for a Set-off upon a Wrongful Act

8.80 It is sometimes suggested that a person may not rely on his or her own wrongful act in order to found a set-off,[355] but statements to that effect are expressed too broadly. A like principle has been applied in the case of misfeasance claims against directors and promoters of companies under the summary procedure set out in the insolvency legislation, and it may extend to a claim against a trustee who disposed of the trust fund in breach of trust. But the application of any such principle beyond those (or analogous) situations is doubtful.

(1) Misfeasance claims against directors and promoters

8.81 If, in the course of a winding up, it appears that any person who has taken part in the promotion, formation or management of the company, or any liquidator, administrative receiver or officer of the company, has misapplied or become accountable for any of the company's money or other property, or if he or she has been guilty of any misfeasance or breach of any fiduciary or other duty in relation to the company, then the Insolvency Act 1986, s. 212[356] provides a summary procedure by which the official receiver, or the liquidator or any creditor or contributory, may apply to the court for an order compelling the person to repay or account for the money or other property. In *Ex p Pelly*,[357] the Court of Appeal held, and it has since been confirmed,[358] that a person liable in misfeasance proceedings to repay money may not bring into account a cross-demand that he or she has against the company.[359] This result has been explained on a number of grounds.

---

[354] *Pro-Image Studios v Commonwealth Bank of Australia* (1991) 4 ACSR 586; *Re Keith Bray Pty Ltd* (1991) 23 NSWLR 430. The courts in each case declined to follow *Re Jarass Pty Ltd* (1988) 13 ACLR 728. In relation to a solvent company, see *Re Harmony and Montague Tin and Copper Mining Co (Spargo's Case)* (1873) LR 8 Ch App 407; *Commissioner of Stamp Duties (NSW) v Perpetual Trustee Co Ltd* (1929) 43 CLR 247, 263–4, 269–70; *Handbury Holdings Pty Ltd v Cmr of Taxation* [2008] FCA 1787 at [72] and [75].

[355] See e.g. Shelford, *The Law of Bankruptcy and Insolvency* (3rd edn, 1862), 522; Doria, *The Law and Practice in Bankruptcy* (1874), 685; Williams and Muir Hunter *The Law and Practice in Bankruptcy* (19th edn, 1979), 197.

[356] In Australia, see the Corporations Act 2001 (Cth), s. 598.

[357] *Re Anglo-French Co-operative Society, ex p Pelly* (1882) 21 Ch D 492.

[358] *Re Exchange Banking Company (Flitcroft's Case)* (1882) 21 Ch D 519; *Re Carriage Co-operative Supply Association* (1884) 27 Ch D 322; *Re Leeds and Hanley Theatres of Varieties Ltd* [1904] 2 Ch 45; *Derek Randall Enterprises Ltd v Randall* [1991] BCLC 379; *Re A Company (No. 1641 of 2003)* [2004] 1 BCLC 210 (loan to director in breach of the Companies Act 1985, s. 330). Compare *Re Toowoomba Welding Works Pty Ltd (No. 2)* [1969] Qd R 337.

[359] In *Ex p Pelly* the directors of a company authorized the payment of the company's funds to a promoter of the company, who used the funds to subscribe for debentures in the company. The company was subsequently wound up. The directors' conduct constituted a breach of duty to the company and accordingly they were liable for misfeasance notwithstanding that the funds had come back to the company through the

Brett LJ in *Ex p Pelly*[360] said that a right of set-off arises only when there is an action **8.82** between parties, whereas a provision such as s. 212 provides a summary remedy without an action. This is not a satisfactory explanation for the rule because, while an action at law is a prerequisite to a set-off under the Statutes of Set-off, it is not necessary for set-off under the insolvency legislation.

The insolvency set-off section does not apply in the case of a debt arising after the liquid- **8.83** ation which is not the result of a prior dealing,[361] and it has been suggested that in a misfeasance proceeding a debt only comes into being as a result of a judgment, which occurs after the liquidation.[362] However, it is difficult to reconcile this as an explanation for the denial of a set-off with the view that the misfeasance section is purely procedural. In other words, as Lord Evershed MR expressed it, the section 'does not create any new cause of action; it only provides a method of litigating particular claims; and, in providing a method, it is not exclusive'.[363] The Master of the Rolls went on to explain that the acts which are covered by the section are acts which are wrongful according to the established rules of law or equity.[364] The section therefore does not bring a debt into being by way of a judgment in a proceeding under the section. Rather, it provides a summary method of enforcing a pre-existing claim.

It has also been suggested that a set-off is denied on the ground of lack of mutuality, given **8.84** that the summons is brought in the name of the liquidator, or other authorized person, rather than in the name of the company.[365] Lack of mutuality may indeed explain the denial of a set-off in some cases, for example where the claim being enforced in misfeasance proceedings is in respect of a disposition of the company's property after the commencement of its winding up[366] or for the recovery of a preference.[367] Set-off in relation to those situations is considered later.[368] In other situations, however, the fact that the claim is

---

subscription for debentures. This was because the debenture-holders were not before the court and they may have retained a valid claim against the company. Compare the circumstances in issue in *Derek Randall Enterprises Ltd v Randall* [1991] BCLC 379. The company in *Ex p Pelly* was indebted to one of the directors, but it was held that the director could not set off the debt against his liability for misfeasance.

[360] (1882) 21 Ch D 492, 507.

[361] See para. 6.63 above.

[362] *Manson v Smith* [1997] 2 BCLC 161, 164–5; *Re SSSL Realisations (2002) Ltd* [2006] Ch 610 at [111]. The passages in the judgment of Hall VC to which Millett LJ referred in *Manson v Smith* (at 164) may have resulted from confusion between the right of set-off under the Statutes of Set-off and set-off under the insolvency legislation. Indeed, in the Court of Appeal in *Ex p Pelly* both Sir George Jessel MR and Brett LJ seem to have assumed that set-off under the Statutes was in issue. See (1882) 21 Ch D 492, 502, 507.

[363] *Re B Johnson & Co (Builders) Ltd* [1955] 1 Ch 634, 647. See also *Cavendish Bentinck v Fenn* (1887) 12 App Cas 652, 669; *Re Asiatic Electric Co Pty Ltd* [1970] 2 NSWR 612, 613; *Re Oasis Merchandising Services Ltd* [1998] Ch 170, 181; *Halsbury's Laws of England* (4th edn, 2004) vol. 7(4), 47, para. 691. There may, however, be cases where the right enforced in a misfeasance proceeding is created only by the winding up. See Halsbury, *loc. cit.*, and *Couve v J Pierre Couve Ltd* (1933) 49 CLR 486, 494–6 (disposition of the company's property after the commencement of winding up); *Re Washington Diamond Mining Co* [1893] 3 Ch 95 (esp at 115) (preference). See also para. 8.84 below.

[364] *Re B Johnson & Co* [1955] 1 Ch 634, 648.

[365] *Re Buena Vista Pty Ltd* [1971] 1 NSWLR 72, 74.

[366] See e.g. *Couve v J Pierre Couve Ltd* (1933) 49 CLR 486.

[367] As apparently occurred in *Re Washington Diamond Mining Co* [1893] 3 Ch 95.

[368] See paras 13.07–13.19 below.

brought in the name of the liquidator does not provide a satisfactory explanation for the principle because, while the liquidator may take out the summons, s. 212 is only procedural, in the sense that it provides a summary procedure for enforcing a liability that the director (or other such person) has to the company.[369] The liability is enforced on behalf of the company, and the proceeds become part of the company's assets.[370] It differs from a claim for repayment of a preference, in relation to which lack of mutuality is properly regarded as a ground for denying a set-off.[371] In the event of misfeasance, where for example the claim is against a director or a person involved in the promotion, formation or management of the company, the company itself will have had a claim against the person before the liquidation, whereas the same cannot be said in relation to a preference.[372]

8.85 There have been occasions when the rule has been discussed in terms suggesting that it is based simply on policy considerations. Thus, it has been said that the liability under the misfeasance section is a liability of a delinquent in breach of a duty in the nature of a breach of trust,[373] and it should not be treated in the delinquent's favour as a debt due from the delinquent to the company so as to entitle him or her to a set-off.[374] It has also been said that, if an innocent contributory liable to pay a call on shares is denied a set-off,[375] then a director or other officer of the company who has misapplied company money certainly should not have the benefit of a set-off.[376] In *Mason v Smith*[377] Millett LJ suggested that the rule is essential to the structure of insolvency. A director who was owed a debt by the company, and who was able to persuade his or her fellow directors to pay the debt in view of the company's impending liquidation, would be faced with the prospect of having the payment avoided as a preference in the liquidation. The director could hardly be in a better position by misappropriating the money from the company and then in subsequent misfeasance proceedings claiming an entitlement to set off the liability to repay the money against the debt due to him or her.

8.86 However, the denial of a set-off has also been justified by reference to the construction of the legislation. In the first place, where the subject of the misfeasance claim is a misappropriation of assets, Millett LJ in *Manson v Smith*[378] said that a misappropriation of assets is not a dealing for the purpose of the insolvency set-off section.[379] Secondly, and more

---

[369] See above.

[370] *Re Bassett, ex p Lewis* (1895) 2 Mans 177, 181.

[371] See para. 13.08 below.

[372] As to the distinction between a misfeasance claim and a preference claim, see *Re Asiatic Electric Co Pty Ltd* [1970] 2 NSWR 612, 613; *Re Fresjac Pty Ltd* (1995) 65 SASR 334, 342; *Re Oasis Merchandising Services Ltd* [1998] Ch 170, 181.

[373] *Cavendish Bentinck v Fenn* (1887) 12 App Cas 652, 669 (Lord Macnaghten); *Re Etic Ltd* [1928] 1 Ch 861 (Maugham J); *Couve v J Pierre Couve Ltd* (1933) 49 CLR 486, 495.

[374] See the earlier judgment of Hall VC referred to in *Ex p Pelly* (1882) 21 Ch D 492, 498. See also *Re Etic Ltd* [1928] 1 Ch 861, 873 ('it would not be right for the officer of the company to be entitled to set up a right of set-off.').

[375] See paras 8.64–8.79 above.

[376] See Jessel MR and Cotton LJ in *Ex p Pelly* (1882) 21 Ch D 492, 503, 509–10.

[377] [1997] 2 BCLC 161, 165.

[378] [1997] 2 BCLC 161, 164.

[379] Assuming that a dealing indeed is always necessary for a set-off. See paras 7.12–7.22 above. A company director is in a fiduciary relationship with the company, and the liability of a director who has misapplied

generally, the point has been made that the power given by the misfeasance section is to compel a person to pay moneys which he or she has applied or retained or for which he or she has become accountable, and if it had been intended that the person should have a right of set-off the section would have said so.[380] Consistent with the view that the rule denying a set-off is based on the construction of the section, Vaughan Williams J in *Re Manson, ex p Lewis*[381] suggested that the rule only applies when the summary procedure conferred by the section is utilized. If, instead, there was an action at law to enforce the liability, he said that there would be a set-off. This derogates from the view that the principle is based simply on policy considerations.

If a director's or a promoter's liability for misfeasance is unable to be employed in a set-off, **8.87** the right of the director or the promoter to receive a dividend on a debt owing to him should be subject to the rule in *Cherry v Boultbee*.[382] *Cherry v Boultbee* is considered later.[383]

(2) Breach of trust in dealing with another's property and fraud

Consider that a trustee ('T') holds property on trust for a beneficiary ('B'), and that T in **8.88** breach of trust disposes of the property or otherwise deals with it so that it is no longer traceable. In such a case, T is obliged to restore the property or pay compensation, the obligation to pay compensation being regarded as an equitable debt or liability in the nature of a debt.[384] If T becomes bankrupt, the equitable debt would be provable in the bankruptcy,[385] and as such it should be capable of being employed in a set-off.[386] If, on the other hand, B is the bankrupt party, it is suggested that T should not be permitted a set-off in the bankruptcy based upon T's own breach of trust,[387] given that, if T had retained

---

company funds is similar to that of a trustee who has misapplied trust funds. It was treated as such in *Ex p Pelly* (1882) 21 Ch D 492, 495, 496 (Hall VC), 500–1 (Jessel MR), 504 (Brett LJ). The trustee's obligation in such a case is to restore the trust estate or to pay compensation, which is regarded as giving rise to an equitable debt as opposed to a liability in damages. See para. 8.62 above. A director, while a fiduciary, admittedly is not a trustee in the strict sense of the words (*Jacobs' Law of Trusts in Australia* (7th edn, 2006), 8–10; *Permanent Building Society v Wheeler* (1992) 10 WAR 109, 142–3), but breach of the fiduciary duty attracts the same remedy of equitable compensation. See *Nocton v Lord Ashburton* [1914] AC 932, 946, 956–8; *Tavistock Pty Ltd v Saulsman* (1990) 3 ACSR 502, 510, and generally Gummow, 'Compensation for Breach of Fiduciary Duty', in Youdan (ed), *Equity, Fiduciaries and Trusts* (1989), ch. 2. The claim against the defaulting director therefore would be for an equitable debt. If a dealing was not necessary where a set-off is sought to be based upon a prior debt (see para. 7.13, but compare paras 7.14–7.22 above), the objection to a set-off raised by Millett LJ would not apply.

[380] *Ex p Pelly* (1882) 21 Ch D 492, 502–3 (Jessel MR) (and see also Hall VC in earlier proceedings referred to at 498). See also *Re A Debtor* [1927] 1 Ch 410, 417–18.

[381] (1895) 2 Mans 177, 181.

[382] (1839) 4 My & Cr 442, 41 ER 171.

[383] See ch. 14 below.

[384] *Ex p Adamson, re Collie* (1878) 8 Ch D 807, 819; *Webb v Stenton* (1883) 11 QBD 518, 530; *Wickstead v Browne* (1992) 30 NSWLR 1, 14–15; *Goodwin v Duggan* (1996) 41 NSWLR 158, 166. See also *Target Holdings Ltd v Redferns* [1996] AC 421, 434; *Coventry v Charter Pacific Corporation Ltd* (2005) 227 CLR 234 at [47] (fraud). Compare *Space Investments Ltd v Canadian Imperial Bank of Commerce Trust Co (Bahamas) Ltd* [1986] 1 WLR 1072, 1074.

[385] Insolvency Act 1986, ss. 322 and 382. See para. 8.62 above.

[386] See para. 7.24 above. Compare the position in relation to some damages claims in tort. See para. 7.26 above.

[387] See also paras 10.10–10.11 below.

the trust property, he or she would have had to account to B's estate without a set-off.[388] The contrary view would mean that the trustee would profit from the breach of trust.[389]

8.89 A claim by an insolvent for fraudulent misrepresentation inducing a contract may be the subject of a set-off,[390] but there is little authority in relation to fraud in other contexts.[391] Fraud did not preclude a set-off in *Ex p Minton, re Green*.[392] An insolvent entered into a composition with her creditors by which each was to receive a rateable dividend, but she agreed with one creditor to pay him in full so as to induce him to sign the composition deed. The payment had been extorted by the creditor, and constituted a fraud upon the other creditors. It was held[393] that the payment was recoverable by the insolvent, and that this claim had passed to her assignees in bankruptcy, but that it could be set off against a separate debt owing to the creditor. However, the case should be considered in the context that the primary question was the liability of the creditor to repay the money, and further that it was the commissioners in the bankruptcy, as opposed to the creditor, who sought to have the liability set off against the separate debt.

(3) Deliberate breach of contract in order to obtain a set-off

8.90 It has been suggested that a set-off might not arise in favour of a creditor of a bankrupt if the creditor purposely broke a contract in order to obtain a set-off in the bankruptcy.[394] In considering that suggestion, however, it should be borne in mind that failure to pay any debt on time constitutes a breach of contract.[395] Set-off constitutes a form of security in the event of the bankruptcy of a party to mutual dealings,[396] and a party to a transaction may breach the contract by refusing to pay a debt arising out of the transaction when the bankruptcy of the other party is imminent, relying instead on the security that the debt would constitute for a separate liability of the other party. A creditor who is aware of the debtor's impending insolvency, and who consequently withholds payment of his or her own separate debt to the debtor as a form of security, would not be denied a set-off, and it is difficult to see why a simple breach of contract in any other form should be treated differently. For example, when a creditor who had purchased goods from an insolvent debtor prior to the debtor's bankruptcy immediately refused to pay the price, offering instead to treat the debt

---

[388] See paras 10.02–10.05 below.

[389] Contrary to the 'strict rule of equity' that forbids a person in a fiduciary position from profiting from his or her position. See *Consul Development Pty Ltd v DPC Estates Pty Ltd* (1975) 132 CLR 373, 397 (Gibbs J).

[390] *Gye v McIntyre* (1991) 171 CLR 609; *Secretary of State for Trade and Industry v Frid* [2004] 2 AC 506 at [24].

[391] Note, however, the discussion in *Re Pollitt, ex p Minor* [1893] 1 QB 175, 179–80 and *Atkinson v Learmouth* (1905) 11 ALR 191, 195 (referring to dishonesty). The decisions in those cases may be explained on the ground that the funds in question were held subject to a trust so as to preclude a set-off. See paras 10.47–10.58 below.

[392] (1834) 3 Deac & Ch 688.

[393] By Erskine CJ, Sir J Cross and Sir George Rose.

[394] *Turner v Thomas* (1871) LR 6 CP 610, 614. See also *Re Pollitt, ex p Minor* [1893] 1 QB 175, 179–80 (decision affirmed [1893] 1 QB 455); *Atkinson v Learmouth* (1905) 11 ALR 191, 195; *Re H E Thorne & Son Ltd* [1914] 2 Ch 438, 450. *Williams and Muir Hunter on Bankruptcy* (19th edn, 1979), 197.

[395] See Maugham J at first instance in *Re City Equitable Fire Insurance Co Ltd* [1930] 2 Ch 293, 302. It is not a 'mere' breach of contract, however. See *Young v Queensland Trustees Ltd* (1956) 99 CLR 560, 567.

[396] See para. 6.21 above.

as satisfaction for the debtor's indebtedness to him, he was allowed a set-off in the debtor's subsequent bankruptcy even though the set-off was based upon his own deliberate breach in not tendering payment.[397] There is also *Bolland v Nash*,[398] in which it was the creditor claiming the benefit of a set-off who had dishonoured his own acceptance and thereby caused the bill to be returned to the bankrupts as indorsers. In other words, the mutuality necessary for the set-off was revived as a result of the creditor's breach of his own engagement as acceptor to pay the bill according to the tenor of his acceptance.[399] In *Willment Brothers Ltd v North West Thames Regional Health Authority*[400] an employer under a building contract stopped payment on a cheque that had been forwarded to the contractor so as to obtain a set-off in the contractor's liquidation, the liquidation having commenced after the cheque was sent to the contractor. The Court of Appeal allowed the set-off.

(4) Breach of contract in not establishing a trust

A contract may stipulate that a sum of money equal in amount to the indebtedness of one   **8.91** of the parties to the other is to be set aside in a separate fund and held on trust. If a trust is established, the trustee would be denied a set-off in the beneficiary's bankruptcy against the obligation to account for the trust fund.[401] It may be, however, that, in breach of contract, the person failed to establish the trust, in which case the question may arise whether a set-off should be allowed in respect of the resulting damages liability. In some cases the maxim that equity deems as done that which ought to be done may apply, so that equity would deem a notional trust to have been created against which there may not be a set-off.[402] In other cases, however, the bankruptcy of the party having recourse to the maxim may make it difficult for him or her to obtain an order for specific performance, and the application of the maxim depends upon the availability of such an order.[403] One possible objection to a set-off is that the person claiming the benefit of the set-off is in breach of contract, in not setting aside a separate fund to which the trust may attach. The contrary argument is that this is no worse than a creditor neglecting to pay, or indeed choosing not to pay, a separate debt owing by him or her to the debtor on the due date,[404] and if a set-off may arise in the

---

[397] *Southwood v Taylor* (1818) 1 B & Ald 471, 106 ER 173, and see also *Holmes v Tutton* (1855) 5 El & Bl 65, 119 ER 405.

[398] (1828) 8 B & C 105, 108 ER 982.

[399] Bills of Exchange Act 1882, s. 54(1).

[400] (1984) 26 BLR 51.

[401] See paras 10.02–10.05 below.

[402] *Re Arthur Sanders Ltd* (1981) 17 BLR 125. Compare *Re ILG Travel Ltd* [1995] 2 BCLC 128, 162, in which ILG acquiesced in the agent's failure to pay the money into a separate account, and also *GPT Realisations Ltd v Panatown Ltd* (1992) 61 BLR 88 (application for mandatory interlocutory injunction to set up a separate trust account refused).

[403] *Re Anstis* (1886) 31 Ch D 596, 605–6; *Re Plumptre* [1910] 1 Ch 609, 619. Similarly, the insolvency of the party against whom it is sought to apply the maxim may prevent its application. See *Mac-Jordan Construction Ltd v Brookmount Erostin Ltd* [1992] BCLC 350. Compare *Re Arthur Sanders Ltd* (1981) 17 BLR 125. The Greater London Council had failed to pay retention money relating to work performed by a contractor (now in liquidation) and various sub-contractors into a separate trust account, despite a contractual obligation to do so. Nourse J said that, in the case of a solvent employer such as the GLC, equity would deem as done that which ought to have been done and would find a notional trust. While the availability of an order for specific performance was not considered, it appears that the remaining work under the contract in fact had been completed by another contractor.

[404] See para. 8.90 above.

one case then, similarly, it should be available in the other. A second possible objection is that, by stipulating for a trust, the parties impliedly had agreed to exclude a set-off, but under the current state of the law that argument would not be tenable[405] given that the House of Lords has held that the parties to mutual dealings cannot contract out of the operation of the mutual credit provision.[406] If neither of these objections would be valid individually, they should not be valid cumulatively, and so, unless equity would deem a notional trust fund to have been set up, it is suggested that a set-off would be available in this situation.[407]

[405] See *Re ILG Travel Ltd* [1995] 2 BCLC 128, 160–1.
[406] *National Westminster Bank Ltd v Halesowen Presswork & Assemblies Ltd* [1972] AC 785. See para. 6.111 above.
[407] See *Mac-Jordan Construction Ltd v Brookmount Erostin Ltd* [1992] BCLC 350, 359.

9

COMMENSURABLE DEMANDS

A. The Requirement of Commensurability

(1) The principle

For the insolvency set-off section to apply, the demands must be commensurable, in other **9.01** words the claim on each side of the account must be a money demand.[1] Set-off under the Statutes of Set-off and equitable set-off are subject to the same requirement.[2] A claim which is not monetary in nature is not susceptible to a set-off even if its value is measurable with precision in money terms.[3] Thus, a set-off has been denied in the context of a claim for the return of specific property in circumstances where the court nevertheless accepted that the property in question had a particular value.[4] In the case of insolvency set-off there are two reasons for the principle. The first, which has been emphasized in the cases, is the perceived

---

[1] *Eberle's Hotels and Restaurant Co Ltd v E Jonas & Brothers* (1887) 18 QBD 459; *Palmer v Day & Sons* [1895] 2 QB 618, 622; *Re Taylor, ex p Norvell* [1910] 1 KB 562, 567; *Hiley v The Peoples' Prudential Assurance Co Ltd* (1938) 60 CLR 468, 490, 497; *Gye v McIntyre* (1991) 171 CLR 609, 623; *Lloyds Bank NZA Ltd v National Safety Council* [1993] 2 VR 506, 510; *Re Parker* (1997) 80 FCR 1, 10. See also *Rose v Hart* (1818) 8 Taunt 499, 129 ER 477; *Re Pen 'Allt Silver Lead Mining Co (Fothergill's Case)* (1873) LR 8 Ch App 270, 275 (shares); *Ex p Roy, re Sillence* (1877) 7 Ch D 70; *Re Winter, ex p Bolland* (1878) 8 Ch D 225; *Peacock v Anderson* (1878) 4 NZ Jur (NS) SC 67; *Lord (Trustee of) v Great Eastern Railway Co* [1908] 2 KB 54 (reversed on other grounds [1909] AC 109); *Ellis and Co's Trustee v Dixon-Johnson* [1925] AC 489; *Re Leeholme Stud Pty Ltd (In Liq)* [1965] NSWR 1649; *Smith v Bridgend County BC* [2002] 1 AC 336 at [36].

[2] For the Statutes of Set-off, see *Tony Lee Motors Ltd v M S MacDonald & Son (1974) Ltd* [1981] 2 NZLR 281, 288; *Grant v NZMC Ltd* [1989] 1 NZLR 8, 11. See also *Air New Zealand Ltd v Wellington International Airport Ltd* [2008] 3 NZLR 87. For equitable set-off, see para. 3.02 above.

[3] Compare Balcombe LJ in the Court of Appeal in *Stein v Blake* [1994] Ch 16, 22 ('measurable in money terms').

[4] See e.g. *Eberle's Hotels and Restaurant Co Ltd v E Jonas & Brothers* (1887) 18 QBD 459; *Ellis and Co's Trustee v Dixon-Johnson* [1925] AC 489 (shares readily available on the stock exchange).

difficulty in producing a balance on the account when one of the demands is not a money claim. As Lord Russell of Killowen CJ once remarked: 'There could not be an "account" as between goods and money, and no balance could be struck.'[5] The second is that the requirement of money demands is inherent in the stipulation in the set-off section that: 'the sums due from one party shall be set off against the sums due from the other.'[6] In so far as the Statutes of Set-off are concerned, the requirement of money demands follows from the very basis of the Statutes, that there must be mutual debts.

(2) *Rolls Razor v Cox* criticized

9.02 A set-off in respect of a claim to recover property was permitted in one case. In *Rolls Razor Ltd v Cox*[7] a salesman employed by a company had been entrusted with goods for the purpose of sale. The company subsequently went into liquidation. When the liquidator brought an action for the return of the goods, the Court of Appeal held that the salesman could retain them as a set-off against the company's debt to him for commissions. For the purpose of the set-off, the goods were valued at the price at which the salesman had been authorized to sell them. It has been suggested that the right enforced in *Rolls Razor* may be explicable as some sort of lien rather than a set-off,[8] but the question of a lien was specifically argued before and rejected by the Court of Appeal. It is clear from the judgments that the right in question was regarded as a set-off. The *Rolls Razor* case should be regarded as wrongly decided.[9] In *Smith v Bridgend County BC*,[10] Lord Hoffmann said that, in the absence of a lien or other security, a defendant could not retain an asset belonging to a plaintiff by way of set-off against a money claim. The comment was made in the context of equitable set-off, but the judgment suggests that it was thought to apply also to insolvency set-off.[11]

9.03 Lord Denning MR in the leading judgment in the *Rolls Razor* case relied on a comment by Gibbs CJ in 1818 in *Rose v Hart*,[12] to the effect that credit may be given for the purpose of the set-off section where there is a delivery of property with a direction to turn it into money. However, the Chief Justice went on to speak in terms of setting off the 'debt' resulting from the direction to turn the property into money, and while it is true that on another occasion he said that credit is created when goods are deposited for the purpose of sale and

---

[5] *Palmer v Day & Sons* [1895] 2 QB 618, 622. See also *Eberle's Hotels v Jonas* (1887) 18 QBD 457, 465, 467, 468, 469; *In re Pen 'Allt Silver Lead Mining Co (Fothergill's Case)* (1873) LR 8 Ch App 270 at 275 ('Shares cannot be set off against a money demand').

[6] See the Insolvency Act 1986, s. 323(2) (bankruptcy) and the Insolvency Rules 1986, r 4.90(3) (company liquidation). The Australian legislation refers to the 'sum due', which imports the same analysis. See the Bankruptcy Act 1966 (Cth), s. 86(1)(b) and the Corporations Act 2001 (Cth), s. 553C(1)(b).

[7] [1967] 1 QB 552.

[8] Wood, *English and International Set-off* (1989), 564.

[9] *Rollx Razor v Cox* nevertheless was accepted as correct by the Court of Appeal (Ackner and Slade LJJ) in *Gromal (UK) Ltd v WT Shipping Ltd* unreported, 13 July 1984. The goods in question in that case were sold by agreement between the parties after the liquidation, on the basis that the proceeds received were to take the place of the goods and the parties were to retain the same rights in respect of the proceeds to which they would have been entitled in respect of the goods.

[10] [2002] 1 AC 336 at [36].

[11] See [2002] 1 AC 336 at [35]. See also *Tony Lee Motors Ltd v M S MacDonald & Son (1974) Ltd* [1981] 2 NZLR 281 in the context of the Statutes of Set-off.

[12] (1818) 8 Taunt 499, 506, 129 ER 477, 480.

not just when the goods are sold,[13] the set-off in *Rose v Hart* nonetheless related to the 'debt' arising from the receipt of the money as a result of carrying out the directions. *Rose v Hart* is considered in greater detail later.[14] The point is there made that Gibbs CJ was concerned to limit the perception that the earlier decision of Lord Hardwicke in *Ex p Deeze*[15] stood as authority for the proposition that there could be a set-off against goods. Lord Hardwicke himself later remarked in *Ex p Ockenden*[16] that in *Ex p Deeze* there had been evidence of a custom of the trade by which packers could retain goods, not only as security for the price of their work upon the goods, but also for the separate debts of the owner. In subsequent cases, however, *Ex p Deeze* had been referred to as an authority on set-off,[17] and Gibbs CJ in *Rose v Hart* was attempting to rationalize the decisions in those cases with the stipulation in the set-off section in the bankruptcy legislation of 1732[18] that 'one debt may be set against another'. In the cases in question the direction to turn the property into money had been carried out, so that in each case there was in fact a debt in existence when the account was to be taken. On the other hand, the debts were not in existence at the relevant date for determining rights of set-off, a problem that Gibbs CJ overcame in *Rose v Hart* by ascribing a wider meaning to mutual credits than to mutual debts. Therefore, a debt which arose after the relevant date could be brought into an account, provided that it was based upon a credit given before that date. Nevertheless, he still required a 'debt' at the taking of the account, so that 'one debt may be set against another' in accordance with the 1732 Act. A proper statement of the principle is that, when goods are deposited for sale, credit is given for any proceeds of sale that *in fact* are received. This is reflected in the marginal note to Moore's report of *Rose v Hart*,[19] that: 'In order to constitute a mutual credit, within 5 Geo 2, c. 30, s. 28, it must be confined to *pecuniary* demands on such credits only as in their nature will terminate in a debt.'

B. Repudiation, and Specific Performance

Consider that A has entered into a contract for the purchase of goods from B, B being a creditor of A on another transaction, but prior to delivery the purchaser (A) goes into liquidation. **9.04**

(1) Insolvency as a repudiation

Insolvency of itself does not generally terminate outstanding contracts to which the insolvent is a party.[20] Nor does it necessarily constitute a repudiation of the contracts so as to **9.05**

---

[13] *Graham v Russell* (1816) 3 Price 227, 231, 146 ER 244, 246.
[14] See paras 10.14–10.35 below.
[15] (1748) 1 Atk 228, 26 ER 146.
[16] (1754) 1 Atk 235, 237, 26 ER 151, 152.
[17] See e.g. *French v Fenn* (1783) 3 Dougl 257, 99 ER 642; *Smith v Hodson* (1791) 4 TR 211, 100 ER 979. Compare *Olive v Smith* (1813) 5 Taunt 56, 128 ER 607.
[18] (1732) 5 Geo II, c. 30, s. 28.
[19] (1818) 2 Moore CP 547 (emphasis added).
[20] See e.g. *Re Sneezum* (1876) 3 Ch D 463, 473; *Shipton Anderson & Co (1927), Ltd v Micks, Lambert & Co* [1936] 2 All ER 1032, 1037; *Official Receiver v Henn* (1981) 40 ALR 569, 572; *Re Palmdale Insurance Ltd* [1982] VR 921, 929.

entitle the other contracting party to elect to treat the contract as terminated.[21] A repudiation may occur if insolvency is coupled with other circumstances. For example, insolvency may have the effect of putting it beyond the insolvent's power to perform his or her obligations under a contract.[22] Thus, an order that an insurance company be wound up because of insolvency has been said to constitute a repudiation by the company of its contracts of insurance, on the basis that the deficiency in the company's funds makes it impossible to pay claims in full.[23] Similarly, if a bank has discounted bills of exchange for a customer prior to the customer's insolvency, the customer has already obtained the benefit of the contract and only has an obligation to reimburse the bank, which the customer could not do in view of his or her insolvency.[24] Repudiation may also occur if the conduct of the insolvent, or of the insolvent's trustee in bankruptcy or liquidator, shows that the contract has been abandoned.[25] In that regard, the courts have indicated that, if one contracting party notifies the other that he or she is insolvent, that may be treated as a notice of repudiation if the first person does not also inform the other that he or she still intends to complete the contract.[26] Generally, though, in the absence of any such circumstances, the courts have shown a marked reluctance to conclude that insolvency of itself constitutes a repudiation of contracts that could return a profit for the insolvent's estate.[27] An example is the case of a contract for the sale of goods. The mere fact that the purchaser becomes insolvent before delivery of the goods is not considered to be a sufficient reason to entitle the vendor to treat the contract as rescinded.[28] In view of the vendor's precarious position, the vendor

---

[21] The ensuing discussion should be distinguished from the situation in which a contract in its terms is such that it is to remain in operation only so long as one of the parties continues in business, so that cessation of business consequent upon insolvency terminates the contract without giving rise to a liability for damages for breach of contract. See e.g. *Rhodes v Forwood* (1876) 1 App Cas 256 and *Re Arawa Dairy Co Ltd* [1938] NZLR 411, although compare *Reigate v Union Manufacturing Co (Ramsbottom) Ltd* [1918] 1 KB 592.

[22] See e.g. the comments of Cotton LJ in *Re Asphaltic Wood Pavement Co. Lee & Chapman's Case* (1885) 30 Ch D 216, 223–4 in relation to the obligation of the company in liquidation to maintain the street for a period of 15 years. See also *Ogdens, Ltd v Nelson* [1905] AC 109, in which the company had sold its business prior to going into voluntary liquidation.

[23] *Re National Benefit Assurance Co Ltd* [1924] 2 Ch 339, 343; *Re Federal Building Assurance Co Ltd* (1934) 34 SR (NSW) 499, 506; *Hiley v The Peoples Prudential Assurance Co Ltd* (1938) 60 CLR 468, 493; *Re Palmdale Insurance Ltd* [1982] VR 921, 929. See also *Re Northern Counties of England Fire Insurance Co (Macfarlane's Claim)* (1880) 17 Ch D 337, 341, but compare the comments of Lord Cairns in the Albert Arbitration (reported as a footnote to *Re English Assurance Co (Holdich's Case)* (1872) LR 14 Eq 72). *Quaere* whether English courts would now reach the same conclusion in relation to insurance companies carrying on long-term business, in view of the liquidator's statutory obligation to carry on the insurer's business so far as it consists of those contracts with a view to its being transferred as a going concern to a person who may lawfully carry out those contracts. See the Financial Services and Markets Act 2000, s. 376, and *MacGillivray on Insurance Law* (11th edn, 2008), 201, paras 7–070 and 7–071.

[24] *Baker v Lloyd's Bank Ltd* [1920] 2 KB 322, 326.

[25] As in *Morgan v Bain* (1874) LR 10 CP 15. See also *Lawrence v Knowles* (1839) 5 Bing (NC) 399, 132 ER 1152; *Re Tru-Grain Co Ltd* [1921] VLR 653.

[26] *Morgan v Bain* (1874) LR 10 CP 15, 25–6. Compare *Mess v Duffus and Co* (1901) 6 Com Cas 165, in which the notice was held not to constitute notice of intention not to perform the contract.

[27] In addition to the cases cited in the next footnote, see *Brooke v Hewitt* (1796) 3 Ves Jun 253, 30 ER 997; *Re Tru-Grain Co Ltd* [1921] VLR 653, 656; *Lindley on Companies* (6th edn, 1902) vol. 2, 1014. See also *Jennings Trustee v King* [1952] 1 Ch 899; *Shipton, Anderson & Co (1927) Ltd v Micks, Lambert & Co* [1936] 2 All ER 1032, 1037.

[28] *Tolhurst v Associated Portland Cement Manufacturers (1900) Ltd* [1902] 2 KB 660 (esp. at 671, referring to *Ex p Chalmers, re Edwards* (1873) LR 8 Ch App 289 and *Morgan v Bain* (1874) LR 10 CP 15). Similarly, the

is entitled to insist that the whole of the price be tendered before delivery, even if the sale was otherwise expressed to be on credit terms.[29] But the purchaser's insolvency itself, without some additional circumstance, is not regarded as a repudiation of the contract. This is based upon a sound policy consideration, that the insolvent's beneficial contracts should be preserved for the benefit of the creditors.[30] If the contract can be performed at a profit, it would make good sense for the purchaser's trustee in bankruptcy or liquidator to use the funds of the estate to pay the price and complete the contract.

(2) Specific performance

If, in the case of a contract for the sale of goods, the purchaser's trustee in bankruptcy or liquidator wishes to proceed with the contract and tenders the price, the vendor could not accept payment and refuse to deliver the goods as a set-off against a separate debt owing by the purchaser, since the contractual obligation to deliver is not a money obligation. The vendor nevertheless may adopt a different approach. The vendor may decide that it would be better to repudiate the contract, on the premise that he or she may thereby incur a monetary damages liability to the purchaser which could be set off against the purchaser's separate debt, and at the same time the vendor would retain the goods for sale elsewhere. In that regard, it should not be an objection to a set-off that the damages liability would be incurred to the purchaser after the commencement of the bankruptcy, since the liability would have arisen out of a prior dealing between the parties.[31] Nor should it be an objection that the set-off would be based upon the vendor's own conduct in deliberately breaching the contract for the express purpose of obtaining a set-off.[32] The vendor's prospect of success may ultimately depend upon whether the purchaser's trustee in bankruptcy or liquidator is able to obtain an order for specific performance of the contract. If specific performance is available, the vendor could be compelled to perform the obligation under the contract to deliver the goods and, since this obligation is not a money obligation, it could not be the subject of a set-off.

9.06

If the article the subject of the sale is unique, the court, subject to other discretionary considerations, ordinarily would decree specific performance. On the other hand, if the contract concerns goods readily available in the market at an ascertainable market price, the courts incline against specific relief. It has been suggested that in such a case specific performance is not available under any circumstances.[33] However, that view seems contrary to principle, and it is of doubtful validity.[34] Specific performance is denied, not on an absolute

9.07

---

insolvency of a vendor is not a sufficient reason to entitle the purchaser to put an end to the contract. See *Mess v Duffus and Co* (1901) 6 Com Cas 165.

[29] *Ex p Chalmers, re Edwards* (1873) LR 8 Ch App 289. See also *Gunn v Bolckow, Vaughan & Co* (1875) LR 10 Ch App 491, 501; *Re Phoenix Bessemer Steel Co* (1876) 4 Ch D 108, 112, 114; *Re Sneezum* (1876) 3 Ch D 463, 473–4; *Grice v Richardson* (1877) 3 App Cas 319. This principle has been codified in the sale of goods legislation. See the Sale of Goods Act 1979, s. 41(1)(c).

[30] *Ex p Chalmers, re Edwards* (1873) LR 8 Ch App 289, 294.

[31] See para. 8.52 above.

[32] See para. 8.90 above.

[33] *Price v Strange* [1978] 1 Ch 337, 369 (Buckley LJ).

[34] It is questioned in Jones and Goodhart, *Specific Performance* (2nd edn, 1996), 278. See also the more cautious approach of Goff LJ in *Price v Strange* [1978] 1 Ch 337, 359.

jurisdictional basis, but rather because in the vast majority of cases damages are an adequate remedy,[35] this being the original foundation of the decree of specific performance.[36] As a corollary, if in a particular case damages at law would not be an adequate remedy, the court in principle should have a discretion to grant specific relief.[37] There is nevertheless a difficulty in relation to contracts for the sale of unascertained goods. The Sale of Goods Act 1979, s. 52 expressly provides for specific performance of a contract to sell specific or ascertained goods, and Atkin LJ in *Re Wait*[38] said of the corresponding provision in earlier legislation[39] that it set out the full extent of equitable remedies in the context of contracts for the sale of goods, so that specific performance is not available where the goods are unascertained. Comments by Lord Brandon of Oakbrook in delivering the judgment of the House of Lords in *Leigh and Sillavan Ltd v Aliakmon Shipping Co Ltd*[40] suggest that he would have agreed with Atkin LJ.[41] On the other hand, Atkin LJ's view has been criticized by commentators.[42]

9.08   Amendments to the Sale of Goods Act 1979[43] have ameliorated to some extent the position in relation to unascertained goods. The definition of 'specific goods' in s. 61 has been amended so as to include within the meaning of that term an undivided share, specified as a fraction or percentage, of goods identified and agreed on at the time a contract of sale was made. This has the effect that, where a specified fraction or percentage of an identified and agreed bulk is sold, the agreement may be specifically enforced pursuant to s. 52.[44] The amendment does not apply when the agreement relates to a sale of a specified quantity to be taken from an identified bulk, as opposed to a fraction or a percentage, although as a result of another amendment to the Act[45] the buyer in such a case, once he or she pays the price, may become the owner of an undivided share in the bulk.[46] If, however, there is no identified bulk, the reforms have no application.

---

[35] *Adderley v Dixon* (1824) 1 Sim & St 607, 610, 57 ER 239, 240; *Falcke v Gray* (1859) 4 Drewry 651, 657–8, 62 ER 250, 252; *Re Clarke* (1887) 36 Ch D 348, 352; *Thomas Borthwick & Sons (Australasia) Ltd v South Otago Freezing Co Ltd* [1978] 1 NZLR 538, 548 (PC) ('A contract for the sale of goods obtainable on the market will not *normally* be specifically enforced' (emphasis added)); Spry, *Equitable Remedies* (8th edn, 2010), 55 n 18, 65–7.

[36] *Harnet v Yeilding* (1805) 2 Sch & Lef 549, 553 (Lord Redesdale).

[37] See in this regard *Sky Petroleum Ltd v VIP Petroleum Ltd* [1974] 1 WLR 576 (esp. at 578–9).

[38] [1927] 1 Ch 606, 630.

[39] Sale of Goods Act 1893, s. 52.

[40] [1986] 1 AC 785, 812.

[41] See also *Re Goldcorp Exchange Ltd* [1995] 1 AC 74, 90–1 in relation to the question of equitable title. In New South Wales, compare *Electrical Enterprises Retail Pty Ltd v Rodgers* (1989) 15 NSWLR 473, 492–3, although the legislation in issue differed from that in England. *Re Wait* has been followed in Victoria. See *King v Greig* [1931] VLR 413, 438–9.

[42] Treitel, 'Specific performance in the sale of goods' [1966] JBL 211, 222–4; Jones and Goodhart, *Specific Performance* (2nd edn, 1996), 147–50. See also Spry, *Equitable Remedies* (8th edn, 2010), 54–5; Pollock, 'Re Wait' (1927) 43 LQR 293. Compare Pettit, *Equity and the Law of Trusts* (11th edn, 2009), 653, n. 41, where it is said that the claim to specific performance in *Re Wait* was based solely on the predecessor of s. 52 of the Sale of Goods Act 1979.

[43] See the Sale of Goods (Amendment) Act 1995.

[44] See *Benjamin's Sale of Goods* (7th edn, 2006), 1107 [17–097].

[45] See s. 20A, introduced by the Sale of Goods (Amendment) Act 1995.

[46] *Benjamin's Sale of Goods* (7th edn, 2006), 1107 [17–097].

(3) The adequacy of damages

In determining whether damages are an adequate remedy, it is not simply a matter of consid‐ **9.09**
ering whether the amount of the loss can be adequately quantified and expressed in a judg‐
ment. This is apparent from the decision of the House of Lords in *Beswick v Beswick*.[47] The
defendant had breached a contract with the plaintiff to make periodic payments to a third
party. A judgment for nominal damages arguably would have constituted an accurate reflec‐
tion of the plaintiff's own loss, but it would not have been adequate to meet the justice of the
case. Accordingly, specific performance was granted. The question is whether a judgment for
damages would put the claimant in a situation as beneficial to him or her as if the agreement
were specifically enforced,[48] or, in other words, whether damages would provide a 'complete
remedy'.[49] Thus, the courts have indicated that it is appropriate to consider whether the
defendant for any reason is unlikely to satisfy a judgment for damages.[50] In that regard, if the
reason that the defendant is unlikely to satisfy the judgment is insolvency, and the defendant
has other creditors, the court may refuse to grant relief on the basis that specific performance
would have the effect of preferring the claimant over the general body of creditors, if in fact
there is no other reason apart from inadequacy of damages for granting relief.[51] But in the
absence of that countervailing circumstance, the actual amount that the claimant is likely to
receive in his or her hands as a result of a judgment for damages, in comparison to what the
position would be if specific performance were granted, is a relevant factor.

In the situation posited,[52] an award of damages would not constitute an adequate remedy **9.10**
to the insolvent purchaser's estate, even where the goods are readily available in the market
at an ascertainable price. If the vendor were to perform his or her obligation and deliver the
goods, the purchaser's estate would have the full benefit of the contract, and at the same
time would only have to pay a dividend on the separate debt owing to the vendor. If, how‐
ever, the purchaser is remitted to a claim for damages against the vendor after the vendor's
repudiation, the vendor's liability for damages ordinarily should be capable of set‐off against
the debt, given that it is not an objection to a set‐off that the vendor may have deliberately
breached a contract in order to obtain a set‐off.[53] The allowance of a set‐off where none
otherwise would be available may have a considerable effect on the funds available for
distribution to the purchaser's creditors, and on that basis an award of damages would not
put the purchaser and his or her creditors in a situation as beneficial as if the contract in
question were specifically performed. As a matter of principle, there is much to be said for
the view that specific performance should be available in this situation, subject to other
relevant discretionary considerations.

---

[47] [1968] AC 58.

[48] *Harnett v Yeilding* (1805) 2 Sch & Lef 549, 556; Spry, *Equitable Remedies* (8th edn, 2010), 59–60.

[49] *Adderley v Dixon* (1824) 1 Sim & St 607, 610, 57 ER 239, 240 (Sir John Leach).

[50] *Hodgson v Duce* (1856) 2 Jur NS 1014; *Evans Marshall & Co Ltd v Bertola SA* [1973] 1 WLR 349,
380–1; *The Oakworth* [1975] 1 Lloyd's Rep 581, 583. See also Horack, 'Insolvency and specific performance'
(1918) 31 *Harvard Law Review* 702; Spry, *Equitable Remedies* (8th edn, 2010), 68.

[51] *Re Wait* [1927] 1 Ch 606. See also *Hewett v Court* (1983) 149 CLR 639, 658; Spry, *Equitable Remedies*
(8th edn, 2010), 55 note 20, 68–9.

[52] See para. 9.06 above.

[53] See para. 8.90 above.

C. Foreign Exchange Contracts[54]

(1) Introduction

9.11 The requirement of commensurability has come into prominence in recent years in the context of foreign exchange contracts.

9.12 For the sake of simplicity, consider the following situation. A bank has entered into two foreign exchange contracts with a customer or with another bank (referred to as the 'counterparty').[55] In the first contract entered into on, say, 1 September, the bank has agreed to provide an amount expressed in currency 1 to the counterparty in consideration of the counterparty's agreement to provide an amount expressed in currency 2. Performance of the contract is to take place on 31 December. Pursuant to a second contract, entered into on 1 October, the counterparty has agreed to provide an amount expressed in currency 3 to the bank in consideration of the bank's agreement to provide an amount expressed in currency 4. This contract is also to be performed on 31 December. However, on 15 November the counterparty goes into liquidation.

9.13 In the event of the liquidation of a counterparty, the liquidator could be expected to disclaim any foreign exchange contract which, because of movements in exchange rates, is considered to be unprofitable,[56] and keep on foot any contract which is profitable to the counterparty. If a contract is disclaimed, a person who sustains consequential loss or damage is deemed by the Insolvency Act[57] to be a creditor of the company to the extent of the loss, and accordingly may prove for the loss in the liquidation. If the liquidator of a counterparty were to disclaim one contract as unprofitable but elect to perform another profitable contract, the bank would wish to set off its obligation arising under the continuing contract against its damages claim against the counterparty in liquidation arising as a result of the disclaimer. The question of where the bank would stand in the event of a liquidation of the counterparty is of paramount concern to banks. It affects dealing limits that banks can set for their counterparties. In addition, where the bank requires cash cover (for example, a margin deposit) as 'security' in the event of default by the counterparty, it may affect the amount of cover or margin deposit required. It also may be important for capital adequacy purposes, that is, in the determination of the amount of capital that the bank is required by the relevant central bank or regulator to have to cover its risk assets.

(2) The nature of the foreign money obligation

9.14 In considering the question, a critical issue is the nature of the foreign money obligation under a foreign exchange contract.

---

[54] The following discussion is adapted from Derham, 'Set-off and netting of foreign exchange contracts in the liquidation of a counterparty' [1991] JBL 463.

[55] Often there will be a large number of contracts with a particular counterparty involving different currencies and performance dates.

[56] Pursuant to the Insolvency Act 1986, s. 178. In Australia, see the Corporations Act 2001 (Cth), s. 568.

[57] Insolvency Act 1986, s. 178(6).

The traditional view, as expressed by Dr Mann,[58] is that foreign money may function either **9.15** as money or as a commodity, depending on the circumstances. He said that foreign money should be regarded as money where it serves monetary functions, for example in the case of a foreign currency debt.[59] However, in the particular situation in which foreign money is dealt in and quoted on the foreign exchange market, he considered that it is the object of commercial intercourse and therefore is a commodity.[60] In other words, it is similar to a contract to deliver so many tons of wheat. Nussbaum[61] and Rabel[62] expressed similar views. Nussbaum justified the conclusion by reference to the distinction between acting as a measure and being measured, between *mensura* and *mensuratum*. Money in a general sense is a standard or measure of the value of goods and services.[63] As a corollary, it is correct to say that the value of goods and services is measured by reference to money. Indeed, money has been described as the common denominator of value.[64] But while money is a measure, it is an abstract unit of measurement (in England, the pound sterling) which cannot be precisely defined.[65] Money as such is not measured by anything else. Money is *mensura*, not *mensuratum*.[66] Yet, when foreign money is sold or exchanged it is being measured. It is measured by its fluctuating exchange value against the fixed unit of account in which domestic money is denominated, the rate of exchange of a foreign currency being the price of that currency in terms of a country's own currency.[67] According to Nussbaum,[68] when foreign money is measured in that manner it has the character of a commodity.[69]

---

[58] Mann, *The Legal Aspect of Money* (5th edn, 1992), 191 *et seq*. Following the views expressed in *Camdex International Ltd v Bank of Zambia* [1997] 6 Bank LR 43, [1997] EWCA Civ 798 (see para. 9.19 below), a different approach is adopted in *Mann on the Legal Aspect of Money* (6th edn (ed. Procter), 2005), 44–9. However, for the purpose of the discussion below of the traditional view advocated by Dr Mann, references to the fifth edition have been retained.

[59] See particularly the comments of Lord Radcliffe in *Re United Railways of Havana and Regla Warehouses Ltd* [1961] AC 1007, 1059–60.

[60] See Mann, *op. cit.* 191. This view was not affected by the decision of the House of Lords in *Miliangos v George Frank (Textiles) Ltd* [1976] AC 443. See Derham, 'Set-off and netting of foreign exchange contracts in the liquidation of a counterparty' [1991] JBL 463, 475–7.

[61] See Nussbaum, *Money in the Law National and International* (1950), 340–4 for a discussion of foreign money in the context of a foreign currency debt, and at 24 (and see also at 319) in relation to foreign money functioning as a commodity when it is purchased or exchanged on the foreign exchange market.

[62] Rabel, *The Conflict of Laws* (2nd edn, 1964) vol. 3, 26.

[63] Nussbaum, *op. cit.* 14, referred to in Mann, *op. cit.* 49.

[64] Nussbaum, *op. cit.* 11.

[65] Mann, *op. cit.* 49, 86. As Nussbaum (*op. cit.* 14) put it in relation to the United States dollar: 'the dollar concept existing at any given time is as little susceptible of definition as, say, the concept of "blue".'

[66] Nussbaum, *op. cit.* 28, and see also the discussion in Mann, *op. cit.* 43–9. Under the Bretton Woods Agreement, the 'par value' of the currency of each member was expressed in terms of gold, in the sense that the par value determined the price for the purchase and sale of gold. See Mann, *op. cit.* 33–6. It is therefore correct to say that the par value constituted a measure. See Mann, *op. cit.* 46. That system effectively had ceased to apply by 1973. See *Lively Ltd v City of Munich* [1976] 1 WLR 1004, 1010–3.

[67] See Mann, *op. cit.* 61.

[68] Nussbaum said (*op. cit.* 24) that: 'in special situations pieces of money are dealt with as commodities. This happens mainly in the market of foreign exchanges. Ever since there has been a theory of money, it has been recognized that money may have a "second use", – namely, to be purchased or exchanged. In the language of Thomas Aquinas, money, if sold or exchanged, is "measured, not a measure;" "*mensuratum*," not "*mensura*". Its intrinsic or exchange value as distinct from the extrinsic or nominal (face) value is controlling in the situation. The latter value is a matter of the law; the former is the result of economic conditions. While the intrinsic value is subject to fluctuations, the extrinsic one is invariable.'

[69] That should not be the case, however, in relation to the periodic payment obligations that arise under a currency and interest rate swap. See Derham, 'Set-off and netting of foreign exchange contracts in the liquidation

9.16 There is some support for that view in the cases.[70] It is consistent with references to foreign exchange contracts in a number of cases in terms of a sale and purchase,[71] although, if the obligation on both sides of the contract is a foreign money obligation, the contract would be more appropriately described as one of exchange, similar to a barter. In *Drexel Burnham Lambert International NV v El Nasr*,[72] Staughton J described Swiss francs the subject of forward contracts of sale and purchase as a commodity, and, in New South Wales, Lee J referred to the opinions of Mann and Nussbaum with evident approval when he held that a foreign exchange contract that made provision for physical delivery was a commodity agreement for the purposes of the Futures Industries Code formerly applicable in that jurisdiction.[73] While 'commodity' admittedly had a particular definition in the Code,[74] his Honour said that, 'it is a natural use of the word to apply it to foreign currency in circumstances in which it is dealt with in commercial transactions of the kind under consideration.'[75] On another occasion, Lord Radcliffe in the House of Lords[76] recognized that there is a distinction between, on the one hand, a contract to pay foreign money abroad in satisfaction of a debt and, on the other, 'a contract to deliver foreign currency in this country or abroad or a true exchange contract', which he defined as a contract to exchange the currency of one country for the currency of another. He specifically rejected the view that foreign currency debts payable abroad give rise to an obligation to deliver a commodity as opposed to an obligation to pay money. On the other hand, he seems to have regarded foreign exchange contracts as contracts for the delivery of a commodity. More recently, the distinction was recognized in New South Wales.[77]

---

of a counterparty' [1991] JBL 463, 468–9. The concept of acting as a measure of the value of goods and services is a general function of money, and Nussbaum's thesis would not require that, if in a particular situation 'money' is not being used specifically for that purpose, it is not money. This would be the case, for example, when money is transferred by way of gift. But where foreign money is being measured, Nussbaum considered that in that circumstance it is not functioning as money. Further, the notion that foreign money when sold or exchanged is measured against domestic money should be distinguished from the situation in which parties have agreed that what is admittedly a foreign currency debt should be converted into domestic money at a specified exchange rate for certain purposes, for example because payment is to be made in domestic money, or in order to ascertain whether security 'top up' is required. The measurement as against domestic money is applied to the debt, which itself is not money. See Mann, *The Legal Aspect of Money* (5th edn, 1992), 5 in relation to bank accounts.

[70] The following authorities are in addition to cases which have dealt with money in a bag, or specific coins. See e.g. *Taylor v Plumer* (1815) 3 M & S 562, 105 ER 721; *Moss v Hancock* [1899] 2 QB 111.

[71] *Re British American Continental Bank Ltd (Goldzieher and Penso's Claim)* [1922] 2 Ch 575, 586 *per* Warrington LJ ('The subjects of these contracts for sale and purchase were sums of foreign currency'); *Bank of India v Patel* [1982] 1 Lloyd's Rep 506, 508, 509, and on appeal [1983] 2 Lloyd's Rep 298, 299, 302; *Isaac Naylor & Sons Ltd v New Zealand Co-operative Wool Marketing Association Ltd* [1981] 1 NZLR 361, 366.

[72] [1986] 1 Lloyd's Rep 356.

[73] *Shoreline Currencies (Aust) Pty Ltd v Corporate Affairs Commission (NSW)* (1986) 10 ACLR 847. See also *Carragreen Currency Corporation Pty Ltd v Corporate Affairs Commission (NSW)* (1986) 11 ACLR 298; *Corporate Affairs Commission (NSW) v Lombard Nash International Pty Ltd* (1986) 11 ACLR 566, 569 ('there is a bet made on the relative price of a commodity, such as *currency*, gold or platinum' (emphasis added)).

[74] 'Commodity' was defined in s. 4 of the Futures Industries Code as: 'a thing that is capable of delivery pursuant to an agreement for its delivery; or . . . an instrument creating or evidencing a thing in action.'

[75] (1986) 10 ACLR 847, 855 (emphasis added).

[76] *Re United Railways of Havana and Regla Warehouses Ltd* [1961] AC 1007, 1059–60.

[77] *Daewoo Australia Pty Ltd v Suncorp-Metway Ltd* (2000) 48 NSWLR 692 at [33].

(3) Set-off consequences if the obligation is not a monetary obligation

If, in accordance with the traditional view, the foreign money obligation in a foreign **9.17** exchange contract was not a money obligation, the set-off consequences would differ depending on which of the parties has that obligation. The situation posited is that a contract has been disclaimed by the counterparty's liquidator because it is considered to be unprofitable. As a result, the bank has a damages claim against the counterparty which may be proved in the liquidation. The liquidator, however, has not disclaimed a second contract, because this contract is considered to be profitable from the counterparty's point of view. In view of the counterparty's insolvency, the bank would not be obliged to perform its obligation under the second contract until the counterparty has first performed its own obligation, despite any term of the contract that may suggest otherwise.[78] If the liquidator accordingly makes available the requisite amount of the currency in question, the bank would wish to set off its resulting obligation to perform its side of the contract against the damages claim that it has against the counterparty arising from the disclaimer of the first contract.

Consider that the counterparty has the foreign money obligation, while the bank's obliga- **9.18** tion is to pay a sum expressed in sterling. It is suggested that the bank in this circumstance ordinarily should be entitled to a set-off in the counterparty's liquidation, since it has a money obligation that arose out of a contract entered into before the liquidation.[79] Alternatively, the bank may have the foreign money obligation. In such a case, if the obligation was not a money obligation,[80] the requirement of commensurability would mean that it could not be employed in a set-off in the counterparty's liquidation. There would not be a 'sum due' for the purpose of the insolvency set-off section. Nor would the fact that the obligation has a readily ascertainable value affect that conclusion.[81]

(4) A recent view – *Camdex v Bank of Zambia*

However, this may no longer be an issue. In *Camdex International Ltd v Bank of Zambia*,[82] **9.19** the Court of Appeal rejected the view that the foreign money obligation under a foreign exchange contract is not a money obligation, Simon Brown LJ commenting:[83]

> When indeed one asks for what purpose it is sought to categorise foreign exchange transactions variously as commodity or as money transactions one is lost for an answer. What in

---

[78] See *Ex p Chalmers, re Edwards* (1873) LR 8 Ch App 289, and para. 9.05 above.

[79] The decision of Watkin Williams J in *Ince Hall Rolling Mills Co Ltd v The Douglas Forge Co* (1882) 8 QBD 179 is authority to the contrary. In that case the liquidator of a supplier delivered goods to a purchaser pursuant to a contract that had been entered into before the liquidation, and it was held that the purchaser was not entitled to a set-off in respect of its resulting liability for the price. The better view, however, is that the *Ince Hall* case was wrongly decided (see paras 13.37–13.57 below), and that a bank with a sterling liability on a foreign exchange contract which becomes due and payable after the counterparty's liquidation should be able to employ that liability in a set-off in the liquidation.

[80] Whether or not it is an obligation to deliver a commodity. See Derham, 'Set-off and netting of foreign exchange contracts in the liquidation of a counterparty' [1991] JBL 463, 470–5.

[81] See para. 9.01 above.

[82] [1997] 6 Bank LR 43, [1997] EWCA Civ 798.

[83] [1997] 6 Bank LR 43, 51–2.

other words is the point of the distinction . . . Of course if one is concerned with rare coins or the manufacture of bank notes or something of that kind, money may indeed be a commodity rather than a medium of exchange. But where, as is the usual case, the obligation in question is simply the payment of a stipulated sum in a stipulated currency, then, whether that obligation arises from a loan, or any other contract or set of circumstances, it is an obligation properly described as one of debt.

Similarly Phillips LJ said:[84]

> In my judgment, where a contract expressly provides for the payment of a sum in a foreign currency, the obligation is a money obligation and breach of it gives rise primarily to a claim in debt, whether the obligation is by way of repayment of money loaned, payment for goods or services or payment for other currencies.

> So far as the last type of contract is concerned, I recognise that an exchange transaction is *sui generis*, but its true nature is the incurring of mutual money obligations, not the barter of commodities.

The analysis in the *Camdex* case has been criticized,[85] but if it is followed it would provide greater certainty to participants in foreign exchange markets.

9.20 But even if the *Camdex* case is not followed, a properly drafted netting agreement should provide protection to a bank against the liquidation of a counterparty. Netting agreements are considered later.[86]

---

[84] [1997] 6 Bank LR 43, 57.

[85] Brindle and Cox (ed.), *Law of Bank Payments* (3rd edn, 2004), 35–41. In Australia, see also *Daewoo Australia Pty Ltd v Suncorp-Metway Ltd* (2000) 48 NSWLR 692 at [33], where Austin J affirmed the view (without reference to the *Camdex* case) that the foreign money obligation under a foreign exchange contract is not a money obligation.

[86] See paras 16.30–16.51 below. In Australia, see paras 16.52–16.67 below in relation to the Payment Systems and Netting Act 1998 (Cth).

10

TRUST FUNDS

A. Introduction

The subject of discussion in this chapter is the question whether, and if so under what **10.01** circumstances, the obligation of a person who holds a fund impressed with a trust to account for the trust fund may be the subject of a set-off against a debt owing to that person in his or her personal capacity. It should be distinguished from the situation in which a beneficiary of a trust is obliged to contribute to the trust fund. That situation is not one of set-off, but rather of the application of a principle known as the rule in *Cherry v Boultbee*,[1] which is considered later.[2]

---

[1] (1839) 4 My & Cr 442, 41 ER 171.
[2] See ch. 14 below.

B. Insolvency Set-off

(1) The general principle

10.02 If T holds a sum on trust for B, and B becomes bankrupt, T must account for the trust fund to B's trustee in bankruptcy without a set-off in respect of an independent debt owing by B to T in T's personal capacity.[3] Thus, a sum held on trust by a solicitor for a bankrupt client cannot be the subject of a set-off in the bankruptcy,[4] and similarly an insurance broker is not entitled to a set-off in respect of subrogation moneys held on trust for a bankrupt underwriter.[5] In an early case,[6] a creditor of a bankrupt was indebted to one of the assignees in bankruptcy in the assignee's personal capacity. When the creditor himself later became bankrupt, the fact of the assignee's trusteeship was held to preclude a set-off in relation to the dividend payable to the creditor and the creditor's own indebtedness to the assignee. The denial of a set-off in these cases is explicable on the basis of lack of mutuality[7] in that, while T has a personal claim against the bankrupt, the bankrupt has a claim *in specie* against a trust fund. It is true that a trustee who has in his hands money to be handed over to the beneficiary has been referred to as an equitable debtor,[8] and the interest of a beneficiary has been described as a right in personam against the trustee.[9] However, it is now accepted that a beneficiary has a proprietary interest in the trust assets,[10] and it is that proprietary interest which destroys mutuality for the purpose of a set-off.

10.03 In considering the principle, two points should be noted. The first is that it applies when the question of set-off arises in relation to an obligation to account for a trust fund to which the beneficiary of the trust is absolutely entitled. If, on the other hand, a creditor has

---

[3] In addition to the cases referred to below, see also *Re The United Ports and General Insurance Co, ex p The Etna Insurance Co* (1877) 46 LJ Ch 403, 406; *Elgood v Harris* [1896] 2 QB 491, 494; *Re McMahon and Canada Permanent Trust Co* (1979) 108 DLR (3d) 71; *Lloyds Bank NZA Ltd v National Safety Council of Australia* [1993] 2 VR 506; *Neptune (Vehicle Washing Equipment) Ltd v Fitzgerald* [1996] Ch 274, 278; *Lehman Brothers International (Europe) v CRC Credit Fund Ltd* [2009] EWHC 3228 (Ch) at [325]–[335]. See also the special purpose payment cases referred to in paras 10.47–10.58 below. In *Hamilton v Commonwealth Bank of Australia* (1992) 9 ACSR 90, 108, Hodgson J queried whether the principle applies in Australia in relation to moneys held by a creditor as fiduciary for the debtor, following *Gye v McIntyre* (1991) 171 CLR 609. It is suggested that the principle is not affected by that case. In relation to Scottish law, see *Melville Dundas Ltd v Hotel Corporation of Edinburgh Ltd* [2006] BLR 474.

[4] *Wright v Watson* (1883) Cab & El 171, and see also *Stumore v Campbell & Co* [1892] 1 QB 314 (Statutes of Set-off). Compare *Shand v M J Atkinson Ltd* [1966] NZLR 551, which was concerned with the construction of the Law Practitioners Act 1955 (NZ).

[5] See *Elgood v Harris* [1896] 2 QB 491, although in that case the trust moneys in any event were received after the bankruptcy.

[6] *Ex p White* (1742) 1 Atk 90, 26 ER 59, and see also *Ex p Bailey, re Howarth* (1840) 1 Mont D & De G 263. Compare *Ex p Nockold* (1734), unreported but noted in Cooke, *The Bankrupt Laws* (8th edn, 1823) vol. 1, 509, which has not been followed. See *Re Henley, Thurgood, & Co* (1863) 11 WR 1021, 1022.

[7] *National Westminster Bank Ltd v Halesowen Presswork & Assemblies Ltd* [1972] AC 785, 821; *Re Arthur Sanders Ltd* (1981) 17 BLR 125, 133; *Lloyds Bank NZA Ltd v National Safety Council of Australia* [1993] 2 VR 506, 515.

[8] *Webb v Stenton* (1883) 11 QBD 518, 526.

[9] Most notably, by Professor Maitland. See Maitland, *Equity* (2nd edn (rev. Brunyate), 1936), 106 *et seq.*

[10] *Archer-Shee v Garland* [1931] AC 212; Pettit, *Equity and the Law of Trusts* (11th edn, 2009), 83–5; Meagher, Gummow and Lehane's *Equity Doctrines and Remedies* (4th edn, 2002), 116–18.

an interest by way of security in a fund in the hands of the debtor,[11] a set-off in some circumstances may occur against the secured debt.[12] To the extent of the set-off the secured debt would be paid, and to that extent the fund would be released from the security.[13] The second point is that the obligation to account for a trust fund, while not susceptible to a set-off under the insolvency set-off section, may be the subject of contractual deductions agreed between the parties in relation to other sums payable under the agreement,[14] or indeed arising on other accounts.[15] The deductions allowed by the contract operate to limit the amount to which the beneficiary is entitled under the trust.[16]

(2) Express stipulation for a trust

In Re ILG Travel Ltd,[17] Jonathan Parker J suggested that a stipulation in a contract between **10.04** T and B, that T is to hold a sum on trust for B, would not preclude a set-off in B's liquidation against a debt owing by B to T under the contract, the reason being that, if insolvency set-off is mandatory and cannot be contracted out of,[18] the parties could not avoid that result by simply using the word 'trust'. That proposition is difficult to accept in cases where there is an identifiable fund impressed with a trust.[19] In that situation, the principle which precludes a set-off against a trust fund should apply. There would be a lack of mutuality, and it should not matter for that conclusion whether the trust in issue is an express trust or a trust arising by operation of law. Nor should it matter for mutuality whether the demands have their source in the same contract or different contracts.[20] It would not be a case of the parties purporting to contract out of the operation of the insolvency set-off section in circumstances where the section otherwise would apply. Rather, the requirements of the section would not be satisfied.

(3) An exception

There is an apparent exception to the general principle which precludes a set-off against an **10.05** obligation to account for a trust fund in the situation in which property has been deposited

---

[11] A trust and a charge are distinct institutions. See *Associated Alloys Pty Ltd v ACN 001 452 106 Pty Ltd* (2000) 202 CLR 588 at [5] and [6].

[12] See paras 6.176–6.179 above.

[13] *Re ILG Travel Ltd* [1995] 2 BCLC 128, 158–60. See para. 6.179 above.

[14] *Re ILG Travel Ltd* [1995] 2 BCLC 128, 157–8; *Obaray v Gateway (London) Ltd* [2001] L & TR 20, [2004] 1 BCLC 555. See also *Re Tout & Finch Ltd* [1954] 1 WLR 178, 186.

[15] See *Re McMahon and Canada Permanent Trust Co* (1979) 108 DLR (3d) 71, 77–8; *Lloyds Bank NZA Ltd v National Safety Council of Australia* [1993] 2 VR 506, 510, 513, 514. See also *Lehman Brothers International (Europe) v CRC Credit Fund Ltd* [2009] EWHC 3228 (Ch) at [326].

[16] It has been suggested that the agreement should be construed as creating a charge on the fund, so that the trustee is not a bare trustee but one whose trust obligation applies only to the balance remaining after deducting the amount due to him or her. See Goode, *Principles of Corporate Insolvency Law* (3rd edn, 2005), 235, and *Obaray v Gateway (London) Ltd* [2001] L & TR 20, [2004] 1 BCLC 555. Compare that view with the analysis in *Associated Alloys Pty Ltd v ACN 001 452 106 Pty Ltd* (2000) 202 CLR 588.

[17] [1995] 2 BCLC 128, 160–1.

[18] See paras 6.111–6.112 above.

[19] See [1995] 2 BCLC 128, 156–7. An entitlement to mix money with one's own ordinarily is regarded as being inconsistent with a trust. See para. 10.19 below.

[20] Compare [1995] 2 BCLC 128, 161. See paras 11.01–11.02 below.

with another with directions or authority to turn it into money. This is considered below in the context of a discussion of *Rose v Hart*.[21]

C. Statutes of Set-off

10.06 A similar principle applies in the case of set-off under the Statutes of Set-off. If T is a trustee of a fund for B, and T is sued by B for payment of the fund, T cannot deduct a separate debt owing by B to T in T's personal capacity.[22] Ordinarily, equity will act by analogy with the right of set-off available at law under the Statutes of Set-off if the demands are equitably, but not legally, mutual.[23] As in the case of insolvency set-off, however, when the claim is for payment of a trust fund there is a lack of mutuality.[24] On the one hand, the trustee has a personal claim against the beneficiary, and on the other the beneficiary has a claim *in specie* against the trust fund.

10.07 Lack of mutuality should be regarded as the proper basis for the early decision in *Whitaker v Rush*.[25] A testator bequeathed £400 to a legatee, who assigned the legacy to the plaintiff. When the plaintiff brought this bill in equity seeking payment of the legacy, the executor asserted that the legatee was indebted to him on a partnership account and for money lent, and that he was not obliged to pay to the plaintiff more than what was due on the balance of accounts. Sir Thomas Clark MR said that there was no case where a debt in one right had been set off against a debt in another right, and he disallowed a set-off. The result seems correct. While the legatee was liable to the executor in the executor's personal capacity, the executor was not personally liable for the legacy, which was payable out of the fund constituted by the proceeds of the testator's estate.

10.08 *Whitaker v Rush* should be contrasted with *Taylor v Taylor*,[26] which concerned an intestacy.[27] The deceased had two sons, the plaintiff and the defendant. Letters of administration were granted to the defendant in 1856. In 1860 he submitted an account to the plaintiff, and in accordance with the terms of the account he paid the plaintiff a sum of money. In 1871 the plaintiff filed this bill, alleging that he had recently discovered that he was entitled to more than had been paid to him under the intestacy. Sir George Jessel MR agreed with him on

---

[21] (1818) 8 Taunt 499, 129 ER 477. See paras 10.14–10.35 below.

[22] *Talbot v Frere* (1878) 9 Ch D 568, 573; *Stumore v Campbell & Co* [1892] 1 QB 314, 316; *Zemco Ltd v Jerrom-Pugh* [1993] BCC 275 (following *Guinness Plc v Saunders* [1988] 1 WLR 863). See also *Re Jeffrey's Policy* (1872) 20 WR 857 (proceeds of life policy deposited as security). Malins VC did not consider the possibility of a trust when he held in *Thomas v Howell* (1874) LR 18 Eq 198 that an agent could set off a sum remaining in his hands on account of rent collected for his principal against the principal's liability for unpaid commission. Compare *Smit Tek International Zeesleepen BV v Selco Salvage Ltd* [1988] 2 Lloyd's Rep 398, 408 in the context of a set-off asserted by the beneficiary of a trust, as opposed to the trustee. Compare also *Sivritas v Sivritas (No. 2)* [2008] VSC 580, which concerned a set-off of judgments and orders under the court's inherent jurisdiction. See paras 2.98–2.122 above.

[23] See para. 3.07 above.

[24] See para. 10.02 above.

[25] (1761) Amb 407, 27 ER 272. See also *Medlicot v Bowes* (1749) 1 Ves Sen 207, 27 ER 985; *Freeman v Lomas* (1851) 9 Hare 109, 68 ER 435.

[26] (1875) LR 20 Eq 155.

[27] An administrator of an intestate's estate, once he or she has completed the administration, holds as trustee for the beneficiaries on the intestacy. See *Re Cockburn's Will Trusts* [1957] 1 Ch 438, 439.

this point, and held that the defendant as administrator was liable to pay the difference. However, he also held that the defendant could set off a debt owing to him in his personal capacity by the plaintiff. The Master of the Rolls said that it was: 'clear, on every principle of equity, on every principle of common sense and common justice, and on every principle derived by analogy from the Statute of Set-off, or otherwise, that the Defendant . . . is entitled to the set-off claimed, and I intend to allow it.'[28] *Whitaker v Rush* was cited in argument, but Sir George Jessel did not mention it in his judgment. While the cases were similar, they differed in the following respect. In *Whitaker v Rush* the claim of the legatee related to a subsisting fund. In *Taylor v Taylor*, on the other hand, it seems clear that there was no longer a fund in existence into which the proceeds of the testator's estate could be traced. The plaintiff only had a personal claim against the defendant for payment of the sum to which he was entitled.[29] Consequently, as Sir George Jessel described the defendant's successful argument, this was a case in which the defendant was saying to the plaintiff: 'You have come into equity for a personal equitable debt due from me to you. I ask to set off a personal legal debt due from you to me.'[30] In fact, the case has been cited as authority for a different proposition. While it is agreed that a debt owing to an executor in his own right cannot be set off against a legacy, it has been suggested, on the authority of *Taylor v Taylor*, that a debt due from one of the next of kin to an administrator may be set off against the next of kin's share in the estate.[31] However, Sir George Jessel did not draw any such distinction between an executor and an administrator, and it would be difficult to justify. The case is better explained on the basis suggested above.

Taylor v Taylor was followed in *Re Jones; Christmas v Jones*.[32] A son had been appointed **10.09** administrator in his mother's intestacy. In addition, he was executor of his father's will. Two people, who were also next of kin of the intestate, brought an action for revocation of the probate of the will. They were unsuccessful, and were ordered to pay the executor's costs. When they demanded payment of their shares of the intestate's estate the administrator paid the proceeds of the estate into court, and said that he was entitled to bring into account the next of kins' indebtedness for costs. Kekewich J held that *Taylor v Taylor* was an authority in favour of a set-off, and that accordingly it should be allowed. This would have been a correct conclusion if *Taylor v Taylor* indeed supports a general proposition that an administrator is in a different position to an executor with respect to set-offs. The contrary view is that the distinguishing feature in that case was the absence of a specific fund in respect of which a claim could have been made. There was merely a personal liability in the administrator. In *Re Jones*, on the other hand, there was still a specific fund, which had been paid into court. The better view is that there was no mutuality for the purpose of a set-off between the next of kin's liability to the administrator for costs and their right to participate in the fund.

---

[28] (1875) LR 20 Eq 155, 160.

[29] Thus, the amount which a defaulting trustee is bound to pay to make good a breach of trust is regarded as an equitable debt. See para. 10.10 below.

[30] (1875) LR 20 Eq 155, 160.

[31] *Withers on Reversions* (2nd edn, 1933), 260. See also *Halsbury's Laws of England* (5th edn, 2009) vol. 11 ('Civil Procedure'), 528, para. 692 (compare para. 690 in relation to executors).

[32] [1897] 2 Ch 190.

D. Dissipation of the Trust Fund

10.10   It is assumed in the preceding discussion that the trustee has retained the trust fund or its traceable proceeds. On that basis, there is a lack of mutuality. Consider, however, that a trustee in breach of trust has dissipated the trust estate. The court in such a case may order the trustee to restore the estate, either by restoring assets that have been lost or by paying sufficient compensation to the trust estate to put it back to what it would have been had the breach not been committed.[33] The trustee should not be entitled to set off against that obligation a separate debt of a beneficiary to the trustee in the trustee's personal capacity. The obligation to restore the trust estate and the trustee's separate claim against the beneficiary personally would not be mutual.[34] Alternatively, the court may order the trustee to pay compensation directly to a beneficiary. An order in that form ordinarily is appropriate in the case of a beneficiary who is absolutely entitled to the trust fund.[35] The obligation to pay compensation for breach of trust is an equitable debt,[36] and as such it would *prima facie* constitute a debt for the purpose of the insolvency set-off section and the Statutes of Set-off.[37] In the circumstances, however, a set-off may be unjust.[38] In particular, if the beneficiary is insolvent, it would be unjust to allow the trustee a set-off based upon his or her own breach of trust, in circumstances where the trustee would otherwise have had to account for the trust fund to the beneficiary without set-off and would have been confined to a dividend on his or her separate claim against the beneficiary.[39] In comparison to that result, a set-off would mean that the trustee would profit from the breach.[40] If instead the court were to order the trustee to restore the trust fund, the order should preclude a set-off.[41]

---

[33] See the discussion in *Target Holdings Ltd v Redferns* [1996] AC 421, 434. See also *Maguire v Makaronis* (1997) 188 CLR 449, 469–70, 473.

[34] See, and compare, *Baillie v Edwards* (1848) 2 HLC 74, 9 ER 1020, discussed in paras 4.79 above and 10.12 below.

[35] *Target Holdings Ltd v Redferns* [1996] AC 421, 434–5.

[36] *Ex p Adamson, re Collie* (1878) 8 Ch D 807, 819; *Webb v Stenton* (1883) 11 QBD 518, 530; *Wickstead v Browne* (1992) 30 NSWLR 1, 14–15; *Goodwin v Duggan* (1996) 41 NSWLR 158, 166; *Coventry v Charter Pacific Corporation Ltd* (2005) 227 CLR 234 at [47] (fraud). See also para. 8.83 above. Compare *Space Investments Ltd v Canadian Imperial Bank of Commerce Trust Co (Bahamas) Ltd* [1986] 1 WLR 1072, 1074.

[37] As in *Taylor v Taylor* (1875) LR 20 Eq 155, for which see para. 10.08 above.

[38] See *Reed v Oury* [2002] EWHC 369 (Ch) at [62].

[39] See para. 10.02 above. *Lloyds Bank NZA Ltd v National Safety Council of Australia* [1993] 2 VR 506 is consistent with this view. A bank held security provided by a customer for a debt. The customer defaulted and the security was sold. After paying the secured debt, a surplus remained, which the bank credited to an account in the name of the customer. The customer was in liquidation, and the question was whether the bank could set off the surplus against a separate debt owing by the customer to the bank. The Appeal Division of the Victorian Supreme Court held that the surplus proceeds from the sale of the security were held on trust for the customer and as such could not be the subject of a set-off in the liquidation. See paras 10.36–10.46 below. An issue that was not addressed was whether there was in fact a traceable and subsisting trust fund. The surplus proceeds were credited to the customer's account, but the credit balance on a bank account is not property held on trust by the bank. It is simply a debt owing by the bank to the customer. It seems to have been assumed, nevertheless, in the *Lloyds Bank* case that there was a subsisting trust. See in particular at 514–15.

[40] Compare *Consul Development Pty Ltd v DPC Estates Pty Ltd* (1975) 132 CLR 373, 397, Gibbs J referring to: 'The strict rule of equity that forbids a person in a fiduciary position to profit from his position . . .' See also para. 8.88 above.

[41] See above.

However, an order in that form ordinarily is not made in the case of a trust which at the time of the action has come to an end, as opposed to a traditional trust in which there is no one beneficiary who is absolutely entitled to the trust property and which is still subsisting,[42] although an order to reconstitute the fund in the former situation has not been wholly ruled out.[43] Alternatively, it may be possible in some cases to invoke the equitable maxim that equity regards as done that which ought to have been done, so that a separate trust fund may be deemed to have been established against which there cannot be a set-off.[44]

In a Western Australian case, *The Bell Group Ltd v Westpac Banking Corporation*,[45] some banks were held to be liable as constructive trustees under the first limb of *Barnes v Addy*[46] for knowing receipt of trust property.[47] In the circumstances of the case, Owen J considered that a personal remedy was sufficient to do justice between the parties and that a proprietary remedy was not necessary. The plaintiffs were in liquidation, and the banks argued that they were entitled under the insolvency set-off section to set off that personal liability against debts owing to them by the plaintiffs. His Honour held that the constructive trust militated against a set-off, notwithstanding that the remedy was personal rather than proprietary.[48] His Honour justified that conclusion on the ground that the constructive trust destroyed mutuality. Mutuality means that cross-demands must be between the same parties and be held in the same capacity or right or interest.[49] The basis of the proposition that there was no mutuality in the case of a purely personal liability as a constructive trustee, where there was no proprietary remedy, was not explained.[50]

10.11

E. Equitable Set-off

Different considerations apply in the case of equitable set-off. Unlike insolvency set-off and set-off under the Statutes of Set-off, the better view, notwithstanding recent statements in the Court of Appeal suggesting the contrary,[51] is that mutuality is not an indispensable

10.12

---

[42] *Target Holdings Ltd v Redferns* [1996] AC 421, 434–6; *Youyang Pty Ltd v Minter Ellison Morris Fletcher* (2003) 212 CLR 484 at [37].

[43] *Target Holdings Ltd v Redferns* [1996] AC 421, 434–5; *Lewis v Nortex Ltd* [2005] NSWSC 482 at [31]. It has been suggested that the same principles should apply in granting relief against a person who is liable as an accessory to a breach of trust. See *Lewis v Nortex Ltd* at [33].

[44] See para. 8.91 above.

[45] [2008] WASC 239.

[46] (1874) LR 9 Ch App 244.

[47] The transfer of the property in the *Bell Group* case was effected through breaches of fiduciary duty owed by directors to various companies, which transfers were subsequently rescinded, as opposed to a transfer of trust property by the trustee in breach of trust. Owen J accepted that the property nevertheless was received subject to a species of trust. See at [2008] WASC 239 at [4797]–[4804].

[48] See [2008] WASC 239 at [9665]–[9676].

[49] See para. 11.01 below.

[50] Compare para. 10.02 above. As support for his conclusion that the constructive trust destroyed mutuality, Owen J referred to *Lloyds Bank NZA Ltd v National Safety Council of Australia* [1993] 2 VR 506. In that case, however, it seems to have been assumed that there was a subsisting trust fund. See the discussion by J. D. Phillips J at 514–15, but note the comment made in relation to that point at para. 10.10n above.

[51] *Muscat v Smith* [2003] 1 WLR 2853 at [42] and [45]; *R (on the Application of Burkett) v London Borough of Hammersmith and Fulham* [2004] EWCA Civ 1342 at [58]; *Edlington Properties Ltd v J. H. Fenner & Co Ltd* [2006] 1 WLR 1583 at [20]. See para. 4.69 above.

requirement of equitable set-off.[52] Therefore, the fact that a claim is proprietary in nature should not suffice to preclude an equitable set-off on the ground of lack of mutuality. The point is illustrated by *Baillie v Edwards*,[53] a decision of the House of Lords in 1848. Baillie had a life interest in an estate. Innes made advances in respect of the estate on terms that Baillie should not be personally liable for them, but rather that Innes would look only to the estate for payment. The effect was that Innes had a charge or lien on the estate but no personal claim against Baillie. In a suit in equity instituted by Baillie to redeem the estate, the House of Lords held that Baillie was entitled to have Innes' claim against the estate paid and satisfied by the application to it of part of a debt owing by Innes to Baillie. The question was regarded as one of set-off.[54] Lord Lyndhurst earlier had refused to allow a set-off, emphasizing lack of mutuality.[55] But in a successful appeal to the House of Lords Baillie's counsel justified the claim on the ground that it was in the nature of an equitable set-off,[56] a submission which the House of Lords appeared to accept. This was an instance of an equitable set-off against a proprietary claim.

10.13   There have been judicial statements which suggest that equitable set-off in principle may be open to a trustee who is obliged to account for a trust fund.[57] However, the circumstances must be such as to support a set-off, and ordinarily a beneficiary's claim to recover a trust fund would not be impeached by the trustee's personal cross-claim against the beneficiary so as to permit an equitable set-off.[58] It was on this basis that a set-off was denied in *Guinness Plc v Saunders*.[59] A director of a company was paid £5.2 million by the company for services in connection with a takeover bid. The Court of Appeal held that the director received the payment in breach of fiduciary duty and that he held it as constructive trustee for the company. The court further held that the director could not set off a claim in *quantum meruit* against the company in respect of the services performed, Fox LJ[60] commenting that the cross-claim for a *quantum meruit* did not impeach or determine the trust which continued to subsist.[61] This was so notwithstanding that the trust and the *quantum meruit* claim arose from the same transaction.[62]

---

[52] See paras 4.67–4.83 above.

[53] (1848) 2 HLC 74, 9 ER 1020. See also para. 4.79 above.

[54] See (1848) 2 HLC 74, 81, 84, 9 ER 1020, 1023, 1024.

[55] *Baillie v Innes* (1845) 14 LJ Ch 341, 343, Lord Lyndhurst commenting: 'I think there was no mutual credit between the parties. Mr Baillie, the plaintiff, trusts Mr Innes – gives credit to Mr Innes; but Mr Innes on his side gives no credit whatever to Mr Baillie; he looked to the estate, and the estate only; and, as there was no mutuality of debt, there is not, also, any mutuality of credit, according to my opinion and my view of the case.'

[56] (1848) 2 HLC 74, 79, 9 ER 1020, 1022. Compare the (unsuccessful) argument of counsel for Mr Innes at 80, 1023.

[57] See *Roxborough v Rothmans of Pall Mall Australia Ltd* (2001) 208 CLR 516 at [67] (Gummow J) and *Pardoe v Price* (1847) 16 M & W 451, 458–9, 153 ER 1266, 1269.

[58] The concept of impeachment of title is the traditional foundation of equitable set-off. See paras 4.02–4.03 above.

[59] [1988] 1 WLR 863, affirming *Guinness Plc v Saunders* [1988] BCLC 43. See also *Zemco Ltd v Jerrom-Pugh* [1993] BCC 275 (CA); *Neptune (Vehicle Washing Equipment) Ltd v Fitzgerald* [1996] Ch 274, 278 *per* Lightman J ('The defendant correctly concedes that he cannot set off any claim for damages against the plaintiff's proprietary claim'); *Lehman Brothers International (Europe) v CRC Credit Fund Ltd* [2009] EWHC 3228 (Ch) at [325]–[335].

[60] Glidewell LJ and Sir Frederick Lawton agreeing.

[61] [1988] 1 WLR 863, 870.

[62] See Browne-Wilkinson VC at first instance [1988] BCLC 43, 51.

F. Authority to Turn Property into Money – *Rose v Hart*

(1) The general principle

Set-off only applies when the claims the subject of the proposed set-off are commensurable, in other words when they are such that they would result in money demands.[63] This was established authoritatively by Gibbs CJ in *Rose v Hart*,[64] when he held that a fuller with whom cloths had been deposited by a person who later became bankrupt could not retain the cloths as a set-off against the bankrupt's indebtedness to him. On the other hand, the Chief Justice recognized that there may be a set-off where goods were deposited with a direction to turn them into money, which has occurred.

10.14

> Something more is certainly meant here by mutual credits than the words mutual debts import; and yet, upon the final settlement, it is enacted merely that one debt shall be set against another. We think this shews that the legislature meant such credits only as must in their nature terminate in debts, as where a debt is due from one party, and credit given by him on the other for a sum of money payable at a future day, and which will then become a debt, or where there is a debt on one side, and a delivery of property with directions to turn it into money on the other; in such case the credit given by the delivery of the property must in its nature terminate in a debt, the balance will be taken on the two debts, and the words of the statute will in all respects be complied with: but where there is a mere deposit of property, without any authority to turn it into money, no debt can ever arise out of it, and, therefore, it is not a credit within the meaning of the statute.[65]

It has been argued[66] that the allowance of a set-off when there is a direction to turn property into money owes its existence to the omission of a relevant fact from the report of Lord Hardwicke's judgment in *Ex p Deeze*.[67] In *Ex p Deeze*, a packer was allowed to retain six bales of cloth sent to him for packing and pressing as against the assignee in bankruptcy of the owner, not only for the cost of his work upon the cloth, but also for the owner's debt to him on a loan. In the course of his judgment, Lord Hardwicke made a number of references to the law of mutual credit, although later, in *Ex p Ockenden*,[68] he said that there had been evidence in *Ex p Deeze* that it was usual for packers to lend money to clothiers, and for a packer to retain cloths as security, not only for the work done upon them, but also for any loans made. The case, then, was not one of set-off at all, but it rather concerned a lien arising from the custom of the trade.[69] Despite this, *Ex p Deeze* was still treated in

10.15

---

[63] See ch. 9 above.

[64] (1818) 8 Taunt 499, 129 ER 477.

[65] (1818) 8 Taunt 499, 506, 129 ER 477, 480.

[66] Bishop, 'Set-off in the administration of insolvent and bankrupt estates' (1901) 1 *Columbia Law Review* 377. See also *Young v Bank of Bengal* (1836) 1 Moore 150, 169–71, 12 ER 771, 779–80.

[67] (1748) 1 Atk 228, 26 ER 146.

[68] (1754) 1 Atk 235, 237, 26 ER 151, 152.

[69] This omission from the report of *Ex p Deeze* inspired Lord Mansfield's condemnation of Atkyn's reports as 'extremely inaccurate'. See *Olive v Smith* (1813) 5 Taunt 56, 64, 128 ER 607, 610. An extract from Lord Hardwicke's notes on *Ex p Deeze* is set out in a note to *Young v Bank of Bengal* (1836) 1 Moore 150, 170, 12 ER 771, 779. Lord Henley inclined to the view that Lord Hardwicke in fact had changed his mind in *Ex p Ockenden* as regards his earlier decision in *Ex p Deeze*, and that Lord Hardwicke took hold of the circumstance of there being evidence of a usage in *Ex p Deeze* in order to reconcile his two decisions. See Henley, *A Digest of the Bankrupt Law* (3rd edn, 1832), 190.

subsequent cases as an authority on set-off.[70] Gibbs CJ in *Rose v Hart* said that he 'could not persuade [himself] to break in upon a class of cases so long established',[71] and his statement of the law represented an attempt to reconcile the cases decided after *Ex p Deeze* with the stipulation in the set-off section in the 1732 bankruptcy legislation[72] that 'one debt may be set against another'. One such case was *French v Fenn*.[73] The bankrupt and the defendant together had purchased a string of pearls, the agreement between them being that the defendant would sell the pearls and that they would then share in any resulting profit. The pearls were sold after the bankruptcy, and it was held that the defendant could set off the bankrupt's share of the profit against the bankrupt's debt to the defendant for the bankrupt's share of the purchase money, which had been advanced by the defendant. There were also the cases of *Parker v Carter*[74] and *Olive v Smith*,[75] in each of which an insurance broker had been entrusted with a policy of insurance with authority to collect the insurance money in the event of a loss. It was held that the broker could set off insurance money received after the insured's bankruptcy against the insured's general indebtedness to him.[76] This included debts which were not a part of the insurance account, and consequently were not within an insurance broker's general lien.

10.16 Since *Rose v Hart*, the principle has been applied in a number of other situations, for example where goods or their documents of title[77] were delivered to a person for the purpose of sale,[78] and where bills of exchange were deposited with a bank to collect and remit the proceeds.[79]

10.17 Gibbs CJ said in *Rose v Hart* that, for mutual credit, the transaction in question must be such that it 'must' end in a debt, and it was on that ground that the Privy Council in *Young v Bank of Bengal*[80] later criticized the decision in *Olive v Smith*. Since *Rose v Hart*, however, the courts have expanded the concept of giving credit, so that it is now regarded as sufficient if the transaction would naturally or in the ordinary course of business end in a debt. It is not necessary that the transaction be such that it must of necessity have that result.[81]

---

[70] See e.g. *French v Fenn* (1783) 3 Dougl 257, 99 ER 642; *Smith v Hodson* (1791) 4 TR 211, 100 ER 979. Compare *Olive v Smith* (1813) 5 Taunt 56, 128 ER 609.

[71] (1818) 8 Taunt 499, 505, 129 ER 477, 480. See also Lord Mansfield in *Olive v Smith* (1813) 5 Taunt 56, 67, 128 ER 607, 611.

[72] (1732) 5 Geo II, c. 30, s. 28.

[73] (1783) 3 Dougl 257, 99 ER 642.

[74] (1788), unreported but noted in Cooke, *The Bankrupt Laws* (8th edn, 1823) vol. 1, 578.

[75] (1813) 5 Taunt 56, 128 ER 607.

[76] See also *Chalmers v Page* (1820) 3 B & Ald 697, 106 ER 816.

[77] *M'Gillivray v Simson* (1826) 2 Car & P 320, 172 ER 145, affirmed 5 LJOSKB 53 (bills of lading).

[78] *Palmer v Day & Sons* [1895] 2 QB 618 (sale by an auctioneer); *Hunter v Official Assignee of Bispham* (1898) 17 NZLR 175 (sale by an auctioneer); *Re Lindsay* (1890) 9 NZLR 192; *Re Rose, ex p Hasluck & Garrard* (1894) 1 Mans 218; *Re Clements* (1931) 7 ABC 255; *Rolls Razor Ltd v Cox* [1967] 1 QB 552 (company salesman). See also *Holmes v Kidd* (1858) 3 H & N 891, 157 ER 729, in which it was agreed that the proceeds of sale of property were to be applied in reduction of the debt, and *New Zealand and Australian Land Co v Watson* (1881) 7 QBD 374, in which the court rejected the proposition that the proceeds in that case were impressed with a trust in favour of the owner.

[79] *Naoroji v The Chartered Bank of India* (1868) LR 3 CP 444.

[80] (1836) 1 Moore 150, 12 ER 771. See also Parke B during argument in *Alsager v Currie* (1844) 12 M & W 751, 754–5, 152 ER 1402, 1403, commenting on *Young v Bank of Bengal*.

[81] See para. 7.04 above.

Moreover, since *Young v Bank of Bengal* the scope of the set-off section has been enlarged to include claims arising out of mutual dealings. The decision in *Olive v Smith* may be objectionable on the ground that the insurance proceeds may have been impressed with a trust, depending on whether it was intended that they be kept separate from the broker's own funds or whether they should form an item in the account between the parties, but this is a difficulty with the *Rose v Hart* cases generally.[82] Apart from that possible objection, and notwithstanding a recent suggestion to the contrary,[83] *Olive v Smith* would appear to be alive and well.

Set-off against a trust fund

In some cases the allowance of a set-off in the circumstances contemplated by *Rose v Hart* **10.18** may produce an anomaly. When property is deposited with a person with directions to turn it into money, the depository's status often is that of a fiduciary, and any money received in respect of the property is impressed with a trust. Accordingly, the allowance of a set-off may conflict with the general principle that a trustee must account for the trust fund without a set-off in respect of an independent debt due to the trustee in his or her personal capacity.[84] In the *Rose v Hart* cases, on the other hand, the depository's authority to turn the property into money and to receive the proceeds has been regarded as a sufficient source of credit to found a set-off in the depositor's bankruptcy, and the question whether there was a trust has not been regarded as critical.[85]

It is not universally accepted that the *Rose v Hart* set-off is anomalous. Professor Goode has **10.19** suggested that these cases constitute instances in which the proceeds are not in fact impressed with a trust.[86] His argument is that the depository extends credit to the depositor in reliance on the prospective receipt of the proceeds of the property, for which the depositor gives credit to the depository. Accordingly, it is suggested that the true basis of *Rose v Hart* is that the depository has implied authority, by virtue of their mutual dealings, to regard him or herself as a debtor for a sum equal to the proceeds, and not as a trustee of the proceeds. This would not explain all the cases, however. It is, of course, correct to say that, while a depository is often a trustee in respect of the proceeds of property deposited with him or her with directions to turn it into money, this is not always the case. For example, if there is an ongoing business relationship between the depositor and the depository such that the depository is regularly entrusted with property to be turned into money, the courts may conclude that it was intended that the nature of the relationship in respect of the proceeds should be one of debt rather than trust.[87] A critical question is whether it was intended

---

[82] See below.
[83] It is suggested in Wood, *English and International Set-off* (1989), 563 that *Olive v Smith* was probably overruled by *Rose v Hart*, although Gibbs CJ in *Rose v Hart* seems to have regarded *Olive v Smith* as consistent with his formulation of the principle.
[84] See para. 10.02 above.
[85] In addition to the cases referred to below, compare *Naoroji v The Chartered Bank of India* (1868) LR 3 CP 444 with *Re Brown, ex p Plitt* (1889) 6 Morr 81 in the context of a bill deposited with a bank to collect and remit the proceeds.
[86] Goode, *Principles of Corporate Insolvency Law* (3rd edn, 2005), 234–5.
[87] Finn, *Fiduciary Obligations* (1977), 105. See e.g. the retention of title cases, *Hendy Lennox (Industrial Engines) Ltd v Grahame Puttick Ltd* [1984] 1 WLR 485 and *Re Andrabell Ltd* [1984] 3 All ER 407, referred to in Goode, *Principles of Corporate Insolvency Law* (3rd edn, 2005), 235.

that the depository should keep the proceeds separate from his or her own money.[88] An obligation to keep moneys in a separate account is a hallmark duty of a trustee.[89] But in the case of the *Rose v Hart* set-off the turning of property into money has not always been the subject of an ongoing business relationship between the parties. Further, in the absence of a relationship of that nature, the argument that the basis of *Rose v Hart* is that the depository extends credit in reliance on his or her prospective receipt of the proceeds would not apply when the depositor's indebtedness to the depository arose before, rather than after, the deposit. In such a case, it could hardly be said that there was reliance by the depository in extending credit.[90]

10.20   Consider *Palmer v Day & Sons*.[91] In September 1894, one Langton gave instructions to the defendant auctioneers to sell some furniture, and also to sell his house. The furniture auction took place on 15 and 19 October. The house was put up for auction on 8 November, but no sale was effected. A sum of approximately £31 was due to the auctioneers in respect of their charges for the auctions, of which approximately £24 related to the unsuccessful attempt to sell the house. Between the date of the furniture auction and the attempted auction of the house, some pictures which had been passed in at the furniture auction were sent to the auctioneers for the purpose of sale. This sale took place after the attempt to sell the house, and also after Langton became bankrupt. Lord Russell of Killowen CJ and Charles J held that the auctioneers could set off against the bankrupt's indebtedness to them for £31 in respect of the unpaid charges their obligation to account for the proceeds of sale of the pictures.[92] However, the instructions to sell the house were given before the pictures were sent to the auctioneers for sale, in which case it would be difficult to argue that the auctioneers gave credit to Langton for their charges in respect of the auction of the house in reliance on their prospective receipt of the proceeds of sale of the pictures. There was no discussion in the judgment as to whether the proceeds were impressed with a trust, which is curious given that the Court of Appeal only some eight years earlier had held that auctioneers

---

[88] *Re Nanwa Gold Mines Ld* [1955] 1 WLR 1080; *Re Bond Worth Ltd* [1980] 1 Ch 228, 260–1; *Chattis Nominees Pty Ltd v Norman Ross Homeworks Pty Ltd* (1992) 28 NSWLR 338, 346 ('one of the tests is whether he is obliged to keep the money in a separate account'); *Westdeutsche Landesbank Girozentrale v Islington LBC* [1996] AC 669, 712; *Royal Trust Bank v National Westminster Bank plc* [1996] 2 BCLC 682, 701; *Triffit Nurseries v Salads Etcetera Ltd* [2000] 1 BCLC 761, 764; Finn, *Fiduciary Obligations* (1977), 103–4; Millett, 'Restitution and Constructive Trusts' (1998) 114 LQR 399, 407. Compare *Stephens Travel Service International Pty Ltd v Qantas Airways Ltd* (1988) 13 NSWLR 331, 349, referred to in *Re ILG Travel Ltd* [1995] 2 BCLC 128, 148–52, 156, *Associated Alloys Pty Ltd v ACN 001 452 106 Pty Ltd* (2000) 202 CLR 588 at [31] and *Walker v Corboy* (1990) 19 NSWLR 382, 389, 397–8. However, the question whether there is an obligation to keep money separate does not conclusively determine the issue. See *Puma Australia Pty Ltd v Sportsman's Australia Ltd (No. 2)* [1994] 2 Qd R 159, 177; Finn, *loc. cit.*

[89] *Puma Australia Pty Ltd v Sportsman's Australia Ltd (No. 2)* [1994] 2 Qd R 159, 162.

[90] The relationships of debt and trust are not mutually exclusive. See *Barclays Bank Ltd v Quistclose Investments Ltd* [1970] AC 567.

[91] [1895] 2 QB 618. See also *Webb v Smith* (1885) 30 Ch D 192 (Statutes of Set-off) and *Hunter v Official Assignee of Bispham* (1898) 17 NZLR 175.

[92] It was held that there were separate contracts for the sale of the house and the furniture (including the pictures), so that the auctioneers' lien on the proceeds did not extend to their charges in respect of the house.

receive proceeds of sale in a fiduciary capacity for their customers.[93] This suggests that the existence or otherwise of a trust was not considered to be relevant to the question of set-off. Nor is there anything in the judgment to suggest that this was a case in which there was an ongoing business relationship such that it may have been intended that the relationship should only be one of debt.

Proceeds received before the bankruptcy

In *Rose v Hart* the proceeds obtained from turning property into money were received after **10.21** bankruptcy,[94] but the same result should follow when the receipt of the proceeds occurred before then. Furthermore, set-off under the Statutes of Set-off would be subject to the same principle.[95]

(2) The circumstances in which the set-off applies

The circumstances in which *Rose v Hart* set-off may apply are considered below. **10.22**

Authority to turn property into money

A person holding chattels without authority to turn them into money, and who is sued **10.23** by the owner's trustee in bankruptcy for their return, cannot bring the value of the chattels into account as a set-off against the bankrupt's indebtedness to him or her. The claims are not commensurable.[96] This has been held to be the case when the chattels are in that person's possession wrongfully,[97] or merely for use,[98] or for the performance of work upon them,[99] or, having been lodged as a security, the secured debt has been paid.[100] It would also apply when a company has granted a charge over chattels to a creditor, but the charge is void as against a liquidator under the applicable companies legislation for non-registration.[101]

The remedies under the Torts (Interference With Goods) Act. The Torts (Interference **10.24** With Goods) Act 1977, s. 2 abolished detinue, which is the action formerly used to obtain the return of goods wrongfully detained. Section 3(2) instead provides that, in proceedings

---

[93] *Crowther v Elgood* (1887) 34 Ch D 691.

[94] See e.g. *French v Fenn* (1783) 3 Dougl 257, 99 ER 642; *Olive v Smith* (1813) 5 Taunt 56, 128 ER 607; *Naoroji v The Chartered Bank of India* (1868) LR 3 CP 444 (it appears more clearly from the report in 37 LJCP 221 that the proceeds in respect of most of the bills were received after the date of the deed of inspectorship); *Astley v Gurney* (1869) LR 4 CP 714; *Palmer v Day & Sons* [1895] 2 QB 618.

[95] In *Webb v Smith* (1885) 30 Ch D 192, the Court of Appeal assumed that the auctioneer had a right of set-off under the Statutes of Set-off in respect of proceeds of sale in his hands.

[96] See ch. 9 above.

[97] *Lord (Trustee of) v Great Eastern Railway Co* [1908] 2 KB 54; *Re Leeholme Stud Pty Ltd* [1965] NSWR 1649. See also *Peacock v Anderson* (1878) 4 NZ Jur (NS) SC 67.

[98] *Ex p Roy, re Sillence* (1877) 7 Ch D 70; *Re Winter, ex p Bolland* (1878) 8 Ch D 225; *Rolls Razor Ltd v Cox* [1967] 1 QB 552.

[99] *Rose v Hart* (1818) 8 Taunt 499, 129 ER 477.

[100] *Eberle's Hotels and Restaurant Co Ltd v E Jonas & Brothers* (1887) 18 QBD 459. See also *Key v Flint* (1817) 8 Taunt 21, 129 ER 289, petition in equity dismissed *Ex p Flint* (1818) 1 Swans 30, 36 ER 285.

[101] See *Smith v Bridgend County BC* [2002] 1 AC 336 in relation to equitable set-off, but it should also apply to insolvency set-off. See in particular at [35] and [36]. The relevant legislation is now the Companies Act 2006, s. 874. In Australia, see the Corporations Act 2001 (Cth), s. 266.

against a person who is in possession or control of the goods of another for wrongful interference with the goods, the relief can take the form of:

(a) an order for delivery of the goods, and for payment of any consequential damages, or

(b) an order for delivery of the goods, but giving the defendant the alternative of paying damages by reference to the value of the goods, together in either alternative with payment of any consequential damages, or

(c) damages.

Relief under (a) is at the discretion of the court, and the claimant may choose between the others.

10.25 The better view is that the Act has not changed the position in relation to set-off. If a claimant claims the return of the goods, it should not make any difference for the purpose of set-off that relief is ordered in accordance with (b) and that the defendant chooses to pay damages. This is consistent with the position formerly applicable in an action in detinue.[102] The form of judgment in a detinue action was for delivery of the chattel or payment of its assessed value together with damages for detention. The defendant in effect had an option, although the Common Law Procedure Act 1854, s. 78 gave the court the power to order delivery up of the chattel, without giving the defendant the option of paying its assessed value. In *Eberle's Hotels and Restaurant Co Ltd v E Jonas & Brothers*,[103] the plaintiff company had deposited some cigars with the defendants as security for a debt. The company was ordered to be wound up and, the debt secured by the cigars having been subsequently paid, the liquidator brought an action in detinue for their return. The defendants claimed that they were entitled to have the value of the cigars assessed and then set off against another unsecured debt owing to them by the plaintiff. The Court of Appeal, however, held that the plaintiff was entitled to the return of the cigars without being subjected to a set-off. An interesting aspect of the case is a comment by counsel during argument, and the responses of Fry LJ and Lord Esher MR. Counsel suggested that, if the judge in a detinue action declined to order delivery of the chattels, so that the defendant instead could pay their assessed value, the claim would be a money claim which could be set off. Fry LJ responded that the application or otherwise of the insolvency set-off section depended on the state of things at the time of the winding up, and at that time there was a right to delivery of the cigars on payment of the secured debt. That was not a right that was susceptible to a set-off.[104] Similarly, Lord Esher asked,[105] 'Can the applicability of [the set-off section] depend on what the judge may do at the trial? Must it not depend on the nature of the respective rights of the parties antecedently to the action?' This suggests that, even if specific restitution had not been ordered, a set-off would have been denied. Similarly, under the regime set out in the Torts (Interference With Goods) Act, if the claimant seeks an order for the delivery of the goods, the availability of a set-off under the insolvency legislation should not depend upon whether the defendant subsequently elects to pay damages in accordance

---

[102] See generally the discussion in *General and Finance Facilities Ltd v Cooks Cars (Romford) Ltd* [1963] 1 WLR 644, 650.

[103] (1887) 18 QBD 459.

[104] (1887) 18 QBD 459, 463. See also Fry LJ at 469 and 470.

[105] (1887) 18 QBD 459, 464.

with the relief ordered. Nor would equity provide relief by way of an equitable set-off in this situation.[106] That conclusion in relation to insolvency set-off is also suggested by cases in which property that initially was in issue was sold with the consent of the parties after the owner's bankruptcy. The courts emphasized that the right at the date of the bankruptcy was to the return of the property, and the fact that the dispute subsequently became one over the proceeds of sale did not let in a set-off.[107]

Destruction of the goods.   Similarly, if the goods deposited with another party were destroyed after the depositor's bankruptcy, so that at the date of the bankruptcy the bankrupt's estate was entitled to the return of the goods, the fact that the only remedy later available to the trustee is to claim damages should not let in a set-off. However, what if the goods were destroyed before the bankruptcy, so that at the date of the bankruptcy specific restitution was not possible, and the trustee accordingly is only in a position to claim damages under s. 3(2)(c) of the Act?[108] A set-off may be available,[109] but it would depend on the circumstances. A set-off can only proceed where there are mutual debts, mutual credits or other mutual dealings. A damages claim is not a debt. Nor does it come within the concept of giving credit.[110] Moreover, in the case of a damages claim for wrongful interference with goods or chattels, the claim often will not arise out of a dealing between the parties, which should have the consequence that there is no set-off in the bankruptcy.[111] In *Re Winter. Ex p Bolland*,[112] Bacon VC said that a mere authority to possess or use particular chattels unaccompanied by a power to sell is not a dealing, although Lord Esher MR adopted a less dogmatic approach in the *Eberle's Hotels* case.[113] In his view, whatever comes within an ordinary business transaction would be a dealing for the purpose of the set-off section,[114] and he suggested that the deposit of the cigars in that case to secure a debt would have constituted a dealing. On the other hand, a wrongful taking of property would not be a dealing for the purpose of the set-off section.[115]

Money claims

The essence of a *Rose v Hart* set-off is that property was deposited with a person with authority to turn it into money, under circumstances not amounting to a preference.[116] The authority must have been acted upon, so that the claim against the depository is for a

10.26

10.27

---

[106]   This is suggested by *Smith v Bridgend County BC* [2002] 1 AC 336, esp. at [36].

[107]   *Re Winter, ex p Bolland* (1878) 8 Ch D 225; *Lord (Trustee of) v Great Eastern Railway Co* [1908] 2 KB 54 (reversed on other grounds [1909] AC 109). See also *Ex p Ockenden* (1754) 1 Atk 235, 26 ER 151.

[108]   Cozens Hardy MR left the question open in *Lord (Trustee of) v Great Eastern Railway Co* [1908] 2 KB 54, 78.

[109]   Compare *Peacock v Anderson* (1878) 4 NZ Jur (NS) SC 67, 70, although the comment by Richmond J was made in the context that a set-off was not available generally against an unliquidated claim. That is no longer the position. See paras 8.51–8.61 above.

[110]   *Palmer v Day & Sons* [1895] 2 QB 618, 621. See paras 7.05 and 7.06 above.

[111]   See para. 8.53 above.

[112]   (1878) 8 Ch D 225, 228.

[113]   (1887) 18 QBD 459, 465.

[114]   See para. 7.08 above.

[115]   *Re Leeholme Stud Pty Ltd* [1965] NSWR 1649, 1650–1; *Manson v Smith* [1997] 2 BCLC 161, 164; *Smith v Bridgend County BC* [2002] 1 AC 336 at [35].

[116]   *Castendyck and Focke v Official Assignee of S A McLellan* (1887) 6 NZLR 67, 75.

sum of money which can be set off against the depositor's own indebtedness to produce a balance on the account. In *Rolls Razor Ltd v Cox*[117] a set-off admittedly was allowed notwithstanding that the authority had not been acted upon, but the better view is that the case was wrongly decided.[118]

Unrevoked authority

10.28   An effective revocation of the authority to turn the property into money should prevent a set-off.[119] However, according to the Court of Appeal in *Rolls Razor v Cox*,[120] a revocation before the bankruptcy or liquidation of the depositor will not always be effective. In that case the authority of the company's salesman to sell the company's goods was revoked after the board of directors publicly announced that the company was insolvent, which occurred before the resolution to wind up the company. The Court of Appeal nevertheless allowed the salesman to set off the value of the goods still in his possession, Lord Denning commenting that: 'this right [of set-off] could not be taken away by the insolvent person at the last moment revoking the power of sale.'[121] The courts should reconsider this decision. The state of the company's solvency before the relevant date may go to the question whether the qualification to the insolvency set-off section would operate to preclude a set-off.[122] However, the qualification merely defines a point beyond which a set-off may not be acquired, as opposed to a point beyond which one party may no longer act so as to deprive the other of a set-off in a subsequent insolvency administration. There is no justification in the language of the set-off section for the view that a company may not act in the interest of its general body of creditors before the commencement of liquidation in order to prevent the depletion of the estate through a set-off. Indeed, Lord Denning's view would appear to conflict with an opinion earlier expressed by Pollock MR in *Re City Life Assurance Co Ltd (Stephenson's Case)*[123] in relation to an earlier insolvency set-off section, in the Bankruptcy Act 1914, s. 31.

> It is suggested that there was an equity between the policy holder and the company that the policy holder should be able to invoke the principle of s. 31 if and when he required to do so, and that the company are not entitled to say that there is no mutuality, because under the dealings between the policy holders and the company the principles of s. 31 ought to have remained available to the policy holder. That argument does not, to my mind, carry weight. There is no equity that the rights which govern the parties, if and when s. 31 applies, should be always available. Sect 31 appears to me to be applicable if and when there is a bankruptcy or winding up of a company, but until that time has come, the law which governs the rights of the parties is not in force and cannot be held to be an inchoate right which the policy

---

[117] [1967] 1 QB 552.

[118] See paras 9.02–9.03 above.

[119] *Palmer v Day & Sons* [1895] 2 QB 618, 623; *Gromal (UK) Ltd v WT Shipping Ltd* unreported, CA (Ackner and Slade LJJ), 13 July 1984.

[120] [1967] 1 QB 552.

[121] [1967] 1 QB 552, 571. The point was not considered by the other member of the majority, Danckwerts LJ, but since he upheld the salesman's right to a set-off he presumably agreed with Lord Denning. Winn LJ in his dissenting judgment said that the revocation of the authority was effective to stop a set-off.

[122] See paras 6.66–6.99 above.

[123] [1926] 1 Ch 191, 217.

holder had as against the company at the time when the winding up of the company had not been commenced or, indeed, thought of.

Pollock MR referred to the time before the winding up had been thought of, but his thesis **10.29** was that there is no equity at any time before the winding up that the possibility of a set-off should be always available. Lord Denning noted that the set-off section sanctions the taking of an account where 'there have been mutual credits'. He said that the use of the past tense indicated that: 'when the mutual dealings *have been* such as to give rise to mutual credits, there is a right of set-off.'[124] If that were a correct interpretation, however, it is difficult to see why it would be that only a 'last moment' revocation would be ineffective. Moreover, if an insolvent debtor may not act at the last moment to take away the possibility of a set-off by revoking a power of sale, the question would arise whether an insolvent debtor could adopt other courses of action which similarly would have the effect of destroying the possibility of a set-off in a future bankruptcy or liquidation, for example an assignment by the debtor to a third party of the benefit of his or her cross-claim against his creditor.[125] But there is no reason why the debtor should be restricted in that regard. The better view is that the set-off section requires not only that there should 'have been' mutual credits at some stage before the bankruptcy or liquidation, but that those mutual credits should still be subsisting at that date. It introduces uncertainty into the law to say that a debtor facing bankruptcy or a winding up may not revoke an authority 'at the last moment'.[126] In *Rolls Razor*, there was a public declaration of insolvency, but in many cases it would be difficult to say when a debtor became aware that bankruptcy or a winding up was unavoidable.

Bankruptcy and liquidation as a revocation of authority. In applying *Rose v Hart*, it **10.30** appears not to matter that the proceeds in question may have been received after the depositor's bankruptcy or liquidation,[127] provided that the deposit of the property occurred before then under circumstances not giving rise to a preference,[128] and provided also that the authority had not been revoked.[129] But, as Dr Oditah has queried,[130] it is not clear why the fact of bankruptcy itself in some cases would not operate as a revocation of an otherwise revocable authority in accordance with normal principles.

---

[124] [1967] 1 QB 552, 571.

[125] Compare *Re City Life Assurance Co Ltd (Stephenson's Case)* [1926] 1 Ch 191, 214. See also paras 17.39–17.40 below in relation to the application of the insolvency set-off section after an assignment.

[126] In the *Rolls Razor* case this meant about a month before the extraordinary resolution to wind up the company.

[127] See e.g. *French v Fenn* (1783) 3 Dougl 257, 99 ER 642; *Olive v Smith* (1813) 5 Taunt 56, 128 ER 607; *Naoroji v The Chartered Bank of India* (1868) LR 3 CP 444 (it appears more clearly from the report at 37 LJCP 221 that the proceeds in respect of most of the bills were received after the date of the deed of inspectorship); *Astley v Gurney* (1869) LR 4 CP 714; *Palmer v Day & Sons* [1895] 2 QB 618.

[128] *Castendyck and Focke v Official Assignee of S A McLellan* (1887) 6 NZLR 67, 75.

[129] See *Naoroji v The Chartered Bank of India* (1868) LR 3 CP 444, 452 (in the context of a deed of inspectorship under the Bankruptcy Act 1861 which, when registered, had an effect equivalent to an adjudication in bankruptcy), and *Palmer v Day & Sons* [1895] 2 QB 618, 623. Compare *Rolls Razor Ltd v Cox* [1967] 1 QB 552 (above).

[130] Oditah, 'Assets and the treatment of claims in insolvency' (1992) 108 LQR 459, 467 n. 55, and also Oditah, *Legal Aspects of Receivables Financing* (1991), 248, n. 72.

10.31 In relation to that issue, the Privy Council in *Elliott v Turquand*[131] suggested that authorities given in the course of mutual dealings and necessary for their continuance are not revoked by bankruptcy:

> Authorities given in the course of mutual dealings, and necessary to the continuance of those dealings, are, by implication, excepted from the rule that authorities are revoked by . . . bankruptcy. They continue and remain unrevoked by virtue of the provision which protects such dealings, in the same way as powers necessary to give effect to protected sales continue and remain unrevoked by . . . bankruptcy. If this were not so, in some cases of mutual credits the protection professed to be given would be illusory.

However, the notion that an authority to sell was necessary for the continuance of the parties' mutual dealings, so as to prevent its revocation by bankruptcy, would not always explain the *Rose v Hart* cases. Consider, for example, *Palmer v Day & Sons*,[132] to which reference was made earlier.[133] There is nothing in the report to suggest that there was an ongoing business relationship such that the deposit was necessary for the continuance of mutual dealings, or that the auctioneer gave credit to the depositor on the strength of the prospective receipt of the proceeds of sale. In that case, the trustee in bankruptcy upon his appointment wrote to the auctioneer requesting him to proceed with the sale of the goods previously deposited with him by the bankrupt. The auctioneer did so, and when he received the proceeds he was allowed to utilize them in a set-off under *Rose v Hart* against a separate debt owing to him by the bankrupt. One would have thought that this was a case in which the auctioneer's original authority to sell was revoked, but that he was then authorized by the trustee to sell as the *trustee's* agent, the goods in question having vested in the trustee upon his appointment. On that analysis, a set-off should have been denied because of lack of mutuality.

10.32 In the absence of an authority coupled with an interest,[134] authority to sell in any event should be revoked when the depositor is a company the subject of a court-ordered winding up. In such a case the Insolvency Act 1986, s. 127 provides that a disposition of the company's property made after the commencement of the winding up is void unless the court otherwise orders. If an authority to sell is not coupled with an interest, s. 127 would seem to revoke any authority that an agent of the depositor, such as an auctioneer,[135] otherwise had to sell the company's property.[136]

10.33 **Demand for the return of the goods by the depositor's trustee in bankruptcy.** In *Palmer v Day & Sons*, the trustee requested the auctioneer to proceed with the sale. However, given that the property deposited with the auctioneer had vested in the trustee upon his appointment, why could not the trustee have demanded its return as the legal owner? He could not have done so if the authority to sell was coupled with an interest, and the comments of the

---

[131] (1881) 7 App Cas 79, 88.
[132] [1895] 2 QB 618.
[133] See para. 10.20 above.
[134] See para. 10.33 below. This would include, for example, the authority of a receiver appointed under a security to sell the secured property.
[135] If the agent is a receiver appointed under a debenture, s. 127 would not affect the authority to sell.
[136] Compare *Rolls Razor v Cox*, which concerned a voluntary liquidation so that the equivalent of s. 127 in force at the time was not applicable.

Privy Council in *Elliott v Turquand* (above) may be said to support the view that an authority given in the course of mutual dealings is of that nature. But is that the case? If the authority to sell is coupled with an interest, it could not be revoked by the depositor before bankruptcy, but the mere fact that authority is given in the course of mutual dealings should not suffice to preclude the depositor from revoking it.[137] There would have to be other circumstances arising from the mutual dealings which establish an interest. *Rolls Razor v Cox* admittedly suggests that a liquidator cannot demand the return of the company's property handed over for sale so as to defeat a set-off. There are, however, difficulties with the reasoning in the case, and it is suggested that it should be re-considered.[138] In any event, it should not be extended to bankruptcy, given that the property of the bankrupt is vested in the trustee. The trustee's reason for demanding its return may not be based solely on a desire to avoid a set-off. He may regard the method or timing of the sale as not being the most beneficial as far as the estate as a whole is concerned, particularly if the debtor before his or her bankruptcy delivered goods for sale on a 'fire sale' basis in order to obtain funds to overcome what was perceived to be a temporary liquidity problem but which culminated in bankruptcy. There may indeed be only a small debt owing to the depository, and in such a case it hardly seems satisfactory that the trustee should be locked into a sale by the depository solely in order to secure that debt.

Deposit of property

In *Rose v Hart*[139] Gibbs CJ said that credit is given when property is deposited with directions to turn it into money. This does not always require an actual deposit of the property concerned. For example, in the case of goods, it would be sufficient if bills of lading are handed over[140] or, as in *Easum v Cato*,[141] if the conduct of the parties is such that it is 'as if' the goods had been put into the person's hands.[142] Moreover, physical delivery is not feasible when the transaction concerns the sale of immoveable property such as land. In such a case, a deposit of the documentation necessary to complete the sale should suffice. In *Elliott v Turquand*,[143] an agent had been authorized to receive the proceeds of sale of land.   **10.34**

---

[137] In *Palmer v Day & Sons* [1895] 2 QB 618, 623, Lord Russell of Killowen assumed that the authority to sell could have been revoked. While he also commented that no action could have been taken by the depositor when the receiving order was made to recover the goods, that was in the context of an argument that the depositor himself could not have maintained an action in detinue for the return of the goods, in which action a set-off admittedly would not have been available, unless he had taken steps to alter the terms on which the goods had been left with the auctioneer. Lord Russell agreed with that view. Since the depositor had not altered the terms, he could not have sued in detinue at the date of the receiving order. See also *Naoroji v Chartered Bank of India* (1868) LR 3 CP 444, 452 (Montague Smith J).

[138] See above, and also paras 9.02 and 10.27 above.

[139] (1818) 8 Taunt 499, 506, 129 ER 477, 480.

[140] *M'Gillivray v Simson* (1826) 2 Car & P 320, 172 ER 145, affirmed 5 LJOSKB 53.

[141] (1822) 5 B & Ald 861, 106 ER 1406.

[142] Prior to their bankruptcy, the bankrupts in *Easum v Cato*, being desirous of making a shipment of goods to Rio de Janeiro for sale, but not in their own names, represented to the merchants through whom the consignment was to be made that the goods belonged to the defendant. When the defendant received the proceeds of sale after the bankruptcy, it was held that he could set off his obligation to account for them to the bankrupts against a separate debt owing by him to the bankrupts, Abbott CJ commenting that: 'this case is to be considered as if the bankrupts had actually put the goods into the hands of the defendant . . .' See (1822) 5 B & Ald 861, 866, 106 ER 1406, 1408.

[143] (1881) 7 App Cas 79.

The Privy Council said that if the agent had been entrusted with the deed of conveyance for the purpose of receiving the purchase money: 'the case would be very like some of the instances referred to in *Rose v Hart*.'[144]

10.35   In *Elliott v Turquand* there was insufficient evidence of a deed of conveyance having been handed over to the agent for the purpose of receiving the proceeds of sale. Nevertheless, the agent had actually received the proceeds under an unrevoked authority before the principal's bankruptcy, and he was allowed to bring them into an account. An agent is often, but not always, a trustee of moneys received in the course of the agency.[145] While the existence or otherwise of a trust was not canvassed by the Privy Council, it did comment[146] that the agent was authorized to receive the purchase money and to credit it to the mutual account existing between them, which indicates that there was no trust. Accordingly, even though the case strictly did not come within the principle discussed in *Rose v Hart*, that did not matter. Because there was no question of a trust, there was nothing objectionable in a set-off.

G. Surplus Proceeds after Realizing a Security

10.36   Consider that a bankrupt or a company in liquidation prior to the insolvency gave security for a debt, and after default in payment of the debt the creditor turned the property constituting the security into money, either through the exercise of a power of sale or, if the security consists of an insurance policy or a negotiable instrument or a debt owing by a third party, by collecting the proceeds. If a surplus remains after the secured debt has been satisfied, the creditor may wish to set off the obligation to account for the surplus against a separate unsecured debt of the bankrupt or the company.

(1) Mortgagee's right of retainer, and tacking

10.37   Before considering that issue, two lines of authority should be distinguished. The first originated in judgments of Sir John Romilly who, instead of relying on the law of set-off, attempted to develop a mortgagee's right of retainer. In both *Spalding v Thompson*[147] and *Re Haselfoot's Estate (Chauntler's Claim)*[148] a policy of life assurance had been mortgaged to secure a debt. When the testator died and the insurance moneys were received, Sir John Romilly held that the mortgagee could retain the surplus against a separate unsecured debt of the testator. In *Re Haselfoot's Estate*[149] he said that the right was not one of set-off, but rather it was a right in the mortgagee to retain a part of the testator's estate in his possession in satisfaction of the testator's debt. Subsequently, Malins VC applied this right of retainer

---

[144] (1881) 7 App Cas 79, 87. See also *Castendyck and Focke v Official Assignee of S A McLellan* (1887) 6 NZLR 67, 74. In the *Castendyck* case the agent was authorized merely to find a purchaser, and not to receive the purchase money, and so he was not allowed to set off the money when it came into his hands.

[145] Compare *Palette Shoes Pty Ltd v Krohn* (1937) 58 CLR 1, 30 (Dixon J), with *Henry v Hammond* [1913] 2 KB 515.

[146] (1881) 7 App Cas 79, 85, 87.

[147] (1858) 26 Beav 637, 53 ER 1044.

[148] (1872) LR 13 Eq 327.

[149] (1872) LR 13 Eq 327, 331.

in a case where there was a surplus remaining after a sale by a mortgagee.[150] In later cases, however, it has been criticized and disregarded,[151] and it would appear that it no longer applies. The second line of authority relates to tacking. When a mortgagor died, equity in a number of cases allowed the mortgagee to tack an unsecured debt onto the mortgage as against the successors in title to the equity of redemption, in so far as the mortgaged property was an asset available for payment of the unsecured debt. However, this was only allowed as a means of preventing circuity of action, and it could not be used to obtain priority over other creditors when the mortgagor's estate was insolvent.[152] In any event, the right appears to have been abolished in relation to mortgages of land as a result of the general abolition of tacking (save in respect of further advances) by the Law of Property Act 1925, s. 94.[153]

(2) Set-off against a trust fund

In the case of set-off, the fundamental point should be that a mortgagee is a trustee for the mortgagor, or as the case may be a subsequent encumbrancer,[154] in respect of any surplus remaining after exercising a power of sale and paying the secured debt.[155] This is not a recent development. Dr Waters[156] has suggested that it would have been obvious to judicial minds at least since *Cholmondeley v Clinton*[157] in 1820. Therefore, the obligation to account for the surplus should not be susceptible to a set-off.[158] *Talbot v Frere*[159] supports that view. Sir George Jessel MR said in that case, in the context of a deceased mortgagor's insolvent estate, that: 'the mortgagee cannot plead set-off. He is a trustee of the money for the estate, and his claim is only a simple contract debt against that estate.'[160] It was also on that ground that the Victorian Supreme Court in *Lloyds Bank NZA Ltd v National Safety Council of Australia*[161] declined to allow a set-off against a surplus obtained from the exercise of a power of sale after the liquidation of the mortgagor. Nor would there appear to be any

10.38

---

[150] *Re General Provident Assurance Co, ex p National Bank* (1872) LR 14 Eq 507. Compare *Pile v Pile* (1872) 23 WR 440, where the sale of the mortgaged property took place under a court order and the proceeds of sale did not come into the mortgagee's hands.

[151] See *Talbot v Frere* (1878) 9 Ch D 568 and *Re Gregson. Christison v Bolam* (1887) 36 Ch D 223.

[152] See e.g. *Irby v Irby* (1855) 22 Beav 217, 52 ER 1091; *Pile v Pile* (1875) 23 WR 440; *Talbot v Frere* (1878) 9 Ch D 568, 572–3. See generally *Fisher and Lightwood's Law of Mortgage* (12th edn, 2006), 773, para. 38.8.

[153] In Australia, see e.g. the Property Law Act 1958 (Vic), s. 94 and the Conveyancing and Law of Property Act 1884 (Tas), s. 38, which are expressed not to apply to mortgages of Torrens title land (see s. 86 of the Victorian Act and s. 91 of the Tasmanian Act), and in Queensland the Property Law Act 1974, s. 82 (which does extend to Torrens land: see s. 5(1)(b)).

[154] *Tanner v Heard* (1857) 23 Beav 555, 53 ER 219.

[155] *Matthison v Clarke* (1854) 3 Drewry 3, 4, 61 ER 801; *Charles v Jones* (1887) 35 Ch D 544; *Lloyds Bank NZA Ltd v National Safety Council of Australia* [1993] 2 VR 506, 510–11, 514; *Sheahan v Carrier Air Conditioning Pty Ltd* (1997) 189 CLR 407, 429–30. See also the Law of Property Act 1925, s. 105.

[156] Waters, *The Constructive Trust* (1964), 207.

[157] (1820) 2 Jac & W 1, 37 ER 527.

[158] This is in the absence of a prior agreement by the mortgagor that the mortgagee may apply the surplus in satisfaction of another debt. See *Lloyds Bank NZA Ltd v National Safety Council of Australia* [1993] 2 VR 506, 508, 510, 513, 514.

[159] (1878) 9 Ch D 568.

[160] (1878) 9 Ch D 568, 573.

[161] [1993] 2 VR 506. See also *Re Parker* (1997) 80 FCR 1, 18.

reason for encouraging a set-off. A secured creditor should not be entitled to use the security to obtain priority over other creditors in relation to a debt that otherwise was unsecured.[162] Apart from *Talbot v Frere* and the *Lloyd's Bank* case, however, the authorities are in an unsatisfactory state.

(3) Deceased's insolvent estate

10.39 In *Talbot v Frere*[163] a testator had mortgaged policies of life assurance to a creditor. The testator died insolvent, and the creditor received the policy moneys which were more than sufficient to pay the mortgage debt. Sir George Jessel held that the creditor could not keep the surplus in payment of another unsecured debt. The creditor was a trustee for the estate,[164] and his obligation to account for the trust fund was not susceptible to a set-off.[165] The same issue arose on similar facts in *Re Gregson. Christison v Bolam*.[166] A set-off was also denied, but on a different ground. North J said that the debt was owing by the testator, whereas the testator himself never had a right to the surplus which first became payable after his death to the use of the executor. Accordingly, there was a lack of mutuality.[167] If, on the other hand, surplus proceeds of security had been received in the testator's lifetime, he suggested that there might have been a set-off.[168] It is difficult, however, to reconcile that view with *Talbot v Frere*. If there is a trust it should prevent a set-off whether the proceeds are received before or after death.[169]

10.40 Those cases concerned a deceased's insolvent estate. More commonly, the issue will arise in the context of a bankruptcy or a liquidation of the mortgagor.

(4) Proceeds received before the debtor's insolvency

10.41 If the security is realized and the proceeds are received before the debtor's bankruptcy, there is support for the view that a surplus can be set off.[170] *Young v Bank of Bengal*[171] concerned a security over some promissory notes. While the security was not realized until after the

---

[162] *Lloyds Bank NZA Ltd v National Safety Council* [1993] 2 VR 506, 522, referring to *Re Pearce* [1909] 2 Ch 492, 499–500 (Buckley LJ) and *Eberle's Hotels and Restaurant Co Ltd v E Jonas & Brothers* (1887) 18 QBD 459, 470 (Fry LJ).

[163] (1878) 9 Ch D 568.

[164] In *Roxburghe v Cox* (1881) 17 Ch D 520, 525, James LJ said of *Talbot v Frere* that, 'That was a case of trustee and *cestui que trust*.'

[165] The set-off in issue in *Talbot v Frere* was pursuant to the Statutes of Set-off, since the deceased had died before the bankruptcy set-off section had been made applicable to deceaseds' insolvent estates by the Supreme Court of Judicature Act 1875, s. 10. See paras 13.130–13.134 below.

[166] (1887) 36 Ch D 223.

[167] See also *Re Gedney; Smith v Grummitt* [1908] 1 Ch 804.

[168] (1887) 36 Ch D 223, 227.

[169] In *Re Gregson* (1887) 36 Ch D 223, 230, North J doubted whether the mortgagees in that case could 'strictly speaking' be said to be trustees. Nevertheless, his judgment suggests that he contemplated that there was a form of trust, commenting that the balance in the hands of the mortgagees was money received 'to the use of the executor'. He may have had in mind what has been termed a quasi-trust (see *Foley v Hill* (1848) 2 HLC 28, 35–6, 9 ER 1002, 1005), or in modern parlance a constructive trust. See Finn, *Fiduciary Obligations* (1977), 89.

[170] See also *Samuel, Samuel & Co v West Hartlepool Steam Navigation Co* (1907) 12 Com Cas 203 (Statutes of Set-off).

[171] (1836) 1 Moore 150, 12 ER 771.

bankruptcy, and a set-off accordingly was denied for the reason explained below, Lord Brougham nevertheless accepted, on the authority of *Atkinson v Elliott*,[172] that a set-off would have been available if the bank had realized the security and received the surplus prior to the bankruptcy: 'for then they would have been debtors in that amount to Palmer and Co, and the case would have been one of mutual debts.'[173]

In *Astley v Gurney*,[174] a set-off was allowed where the proceeds of a security were received **10.42** before bankruptcy, although the circumstances were unusual. As security for two debts, the debtor deposited bills of lading for shipments of cotton and coffee, and also some bills of exchange. Prior to his bankruptcy, and prior to the due date for payment, the debtor agreed that the creditor should sell the cotton and the coffee. The cotton was sold before the bankruptcy, but the sale of the coffee was not effected until later. The proceeds of sale of the cotton, together with an amount received on one of the bills of exchanged that matured before the bankruptcy, were sufficient to pay both debts, leaving a surplus. It was held that this surplus could be set off against a separate unsecured debt. The justification for allowing a set-off was the debtor's assent to a sale before the debt was due and before bankruptcy, which was taken to include also authority to receive the proceeds.[175] Cleasby B in the Exchequer Chamber said that this authority altered the position of the parties so that, as soon as it was given, credit was given to the creditor for the proceeds of sale.[176] He distinguished it from a deposit of property as security, because in that case the deposit is not made for the purpose of being converted into money, but rather with the intention of its being returned.[177] This is not a satisfactory explanation, however. All that occurred as a result of the sale was that one form of security (cotton) was replaced with another, in the form of the proceeds of the sale. The question still should have been how the proceeds were to be treated. In Victoria, Marks J suggested that the authority given to the creditor in *Astley v Gurney* to receive the proceeds of sale was interpreted as authority to apply the proceeds in satisfaction of other debts.[178] While this is not stated expressly in the judgments, it seems the best explanation for the decision.

In neither *Young v Bank of Bengal* nor *Astley v Gurney* was the question of a trust canvassed, **10.43** but it was considered in *Re H E Thorne & Son Ltd*.[179] A company had mortgaged some machinery, the mortgage agreement containing a covenant by the mortgagor to insure. The machinery was destroyed by fire, and the insurance money was paid to the mortgagee. Some two weeks later the company went into liquidation. It was held that the mortgagee could set off the surplus over and above the mortgage debt against a separate unsecured

---

[172] (1797) 7 TR 378, 101 ER 1030.

[173] (1836) 1 Moore 150, 168, 12 ER 771, 778.

[174] (1869) LR 4 CP 714.

[175] See Bovill CJ in the Common Pleas (1869) LR 4 CP 714, 719–20, and Cleasby B on appeal in the Exchequer Chamber at 722–3.

[176] (1869) LR 4 CP 714, 722. The appeal to the Exchequer Chamber was only in respect of the coffee sold after the bankruptcy (see below), but Cleasby B's comments were expressed generally, in relation to both the cotton and the coffee. Indeed, he said (at 723) that it did not matter whether the sale occurred before or after bankruptcy.

[177] (1869) LR 4 CP 714, 721–22.

[178] *Lloyds Bank NZA v National Safety Council* [1993] 2 VR 506, 512.

[179] [1914] 2 Ch 438.

debt of the mortgagor.[180] It was argued that the surplus was held on trust and that therefore it was not susceptible to a set-off, but Astbury J was not persuaded. Instead, he based his decision upon a statement by Lord Esher in *Eberle's Hotels v Jonas*,[181] that: 'wherever in the result the dealings on each side would end in a money claim, [the set-off section] would be applicable.' Astbury J said that the liquidator's argument that there may not be a set-off: 'where a creditor holds the balance of a realized security in trust for his debtor so that the creditor is not entitled to deal with it in his account . . . would form a serious limitation on the general rule in *Eberle's Hotels Co v Jonas*.'[182] However, this view would seem to allow any trust fund arising from a dealing to be employed in a set-off, a conclusion that could hardly be accepted.[183]

(5) Proceeds received after the debtor's insolvency

10.44 Alternatively, the security may be enforced and the proceeds received *after* the debtor's bankruptcy or liquidation. In *Young v Bank of Bengal*,[184] a debtor pledged promissory notes as security for a debt, but became bankrupt prior to default in payment. When default subsequently occurred the bank exercised its security rights and sold the notes. The Privy Council held that a surplus remaining after satisfying the secured debt had to be accounted for without a set-off against a separate unsecured debt. The denial of a set-off has been explained on the ground that the security was deposited only for a particular or special purpose,[185] though this is not in fact the reason that was given in the case. Indeed, it is

---

[180] The insurance money received under a policy taken out pursuant to a covenant to insure would have taken the place of the property destroyed, and would have been held as security until it was applied in payment of the mortgage debt. See *Edmonds v The Hamilton Provident and Loan Society* (1891) 18 OAR 347. Security on a policy of insurance is also security on the proceeds. See *Glahom v Rowntree* (1837) 6 Ad & E 710, 716, 112 ER 273, 275. In Australia, see the Personal Property Securities Act 2009 (Cth), ss. 31(1)(b) and 32(1).

[181] (1887) 18 QBD 459, 465. Astbury J found further support for his conclusion in another statement in Lord Esher's judgment in the *Eberle's Hotels* case (at 466) that: 'These cigars were deposited to secure a debt with power to sell them at once, even before default in payment of the monthly instalments. If the defendants had sold them before the debt was paid, I am disposed to think that the plaintiffs' claim for an account of their proceeds would then have been a mere money claim.' However, this comment should be understood in the context of a letter written by the plaintiffs to the defendants authorizing them to dispose of the cigars and to 'put the proceeds to their credit'. See at 459–60. In other words, it was contemplated that, if the cigars were sold, the proceeds were not to be kept separate but rather were to be credited to the general account between them.

[182] [1914] 2 Ch 438, 453. In *Lloyds Bank NZA v National Safety Council* [1993] 2 VR 506, 512, Marks J distinguished *Re Thorne* on the ground that a credit in fact had been raised at the time of the liquidation, the surplus moneys having been credited to the account of the company before its liquidation. He also suggested that authority to credit proceeds against existing debts was open to implication in *Re Thorne*. It appears that there had been correspondence between the parties in that case prior to the liquidation in which the company's indebtedness was shown after deducting the insurance proceeds. See [1914] 2 Ch 438, 440. However, neither of the matters to which Marks J referred formed part of Astbury J's reasons in *Re Thorne*.

[183] In particular, Astbury J's analysis fails to account for the denial of a set-off in the special-purpose payment cases. These were distinguished, unsatisfactorily, by Astbury J on the ground that the exercise of a right of set-off would have amounted to a breach of a specific contract. See the discussion of these cases in paras 10.47–10.58 below.

[184] (1836) 1 Moore 150.

[185] *Alsager v Currie* (1844) 12 M & W 751, 757–8, 152 ER 1402, 1404; *Naoroji v Chartered Bank of India* (1868) LR 3 CP 444, 448 (Byles J, *arguendo*); *Re Daintrey* [1900] 1 QB 546, 559. See also *MS Fashions Ltd*

difficult to reconcile that explanation with Lord Brougham's view that a set-off would have been available if the security had been enforced before the bankruptcy.[186] The reason given for denying a set-off was that credit had not been given within the meaning ascribed to that expression by Gibbs CJ in *Rose v Hart*.[187] The Privy Council adopted a strict interpretation of *Rose v Hart*, and said that it was necessary to show that the transaction was such that it *must* end in a debt.[188] This could not be said with certainty in *Young v Bank of Bengal*, because default had not occurred at the date of the bankruptcy. Therefore, there was no authority to sell at that time, and indeed the security could have been redeemed by the assignees in bankruptcy.

The question of set-off in this context also arose in *Astley v Gurney*,[189] to which reference **10.45** was made earlier.[190] Briefly, a debtor provided as security bills of lading for shipments of cotton and coffee, and also some bills of exchange. Most of the bills of exchange were collected after the bankruptcy, and the Common Pleas held, on the authority of *Young v Bank of Bengal*, that the surplus proceeds arising in relation to them could not be set off against a separate unsecured debt. It was never intended that the proceeds of the bills of exchange should be applied to anything but the debt for which they were given as security. Credit, therefore, was not given for the surplus.[191] The position was different, however, in relation to the coffee, which was also sold after the bankruptcy. This was the subject of an appeal to the Exchequer Chamber,[192] which held that those surplus proceeds could be set off against a separate unsecured debt. The set-off in this instance was justified on the same ground referred to earlier in relation to the cotton,[193] that the debtor had authorised a sale before the debt had matured and before the bankruptcy, which included authority to receive the proceeds. That authority constituted the giving of credit for the proceeds of sale when they were received.[194]

---

v Bank of Credit and Commerce International SA [1993] Ch 425, 451, and *Key v Flint* (1817) 8 Taunt 21, 23, 129 ER 289, 289–90.

[186] (1836) 1 Moore 150, 168, 12 ER 771, 778, and see para. 10.41 above.

[187] See paras 7.02–7.04 above. Because the security was enforced and the proceeds were obtained *after* the bankruptcy, there was not a 'debt' in existence at the date of the bankruptcy. If therefore, a set-off was to proceed, it was necessary to find that credit was given.

[188] See the discussion at (1836) 1 Moore 150, 168–9, 12 ER 771, 779. In later cases it was said to be sufficient if the transaction would naturally or in the ordinary course of business end in a debt. See e.g. *Naoroji v Chartered Bank of India* (1868) LR 3 CP 444, 451, 452, and para. 7.04 above. In *Naoroji v Chartered Bank of India*, Byles J (at 452) described *Young v Bank of Bengal* as 'a very doubtful authority'.

[189] (1869) LR 4 CP 714.

[190] See para. 10.42 above.

[191] (1869) LR 4 CP 714, 720.

[192] (1869) LR 4 CP 714. The report suggests that the Exchequer Chamber reversed the decision of the Common Pleas, whereas this is not obvious from a reading of the judgments. The discrepancy is explained in a footnote to another report of the case at 38 LJCP 357, 359.

[193] See para. 10.42 above.

[194] Oditah, *Legal Aspects of Receivables Financing* (1991), 249–50 sought to explain the set-off on the ground that the security over the coffee had been released, but this would not solve the problem. It was merely agreed that the creditor could sell the coffee and receive the proceeds. One may assume that it was intended that the proceeds would then form the security.

(6) Criticism of the cases

10.46 The rationale in those cases for denying a set-off when the security was realized after the bankruptcy, in the absence of prior instructions to sell, was that credit had not been given at the date of the bankruptcy. The difficulty with relying on that explanation now is that the set-off section has since been expanded to include claims arising out of mutual dealings.[195] Accordingly, if the question of a trust is left aside, the ostensible reason given in the cases for denying a set-off would no longer apply.[196] The 'debt' in respect of the surplus would be the product of a prior dealing between the parties, and therefore it would be part of their mutual dealings. It would no longer be to the point that it may have been uncertain whether the security would be sold because, as Brett LJ remarked in *Peat v Jones & Co*,[197] mutual dealings was added to the set-off section in order to get rid of questions which might arise as to whether a transaction would end in a debt or not. Therefore, if the courts were to ignore the trust impressed upon the surplus proceeds, it should not matter whether the security was realized before or after bankruptcy. The better approach is to recognize that surplus proceeds from the realization of a security ordinarily are impressed with a trust. Unless in a particular case it is intended that the surplus be credited to an account between the parties, so that there is no trust, a creditor should not therefore be entitled to obtain priority over other creditors in relation to another unsecured debt owing to him or her by setting off the surplus against that debt.[198] This is the position that has been accepted in Victoria.[199] According to this view, it should not matter when the security was realised.[200]

H. Special-Purpose Payments

(1) Failure of the purpose

10.47 If a person ('the depositor') has paid a sum of money to another ('the depository') to be applied for a special purpose which has failed, or which has not been carried into effect, the depositor is entitled to recover the money undiminished by a set-off. This applies when the defence of set-off as between solvent parties under the Statutes of Set-off is in issue,[201] and also, if the depositor has become bankrupt or is a company which has gone into

---

[195] See ch. 7 above.

[196] See Derham, 'Some aspects of mutual credit and mutual dealings' (1992) 108 LQR 99, 109, a point also made by Phillips J in the Victorian Supreme Court in *Lloyds Bank NZA v National Safety Council* [1993] 2 VR 506, 520–2.

[197] (1881) 8 QBD 147, 149.

[198] Compare *Baker v Lloyd's Bank Ltd* [1920] 2 KB 322, although Roche J seems to have accepted (at 328) that the security in that case was not intended to be confined to the specific advance in respect of which it was given.

[199] *Lloyd's Bank NZA Ltd v National Safety Council* [1993] 2 VR 506.

[200] Indeed, an issue for consideration in relation to the surplus produced from the exercise of a power of sale governed by the Law of Property Act 1925 is whether the allowance of a set-off is consistent with s. 105, which provides that any surplus received by a mortgagee, after paying prior claims, 'shall be paid to the person entitled to the mortgaged property'. A similar provision is to be found in the Consumer Credit Act 1974, s. 121(3) in relation to pawnbrokers. In Australia, see e.g. the Property Law Act 1958 (Vic), s. 105.

[201] *Stumore v Campbell & Co* [1892] 1 QB 314.

liquidation, when it is sought to base a defence on the insolvency set-off section. In *Re Pollitt, ex p Minor*,[202] a client was indebted to his solicitor, who refused to act further unless the client deposited a sum of money to cover future costs. The client accordingly placed money in the solicitor's hands for that purpose. Subsequently, the client became bankrupt, after which the solicitor continued to act on his behalf. The Court of Appeal held that the solicitor was only entitled to his costs for the work performed before notice of the act of bankruptcy, when his authority to act was revoked. Therefore, the purpose for which the money had been lodged with him had failed, and he was obliged to return the residue to the bankrupt's trustee without deducting the bankrupt's prior debt to him. The leading judgment in the Court of Appeal was delivered by Lord Esher MR, who said:[203] 'If the money was given to the solicitor for a specific purpose, then, as between him and the bankrupt, there could not be a set-off.'

(2) Residue remaining after the purpose is carried out

Alternatively, the purpose may have been carried out but there is a residue remaining in the hands of the depository. In *Re Mid-Kent Fruit Factory*,[204] a company gave two cheques to its solicitors for the purpose of discharging the claims of its creditors, the solicitors being instructed to settle for less if possible. The solicitors managed to settle for less in some cases, though the company was not informed of this. When the company went into liquidation, the solicitors sought to set off the balance remaining against the company's liability for costs. Vaughan Williams J considered that, when money is deposited for a special purpose, and after the purpose is fulfilled a balance remains with the depository, the depository cannot set off the balance in the depositor's bankruptcy unless the depository can show that he or she retained it with the consent of the depositor.[205] In the case before him the company was not aware of the surplus, and so it could not be said that the company had consented to the solicitors retaining it. A set-off therefore was not available.[206]

10.48

(3) Collection of the proceeds of a negotiable instrument

A similar principle may apply when a negotiable instrument is deposited with a person to collect the proceeds and apply them in a particular way. If the person instead retains the proceeds, and does not apply them as directed, the trustee in bankruptcy of the depositor may recover the proceeds undiminished by a set-off.[207]

10.49

---

[202] [1893] 1 QB 455, affirming [1893] 1 QB 175.
[203] [1893] 1 QB 455, 458.
[204] [1896] 1 Ch 567. See also *Re City Equitable Fire Insurance Co Ltd* [1930] 2 Ch 293, 313–14.
[205] Compare *Buchanan v Findlay* (1829) 9 B & C 738, 749, 109 ER 274, 278, in which the depository would have been entitled under the agreement to retain the surplus if the proceeds of the bills entrusted with him had been applied as directed.
[206] The depository has the onus of showing the depositor's consent.
[207] *Buchanan v Findlay* (1829) 9 B & C 738, 109 ER 274; *Atkinson v Learmouth* (1905) 11 ALR 191. See also *Alder v Keighley* (1846) 15 M & W 117, 153 ER 785 (though this case was decided by reference to the form of action employed).

(4) The justification for denying a set-off

10.50 In some of these special-purpose payment cases the courts, when denying the depository a set-off, have emphasized the proprietary nature of the depositor's claim. Sometimes, the deposit has been said to give rise to a trust,[208] and in other cases a bailment.[209] There is, however, authority which suggests that the rule is based upon a broader concept, and that the depository may be denied a set-off in the depositor's bankruptcy even though the relationship between the parties is only one of debt. In *Re City Equitable Fire Insurance Co Ltd*,[210] a reinsurer under a treaty of reinsurance had agreed to accept a share of all fire insurance policies accepted or renewed by the insurer, and in order to secure the due performance of the reinsurer's obligations under the treaty the insurer was entitled to retain (as a 'deposit') 40 per cent of all premiums credited to the reinsurer in the first year. The reinsurer went into liquidation, and after all its obligations to the insurer under the treaty had been satisfied the insurer still retained a substantial fund. It was held that the deposit constituted money left in the hands of the insurer for a special purpose, and that the balance remaining after the purpose was satisfied had to be returned to the liquidator without a set-off against other debts owing by the reinsurer to the insurer. Counsel for the insurer argued that the deposit was not a trust fund but rather it was a loan with a conditional right to payment, and on that basis it should be able to be employed in a set-off. It is a hallmark of a trust that it should be intended that the moneys in question be kept separate,[211] but it appears that the insurer was not obliged to keep the deposit separate from its own funds. Further, the insurer was required to pay interest to the reinsurer on the deposit,[212] a factor which is usually considered to be a powerful indication of a debt rather than a trust relationship.[213] However, the existence or otherwise of a trust was not treated as critical to the decision. At first instance, Maugham J commented:[214] 'It does not seem to me to matter much whether it is or is not regarded as a trust fund. It is, to my mind, moneys "deposited for a specific purpose" . . .' On appeal, the Court of Appeal failed to mention the presence or absence of a trust. Lord Hanworth MR, with whom Lawrence and Romer LJJ agreed, was content to find that the accumulated fund was intended to be held for a specific purpose, as security for the due performance of the reinsurer's obligations under the treaty, and that therefore it should be set aside from any account between the parties.

---

[208] See *Wright v Watson* (1883) Cab & El 171, and also *Stumore v Campbell & Co* [1892] 1 QB 314.

[209] See *Re Mid-Kent Fruit Factory* [1896] 1 Ch 567, 572, and also *Buchanan v Findlay* (1829) 9 B & C 738, 749, 109 ER 274, 278 (bills of exchange deposited for a specific purpose).

[210] [1930] 2 Ch 293.

[211] See para. 10.19 above.

[212] Since the interest was to be paid to the reinsurer, and not retained by the insurer as part of the retention fund, it was held that it could be set off.

[213] *Pott v Clegg* (1847) 16 M & W 321, 327, 153 ER 1212, 1214 (Parke B, *arguendo*); *Foley v Hill* (1848) 2 HLC 28, 36, 9 ER 1002, 1005; *Re Broad, ex p Neck* (1884) 13 QBD 740; Finn, *Fiduciary Obligations* (1977), 108. An agreement to pay interest is not conclusive evidence of a debt. For example, if the person receiving the money has agreed to invest it for the payer, and to pay the interest that is actually received, a trust is created. See *Scott and Ascher on Trusts* (5th edn, 2006) vol. 1, 90–1, § 2.3.8.1 and *Re Exchange Travel (Holdings) Ltd (No. 3)* [1996] BCLC 524, 534. However, in cases like the *City Equitable Fire* case, where the agreement is to pay interest at a defined rate whether or not the money is invested, that circumstance almost certainly indicates that the payee is to have the use of the money, and that the transaction gives rise to a debt and not a trust. See *Scott on Trusts, loc. cit.*

[214] [1930] 2 Ch 293, 303.

Winn LJ in the Court of Appeal in *Halesowen Presswork & Assemblies Ltd v Westminster* **10.51**
Bank Ltd[215] suggested that the parties to mutual dealings may 'separate out' a particular
debt, so that it is not to be regarded as mutual for the purpose of the insolvency set-off section. However, Lord Kilbrandon on appeal doubted that proposition,[216] and it is inconsistent with the accepted view that the insolvency set-off section cannot be contracted out
of.[217] Mutuality, in truth, is concerned with the status of the parties and their relationship
with each other, not with the circumstances under which a debt arose.[218] Alternatively,
Willes J once suggested[219] that 'some difficulty might arise' in allowing a defendant a set-off
if he has 'purposely broken his contract in order to create the claim', and Astbury J had
recourse to a similar notion in *Re H E Thorne & Son Ltd*[220] in order to explain the special-
purpose payment cases. He said that a depository is denied a set-off in these cases 'if it
involves a breach of the contract under which he obtained the money'.[221] Other judgments
support that view. In *Re Pollitt*[222] Vaughan Williams J said that: 'The attempt to use the
money deposited as security for another purpose than that for which it was deposited is an
attempt to do wrong.' In an Australian case, *Atkinson v Learmouth*,[223] a debtor had handed
a promissory note to the creditor with instructions to collect the proceeds and to pay them
(less a discount) into the debtor's bank account. The creditor duly collected the proceeds,
but instead of applying them as directed he retained them in satisfaction of the debtor's
debt to him. While there are statements in the joint judgment of Hodges and Holroyd JJ
which suggest that the claim brought by the debtor's assignee in bankruptcy for payment
of the proceeds was regarded as proprietary in nature,[224] they commented in disallowing a
set-off that:[225] 'we should expect that the law would not allow a man by dishonestly breaking his contract, and keeping another man's money, to gain any advantage.' The problem
with this as an explanation is that there is no such general principle which precludes a person from basing a set-off upon his own breach of contract, even where the contract is purposely broken in order to bring about that result.[226] For example, failure to pay a debt on
time constitutes a breach of contract,[227] but a creditor who is aware of the debtor's insolvency and who consequently withholds payment of his or her own debt to the debtor is not
for that reason denied a set-off. It is difficult to see why a simple breach of contract in any

---

[215] [1971] 1 QB 1, 43–4, referring to his earlier judgment in *Rolls Razor Ltd v Cox* [1967] 1 QB 552,
575.
[216] *National Westminster Bank Ltd v Halesowen Presswork & Assemblies Ltd* [1972] AC 785, 821.
[217] See paras 6.111–6.112 above.
[218] See para. 11.01 below.
[219] *Turner v Thomas* (1871) LR 6 CP 610, 614.
[220] [1914] 2 Ch 438.
[221] [1914] 2 Ch 438, 450.
[222] [1893] 1 QB 175, 179 (decision affirmed [1893] 1 QB 455).
[223] (1905) 11 ALR 191.
[224] Hodges and Holroyd JJ emphasized (at (1905) 11 ALR 191, 194–5) that the debtor was the owner of
the note and the proceeds. They also said (at 196) that the difference between their approach and that of the
dissentient, Hood J, was the statement by Hood J that the dealing in the note was intended to terminate in a
debt.
[225] (1905) 11 ALR 191, 195.
[226] See para. 8.90 above.
[227] *Re City Equitable Fire Insurance Co Ltd* [1930] 2 Ch 293, 302 (Maugham J). It is not a 'mere' breach of
contract, however. See *Young v Queensland Trustees Ltd* (1956) 99 CLR 560, 567.

other form should be treated differently. But even if there were a general principle to the effect that a set-off may not arise when a contract has been breached for the very purpose of gaining a set-off, it would not be relevant to special-purpose payment cases in which the purpose has failed for some other reason, or when the purpose has been carried out leaving a surplus.

10.52 Nor is the breach of contract theory supported by the old common law cases which established that, when either money or a negotiable instrument was lodged with a depository to be applied to a specific purpose, and the depository instead wilfully retained the money, or the instrument or its proceeds, in purported satisfaction of the depositor's indebtedness to him or her, there could not be a set-off if the depositor brought a special action for breach of duty, although a set-off was allowed if the depositor waived the breach and sued instead for money had and received.[228] These cases are explicable on the basis of the form of action employed. Actions for damages for breach of duty are unliquidated in nature, and before 1861[229] claims of that nature could not be proved in a bankruptcy, and consequently could not be set off.[230] While it was generally considered in these cases that a set-off was available in an action for money had and received,[231] they were decided at common law where the presence or absence of a trust arising out of the stated purpose ordinarily would not have been considered.[232]

10.53 The only justification for denying a set-off to a depository against the obligation to account for the remains of a fund received for a special purpose is that the money was held subject to a trust. If the money was not intended to be kept separate from the depository's own funds before the purpose was carried out, there would not be a trust,[233] in which case a set-off in principle should be available to the depository in the depositor's bankruptcy. This was the view of the Court of Appeal in the context of set-off between solvent parties,[234] and

---

[228] See generally *Colson v Welsh* (1795) 1 Esp 378, 170 ER 391; *Atkinson v Elliott* (1797) 7 TR 378, 101 ER 1030; *Thorpe v Thorpe* (1832) 3 B & Ad 580, 110 ER 211; *Hill v Smith* (1844) 12 M & W 618, 152 ER 1346; *Alder v Keighley* (1846) 15 M & W 117, 153 ER 785; *Bell v Carey* (1849) 8 CB 887, 137 ER 757. Compare *Buchanan v Findlay* (1829) 9 B & C 738, 109 ER 274, in which a set-off was disallowed in an action for money had and received in relation to the proceeds of bills, but in that case the bankrupts prior to their bankruptcy had demanded the return of the bills, so that the defendants had no right to receive the proceeds.

[229] Compare the Bankruptcy Act 1861, s. 153.

[230] *Rose v Sims* (1830) 1 B & Ad 521, 109 ER 881. Compare *Gibson v Bell* (1835) 1 Bing (NC) 743, 131 ER 1303 and *Groom v West* (1838) 8 Ad & E 758, 112 ER 1025. It was held in these cases that, when a purchaser of goods who had agreed to pay the price by accepting a bill of exchange in fact failed to do so, and the vendor's assignees in bankruptcy brought a special action of assumpsit against him for breach of contract, the purchaser could set off in that action an independent indebtedness of the bankrupt vendor to him (but compare *Hutchinson v Reid* (1813) 3 Camp 329, 170 ER 1400 in the context of the Statutes of Set-off). This was justified on the ground that the claim in reality was for the price of the goods themselves, so that effectively it was liquidated in nature. Indeed, Lord Denman CJ in *Groom v West* distinguished the liquidated nature of the demand before him from the case of a claim for unliquidated damages for breach of duty in not applying a special purpose payment in the required manner.

[231] See e.g. *Colson v Welsh* (1795) 1 Esp 378, 380, 170 ER 391, 391–2; *Atkinson v Elliott* (1797) 7 TR 378, 101 ER 1030; *Hill v Smith* (1844) 12 M & W 618, 631, 152 ER 1346, 1351 (in relation to the Statutes of Set-off). Compare *Buchanan v Findlay* (1829) 9 B & C 738, 109 ER 274, explained in *Thorpe v Thorpe* (1832) 3 B & Ad 580, 583–4, 110 ER 211, 212.

[232] Compare para. 2.106 above in relation to set-off of judgments and orders.

[233] See paras 10.19 and 10.50 above.

[234] *Anglo Corporation Ltd v Peacock AG* [1997] EWCA Civ 992.

it should apply equally to insolvency set-off. The *City Equitable Fire* case therefore should only be regarded as correctly decided if, notwithstanding the obligation to pay interest, there was a trust so that the insurer would have been obliged to pay the retention moneys into a separate account. Given that there does not appear to have been an obligation to keep the deposit separate, a set-off should have been available. Subsequently, Lord Kilbrandon and Lord Simon of Glaisdale referred to the *City Equitable Fire* case without criticism in *National Westminster Bank Ltd v Halesowen Presswork & Assemblies Ltd*,[235] but their respective explanations for the special-purpose payment cases each seem to countenance a form of trust fund. Lord Kilbrandon said that the funds in these cases were 'impressed with quasi-trust purposes',[236] a concept that has also been used to explain the status of property held under a fiduciary obligation that is similar to a trust, but which is not a trust in the strict technical sense of the word.[237] Indeed, Lord Kilbrandon referred in his judgment to the 'fund' held by way of guarantee against the non-performance of the obligations in the *City Equitable Fire* case, which suggests that he assumed that there was a trust in that case. The use of the expression 'quasi-trust' was criticized by Lord Simon of Glaisdale as giving 'uncertain guidance in the law'. He preferred to say that: 'money is paid for a special (or specific) purpose so as to exclude mutuality of dealing within [the set-off section] if the money is paid in such circumstances that it would be a misappropriation to use it for any other purpose than that for which it is paid.'[238] It is not clear what he meant by 'misappropriation'. But it suggests that the parties should have intended that there be a separate fund which is not to be misappropriated, and such a fund may be characterized as a trust fund.

(5) Bank accounts, and other debt relationships

In *National Westminster Bank v Halesowen*,[239] a company's current account with a bank was **10.54** overdrawn. It was agreed between the company and the bank that the account should be frozen, and that a new account should be opened through which the company's current business henceforth should pass. It was held that this new account was not precluded from being set off in the company's liquidation against the overdrawn account by virtue of being a special-purpose account. This seems correct. The account had credited to it the company's own money. It was a normal bank account giving rise to a debtor/creditor relationship. There are other cases to a similar effect. In *Pedder v The Mayor, Aldermen, and Burgesses of Preston*,[240] the Corporation of Preston had an account with a bank for the Corporation's general municipal functions. In addition, the Corporation had been constituted the Local Board of Health under the Public Health Act 1848, and for this a separate account was opened with the same bank. The bank entered into an arrangement with its creditors under the Bankrupt Law Consolidation Act 1849, at which time the general account was overdrawn and the Local Board of Health account was in credit. Section 87 of the 1848 Act

---

[235] [1972] AC 785.
[236] [1972] AC 785, 821.
[237] *Foley v Hill* (1848) 2 HLC 28, 35–6, 9 ER 1002, 1005. In modern parlance this is called a constructive trust. See Finn, *Fiduciary Obligations* (1977), 89.
[238] [1972] AC 785, 808. See also *Re Arthur Sanders Ltd* (1981) 17 BLR 125, 133, and the comments of Vaughan Williams J in the Divisional Court in *Re Pollitt* [1893] 1 QB 175, 179.
[239] [1972] AC 785.
[240] (1862) 12 CB(NS) 535, 142 ER 1251.

provided that the money received by the Local Board of Health 'shall be applied . . . in defraying such of the Expenses incurred or to be incurred by the said Local Board in carrying this Act into execution', but it was nevertheless held that the Corporation could set the credit balance on that account against its indebtedness on the other. Another illustration is *Ex p Pearce, re Langmead*.[241] Commissioners had been appointed for the purposes of improving the harbour of Teignmouth and the navigation of the river Teign. The Commissioners opened two accounts with a bank, headed respectively 'No 1 Harbour Account' and 'No 2 River Account'. The Harbour Account was in credit and the River Account in debit. It was held in the bankruptcy of the bank that the two accounts could be set off, notwithstanding that an Act of Parliament provided that the sums standing to the credit of the Harbour Account were to be used in improving Teignmouth Harbour. In the *Pedder* and *Pearce* cases, the debtor on the special purpose account was bankrupt, whereas in *Halesowen* the creditor on the account was the insolvent party, but the principle should be the same. In *MS Fashions Ltd v Bank of Credit and Commerce International SA*[242] the Court of Appeal[243] held that an account into which money had been deposited as security for a third party's debt to the bank was not exempt from set-off on the basis of the special-purpose payment cases.[244]

10.55 A different result occurred in New South Wales in *National Mutual Royal Bank v Ginges*.[245] The case concerned an account opened by a company in similar circumstances to the account in the *Halesowen* case. Brownie J accepted that its purpose was to provide creditors participating in a moratorium with a 'fund' to which they could look for payment, and held that it could not be set off in the company's liquidation. But unless the creditors had an equitable interest in the account,[246] which was not discussed,[247] the purpose for which the account was opened should not have prevented a set-off. As between the bank and the customer the account simply gave rise to a debt.[248]

---

[241] (1841) 2 Mont D & De G 142.

[242] [1993] Ch 425, 448–51.

[243] Dillon, Nolan and Steyn LJJ.

[244] See also *Bank of Credit and Commerce Hong Kong Ltd (in liq) v Mahadumrongkul* (8 May 1997), in which the Privy Council (on appeal from the Court of Appeal of Hong Kong) rejected the view that a deposit made by a director of a company with a bank as security for the company's debt to the bank was held on trust.

[245] Supreme Court of New South Wales, Brownie J, 15 March 1991.

[246] See paras 11.13–11.17 below.

[247] The judgment records that the bank paid the money into court pursuant to Part IV of the Trustee Act 1925 (NSW), and that Waddell CJ in Eq in earlier proceedings (30 April 1990) had ordered that the money be paid to the liquidator. However, the reason for the order does not appear in Brownie J's judgment in the *Ginges* case, in particular whether the question of set-off was raised before Waddell CJ in Eq. Nor was the question of a trust discussed in these proceedings. The bank was suing the defendants as guarantors of the company's overdrawn account, and the guarantors argued unsuccessfully by way of defence that the overdrawn account should have been set off in the company's liquidation against the account in credit.

[248] Nevertheless, Clarke JA referred to *National Mutual v Ginges* without adverse comment in *Central Brake Service (Sydney) Ltd v Central Brake Service (Newcastle) Ltd* (1992) 27 NSWLR 406, 412. Compare also Helsham CJ in Eq's comments in *MPS Constructions Pty Ltd v Rural Bank of New South Wales* (1980) 4 ACLR 835, 845 in relation to the bank account set up in that case for the payment of retention money pursuant to a building contract.

When the relationship is one of debt, for example where money is paid into a bank account **10.56** to be applied to a particular purpose which has not been carried out, other factors nevertheless may affect the availability of a set-off. In the first place, there may have been an agreement (express or implied) that the debt is not to be set off, although this would not be effective to exclude a set-off once bankruptcy or liquidation occurs.[249] Secondly, if the money was paid to the bank under circumstances where it was specifically appropriated to meet a liability owing by the depositor to a third party, the circumstances may be such as to give rise to an equitable assignment or, if the bank has communicated its assent to the arrangement to the third party, possibly it may constitute an attornment so as to entitle the third party to sue on the basis of money had and received,[250] although attornment where there is no fund remains a matter of controversy.[251] In either case this would destroy mutuality for the purpose of set-off against the depositor.

(6) The principle re-phrased

If the existence of a trust is recognized as the reason for denying a set-off in the **10.57** special-purpose payment cases, the statements of law found in *Re Pollitt* and *Re Mid-Kent Fruit Factory*[252] should be re-phrased. The principle is better stated in terms that, if a payment is made for a special purpose, and either the purpose fails or, it if has been carried out, a residue remains, the depository may not set off the obligation to return the money if the depositor has retained a beneficial interest in the money so that it is subject to a trust in his or her favour.[253] In the *Mid-Kent Fruit Factory* case[254] Vaughan Williams J considered that, if there is a balance remaining after the purpose has been carried out, the depository cannot bring the balance into an account unless the depository can show that it remained in his or her hands with the depositor's consent. While the depositor's consent to the money remaining with the depository may militate against a trust, it is not conclusive. The question is the terms upon which the money was to be retained, in particular whether the depositor could mix it with his or her own funds or whether he or she was required to keep it separate for the benefit of the depositor.[255]

The distinction between a debt and a trust is important not only for set-off, but also in the **10.58** determination of the depositor's rights as against the depository where the depository became bankrupt before the money was applied to the purpose. If the fund was deposited subject to a trust, and the purpose has failed, the depositor as the beneficial owner of the money can recover it in full from the bankrupt's estate.[256] If, however, the relationship

---

[249] See paras 6.111–6.112 above.

[250] *W. P. Greenhalgh and Sons v Union Bank of Manchester* [1924] 2 KB 153.

[251] See the criticism of *Shamia v Joory* [1958] 2 QB 448 in Goff and Jones, *The Law of Restitution* (7th edn, 2007), 695–6. See also *Rothwells Ltd v Nommack (No. 100) Pty Ltd* [1990] 2 Qd R 85, 90–1.

[252] See paras 10.47–10.48 above.

[253] See *Barclays Bank Ltd v Quistclose Investments Ltd* [1970] AC 567, 581–2, as explained by Lord Millett in *Twinsectra Ltd v Yardley* [2002] 2 AC 164 at [77] *et seq*.

[254] [1896] 1 Ch 567. See para. 10.48 above.

[255] See paras 10.19 and 10.50 above.

[256] Insolvency Act 1986, s. 283(3). See e.g. *Ex p Dumas* (1754) 2 Ves Sen 582, 28 ER 372; *Re Rogers, ex p Holland & Hannen* (1891) 8 Morr 243; *Barclays Bank Ltd v Quistclose Investments Ltd* [1970] AC 567.

between the parties is simply one of debtor and creditor, as was the case in *Re Barned's Banking Co Ltd (Massey's Case)* where a bank was provided with funds to cover the acceptance of a bill of exchange,[257] the depositor is confined to a proof in the depository's bankruptcy.

See also *Tooke v Hollingworth* (1793) 5 TR 215, 101 ER 121, affirmed (1795) 2 H Bl 501, 126 ER 670 for the position at common law.

[257] (1870) 39 LJ Ch 635. See also *Pott v Clegg* (1847) 16 M & W 321, 153 ER 1212. Compare *Farley v Turner* (1857) 26 LJ Ch 710, where the bank had specifically appropriated the money to the purpose before its bankruptcy.

11

MUTUALITY – INTRODUCTION

A. The Meaning of Mutuality

(1) Mutuality defined

For both the insolvency set-off section and the Statutes of Set-off there must be mutuality.[1] **11.01**
Mutuality does not require that the claims should arise at the same time,[2] nor that there
should be any connection between them.[3] It is irrelevant, moreover, that the claims may be
of a different nature. As the High Court of Australia observed in *Gye v McIntyre*:[4] 'the word
"mutual" conveys the notion of reciprocity rather than that of correspondence.' Thus,
an obligation arising out of an instrument under seal may be set off against a simple

---

[1] Compare paras 4.67–4.83 above in relation to equitable set-off. Lack of mutuality is also a defence to
proceedings for specific performance, but it is there used in a different sense, that as a matter of discretion the
court will not compel a defendant to perform his or her obligations specifically if it cannot at the same time
ensure that any unperformed obligations of the claimant will be specifically performed, unless damages would be
an adequate remedy for any default by the claimant. See *Price v Strange* [1978] 1 Ch 337, 367–8 (Buckley LJ).

[2] *Halsbury's Laws of England* (5th edn, 2009) vol. 11 ('Civil Procedure'), para. 653, n. 2. See also the
reference in *Day & Dent Constructions Pty Ltd v North Australian Properties Pty Ltd* (1981) 34 ALR 595, 600
(Federal Court of Australia) to the submission to that effect in relation to the Statutes of Set–off, which was
not disputed.

[3] *Naoroji v Chartered Bank of India* (1868) LR 3 CP 444, 452; *Re Daintrey* [1900] 1 QB 546.

[4] (1991) 171 CLR 609, 623.

contract debt,[5] and a secured debt may be set off against an unsecured debt.[6] Mutuality means that the demands must be between the same parties and they must be held in the same capacity, or right, or interest.[7] It is concerned with the status of the parties and their relationship to each other. It is not concerned with the nature of the claims themselves. The nature of the claims is dealt with instead by the requirement of 'debts' or, in insolvency set-off, of 'debts', 'credits' or claims arising out of prior 'dealings'.[8] The requirement of same parties means that A's right to sue B cannot be set off against A's debt to C, or that a joint demand cannot be set off against a separate demand.[9] In the case of insolvency set-off, the requirement that the demands be held in the same capacity (or right, or interest) means that each of the parties, who is liable to the other, must be the beneficial owner of the cross-claim against that other.[10] In other words, 'there must be identity between the persons beneficially interested in the claim and the person against whom the cross-claim existed'.[11] The principle differs slightly for the Statutes of Set-off. In that context, mutuality strictly is determined by reference to legal titles, although equity may confer or deny a set-off depending on whether there is mutuality in equity.[12] In the case of a company, a change in control of the company between the dates that the cross-demands were contracted does not affect mutuality, if in truth the same legal entity was the contracting party in both cases.[13]

11.02 The form of the arrangements by which the cross-demands came into existence does not affect mutuality. It is not correct to say, as Lord Denning suggested in the Court of Appeal in *Halesowen Presswork & Assemblies Ltd v Westminster Bank Ltd*,[14] that the nature of the arrangements entered into may be 'so special as to deprive them of mutuality', an approach that Lord Cross of Chelsea on appeal in the House of Lords[15] criticized as placing on the expression a meaning that was too narrow in the light of the decided cases.[16] In *Rolls Razor Ltd v Cox*,[17] Winn LJ advanced the theory that mutuality essentially is concerned

---

[5] See e.g. *Ex p Law, re Kennedy* (1864) De Gex 378.
[6] But see paras 6.176–6.182 above in relation to insolvency set-off.
[7] *Ince Hall Rolling Mills Co Ltd v The Douglas Forge Co* (1882) 8 QBD 179, 183 ('between the same parties and in the same interest'); *Shand v M J Atkinson Ltd* [1966] NZLR 551, 570 ('by and against a person in the same right'); *Peel v Fitzgerald* [1982] Qd R 544, 547 ('between the same parties and in the same right'); *Secretary of State for Trade and Industry v Frid* [2004] 2 AC 506 at [26] ('in the same capacity'). In *Gye v McIntyre* (1991) 171 CLR 609, 623, 625, the Australian High Court suggested that the requirement of commensurability (see ch. 9 above) is an aspect of mutuality, but that requirement is better characterized as being inherent in set-offs generally and, in the case of insolvency set-off, as following from the reference in the insolvency set-off section to setting off 'the sums due' (or, in the Australian legislation, 'the sum due'). See para. 9.01 above.
[8] See ch. 7 above.
[9] See ch. 12 below.
[10] See paras 11.13–11.17 below.
[11] *West Street Properties Pty Ltd v Jamison* [1974] 2 NSWLR 435, 441 (Jeffrey J).
[12] See paras 11.18–11.20 below.
[13] *Central Brake Service (Sydney) Pty Ltd v Central Brake Service (Newcastle) Pty Ltd* (1992) 27 NSWLR 406 (official management).
[14] [1971] 1 QB 1, 36.
[15] *National Westminster Bank Ltd v Halesowen Presswork & Assemblies Ltd* [1972] AC 785, 812.
[16] Compare Viscount Dilhorne, who said (at [1972] AC 785, 806) that the arrangements before him were not of this special character, without offering an opinion in relation to Lord Denning's view.
[17] [1967] 1 QB 552, 574.

with the intentions of the parties. Subsequently, however, Jonathan Parker J in *Re ILG Travel Ltd*[18] rejected the proposition that the subjective intentions of the parties can be decisive of the question whether dealings between them are mutual dealings, and indeed in insolvency set-off the notion that intention is relevant to mutuality is contrary to the proposition that the insolvency set-off section cannot be contracted out of.[19] Later Winn LJ commented that the set-off section in the insolvency legislation 'applies only to cross-claims arising *directly* from dealings between a person who has become a bankrupt and another person all of which are properly called "mutual" '.[20] In essence, this appears to be a restatement of the argument that was rejected in 1798 in *Hankey v Smith*,[21] that for mutual credit the parties should have meant to trust each other in the transaction in question. It was held in that case that an indebtedness of a bankrupt acceptor upon a bill of exchange could be brought into an account by the holder, even though the bankrupt was unaware that the bill had been indorsed to the holder. A similar result has occurred in the context of the Statutes of Set-off.[22] The notion of 'direct' dealings, or of the element of trust, fails to explain the right of set-off in cases like *Hankey v Smith*, or indeed in any case in which one of the parties to the proposed set-off gained a right to sue the other only as a result of an assignment to him or her of the other's indebtedness.[23] Rather, those cases support the view that for mutuality one should look only to the identity of the persons entitled to the benefit and subject to the burden of the cross-demands.

(2) Double insolvency

In *Re SSSL Realisations (2002) Ltd*,[24] the Court of Appeal accepted that the concept of mutuality has a further aspect in a double insolvency situation. Consider that A and B have cross-claims against each other and that they are both in liquidation. Further, A's claim for some reason is not provable in B's liquidation. Because A's claim is not provable, it could not be set off in B's liquidation.[25] In that circumstance, the Court of Appeal accepted that, similarly, there could not be a set-off in A's liquidation. This was justified on the basis of mutuality. In delivering the judgment of the court, Chadwick LJ said:[26]

11.03

> The reason, as it seems to me, why (in a double insolvency case) a debt which cannot be proved by A in the liquidation of B cannot be set off against B's proof of debt in the liquidation

---

[18] [1995] 2 BCLC 128, 160.

[19] See paras 6.111–6.112 above.

[20] *Halesowen Presswork & Assemblies Ltd v Westminster Bank Ltd* [1971] 1 QB 1, 43 (CA) (emphasis added).

[21] (1789) 3 TR 507n, 100 ER 703. There have nevertheless been other occasions when mutuality has been defined in terms of mutual trust. See Story, *Commentaries on Equity Jurisprudence* (14th edn, 1918) vol. 3, 471 (and the cases referred to in note 4), and *Knox v Cockburn* (1862) 1 QSCR 80. See also *Koster v Eason* (1813) 2 M & S 112, 118, 105 ER 324, 326–7, where Lord Ellenborough spoke in terms of 'consent'.

[22] See e.g. *Cornforth v Rivett* (1814) 2 M & S 510, 105 ER 471.

[23] See e.g. *Clark v Cort* (1840) Cr & Ph 154, 41 ER 449; *Mathieson's Trustee v Burrup, Mathieson and Co* [1927] 1 Ch 562; *Southern Cross Construction Ltd v Southern Cross Club Ltd* [1973] 1 NZLR 708; *Kon Strukt Pty Ltd v Storage Developments Pty Ltd* (1989) 96 FLR 43. See also, with respect to the Statutes of Set–off, *Bennett v White* [1910] 2 KB 643.

[24] [2006] Ch 610.

[25] See para. 7.24 above.

[26] [2006] Ch 610 at [90].

of A is that the requirement of mutuality is not satisfied. The provisions as to statutory set-off in the insolvency code require that the same balance in respect of 'the mutual credits, mutual debts or other mutual dealings' be struck between A and B in both liquidations.

In the *SSSL Realisations* case, A was a surety for debts owing by B to C. Both A and B were in liquidation. The creditor (C), not having been paid in full, was entitled to prove for the debts in the liquidation of B, as the principal debtor. Because of the rule against double proof,[27] A could not prove in B's liquidation in competition with C in respect of A's contingent claim for an indemnity arising from the suretyship, and similarly A's contingent claim could not be set off in B's liquidation against a separate debt owing by B to A.[28] If there was no set-off as between A and B in B's liquidation, the Court of Appeal considered that there similarly could not be a set-off in A's liquidation.

11.04 That reasoning negates the principle accepted by the High Court of Australia in *Gye v McIntyre*[29] that, while the insolvency set-off section requires that a creditor's claim against a company in liquidation be provable in the liquidation, there is no requirement that the company's cross-claim against the creditor must be in the nature of a provable debt.[30] However, on the view accepted in *Re SSSL Realisations*, this would be necessary for a set-off in the company's liquidation if the creditor is also insolvent. If the company's cross-claim is not provable in the creditor's liquidation, it could not be the subject of a set-off in that liquidation and hence it could not be the subject of a set-off in the company's own liquidation.

11.05 In the circumstances under consideration in *Re SSSL Realisations*, the denial of a set-off in both liquidations is a just result. Chadwick LJ was considering the rule against double proof. The purpose of that rule is to prevent a situation arising where an insolvent principal debtor has to pay twice in respect of what in substance is the same debt, once in relation to a proof of debt lodged by the creditor and a second time consequent upon a proof lodged by the surety in respect of the surety's contingent claim for an indemnity.[31] There can only be one proof of debt, by the creditor. Further, set-off is equivalent to payment,[32] and if the surety were permitted a set-off in the principal debtor's liquidation the principal debtor would still end up paying twice, once on the creditor's proof of debt and a second time through a set-off against a separate debt owing by the surety to the principal debtor. Therefore, the consideration which underlies the rule against double proof dictates that the surety should not be entitled to a set-off in the principal debtor's liquidation. But the same result, of double payment by the principal debtor, would occur if the surety were also insolvent and a set-off occurred instead in the surety's liquidation. Consequently, when a set-off

---

[27] See paras 8.13 and 8.14 above.
[28] See para. 8.18 above.
[29] (1991) 171 CLR 609, 628–629, referred to in *Re Bank of Credit and Commerce International SA (No. 8)* [1998] AC 214, 228. See also *Coventry v Charter Pacific Corporation Ltd* (2005) 227 CLR 234 at [54]–[55] and [106].
[30] See paras 7.27–7.30 above.
[31] See para. 8.14 above.
[32] See para. 12.34 below.

is denied to a surety in the principal debtor's liquidation because of the rule against double proof, a set-off similarly should be denied in the surety's liquidation.[33]

The first sentence in the quoted passage from Chadwick LJ's judgment[34] referred to the **11.06** particular situation in which a debt cannot be proved in the liquidation of one of the parties. The reason given in the second sentence for denying a set-off in both liquidations rested on a more general proposition, that the same balance must be able to be struck in both liquidations. A set-off may be denied in the liquidation of one of the parties to mutual claims for reasons other than the provability of one of the claims. In so far as the reasoning rested upon that more general proposition, it should be reconsidered.

In the first place, the insolvency set-off section directs attention to the availability of a **11.07** set-off in a particular insolvency. If there are mutual credits, mutual debts or claims arising out of mutual dealings in an insolvency, a set-off *prima facie* may occur in that insolvency. The position in another insolvency is distinct.

Secondly, there is no need for a rule that the same balance be struck in both insolvencies. It **11.08** suffices if a balance may be struck in one insolvency. If a set-off between A and B is available in A's insolvency, that set-off would extinguish the mutual claims the subject of the set-off and it would bind both A's and B's estate. A corresponding set-off in B's insolvency is not necessary.

Thirdly, a general proposition in a double insolvency situation requiring a set-off in both **11.09** insolvencies is inconsistent with cases dealing with unpaid share capital. If a limited liability company is in liquidation and there are partly paid shares, a shareholder who is also a creditor of the company is not entitled to a set-off in the liquidation against the liability to contribute the unpaid share capital.[35] The prohibition against a set-off applies in the

---

[33] See also *Re Fenton* [1931] 1 Ch 85, to which Chadwick LJ referred in *Re SSSL Realisations* [2006] Ch 610 at [84] and [89]. This was a double insolvency situation, and it was held that the rule against double proof precluded a set-off. It is implicit that the denial related to both insolvencies. Indeed, while Lord Hanworth (at 105) and Romer LJ (at 120) referred to the principal debtor's liquidation, Lawrence LJ (at 111) made reference to both insolvencies. The denial of a set-off in both insolvencies may be explained on the basis set out in the text in relation to *Re SSSL Realisations*. But it also may be explained on another ground. Consider the matter first from the perspective of the insolvent principal debtor's estate. The creditor in *Re Fenton* had proved in the insolvency of the surety but had not been paid anything. The surety's claim against the principal debtor's estate therefore was wholly contingent. Apart from the rule against double proof, that contingent liability of the principal debtor would have been provable, and also available for set-off, in the principal debtor's insolvency. See para. 8.14 above. However, when looked at from the perspective of the insolvent surety's estate, the position was different. From that perspective, the issue concerned a contingent claim (as opposed to a contingent liability) of the insolvent surety, and at the time that *Re Fenton* was decided a contingent claim possessed by an insolvent, while it remained contingent, could not be set off in that insolvency. See para. 8.35 above. The position has changed in England in company administration and liquidation by virtue of the Insolvency Rules 1986, rr. 2.85(4)(b) and (5) (administration) and 4.90(4)(b) and (5) (liquidation). Nevertheless, it explains why a set-off was unavailable in *Re Fenton*, not only in the principal debtor's insolvency (on the basis of the rule against double proof), but also in the surety's insolvency. It is not necessary to have recourse to the principle of mutuality referred to in *Re SSSL Realisations* at [90] (see above) in order to explain the absence of a set-off in the surety's insolvency. This may be the point that Chadwick LJ had in mind in *Re SSSL Realisations* at [89].
[34] See para. 11.03 above.
[35] See paras 8.64–8.79 above.

liquidation of the company. If, in addition, the shareholder is bankrupt, it has been held that the shareholder's liability to contribute may be the subject of a set-off *in the bankruptcy*.[36] Thus, a set-off may be available in one insolvency but not in the other.

11.10 As mentioned above, in the particular situation in issue in *Re SSSL Realisations*, there is much to be said for the view that in a double solvency situation a set-off should be denied in both insolvencies, given the operation of the rule against double proof. In other situations, however, there is not the same justification for denying a set-off in both insolvencies where it is denied in one and, for the reasons given above, it is suggested that there is no general principle to the effect that a set-off must be available in both insolvencies in order that a set-off may occur. The cases dealing with calls on shares, to which reference was made,[37] illustrate that proposition. The point may also be relevant in other situations, for example in relation to secured debts. If a creditor has security for a debt owing by a company in liquidation, and the creditor chooses to rely on the security rather than prove in the insolvency, the debt is not the subject of a set-off in the debtor's insolvency.[38] This is because the insolvency set-off section requires that there be a creditor who is 'proving or claiming to prove' in the insolvency, and in the situation posited that requirement is not satisfied. If, on the other hand, the secured creditor, as opposed to the debtor, is in liquidation, the secured debt is not subject to a requirement of proof and it may be set off in the creditor's insolvency.[39] To the extent of the set-off, the security would be freed. In a case in which both the secured creditor and the debtor are insolvent, there could not be a set-off in the debtor's insolvency if the creditor's estate is purporting to rely on the security. But there would appear to be no reason why a set-off should not be permitted in the secured creditor's own insolvency. The secured debt could be set off against a separate debt owing by the secured creditor to the debtor, with a consequent release of the security to that extent.[40]

11.11 There is further point. Consider that A and B have cross-claims against each other which could be set off in B's liquidation but not in A's liquidation. Consider also that A goes into liquidation on day 1 and B goes into liquidation later, on day 2. In this situation, there will not have been a set-off in A's liquidation and, assuming the correctness of the general

---

[36] See para. 8.71 above, explaining *Re Duckworth* (1867) LR 2 Ch App 578. See also *Re Anglo–Greek Steam Navigation and Trading Co. Carralli & Haggard's Claim* (1869) LR 4 Ch App 174; *Ex p Cooper, re A Trust Deed* (1867) 15 LT 637; *Re Universal Banking Corporation, ex p Strang* (1870) LR 5 Ch App 492 (but see the criticism of that case at para. 8.71 above). Compare *Re Auriferous Properties Ltd* [1898] 1 Ch 691, wherein Wright J, while acknowledging the authority of *Re Duckworth*, held that a set-off is not available when the contributory is a company in liquidation. *Quaere* whether *Re Auriferous Properties* was correctly decided. See para. 8.74 above. *Re Duckworth* was decided before the bankruptcy set-off section was extended to company liquidation in 1875 (see para. 6.05 above), but the principle is not affected by that development. This was assumed in *Re GEB, A Debtor* [1903] 2 KB 340, 352, and see also *Re Patrick Corporation & the Companies Act* (1980) ACLC 40–643 at p. 34,272 (NSW SC).

[37] See para. 11.09 above.

[38] See paras 6.177 and 6.178 above.

[39] See para. 6.179 above.

[40] Compare *Brown v Cork* [1985] BCLC 363. The case concerned a secured debt in a double insolvency situation, and the Court of Appeal at 369–71, 374 (referring to the first instance judge) and 376 (approving of the respondent's submissions) appeared to accept an argument that the fact of the security precluded a set-off. However that argument was considered only from the perspective of the liquidation of the debtor (the underpaying surety). The judgment is criticized at paras 8.47–8.50 above for not considering the position in the liquidation of the creditor (the overpaying surety).

principle suggested in *Re SSSL Realisations*, that principle would apply to deny a set-off also in B's later liquidation. That result does not present any practical difficulty.[41] There would also be not be any practical difficulty if A and B go into liquidation at the same time. Consider, however, that B goes into liquidation first, on day 1, and that A's liquidation does not occur until later. Set-offs occur automatically on the date of a liquidation.[42] Therefore, when B went into liquidation, a set-off *prima facie* would have occurred. If, however, A subsequently goes into liquidation, the question would arise as to the position in B's earlier liquidation. Applying *Re SSSL Realisations*, one possibility is that it would be said that, with the benefit of hindsight,[43] there was not in fact a set-off in that liquidation because the circumstances did not support a set-off in A's liquidation. But that would introduce uncertainty into the winding up of B, particularly in relation to the calculation and payment of dividends. Alternatively, the hindsight principle might be said not to apply in this situation, so as not to disturb set-offs in B's liquidation. But if that is the case, the result would then differ depending on which company went into liquidation first. As mentioned above, if A went into liquidation first there would not be a set-off in its liquidation and (on the basis of *Re SSSL Realisations*) there consequently would not be a set-off in B's later liquidation. But if B went into liquidation first, there would be a set-off in its liquidation which would not be unwound by the hindsight principle. Therefore, on either approach in relation to hindsight, the general principle suggested in *Re SSSL Realisations* would give rise to difficulty.

(3) The necessity for mutuality

It is said that mutuality must always be present,[44] but in relation to set-off in insolvency the **11.12** rule is better stated in terms that cross-demands which are not strictly mutual may not be set off 'except under special circumstances'.[45] There are a number of situations in which the courts have allowed a set-off despite an apparent absence of strict mutuality,[46] though some of these are examples of equitable set-off for which the better view is that mutuality is not always a strict requirement.[47]

---

[41] If there is no set-off in the liquidations, the rule in *Cherry v Boultbee* (1839) 4 My & Cr 442, 41 ER 171 (see ch. 14 below) should apply, on the basis set out in paras 14.102–14.104 below. If denial of a set-off in a double insolvency arises because of the rule against double proof, as in *Re SSSL Realisations* where both a surety and the principal debtor were in liquidation, the issue referred to in para. 14.103 below, as to which of the parties should be entitled to the benefit of the *Cherry v Boultbee* principle, should not arise. This is because the rule against double proof has the consequence that the surety could not prove in the liquidation of the principal debtor. *Cherry v Boultbee* therefore could not apply in that liquidation (the surety not having a right to participate in that liquidation) and so the principle could only be applied in the surety's liquidation.

[42] See para. 6.123 above.

[43] See paras 6.132–6.138 above. In *Re Bank of Credit and Commerce International SA (No. 8)* [1996] Ch 243, 269 Rose LJ commented: 'it is now settled that the set-off operates automatically upon the date of bankruptcy, and that the hindsight principle enables debts to be treated as owing or not on that date with the benefit of hindsight . . .'

[44] *Re Mid-Kent Fruit Factory* [1896] 1 Ch 567, 571. See also *Knox v Cockburn* (1862) 1 QSCR 80, 83; *Re City Life Assurance Co Ltd* [1926] 1 Ch 191, 216; *Day & Dent Constructions Pty Ltd v North Australian Properties Pty Ltd* (1981) 34 ALR 595, 601 (Federal Court of Australia).

[45] *Freeman v Lomas* (1851) 9 Hare 109, 113–14, 68 ER 435, 437 (Sir George Turner). See also *West Street Properties Pty Ltd v Jamison* [1974] 2 NSWLR 435, 441 (Statutes of Set-off).

[46] See eg paras 12.08–12.20 below.

[47] See paras 4.67–4.83 above (but compare the recent authorities suggesting the contrary: see para. 4.69 above). Bankruptcy or company liquidation should not affect the availability of equitable set-off. See paras 6.25–6.32 above.

B. Equitable Interests – Insolvency Set-off

(1) Fundamental principle

11.13 A fundamental principle of insolvency set-off is that mutuality is determined by reference to equitable interests rather than bare legal rights.[48] Therefore, if the other requirements of the insolvency set-off section are satisfied, the beneficial owner of a debt may set off the debt against a liability that he or she has to the debtor.[49] Thus, where an equitable assignee of a debt is sued by the debtor's trustee in bankruptcy in respect of a separate liability owed by the assignee to the debtor, the assignee may bring the assigned debt into an account.[50] Conversely, a set-off will be denied under the insolvency set-off section if one of the parties to the proposed set-off holds the claim as a bare trustee for a third party,[51] or if the claim has been assigned to a third party.[52] This emphasis on equitable rights is a consequence of the influence of equity in matters of bankruptcy. The Chancellor more or less assumed control over bankruptcy in the nineteenth century, and since the creation of a separate Court of Bankruptcy in 1831[53] and its subsequent amalgamation with the Supreme Court of Judicature in 1883,[54]

---

[48] *Re Hett, Maylor, and Co* (1894) 10 TLR 412; *Hiley v Peoples Prudential Assurance Co Ltd* (1938) 60 CLR 468, 488, 497; *Popular Homes Ltd v Circuit Developments Ltd* [1979] 2 NZLR 642, 656–8; *Gye v McIntyre* (1991) 171 CLR 609, 623; *Secretary of State for Trade and Industry v Frid* [2004] 2 AC 506 at [26]; *Coventry v Charter Pacific Corporation Ltd* (2005) 227 CLR 234 at [56]. As Byles J remarked during argument in *Watkins v Clark* (1862) 12 CB (NS) 277, 282, 142 ER 1149, 1152: 'The bankrupt law deals with beneficial interests only.'

[49] *Crosse v Smith* (1813) 1 M & S 545, 105 ER 204; *Bailey v Johnson* (1872) LR 7 Ex 263; *Ex p Morier, re Willis, Percival, & Co* (1879) 12 Ch D 491, 496, 500, 502; *Hiley v Peoples Prudential Assurance Co* Ltd (1938) 60 CLR 468, 497. See also *Cochrane v Green* (1860) 9 CB (NS) 448, 142 ER 176. The observations of Sir George Jessel MR in *Middleton v Pollock, Ex p Nugee* (1875) LR 20 Eq 29, 36–7 (and see also *Welton v Harnett* (1886) 7 NSWR 74) on the necessity for some 'special jurisdiction' should not be accepted as correct.

[50] *Mathieson's Trustee v Burrup, Mathieson and Co* [1927] 1 Ch 562; *Daleri Ltd v Woolworths Plc* [2008] EWHC 2891 (Ch) (company liquidation).

[51] E.g. when a creditor of a bankrupt on a negotiable instrument holds the instrument as trustee for a third party, the creditor may not employ the debt arising from the instrument in a set-off. See *Fair v M'Iver* (1812) 16 East 130, 104 ER 1038; *Belcher v Lloyd* (1833) 10 Bing 310, 131 ER 924; *Lackington v Combes* (1839) 6 Bing (NC) 71, 133 ER 28; *Forster v Wilson* (1843) 14 M & W 191, 152 ER 1165; *London, Bombay, and Mediterranean Bank v Narraway* (1872) LR 15 Eq 93; *Tapper v Matheson* (1884) NZLR 3 SC 312; *Re Kaupthing Singer and Friedlander Ltd* [2009] 2 Lloyd's Rep 154 at [9]. In *Re Last, ex p Butterell* (1994) 124 ALR 219, why did the fact that Rawilla Pty Ltd was a trustee of a discretionary trust not preclude a set-off? See para. 17.125n below. Set-offs may nevertheless be available on other grounds in cases involving trusts. See paras 17.122–17.134 below.

[52] *Boyd v Mangles* (1874) 16 M & W 337, 153 ER 1218; *Re Asphaltic Wood Pavement Co. Lee & Chapman's Case* (1885) 30 Ch D 216; *Re W Guthrie and Allied Companies* (1901) 4 GLR 155 (NZSC); *Popular Homes Ltd v Circuit Developments Ltd* [1979] 2 NZLR 642, 656–8. See also *De Mattos v Saunders* (1872) LR 7 CP 570; *Re City Life Assurance Co Ltd (Stephenson's Case)* [1926] 1 Ch 191, 214 (as explained by Dixon J in *Hiley v Peoples Prudential Assurance Co* Ltd (1938) 60 CLR 468, 501–5); *Re Patrick Corporation Ltd and the Companies Act* (1980) ACLC 40–643; *Thomas v National Australia Bank Ltd* [2000] 2 Qd R 448, 455.

[53] See (1831) 1 & 2 Will IV, c. 56. The Bankruptcy Act 1869 replaced the Court of Bankruptcy with the London Bankruptcy Court.

[54] The Supreme Court of Judicature Act 1873, ss. 3 and 16 originally contemplated the consolidation of the London Bankruptcy Court with the newly created Supreme Court of Judicature, but the proposal was abandoned with the enactment of s. 9 of the Supreme Court of Judicature Act 1875, and was not carried into effect until the enactment of the Bankruptcy Act 1883, s. 93.

the court administering bankruptcy has been a court of both common law and equity.[55] As Clauson J aptly remarked:[56]

> The Bankruptcy Act . . . is an Act regulating the proceedings of a Court which has always been a Court of equity, proceeding on equitable principles, recognizing equitable debts, subject of course to such infirmities as are sometimes present, but drawing no distinction between equitable and legal rights for purposes of administering the estate of the bankrupt.

When a debt is held on trust, the notion that the debt may be set off against a cross-claim **11.14** owing by the beneficiary to the debtor assumes that the debt is held on trust only for that beneficiary. If the debt is held on behalf of a number of beneficiaries, a set-off may be denied on the ground that a jointly owned claim may not be set off against a debt owing by one only of the joint claimants.[57]

(2) Beneficial title acquired after the relevant date

For a set-off to proceed under the insolvency legislation, the beneficial title ordinarily **11.15** should have been acquired before the relevant date for determining rights of set-off,[58] so that, for example, a set-off may not be based upon an assignment or other acquisition of title that took place after that date.[59] There may be a set-off, however, if the beneficial title, although not acquired until after the relevant date, nevertheless reverts back to a time before then. This may occur when a bankruptcy is annulled. In *Bailey v Johnson*[60] the defendant had been adjudicated a bankrupt, so that his property vested in his trustee in bankruptcy on trust for his creditors. The trustee realized the estate, and paid the proceeds into a bank account. The bank was also a creditor of the defendant. Subsequently, the bank itself was adjudicated bankrupt, and after that the defendant's bankruptcy was annulled. The bank's trustee in bankruptcy sued the defendant for payment of the debt owing to the bank, whereupon the defendant sought to set off the proceeds of his estate paid into the bank. The annulment took place after the bank's bankruptcy, at which time the defendant's estate was held on trust for his general body of creditors. On the other hand, the bankruptcy legislation provides a mechanism by which, upon an annulment, the property of the debtor may 'revert' to him.[61] This was held to operate retrospectively, so that the money should be considered as having been the defendant's when it was paid into the bank. A set-off therefore was allowed.

---

[55] The Lord Chancellor in 1921, pursuant to the power conferred upon him by the Bankruptcy Act 1914, s. 97, assigned the jurisdiction in bankruptcy to the Chancery Division of the High Court. See the Order of the Lord Chancellor, 15 Aug 1921, No. 1741 (L 21).

[56] *Mathieson's Trustee v Burrup, Mathieson and Co* [1927] 1 Ch 562, 569. See also *Lister v Hooson* [1908] 1 KB 174, 178 *per* Fletcher Moulton LJ ('the jurisdiction in bankruptcy was from the first an equitable jurisdiction').

[57] See paras 12.02–12.07 below. See also *Cathedral Place Pty Ltd v Hyatt of Australia Ltd* [2003] VSC 385 at [44]–[45] in relation to a debt owing by A to a listed unit trust, on the one hand, and on the other a debt owing by one of the unit holders to A.

[58] See paras 6.45–6.65 above. Compare the criticism of *MPS Constructions Pty Ltd v Rural Bank of New South Wales* (1980) 4 ACLR 835 in para. 8.31 above.

[59] *Middleton v Pollock, ex p Nugee* (1875) LR 20 Eq 29.

[60] (1872) LR 7 Ex 263.

[61] See the Insolvency Act 1986, s. 282(4), and in Australia the Bankruptcy Act 1966 (Cth), s. 154(1).

(3) Insolvent assignor or trustee

11.16   When a claimant suing to enforce a debt had assigned the debt in equity to a third party or holds it as trustee for a third party, the debtor in some circumstances is permitted to set off a separate debt owing to him or her by the claimant, notwithstanding the beneficial interest of the third party, on the basis of a principle of taking subject to equities. The circumstances in which this may occur are considered later.[62] If the assignor or the trustee is bankrupt (or is a company in liquidation), the debtor's right of set-off in such a case is not derived from the insolvency legislation.[63] Rather, it is based upon the notion that the beneficial owner should take subject to a legal right of set-off available to the debtor against the assignor under the Statutes of Set-off, or alternatively subject to an equitable set-off when the demands are sufficiently closely connected.[64] This has the consequence that, unless the circumstances are such as to give rise to an equitable set-off, both demands must be liquidated and due and payable at the date of the action.[65] Since the bankrupt is not beneficially interested in the claim, it would not have passed to his or her trustee in bankruptcy as property of the bankrupt, in which case the insolvency set-off section cannot be invoked against the person who is beneficially interested. For example, in *De Mattos v Saunders*,[66] the plaintiff was an insured under a policy of marine insurance, and was suing the underwriter for an indemnity for a total loss on behalf of a third party who had made advances on the shipping documents. A claim under a policy of indemnity insurance is regarded as a claim for unliquidated damages, and accordingly it cannot be set off under the Statutes of Set-off.[67] Therefore, there was no right of set-off under the Statutes to which the third party in *De Mattos v Saunders* could be made to take subject. The plaintiff had executed a deed of inspectorship under the Bankruptcy Act 1861 which incorporated the principles of bankruptcy,[68] but it was held that the insolvency set-off section applicable in bankruptcy did not assist the underwriter. The plaintiff's claim was not available for the benefit of his creditors under the deed, and therefore the section did not apply.

(4) Insolvent beneficial owner

11.17   Alternatively, it may be that the beneficial owner of a claim, as opposed to the legal owner, is bankrupt. In that circumstance, the debtor may assert a set-off under the insolvency set-off section in respect of a separate liability of the bankrupt to the debtor in an action brought by the legal owner on behalf of the bankrupt. In *Thornton v Maynard*,[69] the

---

[62] See ch. 17 below.

[63] *De Mattos v Saunders* (1872) LR 7 CP 570; *Re Asphaltic Wood Pavement Co. Lee & Chapman's Case* (1885) 30 Ch D 216, 225; *Popular Homes Ltd v Circuit Developments Ltd* [1979] 2 NZLR 642, 657. See also *Turner v Thomas* (1871) LR 6 CP 610, 615; *Hoverd Industries Ltd v Supercool Refrigeration and Air Conditioning (1991) Ltd* [1995] 3 NZLR 577. See also para. 17.39 below.

[64] See ch. 4 above. In relation to equitable set-off in the context of a trustee in liquidation, see *Murphy v Zamonex Pty Ltd* (1993) 31 NSWLR 439 (referred to with approval in *Penwith District Council v V P Developments Ltd* [2005] 2 BCLC 607 at [20]–[23]) and *Doherty v Murphy* [1996] 2 VR 553, referred to in para. 17.122 below.

[65] Note that the position in relation to the Statutes of Set–off differs in some Australian states. See paras 2.63–2.86 above.

[66] (1875) LR 7 CP 570.

[67] See para. 2.26 above.

[68] See the Bankruptcy Act 1861, s. 197.

[69] (1872) LR 10 CP 695.

plaintiff as holder of several bills of exchange was suing the acceptor, although he had already been paid a dividend on the bills in the bankruptcy of the drawer. When the acceptor of a bill is bankrupt, the holder in proving in the bankruptcy must give credit for anything that he or she had received from the drawer or an indorser before lodging the proof,[70] but that principle does not apply if the acceptor is solvent. In such a case the holder may sue the acceptor for the full amount of the bill, but to the extent of anything received from the drawer the holder sues as trustee for the drawer. It was held in *Thornton v Maynard* that, because the holder to the extent of the dividend received from the drawer's bankrupt estate was suing as trustee, the acceptor was entitled to that extent to a set-off under the bankruptcy legislation in respect of a debt owing to him by the drawer.[71]

C. Statutes of Set-off

It is sometimes assumed that mutuality for the purpose of determining the availability of a set-off under the Statutes of Set-off similarly is determined by reference to the equitable titles to the cross-demands,[72] but that proposition inaccurately states the position.[73] The Statutes permit a set-off in an action if there is mutuality by reference to legal titles. If there is not mutuality at law but there is in equity, equity nevertheless may act by analogy with the legal right of set-off available pursuant to the Statutes and recognize a set-off.[74] Alternatively, if there is mutuality at law by reference to the legal titles but one of the debts has been assigned in equity or is held on trust for a third party, a court of equity may regard it as unconscionable for a set-off at law to occur and accordingly not permit the set-off.[75] But apart from these instances of equitable intervention, the Statutes themselves were confined to cross-debts at law between the parties to a common law action.[76] Consider the case

11.18

---

[70] *Re Blackburne* (1892) 9 Morr 249, 252; *Re Houlder* [1929] 1 Ch 205, 212.

[71] The claim accruing to the bankrupt estate was still contingent at the date of the bankruptcy, but this is not sufficient to prevent a set-off. See paras 8.35–8.46 above.

[72] See e.g. Russell LJ (with whom Sellers LJ agreed) in *Robbie & Co Ltd v Witney Warehouse Co Ltd* [1963] 1 WLR 1324, 1339. See also in Canada *Coba Industries Ltd v Millie's Holdings (Canada) Ltd* [1985] 6 WWR 14, 28–29; *Telford v Holt* (1987) 41 DLR (4th) 385, 394.

[73] I acknowledge my debt to the discussion in *Meagher, Gummow and Lehane's Equity Doctrines and Remedies* (4th edn, 2002), 943–944 [28–335]. See also *Hoverd Industries Ltd v Supercool Refrigeration and Air Conditioning (1991) Ltd* [1995] 3 NZLR 577, 587.

[74] *Freeman v Lomas* (1851) 9 Hare 109, 116, 68 ER 435, 438; *Cavendish v Geaves* (1857) 24 Beav 163, 53 ER 319; *Cochrane v Green* (1860) 9 CB (NS) 448, 142 ER 176; *Agra and Masterman's Bank Ltd v Leighton* (1866) LR 2 Ex 56, 65; *Union Bank of Australia v Waterston* (1894) 12 NZLR 672; *Barclays Bank Ltd v Aschaffenburger Zellstoffwerke AG* [1967] 1 Lloyd's Rep 387. See paras 3.07–3.09 above in relation to equity acting by analogy. Indeed, it appears that the common law courts in some early cases took notice of a trust for the purpose of recognizing a set-off. Two such cases, *Bottomley v Brooke* and *Rudge v Birch*, both unreported, were mentioned by counsel during argument in *Winch v Keeley* (1787) 1 TR 619, 621–2, 99 ER 1284, 1285–6. Compare, however, *Tucker v Tucker* (1833) 4 B & Ad 745, 110 ER 636. In *Bennett v White* [1910] 2 KB 643 the defendant was an assignee under a statutory assignment, and so there was mutuality at law.

[75] *Re Whitehouse & Co* (1878) 9 Ch D 595, 597; *Re Paraguassu Steam Tramroad Co. Black & Co's Case* (1872) LR 8 Ch App 254, 261; *Mercer v Graves* (1872) LR 7 QB 499, 504 (Blackburn J).

[76] *Re Whitehouse & Co* (1878) 9 Ch D 595, 597 ('when we look at the terms of those Acts of Parliament . . . it is plain they only applied to what was then an action at common law'); *Chitty's Blackstone* (1826) vol. 3, 305, n. 37 ('The debt to be set off must be a *legal* and *subsisting* demand; an equitable debt will not suffice'); *Isberg v Bowden* (1853) 8 Ex 852, 155 ER 1599, as explained by Keating J in *Watkins v Clark* (1862) 12 CB(NS) 277,

of an equitable assignment of a debt. The general rule is that an equitable assignee takes subject to a right of set-off accruing to the debtor against the assignor before the debtor received notice of the assignment.[77] The determinative date is the date of notice, not the date of the assignment.[78] When a cross-debt accrues to the debtor against the assignor after notice, the reason that a set-off is denied to the debtor as against the assignee is not simply that mutuality in equity is absent. There is still mutuality at law as between the debtor and the assignor, and therefore there is a right of set-off at law. The question is whether it is unconscionable for the debtor to rely on the right of set-off otherwise available at law when the equitable title to one of the debts is in someone else.[79] The answer to that question depends on when the cross-debt was acquired. If it was acquired after notice of the assignment, equity regards it as unconscionable for the debtor to rely on the set-off available at law, and equity accordingly will not permit the debtor to do so.[80]

11.19 The correctness of this analysis is apparent if one looks instead at the position that obtains when the debtor acquired the liquidated cross-claim against the assignor after the equitable assignment but before the debtor had notice of the assignment. In such a case it is recognized that the third party assignee takes subject to the debtor's right of set-off, a result that is inconsistent with mutuality being determined solely by reference to equitable interests. The giving of notice is not necessary to complete the title of an equitable assignee.[81] Notice is desirable in order to ensure that the assignee has priority over other assignees in accordance with the rule in *Dearle v Hall*[82] (when it applies[83]) and in order to oblige the debtor to tender payment to the assignee rather than the assignor.[84] Notice is not necessary, however, for the equitable title to pass to the assignee, which occurs at the date of the assignment. Therefore, in the period between the assignment and notice of the assignment, when the cross-debt was incurred, there was not mutuality in equity between the assigned debt and the cross-debt. In equity the assigned debt was owing to the assignee, while the cross-debt was incurred by the assignor. Accordingly, when the question of set-off later arises, it can be seen that there is not, and never has been, mutuality in equity. Why, then,

---

281–2, 142 ER 1149, 1151 ('the Statutes of Set-off are confined to legal debts between the parties'). See also *Popular Homes Ltd v Circuit Developments Ltd* [1979] 2 NZLR 642, 655.

[77] See para. 17.03 below.

[78] See e.g. *Moore v Jervis* (1845) 2 Coll 60, 63 ER 637 and *Brice v Bannister* (1878) 3 QBD 569, 578, and para. 17.19 below.

[79] See *Wilson v Gabriel* (1863) 4 B & S 243, 247–248, 122 ER 450, 452 (Blackburn J), referred to in *Christie v Taunton, Delmard, Lane and Co* [1893] 2 Ch 175, 182. As Bramwell B expressed it in *Higgs v The Northern Assam Tea Co Ltd* (1869) LR 4 Ex 387, 394, the question is: 'taking the set-off to be available at law, would equity restrain the defendants from relying on it?' See also *Watson v Mid-Wales Railway Co* (1867) LR 2 CP 593, 600 (Montague Smith J).

[80] *Hoverd Industries Ltd v Supercool Refrigeration and Air Conditioning* [1995] 3 NZLR 577, 587.

[81] *Gorringe v Irwell India Rubber and Gutta Percha Works* (1886) 34 Ch D 128; *Ward v Duncombe* [1893] AC 369, 392; *Re City Life Assurance Co Ltd (Stephenson's Case)* [1926] 1 Ch 191, 219–20; *Re Trytel* [1952] 2 TLR 32, 34; *Thomas v National Australia Bank Ltd* [2000] 2 Qd R 448. Compare *Mountain Road (No. 9) Ltd v Michael Edgley Corporation Pty Ltd* [1999] 1 NZLR 335.

[82] (1828) 3 Russ 1, 38 ER 475.

[83] See *Goode on Legal Problems of Credit and Security* (4th edn (ed. Gullifer), 2008), 177–8 [5–08]. In Australia, compare the position under the Personal Property Securities Act 2009 (Cth).

[84] *Brice v Bannister* (1878) 3 QBD 569; *Re Trytel* [1952] 2 TLR 32, 34; *Halsbury's Laws of England* (4th edn (Reissue), 2003) vol. 6, 47, para. 71. In Australia, see the Personal Property Securities Act 2009 (Cth), s. 80(7) and (8). The notice must be in writing. See s. 286.

is a set-off allowed? The reason is that the debtor has a right of set-off at law under the Statutes of Set-off, since the position at law is that the assigned debt is still owing to the assignor and accordingly there is mutuality at law. Moreover, it is not unconscionable for the debtor to rely on the legal right to a set-off, since the cross-debt was incurred before the debtor had notice of the equitable assignment. There are admittedly to be found statements in judgments of Sir George Jessel MR[85] and Lord Selborne LC[86] which seem to suggest that equity never permits a set-off under the Statutes where cross-demands are mutual at law but not in equity. However, the allowance of a set-off when the cross-debt is incurred after the assignment but before notice shows that the rule is not inflexible, and that the principle is one of unconscionability.[87] As Jeffrey J remarked in the New South Wales Supreme Court in *West Street Properties Pty Ltd v Jamison*:[88] 'Lack of mutuality in equity can be a reason for denying a right to set-off at law, . . . but that is not to say that its presence is invariably necessary before allowing any right of set-off at all.' This analysis admittedly sits uncomfortably with the view that has been expressed in some quarters, that the principles, as well as the courts, of common law and equity have now been fused.[89] That view is much criticized, however,[90] and it does not provide a satisfactory framework for explaining the allowance of a set-off when a cross-debt arises after the assignment but before notice.

When liquidated cross-demands are mutual having regard to equitable rights, it is not **11.20** necessary for the defendant show some additional 'equity' to support an equitable set-off, since equity in such a case may act by analogy with the legal right under the Statutes. Observations to the contrary[91] should not be accepted.

D. Ascertained Beneficial Interests

It has been said that, in order to achieve mutuality where a debt is held on trust for a benefi- **11.21** ciary, the beneficial ownership must be clear and ascertained without inquiry.[92] This requires an explanation. The early cases referred to as authority for the proposition[93]

---

[85] *Re Whitehouse & Co* (1878) 9 Ch D 595, 597.

[86] *Re Paraguassu Steam Tramroad Co. Black & Co's Case* (1872) LR 8 Ch App 254, 261.

[87] This is also evident from the decision of the Court of Appeal in *Rother Iron Works Ltd v Canterbury Precision Engineers Ltd* [1974] 1 QB 1 in relation to receivership. See para. 17.109 below.

[88] [1974] 2 NSWLR 435, 441–2.

[89] *United Scientific Holdings Ltd v Burnley Borough Council* [1978] AC 904. See also *Bank of Credit and Commerce International SA v Ali* [2002] 1 AC 251 at [17] *per* Lord Bingham ('More than a century and a quarter have passed since the fusion of law and equity . . .'); Burrows, 'We do this at common law but that in equity' (2002) 22 OJLS 1, 4.

[90] Baker, 'The future of equity' (1977) 93 LQR 529; *Meagher, Gummow and Lehane's Equity Doctrines and Remedies* (4th edn, 2002), ch. 2; Martin, 'Fusion, fallacy and confusion; a comparative study' [1994] *The Conveyancer* 13. See also *MCC Proceeds Inc v Lehman Bros International (Europe)* [1998] 4 All ER 675, 690–691 (equitable title not sufficient to found a common law claim in conversion). Sir Peter Millett writing extra–judicially ('Equity – the road ahead' (1995) 9 *Tolley's Trust Law International* 35, 37) commented that the fusion theory is now widely discredited. In *Bank of Boston Connecticut v European Grain and Shipping Ltd* [1989] 1 AC 1056, 1109, the House of Lords remarked that the Judicature Acts: 'while making important changes in procedure, did not alter and were not intended to alter the rights of the parties.'

[91] *Middleton v Pollock, ex p Nugee* (1875) LR 20 Eq 29, 36–37; *Welton v Harnett* (1886) 7 NSWR 74.

[92] Wood, *English and International Set–off* (1989), 779–80, 1081–2.

[93] *Bishop v Church* (1748) 3 Atk 691, 26 ER 1197; *Ex p Morier, re Willis, Percival, & Co* (1879) 12 Ch D 491; *Phillips v Howell* [1901] 2 Ch 773.

concerned either a residuary legatee under a will or a person entitled under an intestacy, where the administration of the estate had not been completed. Prior to completion of the administration, a residuary legatee or a person entitled in an intestacy does not have a beneficial interest in the estate. All that the legatee or the person so entitled has is an equitable chose in action, in the form of a right to require the due administration of the estate. That was confirmed by the Privy Council in *Commissioner of Stamp Duties (Queensland) v Livingston*[94] in relation to a residuary legatee, and the principle is equally applicable in the case of an intestacy.[95] The early set-off cases which have been cited as requiring a clear and ascertained beneficial ownership[96] in fact are authorities for a different proposition, that the court will not take an account of the assets of the estate, and of the debts and charges that still have to be satisfied out of it, so as to allow a present set-off to the extent of the interest that it is anticipated that the legatee or the person entitled in an intestacy will have in the future. This should apply in relation to both insolvency set-off and set-off between solvent parties.

(1) Proof of a presently existing beneficial interest

11.22 Alternatively, it may be that the facts alleged, if proved, would disclose a presently existing beneficial interest in a debt, but the facts are in dispute.

11.23 The question of the availability of a set-off in that circumstance has arisen in the context of nominee bank accounts. In two cases before the Court of Appeal, *Bhogal v Punjab National Bank*[97] and *Uttamchandami v Central Bank of India*,[98] a bank alleged that an account in the name of A in truth was held for the benefit of B. When A sued the bank for payment of the credit balance on the account, and applied for summary judgment, the bank argued that it was entitled to leave to defend on the basis of a set-off arising out of an indebtedness of B on another account. In a third case before the Court of Appeal, *Saudi Arabian Monetary Agency v Dresdner Bank AG*,[99] a bank refused to comply with its customer's instructions to transfer the credit balance on the customer's account to an account with another bank, alleging that the account was a nominee account and that the beneficial owner was separately indebted to the bank. Unlike in the earlier cases, the customer admitted that it was not the beneficial owner of the account. It denied, however, that the debtor to the bank was the beneficial owner. The customer sought an order requiring the bank to effect the transfer and applied for summary judgment. The set-off alleged in those cases was an equitable set-off. Since the cross-debts were unconnected, the equitable set-off could only have been based upon equity acting by analogy with the Statutes of Set-off,[100] as opposed to the

---

[94] [1965] AC 694. See also *Ex p Morier* (1879) 12 Ch D 491, 496 (James LJ), and para. 13.125 below. Similarly, the object of a discretionary trust does not have a legal or a beneficial interest in the trust property. See *Gartside v IRC* [1968] AC 553; *Chief Commissioner of Stamp Duties v ISPT Pty Ltd* (1998) 45 NSWLR 639, 655.

[95] *Re Leigh's Will Trusts* [1970] 1 Ch 277, 281–2.

[96] See above.

[97] [1988] 2 All ER 296 (CA).

[98] Unreported, but noted in (1989) 139 *New Law Journal* 222 (CA).

[99] [2005] 1 Lloyd's Rep 12 (CA).

[100] See paras 3.07–3.09 above. *Cochrane v Green* (1860) 9 CB(NS) 448, 142 ER 176, to which Lloyd LJ referred in the *Uttamchandami* case (1989) 139 *New Law Journal* 222, 222–3 and Neuberger J referred at first instance in the *Saudi Arabian Monetary Agency* case (see Chadwick LJ's judgment in the Court of Appeal [2005] 1 Lloyd's Rep 12 at [5]), concerned that form of equitable set-off.

substantive form of equitable set-off which may arise in relation to closely connected cross-claims.[101] Usually, the defendant in an application for summary judgment will be granted leave to defend if he or she can show an arguable case, but it was accepted in those cases that the bank was not entitled to unconditional leave to defend in the absence of clear and indisputable evidence[102] that the account was merely a nominee account held for the benefit of the debtor to the bank.[103] This is to be ascertained by reference to the reasons given by the bank for refusal to pay at the time when payment ought to have been made.[104]

Three comments may be made in relation to the requirement of clear and indisputable evidence.   **11.24**

The first is that Dillon and Bingham LJJ in their respective judgments in the *Bhogal* case relied on an earlier decision of the Court of Appeal, in *Ex p Morier*,[105] but that case was concerned with a different issue.   **11.25**

In *Ex p Morier*, a brother and sister were executors of their deceased father's will, and accordingly opened an account in their joint names with a bank. The brother, who was the residuary legatee under the will, kept another account of his own with the bank. The bank filed a liquidation petition, at which time there was a balance standing to the credit of the joint account, whereas the brother's separate account was overdrawn. The brother sought to set off the balance due from him to the bank on his overdrawn account against the sum due from the bank on the executors' joint account, on the ground that he was the residuary legatee and the sum standing to the credit of the joint account belonged in equity to him alone. The brother's argument to that effect failed before the Court of Appeal. A number of debts remained to be paid out of the estate, and the Court was not prepared to take an account in relation to the testator's estate in order to ascertain the brother's entitlement as residuary legatee. In a short judgment Brett LJ said:[106]   **11.26**

> My view is this, that, the account standing in the names of the brother and sister, the case could not have been brought within the rules of equitable set-off or mutual credit, unless the brother was so much the person solely beneficially interested that a Court of Equity, without any terms or any further inquiry, would have obliged the sister to transfer the account into her brother's name alone.

---

[101] See ch. 4 above.

[102] See *Bhogal v Punjab National Bank* [1988] 2 All ER 286, 301 (Dillon LJ); *Uttamchandami v Central Bank of India* unreported but noted in (1989) 139 *New Law Journal* 222, 223 (Lloyd LJ); *Saudi Arabian Monetary Agency v Dresdner Bank AG* [2005] 1 Lloyd's Rep 12 at [23] and [33]–[35]. See also *Bank of Credit and Commerce International SA v Al-Saud* [1997] 1 BCLC 457, 465 ('clear evidence'). In *Saudi Arabian Monetary Agency v Dresdner Bank AG* (above) at [35], Longmore LJ noted that the claim in that case in substance was for an order for specific performance against the bank (in the form of a mandatory injunction) requiring the bank to transfer funds in the customer's account to an account with another bank in accordance with the customer's instructions, as opposed an action against the bank for payment. His Lordship suggested that: 'the *Bhogal* test that a defendant bank must be able to say that such beneficial ownership is "indisputable" should apply even more strongly in a case where the claim is for specific performance than in a case where the claimant, as in *Bhogal*, is merely asserting a claim in debt'.

[103] As in *Re Hett, Maylor, and Co* (1894) 10 TLR 412.

[104] *Saudi Arabian Monetary Agency v Dresdner Bank AG* [2005] 1 Lloyd's Rep 12 at [31].

[105] (1879) 12 Ch D 491 (CA).

[106] (1879) 12 Ch D 491, 502.

Both that comment, however, and the decision in *Ex p Morier* should be considered in the context that *Ex p Morier* was concerned with the position of a residuary legatee prior to completion of the administration of the estate. Since there were a number of debts which remained outstanding, it was clear that there was not at the date of the liquidation a presently existing beneficial interest, and the Court of Appeal held that it would not take an account of the assets of the estate and the debts and liabilities payable out of the estate in order to ascertain what the beneficial interest ultimately would be. Thus James LJ, in a judgment with which Brett LJ agreed,[107] commented:

> It is said A and B were executors, and A was also the residuary legatee, and therefore entitled to the whole of the fund. *But the fund had never been liquidated so as to become a trust fund.*[108]

And later:

> I think the Court has never yet taken accounts in order to see how much of a fund standing in the name of two persons in a bank would *ultimately*, upon the balance of the accounts, turn out to be the property of one of them, so as to enable that balance to be a set-off against a sum due by that one to the bank.[109]

That situation should be contrasted with the cases dealing with nominee accounts, in which the facts alleged, if proved, would have established a presently existing interest, and the question was whether the court should investigate those facts. The issue, then, was entirely different, and so *Ex p Morier* did not require the decisions in those cases.[110]

11.27 The second comment is that considerable emphasis was also placed in the *Bhogal* case on the responsibilities of banks to honour their obligations promptly. Both Dillon and Bingham LJJ in the *Bhogal* case quoted with approval a passage from the judgment of Scott J at first instance who, in rejecting the bank's defence, said that:[111] 'The commercial banking commitment that a bank enters into with a person who deposits money with it is just as needful of immediate performance as are a bank's obligations under a letter of credit or bank guarantee.' Scott J said that he was not satisfied that banks should be treated like other debtors in relation to summary judgment.[112] In addition, Dillon LJ emphasized a bank's duty to honour a customer's cheque drawn in accordance with the mandate, provided that the customer has sufficient funds in the account to cover it.[113] Similar views were expressed in *Saudi Arabian Monetary Agency v Dresdner Bank AG*.[114] Chadwick LJ suggested in that case that the principle requiring clear and indisputable evidence can be explained either by reference to an implied term in the contract between a bank and its customer to the effect that the bank will not refuse payment of money deposited with it on the basis merely of an arguable case that some other debtor to the bank has an equitable

---

[107] (1879) 12 Ch D 491, 500.
[108] (1879) 12 Ch D 491, 496 (emphasis added).
[109] (1879) 12 Ch D 491, 499–500 (emphasis added).
[110] A similar explanation of *Ex p Morier* to that set out above was suggested in *Saudi Arabian Monetary Agency v Dresdner Bank AG* [2005] 1 Lloyd's Rep 12 at [21] and [22].
[111] [1988] 2 All ER 296, 299–300, 306.
[112] Also referred to by Bingham LJ [1988] 2 All ER 296, 306.
[113] See [1988] 2 All ER 296, 300, 301.
[114] [2005] 1 Lloyd's Rep 12.

interest in the money, or alternatively on the basis of a proposition that, where the existence of an equitable interest is not clear and indisputable, equity will not override the clear rules on which bankers and customers habitually deal with each other.[115] Thus, banks have been perceived as occupying a special position in relation to their obligations as debtors. If these cases are to be followed, it should be on this ground rather than on the authority of *Ex p Morier*.

The third comment concerns the remedies available to the bank in the event that it has clear **11.28** and indisputable evidence of a trust. In the *Bhogal* case the action was for payment of a debt, in the form of the credit balance on a bank account. The bank sought to defend the action by alleging an entitlement to an equitable set-off. The basis of the alleged set-off was that, having regard to equitable rights, the case was one of mutual debts for the purpose of equity acting by analogy with the Statutes of Set-off.[116] The set-off conferred by the Statutes of Set-off is limited in its operation, in that it merely provides a procedural defence to an action at law for payment of a debt,[117] and the Statutes should have the same construction in equity when they are applied by analogy.[118] In other words, the set-off asserted should merely have provided a defence to an action for payment. Nevertheless, there appears to have been an acceptance of the proposition that, if the bank had succeeded in establishing clear and indisputable evidence of a trust, it would have been entitled to freeze the account and dishonour cheques drawn on it.[119] The question whether the bank would have been entitled to dishonour cheques is considered later in relation to combination of bank accounts.[120]

(2) Mixed account

In the *Bhogal* case, the bank said that accounts in the name of Mr Basna and Mr Bhogal **11.29** were nominee accounts beneficially owned by a Mr Sanger. It asserted that Mr Sanger was either the sole and absolute beneficial owner of the moneys in the accounts or he had a substantial beneficial interest in them. It also asserted that Mr Sanger was liable to the bank on another overdrawn account. The bank contended that those circumstances gave rise to a defence of equitable set-off, and that accordingly it should be granted unconditional leave to defend in summary judgment applications brought by Mr Basna and Mr Bhogal for payment of the account balances. The Court of Appeal rejected the bank's contention, because there was not clear and indisputable evidence that the accounts were nominee accounts. Apart from that ground, Dillon LJ also suggested that, for a set-off to occur in relation to a nominee account, the totality of the money in the account must belong to the

---

[115] [2005] 1 Lloyd's Rep 12 at [23] and [31].
[116] See para. 11.23 above.
[117] See paras 2.34–2.39 above.
[118] See *Ex p Stephens* (1805) 11 Ves Jun 24, 27, 32 ER 996, 997 (Lord Eldon) and paras 3.07–3.09 above. Before the Judicature Acts, an equitable set-off would be given effect by means of an injunction to restrain the plaintiff in an action at law from either proceeding with the action or enforcing a judgment obtained at law unless credit was given for a cross-claim available to the defendant at law, but equitable set-off can now be pleaded directly as a defence in an action at law. See para. 3.01 above.
[119] See Dillon LJ in *Bhogal v Punjab National Bank* [1988] 2 All ER 296, 301, and also the discussion by Lloyd LJ in *Uttamchandami v Central Bank of India* (1989) 139 *New Law Journal* 222, 223.
[120] See paras 15.66–15.71 below.

principal of the nominee, whereas in the case of the Basna account it appeared that at least some of the money in the account belonged to Mr Basna. Therefore, even if the bank had been able to show that the Basna account was a mixed account, fed in part by moneys belonging to Mr Sanger and in part by moneys which belonged to Mr Basna, he said that there could be no equitable set-off in view of Mr Basna's own entitlement.[121] Similarly, Bingham LJ said that he was willing to accept that a bank could challenge its customer's title to money in the customer's account on its own behalf only when its claim is against a sole beneficiary.[122] In his discussion of the point, Dillon LJ referred to *Addis v Knight*,[123] which concerned the joint liability of a partnership. The courts have accepted that a joint debt or a joint claim of a partnership generally cannot be set off against a separate claim by or against one of the partners.[124] However, any analogy with a partnership is not complete, because a partnership contracts on a joint basis, which is not the position when the moneys of a number of persons are deposited in an account held by one of them.

11.30 Subsequently, a differently constituted Court of Appeal considered the question of set-off in the context of a mixed nominee account in *Bank of Credit and Commerce International SA (in liq) v Al-Saud*.[125] The defendant, Prince Fahd bin Salman bin Abdul Aziz Al-Saud, had given a guarantee to the plaintiff bank in respect of a loan made by the bank to a company. The company defaulted, whereupon the bank, which was now in liquidation, sued the Prince on the guarantee and applied for summary judgment. The Prince responded that he was entitled to leave to defend because of a set-off available against the claim, based on three accounts with the plaintiff which were in credit. The accounts were in the name of a third party, one Mr Ghazzawi, but both the Prince and Mr Ghazzawi said that the moneys paid into the accounts belonged to the Prince. It appeared, however, that there had been some intermingling of Mr Ghazzawi's own money in the accounts, and also that Mr Ghazzawi was entitled to defray some expenses from the accounts, so that an inquiry would have been necessary in order to ascertain the precise state of the accounts between the Prince and Mr Ghazzawi.[126] Neill LJ in delivering the judgment of the Court of Appeal accepted, on the authority of *Ex p Morier*, that, unless the Prince's beneficial interest in the three accounts could be established by clear evidence and without the necessity for the taking of an account, there would be a lack of mutuality. On the facts of *BCCI v Al-Saud*, where it was accepted that some inquiry would have been necessary, the Court of Appeal held that there was no arguable defence of set-off. But if the extent of the Prince's interest in the account had been clear and ascertained, the judgment suggests that a set-off may have been available to that extent.[127] That suggestion should be contrasted with the strict

---

121 [1988] 2 All ER 296, 301.
122 [1988] 2 All ER 296, 307.
123 (1817) 2 Mer 117, 35 ER 885.
124 See paras 12.02–12.20 below.
125 [1997] 1 BCLC 457 (Neill, Simon Brown and Waite LJJ).
126 [1997] 1 BCLC 457, 461–2, 465.
127 Neill LJ commented [1997] 1 BCLC 457, 465: 'It is true that Mr Ghazzawi has asserted in his affidavits that the money in the accounts belongs in the main to the Prince, but it seems to be a sensible rule that a beneficial interest has to be established by clear evidence and without the necessity for the taking of an account.' Later he said (at 466): 'In my judgment counsel for BCCI was correct in his submission that unless the Prince's entitlement to the moneys in the three Park Lane accounts can be shown to be clear and

view expressed in *Bhogal v Punjab National Bank*, that there should be a sole beneficiary to whom the totality of the money in the account belongs.

Two points may be made in relation to these respective views.   **11.31**

The first is that the opinions in the *Bhogal* case were justified by reference to passages in the **11.32** judgments of James and Brett LJJ in *Ex p Morier*. Bingham LJ in the *Bhogal* case[128] said that the requirement of a 'sole beneficiary' reflected Brett LJ's short judgment in *Morier*,[129] while Dillon LJ[130] regarded his view in relation to a mixed account as following from a comment by James LJ in *Ex p Morier*, to the effect that it is not sufficient that the result of taking an account would merely show an ultimate balance belonging to the principal of an alleged nominee account holder.[131] However, the passages from *Ex p Morier* should be considered in the context of the circumstances in issue in that case,[132] in particular that the administration of the deceased's estate had not been completed. Therefore, a trust had not yet arisen in favour of the residuary legatee in relation to the executorship account which the residuary legatee was seeking to set off against his overdrawn personal account. Hence Brett LJ's comment in *Ex p Morier*, that the amount standing to the credit of the account could not be set off: 'unless the [residuary legatee] was so much the person solely beneficially interested that a Court of Equity, without any terms or any further inquiry, would have obliged the [co-executor] to transfer the account into the [residuary legatee's] name alone.' In the circumstances of the case, a trust would not have arisen until the completion of the administration, at which time the residuary legatee would have become solely beneficially interested in the account. But until the completion of the administration, it could not be said that the residuary legatee had a beneficial interest. The statements in *Ex p Morier* did not comprehend the situation in which two or more persons have clear and ascertained *present* beneficial interests in a bank account in the name of a nominee.

Secondly, the broader view suggested by *BCCI v Al-Saud* is consistent with cases concern-   **11.33** ing debts other than bank accounts, where the courts have recognized that a set-off may occur in relation to a beneficial interest in a debt that is not the sole beneficial interest.[133]

---

ascertained there is a lack of mutuality or reciprocity between himself and BCCI.' In Northern Ireland, Carswell LJ (with whose judgment Hutton LCJ agreed) left open the question whether a set-off was available to a bank in relation to an account, where the bank could show with sufficient clarity that the person against whom the set-off was sought to be exercised was entitled to a part only of the account, albeit a specific and ascertainable part. Nevertheless, he said that at least an arguable case for a set-off could have been put forward. See *Abbey National plc v McCann* [1997] Northern Ireland Judgments Bulletin 158, 172–3. Compare Capper, 'Deceit, banker's set-off and Mareva undertakings – the Abbey's bad habits' [1999] LMCLQ 21, 24–5.

[128] [1988] 2 All ER 296, 307.
[129] See para. 11.26 above.
[130] [1988] 2 All ER 296, 301.
[131] See (1879) 12 Ch D 491, 496. Dillon LJ paraphrased James LJ's comments in terms that: 'it is not enough if the taking of an account would merely show an ultimate balance, *and not the totality of the money in an account*, to belong to the principal of an alleged nominee account holder.' The italicized words, however, do not appear in the passage in James LJ's judgment to which Dillon LJ referred.
[132] See para. 11.26 above.
[133] It has been suggested that banks should be treated differently to other debtors (see para. 11.27 above), but if the interest of a person in a bank account is clear and ascertained, albeit not extending to the totality of the moneys in the account, that factor should not be paramount.

For example, in *Manley & Sons Ltd v Berkett*,[134] an auctioneer was suing for the price of goods sold to the defendant. The auctioneer had a first claim on the proceeds for his charges and expenses, but to the extent of the proceeds that the auctioneer would have had to hand over to the vendor, and in which the vendor accordingly was beneficially interested, the purchaser was allowed a set-off against a debt owing to him by the vendor. There was in that case an agreement for a set-off between the vendor and the purchaser, but Bankes J nevertheless characterized the set-off advanced by the purchaser as an equitable set-off. There are also examples in the context of insolvency set-off. Thus, when a debt due to a creditor is assigned by the creditor to a third party as security for a debt owing by the creditor to the third party, but the debt owing to the third party is for a smaller amount than the assigned debt, so that there is a residue from the assigned debt to be paid over to the creditor/assignor, and the creditor has gone into liquidation, a cross-demand by the debtor against the creditor in some circumstances may be set off against the residue to which the creditor would be entitled.[135] *Thornton v Maynard*[136] provides another illustration. The holder of some bills of exchange was suing the acceptor for payment. It appeared, however, that the holder had already been paid a dividend in the drawer's bankruptcy in respect of the bills, and to the extent of the dividend he was suing as trustee for the drawer. It was held that the acceptor to that extent was entitled to set off a debt owing to him by the drawer. The drawer was bankrupt, so that the set-off is explicable on the basis of insolvency set-off,[137] but Lord Coleridge CJ, in delivering the judgment of the Common Pleas,[138] nevertheless referred to it as a set-off in equity.

(3) Insolvency set-off

11.34 The form of set-off in issue in *BCCI v Al-Saud* differed from that in *Bhogal v Punjab National Bank*. The *Bhogal* case concerned equitable set-off arising by analogy with the Statutes of Set-off, whereas in the *Al-Saud* case insolvency set-off was in issue. Insolvency set-off raises different considerations.

11.35 In *Ex p Morier*, the residuary legatee seeking a set-off did not have a present beneficial interest in the executors' account. Where, however, the substance of the allegation relates to an alleged present beneficial interest, the extension of a perceived requirement of clear and indisputable evidence of the interest to insolvency set-off is not without difficulty. In the case of insolvency set-off, the set-off section provides that an account 'shall be taken' of what is due from each party to the other in respect of their mutual dealings.[139] The statutory injunction to take an account seems contrary to the view that a set-off should be denied unless the beneficial interest is clear and ascertained. Furthermore, the court in the *Bhogal* case emphasized a bank's responsibilities to honour its obligations to its customers

---

[134] [1912] 2 KB 329.

[135] *Hiley v Peoples Prudential Assurance Co Ltd* (1938) 60 CLR 468, 497–8 (Dixon J), referring to *Re Asphaltic Wood Pavement Co. Lee & Chapman's Case* (1885) 30 Ch D 216. See paras 11.39–11.45 below.

[136] (1875) LR 10 CP 695.

[137] See the Bankruptcy Act 1869, s. 39.

[138] Lord Coleridge CJ, Brett and Archibald JJ.

[139] See the Insolvency Rules, r. 4.90(3) for company liquidation, and for bankruptcy the Insolvency Act 1986, s. 323(2).

promptly,[140] which would not be relevant if the bank or the customer is in liquidation given that the banker/customer relationship would have terminated.[141] The notion of the bank's responsibilities particularly would not have any application if the bank is in liquidation, since the customer in any event would be confined to a proof in the liquidation. Moreover, there may be a question of set-off as between the bank and the alleged nominee. Consider that a bank is in liquidation, and an account in credit in the name of A is alleged to be held wholly or partly for the benefit of B. If a set-off is not permitted as between the bank and B in relation to the account unless the interest of B in the account is clear and ascertained, what is the position if A also happens to be indebted to the bank? If there is not clear and indisputable evidence that B has an interest in the account, it may equally be the case that it is not clear and indisputable that A is the beneficial owner of the account, in which case would A also be denied a set-off? Alternatively, if the principle only operates to deny B a set-off, could A then have a set-off for an amount greater than his or her true beneficial interest in the account? These questions suggest that the court should in fact ascertain the interests of A and B and permit or deny set-offs accordingly.

BCCI v Al-Saud nevertheless is authority for the view that the principle applied in *Bhogal v Punjab National Bank* and *Uttamchandani v Central Bank of India*, requiring clear and indisputable evidence as to title in relation to a nominee bank account, extends also to insolvency set-off. That view should be reconsidered. **11.36**

E. Security Over a Debt

(1) Introduction

A debt owing to a creditor may be the subject of a security given by the creditor in favour of a third party.[142] A security over a debt may take a number of forms, and it is appropriate to consider the results that may follow in relation to each of them. **11.37**

(2) Assignment by way of mortgage

In the first place, a debt may be assigned by way of mortgage. In so far as set-offs between the debtor and the mortgagor/creditor are concerned, the relevant principles essentially are as follows. The assignment has the result that *prima facie* there is not mutuality in equity,[143] and this is so whether or not default has occurred under the mortgage. *Prima facie*, therefore, the insolvency set-off section would not apply. On the other hand, the mortgagee, being an assignee, is subject to the same principle applicable generally in the case of assignments, that an assignee takes subject to an equitable set-off available to the debtor against **11.38**

---

[140] See para. 11.27 above.

[141] See *Halesowen Presswork & Assemblies Ltd v Westminster Bank Ltd* [1971] 1 QB 1, 23, 24 (Roskill J) in relation to the winding up of the customer.

[142] See also paras 6.176–6.182 above.

[143] Compare, however, the discussion below of the situation in which the assigned debt is greater than the secured debt.

the assignor, or to a set-off that accrued to the debtor under the Statutes of Set-off before the debtor had notice of the assignment.[144]

Assigned debt exceeds the secured debt

11.39 What if the debt assigned by way of security exceeds the debt owing by the mortgagor/ creditor to the mortgagee for which it is security, and the debtor has a cross-claim against the creditor? In Australia, Dixon J in *Hiley v The Peoples Prudential Assurance Co Ltd*,[145] said, in the context of a debt owing by a company in liquidation which had been assigned by the creditor by way of security to a third party:

> In the third place, it is settled that if a creditor of a liquidating company, that is, the person entitled to a legal chose in action, has before the winding up assigned it equitably to a third party by way of charge as security for a debt owing by him to the third party but of smaller amount so that there is a residue to be paid over to the assignor, the liquidating company may set off against the residue a cross-demand upon the assignor.

It is difficult to accept this proposition as a general statement of principle. There is an apparent lack of mutuality for the purpose of the insolvency set-off section, since the mortgagee has security over the whole of the debt assigned to him or her and there is no part in which the mortgagor alone is beneficially interested. The question is whether this is an instance in which a set-off nevertheless is appropriate. *Prima facie* it is not. The security in this case is a debt owing to the mortgagor. If the debtor is insolvent, the true value of the security would not be the face value of that debt. It would be less, depending on the dividend payable by the debtor. Accordingly, where a debt of £x owing to a mortgagee by the mortgagor is secured by a mortgage over a debt of £y owing to the mortgagor by a debtor in liquidation, where y is greater than x, it would hardly be fair to allow a set-off as between the mortgagor and the debtor to the extent of £(y-x), since this would deplete the security. Dixon J's proposition assumes that, if £x is still owing by the debtor after the set-off, the mortgagee's position is protected, but the mortgagee would not be protected if the debtor is insolvent.

11.40 It would nevertheless be appropriate to recognize a set-off in the circumstance contemplated by Dixon J if two conditions are satisfied. The first, which Wood has suggested,[146] is that the security should be presently enforceable and it should be in the process of being enforced, so that the mortgagee's position after taking into account the set-off is presently ascertainable. Unless this limitation is imposed, the mortgagee may find when the security is later enforced that it has been depleted by a set-off as between the creditor/mortgagor and the debtor. The second condition is that the debtor on the assigned debt should be solvent so that, after setting off an amount equal to £(y-x) as against the creditor/mortgagor, the remaining £x owing by the debtor in fact is worth £x. In a case where a creditor/mortgagor

---

[144] See paras 17.13–17.15 (Statutes of Set–off) and paras 17.32–17.38 (equitable set-off) below. This can include also a sub-mortgage. See *Popular Homes Ltd v Circuit Developments Ltd* [1979] 2 NZLR 642, and compare *Clairview Developments Pty Ltd v Law Mortgages Gold Coast Pty Ltd* [2007] 2 Qd R 501 at [42].

[145] (1938) 60 CLR 468, 497. See also Rich J at 489 (referring to *Re Asphaltic Wood Pavement Co. Lee & Chapman's Case* (1885) 30 Ch D 216).

[146] Wood, *English and International Set-off* (1989), 782.

is insolvent, there is nothing objectionable in recognizing a set-off as between the creditor and the debtor in relation to the part of the debt which exceeds the amount of the secured debt for which the first-mentioned debt was assigned as security, but there is when the debtor is the insolvent party. Indeed, in the case to which Dixon J referred as authority for his suggested proposition, the creditor rather than the debtor was insolvent. *Lee & Chapman's Case*[147] concerned a charge granted by a company over a debt owing to it by the Commissioners of Sewers. The company later went into liquidation. There was no suggestion that the Commissioners were insolvent, and accordingly there was nothing unfair in the Court of Appeal's decision to allow the Commissioners to set off their debt to the extent of the amount over and above the secured debt owing by the company. While the question of mutuality was not considered in *Lee & Chapman's Case*, when a creditor grants security over the debt to a third party and the creditor also happens to be liable to the debtor, the creditor should be regarded as having a sufficient interest in the surplus over and above the secured debt for the purpose of the requirement of mutuality if the security is being enforced and the debtor is solvent, so that the secured creditor's position is both presently ascertainable and sufficiently protected.

Auctioneer's lien

A similar principle has been recognized in the context of an auctioneer's lien.[148] An **11.41** auctioneer has a lien on the proceeds of sale for his or her charges and expenses. If a purchaser of goods at auction removes the goods before payment in full the auctioneer may sue for the price, but the purchaser is permitted to set off in that action a debt owing by the vendor to the purchaser to the extent that the proceeds would be handed over to the vendor.[149] While the auctioneer would have had a prior interest in the whole of the claim in order to satisfy the lien, mutuality should be satisfied if the purchaser is solvent and the auctioneer's lien accordingly is protected.

Set-off between the mortgagee and the debtor

What about the position as between the mortgagee and the debtor? Wood[150] has suggested **11.42** that, if the mortgagor is not in default, the assigned debt cannot be set off against a debt that the mortgagee owes to the debtor, on the ground that the mortgagor's interest in the assigned debt in the form of the equity of redemption otherwise will have been used to pay the debt owing by the mortgagee. It would mean that the mortgagee will have foreclosed before default by the mortgagor. This seems correct. The fact that the mortgagor still has the equity of redemption means that the mortgagor still has a proprietary interest in the assigned debt which would destroy mutuality as between the mortgagee and the debtor.

---

[147] *Re Asphaltic Wood Pavement Co. Lee & Chapman's Case* (1885) 30 Ch D 216. See also *Union Bank of Australia v Waterston* (1894) 12 NZLR 672 (agreement for set-off between the mortgagor and the debtor).

[148] See para. 13.101 below.

[149] *Manley & Sons Ltd v Berkett* [1912] 2 KB 329 (in which there was an agreement for a set-off between the purchaser and the vendor, although Bankes LJ (at 333–4) nevertheless approached the question on the basis that an equitable set-off was in issue). See also *Holmes v Tutton* (1855) 5 El & Bl 65, 82, 119 ER 405, 412.

[150] Wood, *English and International Set-off* (1989), 780, 916.

As Wood has also pointed out,[151] however, the cases suggest that the result would be different if the mortgagee is enforcing the debt after default. Thus, where a broker took out an insurance policy on account of his principal but in his own name, so that he could sue upon it, and the broker had a lien on the policy for the balance of the insured's account with him exceeding the amount of a claim on the policy, the broker, upon being sued by the underwriter's assignees in bankruptcy for unpaid premiums for which the broker was personally liable, was allowed to set off the underwriter's liability on the policy.[152] Moreover, where an agent selling the goods of his principal was entitled by virtue of a lien on the goods to receive payment of the price, it was held that an agreement between the purchaser and the agent's assignees in bankruptcy by which the price was set off against a debt owing by the agent to the third party was binding on the principal.[153]

Secured creditor has other security

11.43   A creditor may have assigned the debt by way of security to a third party, but the third party has other security from the creditor which is sufficient to satisfy the secured debt. Can the debtor in that circumstance set off the assigned debt against a liability of the creditor in the creditor's bankruptcy or liquidation? A similar issue arose in *Ex p Staddon, re Wise*.[154] The petitioner had borrowed £500 from the bankrupts, who were country bankers, and gave them a promissory note for that amount. The bankrupts in turn had deposited the promissory note, together with other securities, with London bankers for the purpose of securing a debt due from them to the London bankers. After the bankruptcy the London bankers called upon the petitioner to pay the amount of the promissory note, which he did. The securities held by the London bankers were more than sufficient to satisfy the debt due to them, and the surplus securities were returned to the assignees in bankruptcy. Before the bankruptcy, the petitioner had taken up some notes of the bankrupts in the course of business, and he presented a petition to the Court of Bankruptcy against the assignees praying that they might be ordered to pay him the sum that he had paid to the London bankers. Sir James Knight Bruce VC declared in his order that the petitioner, as against the estate of the bankrupts, was entitled to set off the amount of the bankrupts' notes that he had taken up against the amount due on his promissory note, and that he was entitled to a lien for the amount that he had paid on the funds and securities which the assignees in bankruptcy had received from the London bankers after the debt to the London bankers was paid. The Vice Chancellor emphasized in his judgment that the petitioner was ignorant that the bankrupts had parted with his promissory note, and that the petitioner had regulated his dealings on that footing by taking up the bankrupts' own notes in the ordinary course of business. But the case should not be confined to that situation. Sir James Knight Bruce VC commented that, since the securities held by the London bankers were more than sufficient to satisfy the debt to them, in a sense the property in the petitioner's

---

[151] Wood, *English and International Set-off* (1989), 919–21.

[152] *Parker v Beasley* (1814) 2 M & S 423, 105 ER 438 (in which the brokers had a lien by virtue of their having accepted bills of exchange on the credit of the goods insured); *Davies v Wilkinson* (1828) 4 Bing 573, 130 ER 889 (insurance broker).

[153] *Hudson v Granger* (1821) 5 B & Ald 27, 106 ER 1103, and see also *Warner v M'Kay* (1836) 1 M & W 591, 150 ER 571.

[154] (1843) 12 LJ Bcy 39, 3 Mont D & De G 256.

promissory note had never left the bankrupts' hands, and the bankrupts therefore retained such an interest in it that the bankruptcy set-off section would have applied. While he said that he did not put the case mainly or exclusively on that ground, it nevertheless suggests a general application for the decision.

The secured creditor in *Ex p Staddon* had been paid. A set-off should not be available in **11.44** these cases as against the secured creditor unless either the secured debt has been paid or it is presently payable,[155] and in the latter case the remaining security is sufficient to satisfy the secured debt. If a set-off were available before the secured debt was payable, on the ground that the secured creditor has other security sufficient to pay the secured debt, the secured creditor would be exposed to the risk of a later reduction in the value of the remaining security.

In *Ex p Staddon*, the secured creditor was paid by the debtor who later asserted the set-off, **11.45** but where there is other security a similar result should follow if the instrument upon which the debtor is liable is returned to the creditor/mortgagor[156] either because the secured creditor had recourse to the other security or because the creditor's trustee in bankruptcy or liquidator redeemed the security by payment.[157]

(3) Fixed charge

A security over a debt may be constituted by a fixed equitable charge taking effect as a **11.46** mere encumbrance, as opposed to an assignment by way of mortgage. This form of security creates in equity a specific charge on the proceeds of the debt as soon as they are received.[158] However, while the charge also confers a form of proprietary interest in the debt the subject of the charge,[159] in the sense that the chargor no longer has an unfettered title to deal with it, and upon default the chargee is entitled to realize the debt through the appointment of a receiver or by disposing of it without the chargor's consent so as to confer upon the transferee an unencumbered title,[160] it does not purport to transfer the beneficial ownership title in the debt to the chargee.[161] Nevertheless, for the purpose of set-off a fixed equitable

---

[155] See also para. 11.40 above.

[156] When in a case such as *Ex p Staddon* a debtor's instrument is returned to the creditor's trustee in bankruptcy or liquidator, it may be a case in which there was a temporary suspension of mutuality, so as in any event to permit a set-off on that ground. See paras 6.105–6.107 above.

[157] In *Ex p Staddon*, the assignees in bankruptcy paid the balance of the secured debt after the payment by the petitioner and the remaining securities were returned to them. The remaining securities were realized, and the report states (at (1843) 3 Mont D & De G 256, 259) that they produced a 'much larger sum' than the amount paid by the petitioner and the balance paid by the assignees. See also para. 11.51 below in relation to redemption of a security.

[158] *Siebe Gorman & Co Ltd v Barclays Bank Ltd* [1979] 2 Lloyd's Rep 142, 159.

[159] *Re Bank of Credit and Commerce International SA (No. 8)* [1998] AC 214, 226. In *Bland v Ingrams Estate Ltd* [2001] Ch 767 at [19] Nourse LJ characterized a chargee's interest in the property the subject of the charge as a proprietary interest, albeit not an equitable interest.

[160] If the instrument creating the charge has not included an express power of sale or a right to appoint a receiver, the chargee may apply to the court for an order for either remedy.

[161] *Carreras Rothmans Ltd v Freeman Mathews Treasure Ltd* [1985] Ch 207, 227; *Re Bank of Credit and Commerce International SA (No. 8)* [1998] AC 214, 226; *Re Cosslett (Contractors) Ltd* [1998] Ch 495, 508; *Tancred v Delagoa Bay and East Africa Railway Co* (1889) 23 QBD 239, 242; *Morris v Woodings* (1997) 25 ACSR 636, 640–1; Gough, *Company Charges* (2nd edn, 1996), 18–19.

charge has the same effect upon mutuality as a mortgage.[162] The important point is that the charge, while it does not involve a full transfer of the beneficial ownership, nevertheless confers an immediate proprietary interest in the debt.[163] It is not merely a security over the proceeds.[164] If the chargor becomes bankrupt the charged debt does not vest in his or her trustee in bankruptcy for the benefit of creditors generally, in which case it should not be the subject of a set-off under the insolvency set-off section as between the chargor and the debtor.[165] For example, in *Lee & Chapman's Case*[166] the security in issue was described as a charge,[167] and it was held that the charged debt was not available for a set-off as between the debtor and the creditor/chargor in the latter's liquidation to the extent of the amount of the debt that was required to discharge the security. Similarly, when the debtor on the charged debt is bankrupt, any proof in the bankruptcy would be lodged for the benefit of the chargee, not the chargor, and it should not be the subject of a set-off in respect of a debt owing by the chargor to the debtor.

Statutes of Set-off

11.47 In so far as set-off under the Statutes of Set-off is concerned, the availability of a set-off as against a debt the subject of a fixed equitable charge similarly should be determined by the same principle applicable in the case of a mortgage. In other words, the equitable chargee should only take subject to a right of set-off that accrued to the debtor against the chargor before the debtor had notice of the charge.[168] When the cross-debt arose in favour of the

---

[162] In considering mutuality, the New Zealand Court of Appeal in *Hoverd Industries Ltd v Supercool Refrigeration and Air Conditioning (1991) Ltd* [1995] 3 NZLR 577, 587 equated a fixed charge with an equitable assignment. See also *Re Patrick Corporation Ltd and the Companies Act* (1980) ACLC 40–643 (fixed charge destroyed mutuality); *Roadshow Entertainment Pty Ltd v (ACN 053 006 269) Pty Ltd* (1997) 42 NSWLR 462, 482, and the cases dealing with crystallization of a floating charge, for which see para. 11.48 below. Compare Grantham, 'The impact of security on set-off' [1989] JBL 377, 386–8, and *Re Patrick Corporation Ltd and the Companies Act* (1980) ACLC 40–643 at 34,373, though the word 'charge' there seems to have been used in the sense of a floating charge. Mr Grantham referred in his article to views expressed by Professor Goode in 'Centre Point' [1984] JBL 172, 173–4, but Professor Goode subsequently expressed a contrary opinion. See *Goode on Legal Problems of Credit and Security* (4th edn (ed. Gullifer), 2008), 107.

[163] *Agnew v Commissioner of Inland Revenue* [2001] 2 AC 710 at [7]. This immediate and attached security interest should be distinguished from the interest which the holder of a floating security has prior to crystallization. While this is a present security (*Smith v Bridgend County BC* [2002] 1 AC 336 at [61] and [62]; Gough, *Company Charges* (2nd edn, 1996), 97; *Wily v St George Partnership Banking Ltd* (1999) 84 FCR 423, 425–7, 430–4), it is, as Professor Goode has explained ('Charges over book debts: a missed opportunity' (1994) 110 LQR 592, 594; *Goode on Legal Problems of Credit and Security* (4th edn (ed. Gullifer), 2008), 126–8), a security over a fund of assets without attaching to any particular asset. See also *Evans v Rival Granite Quarries Ltd* [1910] 2 KB 979, 999; *Moodemere Pty Ltd v Waters* [1988] VR 215, 228; *Re Spectrum Plus Ltd* [2005] 2 AC 680 at [139]. It has also been said that the interest created by a floating charge, although existing, is dormant until crystallization. See *Smith v Bridgend* at [61]. These analyses may provide a solution to the problem to which Mr Grantham adverted in his article, 'The impact of a security interest on set-off' [1989] JBL 377, 386–7.

[164] Compare an assignment of the proceeds of a debt, for which see paras 17.66–17.67 below.

[165] *De Mattos v Saunders* (1872) LR 7 CP 570, 582; *Re Asphaltic Wood Pavement Co. Lee & Chapman's Case* (1885) 30 Ch D 216, 225; *Popular Homes Ltd v Circuit Developments Ltd* [1979] 2 NZLR 642, 657. See also *Turner v Thomas* (1871) LR 6 CP 610, 615, and paras 17.39 and 17.115 below.

[166] *Re Asphaltic Wood Pavement Co. Lee & Chapman's Case* (1885) 30 Ch D 216.

[167] See the statement of facts, and the judgment of Bacon VC at first instance, at (1881) 26 Ch D 624, 627–8, 634, and on appeal Brett MR (1885) 30 Ch D 216, 220–2, although compare Cotton LJ at 224–6.

[168] See para. 11.38 above. Compare *Rother Iron Works Ltd v Canterbury Precision Engineers Ltd* [1974] 1 QB 1 (see para. 17.109 below) in the context of a receiver who carried on the company's business.

debtor after notice there admittedly would still be mutuality by reference to the legal titles to the debts, so that the Statutes *prima facie* apply.[169] On the other hand, it would be unconscionable for the debtor to base a defence on a cross-debt that accrued after the debtor had notice that a third party had a proprietary interest in his or her indebtedness through a charge,[170] and the debtor accordingly would not be permitted in equity to rely on any such defence in an action to enforce the debt.[171]

This view is consistent with the floating charge cases referred to below.[172] While it was generally said in those cases that crystallization of the security brought about an equitable assignment of the debt in favour of the debenture-holder, in many of them the debenture in fact provided for a charge upon crystallization as opposed to a mortgage,[173] and in that respect they support the view that a charge has an effect similar to an assignment as far as rights of set-off are concerned. Thus, Jeffrey J in the New South Wales Supreme Court in *West Street Properties Pty Ltd v Jamison*[174] referred, in the context of a crystallized floating charge, to the principle: 'which prevents a cross-action for a legal debt from being maintained against a plaintiff suing on behalf of an equitable chargee where the substantial consequence of doing so would be to allow the defendant, as no more than an unsecured creditor of the plaintiff, to defeat the equitable chargee's security.' It has been assumed in New Zealand that the same principle applies in the case of an equitable charge as for a mortgage.[175]   **11.48**

(4) Floating security[176]

A company may grant a floating security over its assets, including over debts owing to it.   **11.49**
Before crystallization, the existence of the floating security has no effect upon rights of set-off accruing to the debtor against the company. The debtor will not be deprived of a set-off by reason of the fact that, at the time that either of the cross-debts was incurred, he or she had notice of the floating security.[177] However, the position changes once crystallization occurs. Upon crystallization, the security attaches to the company's assets, and it is commonly said that any debts owing to the company and coming within the ambit

---

169 See para. 11.18 above.

170 *Hoverd Industries Ltd v Supercool Refrigeration and Air Conditioning (1991) Ltd* [1995] 3 NZLR 577, 587, referring to Meagher, Gummow and Lehane, *Equity Doctrines and Remedies* (3rd edn, 1992), 720–1 para. 2867 (see now *Meagher, Gummow and Lehane's Equity Doctrines and Remedies* (4th edn, 2002), 943–4 [28–335]). The analysis of James LJ in *Roxburghe v Cox* (1881) 17 Ch D 520, 526 would appear to apply equally to an equitable charge.

171 See para. 11.18 above.

172 See para. 11.49 below and paras 17.99–17.118 below.

173 See e.g. *N W Robbie & Co Ltd v Witney Warehouse Co Ltd* [1963] 1 WLR 1324, in which the security took the form of a charge (see the terms of the security at 1326), and the discussion in *Biggerstaff v Rowatt's Wharf Ltd* [1896] 2 Ch 93 (the terms of the security being set out at 94). See also *National Mutual Life Nominees Ltd v National Capital Development Commission* (1975) 37 FLR 404, 408–410 (criticized in Sykes and Walker, *The Law of Securities* (5th edn, 1993), 960).

174 [1974] 2 NSWLR 435, 441.

175 *Dalgety and Co Ltd v National Mortgage and Agency Co Ltd* (1910) 13 GLR 379.

176 See also paras 17.99–17.118 below. In Australia, compare the position under the Personal Property Securities Act 2009 (Cth). See paras 17.102–17.104 below.

177 *Biggerstaff v Rowatt's Wharf Ltd* [1896] 2 Ch 93.

of the security are assigned in equity to the secured creditor.[178] The proposition that crystallization results in an equitable assignment of the company's assets the subject of the security has been described as 'too imprecise',[179] and indeed crystallization of a floating security is often expressed to result in a fixed equitable charge over the assets[180] as distinct from an assignment by way of mortgage. But it has also been said that the appellation 'equitable assignment' is sufficient for some purposes,[181] and the cases suggest that crystallization of a floating security which is in the form of a charge is to be equated with an equitable assignment for the purpose of determining rights of set-off.[182] The principles discussed above in the context of mortgages accordingly are relevant, on the basis that an equitable assignment (or fixed charge) occurs at the date of crystallization.

11.50 If after crystallization the company goes into liquidation, a debt otherwise owing to the company at the date of the liquidation will have become the subject of a fixed security in favour of the secured creditor as a result of the crystallization, whether by way of an assignment or a fixed equitable charge. Accordingly, the debtor could not rely on the insolvency set-off section in the company's liquidation,[183] except, in the circumstances referred to above,[184] to the extent that the debt in question exceeds the amount secured. The question whether the insolvency set-off section would apply if the security is redeemed by the company after its liquidation is considered below.

(5) Redemption of the security

11.51 When a debt is the subject of a security, and the security is redeemed, the full beneficial title to the debt reverts to the creditor/security provider, and rights of set-off should be determined accordingly. Therefore, in a subsequent liquidation of the security provider, the debt should be able to be set off pursuant to the insolvency set-off section against a cross-debt owing by the security provider to the debtor. However, what if the security is redeemed after the security provider's liquidation? If the security provider held the debt before the

---

[178] *Biggerstaff v Rowatt's Wharf Ltd* [1896] 2 Ch 93; *N W Robbie & Co Ltd v Witney Warehouse Co Ltd* [1963] 1 WLR 1324 (referred to in *Security Trust Co v Sovereign Bank of Canada* [1976] AC 503, 518); *George Barker (Transport) Ltd v Eynon* [1974] 1 WLR 462, 467; *National Mutual Life Nominees Ltd v National Capital Development Commission* (1975) 37 FLR 404, 407–10; *Rendell v Doors and Doors Ltd* [1975] 2 NZLR 191; *Business Computers Ltd v Anglo–African Leasing Ltd* [1977] 1 WLR 578, 582; *Hoverd Industries Ltd v Supercool Refrigeration and Air Conditioning (1991) Ltd* [1995] 3 NZLR 577, 587; *Re ELS Ltd* [1995] Ch 11; *Roadshow Entertainment Pty Ltd v (ACN 053 006 269) Pty Ltd* (1997) 42 NSWLR 462, 482.

[179] *Sheahan v Carrier Air Conditioning Pty Ltd* (1997) 189 CLR 407, 422–3 (Brennan CJ). See also *Re Parker* (1997) 80 FCR 1, 17–18; *G & M Aldridge Pty Ltd v Walsh* [1999] 3 VR 601 at [26] (decision affirmed (2001) 203 CLR 662 (HC)).

[180] See above.

[181] *G & M Aldridge Pty Ltd v Walsh* [1999] 3 VR 601 at [26].

[182] See e.g. *N W Robbie & Co Ltd v Witney Warehouse Co Ltd* [1963] 1 WLR 1324; *Business Computers Ltd v Anglo–African Leasing Ltd* [1977] 1 WLR 578, 580, 582; *Hoverd Industries Ltd v Supercool Refrigeration and Air Conditioning (1991) Ltd* [1995] 3 NZLR 577, 587; *Roadshow Entertainment Pty Ltd v (ACN 053 006 269) Pty Ltd* (1997) 42 NSWLR 462, 482.

[183] *Re Parker* (1997) 80 FCR 1, 16–18. This appears from cases such as *Handley Page Ltd v Commissioners of Customs and Excise and Rockwell Machine Tool Co Ltd* [1970] 2 Lloyd's Rep 459; *Rendell v Doors and Doors Ltd* [1975] 2 NZLR 191; *Hoverd Industries Ltd v Supercool Refrigeration and Air Conditioning (1991) Ltd* [1995] 3 NZLR 577, 585 *et seq*. See also para. 11.13 above, and para. 17.115 below.

[184] See para. 11.40 above.

debt became the subject of a fixed security, it should not matter that redemption occurs after liquidation. It would simply be a case of a suspension of mutuality,[185] and *Hiley v The Peoples Prudential Assurance Co Ltd*[186] supports the availability of a set-off in that circumstance. Consider, however, that the security is a floating security over all the assets of the security provider, and the debt the subject of the security was incurred to the security provider after the floating security crystallized.[187] If, as is usually the case, the security extends to future assets, the debt when it came into existence would have been the subject of an immediate equitable assignment to the secured creditor.[188] The situation in that circumstance would differ from that in the *Hiley* case, in which there was merely a suspension of mutuality. The company in the *Hiley* case was owed the debt, it assigned it by way of mortgage, and it redeemed the security after its liquidation. In the situation posited, on the other hand, the security provider prior to the liquidation was never owed the debt free of the security.[189] The secured creditor from the beginning was beneficially interested in the dealing which gave rise to the debt the subject of the security, and so there would not have been mutuality in equity prior to the liquidation. On that basis, it would not be a case of a suspension of mutuality. A set-off nevertheless still be available if the secured creditor had sufficient other security to satisfy the secured debt. In that situation, the security provider should have retained a sufficient interest in the redeemed debt so as to permit a set-off.[190] In a case in which the security was over all the security provider's assets, and the security was redeemed so that the full beneficial interest in the debt reverted to the security provider, ordinarily it would follow that the secured creditor had sufficient other security.

---

[185] See paras 6.105–6.107 above.

[186] (1938) 60 CLR 468.

[187] Chilwell J's *dictum* in *Rendell v Doors and Doors Ltd* [1975] 2 NZLR 191, 202–3 (which is criticized in Wood, *English and Internation Set-off* (1989), 922) should be considered in this context.

[188] *N W Robbie & Co Ltd v Witney Warehouse Co Ltd* [1963] 1 WLR 1324.

[189] The comments of Deane J in *Federal Commissioner of Taxation v Everett* (1978) 21 ALR 625, 644, referring to *Re Lind* [1915] 2 Ch 345, 360 in relation to an assignment of future property, are relevant here.

[190] See paras 11.43–11.45 above.

12

MUTUALITY – SAME PARTIES

A. Introduction

In the absence of an agency or a trust relationship which brings about mutuality in equity **12.01** or, alternatively, before bankruptcy or liquidation, of a set-off agreement between the parties,[1] A's right to sue B may not be set off against A's indebtedness to C.[2] This applies in circumstances where B and C are related companies,[3] and also where C is a director of company B[4] or is the beneficial owner of company B.[5]

---

[1] See ch. 16 below in relation to set-off agreements.

[2] See e.g. *North and South Wales Bank Ltd v Macbeth* [1908] AC 137, 141 (HL). But note paras 4.67–4.83 above in relation to equitable set-off.

[3] *Bank of Credit and Commerce International (Overseas) Ltd v Habib Bank Ltd* [1999] 1 WLR 42; *Meridien BIAO Bank GmbH v Bank of New York* [1997] 1 Lloyd's Rep 437. See also *First National Bank of Chicago v West of England Shipowners Mutual Protection and Indemnity Association (The Evelpidis Era)* [1981] 1 Lloyd's Rep 54. *Aliter* if the corporate veil can be lifted so that C's asset, in the form of the claim against A, can be considered as an asset of B. Compare *Meridien BIAO Bank v Bank of New York* at 446. It makes no difference that B and C are in liquidation and their liquidators have entered into a pooling arrangement. See *BCCI v Habib Bank* at 48–9.

[4] *Re Barker, ex p Michell* (1958) 18 ABC 195.

[5] *Re Bank of Credit and Commerce International SA (No. 8)* [1998] AC 214. See also *Hamilton Ice Arena Ltd v Perry Developments Ltd* [2002] 1 NZLR 309 (equitable set-off).

B. Joint Claims and Liabilities

(1) The general principle

12.02   The requirement of same parties often arises in the context of joint debts and demands. Joint debtors may employ the debt in a set-off against a cross-demand possessed by them jointly against the creditor,[6] but a set-off will not generally arise as between, on the one hand, a joint debt or a joint demand, and on the other a separate cross-claim possessed or a separate debt owing by one of the joint parties.[7] Thus, in the case of a partnership,[8] a joint debt of the partnership generally cannot be set off against a debt owed separately to one of the partners,[9] and a separate debt of one of the partners cannot be set off against an obligation owing to the firm.[10] Further, an agreement between a partner and his or her separate creditor, by which the partner's debt is to be set off against a debt owing by the creditor to the partnership, may be impugned in equity by the other partners to the extent of their interest in the debt to the partnership if the creditor had notice that it was in fact a partnership asset.[11] Even if all the partners separately are indebted to a creditor of the firm, the separate debts give rise to separate claims, and they may not be set off against a liability of the creditor to the partnership.[12] Conversely, in *Ex p Christie*[13] partners were jointly indebted to a creditor, who was indebted to each of the partners separately, and a set-off was denied in the creditor's bankruptcy.

---

[6]   See e.g. *Stackwood v Dunn* (1842) 3 QB 822, 114 ER 723; *Forster v Wilson* (1843) 12 M & W 191, 152 ER 1165.

[7]   In addition to the cases referred to below, see *Arnold v Bainbrigge* (1853) 9 Ex 153, 156 ER 66; *Jones v Fleeming* (1827) 7 B & C 217, 108 ER 704; *Equititrust Ltd v Franks* (2009) 258 ALR 388 (joint debt and separate claim).

[8]   It is now possible to have a limited liability partnership which, unlike a normal partnership, is a separate legal entity from its members. See the Limited Liability Partnerships Act 2000. Mutuality should be determined on the same basis as for a company.

[9]   *M'Gillivray v Simson* (1826) 2 Car & P 320, 172 ER 145, affirmed 5 LJOSKB 53; *Tyso v Pettit* (1879) 40 LT 132; *Re Jane, ex p The Trustee* (1914) 110 LT 556. See also *Addis v Knight* (1817) 2 Mer 117, 35 ER 885; *Vale of Clwydd Coal Co v Garsed* (1885) 2 WN (NSW) 14 (joint debt); *Re Pennington and Owen, Ltd* [1925] 1 Ch 825. Compare *James v Kynnier* (1799) 5 Ves Jun 108, 31 ER 496, in which the sum paid by the partner to the partnership creditor was treated as a payment of the partnership debt, as opposed to giving rise to a separate debt owing by the creditor to the partner.

[10]   *Ex p Riley* (1731) W Kel 24, 25 ER 476; *Ex p Twogood* (1805) 11 Ves Jun 517, 32 ER 1189; *Ex p Soames, re Pestell* (1833) 3 Deac & Ch 320; *France v White* (1839) 6 Bing (NC) 33, 133 ER 13; *Baker v Gent* (1892) 9 TLR 159. See also *Middleton v Pollock, ex p Nugee* (1875) LR 20 Eq 29; *Bowyear v Pawson* (1881) 6 QBD 540; *McEwan v Crombie* (1883) 25 Ch D 175; *Tapper v Matheson* (1884) NZLR 3 SC 312; *Loughnan v O'Sullivan* [1922] 1 IR 103 (affirmed [1922] 1 IR 160) (joint judgment for costs in favour of A and B against C could not be set off in C's bankruptcy against B's separate debt to C). In *Ex p Ross, re Fisher* (1817) Buck 125, a firm consisting of two partners was dissolved though the business was continued by one of the former partners. It was held that a debt due to the former partners could not be set off against a liability incurred by the remaining partner after the dissolution.

[11]   See *Piercy v Fynney* (1871) LR 12 Eq 69, but compare Lord Esher MR in *Harper v Marten* (1895) 11 TLR 368 (see para. 12.18 below). See also para. 16.72 below.

[12]   *Tyso v Pettit* (1879) 40 LT 132.

[13]   (1804) 10 Ves Jun 105, 32 ER 783.

(2) Parties may act to bring about a set-off

The parties may nevertheless act to bring about a set-off. Thus, a partnership may agree **12.03**
with a debtor to the firm that the firm is to be responsible for debts owing separately by its
members to the debtor, and that those separate debts are to be set off against the debt owing
to the firm.[14] Similarly, the conduct of the parties may be such as to indicate an agreement
that a claim possessed by a partner against a third party is to be amalgamated with a debt
owing by himself and his partners to that party.[15] In these cases, however, the agreement
will not be effective in a bankruptcy when it involves an asset of the bankrupt unless the
set-off has occurred prior to the bankruptcy.[16] Alternatively, if a member is a separate creditor, his or her right to sue may be assigned to the firm, which may then set it off against
a joint indebtedness of the firm.[17] A more common situation arises when a partner retires.
A retiring partner remains liable for debts incurred by the firm before the retirement.
But if a creditor has agreed to a novation, so that the firm constituted by the remaining
partners is to be treated as the debtor and the old firm which included the retired partner is
discharged, the debt may be set off against a debt subsequently incurred by the creditor to
the new firm.[18] Without a novation the partnership in debt would be differently constituted from the partnership in credit, and mutuality would be lacking.[19]

(3) Severance of a joint claim

In the case of joint creditors, they may agree that the debt should be severed.[20] If the **12.04**
debtor is a party to the agreement it may take effect by way of novation, by which the
joint claim is extinguished and is replaced by a separate claim in favour of each creditor
for his or her proportion. Each creditor would then be able to employ his or her separate
claim in a set-off against a debt that the creditor owes to the debtor. Alternatively, if
the debtor is not a party, an agreement amongst the creditors to sever the joint claim may
take effect by way of an equitable assignment of part of the debt to each creditor.[21]
The creditors would then hold the debt jointly as trustees for themselves as tenants in
common of distinct portions of the debt,[22] and questions of set-off would be determined
by reference to the same principles applicable generally to equitable assignments

---

[14] *Kinnerley v Hossack* (1809) 2 Taunt 170, 127 ER 1042. There must be evidence of an agreement for
payment by means of a set-off. A mere understanding by one party is not sufficient. See *Ex p Soames, re Pestell*
(1833) 3 Deac & Ch 320, 324, and also *Tyso v Pettit* (1879) 40 LT 132.

[15] *Ell v Harper* (1886) NZLR 4 SC 307.

[16] *British Eagle International Air Lines Ltd v Compagnie Nationale Air France* [1975] 1 WLR 758. See
paras 16.21–16.26 below.

[17] Compare *Watts v Christie* (1849) 11 Beav 546, 50 ER 928, where the assignment took place in circumstances such that a set-off would have constituted a fraudulent preference. See para. 6.101 above.

[18] *Burgess v Morton* (1894) 10 TLR 339, reversed on other grounds [1896] AC 136.

[19] As in *Re Jane, ex p The Trustee* (1914) 110 LT 556.

[20] Compare *Bowyear v Pawson* (1881) 6 QBD 540, in which a creditor entered into an agreement by which
he assigned the claim to himself and another person in equal shares as tenants in common. Watkin Williams
and Mathew JJ held that this was not sufficient to sever the debt so as to entitle the other person to set off his
interest in it against a separate debt that he owed to the debtor.

[21] Since it is not possible to have a legal assignment of part of a debt, the assignment in this situation must
of necessity be an equitable assignment. See *McIntyre v Gye* (1994) 51 FCR 472, 479.

[22] *McIntyre v Gye* (1994) 51 FCR 472, 479.

of debts.[23] Thus, each creditor in respect of his or her portion would take subject to a set-off available to the debtor against the joint creditors before the debtor received notice of the assignment. If the debtor raises the defence against only one of the creditors suing as an equitable assignee, that creditor should be entitled to contribution from the other creditors.

(4) Insolvency set-off and partnerships

12.05 In order for the insolvency set-off section to apply in relation to partnership liabilities,[24] the partnership must be in the process of being wound up under the Insolvent Partnerships Order 1994,[25] either as an unregistered company[26] or in circumstances where a joint bankruptcy petition has been presented by all members of the insolvent partnership.[27] It may also apply if an administrator is appointed to a partnership and the administrator, being authorized to make a distribution to creditors of the partnership, has given notice of intention to do so.[28] But where an action is brought to recover a debt owing to a partnership, the insolvency set-off section will not apply in relation to a cross-claim against the partnership merely because one of the partners has become bankrupt.[29]

(5) Equitable interests

12.06 Since mutuality in insolvency set-off is determined by reference to the equitable interests of the parties,[30] a set-off may proceed notwithstanding that at law one claim may be joint and the other separate if in equity the same parties are interested in the cross-claims. Therefore, a debt owing to a number of creditors (C1 and C2) jointly may be set off against the separate indebtedness of one of the creditors (C1), if C1 and C2 are merely trustees of the debt for C1 so that C1 is the only person beneficially interested in it.[31] Conversely, a set-off may be denied where there is mutuality at law but not in equity.[32]

---

[23] See *Adamopoulos v Olympic Airways SA* (1991) 25 NSWLR 75, 87, and ch. 17 below.

[24] In the case of a limited liability partnership, see para. 6.04 above.

[25] S.I. 1994 No. 2421.

[26] See the Insolvent Partnerships Order 1994, arts 7, 8, 9 and 10, together with Part V (in particular s. 221(1)) of the Insolvency Act 1986 and art. 18 of the Insolvent Partnerships Order (incorporating the Insolvency Rules 1986).

[27] See the Insolvent Partnerships Order 1994, art. 11. In Australia, see the Bankruptcy Act 1966 (Cth), ss. 45, 46 and 56A. In Australia a partnership of more than five members may be wound up under the Corporations Act 2001 as a Part 5.7 body, in which case the set-off section (s. 553C) applies. See s. 583.

[28] Insolvent Partnerships Order 1994, arts 6 (referring to Sch. 2, and see in particular para. 23 of Sch. 2) and 18 (incorporating the Insolvency Rules 1986). See also para. 6.10 above.

[29] *Staniforth v Fellowes* (1814) 1 Marsh 184; *New Quebrada Co, Ltd v Carr* (1869) LR 4 CP 651; *London, Bombay and Mediterranean Bank v Narraway* (1872) LR 15 Eq 93.

[30] See para. 11.13 above.

[31] Compare *Re Imperial Mercantile Credit Association, ex p Smith and Ford* (1867) 15 WR 1069, in which the beneficial entitlement of one of the trustees only related to the interest payable on the debt. Compare also *Ex p Morier, re Willis, Percival, & Co* (1879) 12 Ch D 491, in which the estate had not been fully administered by the executors, and so a trust as yet had not been imposed in favour of the executor who was the residuary legatee. See the discussion of *Ex p Morier* in para. 13.126 below.

[32] *Tapper v Matheson* (1884) NZLR 3 SC 312.

In relation to the Statutes of Set-off,[33] a defence of set-off may arise at law if there is mutual- **12.07**
ity by reference to the legal title to cross-debts, and equity acting by analogy with the
Statutes similarly may recognize a set-off if there is mutuality in equity. Conversely, if a
creditor holds the debt on trust for or if the creditor has assigned it in equity to a third party,
equity may regard it as unconscionable for a set-off at law to occur as between the debtor
and the creditor, and accordingly not permit a set-off. Thus, the same result often (but not
always[34]) follows in relation to the Statutes as if mutuality were determined by reference to
equitable titles.

C. Exceptions

The courts have been reluctant to depart from the principle that a joint demand and a **12.08**
separate demand may not be brought into an account. There are nevertheless a number of
instances in which a set-off has been allowed, despite an apparent absence of strict mutuality. Some of these in truth are not exceptions to a requirement of mutuality in that, properly
regarded, they do not constitute instances in which a set-off was allowed under the insolvency set-off section where there was not mutuality. Rather, they are examples of equitable
set-off, for which the better view is that mutuality is not a strict requirement.[35]

(1) Surety made jointly liable

In *Ex p Hanson*,[36] one of two joint debtors on a bond given as security for a debt had **12.09**
joined in the bond only as a surety. Lord Eldon held that the principal debtor was entitled
in equity to employ the joint debt in a set-off against a separate claim that he had against
the bankrupt creditor. A set-off was allowed because: 'the joint debt was nothing more
than a security for the separate debt; and upon equitable considerations a creditor, who has
a joint security for a separate debt, cannot resort to that security without allowing what
he has received on the separate account.'[37] A similar notion was applied in *Hamp v Jones*.[38]
A judgment had been obtained at law against both Hamp and his bailiff for damages for
wrongful distress. In addition, Hamp had a separate claim against the judgment creditor.
The creditor was insolvent, but not apparently bankrupt. Because the demands were not
mutual they could not be set off at law. Hamp, however, had agreed to indemnify the
bailiff on the judgment, and so Sir Lancelot Shadwell VC held that Hamp could set off the
judgment against his separate claim, the Vice Chancellor commenting:[39] 'If, as the bill
states, Mr Hamp has agreed to indemnify his bailiff, that, it seems to me, is a reason for
the interference of the Court.' In this case, a private agreement for an indemnity provided

---

[33] See paras 11.18–11.20 above.
[34] See para. 11.19 above.
[35] See paras 4.67–4.83 above, and *Bank of New Zealand v Harry M Miller & Co Ltd* (1992) 26 NSWLR
48, 55.
[36] (1811) 18 Ves Jun 232, 34 ER 305, affirming (1806) 12 Ves Jun 346, 33 ER 131. See also *Ex p Hippins,
re Sikes* (1826) 2 Gl & J 93, 4 LJOS Ch 195; *Clarkson v Smith & Goldberg* [1926] 1 DLR 509, 511.
[37] (1811) 18 Ves Jun 232, 233–4, 34 ER 305 *per* Lord Eldon.
[38] (1840) 9 LJ Ch 258.
[39] (1840) 9 LJ Ch 258.

the basis for a set-off. If, on the other hand, an agreement for an indemnity in truth is nothing more than a device to obtain an advantage over other creditors by means of a set-off, an equitable set-off should not be permitted.

(2) Judgments

12.10   The common law courts, in the exercise of what has been described as a form of equitable jurisdiction for the purpose of preventing absurdity or injustice,[40] will permit a set-off of judgments in appropriate cases.[41] In exercising this jurisdiction the courts have been prepared in some cases to allow a set-off where A has a judgment against B and C, and B has a separate judgment against A.[42] In those cases, however, there was no question of bankruptcy. If there is a bankruptcy, a set-off of judgments generally will not be permitted in circumstances extending beyond the insolvency set-off section.[43]

(3) Fraud

12.11   Equity will permit D1, one of two joint debtors D1 and D2, to set off the joint debt in the creditor's bankruptcy against the creditor's separate debt to D1, if the creditor's debt arose as a result of the creditor's fraud and D1 was unaware of the fraud at the time when the joint debt was incurred. This proposition is based on two decisions of Lord Eldon. In *Vulliamy v Noble*[44] a customer (D1) had deposited some stock with a bank as security for a loan. The customer paid off the loan, but neglected to request a retransfer of the security. In the meantime he had become a joint debtor with D2 to the bank in a separate transaction. After the bank's bankruptcy, D1 discovered that the bank had sold the stock, so that, instead of being the owner of stock, he was merely a creditor of the bank for its value.[45] Lord Eldon held that D1 could set off the bank's indebtedness to him in his separate capacity against his and D2's joint debt to the bank.[46] In doing so, he referred to his earlier decision

---

[40] *Edwards v Hope* (1885) 14 QBD 922, 926.

[41] See paras 2.98–2.122 above.

[42] *Roberts v Biggs* Barnes 146, 94 ER 848; *Mitchell v Oldfield* (1791) 4 TR 123, 100 ER 929; *Dennie v Elliott* (1795) 2 H Bl 587, 126 ER 719. See para. 2.107 above.

[43] See paras 2.111–2.113 above.

[44] (1817) 3 Mer 593, 36 ER 228.

[45] When a secured debt is paid but the security is not returned, the security is held on trust for the former debtor. See *Pearce v Morris* (1869) LR 5 Ch App 227, 230; *Holme v Fieldsend* [1911] WN 111. If the property constituting the security is sold by the trustee, the beneficial owner may trace it to the proceeds of sale, and if the proceeds have been mixed with the trustee's own funds the beneficial owner has a charge on the whole of the blended fund, the onus being on the trustee to prove which part of it is his or hers. See *Re Hallett's Estate. Knatchbull v Hallett* (1880) 13 Ch D 696; *Re Tilley's Will Trusts (Burgin v Croad)* [1967] 1 Ch 1179. Ordinarily, then, someone in the position of the customer in *Vulliamy v Noble* would have effective real rights for the recovery of the sum owing to him or her, and a set-off would only be required if the proceeds cannot be traced or, having been traced, if the fund with which it is mixed is insufficient to satisfy the charge.

[46] In *Middleton v Pollock, ex p Knight and Raymond* (1875) LR 20 Eq 515, 521–3 Sir George Jessel MR sought to explain *Vulliamy v Noble* on the ground that the stock was retained by the bank under an agreement that it should constitute security for the joint debt. Therefore, it was said that the case was not concerned with set-off at all, because equity would have applied the proceeds of sale in reduction of the joint debt for which it was security so that only the balance would have been payable. It is suggested, however, that the case cannot be explained on that ground, and that in truth it is an authority on equitable set-off. See paras 4.71–4.76 above.

in *Ex p Stephens*.[47] The separate debt of the bankrupt creditors in that case to one of their two joint and several debtors (D1) similarly had arisen as a result of the creditors' own fraud, in retaining D1's money for their own use rather than using it to purchase annuities as instructed. Lord Eldon enjoined the creditors' assignees in bankruptcy from suing the other joint and several debtor (D2) for payment of the debt, and ordered that D1 should be allowed to set off the joint and several debt of herself and D2 against her separate claim arising as a result of the creditors' fraud.

Ex p Stephens is generally regarded as having turned on the element of fraud,[48] and indeed Lord Eldon later doubted whether the decision would have been right but for the fraud.[49] It would not be crucial in a similar case today, however.[50] The liability in *Ex p Stephens* was several as well as joint, and the view now would be that the several liability of D1 and D1's cross-claim constitute mutual debts or claims arising out of mutual dealings which are capable of set-off under the insolvency set-off section.[51] The case nevertheless is still relevant as illustrating circumstances in which a set-off may be available against a joint debt.[52]

12.12

In discussing *Ex p Stephens* in *Vulliamy v Noble*,[53] Lord Eldon emphasized that, when D1 in *Ex p Stephens* incurred the liability to the bankers, she was unaware that they had her money in their hands for which they were accountable.[54] If D1 in a similar case was aware of the fraud at the time of entering into a joint debt, so that D1 was cognizant of the position, it would not generally be appropriate to give D1 a preference over other creditors by means of a set-off.

12.13

The situation would be different if the fraudulent conduct of a bankrupt has resulted in a debt owing to two creditors (C1 and C2) jointly, one of whom (C1) is a separate debtor of the bankrupt. A joint owner of property may not apply the property to his or her own exclusive use. The joint property in this case consists of the claim arising from fraud, and if C1 would not have had the right to apply it to his or her own exclusive use before the bankruptcy, C1 should not be entitled to do so after the bankruptcy. C1 therefore should not be entitled to set off the joint claim in the bankruptcy against C1's separate

12.14

---

[47] (1805) 11 Ves Jun 24, 32 ER 996.

[48] *Ex p Hanson* (1806) 12 Ves Jun 346, 348–9, 33 ER 131, 132; *Ex p Blagden* (1815) 19 Ves Jun 465, 467, 34 ER 589, 590; *Jones v Mossop* (1844) 3 Hare 568, 573, 67 ER 506, 509; *Ex p Staddon, re Wise* (1843) 12 LJ Bcy 39, 40; *Middleton v Pollock, ex p Knight and Raymond* (1875) LR 20 Eq 515, 519–20; *McIntyre v Perkes* (1990) 22 FCR 260, 271; *Lord v Direct Acceptance Corporation Ltd* (1993) 32 NSWLR 362, 369–70; *Re Bank of Credit and Commerce International SA (No 8)* [1996] Ch 245, 267–8. See also *Strong v Foster* (1855) 17 CB 201, 217, 139 ER 1047, 1053.

[49] *Ex p Blagden* (1815) 19 Ves Jun 465, 467, 34 ER 589, 590.

[50] *MS Fashions Ltd v Bank of Credit and Commerce International SA* [1993] Ch 425, 438 (Hoffmann LJ). See also the discussion and explanation of *Ex p Stephens* in paras 12.29–12.39 below.

[51] See para. 12.21 below.

[52] In *Vulliamy* (1817) 3 Mer 593, 621, 36 ER 228, 239 Lord Eldon regarded it as relevant in that context.

[53] (1817) 3 Mer 593, 621, 36 ER 228, 239.

[54] See also *Re Bank of Credit and Commerce International SA (No. 8)* [1996] Ch 245, 266 (CA).

indebtedness. *Middleton v Pollock, ex p Knight and Raymond*[55] illustrates the point. The joint creditors in that case admittedly were trustees for third parties, and it was emphasized that payment could not properly have been tendered to one of the trustees alone. But even if there were no trust, the result should have been the same. Further, the fact of the trust should have sufficed to preclude a set-off irrespective of the joint legal ownership. Mutuality in bankruptcy is determined by reference to the equitable interests of the parties, and fraud would not justify joint creditors applying the debt owing to them as trustees in satisfaction of the indebtedness of one of them, when the equitable ownership of the joint creditors' claim is in someone else.

(4) Dormant partner

12.15 In *Stracey, Ross, et al v Deey*,[56] a partnership carried on trade as grocers. However, only one partner was active in the business, the other partners being dormant. A debtor of the business had also dealt separately with the active partner, who in the course of those dealings became indebted to the debtor. When the partnership sued the debtor on the grocery account, Lord Kenyon allowed the debtor to set off the active partner's separate debt to him. The decision in *Stracey* appears as a note to the report of *George v Clagett*,[57] the seminal authority on the right of a person dealing with someone acting as an agent for an undisclosed principal to set off a separate debt owing by the agent to that person against the person's liability to the principal on the dealing.[58] But while the position of a dormant partner has been said to be analogous to that of an undisclosed principal,[59] the analogy has been criticized on the ground that the dormant partner's right to sue and his or her liability to be sued[60] do not arise because he or she is an undisclosed principal intervening on the agent's contracts, but rather because the dormant partner is a party to the contracts.[61] Accepting that distinction, the decision in *Stracey* nevertheless should still be followed.[62] If a partnership acts in such a way as to conceal the interest of a dormant partner in the business, and consequently it gives the impression that it consists only of the active partners, it should not be allowed to deny a third party a set-off that would have arisen if the partnership had in fact been so constituted. However, the availability of a set-off may be subject to the same limitation which applies to undisclosed principals, that it is confined to the case of mutual debts under the Statutes of Set-off or, in an appropriate case, to equitable set-off, as opposed to the wider right of set-off conferred by the insolvency legislation.[63]

---

[55] (1875) LR 20 Eq 515.
[56] (1789) 7 TR 361n, 101 ER 1021, 2 Esp 469n, 170 ER 422.
[57] (1797) 7 TR 359, 101 ER 1019.
[58] See paras 13.79–13.99 below.
[59] *Beckham v Drake* (1841) 9 M & W 79, 85, 152 ER 35, 37 (Parke B), and see also *Watteau v Fenwick* [1893] 1 QB 346, 349.
[60] Together with the active partners.
[61] See Pollock, Note (1893) 9 LQR 111; Montrose. 'Liability of principal for acts exceeding actual and apparent authority' (1939) 17 Canadian Bar Review 693, 703–4. See also *Bowstead and Reynolds on Agency* (18th edn, 2006), 380; Stoljar, *The Law of Agency* (1961), 57. Compare *Construction Engineering (Aust) Pty Ltd v Hexyl Pty Ltd* (1985) 155 CLR 541.
[62] See e.g. *Muggeridge's v Smith and Co* (1884) 1 TLR 166.
[63] *Turner v Thomas* (1871) LR 6 CP 610, and see para. 13.82 below.

The converse situation instead may apply. A partnership may conduct business under the **12.16** name of A and B, although B is an employee and not a partner. A third party who deals with the firm in ignorance of the true situation would contract with A and B jointly, but A and B nevertheless would enter into the contract as agent for A as an undisclosed principal. If A intervenes on the contract and sues the third party, the third party may set off in that action a debt owing to him or her by A.[64]

The set-off in a case such as *Stracey* is based upon the third party's belief that the active **12.17** partner was the only principal in the business. In that regard, the circumstances must not have been such as to put the third party on inquiry as to whether there was a dormant partner. In *Baker v Gent*[65] a partnership consisted of two partners, Lachmann and Phillips, but the interest of Phillips in the business was concealed. The business traded under the name of Lachmann and Co. This was held to constitute notice to the defendant that someone else may have been involved in the firm, and accordingly he was not allowed to set off his indebtedness to the firm against Lachmann's separate debt to him. On the other hand, a name such as Lachmann and Co should not put a person dealing with the firm upon inquiry as to the existence of a dormant partner if there were two or more active partners involved in the business.

The generally accepted explanation for the set-off in the undisclosed principal cases is that **12.18** it is based upon representation and estoppel. In the same way, whether or not the partnership cases are thought to involve an undisclosed principal, the set-off in those cases is said to arise from 'some default in the other partners, or some assent on their part'.[66] It is not sufficient that a person dealt with one member of a partnership in the erroneous belief that that member was the only principal in the business.[67] In *Harper v Marten*[68] two partners, Forster and Peake, traded under the name of Forster, Peake, and Co. The defendant dealt only with Peake, and assumed that Peake was trading on his own account. The defendant entered into an agreement with Peake by which her indebtedness resulting from those dealings should be set off against a claim that she had against Peake alone. The Court of Appeal upheld the agreement despite the express reference to Forster in the partnership name. Two points should be noted, however. The first is that the defendant had inquired of Peake as to from whom she was ordering the goods, and he replied himself. The second is the court's finding that Forster had placed the most implicit confidence in Peake and had allowed him to have the whole control and management of the business, and moreover Forster had refrained from making any demand on the defendant for payment of her account when he might reasonably have been expected to do so. Therefore, as Lord Esher MR remarked, while Forster had not authorized Peake to tell a lie, he had enabled Peake to do so and had allowed it to look like the truth.

---

[64] *Spurr v Cass* (1870) LR 5 QB 656.

[65] (1892) 9 TLR 159.

[66] *Gordon v Ellis* (1846) 2 CB 821, 828–9, 135 ER 1167, 1170 *per* Tindal CJ *(arguendo)*.

[67] *Gordon v Ellis* (1846) 2 CB 821, 135 ER 1167. Compare *Harper v Marten* (1895) 11 TLR 368 (Lord Esher MR).

[68] (1895) 11 TLR 368.

(5) Common partners in two partnerships

12.19 Another Lord Kenyon judgment has provided a further possible exception. In *Puller v Roe*,[69] a partnership consisting of four partners, A, B, C and D (known as A & Co), held a promissory note made by the defendants. C and D were also partners in another firm. A & Co were indebted to this other partnership, and so the note was indorsed by A & Co to C and D in satisfaction of that debt. Subsequently, A, B, C and D all became bankrupt. The assignees in bankruptcy of the second partnership of C and D sued the defendants on the note, whereupon Lord Kenyon held that the defendants could set off some debts owing to them by A & Co, his Lordship commenting that partners: 'cannot as between themselves raise a distinct account, though they might indorse to a third person. The affairs of the company are in presumption of law known to all the partners, and all are equally liable.'[70] Nevertheless, while the decision appears to represent a commonsense result, unless C and D in truth held the note as trustees for A & Co it is not easy to explain the set-off. The holder in due course of a negotiable instrument takes free of equities, including rights of set-off.[71] In order to be a holder in due course, a person *inter alia* must have taken the instrument in good faith and for value, and at the time that it was indorsed to him or her the person must not have had notice of any defect in the title of the person who negotiated it.[72] Mere knowledge of a possible right of set-off between prior parties does not affect the negotiability of an instrument,[73] and therefore the partners' presumed knowledge of the state of the account between A & Co and the defendants should not have impugned their good faith. Nor indeed is it regarded as fraud for an indorser and an indorsee to agree to the negotiation of the instrument in order to defeat a right of set-off otherwise available against the indorser.[74] *Puller v Roe* possibly may be explained on the basis of the old common law rule that one partnership could not sue another if one or more of the partners were common to both firms, since those partners in effect would be both plaintiffs and defendants in the one suit.[75] Consequently, the discharge of A & Co's debt to C and D in *Puller v Roe* may not have been perceived as value given for taking the note.[76] The fact of common partners, however, should no longer be an objection to an action between two firms.[77] Moreover, the debt may be the subject of an account in equity between the partners,[78] in which case its discharge should be sufficient value. Thus, an antecedent debt which has been rendered unenforceable by statute may afford sufficient consideration for a negotiable instrument.[79]

---

[69] (1793) Peake 260, 170 ER 149.

[70] (1793) Peake 260, 263, 170 ER 149, 150.

[71] Bills of Exchange Act 1882, s. 38.

[72] Bills of Exchange Act 1882, s. 29.

[73] *Oulds v Harrison* (1854) 10 Ex 572, 576, 156 ER 566, 568 (Parke B, *arguendo*).

[74] See *Oulds v Harrison* (1854) 10 Ex 572, 156 ER 566 in relation to the more unlikely case of an overdue bill (see para. 17.70 below), and also *Metropolitan Bank v Snure* (1860) 1O UC (CP) 24.

[75] See *Bosanquet v Wray* (1815) 6 Taunt 597, 128 ER 1167 and *Mainwaring v Newman* (1800) 2 Bos & Pul 120, 126 ER 1190.

[76] Normally an antecedent debt or liability may constitute valuable consideration for a bill of exchange or promissory note. See the Bills of Exchange Act 1882, s. 27(1)(b).

[77] See *Lindley & Banks on Partnership* (18th edn, 2002), 430 [14.13].

[78] See e.g. *Meyer and Company v Faber (No. 2)* [1923] 2 Ch 421, 439.

[79] *Sharpe v Ellis* (1971) 20 FLR 199, 208.

(6) Setting off a joint creditor's interest in the debt

There is early Chancery support for the view that when C1, one of a number of partners **12.20** C1 and C2, is bankrupt, and a debtor to C1 and C2 has a separate claim against the bankrupt, the debtor may set off the bankrupt's *interest* in his or her indebtedness to the bankrupt and C2 jointly against the bankrupt's separate debt to the debtor,[80] provided that the extent of the bankrupt's interest in the joint claim is not disputed, and provided also that the partnership assets are otherwise sufficient to satisfy the partnership debts.[81] In *Lord Lanesborough v Jones*[82] Lord Cowper suggested (*obiter*) that a debtor to C1 and C2 who has a separate claim against C1 may bring into an account, in C1's bankruptcy, C1's interest in the debtor's indebtedness to them, 'if there be a surplus beyond what will pay the partnership debts'. The principle was subsequently applied in *Ex p Quintin*,[83] where Lord Loughborough emphasized that the solvent partner (C2) had paid all the partnership debts, and had also agreed that he was only interested to the extent of a quarter in the debts due to the partnership.[84] However, Lord Eldon effectively overruled the *Quintin* case in *Ex p Twogood*,[85] the Lord Chancellor expressing concern that the administration of the bankruptcy would be delayed unduly until the state of the partnership accounts could be ascertained.[86] Nevertheless, despite Lord Eldon's condemnation of *Ex p Quintin*, the possibility of a set-off has been kept alive in Victoria by *Re John Sloss, ex p Robison Brothers, Campbell & Sloss Ltd*,[87] in which the Supreme Court seemed to accept that *Quintin* was still good law. In fact a set-off was denied in *Re Sloss* because of lack of evidence as to the extent of the entitlement of the bankrupt partner in the debt owing to the partnership. On the other hand, Madden CJ cited *Ex p Quintin* with evident approval, and although he made no mention of *Ex p Twogood* in his judgment, that case had been brought to the attention of the court during argument. Perhaps the courts may be inclined to apply *Ex p Quintin* when the partnership accounts are relatively simple, or when the assets of the partnership are patently sufficient to satisfy the partnership debts, so that the administration of the bankruptcy would not be unduly delayed. However, it would be unsatisfactory if the question whether a debtor to a partnership is entitled to a set-off were to depend on the state of the partnership accounts, and the better view is that a set-off is not be available in this situation, in accordance with Lord Eldon's judgment in *Ex p Twogood*.

---

[80] See, and compare, *McEwan v Crombie* (1883) 25 Ch D 175, in which the claim was not truly joint.

[81] The second proviso would be required to protect the creditors of the partnership in the event of its bankruptcy, because the debts owing to the partnership would be joint property distributable in the first instance amongst the joint creditors. See Part II of Sch. 4 (s. 175A) and Sch. 7 (s. 328A) of the Insolvent Partnerships Order 1994 (S.I. 1994 No. 2421). In Australia this restriction would apply whether or not the joint creditors are partners. See the Bankruptcy Act 1966 (Cth) s. 110.

[82] (1716) 1 P Wms 325, 326–7, 24 ER 409, 410.

[83] (1796) 3 Ves Jun 248, 30 ER 994.

[84] Lord Loughborough referred to *Ex p Edwards* (1745) 1 Atk 100, 26 ER 66, in which Lord Hardwicke ordered that an action against a debtor to a partnership should be stayed pending the taking of an account as to how much was owing to the partnership, and how much was owing to the debtor by one of the partners. However, the report is silent as to whether a set-off eventually was allowed.

[85] (1805) 11 Ves Jun 517, 32 ER 1189. See also *Addis v Knight* (1817) 2 Mer 117, 122, 35 ER 885, 887.

[86] Lord Eldon also remarked that the effect of a set-off would be to prefer the particular creditor over the general body of the bankrupt partner's separate creditors, but every set-off in insolvency has that effect.

[87] (1893) 19 VLR 710.

D. Several Persons Separately Liable

(1) Joint and several debt

12.21 In the case of a joint and several debt,[88] each of the debtors is severally as well as jointly liable.[89] The creditor in such a case may sue all the debtors in the one action, or he or she may proceed against one or more of them separately.[90] The indebtedness of a truly joint and several debtor, and a debt owing by the creditor to that debtor, constitute mutual debts, and may be set off.[91] The occurrence of the set-off would bring about a *pro tanto* reduction in the joint and several debt, and would discharge the other debtors as well.[92] In that regard, when debtors are jointly and severally liable, and either the creditor or one of the debtors is bankrupt, a set-off under the insolvency set-off section would occur automatically at the date of the bankruptcy.[93] If the creditor is the bankrupt party, and two or more of the debtors have cross claims eligible for a set-off, a set-off should take effect on a *pro rata* basis.[94] Insolvency set-off should be compared to set-off under the Statutes of Set-off, which is not automatic but rather operates as a procedural defence to an action at law.[95] The creditor could sue whichever of the debtors the creditor chooses. In such a case the joint and several debtor being sued could not bring into account an indebtedness of the creditor to one of the other joint and several debtors. The debts would not be mutual. A right of contribution between the debtors does not justify a set-off in that circumstance.[96] If, on the other hand, joint and several debtors are sued together, judgment for a set-off in favour of one of the debtors to that extent would discharge the debt, and therefore the judgment against the other debtors should also be reduced accordingly.[97]

---

[88] This includes the case of a breach of trust where there is more than one trustee. The liability of trustees for breach of trust is joint and several, and gives rise to an equitable debt. See *Goodwin v Duggan* (1996) 41 NSWLR 158. The term 'joint and several' may also find application in the construction of covenants or other contractual promises, in partnership law and in the law dealing with the liability to account and with joint and several tortious liability. However, it is not apt in the case of property interests. See *Kendle v Melsom* (1998) 193 CLR 46 at [20].

[89] See generally Glanville Williams, *Joint Obligations* (1949), 34–5.

[90] Glanville Williams, *Joint Obligations* (1949), 59–62.

[91] *Fletcher v Dyche* (1787) 2 TR 32, 100 ER 18; *Owen v Wilkinson* (1858) 5 CB(NS) 526, 141 ER 213; *Re Last, ex p Butterell* (1994) 124 ALR 219; *Re Kolb* (1994) 51 FCR 31; *Re Bank of Credit and Commerce International SA (No. 8)* [1998] AC 214, 224–5. See also *Paulson v Murray* (1922) 68 DLR 643 (set-off of judgments), and *Ferrum Inc v Three Dees Management Ltd* (1992) 7 OR (3d) 660, 669.

[92] *Owen v Wilkinson* (1858) 5 CB(NS) 526, 527, 141 ER 213 (Willes J, referring to *Pothier on Obligations*, by Evans, vol. 2, 68); *Goodwin v Duggan* (1996) 41 NSWLR 158, 167; *Re Bank of Credit and Commerce International SA (No. 8)* [1998] AC 214, 224–5; *Handberg v Smarter Way (Aust) Pty Ltd* (2002) 190 ALR 130 (judgment for costs); *Krishell Pty Ltd v Nilant* (2006) 32 WAR 540 at [84]–[85] (set-off of judgments and orders).

[93] See para. 6.119–6.146 above.

[94] This would be consistent with the approach adopted when a debtor owes two debts to a creditor, one of which has priority in the debtor's bankruptcy or liquidation. See para. 6.168–6.173 above.

[95] See para. 2.34–2.49 above. In New South Wales, see the Civil Procedure Act 2005 (NSW), s. 21 (see paras 2.66–2.73 above).

[96] *Bowyear v Pawson* (1881) 6 QBD 540; *Lord v Direct Acceptance Corporation Ltd* (1993) 32 NSWLR 362, 371–2; *Goodwin v Duggan* (1996) 41 NSWLR 158, 166, 167–8; *Equititrust Ltd v Franks* (2009) 258 ALR 388 at [49]; *Tatlers.com.au Pty Ltd v Davis* [2007] NSWSC 835 at [44]–[45].

[97] *Goodwin v Duggan* (1996) 41 NSWLR 158; *Equititrust Ltd v Franks* (2009) 258 ALR 388 at [48].

A different view was adopted in relation to insolvency set-off in *Archer Structures Ltd v* **12.22**
Griffiths.[98] The defendant was jointly and severally liable, with a company (MPJ Contractors
Ltd) of which he was a director, to the claimant pursuant to the Insolvency Act 1986, s. 217
for a debt owed by that company to the claimant, as a consequence of a breach by the
defendant of s. 216 of the Act relating to the re-use of the name of another company that
had gone into liquidation. MPJ Contractors was also in liquidation and it had asserted
a cross-claim against the claimant. The defendant argued that MPJ Contractors' debt and
its cross-claim were automatically set off in the liquidation pursuant to r. 4.90 of the
Insolvency Rules 1986[99] and to the extent of the set-off he was also released. The argument
failed. The judge[100] acknowledged that MPJ Contractors was only liable to the claimant
for the balance after the operation of the insolvency set-off rule, but she said that that did
not affect the position as between the defendant and the claimant. The decision should
be re-considered. It had the effect that the claimant would be paid twice, once as a consequence of the cancellation of its liability to the company through a set-off and a second
time by the defendant.

(2) Guarantees and bills of exchange

Apart from joint and several debts, there are other situations in which a number of persons **12.23**
may be sued separately in respect of what in substance is the same debt. This may arise, for
example, when a guarantee is given in respect of another person's debt, or in the case of a
bill of exchange on which the drawer or an indorser is liable as well as the acceptor. Further,
while in some cases of joint and several liability none of the parties may be principally liable
inter se, in others one party may be the principal debtor, with the liability of the other joint
and several debtors intended to be secondary. The contract in that circumstance effectively
is one of suretyship. Similarly, in the case of a bill of exchange the acceptor has the principal
liability and the liability of the drawer and the indorsers is secondary, unless it is an accommodation acceptance in which case, as between the drawer and the acceptor, equity regards
the drawer as the person principally liable.[101] In those situations, one of the parties may
have a separate claim against the creditor, and the creditor may have become bankrupt or
is a company in liquidation. In a number of early cases the question arose as to whether the
creditor's trustee (or assignees) in bankruptcy could avoid a set-off by proceeding against
one party rather than another for payment, or alternatively whether there was an obligation
to facilitate a set-off by proceeding against a particular party. The cases established the
following propositions.

1. If one of the debtors was principally liable *inter se*, so that ultimately he or she was to pay
   the debt, that debtor could insist that the creditor's trustee in bankruptcy proceed
   against him or her so as to enable that debtor to have the benefit of a set-off.[102] Thus, in

---

[98] [2004] 1 BCLC 201.
[99] See paras 6.06 and 6.123 above.
[100] Her Honour Judge Frances Kirkham, Chancery Division, Birmingham District Registry.
[101] The common law, on the other hand, considered that the accommodation acceptor was principally
liable. See *Coles Myer Finance Ltd v Commissioner of Taxation* (1993) 176 CLR 640, 657, 683–9.
[102] *Ex p Hanson* (1811) 18 Ves Jun 232, 34 ER 305; *Ex p Hippins, re Sikes* (1826) 2 Gl & J 93, 4 LJOS Ch
195; *Ex p Banes, re The Royal British Bank* (1857) 28 LTOS 296, 297.

Ex p Hippins, re Sikes[103] Lord Eldon held that the drawer of an accommodation bill, as the person principally liable in equity, could demand that the bill be delivered up in part discharge of a debt owing to him by the bankrupt holders.

2. A trustee in bankruptcy holding a bill of exchange that had been dishonoured by the acceptor could not be compelled to have recourse to the drawer or an indorser of the bill who was also a creditor of the bankrupt, and who therefore would have had a set-off against his or her liability on the bill, but instead could insist on suing the acceptor as the party principally liable. Commissioner Holroyd adopted that view in *Ex p Banes, re The Royal British Bank*,[104] following an earlier decision by Lord Eldon to the same effect in *Ex p Burton, Franco and Corea, re Kensington*.[105] Conversely, a bankrupt acceptor's trustee could not require the holder to have recourse to an indorser so as to avoid a set-off.[106]

12.24 The courts have now accepted that the insolvency set-off section takes effect automatically upon the occurrence of a bankruptcy or a liquidation.[107] On that basis, the question should not be whether a trustee in bankruptcy or a liquidator can avoid a set-off by proceeding against one party rather than another, or whether the trustee or the liquidator is obliged to facilitate a set-off by having recourse to a debtor who has a cross-claim, but whether a set-off has or has not occurred. The point is illustrated by *MS Fashions Ltd v Bank of Credit and Commerce International SA*.[108] The case concerned a bank which had gone into liquidation. Prior to its liquidation the bank had provided loans to various companies, in each case secured by a cash deposit made by a director as surety. The deposit was charged in favour of the bank as security for the company's debt, and the charge in each case provided that the director was liable as a principal debtor. In addition, the directors executed personal guarantees. In each case the liquidator adopted the stance that he was entitled to proceed against the company for repayment of the advance, and to confine the surety to a dividend in the liquidation in respect of the deposit. However, the Court of Appeal held that a set-off occurred automatically in the liquidation as between the bank's debt to the surety on the deposit and the surety's liability to the bank, and that this also operated to extinguish the principal debt owed by the company.[109]

12.25 Under the guarantees in the *MS Fashions* case, the surety's liability was expressed to be payable on demand. In the case of some of the companies, demands had not been made on the sureties.[110] The liquidator argued that, in the absence of a demand, the bank's claim against the surety was still contingent. A contingent debt owing by a company in liquidation may

---

[103] (1826) 2 Gl & J 193, 4 LJOS Ch 195.

[104] (1857) 28 LTOS 296.

[105] (1812) 1 Rose 320. In *Ex p Hippins, re Sikes* (1826) 2 Gl & J 93, 96 Lord Eldon said that, after examining the secretary's book, it appeared that the bill in *Ex p Burton* was not an accommodation acceptance.

[106] *McKinnon v Armstrong Brothers & Co* (1877) 2 App Cas 531. See also *Crosse v Smith* (1813) 1 M & S 545, 105 ER 204, in which it was held that a bankrupt drawer could not compel the holder to proceed against the acceptor, and thereby avoid a set-off in the drawer's bankruptcy.

[107] See paras 6.119–6.146 above.

[108] [1993] Ch 425. See also *Handberg v Smarter Way (Aust) Pty Ltd* (2002) 190 ALR 130 at [47].

[109] [1993] Ch 425, 448. See also Hoffmann LJ at first instance at 439.

[110] In the case of *MS Fashions Ltd* the liquidator had made a demand on both the company and the surety, but that matter was not the subject of an appeal to the Court of Appeal.

be the subject of a set-off,[111] but under the insolvency legislation then in force there could not be a set-off in relation to a contingent claim possessed by the company if the contingency had not occurred.[112] Therefore, if indeed the claim of the bank in liquidation had been contingent, the liquidator's argument would have been correct.[113] The Court of Appeal referred, however, to earlier authority to the effect that, where a surety contracted on the basis of being liable as a principal debtor, the surety could be sued on his or her engagement without a demand having been made, notwithstanding that the agreement may have provided for a demand.[114] This had the consequence that the surety's liability to the bank in liquidation was not contingent, and it was held that it could be the subject of an automatic set-off.

Two comments may be made in relation to the *MS Fashions* case.   **12.26**

In the first place, it is doubtful whether in truth the circumstances in issue were such as to   **12.27**
support a set-off. It was not simply a case of a surety having a cross-claim against a creditor in liquidation. Rather, the cross-claim took the form of a deposit which was charged in favour of the creditor, and the charge should have had the effect of destroying mutuality for the purpose of a set-off.[115] This aspect of the case is considered later.[116]

Secondly, it is no longer the law in company liquidation in England that a contingent claim   **12.28**
possessed by the company is not susceptible to a set-off until the contingency has occurred.[117] As a result of amendments to the Insolvency Rules in 2005,[118] a sum is to be regarded as due to (or from) a company in liquidation for the purpose of set-off whether the obligation by virtue of which it is payable is certain or contingent, and the power to estimate the value of a contingent debt has been extended to contingent obligations owing to the company.[119] On that basis, where a director of a company has guaranteed the company's debts to a bank and the bank has gone into liquidation, the director's liability on the guarantee should be able to be set off in the liquidation against a deposit made by the director with the bank notwithstanding that a demand has not been made under the guarantee. It would not be

---

[111] See paras 8.19–8.28 above.

[112] See para. 8.35 above.

[113] Compare Calnan, 'The insolvent bank and security over deposits' (1996) 11 *Journal of International Banking and Financial Law* 185, 188–9. It is suggested that Calnan's reference to *Stein v Blake* [1996] AC 243 does not assist the argument in favour of a set-off, since it begs the question as to whether the requirements of the insolvency set-off section have been satisfied, in particular that there must be a sum 'due' on each side of the account.

[114] [1993] Ch 425, 447–8, referring to *Rowe v Young* (1820) 2 Bligh 391, 465–6, 4 ER 372, 404–5. See also Hoffmann LJ at first instance in the *MS Fashions* case [1993] Ch 425, 436, referring to *Esso Petroleum Co Ltd v Alstonbridge Properties Ltd* [1975] 1 WLR 1474, 1483, and *General Produce Co v United Bank Ltd* [1979] 2 Lloyd's Rep 255, 259. In Australia, compare *Re Taylor, ex p Century 21 Real Estate Corporation* (1995) 130 ALR 723.

[115] In *Re Bank of Credit and Commerce International SA (No. 8)* [1998] AC 214, 225 the House of Lords left open the question whether the existence of the charge would have affected mutuality. The Court of Appeal in that case [1996] Ch 245, 273 suggested that the *MS Fashions* case may require reconsideration, although not specifically on this ground.

[116] See paras 16.83–16.88 below.

[117] See para. 8.35 above.

[118] Insolvency (Amendment) Rules 2005 (S.I. 2005 No. 527). See para. 6.06 above.

[119] Insolvency Rules 1986, r. 4.90(4)(b) and (5), referring to r. 4.86. In relation to a company in administration (see para. 6.10 above), see r. 2.85(4)(b) and (5), referring to r. 2.86.

necessary in such a case for the director to have contracted as a principal debtor.[120] However, the amendment applicable in company liquidation has not been extended to bankruptcy, where the principle remains that a bankrupt's contingent claim can only be included in a set-off after the contingency has occurred.[121] Therefore, where a surety has not contracted as a principal debtor and liability under the guarantee is expressed to be conditional upon a demand being made, there could not be a set-off as between the surety and the creditor in the creditor's bankruptcy until a demand has been made. This also remains the position in Australia, in both bankruptcy and company liquidation.[122]

(3) *Re BCCI (No. 8)* – a choice of remedy?

12.29   The issue of set-off in the liquidation of a creditor, in circumstances where there is a surety for the debt and the surety has a cross-claim against the creditor available by way of set-off in the liquidation, was the subject of further analysis by the Court of Appeal[123] in *Re Bank of Credit and Commerce International SA (No. 8)*.[124] In delivering the judgment of the court, Rose LJ acknowledged the self-evident proposition that the creditor's liquidator could not both set off against the surety and recover from the principal debtor.[125] On the other hand, he canvassed the possibility that the liquidator may have a choice as to which remedy to pursue, notwithstanding the automatic nature of insolvency set-off.[126]

12.30   The impetus for that view was a perceived need to reconcile *Ex p Stephens*[127] with the automatic theory of insolvency set-off that has now been accepted by the courts. In *Ex p Stephens*, Miss Stephens and her brother had given a joint and several promissory note to bankers in respect of a loan to the brother of £1,000, Miss Stephens signing as surety. In addition, Miss Stephens had a cross-claim against the bankers, arising from their failure to comply with her instructions to invest the proceeds obtained from realizing certain securities in the purchase of other securities, and their concealment of that fact. The bankers subsequently became bankrupt. Their assignees in bankruptcy brought an action on the promissory note against the brother alone, thereby attempting to avoid the set-off that was available to Miss Stephens. Miss Stephens and her brother then brought this proceeding in equity to prevent that occurring. Lord Eldon held that Miss Stephens was entitled to set off the bank's liability to her against her liability on the joint and several note. He ordered that the assignees be restrained from suing either Miss Stephens or her brother on the note, and that the note be delivered up to her.

---

[120] Unlike in the *MS Fashions* case. See para. 12.24 above.
[121] See paras 8.35–8.36 above.
[122] See paras 8.35–8.36 above.
[123] Rose, Saville and Millett LJJ.
[124] [1996] Ch 245, 265–9. The decision was affirmed by the House of Lords: see [1998] AC 214.
[125] [1996] Ch 245, 269.
[126] The argument was noted, but not commented upon, by the House of Lords on appeal. See [1998] AC 214, 225.
[127] (1805) 11 Ves Jun 24, 32 ER 996. See para. 12.11 above.

It has been said that *Ex p Stephens* turned on the bankers' fraud, in failing to carry out **12.31** Miss Stephens' instructions and concealing their failure from her,[128] and indeed Lord Eldon later commented that, but for the fraud, he doubted much whether the decision would have been right.[129] The case, as Rose LJ noted in *Re BCCI (No. 8)*,[130] proceeded on the basis that a joint and several debtor could set off a debt owing to him or her by the creditor, but that, in the absence of a special circumstance such as fraud, the creditor could avoid the set-off by proceeding against another joint and several debtor. But on the basis of the automatic theory of insolvency set-off, the presence or absence of fraud should not have mattered.[131] There were mutual debts as between Miss Stephens and the bankers which would have given rise to a set-off between them at the date of the bankruptcy, thereby resulting in payment of the joint and several note.[132] In order to attempt to reconcile *Ex p Stephens* with the automatic theory, Rose LJ sought to draw a distinction between, on the one hand, a discharge of the surety as against the creditor which is based upon a set-off as between those parties, and on the other a discharge which arises as a result of payment by the surety to the creditor.[133] He accepted that discharge *of the principal debtor*, whether by payment by the principal debtor or by way of set-off as between the principal debtor and the creditor, necessarily discharges the surety.[134] Further, discharge of the surety as a result of actual payment by the surety would also discharge the principal debtor.[135] On the other hand, he suggested that the principal debtor is not discharged when the surety is discharged by way of set-off. In *Ex p Stephens*, Miss Stephens had joined in the promissory note as surety for her brother, and on Rose LJ's analysis a discharge of Miss Stephens as surety by way of a set-off as between her and the bankers was not sufficient to discharge the brother as principal debtor. Only *actual* payment by Miss Stephens would have had that effect. As a consequence of that analysis, Rose LJ postulated that the creditor has a choice of which remedy to pursue. The creditor can rely on the set-off against the surety. Alternatively, Rose LJ suggested that, in the absence of fraud by the creditor, the surety's set-off would not prevent the creditor from suing the principal debtor, since the principal debtor has not been discharged by the set-off. If the creditor sued the principal debtor, Rose LJ said that

---

[128] *Ex p Hanson* (1806) 12 Ves Jun 346, 348–9, 33 ER 131, 132; *Ex p Blagden* (1815) 19 Ves Jun 465, 467, 34 ER 589, 590; *Jones v Mossop* (1844) 3 Hare 568, 573, 67 ER 506, 509; *Ex p Staddon, re Wise* (1843) 12 LJ Bcy 39, 40; *Middleton v Pollock, ex p Knight and Raymond* (1875) LR 20 Eq 515, 519–20; *McIntyre v Perkes* (1990) 22 FCR 260, 271; *Lord v Direct Acceptance Corporation Ltd* (1993) 32 NSWLR 362, 369–70; *Re Bank of Credit and Commerce International SA (No. 8)* [1996] Ch 245, 267–8. See also *Strong v Foster* (1855) 17 CB 201, 217, 139 ER 1047, 1053.

[129] *Ex p Blagden* (1815) 19 Ves Jun 465, 467, 34 ER 589, 590.

[130] [1996] Ch 245, 268.

[131] See Hoffmann LJ (as he then was) in *MS Fashions Ltd v Bank of Credit and Commerce International SA* [1993] Ch 425, 438.

[132] See para. 12.21 above.

[133] See the discussion at [1996] Ch 245, 268–9.

[134] [1996] Ch 245, 268, referring to *Ex p Hanson* (1806) 12 Ves Jun 346, 33 ER 131 (affirmed (1811) 18 Ves Jun 232, 34 ER 305). In Australia, see also counsel's submission to which Sheller JA referred without adverse comment in *Lord v Direct Acceptance Corporation Ltd* (1993) 32 NSWLR 362, 368–9, and generally *McDonald v Dennys Lascelles Ltd* (1933) 48 CLR 457, 479–80. Compare *Bank of Credit and Commerce International (Overseas) Ltd v Habib Bank Ltd* [1999] 1 WLR 42 (assumption of a debtor's liability by way of novation after the debtor's liquidation), for which see paras 6.139–6.141 above.

[135] But note para. 8.16 above in relation to a part payment of the debt by a surety where the principal debtor is insolvent.

the recovery from the principal debtor would be treated as notionally taking place at the date of the bankruptcy. It could then be said, with hindsight, that nothing in fact was due from the surety at the date of the bankruptcy. Therefore, there would not have been a set-off as against the surety, so that the surety would be entitled to prove in the creditor's insolvency for the creditor's indebtedness to him or her.[136]

12.32 The Court of Appeal's comments on this point were *obiter*, since it was held that the depositors in *Re BCCI (No. 8)* had not assumed a personal obligation to the bank to pay the principal debt, and so there was no personal covenant against which the deposits could be set off.[137] But apart from that, there are difficulties with the analysis, and the better view is that discharge of the surety by way of set-off also discharges the principal debtor.

12.33 In the first place, the *MS Fashions* case supports the contrary view to that suggested in *Re BCCI (No. 8)* in the situation in which a guarantee has a principal debtor clause. The sureties in the *MS Fashions* case had assumed the obligation of a principal debtor, and the case stands as authority for the proposition that the creditor's trustee in bankruptcy or liquidator in that circumstance cannot sue the 'true' principal debtor to the extent that the debt has been extinguished by the surety's set-off.

12.34 Further, the suggested distinction between discharge by set-off and discharge by payment is contrary to the generally accepted view that set-off is equivalent to payment.[138] Dillon LJ assumed the correctness of that proposition in the Court of Appeal in the *MS Fashions* case, wherein he equated a set-off as between a surety and the creditor with a payment by the surety, which he regarded in turn as operating in reduction of the principal debt. Speaking of the effect of a set-off under the insolvency set-off section, he said that:[139]

> The statutory set-off . . . operates to reduce or extinguish the liability of the guarantor and necessarily therefore operates as in effect a payment by him to be set against the liability of the principal debtor. A creditor cannot sue the principal debtor for an amount of the debt which the creditor has already received from a guarantor.

---

[136] Rose LJ said: 'The only question is whether the principal debtor is discharged by the set-off simultaneously available to the surety or whether the creditor can recover from the principal debtor and, having recovered, submit to a proof from the surety without any discount on the basis that, with hindsight, it has appeared that nothing was due from the surety at the date of bankruptcy. The mischief against which bankruptcy set-off is directed would indicate that the correct approach is in the latter sense.' [1996] Ch 245, 269.

[137] See para. 12.41 below.

[138] *Ex p Barnett, re Deveze* (1874) LR 9 Ch App 293, 297; *Inland Revenue Commissioners v John Dow Stuart Ltd* [1950] AC 149, 164 *per* Lord Porter ('Set-off is payment . . .'); *Re Loteka Pty Ltd* [1990] 1 Qd R 322, 324; *MS Fashions Ltd v Bank of Credit and Commerce International SA* [1993] Ch 425, 439 (Hoffmann LJ), 448 (CA). The House of Lords in *Re Bank of Credit and Commerce International SA (No. 8)* [1998] AC 214, 225 referred in the context of r. 4.90 of the Insolvency Rules (the insolvency set-off provision in company liquidation) to 'payment or deemed payment'. See also *Gye v Davies* (1995) 37 NSWLR 421, 431–2 ('moneys deemed paid by them in consequence of the set-off'); *Krishell Pty Ltd v Nilant* (2006) 32 WAR 540 at [72] ('equivalent to discharge'); *Veolia Water Solutions v Kruger Engineering (No. 3)* [2007] NSWSC 459 at [24] ('satisfied by set-off' and 'payment'); *Reed Constructions Australia Pty Ltd v DM Fabrications Pty Ltd* (2007) 25 ACLC 1463 at [37]–[38]. Compare *Mellham Ltd v Burton* [2003] STC 441 at [16], which was concerned with the construction of particular provisions in tax legislation. The decision in the *Mellham* case was reversed on appeal. See *Burton v Mellham Ltd* [2006] 1 WLR 2820 (see in particular at [29]).

[139] [1993] Ch 425, 448.

This reflects a similar view expressed by Hoffmann LJ at first instance.[140] While in the *MS Fashions* case the sureties had contracted as principal debtor, that circumstance does not alter the acceptance of the basic proposition that set-off is equivalent to payment. Once that equivalence is recognized, it should have the consequence that, if a surety's liability is in respect of the same debt as that owed by the principal debtor, payment by the surety (through set-off) should also extinguish the principal debtor's debt to the same extent.[141] This is consistent with the position adopted in relation to joint and several debts.[142]

(4) *Ex p Stephens* explained

The point that should be borne in mind when considering cases such as *Ex p Stephens* is that **12.35** it is only in recent times that the automatic theory of insolvency set-off has gained acceptance by the courts.[143] It was not current when *Ex p Stephens* was decided. This is apparent from the form of pleading used in the nineteenth century when a defendant in an action brought by assignees in bankruptcy sought to rely on a set-off. The defendant in such a case would not deny that he or she was indebted on the basis of a set-off that had already occurred at the date of the bankruptcy. Rather, the defence was pleaded by way of an allegation that the bankrupt 'was, *and still is*, indebted to the defendant'.[144] The pleading assumed that the cross-demands still retained their separate identities after the bankruptcy, when the action was brought, and that a set-off was effected by an order of the court.[145] Further, when Sir George Jessel MR in 1881[146] sought to explain why the insolvency set-off section could be relied on as a defence to an action at law brought by a trustee in bankruptcy for payment of a debt owing to the bankrupt, as opposed to the set-off being given effect in the Bankruptcy Court, he did not do so, as one would have expected if it was thought to be the case, by reference to a notion that the cross-demands had already been discharged by a set-off that had occurred automatically at the bankruptcy date, so that to that extent there was no debt remaining which could be the subject of a common law action. On the contrary, he said that the bankruptcy legislation contemplated the set-off being allowed in the Bankruptcy Court, and that if a debtor were sued instead in a common law court the debtor could apply to the Court of Bankruptcy for an injunction to restrain the assignees in bankruptcy from suing. He said that the common law courts, having regard to 'the equity

---

[140] [1993] Ch 425, 439 ('the set-off is equivalent to payment').

[141] See the reasoning of Hoffmann LJ at [1993] Ch 425, 439. Of course, this assumes that there is a set-off as between the surety and the creditor. See para. 12.27 above.

[142] See para. 12.21 above.

[143] See also paras 6.126–6.127 above.

[144] See e.g. *Hulme v Muggleston* (1837) 3 M & W 30, 31, 150 ER 1043, 1044; *Russell v Bell* (1841) 8 M & W 277, 278, 151 ER 1042, 1043; *Bittleston v Timmis* (1845) 1 CB 389, 391, 135 ER 591, 592. See also *West v Baker* (1875) 1 Ex D 44, 45. In *Gibson v Bell* (1835) 1 Bing NC 743, 131 ER 1303 the defendant pleaded (at 746, 1305) that: 'the said sum of money still remained unpaid and unsatisfied to the Defendant.' In Bullen and Leake, *Precedents of Pleading* (2nd edn, 1863), 580, the plea was expressed in terms that a debt owing by the bankrupt 'at the commencement of this suit was and still is due to the defendant'. Later editions set out the pleading in similar terms. See para. 6.126n above.

[145] See para. 6.120 above.

[146] *Peat v Jones & Co* (1881) 8 QBD 147, 149.

of the statute',[147] then went a step further and allowed the debtor to plead the set-off in the common law court itself, without the necessity of applying for an injunction.[148] That explanation is hardly consistent with the set-off being thought of as operating by way of an automatic discharge at the bankruptcy date. If the set-off were thought of as operating automatically at that date, it would not have been necessary to have recourse to a concept such as the equity of the statute.

12.36 Consistent with that view, Lord Eldon's judgment in *Ex p Stephens* itself suggests that he did not regard a set-off as having already occurred between Miss Stephens and the bankers under the bankruptcy legislation. In the course of his judgment he referred to: 'the balance, for which she would have been creditor, *if* the assignees had sued her, or arranged the account upon the principle of mutual debt and credit.'[149] This suggests that, until an account was taken, either by the court in an action by the assignees against Miss Stephens, or as a result of the assignees themselves arranging the account on the basis of mutual credit, the cross-demands between her and the bankers were regarded as retaining their separate identities.

12.37 Once it is appreciated that, when *Ex p Stephens* was decided, it was not the prevailing view that set-off under the bankruptcy legislation occurred automatically at the date of the bankruptcy, the importance of the element of fraud in the case becomes apparent. The promissory note was joint and several. The bankers' assignees in bankruptcy accordingly could have sued either Miss Stephens or her brother or both. They chose to sue the brother alone. When the action was commenced the note had not been discharged, either by payment or by way of set-off. Miss Stephens had a *right* of set-off, which would have provided her with a defence, but she was not being sued. A set-off had not taken place pursuant to that right, so that it had not operated to discharge either Miss Stephens or her brother. Further, the brother was not possessed of a cross-claim against the bankers, so that he did not have a defence to the action. Hence the importance of fraud. It provided the justification for equity to intervene in the assignees' action against the principal debtor, by restraining the action and ensuring that Miss Stephens obtained the benefit of her set-off.

12.38 *Ex p Stephens* therefore is explicable on the basis that a set-off was not regarded as having taken place in the bankruptcy at the time when Miss Stephens presented her petition in equity, and the effect of Lord Eldon's order was to allow a set-off in equity in her favour by way of a common injunction restraining an action on the promissory note.[150] It will be

---

[147] For a discussion of the concept of the equity of a statute, see *Nelson v Nelson* (1995) 184 CLR 538, 552–4.

[148] See also Sir George Jessel's later discussion in *Mersey Steel and Iron Co v Naylor, Benzon, & Co* (1882) 9 QBD 648, 664 (CA).

[149] (1805) 11 Ves Jun 24, 27, 32 ER 996, 997 (emphasis added).

[150] In *Re BCCI (No. 8)* [1996] Ch 245, 269 Rose LJ offered a different interpretation of the order in *Ex p Stephens*. He said that Lord Eldon's order was not that Miss Stephens was discharged by set-off (which, he said, was never in dispute), but rather that: 'the assignees [in bankruptcy] held £1,000 of her money on trust to discharge the note.' On that basis, the discharge of the principal debtor in *Ex p Stephens* could be regarded as occurring by way of a payment, rather than by way of a set-off available to Miss Stephens as surety. Two comments may be made in relation to that interpretation. The first is the point already made, that it is not

recalled that an injunction restraining common law proceedings was the method by which courts of equity gave effect to equitable set-offs before the Judicature Acts.[151] Thus, Sir William Grant in *Addis v Knight*[152] referred to *Ex p Stephens* as having established that: 'under certain circumstances, there may be a set-off in Equity when there can be none at Law.'

In the Court of Appeal's judgment in *Re BCCI (No. 8)*,[153] Miss Stephen is variously described as having had a 'right of set-off' and as having been 'discharged' by set-off. These expressions appear to have been used inter-changeably. In truth, while Miss Stephens had a 'right of' set-off, Lord Eldon did not regard her as having been 'discharged' by set-off. Because *Ex p Stephens* proceeded on the assumption that a creditor on a joint and several debt normally could avoid a set-off available to one debtor by proceeding against another debtor, the Court of Appeal in *BCCI (No. 8)* opined that this could only be on the basis that, in a three-party situation, discharge by set-off is not to be equated with discharge by payment.[154] That in turn formed the basis of the proposition that a creditor, faced with an automatic set-off available to a surety, could still sue the principal debtor. In fact, *Ex p Stephens* provides no support for that proposition. It does not stand as authority for the view that a discharge by way of set-off as between a creditor and a surety does not discharge the debtor, because on the view of the operation of the insolvency set-off section then current, the surety had not been discharged by way of set-off. It was Lord Eldon's order which was regarded as bringing about a set-off, in the manner in which that was done by courts of equity at the time, by way of an injunction restraining common law proceedings and an order for delivery up of the promissory note. **12.39**

(5) Set-off between the creditor and the principal debtor as a discharge of the surety

On the other hand, the Court of Appeal in *Re BCCI (No. 8)* accepted that a set-off of debts between the creditor and the principal debtor under the insolvency set-off section would discharge the surety.[155] It should be compared in that regard to *Bank of Credit and Commerce International (Overseas) Ltd v Habib Bank Ltd*.[156] In that case a third party assumed liability **12.40**

---

correct to say that it was 'never in dispute' that Miss Stephens herself was 'discharged by set-off'. She had a right of set-off, but it was not thought that she had been discharged by it. Secondly, it is true that Lord Eldon commented in his judgment (at (1805) 11 Ves Jun 24, 28, 32 ER 996, 998) that Miss Stephens 'has a clear right to say, they shall hold £1000 of her money in discharge of the note; and shall deliver up the note'. But, as Sir George Jessel MR's discussion of *Ex p Stephens* in *Middleton v Pollock, ex p Knight and Raymond* (1875) LR 20 Eq 515, 520–1 makes plain, that referred simply to a right of set-off, which indeed is reflected in the order that was made. The order, as summarized in the final paragraph of the report of *Ex p Stephens* (at 28), was not that £1,000 be held on trust to discharge the debt, but rather that Miss Stephens 'be at liberty to set off the amount of the promissory note against the demand she has upon the bankrupts', with consequential orders that the promissory note be delivered up to her and the assignees be restrained from suing either her or her brother. See also the discussion of *Ex p Stephens* in *Lord v Direct Acceptance Corporation Ltd* (1993) 32 NSWLR 362, 369–70.

[151] See para. 3.01 above.
[152] (1817) 2 Mer 117, 121, 35 ER 885, 887.
[153] [1996] Ch 245, 266–9.
[154] [1996] Ch 245, 268.
[155] [1996] Ch 245, 268. See para. 12.31 above.
[156] [1999] 1 WLR 42.

for the debts of a debtor after the debtor's liquidation, apparently by way of a novation, and Park J accepted that payments made by the third party to a creditor precluded a set-off as between the debtor and the creditor at the date of the liquidation. That aspect of the case was considered, and criticized, earlier.[157]

E. Separate Depositor does not Assume a Personal Obligation

12.41 In the *MS Fashions* case,[158] the person who provided the bank with a deposit as security for the company's liability on the loan had also assumed a personal liability for the loan. The assumption of a personal liability was crucial to the decision to recognize a set-off as between the depositor and the bank in the bank's liquidation, because it provided the means of bringing about mutuality. Where, however, a depositor has not assumed a personal liability but merely provided the deposit by way of collateral security for a loan to a company, there is no mutuality between, on the one hand, the bank's indebtedness to the depositor in relation to the deposit, and on the other the bank's claim against the company.[159] In that circumstance, the House of Lords in *Re Bank of Credit and Commerce International SA (No. 8)*[160] confirmed that the deposit and the loan will not be the subject of a set-off under the insolvency set-off section in the event of the bank's liquidation.[161] The liquidator can proceed against the company for repayment of the loan, and confine the depositor to a proof in the liquidation in respect of the deposit.[162]

12.42 *Re BCCI (No. 8)* should be contrasted with *Clarkson v Smith & Goldberg*,[163] a decision of the Appellate Division of the Ontario Supreme Court. A bank had provided an overdraft to a partnership, taking as security a charge over a separate deposit made by one of the partners. The bank went into liquidation, and the liquidator sought to recover the debt from the partnership without allowing a set-off in respect of the deposit charged as security. The Appellate Division rejected the liquidator's approach and allowed an equitable set-off. In addition to his liability as a partner the depositor had assumed a separate personal liability,[164] but that was not the basis of the set-off. It was based upon the partnership debt.[165] The partners were jointly liable for the partnership debt, and a judgment against

---

[157] See paras 6.139–6.141 above.

[158] [1993] Ch 425. See para. 12.24 above.

[159] The charge on the deposit in favour of the bank is an additional reason for finding a lack of mutuality. See paras 16.83–16.85 below. In *Re Bank of Credit and Commerce International SA (No. 8)* [1998] AC 214, 225 the House of Lords left open the question whether the existence of the charge has that effect.

[160] [1998] AC 214.

[161] See also *Lord v Direct Acceptance Corporation Ltd* (1993) 32 NSWLR 362; *Tam Wing Chuen v Bank of Credit and Commerce Hong Kong Ltd* [1996] 2 BCLC 69 (PC). Nor is this a ground for an equitable set-off. See paras 4.88–4.90 above.

[162] If the customer had also provided a separate security to the bank in the form of a mortgage, the doctrine of marshalling would not apply so as to compel the bank to have recourse first to the deposit. See *Re Bank of Credit and Commerce International SA (No. 8)* [1996] Ch 245, 271–2 (CA), [1998] AC 214, 230–1 (HL).

[163] [1926] 1 DLR 509.

[164] The partner drew a cheque on his account and gave it to the bank as security.

[165] The point was made in the judgment that a right of set-off ordinarily does not exist between a debt due by a firm and an amount due to a separate partner, but even apart from that principle the charge over the separate partner's deposit would have destroyed mutuality. See paras 16.83–16.85 below.

the partnership could be levied against the firm's assets or the separate assets of the partners. Since the partner who provided the security could be required to pay the whole debt out of his personal assets, or to contribute to payment through his interest in the firm assets, it was regarded as manifestly unjust that he should be refused the use of his deposit to pay the debt. In *Re BCCI (No. 8)*, on the other hand, the depositor had no liability, other than as security provider, to contribute to the payment of the principal debt, so that the reasoning adopted by the Ontario Supreme Court is not applicable to that case.

The denial of a set-off in *Re BCCI (No. 8)*, when compared to the allowance of a set-off in the *MS Fashions* case, has been described as anomalous and paradoxical, because it means that a bank's position is better in its own liquidation when it had not obtained a personal guarantee from the depositor than when it had.[166] In truth, there is no paradox. When a surety provides a security deposit to a bank, the bank may also require a personal covenant from the depositor in order to give it an additional avenue for obtaining repayment of the debt in the event that the borrower defaults. But if there is a set-off the bank obtains repayment in full. The purpose of taking the security therefore is achieved. It would be commercially unrealistic to suggest that a lender in structuring security arrangements is concerned additionally with the position that may apply in its own liquidation. In any event, there should not have been a set-off under the insolvency set-off section in the *MS Fashions* case. This is because the charge over the deposit in favour of the bank should have prevented mutuality arising in relation to the deposit and the depositor's personal liability to the bank. This aspect of the *MS Fashions* case is considered later.[167]

12.43

(1) Obligation to set off

The Court of Appeal in *Re BCCI (No. 8)*[168] noted that the terms of the deposit in that case merely authorised the bank to set off the deposit against the loan to the company. The bank was not obliged to do so. But what if the terms had been such as to require a set-off, and a set-off had not occurred at the date of the bank's liquidation? That was the situation in *Bank of Credit and Commerce Hong Kong Ltd (in liq) v Mahadumrongkul*,[169] a decision of the Privy Council on appeal from the Court of Appeal of Hong Kong. As in *Re BCCI (No. 8)*, a shareholder had placed a deposit with a bank to secure a loan to the company, apparently without having assumed a personal liability as a guarantor. In a letter to the depositor, the bank said that, upon default by the borrower, 'we shall . . . automatically apply any monies standing to the credit of the [Deposit] Account' in settlement of the principal, interest and margin owing in respect of the loan. Subsequently, the bank went into liquidation, and after that the borrower defaulted. The point in issue was the date upon which the deposit was required to be applied in reduction of the loan pursuant to the agreement. The question whether a set-off in fact occurred on that date was not

12.44

---

[166] See *Re Bank of Credit and Commerce International SA (No. 8)* [1996] Ch 245, 253, 273 (CA), [1998] AC 214, 224–5 (HL); *Tam Wing Chuen v Bank of Credit and Commerce Hong Kong Ltd* [1996] 2 BCLC 69, 71–2 (PC); Millett, 'Pleasing paradoxes' (1996) 112 LQR 524.

[167] See paras 16.83–16.85 below.

[168] [1996] Ch 245, 273.

[169] [1997] UKPC 20 (Lord Goff of Chieveley, Lord Slynn of Hadley, Lord Lloyd of Berwick, Lord Nicholls of Birkenhead and Lord Hoffmann).

specifically addressed, but it seems to have been assumed that a set-off would then have occurred.[170] At least in England,[171] however, an agreement in those terms should not result in a set-off after the liquidation if a set-off was not available in any event under the insolvency set-off section,[172] and in this case there was a lack of mutuality as between the bank's indebtedness to the depositor and its claim against the borrower. As the Court of Appeal remarked in *BCCI (No. 8)*[173] in relation to the deposit in that case:

> The appellants were indebted to the bank. Their controlling shareholders deposited moneys with the bank. If the case had stopped there, there could have been no question of set-off in the bank's insolvency. The bank could not have set off the debts which it owed to the depositors against the debts which their companies owed to the bank. The requirement of mutuality would have been absent. *Even if all parties agreed that the bank should set off the amounts in question*, it could not have done so after the bankruptcy. In the absence of the necessary mutuality, the set-off would have contravened the statutory scheme of distribution in insolvency. Once insolvency supervenes, rule 4.90 of the Insolvency Rules 1986 requires set-off in the situations in which it is applicable and public policy forbids it where it is not.

This should apply whether the agreement is couched in terms that a set-off is to occur automatically in the event of a default, which occurs after liquidation, or whether an act by the bank is required in order to effect the set-off.

F. Deceased Insolvent Partner

12.45 The Partnership Act 1890, s. 9 provides that the estate of a deceased partner is severally as well as jointly liable for the debts of the firm, though this is expressed to be subject to the prior payment of his or her separate debts. In keeping with that priority, a debtor to a deceased partner cannot set off a debt owing to the debtor by the partnership,[174] at least if the deceased's estate has insufficient assets to pay the deceased's separate debts.[175] If it were otherwise, an asset of the deceased partner (the debt owing by the debtor) would be used to pay the firm's debts before the deceased partner's separate debts had been paid.

12.46 Where two or more partners jointly own the beneficial interest in a claim, and all except one die, the common law courts applied the principle that the claim passed to the survivor, so

---

[170] The borrower was ordered to be wound up on 2 March 1992. The depositor and the borrower (a company of which the depositor was a director) asserted that the agreement required that a set-off be effected against outstanding principal twenty days after 28 June 1991, whereas the liquidator said that the relevant date under the agreement was 16 July 1992. The significance of the date of the set-off was that the continued accrual of interest on the loan until the later date, together with the cessation of the bank's liability to pay interest on the deposit as from the commencement of the winding up, would have meant that the money owing to the bank exceeded the amount owing on the deposit. The Privy Council held that the later date was correct, referring to it as 'the effective date for the set-off', which suggests that a set-off was regarded as having occurred on that date in accordance with the agreement.

[171] And also in Australia.

[172] *British Eagle International Air Lines Ltd v Compagnie Nationale Air France* [1975] 1 WLR 758. See paras 16.21–16.26 below.

[173] [1996] Ch 245, 272 (emphasis added).

[174] *Addis v Knight* (1817) 2 Mer 117, 35 ER 885.

[175] *Lindley & Banks on Partnership* (18th edn, 2002), 451 [14–79].

that there was mutuality for the purpose of a set-off between the original joint claim and a separate debt owing by the survivor.[176] In equity, however, the claim must be brought into account in determining the entitlement of the deceased partners' estates in relation to the partnership.[177] The better view is that this entitlement of the deceaseds' estates destroys mutuality in equity for the purpose of a set-off.[178]

---

[176] *Slipper v Stidstone* (1794) 5 TR 493, 101 ER 277, and see also *French v Andrade* (1796) 6 TR 582, 101 ER 715.

[177] See e.g. *McClean v Kennard* (1874) LR 9 Ch App 336, and generally *Lindley on the Law of Partnership* (15th edn, 1984), 521 (where the explanation of the historical position is more clearly set out than in *Lindley & Banks on Partnership* (18th edn, 2002), 515 [18–66]). See also the Insolvency Act 1986, s. 421A.

[178] See *Lindley & Banks on Partnership* (18th edn, 2002), 451 [14–79]. Compare Wood, *English and International Set-off* (1989), 1034–5. *Aliter* if the debt owing is a partnership debt as opposed to a separate debt of the survivor. See Lindley and Banks, *loc. cit.*

13

MUTUALITY – SAME RIGHT

A. Introduction

13.01   In the case of insolvency set-off, the requirement that the demands be held in the same right means that each of the parties, who is liable to the other, should be the beneficial owner of a cross-demand against the other.[1] It should be compared to the Statutes of Set-off, which contemplate mutuality by reference to the legal title to the debts. Equity, on the other hand, may allow a set-off by analogy with the Statutes if there is mutuality in equity but not at law, or alternatively it may refuse to allow a set-off if there is mutuality at law but not in equity, so that the same result usually would follow in the case of the Statutes as if mutuality were determined by reference to equitable interests.[2]

(1) Different personal capacities

13.02   As long as the demands in that sense are mutual, the dealings are not considered to be in a different right merely because each may relate to a different personal status or capacity possessed by one of the parties.[3] For example, in an action brought by a trustee against a beneficiary of the trust for an indemnity as to costs and expenses incurred in connection with the trust, the Queensland Supreme Court held that the beneficiary could set off an indebtedness of the trustee in his personal capacity.[4] On another occasion an executor was the sole person interested in the estate of the testator, and all claims against the estate had been satisfied. When the executor brought an action to recover a debt owing to the estate, the debtor was allowed to set off a personal indebtedness of the executor to him in a matter unrelated to the estate.[5] Neither of these cases concerned a bankruptcy or a company liquidation, but they should apply equally to insolvency set-off. A further illustration is to be found in the cases which support the proposition that a local authority which has vested in it a number of statutory functions may set off a credit balance arising on a bank account which relates to one function against its indebtedness on an account relating to another.

---

[1] See para. 11.01 above.
[2] See paras 11.18–11.20 above.
[3] See *Gye v McIntyre* (1991) 171 CLR 609, 625–6.
[4] *Peel v Fitzgerald* [1982] Qd R 544.
[5] *Williams v MacDonald* [1915] VLR 229. See also, and compare, *Knowles v Maitland* (1825) 4 B & C 173, 107 ER 1024, in which the cross-demands both related to the capacity of colonel of the regiment.

In *Pedder v The Mayor, Aldermen, and Burgesses of Preston*,[6] the Corporation of Preston had an account with a bank for the corporation's general municipal functions. In addition, the Corporation had been constituted the Local Board of Health under the Public Health Act 1848, and for this a separate account was opened with the same bank. The bank entered into an arrangement with its creditors under the Bankrupt Law Consolidation Act 1849, at which time the general account was overdrawn and the Local Board of Health account was in credit. Though s. 87 of the 1848 Act provided that the money received by the Local Board of Health 'shall be applied . . . in defraying such of the Expenses incurred or to be incurred by the said Local Board in carrying this Act into execution', it was held that the Corporation could set the credit balance on that account against its indebtedness on the other.

(2) Trustees in bankruptcy

A right accruing to, or a liability incurred by, a trustee in bankruptcy in his or her own right **13.03** as trustee may not be the subject of a set-off in the bankruptcy.[7] Nor can the trustee set off the dividend payable to a creditor against the creditor's indebtedness to the trustee in the trustee's private capacity.[8]

A liability incurred by the trustee in his or her own right as trustee is a liability which gives **13.04** rise to a direct claim against the trustee personally, as opposed to a provable debt. A right accruing to the trustee in the trustee's own right as trustee is a right founded solely upon the trustee's title as trustee of the estate, as opposed to the title of the bankrupt. It includes a right arising in favour of the estate against another person after the bankruptcy which is not based upon an obligation incurred by that person or a transaction entered into by that person with the debtor before the debtor's bankruptcy. Thus, there may be an award of costs made in favour of the trustee in an action brought to recover a debt owing to the bankrupt's estate. The defendant's obligation to pay the costs only arises after the bankruptcy as a result of his or her failure to pay the debt to the trustee upon demand, and as such it may not be brought into account as a set-off against a liability of the bankrupt.[9] Another illustration is *Ex p Young, re Day & Sons*.[10] The trustee in bankruptcy of a firm opened an account with a bank, and paid into it a sum of money received on behalf of the estate. Subsequently, the bank filed a liquidation petition. It was held that the firm's trustee could not set off the bank's debt to him for the money deposited against an independent indebtedness of the bankrupt firm to the bank for which a proof had been lodged.[11]

---

[6] (1862) 12 CB (NS) 535, 142 ER 1251. See also *Ex p Pearce, re Langmead* (1841) 2 Mont D & De G 142.

[7] *Re A Debtor, ex p The Peak Hill Goldfield Ltd* [1909] 1 KB 430, 437.

[8] *Ex p White* (1742) 1 Atk 90, 26 ER 59; *Ex p Bailey, re Howarth* (1840) 1 Mont D & De G 263; *Ex p Saunders, re Innes* (1842) 2 Mont D & De G 529, 530–1. One reason is that the demands are due in different rights. See *Ex p Alexander, re Elder* (1832) 1 Deac & Ch 513, 524 (Erskine CJ). A second reason is that the creditor is a *cestui que trust* of the trustee, and so is entitled to receive the dividend undiminished by a set-off. See *Re Henley, Thurgood, & Co* (1863) 11 WR 1021, 1022, and para. 10.02 above.

[9] *West v Pryce* (1825) 2 Bing 455, 130 ER 382.

[10] (1879) 41 LT 40.

[11] Similarly, it has been held that a sum of money received by a creditor of a bankrupt on behalf of the estate may not be brought into an account. See *Groom v Mealey* (1835) 2 Bing (NC) 138, 132 ER 54; *Elgood v Harris* [1896] 2 QB 491. Compare *Bailey v Johnson* (1872) LR 7 Ex 263, in which the bankruptcy under which the trustee paid the money into the bank was annulled after the bank's bankruptcy. See para. 11.15 above.

However, while the decision was correct in relation to set-off, it is suggested that the trustee should have been able to invoke an independent principle known as the rule in *Cherry v Boultbee*,[12] and on that basis refuse to pay a dividend to the bank until the bank had accounted for the money received.[13] *Cherry v Boultbee* is considered later.[14]

(3) The effect of company liquidation

13.05   In so far as companies are concerned, a liquidation does not affect the corporate personality of the company.[15] Nor generally does it result in a *cessio bonorum* in favour of the liquidator. In contrast to bankruptcy,[16] the legal title to the company's assets remains with the company.[17] A liquidator 'is principally and really an agent for the company but occupies a position which is fiduciary in some respects and is bound by the statutory duties imposed upon him by the [Insolvency] Act'.[18] However, the making of a winding-up order in a compulsory winding up, or the passing of a resolution for a voluntary liquidation, should have the same effect upon mutuality as far as the company's claims accruing after the winding up are concerned as the appointment of a trustee has in a bankruptcy. In *Ayerst v C & K (Construction) Ltd*,[19] the House of Lords held that, while a winding-up order in a compulsory liquidation does not divest the company of the legal title to its assets, it does deprive it of the beneficial title.[20] This is a consequence of the vesting of the custody and control of the company's property in the liquidator to be applied by him or her in discharge of the company's liabilities and, in the case of a surplus, to be distributed amongst the members. Admittedly, uncertainty as to the property divisible amongst the creditors, as well as uncertainty as to the creditors entitled to share in the realization of the property, means that a creditor who is entitled to share in the proceeds is not invested with the

---

[12] (1839) 4 My & Cr 442, 41 ER 171.

[13] As in *Ex p Bebb* (1812) 19 Ves Jun 222, 34 ER 501 and *Ex p Graham* (1814) 3 V & B 130, 35 ER 428. See para. 14.40 below.

[14] See ch. 14 below.

[15] See the Insolvency Act 1986, s. 87(2) in relation to a voluntary winding up. This is also the case in a compulsory liquidation. See *Reigate v Union Manufacturing Co (Ramsbottom) Ltd* [1918] 1 KB 592, 606.

[16] A trustee in bankruptcy upon his or her appointment has vested in him or her the property belonging to the bankrupt at the commencement of the bankruptcy. See the Insolvency Act 1986, ss. 283(1) and 306. This includes things in action. See the definition of 'property' in s. 436.

[17] *Re A Debtor* [1927] 1 Ch 410, 420; *John Mackintosh and Sons Ltd v Baker's Bargain Stores (Seaford) Ltd* [1965] 1 WLR 1182; *Re Northside Properties Pty Ltd* [1971] 2 NSWLR 320, 326; *National Westminster Bank Ltd v Halesowen Presswork & Assemblies Ltd* [1972] AC 785, 796. When a company is being wound up by the court, there is provision for the liquidator to apply to the court for an order vesting the company's property in him or her. See the Insolvency Act 1986, s. 145. The effect of such an order is to vest the company's property in the liquidator in the liquidator's official, as opposed to personal, capacity. See *Graham v Edge* (1888) 20 QBD 683. The section is rarely invoked. See *Buckley on the Companies Act* (14th edn, 1981) vol. 1, 597–8.

[18] *Thomas Franklin & Sons Ltd v Cameron* (1935) 36 SR (NSW) 286, 296 (Davidson J), referred to with approval in *FCT v Linter Textiles Australia Ltd* (2005) 220 CLR 592 at [33]. See also *Re Windsor Steam Coal Co (1901) Ltd* [1928] 1 Ch 609. A liquidator is entitled to examine a proof lodged in the winding up in the light of any possible right of set-off. See *Re National Wholemeal Bread and Biscuit Co* [1892] 2 Ch 457.

[19] [1976] AC 167. See also *Mitchell v Carter* [1997] 1 BCLC 673, 686 (Millett LJ); *Wight v Eckhardt Marine GmbH* [2004] 1 AC 147 at [22] (PC); *Buchler v Talbot* [2004] 2 AC 298 at [28] (Lord Hoffmann); *Cambridge Gas Transportation Corpn v Official Committee of Unsecured Creditors of Navigator Holdings plc* [2007] 1 AC 508 at [14] (PC); *Re HIH Casualty and General Insurance Ltd* [2008] 1 WLR 852 at [68] (Lord Neuberger of Abbotsbury).

[20] This also applies to a voluntary winding up. See [1976] AC 167, 176.

beneficial title to any part of the company's property while it is still being administered by the liquidator.[21] Nevertheless, the House of Lords concluded that it could still be said that the company itself is not possessed of the beneficial title. If a company does not have the beneficial title to its assets after the commencement of its liquidation, for the purpose of mutuality in equity the effect, as far as claims accruing subsequently to the company are concerned, accordingly should be the same as in the case of the appointment of a trustee in bankruptcy. That proposition brings into question *Monkwearmouth Flour Mill Co v Lightfoot*.[22] The defendant was appointed after the commencement of the plaintiff company's liquidation to collect outstanding debts due to the company. When he was sued for the money he had received he was allowed to set off the company's prior indebtedness to him. At no stage, however, could it be said that the company itself was the beneficial owner of any right against him. Nor was his liability the result of a dealing entered into with the company before the commencement of its liquidation.[23] A set-off, therefore, should have been denied on the ground of lack of mutuality.[24]

13.06 Courts in Australia have adopted a different view as to the effect of a winding up, the Australian High Court having rejected the proposition accepted in the *Ayerst* case that a company upon going into liquidation ceases to be the beneficial owner of its assets.[25] The change in control of the affairs of the company upon commencement of liquidation is not regarded as affecting beneficial ownership. But on that view the *Monkwearmouth* case would still be difficult to explain, since the company's claim accrued after the relevant date for determining rights of set-off,[26] without it being related to a prior transaction.

B. Transactions Impugned by an Insolvency Office-Holder

(1) Preferences

Bankruptcy

13.07 If, within the period of six months[27] prior to the presentation of a petition against a debtor, the debtor did anything or suffered anything to be done which had the effect of putting a particular creditor into a better position in the debtor's bankruptcy than the creditor would otherwise have been, the court on the application of the trustee may make such order as it thinks fit for restoring the position to what it would have been if the debtor had not given the preference.[28] A creditor who is liable to return a preferential payment is not entitled to set off against that liability the debt for which the payment was intended to be satisfaction,[29]

---

[21] [1976] AC 167, 178–9.

[22] (1897) 13 TLR 327.

[23] See paras 7.07–7.10 above.

[24] See in this regard *Sankey Brook Coal Co Ltd v Marsh* (1871) LR 6 Ex 185.

[25] *FCT v Linter Textiles Australia Ltd* (2005) 220 CLR 592.

[26] See paras 6.63–6.65 above.

[27] Or two years for a person associated with the bankrupt. See the Insolvency Act 1986, s. 341(1).

[28] Insolvency Act 1986, s. 340. In Australia see the Bankruptcy Act 1966 (Cth), s. 122.

[29] *Courtney v King* (1870) 1 VR (L) 70; *Re A Debtor* [1927] 1 Ch 410; *Re Grezzana; Painter & Anor v Charles Whiting & Chambers Ltd* (1932) 4 ABC 203: *Re Smith, ex p The Trustee; J Bird Pty Ltd and Tully*

or indeed any other liability of the bankrupt.[30] The trustee's right to the return of the preference accrues in his or her own right as trustee, and is not derived from an obligation incurred by the creditor to the bankrupt. The creditor's liability and the creditor's claim against the bankrupt are, accordingly, not mutual.[31] In any event, public policy would dictate that a transaction which Parliament has said should be avoided as a preference should not be able to ground a set-off, because otherwise the efficacy of preference provision would be severely limited.[32] In Australia, the courts have also had regard to the qualification to the set-off section[33] as a reason for denying a set-off.[34] The creditor's notice of the debtor's insolvency, which under the Australian Bankruptcy Act would operate to deny to the creditor the defence of purchaser, payee or encumbrancer in good faith in a preference action,[35] would also often preclude a set-off.

Company liquidation

13.08   The same principle applies in the liquidation of an insolvent company,[36] so that a creditor of the company is not entitled to a set-off against an obligation to repay a preference.[37] It has been said that it is more likely that the denial of a set-off in the case of a company liquidation is attributable to considerations of policy rather than of strict logic,[38] but the fact that the creditor's obligation only arises after the liquidation, and therefore after

---

(Respondents) (1933) 6 ABC 49. See also *Calzaturificio Zenith Pty Ltd v NSW Leather & Trading Co Pty Ltd* [1970] VR 605. Compare *Morris v Flower* (1863) 2 SCR (NSW) 196.

[30] *Wood v Smith* (1838) 4 M & W 522, 527, 150 ER 1536, 1538; *Hamilton v Commonwealth Bank of Australia* (1992) 9 ACSR 90, 107; *Re Armour* (1956) 18 ABC 69, 74–6. See also *Re K B Docker* (1938) 10 ABC 198, 238–9 (in relation to the alternative ground). A similar principle applied when a voluntary settlement was avoided by a trustee in bankruptcy, in circumstances where money the subject of the settlement was not paid in satisfaction of a debt owing by the bankrupt. The recipient was required to return the settlement without a set-off in respect of a debt owing to him or her. See *Lister v Hooson* [1908] 1 KB 174; *Re Hermann, ex p The Official Assignee* (1916) 16 SR (NSW) 264.

[31] *Courtney v King* (1870) 1 VR (L) 70, 73; *Lister v Hooson* [1908] 1 KB 174 (voluntary settlement); *Re Armour* (1956) 18 ABC 69, 75–6. A similar analysis formerly applied under the doctrine of relation back, when the trustee's title related back to encompass a sum of money paid by the bankrupt to a creditor before the sequestration order. See *Re Pollitt* [1893] 1 QB 455, and also *Tamplin v Diggins* (1809) 2 Camp 312, 170 ER 1167; *Thomason v Frere* (1809) 10 East 418, 103 ER 834; *Kinder v Butterworth* (1826) 6 B & C 42, 108 ER 369. Mutuality was lacking only when the obligation of the creditor to account for a sum of money was based *solely* upon relation back, as opposed to an indebtedness that the creditor had incurred to the bankrupt. Compare *Elliott v Turquand* (1881) 7 App Cas 79; *Re Jackson, ex p The Official Assignee* (1888) 6 NZLR 417. The doctrine of relation back no longer applies in England under the Insolvency Act 1986.

[32] See *Re Grezzana* (1932) 4 ABC 203, 206. This is particularly so when the argument for a set-off is based upon the original debt for which the preferential payment was intended to be satisfaction. See *Courtney v King* (1870) 1 VR (L) 70, 73; *Re A Debtor* [1927] 1 Ch 410, 415–16, 419–20; *Re Grezzana* (above).

[33] See paras 6.66–6.99 above.

[34] *Re Hardman* (1932) 4 ABC 207; *Re Smith* (1933) 6 ABC 49; *Re Pitts and Lehman Ltd* (1940) 40 SR (NSW) 614; *Re K B Docker* (1938) 10 ABC 198, 238–9. See also *Russell Wilkins & Sons Ltd v The Outridge Printing Co Ltd* [1906] St R Qd 172.

[35] Bankruptcy Act 1966 (Cth), s. 122(4)(c).

[36] See the Insolvency Act 1986, ss. 239 and 240. In Australia see the Corporations Act 2001 (Cth), ss. 588FA, 588FC, 588FE and 588FF.

[37] *Re A Debtor* [1927] 1 Ch 410; *Calzaturificio Zenith Pty Ltd v NSW Leather & Trading Co Pty Ltd* [1970] VR 605; *Re Exchange Travel (Holdings) Ltd (No. 3)* [1997] 2 BCLC 579, 594. The absence of a *cessio bonorum* in a company liquidation makes no difference. See *Re A Debtor* at 420 (Clauson J).

[38] *McPherson's Law of Company Liquidation* (5th edn, looseleaf), [12.1090].

the relevant date for determining rights of set-off, should be a sufficient justification for denying a set-off.[39] There is also a lack of mutuality.[40] While the proceeds of a preference action form part of the fund of assets that is available for payment of the claims of unsecured creditors,[41] in England neither the right to recover a preferential payment nor the proceeds of the action is regarded as the property of the company.[42] Rather, it is a statutory right given to the liquidator for the purpose of the winding up[43] and for the benefit of the general body of creditors.[44] Thus, a right to recover a preferential payment is not caught by a debenture granted by the company over its present and future assets.[45] Since the right is not the property of the company, there is not mutuality in equity as between it and a debt owing by the company to the creditor.[46]

Administration order in relation to a company

The preference provision in the Insolvency Act also applies when an administration order **13.09** is made in relation to a company.[47] The principle should be the same in administration as for liquidation. A set-off[48] should not, therefore, be available against a claim by the administrator to recover a preference.

---

[39] See *Re A Debtor* [1927] 1 Ch 410, and para. 6.63 above. The occurrence of the liquidation is a new and independent transaction intervening after the preferential payment. See *Hiley v Peoples Prudential Assurance Co Ltd* (1938) 60 CLR 468, 487 ('without any new transaction') (Rich J), ('no new and independent transaction') (Dixon J).

[40] See, in a different context, *FCT v Linter Textiles Australia Ltd* (2005) 220 CLR 592 at [40]–[41]. In relation to the position in Australia, see paras 13.15–13.16 and 13.25–13.27 below.

[41] *Re Starkey* [1994] 1 Qd R 142, 154.

[42] *Re M. C. Bacon Ltd* [1991] Ch 127, 136–7; *Re Oasis Merchandising Services Ltd* [1998] Ch 170, 181–3 (and the cases there referred to); *Lewis v Commissioner of Inland Revenue* [2001] 3 All ER 499 (see in particular at [36]–[37]); Gough, *Company Charges* (2nd edn, 1996), 122. Compare para. 13.15 below in relation to Australia.

[43] *Re Fresjac Pty Ltd* (1995) 65 SASR 334, 347.

[44] *Willmott v London Celluloid Co* (1886) 34 Ch D 147, 150; *Re Yagerphone Ltd* [1935] 1 Ch 392, 396; *Re M. C. Bacon Ltd* [1991] Ch 127, 137; *Sheahan v Carrier Air Conditioning Pty Ltd* (1997) 189 CLR 407, 428. Similarly, in the context of a voluntary settlement in bankruptcy, Fletcher Moulton LJ in *Lister v Hooson* [1908] 1 KB 174, 179 explained the denial of a set-off against the obligation to account to the trustee on the ground that the proceeds are 'considered to be due to the estate for the purposes of the bankruptcy, i.e., for paying the creditors of the estate'.

[45] *Re Yagerphone Ltd* [1935] 1 Ch 392; *N. A. Kratzmann Pty Ltd v Tucker (No. 2)* (1968) 123 CLR 295, 299–301; *N. W. Robbie & Co Ltd v Witney Warehouse Co Ltd* [1963] 1 WLR 1324, 1338; *Re Fresjac Pty Ltd* (1995) 65 SASR 334, 346–7; *Re Oasis Merchandising Services Ltd* [1998] Ch 170, 181–2; *Sheahan v Carrier Air Conditioning Pty Ltd* (1997) 189 CLR 407, 428; *Hamilton v National Australia Bank Ltd* (1996) 66 FCR 12, 37; *Re Exchange Travel (Holdings) Ltd* [1997] 2 BCLC 579, 596; *Tolcher v National Australia Bank Ltd* (2003) 44 ACSR 727. Compare the situation in which the subject of the action is the recovery of specific property. See Walters and Armour, 'The proceeds of office-holder actions under the Insolvency Act: charged assets or free estate?' [2006] LMCLQ 27, and in Australia *Kratzmann's* case at 301–2 and *Re Fresjac* at 340, 344–5. In the case of a company limited by guarantee, where the obligation to contribute arose only in the event of a winding up, a charge over the company's assets and undertaking was held not to extend to the amounts guaranteed. See *Re Irish Club Co Ltd* [1906] WN 127.

[46] See para. 11.13 above. Similarly, an equitable set-off ordinarily should not be available. See *Re Buchanan Enterprises Pty Ltd* (1982) 7 ACLR 407.

[47] See the Insolvency Act 1986, s. 239(1), referring to s. 238(1). *Aliter* in Australia. See the Corporations Act 2001 (Cth), ss. 588FE and 588FF ('on the application of a company's liquidator').

[48] Under the Insolvency Rules 1986, r. 2.85. See paras 6.10–6.11 above.

No preference if a set-off would have been available

13.10 If A and B are indebted to each other, and A makes a payment to B in satisfaction of A's debt
in circumstances where B similarly discharges its debt by payment to A, or if A and B
merely agree that the cross-demands should be set one against the other and cancelled,[49]
then A's payment, or the agreement for a set-off, will not be construed as a preference in A's
subsequent insolvency if the cross-demands were such that they would have given rise to a
set-off in any event. The fact that the debts would have been set off in the insolvency means
that the arrangement has not worked to the detriment of A's other creditors. 'You cannot
prefer a man . . . by merely putting him in the very position in which he would be if a bankruptcy followed.'[50] That was not the case, however, in *Re Washington Diamond Mining
Co.*[51] A director of a company was owed directors' fees. At the same time he held shares in
the company which were not fully paid up, so that he had a potential liability to contribute
the amount unpaid on the shares. The company went into liquidation. Before the liquidation, but during the preference period, the director gave a cheque to the company for the
amount remaining unpaid on his shares, and received at the same time a cheque from the
company for a like amount on account of his fees.[52] Lindley LJ in the Court of Appeal
characterized the arrangement as an attempt by the director to pay up his shares in full
without really parting with any money,[53] and said that the exchange of cheques was simply
a mode for setting off the amount due for fees against the amount due on the shares.[54] If the
debts could have been set off in any event in the liquidation, the arrangement would not
have been a preference. But while there may be a set-off in an action at law by a solvent
company to enforce a call on shares, a call for unpaid capital is not such a claim that may

---

[49] It should not be necessary for a preferential 'payment' that money changed hands. See Lindley LJ in
Re Washington Diamond Mining Co [1893] 3 Ch 95, 109–10.

[50] *Re Washington Diamond Mining Co* [1893] 3 Ch 95, 104 *per* Vaughan Williams J. See also *Hamilton
v Commonwealth Bank of Australia* (1992) 9 ACSR 90, 106–8; *Wily v Rothschild Australia Ltd* (1999) 47
NSWLR 555, 566; *Wily v St George Partnership Banking Ltd* (1999) 84 FCR 423, 435–6 (mutual payments);
Minister for Transport v Francis (2000) 35 ACSR 584, 594; *Re Mistral Finance Ltd* [2001] BCC 27 at [53];
Jetaway Logistics Pty Ltd v DCT (2008) 68 ACSR 226 at [14] (reversed on other grounds (2009) 76 ACSR
404). Compare *Wily v Bartercard Ltd* (2000) 34 ACSR 186 (esp. at 197), in which there would not have
been a set-off if the transaction were set aside. The decision in the *Bartercard* case was affirmed on appeal.
See (2001) 39 ACSR 94. Compare also *Re B P Fowler Ltd* [1938] 1 Ch 113, in which Crossman J held that
the payments constituted a preference notwithstanding that he left open (at 120) whether there would have
been a set-off in the liquidation. In that respect the judgment is unsatisfactory. In *Trans Otway Ltd v Shephard*
[2006] 2 NZLR 289, the New Zealand Supreme Court held that a payment by way of set-off constituted a
preference in circumstances where the qualification to the insolvency set-off section would have operated to
preclude a set-off in the liquidation. In considering whether the qualification to the set-off section (see paras
6.66–6.99 above) would have precluded a set-off, the question of notice is to be determined by reference to
the circumstances at the time of the incurring of the obligations, as opposed to the time of effecting a set-off
pursuant to the agreement, because the question of a preference is to be determined on the assumption that
the agreement is set aside. See *Minister for Transport v Francis* (above).

[51] [1893] 3 Ch 95. See also *Re Land Development Association. Kent's Case* (1888) 39 Ch D 259; *Re Atlas
Engineering Co (Davy's Case)* (1889) 10 LR (NSW) Eq 179, 6 WN (NSW) 64; *Mitchell v Booth* [1928] SASR
367. Compare *Re Masons' Hall Tavern Co. Habershon's Case* (1868) LR 5 Eq 286.

[52] The company's account was in credit only for a trifling amount. The cheque given to the company was
deposited first, and it was only after the amount of the cheque was received by the company's bankers that the
cheque given to the director was cashed.

[53] [1893] 3 Ch 95, 109.

[54] [1893] 3 Ch 95, 110.

give rise to a set-off in a liquidation.[55] The Court of Appeal, therefore, held that the arrangement constituted a preference, with the result that the director was required to contribute the full amount of the unpaid capital to the company and to lodge a proof in the liquidation in respect of his claim for fees. When an agreement for a set-off is set aside as a preference, the parties should be put in the same position as if the demands had not been set against each other.[56]

Other arrangements constituting preferences

A preference also may take the form of an arrangement between a creditor and a debtor by which the creditor is to become indebted to the debtor, so that a possible set-off situation may arise. In such cases the preference provision will override any right to a set-off.[57] For example, there may be a preference in the bankruptcy of a debtor where the debtor sold goods or other property on credit to a creditor, the preference arising from the possibility of the creditor setting off the purchase price against the debtor's indebtedness.[58] An alternative to a credit sale is a delivery of goods to the creditor with authority to sell and to receive the proceeds,[59] or merely an authority to receive the proceeds of a sale conducted by someone else.[60] In such a case the creditor may be ordered to return the proceeds of sale undiminished by a set-off.[61]

13.11

Desire to produce a preference

The preference provision in the English Insolvency legislation stipulates that the debtor should have been 'influenced' by a 'desire to produce' a situation in which the creditor may be preferred.[62] There should have been some desire to confer a preference, so that an arrangement involving a sale of goods on credit or a delivery of property for sale will only be held to constitute a preference, with the consequent denial of a set-off against the purchase price or the obligation to pay the proceeds of sale, if the debtor was influenced by a desire that the creditor should set off the purchase price or the proceeds of sale against the debtor's indebtedness.[63] It should be contrasted with the position in Australia, where

13.12

---

[55] See paras 8.64–8.79 above.

[56] See the Insolvency Act 1986, ss. 239(3) and 340(2), and the discussion in *Hamilton v Commonwealth Bank of Australia* (1992) 9 ACSR 90, 107. In Australia, see the Bankruptcy Act 1966 (Cth), s. 122(5).

[57] *Re Clements* (1931) 7 ABC 255, 268–9. See also *Trans Otway Ltd v Shephard* [2006] 2 NZLR 289.

[58] *Sempill v Vindin* (1868) 7 SCR (NSW) 361. Compare *Smith v Hodson* (1791) 4 TR 211, 100 ER 979 and *Donaldson v Couche* (1867) 4 WW & A'B (L) 41, in which the assignees in bankruptcy affirmed the sale by suing for the price.

[59] The provision of property by a debtor to a creditor for sale and to retain the proceeds, or a credit given in an account, may be characterized as a 'payment made' by the debtor. See *Findlay v Trevor* (1993) 11 ACLC 483, 490, 499.

[60] There would not be a set-off in any event if the proceeds are received subject to a trust. See ch. 10 above.

[61] *Castendyck and Focke v The Official Assignee of S. A. McLellan* (1887) 6 NZLR 67; *Re Hardy* (1901) 19 NZLR 845; *Re Clements* (1931) 7 ABC 255; *Re Wade (Deceased)* (1943) 13 ABC 116. See also *Re Grezzana* (1932) 4 ABC 203. Compare *Re Smith* (1933) 6 ABC 49 and *Re McConnell* (1911) 18 ALR 90, [1912] VLR 102, in which the creditor acted in good faith, for valuable consideration, and in the ordinary course of business, and therefore was protected. Compare also *Simson v Guthrie* (1873) 4 AJR 182; *Re Lindsay* (1890) 9 NZLR 192.

[62] See the Insolvency Act 1986, s. 340(4), and for company liquidation s. 239(5).

[63] See also in New Zealand *Re Reimer* (1896) 15 NZLR 198 and *Hunter v The Official Assignee of Bispham* (1898) 17 NZLR 175.

the preference provision merely looks to the *effect* of the transaction. A transfer of property[64] in favour of a creditor is void as against the debtor's trustee in bankruptcy if it had the effect of giving the creditor a preference.[65] The intention of the debtor to prefer is irrelevant.[66] On the other hand, in a case in which a debtor deposited goods with his or her creditor for the purpose of sale by the creditor, it was said that any retainer of the proceeds of sale by the creditor would not be a 'payment' for the purpose of the preference section unless the debtor had authorized the creditor, either expressly or impliedly, to satisfy the debt from the proceeds.[67]

Acting inconsistently with a right to avoid a transaction

13.13   Formerly, the preference provision in the the bankruptcy legislation entitled the trustee in bankruptcy to avoid the payment or transfer of property.[68] It was not necessary for the trustee to apply for an order from the court. When there had been a transfer of property, the denial of a set-off was premised on the assumption that the trustee did not adopt a course of action that was inconsistent with the statutory right to avoid the transfer and to seek either a return of the property or damages for its conversion. In *Smith v Hodson*,[69] the preference took the form of a sale of goods on credit to a creditor, thereby leaving open the possibility of the creditor obtaining an advantage over other creditors by means of a set-off against his indebtedness for the purchase price. The bankrupt's assignees in bankruptcy had a choice. They could either have avoided the contract of sale as a preference and sued for the recovery of the property, or they could have affirmed the transaction and sued for the purchase price. Since they adopted the latter course they let in a set-off.[70] Under the current preference provision in the Insolvency Act 1986,[71] a trustee in bankruptcy cannot avoid a preference by unilateral action. The trustee must apply to the court for an order to that effect. But if in a *Smith v Hodson* situation the trustee fails to seek an order and instead sues for the price, a set-off ordinarily should be available to the creditor.[72]

---

[64] This includes a payment of money. See the Bankruptcy Act 1966 (Cth), s. 122(8)(a).

[65] Bankruptcy Act 1966 (Cth), s. 122(1). For company liquidation, see the Corporations Act 2001 (Cth), ss. 588FA(1) and 588FC.

[66] *S. Richards and Co Ltd v Lloyd* (1933) 49 CLR 49.

[67] *Re Clements* (1931) 7 ABC 255, 270. Therefore, Paine J held in *Re Clements* that the creditor in that case was not precluded from setting off the obligation to account for the proceeds against the debt. In *Hamilton v Commonwealth Bank of Australia* (1992) 9 ACSR 90, 108 Hodgson J criticized the availability of a set-off in *Re Clements* in that circumstance. He said that it was difficult to see why, as a matter of justice, a creditor should be better off where it received the proceeds of sale not as a payment, but merely because it was given authority by the debtor to sell the goods and receive the proceeds as agent. That criticism is well-founded. Hodgson J suggested that Paine J should have found that the money was received by the agent as a fiduciary for the debtor, and accordingly it should have been accounted for to the trustee. The difficulty with that suggestion is that a set-off in relation to sale proceeds is based upon *Rose v Hart* (1818) 8 Taunt 499, 129 ER 477, which seems to apply regardless of whether the proceeds are impressed with a trust. See paras 10.18–10.20 above.

[68] See e.g. the Bankruptcy Act 1914, s. 44(1). This is still the case in Australia in relation to bankruptcy (see the Bankruptcy Act 1966 (Cth), s. 122), but not in company liquidation. See the Corporations Act 2001 (Cth), s. 588FF.

[69] (1791) 4 TR 211, 100 ER 979. See also *Holmes v Tutton* (1855) 5 El & Bl 65, 119 ER 405.

[70] See also *Donaldson v Couche* (1867) 4 W W & A'B (L) 41.

[71] See s. 340 for bankruptcy, and s. 239 for corporate insolvency.

[72] In bankruptcy in England, the qualification to the set-off section only applies in relation to sums becoming due *from* the bankrupt. See para. 6.73 above. In Australia, on the other hand, the qualification is drafted in terms of both giving and receiving credit, and so it may apply so as to prevent a set-off in this situation.

Right of proof

Where a payment is avoided as a preference, the Insolvency Act[73] provides that the court **13.14** may make such order as it thinks fit with respect to the rights of the recipient of the avoided payment to prove for the debt which was discharged by it. In Australia, the High Court has held that the recipient may not prove until the preference has been repaid in full.[74]

(2) Australia – preferences in company liquidation

In Australia, the view as to the nature and effect of the right to take action in respect of **13.15** a preference differs in some respects from that in England. English courts have said that the proceeds of a preference when recovered by a liquidator are impressed with a trust in the liquidator's hands for those creditors amongst whom the liquidator has to distribute the assets.[75] In Australia, on the other hand, the notion of a trust, in the full sense of the word, has been doubted.[76] Further, at least for the purpose of a liquidator's power to sell all or part of the company's property pursuant to s. 477(2)(c) of the Corporations Act 2001 (Cth), it has been held in Australia that the proceeds of a successful claim to recover a preference constitute property of the company,[77] whereas in England the right to recover is not regarded as the property of the company.[78] In adopting that view in Australia, particular significance has been attached to s. 588FF(1) of the Corporations Act, which provides that the court may order the recipient of a preference to pay the amount in question 'to the company'.[79] None of those matters, however, should affect the principle that a set-off is not available against an obligation to repay a preference.[80] In the case of the debt the subject of the preferential payment, one reason for denying a set-off as against that debt is that it is not

---

See paras 6.85 and 6.87 above. This would also now appear to be the position in company administration and liquidation in England. See paras 6.77 and 6.83 above.

[73] See s. 241(1)(g) for company liquidation and administration, and s. 342(1)(g) for bankruptcy. In Australia, see the Corporations Act 2001 (Cth), s. 588FF(1)(g) in the context of company liquidation.

[74] *N. A. Kratzmann Pty Ltd v Tucker (No. 2)* (1968) 123 CLR 295. See now the Corporations Act 2001 (Cth), s. 588FI.

[75] *Re Yagerphone Ltd* [1935] Ch 392, 396; *Re M. C. Bacon Ltd* [1991] Ch 127, 137.

[76] *Re Starkey* [1994] 1 Qd R 142, 154; *Re Fresjac Pty Ltd* (1995) 65 SASR 334, 348.

[77] *Re Tosich Construction Pty Ltd* (1997) 73 FCR 219; *Elfic Ltd v Macks* [2003] 2 Qd R 125. See also *Re Addstone Pty Ltd* (1998) 83 FCR 583, 588. In other contexts, however, Australian courts have expressed views similar to those expressed by English courts (see below), that neither the right to recover a preference nor the proceeds recovered form part of the property of the company. In relation to the claim itself, see *Bibra Lake Holdings Pty Ltd v Firmadoor Australia Pty Ltd* (1992) 7 WAR 1, 7; *Re Fresjac Pty Ltd* (1995) 65 SASR 334, 346–7. In relation to the proceeds when recovered, see *Bibra Lake v Firmadoor* above at 5, 6–7 (referring to *Horn v York Paper Co Ltd* (1991) 23 NSWLR 622, 623); *Re Starkey* [1994] 1 Qd R 142, 154; *Geneva Finance Ltd v Resource and Industry Ltd* (2002) 169 FLR 152 at [17].

[78] See para. 13.08 above. Similarly, the fruits of the action are not regarded as the property of the company. See *Re Oasis Merchandising Ltd* [1998] Ch 170, 181.

[79] *Re Tosich Construction Pty Ltd* (1997) 73 FCR 219, 235; *Elfic Ltd v Macks* [2003] 2 Qd R 125 at [205].

[80] *Re A Debtor* [1927] 1 Ch 410; *Calzaturificio Zenith Pty Ltd v NSW Leather & Trading Co Pty Ltd* [1970] VR 605; *Re Exchange Travel (Holdings) Ltd (No. 3)* [1997] 2 BCLC 579, 594. Indeed, prior to the introduction of s. 588FF it was said that the appropriate order in the case of a preference was that payment be made to the company, as opposed to the liquidator. See *Octavo Investments Pty Ltd v Knight* (1979) 144 CLR 360, 372; *Bibra Lake Holdings Pty Ltd v Firmadoor Australia Pty Ltd* (1992) 7 WAR 1, 6–7; *Re Fresjac Pty Ltd* (1995) 65 SASR 334, 343. Therefore, the inclusion of the stipulation in s. 588FF that payment is to be made 'to the company' simply reflects the pre-existing view as to the appropriate order.

provable until the preference has been repaid in full.[81] More generally, the obligation arises after the liquidation[82] and there is a lack of mutuality.[83]

13.16 An application to set aside a preference is made by the liquidator, not the company,[84] and it is made for the benefit of unsecured creditors and for the purpose of the winding up.[85] Courts in Australia, like those in England,[86] have accepted that a charge granted by a company over its present and future assets does not attach to a right to recover a preferential payment or the proceeds of recovery.[87] Similarly, neither a right to set aside a preferential payment in a liquidation nor the proceeds of recovery could be assigned by the company prior to its liquidation as future property.[88] Those propositions should not be affected by the stipulation in s. 588FF that payment is to be made 'to the company'.[89] The reason why a security granted by a company does not attach to the proceeds of a preference claim is that the right to apply for relief in relation to a preference is given for the benefit of the general body of creditors and for the purpose of the winding up.[90] This is still the case under

---

[81] See the Corporations Act 2001 (Cth), s. 588FI and para. 13.14 above. In relation to the requirement of a provable debt, see para. 7.24 above.

[82] See para. 6.63 above and *Re A Debtor* [1927] 1 Ch 410. The occurrence of the liquidation is a new and independent transaction intervening after the preferential payment. Compare *Hiley v Peoples Prudential Assurance Co Ltd* (1938) 60 CLR 468, 487 ('without any new transaction') (Rich J), ('no new and independent transaction') (Dixon J).

[83] See also Bennetts, 'Voidable transactions: consequences of removing avoidance powers from the liquidator and vesting them in the court' (1994) 2 *Insolvency Law Journal* 136, 137–9.

[84] See the Corporations Act 2001 (Cth), s. 588FF ('on the application of a company's liquidator'), and also *Olsen v Nodcad Pty Ltd* (1999) 32 ACSR 118 at [7]; *Carob Industries Pty Ltd v Simto Pty Ltd* (2000) 23 WAR 515 at [42]; *Re Harris Scarfe Ltd* (2006) 203 FLR 46 at [27]. Compare *SJP Formwork (Aust) Pty Ltd v DCT* (2000) 34 ACSR 604. Before the introduction of s. 588FF, the liquidator was regarded as the proper plaintiff in the action. See *Bibra Lake Holdings Pty Ltd v Firmadoor Australia Pty Ltd* (1992) 7 WAR 1; *Re Fresjac Pty Ltd* (1995) 65 SASR 334, 343.

[85] *Sheahan v Carrier Air Conditioning Pty Ltd* (1997) 189 CLR 407, 428; *Re Fresjac Pty Ltd* (1995) 65 SASR 334, 347; *Willmott v London Celluloid Co* (1886) 34 Ch D 147, 150; *Re M. C. Bacon Ltd* [1991] Ch 127, 137.

[86] See para. 13.08 above.

[87] *N. A. Kratzmann Pty Ltd v Tucker (No. 2)* (1968) 123 CLR 295, 299–301; *Re Fresjac Pty Ltd* (1995) 65 SASR 334, 346–7; *Sheahan v Carrier Air Conditioning Pty Ltd* (1997) 189 CLR 407, 428; *Hamilton v National Australia Bank Ltd* (1996) 66 FCR 12, 37; *Tolcher v National Australia Bank Ltd* (2003) 44 ACSR 727.

[88] *UTSA Pty Ltd v Ultra Tune Australia Pty Ltd* [1997] 1 VR 667, 698.

[89] This was assumed in *Hamilton v National Australia Bank Ltd* (1996) 66 FCR 12, 37 (Lehane J). See also *Tolcher v National Australia Bank Ltd* (2003) 44 ACSR 727. Compare *Jonsson, Milner & Riaps Pty Ltd v Tim Ferrier Pty Ltd* [2001] QSC 010 at [16] (not followed in the *Tolcher* case), and Bennetts, 'Voidable Transactions: consequences of removing avoidance powers from the liquidator and vesting them in the court' (1994) 2 *Insolvency Law Journal* 136, 139–40. Bennetts has referred to some comments by Knox J in *Re Produce Marketing Ltd (No. 2)* [1989] BCLC 520 in the context of a claim for wrongful trading under s. 214 of the English Insolvency Act 1986 as supporting the contrary view. However, those comments no longer reflect the position in England. In *Re Oasis Merchandising Services Ltd* [1998] Ch 170, 181 the Court of Appeal accepted that a right of action by a liquidator for fraudulent (s. 213) or wrongful trading, and the fruits of such an action, are not property of the company and are not caught by a debenture. See also *Re M. C. Bacon Ltd* [1991] Ch 127, 138 and *Lewis v Commissioner of Inland Revenue* [2001] 3 All ER 499 (preference).

[90] In *Sheahan v Carrier Air Conditioning Pty Ltd* (1997) 189 CLR 407, 428 Dawson, Gaudron and Gummow JJ said that: 'The right to have such preferential dealings set aside, statutory in nature, is given for the benefit of the general body of creditors. Hence, the security would not attach to the proceeds of the judgments the appellant recovered at first instance in the present litigation.'

s. 588FF, notwithstanding the stipulation as to payment.[91] If the company cannot charge the right to make an application to the court in relation to a preference because the right is one given for the benefit of unsecured creditors, and if the company similarly cannot assign it prior to liquidation, it is evident that, while the stipulation as to payment in s. 588FF may result in the company having the legal title to the recovery received, it is not the beneficial owner of the claim itself.[92] If it is not the beneficial owner, there would not be mutuality in equity in relation to the obligation to repay a preference and a debt owing to the creditor by the company for the purpose of a set-off under the insolvency set-off section.[93]

(3) Other impugned transactions

There are other provisions in the insolvency legislation which enable a trustee in bank-   **13.17**
ruptcy or a liquidator or an administrator of a company to take action in relation to certain transactions, for example in relation to transactions at an undervalue,[94] transactions defrauding creditors,[95] and (in company liquidation) where there has been fraudulent trading[96] or wrongful trading.[97] Moreover, a disposition of a company's property made after the commencement of a court-ordered winding up is void without the consent of the court.[98] An obligation to make or return a payment under those provisions should be subject to the same rule which obtains in the case of a preference,[99] that it cannot be the subject of a set-off. A similar comment may be made in respect of the obligation to account for the proceeds of an execution or attachment completed after the bankruptcy or liquidation of the debtor.[100] In Australia, it has been said that the rationale which precludes set-off

---

[91] In *Re Fresjac Pty Ltd* (1995) 65 SASR 334, 343 Doyle CJ noted, in relation to the position prior to the introduction of s. 588FF into the Corporations Law in 1992, that the appropriate order in the case of a preference was for the payment of any sum recovered to be made to the company, and commented that this: 'suggests that the fact that money is received by the company is not sufficient of itself to enable a charge to attach to the money, because it is clear that in the case of the recovery of a preferential payment such recovery is for the benefit of the general creditors and not for the benefit of a secured creditor.'

[92] See also para. 13.26 below. Thus, when it was said prior to the enactment of s. 588FF in 1992 that the appropriate order in a preference action was for payment to the company rather than the liquidator, this was explained on the ground that the *legal* title to the assets of a company being wound up remained with the company. See *Bibra Lake Holdings Pty Ltd v Firmadoor Australia Pty Ltd* (1992) 7 WAR 1, 7; *Amatek Ltd v Botman* (1995) 127 FLR 160, 172.

[93] See para. 11.13 above.

[94] Insolvency Act 1986, s. 238, and for bankruptcy s. 339. Section 238 also applies when an administration order is made in relation to a company. As in the case of a preference (see para. 13.09 above), a set-off should not be available pursuant to the Insolvency Rules 1986, r. 2.85 (see para. 6.10 above) in response to an application by an administrator for an order in relation to a transaction at an undervalue.

[95] Insolvency Act 1986, s. 423.

[96] Insolvency Act 1986, s. 213.

[97] Insolvency Act 1986, s. 214.

[98] Insolvency Act 1986, s. 127. See also s. 284 with respect to individuals, which applies to dispositions in the period beginning with the presentation of the petition and ending with the vesting of the bankrupt's estate in the trustee.

[99] See paras 13.07–13.14 above.

[100] See the Insolvency Act 1986, ss. 183 and 346. Compare the exceptional case of *Ex p Elliott, re Jermyn* (1838) 3 Deac 343. The petitioner had paid a sum of money in order to prevent a distress being levied on the bankrupt's goods. The petitioner sold some of the goods, and was sued by the bankrupt's assignees for the proceeds. It had been held in a previous action ((1837) 2 Deac 179) that the sum paid on behalf of the bankrupt to prevent the distress was not a provable debt, but the court in the present case said that the assignees could not recover the proceeds without giving credit for the sums paid by the petitioner.

against an obligation to repay a preference[101] must apply also to a transaction which is a voidable uncommercial transaction.[102]

13.18 The view that a set-off is not available in those situations is a reflection of the distinction which English courts have drawn in company liquidation between assets which are the property of the company at the commencement of the liquidation, including rights of action which arose and might have been pursued by the company itself prior to the liquidation, and assets which only arise after the liquidation and which are recoverable only by the liquidator through the exercise of rights conferred on him or her alone by statute.[103] A claim by the liquidator within the latter category is not regarded as constituting property of the company, and accordingly it would not be caught by a charge granted by the company over its present and future assets.[104] Thus, in England, a claim to recover a fraudulent preference is not considered to be property of the company,[105] and nor is a claim for fraudulent or wrongful trading,[106] or a right to assert that a disposition of the company's property after the commencement of its winding up is void.[107] English courts have therefore held that a right to recover a void disposition cannot be assigned by the liquidator pursuant to a power to sell any of the company's property.[108] Similarly, in South Australia,[109] Doyle CJ (with whom Matheson J agreed) concluded that the right to recover property the subject of a void disposition is not property of the company,[110] and consequently it is not a right to which a charge granted by the company would attach.[111] As in the case

---

However, this was not justified on the basis of the principles of set-off. Rather, the action to recover the proceeds was characterized as an action for money had and received. The action for money had and received, although founded in the common law, is of an equitable nature. See *Roxborough v Rothmans of Pall Mall Australia Ltd* (2001) 208 CLR 516 at [96]–[99] (Gummow J), [202]–[203] (Callinan J). It only entitles the claimant to recover what in conscience he or she is entitled to. In particular, the claimant must give credit for any benefits that he or she has received. See *Westdeutsche Landesbank Girozentrale v Islington LBC* [1994] 4 All ER 890, 940–1 (Hobhouse J).

[101] See paras 13.15–13.16 above.

[102] *Cashflow Finance Pty Ltd v Westpac Banking Corporation* [1999] NSWSC 671 at [574]. See the Corporations Act 2001 (Cth), ss. 588FB and 588FE(3).

[103] *Re Oasis Merchandising Services Ltd* [1998] Ch 170, 181–3 (CA); *Re Ayala Holdings Ltd (No. 2)* [1996] 1 BCLC 467, 480–1, 483.

[104] *Re Oasis Merchandising Services Ltd* [1998] Ch 170, 181–2.

[105] See para. 13.08 above. The contrary view has been expressed in Australia. See para. 13.15 above.

[106] *Re Oasis Merchandising Services Ltd* [1998] Ch 170, 181; *Re M. C. Bacon Ltd* [1991] Ch 127, 138 (referring to the Insolvency Act 1986, s. 214). In Australia, compare the Corporations Act 2001 (Cth), ss. 588M and 588W in relation to insolvent trading, which provide for recovery by the liquidator 'as a debt due to the company'. But this should not suffice to establish mutuality for the purpose of a set-off. See paras 13.20–13.29 below. On the other hand, a claim against directors for misfeasance is property of the company which can be charged, since the right of action in such a case arises and was available to the company before the winding up. See *Re Oasis Merchandising Services Ltd* [1998] Ch 170, 181; *Re Fresjac Pty Ltd* (1995) 65 SASR 334, 342 (referring to *Re Asiatic Electric Co Pty Ltd* [1970] 2 NSWLR 612).

[107] Insolvency Act 1986, s. 127.

[108] *Re Ayala Holdings Ltd* [1996] 1 BCLC 467.

[109] *Re Fresjac Pty Ltd* (1995) 65 SASR 334.

[110] Compare *Elfic Ltd v Macks* [2003] 2 Qd R 125 in relation to a preference. See para. 13.15 above.

[111] (1995) 65 SASR 334, 345. Similarly, Doyle CJ said that the *proceeds* of the exercise of the right do not fall to be treated as property of the company caught by a pre-existing charge. On the other hand, the Chief Justice (at 340, 344–5) accepted that, when the property disposed of is specific property the subject of a charge, as opposed to money, that property, if recovered, would again become subject to the charge. See also Walters and Armour, 'The proceeds of office-holder actions under the Insolvency Act: charged assets or free estate?' [2006] LMCLQ 27.

of a preference,[112] there would not in these situations be mutuality in equity for the purpose of the insolvency set-off section in relation to the right in question and a separate debt owing by the company.[113]

In Australia, *Shirlaw v Lewis*[114] suggests that in some circumstances there may be a set-off **13.19** in relation to a void disposition. Two companies entered into a contract for the sale of a business. The purchaser went into possession prior to completion, but the contract provided that if the purchaser defaulted the vendor was entitled to terminate the purchaser's licence to conduct the business and to resume possession, whereupon the vendor would purchase all of the purchaser's goods and saleable stock in trade used in the business. The purchaser repudiated the contract, so as to give rise to a liability in damages to the vendor. The vendor accepted the repudiation, thereby terminating the contract, and Hodgson J in the New South Wales Supreme Court accepted that a sale of the goods and stock in trade was intended to take effect in that circumstance. A winding up of the purchaser commenced, after which the vendor re-took possession. It then proceeded on the basis that it was the purchaser of the stock pursuant to the contract and on-sold it. The liquidator of the purchaser asserted that the sale of the stock to the vendor after the commencement of the winding up was a void disposition, and sought damages for conversion from the vendor because of the on-sale. Hodgson J held that, whether the claim against the vendor was characterized as being in the nature of a claim for unjust enrichment or a claim in conversion,[115] the vendor was entitled to set off its damages claim arising from the repudiation, since the taking of the stock arose out of the pre-liquidation dealings of the parties. It is difficult to support that view. The purpose of the statutory power to avoid a disposition of property is to enable the recovery of the property with a view to a rateable distribution among the general creditors,[116] and if a particular creditor who is a recipient of the property could set off the debt owing to him or her against a liability in damages for converting the property, the purpose of the section would be defeated. If the power to avoid the disposition is exercisable for the benefit of creditors generally, so should the right to sue in conversion. The company, therefore, should not itself be the beneficial owner of the claim in conversion so as to satisfy the requirement of mutuality in equity in relation to that claim and the debt owing by the company to the creditor.[117] In view of the set-off, Hodgson J said

---

[112] See paras 13.08 and 13.15–13.16 (Australia) above.

[113] Similarly, equitable set-off ordinarily would not be available. See *Re Buchanan Enterprises Pty Ltd* (1982) 7 ACLR 407. Compare *Thomas v Hatzipetros* (1997) 24 ACSR 286, which concerned a different question, whether a disposition of property should be validated on the ground that the company was no worse off by the disposition because the bank as the disponee in any event would have claimed a set-off.

[114] (1993) 10 ACSR 288.

[115] Hodgson J in fact doubted (at (1993) 10 ACSR 288, 295) that a retrospective avoidance of a disposition can retrospectively make a disposal of goods a wrongful act of conversion. See also *Perpetual Trustees Australia Ltd v Heperu Pty Ltd* [2009] NSWCA 84 at [75]–[81], but compare *Sydlow Pty Ltd v Melwren Pty Ltd* (1994) 13 ACSR 144, 147.

[116] *Re Fresjac Pty Ltd* (1995) 65 SASR 334, 343, 344–5; *Re Loteka Pty Ltd* [1990] 1 Qd R 322, 324; *Rose v AIB Group (UK) plc* [2003] 1 WLR 2791 at [14].

[117] In relation to a claim in conversion, Doyle CJ in *Re Fresjac Pty Ltd* (1995) 65 SASR 334, 347 referred to *Re Quality Camera Co Pty Ltd* [1965] NSWR 1330 as illustrating the proposition that money recovered as a preference is not caught by a charge over the company's assets, even when the money is the value of specific goods which themselves were caught by the charge. The Chief Justice considered (see in particular at 349) that the same conclusion applied in the case of a void disposition.

that it was unnecessary to consider an alternative argument, that the disposition should be validated by the court,[118] but that would have been a preferable basis for a decision in favour of the vendor.

(4) Insolvent trading in Australia

13.20 Two decisions in Australia in relation to insolvent trading would also benefit from reconsideration.

13.21 The first case, *Re Parker*,[119] was a decision of Mansfield J in the Federal Court. It concerned ss. 588V and 588W of the Corporations Law,[120] which imposed liability on a holding company for insolvent trading by a subsidiary. In essence, s. 588V provides that a holding company contravenes the section if its subsidiary incurred debts when it was insolvent and, having regard to the nature and extent of the holding company's control over the subsidiary's affairs, it is reasonable to expect that the holding company would have been aware that there were reasonable grounds for suspecting the subsidiary's insolvency. If the subsidiary goes into liquidation, and the holding company has contravened s. 588V, s. 588W provides that the liquidator may recover from the holding company, 'as a debt due to the company', the amount of any loss or damage suffered by unsecured creditors because of the subsidiary's insolvency.

13.22 In *Re Parker*, the liquidator of a subsidiary alleged that the holding company was liable under s. 588W. In addition, the subsidiary was indebted to the holding company, and the liquidator said that the subsidiary's debt should be set off pursuant to s. 553C of the Corporations Law against the holding company's liability under s. 588W. The impetus for this was that the holding company was in receivership, and its assets (including any dividend payable to the holding company) were expected to be absorbed in satisfying the charge to the secured creditor. Therefore, in the absence of a set-off, the holding company would have received a dividend in the subsidiary's liquidation in respect of the debt due to it and at the same time there would not have been any assets available to satisfy the holding company's liability under s. 588W.[121] Mansfield J accepted the liquidator's argument, and held that a s. 588W claim could be the subject of a set-off.[122]

---

[118] Pursuant to the Corporations Law, s. 468. See now the Corporations Act 2001 (Cth), s. 468.

[119] (1997) 80 FCR 1. See also *BGC Contracting Pty Ltd v Kimberly Gold Pty Ltd* (2000) 35 ACSR 633 at [96] (Master Bredmeyer).

[120] Now, the Corporations Act 2001 (Cth).

[121] Normally, if a floating charge granted by a company crystallized before the company's liquidation, a debt owing to the company and coming within the ambit of the charge would have become the subject of a fixed security in favour of the secured creditor, so that there would not have been mutuality in equity at the date of the liquidation as between the charged debt and a debt owing by the company to the debtor. See para. 11.50 above. In *Re Parker*, however, an administrator had been appointed to the subsidiary prior to crystallization of the charge, and Mansfield J accepted that s. 513B of the Corporations Law had the effect that the date of the administration was the relevant date for determining rights of set-off. See paras 6.52–6.62 above, where that view is criticized. Since the administrator was appointed before crystallization, Parker J accepted that there was mutuality in equity at the relevant date for the purpose of a set-off under the insolvency set-off section. Furthermore, the fact that the charge crystallized before the winding up would have had the consequence that the liquidator could not have invoked the rule in *Cherry v Boultbee* (1839) 4 My & Cr 442, 41 ER 171. See paras 14.23–14.26 below.

[122] One of the conditions for liability under ss. 588V and 588W is that, at the time when the subsidiary incurred the debts, the holding company or one of its directors was aware, or it was reasonable to expect that

The question of the availability of a set-off involved the determination of two issues. The **13.23** first was whether the holding company's liability under s. 588W constituted a debt or a credit or a claim arising out of a dealing for the purpose of the insolvency set-off section, and the second was whether there was mutuality.

In relation to the first issue, a claim pursuant to s. 599W does not exist prior to the liquid- **13.24** ation. On the contrary, liquidation is a pre-condition to it. Mansfield J was also prepared to accept in *Re Parker* that the claim might not arise from a prior dealing between the holding company and the subsidiary, or at least he declined to decide the case on that basis.[123] On the other hand, he pointed out that the events which constituted the contravention occurred before the commencement of the subsidiary's liquidation. Mansfield J said that the claim under s. 588W was the 'natural outcome' of those events, which justified the application of the set-off section.[124] He derived support for that view from an earlier comment by Bigham J in *Re Daintrey*,[125] which was quoted by Rich J in *Hiley v Peoples Prudential Assurance Co Ltd*,[126] and to which the High Court referred with approval in *Gye v McIntyre*.[127] Bigham J said of the appellants in *Re Daintrey* that they: 'are not seeking to alter the rights of the parties by reference to subsequent transactions, but are seeking to ascertain them by reference to the natural outcome of previous transactions…'.[128] However, in the *Hiley* case both Rich and Dixon JJ also emphasized that the company's right to the debt which it was sought to include in a set-off in that case[129] arose out of subsisting rights in the company when the winding up began,[130] and Rich J in particular emphasized the importance generally of prior rights when it is sought to include a claim arising after the liquidation in a set-off:

> But this … does not mean that at the time when the winding up commences there must exist claims which then and there can be made the subject of account and set-off … Rights must

---

the holding company or one of its directors would have been aware, that there were reasonable grounds for suspecting that the subsidiary was insolvent. Often, that notice would bring into effect the qualification to the insolvency set-off section, in s. 553C(2), so as to preclude a set-off in the subsidiary's liquidation. See paras 6.87–6.89 above. On the other hand, s. 553C(2) is drafted in terms of the person claiming the benefit of the set-off having the requisite notice. The context suggests that this contemplates the creditor of the company and not the company itself. Since in *Re Parker*, the liquidator, as opposed to the holding company, was claiming the set-off, the qualification arguably did not apply. The point may be made, however, that it seems inconsistent with the mandatory and automatic nature of insolvency set-off that the question whether a set-off occurs should depend on which party is claiming it. See para. 6.90 above.

123 (1997) 80 FCR 1, 10–11.
124 (1997) 80 FCR 1, 12.
125 [1900] 1 QB 546.
126 (1938) 60 CLR 468, 487.
127 (1991) 171 CLR 609, 630.
128 [1900] 1 QB 546, 568.
129 An insurance company prior to its liquidation had assigned a debt owing to it to a third party by way of security, and after the winding up began the debt was transferred back to the company. Since the debt had come back to the company, the High Court held that the debtor could employ it in a set-off in the liquidation, notwithstanding that at the date of the liquidation it was held by the third party. The important point was that the company had an equity of redemption, and the debt was got back by virtue of rights subsisting at the commencement of the winding up. See para. 6.105 above.
130 (1938) 60 CLR 468, 489 (Rich J), 499 (Dixon J). Similarly, in *Re Daintrey* [1900] 1 QB 546, to which Rich J referred in *Hiley* (see above), there were subsisting rights at the date of the bankruptcy arising out of the contract for the sale of the business.

be vested in the creditor and in the company which, without any new transaction, grow in the natural course of events into money claims capable of forming items in an account or capable of settlement by set-off.[131]

In *Re Parker*, on the other hand, the subsidiary had no rights against its holding company prior to the liquidation. Section 588V describes certain events which must have occurred before the liquidation in order to support a claim in the liquidation under s. 588W. Those events themselves, however, do not confer any rights on the subsidiary prior to its liquidation. They are simply pre-conditions to the statutory right coming into being.[132] For a set-off to occur, there must have been mutual debts, mutual credits or mutual dealings. The s. 588W claim arose after the liquidation, and therefore the set-off could not have been based upon mutual debts in existence at the date of the liquidation.[133] Moreover, Mansfield J proceeded on the basis that the s. 588W claim did not arise out of a prior dealing. The justification for the set-off, therefore, must have been that the subsidiary gave credit to the holding company prior to the liquidation. But if the subsidiary had no 'rights' against the holding company prior to the liquidation, whether arising from a prior transaction or otherwise, it is difficult to see how it could be said that the subsidiary ever gave credit to the holding company before the liquidation.[134] This view is not affected by the proposition accepted by Mansfield J, that it is not necessary for a set-off that the claims should have arisen out of prior dealings between the parties.[135] In the cases to which Mansfield J referred for that proposition,[136] a creditor of a bankrupt had acquired the debt before the bankruptcy, as a result of a third party having negotiated to the creditor an instrument upon which the bankrupt was liable. That did not involve a dealing between the bankrupt and the creditor, but there was nevertheless an existing debt owing to the creditor on the instrument at the date of the bankruptcy, and the creditor gave credit in relation to that debt before the bankruptcy. The credit, therefore, was founded upon the prior rights that the creditor had pursuant to the instrument negotiated to it. In *Re Parker*, on the other hand, there were no prior rights which could be said to have constituted the giving of credit in relation to the subsequent s. 588W claim.

13.25   In any event, there was a lack of mutuality.[137] Mansfield J did not consider that mutuality presented a problem. He noted that s. 588W is expressed in terms that the subsidiary's liquidator may recover from the holding company 'as a debt due to the company'. He regarded this as sufficient to establish mutuality as between the subsidiary's s. 588W claim and the holding company's claim against the subsidiary.[138] Section 588W should not have that effect, however.

---

[131] (1938) 60 CLR 468, 487.

[132] Compare *Secretary of State for Trade and Industry v Frid* [2004] 2 AC 506, in which the Secretary of State had a contingent statutory obligation to pay before the employer's liquidation in that case. See Lord Hoffmann at [17] and [19], and para. 8.12 above.

[133] See para. 7.02 above.

[134] See para. 7.04 above.

[135] (1997) 80 FCR 1, 10–11. But see paras 7.12–7.22 above.

[136] *Hankey v Smith* (1789) 3 TR 507n, 100 ER 703 and *Forster v Wilson* (1843) 12 M & W 191, 152 ER 1165.

[137] The reasoning referred to in *FCT v Linter Textiles Australia Ltd* (2005) 220 CLR 592 at [40]–[41], though in a different context, is consistent with this view.

[138] (1997) 80 FCR 1, 11.

The stipulation that a claim under s. 588W is recoverable 'as a debt due to the company' **13.26** may have the consequence that the subsidiary has the legal title to the claim.[139] In insolvency set-off, however, mutuality is determined by reference to equitable interests,[140] and it seems difficult to say that the subsidiary itself is the beneficial owner of any claim that may accrue to it under s. 588W. For example, the subsidiary prior to its liquidation could not charge any subsequently accruing claim under s. 588W.[141] In the first place, that proposition arises by implication from s. 588Y, which states that an amount paid to a company under s. 588W is not available to pay a secured debt of the company unless all the company's unsecured debts have been paid in full. Further, the Explanatory Memorandum circulated with the Corporate Law Reform Bill 1992, which introduced ss. 588V and 588W, made it clear that the purpose of the action is to benefit unsecured creditors,[142] in which case the comment of the High Court in *Sheahan v Carrier Air Conditioning Pty Ltd*[143] in the context of a right to have a preference set aside should be equally applicable to s. 588W: 'The right to have such preferential dealings set aside, statutory in nature, is given for the benefit of the general body of creditors. *Hence*, the security would not attach to the proceeds of the judgments . . .'[144] Similarly, because of the interest of unsecured creditors, the subsidiary prior to its liquidation could hardly assign for its own benefit a potential claim under s. 588W as future property.[145] These factors suggest that the company is not the beneficial owner of the claim.[146] If the company is not the beneficial owner, there would not be mutuality for the purposes of a set-off as between the claim and a debt owing by the company. It is true that in *Re Parker* the allowance of a set-off benefited the unsecured creditors, since it removed the holding company as a proving creditor in circumstances where the cross-claim against the holding company pursuant to s. 588W would not have yielded anything. But that is not the point. If a set-off is available to one party it should be equally available to the other, and in other cases it would be contrary to the interests of unsecured creditors if the holding company were permitted to set off its liability under s. 588W against a separate debt owing to it by the subsidiary.

There is admittedly authority for the view that a claim under s. 588W is property of the **13.27** company for the purpose of a liquidator's power to sell pursuant to s. 477(2)(c) of the

---

[139] Notwithstanding authority suggesting that the liquidator is the proper plaintiff in an insolvent trading action. See *Re Parker* (1997) 80 FCR 1, 11; *Fryer v Powell* (2002) 37 ACSR 589; *Tolcher v National Australia Bank Ltd* (2003) 44 ACSR 727 at [16]. Compare *Ariss v Express Interiors Pty Ltd* [1996] 2 VR 507, 519.

[140] See paras 11.13–11.17 above.

[141] See *Tolcher v National Australia Bank Ltd* (2003) 44 ACSR 727 in relation to the insolvent trading claim against the shadow director under the Corporations Act 1981 (Cth), s. 588M(2). See also para. 13.08 above in relation to preferences.

[142] The Explanatory Memorandum stated (in para. 1128) that the liquidator 'may take proceedings against the holding company to recover, for the benefit of unsecured creditors, loss or damage suffered by unsecured creditors as a result of the holding company's contravention of 588V'.

[143] (1997) 189 CLR 407.

[144] (1997) 189 CLR 407, 428 (emphasis added).

[145] In *UTSA Pty Ltd v Ultra Tune Australia Pty Ltd* [1997] 1 VR 667, 698 Hansen J at first instance accepted that a claim under the Corporations Law, s. 588FF is not assignable by the company.

[146] See also para. 13.16 above in relation to preferences.

Corporations Act 2001 (Cth).[147] But while the claim may be property of the company for the purpose of enabling the liquidator to deal with it as a saleable asset pursuant to s. 477(2)(c), that proposition does not require the conclusion that the company itself is the beneficial owner. The company would hold the claim for the benefit of unsecured creditors. There is not a trust in the full sense of the word,[148] but that does not matter. The important point for mutuality is that the company itself is not the beneficial owner. An analogy may be drawn with the position of an executor of a deceased's estate prior to completion of the administration.[149] Before the completion of the administration a legatee does not have a beneficial interest in the assets the subject of the bequest,[150] and nor does the executor. The testator's property comes to the executor in full ownership, in the sense that he or she has the whole right of property, to the extent that there are property rights. Nevertheless, the executor holds it for the purpose of carrying out the functions and duties of administration, not for his or her own benefit. The executor, therefore, is not the beneficial owner of the estate.[151]

13.28 The second case, *Hall v Poolman*,[152] was similar to *Re Parker*, though it concerned director liability for insolvent trading contrary to ss. 588G and 588M of the Corporations Act 1981 (Cth), as opposed to holding company liability. Palmer J in the New South Wales Supreme Court reached a similar decision to that of Mansfield J in *Re Parker*, that a director's insolvent trading liability could be the subject of a set-off in the company's liquidation,[153] though without reference to *Re Parker*. Palmer J noted that 'mutual dealings' in s. 553C is a phrase of the 'widest import'.[154] Unlike Mansfield J in *Re Parker* in relation to a holding company, he accepted that a director of a company acting in the course of his or her duties as such is 'dealing' with the company and that the company similarly is 'dealing' with the director even though, as an incorporeal creature, the company is passive in the relationship. He further accepted that the insolvent trading claim and the director's separate claim against the company in that case were mutual.[155]

---

[147] *Re Movitor Pty Ltd* (1996) 64 FCR 380, 392. Compare para. 13.18 above in relation to the view adopted by English courts. The question in *Re Movitor* was whether the fruits of an action under s. 588W were property of the company for the purpose of the Corporations Law, s. 477(2)(c). Drummond J also said, however (at 392) that the 'debt' can properly be regarded as property of the company which the liquidator is empowered to sell. In England, the Court of Appeal in *Re Oasis Merchandising Services Pty Ltd* [1998] Ch 170, 184–5 distinguished *Re Movitor* on the basis of the different language in the Australian insolvent trading provision. See also *Re William Felton Co Pty Ltd* (1998) 28 ACSR 228, 235–6; *Re Addstone Pty Ltd* (1998) 83 FCR 583, 592.

[148] See *Re Starkey* [1994] 1 Qd R 142, 154 (McPherson JA) and *Re Fresjac Pty Ltd* (1995) 65 SASR 334, 348 (Doyle CJ) in relation to preferences.

[149] See *Re Starkey* [1994] 1 Qd R 142, 154 in relation to preferences, and para. 13.125 below.

[150] *Official Receiver in Bankruptcy v Schultz* (1990) 170 CLR 306, 312, 314.

[151] *Commissioner of Stamp Duties (Queensland) v Livingston* [1965] AC 694, 707–8; *Ayerst v C & K (Construction) Ltd* [1976] AC 167, 177–8.

[152] (2007) 65 ACSR 123.

[153] Set-off was considered at (2007) 65 ACSR 123 at [405]–[434].

[154] (2007) 65 ACSR 123 at [425], referring (at [424]) to *Gye v McIntyre* (1991) 171 CLR 609, 625 ('very wide scope'). See para. 7.08 above.

[155] (2007) 65 ACSR 123 at [422].

For the reason given above in relation to holding company liability, it is suggested that the **13.29** claims were not mutual in equity and that a set-off, therefore, should have been denied in *Hall v Poolman*.

(5) Assignment of book debts

The Insolvency Act, s. 344 provides that an assignment of book debts by a person engaged **13.30** in any business is void as against the person's trustee in bankruptcy as regards book debts which were not paid before the presentation of the petition, unless the assignment has been registered under the Bills of Sale Act 1878. Where an assignment is void the purchaser may be liable to account to the vendor's trustee for the proceeds of debts received. In Victoria a purchaser of book debts was permitted to set off a cross-claim against his or her liability to account for proceeds under the insolvency set-off section,[156] but the case in question should be understood in the context of the legislation in issue. The Book Debts Act 1896 (Vic) provided that an assignment of book debts had no validity at law or in equity until it was registered. The Victorian legislation should be compared to the English Insolvency Act, which provides that the assignment is void *as against the trustee*.[157] The only obligation to account for the proceeds is to a trustee in bankruptcy. In such a case a question of mutuality would arise which was not in issue in Victoria.

(6) Set-off, after the avoidance of an assignment of a debt

A bankrupt prior to the bankruptcy may have assigned to X a debt owing to the bankrupt **13.31** by Y. If the assignment is subsequently avoided, for example as a transaction at an under-value or a transaction defrauding creditors, so that the debt reverts to the bankrupt, there is then the possibility of the debt forming the basis of a set-off as between the bankrupt and Y.[158] The issue of mutuality, when the effect of avoiding a transaction is that a payment must be made to the trustee, would not arise.

C. Performance of Contracts after Insolvency

(1) Disclaimer

The fact that one of the parties to a contract has become bankrupt or has gone into liquidation **13.32** may constitute a repudiation of the contract, but insolvency is not always a repudiation.[159] If a contract is not repudiated, any rights arising under it in favour of the insolvent will become an asset of the estate available for distribution amongst creditors. If the insolvent's side of the contract still requires performance, the trustee or the liquidator may choose to

---

[156] *Savage v Thompson* (1903) 29 VLR 436.

[157] After the assignment is avoided any proceeds received by the purchaser may be subject to a constructive trust, and therefore not be susceptible to a set-off in any event on that ground. See ch. 10 above.

[158] *Re Last, ex p Butterell* (1994) 124 ALR 219. Why did the fact that Rawilla Pty Ltd was a trustee of a discretionary trust not have the consequence that there was no mutuality in equity? See para. 17.125n below.

[159] See e.g. *Brooke v Hewitt* (1796) 3 Ves Jun 253, 30 ER 997; *Jennings' Trustee v King* [1952] 1 Ch 899; *Official Receiver v Henn* (1981) 40 ALR 569. See also para. 9.05 above.

disclaim it as an unprofitable contract.[160] Alternatively, the contract may be regarded as profitable and not be disclaimed. In that circumstance, the question may arise whether rights and liabilities arising pursuant to the contract as a result of later performance or non-performance may be the subject of a set-off.

Bankruptcy

13.33   Consider first the case of a bankruptcy. A trustee in bankruptcy ordinarily is not liable personally for a breach of the bankrupt's contracts occurring after the bankruptcy, including as a result of a disclaimer. Rather, the other contracting party is remitted to a proof in the bankruptcy for the resulting damages claim,[161] and since the claim arises out of a prior dealing with the bankrupt it should also be capable of being used in a set-off.[162] Often, though, when a contract imposing onerous obligations on a bankrupt is in issue,[163] the other contracting party will serve a notice on the bankrupt's trustee requiring the trustee to decide within twenty-eight days whether or not he or she is going to disclaim the contract, and if the trustee does not disclaim, the Insolvency Act states that the trustee is deemed to have adopted the contract.[164] Two interpretations of this provision have been suggested.[165] The first is that the trustee is deemed to have adopted the contract in the trustee's personal capacity, so that the trustee becomes personally liable for any subsequent breach of the contract, subject only to a possible right of indemnity from the estate.[166] Since the burden of a contract, as distinct from the benefit, cannot be assigned, this interpretation contemplates a form of novation of the contract, by which the trustee in his or her personal capacity replaces the bankrupt as the party responsible for carrying out the contract. The second interpretation is also based on a novation, but in this case the trustee representing the estate

---

[160] See the Insolvency Act 1986, s. 315, and, for company liquidation, s. 178. In Australia see the Bankruptcy Act 1966 (Cth), s. 133, and for companies the Corporations Act 2001 (Cth), ss. 568–568F. *Quaere* whether, in the determination of whether a contract is unprofitable, a trustee in bankruptcy or liquidator may take into account the effect of any set-off that may be available to the other party. In *Old Style Confections Pty Ltd v Microbyte Investments Pty Ltd* [1995] 2 VR 457, 466–7 Hayne J considered that the availability of a set-off against contract payments is not a relevant consideration. This is the preferred view. It is consistent with the view that the power to disclaim exists so that a liquidator is not impeded or prejudiced in discharging the obligation to realise the company's property and pay a dividend to creditors within a reasonable time. See *Re SSSL Realisations (2002) Ltd* [2006] Ch 610 at [33]–[54]. Note that in Australia a liquidator or trustee can disclaim any contract, though if it is not an unprofitable contract the leave of the court is required. See the Bankruptcy Act 1966 (Cth), ss. 133(1A) and 133(5A), and the Corporations Act 2001 (Cth), ss. 568(1)(f) and 568(1A).

[161] *Re Sneezum, ex p Davis* (1876) 3 Ch D 463. See also *Stead Hazel and Co v Cooper* [1933] 1 KB 840 for companies. In the event of a disclaimer, the Insolvency Act 1986, ss. 178(6) and 315(5) confer a right of proof for loss suffered as a result of the disclaimer.

[162] In relation to set-off consequent upon a disclaimer, see *Re Anderson* [1924] NZLR 1163. See generally paras 8.51–8.52 above.

[163] For a discussion of onerous contracts, see Melville, 'Disclaimer of contracts in bankruptcy' (1952) 15 MLR 28.

[164] Insolvency Act 1986, s. 316(2). In Australia see the Bankruptcy Act 1966 (Cth), s. 133(6).

[165] Melville, 'Disclaimer of contracts in bankruptcy' (1952) 15 MLR 28, 33–4; Williams and Muir Hunter, *The Law and Practice in Bankruptcy* (19th edn, 1979), 394–5.

[166] Robson, *Law of Bankruptcy* (7th edn, 1894), 473–4. In the case of a lease, if a trustee does not disclaim he or she becomes personally liable for rent. The basis of the liability is privity of estate. See e.g. *Ex p Dressler, re Solomon* (1878) 9 Ch D 252, and paras 13.64–13.68 below.

and the creditors generally becomes liable. On this interpretation, it has been suggested[167] that the other contracting party would be a first priority creditor entitled to be paid ahead of the other creditors. Either interpretation, however, should mean that the other contracting party could not bring a prior debt that he or she owes to the bankrupt into an account. Mutuality would be lacking in relation to that debt and the claim against the trustee either in his or her personal capacity or as representing the estate. Usually this would not be significant, because the right of the other contracting party to proceed against the trustee personally, or to have a direct claim against the estate, would obviate the necessity for a set-off. Indeed, if the value of the claim of the other contracting party is greater than his or her indebtedness to the bankrupt, both alternatives would be preferable to a set-off, because set-off only enables a creditor to obtain the full value of the claim to the extent of the creditor's indebtedness. On the other hand, the other contracting party could suffer from the loss of a set-off if the section is interpreted as imposing personal liability on the trustee and the trustee is also insolvent.

Company liquidation

Disclaimer has a similar operation in company liquidation. If the liquidator disclaims a contract the resulting damages claim should be able to be the subject of a set-off, since it arises out of a prior dealing with the company.[168] Liquidation differs from bankruptcy, however, in that the company's property does not vest in the liquidator as the person administering the estate.[169] Consistent with that distinction, if a notice is served upon a liquidator requiring the liquidator to decide whether or not he or she is going to disclaim a contract, and the liquidator fails to disclaim within the twenty-eight-day period, the Insolvency Act 1986 does not provide (as in bankruptcy) that the liquidator is deemed to have adopted the contract.[170] Any subsequent breach of contract would be a liability of the company, and in accordance with normal principles it should be able to be the subject of a set-off.

13.34

(2) Contract by insolvent to sell property or perform work

A person may have contracted to sell property or to perform work, but have become bankrupt or gone into liquidation before the contract has been performed.[171] If the trustee in bankruptcy or the liquidator subsequently performs the contract, so that the price becomes payable, the other contracting party may wish to set off a separate debt of the bankrupt or the company against the obligation to pay the price.

13.35

Beneficial ownership had vested in the purchaser before the vendor's insolvency

If the contract is for the sale of real property, and the beneficial ownership of the property had vested in the purchaser prior to the vendor's bankruptcy or liquidation, the purchaser

13.36

---

[167] Melville, 'Disclaimer of contracts in bankruptcy' (1952) 15 MLR 28, 34.

[168] See *Re Anderson* [1924] NZLR 1163 (disclaimer of shares). See generally paras 8.51–8.52 above.

[169] See para. 13.05 above.

[170] Compare in Australia the Corporations Act 2001 (Cth), s. 568(8), which provides that, if the liquidator does not disclaim within the appointed time, 'he or she' shall be taken to have adopted it.

[171] Compare *Shirlaw v Lewis* (1993) 10 ACSR 288, in which the sale occurred after the winding-up summons was filed but before the winding-up order.

ordinarily would be entitled to specific performance of the contract, subject to the usual requirement of being able to show that he or she is ready and willing to perform his or her own essential obligations under the contract. If the vendor happens to be separately indebted to the purchaser, and the debt is otherwise capable of being included in a set-off under the insolvency set-off section, the Court of Appeal in *Re Taylor, ex p Norvell*[172] held that specific performance may be decreed on terms that the purchaser pay the balance (if any) in favour of the vendor. Similarly, in *Re Mistral Finance Ltd*[173] it was accepted that a contract for the sale of a yacht was specifically enforceable against the liquidator of the seller[174] and that the price could be set off in the liquidation against a separate debt of the seller to the purchaser.

Beneficial title had not passed before the vendor's insolvency

13.37   Consider that the contract is for the sale of property the beneficial ownership of which had not vested in the purchaser prior to the vendor's insolvency. This may occur, for example, in the case of a contract for the sale of a quantity of unascertained goods for delivery at a future date. Often in such a case the price is not payable until delivery occurs. If in the interim the vendor has become bankrupt or has gone into liquidation, the trustee in bankruptcy or the liquidator may disclaim the contract if it is unprofitable.[175] Alternatively, if the contract is profitable, the trustee or the liquidator may decide to complete it for the benefit of the unsecured creditors and deliver the goods in question. There should not be any difficulty if the goods are delivered and accepted on a 'cash on delivery' basis. If, however, delivery takes place without immediate payment, the purchaser may assert that he or she is entitled to a set-off against the debt for the price. The same issue may arise in the context of a prior contract for the performance of work. If the trustee or the liquidator decides to complete the contract because it is profitable and performs the work, the question may arise whether the resulting payment obligation may be the subject of a set-off.

13.38   The argument in favour of a set-off is as follows. A debt which arises in favour of a bankrupt or a company in liquidation after the bankruptcy or the liquidation but pursuant to a prior contract is capable of being employed in a set-off.[176] The debt for the price is a natural result of the prior transaction and so it should be a case of giving credit for the purpose of the set-off section,[177] though in any event the debt is a money demand arising out of a prior dealing between the parties to the proposed set-off and on general principles it should be available for a set-off on that ground.[178] Further, the requirement of mutuality *prima facie* should be satisfied. For mutuality, the cross-demands must be between the same parties and they must be held in the same right and interest[179] The fact that a debt for the price first arises after the bankruptcy or liquidation by itself should not affect mutuality, notwithstanding

---

[172] [1910] 2 KB 562.
[173] [2001] BCC 27.
[174] See [2001] BCC 27 at [61] and [62].
[175] Pursuant to the Insolvency Act 1986, s. 315 or, for company liquidation, s. 178. As to set-off consequent upon a disclaimer, see *Re Anderson* [1924] NZLR 1163.
[176] See paras 8.35–8.46 above.
[177] See para. 7.04 above.
[178] See paras 7.07–7.10 above.
[179] See para. 11.01 above.

that the debt from the time that it accrued would have been vested in the trustee or, in the case of a company liquidation in which there is no *cessio bonorum*, notwithstanding that the company itself would never have had a beneficial interest in the accrued debt.[180] The critical point is that the debt arose out of a prior contract between the parties to the proposed set-off, and mutuality *prima facie* should be satisfied as at the relevant date for determining rights of set-off in relation to that debt and a cross-claim between the parties.[181] As Dixon J expressed the principle in the High Court of Australia in *Hiley v The Peoples Prudential Assurance Co Ltd*:[182]

> It is enough that at the commencement of the winding up mutual dealings exist which involve rights and obligations of such a nature that afterwards in the events that happen they mature or develop into pecuniary demands capable of set-off. If the end contemplated by the transaction is a claim sounding in money so that, in the phrase employed in the cases, it is commensurable with the cross-demand, no more is required than that at the commencement of the winding up liabilities shall have been contracted by the company and the other party respectively from which cross money claims accrue during the course of the winding up . . .

Nevertheless, the decision of Watkin Williams J in *Ince Hall Rolling Mills Co Ltd v The Douglas Forge Co*[183] stands as authority against the availability of a set-off.

The Ince Hall *case*

The *Ince Hall* case concerned a contract for the sale of a quantity of unascertained goods, where the contract was entered into before the liquidation of the supplier. After the liquidation the liquidator was authorized by the court to carry on the business for the purpose of winding up the company, whereupon the liquidator determined to complete the contract and to deliver the goods contracted for. Payment did not take place upon delivery, and when the liquidator subsequently sued for the price the purchaser sought to set off a separate debt owing to it by the company. Watkin Williams J held that the debt for the price could not be the subject of a set-off. He said that there was a lack of mutuality, the reason being that, when a company completes a transaction after the commencement of its liquidation, albeit pursuant to a prior contract, it does so in a new interest and a new capacity:[184]

13.39

> Every transaction entered into by the company from [the commencement of liquidation] is void unless sanctioned by the Court; no contracts can be executed nor can the business of the company be carried on in a single particular except for the purposes of winding-up and for the benefit of the creditors, and, although the company continues in existence and under the same name, and may, if allowed by the Court, continue to carry on its business and enter into or complete transactions, it does so in a new interest and a new capacity, and solely for the purpose of winding-up its affairs in the interest of its creditors and shareholders . . . The practical

---

[180] See para. 13.05 above. A different view has been adopted in Australia, that liquidation does not deprive a company of the beneficial title to its assets. See para. 13.06 above, referring to *FCT v Linter Textiles Australia Ltd* (2005) 220 CLR 592. On that basis, lack of mutuality is even less likely to be an objection in Australia in company liquidation.

[181] This is implicit in the cases referred to in paras 8.36–8.46 above.

[182] (1938) 60 CLR 468, 497. This has since been accepted as a correct statement of the law. See *Re Charge Card Services Ltd* [1987] 1 Ch 150, 178 (Millett J); *Gye v McIntyre* (1991) 171 CLR 609, 624; *Old Style Confections Pty Ltd v Microbyte Investments Pty Ltd* [1995] 2 VR 457, 463, 464 (Hayne J).

[183] (1882) 8 QBD 179.

[184] (1882) 8 QBD 179, 184.

effect of the defendants' contention would be that the company by a transaction which is void, unless sanctioned and ratified by the Court, would be paying one creditor in full out of the assets of the insolvent company in preference to the other creditors; such a result may well make one pause before giving effect to such a contention.

Criticism of Ince Hall

13.40   If goods are supplied to a purchaser pursuant to a contract entered into before the supplier's liquidation, the purchaser may ask why the fact that delivery takes place after liquidation rather than before should affect his or her position. A debt for the price arises upon delivery, and the question whether delivery will occur is in the hands of the supplier's liquidator, not the purchaser. If the liquidator, instead, had disclaimed the contract, the resulting damages claim against the company would have been a provable debt in the liquidation,[185] and similarly it would have been able to be the subject of a set-off.[186]

13.41   The decision in the *Ince Hall* case nevertheless has been referred to in later cases, generally without criticism.[187] Moreover, an explanation that has been suggested for the decision of the Court of Appeal in *Re A Debtor (No. 66 of 1955)*[188] would support the *Ince Hall* case, at least in the context of bankruptcy.[189] In *Re A Debtor (No. 66 of 1955)*, a surety's trustee in bankruptcy paid the creditor under the guarantee in order to obtain the release of security given to the creditor, and it was held that the surety's resulting claim for an indemnity from the debtor could not be the subject of a set-off in the surety's bankruptcy. The ostensible reason for the decision was that at the relevant date for determining rights of set-off[190] the surety merely had a contingent right to an indemnity, the creditor not having been paid at that date, and it was not considered to be possible to base a set-off upon a claim that was merely contingent, and consequently not due, at that date. The decision on that ground can no longer be supported.[191] Nevertheless, in *Secretary of State for Trade and Industry v Frid*,[192] Lord Hoffmann, in a judgment with which the other members of the House agreed,[193] referred to a justification suggested by Danckwerts J in the Divisional Court

---

[185] See the Insolvency Act 1986, s. 178(6). The equivalent provision for bankruptcy is s. 315(5).

[186] See para. 13.34 above. In the converse case of a company which failed to purchase goods after its liquidation notwithstanding a prior agreement to do so, it was held that the resulting damages claim against the company could be set off. See *Telsen Electric Co Ltd v J J Eastick & Sons* [1936] 3 All ER 266.

[187] *Ince Hall* was referred to with evident approval by the Western Australian Supreme Court in *Re The West Australian Lighterage, Stevedoring and Transport Co Ltd* (1903) 5 WAR 132, 138. Further, the New South Wales Court of Appeal in *Central Brake Service (Sydney) Ltd v Central Brake Service (Newcastle) Ltd* (1992) 27 NSWLR 406, 409 noted the decision without adverse comment. In *Re Taylor, ex p Norvell* [1910] 1 KB 562, 575 (and see also at 576) Fletcher Moulton J in his dissenting judgment said (without referring to the *Ince Hall* case) that 'it cannot be doubted' that a trustee in bankruptcy electing to perform a prior contract to sell goods would be entitled to be paid the price in cash and not by a set-off. On the other hand, Hayne J in *Old Style Confections Pty Ltd v Microbyte Investments Pty Ltd* [1995] 2 VR 457, 462–3, 464 left open the question whether the *Ince Hall* case was correctly decided.

[188] [1956] 1 WLR 1226. See paras 8.20 and 8.42–8.43 above.

[189] But see para. 13.56 below.

[190] The date of the receiving order. See para. 6.43 above.

[191] See paras 8.22 and 8.42 above.

[192] [2004] 2 AC 506 at [15]–[16].

[193] Lord Nicholls of Birkenhead, Lord Hope of Craighead, Lord Phillips of Worth Matravers and Lord Brown of Eaton-under-Heywood.

in *Re A Debtor (No. 66 of 1955)*[194] for the denial of a set-off in that case. Danckwerts J reasoned that a debt only became due from the debtor after the relevant date for determining rights of set-off in the surety's bankruptcy, by payment to the creditor. That payment was not made by the surety but by the trustee in bankruptcy, out of assets that were no longer vested in the surety but in the trustee for the benefit of creditors. There was no mutuality at the relevant date and the debt on which the action was founded was not due to the surety but to the trustee. Lord Hoffmann said that he found Danckwerts J's reasoning 'convincing', though declining to express a concluded view on the subject. Earlier, Gibbs CJ in the High Court of Australia in *Day & Dent Constructions Pty Ltd v North Australian Properties Pty Ltd*[195] had suggested (similarly without deciding) that the fact that the surety in *Re A Debtor (No. 66 of 1955)* was bankrupt, and the payments were made by the trustee to enable him to obtain the bankrupt's property, may justify a conclusion that there were no mutual dealings between the trustee and the debtor.

The comments of Lord Hoffmann and Gibbs CJ were made in the context of bankruptcy, **13.42** where the assets of a bankrupt vest in the trustee. The *Ince Hall* case, on the other hand, concerned a company liquidation. Unlike in bankruptcy, company liquidation does not generally result in a *cessio bonorum* in favour of the liquidator.[196] Nevertheless, Philip Wood[197] has sought to explain the *Ince Hall* case on the basis of a suggested general principle applicable to both bankruptcy and company liquidation, that if an insolvency representative 'earns' a payment under a contract by the use of the insolvent's assets, e.g. by delivering property or performing work or continuing a lease of the insolvent's property, the price or the rent which is then earned is non-mutual with a separate debt of the insolvent, and so it is not available for a set-off. The reason for this is said to be that the assets of the estate available for distribution generally in effect would be used to pay one creditor in full. The insolvent would be divested of the assets used to perform the contract, and the estate would also lose the entitlement to the price or the rent as a result of the set-off.

A number of points can be made in relation to those views. **13.43**

In the first place, the lease cases to which Wood referred[198] in support of the suggested **13.44** general proposition were concerned with bankruptcies, and in that context the denial of a set-off in respect of post-insolvency rent where the landlord had become bankrupt is explicable on the basis that the land had vested in the trustee who accordingly had become the new landlord.[199]

Secondly, in the context of company liquidation, the denial of a set-off in the *Ince Hall* **13.45** case gives rise to difficulty when considered in light of other cases.[200]

---

[194] [1956] 1 WLR 480, 487.
[195] (1982) 150 CLR 85, 94.
[196] See para. 13.05 above.
[197] Wood, *English and International Set-off* (1989), 326, 329.
[198] Wood, *English and International Set-off* (1989), 342–4.
[199] See paras 13.64–13.68 below.
[200] In addition to the following cases, see *Old Style Confections Pty Ltd v Microbyte Investments Pty Ltd* [1995] 2 VR 457 (Hayne J), which suggests that it is not an objection to a set-off that a post liquidation payment obligation was 'earned' by the use of the company's property after the liquidation. See para. 13.72 below.

13.46   One such case is *Hiley v The Peoples Prudential Assurance Co Ltd*,[201] a decision of the High Court of Australia. It concerned a policy-holder in a life insurance company who had borrowed money from the company secured by a mortgage over property. The company then transferred the mortgage, including the policy-holder's debt, to an assignee by way of security. After the company went into liquidation, the liquidator redeemed the mortgage, whereupon it was held[202] that the policy-holder could employ the debt in a set-off in the liquidation. The redemption of the security occurred as a result of a compromise of rights involving the life company and the assignee,[203] but the tenor of the judgments suggests that the same result would have followed if the redemption had occurred as a result of a payment of money by the liquidator.[204] In the case of a payment of money the liquidator would have used the company's funds to redeem the mortgage, and in the case of the compromise an asset of the company, or at least a potential asset, in the form of the compromised rights was used for that purpose. But that circumstance was not regarded as fatal to a set-off. While the compromise was not with the person claiming the benefit of the set-off, looked at from the perspective of a liquidator, who used an asset which was otherwise potentially available for the benefit of creditors generally, that factor should not be significant.

13.47   The *Ince Hall* case is also difficult to reconcile with *Re Asphaltic Wood Pavement Co. Lee & Chapman's Case*.[205] *Lee & Chapman's Case* concerned a contract for the performance of work.[206] A company had contracted with the Commissioners of Sewers to pave a street for a stated price. In addition the contract provided that, if within two years following completion the Commissioners by notice in writing to the company should so require, the company had to keep the road in repair for a period of fifteen years, for which the company was to be paid at a fixed annual rate. The company went into liquidation before the completion of the work. The liquidator was empowered by the court to complete the contract, and for that purpose to expend all necessary moneys for wages, materials and incidental expenses, which he duly did.[207] On the other hand, given the liquidation, the company was not in

---

[201] (1938) 60 CLR 468.

[202] Rich, Starke and Dixon JJ, Latham CJ dissenting.

[203] A number of mortgages had been transferred by way of security to the assignee. The liquidator alleged that the transfers were void and sought declarations to that effect. The dispute was compromised on the basis that some of the disputed mortgages, including Hiley's, would be transferred back to the company and the remainder would be retained by the assignee as its absolute property.

[204] See e.g. Rich J's general reference (at 489) to the liquidator, without any new transaction, having managed to get rid of the encumbrance and to reduce the mortgage into the company's possession, Starke J's reference to payment at 491, and Dixon J's reference (at 499) to the liquidator clearing off the encumbrance and (at 505) to redemption of the mortgages.

[205] (1885) 30 Ch D 216, referred to with evident approval in *Hiley v The Peoples Prudential Assurance Co Ltd* (1938) 60 CLR 468, 497–8 (Dixon J).

[206] In relation to contracts for the performance of work, compare Wood, *English and International Set-off* (1989), 336. As Wood noted, *Alloway v Steere* (1882) 10 QBD 22 was concerned with a lease, for which special considerations apply. See para. 13.65 below.

[207] The contract was entered into on 22 September 1882. On 9 December 1882 the company presented a petition for a winding-up order, and by orders made on 12 and 16 December 1882 the provisional official liquidator appointed to the company was empowered to complete the contract. On 13 January 1883 the company was ordered to be wound up, and on 29 January the official liquidator, having completed the work, forwarded an account to the Commissioners. On 8 March 1883 the Commissioners' engineer certified that the work was complete. On 25 May 1883 the Commissioners served the company with a formal notice that they required the company to repair and maintain the street for the further period of fifteen years.

a position to fulfil its obligation to repair for the fifteen-year period, the Commissioners having served the requisite notice. Prior to the liquidation the company had granted a charge to a third party which encompassed part of the moneys payable under the contract, but the Court of Appeal[208] held that the residue of the contract sum owing by the Commissioners could be set off against the Commissioners' claim for damages for anticipatory breach of contract arising from failure to keep the road in repair for fifteen years. This was so notwithstanding that the Commissioners' debt to the company for the price only arose after the liquidation when the work was completed. The company's money would have been used after the liquidation to complete the contract for the benefit of the company's creditors, in buying materials, paying wages etc, and in that sense *Lee & Chapman's Case* is similar to the *Ince Hall* case. Yet a set-off was allowed. The *Ince Hall* case was mentioned in argument before the Court of Appeal, but Brett LJ responded that the decision in that case had no bearing upon the case before him.[209] It is not clear what he meant by that. It is true that in *Lee & Chapman's Case* a great part of the work had been completed before the liquidation, whereas in the *Ince Hall* case performance by the company occurred entirely after the liquidation. However, to the extent that the company's funds were expended after the liquidation, and the expenditure of those funds was necessary in order for the company's creditors to obtain the benefit of the contract,[210] the cases would appear to be similar.[211]

In *Lee & Chapman's Case*, the Commissioners' claim was based upon a breach by the company of an obligation that arose out of the same contract as the Commissioners' liability to pay the contract sum, and for that reason Wood has suggested that the set-off enforced in *Lee & Chapman's Case* is an example of an equitable (or a transaction) set-off, as opposed to a set-off under the bankruptcy legislation.[212] Nevertheless, equitable set-off was not mentioned in any of the judgments. The only right of set-off that was discussed was the right arising under the mutual credit provision in the bankruptcy legislation,[213] and it is clear that this was the form of set-off that was considered to be in issue. In other words, it must have been accepted that there was mutuality for the purpose of the bankruptcy set-off section, even though the contract was completed after the liquidation for the benefit of creditors. **13.48**

Given that *Lee & Chapman's Case* in truth was concerned with insolvency set-off, is there a satisfactory basis for distinguishing it from the *Ince Hall* case? In each case a claim accrued to a company after the commencement of its liquidation as a result of the use by the liquidator of the company's assets or funds. In the *Ince Hall* case, the person liable on **13.49**

---

[208] Brett MR, Cotton and Lindley LJJ.

[209] (1885) 30 Ch D 216, 219.

[210] See Bacon VC at first instance (1884) 26 Ch D 624, 634.

[211] Indeed, the analysis of Watkin Williams J in the *Ince Hall* case in relation to the question of mutuality is at odds with the tenor of Cotton LJ's judgment in *Lee & Chapman's Case* (1885) 30 Ch D 216, 224 (and see also Brett MR at 220), although the context admittedly was different. In *Old Style Confections Pty Ltd v Microbyte Investments Pty Ltd* [1995] 2 VR 457, 462 Hayne J commented that the *Ince Hall* case 'may well be said' to be inconsistent with *Lee & Chapman's Case*, but without deciding the point. In relation to the *Old Style Confections* case, see para. 13.72 below.

[212] Wood, *English and International Set-off* (1989), 331, 337.

[213] See, in particular, (1885) 30 Ch D 216, 222 (Brett MR), 224 (Cotton LJ), referring to the Bankruptcy Act 1869, s. 39.

the claim was the direct recipient of property of the company that would otherwise have been available for distribution generally, whereas in *Lee & Chapman's Case* the company's funds would have been remitted to third parties (suppliers of materials, employees receiving wages etc). But that distinction is insubstantial.[214] In *Lee & Chapman's Case* the party claiming the set-off nevertheless benefited directly from the performance of the contract. In both cases, the person asserting a set-off against the debt to the company arising from performance of the contract received full consideration for the debt, in the *Ince Hall* case as a result of the delivery of the goods the subject of the contract of sale, and in *Lee & Chapman's Case* by reason of the street having been paved. But the circumstance that full consideration has been received is not a reason for denying a set-off. It has never been a principle of insolvency set-off that a person indebted to a bankrupt or a company in liquidation should be precluded from employing the debt in a set-off if that person otherwise had received full consideration from the bankrupt or the company. This is apparent from cases in which goods were delivered by a vendor to a purchaser on credit terms before the vendor became bankrupt, and the price was not payable until after the bankruptcy. It was held in those cases that the purchaser was entitled to a set-off against the price even though the purchaser already had the goods.[215] Indeed, in the case of a loan the borrower receives full consideration, in the form of the money the subject of the loan, and is not precluded by that fact from subsequently asserting the debt in a set-off.

13.50 **Receivership.**   The *Ince Hall* case also produces a different result to that which applies in a receivership, as a consequence of the decision of the Court of Appeal in *Rother Iron Works Ltd v Canterbury Precision Engineers Ltd*.[216] Apart from the fact that *Ince Hall v Douglas Forge Co* concerned a liquidation and *Rother Iron Works v Canterbury Precision Engineers* a receivership, the similarity between the cases is striking. In both cases a company had contracted to sell goods to a person who was a creditor on another transaction. The purchaser became indebted for the price when the goods were delivered, which in each case occurred after the relevant event (liquidation in the *Ince Hall* case, and receivership in the *Rother Iron Works* case). Yet, while a set-off was denied in *Ince Hall v Douglas Forge Co*, the purchaser in *Rother Iron Works v Canterbury Precision Engineers* was permitted to set off the debt for the price against a prior cross-debt owing by the company. Russell LJ in the *Rother Iron Works* case referred to the *Ince Hall* case, but distinguished it on the ground that the liquidation of a company produces a vital change in the status of the company and does not operate only as an equitable assignment by way of charge. It is undoubtedly true that liquidation and receivership are different, and it is also true that different set-off rules apply in each case,[217] but there is nevertheless some similarity between them. When the

---

[214] See the similar point made in para. 13.46 above in relation to *Hiley v The Peoples Prudential Assurance Co Ltd* (1938) 60 CLR 468.

[215] *Smith v Hodson* (1791) 4 TR 211, 100 ER 979; *Groom v West* (1838) 8 Ad & E 758, 112 ER 1025 (in which it was specifically argued, unsuccessfully, that a set-off should be denied because the purchaser already had the goods); *Gibson v Bell* (1835) 1 Bing (NC) 743, 131 ER 1303; *Russell v Bell* (1841) 8 M & W 277, 151 ER 1042.

[216] [1974] 1 QB 1. See para. 17.109 below.

[217] As Templeman J noted in *Business Computers Ltd v Anglo-African Leasing Ltd* [1977] 1 WLR 578, 585. The insolvency set-off section applies in a liquidation, whereas in receivership rights of set-off are governed by the Statutes of Set-off and the principles of equitable set-off. See paras 17.99–17.118 below.

floating charge crystallized in the *Rother Iron Works* case, the goods which were later sold became subject to a fixed charge in favour of the secured creditor, and were set aside to satisfy the debt owing to the creditor. Similarly, the view of English courts is that a winding up divests the company of the beneficial title to its assets, which are collected and applied in the first instance for the benefit of creditors in discharge of the company's debts.[218] In both cases, then, the company was not the full beneficial owner of the goods delivered. There are indications that Russell LJ was not comfortable with the decision in the *Ince Hall* case. In response to the argument that the allowance of a set-off in the *Rother Iron Works* case would produce an illogical distinction between liquidation and receivership, his Lordship remarked that he was 'not satisfied that the *Ince Hall* case does necessarily show such an illogical distinction',[219] which is not a particularly confident assertion as to the perceived differences between the two cases. Moreover, as an alternative basis for distinguishing the earlier case, Russell LJ referred to a statement by Lindley LJ in *Mersey Steel & Iron Co v Naylor, Benzon & Co*[220] to the effect that *Ince Hall v Douglas Forge Co* was a case where the liquidator, after the winding up had commenced, entered into a new contract. In fact this is not a proper interpretation of the *Ince Hall* case, because Watkin Williams J in that case proceeded on the basis that the goods were supplied after the liquidation in execution of a contract entered into by the company before then.[221]

Assignment of future business receipts.   There is a line of cases which, it has been   **13.51**
suggested,[222] is consistent with the decision in the *Ince Hall* case. The cases established the principle that an assignment by a trader of the future receipts of his or her business is, as regards receipts which accrue after the commencement of the trader's bankruptcy, inoperative as against the title of the trustee in bankruptcy.[223] The basis of the principle, as explained by Lord Esher MR in *Re Davis & Co, ex p Rawlings*,[224] is that the payments:

> would only arise in case the business of the bankrupts should be carried on, and in case, by reason of its being carried on, payments should be made to the person who was carrying it on. If the business was being carried on by the trustee the payments would never become due to the bankrupts, they would become due to the trustee.

---

[218] *Ayerst v C & K (Construction) Ltd* [1976] AC 167. A different view has been adopted in Australia, that a company upon going into liquidation does not cease to have the beneficial title to its assets. See para. 13.06 above. On that approach, the *Ince Hall* case should have even less merit in company liquidation in Australia than in England.

[219] [1974] 1 QB 1, 5 (emphasis added).

[220] (1882) 9 QBD 648, 669.

[221] See the question framed by Watkin Williams J in the opening paragraph of his judgment at (1882) 8 QBD 179.

[222] See Wood, *English and International Set-off* (1989), 326, 334–6.

[223] *Ex p Nichols, re Jones* (1883) 22 Ch D 782; *Wilmot v Alton* [1897] 1 QB 17; *Re Irvine* [1919] NZLR 351; *Re Collins* [1925] Ch 556. Compare *Drew & Co v Josolyne* (1887) 18 QBD 590, *Official Assignee of Palmer v Sharpe* [1921] NZLR 460 and *Re Tout and Finch Ltd* [1954] 1 WLR 178, in which the debt assigned represented retention moneys already earned but not yet payable at the date of the bankruptcy or liquidation. Similarly, in *Re Davis & Co*, ex p *Rawlings* (1888) 22 QBD 193 and *Ex p Moss, re Toward* (1884) 14 QBD 310 the debt assigned was in existence at the date of the bankruptcy although not payable until a future date, and so the title of the assignee took precedence over that of the trustee in bankruptcy.

[224] (1888) 22 QBD 193, 198. See also *Ex p Nicholls, re Jones* (1883) 22 Ch D 782, 785–6 (Jessel MR); *Re Green* [1979] 1 WLR 1211, 1220–1.

Since payments arising from the carrying on of the business after bankruptcy do not become due to the bankrupt, they cannot be assigned before the bankruptcy so as to defeat the trustee's title. The earnings received as a result of the trustee operating the business after the bankruptcy are regarded as the earnings of the trustee, not the bankrupt.[225]

13.52 The trustee's title to receipts is readily apparent when the trustee in carrying on the business enters into new contracts,[226] and it is clear that sums payable under those contracts could not be set off in the bankruptcy against debts owing by the bankrupt. But what if the trustee simply performs a contract made with the bankrupt prior to the bankruptcy? The courts have accepted that the principle applies in that circumstance.[227] The contract receipts are regarded as having been earned by the trustee in carrying out the contract. However, the question of set-off raises a different issue.[228] Though the contract is performed by the trustee, the receipts still arise out of the bankrupt's contract, and an action to enforce payment would be based on that contract. This is critical for insolvency set-off, which is concerned with debts and credits and claims arising from mutual dealings.[229] A debt which accrues after a bankruptcy, but which relates to a prior contract with the bankrupt, arises out of a prior dealing with the bankrupt, and claims arising from prior mutual dealings give rise to an equity pursuant to the insolvency set-off section to which the bankrupts' trustee takes subject. As Dixon J in the Australian High Court expressed the principle in *Hiley v Peoples Prudential Assurance Co*[230] in the context of company liquidation: 'If the end contemplated by the transaction is a claim sounding in money . . . *no more is required* than that at the commencement of the winding up liabilities shall have been contracted by the company and the other party respectively from which cross money claims accrue during the course of the winding up.'

---

[225] *Re Green* [1979] 1 WLR 1211, 1223–4; *Official Assignee of Palmer v Sharpe* [1921] NZLR 460, 462.

[226] See e.g. *Ex p Moss, re Toward* (1884) 14 QBD D 310, 316–17.

[227] *Wilmot v Alton* [1897] 1 QB 17; *Re Collins* [1925] 1 Ch 556. The principle does not apply, however, where the bankrupt had wholly executed his or her part of the contract before the bankruptcy, so that nothing by way of further performance was required of the bankrupt. See *Wilmot v Alton* at 22–3 (Rigby LJ); *Re Trytel* [1952] 2 TLR 32.

[228] A security granted by a company over its present and future assets does not catch a right to recover a preferential payment, a proposition that was referred to earlier as indicating a lack of mutuality in equity in relation to the right of recovery and a debt owing by the company to the preferred creditor. See paras 13.08 and 13.16 above. That situation differs, however, from the principle applicable in the case of business receipts after bankruptcy. In the case of a preference, the statutory right to recover is given for the benefit of the general body of creditors, and not for the benefit of the company itself. See *Re M. C. Bacon Ltd* [1991] Ch 127, 137 (Millett J). On the other hand, when a bankrupt prior to the bankruptcy entered into a contract which produces business receipts after bankruptcy, the bankrupt would have entered into it for his or her own benefit. Further, a right to recover a preference in its nature is such that it cannot be charged. Business receipts, on the other hand, are capable of being charged; it is only in the situation in which the trader becomes bankrupt that the charge is ineffective as against the title of the trustee in bankruptcy.

[229] See also the cases in which a claim in favour of a bankrupt's estate which was contingent at the date of the bankruptcy but which subsequently vested was held to give rise to a set-off. See paras 8.36–8.46 above.

[230] (1938) 60 CLR 468, 497 (emphasis added), referred to with approval in *Re Charge Card Services Ltd* [1987] 1 Ch 150, 178 (Millett J) and *Gye v McIntyre* (1991) 171 CLR 609, 624. In *Old Style Confections Pty Ltd v Microbyte Investments Pty Ltd* [1995] 2 VR 457, 463 Hayne J said that: 'the mere fact that performance of the contract made before liquidation may not take place until after liquidation does not determine whether the debt due under that contract may be set-off against other dealings with the company.'

The view that the cases concerning assignments of future business receipts do not impact **13.53** upon rights of set-off is suggested by *Lee & Chapman's Case*.[231] The Court of Appeal in that case upheld a set-off in the liquidation of a company in respect of a claim that accrued after the commencement of the liquidation but pursuant to a prior contract, as a result of the liquidator having carried on the company's business. Lindley LJ was one of the judges in the Court of Appeal in that case. Two years earlier he was also one of the judges in the Court of Appeal in *Ex p Nichols*[232] who had upheld the principle applicable to assignments of future business receipts after bankruptcy, and yet he appears not to have regarded that case as deserving mention when, along with Brett MR and Cotton LJ, he upheld the claim for a set-off in *Lee & Chapman's Case*. Further, when the Court of Appeal in *Wilmot v Alton*[233] subsequently followed *Ex p Nichols*, Brett MR, who by then was Lord Esher MR, seemingly did not consider it necessary to explain his earlier judgment in *Lee & Chapman's Case*. This suggests that the principle relating to assignments of future business receipts was not regarded as relevant to the question of set-off.

A possible explanation for *Lee & Chapman's Case* is that the assignment principle does not **13.54** apply in the case of a company liquidation,[234] although it has been assumed otherwise.[235] In *Re Green*[236] Walton J explained the principle on the ground that, in a bankruptcy, the business and its profit-making apparatus vest in the trustee,[237] so that when profits from carrying on the business arise they are profits of a business vested in the trustee. In a company liquidation, on the other hand, the assets of the company ordinarily do not vest in the liquidator.[238] But distinguishing *Lee & Chapman's Case* on that basis would not assist in explaining the *Ince Hall* case, since that case also concerned a company liquidation.

In any event, set-off and the principle which impacts upon an assignment of business **13.55** receipts after bankruptcy attract different considerations. In the latter case, when a person in the course of his or her business enters into a contract which requires performance in the future, and the person becomes bankrupt before the contract has been performed, the trustee in bankruptcy, if he or she regards it as being for the benefit of the estate, may

---

[231] *Re Asphaltic Wood Pavement Co. Lee & Chapman's Case* (1885) 30 Ch D 216 (see para. 13.47 above), referred to with evident approval in *Hiley v The Peoples Prudential Assurance Co Ltd* (1938) 60 CLR 468, 497–8 (Dixon J). See also *Clarke v Fell* (1833) 4 B & Ad 404, 110 ER 507, in which the bankrupt completed the repairs to the carriage after the bankruptcy, and the tenor of the judgments suggests that a set-off would have been allowed to the owner of the carriage against the cost of the repairs but for the agreement to pay in ready money.

[232] *Ex p Nichols, re Jones* (1883) 22 Ch D 782.

[233] [1897] 1 QB 17.

[234] *Lee & Chapman's Case* itself lends support to that view. Ninety per cent of the earnings under the contract in that case had been charged to a third party, so that the set-off only related to the ten per cent to which the company itself remained entitled. Not only was the set-off upheld, but the charge was also regarded as effective notwithstanding that the contract was completed after liquidation.

[235] See Wynn-Parry J in *Re Tout and Finch Ltd* [1954] 1 WLR 178, 186–9 (although in the circumstances the assignment principle was held not to apply because the retention moneys had been earned before the liquidation, notwithstanding that they were not payable until later), and Goode, *Principles of Corporate Insolvency Law* (3rd edn, 2005), 163–4.

[236] [1979] 1 WLR 1211, 1220–1, 1224.

[237] Thus, Walton J held in *Re Green* that the principle does not apply to an assignment of the future personal earnings of a bankrupt.

[238] See para. 13.05 above.

perform the contract. But the trustee is not obliged to do so. The trustee could decide not to perform the contract, in which case nothing would be payable under it to an assignee of business receipts. If, on the other hand, the trustee elects to go on with the contract, the trustee would do so for the benefit of the estate, and under the assignment principle any moneys when they become due would belong to the estate.[239] The assignee once again would not receive anything, so that the assignee is put in the same position in the event that the contract is performed that he or she would have been in if the trustee had decided not to perform the contract. However, this would not reflect the position of a party to a contract with a bankrupt in relation to set-off, if the rule were that that party is denied a set-off in relation to sums payable to the trustee through performance of the contract. This is because, if the trustee had elected not to perform, the other contracting party in that circumstance would have had a provable claim in the bankruptcy for any damage suffered consequent upon the bankrupt's breach of contract, and that claim could have been employed in a set-off.[240] Thus, unlike in the case of the assignment principle, the position in relation to set-off would differ depending on whether or not the trustee performed the contract. There is another point. If a trustee elects to carry on the business after the bankruptcy for the benefit of the estate, but business receipts after the bankruptcy were to go to a prior assignee, the estate would not benefit from the performance. A set-off, on the other hand, would not have that result. If a set-off were allowed it would not be a case of the estate obtaining no benefit from the contract. The contract sum would still enure to the benefit of the estate, although not by way of a cash payment. Rather, payment would be effected by a set-off against a debt which otherwise would have been provable in competition with the other creditors.[241]

Conclusion in relation to the Ince Hall *case*

13.56   Reference was made earlier[242] to views expressed by Lord Hoffmann in the House of Lords and Gibbs CJ in the High Court of Australia in relation to *Re A Debtor (No. 66 of 1955)*,[243] which provide some support for the *Ince Hall* case. They were not expressed as concluded views, however, and there is much to be said for the proposition that a sale of goods by a trustee in bankruptcy or a liquidator pursuant to a prior contract should be capable of giving rise to a set-off against the resulting debt for the price. Performance takes place pursuant to a contract made with the bankrupt or the company before the insolvency administration,[244] and that contract constitutes a prior dealing with the bankrupt or the company for the purpose of the insolvency set-off section. There may therefore be said to be mutuality of dealing in relation to that dealing and a separate dealing between the parties which gives rise to a cross-claim against the insolvent. But in any event, Lord Hoffmann and Gibbs CJ spoke in the context of bankruptcy, where the bankrupt's assets vest in the

---

[239] *Wilmot v Alton* [1897] 1 QB 17, 20–1 (Lord Esher MR), 23 (Rigby LJ).

[240] See para. 13.33 above.

[241] See the comments of Hayne J (in a different context) in *Old Style Confections Pty Ltd v Microbyte Investments Pty Ltd* [1995] 2 VR 457, 466.

[242] See para. 13.41 above.

[243] [1956] 1 WLR 1226.

[244] Compare Lindley LJ's explanation of the *Ince Hall* case in *Mersey Steel and Iron Co v Naylor, Benzon & Co* (1882) 9 QBD 648, 669 (CA). See below.

trustee in bankruptcy. The trustee in that situation uses assets vested in him or her, as opposed to the bankrupt's assets, for the purpose of completing the contract for the benefit of creditors.[245] In company liquidation, on the other hand, there is generally no such transfer of assets. *Hiley's* case and *Lee & Chapman's Case* (above) both support the availability of a set-off in company liquidation in circumstances such as those in issue in the *Ince Hall* case, and the decisions in those cases have not been questioned.[246] Those cases are also consistent with the position which applies in company receivership.[247] If, therefore, the tentative views of Lord Hoffmann and Gibbs CJ are to be adopted, they should be confined to bankruptcy. The *Ince Hall* case, which concerned a company liquidation, should be regarded as wrongly decided.

The relevance of the time that property passed

In the case of a contract for the sale of land or goods where the seller has become insolvent   **13.57**
prior to completion, it has been suggested that the availability of set-off depends upon whether the beneficial ownership of the property in question passed before the insolvency date.[248] A set-off may be available if the beneficial ownership passed before that date, and conversely it is said that a set-off is denied if it had not passed. As authority for the latter proposition, reference is made to the *Ince Hall* case.[249] However, set-off is not concerned with property rights as such, but with money claims arising from the giving of credit or from prior dealings between the parties. The time of passing of the beneficial interest should only be incidentally relevant, in the sense that it can affect the parties' remedies. If the beneficial ownership has already passed, the vendor's trustee in bankruptcy or liquidator could not disclaim the contract.[250] Further, the court ordinarily would order specific performance of the contract on the application of the purchaser, on terms that the purchaser pay the balance of the price after deducting a debt owing by the insolvent vendor.[251] If, on the other hand, the beneficial ownership has not passed, the contract may be able to be disclaimed as an unprofitable contract,[252] in which case it could not be specifically enforced.[253] The purchaser would then be left to his or her remedy in damages, which in

---

[245] *Secretary of State for Trade and Industry v Frid* [2004] 2 AC 506 at [15].

[246] *Hiley v Peoples Prudential Assurance Co* (see para. 13.46 above) was referred to with evident approval in *MS Fashions Ltd v Bank of Credit and Commerce International SA* [1993] Ch 425, 446 (CA). See also, in the Australian High Court, *Day & Dent Constructions Pty Ltd v North Australian Properties Pty Ltd* (1982) 150 CLR 85 and *Gye v McIntyre* (1991) 171 CLR 609, 619, 624. In *Hiley's* case (1938) 60 CLR 468, 497–8, Dixon J accepted the correctness of *Lee & Chapman's Case* (see paras 13.47–13.49 above). *Lee & Chapman's Case* was also cited without criticism by the Court of Appeal in *Sovereign Life Assurance Co v Dodd* [1892] 2 QB 573 and in *Re City Life Assurance Co Ltd. Grandfield's Case* [1926] 1 Ch 191. See also *Secretary of State for Trade and Industry v Frid* [2004] 2 AC 506 at [9] and *Day & Dent Constructions v North Australian Properties* at 104.

[247] See para. 13.50 above.

[248] Wood, *English and International Set-off* (1989), 327–6.

[249] See above.

[250] *Re Bastable, ex p The Trustee* [1901] 2 KB 518.

[251] *Re Taylor, ex p Norvell* [1910] 1 KB 562. See para. 13.36 above.

[252] In determining whether a contract is unprofitable, the availability of a set-off to the other contracting party should not be a relevant consideration. See *Old Style Confections Pty Ltd v Microbyte Investments Pty Ltd* [1995] 2 VR 457, 466–7 (Hayne J) and the general discussion of the power to disclaim in *Re SSSL Realisations (2002) Ltd* [2006] Ch 610 at [33]–[54].

[253] See Jones and Goodhart, *Specific Performance* (2nd edn, 1996), 221.

turn should be able to be the subject of a set-off.[254] But if in a case such as *Ince Hall v Douglas Forge Co*[255] the contract is performed, the availability of a set-off should not be confined to the situation in which the beneficial ownership of the property in question passed to the purchaser prior to the vendor's bankruptcy or liquidation.[256]

(3) Contract to sell property to or to perform work for an insolvent

13.58 The converse of the situation considered above is that the purchaser (as opposed to the seller) of property to be delivered or of work to be performed becomes bankrupt or goes into liquidation before completion of the contract. Once again, if the contract is disclaimed a resulting damages claim would be provable,[257] and it should also be capable of being employed in a set-off.[258] Consider, however, that the contract remains on foot. In the first place, questions of set-off are unlikely to arise in this situation because, in the case of a contract to sell goods, if the purchaser has become insolvent the vendor is entitled to insist that the price be tendered before delivery, even if the sale was otherwise expressed to be on credit terms.[259] A similar principle would appear to apply to contracts for the performance of work.[260] But if in a particular case the goods are delivered without payment having first been received, or the work is performed without the price having first been secured, the better view, for reasons similar to those given above in criticizing the decision in the *Ince Hall* case,[261] is that the resulting debt should be able to be employed in a set-off,[262] given that it resulted from a prior contract and it would be provable in the bankruptcy or the liquidation.

(4) Options

13.59 The preceding discussion concerned the situation in which there is an unconditional contract for the sale of goods or for the performance of work, and bankruptcy or liquidation intervenes before the contract has been performed. Alternatively, a creditor may have an option to purchase the debtor's property, and upon exercise of the option the creditor may wish to set off the resulting debt for the price against the debt owing by the debtor. If the option is exercised before the debtor becomes bankrupt or goes into liquidation there should not be any difficulty. The debt for the price should be capable of giving rise to a set-off against the debt due to the creditor.[263] Consider, however, that the option is not exercised until after the debtor's bankruptcy or liquidation. For the reasons given above

---

[254] See paras 13.33–13.34 above.

[255] See paras 13.37–13.56 above.

[256] The contrary argument is stronger in bankruptcy than in company liquidation. See paras 13.41–13.42 and 13.56 above.

[257] See the Insolvency Act 1986, ss. 178(6) and 315(5).

[258] See paras 13.33–13.34 above.

[259] *Ex p Chalmers* (1873) LR 8 Ch App 289; Sale of Goods Act 1979, s. 41(1)(c).

[260] *Re Sneezum, ex p Davies* (1876) 3 Ch D 463, 473–4.

[261] (1882) 8 QBD 179. See paras 13.37–13.56 above.

[262] Compare Wood, *English and International Set-off* (1989), 308–9.

[263] See e.g. *Shirlaw v Lewis* (1993) 10 ACSR 288, in which the purchase of the goods and stock in trade pursuant to the prior agreement occurred after the winding up summons was filed but before the winding-up order, when the vendor of the business re-took possession, and Hodgson J accepted that it could be the subject of a set-off.

in the context of the discussion of the *Ince Hall* case,[264] the better view is that the circumstance that the property sold pursuant to the option otherwise would have been available for distribution amongst creditors should not suffice to preclude a set-off.[265] Nor should the creditor be denied a set-off simply because he or she will have received full consideration for the debt for the price, in the form of the property the subject of the option.[266] In Australia it has been held that a creditor exercising an option to purchase after the debtor's liquidation may set off the resulting debt for the price against the debtor's indebtedness to the creditor.[267] That view is contrary to two earlier cases, but there are difficulties with the reasoning in those cases.

In *Re Kidsgrove Steel, Iron, and Coal Co*[268] the owner of a colliery and iron works leased them **13.60** to a company, the lease giving the owner the option, after the end or determination of the lease, of purchasing at a valuation all plant and fixtures that might be erected by the company as lessee. The company went into liquidation, after which the lease was determined. The owner thereupon exercised the option to purchase the plant and fixtures erected on the premises. Chitty J held that the resulting debt for the price could not be the subject of a set-off, since the contract to purchase was not in existence at the date of the liquidation. He said that the contract only arose subsequently, when the option was exercised. More recently, the New Zealand Court of Appeal in *Paganini v The Official Assignee*[269] also held against a set-off in similar circumstances, though without referring to *Re Kidsgrove*. The Court of Appeal justified its decision on a number of grounds, but the principal ground was that, since the option was not exercised until after the liquidation of the debtor/vendor, there was not at the date of the liquidation a debt owing to the debtor for the price and nor had the parties at that date engaged in mutual dealings.[270]

---

[264] (1882) 8 QBD 179. See paras 13.37–13.57 above.

[265] The contrary argument may be stronger in bankruptcy than in company liquidation. See paras 13.41–13.42 and 13.56 above.

[266] See para. 13.49 above.

[267] *JLF Bakeries Pty Ltd v Baker's Delight Holdings Ltd* (2007) 64 ACSR 633 at [23]–[31].

[268] (1894) 38 Sol Jo 252.

[269] Unreported, Gault, Thomas and Keith JJ, CA308/98, 22 March 1999, affirming *Paganini v Official Assignee* (1999) 8 NZCLC 261,811. See also *Re Proudfoot* [1961] NZLR 268, 282, referred to in the Court of Appeal in the *Paginini* case at [12]. To the extent that reliance was placed in *Re Proudfoot* (at 282) and the *Paginini* case (at [12]) on *Re A Debtor (No. 66 of 1955)* [1956] 1 WLR 1226, that case has been criticized. See paras 8.20–8.23 above. The *Paganini* case was referred to in *Stotter v Equiticorp Australia Ltd* [2002] 2 NZLR 686 at [39]. For a discussion of the *Paginini* case, see Taylor, 'The year in review – New Zealand insolvency law in 1999' [1999] *Insolvency Law Journal* 212.

[270] See at [13] in the judgment. In addition, Keith J in delivering the judgment of the Court of Appeal referred (at [13]–[17]) to the requirement of mutuality. The essence of the argument was that the debt for the price arose after the liquidation, when the company no longer had the beneficial interest in its property. See para. 13.05 above (but compare para. 13.06 above in relation to Australia). But if the relevant dealing were characterized as the entry into the agreement which gave rise to the option as opposed to the exercise of the option (see below), there would have been mutuality since the dealing was entered into before the liquidation. The Court of Appeal also considered that policy considerations supported its conclusion. See below. At first instance ((1999) 8 NZCLC 261,811) Robertson J relied on the decision of Richmond J in *Felt and Textiles of New Zealand Ltd v R Hubrich Ltd* [1968] NZLR 716. The *Felt and Textiles* case, however, was concerned with set-off under the Statutes of Set-off in the context of a receivership, as opposed to set-off in company liquidation. See para. 17.112 below. The Statutes of Set-off were confined to mutual debts. They did not extend to claims arising out of prior mutual dealings, as in the case of insolvency set-off. In the case of an option, the relevant dealing may be characterized as the entry into the option itself.

13.61 The New Zealand Court of Appeal treated the exercise of the option as the relevant dealing, which occurred after the liquidation. An alternative view is that the dealing was the entry into the contract containing the option before the liquidation. The creditor in exercising the option was simply pursuing rights conferred by the earlier contract, and the exercise of the option itself did not involve a new and independent transaction. In Australia, Dixon J employed similar language in allowing a set-off in *Hiley v Peoples Prudential Assurance Co Ltd*.[271] At the date of the liquidation the debt for the price was contingent upon the option being exercised, but a contingent indebtedness to a company, where the contingency occurs after the company's liquidation, can be the subject of a set-off in the liquidation.[272] In the *Paganini* case the exercise of the option seems to have been regarded as a separate transaction or dealing, notwithstanding that it had its source in an earlier contract. That view also seems to have informed Chitty J's reason for refusing a set-off in *Re Kidsgrove*, that the contract to purchase arose after the date of the liquidation. An option is sometimes described as an irrevocable offer,[273] and on that basis the exercise of the option can be characterized as giving rise to a new contract. But even if that analysis of an option is accepted, that contract is not a new and independent transaction. It is the result of pursuing prior rights granted by the option. This is consistent with the proposition that the grant of an option ordinarily gives rise to an interest in the property the subject of the option[274] (albeit that it does not make the grantor of the option a trustee[275]). In any event, the view that a new contract is formed is not universally accepted. Another analysis has been proposed, that an option is a conditional contract,[276] and on that view the contract of sale would be formed before the debtor's bankruptcy or liquidation.

13.62 It may be sought to justify the decisions in *Re Kidsgrove* and the *Paganini* case on the basis of a perceived policy consideration, that it should not be open to a creditor who holds an option over the debtor's property to improve his or her position at the expense of the other creditors, by choosing to exercise the option after the debtor's bankruptcy or liquidation and then setting off the debt for the price against a debt in respect of which the creditor

---

[271] (1938) 60 CLR 468, 499 ('this was the consequence of pursuing rights subsisting at that time and involved no new and independent transaction'). See also Rich J at 487 ('Rights must be vested in the creditor and in the company which, without any new transaction, grow in the natural course of events into money claims . . .'). In *MS Fashions Ltd v Bank of Credit and Commerce International SA* [1993] Ch 425, 446 Dillon LJ (with whom Nolan and Steyn LJJ agreed) referred to the *Hiley* case with evident approval.

[272] See paras 8.36–8.46 above, and *JLF Bakeries Pty Ltd v Baker's Delight Holdings Ltd* (2007) 64 ACSR 633 at [12]–[31]. Pursuant to the Insolvency Rules 1986, r. 4.90(4) and (5) (and see also r. 2.85(4) and (5) in relation to administration), it is no longer necessary for a set-off, in the case of a contingent liability to a company in liquidation, that the contingency should have occurred. However, the old rules still apply in bankruptcy, and in both bankruptcy and liquidation in Australia. See para. 8.35 above.

[273] *Helby v Mathews* [1895] AC 471, 477 (Lord Herschell LC), 479–80 (Lord Watson).

[274] *London and South Western Railway Co v Gomm* (1882) 20 Ch D 562, 581 (Sir George Jessel MR); *Spiro v Glencrown Properties Ltd* [1991] Ch 537, 543; *Michaels v Harley House (Marleybone) Ltd* [1997] 1 WLR 967, 977. In Australia see *Laybutt v Amoco Australia Pty Ltd* (1974) 132 CLR 57, 75–6; *GPT Re Ltd v Lend Lease Real Estate Investments Ltd* (2005) 12 BPR 23,217 at [51]; Farrands, *The Law of Options and other Pre-Emptive Rights* (2010), 37–48. Compare *Dekala Pty Ltd v Perth Land & Leisure Ltd* (1989) 17 NSWLR 664.

[275] *Michaels v Harley House (Marleybone) Ltd* [1997] 1 WLR 967, 977.

[276] *Griffith v Pelton* [1958] 1 Ch 205, 225; *Laybutt v Amoco Australia Pty Ltd* (1974) 132 CLR 57, 75–6; *JLF Bakeries Pty Ltd v Baker's Delight Holdings Ltd* (2007) 64 ACSR 633 at [20]. In *Spiro v Glencrown Properties Ltd* [1991] Ch 537, 544, Hoffmann J (as he then was) rejected the view that an option strictly speaking is either an offer or a conditional contract, and suggested instead that it is a relationship *sui generis*.

otherwise would only have received a dividend. The creditor has the choice whether to purchase the property the subject of the option, and that choice available to the option-holder distinguishes this situation from the *Ince Hall* case, which was criticized above.[277] In the *Ince Hall* case, it was the vendor's liquidator, rather than the purchaser, who decided to complete the contract. In truth, however, when one considers this perceived policy consideration, it does not provide a compelling reason for denying a set-off. In the first place, if the sale pursuant to the option would be unprofitable for the vendor, the vendor's trustee in bankruptcy or liquidator could disclaim the contract. More importantly, there is no general principle which precludes a creditor from acting in order to bring about a situation in which a set-off would be available in the debtor's bankruptcy or liquidation, save to the extent that the qualification to the insolvency set-off section may apply.[278] Consider in that regard *Re The Moseley Green Coal and Coke Co Ltd. Barrett's Case*.[279] A debt was secured by a promissory note given by the debtor to the creditor and by a guarantee given by a surety. After the debtor had been ordered to be wound up the surety's sister paid the creditor, and the promissory note was indorsed and delivered to her. Subsequently, the sister agreed to hand over the promissory note to the surety in exchange for his own promissory note. Lord Westbury held that the surety could bring the claim on the promissory note into an account with a debt that he owed to the debtor, since his acquisition of the promissory note related to the prior obligation that he had assumed as surety. It appears, however, that the sister was not pressing the surety for reimbursement, and that the arrangement was entered into with the sister at the suggestion of the surety's own legal advisers for the specific purpose of obtaining a set-off for the surety.[280] Consider also *Re Inglis; ex p The Trustee*,[281] a decision of Paine J in the South Australian Insolvency Court. A debtor delivered wheat to the creditor for storage on terms that the creditor had the option of either purchasing the wheat at market price or delivering to the debtor or to his order wheat of the same quality. The debtor became bankrupt after delivering the wheat but before an election was made. Paine J accepted that the creditor could choose to purchase the wheat at market price and thereby obtain a set-off against the resulting debt.

Lee & Chapman's Case[282] is also relevant. The contract in that case provided that the   **13.63**
Commissioners of Sewers could give a notice to the company requiring it to keep the road in repair for a period of fifteen years at a stated price. The notice was given after the company's liquidation, and it was the company's resulting liability for damages to the Commissioners for anticipatory breach of contract in relation to that obligation that was the subject of the set-off. The set-off was allowed notwithstanding that it was the result of the exercise of an option after liquidation. The circumstances admittedly differed from

---

[277] See paras 13.37–13.57 above.
[278] See paras 6.66–6.99 above.
[279] (1865) 4 De G J & S 756, 46 ER 1116, 34 LJ Bcy 41.
[280] See the statement of the facts at (1865) 34 LJ Bcy 41, 42. See also paras 6.105–6.107 above in relation to temporary suspension of mutuality. It has been queried whether the surety's payment to his sister could properly be characterized as a payment under the guarantee, so as to support a set-off. See *Secretary of State for Trade and Industry v Frid* [2004] 2 AC 506 at [12].
[281] (1932) 5 ABC 255.
[282] *Re Asphaltic Wood Pavement Co. Lee & Chapman's Case* (1885) 30 Ch D 216. See para. 13.47 above.

those in *Re Kidsgrove* and the *Paganini* case. In *Lee & Chapman's Case* the party exercising the option was a debtor of the company (for the price of services performed), and it was the claim against the company resulting from the exercise of the option (for damages, for failure to carry out the repair obligation) that was set off against the debt owing to the company. In *Re Kidsgrove* and the *Paganini* case, on the other hand, the option-holder was a creditor. The creditor incurred a debt for the price as a result of exercising the option, and sought to set off that liability against a debt that otherwise would only have yielded a dividend. But that point should not be significant. *Lee & Chapman's Case* suggests that it is not fatal to a set-off that it is based upon the exercise of an option by the party asserting a set-off after the bankruptcy or liquidation of the other party.

D. Leases

(1) Bankruptcy

13.64 Bankruptcy does not result in a vesting of the bankrupt's contracts in the trustee in bankruptcy, but rather a vesting of the bankrupt's rights under the contracts. A contract is still the contract of the bankrupt. Any action by the trustee to obtain a benefit which accrued under the contract prior to the bankruptcy would be an action on the original contract. Similarly, if the trustee decides to carry on the contract after the bankruptcy for the benefit of the estate, then, apart from the possible statutory novation which may be brought about by serving a notice on the trustee requiring the trustee to decide whether or not he or she will disclaim the contract,[283] any rights subsequently obtained or obligations subsequently incurred would still relate to the bankrupt's contract, and any action by or against the estate would be based upon the privity that the bankrupt has in the contract. Mutuality, therefore, should still be present in relation to that claim and a cross-debt arising pursuant to a prior independent dealing between the bankrupt and the other contracting party.[284] A different analysis applies when the relationship between the bankrupt and the other party was that of landlord and tenant. Any claims possessed or liabilities incurred by the bankrupt pursuant to a lease of real property prior to the bankruptcy, whether as landlord or tenant, ordinarily would be capable of giving rise to a set-off as against the other party to the lease.[285] On the other hand, upon the appointment of the trustee in bankruptcy the bankrupt's interest in the land vests in the trustee,[286] and the trustee becomes the landlord or the tenant, as the case may be. The trustee may disclaim the interest under the Insolvency Act, s. 315 as onerous property, in which case the trustee is relieved from personal liability for breach of the terms of the lease as from the commencement of the trusteeship.[287] If, however, the trustee fails to disclaim, any rights or liabilities subsequently obtained or incurred by the trustee under covenants annexed to the land[288] accrue in his or her own

---

[283] Pursuant to the Insolvency Act 1986, s. 316. See para. 13.33 above.

[284] See para. 11.01 above.

[285] See e.g. *Ex p Hope, re Hanson* (1858) 3 De G & J 92, 44 ER 1203, in which a set-off was allowed against rent overdue before the tenants' bankruptcy.

[286] Insolvency Act 1986, s. 306.

[287] See the Insolvency Act 1986, s. 315(3), and in Australia the Bankruptcy Act 1966 (Cth), s. 133(2).

[288] See the Landlord and Tenant (Covenants) Act 1995, s. 3.

right as trustee, *as the landlord or tenant*. This includes, in the case of the landlord, the right to payment of rent. Privity of estate, as opposed to privity of contract, enables the trustee and the other party to enforce *inter se* their rights under the covenants.[289]

Mutuality

When the property of a bankrupt vests in the trustee, so that in the case of a lease the trustee becomes the landlord or the tenant, as the case may be, there is a lack of mutuality between any claim accruing to, or any liability incurred by, the trustee in his or her own right as trustee under a covenant annexed to the land and an independent cross-demand between the bankrupt and the other party to the lease.[290] This is consistent with the principle that, unlike an assignee of a chose in action who sues under the assignor's privity of contract, an assignee of an estate or interest in land who sues does not take subject to personal defences that the defendant would have had against the assignor.[291] For example, in *Alloway v Steere*[292] a debtor was the tenant of a farm. There was a local custom by which the person who was the tenant of farmland was entitled at the expiration of the tenancy to an allowance for any tillages and cultivation. During the currency of the tenancy the debtor instituted proceedings under the Bankruptcy Act 1869 for liquidation of his affairs by arrangement or composition with his creditors, with the result that the tenancy vested in his trustee. When the trustee subsequently claimed the allowance, the landlord was not allowed to set off arrears of rent owing by the debtor from the period before the liquidation proceedings.[293] As Manisty J remarked:[294]

> The relative rights and liabilities of the landlord and the trustee appear clearly from the case of *Titterton v Cooper* ((1882) 9 QBD 473), where the whole question was fully considered, and the conclusion arrived at by the Court of Appeal was that a trustee in bankruptcy, not disclaiming, was in the position of an ordinary assignee of the lease, and as such liable for the rent, and for the performance of the covenants during the time the lease was vested in him. No one could suggest that an ordinary assignee could be made liable for breaches of covenant, or of the contract of tenancy, which occurred before the assignment to him, and the breach of contract in respect of which the landlord claims a set-off in the present case is such a breach.

13.65

---

[289] The covenants which are binding on and which accrue to the benefit of an assignee of the lease or the reversion formerly were limited to those which 'touch and concern' the land, but (subject to s. 3(6)) that limitation no longer applies in relation to new tenancies under the Landlord and Tenant (Covenants) Act 1995. See s. 3, and the definitions of 'landlord covenant' and 'tenant covenant' in s. 28.

[290] While the trustee in bankruptcy of a tenant from the time of the appointment is liable personally on the basis of privity of estate for the payment of rent and the performance of other covenants annexed to the land, he or she usually would be entitled to an indemnity from the estate. See *Lowrey v Barker & Sons* (1880) 5 Ex D 170, 173, 175 and *Titterton v Cooper* (1882) 9 QBD 473, 492, but compare *Re Page Brothers, ex p Mackay* (1884) 14 QBD 401.

[291] *David v Sabin* [1893] 1 Ch 523.

[292] (1882) 10 QBD 22. See also *Ex p Sir W Hart Dyke, re Morrish* (1882) 22 Ch D 410; *Titterton v Cooper* (1882) 9 QBD 473. Compare *Re Wilson, ex p Lord Hastings* (1893) 10 Morr 219, in which Vaughan Williams J found a custom in the county of Norfolk by which the landlord could deduct any arrears of rent, including arrears owing by the bankrupt as a previous tenant, from an allowance payable to the bankrupt's trustee for fixtures, growing crops etc left in the hands of the landlord. A similar custom may exist in a number of other counties. See Williams and Muir Hunter, *The Law and Practice in Bankruptcy* (19th edn, 1979), 198 n 98.

[293] Compare *Ex p Hope, re Hanson* (1858) 3 De G & J 92, 44 ER 1203, in which the assignees in bankruptcy elected not to continue the tenancy.

[294] (1882) 10 QBD 22, 29.

Bankrupt landlord

13.66   Similarly, when the landlord in *Kitchen's Trustee v Madders*[295] became bankrupt, the tenants were not permitted to set off a damages claim against the bankrupt landlord for which they had obtained judgment against their obligation to pay rent to the landlord's trustee in bankruptcy relating to the period after the trustee's appointment.[296]

13.67   The principle applied in *Kitchen's Trustee v Madders* is that a landlord's trustee in bankruptcy is in the same position with regard to the tenant as any other assignee of the property from the landlord, and as such becomes the landlord.[297] This principle was not applied three years later in *Bradley-Hole v Cusen*,[298] but, while that case has enjoyed the support of text-writers,[299] the decision is questionable. The rent paid by the tenant of a dwelling-house to the landlord before the landlord's bankruptcy was greater than the rent lawfully recoverable by the landlord under the Rent Restriction Acts. The legislation conferred upon the tenant the right to recover the overpayment from the landlord who received it, or to deduct it from rent payable by the tenant to the landlord.[300] The issue was whether the deduction could be made from rent payable to the landlord's trustee in bankruptcy for the period after the bankruptcy. Jenkins LJ delivered the judgment of the Court of Appeal. He was prepared to assume, though without finally deciding, that the deduction could not have been made from rent payable to an ordinary assignee of the landlord. He referred, however, to *Bendall v McWhirter*,[301] in which Somervell and Romer LJJ held that a deserted wife had a personal licence to remain in occupation of the matrimonial home owned by the husband, and that the husband's trustee in bankruptcy was no more entitled to revoke this licence than was the husband himself.[302] Jenkins LJ concluded from that decision that a trustee in bankruptcy must be something other than an ordinary assignee, because an ordinary assignee of the husband's property would not have taken subject to the husband's personal obligations. By analogy, he thought that a landlord's trustee should take subject to the tenant's right of deduction in the case before him. Subsequently, the House of Lords in *National Provincial Bank Ltd v Ainsworth*[303] overruled *Bendall v McWhirter*, and in doing so rejected the notion that *Bendall v McWhirter* could be supported on the ground

---

[295] [1950] 1 Ch 134.

[296] See also *Graham v Allsopp* (1848) 3 Ex D 186, 154 ER 809 (in relation to the quarter's rent due after Christmas). Compare *Booth v Hutchinson* (1872) LR 15 Eq 30, in which Sir Richard Malins VC permitted a set-off in respect of rent accruing due after the date of the landlord's deed of assignment, although the question of mutuality appears not to have been considered.

[297] See the discussion of *Kitchen's Trustee v Madders* in *Old Syle Confections Pty Ltd v Microbyte Investments Pty Ltd* [1995] 2 VR 457, 463.

[298] [1953] 1 QB 300.

[299] See Megarry, *The Rent Acts* (10th edn, 1967) vol. 1, 346; *Woodfall's Law of Landlord and Tenant* (loose-leaf edn, 1994) vol. 3, para. 23.004; *Hill and Redman's Law of Landlord and Tenant* (17th edn, 1982) vol. 1, 988; *Halsbury's Laws of England* (4th edn (reissue), 2006) vol. 27(2), 219 para. 903 n 4. The decision was also referred to without adverse comment in *Mulvey v Secretary of State for Social Security* [1997] UKHL 10 and by the Divisional Court in *R (Balding) v Secretary of State for Work and Pensions* [2007] 1 WLR 1805 at [36].

[300] The relevant provision was the Increase of Rent and Mortgage Interest (Restrictions) Act 1920, s. 14(1), which was in similar terms to the Rent Act 1977, ss. 57(1) and (2).

[301] [1952] 2 QB 466.

[302] Lord Denning went further, and said that the deserted wife had an equity which was binding not only on the husband's trustee but also on third parties generally.

[303] [1965] AC 1175.

that a trustee in bankruptcy is in any special position,[304] or that a distinction could be drawn between trustees in bankruptcy on the one hand and purchasers and mortgagees on the other.[305] As Lord Upjohn remarked: 'a trustee in bankruptcy succeeds only to the property of the bankrupt in its then plight and condition and is not concerned with personal rights that do not affect that property.'[306] That effectively rejects the reasoning employed by Jenkins LJ, and so the decision in *Bradley-Hole v Cusen* could only be correct if the deduction could have been made against an ordinary assignee of the landlord. While Lord Wilberforce in *National Provincial Bank v Ainsworth* was prepared to accept that *Bradley-Hole v Cusen* was correctly decided,[307] Jenkins LJ in that case would seem to have been correct in his assumption that an ordinary assignee would not have been so bound, which brings into question the basis for making the deduction from rent payable to the trustee. The definition of 'landlord' in the Rent Restriction Acts,[308] as including any person deriving title under the original landlord, is expressed not to apply when the context requires otherwise. The stipulation in the legislation that the tenant may recover the overpayment from the landlord who received it[309] would seem to indicate that 'landlord' indeed is used in a narrower sense in this context,[310] because a person who derived his or her title from the landlord who received the money would not be the landlord who received it.

It has been suggested that *Bradley-Hole v Cusen* is, in truth, an example of an equitable set-off, and that on that basis it was correctly decided.[311] However, there are two difficulties with that view. The first is that equitable set-off was not mentioned in the judgment. The second is that the demands in any event would not have been sufficiently closely connected to give rise to an equitable set-off.[312] Given that a trustee in bankruptcy is in the same position as any other assignee of the reversion, a claim for rent by an assignee in relation to a period after the assignment would not be impeached, for the purpose of an equitable set-off,[313] by the tenant's claim for an overpayment to the original landlord.[314]

13.68

---

[304] See Lord Hodson at 1226.
[305] See Lord Wilberforce at 1256.
[306] [1965] AC 1175, 1240.
[307] [1965] AC 1175, 1258.
[308] See now the Rent Act 1977, s. 152.
[309] Recovery could also be had from the landlord's personal representative. A personal representative ordinarily means an executor or an administrator (see *Re Best's Settlement Trusts* (1874) LR 18 Eq 686, 691), as opposed to a trustee in bankruptcy.
[310] See *Murray v Webb* (1925) 59 Ir LT 41.
[311] Wood, *English and International Set-off* (1989), 343. Wood uses 'transaction set-off' as a generic term encompassing both equitable set-off and common law abatement.
[312] The suggestion in Wood, *English and International Set-off* (1989), 343, that the set-off in *Booth v Hutchinson* (1872) LR 15 Eq 30 against rent accruing after the deed of assignment similarly may be explained on the basis of equitable set-off, is open to the same objection.
[313] See paras 4.02–4.03 above. Applying the formulation approved by the House of Lords in *Bank of Boston Connecticut v European Grain and Shipping Ltd* [1989] 1 AC 1056 (see para. 4.13 above), the cross-claim could not be said to have arisen out of the same transaction as the trustee's claim for rent due to him or her as an assignee of the reversion.
[314] See the analogous situations in *Reeves v Pope* [1914] 2 KB 284 and *Edlington Properties Ltd v J H Fenner & Co Ltd* [2006] 1 WLR 1583, and the discussion in paras 17.62–17.89 below.

(2) Company liquidation

13.69 In company liquidation, the company's interest in a leasehold property does not vest in the liquidator.[315] If the lease is not disclaimed or otherwise terminated, the company itself remains as the landlord or the tenant, as the case may be, and the concept of privity of estate applicable to trustees in bankruptcy does not apply.[316] Therefore, when the company is the tenant, the landlord cannot proceed against the company's liquidator personally for payment of rent. The landlord may be entitled to be paid in full for rent which has accrued after liquidation as an expense of the liquidation, if the liquidator has retained possession for the benefit of the winding up.[317] But if that is not the case, the landlord's only remedy is to prove in the liquidation.

Extent of the right of proof for rent

13.70 The Insolvency Rules 1986, r. 4.92[318] provides that, in the case of rent and other payments of a periodical nature, the creditor may prove for any amounts due and unpaid up to the date when the company went into liquidation and, where at that date any payment was accruing due, the creditor may prove for so much as would have fallen due at that date, if accruing from day to day.[319] This does not mean that a landlord cannot prove for rent which accrues after the liquidation.[320] The rule is permissive in its operation, not prohibitory. It originally was introduced into the bankruptcy legislation in order to give a landlord a right of proof that he or she did not otherwise have.[321] A provision to this effect first appeared in the Bankruptcy Act 1861.[322] Prior to that Act, a landlord could only prove in the tenant's bankruptcy for rent which had accrued due at the time of the filing of the petition for adjudication. The landlord could not prove for a proportionate part of a payment that had as yet not accrued due. It was in order to remedy that situation that s. 150 of the 1861 Act was introduced, so as to allow a right of proof for a proportionate part of rent and other periodic payments up to the date of adjudication.[323] It is now accepted that, if a lease is not disclaimed or otherwise terminated, the landlord may prove for rent which relates to the period after the bankruptcy or liquidation,[324] but there are conflicting views as to the extent of the right.[325] The preferred approach is that the provisions in the insolvency legislation dealing with estimating the value of contingent and other uncertain claims[326] apply to

---

[315] See para. 13.05 above.

[316] *Old Style Confections Pty Ltd v Microbyte Investments Pty Ltd* [1995] 2 VR 457, 463.

[317] *Re ABC Coupler & Engineering Co Ltd (No. 3)* [1970] 1 WLR 702; *Re Downer Enterprises Ltd* [1974] 1 WLR 1460; *Re H. H. Realisations Ltd* (1975) 31 P & C R 249; *Re Toshoku Finance UK plc* [2002] 1 WLR 671 at [20]–[38] (HL).

[318] In the case of a company in administration, see r. 2.87. The equivalent provision in bankruptcy is set out in r. 6.112.

[319] In Australia, see the Corporations Regulations, reg. 5.6.43(1). For bankruptcy, see the Bankruptcy Act 1966 (Cth), s. 96.

[320] *Re Toshoku Finance UK plc* [2002] 1 WLR 671 at [24]–[25]. In Australia, see the Corporations Regulations, reg. 5.6.43(2). Compare Wood, *English and International Set-off* (1989), 309, 310–11.

[321] See Cotton LJ in *Ex p Dressler, re Solomon* (1878) 9 Ch D 252, 259 in relation to the Bankruptcy Act 1869, s. 35.

[322] Bankruptcy Act 1861, s. 150.

[323] Robson, *A Treatise on the Law of Bankruptcy* (3rd edn, 1876), 260.

[324] In addition to the cases referred to below, see *Re H. H. Realisations Ltd* (1975) 31 P & C R 249.

[325] See the discussion in *Brash Holdings Ltd v Katile Pty Ltd* [1996] 1 VR 24, 35–6.

[326] See the Insolvency Rules 1986, rr. 4.86 (liquidation) and 2.81 (administration). For bankruptcy, see the Insolvency Act 1986, s. 322(3). In Australia, see the Corporations Act 2001 (Cth), s. 554A and the Bankruptcy Act 1966 (Cth), s. 82(4).

a periodical obligation to pay rent, so that an estimate should be made for the purpose of proof of the landlord's loss as a result of the tenant's liquidation and subsequent dissolution.[327] There is an alternative view that, while the landlord is entitled to claim for the whole of the rent to the end of the term, he or she can only prove for rent which in fact has become due and payable.[328] But whatever the extent of the right of proof, a set-off should be available to the landlord in relation to the provable debt and a separate debt owing to the tenant.

Landlord in liquidation

In the situation in which a landlord is a company that has gone into liquidation, and privity **13.71** of estate accordingly is not relevant, it has been suggested that rent payable after the insolvency is not normally available for set-off against a pre-insolvency debt owed by the landlord to the tenant, the reason being that the rent is 'earned' by the landlord's estate and, since it is payable for the benefit of the general body of creditors, there is a lack of mutuality in relation to it and a pre-insolvency debt incurred by the insolvent to the lessee.[329] The better view is that there is no general principle in company liquidation that precludes a set-off when a debt is earned by the use after the liquidation but pursuant to a prior contract of property otherwise available for distribution generally.[330] If privity of estate does not apply, it is difficult to see why rent accruing to a company in liquidation should not be available for a set-off if it arises out of a prior lease, on the basis of the principles referred to below in relation to periodical payments. In the language of Rich J in the High Court of Australia in *Hiley v The Peoples Prudential Assurance Co Ltd*,[331] it is a case where rights are vested in the tenant and in the company which, without any new transaction, grow in the natural course of events into money claims capable of forming items in an account. Dixon J commented in similar terms in that case.[332] In the case of a lease, rent becomes payable without the intervention of a new transaction.

E. Periodical Payment Obligations after Insolvency

A common form of periodical payment obligation is the payment of rent pursuant to a **13.72** lease of land. Set-off in that context was considered above. In the case of periodical payment obligations generally, it is not a sufficient objection that the payment arises after the insolvency of one of the parties. Thus, Hayne J in the Victorian Supreme Court in *Old Style*

---

[327] *Re Lucania Temperance Billboard Halls (London) Ltd* [1966] 1 Ch 98, 106; *James Smith & Sons (Norwood) Ltd v Goodman* [1936] 1 Ch 216; *Lam Soon Australia Pty Ltd v Molit (No. 55) Pty Ltd* (1996) 70 FCR 34, 43–4 (and see also at first instance (1996) 63 FCR 391, 398–401).

[328] *Metropolis Estates Co Ltd v Wilde* [1940] 2 KB 536, 541–2, referring to *Re New Oriental Bank Corporation (No. 2)* [1895] 1 Ch 753; *Re Oak Pitts Colliery Co* (1882) 21 Ch D 322, 329; Williams and Muir Hunter, *The Law and Practice in Bankruptcy* (19th edn, 1979) 154; Hill and Redman's *Law of Landlord and Tenant* (17th edn, 1982) vol. 1, 595; *Buckley on the Companies Act* (14th edn, 1981), vol. 1, 717–18; *Palmer's Company Law* (1997, looseleaf) vol. 4, para. 15.432.

[329] Wood, *English and International Set-off* (1989), 342.

[330] See para. 13.39–13.57 above. See in particular para. 13.56 above in relation to company liquidation.

[331] (1938) 60 CLR 468, 487.

[332] (1938) 60 CLR 468, 499.

Confections Pty Ltd v Microbyte Investments Pty Ltd[333] held that a periodical licence fee accruing to a company after its liquidation pursuant to a prior licence agreement for the use of the company's equipment could be the subject of a set-off. This was on the basis that the post-liquidation licence fee existed as a contingent obligation at the date of the liquidation. Further, the *Old Style Confections* case illustrates that it is not an objection to a set-off that the post-liquidation payment obligations were earned by the use of the company's property after the liquidation, in circumstances where they arose out of a prior contract.[334]

13.73   In the case of a contract providing for periodical payments *by* an insolvent, the insolvency legislation provides that the creditor may prove for any amounts due and unpaid up to the date of the insolvency, and where at that date any payment was accruing due the creditor may prove for so much as would have fallen due if accruing from day to day.[335] In bankruptcy, the date of the insolvency means the date of the bankruptcy order,[336] in company liquidation, the date when the company went into liquidation (or, if the liquidation was immediately preceded by an administration, the date that the company entered administration)[337] and in administration under the English legislation, the date that the company entered administration (or, if the administration was immediately preceded by a winding up, the date that the company went into liquidation).[338] This does not mean that a creditor cannot prove for amounts which become due and payable after that date.[339] The better view is that the provisions of the insolvency legislation which provide for an estimate to be made of the amount of a contingent claim for the purpose of proof[340] apply, and that should also be the case for the purpose of set-off.[341]

13.74   Consider a periodical payment obligation on the other side of the account, being an obligation *to* the insolvent. In bankruptcy, there is no power under the insolvency legislation for a trustee in bankruptcy to estimate the value of a contingent debt owing to the bankrupt. Therefore, a set-off could only occur in bankruptcy in respect of periodical payment amounts that have become presently due.[342] This is also the case in Australia, in both bankruptcy and company liquidation. The position is different under the English legislation in company liquidation and administration. The power of a liquidator or administrator to estimate the value of a contingent or other uncertain claim has been

---

[333] [1995] 2 VR 457.

[334] See also paras 13.39–13.57 above. Compare Wood, *English and International Set-off* (1989), 342 (and see also at 309 and 329).

[335] See the Insolvency Rules 1986, r. 6.112 (bankruptcy), r. 4.92 (company liquidation) and r. 2.87 (administration). In Australia, see the Bankruptcy Act 1966 (Cth), s. 96 (bankruptcy) and the Corporations Regulations, reg. 5.6.43(1).

[336] Insolvency Rules 1986, r. 6.112. In Australia, see the Bankruptcy Act 1966 (Cth), s. 96 and the definition of 'the date of the bankruptcy' in s. 5.

[337] Insolvency Rules 1986, r. 4.92. In Australia, see the Corporations Regulations, reg. 5.6.43(1) (date of the winding-up order or resolution).

[338] Insolvency Rules 1986, r. 2.87.

[339] See para. 13.70 above.

[340] See the Insolvency Rules 1986, rr. 4.86 (liquidation) and 2.81 (administration). For bankruptcy, see the Insolvency Act 1986, s. 322(3). In Australia, see the Corporations Act 2001 (Cth), s. 554A and the Bankruptcy Act 1966 (Cth), s. 82(4).

[341] *Old Style Confections Pty Ltd v Microbyte Investments Pty Ltd* [1995] 2 VR 457.

[342] See paras 8.35 and 8.36 above.

extended to obligations owing to, as well as from, the company.[343] This should apply to periodical payment obligations accruing to the company after commencement of the liquidation or administration.

F. Agency

(1) Introduction

In an agency situation mutuality is generally determined by the principal/third party rela-   **13.75**
tionship, as opposed to that of the agent and the third party. For example, when a bill of exchange is indorsed to an agent for the purpose of collection, the acceptor generally may bring his or her indebtedness on the bill into an account with a cross-claim against the indorser.[344] Conversely, a person holding a bill as agent for another generally cannot employ the bill in a set-off against the agent's separate debt to the acceptor. A similar rule applies when an agent entering into a contract with a third party discloses that he or she is acting on behalf of a principal.[345] The principal is the contracting party, and lack of mutuality would operate to deny the third party a right to set off a debt of the agent to the third party against the third party's payment obligation under the contract to the principal.[346] The same result would often follow in cases where an agent discloses that he or she is acting on behalf of a principal but without disclosing the principal's identity. Depending on the circumstances, the third party in that situation may be regarded as having agreed to treat as a party to the contract anyone on whose behalf the agent may have been authorized to contract,[347] and in an action by the principal the third party could not set off a liability of the agent to him or her.[348]

(2) Set-off agreement between the agent and the third party[349]

An agent may be authorized to receive payment of a sum of money from a third party on   **13.76**
behalf of the principal. The mere existence of authority to that effect would not justify an attempt by the third party to obtain payment of a debt owing to him or her by the agent

---

[343] Insolvency Rules 1986, rr. 2.85(5) (administration) and 4.90(5) (liquidation). The rules relating to periodical payments (rr 2.87 (administration) and 4.92 (liquidation) also apply, for the purpose of set-off, to sums due to the company. See rr. 2.85(6) and 4.90(6).

[344] See *Re Anglo-Greek Steam Navigation and Trading Co (Caralli & Haggard's Claim)* (1869) LR 4 Ch App 174. The agent for collection in that case admittedly had indorsed the bill back to the inspectors of the indorser appointed under the indorser's deed of inspectorship. Nevertheless, Giffard LJ said that it was immaterial whether the bills had been got back. See also *Barclays Bank Ltd v Aschaffenburger Zellstoffwerke AG* [1967] 1 Lloyd's Rep. 387.

[345] Compare the case of an undisclosed principal. See paras 13.79–13.99 below.

[346] *Richardson v Stormont, Todd & Co Ltd* [1900] 1 QB 701. See also *Moore v Clementson* (1809) 2 Camp 22, 170 ER 1068; *Dorf v Neumann, Luebeck and Co* (1924) 40 TLR 405.

[347] See *Teheran-Europe Co Ltd v s. T Belton (Tractors) Ltd* [1968] 2 QB 545, 555 (Diplock LJ). See also *N & J Vlassopulos Ltd v Ney Shipping Ltd (The Santa Carina)* [1977] 1 Lloyd's Rep. 478, 481, 484; *Marsh & McLennan Pty Ltd v Stanyers Transport Pty Ltd* [1994] 2 VR 232; Goodhart and Hamson, 'Undisclosed principals in contract' (1932) 4 CLJ 320, 339. Compare *Bowstead and Reynolds on Agency* (18th edn, 2006), 510.

[348] *Hornby v Lacy* (1817) 6 M & S 166, 105 ER 1205. For set-off as between the agent and the third party, see paras 13.107–13.109 below.

[349] See ch. 16 below in relation to set-off agreements.

by way of a set-off against the debt to the principal.[350] Nor, ordinarily, would it authorize the agent to enter into an agreement for a set-off against his or her own debt to the third party.[351] Moreover, an alleged custom to that effect would be unreasonable,[352] so that it would not bind the principal unless the principal knew of the custom and had agreed to be bound by it.[353]

13.77 There are, nevertheless, some situations in which a set-off agreement between the agent and the third party involving the principal's claim would be valid. If the principal is indebted to the agent, and has authorized the agent to obtain payment out of the proceeds of the third party's debt to the principal, the agent may receive payment by means of a set-off against a debt that he or she owes to the third party.[354] Further, an agent selling the goods of the principal may be entitled by virtue of a lien to receive payment of the price. In such a case an agreement between the purchaser and the agent[355] to set off the price against a debt owing by the agent to the purchaser would be binding upon the principal to the extent of the principal's indebtedness to the agent secured by the lien.[356] In addition, where the principal is undisclosed, an agreement for a set-off between the agent and the third party entered into before the third party had notice that the person with whom he or she was dealing was merely an agent ordinarily would be binding on the principal,[357] although a set-off may be available to the third party at common law in that circumstance even apart from the agreement.[358]

13.78 Consider that the principal has authorized the agent to employ the third party's liability to the principal in a set-off against the agent's personal debt to the third party. If a set-off is effected before any of them becomes bankrupt or goes into liquidation, there would not ordinarily be a problem.[359] Where, however, the principal becomes bankrupt before a set-off has occurred, a subsequent set-off would not be valid unless the source of the

---

[350] *Bartlett v Pentland* (1830) 10 B & C 760, 109 ER 632; *Pearson v Scott* (1878) 9 Ch D 198; *Stolos Compania SA v Ajax Insurance Co Ltd (The Admiral C)* [1981] 1 Lloyd's Rep 9.

[351] *Jell v Pratt* (1817) 2 Stark 67, 171 ER 575; *Young v White* (1844) 7 Beav 506, 49 ER 1162; *Wrout v Dawes* (1858) 25 Beav 369, 53 ER 678; *Coupe v Collier* (1890) 62 LT 927. See also *Trading & General Investment Corp v Gault Armstrong & Kemble Ltd (The Okeanis)* [1986] 1 Lloyd's Rep 195, 199.

[352] See *Pearson v Scott* (1878) 9 Ch D 198; *Crossley v Magniac* [1893] 1 Ch 594; *Blackburn v Mason* (1893) 68 LT 510; *Anderson v Sutherland* (1897) 13 TLR 163. See also *Cooke & Sons v Eshelby* (1887) 12 App Cas 271, 280 with respect to the alleged custom.

[353] *Blackburn v Mason* (1893) 68 LT 510. There is a custom at Lloyd's by which a broker may set off the amount of a loss against his or her debt for premiums due to the underwriter. This method of payment will bind the insured if it can be shown that the broker was authorized to settle losses in accordance with the custom. See *Stewart v Aberdein* (1838) 4 M & W 211, 150 ER 1406, and *Stolos Compania SA v Ajax Insurance Co Ltd (The Admiral C)* [1981] 1 Lloyd's Rep. 9, 10, and generally *Arnould's Law of Marine Insurance and Average* (17th edn, 2008), 143–6.

[354] *Barker v Greenwood* (1837) 2 Y & C Ex 414, 160 ER 458. See also *Pariente v Lubbock* (1856) 8 De G M & G 5, 44 ER 290.

[355] Or the agent's trustee in bankruptcy, as in *Hudson v Granger* (1821) 5 B & Ald 27, 106 ER 1103.

[356] *Hudson v Granger* (1821) 5 B & Ald 27, 106 ER 1103. See also *Warner v M'Kay* (1836) 1 M & W 591, 150 ER 571, and paras 13.107–13.109 below.

[357] See also *Bowstead and Reynolds on Agency* (18th edn, 2006), 402–403.

[358] See below.

[359] This is subject to the set-off not being impugned in a subsequent insolvency on the ground that it is a transaction at an undervalue or a transaction defrauding creditors. See the Insolvency Act 1986, ss. 238, 339 and 423.

agent's authority is a security over the principal's claim so that to that extent it is not an asset available for distribution amongst the principal's creditors. Apart from that exception, authority conferred by the principal in favour of the agent would not bind the principal's trustee in bankruptcy in whom the claim is vested as part of the principal's estate. This should also be the case when the third party has become bankrupt. The use of the third party's asset in the form of the claim against the agent, in order to satisfy the third party's liability to the principal in circumstances where the insolvency set-off section does not apply, would be contrary to the requirement of a *pari passu* distribution of the bankrupt's estate, and the agreement accordingly would not be binding as against the trustee.[360] Consider, however, that the agent is the party who has become bankrupt. If the occurrence of the bankruptcy terminated the authority, a set-off could not occur. But if the authority is not terminated, the bankruptcy should not affect the position.[361] A set-off should only be objectionable if it involves the use of an asset otherwise available for distribution amongst the insolvent's creditors. This is not the case in relation to the agent, since the set-off is against the agent's liability. This admittedly is contrary to the view expressed by the Court of Appeal in *Re Bank of Credit and Commerce International SA*,[362] that: 'if A owes B £x and B owes C £y *and any of them becomes insolvent* the two debts cannot be set off even if there is an express agreement by the three of them that B may set them off; such an agreement is contrary to the scheme of distribution on insolvency and cannot prevail over the rules which require pari passu distribution . . .' However, to the extent that this statement includes the situation in which A is the insolvent party, it is difficult to see what the objection is.[363]

(3) Undisclosed principals

A person may contract in his or her own name but as agent for an undisclosed principal.[364] **13.79** The status of an undisclosed principal is anomalous in English law. A principal whose existence is unknown to a third party could hardly be said to be a party to a contract with the third party. The agent is the contracting party, and therefore the agent may sue and be sued on the contract. But, in addition, the principal may sue and be sued if there is nothing in the contract which is inconsistent with someone other than the agent being the 'principal'.[365] This right of the principal to sue and the liability to be sued is not based upon privity of contract, because the principal is not a contracting party. Rather, the undisclosed principal is treated as having a right to intervene on the agent's contract.[366] This intervention was described by Sir Frederick Pollock as being 'inconsistent with the elementary doctrines of

---

[360] See the discussion of *British Eagle International AirLines Ltd v Compagnie Nationale Air France* [1975] 1 WLR 758 in paras 16.21–16.26 below.

[361] Compare Wood, *English and International Set–off* (1989), 1001–2, 1010.

[362] [1996] Ch 245, 257 (emphasis added). See also on appeal in the House of Lords [1998] AC 214, 223.

[363] See para. 16.29 below.

[364] For a discussion of the situations in which the undisclosed principal doctrine applies, see Reynolds, 'Practical problems of the undisclosed principal doctrine' (1983) 36 *Current Legal Problems* 119.

[365] *Dunlop Pneumatic Tyre Co Ltd v Selfridge and Co Ltd* [1915] AC 847, 864; *Siu Yin Kwan v Eastern Insurance Co Ltd* [1994] 2 AC 199, 207–9. See generally Powell, *The Law of Agency* (1952), 130–1 and *Bowstead and Reynolds on Agency* (18th edn, 2006), 384.

[366] *Welsh Development Agency v Export Finance Co Ltd* [1992] BCLC 148, 173, 182. See generally Goodhart and Hamson (1932) 4 CLJ 320, 345 *et seq.*, criticizing McCardie J in *Said v Butt* [1920] 3 KB 497, 500.

the law of contract'.[367] Various writers over the years have made a number of attempts to provide a theoretical justification for it,[368] but none has been entirely successful. It is probably best to regard the doctrine as an anomaly introduced by the common law for reasons of mercantile convenience.[369]

13.80   If the undisclosed principal, when discovered, is sued on the contract by the third party, the principal could not set off in that action a claim that he or she has against the agent.[370] Nor could the principal bring into account a claim that the agent has against the third party, though a set-off may be available in accordance with normal principles if the third party is liable to the principal.[371] Alternatively, it may be that the principal is the party who takes action by intervening on the contract and enforcing it against the third party.[372] In such a case there is the possibility of a set-off in relation to a cross-demand available to the third party against the principal. In addition, however, the third party may bring into account a debt of the agent to the third party that arose before the third party had notice that the person with whom he or she was dealing in fact was acting as an agent. The leading case is *George v Clagett*.[373] A factor sold goods for his principal in his own name without disclosing that he was an agent. When the principal sued the third party purchaser for the price,[374] the third party was allowed to set off the agent's separate debt to him. The set-off is not limited to cases involving a sale of goods, but is of general application. Bowen LJ, in *Montagu v Forwood*,[375] described its scope in the following terms:

> If A employs B as his agent to make any contract for him, or to receive money for him, and B makes a contract with C, or employs C as his agent, if B is a person who would be reasonably supposed to be acting as a principal, and is not known or suspected by C to be acting as an agent for any one, A cannot make a demand against C without the latter being entitled to

---

Compare, however, Glanville Williams, 'Mistake as to party in the law of contract' (1945) 23 *Canadian Bar Review* 380, 404.

[367] (1887) 3 LQR 358, 359. See also *Siu Yin Kwan v Eastern Insurance Co Ltd* [1994] 2 AC 199, 207.

[368] See the discussion in Stoljar, *The Law of Agency* (1961), 228–233. See also *Bowstead and Reynolds on Agency* (18th edn, 2006), 372–374; Fridman, *The Law of Agency* (7th edn, 1996), 257.

[369] Fridman, *The Law of Agency* (7th edn, 1996), 258; *Siu Yin Kwan v Eastern Insurance Co Ltd* [1994] 2 AC 199, 207. See also *Bowstead and Reynolds on Agency* (18th edn, 2006), 374.

[370] *Waring v Favenck* (1807) 1 Camp 85, 170 ER 886; *Kymer v Suwercropp* (1807) 1 Camp 109, 170 ER 894.

[371] See e.g. *Spurr v Cass* (1870) LR 5 QB 656.

[372] If the agent has a direct pecuniary interest in enforcing the contract, in the form of a 'lien' over the proceeds for his or her charges and expenses, or for the balance of the agent's general account with the principal, payment by the third party to the principal when the third party has notice of the lien would not be a defence to a later action brought by the agent for payment. See *Robinson v Rutter* (1855) 4 El & Bl 954, 119 ER 355. In relation to an insurance broker's lien, see *Arnould's Law of Marine Insurance and Average* (17th edn, 2008), 160. If the third party is uncertain as to whether to pay the principal, the appropriate course is to interplead. See Powell, *The Law of Agency* (1952), 223, n. 2.

[373] (1797) 7 TR 539, 101 ER 1019.

[374] The question of a set-off, in the proper sense of that word, usually would only arise when the principal sues for the price. It should be distinguished from the situation in which the principal disputes the title of the purchaser to goods bought through the principal's agent on the ground that the agent exceeded his or her authority in selling in a particular manner, for example by setting off the price against a debt owing by the agent to the purchaser. See e.g. *Lloyds & Scottish Finance Ltd v Williamson* [1965] 1 WLR 404; *Tingey and Co Ltd v John Chambers and Co Ltd* [1967] NZLR 785.

[375] [1893] 2 QB 350.

stand in the same position as if B had in fact been a principal. If A has allowed his agent B to appear in the character of a principal he must take the consequences.[376]

The plaintiff in that case had employed an agent to collect a general average loss from Lloyd's underwriters. The agent in turn employed Lloyd's brokers as sub-agents. The policy had been effected in the name of the agent,[377] and the sub-agents thought that the loss was payable to the agent on his own account. When the sub-agents were sued by the plaintiff as an undisclosed principal for the money received from the underwriters, they were allowed to set off the agent's debt to them.[378]

As a preliminary point, it is assumed in the following discussion that the third party would have a right of set-off against the agent in accordance with normal principles. This would not be the case if the third party, instead of being a debtor, is holding a fund on trust, the obligation to account for which is not susceptible to a set-off.[379] **13.81**

Insolvency set-off

In the event of the bankruptcy or liquidation of the agent, the set-off to which the principal takes subject is not that conferred by the insolvency set-off section. Rather, it is confined to defences of set-off available as between solvent parties, in other words set-off under the Statutes of Set-off and equitable set-off. In *Turner v Thomas*[380] an agent for an undisclosed principal contracted to sell goods to a third party. The agent was separately indebted to the third party, and later became bankrupt, whereupon the third party refused to proceed with the contract. He was then sued by the principal for damages for breach of contract. While the third party's damages liability could have been set off in the agent's bankruptcy if the agent had contracted as principal, it could not have formed the basis of a defence to an action at law under the Statutes of Set-off, since the Statutes required mutual debts. Accordingly, it was held that the agent's debt could not be set off in accordance with *George v Clagett* against the damages liability in the principal's action. One reason given for the limitation on the third party's right of set-off was that the possibility of the agent's bankruptcy would not have been contemplated by the third party when deciding whether or not to deal with the agent, although that generalization may not always hold true.[381] A second, more substantial, reason given for the limitation was that the bankruptcy set-off section is only intended for the settlement of accounts between a bankrupt and a person dealing with the bankrupt, as opposed to accounts between that person and some other party such as an undisclosed principal who stands outside the bankruptcy. The principal, by intervening on the contract and suing in his or her own name, takes the claim outside the operation **13.82**

[376] [1893] 2 QB 350, 355–356.
[377] This only appears from the report of the case at 69 LT 371.
[378] For other sub–agency cases involving a sale of goods, see *New Zealand and Australian Land Co v Watson* (1881) 7 QBD 374 and *Knight v Matson & Co* (1902) 22 NZLR 293, although compare *Kaltenbach, Fischer & Co v Lewis & Peat* (1885) 10 App Cas 617, 626–7. See also *Bowstead and Reynolds on Agency* (18th edn, 2006), 155–160 in relation to the principal and sub–agent relationship.
[379] See ch. 10 above.
[380] (1871) LR 6 CP 610. See also *Thornton v Maynard* (1875) LR 10 CP 695, 700; *Montagu v Forwood* [1893] 2 QB 350. 354 (Lord Esher MR, and see also Bowen LJ in the report of the case at 69 LT 371, 373).
[381] See e.g. *Cooke & Sons v Eshelby* (1887) 12 App Cas 271, 280.

of the insolvency legislation, in which case the insolvency set-off section should not be relevant.[382]

Equitable set-off

13.83 The doctrine of the undisclosed principal is a common law doctrine, and *George v Clagett* was decided at common law. Consistent with its origin, the right of set-off that the courts have enforced in these cases is the defence available in the common law courts under the Statutes of Set-off. In an appropriate case, however, there is no reason why the third party could not assert equitable defences of set-off against the undisclosed principal. Similarly, when the third party is suing on the contract, and there is a cross-claim against the third party arising out of the contract which is sufficiently closely connected to give rise to an equitable set-off, the third party's title to sue would be impeached, whether the action is against the principal or the agent

Existing debts before notice

13.84 Set-off under the Statutes of Set-off requires that both debts be due and payable.[383] It is clear from *George v Clagett*, however, that it is not necessary that both debts should have been payable when the third party received notice of the principal. The purchase in that case took place before the date of notice, but the price was not payable until a later date, while the indebtedness of the agent was based upon a bill of exchange accepted by the agent but not payable until four days after notice. On the other hand, there must be existing debts (whether or not presently payable) before notice.[384] In *Kaltenbach, Fischer & Co v Lewis & Peat*[385] merchants employed an agent to sell goods, and the agent in turn employed a firm of brokers as sub-agents. The brokers sold the goods to a purchaser who was allowed six months' credit for the price. Before the period had elapsed, and while the brokers were still in possession of the goods, the merchants gave notice of their interest in the transaction to the brokers, and claimed the return of the goods or their net proceeds. The agent had pledged the goods to the brokers to secure a debt, and it was accepted that the brokers' interest was protected by the Factors Act, so that they were entitled to a lien for that amount and to deduct it from the proceeds of sale. But the brokers asserted that they were also entitled to set off the balance of the proceeds against other amounts due to them by the agent, and they accordingly credited the balance to the agent's account. The House of Lords held that they were not entitled to do so. Lord Bramwell dealt with the case on the basis that it involved a claim for property.[386] The brokers still retained the goods when notice was given to them, and the merchants as principals had a right to possession at that time, subject to the lien. Accordingly, the principals' claim was proprietary in nature, and therefore it was not susceptible to a set-off. Lord Watson proceeded on a different analysis,[387]

---

[382] Similarly, the insolvency set-off section cannot be invoked against an assignee of a debt when the assignor has become bankrupt. See para. 17.39 below.

[383] See para. 2.29 above.

[384] The requirement of existing debts at the time of notice also applies to a debtor's right to set off a debt owing to him or her by the creditor in an action brought against the debtor by an assignee of the debt. See para. 17.15 below.

[385] (1885) 10 App Cas 617, discussed in Goodhart and Hamson, Note (1932) 4 CLJ 320, 333–4.

[386] (1885) 10 App Cas 617, 635–637.

[387] (1885) 10 App Cas. 617, 626–628.

emphasizing instead that there was no debt owing by the brokers when they received notice of the true ownership. A debt did not arise until later, when the price was received from the purchaser, and his Lordship said that the brokers could not avail themselves of a set-off arising in that manner after notice.[388] The principle in relation to set-off should be contrasted with the situation in which an insurance broker with a general lien on the policy for the balance of the insured's account discovers that the nominal insured is only an agent. In such a case the broker is still allowed to exercise a lien over any money received from the insurer after notice of the agency, provided that the broker held the policy before notice and provided also that the lien can only be exercised in respect of the amount due to the broker at the date of notice.[389]

Knowledge of the agency

The set-off only arises if the third party believed that the agent was the principal when the   **13.85**
third party became indebted under the transaction[390] or, if the cross-debt owing by the agent to the third party arose after the entry into the transaction on behalf of the undisclosed principal,[391] if the third party still held the belief at that time.[392] Knowledge of the agency sufficient to preclude a set-off need not point to the agent as being the agent of the claimant. It suffices if it points to the person as being an agent, whether for the claimant or for anyone else.[393] Furthermore, it is not necessary that the third party personally should know of the agency. It would suffice if his or her own agent is aware of it in circumstances where that knowledge would be imputed to the third party.[394]

Duty of inquiry

If the circumstances are such as to put the third party on inquiry as to the status of the   **13.86**
agent, and the third party fails to make an inquiry, he or she may be denied a set-off.[395] In effect this is the same as saying that the third party's belief should be reasonable,[396] or that there should be 'nothing to lead the person who deals with [the agent] to suppose, and

---

[388] If the brokers had received the price before they had notice of the undisclosed principals, Lord Watson said that it was possible that they might have been entitled to set it off against the agent's balance, but that in the circumstances it was not necessary to offer an opinion on the point. See (1885) 10 App Cas. 617, 627. Lord Fitzgerald (at 640–1) appears to have proceeded on the same basis as Lord Watson, though his judgment is not clear on this point.

[389] *Mann v Forrester* (1814) 4 Camp 60, 171 ER 20; *Near East Relief v King, Chasseur and Co Ltd* [1930] 2 KB 40, 46. See generally *Arnould's Law of Marine Insurance and Average* (17th edn, 2008), 154–155.

[390] *Carr v Hinchliff* (1825) 4 B & C 547, 107 ER 1164; *Fish v Kempton* (1849) 7 CB 687, 137 ER 272. See also *Kaltenbach, Fischer & Co v Lewis & Peat* (1885) 10 App Cas 617, discussed above.

[391] See *Moore v Clementson* (1809) 2 Camp. 22, 170 ER 1068, as explained by Parke B in *Warner v M'Kay* (1836) 1 M & W 591, 596, 150 ER 571, 573.

[392] See e.g. *Borries v Imperial Ottoman Bank* (1873) LR 9 CP 38; *Salter v Purchell* (1841) 1 QB 209, 213–214, 113 ER 1110, 1111 (Parke B, *arguendo*).

[393] *Semenza v Brinsley* (1865) 18 CB (NS) 467, 144 ER 526; *Maspons y Hermano v Mildred, Goyeneche & Co* (1882) 9 QBD 530, affirmed (1883) 8 App Cas 874. See also *Walshe v Provan* (1853) 8 Ex 843, 155 ER 1595; *Busby v MacLurcan and Lane Ltd* (1930) 48 WN (NSW) 2, 5.

[394] *Dresser v Norwood* (1864) 17 CB (NS) 466, 144 ER 188.

[395] *Baring v Corrie* (1818) 2 B & Ald 137, 144, 106 ER 317, 320; *Pratt v Willey* (1826) 2 Car & P 350, 172 ER 158. See also *Pearson v Scott* (1879) 9 Ch D 198, 202; *Cooke & Sons v Eshelby* (1887) 12 App Cas 271, 277–278; *Montagu v Forwood* [1893] 2 QB 350, 356. For an analogous case concerning a dormant partner, see *Baker v Gent* (1892) 9 TLR 159 (see para. 12.17 above).

[396] *Cooke & Sons v Eshelby* (1887) 12 App Cas 271, 278; *Montagu v Forwood* [1893] 2 QB 350, 355.

he does not in fact know, that he is acting as an agent'.[397] It has been said that: 'the only question to be decided is whether the defendant really dealt with the agent in the honest belief that he was dealing with a principal.'[398] Nevertheless, the cases suggest that an honest belief will not suffice if the third party failed to make an inquiry when one was called for. This duty of inquiry has a common law origin, and it is, therefore, independent of the equitable doctrine of constructive notice.

13.87   The circumstances in which the agent contracted may be such as to indicate that he or she must have been acting only as an agent. In *Maanns v Henderson*,[399] an English subject in time of war, although acting for a neutral foreigner, opened a policy of insurance in his own name with a broker, and informed the broker that the property was neutral. This was held to be a sufficient indication to the broker that the English subject was acting as an agent and not on his own account. In some cases documents accompanying a sale may indicate that the sale is being made on behalf of another person. In one case the principal was named as the seller on a ticket accompanying the goods being sold by the agent in the agent's own name, and accordingly it was held that the third party ought to have inquired into the nature of the situation of the agent.[400] That case should be compared to *Cooper v Strauss and Co*.[401] A sale note contained the words 'Sold for and on account of', but without the insertion of the name of a principal. Kennedy J said that those words appeared in the sale note because factors sometimes sold on their own account, but more generally for a principal. While a set-off was disallowed because the agent in fact had informed the third party that he was selling on behalf of the real owners, the contents of the sale note evidently were not considered to be sufficient to achieve that result. The sale note did mention the name and address of the real principal. However, this information was only included as a description of the goods being sold, and Kennedy J did not consider that it would convey to a purchaser that the contract of sale was being made on behalf of that person as owner. Similarly, in *Knight v Matson & Co*[402] a cattle-dealer sold cattle with the brand of the real owner upon them. However, a cattle-dealer buying cattle would not obliterate or change the existing brands, and so the presence of a brand upon cattle being sold by a dealer was not considered to be sufficient to put the third party on inquiry as to their true ownership.

13.88   In the case of a sale of goods, where the sale concerns goods presently owned and existing,[403] the third party could not deny that he or she was put on inquiry if the agent at the time of the sale did not have actual possession of the goods or of their *indicia* of title.[404] Indeed, it

---

[397] *Montagu v Forwood* [1893] 2 QB 350, 355 *per* Lord Esher MR.
[398] *Knight v Matson & Co* (1902) 22 NZLR 293, 309 *per* Williams J. See also *Fish v Kempton* (1848) 7 CB 687, 691–2, 693, 137 ER 272, 274, 275.
[399] (1802) 1 East 335, 102 ER 130.
[400] *Pratt v Willey* (1826) 2 Car & P 350, 172 ER 158. Compare *Greer v Downs Supply Co* [1927] 2 KB 28, in which the third party raised the matter with the agent.
[401] (1898) 14 TLR 233.
[402] (1902) 22 NZLR 293.
[403] Compare e.g. *Cooke & Sons v Eshelby* (1887) 12 App Cas 271.
[404] See *Baring v Corrie* (1818) 2 B & Ald 137, 106 ER 317. In cases such as *Montagu v Forwood* [1893] 2 QB 350, in which an agent is employed to collect a sum of money from a third party, the agent should have possession of any requisite documents.

has been said that in order to make a valid defence under *George v Clagett*, the plea should show that the contract was made by a person whom the principal had entrusted with possession.[405] In *Wynen v Brown*[406] the goods had been entered in the name of the brokers at the Custom House, they had been warehoused in the brokers' name, and the order to the wharfinger for their delivery had also been in the brokers' name. Those circumstances were regarded as sufficient to give rise to a set-off, even though the brokers did not have the bills of lading or other *indicia* of title and even though the goods had been wharfed in the principal's name. The case is inadequately reported, but it may be queried whether, on the facts as disclosed, the third party should have questioned the brokers or the wharfinger as to the ownership of the goods.

It may be that the third party is aware that the person with whom he or she is contracting **13.89** sometimes deals as an agent for other persons. The cases in point are noticeable for their lack of consistency. Lord Ellenborough, in *Moore v Clementson*,[407] considered that a mere general knowledge possessed by the third party that the other contracting party was a factor by itself would not deprive the third party of a set-off. It appears from the headnote to *Wynen v Brown*[408] that the person selling was known to be a broker, but a set-off was allowed without any indication of an inquiry having been made.[409] Similarly, in *Dresser v Norwood*,[410] the Common Pleas allowed the third party a set-off even though he himself had employed the other party as a selling agent on two occasions. The jury's finding that the third party believed that he was dealing directly with the owner was considered to be sufficient for a set-off.[411] On the other hand, in *Baring v Corrie*,[412] the third party knew that the persons with whom they were dealing acted both as brokers and merchants, and Abbott CJ said that the third party should have inquired. In *Pearson v Scott*,[413] a solicitor had been instructed to sell some stock. He in turn employed a stockbroker. When the sale was completed, the stockbroker forwarded the proceeds to the solicitor, less a deduction to cover an indebtedness of the solicitor to him on a separate transaction. While the solicitor was known as a person who speculated in stock on his own account, Fry J held that, since the stockbroker knew that the person who employed him was a solicitor, he should have realized that he was dealing with a person who may have been acting upon the instructions of a client, and therefore he should have made some inquiry. Since the stockbroker had not initiated an inquiry, he could not be heard to say that he dealt with the solicitor in

---

[405] *Semenza v Brinsley* (1865) 18 CB (NS) 467, 477, 144 ER 526, 530. See also *Borries v The Imperial Ottoman Bank* (1873) LR 9 CP 38.

[406] (1826) 4 LJOSKB 203.

[407] (1809) 2 Camp 22, 170 ER 1068.

[408] (1826) 4 LJOSKB 203.

[409] See also *Garrett v Bird* (1872) 11 SCR (NSW) 97, which was concerned with the agent's standing to sue.

[410] (1863) 14 CB (NS) 574, 143 ER 570.

[411] Subsequently, the Exchequer Chamber reversed the decision, but on the ground that the third party himself had acted through an agent who was aware of the identity of the real owner. This knowledge was imputed to the third party. There is nothing in the report, however, to indicate that the third party's own awareness that the other contracting party was in the habit of selling as a factor was thought to prevent a set-off. See *Dresser v Norwood* (1864) 17 CB (NS) 466, 144 ER 188.

[412] (1818) 2 B & Ald 137, 106 ER 317.

[413] (1878) 9 Ch D 198.

any other character than as agent for the principals now suing for the proceeds, and so his act of crediting part of the proceeds to the solicitor's account with him was held not to discharge him from liability to the principals. In *Knight v Matson & Co*,[414] the agent was a dealer in cattle, but the third party had been informed in a prior transaction that the dealer on that occasion was acting as an agent. While one of the members of the majority, Williams J, said that the only question was whether the third party really dealt with the agent in the honest belief that they were dealing with a principal,[415] Edwards J decided the case on the basis that the third party had not been put on inquiry.[416] The dealer was in the business of selling cattle on his own account, and knowledge of a single isolated occasion on which he had acted as an agent was not regarded as sufficient to deny the third party a set-off on the ground of failure to inquire as to the ownership of the cattle. Stout CJ dissented. He said that the third party should have known from the previous transaction that the dealer might have been acting as an agent, and he considered that the third party's failure to inquire into the dealer's status in the second dealing should deprive them of a set-off.[417]

13.90   The imposition of a duty of inquiry when the third party is aware that the other contracting party has dealt in the past as an agent becomes important when the third party asserts that he or she believed that the other party on this occasion was dealing as a principal, but in the circumstances that belief was unreasonable. The cases suggest that this may give rise to a duty to inquire, but its imposition, and the reasonableness of the belief, would depend upon the facts of each case. Lord Ellenborough's opinion in *Moore v Clementson*, that a mere general knowledge that the other party is a factor will not result in the loss of a set-off, is almost certainly too wide. When the third party is aware that the nature of the business of the person with whom he or she is dealing is such that the person often acts as an agent for others,[418] it is unlikely that his or her expressed belief that the person was acting as a principal in the particular transaction in issue would be reasonable in the absence of an inquiry. On the other hand, the belief would generally be reasonable in a case like *Knight v Matson*, or *Dresser v Norwood*, where the agent as a matter of business usually deals on his or her own account, although he or she is known to have dealt occasionally in the past as an agent for others.

Basis of the set-off

13.91   In the absence of a proper theoretical justification for the intervention of an undisclosed principal on the agent's contract,[419] it is difficult to explain the basis for the third party's right of set-off against the principal. There have been statements suggesting that the set-off may be based upon a notion that an undisclosed principal takes subject to equities or

---

[414] (1902) 22 NZLR 293.
[415] (1902) 22 NZLR 293, 309, 311.
[416] (1902) 22 NZLR 293, 315–17.
[417] See also *Cooke & Sons v Eshelby* (1887) 12 App Cas 271; *London Joint Stock Bank v Simmons* [1892] AC 201, 229–30.
[418] As in *Cooke & Sons v Eshelby* (1887) 12 App Cas 271.
[419] See para. 13.79 above.

582

defences available to the third party against the agent before notice.[420] In other words, an undisclosed principal should be treated in the same way as an assignee of a chose in action.[421] Goodhart and Hamson[422] sought to explain the doctrine of the undisclosed principal as being a primitive form of assignment, although there are differences between the concepts.[423] An assignment results from an act of the parties, whereas the rights and liabilities of an undisclosed principal arise as a matter of law. Moreover, an assignment usually occurs after the relationship between the assignor and the debtor has come into existence, whereas the interest of an undisclosed principal in the agent's contract arises contemporaneously with the entry into that contract. Further, a contract which provides that it is not assignable cannot be assigned, but such a provision does not preclude intervention by an undisclosed principal.[424] In any event, before the enactment of the Judicature Acts a chose in action generally was not assignable at common law,[425] and so an analogy between assignments and the common law treatment of the undisclosed principal would not have a strong historical foundation. Perhaps reflecting those difficulties with the assignment theory, the generally accepted explanation for the set-off is that it is based, not upon a notion of taking subject to equities, but estoppel.

The leading case is *Cooke & Sons v Eshelby*.[426] Brokers sold goods to Cooke & Sons in their **13.92** own name, but acting on behalf of a principal. The principal gave notice that the sale was made on his behalf, and sued the purchasers for the price. The purchasers sought to set off in that action a debt due to them from the brokers. The purchasers were asked in interrogatories as to whether they did not believe that the brokers in the transaction were acting on behalf of principals, and they replied that they 'had no belief on the subject', and that they dealt with the brokers 'not knowing whether they were acting as brokers on behalf of principals, or on their own account as the principals'. The House of Lords held that, because the purchasers had not been led to believe that the brokers were acting as principals rather than as agents, they were not entitled to a set-off.[427] The set-off was regarded as being based

---

[420] See *Isberg v Bowden* (1853) 8 Ex 852, 859, 155 ER 1599, 1602; *Dresser v Norwood* (1863) 14 CB (NS) 574, 588–9, 143 ER 570, 576; *Turner v Thomas* (1871) LR 6 CP 610, 613; *Montgomerie v United Kingdom Mutual Steamship Association Ltd* [1891] 1 QB 370, 372. See also the early judgments in *Rabone v Williams* (1785) 7 TR 360n, 101 ER 1020 and *Stracey, Ross, et al. v Deey* (1789) 7 TR 361n, 101 ER 1021. The Privy Council in *Browning v Provincial Insurance Co of Canada* (1873) LR 5 PC 263, 272 said that 'an undisclosed principal may sue and be sued upon mercantile contracts made by his agent in his own name, subject to any defences or equities which without notice may exist against the agent'.

[421] See ch 17 below.

[422] Goodhart and Hamson, (1932) 4 CLJ 320.

[423] See Glanville Williams, 'Mistake as to party in the law of contract' (1945) 23 *Canadian Bar Review* 380, 408; Powell, *The Law of Agency* (1952), 138–9; Stoljar, *The Law of Agency* (1961), 232; *Siu Yin Kwan v Eastern Insurance Co Ltd* [1994] 2 AC 199, 210.

[424] *Siu Yin Kwan v Eastern Insurance Co Ltd* [1994] 2 AC 199, 210. In relation to a prohibition on assignment, see *Linden Gardens Trust Ltd v Lenesta Sludge Disposals Ltd* [1994] 1 AC 85, though in Australia compare the Personal Property Securities Act 2009 (Cth), s. 81.

[425] See *Lampet's Case* (1612) 10 Co Rep 46b, 48a, 77 ER 994, 997.

[426] (1887) 12 App Cas 271.

[427] Compare Reynolds, who has argued that this may have been a case of an unnamed, as opposed to an undisclosed, principal. See Reynolds, 'Practical problems of the undisclosed principle doctrine' (1983) 36 *Current Legal Problems* 119, 133.

upon an estoppel,[428] and before the principal could be estopped from denying the set-off there had to be a representation and reliance upon that representation. As Lord Watson remarked:[429]

> These decisions appear to me to establish conclusively that, in order to sustain the defence pleaded by the appellants, it is not enough to shew that the agent sold in his own name. It must be shewn that he sold the goods as his own, or, in other words, that the circumstances attending the sale were calculated to induce, and did induce, in the mind of the purchaser a reasonable belief that the agent was selling on his own account and not for an undisclosed principal; and it must also be shewn that the agent was enabled to appear as the real contract-ing party by the conduct, or by the authority, express or implied, of the principal. The rule thus explained is intelligible and just: and I agree . . . that it rests upon the doctrine of estoppel.

Similarly, Lord Halsbury, while not actually mentioning estoppel, nevertheless explained the undisclosed principal cases in terms embodying the elements of that doctrine.[430] The answer to the interrogatory indicated that the element of reliance was absent.

13.93   The requirement of showing reliance upon a representation is inconsistent with the view that the set-off is based simply on a notion of taking subject to equities. Nevertheless, it provides a sound approach to the issue.[431] There is no justification for shifting the burden of the liability for the agent's indebtedness onto the undisclosed principal unless the third party had been led to believe, erroneously, that he or she was dealing directly with a princi-pal. A third party in a case such as *Cooke v Eshelby*, who had no belief as to whether the person with whom he or she was dealing was a principal, may be taken to have assumed the risk that there may have been an undisclosed principal who could intervene, in which case the possibility of a set-off against the agent is unlikely to have been a factor influencing the decision to deal with the agent.[432] Having said that, estoppel does not explain the allowance of a set-off in all the undisclosed principal cases, irrespective of whether the estoppel is thought to be based upon conduct of the principal as constituting a representation,

---

[428] See also *Montagu v Forwood* [1893] 2 QB 350, 355 (Bowen LJ); *Cooper v Strauss and Co* (1898) 14 TLR 233; *Farquharson Brothers and Co v King* (1901) 70 LJKB 985, 987 (Vaughan Williams LJ, *arguendo*); *Tingey and Co Ltd v John Chambers and Co Ltd* [1967] NZLR 785. In *Fish v Kempton* (1849) 7 CB 687, 691, 137 ER 272, 274 Wilde CJ explained the set-off in terms savouring of estoppel, and see also the judgments in *Baring v Corrie* (1818) 2 B & Ald 137, 106 ER 317.

[429] (1887) 12 App Cas 271, 278.

[430] 'The ground upon which all these cases have been decided is that the agent has been permitted by the principal to hold himself out as the principal, and that the person dealing with the agent has believed that the agent was the principal, and has acted on that belief.' (1887) 12 App Cas 271, 275. Compare Lord Fitzgerald, who said (at 282–3) that he had 'some hesitation' in accepting the view that the set-off rests upon estoppel. However, as noted in Spencer Bower and Turner, *The Law Relating to Estoppel by Representation* (3rd edn, 1977), 25 (but not repeated in the 4th edition), he then proceeded to state the proposition in terms of his own choosing which differed in no substantial respect from those in which estoppel by representation are usually expressed.

[431] Compare Pollock (1887) 3 LQR 358, 359, who doubted the wisdom of extending the anomalous rights of an undisclosed principal.

[432] Compare the evidence to the contrary referred to by Lord Fitzgerald in *Cooke v Eshelby* (1887) 12 App Cas 271, 280, based upon an alleged custom in the Liverpool Cotton Market which was not proved, that the third party may set off the broker's indebtedness against any obligation to pay the price to an undisclosed principal, even when aware of the possibility of the existence of such a principal.

or whether the representation is thought to be made by the agent which then becomes binding upon the principal.[433]

Consider first the possibility of the principal's own conduct as constituting a representation, in the context of a sale of goods. A representation sufficient to induce the belief that the agent is contracting as principal should suggest that the agent is the owner of the goods in question. In other words, the representation should be sufficient to satisfy the doctrine of apparent ownership.[434] This doctrine, as *Bowstead and Reynolds on Agency*[435] explains, is concerned with the validity of a disposition of property and with overcoming the *nemo dat* principle, whereas in the set-off cases the validity of the disposition is conceded. However, unless the agent has been held out as the owner of the goods, and as such able to transfer a good title in his or her own right, it can hardly be said that anything done by the undisclosed principal has constituted a representation that the agent is selling as a principal. The difficulty, as *Bowstead and Reynolds* also points out in criticizing the estoppel theory,[436] is that, while the third party evidently may found a set-off upon the mere fact of the agent having had possession of the goods for sale, or of their *indicia* of title,[437] possession is not sufficient to create a situation of apparent ownership.[438] Something further is required,[439] for example that the real owner has allowed the goods to stand in another's name,[440] or that the real owner has given another person an acknowledgement in writing that the other person has bought and paid for the goods,[441] or that the real owner has signed a document offering to buy the goods from the other person.[442] It seems then that the set-off in these cases may be based upon conduct that would not be sufficient to constitute a representation by the undisclosed principal that the agent is owner of the goods being sold.

There is another way of approaching the estoppel theory, and that is that the agent, by contracting in his or her own name, represents that he or she is the principal in the transaction, and if the undisclosed principal has authorized this the principal becomes bound by

13.94

13.95

---

[433] I acknowledge my debt in the following discussion to *Bowstead and Reynolds on Agency* (18th edn, 2006), 401–5.

[434] While the doctrine of apparent ownership is also said to be based upon an estoppel (see e.g. *Mercantile Credit Co Ltd v Hamblin* [1965] 2 QB 242, 271), the fact that it confers a real title, as opposed to operating merely between the parties themselves, has been said to create a difficulty with an estoppel analysis, or at least against the traditional view that an estoppel does not establish a title. See *Bowstead and Reynolds on Agency* (18th edn, 2006), 420–1, 424 and compare Spencer Bower, *The Law Relating to Estoppel by Representation* (4th edn, 2004), 16.

[435] *Bowstead and Reynolds on Agency* (18th edn, 2006), 402–3.

[436] *Bowstead and Reynolds on Agency* (18th edn, 2006), 403, 421, 425.

[437] See *Semenza v Brinsley* (1865) 18 CB (NS) 467, 477, 144 ER 526, 530, and also *Borries v The Imperial Ottoman Bank* (1873) LR 9 CP 38.

[438] *Rimmer v Webster* [1902] 2 Ch 163, 169; *Motor Credits (Hire Finance) Ltd v Pacific Motor Auctions Pty Ltd* (1963) 109 CLR 87, 99. Compare *Lloyds & Scottish Finance Ltd v Williamson* [1965] 1 WLR 404, criticized, and possibly explained, in *Bowstead and Reynolds on Agency* (18th edn, 2006), 425 n 53, and see also Fridman, *The Law of Agency* (7th edn, 1996), 279–80.

[439] *Bowstead and Reynolds on Agency* (18th edn, 2006), 425.

[440] See e.g. *Henderson & Co v Williams* [1895] 1 QB 521 (goods warehoused in another's name).

[441] *Rimmer v Webster* [1902] 2 Ch 163.

[442] *Eastern Distributors Ltd v Goldring* [1957] 2 QB 600.

the representation.[443] This approach avoids the difficulty that the principal's conduct may not have been sufficient to constitute a representation that the agent was contracting as a principal in his or her own right. However, even if it is accepted that the agent makes such a representation by contracting in his or her own name,[444] it still fails to explain the right of set-off in cases in which the agent had been instructed to reveal the fact of the agency, or at least had not been authorized to use his or her own name when contracting.[445] There have been statements which assume that the set-off only applies when the principal has authorized the agent to contract as though he or she were the principal.[446] Indeed, in *Baring v Corrie*,[447] a third party who bought goods from a broker selling in his own name was denied a set-off against the undisclosed principal, *inter alia* because a broker's authority was confined to selling in the name of the principal.[448] Nevertheless, it was held by the Court of Appeal in *Ex p Dixon, re Henley*,[449] and again by the New Zealand Court of Appeal in *Knight v Matson & Co*,[450] that an express direction to the agent to reveal the fact of the agency will not deprive the third party of a set-off if the agent ignores the direction and contracts in his or her own name without disclosing that he or she is an agent.[451] It may be thought unfair that the principal should be subjected to a set-off that would not have arisen if the agent had acted in accordance with the principal's instructions. Equally, though, it is unfair that a private communication from the principal to the agent should have the effect of depriving the third party of a set-off when the possibility of a set-off may have been an inducement for the third party to contract with the agent. If the principal chooses to deal through an agent, the principal should be expected to take the risk that the agent may exceed his or her authority and act as though he or she is transacting as a principal.[452]

13.96   Before discussing these cases in the context of the agent's authority to make the representation, it should be noted that *Knight v Matson* may be explained on another ground. Edwards J

---

[443] See Spencer Bower, *The Law Relating to Estoppel by Representation* (4th edn, 2004), 143. In *Borries v The Imperial Ottoman Bank* (1873) LR 9 CP 38, 47 Brett J referred to the agents as representing themselves to be the real owners.

[444] Compare Goodhart and Hamson's view ((1932) 4 CLJ 320, 344), that 'normally a person contracting in his own name does not, by that mere fact, make any representation that he is not contracting as trustee for, or for the benefit of, another'. As support for that proposition, Goodhart and Hamson referred to two cases, *Nash v Dix* (1898) 78 LT 445 and *Dyster v Randall and Sons* [1926] Ch 932, although these may have been concerned with the materiality of the representation (as defined in Spencer Bower, Turner and Handley. *Actionable Misrepresentation* (4th edn, 2000), 75–6), as opposed to whether there had been any representation.

[445] The mere fact that the agent was authorized not to reveal the name of the principal does not mean that the agent was authorized to contract as though he or she was the principal. See *Cooke v Eshelby* (1887) 12 App Cas 271, 281–2 (Lord Fitzgerald).

[446] E.g. Lord Halsbury LC in *Cooke v Eshelby* (1887) 12 App Cas 271, 275 spoke of the 'permission of the real principal to the agent to assume his character'. In *Dresser v Norwood* (1863) 14 CB (NS) 574, 143 ER 570, the authority given to the agent to sell in his own name was emphasized. See also *Fish v Kempton* (1849) 7 CB 687, 691, 137 ER 272, 274 (Wilde CJ, *arguendo*); *Semenza v Brinsley* (1865) 18 CB (NS) 467, 477, 144 ER 526, 530.

[447] (1818) 2 B & Ald 137, 106 ER 317.

[448] For the distinction formerly drawn between brokers and factors, see *Bowstead and Reynolds on Agency* (18th edn, 2006), 34–5.

[449] (1876) 4 Ch D 133, explaining *Semenza v Brinsley* (1865) 18 CB (NS) 467, 144 ER 526.

[450] (1902) 22 NZLR 293.

[451] The agent's failure to reveal the agency would not affect his or her authority to sell. This is clear from the *Dixon* and *Matson* cases, and see also *Stevens v Biller* (1883) 25 Ch D 31.

[452] See Powell, *The Law of Agency* (1952), 148–9, where this point is made without reference to either *Ex p Dixon* or *Knight v Matson*.

found that a situation of apparent ownership had been created. The agent in that case was a dealer in cattle in his own right. It has been suggested that a deposit of goods with a person who in the normal course of business is known to sell goods of that type on his or her own account may be sufficient to satisfy the doctrine of apparent ownership.[453] Therefore, the conduct of the undisclosed principal in *Knight v Matson* in entrusting his cattle for sale with a person who bought and sold cattle in his own right in the normal course of his business may have constituted a representation to those dealing with that person that he in fact was the owner of the cattle. Since an estoppel may be explained on the basis of the principal's own representation, the agent's disregard for the instructions given to him as to the disclosure of the agency would lose its significance. That explanation, however, was not the basis of the decision in *Ex p Dixon*.[454] The agent was an iron and metal merchant. In the transaction in question, he sold a particular type of pig iron to the third party on behalf of an undisclosed principal. While it may be accepted that an iron and metal merchant would buy and sell pig iron in his or her own right in the normal course of business, this was not emphasized either in the statement of facts set out in the report or in the judgments, which suggests that the case did not turn on that circumstance. Rather, the Court of Appeal in allowing a set-off had recourse to the scope of the authority usually possessed by a factor.

If an agent has been instructed to reveal the fact of his or her agency, it is difficult to see how it could be said that the principal has authorized the agent to represent that he or she is the principal. Clearly the agent does not possess actual authority. Moreover, an argument based upon apparent authority would not be open to the third party seeking a set-off. Apparent authority arises when a person by words or conduct represents or permits it to be represented that another has authority to act on his or her behalf.[455] However, the essence of the set-off in these cases is that the third party believed that the person with whom he or she was dealing was contracting as a principal. The third party could hardly argue that the person was held out as having authority to contract in that person's own name though on behalf of the real principal, and at the same time assert that he or she believed that the person with whom he or she was dealing was the principal in the transaction. As Scrutton LJ once remarked:[456] 'you cannot rely on the apparent authority of an agent who did not profess in dealing with you to act as agent.' While this may seem clear, the Court of Appeal in *Ex p Dixon*[457] nevertheless based its decision to allow a set-off upon the notion that the agent could be taken as having had authority to sell in his own name. Thus Brett JA said:[458]

13.97

> Now, the rule of law is, that the extent of an agent's authority as between himself and third parties is to be measured by the extent of his usual employment. That being so, the very fact of entrusting your goods to a man as a factor, with the right to sell them, is *prima facie* authority from you to him to sell in his own name.

---

[453] See *Bowstead and Reynolds on Agency* (18th edn, 2006), 425, referring to *Motor Credits (Hire Finance) Ltd v Pacific Motor Auctions Pty Ltd* (1963) 109 CLR 87, 99.

[454] However, Edwards J in *Knight v Matson* (1902) 22 NZLR 293, 315 seemed to regard *Ex p Dixon* as a case of apparent ownership.

[455] *Bowstead and Reynolds on Agency* (18th edn, 2006), 335–6.

[456] *Underwood Ltd v Bank of Liverpool and Martins* [1924] 1 KB 775, 792.

[457] (1876) 4 Ch D 133.

[458] (1876) 4 Ch D 133, 137, referred to with approval by Williams J in *Knight v Matson* (1902) 22 NZLR 293, 308–9.

Similarly, James LJ in deciding in favour of the set-off said that:[459] 'As regards third parties, the powers of an agent are measured by the apparent scope of his authority, and cannot be limited by any private communication with him.'

13.98 There was no mention in *Ex p Dixon* of the apparent inconsistency of basing the third party's right of set-off upon the authority usually possessed by a factor, when the set-off is only allowable if the third party did not know that the person with whom he or she was dealing was a factor.[460] This aspect of the decision in *Ex p Dixon* is reminiscent of the later case of *Watteau v Fenwick*,[461] in which it was held that the owner of a business was liable on contracts entered into by an agent who was the manager of the business but who appeared to be the principal, even though the agent had been instructed not to enter into that type of transaction. Wills J said that, 'the principal is liable for all the acts of the agent which are within the authority usually confided to an agent of that character, notwithstanding limitations, as between the principal and the agent, put upon that authority.'[462] This case has often been criticized on the same ground as that mentioned above, that the agent had neither actual nor apparent authority, and therefore the principal should not have been liable on the contract.[463] But even apart from that criticism, *Watteau v Fenwick* does not support the approach adopted in *Ex p Dixon*. In *Watteau v Fenwick* the third party did not know that the other contracting party was only an agent. Nevertheless, the decision in that case is still consistent with the result that would have followed if the third party had been informed of that fact, in other words, the principal would have been liable on the contract. This is not so in relation to *Ex p Dixon*, however. If the third party had been aware that he was dealing with a factor, he would have been denied the relief that was granted by the Court of Appeal, that is, a right to set off the agent's debt to him against his liability to the principal. Therefore, the form of authority which the court found in *Ex p Dixon* has an even more tenuous basis for the decision in that case than the authority found in *Watteau v Fenwick*.

13.99 Unless possibly *Ex p Dixon* is treated as a case in which the goods had been delivered to an agent who was accustomed to deal in goods of that type on his or her own account in the normal course of that person's business, so as to come within the doctrine of apparent ownership, it is difficult to explain the allowance of a set-off on the basis of an estoppel. The notion that the agent dealt in goods of that type on his own account was not emphasized in the judgments, and it seems that the decision did not turn on it. Leaving aside that

---

[459] (1876) 4 Ch D 133, 136.

[460] Brett JA in *Ex p Dixon* seemed to contemplate the situation in which the agent is a factor in the traditional sense of the word, so that the person's 'usual employment' is to sell the goods of others in his or her own name. However, Williams J in *Knight v Matson* (1902) 22 NZLR 293, 308–9, in applying Brett JA's statement, evidently considered that the analysis should not be limited to that type of agent.

[461] [1893] 1 QB 346.

[462] [1893] 1 QB 346, 348–9.

[463] See *Bowstead and Reynolds on Agency* (18th edn, 2006), 108–11, 379–83 and Fridman, *The Law of Agency* (7th edn, 1996), 72–6. Bingham J doubted the authority of *Watteau v Fenwick* in *Rhodian River Shipping Co SA v Halla Maritime Corporation (The Rhodian River)* [1984] 1 Lloyd's Rep 373, and the British Columbia Court of Appeal declined to follow it in *Sign-O-Lite Plastics Ltd v Metropolitan Life Insurance Co* (1990) 73 DLR (4th) 541. See also *McLaughlin v Gentles* (1919) 51 DLR 383 and *International Paper Co v Spicer* (1906) 4 CLR 739, 763.

explanation, the case may be regarded as wrongly decided on the ground that the representation made by the agent was not authorized by, and consequently was not binding upon, the undisclosed principal. That would not be a welcome result, however, because a private communication between the principal and the agent should not have the effect of denying the third party a set-off that he or she otherwise may have expected to have, particularly when it was the principal who chose to deal through an agent. Alternatively, the courts may come to recognize that the estoppel theory put forward by the House of Lords in *Cooke v Eshelby*,[464] which was decided only eleven years after *Ex p Dixon*[465] without any mention being made of that case, is not a satisfactory explanation for the *George v Clagett* set-off,[466] and that, as the principal's very right of intervention on his agent's contract is an anomaly without a proper juristic explanation,[467] so is the third party's right of set-off.

(4) Set-off between the principal and the third party

When a contract is effected through an agent, the parties to the contract usually are the principal and the third party.[468] The agent is not a party, and accordingly the agent may not enforce the contract in an action brought in his or her own name.[469] This is not an invariable rule, however, because there are a number of situations in which an agent contracts personally, and in which he or she may sue.[470] This is the case when the agent contracts for an undisclosed principal. It may also apply, depending on the circumstances, in the case of an agent for an unnamed principal,[471] that is, when the agent discloses that he or she is acting as an agent but without disclosing the principal's identity, and when a person enters into a contract in his or her own name but is expressed to do so 'and/or as agent', so that the person may or may not be contracting as a principal.[472] Similarly, a factor,[473] an auctioneer

13.100

---

[464] (1887) 12 App Cas 271.

[465] (1876) 4 Ch D 133.

[466] The statement of the principle in terms of estoppel is criticized in Powell, *The Law of Agency* (1952), 147–8, and in *Bowstead and Reynolds on Agency* (18th edn, 2006), 402–3.

[467] See para. 13.79 above.

[468] Compare the case of an undisclosed principal, who is not a party to the agent's contract. See para. 13.79 above.

[469] See e.g. *Storaker v Southouse & Long Ltd* (1920) 20 SR (NSW) 190. The fact that the agent may be on a *del credere* commission does not affect this conclusion. See *Bramwell v Spiller* (1870) 21 LT 672. Nor would it make any difference if the agent paid the contract sum to the principal under the terms of the commission. See *Jordeson and Co and Simon Kahn v London Hardwood Co* (1913) 19 Com Cas 161; *Coghlan v McKay* (1902) 8 ALR 155. See also *Flatau, Dick & Co v Keeping* (1931) 39 Ll L Rep 232 (advances made by the agent to his principal on the goods).

[470] See generally *Bowstead and Reynolds on Agency* (18th edn, 2006), 505 *et seq.*

[471] In *Teheran-Europe Co Ltd v s. T Belton (Tractors) Ltd* [1968] 2 QB 545, 558 Diplock LJ contemplated the situation in which both the principal and the agent may be entitled to sue on the contract. See generally *Bowstead and Reynolds on Agency* (18th edn, 2006), 510–12.

[472] See *Lee v Bullen* (1858) 27 LJQB 161. See also *Greater Britain Insurance Corporation Ltd v C T Bowring & Co (Insurance) Ltd* (1925) 22 Ll L Rep 538, in which Greer J allowed brokers a set-off in respect of policies effected by them 'and/or as agents'. For the terms of the policy, see (1925) 23 Ll L Rep 285. Greer LJ's reliance on *Koster v Eason* (1813) 2 M & S 112, 105 ER 324 and *Parker v Beasley* (1814) 2 M & S 423, 105 ER 438 suggests that he considered that the brokers could have sued in their own name. His decision was subsequently affirmed by the Court of Appeal ((1926) 24 Ll L Rep 7), but on the alternative ground that the agreement between the parties modified their relationship.

[473] *Drinkwater v Goodwin* (1775) 1 Cowp 251, 98 ER 1070.

of goods,[474] and an agent who effects insurance in his or her own name on behalf of another with that other's authority[475] may each sue. If the case is one in which the agent rather than the principal sues, the question whether the third party may set off in that action a debt owing to him or her by the principal *prima facie* should depend on whether it can be said that the agent in bringing the action does so as trustee for the principal, because otherwise the demands would not be mutual in equity.[476] In fact, it is not easy to find a trust in all cases.

Auctioneer's lien

13.101 Consider the case of a sale of goods by auction. The purchaser may have removed the goods without immediate payment and subsequently been sued by the auctioneer for the price, the auctioneer's entitlement to sue arising either by virtue of a special property that he or she has in the goods, or alternatively from a contract implied by law between the auctioneer and the purchaser whereby the purchaser has agreed to pay the price to the auctioneer.[477] The purchaser may set off in that action a debt owing to him or her by the vendor/principal, provided that the auctioneer is adequately protected in respect of the auctioneer's lien[478] for his or her expenses and charges in auctioning the goods,[479] and for any other right of deduction previously agreed to by the vendor in respect of other debts owing to the auctioneer by the vendor.[480] The use of the word 'lien' to describe the auctioneer's rights in respect of the proceeds of sale is criticized in *Bowstead and Reynolds on Agency*[481] on the same basis that the term 'banker's lien' has been said to be inappropriate to describe a banker's right to treat accounts as combined.[482] In other words, it is difficult to see how a lien can be exercised over money, which normally would become the property of the holder

---

[474] See *Williams v Millington* (1788) 1 H Bl 81, 126 ER 49; *Chelmsford Auctions Ltd v Poole* [1973] 1 QB 542. This is not the case, however, in relation to an auctioneer of land. See *Cherry v Anderson* (1876) Ir R 10 CL 204.

[475] *Provincial Insurance Co of Canada v Leduc* (1874) LR 6 PC 224, 244.

[476] Compare *Atkyns and Batten v Amber* (1796) 2 Esp 493, 170 ER 431, in which a set-off was denied, although the broker in that case had made advances to the principal on the goods sold so that he would have been suing on his own account. *Quaere* whether the agent in that case should have been allowed to sue in his own name. See *Bramwell v Spiller* (1870) 21 LT 672. The sale note in *Atkyns v Amber* said that the goods were sold by the agent 'on account of' the principal, so that the agent himself would not appear to have been a party to the contract. See e.g. *Jordeson and Co and Simon Kahn v London Hardwood Co* (1931) 19 Com Cas 161 ('as agents for'); *Flatau, Dick & Co v Keeping* (1931) 39 Ll L Rep 232 ('sold for account of our principals').

[477] *Chelmsford Auctions Ltd v Poole* [1973] 1 QB 542, 549, 550, referring to *Benton v Campbell, Parker and Co* [1925] 2 KB 410, 416.

[478] An auctioneer has only a particular lien over goods for his or her charges and expenses in respect of those particular goods. See *Webb v Smith* (1885) 30 Ch D 192. The auctioneer's position should be compared to that of a factor, who has a general lien for the balance of his or her account with the principal. See *Kruger v Wilcox* (1755) Amb 252, 27 ER 168; *Baring v Corrie* (1818) 2 B & Ald 137, 148, 106 ER 317, 321.

[479] *Jarvis v Chapple* (1815) 2 Chit 387; *Holmes v Tutton* (1855) 5 El & Bl 65, 82, 119 ER 405, 412; *Manley & Sons Ltd v Berkett* [1912] 2 KB 329. See also *Bulgin v McCabe* (1859) unreported but mentioned at 1 QSCR 83–4; *Grice v Kenrick* (1870) LR 5 QB 340, 345; *Benton v Campbell, Parker and Co Ltd* [1925] 2 KB 410, 416; *Chelmsford Auctions Ltd v Poole* [1973] 1 QB 542, 549. Compare *Coppin v Craig* (1816) 7 Taunt 243, 129 ER 97, in which the auctioneer had sold the goods of one person under another's name.

[480] *Manley & Sons Ltd v Berkett* [1912] 2 KB 329.

[481] *Bowstead and Reynolds on Agency* (18th edn, 2006), 312. See also *Re Clune* (1988) 14 ACLR 261, 267. Compare Dal Pont, *Law of Agency* (12th edn, 2008), 463–4.

[482] See para. 15.03 below.

subject to an obligation to account for it. It is suggested in *Bowstead* that the auctioneer's lien over the proceeds may refer to a number of rights. Thus, it may be explained as a right of set-off when the auctioneer is sued by the principal, or it may refer to the auctioneer's right to sue the purchaser for the price and then retain the proceeds, or it may refer to the rule that the purchaser, to the extent of the lien, may not set off against the auctioneer a claim that he or she has against the vendor. But in considering the auctioneer's position, it should also be appreciated that it differs from that of a banker in that the auctioneer holds the proceeds of sale subject to a trust.[483] When the price is received there is therefore a fund which is to be kept separate, and from which the amount secured by the lien can be retained. A bank, on the other hand, is a debtor, not a trustee.[484] However, the essence of the view in *Bowstead* would appear to be correct, that an auctioneer's lien should be regarded as a package or rights, including the right to sue the purchaser for the price and to retain from the trust fund representing the proceeds an amount sufficient to satisfy the auctioneer's entitlement.

In *Benton v Campbell, Parker and Co*,[485] Salter J suggested that a set-off in respect of a debt **13.102** owing by the vendor is not available in the auctioneer's action before the debt secured by the lien has been paid, but the better view is that it is sufficient if allowance is given for the auctioneer's entitlement in the set-off, by only permitting the purchaser to set off the price less an amount equal to the sum necessary to protect the auctioneer's entitlement.[486] This right of set-off available to the purchaser in the auctioneer's action has been described as a right in equity by way of equitable defence.[487]

Consider, however, the position in relation to insolvency set-off. When the vendor is bank- **13.103** rupt or is a company in liquidation, there is a conceptual difficulty in allowing a set-off as between the purchaser and the vendor before the auctioneer's charges and expenses have been met, and that is that the demands in such a case strictly would not be mutual. Once the auctioneer has received the sale proceeds, a trust may arise in favour of the principal after the auctioneer has made the necessary deduction in order to obtain reimbursement.[488] However, the insolvency legislation is cast in terms of mutual debts, credits, and dealings, and mutuality is determined by reference to the equitable title to the demands,[489] as opposed to the eventual equitable title to the proceeds of the demands. The difficulty is that, until the auctioneer's lien has been satisfied, it could hardly be said that the auctioneer holds the right to sue solely as trustee for the principal, since the auctioneer at that stage will have the prior right to look to anything that may be recovered in order to satisfy the lien.

---

[483] *Crowther v Elgood* (1887) 34 Ch D 691; *Re Cotton (deceased); Ex p Cooke* (1913) 108 LT 310.

[484] *Foley v Hill* (1848) 2 HLC 28, 9 ER 1002.

[485] [1925] 2 KB 410, 416. See also *Holmes v Tutton* (1855) 5 El & Bl 65, 82, 119 ER 405, 412.

[486] *Manley & Sons Ltd v Berkett* [1912] 2 KB 329. A set-off should be denied, however, if the auctioneer previously had tendered the sale price to the vendor, so that the auctioneer is suing entirely on his or her own account, as in *Chelmsford Auctions Ltd v Poole* [1973] 1 QB 542.

[487] *Manley & Sons Ltd v Berkett* [1912] 2 KB 329, 333. See also *Holmes v Tutton* (1855) 5 El & Bl 65, 82, 119 ER 405, 412. In *Chelmsford Auctions Ltd v Poole* [1973] 1 QB 542, 549 Lord Denning referred to the set-off as an 'equity'.

[488] *Re Cotton (deceased), ex p Cooke* (1913) 108 LT 310.

[489] See paras 11.13–11.17 above.

The auctioneer may be a trustee, first for him or herself, and, after that, for the principal. Nevertheless, the auctioneer would be the first beneficiary, and the auctioneer's beneficial interest would extend to the whole claim as the source from which the lien is to be satisfied. While the principal may be said to have a beneficial interest in the remainder, that interest would be subject to the interest of the auctioneer, and strictly it should not suffice to render the claim mutual with an indebtedness of the principal to the purchaser. However, at least if the purchaser is solvent, this objection is unlikely to prevail. An analogous situation occurred in *Lee & Chapman's Case*.[490] A debt owing to a company was charged to a third party. The company went into liquidation, and it was held that the debtor was entitled to a set-off in the liquidation against the part of the debt over and above the amount required to satisfy the secured debt owing to the third party as chargee. On the other hand, a set-off ordinarily should not be available as between the vendor and the purchaser if the purchaser is insolvent, unless the auctioneer's prior interest is otherwise secured.[491] If the purchaser is insolvent, a set-off would reduce the debt over which the auctioneer has a 'lien' without any certainty that the proceeds eventually received in respect of the remainder of the debt would be sufficient to satisfy the lien.

13.104 The effectiveness as against the auctioneer of an agreement for a set-off between the vendor and the purchaser should be determined by reference to similar principles. The agreement will not provide a defence to an action by the auctioneer unless the auctioneer's charges and expenses have been paid,[492] or at least, if the purchaser is solvent, the set-off may be reduced so as to leave an amount sufficient to cover them.[493] In *Grice v Kenrick*,[494] the auctioneer's lien had been satisfied, and although he was aware of a set-off agreement between the vendor and the purchaser, the auctioneer himself paid the price to the vendor and proceeded to sue the purchaser. The set-off agreement was held to constitute a defence to the auctioneer's action, although the court suggested that the auctioneer would have succeeded if he had been deceived by the purchaser, or if there had been anything accompanying the receipt of the goods from which a promise on the purchaser's part to pay the auctioneer could have been inferred.

Undisclosed principal

13.105 A similar analysis should apply when an agent who contracted on behalf of an undisclosed principal sues the other contracting (third) party,[495] and the third party, having discovered the identity of the principal, wishes to set off in that action a debt owing to him or her by the principal. While the agent ordinarily would hold any proceeds received under the contract on trust for the principal,[496] the Privy Council in *Allen v F O'Hearn and Co*[497]

---

[490] *Re Asphaltic Wood Pavement Co. Lee & Chapman's Case* (1885) 30 Ch D 216.
[491] See paras 11.39 and 11.40 above.
[492] *Grice v Kenrick* (1870) LR 5 QB 340.
[493] *Manley & Sons Ltd v Berkett* [1912] 2 KB 329.
[494] (1870) LR 5 QB 340.
[495] The agent as the contracting party is entitled to sue on the contract. See *Garrett v Bird* (1872) 11 SCR (NSW) 97. See also *Sims v Bond* (1833) 5 B & Ad 389, 393, 110 ER 834, 835–6, and generally *Bowstead and Reynolds on Agency* (18th edn, 2006), 507–8.
[496] *Pople v Evans* [1969] 2 Ch 255, 261, and see also *Allen v F O'Hearn and Co* [1937] AC 213, 218.
[497] [1937] AC 213, 218.

considered that, as regards the third party, the agent is not a trustee for the undisclosed principal.[498] *Prima facie* that should have the consequence that, as between the agent and the third party in the agent's action, there is a lack of mutuality in relation to the cross-demands. There was a similar lack of mutuality, however, in the auctioneer cases, and they suggest that this objection is unlikely to prevent a set-off given that the principal is the party who will benefit from the claim. If the principal intervened and sued the third party there would be mutuality, and the existence or otherwise of a right of set-off should not depend on whether the principal or the agent sues. Furthermore, if either the principal or the third party is bankrupt or in liquidation, a set-off may occur between them in any event under the insolvency set-off section without the necessity for an action.[499]

Unnamed principal

Alternatively, the agent may have informed the third party that he or she was acting **13.106** on behalf of a principal, but without naming the principal. In other words, the case may concern a disclosed principal who nevertheless is unnamed. Sometimes the agent in these cases will contract personally and therefore will be liable on the contract, this liability being in addition to that of the principal,[500] in which case the agent also may be entitled to bring proceedings.[501] If the agent sues, the position once again should be that the third party generally can set off a cross-demand that he or she has against the principal. However, whether the principal is undisclosed or merely unnamed, the availability of a set-off should be subject to the same principle applicable to auctioneers (above), that a set-off should not be available if it would prejudice a prior interest that the agent has in the action.

(5) Set-off between the agent and the third party, where the agent can enforce the contract[502]

When an agent is entitled to enforce a contract made on behalf of the principal,[503] and the **13.107** agent is independently indebted to the third party, a set-off should be permissible as between them to the extent that the agent has a prior interest in the action, for example as a result of an lien for his or her charges and expenses. This is implicit in *Hudson v Granger*.[504] In that case, an agent who sold the principal's goods was entitled by virtue of a lien on the goods to receive the price. It was held that an agreement between the purchaser and the agent's assignees in bankruptcy, by which the price was set off against a debt owing by the agent to the third party, was binding on the principal. On the other hand, to the

---

[498] See also *Pople v Evans* [1969] 2 Ch 255. Compare Ames, 'Undisclosed principal – his rights and liabilities' (1909) 18 *Yale Law Journal* 443, 446, 448, and Higgins, 'The equity of the undisclosed principal' (1965) 28 MLR 167. Compare also Wood, *English and International Set-off* (1989), 980–1.

[499] *Stein v Blake* [1996] AC 243. See paras 6.119–6.146 above.

[500] *Bowstead and Reynolds on Agency* (18th edn, 2006), 510. Compare *N & J Vlassopulos Ltd v Ney Shipping Ltd (The Santa Carina)* [1977] 1 Lloyd's Rep 478.

[501] As in *Short v Spackman* (1831) 2 B & Ad 962, 109 ER 1400. See Fridman, *The Law of Agency* (7th edn, 1996), 249–50, though compare Stoljar, *The Law of Agency* (1961), 250–1. In *Teheran-Europe Co Ltd v s. T Belton (Tractors) Ltd* [1968] 2 QB 545, 558 Diplock LJ contemplated the situation in which both the principal and the agent may be entitled to sue, and may be liable to be sued, on the contract.

[502] See also para. 13.76–13.78 above.

[503] See para. 13.100 above.

[504] (1821) 5 B & Ald 27, 106 ER 1103. See also *Warner v M'Kay* (1836) 1 M & W 591, 150 ER 571.

extent that the principal is the party interested in the claim, a debt owing to the agent personally should not be able to be set off.[505]

Insurance brokers in marine insurance

13.108 The question of a set-off as between an agent and a third party has arisen in the context of marine insurance. As a result of a mercantile custom, which has since received statutory recognition,[506] a broker who effects a policy of marine insurance on behalf of an insured is directly responsible as a principal to the underwriter for the premium.[507] In a number of cases in which a broker was being sued by an underwriter's trustee (or, formerly, assignees) in bankruptcy for premiums, the broker sought to set off the underwriter's liability to the insured for losses on policies effected through the broker.[508] The *prima facie* rule is that, unless the broker effected the policy on his own account,[509] the underwriter's liability to the insured and the broker's indebtedness to the underwriter are not mutual, so that a set-off against the broker's debt is not permitted.[510] That would also apply in a case where the underwriter is being sued by the insured in respect of a loss.[511] Nor would an agreement for a set-off between the broker and the underwriter bind the insured.[512] Consider, however, that the policy is taken out in the broker's name,[513] so that the broker may sue upon it,[514] and moreover that the broker has an interest in the claim on the policy as a result of a lien for an amount owing to him or her by the insured.[515] In those circumstances, if the broker is sued by the underwriter's trustee in bankruptcy for unpaid premiums, it has been held that the broker may set off the insured's claim on the policy.[516] In the cases in question, the amount owing to the broker secured by the lien exceeded the claim on the policy. If, on the other hand, the lien is for an amount less than the loss, a set-off should only be permitted to the extent of the lien. The contrary conclusion would mean that the

---

[505] Compare the contrary view expressed at common law by Denman CJ in *Gibson v Winter* (1833) 5 B & Ad 96, 102, 110 ER 728, 730.

[506] Marine Insurance Act 1906, s. 53(1). In Australia, the Marine Insurance Act 1909 (Cth), s. 59(1) was repealed by the Financial Services Reform (Consequential Provisions) Act 2001 (Cth).

[507] See generally *Arnould's Law of Marine Insurance and Average* (17th edn, 2008), 139. It appears that this is not so in non-marine insurance, although an agent authorized to receive payment on behalf of an insurer will be liable to account for premiums actually received. See *Re Palmdale Insurance Ltd* [1982] VR 921.

[508] The cases are collected and discussed in *Arnould on the Law of Marine Insurance and Average* (12th edn, 1939) vol. 1, 163 *et seq.* In Australia, note the Insurance (Agents and Brokers) Act 1984 (Cth), s. 37, which provides that moneys paid to a person (not being a registered insurance broker) as agent of an insurer are subject to a trust in favour of the insurer and are not capable of being made subject to a set-off.

[509] See *Koster v Eason* (1813) 2 M & S 112, 105 ER 324, although this is unlikely to be the case in modern business. See *Arnould's Law of Marine Insurance and Average* (17th edn, 2008), 150 n 78.

[510] See e.g. *Wilson v Creighton* (1782) 3 Dougl 132, 99 ER 576; *Bell v Auldjo* (1784) 4 Dougl 48, 99 ER 761.

[511] *Stolos Compania SA v Ajax Insurance Co Ltd (The Admiral C)* [1981] 1 Lloyd's Rep 9.

[512] *Jell v Pratt* (1817) 2 Stark 67, 171 ER 575.

[513] The name inserted in the policy is 'frequently – perhaps usually – that of the brokers acting on behalf of others'. *The Yasin* [1979] 2 Lloyd's Rep. 45, 53 *per* Lloyd J.

[514] See *Provincial Insurance Co of Canada v Leduc* (1874) LR 6 PC 224, 244.

[515] For a discussion of an insurance broker's lien, see *Arnould's Law of Marine Insurance and Average* (17th edn, 2008), 154–60.

[516] *Davies v Wilkinson* (1828) 4 Bing 573, 130 ER 889; referring to *Parker v Beasley* (1814) 2 M & S 423, 105 ER 438 (in which the brokers were not insurance brokers but they had a lien on a policy taken out in their own names by virtue of their accepting bills on the credit of the goods insured).

insured's asset would be used to pay the broker's liability.[517] Moreover, a claim on a policy of marine insurance is regarded as being unliquidated in nature, even after the loss has been adjusted,[518] so that a set-off would not appear to be available under the Statutes of Set-off if both the broker and the underwriter are solvent.[519]

Non-marine insurance

In non-marine insurance, a broker effecting a policy of insurance on behalf of a client would not ordinarily do so in the broker's own name. Therefore, the preceding discussion of the broker's right to set off losses when the name inserted in the policy is that of the broker would not be relevant. On the other hand, an attempt was made in New South Wales to introduce a right of set-off between the insurer and the broker in relation to premiums and commissions based upon custom or usage. In *Re Colin Williams (Insurance) Pty Ltd*,[520] an insurance company and an insurance broker had adopted a practice by which the company would debit the broker in its accounts with the amount of the premium,[521] and credit the broker with the appropriate commission. If a policy was cancelled so that a proportion of the premium was returnable, the insurance company would credit the broker's account with the rebate of premium, and debit that account with a rateable proportion of the commission.[522] Both the insurer and the broker went into liquidation. The insurer cancelled all its policies, and as a result became liable for returns of premium. The insurer's liquidator proposed to credit the broker with the returns, and debit it with the rebate of commission together with the sums owing by the broker for premiums. The broker's liquidator, on the other hand, said that the return premiums were payable to the policy-holders, and so could not be set off against the sums owing by the broker. Evidence was given of a practice in the insurance industry by which an insurance broker is credited with any return premium on a policy arranged through the broker and subsequently cancelled. Helsham J pointed out, however, that the policies all had provisions to the effect that, if the policy were cancelled, the unearned premium would be refunded *to the insured*. His Honour said that any alleged usage would be unreasonable if it was inconsistent with the terms of the contract between the insurer and the insured. In any event, even apart from the wording of the policies, he said that a usage by which

13.109

---

[517] See Lord Ellenborough in *Koster v Eason* (1813) 2 M & S 112, 119–20, 105 ER 324, 327.

[518] *Luckie v Bushby* (1853) 13 CB 864, 138 ER 1443; *Jabbour v Custodian of Israeli Absentee Property* [1954] 1 WLR 139, 143.

[519] See para. 2.26 above.

[520] [1975] 1 NSWLR 130. See also *Re Palmdale Insurance Ltd* [1982] VR 921.

[521] In non-marine insurance a broker ordinarily is not principally liable for the premium, though an agent of the insurer authorized to receive premiums on behalf of the insurer will be liable to account for premiums actually received. See *Re Palmdale Insurance Ltd* [1982] VR 921. Compare the custom at Lloyd's in relation to marine insurance, which renders the broker principally liable. See *MacGillivray on Insurance Law* (11th edn, 2008), 1121, para. 35–013. There is no authority establishing the existence of a similar custom in non-marine insurance in Australia. See *Norwich Fire Insurance Society Ltd v Brennans (Horsham) Pty Ltd* [1981] VR 981, 989, and also, in England, *Wilson v Avec Audio-Visual Equipment Ltd* [1974] 1 Lloyd's Rep 81. *Quaere* whether, in the absence of an agreement between the parties, the broker in *Re Colin Williams* in fact would have been liable to the insurance company for premiums. See *Norwich Winterthur Insurance (Australia) Ltd v Con-Stan Industries of Australia Pty Ltd* [1983] 1 NSWLR 461, 474 (result affirmed (1986) 160 CLR 226).

[522] Helsham J accepted that there was a usage by which an insurer, upon cancelling a policy in respect of which a broker's commission had been paid, could claim a proportionate part of the commission. He further held that this usage was not unreasonable. See also *Re Palmdale Insurance Ltd* [1982] VR 921.

an underwriter credits a broker's account with return premiums would be unreasonable, and consequently would not be binding upon the insured, unless the insured had knowledge of the practice when he or she entered into the contract.[523]

(6) Set-off against an agent with a lien, where the agent cannot sue

13.110 We have seen that, where an insurance broker has taken out a policy of insurance on behalf of an insured but in the broker's own name, so that the broker can sue upon it, and the broker is indebted to the underwriter, the courts have permitted the broker to employ an accrued claim on the policy in a set-off in the underwriter's bankruptcy against the debt to the extent that the broker has a lien on the policy.[524] In the cases in question, it was crucial to the set-off that the policy was in the broker's own name. As Lord Ellenborough remarked,[525] the underwriter in such a case: 'had consented that [the brokers] should be at liberty to stand in the character and situation of principals, that in case of loss they should be entitled to act in all respects as his creditors, and that they should be considered as giving him credit upon the policy at their own risk, and on their account.' If, on the other hand, the policy was not in the broker's name, the broker was not entitled to a set-off, notwithstanding that the broker had a lien. The important point as far as mutuality for a set-off is concerned is that a broker's lien is not equitable in origin, but rather it has its source in the common law.[526] The common law gave effect to the lien by allowing the broker to retain possession of the policy and to apply any proceeds of a claim that the broker in fact received in reduction of the debt secured by the lien.[527]

13.111 But, consistent with the view that the lien is not equitable in nature and that therefore it does not confer an equitable proprietary interest in the insured's claim,[528] it was held that, where the broker could not sue, there was a lack of mutuality between the insured's claim against the underwriter on the policy and the underwriter's demand against the broker for premiums, and consequently no set-off.[529]

---

[523] Helsham J referred to similar cases in marine insurance in which it was held that a usage at Lloyd's, by which an underwriter could settle a loss by setting it off against a broker's liability for premiums, would not bind the insured, unless the insured had knowledge of the existence of the usage, or in any event the broker from the course of dealing between him or herself and the insured had authority to settle losses in accordance with it. See *Sweeting v Pearce* (1859) 7 CB (NS) 449, 141 ER 890, (1861) 9 CB (NS) 534, 142 ER 210, and generally *Arnould's Law of Marine Insurance and Average* (17th edn, 2008), 143–6.

[524] See para. 13.108 above.

[525] *Koster v Eason* (1813) 2 M & S 112, 118, 105 ER 324, 326–7.

[526] Apart from the intervention of statute in the form of the Judicature Acts, the common law courts generally would not enforce an assignment of a debt, in which case there is little attraction in an argument that the lien operates as a form of assignment. Compare Wood, *English and International Set-off* (1989), 919.

[527] See e.g. *Mann v Forrester* (1814) 4 Camp 60, 171 ER 20; *Eide UK Ltd v Lowndes Lambert Group Ltd* [1999] QB 199, 208–11.

[528] Compare Wood, *English and International Set-off* (1989), 1004–5. The comments of the Privy Council in *Allen v F O'Hearn* [1937] AC 213, 218, in relation to whether an agent for an undisclosed principal is a trustee of the claim, should also be considered in this context. See para. 13.105 above.

[529] See *Koster v Eason* (1813) 2 M & S 112, 105 ER 324; *Xenos v Wickham* (1863) 14 CB (NS) 435, 465–6, 143 ER 515, 528; *Wilson v Creighton* (1782) 3 Dougl 132, 99 ER 576. See also *Cumming v Forester* (1813) 1 M & S 494, 105 ER 185 (set-off between solvent parties). Nor did it matter whether or not the broker acted on a *del credere* commission. See *Peele v Northcote* (1817) 7 Taunt 478, 129 ER 192. Compare Wood, *English and International Set-off* (1989), 918–19, 1006–7.

(7) *Del credere* commissions

There are a number of old set-off cases concerning agents who contracted on the basis of **13.112** a *del credere* commission, in other words where the agent undertook to indemnify the principal against loss arising from the failure of persons with whom the principal contracted to carry out their contracts.[530] In *Grove v Dubois*,[531] an insurance broker on a *del credere* commission took out policies in his own name on behalf of foreign correspondents. When he was sued by an underwriter's assignees in bankruptcy for unpaid premiums, it was held that he could set off claims that had accrued on the policies. The Court of King's Bench in allowing a set-off laid considerable emphasis on the fact of the commission, and indeed Lord Mansfield in his judgment said that the 'whole turns on the nature of a commission *del credere*'.[532] The view seems to have been that, if the broker had made himself liable to the principal for the loss, the broker in turn must have given credit to, or trusted, the underwriter for the amount of the loss.[533] That basis for the decision has been criticized, however, particularly by Lord Ellenborough, on the ground that a contract between the insured and the broker for a *del credere* commission ought not vary the rights between the broker and the underwriter, who is a stranger to it, and empower the broker to set up a claim against the underwriter that is derived from the contract.[534] Nevertheless, despite that criticism, the case has not been overruled. Rather, it has been suggested that the dealing in *Grove v Dobois* was with the broker as a principal,[535] the broker having insured for foreign correspondents who were unknown to the underwriter. In truth this is not the basis on which the judgments in *Grove v Dubois* proceeded.[536] A more fundamental question was in issue, whether a *del credere* agent assumed a primary or a secondary obligation.[537] Lord Mansfield in *Grove v Dubois*[538] said that it was primary. Lord Ellenborough, on the other hand, considered that it took effect as a guarantee,[539] and therefore was secondary.

---

[530] *Halsbury's Laws of England* (4th edn (reissue), 2003), vol. 2(1) ('Agency'), 11, para. 13. See generally Chorley, 'Del credere' (1929) 45 LQR 221, (1930) 46 LQR 11.

[531] (1786) 1 TR 112, 99 ER 1002. See also *Bize v Dickason* (1786) 1 TR 285, 99 ER 1097; *Wienholt v Roberts* (1811) 2 Camp 586, 170 ER 1260.

[532] (1786) 1 TR 112, 115, 99 ER 1002, 1004.

[533] See the discussion in the note to the report of *Baker v Langhorn* (1816) 4 Camp 396, 399, 171 ER 126, 127. In *Lee v Bullen* (1858) 27 LJQB 161 the *del credere* commission was said to give the broker an 'interest' in the contract of insurance. See also *Tapper v Matheson* (1884) NZLR 3 SC 312, 314.

[534] *Cumming v Forester* (1813) 1 M & S 494, 499, 105 ER 185, 186; *Koster v Eason* (1813) 2 M & S 112, 119, 105 ER 324, 327; *Hornby v Lacy* (1817) 6 M & S 166, 171, 105 ER 1205, 1207 *per* Lord Ellenborough (although compare Lord Ellenborough's earlier judgment in *Wienholt v Roberts* (1811) 2 Camp 586, 170 ER 1260). See also *Baker v Langhorn* (1816) 6 Taunt 519, 521, 128 ER 1136, 1137 (Gibbs CJ); *Peele v Northcote* (1817) 7 Taunt 478, 480, 485, 129 ER 192, 193, 195 (Gibbs CJ); *Hornby v Lacy* at 172, 1207 (Abbott CJ). *Quaere* whether this is a satisfactory ground for criticism. For example, an assignment by A to B of a debt owing by C may provide B with a defence under the Statutes of Set-off to an action brought against him or her by C for payment of a debt arising on another transaction. See paras 3.07–3.09 above.

[535] *Cumming v Forester* (1813) 1 M & S 494, 499, 105 ER 185, 187 (Lord Ellenborough). In *Parker v Smith* (1812) 16 East 382, 385–6, 104 ER 1133, 1135 Lord Ellenborough said that *Grove v Dubois* was determined on the ground that there were 'dealings virtually had with the assured themselves'. See also *Arnould on the Law of Marine Insurance and Average,* (12th edn, 1939) vol. 1, 164–5.

[536] Chorley, 'Del Credere' (1929) 45 LQR 221, 227.

[537] Chorley, 'Del Credere' (1929) 45 LQR 221, 229–30.

[538] (1786) 1 TR 112, 115, 99 ER 1002, 1004.

[539] *Morris v Cleasby* (1816) 4 M & S 566, 574, 105 ER 943, 947; *Hornby v Lacy* (1817) 6 M & S 166, 171, 105 ER 1205, 1207.

This is the view that has prevailed. A *del credere* commission is regarded as an agreement to indemnify the principal if the third party fails to pay through insolvency, or something that makes it impossible to recover as in the case of insolvency.[540]

13.113 Given this characterization of a *del credere* agency, if the agent has paid the principal in accordance with the commission, and the case is one in which the agent in any event can sue the third party in the agent's own name, for example because the agent acted for an undisclosed principal or (in some cases) an unnamed principal,[541] the position is simple. There is mutuality both at law and in equity as between the agent and the third party.[542] Since the agent after payment under the *del credere* commission holds the claim for his or her own benefit and not for the benefit of the principal, there is no other beneficial interest which can affect mutuality. Where the third party has become bankrupt or has gone into liquidation, so that the insolvency set-off section governs the question, the availability of a set-off would depend on the principles discussed earlier in relation to contingent debts and guarantees.[543] Thus, the agent would not be entitled to a set-off if payment has not been made under the commission.[544] The principal in such a case would still have a right of proof in the insolvency, and the rule against double proof would prevent a set-off as between the agent and the third party.[545]

13.114 Consider that the case is one in which the agent does not have standing to sue, and the third party is insolvent. Usually the *del credere* commission would not have been given at the request of the third party, in which case *Owen v Tate*[546] suggests that after payment the agent as a surety would not have a claim for reimbursement from the third party which could be set off. That view is consistent with some of the early common law cases in which *Grove v Dubois* was criticized and a set-off was denied.[547] However, *Owen v Tate* has not been favourably received by commentators,[548] and it might not be followed. Moreover, it might not have the effect of precluding a remedy to the *del credere* agent by way of subrogation to the principal's rights against the third party, either on the basis of the equitable

---

[540] *Thomas Gabriel & Sons v Churchill & Sim* [1914] 3 KB 1272, affirming [1914] 1 KB 449.

[541] See *Teheran-Europe Co Ltd v S T Belton (Tractors) Ltd* [1968] 2 QB 545, 558 in relation to an agent for an unnamed principal, and para. 13.106 above.

[542] See *Koster v Eason* (1813) 2 M & S 112, 105 ER 324, in which Lord Ellenborough emphasized (at 118, 326–7) the title to sue. This is the proper explanation of *Lee v Bullen* (1858) 27 LJQB 161, in which the brokers contracted in their own names 'and/or as agents'. Wightman J emphasized that the brokers might have sued and recovered in their own names, but compare Compton J at 162.

[543] See paras 8.10–8.34 (contingent debt owing by the insolvent) and paras 8.35–8.46 (contingent debt owing to the insolvent) above. In particular, a guarantor who pays the creditor after the creditor has proved in the debtor's bankruptcy or liquidation should be subrogated to the creditor's proof, and because of that beneficial interest in the proof the guarantor should be entitled to a set-off. See para. 8.29 above, and the discussion of subrogation below. Accordingly, it should not be fatal to a set-off that the agent paid under the *del credere* commission after the principal had lodged a proof in the third party's bankruptcy or liquidation. Compare Wood, *English and International Set-off* (1989), 1007.

[544] *Koster v Eason* (1813) 2 M & S 112, 119–20, 105 ER 324, 327.

[545] See paras 8.13–8.18 above.

[546] [1976] 1 QB 402. Compare *The 'Zuhal K'* [1987] 1 Lloyd's Rep 151.

[547] See e.g. *Cumming v Forrester* (1813) 1 M & S 494, 105 ER 185; *Morris v Cleasby* (1816) 4 M & S 566, 105 ER 943; *Peele v Northcote* (1817) 7 Taunt 478, 129 ER 192.

[548] Goff and Jones, *The Law of Restitution* (7th edn, 2007), 138–9; Birks, *An Introduction to the Law of Restitution* (1989), 311–12; Burrows, *The Law of Restitution* (1993), 213–16.

right[549] or pursuant to the statutory right conferred on a surety by s. 5 of the Mercantile Law Amendment Act 1856.[550] Even if it is the case, on the authority of *Owen v Tate*, that the agent has no direct right of reimbursement from the third party, but subrogation is available, the interest obtained in the principal's action consequent upon the right of subrogation may provide a sufficient basis for a set-off.[551] Nor should it make any difference that the interest is acquired after the third party's bankruptcy by payment to the principal, since it still arises out of a prior obligation in the form of the *del credere* agency.[552] The basis of the set-off would be the giving of credit, in that the *del credere* commission would naturally or in the ordinary course of business end in a debt[553] owing by the third party to the agent as a result of the right of subrogation. In that situation, the circumstance that there is no direct dealing between the *del credere* agent and the third party should not preclude a set-off.[554] The position is more complicated in Australia, given some views that have been expressed by the Australian High Court,[555] but the better view is that insolvency set-off does not require a dealing between the parties to the proposed set-off where the claim sought to be set off is a mutual debt or credit.[556]

(8) Set-off between the agent and the third party, where the agent is personally liable as agent

An agent contracting for a principal may undertake a personal liability to the third party,[557] **13.115** which should be capable of being set off against a personal claim that the agent has against the third party.[558] On the other hand, the agent should not be entitled to bring into an account a liability of the third party to the principal. While the principal may be obliged to indemnify the agent, this would be of no concern to the third party, and it should not be sufficient to bring about mutuality between the agent's personal liability to the third party and a claim possessed by the principal against the third party.[559] A set-off may nevertheless be available if the principal in truth had contracted only as a surety, rather than as a principal debtor in his or her own right. In that circumstance, if the third party proceeds against the agent/surety, the agent may be able to defend the action on the basis of a set-off that would have been available to the principal debtor.[560]

---

[549] Goff and Jones, *The Law of Restitution* (7th edn, 2007), 138–9; Beatson, *The Use and Abuse of Unjust Enrichment* (1991), 199. Compare Mitchell, *The Law of Subrogation* (1994), 166–7.

[550] Burrows, *The Law of Restitution* (1993), 215; O'Donovan and Phillips, *Modern Contract of Guarantee* (looseleaf) [12.2670].

[551] See para. 8.29 above.

[552] See paras 8.30–8.31 above, criticizing *MPS Constructions Pty Ltd v Rural Bank of New South Wales* (1980) 4 ACLR 835.

[553] See para. 7.04 above.

[554] See paras 7.12–7.19 and 8.24–8.28 above.

[555] See paras 7.20–7.22 above, referring to *Gye v McIntyre* (1991) 171 CLR 609, 623, 626 and *Coventry v Charter Pacific Corporation Ltd* (2005) 227 CLR 234.

[556] See paras 7.13 and 7.26 above.

[557] See generally *Bowstead and Reynolds on Agency* (18th edn, 2006), 501 *et seq.*

[558] See *Kent v Munroe* (1904) 8 OLR 723 in relation to McDiarmid.

[559] See *Nelson v Roberts* (1893) 69 LT 352, and Angas Parsons J in *Rex v Ray, ex p Chapman* [1936] SASR 241, 249 (liability of personal representative for costs). See also *Kent v Munroe* (1904) 8 OLR 723.

[560] See paras 18.07–18.39 below.

(9) Set-off between the principal and the agent

13.116 If the agent incurs a liability to the third party for which he or she is entitled to be reimbursed by the principal, there may be a set-off as between the principal and the agent in respect of the agent's right of reimbursement and a separate indebtedness of the agent to the principal.[561]

13.117 An agent may be obliged to account to the principal for sums received in the course of the agency. The question whether the agent is entitled to a set-off may depend on whether the sums in question are impressed with a trust.[562]

G. The Crown

(1) General principle

13.118 Prior to the enactment of the Crown Proceedings Act 1947, it was not possible for the defendant in an action at law brought by the Crown to set off a cross-demand against the Crown. A subject could only make good a claim against the Crown by means of a petition of right, and that procedure could not be avoided by the subject refusing to pay a debt to the Crown and then asserting his or her own claim as a set-off.[563] The inability to rely on a set-off against the Crown was remedied by s. 13 of the Crown Proceedings Act,[564] which provided that all civil proceedings by or against the Crown were to be instituted and proceeded with in accordance with the rules of court and not otherwise. However, CPR r. 66.4 contains a number of restrictions on the availability of set-off and counterclaim in proceedings by or against the Crown. Briefly, a person cannot raise a defence of set-off or make a counterclaim in proceedings by the Crown if the proceedings are for the recovery of, or the proposed set-off or counterclaim is based upon a claim for repayment of, taxes, duties or penalties. Further, a counterclaim cannot be made or a defence of set-off raised without the permission of the court:

(a) in proceedings by or against the Crown in the name of the Attorney-General, or

(b) in proceedings by or against the Crown in the name of a Government department unless the subject-matter of the counter-claim or set-off relates to that department.

13.119 The Civil Procedure Rules do not apply to insolvency proceedings under the Insolvency Act 1986. On the other hand, r. 7.51 of the Insolvency Rules 1986 provides that, except so far as they are inconsistent with the Insolvency Rules, the Civil Procedure Rules and the

---

[561] *Cropper v Cook* (1868) LR 3 CP 194.

[562] See ch. 10 above.

[563] *Attorney-General v Guy Motors Ltd* [1928] 2 KB 78. Compare *Hettihewage Siman Appu v The Queen's Advocate* (1884) 9 App Cas 571, in which there was a right to sue the Crown under the laws of Ceylon. In *Re Ind, Coope & Co Ltd* [1911] 2 Ch 223, 235–6 Warrington J left open the question whether a set-off could have been exercised against the Crown. The Crown, on the other hand, could plead a set-off in answer to a petition of right. See *De Lancey v The Queen* (1871) LR 6 Ex 286, 288 (Kelly CB), referring to (1860) 23 & 24 Vict, c. 34, s. 7.

[564] For the County Court, see s. 15. In relation to equitable set-off, see *Saitta v Commissioner of Taxation* (2002) 125 FCR 388 (Australia). For set-off against an order for costs made against the Crown, see *Revenue and Customs Commissioners v Xicom Systems Ltd* [2008] EWHC 1945 (Ch).

practice and procedure of the High Court apply to insolvency proceedings in that court. However, that does not import the restrictions in CPR r. 66.4 into insolvency set-off. Insolvency set-off takes effect automatically upon the occurrence of a bankruptcy or a liquidation.[565] It does not require a proceeding or the making of a claim, and therefore CPR r. 66.4 can have no application. Thus, obligations to pay tax to and rights to tax refunds from revenue authorities can be the subject of set-off in bankruptcy and company liquidation.[566]

(2) Government departments

The Crown includes government departments that are headed by a Minister.[567] Debts **13.120** arising from dealings with the one government department would be mutual for the purpose of a set-off. An analogous case is *Knowles v Maitland*,[568] in which the colonel of a regiment was both debtor and creditor in that capacity, and a set-off was allowed. However, a person may be liable to one government department and have a claim against another. Because of the theory that the Crown is one and indivisible the demands would be mutual[569] although, where the debtor is neither bankrupt nor a company in liquidation, a set-off would be subject to CPR r. 66.4.

The fact that legislation may provide that a department is entitled to enforce rights acquired **13.121** in the exercise of its functions and is liable in respect of liabilities 'as if it were acting as a principal' does not mean that the rights or liabilities are not those of the Crown so as to destroy mutuality. A provision to that effect may be purely procedural, in the sense that the department is capable of suing and being sued as a principal, but in the eyes of the law it is still an agent of the Crown.[570]

(3) Criticism of Crown set-off

The Cork Committee,[571] following similar comments by the Blagden Committee in **13.122** 1957,[572] considered that this right of set-off available to the Crown conferred upon it an unwarranted preference in the bankruptcy of a subject. Accordingly, it recommended that government departments should be treated as separate entities for the purpose of set-off, and moreover that there should not be any right of set-off between contractual and statutory obligations. On the other hand, it also recommended that set-off in relation to one statutory obligation and another, and in relation to one contractual obligation and another, in each case relating to the same government department, should be allowed in accordance

---

[565] See paras 6.119–6.146 above.
[566] *Re D. H. Curtis (Builders) Ltd* [1978] 1 Ch 162; *Re Cushla Ltd* [1979] 3 All ER 415; *Re Unit 2 Windows Ltd* [1985] 1 WLR 1383; *Secretary of State for Trade and Industry v Frid* [2004] 2 AC 506.
[567] Hogg and Monahan, *Liability of the Crown* (3rd edn, 2000), 11.
[568] (1825) 4 B & C 173, 107 ER 1024, as explained by Lord Tenterden CJ in *Earl of Dalhousie v Chapman* (1829) 7 LJOSKB 233.
[569] See e.g. *Re D. H. Curtis (Builders) Ltd* [1978] 1 Ch 162; *Secretary of State for Trade and Industry v Frid* [2004] 2 AC 506 (claim against Customs and Excise and a cross-claim by the Secretary of State for Trade and Industry).
[570] *Cullen v Nottingham Health Authority* [1986] BCC 99,368.
[571] *Cork Committee Report*, 306–7, 309.
[572] *Blagden Committee Report*, 29.

with the principle of mutuality. Those recommendations were not included in the Insolvency Act 1986, but there is much to commend them, though it is debatable whether the Crown should be permitted to set off one statutory obligation against another when the one government department is involved. Statutory rights and obligations arise independently of any desire by the parties to deal with each other. If the possibility of a right of set-off could not have acted as a stimulus for parties to deal with each other, there is no real justification for allowing either of them preferential treatment by means of a set-off in the event of the insolvency of the other.[573]

(4) Public corporations

13.123   It may be that a public corporation, as opposed to a department of state, is liable to a bankrupt or a company in liquidation, or that a public corporation has a claim against the bankrupt or the company. The question then may arise whether there is mutuality in relation to that demand and a cross-demand that relates to a department of state, or another public corporation. In Australia, it has been held that the fact that a public corporation is a party to one of the demands does not destroy mutuality as long as the corporation may be considered to be an agent of the Crown, a concept that is determined by the measure of control that the Crown, through its Ministers, has over the body in question.[574] This should also apply in England. An illustration is *Re Duncan and Wakefield's Assignment*, a decision of the Western Australian Supreme Court.[575] Debtors who had executed a deed of assignment were owed money by the Minister of Lands, but were also indebted to the State Saw Mills. Dwyer J noted that the State Saw Mills:[576]

> is a trading concern created to carry on a profit making business, it is administered by one of the State Ministers as part of his normal ministerial duties, the property it holds belongs to the State and has always so belonged, its funds are provided from time to time out of the consolidated revenue, and its profits go into consolidated revenue, there is no special beneficiary or group of beneficiaries to be advantaged, the benefit from its operations is for the State as a whole and not for any particular class or restricted number of persons, and any loss must be borne similarly.

His Honour concluded that the corporation was an agent of the Crown, and accordingly it could bring into account the Minister's liability to the debtor. In *Re Mathrick*,[577] two public corporations were involved. The Board of Land and Works owed a sum of money to a bankrupt, while the Forests Commission was a creditor of the bankrupt. Lukin J held that both bodies were agents of the Crown. In each case the corporation was financed out of consolidated revenue, and all moneys were received on account of consolidated revenue. Moreover, each was subject to a large amount of ministerial control. Because they were both agents of the Crown, a set-off could proceed.[578] If, on the other hand, a public corporation

---

[573] See paras 6.20 and 6.21 above.
[574] Hogg and Monahan, *Liability of the Crown* (3rd edn, 2000), 333–4.
[575] (1932) 34 WALR 138.
[576] (1932) 34 WALR 138, 139.
[577] (1941) 12 ABC 212.
[578] Lukin J overruled an earlier decision of his own in *Re McCann & Edwards' Deed of Arrangement* (1932) 4 ABC 145, in which a set-off had been denied in similar circumstances.

is independent of the government, with independent powers and discretions, it does not represent the Crown,[579] and mutuality would be lacking where a cross-demand relates to another public corporation or the Crown.

(5) The federal system in Australia

In a federal system such as Australia, a person may be a debtor to the Crown in right of one **13.124** state and a creditor of the Crown in right of another state, or of the Commonwealth, and vice versa. The aphorism that 'the Crown is one and indivisible'[580] would suggest that the demands are mutual and may be set off. However, as Latham CJ once observed, when this aphorism is 'stated as a legal principle, it tends to dissolve into verbally impressive mysticism'.[581] In truth, the Crown in right of each state and of the Commonwealth represents a separate government and a separate legal person. The better view is that the demands are not mutual, and that a set-off should not be allowed.[582] Nor, one imagines, would a government of one state be happy that its claim against a person could be used to satisfy the liability of another state.

H. Set-off in Relation to a Deceased's Estate

(1) Executors and administrators

An executor or administrator of a deceased's estate still in the course of administration is **13.125** not a trustee of the deceased's property, which includes any debts owing to the estate. A trust requires that there should be specific subjects identifiable as the trust fund, and while the estate is still being administered it is impossible to identify, in the case of residuary legatees and persons entitled upon an intestacy, the person in whom the beneficial ownership of any particular asset forming part of the estate is vested.[583] An executor has various fiduciary obligations in relation to the assets that come into his or her hands in right of the office of executor, but the residuary legatees do not have a beneficial property interest in those assets before the completion of the administration.[584] Their only right consists of a chose in action to have the estate properly administered. Those principles were

---

[579] *Skinner v Commissioner for Railways* (1937) 37 SR (NSW) 261, 270; *Grain Elevators Board (Victoria) v Dunmunkle Corporation* (1946) 73 CLR 70, 76.
[580] See e.g. *Amalgamated Society of Engineers v Adelaide Steamship Co Ltd* (1920) 28 CLR 129, 152.
[581] *Minister for Works for Western Australia v Gulson* (1944) 69 CLR 338, 350.
[582] See *Vass v Commonwealth* (2000) 96 FCR 272, 288–9, although that was not simply a case of different governments.
[583] *Ayerst v C & K (Construction) Ltd* [1976] AC 167, 178, referring to *Commissioner of Stamp Duties (Queensland) v Livingston* [1965] AC 694, 707–8 (PC). This applies equally in the case of a specific bequest. See *Official Receiver in Bankruptcy v Schultz* (1990) 170 CLR 306, 312.
[584] 'What equity did not do was to recognise or create for residuary legatees a beneficial interest in the assets in the executor's hands during the course of administration. Conceivably, this could have been done, in the sense that the assets, whatever they might be from time to time, could have been treated as a present, though fluctuating, trust fund held for the benefit of all those interested in the estate according to the measure of their respective interests. But it never was done. It would have been a clumsy and unsatisfactory device from a practical point of view; and, indeed, it would have been in plain conflict with the basic conception of equity that to impose the fetters of a trust upon property, with the resulting creation of equitable interests in that property, there had to be specific subjects identifiable as the trust fund.' *Commissioner of Stamp Duties (Queensland) v Livingston* [1965] AC 694, 707–8 *per* Viscount Radcliffe (PC).

accepted by the Privy Council in *Commissioner of Stamp Duties (Queensland) v Livingston*.[585] In delivering their Lordships' judgment, Viscount Radcliffe also said that a testator's property comes to the executor: 'in full ownership, without distinction between legal and equitable interests. The whole property was his.'[586] This does not mean that an executor is the beneficial owner of the assets. The executor has the 'full ownership', but in the sense that the executor has vested in him or her 'the whole right of property'[587] to the extent that there are property rights in those assets. As Lord Diplock later remarked: 'No one would suggest that an executor, who was not also a legatee, was beneficial owner as well as legal owner of any of the property which was in the full ownership of the deceased before his death.'[588] It would seem then that, during the administration of the estate, neither the executor nor a residuary legatee is regarded as the beneficial owner of a debt which constitutes an asset of the estate. This concept also applies in the case of an intestacy, so that neither the administrator nor any person entitled on the intestacy is the beneficial owner of an asset which forms part of the unadministered estate.[589] An unadministered estate is similar in that regard to a valid non-charitable purpose trust, for example a trust for a monument. There is no beneficiary who it can be said is the beneficial owner of the trust fund, but that does not mean that the trustee is the beneficial owner. Given these principles, consider the case of a debtor to an estate who is being sued by an executor or an administrator. In the first place, the debtor could not set off a claim that he or she has against the executor or administrator in that person's personal capacity. Nor, if the estate has not been administered, could the debtor bring the debt into an account in a bankruptcy with a debt owing to him or her by a residuary legatee personally, or, as the case may be, by a person entitled to a share of the intestate's estate.[590] Mutuality in equity would be lacking.

13.126 Once an executor or an administrator has completed the administration of the estate, he or she becomes a trustee holding for the beneficiaries under the terms of the will or on an intestacy.[591] If in that situation the executor is the sole person beneficially interested in the

---

[585] [1965] AC 694. In Australia, see *Official Receiver in Bankruptcy v Schultz* (1990) 170 CLR 306, 312–14 (although the Australian High Court (at 314) left open the question whether the estate is held on trust for the beneficiaries *as a class*, so as to confer a proprietary interest on all beneficiaries); *Barns v Barns* (2003) 214 CLR 169 at [50].

[586] [1965] AC 694, 707.

[587] [1965] AC 694, 712.

[588] *Ayerst v C & K (Construction) Ltd* [1976] AC 167, 178. Even when a person is solely entitled to the full beneficial ownership of property, both at law and in equity, it is not correct to say that the person enjoys an 'equitable interest' in the property. Rather, the legal title carries with it all rights. Therefore, if the person disposes of the property in circumstances which give rise to a trust in his or her favour, it is not correct to say that the person 'retains' the equitable interest. See *Westdeutsche Landesbank Girozentrale v Islington LBC* [1996] AC 669, 706, 714.

[589] *Re Leigh's Will Trusts* [1970] 1 Ch 277, 281–2. Similarly, a beneficiary in a discretionary trust has no proprietary interest in the trust assets. See *Gartside v IRC* [1968] AC 553; *Chief Commissioner of Stamp Duties v ISPT Pty Ltd* (1997) 45 NSWLR 639, 655; *Commissioner of State Revenue v Serana Pty Ltd* [2008] WASCA 82 at [121]–[127]. Compare *Kennon v Spry* (2008) 238 CLR 366 at [74]–[80], [125]–[126] in relation to the Family Law Act 1975 (Cth).

[590] See *Bishop v Church* (1748) 3 Atk 691, 26 ER 1197; *Phillips v Howell* [1901] 2 Ch 773.

[591] *Re Cockburn's Will Trusts* [1957] 1 Ch 438, 439.

estate, a debt owing by the executor may be set off against a debt due to the estate.[592] Until the administration has been completed, however, a court of equity generally will not inquire whether the estate has sufficient assets to satisfy the testator's debts and testamentary expenses, and the expenses of the administration, in order to facilitate a set-off either by or against the residuary legatee or person entitled on an intestacy.[593] As Sir George Jessel MR once remarked: 'for the mere purpose of set-off the Court will not take the account.'[594] In *Ex p Morier, re Willis, Percival, & Co*,[595] a brother and sister were executors of their deceased father's will, and accordingly opened an executorship account with a bank in their joint names. The son, who was the sole residuary legatee, also kept a separate account with the bank in his personal capacity. The bank stopped payment and entered into an arrangement with its creditors for its liquidation,[596] at which time the executorship account was in credit and the son's personal account in debit. Securities had been set aside to answer the specific legacies bequeathed by the will, and the testator's debts and funeral and testamentary expenses had all been paid. At the date of the arrangement, however, the executors were still jointly liable for some rates and taxes, and in addition a solicitor's bill of costs had not been paid. The administration, therefore, had not been completed at that date, with the result that a trust had not arisen in favour of the son as the residuary legatee so as to enable him to employ the bank's debt in a set-off. Nor was the Court of Appeal prepared to take an account of the testator's estate in order to ascertain whether there would be a surplus accruing to the residuary legatee.

Two cases in which a set-off was permitted

There are nevertheless two cases in which a debt constituting an asset of a deceased's estate was allowed to be brought in as a set-off against a separate indebtedness of the residuary legatee before the completion of the administration, although neither decision is free of difficulty. **13.127**

The first case, *Jones v Mossop*,[597] concerned an assent in an intestacy. An assent is a method by which a personal representative indicates that he or she does not require certain property for the discharge of the liabilities of the estate, and that therefore it may pass to the legatee.[598] After the assent, the beneficial interest in the property concerned vests in the legatee. The legatee may bring an action to recover it, including against the personal representative.[599] The facts of *Jones v Mossop* are complicated, but may be summarized as follows. Jones was indebted on a bond to John Reed. John Reed died intestate, leaving **13.128**

---

[592] *Williams v MacDonald* [1915] VLR 229. For a discussion of the question whether an executor is required to make an assent in his or her own favour in this situation, see *Williams, Mortimer and Sunnucks on Executors, Administrators and Probate* (19th edn, 2008), 1160. Assuming that the administration of the estate had been completed, *quaere* why a set-off was not allowed in *Harvey v Wood* (1821) 5 Madd 459, 56 ER 971.

[593] *Bishop v Church* (1748) 3 Atk 691, 26 ER 1197.

[594] *Middleton v Pollock, ex p Nugee* (1875) LR 20 Eq 29, 34.

[595] (1879) 12 Ch D 491.

[596] See the Bankruptcy Act 1869, s. 125.

[597] (1844) 3 Hare 568, 67 ER 506.

[598] Williams, *The Law Relating to Assents* (1947), 1.

[599] *Williams, Mortimer and Sunnucks on Executors, Administrators and Probate* (19th edn, 2008), 1164.

Richard Reed his only child and next of kin, and as such entitled to a clear residue of his personal estate. Richard Reed obtained a grant of administration of his father's estate. Before he could undertake the administration, however, he became insolvent, and he later died. Mossop was appointed assignee in his insolvency. After the death of Richard Reed, Mossop obtained letters of administration *de bonis non* of John Reed, and commenced an action against Jones on the bond. Jones was a creditor of Richard Reed, and accordingly he sought to have his claim set off against his debt to John Reed's estate, the residue of which after payment of John Reed's debts would vest in Richard Reed. A number of the debts of John Reed still remained unpaid, but Wigram VC nevertheless allowed a set-off because of some admissions made by Mossop as administrator. Mossop said that he believed that the personal estate exclusive of the bond was more than sufficient to pay John Reed's debts, that the money due upon the bond was part of the net residue of the estate, and that it had become legally and equitably the absolute property of Richard Reed. The Vice Chancellor said that the case: 'is the same in principle as where an assent has been given to a legacy whereby the property has passed to the legatee, being himself an executor, in which case the legacy is separated from the estate of the testator, and becomes the property of the legatee.'[600] But notwithstanding the admissions, the decision is still open to question on the basis of the view that has been expressed, that an administrator, as opposed to an executor, cannot assent in respect of pure personalty which passes on an intestacy,[601] and a debt owing to the deceased is personalty.

13.129   The second case is *Bailey v Finch*.[602] The defendant was the sole executor of a testatrix's will, and was also the residuary legatee. An executorship account opened by him with a banking firm showed a credit balance of £500 when the firm was adjudged bankrupt. At the date of the bankruptcy the defendant had not provided specifically for two bequests, but there were in the hands of the defendant, besides the credit balance with the firm, other personal assets of the testatrix which would have been more than sufficient to provide for the bequests. The defendant also had his own personal account with the firm, which was overdrawn to the extent of £300. It was held in this action brought against him on the overdrawn account by the trustee of the bankrupts' estate that he could set off the credit balance on the executorship account, even though the administration had not been completed at the time of the bankruptcy, and even though there had not been a prior assent in respect of any part of the residuary estate. The set-off was based upon the court's finding that there was a right of set-off at law.[603] The defendant was the sole creditor on the executorship account. Therefore, at law there was mutuality between that claim and his personal debt to the bank. The executorship account had not been set aside to answer any other specific bequest. Therefore, there was no other person who could be identified as having the equitable title to it. Moreover, the rest of the estate was more than sufficient to satisfy the specific bequests, and so it was considered that there was no reason in equity for disallowing this

---

[600] (1844) 3 Hare 568, 576, 67 ER 506, 510.

[601] See *Williams, Mortimer and Sunnucks on Executors, Administrators and Probate* (19th edn, 2008), 1159. Compare Parry and Kerridge, *The Law of Succession* (12th edn, 2009), 582–3 [24–37].

[602] (1871) LR 7 QB 34.

[603] See Blackburn J (1871) LR 7 QB 34, 36 (arguends), 44–5, and Cockburn CJ at 39–40.

set-off permitted at law. The fact of mutuality at law was the ground upon which James and Cotton LJJ later distinguished *Bailey v Finch* in *Ex p Morier, re Willis, Percival & Co*.[604] In *Ex p Morier*, the executorship account was in the joint names of the two executors. Therefore, in contrast to *Bailey v Finch*, there was a lack of mutuality at law between the executors' joint demand against the bank and the bank's separate claim against the executor who was the residuary legatee, so that a set-off would not have been available at law. Nevertheless, the analysis in *Bailey v Finch* is not without difficulty, and indeed Cotton LJ in *Ex p Morier*[605] appears to have been uncomfortable with the decision. The firm had been made bankrupt, in which case the set-off section in the insolvency legislation alone should have determined the availability of a set-off.[606] Mutuality under the insolvency set-off section is determined by reference to the equitable interests of the parties rather than dry legal rights.[607] While an estate is still in the course of administration it is impossible to identify, at least in the case of residuary legatees, the person in whom the beneficial ownership in any particular property forming part of the estate is vested.[608] Since the administration had not been completed at the time of the bankruptcy in *Bailey v Finch*, and nor had there been an assent, it was not possible to say at that date that the defendant himself was the beneficial owner of the executorship account.[609] On that basis, a set-off should not have been allowed. The distinction is between a set-off at law, which may take effect when the demands are mutual at law unless there is another person whom it can be said has an equitable title to either of the demands sufficient to prevent a set-off, or there is some other reason in equity as to why a set-off should not proceed,[610] and a set-off in insolvency, in which it must be shown that the parties themselves to the proposed set-off have the equitable titles to the demands.

(2) Set-off between a third party and a deceased's estate

If a creditor of a deceased proceeds against the estate for payment, the executor or administrator of the estate cannot set off a debt owing by the creditor to the executor or administrator in that person's personal capacity.[611] Alternatively, the creditor may be indebted separately to the estate as a result of a liability incurred to the deceased, in which case the creditor may wish to set the debts against each other, particularly if the estate is insolvent.

13.130

---

[604] (1879) 12 Ch D 491, 498–9 (James LJ), 501–2 (Cotton LJ). See para. 13.126 above.

[605] (1879) 12 Ch D 491, 501–2.

[606] See paras 6.22–6.24 above.

[607] See paras 11.13–11.17 above.

[608] *Ayerst v C & K (Construction) Ltd* [1976] AC 167, 178. This applies also in the case of a specific bequest. See *Official Receiver in Bankruptcy v Schultz* (1990) 170 CLR 306, 312.

[609] See Blackburn J (1871) LR 7 QB 34, 45 ('this money, which at the time of the bankruptcy was legally in the defendant, and not also equitably only because some other persons had a small claim on it'), although compare Cockburn CJ at 40 and Mellor J at 46.

[610] See paras 11.18–11.20 above.

[611] *Medlicot v Bowes* (1749) 1 Ves Sen 207, 208, 27 ER 985, 986. Similarly, in an action by an executor or administrator for money had and received after the death to the use of the executor or the administrator, the defendant cannot set off a debt owing to him or her by the deceased. See *Schofield v Corbett* (1836) 11 QB 779, 116 ER 666.

Equitable set-off, and the Statutes of Set-off

13.131 Consider first the question of set-off when the estate is not being administered in bankruptcy. In such a case, if the demands are sufficiently closely connected there is no reason why an equitable set-off should not be available.[612] Further, the Statutes of Set-off may apply. The first Statute, (1729) 2 Geo II, c. 22, s. 13, provided that: 'where there are mutual debts between the plaintiff and defendant, or if either party sue or be sued as executor or administrator, where there are mutual debts between the testator or intestate and either party, one debt may be set against the other.'[613] This has been interpreted as requiring that the debts the subject of a set-off originally should have existed between two living persons.[614] In other words, there must have been cross-debts between the testator (or the intestate) and the creditor before the death.[615] *Wilkinson v Cawood*[616] is not inconsistent with that view. A sub-lessee paid rent to the wife of his deceased landlord after the death, and she in turn paid ground rent to the superior landlord. When she was sued by the deceased's executor in respect of the rent that she had received, it was held that she could set up the payments she had made for ground rent that had accrued due before (but not after) the death, even though those payments did not give rise to a debt owing to her by the deceased before the death. *Wilkinson v Cawood* should be compared to *Shipman v Thompson*.[617] A testator had appointed an agent to collect rent. After the testator's death, the agent received payments of rent that were due and payable before the death, and it was held that he had to account for them to the estate without set-off in respect of a debt owing to him by the testator. *Shipman v Thompson* accords with the traditional interpretation of the Statutes. The agent was not indebted to the testator before the death, so that the Statutes did not apply. The rent was not received by the agent to the use of the testator, but rather to the use of the executor. There is no inconsistency, however, between *Wilkinson v Cawood* and *Shipman v Thompson*, because the former case in truth did not concern set-off under the Statutes of Set-off. Rather, the payments of ground rent to the superior landlord were treated as a discharge *pro tanto* of the rent due to the intermediate landlord,[618] so that there was no longer an obligation to account for it.

---

[612] See ch. 4 above.

[613] In New South Wales, see the Civil Procedure Act 2005, s. 21(1) and (2).

[614] *Rees v Watts* (1855) 11 Ex 410, 414, 156 ER 891, 893.

[615] *Lambarde v Older* (1853) 17 Beav 542, 51 ER 1144; *Rees v Watts* (1855) 11 Ex 410, 156 ER 891 (in which the early cases are discussed); *Allison v Smith* (1869) 10 B & S 747, 148 RR 589; *Newell v The National Provincial Bank of England* (1876) 1 CPD 496; *Hallett v Hallett* (1879) 13 Ch D 232; *Re Gregson; Christison v Bolam* (1887) 36 Ch D 223; *Re Wickham's Will. Grant v Union Trustee Co of Australia Ltd* (1898) 9 QLJ 102 (though note the discussion of *Wickham* in para. 14.42 below in the context of the rule in *Cherry v Boultbee* (1839) 4 My & Cr 442, 41 ER 171). See also *Beckwith v Bullen* (1858) 8 El & Bl 683, 120 ER 254 (deceased underwriter's liability on policy still unliquidated at the date of death), and *Mardall v Thellusson* (1856) 6 El & Bl 976, 119 ER 1127. Compare *Parker v Jackson* [1936] 2 All ER 281, which is criticized in paras 2.40–2.45 above, and also *Blakesley v Smallwood* (1846) 8 QB 538, 115 ER 978, which is discussed in *Rees v Watts* (1855) 11 Ex 410, 415–16, 156 ER 891, 893–4. The relevant date is the date of death, as opposed to the date of notice of death, though compare Wood, *English and International Set-off* (1989), 1104 in relation to the debt owing by the deceased. In *Rogerson v Ladbroke* (1822) 1 Bing 93, 130 ER 39 the banker's right of combination was in issue, as opposed to set-off under the Statutes of Set-off. See ch. 15 below.

[616] (1797) 3 Anst 905, 145 ER 1077.

[617] (1738) Willes 103, 125 ER 1078.

[618] See also *Sapsford v Fletcher* (1792) 4 TR 511, 100 ER 1147, to which MacDonald CB referred in *Wilkinson v Cawood*.

It is not clear from the cases whether the debts should not only have been in existence but **13.132** also have been due and payable before death, although the Statutes of Set-off point to the latter as being the correct principle. The Statutes allowed a set-off between two living persons in the case of mutual debts, and 'debts' has been interpreted in that context as referring to debts which are not only in existence but also due and payable.[619] In the case of an action by or against an executor or administrator the Statutes similarly provided that there could be a set-off if there were mutual debts between the testator and the other party to the proposed set-off. Ordinary rules of statutory interpretation suggest that 'debts' should be given the same meaning in this context, in which case it would refer to debts due and payable between those parties. This has been held to be the case in Canada,[620] while North J, in discussing the availability of a set-off where one of the parties had died in *Re Gregson*,[621] framed the relevant question in terms of a debt *payable* to the testator in his lifetime.[622] It is not clear, however, that the courts will adopt that position.[623] The tendency of the courts in recent times has been to enlarge the circumstances in which set-off is available, which suggests that they would be sympathetic to the broader interpretation.

Bankruptcy

In 1875 the rules of bankruptcy, including the insolvency set-off section, were incorpor- **13.133** ated for the first time into the administration of a deceased's estate when it is insolvent.[624] Prior to 1875, rights of set-off were only available under the Statutes of Set-off, and accordingly were subject to the limitation inherent in the Statutes, that both debts had to be owing, and possibly also be due and payable,[625] between the parties before the deceased's death. However, since the administration of insolvent estates has been brought within the ambit of the insolvency legislation,[626] that restriction would no longer apply. Rather, the demands which may be brought into an account are regulated by the terms of the insolvency set-off section, so that it is sufficient if the credits or dealings in question were mutual in their origin.[627] Thus, claims which are contingent at the relevant date, or which

---

[619] See para. 2.29 above. In New South Wales, see the Civil Procedure Act 2005, s. 21(1).

[620] *Trusts & Guar Co v Royal Bank* [1931] 2 DLR 601. Compare *Ontario Bank v Routhier* (1900) 32 OR 67 and *Royal Trust Co v Molsons Bank* (1912) 8 DLR 478, in which it was accepted that the bank could have applied the testator's deposit against the promissory notes maturing after the death, although these cases appear to have been concerned with a banker's right of combination of accounts (see ch. 15 below) rather than set-off under the Statutes.

[621] (1887) 36 Ch D 223, 226–7.

[622] See also *Newell v The National Provincial Bank of England* (1876) 1 CPD 496, although the promissory note in that case was given as surety.

[623] While there is a presumption that a word appearing in different parts of the same section in an Act of Parliament has the same meaning, this is not an invariable rule. See e.g. *Doe d Angell v Angell* (1846) 9 QB 328, 355, 115 ER 1299, 1309; *Re Smith; Green v Smith* (1883) 24 Ch D 672, 678; *Clyne v Deputy Commissioner of Taxation* (1982) 150 CLR 1, 10, 15.

[624] See the Supreme Court of Judicature Act 1875, s. 10.

[625] See above.

[626] See now the Administration of Insolvent Estates of Deceased Persons Order 1986 (S.I. 1986 No. 1999), made pursuant to the Insolvency Act 1986, s. 421. For Australia, see the Bankruptcy Act 1966 (Cth), Pt XI, and also the various state laws regarding the administration of insolvent estates, e.g. the Probate and Administration Act 1898 (NSW), s. 46C.

[627] *Watkins v Lindsay and Co* (1898) 67 LJQB 362, 364.

only become due and payable after that date, may be included in a set-off, in accordance with principles applicable generally to insolvency set-off.

13.134 If a debtor by or against whom a bankruptcy petition has been presented dies, the proceedings in the matter are continued as if he or she were still alive, unless the court orders otherwise.[628] If, on the other hand, the deceased died before presentation of the petition, the Administration of Insolvent Estates of Deceased Persons Order 1986 now stipulates that the equivalent of the commencement of the bankruptcy, which is the relevant date for determining rights of set-off under the Insolvency Act, is the date of the insolvency administration order, this being an order for the administration in bankruptcy of the insolvent estate of a deceased debtor.[629] This should not mean, however, that the date of the order is the relevant date for determining rights of set-off.[630] In so far as the claim against the deceased is concerned, the Order also provides that, in the definition of 'bankruptcy debt' in the Insolvency Act 1986, the date of death of the deceased debtor is to be substituted for the commencement of the bankruptcy,[631] so that the provability of a claim is to be determined by reference to that date. Since the set-off section requires that there be a creditor proving or claiming to prove for a bankruptcy debt, in practice the date of death should be the relevant date for the claim against the estate.[632] In substance this should also be the position in relation to the cross-demand possessed by the estate. If a creditor becomes indebted to the deceased's estate after the date of death but before the order, and the debt does not arise out of a prior dealing that the creditor had with the deceased, there would be a lack of mutuality between that debt and the debt owing by the deceased to the creditor, so that a set-off would not be available on that ground. In *Re Gedney; Smith v Grummitt*[633] a person purchased some simple contract debts and a mortgage owing by the deceased, the purchase taking place after the death but before an order for the administration of the estate in bankruptcy. The purchaser realized the

---

[628] See art. 5 of the Administration of Insolvent Estates of Deceased Persons Order 1986 (S.I. 1986 No. 1999). In Australia, see the Bankruptcy Act 1966 (Cth), ss. 63 and 245.

[629] See Part 1 of Sch. 1 to the Order.

[630] Compare the position in Australia. The date of the sequestration order is the relevant date for the purpose of the set-off section (see para. 6.51 above), and s. 248(3)(a) of the Bankruptcy Act 1966 (Cth) provides that 'a reference to a sequestration order shall be read as a reference to an order for administration of an estate' under Part XI. An order that the estate of a deceased person should be administered under the bankruptcy legislation is not made on the basis of an act of bankruptcy. It is not altogether clear, then, how the qualification to the set-off section in s. 86(2) of the Bankruptcy Act dealing with notice of an act of bankruptcy would operate under the Australian legislation when a debt owing by the deceased is acquired after the date of death but before the order. If in fact the creditor had notice of an act of bankruptcy committed by the deceased within the six-month period before the date of the order, there is no reason why the proviso should not apply in the normal way. This is consistent with s. 247A (relation back under Part XI). In other cases, where a person acquires a debt owing by the deceased between the date of death and the date of the order, the courts may apply the qualification on the basis that the person should not be entitled to employ the debt in a set-off if at the time of acquisition he or she was aware that the estate was insolvent. See e.g. *Law v James* [1972] 2 NSWLR 573 and *Wily v Rothschild Australia Ltd* (1997) 47 NSWLR 555, 566 in relation to companies. This is not an issue in England, where the qualification to the set-off section is now drafted in terms of notice of the petition rather than notice of an act of bankruptcy. See para. 6.72 above.

[631] See para. 31 of Part II of Sch. I to the Order.

[632] Under the Bankruptcy Act 1914, the date of death seems to have been the relevant date. See *Re Bailey, deceased; Duchess Mill Ltd v Bailey* (1932) 76 Sol Jo 560.

[633] [1908] 1 Ch 804.

mortgage and, having applied the proceeds in satisfaction of the mortgage debt, held a surplus which he claimed to set off against the other debts due to him. Even apart from the question whether a set-off should have been denied because the surplus was impressed with a trust,[634] Warrington J held that the surplus never belonged to the testator and accordingly there was never a debt due to him. Nor did it arise out of a dealing with the testator. There was no basis, therefore, for a set-off.[635] On the same principle, the proceeds of a deceased's estate deposited with a bank may not be brought into an account with an indebtedness of the deceased to the bank,[636] and an order for costs made against a creditor of the estate in favour of the executor for successfully defending an action by the creditor against the estate cannot be set off against the debt owing to the creditor.[637] Similarly, if an executor or administrator sells an asset of the estate to a person who is a creditor of the deceased, the creditor cannot set off the price against the debt owing to him or her, in the absence of an agreement to that effect.[638]

Debts incurred by the personal representative

It may be that a personal representative carried on the deceased's business, and in doing so incurred some debts. A personal representative who carries on the deceased's business is personally liable for all debts which he or she contracts in so doing, although if that person was authorized to conduct the business he or she is entitled as against the beneficiaries to be indemnified out of that part of the testator's estate which he or she was authorized to employ in the business.[639] *Nelson v Roberts*[640] is authority for the proposition that this personal liability of the personal representative to a creditor and a debt owing by the creditor to the estate are not mutual.[641]

13.135

Charge on the estate for costs and expenses

A personal representative is entitled to an indemnity for costs and expenses incurred in performing his or her duties. If the assets are insufficient to pay the creditors of the deceased, these costs are a first charge on the estate. Nevertheless, a charge on the estate is not a personal claim, and it generally cannot be the subject of a set-off.[642]

13.136

(3) Set-off by a beneficiary of the estate

If a beneficiary of the estate is also indebted to the estate, so that the beneficiary has a right to participate as well as an obligation to contribute to the fund constituting

13.137

---

[634] See paras 10.36–10.46 above.
[635] See also *Re Gregson; Christison v Bolam* (1887) 36 Ch D 223.
[636] *National Bank of Australasia v Swan* (1872) 3 VR (L) 168. In *National Bank v Swan* the deceased's debt arose pursuant to a guarantee, although default by the principal debtor did not occur until after the death. Stawell CJ (at 171) rejected an argument that, because the debt arose after the death, it was the administrator's, and not the intestate's, debt.
[637] *Re Dickinson. Marquis of Bute v Walker, ex p Hoyle, Shipley and Hoyle* [1888] WN 94.
[638] *Lambarde v Older* (1853) 17 Beav 542, 51 ER 1144.
[639] *Labouchere v Tupper* (1857) 11 Moore 198, 14 ER 670.
[640] (1893) 69 LT 352. See also *Staniar v Evans* (1886) 34 Ch D 470, 476–7; *Rex v Ray, ex p Chapman* [1936] SASR 241, 249.
[641] *Quaere* whether *Nelson v Roberts* should be followed. See paras 17.124–17.126 below.
[642] *Monypenny v Bristow* (1832) 2 Russ & M 117, 39 ER 339. Compare para. 3.05 above.

the estate, the rule in *Cherry v Boultbee*[643] may apply, with the consequence that the obligation to contribute may be appropriated as satisfaction of the right to participate as beneficiary.[644]

13.138 An executor or administrator may be personally liable to a beneficiary if he or she fails to apply the estate in accordance with his or her duties. There is authority which suggests that the executor or administrator can set off against that liability a debt owing by the beneficiary to the executor or administrator in that person's personal capacity,[645] though this may depend on the circumstances.[646]

---

[643] (1839) 4 My & Cr 442, 41 ER 171.
[644] See ch. 14 below.
[645] See *Taylor v Taylor* (1875) LR 20 Eq 155, which is explained in paras 10.08 and 10.09 above.
[646] See paras 10.10–10.11 above.

14

THE RULE IN *CHERRY v BOULTBEE*

A. Introduction

14.01 The notion which underlies the equitable principle (commonly called the rule) in *Cherry v Boultbee*[1] is that: 'where a person entitled to participate in a fund is also bound to make a contribution in aid of that fund, he cannot be allowed so to participate unless and until he has fulfilled his duty to contribute.'[2] It is an illustration of a more fundamental principle of equity, that he who seeks equity must do equity.[3] Many of the cases concerned with *Cherry v Boultbee* have involved a debtor of a deceased person who is entitled to a pecuniary legacy under the will. Unless an intention has been manifested to exclude the operation of the *Cherry v Boultbee* principle,[4] the executor may decline to hand over anything in satisfaction of the legacy to the extent of the debt. The executor would wish to exercise this right if the debtor is insolvent or if for some other reason the debtor is unlikely to satisfy the liability.

14.02 The principle was applied by the courts a long time before 1839, when *Cherry v Boultbee*[5] was decided.[6] However, it was not until Lord Cottenham's judgment in that case that it was expressly distinguished from the right of set-off.[7] The Lord Chancellor commented:[8]

> It must be observed that the term 'set-off' is very inaccurately used in cases of this kind. In its proper use, it is applicable only to mutual demands, debts and credits. The right of an executor of a creditor to retain a sufficient part of a legacy given by the creditor to the debtor, to pay a debt due from him to the creditor's estate, is rather a right to pay out of the fund in hand, than a right of set-off.

Since then the courts have emphasized that *Cherry v Boultbee* has a wider application than set-off, and that it rests upon quite different principles.[9] Thus, *Cherry v Boultbee* applies in

---

[1] (1839) 4 My & Cr 442, 41 ER 171.

[2] *Re Peruvian Railway Construction Co Ltd* [1915] 2 Ch 144, 150 *per* Sargant J (affirmed [1915] 2 Ch 442). See also *Re Akerman* [1891] 3 Ch 212, 219; *Re Rhodesia Goldfields Ltd; Partridge v Rhodesia Goldfields Ltd* [1910] 1 Ch 239, 247; *Re Fenton (No. 2)* [1932] 1 Ch 178, 186; *Re Davies Chemists Ltd* [1993] BCLC 544, 546; *Otis Elevator Co Pty Ltd v Guide Rails Pty Ltd* (2004) 49 ACSR 531 at [33] and [35]; *Gray v Gray* (2004) 12 BPR 22,755, [2004] NSWCA 408 at [90]; *Re SSSL Realisations (2002) Ltd* [2006] Ch 610 at [79] ('a person cannot take an aliquot share out of the fund unless he first brings into the fund what he owes').

[3] *Courtenay v Williams* (1844) 3 Hare 539, 553–4, 67 ER 494, 500; *Stephenson Nominees Pty Ltd v Official Receiver* (1987) 16 FCR 536, 558; *Gray v Gray* (2004) 12 BPR 22,755, [2004] NSWCA 408 at [91].

[4] *Harvey v Palmer* (1851) 4 De G & Sm 425, 64 ER 897. See also *Re Eiser's Will Trusts* [1937] 1 All ER 244; *Cattles Plc v Welcome Financial Services Ltd* [2009] EWHC 3027 (Ch) at [50]–[60] (appeal dismissed *Cattles Plc v Welcome Financial Services Ltd* [2010] EWCA Civ 599 without considering *Cherry v Boultbee*). Compare *Re Kowloon Container Warehouse Co Ltd* [1981] HKLR 210, in which it was held that a provision in a company's articles, to the effect that the company should have a lien upon the shares of a member for his debts owing to the company, did not purport to exclude *Cherry v Boultbee*, and *Mills v HSBC Trustee (CI) Ltd* [2009] EWHC 3377 (Ch). The intention to exclude the principle must be clear. See *Mills v HSBC Trustee (CI) Ltd* at [26].

[5] (1839) 4 My & Cr 442, 41 ER 171.

[6] The earliest reported example appears to be *Jeffs v Wood* (1732) 2 P Wms 128, 24 ER 668.

[7] Compare e.g. Lord Cottenham's earlier judgment in *Houlditch v Wallace* (1838) 5 Cl & Fin 629, 666, 7 ER 543, 557. In subsequent cases the right occasionally was still referred to as a set-off. See e.g. *Freeman v Lomas* (1851) 9 Hare 109, 68 ER 435 (Sir George Turner).

[8] (1839) 4 My & Cr 442, 447, 41 ER 171, 173.

[9] *Re Rhodesia Goldfields Ltd; Partridge v Rhodesia Goldfields Ltd* [1910] 1 Ch 239, 246–7; *Re Smelting Corporation; Seaver v The Company* [1915] 1 Ch 472, 476; *Re National Live Stock Insurance Co Ltd* [1917]

relation to a right to participate in a trust fund, whereas the general rule with respect to set-off is that a set-off may not be based upon an obligation to account for a sum held on trust.[10]

(1) The nature of the principle

Lord Cottenham described the operation of the principle as a right in the executor to 'retain' a part of a legacy as payment of the debt, but the courts on a number of occasions have rejected retainer as a description of the right.[11] As Kekewich J once remarked:[12] 'Nothing is in truth retained by the representative of the estate; nothing is in strict language set off.' There has still nevertheless been a tendency to refer to the principle in terms of retainer,[13] and indeed in a later case Sargant J criticized the rejection of that epithet by Kekewich J.[14] Kekewich J would appear to have been correct, however. The more popular explanation, which can be traced back to the judgment of Sir Joseph Jekyll in 1723 in *Jeffs v Wood*,[15] is that the principle in effect provides a method of payment. The administrator of the fund[16] asserts that a person who is entitled to participate in the fund and who is also a debtor to the fund already has an asset of the fund in his or her own hands, in the form of the debt, which should be appropriated as *pro tanto* payment of the right to participate.[17]

14.03

---

1 Ch 628, 632; *Re Melton; Milk v Towers* [1918] 1 Ch 37, 58–9; *Re Fenton (No. 2), ex p Fenton Textile Association Ltd* [1932] 1 Ch 178, 188; *Selangor United Rubber Estates Ltd v Cradock (No. 4)* [1969] 1 WLR 1773, 1778; *Re Davies Chemists Ltd* [1993] BCLC 544, 548 *Gray v Gray* (2004) 12 BPR 22,755, [2004] NSWCA 408 at [91]. See also *Re SSSL Realisations (2002) Ltd* [2006] Ch 610 at [12]–[13].

[10] See ch. 10 above.

[11] *Re Akerman* [1891] 3 Ch 212, 219; *Smith v Smith* (1861) 3 Giff 263, 271, 66 ER 408, 411; *Re Melton; Milk v Towers* [1918] 1 Ch 37, 59 (Scrutton LJ rejecting the epithets 'retainer' and 'lien', but compare Warrington LJ at 55); *In the Will of Bickerdike, decd; Bickerdike v Hill* [1918] VLR 191, 196; *Gray v Gray* (2004) 12 BPR 22,755, [2004] NSWCA 408 at [91]. See also *Re Rhodesia Goldfields Ltd; Partridge v Rhodesia Goldfields Ltd* [1910] 1 Ch 239, 245–6; *Re National Live Stock Insurance Co Ltd* [1917] 1 Ch 628, 631–2. Therefore, it is not properly described as a security. See *Mills v HSBC Trustee (CI) Ltd* [2009] EWHC 3377 (Ch) at [34]–[35], where the point nevertheless was left open.

[12] *Re Akerman* [1891] 3 Ch 212, 219.

[13] See e.g. *Corr v Corr* (1879) 3 LR Ir 435, 446, 448; *Re Taylor; Taylor v Wade* [1894] 1 Ch 671; *Re Watson; Turner v Watson* [1896] 1 Ch 925; *Jackson v Yeats* [1912] 1 IR 267; *Re Lennard; Lennard's Trustee v Lennard* [1934] 1 Ch 235, 241; *Stephenson Nominees Pty Ltd v Official Receiver* (1987) 16 FCR 536, 558. Compare Sargant J in *Re Peruvian Railway Construction Co Ltd* [1915] 2 Ch 144, 151 ('right of retainer or quasi-retainer').

[14] *Re Savage; Cull v Howard* [1918] 2 Ch 146.

[15] (1732) 2 P Wms 128, 130, 24 ER 668.

[16] Henceforth, the term 'administrator' is used generally to describe a person charged with the responsibility of collecting assets into a fund and distributing the fund amongst a group of persons. There may be more than one such person. See e.g. *Russell-Cooke Trust v Richard Prentis* [2003] EWHC 1206 (Ch).

[17] See e.g. *Campbell v Graham* (1831) 1 Russ & M 453, 39 ER 175; *Courtnay v Williams* (1846) 15 LJ Ch 204, 208; *Re Akerman; Akerman v Akerman* [1891] 3 Ch 212, 219–20; *Re Goy & Co Ltd; Farmer v Goy & Co Ltd* [1900] 2 Ch 149, 153; *Turner v Turner* [1911] 1 Ch 716, 719; *Re Pennington and Owen Ltd* [1925] 1 Ch 825, 830, 832–3; *Picken v Lord Balfour of Burleigh* [1945] 1 Ch 90, 104. See also *Dingle v Coppen* [1899] 1 Ch 726, 740; *Re Melton* [1918] 1 Ch 37, 54, 58–9; *Otis Elevator Co Pty Ltd v Guide Rails Pty Ltd* (2004) 49 ACSR 531 at [33]–[34], and the second formulation of the principle applicable to defaulting trustees referred to in para. 14.83 below. This accords with the accounting treatment of the rule described in *Re SSSL Realisations (2002) Ltd* [2006] Ch 610 at [12], [79] and [103]–[105]. Compare *Dodson v Sandhurst & Northern District Trustees Executors and Agency Co Ltd* [1955] VLR 100, 104.

The administrator in truth does not 'retain' anything as payment of the debt.[18] Rather, the administrator directs the debtor to satisfy the entitlement to a share of the fund from a particular fund asset. The principle is better described as a right to appropriate a particular asset as payment, as opposed to a right of set-off or a right of retainer.[19]

B. Executor's Right of Retainer

14.04 *Cherry v Boultbee* should be distinguished from an executor's right of retainer. The common law developed the principle that an executor or an administrator of a deceased's estate could retain from the estate an amount sufficient to cover any debts owing to him or her by the deceased[20] in priority to the costs of the administration,[21] and also in priority to the claims of creditors of an equal or lower degree.[22] This right was not in the nature of a right of set-off, in the sense that the word is used to describe the process by which cross-demands are brought into an account so as to produce a balance, but rather it was a right to retain assets in payment of a debt. Thus, while it is a prerequisite to the common law defence of set-off under the Statutes of Set-off that the debt sought to be set off must be enforceable by action,[23] an executor could exercise a right of retainer in respect of a debt which, though existing, was unenforceable as a result of a time bar.[24] The executor's right of retainer is also distinct from *Cherry v Boultbee*, which is not properly described as a right of retainer.[25] They had different origins. The executor's right of retainer was developed by the common law courts,[26] whereas *Cherry v Boultbee* is an equitable doctrine.

14.05 The executor's right of retainer has now been abolished in England, although a personal representative who pays him or herself from the estate is not required to account for the

---

[18] Compare *Re Hurburgh; National Executors and Trustees Co of Tasmania Ltd v Hurburgh* [1959] Tas SR 25, 40–2, where Crawford J suggested that *Cherry v Boultbee* confers a right *in rem*. However, the two reasons adduced to support that contention may be explained on other grounds. The first reason, regarding the effect of a bankruptcy or an assignment, may be explained by reference to the principle that a trustee in bankruptcy or an assignee takes subject to equities. See paras 14.63–14.68 below. The second reason regarding the effect of proving for the debt in the bankruptcy may be explained on the basis of a waiver of the right conferred by *Cherry v Boultbee*. See para. 14.58 below.

[19] The corresponding passage in the third edition (p. 587) was quoted and adopted (as an extract from counsel's submissions) in *Cattles Plc v Welcome Financial Services Ltd* [2009] EWHC 3027 (Ch) at [52]. See also, in Canada, *Re Olympia & York Developments Ltd* (1993) 103 DLR (4th) 129, 141, referred to in *Re Attorney General of Canada and Standard Trust Co* (1995) 128 DLR (4th) 747, 750 and *Canada (Attorney General) v Confederation Life Insurance Co* (2002) 39 CBR (4th) 182 at [39].

[20] If the debts were owing by the deceased, they would be unconnected with the administration of his or her estate. They would not therefore come within the right of a trustee to an indemnity from the capital and income of the trust for costs properly incurred in the administration of the trust. See *Stott v Milne* (1884) 25 Ch D 710.

[21] *Re Wester Wemyss; Tilley v Wester Wemyss* [1940] Ch 1.

[22] *Attorney-General v Jackson* [1932] AC 365.

[23] See paras 2.46–2.50 above.

[24] *Hill v Walker* (1858) 4 K & J 166, 70 ER 69.

[25] See above.

[26] *Attorney-General v Jackson* [1932] AC 365, 370. Since this right of retainer was developed by the common law, originally it could only be exercised against the legal, and not the equitable, assets of the estate, and moreover the executor's right was not prejudiced if he or she was a trustee of the debt for a third party. See, however, the Administration of Estates Act 1925, s. 34(2), discussed in *Re Rudd. Royal Exchange Assurance v Ballantine* [1942] 1 Ch 421. See also, in Tasmania, the Administration and Probate Act 1935, s. 34(2).

sum so paid if he or she acted in good faith and at the time had no reason to believe that the deceased's estate was insolvent.[27] It has also been abolished in Western Australia,[28] New South Wales,[29] South Australia,[30] Victoria,[31] Queensland[32] and New Zealand,[33] in each case (apart from Queensland) without a similar saving provision. While it has attracted a considerable amount of case law, in view of its now limited application[34] it is not proposed to discuss it further.[35]

C. The Scope of the Rule

Cherry v Boultbee has been described as a principle of wide utility and broad equity, and not dependent upon refined or technical considerations.[36] It is not confined to cases in which a legatee who was indebted to the testator is the beneficiary of a 'bounty' from the testator in the form of a legacy,[37] but applies generally whenever a person who is entitled to a share of a fund is also liable to contribute to the fund.[38] Thus, it may be invoked by an administrator of an intestate's estate against a next of kin,[39] and it may apply to a person with a derivative title to a legacy, being a person who obtained a right to the legacy under the will or as a result of the intestacy of another originally entitled to it.[40] It can also apply when the beneficiary of a trust is indebted to the trust,[41] including in one instance where resulting trusts impressed upon matrimonial property in proportion to the expenditure incurred by the husband and wife respectively were being dissolved,[42] and when a defaulting trustee is entitled to an indemnity from the trust fund for expenses and liabilities properly incurred.[43]

14.06

---

[27] Administration of Estates Act 1971, s. 10.

[28] Administration Act 1903 (WA), s. 10(2).

[29] Probate and Administration Act 1898 (NSW), s. 82(2), which amendment was introduced by Act No 14 of 1906, s. 4.

[30] Administration and Probate Act 1919 (SA), s. 62.

[31] Administration and Probate Act 1958 (Vic), s. 36(3).

[32] Succession Act 1981 (Qld), s. 58(1).

[33] Administration Act 1969 (NZ), s. 40.

[34] It still applies in Tasmania.

[35] For a discussion of the executor's right of retainer, see *Meagher, Gummow and Lehane's Equity Doctrines and Remedies* (4th edn, 2002), 1067–9.

[36] *Stephenson Nominees Pty Ltd v Official Receiver* (1987) 16 FCR 536, 558 (Gummow J), referring to *Re Jewell's Settlement* [1919] 2 Ch 161, 174, 177.

[37] Compare *Dingle v Coppen* [1899] 1 Ch 726, 739, 740. For an application of the principle in the case of a *power* to pay moneys to a person indebted to the testator, see *Re Bleechmore; Public Trustee v Bleechmore* [1922] SASR 399.

[38] *Pyrenees Vineyard Management Ltd v Russell Frajman* (2008) 69 ACSR 95 at [39] ('the person controlling a fund, whether as trustee, liquidator or in some other capacity . . .').

[39] *Re Cordwell's Estate; White v Cordwell* (1875) LR 20 Eq 644.

[40] *Dodson v Sandhurst & Northern District Trustees Executors and Agency Co Ltd* [1955] VLR 100; *Re Milnes; Milnes v Sherwin* (1885) 53 LT 534. See also with respect to defaulting trustees (see paras 14.79–14.91 below) *Re Dacre; Whitaker v Dacre* [1916] 1 Ch 344.

[41] See e.g. *Priddy v Rose* (1817) 3 Mer 86, 36 ER 33; *Re Akerman* [1891] 3 Ch 212.

[42] *Cowcher v Cowcher* [1972] 1 WLR 425.

[43] *Lewis v Trask* (1882) 21 Ch D 862; *Re Johnson. Shearman v Robinson* (1880) 15 Ch D 548 (creditor subrogated to a defaulting trustee's right of indemnity out of the trust estate was in no better position than the trustee); *Staniar v Evans* (1886) 34 Ch D 470 (see para. 14.14 below); *RWG Management Ltd v Commissioner for Corporate Affairs* [1985] VR 385, 397–9. See also, *Re British Power Traction and Lighting Co Ltd* [1910]

(1) Bankruptcy and company liquidation

14.07 *Cherry v Boultbee* may be relevant when a trustee in bankruptcy or a liquidator is administering the fund represented by the estate available for distribution.[44] Normally, it is not in the interests of the general body of creditors that a claim against the estate should be set off against a liability of the estate, because this reduces the dividend payable generally. Consider, however, that a creditor of a company in liquidation is also liable to the company,[45] but that the liability for some reason cannot be employed by the creditor in a set-off.[46] The creditor is entitled to receive a dividend in the liquidation,[47] but is also required to make a contribution to the extent of the liability. The liquidator may assert that the creditor should satisfy the right to receive the dividend from the obligation to contribute. For example, *Cherry v Boultbee* may entitle the liquidator of a company to refuse to pay a dividend to a creditor who is liable for damages for misfeasance,[48] or who is liable for unpaid calls,[49] neither of which may be employed in a set-off in a winding up.[50] In *Re SSSL Realisations (2002) Ltd*[51] the Court of Appeal considered a situation where

---

2 Ch 470 (receiver and manager appointed in a debenture-holders action). Compare the situation in which a defaulting trustee is a beneficiary of the trust. See paras 14.79–14.91 below.

[44] In addition to the cases referred to below, see *Rowe v Anderson* (1831) 4 Sim 267, 58 ER 100. In *Fused Electrics Pty Ltd v Donald* [1995] 2 Qd R 7, 8–9, Williams J doubted whether *Cherry v Boultbee* is applicable in the case of a company liquidation, on the ground that it may not be correct to categorize the assets of a company in liquidation as a fund. Similarly, Lindsay J in *Russell-Cooke Trust v Richard Prentis* [2003] EWHC 1206 (Ch) at [12] left open the question whether *Cherry v Boultbee* applies in corporate or personal insolvency. However, those doubts are contrary to the cases referred to below, and the suggestion that the principle does not apply in company liquidation was rejected by the Court of Appeal in *Re SSSL Realisations (2002) Ltd* [2006] Ch 610 at [98]–[100]. Liquidation gives rise to an entitlement in creditors to share in the proceeds of realization of the company's property (see *Ayerst v C & K (Construction) Ltd* [1976] AC 167, 178–9), and those proceeds constitute a fund for the purpose of the equitable principle. See para. 14.11 below. See also *Re Saltergate Insurance Co Ltd (No. 2)* [1984] 3 NSWLR 389 (proceeds of a reinsurance treaty received by the liquidator of an insurance company constituting a separate fund in the winding up, pursuant to legislation having a similar effect to the Corporations Act 2001 (Cth), s. 562A).

[45] In Australia, note that when the creditor is a member of the company, and the debt is owed by the company to the creditor in the creditor's capacity as a member, whether by way of dividends, profits or otherwise, the Corporations Act 2001 (Cth), s. 553A provides that the debt is not admissible to proof against the company unless the creditor has paid all amounts that the creditor is liable to pay as a member of the company. See also the Corporations Act 2001 (Cth), s. 563A, and in England the Insolvency Act 1986, s. 74(2)(f).

[46] If set-off is available in a liquidation, the rule in *Cherry v Boultbee* does not apply. See *Re SSSL Realisations (2002) Ltd* [2006] Ch 610 at [13].

[47] *Cherry v Boultbee* would have no application in relation to a creditor who had agreed not to prove in the liquidation. See *Re SSSL Realisations (2002) Ltd* [2006] Ch 610 at [68].

[48] *Re Leeds and Hanley Theatres of Varieties Ltd* [1904] 2 Ch 45. See also *Re Bailey Cobalt Mines Ltd* (1919) 45 DLR 585, 590–1; *Re Jewell's Settlement; Watts v Public Trustee* [1919] 2 Ch 161, 175–6; *Re VGM Holdings Ltd* [1942] 1 Ch 235; *Selangor United Rubber Estates Ltd v Cradock (No. 4)* [1969] 1 WLR 1773. Cotton LJ expressed a tentative view to that effect in *Re Milan Tramways Co, ex p Theys* (1884) 25 Ch D 587, 592–3 (discussed in *Re Jewell's Settlement* [1919] 2 Ch 161, 174–6).

[49] *Re Auriferous Properties Ltd (No. 2)* [1898] 2 Ch 428; *Re National Live Stock Insurance Co Ltd* [1917] 1 Ch 628; *Re Hattons Confectionery Co Ltd* [1936] NZLR 802; *Re White Star Line Ltd* [1938] 1 Ch 458.

[50] See paras 8.81–8.87 (misfeasance) and 8.64–8.79 (unpaid calls) above. See also, in relation to an obligation to repay a preference, paras 13.07–13.16 above (set-off) and *N A Kratzmann Pty Ltd v Tucker (No. 2)* (1968) 123 CLR 295.

[51] [2006] Ch 610. See further the discussion of the case at paras 14.35 and 14.53 below. See also *Mills v HSBC Trustee (CI) Ltd* [2009] EWHC 3377 (Ch). Compare *Cattles v Welcome Financial Services Ltd* [2009] EWHC 3027 (Ch) (appeal dismissed *Cattles Plc v Welcome Financial Services Ltd* [2010] EWCA Civ 599 without considering *Cherry v Boultbee*).

an insolvent surety's estate was precluded by the rule against double proof from proving in the liquidation of the principal debtor in respect of the surety's claim for an indemnity from the principal debtor,[52] and the principal debtor had a provable debt in the surety's liquidation.[53] If a surety's claim for an indemnity is not provable in the principal debtor's liquidation, there would not be a set-off under the insolvency set-off section.[54] In the absence of a set-off,[55] the court considered that *Cherry v Boultbee* would apply so that, in determining the principal debtor's right to share in the fund distributable in the surety's liquidation, the principal debtor would have to bring into account its obligation to indemnify the surety as a contribution required to be made to that fund.

Cherry v Boultbee may also be invoked to prevent a shareholder of a company which is in liquidation, but which has a surplus available for distribution amongst the shareholders, from receiving a rateable proportion of the surplus without satisfying a debt that he or she owes to the company.[56]   **14.08**

It may be that a creditor of a bankrupt has become indebted to the bankrupt's trustee for costs in litigation conducted on behalf of the estate. While lack of mutuality would prevent a set-off,[57] the liability for costs is still a contribution required to be made in aid of the fund,[58] and so the dividend payable to the creditor may be regarded as paid to the extent of the costs liability pursuant to the *Cherry v Boultbee* principle.[59] A similar result applies in company liquidation.[60]   **14.09**

(2) Equitable principle

On the other hand, *Cherry v Boultbee*, being an equitable principle, will not apply where it is contrary to statute or contrary to the agreement of the parties, or where the circumstances otherwise show that it would not be in accordance with good conscience that   **14.10**

---

[52] See paras 8.13–8.18 above.

[53] In fact, the Court of Appeal held that the principal debtor had contracted out of the right to prove in the surety's liquidation. The *Cherry v Boultbee* point nevertheless has been said to be part of the ratio. See *Cattles Plc v Welcome Financial Services Ltd* [2010] EWCA Civ 599 at [47]–[48].

[54] See para. 7.24 above. Because of the rule against double proof, a set-off would have been denied in both insolvencies. See paras 11.03 and 11.05 above.

[55] The Court of Appeal considered (see [2006] Ch 610 at [90]) that, in a double insolvency situation, there can be no set-off in either liquidation unless it is available in both liquidations. In the circumstances in issue, where the rule against double proof applied, that view seems correct, but expressed as a general proposition it is suggested that it should be reconsidered. See paras 11.03–11.11 above.

[56] *Re Peruvian Railway Construction Co Ltd* [1915] 2 Ch 144, 151; *Re 3 Ernest Street Pty Ltd* (1980) CLC 40–619 at p 34,146 (Needham J, NSW SC); *Re Kowloon Container Warehouse Co. Ltd* [1981] HKLR 210; *Otis Elevator Co Pty Ltd v Guide Rails Pty Ltd* (2004) 49 ACSR 531. Compare *FAI General Insurance Co Ltd v FAI Car Owners Mutual Insurance Co Ltd* [2009] NSWSC 1350 at [61]–[73] where there was only one shareholder.

[57] *West v Pryce* (1825) 2 Bing 455, 130 ER 382.

[58] See para. 14.39 below.

[59] *Re Mayne, ex p The Official Receiver* [1907] 2 KB 899.

[60] *Re Davies Chemists Ltd* [1993] BCLC 544. The circumstance that the costs order is made after the liquidation would preclude set-off. See para. 6.63 above, and also para. 8.11 above in relation to a costs order made after a bankruptcy or liquidation in respect of proceedings commenced before the bankruptcy or liquidation.

it should apply.[61] In a case in Queensland, a person who was liable to a company which had gone into liquidation was awarded costs in proceedings brought against him by the liquidator on behalf of the company, and the entitlement to the costs was accorded priority by the applicable companies legislation on the basis that they were costs, charges and expenses of the winding up. Because of the statutory priority, the liquidator was not permitted to invoke *Cherry v Boultbee*.[62]

(3) The requirement of a fund

14.11 The essence of *Cherry v Boultbee* is that there is a right to participate in, and an obligation to contribute to, a fund.[63] The concept of a 'fund' is flexible;[64] it includes a trust fund,[65] an estate administered under a will or in an intestacy, and the pool of assets of a bankrupt or a company in liquidation[66] which is administered in accordance with the relevant statutory scheme.[67] In a case in Australia, it was held to include a statutory fund set up to compensate victims of crime.[68] It does not include, however, a company's assets while the company is still a going concern.[69] On the other hand, it is not necessary that the fund should consist of anything of value other than the obligation in respect of which the principle is sought to be invoked.[70]

(4) As a condition of equitable relief

14.12 While the principle in *Cherry v Boultbee* is concerned with a right to participate in and an obligation to contribute to a fund, the equitable principle which underlies it may be

---

[61] *Perpetual Trustees (WA) Ltd v Equus Corp Pty Ltd* (NSWSC, Young J, 5 March 1998, BC9800921 at 7); *Wenkert v Pantzer* [2010] FCA 866 at [76]–[77]. See also *Northern Territory of Australia v Piper* (2002) 169 FLR 483 at [12] (statute). In *Perpetual Trustees*, the fact that the rights of the beneficiaries of a trust to receive moneys pursuant to the trust were set out in great detail in the trust deed was not regarded as negativing the operation of *Cherry v Boultbee*.

[62] *Fused Electrics Pty Ltd v Donald* [1995] 2 Qd R 7. See also *Process Engineering Pty Ltd v Derby Meat Processing Co. Ltd* [1977] WAR 145. *Re Bank of Hindustan, China and Japan, ex p Smith* (1867) LR 3 Ch App 125, to which Williams J referred in the *Fused Electrics* case, may be distinguished on the ground that the solicitor's lien would have prevented the application of *Cherry v Boultbee*.

[63] See e.g. *Re Peruvian Railway Construction Co Ltd* [1915] 2 Ch 144, 150; *Re Melton* [1918] 1 Ch 37, 55 (Warrington LJ).

[64] *Perpetual Trustees (WA) Ltd v Equus Corp Pty Ltd* (NSWSC, Young J, 5 March 1998, BC9800921 at 9).

[65] In *Perpetual Trustees (WA) Ltd v Equus Corp Pty Ltd* (NSWSC, Young J, 5 March 1998, BC9800921) this was held to include a pool of fees received by a trustee, where the trustee was obliged simply to distribute them (less authorised deductions) within thirty days.

[66] Or, in England, the assets of a company in administration where the administrator has given notice of his or her intention to declare and distribute a dividend under the Insolvency Rules 1986, r. 2.68. See *Mills v HSBC Trustee (CI) Ltd* [2009] EWHC 3377 (Ch) at [5].

[67] In relation to company liquidation, see *Hiley v The Peoples Prudential Assurance Co Ltd* (1938) 60 CLR 468, 496; *Linter Textiles Australia Ltd v Commissioner of Taxation* (2002) 20 ACLC 1708 at [15]. See also paras 14.07–14.09 above. This includes the surplus assets of a company in liquidation which are available for distribution amongst shareholders. See para. 14.08 above.

[68] *Northern Territory of Australia v Piper* (2002) 169 FLR 483.

[69] *Re Peruvian Railway Construction Co Ltd* [1915] 2 Ch 144, 151; *Selangor United Rubber Estates Ltd v Cradock (No. 4)* [1969] 1 WLR 1773, 1779 *Ansett Australia Ltd v Travel Software Solutions Pty Ltd* (2007) 65 ACSR 47 at [101]–[102].

[70] As may have been the case in *Re VGM Holdings Ltd* [1942] 1 Ch 235. See also *Ex p Turpin, re Brown* (1832) Mont 443, for which see para. 14.60 below.

relevant in other circumstances. For example, if A is claiming a constructive trust remedy against B, and A in breach of a fiduciary duty to B has misapplied B's funds, it may be made a condition of equitable relief that A must first do equity by accounting for the misapplied funds.[71]

D. Who May Invoke the Rule?

The principle considered in *Cherry v Boultbee* operates in favour of the fund, and generally **14.13** it can only be invoked by the person administering the fund.[72] Accordingly, a person obliged to contribute to a fund who also has a right to participate which for some reason is unenforceable could not insist that the obligation to contribute be satisfied by his or her unenforceable right.[73] There is nevertheless an exception in the situation in which the administrator of the fund is the person against whom the principle may be invoked. For example, a trustee who is also a beneficiary of the trust may have acted in breach of trust. In that circumstance the other beneficiaries may apply for an order that the principle should apply in respect of the trustee's entitlement, if their own entitlements would be affected.[74]

(1) Can the contributor be required to pay in full?

What if the administrator of the fund does not invoke *Cherry v Boultbee* against a contribu- **14.14** tor, so as to appropriate a right to participate in satisfaction of the obligation to contribute? Can the contributor be compelled to contribute before claiming a distribution from the fund in respect of the right to participate? It has been said that a person should not be ordered to pay that part of a liability which would come back to him or her on a distribution.[75] However, in *Staniar v Evans*[76] North J said that an order for payment of the full amount of the liability to contribute is the usual order, and that an order for payment only of the balance after deducting the entitlement to participate may be made as a matter of favour only. He said that, in order to obtain an order for payment of the balance, the contributor should be 'perfectly able, and ready, and willing' to pay the contribution.[77] If, as was the case in *Staniar v Evans*, the contributor cannot show his or her ability and readiness

---

[71] *Stephenson Nominees Pty Ltd v Official Receiver* (1987) 16 FCR 536, 538 (Gummow J). This may be what Young J in the New South Wales Supreme Court had in mind when he suggested in *Perpetual Trustees (WA) Ltd v Equus Corp Pty Ltd* (5 March 1998, BC9800921) that a fund may not be a prerequisite for the application of *Cherry v Boultbee*.

[72] Thus, Gibson J in *Re Hurburgh* [1959] Tas SR 25, 37 said of the principle in *Cherry v Boultbee* that it 'does not operate to quantify the share to be paid to a legatee until the executors (or trustees) choose to assert it'.

[73] Compare paras 14.17–14.22 below in relation to an unenforceable obligation to contribute.

[74] See e.g. *Fox v Buckley* (1876) 3 Ch D 508.

[75] *Re VGM Holdings Ltd* [1942] 1 Ch 235; *Selangor United Rubber Estates Ltd v Cradock (No. 4)* [1969] 1 WLR 1773; *RWG Management Ltd v Commissioner for Corporate Affairs* [1985] VR 385, 397–9 (defaulting trustee); *Fitzwood Pty Ltd v Unique Goal Pty Ltd* [2002] FCAFC 285 at [138] (defaulting trustee). See also *Cumming v Sands* [2001] NSWSC 706.

[76] (1886) 34 Ch D 470.

[77] (1886) 34 Ch D 470, 473–4.

and willingness to pay, for example because of insolvency, the order instead should be in terms that the full amount of the contribution must be paid before the right to participate can be exercised.[78] *Staniar v Evans* concerned a defaulting trustee who was entitled to costs out of the estate,[79] but North J indicated that the principle is equally applicable where the right to participate consists of a right to a share of the trust estate as a beneficiary.[80] Special considerations apply to cases involving defaulting trustees in that situation,[81] and the principle is considered later in that context.[82] Nevertheless, the courts have adopted a similar approach to that suggested by North J in other cases not concerned with defaulting trustees.[83]

14.15 In *Staniar v Evans* the obligation to contribute exceeded the right to participate. North J's order benefited the trust estate, because in a bankruptcy of the defaulting trustee the trust estate could have proved and received a dividend on the whole debt, as opposed to proving and receiving a dividend only in relation to the balance. On the other hand, Lord Eldon's earlier judgment in *Ex p Graham*[84] suggests that, if the person obliged to contribute pays an amount such that the remaining obligation to contribute equals the obligor's entitlement to participate, the debt may then be regarded as paid. The fund in *Ex p Graham* arose in the bankruptcy of a firm. The firm's assignees in bankruptcy deposited £28,079 19s. 10d. with bankers, Kensington and Co, who themselves later became bankrupt. Prior to their bankruptcy, Kensington and Co had lodged a proof in the firm's bankruptcy for a debt due to them, in the amount of £8,247 18s. The assignees in bankruptcy of the firm initially lodged a proof in Kensington and Co's bankruptcy for the amount of the deposit less a dividend of £1,649 11s. 7d. that had been declared in the firm's bankruptcy in favour of Kensington and Co. Subsequently, however, the assignees brought this petition praying that they might in addition be permitted to prove in Kensington and Co's bankruptcy for the amount by which they had reduced their proof, and that the assignees in bankruptcy of Kensington and Co might be restrained from receiving a dividend in the firm's bankruptcy until the

---

[78] See e.g. the order in *N A Kratzmann Pty Ltd v Tucker (No. 2)* (1968) 123 CLR 295, and see also *Cumming v Sands* [2001] NSWSC 706 at [9]. Compare *Re British Power Traction and Lighting Co Ltd* [1910] 2 Ch 470 (in which the receiver was insolvent, though in that case there were sureties for the default and in any event the debenture-holders who were entitled to the estate had asked for a declaration that only the balance should be payable). There is Australian authority to the contrary in relation to defaulting trustees. See *RWG Management Ltd v Commissioner for Corporate Affairs* [1985] VR 385, 397–9 (in relation to an insolvent trustee), referred to in *Fitzwood Pty Ltd v Unique Goal Pty Ltd* [2002] FCAFC 285 at [138] (in which the trustee was in liquidation).

[79] See also North J's earlier judgment in *Lewis v Trask* (1882) 21 Ch D 862, and generally para. 14.06 above.

[80] (1886) 34 Ch D 470, 473. See also *Re Gloag's Estate* (1892) 11 NZLR 90.

[81] See paras 14.79–14.91 below.

[82] See paras 14.87–14.91 below.

[83] *Ex p Bebb* (1812) 19 Ves Jun 222, 34 ER 501; *Ex p Graham* (1814) 3 V & B 130, 35 ER 428; *Ex p Bignold, re Charles* (1817) 2 Madd 470, 56 ER 408; *Re Auriferous Properties Ltd (No. 2)* [1898] 2 Ch 428 (obligation to contribute unpaid capital); *Re White Star Line Ltd* [1938] 1 Ch 458 (obligation to contribute unpaid capital); *N A Kratzmann Pty Ltd v Tucker (No. 2)* (1968) 123 CLR 295 (obligation to repay a preference). See also *Ex p Turpin, re Brown* (1832) Mont 443 (see para. 14.60 below); *Ex p Young, re Prior* (1835) 4 Deac & Ch 645; *Ex p Crofts, re Last & Casey* (1837) 2 Deac 102; *Ex p King, re Severn* (1835) 1 Deac 143; *Re Walter. Ex p Walter's Assignees* (1859) 32 LTOS 396; *Ex p Gonne, re March* (1837) 6 LJ Bcy 57.

[84] (1814) 3 V & B 130, 35 ER 428.

amount deposited with Kensington and Co had been repaid.[85] Lord Eldon said in his judgment that:

> until that Sum of £28,079, 19s 10d has been paid *minus* all the Dividends, to which Kensington and Co would have a Claim under their Proof, they are not entitled to those Dividends: but, whenever so much of that Sum of £28,079, 19s 10d is paid as leaves no more with Kensington and Co than the Amount of their Dividend upon the £8247, 18s then that Sum of £28,079, 19s 10d is paid.[86]

Lord Eldon made an order in accordance with the prayer in the petition, but with liberty to the assignees of Kensington and Co to apply whenever they shall have furnished to the firm's estate the sum of £28,079, 19s. 10d. minus the amount of the dividends to which Kensington and Co would be entitled upon their proof. This approach is consistent with the view that a person should not be required to pay when the payment would come back to him or her in a distribution.[87]

If the person the subject of the order is a trustee of a trust, and the right to participate takes **14.16** the form of an indemnity from the fund for his or her expenses, an order for payment of the balance may be made in the circumstances contemplated in *Staniar v Evans* notwithstanding that the fund may be insufficient to make all the required distributions out of the trust. This is because the trustee in any event has a first charge on the trust fund for his or her expenses incurred in the administration of the trust.[88] In other circumstances, however, the court should consider whether there are any prior ranking claims on the trust fund which may require that payment of all or part of the obligation to contribute to the fund should be made, and also the effect that an order for payment of the balance may have on the entitlements of other parties. This may be the case, for example, when the person the subject of the order is the beneficiary of a trust, and the trustee has a first charge on the trust estate for expenses incurred. If the beneficiary has an obligation to contribute, an order that he or she need only tender the balance after deducting the entitlement to participate in the trust would prejudice the trustee if it would mean that the fund in hand would be insufficient to reimburse the trustee for his or her expenses. If a fund is insolvent, the person obliged to contribute would only receive a dividend in respect of the right to participate,[89] and so an order for payment of the balance should only be made if the dividend is presently ascertainable.[90] When a person liable to contribute to a fund is entitled to a percentage of the fund, as opposed to a fixed entitlement, and it is otherwise appropriate that an order be made for payment of the balance, the court in making the order should ascertain the

---

[85] When a fund consists of a bankrupt's estate, a creditor's (in that case, Kensington and Co's) right to participate for the purpose of *Cherry v Boultbee* is the dividend payable on the debt. See para. 14.94 below. On the other hand, Kensington and Co, having become bankrupt after the deposit was made with them, was liable to contribute the full amount of the deposit. See para. 14.96 below. *Cherry v Boultbee* was applied in the bankruptcy of the firm, as opposed to the bankruptcy of the bankers with whom the proceeds of the firm's estate were deposited. See para. 14.103 below.

[86] (1814) 3 V & B 130, 132, 35 ER 428, 429.

[87] See above.

[88] *Stott v Milne* (1884) 25 Ch D 710.

[89] See para. 14.94 below.

[90] Compare *Ex p Graham* (1814) 3 V & B 130, 35 ER 428 above, and *Cumming v Sands* [2001] NSWSC 706 at [9].

person's share by first taking into account any expenses that will have to be met from the fund, for example costs incurred in litigation in order to establish the liability. Once the fund actually available for distribution has been ascertained in this way, the court in its discretion may order that only the excess of the obligation to contribute over the right to participate in the fund is required to be paid.[91]

E. Enforceable Rights and Obligations

(1) Unenforceable obligation to contribute

14.17   The distinction between a right of set-off and the principle in *Cherry v Boultbee* may be illustrated by the different treatment accorded by each to the usual form of statute of limitation, which takes away a creditor's right to enforce the debt but does not affect the existence of the debt. It is a prerequisite to a set-off under the Statutes of Set-off that the debts the subject of the set-off be enforceable by action,[92] but the fact that the liability to contribute to a fund is time-barred, and consequently unenforceable, generally does not preclude the right to invoke *Cherry v Boultbee*.[93] The administrator of the fund does not set up the liability as a form of cross-action. Rather, the administrator says that, although the claim against the contributor is unenforceable, it is still an existing asset of the estate. Since the person claiming a share of the fund holds an asset constituting a part of the fund, that person should pay him or herself *pro tanto* out of that asset. A right under *Cherry v Boultbee* is similar in that regard to the right of a lienee at law to withhold possession even when the debt upon which the lien is based is existing but unenforceable as a result of a time bar.[94] There is one case in which it was held that *Cherry v Boultbee* could not be invoked in respect of an unenforceable obligation to contribute. In *Dingle v Coppen*,[95] a person indebted to a testatrix obtained judgment against the estate for damages for waste committed by the testatrix during her lifetime. When the testatrix died, the limitation period for the debt owing to her had expired. Byrne J held that the executors could not apply *Cherry v Boultbee* so as to oblige the debtor to satisfy his claim for damages by appropriating the estate's asset

---

[91] *Selangor United Rubber Estates Ltd v Cradock (No. 4)* [1969] 1 WLR 1773; *Public Trustee v Gittoes* [2005] NSWSC 373 at [138].

[92] See paras 2.46–2.50 above.

[93] *Courtnay v Williams* (1846) 15 LJ Ch 204; *Smith v Smith* (1861) 3 Giff 263, 66 ER 408; *Coates v Coates* (1864) 33 Beav 249, 55 ER 363; *Gee v Liddell (No. 2)* (1866) 35 Beav 629, 55 ER 1041; *Re Cordwell's Estate; White v Cordwell* (1875) LR 20 Eq 644; *Re Knapman; Knapman v Wreford* (1881) 18 Ch D 300, 304; *Re Milnes; Milnes v Sherwin* (1885) 53 LT 534; *Re Akerman* [1891] 3 Ch 212; *Re Langham; Otway v Langham* (1896) 74 LT 611; *Re Allison* (1900) 1 Tas LR 169; *Gray v Gray* (2004) 12 BPR 22,755, [2004] NSWCA 408 at [13], [86]–[101]. See also *Rose v Gould* (1852) 15 Beav 189, 51 ER 509; *Poole v Poole* (1871) LR 7 Ch App 17. Compare the Limitation Act 1969 (NSW), s. 63 pursuant to which a time-barred debt is extinguished. See *Gray v Guardian Trust Australia Ltd* [2002] NSWSC 1218 at [110], and paras 14.20–14.22 below. If a debt is time-barred, an action cannot be brought in respect of it, and so damages in the form of interest cannot be awarded at a trial. Consequently, interest cannot be deducted under *Cherry v Boultbee*. See *In the Will of Bickerdike, deceased; Bickerdike v Hill* [1918] VLR 191, 197.

[94] *Spears v Hartly* (1800) 3 Esp 81, 170 ER 545; *Higgins v Scott* (1831) 2 B & Ad 413, 109 ER 1196; *Australia and New Zealand Banking Group Ltd v Douglas Morris Investments Pty Ltd* [1992] 1 Qd R 478, 497. See generally, as to the exercise of rights by a creditor in relation to a time-barred debt which do not require recourse to the courts, *Commonwealth v Mewett* (1997) 191 CLR 471, 535.

[95] [1899] 1 Ch 726.

represented by his unenforceable indebtedness. In *Dingle v Coppen*, there were two cross-demands, each of which in its nature was such that, when it arose, it could have been made the subject of an action at law between the debtor and the testatrix personally. However, because of the expiration of the limitation period, the testatrix at the time of her death could not have enforced the debt owing to her. Nor could she have employed it as a defence to an action brought against her in respect of the waste.[96] In those circumstances, Byrne J considered that the fact of her death should not make any difference, and that the estate should not be able to achieve the same effect as a set-off by means of *Cherry v Boultbee*. He distinguished the case from the situation in which a person is given a bounty in the form of a legacy under a will. In that situation, there is nothing inequitable in applying *Cherry v Boultbee* on the basis that a time-barred obligation to contribute should be taken into account.

Cherry v Boultbee should similarly be available as a general rule when the obligation to contribute to the fund is unenforceable for any other reason,[97] for example because of failure to comply with the requirements of the Statute of Frauds. The Court of Appeal in *Re Rownson; Field v White*[98] admittedly held that, while an executor or an administrator may exercise a right of retainer in satisfaction of a debt owing to him or her by the deceased that has become unenforceable because of a time bar, the executor or administrator is not entitled to a similar right of retainer when the debt is unenforceable because of failure to comply with the Statute of Frauds. However, the principle in *Cherry v Boultbee* is separate and distinct from an executor's right of retainer,[99] and indeed there is a sound reason for distinguishing the two in this respect. The Court of Appeal in *Re Rownson* regarded the right of a personal representative to pay any creditor of the deceased, including him or herself, in respect of a debt that has become time-barred, as an exception to the personal representative's general duty not to waste an estate that is not his or her own. The Court was not prepared to extend that exception to the case of a debt owing to the personal representative that is unenforceable instead under the Statute of Frauds. That consideration does not apply, however, when *Cherry v Boultbee* is in issue. Rather, the personal representative acts in the interests of the estate by directing a person, who otherwise would deplete the estate by withdrawing his or her own entitlement, to obtain payment from an asset of the estate in his or her own hands that otherwise would have no value because of its unenforceability.

14.18

(2) Right to participate must be due and payable

In order to invoke *Cherry v Boultbee*, the right to share in the fund must be due and payable.[100] By this it is meant that, until the right to participate has become payable, the administrator may not assert the equity by appropriating an obligation to contribute as

14.19

---

[96] This was apart from the question whether the nature of the demands was such that a set-off would have been available in any event.

[97] See also *Herskope v Perpetual Trustees (WA) Ltd* (2002) 41 ACSR 707 (covenant not to sue).

[98] (1885) 29 Ch D 358.

[99] See para. 14.04 above.

[100] See *Campbell v Graham* (1831) 1 Russ & M 453, 465, 39 ER 175, 179 (affirmed *Campbell v Sandford* (1834) 8 Bligh NS 622, 5 ER 1073). See also para. 14.44 below in relation to a periodic right to participate.

satisfaction of the right to participate.[101] For example, the principle may not be invoked in respect of a legacy while that legacy is still only a right in reversion[102] or, in the case of a residuary legacy, until the residue is ascertained.[103]

(3) Obligation to contribute must not have ceased to exist

14.20 While the circumstance that the obligation to contribute is not enforceable by action does not preclude the application of the *Cherry v Boultbee* principle,[104] *Cherry v Boultbee* does not apply if the obligation has ceased to exist when the share of the fund becomes payable and the equity is asserted,[105] unless in a particular case the terms governing the fund provide otherwise.[106] Thus, *Cherry v Boultbee* has been said not to apply if the debt is one for which the person claiming the share has been released as a result of a discharge from bankruptcy,[107] or pursuant to a composition or deed of arrangement,[108] or if the debt has been extinguished by moratorium legislation.[109]

14.21 In relation to discharge from bankruptcy, the Insolvency Act 1986, s. 281 provides that the discharge releases the bankrupt from all bankruptcy debts but has no effect on the

---

[101] Thus, interest still accumulates on the debt until the share becomes payable. See *Re Akerman* [1891] 3 Ch 212; *Re Watson* [1896] 1 Ch 925.

[102] See *Re Batchelor. Sloper v Oliver* (1873) LR 16 Eq 481, 483–484 (referred to with evident approval in *Re Watson* [1896] 1 Ch 925, 932); *Re Baird (Decd), Hall v Macky* [1935] NZLR 847, 852. See also *Re Hurburgh* [1959] Tas SR 25, 43–46 (Crawford J), criticizing *Richards v Richards* (1821) 9 Price 219, 147 ER 72, and seeking to explain *Burridge v Row* (1842) 1 Y & C CC 183, 62 ER 846, affirmed (1844) 13 LJ Ch 173, on the basis of set-off. Certainly Lord Lyndhurst in *Burridge v Row* based his decision on both set-off and the principle in *Cherry v Boultbee*. However, the insolvency legislation only allows a trustee in bankruptcy to estimate the value of a liability of the bankrupt, so that a dividend in respect of it may be paid immediately. See the Insolvency Act 1986, s. 322(3). There is no corresponding power to put a present value on a sum payable to the bankrupt in the future and to demand payment of that sum immediately. Consequently, it should not be possible for a set-off to proceed while the right of the bankrupt is still only a right in reversion. However, in England a different position now applies in company liquidation and administration. See para. 8.35 above.

[103] See *Re Hurburgh* [1959] Tas SR 25, 32–3.

[104] See para. 14.17 above.

[105] *Re Sewell; White v Sewell* [1909] 1 Ch 806, 808 ('the liability must exist when the equity is asserted'). In addition to the cases cited below, see also *Re Palmer; Palmer v Clarke* (1894) 13 R 233 (with respect to the disclaimed contract); *Re Wheeler. Hankinson v Hayter* [1904] 2 Ch 66; *In the Will of Bickerdike, decd; Bickerdike v Hill* [1918] VLR 191; *Woodcock v Eames* (1925) 69 Sol Jo 444. Compare *Re Pink. Pink v Pink* [1912] 1 Ch 498. *Quaere* whether there should be an existing debt at that date, or whether it is sufficient that the liability is contingent. See paras 14.35–14.38 below.

[106] See *Re Ainsworth; Millington v Ainsworth* [1922] 1 Ch 22, in which a direction in a will, that a debt due to the testator from his son should be deducted from the moiety of the residuary estate bequeathed to the son, was held not to be affected by the son's discharge from bankruptcy.

[107] *Re Akerman* [1891] 3 Ch 212, 217; *Re Watson* [1896] 1 Ch 925, 933; *Re Baird* [1935] NZLR 847. Compare *Re Hope; De Cetto v Hope* [1900] WN 76, which is explained on other grounds in *Re Hurburgh* [1959] Tas SR 25, 48. *Re Melton* [1918] 1 Ch 37 is cited as authority to the contrary in *Withers on Reversions* (2nd edn, 1933), 246, but it appears from the statement of the facts in *Re Melton* (at 38) that the bankrupt in that case had never obtained his discharge. *Quaere* why the fact of the debtor's discharge from bankruptcy in *Re Palmer* (1894) 13 R 233 did not take away the executor's right to invoke *Cherry v Boultbee* in relation to the £700.

[108] See *Re Sewell; White v Sewell* [1909] 1 Ch 806, and the cases cited therein, and also *Re Hurburgh* [1959] Tas SR 25. Compare *Re Powell; Powell v Powell* (1904) 20 TLR 374. However, *Cherry v Boultbee* may be invoked in respect of any sum payable as a dividend under the composition or scheme. See *Re Orpen. Beswick v Orpen* (1880) 16 Ch D 202.

[109] *Parkes Property and Stock Co Ltd v Perpetual Trustee Co Ltd* (1936) 36 SR (NSW) 457.

functions of the trustee in bankruptcy or on the operation of the provisions of Part IX of the Act for the purpose of carrying out those functions. In particular, discharge does not affect the right of a creditor to prove in the bankruptcy for any debt from which the bankrupt is released. In *Law Society v Shah*,[110] Floyd J considered that discharge under s. 281 extinguishes only the remedy of enforcement as against the bankrupt and that the underlying cause of action remains. In discussing the point, he referred to the operation of a limitation defence which normally bars only the remedy and not the right.[111] But that result is a consequence of the clear language of the limitation legislation, which ordinarily is drafted in terms that an action may not be brought after the expiration of the limitation period.[112] Section 281, on the other hand, specifically states that a discharge 'releases' the bankrupt from all bankruptcy debts. The better view is that a discharge from bankruptcy has the effect of extinguishing the debts,[113] albeit that for the purpose of the administration of the estate the debts are to be regarded as preserved. On that basis, the principle outlined above in relation to *Cherry v Boultbee* should still apply.[114]

Consider that a debtor to a deceased testator has become bankrupt while the debtor's right **14.22** to a legacy under the will is still only a right in reversion.[115] If the executor chooses to prove for the debt in the bankruptcy, the executor waives the right to invoke *Cherry v Boultbee*.[116] If, on the other hand, the executor decides to wait until the debtor's legacy falls into possession and then to rely on *Cherry v Boultbee* as a means of obtaining the full value of the debt, he or she runs the risk that the debtor may be discharged from bankruptcy while the right to the legacy is still only in reversion. If that were to happen, the fact that the debtor has been released from liability on the debt as a result of the discharge[117] would mean that the principle could not be invoked against the debtor, and so the testator's estate will have lost the chance of receiving anything in respect of the debt. However, the provision in the Insolvency Act, by which a bankrupt may be discharged automatically after one year from the date of the bankruptcy,[118] offers some guidance to an executor faced with the choice of which approach to adopt in this situation.

F. Mutuality

In order for the principle in *Cherry v Boultbee* to apply, there must at one time have been **14.23** a person who was both entitled to participate in, and also liable to contribute to, a fund. The administrator of the fund may not invoke the principle in respect of a debt due to

---

[110] [2009] Ch 223 at [31]–[38].

[111] See para. 14.17 above.

[112] See e.g. the Limitation Act 1980, s. 5, which is expressed in terms that 'an action shall not be brought' after the expiration of the limitation period'.

[113] *Wight v Eckhardt Marine GmbH* [2004] 1 AC 147 at [27]. See also the cases referred to in para. 14.20 above.

[114] This is consistent with *R (Balding) v Secretary of State for Work and Pensions* [2008] 1 WLR 564 (affirming [2007] 1 WLR 1821) in relation to a statutory right of deduction.

[115] See *Re Hurburgh* [1959] Tas SR 25, 50–51.

[116] See para. 14.58 below.

[117] See above.

[118] Insolvency Act 1986, s. 279. Compare the former Bankruptcy Act 1914, s. 26. In Australia, see the Bankruptcy Act 1966 (Cth), s. 149.

some other person, rather than to the fund,[119] and similarly it is not sufficient that the person entitled to participate is indebted to a third party who is under an obligation to contribute.[120]

(1) Bankruptcy[121]

14.24 The requirement of a person being at the one time entitled to participate in and obliged to contribute to the fund may come into issue in the event of the bankruptcy of the person entitled to participate.[122] This was the case in *Cherry v Boultbee*.[123] A legatee under a will was indebted to the testatrix. After incurring the debt, but before the testatrix died, the legatee became bankrupt. The bankruptcy did not affect the liability on the debt, which remained the liability of the legatee. On the other hand, since the legatee had become bankrupt during the lifetime of the testatrix, and had not obtained a discharge from bankruptcy,[124] the legatee himself never had a right to the legacy. Rather, the right to it was vested at all times in his assignee in bankruptcy on behalf of the estate.[125] Consequently: 'there never was a time at which the same person was entitled to receive the legacy and liable to pay the entire debt; the right, therefore, of retaining a sufficient sum out of the legacy to pay the debt can never have been vested in anyone.'[126] If, on the other hand, the legatee's bankruptcy had occurred after the death, the executors would have been permitted to invoke the principle.[127] The legatee himself at one time would have been entitled to share in the fund. Moreover, since the bankrupt's assignees in bankruptcy could claim no better title than the bankrupt himself, the principle could have been invoked against them also.[128]

---

[119] See *Re Watson* [1896] 1 Ch 925, 937, and also *Stammers v Elliott* (1868) LR 3 Ch App 195, 199 (with respect to the £150). Compare *Pyrenees Vineyard Management Ltd v Russell Frajam* (2008) 69 ACSR 95 in relation to a managed investment scheme under Chapter 5C of the Australian Corporations Act 2001 (Cth).

[120] See *Avison v Holmes* (1861) 1 J & H 530, 70 ER 855, and also *Smee v Baines* (1861) 29 Beav 661, 54 ER 784.

[121] See further paras 14.95–14.101 below in relation to the question whether, in the case of an insolvent contributor, *Cherry v Boultbee* should be applied to the extent of the full face value of the debt or merely to the extent of the dividend payable on the debt.

[122] Compare paras 14.98–14.101 below in relation to company liquidation. Unlike in a bankruptcy, where the assets of the bankrupt vest in the trustee in bankruptcy, the assets of a company in liquidation ordinarily are not vested in the liquidator. See paras 13.05–13.06 above.

[123] (1839) 4 My & Cr 442, 41 ER 171, not following *Ex p Man* (1829) Mont & M 210. See also *Bell v Bell* (1849) 17 Sim 127, 60 ER 1077; *Re Hodgson, Decd. Hodgson v Fox* (1878) 9 Ch D 673; *Re Orpen. Beswick v Orpen* (1880) 16 Ch D 202; *Re Peruvian Railway Construction Co Ltd* [1915] 2 Ch 144; *Re Lussier* [1927] 4 DLR 637; *Re Reiter, ex p Hislop* (1932) 5 ABC 98. Sir George Turner in *Freeman v Lomas* (1851) 9 Hare 109, 115–16, 68 ER 435, 438 had reservations about the decision in *Cherry v Boultbee*.

[124] If the legatee had obtained a discharge from bankruptcy the terms of the will were such that he would have obtained an absolute right to the legacy, but he died before obtaining the discharge. See Lord Langdale at first instance (1838) 2 Keen 319, 325, 48 ER 651, 654.

[125] See now the Insolvency Act 1986, ss. 283 and 306, and s. 436 for the definition of property. See also s. 307 with respect to after acquired property. In Australia, see the Bankruptcy Act 1966 (Cth), ss. 58 and 116.

[126] (1839) 4 My & Cr 442, 448, 41 ER 171, 173 *per* Lord Cottenham.

[127] In this situation the principle can be invoked in respect of the full face value of the debt. See para. 14.96 below.

[128] *Jeffs v Wood* (1723) 2 P Wms 128, 24 ER 668; *Bousfield v Lawford* (1863) 1 De G J & S 459, 46 ER 182; *Ranking v Barnard* (1820) 5 Madd 32, 56 ER 806; *Richards v Richards* (1821) 9 Price 219, 147 ER 72.

While it was held in *Cherry v Boultbee* that the executors could not apply the principle in **14.25** respect of the full amount of the debt owing to the fund, Lord Cottenham nevertheless accepted that it could be invoked in respect of the dividend payable in the bankruptcy.[129] In other words, the executors could insist that the legacy should be considered as paid to the extent of the dividend payable on the debt. The one party, in the form of the assignee in bankruptcy, was entitled to participate in the fund, by receiving the legacy on behalf of the insolvent estate, and was also obliged to contribute to the fund, by paying a dividend out of the insolvent estate.[130]

(2) The relevant date

The relevant date in these insolvent debtor cases is the date of the event which precipitates **14.26** the setting up of the fund. Thus, where the fund consists of a deceased's estate, the precipitating event is the death.[131] In a bankruptcy or a company liquidation, it is the commencement of the bankruptcy or the liquidation. The principle may be invoked by the administrator of the fund as long as the person liable to contribute to the fund was also possessed of a right to participate at some time after the precipitating event. For example, when a company in liquidation had a surplus available for distribution amongst its shareholders, and one of the shareholders, who was indebted to the company, died insolvent, Sargant J considered that the liquidator could only have invoked the principle if the death had occurred after the commencement of the liquidation. He said that, when the liquidation commenced, 'the rights in respect of the shares may be considered to have been converted into a right or expectation of receiving a rateable proportion of the surplus moneys remaining after satisfying the liabilities of the company'.[132] The precipitating event, as Sargant J also remarked, is the '*earliest* possible moment at which any right of retainer or set-off or the like could arise'.[133] It means that the principle in *Cherry v Boultbee* may not be invoked if the debtor to the fund did not have a right to share in it personally some time after the precipitating event.[134] In the case in issue, the shareholder had died before the liquidation. At the date of the liquidation, the deceased shareholder was still the person indebted to the company, but the shares, and the right to participate in the surplus, had vested in the executor. The liquidator therefore was not entitled to apply the principle in relation to the debt owing to the company. On the other hand, consistent with *Cherry v Boultbee*,[135] Sargant J recognized that the principle could be invoked in respect of

---

[129] (1839) 4 My & Cr 442, 448, 41 ER 171, 173 (referring to the judgment of the Master of the Rolls, whose decision Lord Cottenham affirmed).

[130] See also in this regard *Re Orpen* (1880) 16 Ch D 202; *Re Peruvian Railway Construction Co Ltd* [1915] 2 Ch 144; *Re Fenton (No. 2), ex p Fenton Textile Association Ltd* [1932] 1 Ch 178, 187. Compare *Re Hodgson* (1878) 9 Ch D 673, in which a dividend had not been declared in the bankruptcy. *Quaere* whether a foreign bankruptcy of the debtor to the fund may be recognized for the purpose of *Cherry v Boultbee*. See the discussion in *Re Kowloon Container Warehouse Co Ltd* [1981] HKLR 210 with respect to a foreign liquidation.

[131] *Re SSSL Realisations (2002) Ltd* [2006] Ch 610 at [108].

[132] *Re Peruvian Railway Construction Co Ltd* [1915] 2 Ch 144, 151 (affirmed [1915] 2 Ch 442). Compare *FAI General Insurance Co Ltd v FAI Car Owners Mutual Insurance Co Pty Ltd* [2009] NSWSC 1350 at [61]–[73], where the company had only one member.

[133] [1915] 2 Ch 144, 151 (emphasis added).

[134] See also *Re SSSL Realisations (2002) Ltd* [2006] Ch 610 at [108].

[135] See para. 14.25 above.

the dividend payable by the executors out of the deceased's insolvent estate to the company. Further, it is not an objection that the obligation to contribute to a fund only arose after the precipitating event.[136]

14.27 While the same person at some time at least must have been entitled to share in the fund and also liable to contribute to it, it is not necessary that the right and the liability should each have been presently payable, or indeed vested, at that time. For example, if a legatee becomes bankrupt after the testator's death, the executors may invoke the principle when the legacy becomes due and payable even if the legatee only had an interest in reversion at the time of the bankruptcy,[137] or if the right to participate otherwise was payable *in futuro* when the bankruptcy occurred. Similarly, it is sufficient if the obligation to contribute was merely contingent at the date of the legatee's bankruptcy, for example when the testator had guaranteed the legatee's debts and the executors were not called upon to make a payment under the guarantee until after the legatee had become bankrupt. The legatee's obligation to indemnify the estate was contingent (upon payment under the guarantee) when the bankruptcy occurred, but that did not preclude the application of the principle.[138] As long as there has been in this sense a situation in which the one person had both a right to participate and an obligation to contribute before that person's bankruptcy, an equity to invoke the principle arises in favour of the administrator of the fund to which the trustee in bankruptcy takes subject.[139] A judgment creditor is in the same position in that regard as a trustee in bankruptcy, and accordingly takes subject to the equity in the form of the right to invoke the principle.[140]

(3) Mutuality is concerned with the relationship to the fund

14.28 Mutuality for the purpose of *Cherry v Boultbee* is concerned with the relationship between the fund and the person indebted to the fund.[141] Generally, it should be determined by reference to principles similar to those applicable to set-off. They differ in one respect, however. Set-off applies where A is indebted to B and B is indebted to A, whereas in the case of *Cherry v Boultbee* it is not necessary that the debt should have been incurred to the person in respect of whose estate the fund was set up. It is sufficient if the debt is incurred to the administrator of the fund, as long as the proceeds of the debt will be in aid of the fund.[142] In other respects, similar principles apply. *Cherry v Boultbee* can be invoked when the

---

[136] See e.g. the cases referred to in paras 14.39–14.42 below in relation to the proposition that the contribution need only be in aid of the fund. See also *Re Palmer; Palmer v Clarke* (1894) 13 R 233, in which an option to purchase the testator's property was exercised after the testator's death, and *Stephen v Venables (No. 1)* (1862) 30 Beav 625, 54 ER 1032, in which executors granted a lease of part of the testator's property to a residuary legatee.

[137] See *Re Watson; Turner v Watson* [1896] 1 Ch 925; *Re Lennard; Lennard's Trustee v Lennard* [1934] 1 Ch 235. See also *Re Melton; Milk v Towers* [1918] 1 Ch 37; *Re Hurburgh* [1959] Tas SR 25, 40 *per* Crawford J ('the legatee is entitled in possession or in reversion or even contingently to a general legacy or a share of residue').

[138] *Willes v Greenhill (No. 1)* (1860) 29 Beav 376, 54 ER 673; *Re Whitehouse; Whitehouse v Edwards* (1887) 37 Ch D 683; *Re Watson; Turner v Watson* [1896] 1 Ch 925; *Re Melton* [1918] 1 Ch 37.

[139] The obligation to contribute nevertheless must still be in existence when the right to participate becomes due and payable. See para. 14.20 above.

[140] *Kilworth v Mountcashell* (1864) 15 Ir Ch Rep 565, 581.

[141] The principle 'is applied only where there is a direct and specific mutuality between the mass and the particular debtor'. See *Re Pennington and Owen Ltd* [1925] 1 Ch 825, 830 *per* Pollock MR.

[142] See paras 14.39–14.42 below.

person liable to contribute is the same as the person entitled to participate,[143] having regard to equitable rights. For example, if A holds his or her right to participate in the fund merely as a trustee, the administrator of the fund could not appropriate the share of the fund as payment of a debt owing by A personally.[144] On the other hand, the administrator may appropriate as payment a debt owing by a person who is the beneficial owner of the right to participate.[145] Conversely, *Cherry v Boultbee* will not apply if the testator was only a trustee of a legatee's indebtedness,[146] or if the debt is owing to the administrator of the fund in his or her personal capacity, even though the administrator may be entitled to the residue of the fund and consequently would be benefited by the deduction.[147] In *Re Binns*,[148] a will stipulated that the residuary estate was to be held on trust for the children of the deceased, but if any child died the children of that child were to take his share. It was held that a grandchild claiming under the will after the death of his parent, who in turn was a child of the testator, was not liable to have his interest reduced to the extent of a debt owing by his deceased parent to the testator. While *Cherry v Boultbee* would have applied if the deceased parent himself had claimed under the will, the child of that deceased parent was entitled in his own right.

(4) Same fund

Similarly, the obligation to contribute and the right to participate ordinarily should relate to the same fund.[149] In *Re Towndrow; Gratton v Machen*[150] a person appointed executor under a will was entitled to a legacy, for which an assent had been given by the executors. In addition he was appointed trustee of the residuary personal estate, although he himself had no beneficial interest in that estate. While acting in his capacity of trustee, he mis-appropriated a part of the residue. Because of the assent, the specific legacy was held on a trust which was separate and distinct from the trusts upon which the rest of the estate were held.[151] Therefore, Parker J held that the trustee was not required to make good his default to the residuary estate before he (or the person to whom he had mortgaged his right to the legacy) could claim the legacy. Parker J correctly applied the principle in *Cherry v Boultbee* on the assumption that the legacy was the subject of a valid assent,[152] but it has been doubted whether the case nevertheless was correctly decided. Younger J in *Re Jewell's*

14.29

---

[143] *Reeve v Richer* (1847) 1 De G & Sm 624, 63 ER 1224; *Re Bruce; Lawford v Bruce* [1908] 2 Ch 682.

[144] If, however, the trust is created after the precipitating event, the person acquiring the beneficial title would take subject to equities. See paras 14.63–14.68 below.

[145] *Re Kent County Gas Light and Coke Co Ltd* [1913] 1 Ch 92, 97; *Re Kowloon Container Warehouse Co. Ltd* [1981] HKLR 210.

[146] *Richardson v Richardson* (1867) LR 3 Eq 686, 695.

[147] *Freeman v Lomas* (1851) 9 Hare 109, 68 ER 435.

[148] [1929] 1 Ch 677.

[149] In addition to the cases cited below, see *Price v Loaden* (1856) 21 Beav 508, 52 ER 955 and *Re Saltergate Insurance Co Ltd (No. 2)* [1984] 3 NSWLR 389, 393–594 (proceeds of a policy of reinsurance distributable as a separate fund in the liquidation of an insurance company, pursuant to legislation similar in effect to the Corporations Act 2001 (Cth), s. 562A).

[150] [1911] 1 Ch 662.

[151] As soon as executors assent to a bequest it ceases to be a part of the testator's assets. See *Dix v Burford* (1854) 19 Beav 409, 412, 52 ER 408, 410, and also para. 13.128 above.

[152] See also *Ballard v Marsden* (1880) 14 Ch D 374 and *Re Milnes; Milnes v Sherwin* (1885) 53 LT 534, 535. Compare *Cole v Muddle* (1852) 10 Hare 186, 68 ER 892, the correctness of which is doubted in *Withers on Reversions* (2nd edn, 1933), 241, fn. a, on the ground that one of several executors should be able to assent

Settlement. Watts v Public Trustee[153] said that *Re Towndrow* might have been decided differently if *Morris v Livie*[154] had been cited to the court. *Morris v Livie* is considered later in the context of defaulting trustees.[155] Knight Bruce VC in that case put forward the view that, when a trustee appointed under a will is also named as a legatee, the legacy is presumed to be consideration for his for her performance of the duties of trustee. *Cherry v Boultbee* specifically contemplates the existence of a right to participate, but dictates that a particular asset may be appropriated as payment of that right. The effect of *Morris v Livie*, on the other hand, is that the trustee is deprived of a right to participate while he or she is in default. In *Re Towndrow* there was an assent. An executor could only assent to a legacy in favour of the legatee to whom it is given, and not in favour of a stranger.[156] Similarly, while it is has been said that an assent is irrevocable,[157] it may be that an assent made in favour of a trustee would not be binding if in truth the result of the trustee's conduct was that he or she was not entitled to the legacy while he or she remained in default. The assent should be binding, however, as against a purchaser of the legacy for value and in good faith from the defaulting trustee on the faith of the assent.[158]

(5) Settlement involving two or more funds

14.30 An apparent exception to the requirement of a single fund exists in the case of a settlement. Two or more funds may be settled under the one settlement but on different trusts. Nevertheless, the courts 'consider everything that is brought or expressed to be brought into settlement by anybody from any source as one aggregate trust fund'.[159] Consequently, the trustees may invoke *Cherry v Boultbee* against a person seeking to participate in the settlement if he or she is also obliged to contribute to it,[160] even though the 'right' and the 'obligation' may relate to different funds encompassed by the settlement.[161] Similarly,

---

to a legacy in which he or she is interested. Compare also *Hastie v Hastie* (1876) 24 WR 242, in which there was a strong case of fraud.

[153] [1919] 2 Ch 161.

[154] (1842) 1 Y & C CC 380, 62 ER 934.

[155] See para. 14.81 below.

[156] *Re West; West v Roberts* [1909] 2 Ch 180, 186.

[157] See e.g. Williams, *The Law Relating to Assents* (1947), 98, though compare *Williams, Mortimer, and Sunnucks on Executors, Administrators and Probate* (19th edn, 2008), 1165.

[158] *Williams, Mortimer and Sunnucks on Executors, Administrators and Probate* (19th edn, 2008), 1164. See also *Edgar v Plomley* [1900] AC 431, which concerned a fund in court in an administration suit ordered to be carried to a separate account in the name of a trustee whom it was later discovered was in default.

[159] *Codrington v Lindsay* (1873) LR 8 Ch App 578, 592 *per* James LJ. See generally *Withers on Reversions* (2nd edn, 1933), 241.

[160] See e.g. *Priddy v Rose* (1817) 3 Mer 86, 36 ER 33; *Kilworth v Mountcashell* (1861) 12 Ir Ch Rep 43 (subsequent proceedings (1864) 15 Ir Ch Rep 565); *Corr v Corr* (1879) 3 LR Ir 435; *Ballard v Marsden* (1880) 14 Ch D 374, 377; *Re Weston; Davies v Tagart* [1900] 2 Ch 164. The liability to contribute need not arise out of the terms of the settlement, but may arise subsequently as a result of a misappropriation. See e.g. *Woodyatt v Gresley* (1836) 8 Sim. 180, 59 ER 72. Moreover, it makes no difference that the settlement may be voluntary, provided that it has been so completed as to be enforceable by the court. See *Re Weston.* Compare *Hallett v Hallett* (1879) 13 Ch D 232, in which the fund for which the action was brought was expressly excluded from the settlement.

[161] See *Burridge v Row* (1844) 13 LJ Ch 173 (affirming 1 Y & C CC 183, 62 ER 846); *Re Jewell's Settlement; Watts v Public Trustee* [1919] 2 Ch 161. The courts seem to incline in favour of finding that there is a single settlement. See e.g. *Woodyatt v Gresley* (1836) 8 Sim 180, 59 ER 72.

separate trusts, or bequests, under the one will may be treated as constituting the one fund, unless the executors have already set apart a particular legacy so that the estate is no longer in bulk.[162]

(6) Joint and separate rights and obligations

The prohibition against setting off joint demands and separate demands[163] also applies to **14.31** *Cherry v Boultbee*.[164] Thus, an executor may not appropriate as payment of a legacy a debt owing to the fund by a number of joint debtors of whom the legatee is one.[165] Similarly, in Ireland a legatee was indebted to a firm in which the testator was a partner, and it was held that the executor could not appropriate the joint claim as payment of the legacy.[166] There was, on the other hand, a curious decision by Stuart VC in *Smith v Smith*.[167] A residuary legatee under a will was a partner in a firm that was indebted to the testator. The firm became bankrupt. Stuart VC held that the executors could appropriate the joint debt of the firm as payment of the legacy due to the partner in his separate capacity. Cozens-Hardy MR in *Turner v Turner*[168] offered a possible explanation for the decision, but without finally deciding whether the case was correctly decided. He said that in *Smith v Smith* the assignees in bankruptcy were seeking payment of the legacy in their capacity of assignees of the separate estate of the partner, rather than as assignees of the joint estate of the firm, and moreover he said that the legatee's separate estate was liable to the testator's estate for the debt. Since the testator's executors in *Smith v Smith* could have proved for the debt against the separate estate of the legatee, which estate was vested in the assignees, the executors could appropriate the debt as payment of the legacy owing to the partner.[169] That explanation is doubtful. Formerly, when a partnership became bankrupt, the principle was that the joint estate was applicable in the first instance in payment of the joint debts and the separate estate of each partner was applicable in the first instance in payment of his or her separate debts. If there was a surplus of the separate estates, it was dealt with as part of the joint estate, and if there was a surplus of the joint estate, it was dealt with as part of the

---

[162] *In the Estate of Tolley, Decd* (1972) 5 SASR 466, and see also *MacPhillamy v Fox* (1932) 32 SR (NSW) 427. Harvey CJ in Eq in *MacPhillamy v Fox* criticized *Re Towndrow* [1911] 1 Ch 662 (see para. 14.29 above), although the criticism would appear to be misplaced, except possibly to the extent that the case concerned a defaulting trustee. *Re Towndrow* is not inconsistent with the Chief Justice's contention that the whole of the funds held by a trustee under a will constitute one fund for the purpose of adjustment, because an assent has the effect of setting apart the particular fund in question from the fund in bulk. In *MacPhillamy v Fox* there had not been an assent in respect of the bequest in issue.

[163] See paras 12.02–12.07 above.

[164] See e.g. *Re Pennington and Owen Ltd* [1925] 1 Ch 825. Note also *McEwan v Crombie* (1883) 25 Ch D 175, which appears to have been a case involving *Cherry v Boultbee* rather than set-off.

[165] *Turner v Turner* [1911] 1 Ch 716.

[166] *Jackson v Yeats* [1912] 1 IR 267.

[167] (1861) 3 Giff 263, 66 ER 408.

[168] [1911] 1 Ch 716.

[169] Cozens-Hardy MR in *Turner v Turner* [1911] 1 Ch 716, 721 said with regard to *Smith v Smith* that the case: 'is consistent with the principle in *Cherry v Boultbee* because the testatrix's executors could have proved against the separate estate of William Smith, whose separate estate was vested in the assignees, and that brings us practically to the same position as though there had never been a firm and the debt had originally been due from the legatee.'

respective separate estates in proportion to the interest of each partner in the joint estate.[170] Thus, the separate estate of each partner was only liable to be applied in payment of a partnership debt to the extent of any surplus remaining after the partner's separate creditors had been paid in full. The principle has been modified under the Insolvent Partnerships Order 1994, so that, to the extent of any deficiency in the joint estate, a claim may now be made against the separate estates *pari passu* with other separate creditors.[171] Nevertheless, it is still the case that the separate estate of each partner is only liable to be applied in payment of partnership debts to the extent that those debts are not capable of being satisfied from the partnership assets. The order in *Smith v Smith* had the effect of allowing a separate asset of a partner to be used to satisfy a partnership debt before the joint estate had been taken into account, which could have disadvantaged the separate creditors of that partner. This potential disadvantage to separate creditors is still relevant under the new partnership distribution rules.

14.32 On the other hand, *Cherry v Boultbee* may apply when the liability to contribute is joint and several rather than joint.[172] If there are joint and several debtors to a fund, and the administrator of the fund appropriates the debt as *pro tanto* payment of the right of one of the debtors to participate, all the debtors are discharged to the extent of the right to participate, although the debtor whose right was appropriated should be entitled to contribution from the other debtors.[173]

G. The Obligation to Contribute

(1) Damages liability

14.33 *Cherry v Boultbee* is not confined to cases in which the obligation to contribute to the fund is for a liquidated sum enforceable either as a debt or by means of an order for specific performance.[174] It may encompass also a liability sounding in damages,[175] for example a liability for breach of contract for failure to keep up a policy of life insurance settled on trust[176] or a liability for damages for misfeasance.[177]

---

[170] See e.g. art. 10 of the Insolvent Partnerships Order 1986 (S.I. 1986 No. 2142). In Australia, see the Bankruptcy Act 1966 (Cth), s. 110.

[171] See Part II of Sch. 4 (s. 175A) and Sch. 7 (s. 328A) of the Insolvent Partnerships Order 1994 (S.I. 1994 No. 2421).

[172] *Selangor United Rubber Estates Ltd v Cradock (No. 4)* [1969] 1 WLR 1773. See also para. 12.21 above in relation to set-off.

[173] This seems to have been recognized in *Selangor United Rubber Estates Ltd v Cradock (No. 4)* [1969] 1 WLR 1773, 1776.

[174] For specific performance, see *Re Palmer; Palmer v Clarke* (1894) 13 R 233, 236.

[175] *Stephenson Nominees Pty Ltd v Official Receiver* (1987) 16 FCR 536, 558. In Canada, compare *Re Attorney General of Canada and Standard Trust Co* (1995) 128 DLR (4th) 747 and *Canada (Attorney General) v Confederation Life Insurance Co* (2002) 39 CBR (4th) 182 (at [51], distinguishing *Re Jewell's Settlement* [1919] 2 Ch 161) in relation to the right of an administrator of a fund to withhold payment to a beneficiary pending the determination of a damages claim. See para. 14.34 below.

[176] *Re Jewell's Settlement; Watts v Public Trustee* [1919] 2 Ch 161, distinguishing *Re Smelting Corporation; Seaver v The Company* [1915] 1 Ch 472.

[177] See the discussion of *Re Milan Tramways Co, ex p Theys* (1884) 25 Ch D 587 in *Re Jewell's Settlement* [1919] 2 Ch 161, 174–6. See also *Re Leeds and Hanley Theatres of Varieties Ltd* [1904] 2 Ch 45.

(2) Contingent, or not presently payable

There is authority for the proposition that the administrator of a fund may not invoke **14.34** *Cherry v Boultbee* when the liability of the person seeking to share in the fund is not payable until a future date. Thus, when a residuary legatee was indebted to the testator on a debt payable by instalments, the executors were not permitted to invoke the principle in respect of instalments payable in the future.[178] This result was justified on the ground that, if the debt could be appropriated as payment of the right to participate before the debt was presently payable, the contract under which the debt arose would have been altered.[179] *Re Rhodesia Goldfields Ltd*[180] is not inconsistent with that view. In that case, neither the existence nor the amount of a debt to a fund had been established or ascertained, but if there was a debt it would have been presently payable. Swinfen Eady J held that, pending the ascertainment and establishment of the amount (if any) due to the fund, the share of the fund for which payment was sought should be retained and carried to a separate account.[181]

Confusingly, there is other authority which suggests that the principle may apply when the **14.35** obligation to contribute is contingent upon the happening of an event. In other words, the liability is not only not presently payable, it is not even presently existing. In *Re Melton; Milk v Towers*[182] a testator guaranteed the debts owing to a bank by a residuary legatee under the will. The testator died and the legatee later became bankrupt. The bank then sought and obtained payment from the testator's estate pursuant to the guarantee. As a result, the testator's estate had a provable claim in the bankruptcy for an indemnity in respect of the sum paid. The point immediately in issue was whether the rule against double proof precluded the application of the *Cherry v Boultbee* principle in relation to a claim for payment of the bankrupt legatee's entitlement under the will, and the case is considered later in that context.[183] But there were also some observations relevant to the application of the principle to a contingent debt. Before the testator's estate had paid the bank, the estate merely had a contingent entitlement to an indemnity from the legatee.[184] Warrington LJ nevertheless accepted that, at 'the death of the testator',[185] the executors 'had a right to be indemnified against any claim which they *might ultimately have to satisfy* as the result of the guarantee; and to retain in their hands so much of [the legatee's] share as

---

[178] *Re Abrahams; Abrahams v Abrahams* [1908] 2 Ch 69. See also *Re Rees; Rees v Rees* (1889) 60 LT 260; *Jeffryes v Agra and Masterman's Bank* (1866) LR 2 Eq 674, 680; *Re Watson* [1896] 1 Ch 925, 933–934; *Re Rhodesia Goldfields Ltd* [1910] 1 Ch 239, 242 (Swinfen Eady J, *arguendo*).

[179] *Re Abrahams* [1908] 2 Ch 69, 72.

[180] [1910] 1 Ch 239. In Australia, see *Kenway Investments (Aust) Pty Ltd v Teamda Developments Pty Ltd* [2007] NSWSC 48 at [63]–[64], referring to a 'precautionary or anticipatory' application of *Cherry v Boultbee*.

[181] In Canada the courts have declined to adopt the approach in the *Rhodesia Goldfields* case in the case of a damages claim which had yet to be determined. See *Re Attorney General of Canada and Standard Trust Co* (1995) 128 DLR (4th) 747, 752 and *Canada (Attorney General) v Confederation Life Insurance Co* (2002) 39 CBR (4th) 182 (at [51]: 'the claim . . . is far from liquidated, and many years from determination').

[182] [1918] 1 Ch 37.

[183] See paras 14.52–14.56 below. See also the discussion of *Re Melton* at paras 14.72–14.74 below.

[184] See para. 8.14 above.

[185] This being before payment to the bank.

was sufficient to provide for that indemnity'.[186] Later in his judgment he said that: 'if the right of the executors *at the testator's death* was to pay out of the share sufficient to discharge and satisfy the claim to be indemnified, then so much of that fund as was necessary to make good the trustees' claim never formed part of [the legatee's] estate so as to become divisible in bankruptcy amongst his creditors.'[187] Those statements suggest that a principal debtor's obligation to indemnify the surety can be the subject of *Cherry v Boultbee* while it is still contingent. That proposition was endorsed in *Re SSSL Realisations (2002) Ltd.*[188] The Court of Appeal in that case considered a situation where a creditor (Y) has a guarantee from S in respect of the debts of X, and S is in insolvent liquidation. The point under discussion was the application of *Cherry v Boultbee* in the administration of the fund in the liquidation of S,[189] in circumstances where S's liability to Y under the guarantee has not been and would not be met in full, and in addition X has a separate provable debt in the liquidation.[190] Chadwick LJ, who delivered the judgment of the court,[191] accepted that *Cherry v Boultbee* can apply in that situation, commenting that: 'it is not necessary that the liability to the creditor has been satisfied out of the fund: it is enough that it may have to be satisfied in the future . . .'[192] He also concluded that the amount that X has to contribute for the purpose of the application of the principle is not the amount of the dividend which S has paid or will be required to pay to the creditor, but the full amount of S's liability as surety for which the creditor is entitled to prove in the liquidation.[193]

14.36   There is an anomaly in applying *Cherry v Boultbee* in the circumstances in issue in *Re SSSL Realisations*. This is a consequence of the nature of a surety's right as against the principal debtor before the surety has paid the creditor. The surety's right in such a case is not that he or she can require the principal debtor to pay a sum of money to the surety as an indemnity against the surety's unsatisfied liability to the creditor,[194] but rather that the surety may apply for *quia timet* relief from a court of equity in the form of an order compelling the debtor to relieve the surety from liability by paying the creditor.[195] The view accepted

---

[186] [1918] 1 Ch 37, 54–5 (emphasis added).

[187] [1918] 1 Ch 37, 55–6 (emphasis added). See also Scrutton LJ at 59, referring to an entitlement in the surety to keep as against the debtor the amount that the trustee has paid 'or is liable to pay'.

[188] [2006] Ch 610 at [81], [101]–[105]. See also *Mills v HSBC Trustee (CI) Ltd* [2009] EWHC 3377 (Ch) at [24]. Compare *Cattles Plc v Welcome Financial Services Ltd* [2009] EWHC 3027 (Ch), in which the operation of *Cherry v Boultbee* in a guarantor's liquidation was held to have been excluded by reason of an agreement by the principal debtor not to claim against the guarantor in competition with the creditor in respect of an inter-company debt. An appeal from the decision in relation to the construction of the agreement was dismissed: *Cattles Plc v Welcome Financial Services Ltd* [2010] EWCA Civ 599.

[189] *Cherry v Boultbee* may apply in relation to the fund available for distribution in the liquidation of a company. See para. 14.07 above.

[190] In the *SSSL Realisations* case the principal debtor (X) was also in liquidation, which raised the question of the effect of the rule against double proof. See paras 14.50–14.57 below.

[191] Jonathan Parker LJ and Etherton J agreeing.

[192] [2006] Ch 610 at [102], referring to Warrington LJ in *Re Melton* [1918] 1 Ch 37, 55. See also [2006] Ch 610 at [79](2).

[193] [2006] Ch 610 at [103]–[105]. Where the contributor to the fund (in the situation under the discussion, the principal debtor X) is insolvent, a further issue is whether *Cherry v Boultbee* is to be applied on the basis that the obligation to contribute is the full face value of the liability in question or the dividend payable in the contributor's insolvency. This issue is considered in paras 14.95–14.101 below.

[194] *Re Fenton* [1931] 1 Ch 85, 114.

[195] *Thomas v Nottingham Incorporated Football Club Ltd* [1972] 1 Ch 596; *Woolmington v Bronze Lamp Restaurant Pty Ltd* [1984] 2 NSWLR 242. The passage in *Re Mitchell; Freelove v Mitchell* [1913] 1 Ch 201,

in *Re SSSL Realisations*, on the other hand, in effect treats the surety as having an entitle-ment to payment from the principal debtor before the surety has paid the creditor.[196] In the particular circumstances under consideration in *Re SSSL Realisations*, the approach adopted by the Court of Appeal nevertheless produces a workable and a just solution.[197] In other contexts, however, that might not be the case.

Consider a case such as *Re Melton* (above), which concerned the distribution of a deceased surety's estate in circumstances where the principal debtor was one of the residuary legatees. Warrington LJ in that case suggested that the executors of the estate were entitled to apply *Cherry v Boultbee* as against the legatee as from the time of the surety's death,[198] this being before the surety had paid the creditor, and the Court of Appeal appeared to accept that proposition in *Re SSSL Realisations*.[199] However, the application in that context of the principle applied in *Re SSSL Realisations* could produce injustice. *Re SSSL Realisations* concerned the calculation of dividends payable in the liquidation of an insolvent surety to the creditor and the principal debtor on provable debts. Those calculations would essen-tially be contemporaneous. In a case such as *Re Melton*, on the other hand, a claim against the surety's estate under the guarantee may not have been made at the time that a distribu-tion is to be made to the legatee. Consider that a legacy is presently payable but the debt the subject of the guarantee has not matured. In *Re SSSL Realisations*, the Court of Appeal accepted that the amount which has to be brought into account in the application of *Cherry v Boultbee*, as the principal debtor's contribution to the whole fund, is the full amount of the fund's liability (as surety) to the creditor. The problem with applying *Cherry v Boultbee* on that basis as against a legatee/principal debtor is that the application of the principle would not relieve the debtor from liability to the creditor when the debt later becomes due and payable. The creditor would still be entitled to look to the principal debtor for pay-ment, even though the debtor in effect has paid the surety's estate[200] through the operation of *Cherry v Boultbee*. **14.37**

The difficulty would arise from the application of *Cherry v Boultbee* as against the legatee before the surety's estate has made any payment under the guarantee, in that the executors could require the legatee to bring into account the full amount of the fund's liability as surety as a contribution to the fund in the determination of the legatee's entitlement to share in the fund. That difficulty is a consequence of the nature of the *Cherry v Boultbee* principle, which operates by way of an entitlement in the person administering the fund to appropriate a particular asset as payment of a right to participate.[201] An alternative approach would be to permit the executors in an appropriate case to withhold payment of **14.38**

206, to which Chadwick LJ referred in *Re SSSL Realisations* [2006] Ch 610 at [102], is consistent with this proposition.

[196] That entitlement could not be said to arise from the right to prove a contingent debt in a liquidation, because if the principal debtor is in liquidation the rule against double proof would prevent a proof by the surety in the liquidation in competition with the creditor. See paras 8.13–8.18 above and 14.50–14.57 below.

[197] See the calculations set out at [2006] Ch 610 at [104].

[198] See para. 14.35 above.

[199] [2006] Ch 610 at [102], referring to [77].

[200] See *Re Fenton* [1931] 1 Ch 85, 114 in relation to a direct payment by a principal debtor to a surety.

[201] See para. 14.03 above.

the legatee's interest until it is determined whether the surety's estate will be called upon to pay the creditor.[202] This would be consistent with the approach adopted in *Re Rhodesia Goldfields Ltd*[203] in the situation in which the neither the existence nor the amount of a liability has been established but if there is a liability it would be a present liability. It would represent what has been termed in Australia a 'precautionary' or 'anticipatory' application of *Cherry v Boultbee*.[204]

(3) Contribution need only be 'in aid of' the fund

14.39   It is not necessary that the contribution should directly form a part of the fund in question. It is sufficient if it is 'in aid of' the fund.[205] For example, *Cherry v Boultbee* may be invoked when the liability to contribute is based upon an award of costs made in favour of the person administering the fund as a result of litigation conducted on behalf of the fund.[206] The administrator ordinarily would have a right of indemnity from the fund in respect of his or her costs. If the administrator has already exercised the right, anything received under the award of costs would be paid into the fund. If, on the other hand, the administrator has not been indemnified from the fund, the costs payable to him or her would still be in aid of the fund because they would relieve the fund of the burden of indemnifying the administrator.[207] When the fund is constituted by an estate being administered in bankruptcy, lack of mutuality would operate to deny the debtor for costs the right to set off the costs against a debt owing to him or her by the bankrupt.[208] The bankrupt's trustee, on the other hand, could invoke *Cherry v Boultbee* in relation to the debtor's right to receive a dividend on the debt.[209]

14.40   The notion that it is sufficient that the obligation to contribute is in aid of the fund explains two early decisions of Lord Eldon. In each of *Ex p Bebb*[210] and *Ex p Graham*,[211] a banking

---

[202] Consistent with *Re Melton* [1918] 1 Ch 37, 51–52 (Swinfen Eady LJ), referring to *Re Binns; Lee v Binns* [1896] 2 Ch 584, 587, 588 (North J).

[203] [1910] 1 Ch 239. See para. 14.34 above.

[204] *Kenway Investments (Aust) Pty Ltd v Teamda Developments Pty Ltd* [2007] NSWSC 48 at [63]–[64] (McDougall J).

[205] See Sargant J's formulation of the principle in *Re Peruvian Railway Construction Co Ltd* [1915] 2 Ch 144, 150. See also *Re Saltergate Insurance Co Ltd (No. 2)* [1984] 3 NSWLR 389, 393–4. This may explain *Irby v Irby (No. 3)* (1858) 25 Beav 632, 53 ER 778.

[206] *Re Knapman* (1881) 18 Ch D 300 (but note the explanation of the case in *Re Pain; Gustavson v Haviland* [1919] 1 Ch 38; *Re Mayne, ex p The Official Receiver* [1907] 2 KB 899; *Dodson v Sandburst & Northern District Trustees Executors and Agency Co Ltd* [1955] VLR 100. *Cherry v Boultbee* may also apply in the converse situation, in which a person who is liable to contribute to a trust fund has obtained an order for payment of costs out of the trust fund. See *Re Harrald; Wilde v Walford* (1884) 51 LT 441.

[207] *Dodson v Sandhurst & Northern District Trustees Executors and Agency Co Ltd* [1955] VLR 100, 102–103.

[208] *West v Pryce* (1825) 2 Bing 455, 130 ER 382. An additional reason for denying a set-off, relevant to both bankruptcy and company liquidation, is that the debt for costs arises after the relevant date for determining rights of set-off. See para. 6.63 above, and also para. 8.11 above in relation to a costs order made after a bankruptcy or liquidation in respect of proceedings commenced before the bankruptcy or liquidation.

[209] *Re Mayne* [1907] 2 KB 899. Compare *Ex p Whitehead, re Kirk* (1821) 1 Gl & J 39, in which the debtor for costs had assigned his estate, including his claim against the bankrupt, to trustees for the benefit of his creditors before the liability for costs arose. Therefore, at no time was the right to participate and the liability to contribute vested in the same person. See the discussion of mutuality in paras 14.23–14.32 above.

[210] (1812) 19 Ves Jun 222, 34 ER 501.

[211] (1814) 3 V & B 130, 35 ER 428.

firm was appointed to act as bankers for the estate of a customer being administered in bankruptcy, the bank being a creditor of the customer. The customer's assignees in bankruptcy paid the proceeds of the estate into the bank, which subsequently itself became bankrupt. It was held that the bankers' estate was not entitled to receive a dividend in the customer's bankruptcy until the whole of the sum received as bankers under the commission had been repaid. This sum was owing to the customer's assignees in bankruptcy, who had deposited the proceeds in the bank, rather than to the customer. However, the bank's liability still represented a contribution required to be made in aid of the customer's estate.[212] Subsequently, Sir Thomas Plumer in *Ex p Bignold, re Charles*[213] considered that the same result should follow in the case of an assignee of a bankrupt who was a creditor of the bankrupt, and who himself became bankrupt while holding proceeds of the estate in his capacity as assignee. Once again, the assignee was not indebted to the bankrupt personally, but rather to the other assignees in bankruptcy. Nevertheless, his required contribution was still in aid of the bankrupt's estate.[214] Consistent with those cases, it should not be an objection to the operation of *Cherry v Boultbee* that a legatee's liability arises as a result of a dealing with the executor of a testator's estate, as opposed to the testator, as long as the fruit of the liability will be in aid of the estate rather than accruing to the executor personally.[215]

The principle that the obligation to contribute need only be in aid of the fund brings **14.41** into question the decision in *Re Henley, Thurgood, & Co*.[216] Henley & Co ('Henleys') were trade creditors of Fairhead & Son ('Fairheads'), who executed an inspectorship deed under the Bankruptcy Act 1861. The inspectors of the deed continued to trade with Henleys, and as a result a balance became due to the inspectors in respect of those dealings. Henleys themselves later became bankrupt, whereupon the inspectors asserted that they could 'retain or set off' the dividend payable to Henleys' assignee in bankruptcy against the debt owing to the inspectors as a result of their own dealings with Henleys. Clearly, there could not be a set-off. There was a lack of mutuality.[217] Moreover, the creditors under the deed, including Henleys, were *cestuis que trust* of the inspectors for the dividend, and an obligation to account for a share of a trust fund is not susceptible to a set-off.[218]

---

[212] See also *Fuller v Knight* (1843) 6 Beav 205, 49 ER 804 in the context of a loan of trust moneys. Compare *Re Wickham's Will; Grant v Union Trustee Co of Australia Ltd* (1898) 9 QLJ 102, which is considered in para. 14.42 below, and *Ex p Young, re Day & Sons* (1879) 41 LT 40, for which see para. 13.04 above.
[213] (1817) 2 Madd 470, 56 ER 408.
[214] Compare *Ex p Alexander, re Elder* (1832) 1 Deac & Ch 513, in which a creditor of a bankrupt had been employed to liquidate the bankrupt's estate and effects. The creditor retained from the proceeds a sum more than sufficient to cover his reasonable commission and expenses. It was held that the official assignee could not direct the creditor to look to the excess still in his hands as payment of his right to receive a dividend on the debt owing to him by the bankrupt. The case, however, turned on the extent of the duties of the official assignee, and it should not be regarded as authority for the view that *Cherry v Boultbee* could not have been invoked in this situation.
[215] A comment by Sir John Romilly in *Smee v Baines* (1861) 29 Beav 661, 663, 54 ER 784, 785, suggesting that there should have been a transaction with the testator, should be considered in the context of the facts in issue in that case.
[216] (1863) 11 WR 1021.
[217] The dealing was with the inspectors themselves rather than Fairheads, while Henleys were creditors of Fairheads.
[218] See ch. 10 above.

But Commissioner Holroyd also concluded that 'retainer' (a term evidently intended to refer to *Cherry v Boultbee*) did not apply, with the consequence that the inspectors could not appropriate Henleys' liability to them on the dealings transacted after the deed as satisfaction of Henleys' right to receive a dividend on Fairheads' debt incurred before the deed. It is suggested that the case was wrongly decided on this point. While Henleys became indebted to the inspectors rather than to Fairheads, the debt was due to the inspectors in their capacity as such. The proceeds would have swelled the fund available for distribution amongst Fairheads' creditors, and accordingly the liability was in aid of the fund. *Cherry v Boultbee* admittedly could not have been invoked by Henleys' assignee in bankruptcy. In so far as the assignee was concerned, the right to participate in Henleys' estate was vested from the commencement of the bankruptcy in Fairheads' inspectors, while Fairheads themselves were the party indebted to Henleys. It was not then a case of the one person being entitled to participate and liable to contribute.[219] But Fairheads' inspectors had a different perspective. The Henleys' bankruptcy occurred after the inspectorship deed and after the dealings between Henleys and the inspectors. From the perspective of the inspectors, Henleys prior to their bankruptcy had a right to participate in and were also liable to make a contribution in aid of Fairheads' fund, which should have given rise to an equity to invoke *Cherry v Boultbee* to which the assignee in bankruptcy of Henleys should have taken subject.[220]

14.42   One may also query the decision of the Queensland Supreme Court in *Re Wickham's Will, Grant v Union Trustee Co of Australia Ltd*.[221] The widow of a testator borrowed a sum of money from the plaintiffs as trustees of her husband's estate. Subsequently, she purchased a share of one of the residuary legatees under the will. Griffith CJ, with whom Chubb J concurred, held that the trustees could not set off the loan against the share of the residuary estate when that share became payable. As far as set-off was concerned, the decision was undoubtedly correct. The demands were not mutual for the purpose of a set-off.[222] However, no consideration was given in the judgment to *Cherry v Boultbee*.[223] In that regard, if assignees in bankruptcy could invoke the principle against a bank with whom they had deposited the proceeds of the estate,[224] the principle should also be relevant when trust funds are lent to a person who acquires a right to participate.[225] The concepts

---

[219] See the discussion of mutuality in paras 14.23–14.32 above.
[220] See para. 14.24 above.
[221] (1898) 9 QLJ 102.
[222] The widow's debt did not arise out of a dealing with the husband himself.
[223] Griffith CJ based his decision as to set-off upon *Hallett v Hallett* (1879) 13 Ch D 232, though Fry J in that case considered both set-off and *Cherry v Boultbee*. Fry J similarly held that lack of mutuality prevented a set-off, but he denied the operation of *Cherry v Boultbee* on a different ground, that the sum claimed from the trustees was never intended to be a part of the settlement. Therefore, while there was an obligation to contribute to the fund, the sum claimed was not based upon a right to participate in the fund.
[224] See *Ex p Bebb* (1812) 19 Ves Jun 222, 34 ER 501 and *Ex p Graham* (1814) 3 V & B 130, 35 ER 428, referred to in para. 14.40 above. Compare *Ex p Young, re Day & Sons* (1879) 41 LT 40, for which see para. 13.04 above.
[225] In fact, the widow in *Re Wickham's Will* had mortgaged the share of the residuary estate to a bank. The share took the form of a reversionary interest in a trust fund which was subject to her own life interest. The widow had died, and so the bank was claiming payment of this share. Before the mortgage the one person, the widow, had both an obligation to contribute to, and a right to participate in, the fund. Moreover, it is not a valid objection to a claim to invoke *Cherry v Boultbee* against an assignee of the right to participate that

of mutuality in set-off and under *Cherry v Boultbee* differ in this respect. For set-off one looks only to the persons possessed of the legal and equitable titles to the demands. In the case of *Cherry v Boultbee*, on the other hand, mutuality is concerned with the relationship between the fund and the person entitled to participate in the fund. Mutuality is preserved as long as the person is under an obligation to make a payment which will go to swell, or will be in aid of, the fund.

(4) There must be an obligation

Cherry v Boultbee may not be invoked if the obligation to contribute was extinguished **14.43** before the right to participate became due and payable.[226] Similarly it does not apply when there never has been an obligation to contribute. This does not require an obligation which is enforceable by action for payment. Thus, the equitable principle has been held to extend to an obligation to contribute to a pension scheme that was enforceable only by way of a deduction from wages.[227] Moreover, in *Brazzil v Willoughby*[228] the bank's obligation to contribute to the trust fund in that case was not enforceable by the beneficiaries, but arose under a notice served on the bank by the Financial Services Authority. If, however, there is no obligation to contribute to the relevant fund, *Cherry v Boultbee* does not apply.[229] This was held to be the case when a sum of money was paid by mistake out of a fund to a person who incidentally was also entitled to participate in the fund, and that sum was not recoverable because the mistake was a mistake of law rather than of fact.[230] The House of Lords has now accepted that the principle by which sums paid under a mistake of law are not recoverable no longer forms part of English law.[231] But even before that development, the courts recognized an exception in the case of a trustee who, acting under an honest mistake of law, made a payment to a beneficiary in excess of the beneficiary's entitlement. The trustee in such a case could deduct the overpayment from future trust payments to the beneficiary.[232]

---

the right was only a right in reversion when the administrator received notice of the assignment. See *Willes v Greenhill (No. 1)* (1860) 29 Beav 376, 54 ER 673, and generally para. 14.69 below. Griffith CJ considered that, even if a right of 'set-off' otherwise had been available to the trustees as against the administrators of the widow's estate, the bank would not have taken subject to it. It is suggested, however, that that would not have been the result under *Cherry v Boultbee*. In support of his view that the bank in any event would not have taken subject to a set-off, Griffith CJ referred to *Watson v Mid Wales Railway Co* (1867) LR 2 CP 593, in which it was held that a set-off could not be based upon a debt arising after notice though as a result of a contract entered into before notice. However, *Watson v Mid Wales Railway* is distinguishable from *Re Wickham's Will*. The *Watson* case concerned a debt which did not exist before notice, whereas the reversionary interest in the fund in *Re Wickham's Will* was a present interest, although one which was not payable until a future day. Similarly, a set-off may be based upon a debt which is in existence before notice but which is not payable until after notice. See *Re Pinto Leite and Nephews, ex p Visconde des Olivaes* [1929] 1 Ch 221, and para. 17.14 below.

[226] See para. 14.20 above.
[227] *Lord Balfour of Burleigh* [1945] 1 Ch 90, 103–4. The decision in that case is also explicable on the ground that the right to a pension was conditional on the required contributions having been paid. See at 102.
[228] [2010] EWCA Civ 561 (see esp at [71]–[83]).
[229] See *Re Morley; Morley v Saunders* (1869) LR 8 Eq 594. See also *Wenkart v Pantzer* [2010] FCA 866 at [74].
[230] *Re Hatch; Hatch v Hatch* [1919] 1 Ch 351.
[231] *Kleinwort Benson Ltd v Lincoln City Council* [1999] 2 AC 349. In Australia, see *David Securities Pty Ltd v Commonwealth Bank of Australia* (1992) 175 CLR 353.
[232] *Re Ainsworth; Finch v Smith* [1915] 2 Ch 96; *Re Reading; Edmands v Reading* [1916] WN 262; *Re Musgrave. Machell v Parry* [1916] 2 Ch 417; *Re Wooldridge; Wooldridge v Coe* [1920] WN 78; *IVS Enterprises v*

This also applied when a trustee in bankruptcy overpaid a creditor in the first dividend.[233] Neville J stated the principle in terms that: 'the Court in a proper case – of course there may be cases in which it would be most inequitable to do it – will adjust the rights between the *cestui que trust* and the trustee who has overpaid through an honest and, so to speak, permissible mistake of construction, or of fact.'[234] This was not strictly an application of the *Cherry v Boultbee* principle, but was a principle *sui generis*. It applied even though the beneficiary was not liable to refund the overpayment,[235] so that it was not based upon the notion underlying *Cherry v Boultbee*, of a person being both entitled to participate in and also obliged to contribute to a fund. Given, however, that moneys paid under a mistake may now be recovered notwithstanding that the mistake was one of law, the trustee's right would now be regarded as coming within the ambit of *Cherry v Boultbee*.

(5) Interest

14.44 *Cherry v Boutblee* may apply in respect of an obligation to pay interest.[236] When the obligation to contribute is an interest-bearing debt, it has been held that *Cherry v Boultbee* should be applied first as against accrued interest, and then as against the principal sum.[237]

H. The Right to Participate

14.45 In order to invoke *Cherry v Boultbee*, the right to participate must be due and payable.[238] It may be that the right of a person indebted to a fund to participate in the fund is periodic in nature. In such a case, the administrator may appropriate a part of the debt to the fund as payment of each right to participate as it accrues due, until such time as the asset of the estate represented by the debt has been exhausted.[239]

14.46 *Cherry v Boultbee* only applies when the right to participate in the fund is for a sum of money.[240] The principle may not be invoked when a debtor to a testator's estate is entitled to a specific bequest of freeholds or leaseholds, or of chattels, because in such a case the right

---

Chelsea Cloisters Management Court of Appeal, 27 January 1994, discussed in Mathews, 'Restitution 0, Trusts 0 (after extra time) – a case of set-off' [1994] *Restitution Law Review* 44.

[233] *Re Searle, Hoare and Co* [1924] 2 Ch 325.

[234] *Re Musgrave* [1916] 2 Ch 417, 425.

[235] *Hilliard v Fulford* (1876) 4 Ch D 389. In relation to an overpaid creditor in a bankruptcy, see *Re Searle, Hoare and Co* [1924] 2 Ch 325, 328.

[236] *Re Akerman* [1891] 3 Ch 212; *Gray v Gray* (2004) 12 BPR 22,755, [2004] NSWCA 408 (see at [94]).

[237] *Campbell v Graham* (1831) 1 Russ & M 453, 39 ER 175, affirmed *Campbell v Sandford* (1834) 8 Bligh NS 622, 5 ER 1073.

[238] See para. 14.19 above.

[239] See *Priddy v Rose* (1817) 3 Mer 86, 36 ER 33; *Skinner v Sweet* (1818) 3 Madd 244, 56 ER 499; *Ex p Turpin, re Brown* (1832) Mont 443; *Smith v Smith* (1835) 1 Y & C Ex 338, 160 ER 137; *Kilworth v Mountcashell* (1864) 15 Ir Ch Rep 565; *Re Jewell's Settlement; Watts v Public Trustee* [1919] 2 Ch 161; *Dodson v Sandhurst & Northern District Trustees Executors and Agency Co Ltd* [1955] VLR 100. Compare the order made by Lord Thurlow in *Ex p Mitford* (1784) 1 Bro CC 398, 28 ER 1202 (the terms of which are set out in *Priddy v Rose* at 105–6, 40).

[240] This includes the case of a trustee's right of indemnity from the trust estate for costs incurred. See e.g. *Staniar v Evans* (1886) 34 Ch D 470, referred to in para. 14.14 above.

to participate cannot be measured against a monetary obligation to contribute.[241] It makes no difference that the bequest may be in respect of property that could easily be converted into money,[242] although, if the testator directs that his or her real and/or personal property is to be sold and the proceeds divided, *Cherry v Boultbee* may be invoked in relation to a right to participate in the proceeds.[243] It is no objection that the debtor is a specific legatee if the legacy is pecuniary in nature.[244]

There is, nevertheless, a situation in which a failure to satisfy an obligation will affect a non-monetary entitlement to participate in a fund. When there is an obligation arising under the terms of a settlement to contribute to the trusts of the settlement, and this has not been done, the person obliged will not be permitted to claim any property to which he or she would otherwise have been entitled pursuant to the settlement.[245] In contrast to *Cherry v Boultbee*,[246] this may be described as a right of retainer. **14.47**

I. Discretionary Relief

Since *Cherry v Boultbee* is an equitable remedy, the conduct of the party claiming the benefit of the principle is relevant to the question whether he or she should be permitted to do so. In *Houlditch v Wallace*,[247] a beneficiary of a trust was entitled to an annuity under the trust. Over a period of some twelve years, before the beneficiary assigned the annuity to the plaintiff, the beneficiary had appropriated income of the trust to his own use in excess of the amount to which he was entitled under the annuity. The other beneficiaries were aware of this, but took no steps to remedy their loss.[248] Lord Cottenham held that the other beneficiaries could not arrest future payments of the annuity as satisfaction of the sums owing by the assignor for the period before the assignment, *inter alia* because of their laches in not enforcing their equity immediately. **14.48**

In *Re Pain; Gustavson v Haviland*[249] the usual principle by which an assignee of an interest in a trust fund takes free of equities arising after notice of the assignment[250] was held not to apply. The assignees in that case had stood by and allowed the assignor to commence proceedings against the trustee. The assignor lost, and was the subject of an order for costs. This was an equity against the assignor which arose after notice of the assignment, but **14.49**

---

[241] *Re Akerman* [1891] 3 Ch 212. See also *Re Taylor; Taylor v Wade* [1894] 1 Ch 671, 674; *Dodson v Sandburst & Northern District Trustees Executors and Agency Co Ltd* [1955] VLR 100, 104.

[242] *Re Savage; Cull v Howard* [1918] 2 Ch 146.

[243] See e.g. *Re Akerman* [1891] 3 Ch 212; *Re Melton* [1918] 1 Ch 37. Compare *Re Milnes; Milnes v Sherwin* (1885) 53 LT 534, which concerned the old rule in *Ackroyd v Smithson* (1780) 1 Bro CC 503, 28 ER 1262 that, when a legacy of a share of the proceeds of sale of real estate has failed, for example because the person named as legatee died before the testator, the share should be treated as real property rather than personalty.

[244] *Re Taylor* [1894] 1 Ch 671; *Re Baird* [1935] NZLR 847. Earlier observations to the contrary by Kekewich J in *Re Akerman* [1891] 3 Ch 212 have not been followed.

[245] *Re Weston; Davies v Tagart* [1900] 2 Ch 164.

[246] See para. 14.03 above.

[247] (1838) 5 Cl & Fin 629, 7 ER 543.

[248] An injunction had been obtained to restrain the beneficiary from receiving the income of the trust, but the order was not acted upon.

[249] [1918] 1 Ch 38.

[250] See paras 14.63–14.78 below.

Younger J held that it could be asserted against the assignees. They had allowed the action to proceed when they might have stopped it, knowing that they would have benefited if it had been successful.

J. Suretyship, and the Rule against Double Proof

14.50 The rule against double proof provides that an insolvent's estate ought not to pay twice in respect of what is substantially the same debt.[251] Consider, for example, that a surety has guaranteed payment of a debt to a creditor and the debtor is bankrupt. The creditor proves in the debtor's bankruptcy and receives or is entitled to receive a dividend. In addition, the surety has a contingent claim against the debtor for an indemnity to the extent that the surety remains liable under the guarantee, the claim being contingent upon payment by the surety in accordance with the guarantee. Contingent debts can be proved in bankruptcy. In substance, however, the surety's claim for an indemnity is in respect of the same debt as that the subject of the creditor's proof, and if both the surety and the creditor could prove the bankrupt's estate would be subjected to two proofs in respect of the same debt. In order to prevent that occurring, the rule against double proof operates to preclude a proof by the surety.[252] Moreover, since the surety cannot prove for an indemnity, the claim for an indemnity cannot be the subject of a set-off.[253] The same result would follow if the creditor has not proved in the debtor's bankruptcy. The rule against double proof would operate to preclude a proof by the surety in circumstances where the creditor was entitled to prove, and it would also preclude a set-off in respect of the surety's contingent claim for an indemnity.[254] On the other hand, the principle in *Cherry v Boultbee* may apply in such cases.

14.51 Luxmoore J adopted the contrary view in *Re Fenton (No. 2), ex p Fenton Textile Association Ltd.*[255] Fenton, who had guaranteed advances by some banks to the Fenton Textile Association, executed two deeds of arrangement in favour of his creditors. Subsequently, the Association was ordered to be wound up. After the winding-up order the banks proved under the deeds for the full amount of the guarantees. Fenton was a debtor of the Association, to which a dividend accordingly was also payable. In earlier proceedings, the Court of Appeal had held that the trustee under the deeds could not set off against the Association's provable debt a claim by Fenton's estate for an indemnity from the Association consequent upon the giving of the guarantees, because of the rule against double proof.[256] After that decision, the trustees declared an interim dividend which was paid to the banks. In the present case, Luxmoore J held that the rule against double proof also precluded the application of *Cherry v Boultbee* as against the Association in relation to the fund being administered under the deeds of arrangement, so that the trustee of the deeds could not 'retain' out of the dividend payable to the Association a sum equal to the

---

[251] See paras 8.13–8.18 above.
[252] See para. 8.14 above.
[253] See para. 8.18 above.
[254] *Re Fenton* [1931] 1 Ch 85, and see para. 8.18 above.
[255] [1932] 1 Ch 178.
[256] *Re Fenton, ex p Fenton Textile Association Ltd* [1931] 1 Ch 85. See para. 8.18 above.

dividend paid to the banks under the guarantees.[257] The rule against double proof was said to apply because the banks had only received a dividend from Fenton's estate, and so they were still entitled to prove against the assets of the Association for the full value of the debt.[258]

However, there was no mention in the judgment in *Re Fenton (No. 2)*[259] of the earlier **14.52** Court of Appeal decision in *Re Melton; Milk v Towers*.[260] *Re Melton* concerned the estate of a testator who had bequeathed a one-fourth reversionary share in a residuary fund to a legatee. The legatee was indebted to a creditor, and the testator was a surety for the debt up to a limited specified amount. The testator/surety died, and the legatee/debtor later became bankrupt. The creditor proved in the debtor's bankruptcy and received a dividend. The creditor then proceeded against the surety's estate under the contract of suretyship for the sum for which the surety had agreed to be liable, and received payment in full of that amount from the estate. When the bankrupt debtor's right to a share of the residuary estate later became payable, the Court of Appeal[261] held[262] that the executors of the surety could invoke the principle in *Cherry v Boultbee* in respect of the right of the surety's estate to an indemnity for the sum paid to the creditor, notwithstanding that the executors could not have proved for that amount in the debtor's bankruptcy because of the rule against double proof. Warrington LJ proceeded on the basis that *Cherry v Boultbee* operates as a right of retainer, and for that reason his judgment is not entirely satisfactory.[263] In his view, *Cherry v Boultbee* conferred upon the surety's executors the right to retain the debtor's entitlement, and to use it to satisfy the claim for an indemnity under the guarantee. This was an equity that came into existence at the date of the death, which was prior to the bankruptcy. The amount necessary to make good the claim accordingly never formed part of the debtor's estate, with the result that the rule against double proof did not apply.[264] That analysis should be compared to the approach of Scrutton LJ, which conformed with the preferred explanation of the *Cherry v Boultbee* principle.[265] As Scrutton LJ remarked: 'how in any way does it infringe the rule against double proof that, when the bankrupt

---

[257] Luxmoore J said (at [1932] 1 Ch 178, 187) that, because the Association had gone into liquidation before the surety's estate had paid anything to the creditor, *Cherry v Boultbee* (1839) 4 My & Cr 442, 41 ER 171 (see paras 14.24–14.25 above) was authority for the proposition that the principle in any event could only have been invoked in respect of a sum equal to the appropriate *dividend* payable in the liquidation on the obligation to indemnify the surety's estate. *Cherry v Boultbee* was a case in which the bankruptcy of the legatee pre-dated the event which precipitated the setting up of the fund. In *Re Fenton*, on the other hand, the liquidation of the Association (being the claimant on the fund) occurred after the surety had executed the deeds of arrangement. For that reason, *Cherry v Boultbee* was not on point. But even if the claimant's insolvency in *Re Fenton* had pre-dated the deeds of arrangement, *Cherry v Boultbee* would still have been distinguishable since the claimant in *Re Fenton* was a company in liquidation rather than a bankrupt. See paras 14.95–14.101 below. In *Re SSSL Realisations (2002) Ltd* [2006] Ch 610 at [115]–[116], Chadwick LJ considered that *Re Fenton* was wrong on this point.

[258] See *Re Sass, ex p National Provincial Bank of England Ltd* [1896] 2 QB 12, and para. 8.16 above.

[259] Though it was referred to during argument.

[260] [1918] 1 Ch 37. See also the further discussion of *Re Melton* at paras 14.35–14.38 above and 14.72–14.74 below.

[261] Swinfen Eady, Warrington and Scrutton LJJ.

[262] Overruling *Re Binns; Lee v Binns* [1896] 2 Ch 584.

[263] See para. 14.03 above.

[264] See Warrington LJ's judgment at [1918] 1 Ch 37, 55–6.

[265] See para. 14.03 above.

claims his share, the representatives of the surety should say, "Certainly, but you must ascertain your share in the proper way"?'[266] The principal debtor in *Re Melton* was entitled to a percentage of the residuary estate. The value of the residue was the sum actually held by the executors in their hands, plus the indemnity obligation owing to the fund. There was no infringement of the rule against double proof, because it was not a question of the debtor's estate being called upon to pay twice in respect of the same debt. Rather, the surety's executors were acknowledging their obligation to pay the debtor's share, but in paying that share they were exercising their right to take into account that the debtor already held an asset forming a part of the fund. Swinfen Eady LJ expressed the matter in similar terms.[267]

14.53　In *Re SSSL Realisations (2002) Ltd*,[268] the Court of Appeal confirmed the correctness of this aspect of the decision in *Re Melton*. As Chadwick LJ observed in the principal judgment,[269] the object of the rule against double proof is not to swell the assets available for distribution in the liquidation of the principal debtor. Rather, it is to limit the claims that can be made in the distribution of those assets by ensuring that there is no more than one proof in respect of each debt. There is no reason why the rule against double proof should have the effect of enabling the liquidator of the principal debtor to collect an asset that could not have been collected under the general law. In particular, Chadwick LJ said that there is no reason why the rule should have the effect of enabling the liquidator of the principal debtor to collect an asset the collection of which would otherwise be subject to the *Cherry v Boultbee* principle.

14.54　Wood has sought to reconcile the decisions in *Re Melton* and *Re Fenton (No. 2)*.[270] In *Re Melton* it appears that the creditor had been fully paid,[271] whereas this was not the case in *Re Fenton (No. 2)*. Because the creditor had been fully paid, the surety's estate would have been subrogated to the creditor's proof in the debtor's bankruptcy,[272] and Wood has suggested that the debtor's legacy could have been 'retained' in respect of this proof, up to the amount of the proof less any dividends paid to the creditor, as opposed to being in respect of the surety's own right to an indemnity. However, this is not the basis upon which the Court of Appeal decided the case. The reasoning of the court proceeded along the lines that the rule against double proof was irrelevant to *Cherry v Boultbee* given the nature of the right that arises under it, rather than that the rule against double proof did not apply to prevent the operation of *Cherry v Boultbee* because the surety's estate had the benefit of the creditor's proof by way of subrogation. It was not crucial that the creditor was fully paid.

---

[266] [1918] 1 Ch 37, 61.

[267] See the last sentence of Swinfen Eady LJ's judgment at [1918] 1 Ch 37, 54 and his summary of the competing claims at 46.

[268] [2006] Ch 610. See in particular at [94]–[97]. See also the discussion of *Re SSSL Realisations* in paras 14.35–14.38 above in relation to the application of *Cherry v Boultbee* to contingent debts.

[269] [2006] Ch 610 at [94]. Jonathan Parker LJ and Etherton J agreed with Chadwick LJ's judgment.

[270] Wood, *English and International Set-off* (1989), 440–1.

[271] Compare, however, Warrington LJ at [1918] 1 Ch 37, 55.

[272] See para. 8.14 above.

The judgments in *Re Fenton (No. 2)* and *Re Melton* in fact are difficult to reconcile.[273] In so far as *Re Fenton (No. 2)* held that the rule against double proof prevented the application of *Cherry v Boutlbee* in that case, Chadwick LJ in *Re SSSL Realisations*[274] said that it was wrong.

Clauson J applied *Re Melton* in *Re Lennard. Lennard's Trustee v Lennard.*[275] The facts in **14.55** *Re Lennard* were similar to those in *Re Melton*, but the case illustrates the further proposition that the surety's executors cannot discharge the surety's obligation as guarantor in a more liberal manner than is strictly necessary, and expect to be able to charge the overpayment as against the principal debtor's trustee in bankruptcy. The guarantee was in respect of an annuity. The creditor valued the annuity, and proved in the debtor's bankruptcy for that value. The surety's executors, however, ignored the fact of the proof altogether. They made a number of payments to the creditor, and then purchased another annuity for her. Clauson J held that the executors could exercise their rights under *Cherry v Boultbee* against the principal debtor's right to share in the residue, but only to the extent of the difference between the value placed on the annuity in the bankruptcy and the dividend paid on that value, as opposed to the amount that they paid in instalments and in purchasing a new annuity. Because the creditor had elected to value the annuity and to prove in the bankruptcy, the surety's executors were entitled to pay the creditor the amount of the valuation and to take over the proof. This would have discharged the surety's estate from further liability under the contract of suretyship. In so far as they had spent a larger sum than was strictly necessary, they could not employ *Cherry v Boultbee* in respect of the surplus.

It may be that the sum brought into account by the representatives of the surety's estate **14.56** under *Cherry v Boultbee*, together with any dividend paid by the debtor to the creditor, is greater than the principal debt itself. In such a case Scrutton LJ, in *Re Melton*,[276] said that: 'If in the end it turns out that the debtor has paid more than 20s in the pound he will get this overpayment back from either the principal creditors or the representatives of the surety. If in the end it turns out that the creditors have got more than 20s in the pound the surplus will be returned to the surety or the debtor, whichever ought to have it.'

A surety and a principal debtor may each have agreed not to prove in the liquidation of the **14.57** other in competition with the creditor. Depending on its terms, the agreement may preclude the application of the *Cherry v Boultbee* principle as between the principal debtor and the surety in relation to the surety's right of indemnity.[277]

---

[273] The cases differed in that, in *Re Melton*, the creditor had proved in and received a dividend from the principal debtor's estate, whereas in *Re Fenton (No. 2)* the rule against double proof was said to be relevant because the creditor was entitled to prove in the principal debtor's bankruptcy for the full debt. However, there is nothing of substance in that distinction.

[274] [2006] Ch 610 at [91].

[275] [1934] 1 Ch 235. *Re Fenton (No. 2)* was not referred to.

[276] [1918] 1 Ch 37, 61.

[277] See *Re SSSL Realisations (2002) Ltd* [2006] Ch 610 at [68]; *Cattles Plc v Welcome Financial Services Ltd* [2009] EWHC 3027 (Ch) (appeal dismissed on the question of the construction of the agreement: *Cattles Plc v Welcome Financial Services Ltd* [2010] EWCA Civ 599). Compare *Mills v HSBC (CI) Ltd* [2009] EWHC 3377 (Ch).

K. Waiver, and Proof of Debt

14.58 *Cherry v Boultbee* cannot be invoked if the person entitled to participate in the fund has been released from the liability to contribute as a result of an order of discharge from bankruptcy.[278] In addition, the administrator of the fund ordinarily[279] would be denied recourse to the principle if he or she has proved the debt in the debtor's bankruptcy and received a dividend,[280] or, if the fund is entitled to be subrogated to someone else's proof,[281] if the administrator has elected to rely on that proof.[282] The leading case is *Stammers v Elliott*.[283] In the course of his judgment in that case, Lord Chelmsford said: 'If he [the executor], therefore, proves a debt under a bankruptcy . . . the debt must be held to be satisfied.'[284] However, the notion that proof constitutes satisfaction or payment of the debt[285] requires an explanation. As Stirling LJ commented in giving the judgment of the Court of Appeal[286] in *Re West Coast Gold Fields Ltd. Rowe's Trustee's Claim*:[287] 'No doubt it is true that proof deprives the creditor of any other remedy against the debtor or his estate, and in that sense proof is payment.'[288] Similarly, Lord Westbury once remarked that: 'Proof against a bankrupt's estate is payment in this sense, that the party making proof could not afterwards have a personal remedy against the bankrupt.'[289] Proof does not constitute payment in an absolute sense so that, as in the *West Coast Gold Fields* case, the mere fact that a company in voluntary liquidation has received a dividend in a shareholder's bankruptcy for a call in relation to partly paid shares does not mean that the shares are considered to be fully paid for the purpose of a distribution of the surplus assets of the company.[290] Rather, those observations suggest that the creditor, by proving, abandons or waives any other remedy that he or she has against the debtor.[291]

---

[278] See e.g. *Re Akerman* [1891] 3 Ch 212, 217, and para. 14.20 above.

[279] Compare the various situations referred to below.

[280] *Stammers v Elliott* (1868) LR 3 Ch App 195; *Re Watson* [1896] 1 Ch 925, 933; *Armstrong v Armstrong* (1871) LR 12 Eq 614. See also *Re Kent County Gas Light and Coke Co Ltd* [1913] 1 Ch 92; *Re Lussier* [1927] 4 DLR 637. The administrator should be able to withdraw a proof before a dividend has been received and rely instead on *Cherry v Boultbee*. This is suggested by *Re Dicken, ex p Dicken* (1817) Buck 115, as explained in *Re Sewell* [1909] 1 Ch 806, 809. See also (and compare) *Re Harvey, ex p Man* (1829) Mont & M 210.

[281] E.g. when a testator guaranteed a beneficiary's debts and the testator's estate has paid the creditor under the guarantee.

[282] *Re Whitehouse* (1887) 37 Ch D 683.

[283] (1868) LR 3 Ch App 195.

[284] (1868) LR 3 Ch App 195, 200.

[285] See e.g. *Ex p Hornby, re Tarleton* (1817) Buck 351, 354 ('proof is equivalent to payment').

[286] Vaughan Williams, Stirling and Cozens-Hardy LJJ.

[287] [1906] 1 Ch 1.

[288] [1906] 1 Ch 1, 8, referred to with evident approval in *Re Hurburgh* [1959] Tas SR 25, 41–2.

[289] *Ewart v Latta* (1865) 4 Macq 983, 990.

[290] The court appeared to accept ([1906] 1 Ch 1, 8, and see also Buckley J at first instance [1905] 1 Ch 597, 602) that the holders of the other shares which were fully paid were alone entitled to share in the surplus assets until the amount paid on their shares was reduced to that which in fact had been paid on the bankrupt's shares.

[291] Crawford J in *Re Hurburgh* [1959] Tas SR 25 41–2 noted that a secured creditor who proves the debt loses the benefit of the security, and so he concluded that *Cherry v Boultbee* similarly must take effect as a right in security. However, the principle may be explained instead on the basis of an abandonment or a waiver of a personal right against the debtor available to the fund.

The foundation of waiver (in the sense used above) is an election between alternative rights **14.59** inconsistent with each other.[292] For it to apply, a person must have knowledge of the facts which give rise in law to the alternative rights and must act in a manner which is consistent only with his or her having chosen to rely on one of them.[293] There must therefore be knowledge of the material facts upon which the right to apply *Cherry v Boultbee* depends. In the absence of such knowledge, the lodgement of a proof of debt would not constitute an election to abandon the right to apply the rule.[294]

The conduct of the administrator of the fund in proving in the bankruptcy could only be **14.60** said to constitute an abandonment of the right to invoke *Cherry v Boultbee* if the debt could have been satisfied by means of the principle had the administrator decided not to prove. It could be said that this would not have been the case if the sole asset of the estate was the debt owing by the bankrupt, because until the debt was paid there would not have been a fund in respect of which *Cherry v Boultbee* could have been invoked. This provides a possible explanation for the decisions in cases such as *Ex p Turpin, re Brown*.[295] *Ex p Turpin* concerned a husband who, upon his marriage, gave a bond for £3,000 to trustees to be settled upon trust for himself for life, with the remainder to the wife and children. The husband became bankrupt without ever having paid anything under the bond, and so the trustees proved in the bankruptcy and obtained a dividend on the debt. It was held that the husband's assignees in bankruptcy were not entitled to the income received by the trustees on the proceeds of the dividend during the husband's life, but rather the trustees could retain and accumulate the income as part of the fund consisting of the dividend until the full debt of £3,000 had been realized.[296] However, there is nothing in the judgment in *Ex p Turpin*, or in other similar cases, to indicate that they were decided upon the ground suggested above,[297] and indeed later cases seem to support the view that the same result would have ensued if the trustees in any event had been possessed of a fund at the time that they lodged a proof in respect of the debt.[298] There was no mention of this line of cases in

---

[292] *Kammins Ballrooms Co Ltd v Zenith Investments (Torquay) Ltd* [1971] AC 850, 882–3; *Sargent v ASL Developments Ltd* (1974) 131 CLR 634, 641, 655.

[293] *Kammins Ballrooms Co Ltd v Zenith Investments (Torquay) Ltd* [1971] AC 850, 883; *Sargent v ASL Developments Ltd* (1974) 131 CLR 634, 641, 642. It is unclear whether there must also be knowledge of the right to elect. Compare Wilken and Villiers, *The Law of Waiver, Variation and Estoppel* (2nd edn, 2002), 54–7 and Handley, *Estoppel by Conduct and Election* (2006), 238–4.

[294] *Otis Elevator Co Pty Ltd v Guide Rails Pty Ltd* (2004) 49 ACSR 531 at [48]–[59].

[295] (1832) Mont 443.

[296] See also *Ex p Young, re Prior* (1835) 4 Deac & Ch 645 (explaining *Ex p Shute, re Shute* (1833) 3 Deac & Ch 1); *Ex p Crofts, re Last & Casey* (1837) 2 Deac 102 (in which the debtor was jointly and severally, and not just jointly, liable); *Re Walter, ex p Walter's Assignees* (1859) 32 LTOS 396. In addition, see *Ex p King, re Severn* (1835) 1 Deac 143, although it is not clear whether the fund in that case consisted of anything other than the dividends.

[297] Indeed, it may be said that there was a subsisting fund before payment, the obligation to pay under the bond constituting a fund asset.

[298] See *Ex p Smith, re Manning* (1836) 1 Deac 385, and note also *Ex p Gonne, re March* (1837) 6 LJ Bcy 57. In *Fuller v Knight* (1843) 6 Beav 205, 49 ER 804, a trustee acted in breach of trust in lending part of the trust fund to the tenant for life. The tenant for life subsequently executed a creditor's deed, to which the trustee was a party, which provided for his assets, including his interest under the settlement, to be applied in payment of certain debts. It was held that the trustee was not precluded from applying the income otherwise available to the life tenant to make good the breach of trust. The agreement embodied in the creditor's deed could not be brought forward in order to prevent the trustee from acting to remedy his breach of trust.

Stammers v Elliott,[299] but they may be distinguished on the following ground.[300] In *Stammers v Elliott*, and the cases following it, the obligation to contribute took the form of a debt that arose independently of the terms of the trust governing the fund. In the *Ex p Turpin* line of cases, on the other hand, the obligation to contribute to the settlement was undertaken as part of the terms of the settlement itself, so that both the obligation to contribute and the right to participate were a part of the same transaction. Equity in this latter situation is more rigorous in ensuring that the estate of the bankrupt does not derive any benefit from the trust until the bankrupt's liability has been satisfied in full.[301] In other words: 'the Court, on looking at the settlement, and finding that the bankrupt had not fulfilled the covenants of the settlement, says, No, if you come here for equity, you must do equity first; and the Court will retain the dividend until the deficiency has been supplied.'[302]

14.61   Other exceptions have been recognized to the principle that proof constitutes a waiver of the right to invoke *Cherry v Boultbee*. One concerns an obligation to account for the proceeds of an insolvent estate. In an early nineteenth-century case,[303] the bank in which the proceeds of a bankrupt customer's estate had been deposited itself became bankrupt. The bank was also a creditor of the customer. It was held that the bank was not entitled to receive a dividend in the customer's bankruptcy on the debt owing to it until its liability to the customer's estate on the deposit had been paid *in toto*. This was not affected by a proof lodged in the bank's bankruptcy. The bank remained liable to contribute the residue of its indebtedness, after paying a dividend to the customer's estate, before it could exercise its own right to participate in the customer's bankruptcy in respect of the debt owing to it.[304] A similar principle was applied in the case of an assignee in bankruptcy who was also a creditor of the bankrupt, and who himself became bankrupt after having received proceeds of the estate.[305]

14.62   Another exception has been recognized in Australia in relation to a situation where a payment to a creditor has been set aside as a preference in the liquidation of the payer and the recipient is also in liquidation. It has been held that the liquidator of the payer may prove for the full amount of the preference in the recipient's liquidation and the recipient cannot prove in the payer's liquidation for the debt the subject of the preferential payment until the preference has been repaid in full.[306]

---

[299] (1868) LR 3 Ch App 195.

[300] The distinction that Lord Chelmsford drew in *Stammers v Elliott* (1868) LR 3 Ch App 195, 200 between an executor and a trustee seems doubtful. See *Re Sewell* [1909] 1 Ch 806, 809 (Parker J).

[301] *Cherry v Boultbee* should no longer be available, however, once the bankrupt is discharged from bankruptcy, so that the bankrupt is released from his or her debt. See *Re Sewell* [1909] 1 Ch 806, 808 (defaulting trustee's debt released by composition), and para. 14.20 above.

[302] *Ex p Gonne* (1837) 6 LJ Bcy 57, 59 *per* Erskine CJ (*arguendo*).

[303] *Ex p Bebb* (1812) 19 Ves Jun 222, 34 ER 501. See also *Ex p Graham* (1814) 3 V & B 130, 35 ER 428, discussed at para. 14.15 above.

[304] But note the order made in *Ex p Graham* (1814) 3 V & B 130, 35 ER 428. See para. 14.15 above.

[305] *Ex p Bignold, re Charles* (1817) 2 Madd 470, 56 ER 408.

[306] *N A Kratzmann Pty Ltd v Tucker (No. 2)* (1968) 123 CLR 295. See para. 13.14 above.

L. Assignments

(1) The general principle

The leading authority on the effect of an assignment or a security interest upon rights under **14.63**
Cherry v Boultbee is *Stephens v Venables (No. 1)*.[307] Executors and trustees granted a lease of
part of the testator's property to a residuary legatee. Subsequently, the legatee charged his
legacy to the plaintiff, and notice of the charge was given to the trustees. When the plaintiff
as chargee claimed the legatee's interest after completion of the administration, a question
arose as to whether the trustees could invoke the principle in *Cherry v Boultbee* against the
plaintiff in respect of arrears of rent owing by the legatee to the estate. Consistent with
the principle applicable to set-off,[308] Sir John Romilly MR held that the plaintiff took
subject to equities, including rights under the principle in *Cherry v Boultbee*, which were
in existence at the date that the trustee received notice of the charge.

> When a trustee or executor receives notice that a legatee has charged his legacy in favor of
> a stranger, the trustee is bound to withhold all further payments to that legatee, unless
> made with the consent of the mortgagee of the legacy. All rights of set-off and adjustment of
> equities between the legatee and the executor already existing at the date of the notice have
> priority over the charge, and may properly be deducted from the amount coming to the
> mortgagee; but the trustees can create no new charge or right of set off after that time. A debt
> due to the trustees before the notice of charge received by him may be set off against the
> share of the legatee, but no debt which accrued due subsequently to that period can be
> allowed to work any deduction from the share charged to the mortgagee.[309]

The trustees therefore could invoke the principle in respect of arrears of rent as at the date
they were given notice of the charge, but not in respect of subsequently accruing rent.[310]

Stephens v Venables concerned a charge, but the same principle applies in the case of **14.64**
an absolute assignment or an assignment by way of mortgage.[311]

Exceptions

The general principle is that an assignee takes free of equities arising after notice, but there **14.65**
are exceptions[312] in the case of defaulting trustees and executors, and also, in some circumstances, where a beneficiary becomes liable to the estate for costs. These exceptions are
considered later.[313]

---

[307] (1862) 30 Beav 625, 54 ER 1032.
[308] See ch. 17 below. Indeed, the Master of the Rolls referred to rights of 'set-off' in his judgment, although
in truth rights under *Cherry v Boultbee* were in issue. The obligation to contribute should not have ceased to
exist when the right to participate becomes due and payable. See e.g. *Re Baird* [1935] NZLR 847, and para.
14.20 above.
[309] (1862) 30 Beav 625, 627, 54 ER 1032, 1033.
[310] See the further discussion of *Stephen v Venables* in para. 14.70 below.
[311] See paras 11.46–11.47 above, and para. 17.100 below.
[312] See also paras 17.32–17.38 below in relation to equitable set-off.
[313] For defaulting executors and trustees, see paras 14.79–14.84 below, and for costs see para. 14.49 above
and 14.75 below.

A competing principle

14.66 Sir John Romilly spoke in terms of a trustee. In *Stephens v Venables*, however, the administration of the estate had not been completed at the date of the assignment of the interest in
the residuary estate.[314] The assignment therefore did not involve an existing equitable
interest under a trust. All that the residuary legatee was entitled to was: 'a chose in action,
capable of being invoked for any purpose connected with the proper administration of his
estate.'[315] In other words, the subject of the assignment in equity was a presently existing
chose in action against the executor, together with the right to receive the fruits of that
chose in action when they matured.[316] Consider a case in which the subject of an assignment instead is an existing equitable interest under a trust. There is a competing equitable
principle, that an assignee of an equitable interest takes subject to prior equities,[317] although
the court will not interfere with the assignee's title if he or she is a purchaser of the equitable
interest for valuable consideration without notice of the prior equity.[318] This differs from
the principle applied in *Stephens v Venables*, and also in the case of set-off, in two respects.
It allows an exception of purchaser for value without notice, and in addition the dividing
line is the date of the assignment as opposed to the date of notice of the assignment. While
it is usually stated in terms of an equitable estate or interest in land, as opposed to a trust
fund, there would appear to be a sound reason for distinguishing between an assignment of
a personal chose in action and an assignment of a beneficial interest in a trust fund. The rule
that an equitable assignee of a chose in action takes subject to equities in existence at the
date of notice is based upon the notion that the assignee steps into the shoes of the assignor.[319] The subject of the assignment is the personal rights possessed by the assignor against
the other party (usually, a debtor), together with the fruits of those rights. Therefore, the
general rule is that the assignee is bound by all equities and defences available against
the assignor whose personal rights the assignee is enforcing.[320] As an exception, however,
equity will not allow the debtor to diminish the rights of the assignee by relying on events
occurring after the debtor has become aware of the assignment.[321] For that reason, the date

---

[314] This appears more clearly from the report of subsequent proceedings in *Stephens v Venables (No. 2)*
(1862) 31 Beav 124, 54 ER 1084.

[315] *Commissioner of Stamp Duties (Queensland) v Livingston* [1965] AC 694, 717 (PC). See para. 13.125
above.

[316] *Re Leigh's Will Trusts* [1970] 1 Ch 277, 282.

[317] For this competing equitable principle, the prior equity should be 'ancillary to or dependent upon' an
equitable title. An equity that is purely personal between the original parties will not suffice. See *National
Provincial Bank Ltd v Ainsworth* [1965] AC 1175, 1238 (Lord Uphohn). This should encompass *Cherry
v Boultbee*. The administrator of the fund says that the person claiming an interest in the fund already has
an asset of the fund in his or her own hands, and therefore to that extent the person's right to participate is
satisfied.

[318] *Westminster Bank Ld v Lee* [1956] 1 Ch 7; *Phillips v Phillips* (1861) 4 De G F & J 208, 218, 45 ER 1164,
1167. Note that a disposition of an equitable interest or trust subsisting at the time of the disposition must
be in writing. See the Law of Property Act 1925, s. 53(1)(c). In Australia, see e.g. the Conveyancing Act 1919
(NSW), s. 23(1)(c).

[319] Tudsbery, *Equitable Assignments* (1912), 87.

[320] Compare the case of a statutory assignment under the Law of Property Act 1925, s. 136(1). If the
requirements of the section are satisfied, the legal right to the debt is transferred. See *Read v Brown* (1888)
22 QBD 128, 132. The date of notice is still the dividing line, however. While the assignee takes subject to
equities, notice is essential for the validity of the statutory assignment.

[321] *Roxburghe v Cox* (1881) 17 Ch D 520, 526. See para. 17.03 below.

of notice to the debtor is the important date. On the other hand, the subject of an assignment of an equitable interest in a trust fund is not just the assignor's personal rights but a share of a specific fund. A proprietary interest in the fund is assigned. The assignee can rely upon his or her own equitable title, as opposed to that of the assignor. Moreover, the assignee of an equitable interest in a trust fund becomes the beneficiary as soon as the assignment takes place. Notice may be important for the question whether the trustee discharges his or her obligation by tendering payment to the assignor. Notice is not necessary, however, in order to perfect the title of the assignee.[322] Therefore, as from the time of the assignment, the assignee's interest in the trust is based upon his or her own title, and not that of the assignor, and anything that occurs after the assignment between the trustee and the assignor should not affect the assignee's title.

There is some support for the view that the purchaser for value without notice principle **14.67** applies in the case of an assignment of a right to participate in a trust fund.[323] Thus, *Lewin on Trusts* states that, if a beneficiary joins in a breach of trust, all the benefit that would have accrued to that beneficiary from the trust fund may be stopped by the other beneficiaries as against the first-mentioned beneficiary, and also against those claiming under him or her, except so far as the defence of purchase for value may be applicable.[324] The proposition is also consistent with a comment by Sir John Romilly MR in *Irby v Irby (No. 3)*,[325] a case decided some four years before *Stephens v Venables*. Herbert de Crespigny was a beneficiary under his father's marriage settlement. He was also in default in his capacity of executor of his father's will, which gave rise to a right in the trustees to impound his entitlement under the settlement. The Master of the Rolls said:[326] that 'this equity would be good against all persons who had taken an assignment of a charge upon Herbert de Crespigny's share, after having had notice of the claim of the trustees upon him.' The case concerned an equitable

---

[322] *Ward v Duncombe* [1893] AC 369, 392. See also *Gorringe v Irwell India Rubber and Gutta Percha Works* (1886) 34 Ch D 128; *Re City Life Assurance Co Ltd. Stephenson's Case* [1926] 1 Ch 191, 219–20; *Re Trytel* [1952] 2 TLR 32, 34; *Thomas v National Australia Bank Ltd* [2000] 2 Qd R 448.

[323] In addition to the following, see *Houlditch v Wallace* (1838) 5 Cl & Fin 629, 7 ER 543 and *Cloutte v Story* [1911] 1 Ch 18, 24. In *Houlditch v Wallace*, an estate was conveyed by its owner to trustees upon trust to pay to himself an annual sum, and to pay the surplus rent to his creditors in satisfaction of his debts. Subsequently, he assigned a part of his right to the annuity by way of security. Both before and after the assignment the owner appropriated income of the estate in excess of the annual sum payable to himself. In relation to sums misappropriated after the assignment, the assignee took free from any equity that the owner's creditors, as the other trust beneficiaries, otherwise would have had to make a deduction from the annual payments. See (1838) 5 Cl & Fin 629, 665, 7 ER 543, 557. In relation to misappropriations before the assignment, Lord Cottenham held that the creditors were precluded by their laches from asserting their equity against the assignee. See para. 14.48 above. Apart from that, the question whether there could have been a deduction from future payments under the annuity was thought to depend upon whether the assignee had notice of the equity. The annuity was payable out of the estate, and counsel for the assignee argued (though without the point being addressed specifically by Lord Cottenham, and compare counsel for the creditors at 660, 555) that it created an interest charged upon the land. See at 652–3, 552. If that were the case, the subject of the assignment itself would have been an interest in the land.

[324] *Lewin on Trusts* (18th edn, 2008), 1625. In *Kilworth v Mountcashel* (1864) 15 Ir Ch Rep 565, 578, 580, Sir Thomas Smith MR adopted a similar statement in an earlier edition of *Lewin*, although he held (at 581) that a judgment creditor is not a purchaser and therefore is not entitled to the benefit of the exception of purchaser for value.

[325] (1858) 25 Beav 632, 53 ER 778.

[326] (1858) 25 Beav 632, 638, 53 ER 778, 780.

interest in a trust, and prior notice would only have been important if the defence of purchaser of an equitable interest for value without notice was relevant.

14.68 The weight of opinion, however, favours the view that the principle applied in the case of an assignment of a personal chose in action is also relevant when a chose in equity, in the form of an equitable interest in a trust fund, is assigned.[327] In accepting this view, the courts and text-writers have not considered the difference between an assignment of a personal chose in action and an assignment of an equitable proprietary interest in a fund.

(2) Presently existing rights and obligations

Not presently payable at the date of notice

14.69 It is not necessary that the right to participate and the obligation to contribute should be presently payable at the date of notice, if indeed they are existing at that date. The administrator of the fund cannot appropriate an obligation to contribute as payment of a right to participate until the right has become due and payable.[328] However, the administrator will not be denied the right to invoke *Cherry v Boultbee* against an assignee of the right to participate merely because the right was still only a right in reversion when the administrator received notice of the assignment,[329] or if it was otherwise still contingent.[330]

Contingent obligation to contribute

14.70 An assignee of a debt does not take subject to a set-off in respect of a cross-debt owing by the assignor to the debtor when the cross-debt arose after notice, albeit that it was the result of a contract entered into before notice.[331] This notion is criticized in the discussion of assignments in relation to set-off[332] on the ground that the existence or otherwise of a right of set-off should depend on when the debtor and the assignor entered into a binding

---

[327] See *Phipps v Lovegrove* (1873) LR 16 Eq 80, 88; *Cumming v Austin* (1902) 28 VLR 347, affirmed (1903) 28 VLR 622; *Re Pain; Gustavson v Haviland* [1919] 1 Ch 38 (esp at 46); *Southern British National Trust Ltd v Pither* (1937) 57 CLR 89, 105 (Rich J); *White & Tudor's Leading Cases in Equity* (9th edn, 1928) vol. 1, 136 (referred to with evident approval by Latham CJ in *Pither* at 102); *Halsbury's Laws of England* (4th edn (reissue), 2003) vol. 6, 42, para. 61 (referring to a 'fundholder'), 44, para. 66; *Withers on Reversions* (2nd edn, 1933), 239 (although neither of the cases cited in *Withers* concerned an equitable interest in a trust, or indeed commented upon an assignment of such an interest). See also *Cockell v Taylor* (1852) 15 Beav 103, 118, 51 ER 475, 481. In Underhill and Hayton, *Law Relating to Trusts and Trustees* (17th edn, 2006), 1205 the principle that a *bona fide* purchaser of the interest of a trustee/beneficiary in default takes subject to a deduction to make good the default, even when the purchaser is without notice, is explained by the notion that 'the equitable interest in question was a chose in action, and purchasers of choses in action take subject to all equities'. In fact, the defaulting trustee cases have been explained on either of two grounds, neither of which is based on the principle that a purchaser of a chose in action takes subject to all equities. See paras 14.79–14.84 below. The second of those grounds, regarding a payment in advance, would also explain *Dibbs v Goren* (1849) 11 Beav 483, 50 ER 904. See *Livesey v Livesey* (1827) 3 Russ 287, 296, 38 ER 583, 587.

[328] See para. 14.19 above.

[329] See *Willes v Greenhill (No. 1)* (1860) 29 Beav 376, 54 ER 673; *Re Batchelor. Sloper v Oliver* (1873) LR 16 Eq 481, 484. Compare *Re Wickham's Will; Grant v Union Trustee Co of Australia Ltd* (1898) 9 QLJ 102 (see para. 14.42 above), in which the judgment proceeded on the basis of set-off rather than *Cherry v Boultbee*.

[330] See *Re Batchelor* (1873) LR 16 Eq 481, 483–4, and also *Re Hurburgh* [1959] Tas SR 25, 31, 40.

[331] *Watson v Mid Wales Railway Co* (1867) LR 2 CP 593, and see also *Business Computers Ltd v Anglo-African Leasing Ltd* [1977] 1 WLR 578.

[332] See para. 17.15 below.

contract, as opposed to when a debt arose pursuant to the contract. That criticism is equally relevant to the principle in *Cherry v Boultbee*, but *Stephens v Venables (No. 1)*[333] is authority for the proposition that the restriction nevertheless also applies in that context. The case concerned a legatee who was granted a lease of part of the testator's property by the executors and trustees of the will for a period of twenty-one years. Subsequently, he charged his right to the legacy, and notice of the charge was given to the trustees. When the legacy became payable, Sir John Romilly MR held that the trustees could invoke the principle in respect of the rent due from the legatee up to the date of notice, but that the chargees in enforcing their security took free from the legatee's indebtedness for rent arising after notice.[334] It made no difference that the liability for rent was based upon an obligation incurred under a lease entered into before notice. Sir John Romilly, in holding that only debts arising before notice could be taken into account, said:[335] 'Were it otherwise, the charge made by the legatee, whether residuary or pecuniary, would be worth nothing, the trustees might, after the receipt of notice of the charge, embark in a speculation with the legatee, and if, in the course of it, a balance accrued due to the trustee from the legatee, he might set it off against the legacy. and leave the mortgagee with nothing.' This would not be a valid objection, however, if the debt, although arising after notice, is based upon a contract entered into before notice.

Furthermore, *Stephens v Venables* seems difficult to reconcile with other cases which support the proposition that an assignee of a legacy takes subject to the principle in *Cherry v Boultbee* in circumstances where the legatee became liable after the testator's death to indemnify the estate for a sum paid on the legatee's behalf under a guarantee given by the testator in relation to the legatee's debts, even though the trustees of the estate tendered payment to the creditor after they had notice of the assignment. In other words, the liability of the legatee/assignor to indemnify the estate was only contingent at the date of notice, and the essence of a contingent liability is that there is no actual liability until the occurrence of the event upon which the contingency depends, in this case payment by the surety's estate to the creditor.[336] Curiously, the first of the cases is a decision of Sir John Romilly MR himself. In *Willes v Greenhill (No. 1)*,[337] the testator was a surety on two promissory notes for a legatee to whom the testator had bequeathed a reversionary share in his residuary estate. The testator's death occurred before the notes became payable. Subsequently, the trustees of the estate paid the creditor on the notes, but prior to the payment the legatee had assigned his legacy by way of mortgage to one of the trustees. This particular trustee, as assignee, obviously had notice of the assignment, and Sir John Romilly held that the notice that he had also constituted notice to the other trustees. Apparently, it was not considered to be an objection to the trustees' right to invoke *Cherry v Boultbee* when the legacy became payable, that the legatee's obligation to indemnify the estate for the sum paid on his behalf was only contingent at the date of the assignment, and therefore at the date of notice.

14.71

---

[333] (1862) 30 Beav 625, 54 ER 1032. See para. 14.63 above. See also *Re Pain; Gustavson v Pain* [1919] 1 Ch 38, 47–8.

[334] See also *Hill v Hicken* [1897] 2 Ch 579.

[335] (1862) 30 Beav 625, 627–8, 54 ER 1032, 1033–4.

[336] See para. 8.14 above.

[337] (1860) 29 Beav 376, 54 ER 673.

Admittedly, the question in *Willes v Greenhill* arose in the context of a priorities dispute between two mortgages, the legatee subsequently also having mortgaged the legacy to the trustees generally in order to secure the moneys to be paid on his behalf on the two notes. Priority depended on which of the mortgages first gave notice to the debtor[337a] (in the present case, the trustees). The Master of the Rolls, in following *Browne v Savage*,[338] said that it was in the interest of the single trustee taking the first mortgage to disclose the mortgage to his fellow trustees in order to obtain priority over any subsequent assignments, and so it could be assumed that in fact he had done this. Therefore, it was held that his mortgage had priority over the subsequent mortgage to the trustees generally. But the same reasoning should also have been relevant to the priorities dispute between the mortgage to the single trustee and the right of the trustees generally to invoke *Cherry v Boultbee*. In other words, it could be assumed that the trustees had notice of the assignment when they paid the creditor, and yet they were not precluded by that notice from invoking *Cherry v Boultbee* against the assignee notwithstanding that the legatee's obligation to contribute was still contingent at the date of notice. *Willes v Greenhill* is consistent in that regard with the principle applied in the case of a bankrupt legatee/principal debtor. The fact that the testator's estate pays the creditor after the bankruptcy, but under a contract of suretyship entered into by the testator before the bankruptcy, will not deprive the executors of the right to invoke the principle against the bankrupt's trustee in bankruptcy.[339] Similarly, it does not seem to be an objection to the operation of *Cherry v Boultbee* that an assignment may have taken place when the right to participate was still only contingent.[340]

14.72   Consider also *Re Melton; Milk v Towers*,[341] which was referred to earlier in the context of suretyship and the rule against double proof.[342] Some additional facts should be noted. The principal debtor in *Re Melton* had mortgaged his interest in the legacy to the creditor after the testator's death, but before his own bankruptcy. Notice of the mortgage was given to the surety's executors before they paid the creditor. The creditor had valued the security, and only proved in the debtor's bankruptcy for the balance of the debt. The creditor therefore retained the benefit of the security. After payment by the executors of the amount required under the suretyship agreement, the creditor realized the security by assigning it to the appellant and applied the proceeds in further reduction of the principal debt.[343] The appellant, as assignee from the creditor, had no better title than the creditor itself had. It was held that the rule against double proof did not deprive the surety's executors of the right to invoke *Cherry v Boultbee* in respect of the sum paid on behalf of the principal debtor. But the principal debtor was only contingently liable to indemnify the estate at the date of notice to the executors, payment to the creditor not yet having taken place, and it is implicit

---

[337a] Under the rule in *Dearle v Hall* (1828) 3 Russ 1, 38 ER 475. In Australia, compare the position under the Personal Property Securities Act 2009 (Cth).

[338] (1859) 4 Drewry 635, 62 ER 244.

[339] *Re Watson* [1896] 1 Ch 925; *Re Lennard* [1934] 1 Ch 235. See para. 14.27 above.

[340] See *Re Batchelor* (1873) LR 16 Eq 481, 483–4, and also *Re Hurburgh* [1959] Tas. SR 25, 31, 40.

[341] [1918] 1 Ch 37. *Re Melton* was discussed at length with approval in *Re SSSL Realisations (2002) Ltd* [2006] Ch 610, but the issue presently under discussion was not emphasized.

[342] See para. 14.52 above. See also the discussion of *Re Melton* at paras 14.35–14.38 above.

[343] See Warrington LJ at [1918] 1 Ch 37, 55.

in the decision that the fact that the obligation to contribute to the estate was only contingent at that date was not considered to be an objection to the operation of the principle.

Wood[344] has sought to explain *Willes v Greenhill* and *Re Melton* on the ground that in both **14.73** cases the beneficiary who assigned the interest was also an executor. In the context of assignments, special rules apply to trustees and executors who are entitled to participate in the estate but who have defaulted in the performance of their duties as such.[345] An assignee of the trustee's or the executor's interest takes subject to a deduction for an amount required to remedy the default even where the default occurred after notice of the assignment. The basis of the principle is default in the performance of a fiduciary obligation, and an assignee from an executor or a trustee takes the risk of a subsequent breach of fiduciary duty.[346] In neither *Willes v Greenhill* nor *Re Melton*, however, was there any question of a default of that nature, and so the fact that the beneficiary assigning the interest also happened to be an executor does not explain the decisions.

It is difficult to see why *Cherry v Boultbee* should have been available in cases such as *Willes* **14.74** *v Greenhill* and *Re Melton*, in which the debtor's liability to the fund arose after notice of the assignment but as a result of a contract of suretyship entered into before notice, but that it should not have been available in a case such as *Stephens v Venables*, where the indebtedness for rent came into existence after notice but as a result of a lease entered into before notice. *Stephens v Venables* is consistent with the principle applied in the law of set-off,[347] while in the suretyship cases the fact that a liability only vested after the notice was not emphasized. The principle enunciated in *Stephens v Venables* is generally regarded as representing the current state of the law.[348] Nevertheless, it constitutes an unwarranted restriction on the operation of *Cherry v Boultbee*, as well as on the right of set-off, and there is much to commend the view that the approach evidenced by the suretyship cases should be applied generally whenever a debt arises after notice although as a result of a contract entered into before notice.

(3) Costs in pending proceedings

If a beneficiary of a trust commences a suit against a trustee and, while the proceedings are **14.75** still pending, the beneficial interest is assigned, the assignee will take subject to any order for costs ultimately made against the beneficiary if the suit fails.[349] Where, however, the suit was commenced after the trustee was notified of the assignment, the assignee ordinarily will take free of a costs order made against the assignor, except to the extent of the trustee's usual right of indemnity out of the *entire* trust fund for all costs and expenses properly incurred

---

[344] Wood, *English and International Set-off* (1989), 449–50.
[345] See paras 14.79–14.91 below.
[346] *Cock v Aitken* (1912) 15 CLR 373, 384 (Isaacs J).
[347] Indeed, Sir John Romilly seemed to treat the case as one of set-off, although in truth rights under *Cherry v Boultbee* were in issue.
[348] See e.g. *Re Milan Tramways Co, ex p Theys* (1884) 25 Ch D 587 (esp Fry LJ at 594).
[349] See *Re Pain; Gustavson v Haviland* [1919] 1 Ch 38, 48–9, explaining *Re Knapman; Knapman v Wreford* (1881) 18 Ch D 300. See also *Re Mayne, ex p The Official Receiver* [1907] 2 KB 899, and *Re Jones; Christmas v Jones* [1897] 2 Ch 190 (esp. at 203–4).

in relation to the trust.[350] On the other hand, the assignee may lose his or her priority if the assignee stands by and allows costs to be incurred that he or she could have prevented.[351]

(4) Assignee has an obligation to contribute

14.76 The assignee of a right to participate takes subject not only to equities available against the assignor, but also to equities available against him or herself. If the assignee is liable to contribute to the fund, that obligation may be appropriated as payment of the right to participate when the right becomes due and payable.[352] *Cherry v Boultbee* is an equitable principle, and it may be applied by a court of equity as against the person with the equitable title to the right to participate, whoever that person may be.

(5) Agreement not to assert equities against assignees

14.77 While an assignee of a chose in action generally takes subject to prior equities available to the debtor against the assignor, a debtor may contract with the creditor on terms that the debtor will not raise against an assignee any rights which he or she may possess against the creditor. For example, debentures issued by a company may provide that the principal and interest secured by the debentures will be paid without regard to any equities between the company and the original or any intermediate holder thereof. This clause will be effective in the winding up of the company when there is a fund available for payment of the debentures, so that a registered transferee who is a *bona fide* purchaser for value will be entitled to receive the sum payable in the winding up in respect of the debentures without any deduction under *Cherry v Boultbee*.[353] On the other hand, a transferee who is not a *bona fide* purchaser for value cannot rely on the clause.[354] In that regard, a trustee under a creditors' deed executed by a debtor was held not to be a purchaser of debentures assigned by the debtor to the trustee pursuant to the deed, the trustee having become the registered holder. Therefore, the trustee took subject to equities available to the company against the debtor notwithstanding that the debentures provided that they were to be paid without regard to equities between the company and the original holder.[355] Similarly, neither a trustee in bankruptcy nor a judgment creditor is considered to be a purchaser.[356]

---

[350] *Re Pain; Gustavson v Haviland* [1919] 1 Ch 38, 49, and see also Isaacs J in the High Court of Australia in *Cock v Aitken* (1912) 15 CLR 373, 383–4.

[351] *Re Pain; Gustavson v Haviland* [1919] 1 Ch 38. See para. 14.49 above.

[352] *Burridge v Row* (1844) 13 LJ Ch 173. See also *Re Milan Tramways Co, ex p Theys* (1884) 25 Ch D 587, 592–3 (Cotton LJ). Compare *Campbell v Graham* (1831) 1 Russ & M 453, 39 ER 175 (and on appeal *Campbell v Sandford* (1834) 8 Bligh NS 622, 5 ER 1073), in which the assignee of the legacies was not personally liable on the bonds.

[353] *Re Goy & Co Ltd; Farmer v Goy & Co Ltd* [1900] 2 Ch 149 (esp at 153, where Stirling J emphasized that the transfer was for value and in good faith, as to which see also *Re Blakely Ordnance Co* (1867) LR 3 Ch App 154, 159). *Aliter* if the debentures do not contain a clause to that effect. See *Re Rhodesia Goldfields Ltd* [1910] 1 Ch 239.

[354] *Re Brown & Gregory Ltd. Shepheard v Brown & Gregory Ltd* [1904] 1 Ch 627, affirmed [1904] 2 Ch 448.

[355] *Re Brown & Gregory Ltd* [1904] 1 Ch 627, affirmed [1904] 2 Ch 448.

[356] *Kilworth v Mountcashell* (1864) 15 Ir Ch Rep 565, 581; *Re Marquis of Anglesey* [1903] 2 Ch 727, 732.

(6) Successive assignments

Consider that A, who has a right to participate in a fund, assigns the right to B, who in turn **14.78** assigns it to C. Subject to the principles discussed above, the administrator of the fund may invoke *Cherry v Boultbee* in respect of an obligation that A has to contribute to the fund. However, the question may arise whether *Cherry v Boultbee* may be invoked when B instead has the obligation to contribute. The issue of successive assignments is considered later.[357]

M. Defaulting Trustee who is also a Beneficiary

Consider the case of a trustee who is also a beneficiary under the trust.[358] In relation to that **14.79** situation, it has been said that: 'It has always been a rule of the Court of Chancery that, if a trustee misappropriates trust money, and has an equitable interest under the trust deed, the Court will not allow him to receive any part of the trust fund in which he is equitably interested under the trust until he has made good his default as trustee.'[359]

A possible explanation for the principle is *Cherry v Boultbee*. It could be said that a default- **14.80** ing trustee (or executor[360]) is directed to satisfy his or her beneficial entitlement from the trust asset in his or her own hands in the form of the obligation to compensate the trust for the breach. In fact, two slightly different formulations have been adopted. The principle is often called a right to impound, or stop, the beneficial interest of the defaulting trustee,[361] although in truth this is not an accurate description of either of the formulations. Moreover, both formulations have been said to give a wider remedy in the case of an assignment than that otherwise available against an assignee under *Cherry v Boultbee*. An assignee ordinarily takes subject to equities in existence before notice. But the courts have said that there is no similar limitation in the case of a defaulting trustee, so that the assignee of the trustee's beneficial interest under the trust may take subject to a deduction to the extent required to remedy the breach irrespective of whether the assignment occurred before or after default.[362] This applies also to a trustee's liability to pay costs to the estate consequent upon the trustee's misconduct.[363] An important limitation, however, is that this extended principle

---

[357] See paras 17.60–17.63 below.

[358] Compare the case of a trustee who is entitled to an indemnity from the trust estate for expenses or liabilities properly incurred. That situation is governed by the rule in *Cherry v Boultbee*, as opposed to the principles discussed below. See paras 14.06 and 14.14 above.

[359] *Re Brown; Dixon v Brown* (1886) 32 Ch D 597, 600 *per* Kay J. In addition to the cases cited below, see *Skinner v Sweet* (1818) 3 Madd 244, 56 ER 499; *Woodyatt v Gresley* (1836) 8 Sim 180, 59 ER 72. Compare *Hallett v Hallett* (1879) 13 Ch D 232, in which the trustee's beneficial interest related to a trust which was separate and distinct from the settlement in respect of which he was in default.

[360] This same principle applies to a defaulting executor. See *Sims v Doughty* (1800) 5 Ves Jun 243, 31 ER 567; *Re Dacre* [1916] 1 Ch 344.

[361] See e.g. *Courtenay v Williams* (1844) 3 Hare 539, 554, 67 ER 494, 500; *Fox v Buckley* (1876) 3 Ch D 508, 509 (Little VC, at first instance).

[362] See e.g. *Re Pain; Gustavson v Haviland* [1919] 1 Ch 38, 47. See para. 14.81 below, but compare para. 14.83 below in relation to the second formulation.

[363] An assignee of a trustee's right to participate will take subject to a deduction in respect of costs payable by the trustee consequent upon misconduct even if the assignment took place before the order for costs. See *Hopkins v Gowan* (1828) 1 Mol 561, 562 (IR), referred to in *Re Pain; Gustavson v Haviland* [1919] 1 Ch 38, 47. This is not the case, however, for a beneficiary who is not also an executor or a trustee, and who is liable

in relation to assignments is only relevant when the assignor was a trustee or an executor at the time of the assignment of the beneficial interest. If the assignor subsequently becomes a trustee or an executor, and then defaults, it does not apply.[364] Moreover, it only applies when the obligation to contribute arises out of a default in the performance of a fiduciary obligation.[365] An obligation to contribute which is derived from another source will not suffice.[366]

(1) First formulation

14.81 The first formulation is set out in *Morris v Livie*.[367] A person appointed trustee under a will committed a breach of trust after he had assigned a right that he had in reversion as a residuary legatee to participate in the trust. When the assignee later sought payment of the legacy, it was held that he took subject to the trustee's obligation to reimburse the trust for the breach. Knight Bruce VC said that the right to participate was given subject to a condition that the trustee would properly perform the duties of trustee. If the trustee acted in breach of trust, the right to participate could not be exercised until the breach had been remedied:

> It may, I conceive, be properly said that [the trustee's] legacy was given under a condition raised and implied by law, that undertaking he should duly fulfil the duties and obligations imposed on him by the instrument giving it. This he could not do without performing the trust as to the stock legacy, which, before his own legacy became due, he had, by his own misconduct, disabled himself from performing. The condition, if existing, accompanied his legacy until its discharge, and applied to it as much after as before its assignment.[368]

Cherry v Boultbee specifically contemplates the existence of a right to participate, but allows the administrator of the fund to appropriate a particular asset as payment of the right. Under *Morris v Livie*, on the other hand, the trustee's breach impugns his or her very entitlement to participate in the trust to the extent of the breach. Strictly, this is not a case of the trustee's interest being impounded. Rather, it is said that, in the event of a breach, the trustee does not have an interest. Since an assignee can only claim what the trustee could claim, the assignee should also take subject to the obligation to remedy the breach, regardless of when the breach may have occurred.

---

for costs incurred after notice of an assignment of his or her interest. The assignee does not take subject to a deduction, except to the extent of the trustee's usual right to indemnity out of the *entire* trust fund for all costs and expenses properly incurred by the trustee in relation to the trust. See *Re Pain*, explaining *Re Knapman; Knapman v Wreford* (1881) 18 Ch D 300. See also *Cock v Aitken* (1912) 15 CLR 373, 383–4 (Isaacs J). On the other hand, it was held in *Re Pain* that the assignee may lose priority if he or she stands by and allows the assignor to incur costs that the assignee could have prevented. See also para. 14.77 above.

[364] *Re Pain; Gustavson v Haviland* [1919] 1 Ch 38, 47; *White & Tudor's Leading Cases in Equity* (9th edn, 1928) vol. 1, 139, citing *Irby v Irby (No. 3)* (1858) 25 Beav 632, 53 ER 778. Compare *Cumming v Austin* (1903) 28 VLR 622, 629.

[365] See *Cock v Aitken* (1912) 15 CLR 373, 384 (Isaacs J).

[366] Compare the discussion of *Willes v Greenhill (No. 1)* (1860) 29 Beav 376, 54 ER 673 and *Re Melton* [1918] 1 Ch 37 in para. 14.73 above.

[367] (1842) 1 Y & C CC 380, 62 ER 934. See also *Wilkins v Sibley* (1863) 4 Giff 442, 445–6, 66 ER 780, 781–2; *Cock v Aitken* (1912) 15 CLR 373, 384; *Re Pain; Gustavson v Haviland* [1919] 1 Ch 38, 46–7.

[368] (1842) 1 Y & C CC 380, 388–9, 62 ER 934, 938.

Morris v Livie is not confined to the case of a trustee who is also a residuary legatee.[369] It has **14.82** been cited as authority for the general proposition that: 'every person taking an assignment from a cestui que trust of a portion of the testator's estate, at all events takes it subject to the liability to make good all breaches of trust on the part of the assignor if he fill the fiduciary position of a trustee, even though the breaches of trust be subsequent to the assignment.'[370] Nevertheless, *Morris v Livie* should not be relevant if it is clear that the bequest was intended to be independent of the office of trustee,[371] because it could not be said in such a case that the bequest was conditional upon the trustee properly performing the duties. On that basis, it is difficult to explain the decision in *Re Hervey; Short v Parratt*[372] by reference to *Morris v Livie*. The case concerned an intestacy. The administratrix was one of the next of kin of the intestate, and as such was entitled, after payment of the debts, to one moiety of the residue. She committed a breach of trust,[373] and so she herself could take nothing out of the personal estate until the amount which she was liable to replace had been made good. Prior to the default she had settled all her property, which included after-acquired property,[374] but it was held, on the authority of *Morris v Livie*, that the trustees of the settlement were subject to the same equity, even though the default occurred after the assignment. In an intestacy, however, nothing is 'given' by the intestate as such, and nor is the administrator appointed by the intestate. It is difficult then to see the basis for suggesting that the administrator's right to participate in the estate was given subject to a condition of properly performing the office, in accordance with *Morris v Livie*.

(2) Second formulation

The second formulation of the principle in these defaulting trustee or executor cases is **14.83** similar to, but is nonetheless distinct from, *Cherry v Boultbee*. Instead of saying that the trustee's obligation to contribute should be appropriated as payment of the right to participate when the right becomes due and payable, it is said that the trustee is deemed to have paid him or herself in advance, or in anticipation, from the money in his or her hands constituted by the misappropriated funds.[375] Strictly, this is not a case of impounding the

---

[369] Compare *Withers on Reversions* (2nd edn, 1933), 242. For example, the trustee in *Barnett v Sheffield* (1852) 1 De G M & G 371, 42 ER 595 was entitled to a specific legacy in the form of an annuity, but because of a misappropriation of trust funds it was held that he could not demand that anything be paid to him under the annuity. Knight Bruce VC (at 382, 599) described the annuity as: 'a guarantee for a full account on his part as to all the transactions in which he as a trustee should be engaged in respect of the trust.'

[370] *Re Knapman* (1881) 18 Ch D 300, 307 *per* Hall VC. It is not necessary that the defaulting trustee should be the only trustee of the trust. See *Barnett v Sheffield* (1852) 1 De G M & G 371, 42 ER 595.

[371] See Little VC at first instance in *Fox v Buckley* (1876) 3 Ch D 508, 509. Compare *Barnett v Sheffield* (1852) 1 De G M & G 371, 42 ER 595, in which the court rejected the argument that the will in that case specifically contemplated that the legacy should be paid despite any misappropriation. For a discussion of when a legacy may be said to be attached to the office of executor, see *Williams on Wills* (9th edn, 2008) vol. 1, 297–8.

[372] (1889) 61 LT 429.

[373] An administrator of an intestate's estate becomes a trustee as soon as the administration is completed. See *Re Cockburn's Will Trusts* [1957] 1 Ch 438, 439.

[374] The assignment of the beneficial interest would have become effective as soon as the trust was created and a beneficial interest was acquired. See *Palette Shoes Pty Ltd v Krohn* (1937) 58 CLR 1, 27.

[375] *Irby v Irby (No. 3)* (1858) 25 Beav 632, 638, 53 ER 778, 780; *Re Carew* [1896] 1 Ch 527, 535; *Edgar v Plomley* [1900] AC 431, 443; *Re Towndrow* [1911] 1 Ch 662, 668; *Re Dacre* [1916] 1 Ch 344; *RWG Management Ltd v Commissioner for Corporate Affairs* [1985] VR 385, 398.

trust fund; rather, the trustee is treated as if he or she has already received the entitlement.[376] It is not important for this formulation that there should be any connection between the beneficial entitlement and the proper performance by the trustee of the trust duties. In this respect it is wider than *Morris v Livie*.[377] For example, it applies even if the trustee acquired a beneficial interest only derivatively.[378] It has been said that it still applies when the breach of trust is committed after the assignment.[379] If indeed that were correct, it would justify a deduction in a case such as *Re Hervey*,[380] in which there was no connection between the office of administratrix and the right to share in the estate. It is questionable, however, whether the terms of this second formulation are apt to allow a deduction in respect of a breach occurring after the assignment or, at any rate, if there are other trustees of the trust, after they received notice of the assignment. The point is that, if a trustee has notice of an assignment of an equitable interest under the trust, the trustee could not discharge his or her obligation by paying the assignor. The trustee must tender payment to the assignee.[381] This should also apply when the assignor is the trustee. Payment by the trustee to him or herself after notice would not discharge the trust obligation to the assignee, and so it is difficult to see how a notion of a payment in advance to a defaulting trustee could bind the assignee if default occurred after notice of the assignment. There must, of course, be a valid notice. In that regard, if there are a number of trustees an assignee need give notice to only one of them, although when the assignor is a trustee the notice that the assignor/trustee obviously has is not considered to be sufficient for that purpose.[382] The assignee should protect his or her interest by giving notice to another trustee. Alternatively, the assignor may be a sole trustee. In the context of a priorities dispute under the rule in *Dearle v Hall*[383] between successive assignees, it has been said that notice to, or the knowledge possessed by, a sole assignor/trustee is not effective to alter priorities.[384] This should not apply, however, when a question of payment is in issue. Notice is not necessary in order to perfect the title of the assignee. The assignee becomes the trust beneficiary as from the date of the assignment.[385] A sole assignor/trustee could hardly discharge the trust obligation to the assignee by paying a stranger whom the trustee knows is not the beneficiary, and equally the assignor/trustee should not be able to discharge that obligation by paying him

---

[376] *Jacubs v Rylance* (1874) LR 17 Eq 341, 342.

[377] On the other hand, *Morris v Livie* would still apply when the trustee personally has not derived any advantage from the breach, but *quaere* whether this second formulation would be relevant in that case. See *Re Pain; Gustavson v Haviland* [1919] 1 Ch 38, 46–7.

[378] *Jacubs* v *Rylance* (1874) LR 17 Eq 341; *Doering v Doering* (1889) 42 Ch D 203; *Cumming v Austin* (1903) 28 VLR 622; *Re Dacre* [1916] 1 Ch 344. See also *Brandon v Brandon* (1859) 3 De G & J 524, 44 ER 1371 with respect to the purchased shares.

[379] *Doering v Doering* (1889) 42 Ch D 203, 207; *Cumming v Austin* (1903) 28 VLR 622; *Re Dacre* [1916] Ch 344, 347.

[380] (1889) 61 LT 429.

[381] *Brice v Bannister* (1878) 3 QBD 569.

[382] *Browne v Savage* (1859) 4 Drewry 635, 62 ER 244; *Cumming v Austin* (1902) 28 VLR 347, affirmed (1903) 28 VLR 622. Compare the case of an assignment *to* a trustee. See para. 14.71 above.

[383] (1828) 3 Russ 1, 38 ER 475.

[384] *Re Dallas* [1904] 2 Ch 385, and compare *Ipswich Permanent Money Club Ltd v Arthy* [1920] 2 Ch 257.

[385] *Ward v Duncombe* [1893] AC 369, 392. See also *Gorringe v Irwell India Rubber and Gutta Percha Works* (1886) 34 Ch D 128; *Re City Life Assurance Co Ltd. Stephenson's Case* [1926] 1 Ch 191, 219–20; *Re Trytel* [1952] 2 TLR 32, 34; *Thomas v National Australia Bank Ltd* [2000] 2 Qd R 448.

or herself when the assignor knows that he or she ceased to be the beneficiary as from the time of the assignment.

(3) Consequences of the formulations

It would seem, then, that neither *Morris v Livie* nor the second theory of a payment **14.84** in advance offers a satisfactory explanation as to why an assignee of a defaulting trustee's beneficial interest should take subject to a deduction to make good the breach if, as in *Re Hervey*, the trustee's entitlement was not dependent upon the proper performance of the office of trustee, and moreover if the breach occurred after the trustees received notice of the assignment, or, in the case of a sole trustee, after the assignment itself.

One consequence of both formulations is that, unlike under *Cherry v Boultbee*, it should **14.85** not make any difference that the liability to contribute otherwise ceased to exist before the right to participate became due and payable, for example because of a discharge from bankruptcy, or as a result of a composition or scheme of arrangement.[386] The discharge should not be relevant, because the breach would mean that the right to participate has already been impugned (under *Morris v Livie*), or it has already been satisfied by a notional payment in advance to the defaulting trustee.[387] Similarly, in the case of *Morris v Livie*, the fact of proving the debt and receiving a dividend in the defaulting trustee's bankruptcy should not constitute a waiver of the right to invoke the principle either before or after discharge,[388] since the trustee's right should still be impugned until such time as the default is remedied *in toto*. While *Re Sewell*[389] is authority to the contrary, the point may be made that Parker J did not analyze the case in terms of the defaulting trustee formulations.

(4) Non-monetary bequest

Cherry v Boultbee is confined to the situation in which a right to participate is for a sum **14.86** of money. It is not available against a legatee entitled to a specific bequest of freeholds or leaseholds, or of chattels.[390] This restriction should not apply, however, in the case of a defaulting executor or trustee under the *Morris v Livie* formulation. It is doubtful whether the second formulation could be invoked in this situation. If an executor or a trustee entitled to a specific bequest of that nature misappropriates funds of the estate, it would not be appropriate to characterize the misapplied funds as a 'payment' of the bequest in advance, because a person to whom specific property has been bequeathed could not claim instead a sum of money. With respect to *Morris v Livie*, on the other hand, if the bequest was conditional upon the executor or trustee properly performing the duties ancillary to the office, failure to perform those duties should impugn the right to the bequest.[391] Admittedly, there have been cases in which a trustee appointed under a will was given a life interest in realty, and it was held that the interest was not liable to be appropriated to make

---

[386] Compare para. 14.20 above in relation to *Cherry v Boultbee*.
[387] Compare the comments of Parker J in *Re Sewell; White v Sewell* [1909] 1 Ch 806, 808–9.
[388] Compare para. 14.58 above in relation to *Cherry v Boultbee*.
[389] [1909] 1 Ch 806.
[390] See para. 14.46 above.
[391] *Palmer v The Permanent Trustee Co* (1915) 16 SR (NSW) 162.

good deficiencies in the trust caused by his own breach.[392] But that was because a devise of realty formerly took place outside the will, so that it was not bound by the trust.[393] Moreover, since the devise took place outside the will, it could not be said that it was connected with the office of trustee, so as to support an argument that it was subject to a condition that the devisee would properly perform the duties of executor and trustee.[394] However, real estate now devolves on the personal representative,[395] and so the old rule should no longer apply.

(5) Bankrupt defaulting trustee

14.87 The preceding discussion concerned the situation in which the defaulting trustee, or an assignee, seeks payment of the trustee's beneficial entitlement under the trust. Consider the converse situation, in which the defaulting trustee is bankrupt and other trustees of the trust wish to prove in the bankruptcy in respect of the breach. For what amount, if any, can they prove? In considering this question, a distinction can be drawn between the two defaulting trustee formulations.

14.88 Under the second formulation, the defaulting trustee is deemed to have paid him or herself in advance, or in anticipation, from the misappropriated funds. Since payment is deemed to have occurred, this would seem to require the striking of a balance between what was due from the defaulting trustee by way of compensation and what was due to the defaulting trustee, so that the claim against the defaulting trustee should be limited to the balance. In Victoria, comments by Brooking J in *RWG Management Ltd v Commissioner for Corporate Affairs*[396] support this approach in the context of an insolvent defaulting trustee with a right of indemnity from the estate. However, it is contrary to views expressed by North J in *Staniar v Evans*.[397] *Staniar v Evans* concerned a defaulting trustee who was entitled to costs out of the estate. North J said that the usual order in such a case is that the trustee cannot receive any costs until the default has been made good. He said that an order may be made for payment of the balance only, but that an order in that form is made as a matter of favour only in circumstances where the trustee in any event is perfectly able and ready and willing to pay what he or she owes. If the trustee is not able and ready and willing to pay, the order should be for payment of the full amount necessary to make good the default. On this view, if the trustee is bankrupt and therefore is unable to pay what he or she owes, the proof should be for the full amount. *Staniar v Evans* concerned a claim for costs out of the trust estate, but North J indicated that the principle is also relevant when the trustee is entitled to a share of the trust estate as a beneficiary.[398] A similar approach has been adopted in other

---

[392] *Egbert v Butter* (1856) 21 Beav 560, 52 ER 976; *Fox v Buckley* (1876) 3 Ch D 508. See also *Re Milnes; Milnes v Sherwin* (1885) 53 LT 534, 535.

[393] See *Re Brown; Dixon v Brown* (1886) 32 Ch D 597, 600.

[394] See Little VC at first instance in *Fox v Buckley* (1876) 3 Ch D 508, 509.

[395] Administration of Estates Act 1925, s. 1(1), and see generally *Williams, Mortimer and Sunnucks on Executors, Administrators and Probate* (19th edn, 2008), 514–15, 1123 n. 33.

[396] [1985] VR 385, 397–8, referred to with approval in *Fitzwood Pty Ltd v Unique Goal Pty Ltd* [2002] FCAFC 285 at [138] (in which the trustee was in liquidation).

[397] (1886) 34 Ch D 470. See also *Lewis v Trask* (1882) 21 Ch D 862, and para. 14.14 above.

[398] (1886) 34 Ch D 470, 473.

situations.[399] It would seem to be particularly apt in the case of the first formulation. If a bequest is given to a trustee of an estate under an implied condition that he or she should fulfil the duties and obligations imposed on him or her by the instrument, the trustee, having defaulted, would not be entitled to the bequest until the breach is remedied. It could therefore be said that the other trustees should be entitled to prove for the full amount of the breach, and that the bankrupt's estate should not be entitled to participate in the trust until the default has been remedied *in toto*.[400]

In fact, the courts have not always proceeded on the *Staniar v Evans* approach when the first **14.89** formulation would apply, at least when the bankrupt otherwise would have had a present right to a definite part of the trust fund at the date of bankruptcy.[401] Rather, the right of proof in the bankruptcy has been limited to the difference between the defaulting trustee's liability and the trustee's beneficial interest in the trust estate, which includes the trust asset represented by his or her own liability. This has the consequence that the other beneficiaries of the trust effectively are deprived of the benefit of *Morris v Livie*. It has been justified on the basis of set-off. In *Ex p Turner, re Crosthwaite*,[402] a trustee appointed under a will was one of two residuary legatees. He misapplied trust funds, and became bankrupt. The other residuary legatee was also appointed a trustee. He sought to prove in the bankruptcy for the full amount of the default, and to retain the dividends and not pay anything to the defaulting trustee until the default was made good. Lord Cranworth and Knight Bruce LJ rejected that approach, and held that set-off applied. Lord Cranworth commented that: 'being one of the residuary legatees, he or his estate is entitled, on the doctrine of mutual credit, to set off against the sum due from him his share of whatever is due to him.'[403] He analysed the position as follows. He said that, if before the bankruptcy, the defaulting trustee had tendered the value of the residue of his liability after setting off his own beneficial interest in the trust, the question between the parties would have been settled. Therefore, the trustees should be remitted to a proof for the difference remaining after the set-off. The decision in *Ex p Turner* was followed in *Re Chapman, ex p Parker*,[404] Mathew J commenting: 'We should be flying in the face of [the insolvency set-off section[405]] if we did not ascertain what the exact liability of the bankrupt was, and that exact liability can only be ascertained by giving the bankrupt credit for his share.'[406]

With respect, it is not easy to see how the insolvency set-off section can be said to apply. In **14.90** the first place, the defaulting trustee's right to participate in the trust is a claim *in specie* for a share of a trust fund, and so it should not be within the ambit of the set-off section.[407]

---

[399] See para. 14.103 below.

[400] The proof in the bankruptcy should not constitute a waiver of the right to invoke *Morris v Livie*, or indeed *Cherry v Boultbee*, since the right to participate and the obligation to contribute both arise out of the trust itself. See *Ex p Turpin* (1832) Mont 443, and para. 14.60 above.

[401] Compare *Re Gloag's Estate* (1892) 11 NZLR 90 (esp at 94), discussed below.

[402] (1852) 2 De G M & G 927, 42 ER 1134.

[403] (1852) 2 De G M & G 927, 932, 42 ER 1134, 1136. Knight Bruce LJ adopted a similar analysis.

[404] (1887) 4 Morr 109.

[405] The relevant provision was the Bankruptcy Act 1883, s. 38.

[406] (1887) 4 Morr 109, 112.

[407] See paras 10.02–10.05 above.

Secondly, the essence of a set-off is the existence of cross-demands between the parties. The bankrupt defaulting trustee in *Ex p Turner* was allowed a deduction in respect of his interest in the total trust estate, which included the trust asset represented by his own liability. Yet it could hardly be said that the bankrupt had a cross-demand against the other trustees in respect of his 'interest' in his own unsatisfied liability. Thirdly, according to *Morris v Livie*, the defaulting trustee's entitlement is conditional upon the breach being remedied. Until that occurs, the bankrupt's entitlement, and any demand in relation to it, would be contingent. Unlike a contingent liability of a bankrupt, a contingent claim possessed by a bankrupt cannot be the subject of a set-off until the contingency has occurred and an amount accordingly has become due to the bankrupt.[408] In the situation under discussion, the contingency would not occur until the default has been remedied. In truth, it is not easy to see how the doctrine of mutual credit in bankruptcy can be said to be relevant to a case such as *Ex p Turner*.

14.91   *Ex p Turner* was not applied in a case in New Zealand. In *Re Gloag's Estate*,[409] a trustee was entitled to a life interest in the whole of the trust fund and, having misapplied the fund, she became bankrupt. Williams J held[410] that the representative of the trust estate in the interest in reversion of the other beneficiaries was entitled to prove for the whole of the misapplied fund, and that the bankrupt's estate could not participate in the income obtained from the dividend payable on the proof until the original fund had been replaced *in toto*. His Honour distinguished *Ex p Turner* on the ground that the defaulting trustee in that case had a present right to a definite share of the trust fund. The trustee before the bankruptcy could have discharged his obligation to the other beneficiary by paying him a certain sum after deducting his immediate share. That was not the case in *Re Gloag's Estate*, however. The defaulting trustee could not have discharged herself by paying to the other beneficiaries the present value of their reversionary interests after her life interest. She could only discharge herself by replacing the corpus, and there was nothing which could be set against that obligation.[411]

N. The Method of Application of *Cherry v Boultbee*

14.92   *Cherry v Boultbee* entitles the administrator of a fund to assert that a debtor to the fund should appropriate a particular asset of the fund, in the form of the debtor's own indebtedness, as *pro tanto* payment of his or her right to participate. The application of this principle is straightforward when the right to participate is for a fixed sum.[412]

---

[408] See paras 8.35–8.46 above. A different position now applies in company liquidation and administration in England. See para. 8.35 above.

[409] (1892) 11 NZLR 90.

[410] Following *Ex p King, re Severn* (1835) 1 Deac 143.

[411] See also *Ex p Stone, re Welch* (1873) LR 8 Ch App 914 (no set-off in respect of debtor/trustee's reversionary interest).

[412] If there are a number of fixed sum legacies, but there is a deficiency in the fund, an abatement may be necessary in order to calculate the amount of the right to participate in respect of which *Cherry v Boultbee* can operate. See *Re King; King v King* (1914) 31 WN (NSW) 55. Compare *Re Richardson, ex p Thompson v Hutton* (1902) 86 LT 25, although it is not clear from the report how the amount due on abatement was calculated.

(1) Right to participate is for a percentage of the fund

Alternatively, a person liable to contribute to a fund may be entitled to a percentage of the fund. In that situation, the administrator in invoking the principle calculates the claimant's share on the basis that the fund has been increased by the value of the claimant's indebtedness, and the claimant becomes entitled to the requisite percentage of the total fund, which includes the debt. The administrator then directs the claimant to appropriate the debt as *pro tanto* payment of his or her share, and so the net sum (if any) payable to the claimant is the difference between the share calculated in this manner and the indebtedness to the fund.[413] In *Re SSSL Realisations (2002) Ltd*,[414] the Court of Appeal expressed the calculation in the form: $D = 1/n$ of $(A + C) - C$, where $1/n$ is the proportion which the claimant's share of the fund bears to the whole,[415] A is the amount of assets to be distributed before taking account of the contribution due to the fund from the claimant, C is the amount of the claimant's contribution and D is the amount which the claimant is entitled to receive in the distribution.

14.93

The point may be illustrated by the case of a fund represented by a bankrupt's estate or the assets of a company in liquidation. In such cases, creditors are confined to a dividend payable out of the insolvent estate.[416] If a creditor is also indebted to the estate, and the circumstances are not such as to give rise to a set-off in the bankruptcy or liquidation,[417] the rule in *Cherry v Boultbee* may apply,[418] in the following manner. The dividend rate payable by the fund is calculated by dividing the total assets of the fund, which include the creditor's liability to the bankrupt or the company, by the total provable debts of the fund, including the debt owing to the creditor.[419] The dividend payable to the creditor is the product of this dividend rate and the creditor's provable claim. The creditor's liability to the bankrupt or the company is then appropriated as *pro tanto* payment of this sum, and the net amount (if any) payable to the creditor is the remainder of the dividend after subtracting the amount of the creditor's liability.[420]

14.94

(2) Insolvent contributor

Consider that a person who is both entitled to participate in, and liable to contribute to, a fund is bankrupt or is a company in liquidation, so that the claimant/contributor would only pay a dividend to creditors, and the trustee in bankruptcy or liquidator is making a claim on the fund. The question arises whether the rule in *Cherry v Boultbee* is to be applied as against the contributor's estate on the basis that the obligation to contribute is the full

14.95

---

[413] *Willes v Greenhill (No. 1)* (1860) 29 Beav 376, 383, 54 ER 673, 675–6; *Re Melton* [1918] 1 Ch 37, 46, 54, 59; *Public Trustee v Gittoes* [2005] NSWSC 373 at [138].

[414] [2006] Ch 610 at [79] (and see also at [12] and [104]).

[415] The numerator often would not be 1, depending on the fractional share of the fund to which the claimant is entitled.

[416] See e.g. *Ex p Graham* (1814) 3 V & B 130, 35 ER 428; *Re Mayne, ex p The Official Receiver* [1907] 2 KB 899.

[417] *Re SSSL Realisations (2002) Ltd* [2006] Ch 610 at [13].

[418] See paras 14.07–14.09 above.

[419] Obviously there can never be a dividend rate greater than one.

[420] In some cases the estate in fact may be able to pay a full dividend when the creditor's obligation to contribute is taken into account in this manner. If in such a case the creditor's liability exceeds the dividend notionally payable to him or her, the difference will represent a subsisting liability still owing by the creditor.

amount of the debt to the fund, or whether the obligation is limited to the dividend payable in the contributor's insolvency.

14.96 Consider first that the insolvency occurred *after* the event which precipitated the establishment of the fund.[421] The administrator of the fund in such a case may bring into account the full face value of the liability to the fund, notwithstanding the contributor's insolvency, since the bankrupt's trustee or the company's liquidator is not considered to be in any better position than the insolvent.[422] Thus *Cherry v Boultree* in this situation operates substantively, in the sense that it allows the administrator to treat the debt owing to the fund as payment of a right to participate to the extent of the full value of the debt, even though the fund otherwise would only have received a dividend on the debt. In effect the same result is achieved as for a set-off in the bankruptcy or the liquidation. If the administrator of the fund mistakenly pays the trustee in bankruptcy or the liquidator without invoking *Cherry v Boultbee*, the rule in *Ex p James*[423] may provide relief.[424]

14.97 Different considerations apply if the contributor is an individual who became bankrupt *before* the event which precipitated the establishment of the fund. This was the situation in *Cherry v Boultbee*.[425] In that case, a debtor became bankrupt before the death of a testatrix to whom he owed money and under whose will he was entitled to a legacy. Upon the occurrence of the bankruptcy, the debtor's estate vested in the assignees in bankruptcy. When the event later occurred which precipitated the establishment of the fund, being the death, the right to the legacy was vested in the assignees. The debtor remained liable to the fund for the full debt, but the debtor was never entitled to receive the legacy. Therefore, the principle, which now bears the name of that case, was not available, at least in relation to the full debt. There never was a time at which the same person was entitled to receive the legacy and liable to pay the entire debt. On the other hand, the assignees in bankruptcy, in whom the right to participate in the fund was vested, were liable to pay a dividend out of the bankrupt estate to the fund, and so the principle could be applied as against the assignees on the basis that the obligation to contribute was limited to the dividend payable on the debt.

14.98 In *Cherry v Boultbee*, the contributor's bankruptcy preceded the event which precipitated the establishment of the fund, and the principle was applied only to the extent of the dividend payable by the contributor's bankrupt estate on the debt to the fund. That result was a consequence of the vesting of the bankrupt's property in the assignees in bankruptcy, whose own obligation was limited to the payment of a dividend. Bankruptcy is

---

[421] See para. 14.26 above.
[422] *Corr v Corr* (1879) 3 LR Ir 435; *Re Weston; Davies v Tagart* [1900] 2 Ch 164; *Re Melton* [1918] 1 Ch 37 (see para. 14.52 above) (explained in *Re SSSL Realisations (2002) Ltd* [2006] Ch 610 at [106]). See also *Jeffs v Wood* (1723) 2 P Wms 28, 24 ER 668; *Ex p Metcalfe* (1805) 11 Ves Jun 404, 408, 32 ER 1143, 1144–5; *Re Brown; Dixon v Brown* (1886) 32 Ch D 597; *Re Whitehouse; Whitehouse v Edwards* (1887) 37 Ch D 683; *Re Watson; Turner v Watson* [1896] 1 Ch 925; *Re Lennard; Lennard's Trustee v Lennard* [1934] 1 Ch 235; *Re Kowloon Container Warehouse Co Ltd* [1981] HKLR 210. Compare *Re Fenton (No. 2)* [1932] 1 Ch 178, which was criticized in *Re SSSL Realisations* at [115]–[116].
[423] (1874) LR 9 Ch App 609. See para. 6.164 above.
[424] See *Re Brown* (1886) 32 Ch D 597, and note also *Ex p Bignold, re Charles* (1817) 2 Madd 470, 56 ER 408.
[425] (1839) 4 My & Cr 442, 41 ER 171. See paras 14.24 and 14.25 above

fundamentally different in that respect to company liquidation. The assets of the company ordinarily do not vest in the liquidator but remain with the company.[426] Where a contributor to a fund is a company which went into liquidation before the establishment of the fund, the question is whether, given that distinction, the *Cherry v Boultbee* principle should be applied to the full face value of the debt or whether it should limited in its application, as in the case of bankruptcy, to the dividend payable on the debt.

14.99 The question arose for consideration in *Re SSSL Realisations (2002) Ltd.*[427] Chadwick LJ[428] in that case accepted that, when the contributor went into liquidation *after* the constitution of the fund, the full amount of the debt is brought into account in the application of *Cherry v Boultbee*,[429] and he held that the same principle applies when the liquidation of the contributor occurred *before* the fund was constituted (in that case, by the liquidation of another company). The position in company liquidation in the latter circumstance was distinguished from that in bankruptcy[430] on the ground that, unlike in bankruptcy, the assets of a company in liquidation, including the claim on the fund, remain with the company, and the identity of the person liable to contribute to the fund (the company) does not change.

14.100 The contrary view has been adopted at first instance in Australia. In *Otis Elevator Co Pty Ltd v Guide Rails Pty Ltd*,[431] the claimant/contributor was a company in liquidation. Palmer J in the New South Wales Supreme Court considered that the principle applicable in bankruptcy also sets out the position in company liquidation, and that, since the liquidation of the contributor in that case began before the fund was established,[432] the *Cherry v Boultbee* principle was to be applied on the basis that the contribution was the dividend on the debt, not its full value. That reasoning was followed in Victoria, in *Ansett Australia Ltd v Travel Software Solutions Pty Ltd*,[433] in relation to an insolvent corporate contributor that had executed a deed of company arrangement under the Australian Corporations Act 2001 (Cth).[434]

14.101 It is suggested that *Re SSSL Realisations* was correctly decided on this point and that the Australian authorities should not be followed. The view adopted in *Re SSSL Realisations* is supported by other authority.[435] It is also consistent with the proposition that a winding up

---

[426] See paras 13.05 and 13.06 above.

[427] [2006] Ch 610 at [106]–[117].

[428] Jonathan Parker LJ and Etherton J agreeing.

[429] Not following *Re Fenton (No. 2)* [1932] 1 Ch 178. See [2006] Ch 610 at [115]–[116].

[430] Chadwick LJ referring ([2006] Ch 610 at [109]) to *Re Kowloon Container Warehouse Co Ltd* [1981] HKLR 210, 217–18, 225–6.

[431] (2004) 49 ACSR 531.

[432] The fund consisted of the surplus available for distribution among the shareholders of a company in its liquidation.

[433] (2007) 65 ACSR 47 at [98] and [106]–[108]. See also *FAI General Insurance Co Ltd v FAI Car Owners Mutual Insurance Co Pty Ltd* [2009] NSWSC 1350 at [64].

[434] Hargrave J's discussion of this point was *obiter*, since he held that there was no fund.

[435] See Chadwick LJ's explanation in *Re SSSL Realisations* [2006] Ch 610 at [110]–[114] of *Re Leeds and Hanley Theatres Of Varieties Ltd* [1904] 2 Ch 45, discussed below at paras 14.102–14.104. Chadwick LJ's analysis of that case is equally pertinent to *Re Mitchell, Houghton Ltd* (1970) 14 CBR (NS) 301, a decision of the Ontario Supreme Court which followed the *Leeds and Hanley* case. Two companies, called the Ontario company and the Quebec company, had claims against each other. The Ontario company filed an assignment in bankruptcy on 22 December 1969, and the Quebec company was adjudged bankrupt on 19 January 1970.

leaves the debts of the company untouched and simply affects the way in which the debts can be enforced.[436] In that regard, *Cherry v Boultbee* can apply notwithstanding that a contributor's debt to a fund has become unenforceable because of the expiration of a limitation period,[437] or because it is the subject of a covenant not to sue.[438] Despite the unenforceability of the debt, the fund is permitted to apply *Cherry v Boultbee*. This is because the debt is still an existing asset of the fund, albeit that it is unenforceable by action. Since the debt remains an existing asset, when the contributor claims a right to share in the fund he or she can be directed to pay him or herself *pro tanto* out of the asset of the fund in the contributor's own hands, in the form of the debt. If *Cherry v Boultbee* can be invoked to the full extent of the face value of an obligation to contribute when the obligation is unenforceable by action, the position should be the same when a contributor has gone into liquidation, given that liquidation affects only enforcement of the company's debts and not the debts themselves.

(3) Two insolvent estates

14.102 The problem becomes more complex when there are two *prima facie* insolvent estates, each of which has a claim against the other, and the situation is such that the cross-demands may not be employed in a set-off. For example, it may be that a company in liquidation is liable in the liquidation of a second company to pay a call on shares,[439] or is liable for misfeasance,[440] and the first company is also a creditor of the second on a separate transaction. The liquidator of the second company may assert that the first company should not be allowed to participate in the liquidation by receiving a dividend on the debt owing to it until the first company has made its required contribution in the form of a call,[441] or has satisfied its misfeasance liability, and the liquidator of the first company may adopt a similar stance. The problem is that neither company in fact may have sufficient assets to satisfy its liability *in toto*. That was the case in *Re Leeds and Hanley Theatres Of Varieties Ltd*.[442] Two companies, the Finance Company (F) and the Theatres Company (T), were in liquidation. F was

---

The claims could not be set off under the applicable insolvency legislation, and so Houlden J applied the *Leeds and Hanley* case in the winding up of the Quebec company. The relevant fund therefore was regarded as the assets of the Quebec company and the Ontario company was treated as the claimant on that fund. In performing the calculation dictated by the *Leeds and Hanley* case, Houlden J applied the dividend payable out of that fund to the Ontario company in reduction of the full face amount of the Ontario company's debt to the Quebec company, notwithstanding that the Ontario company had filed its assignment in bankruptcy before the Quebec company's bankruptcy.

[436] *Wight v Eckhardt Marine GmbH* [2004] 1 AC 147 at [27] (PC); *Hague v Nam Tai Eletronics Inc* [2007] 2 BCLC 194 at [17]; *Gertig v Davies* (2003) 85 SASR 226 at [33]. In Australia, this is also the effect of a deed of company arrangement under the Corporations Act 2001 (Cth). See *Helou v P D Mulligan Pty Ltd* (2003) 57 NSWLR 74.

[437] See para. 14.17 above. Compare the situation in which the debt is extinguished upon the expiration of the limitation period so that it ceases to exist. See the Limitation Act 1969 (NSW), s. 63 (referred to in *Gray v Guardian Trust Australia Ltd* [2002] NSWSC 1218 at [110]), and generally paras 14.20–14.22 above.

[438] *Herskope v Perpetual Trustees (WA) Ltd* (2002) 41 ACSR 707.

[439] See paras 8.64–8.79 above.

[440] See paras 8.81–8.87 above.

[441] See *Re Auriferous Properties Ltd (No. 2)* [1898] 2 Ch 428; *Re National Live Stock Insurance Co Ltd* [1917] 1 Ch 628; *Re White Star Line Ltd* [1938] 1 Ch 458.

[442] [1904] 2 Ch 45.

a creditor of T for £5,100 on debentures issued by T, while T had a claim against F for £4,323 as a result of a judgment obtained against F for damages for misfeasance. Because of the nature of the latter claim, the two demands could not be set off.[443] Moreover, neither company had sufficient assets in hand with which to pay its own liability in full. F had no assets other than the dividend payable by T on the debentures, but had other creditors to the extent of £5,490. T had other assets totalling in value £8,277, and other liabilities of £4,685. Buckley J adopted the following procedure for settling the rights of the parties:

> The proper administration in my judgment, therefore, is this. Notionally treat the Finance Company as having paid the £4,323 to the Theatres Company; take the aggregate notional sum thus arrived at and treat it as applied in payment of a dividend upon all the debts of the Theatres Company — that is to say, upon the £5,100 due to the Finance Company and the £4,685 due to other people. That will attribute to the Finance Company a certain sum. If that sum be greater than the £4,323 that they owe, they will get the difference. If it be less, or equal, they will receive nothing. If the dividend thus arrived at on the £4,685 cannot be satisfied in full (because the notional sum, of course, is not really paid), then the £4,685 would take the whole of the assets of the Theatres Company, although it be less than the notional dividend calculated upon the footing that the Finance Company have paid that which they have not paid.[444]

In essence, this is an application in favour of T of the method outlined above for calculating the net sum payable when a creditor of a bankrupt or a company in liquidation is also liable to make a contribution.[445] A notional payment of £4,323 by F to T would have produced an aggregate fund in T of £12,600. Its total liabilities were only £9,785 (being £5,100 plus £4,685), and so T could pay a full dividend of 100p in the £. Therefore, F was entitled to receive £5,100 from T, but since F was indebted to T for £4,323 the net sum payable was reduced to £777.

---

[443] *Ex p Pelly* (1882) 21 Ch D 492. See paras 8.81–8.87 above.

[444] [1904] 2 Ch 45, 51–2. Compare *Re National Live Stock Insurance Co Ltd* [1917] 1 Ch 628, in which Astbury J (at 633) referred to evidence that neither company would be in a position to receive a cash dividend in the winding up of the other, and ordered that the assets of each company be distributed amongst its creditors but excluding the claim of the other company.

[445] See para. 14.94 above. Buckley J's approach has been approved in other cases. See *Re National Live Stock Insurance Co Ltd* [1917] 1 Ch 628, 632; *Re Hattons Confectionery Co Ltd* [1936] NZLR 802; *Re Mitchell, Houghton Ltd* (1970) 14 CBR (NS) 301; *Re SSSL Realisations (2002) Ltd* [2006] Ch 610 at [110]–[114] (note that *Cherry v Boultbee* could only have applied in the liquidation of the surety in that case, since the surety could not have proved in the liquidation of the principal debtor because of the rule against double proof). Compare *West Mercia Safetywear Ltd v Dodd* [1988] BCLC 250. It has also been criticized, however. See Luckett and Dean, 'Cross debts: notional calculations in liquidations' (1983) 11 *Australian Business Law Review* 69. They noted that, as a result of the order, F received £777 from T for distribution amongst its other creditors, who each would have received a resulting dividend of 2s. 10d. in the pound, whereas T as a creditor of F in effect received payment in full for its own claim against F. Accordingly, they proposed an alternative procedure which would have the effect of treating all the creditors of each company in an equal manner. See also Dean, Luckett and Houghton, 'Notional calculations in liquidations revisited' (1993) 11 *Companies and Securities Law Journal* 204. However, a feature of *Cherry v Boultbee* in the situation in which the debtor/creditor of the fund has gone into liquidation is that it may have the effect of enabling the fund to obtain the full value of the debt owing to it to the extent of the right to participate. See para. 14.96 above. This is a consequence of the right of the administrator of the fund to direct the debtor to satisfy his or her right to participate from the debtor's own obligation to contribute.

14.103   Buckley J only notionally treated F as having paid its debt. Consequently, only T obtained
the benefit of the operation of *Cherry v Boultbee*. A greater sum would have been payable
by T if instead F had been treated as the recipient of the notional payment.[446] Buckley J's
decision to give T the benefit of the principle in *Cherry v Boultbee* may have been prompted
by the fact that the summons was taken out in the winding up of T, and so he was only
called upon to consider the position as between T and its creditors.[447] It also may be justified, however, on another ground, that a party such as F which is liable for misfeasance not
only may not employ the liability in a set-off against a cross-demand, but in addition it
should be required to satisfy the liability *in toto* before a right to receive a dividend on the
cross-demand accrues. The courts have applied a similar principle where a company in
liquidation was liable in the liquidation of another company to pay a call on shares,[448] and
where a company in liquidation was obliged to return a payment invalidated as a preference
in the liquidation of the payer, so that the first-mentioned company had to repay the preference in full before it could receive a dividend on the original debt for which the payment
was intended to constitute satisfaction.[449] There have also been cases in which a banker, or
an assignee in bankruptcy, who received proceeds from the realization of a bankrupt's
estate, and who happened to be a creditor of the bankrupt, later also became bankrupt. The
banker's, or the assignee's, estate was held not to be entitled to receive a dividend on the
bankrupt's indebtedness until the proceeds had been repaid.[450] A person liable for misfeasance is unlikely to be treated more leniently than, for example, an innocent contributory
liable to pay a call on shares,[451] and so it is understandable that F, the party liable for
misfeasance, should have been chosen as the party to make a notional payment, rather
than T.

---

[446] The dividend rate payable by F, on the assumption that T has notionally paid its debt, would have
been obtained by dividing its total assets, including T's debt, by its total liabilities, which would have equalled
(5,100 + 0)/(5,490 + 4,323). This produces a dividend rate of .5197. Thus the value of T's right of partici-
pation would have been the product of .5197 and £4.323, being £2,246.74. Under *Cherry v Boultbee*, F's
liquidator would have been entitled to direct T to appropriate a part of its own liability to contribute (being
£5,100) in satisfaction of this right to participate, after which T would still have had a residual liability to
F of £2,853.26. The dividend rate payable by T on this debt, being its total assets divided by its liabilities (the
assets of T would no longer include F's liability for £4,323), would have been 8,277/(4,685 + 2,853.26). Since
this is greater than one, T could have paid a full dividend to its creditors, so that F would have received the full
value of the residue of T's debt for £2,853.26. The end result is that, while the judgment of Buckley J obliged
T to pay to F £777, T would have been required to pay the greater sum of £2,853.26 if the notional payment
had been deemed to have been made by T rather than F.

[447] See Buckley J at [1904] 2 Ch 45, 51. Compare *Re Auriferous Properties Ltd (No. 2)* [1898] 2 Ch 428
and *Re National Live Stock Insurance Co Ltd* [1917] 1 Ch 628, in which a summons was taken out in both
liquidations.

[448] *Re Auriferous Properties Ltd (No. 2)* [1898] 2 Ch 428; *Re Hattons Confectionery Co Ltd* [1936] NZLR
802; *Re White Star Line Ltd* [1938] 1 Ch 458. Compare *Re National Live Stock Insurance Co Ltd* [1917] 1 Ch
628.

[449] *N A Kratzmann Pty Ltd v Tucker (No. 2)* (1968) 123 CLR 295. In Australia, see also the Corporations
Act 2001 (Cth), s. 588FI.

[450] *Ex p Bebb* (1812) 19 Ves Jun 222, 34 ER 501; *Ex p Graham* (1814) 3 V & B 130, 35 ER 428; *Ex p
Bignold, re Charles* (1817) 2 Madd 470, 56 ER 408. See, however, the order made in *Ex p Graham*, discussed
in para. 14.15 above.

[451] See *Ex p Pelly* (1882) 21 Ch D 492, 503, 509–10.

The calculation of the notional dividend rate in the *Leeds and Hanley* case was premised on **14.104** the assumption that T had a valuable asset to the full extent of F's liability. This was a valid assumption in that case, since the dividend payable by T to F was greater than F's liability to T, and therefore all of the asset represented by F's liability was employed in order to reduce the sum otherwise payable to F. It would not have been the case, however, if F's liability had been greater than the dividend notionally payable in T's liquidation. F would have had a residual liability remaining after the application of *Cherry v Boultbee*, and if F was insolvent it would only have been able to pay a fractional dividend on this residue. This means that F in effect would have received credit for a higher dividend rate in the *Cherry v Boultbee* calculation than that payable to T's other creditors, who would have been paid a dividend calculated on the basis of the true resulting asset value of the company. However, the effect on the dividend rate in a case such as this often would be marginal.

15

COMBINATION OF BANK ACCOUNTS

A. Introduction

15.01 When a customer has more than one account with a bank, one of which is in credit and another in debit, it is said that the bank may in some circumstances combine, or consolidate, the accounts and proceed on the basis that there is only one debt for the balance.[1] The accounts need not be at the same branch.[2] Nor is it necessary that the account in credit should have resulted from a deposit by the customer. A combination may arise in relation to an account that originally was opened in the name of a third party but which became payable to the customer.[3]

15.02 Combination is important if the bank is suspicious of the customer's solvency, because it provides the bank with a means by which it can obtain the benefit of the account in credit, by setting it against the account in debit, before the customer has dissipated the credit balance. For example, if combination applies, a bank may refuse to honour a cheque drawn by a customer on an account in credit if the customer has a debit balance on another account, unless the overall credit balance on the two accounts taken together is sufficient to satisfy the cheque or the balance in any event is within an agreed overdraft limit.[4] In this sense, it has been said that combination may be used as a sword as well as a shield.[5]

B. The Nature of the Right of Combination

(1) Distinguished from lien and set-off

15.03 A bank has a lien on all securities deposited with it as banker unless there is an express contract, or circumstances showing an implied contract, inconsistent with a lien.[6] On occasions it has been assumed that combination of accounts is merely an aspect of the banker's lien,[7] though the courts have been critical of the use of the term 'lien' in

---

[1] The question whether accounts are combined may also arise in relation to accounts each of which is in debit. See e.g. *Stannard v National Bank of New Zealand Ltd* (1986) 3 NZCLC 99,510, in which the issue was whether security provided to a bank extended to term loans as well as to an overdrawn current account.

[2] *Garnett v M'Kewan* (1872) LR 8 Ex 10, and see para. 15.33 below.

[3] See Bacon VC in *Roxburghe v Cox* (1881) 17 Ch D 520, who (incorrectly) characterized the right in question as a lien. See below. While James and Lush LJJ on appeal decided the case instead by reference to the principles of set-off under the Statutes of Set-off, Baggallay LJ (at 527–8) said that he did not dissent from Bacon VC's conclusion.

[4] *Garnett v M'Kewan* (1872) LR 8 Ex 10.

[5] *Barclays Bank Ltd v Okenarhe* [1966] 2 Lloyd's Rep 87, 97. See also *National Bank of New Zealand v Heslop* (1882) NZLR 1 CA 47; *Royal Trust Co v Molsons Bank* (1912) 8 DLR 478, 480.

[6] *Brandao v Barnett* (1846) 3 CB 519, 531, 136 ER 207, 212–13.

[7] See e.g. *Misa v Currie* (1876) 1 App Cas 554, 569 *per* Lord Hatherley ('all monies paid into a bank are subject to a lien'); *Bower v Foreign and Colonial Gas Co* (1874) 22 WR 740; *Roxburghe v Cox* (1881) 17 Ch D 520; *T. and H. Greenwood Teale v William Williams Brown and Co* (1894) 11 TLR 56; *Baker v Lloyd's Bank Ltd* [1920] 2 KB 322, 327; *Greenhalgh and Sons v Union Bank of Manchester* [1924] 2 KB 153, 164; *Halesowen Presswork & Assemblies Ltd v Westminster Bank Ltd* [1971] 1 QB 1, 19 (Roskill J). Ungoed-Thomas J in *Re Keever* [1967] 1 Ch 182 referred to a lien, but that was in the context of the bank's lien on the cheque (and its proceeds) which was security for the balance on the customer's account (see at 190), as opposed to combination of the accounts in order to ascertain the balance secured.

this context.[8] The lien to which a bank is entitled is a common law possessory lien. This form of lien merely confers upon a creditor the right to retain possession of tangible property held by the creditor until such time as the debtor pays the debt. Once the creditor loses possession, the lien is lost. Thus, a cheque or other negotiable security deposited with a bank for collection may be the subject of a lien while it remains in the possession of the bank. But when the cheque is cleared the bank loses possession of it, with the result that the lien comes to an end. Since the relationship of banker and customer is one of debt rather than of trustee and beneficiary,[9] the proceeds of the cheque received by the bank become the property of the bank, and it can hardly be correct to say that the bank has a lien on its own property. The bank is a debtor in relation to the proceeds, including where the proceeds are paid into an account in credit in the name of the customer. A debt is not tangible property, however, and so the use of the word 'lien' to describe the bank's rights in relation to the account is inappropriate.[10]

Lord Denning in the Court of Appeal in *Halesowen Presswork & Assemblies Ltd v Westminster Bank Ltd*[11] said that, 'we should discard the use of the word "lien" in this context and speak simply of a banker's "right to combine accounts": or a right to "set off" one account against the other.'[12] However, the term 'set-off' similarly does not convey the true nature of combination of accounts. It suggests that there are independent debts in existence which the bank may set off by the exercise of a right so as to produce a single debt for the balance, but that is not the traditional basis of combination. Rather, the explanation found in the cases is that, unless a particular account is separated out by agreement (express or implied) or it is separate as a matter of law, the debt owing by either party to the other at any particular time can only be ascertained by looking at the balance of all the accounts together. In other words, it is not so much a right to set off independent debts as a recognition that the debt owing is the balance of all the accounts. Expressed more concisely, combination is an accounting situation rather than a set-off situation.[13] On that basis, a specific act of combination should not be required.[14] The accounting does not bring about the single debt, but rather it is undertaken in order to ascertain what the debt is. When combination is referred

15.04

---

[8] *Re Morris, deceased; Coneys v Morris* [1922] 1 IR 136; *Halesowen Presswork & Assemblies Ltd v Westminster Bank Ltd* [1971] 1 QB 1, 33–4 (Lord Denning MR), 46 (Buckley LJ), which view was endorsed on appeal by Viscount Dilhorne ([1972] AC 785, 802) and by Lord Cross of Chelsea (at 810). See also *Royal Trust Co v Molsons Bank* (1912) 8 DLR 478, 480–1; *Broad v Commissioner of Stamp Duties* [1980] 2 NSWLR 40; *MPS Constructions Pty Ltd v Rural Bank of New South Wales* (1980) 4 ACLR 835, 840–1; *Duke Finance Ltd v Commonwealth Bank of Australia* (1990) 22 NSWLR 236, 251.

[9] *Foley v Hill* (1848) 2 HLC 28, 9 ER 1002.

[10] *Halesowen Presswork & Assemblies Ltd v Westminster Bank* Ltd [1971] 1 QB 1, 46 (Buckley LJ). See also on appeal in the House of Lords [1972] AC 785, 802 (Viscount Dilhorne), 810 (Lord Cross of Chelsea).

[11] [1971] 1 QB 1.

[12] [1971] 1 QB 1, 34.

[13] *Halesowen Presswork & Assemblies Ltd v Westminster Bank Ltd* [1971] 1 QB 1, 46 (Buckley LJ); *Re Charge Card Services Ltd* [1987] 1 Ch 150, 173–4 (Millett J); *Re Shoreville Mandalay Ltd* [1993] MCLR 122, 135 (NZ CA).

[14] Even on the view that combination operates as a set-off of independent accounts (see below), a physical combination of the accounts in the bank's books may not be necessary if the right is otherwise properly asserted. See Roskill J at first instance in *Halesowen Presswork & Assemblies Ltd v Westminster Bank Ltd* [1971] 1 QB 1, 19, and also *Direct Acceptance Corporation Ltd v Bank of New South Wales* (1968) 88 WN (Pt 1) (NSW) 498, 502.

to as a set-off, that expression is not inapt if it is meant to convey a set-off of debits against credits[15] in order to calculate the debt, but it is inaccurate if it is intended to mean a set-off of independent obligations. The foundation of the principle is a single banker/customer relationship,[16] and it has its justification in the notion that, no matter how many accounts belonging to a customer a bank may have entered in its books, there is still only one relationship.[17] As Kelly CB expressed it, in a case where a customer had a credit balance at one branch which was almost exactly equalled by a debit balance at another branch:[18] 'The defendant's bank, therefore, had scarcely a shilling of his money, and I cannot see why they were bound to honour his cheque at Leighton Buzzard just because there was a balance at that branch in his favour.'

15.05   While this analysis has its supporters,[19] it also has its critics.[20] In Wood's opinion, the right in question, which he calls current account set-off, is indeed a set-off, in the sense that it requires an act by the bank to set what are otherwise distinct reciprocal claims against one another.[21] Wood regards the various judicial statements which suggest that there is only one amount owing as being no more than an expression of the fact that, in the absence of an agreement to the contrary, the bank at any time may set off accounts without notice to the customer and accordingly treat divided accounts as a single blended account.[22] However, this does not appear to be what the judges had in mind. But the rejection of that view does not mean that nothing follows from the fact that separate accounts are recorded in the bank's books. It is unlikely that the courts in saying that a number of accounts form one entire account intended to refer to the operation of the accounts themselves. Rather, they appear to have had in mind the question whether, and to what extent, a debt is owing at any particular time by the bank or the customer to the other. Accordingly, for certain purposes the accounts should indeed be treated as separate, for example for the calculation and payment of interest, and for questions relating to the order and appropriation of payments in accordance with *Clayton's Case*.[23] In truth, as Byrne J remarked at first instance in *Mutton v Peat*,[24] in response to an argument that as between banker and

---

[15] See *Matthews v Geraghty* (1986) 43 SASR 576, 580.

[16] Accounts of different customers cannot be combined without authority. See *Re Shoreville Mandalay Ltd* [1993] MCLR 122, 135 (NZ CA).

[17] See *Halesowen Presswork & Assemblies Ltd v Westminster Bank Ltd* [1971] 1 QB 1, 46 *per* Buckley LJ ('When the relationship of the banker and customer is a single relationship such as I have already mentioned, albeit embodied in a number of accounts . . .'), and *Welsh Development Agency v Export Finance Co Ltd* [1992] BCLC 148, 167 *per* Dillon LJ (' . . . was more accurately to be described as a right of the banker to combine accounts because there was only one banker and customer relationship . . .').

[18] *Garnett v M'Kewan* (1872) LR 8 Ex 10, 12.

[19] Shea, 'Statutory set-off' (1986) 3 *Journal of International Banking Law* 152, 154; Wadsley and Penn, *The Law Relating to Domestic Banking* (2nd edn, 2000), 352 [11–039]; McCracken, *The Banker's Remedy of Set-off* (3rd edn, 2010), Ch 1; Cranston, *Principles of Banking Law* (2nd edn, 2002), 165.

[20] See Wood, *English and International Set-off* (1989), 92–4; Salter, 'Remedies for banks: an outline of English law' in Blair (ed.), *Banks and Remedies* (2nd edn, 1999), 49–52; Goode, *Principles of Corporate Insolvency Law* (3rd edn, 2005), 216. *Ellinger's Modern Banking Law* (4th edn, 2006), 231, 233 also suggests this view. Compare *Paget's Law of Banking* (13th edn, 2007), 714–15, 720–1.

[21] Wood, *English and International Set-off* (1989), 92, 94.

[22] Wood, *English and International Set-off* (1989), 92.

[23] (1816) 1 Mer 572, 35 ER 781.

[24] [1899] 2 Ch 556, 560. .

---

customer all accounts form but one account, this 'is true for certain purposes'. On the other hand, unless there is an express or implied agreement to the contrary which would preclude a combination in any event, the courts have recognized that a bank is entitled to give effect to the principle of combination in its books by moving debits or credits from one account to another.[25] When that occurs the accounts cease to be separate for those purposes as well. But as Canadian courts have emphasized, the book-keeping entry itself does not constitute a payment of the account in debit, since there was in any event only one debt.[26]

(2) The cases

An early case suggesting that combination is an accounting situation is *Ex p Pearce, re Langmead.*[27] Commissioners appointed under an Act of Parliament had two accounts with a bank, designated respectively the river account and the harbour account. The river account was overdrawn, but the harbour account had a credit balance exceeding the debit balance on the river account. The bank became bankrupt, whereupon the assignees in bankruptcy commenced proceedings at law against the customer for payment of the debit balance on the river account. Sir John Cross granted an injunction restraining the action, commenting that: 'There was only one account of banker and customer between the bank and the commissioners.'[28] The assignees therefore had no just cause to bring the action. It is true that he referred later in his judgment to set-off, and to the 'debts' on each of the accounts, but those expressions may not have been used in their technical sense. Nor could his reference to a single account be explained as a recognition of the concept that the bank at any time could have combined without notice,[29] because the bank (or at least its assignees in bankruptcy) was the party attempting to treat the accounts as separate.

15.06

Bailey v Finch[30] also concerned the bankruptcy of a bank. The defendant as executor under a will had an executorship account with the bank. In addition, he had three accounts in his personal capacity, two of which were overdrawn and the third of which was in credit. On the three accounts there was an overall balance against him. The question was whether the defendant could set off the executorship account against the overall debit balance on the three accounts, and the case was discussed earlier in that context.[31] For present purposes

15.07

---

[25] In the *Halesowen* case, see Roskill J at first instance [1971] 1 QB 1, 20–1, Lord Denning MR in the Court of Appeal at 35 and Lord Kilbrandon in the House of Lords [1972] AC 785, 819, each criticizing a *dictum* by Swift J to the contrary in *Greenhalgh and Sons v Union Bank of Manchester* [1924] 2 KB 153, 164. See also *Garnett v M'Kewan* (1872) LR 8 Ex 10 (esp. Kelly CB at 13); *Re Sutcliffe & Sons Ltd, ex p Royal Bank* [1933] 1 DLR 562 (esp. at 569); *Re T. C. Marines Ltd* (1973) 34 DLR (3d) 489; *Re Plasky* (1981) 39 CBR 186, 194; *Deep v Bank of Montreal* (1991) 47 OAC 319. In *Clark v Ulster Bank Ltd* [1950] NILR 132, 143 Black LJ referred to this as crystallizing the position.

[26] *Re Sutcliffe & Sons Ltd, ex p Royal Bank* [1933] 1 DLR 562 (esp. at 569); *Ross v Royal Bank of Canada* (1965) 52 DLR (2d) 578; *Re Plasky* (1981) 39 CBR 186; *Re T. C. Marines Ltd* (1973) 34 DLR (3d) 489. See also, and compare, *Re Shibou* (1983) 3 DLR (4th) 723, 726–7 (decision affirmed *Guttman v Toronto-Dominion Bank* [1984] 5 WWR 529). For the same reason, the book-keeping entry does not constitute a seizure of assets. See *Deep v Bank of Montreal* (1991) 47 OAC 319.

[27] (1841) 2 Mont D & De G 142.

[28] (1841) 2 Mont D & De G 142, 145.

[29] Compare para. 15.05 above.

[30] (1871) LR 7 QB 34.

[31] See para. 13.129 above.

the interesting point is the characterization by Blackburn J of the position in relation to the three accounts. He said that:[32]

> [W]hat we have to look to is, what were the facts at the time of the bankruptcy; and the rights of the parties must be regulated by what those facts were. It appears that at that time Mr Finch, the defendant, had an account with the bank, or rather several accounts, which for convenience he had called by different names; it matters not what they were, he had for convenience three accounts. There is no doubt whatever, as between him and the bank, those three accounts all formed in reality one account; and that a debt was owing by him to the bank upon those three accounts, being the balance of the whole three taken together. That would have been independent of any question of set-off and mutual credit.

Blackburn J was speaking of the position at the time of the bankruptcy. At that time he considered that there was one debt for the balance of the three accounts, and this was independent of any question of set-off under the bankruptcy legislation. Moreover, there is nothing in the report to suggest that there had been an act of combination at that time. On the contrary, the comments of Blackburn J suggest otherwise. Nor, one imagines, would the trustee in bankruptcy have regarded it as being in the interests of the estate to effect a combination, if indeed an act of combination was thought to be necessary in order to produce a single debt, since the bank rather than the customer was insolvent.

15.08   Subsequently, James LJ considered *Bailey v Finch* in *Ex p Morier, re Willis, Percival, & Co*,[33] his Lordship commenting in relation to that case:[34]

> There all the judges start with this . . . that really *in point of law* there was but one account, and there was no debt except upon taking the two accounts together. The mere fact of the two accounts being put upon different pages of the ledger could have no more effect than if an account had gone over from one page of the bank's ledger to another, or than if a man, as a mere matter of account, had kept different accounts, such as a farm account, a colliery account, or a house account, merely for his own convenience for ascertaining how moneys came in and how they had been applied.

James LJ described the notion, that there was no debt except upon taking the two accounts together, as the position 'in point of law'. It was not intended to be a description of the position that applied as a matter of substance, based on a notion that the bank could have set off the accounts at any time without notice to produce a single account.[35] Nor was James LJ's opinion on the point recently formed. Some seven years earlier, in *Re European Bank. Agra Bank Claim*,[36] he said, in a judgment with which Mellish LJ agreed, that: 'It was only for convenience that the loan account was kept separately . . . In truth, as between banker and customer, whatever number of accounts are kept in the books, the whole is really but one account . . .'

---

[32] (1871) LR 7 QB 34, 40.
[33] (1879) 12 Ch D 491.
[34] (1879) 12 Ch D 491, 498–9 (emphasis added).
[35] Compare para. 15.05 above.
[36] (1872) LR 8 Ch App 41, 44, referred to with approval in *Re Keever* [1967] 1 Ch 182, 190, *Pertamina Energy Trading Ltd v Credit Suisse* [2006] SGCA 27 at [43] and *Re Shoreville Mandalay Ltd* [1993] MCLR 122, 135 (NZ CA).

In *Ex p Douglas*,[37] Luxmoore J adopted James LJ's statement in *Ex p Morier*, although not **15.09**
in the context of banker and customer. A partnership had lent some money to a second
partnership, the amount of the loan being carried to a loan account. James Douglas was a
member of both firms, and when he died a general trading account between them showed
a credit balance in favour of the second partnership. Luxmoore J referred to James LJ's judgment as support for the proposition that,[38] 'In law there was in fact at James Douglas's death
but one account between the two firms, and taking the two accounts together, there was no
debt.' Once again, that was regarded as the position *in law*. At the date of the death, when
there had not been any purported act of combination, there was nevertheless only one debt
for the balance.

Consider *Mutton v Peat*.[39] Stockbrokers had two accounts with a bank, a current account **15.10**
with a credit balance of £1,362 10s. and a loan account upon which they owed £7,500. In
addition, the brokers had deposited some bonds by way of security for their indebtedness
to the bank. When the brokers ceased trading the bank made a point of carrying the credit
balance on the current account to a separate liquidation account, rather than applying it in
reduction of the loan account, and it was argued that the security applied only to the loan
account without taking into account the credit account.[40] In this case the bank had gone
out of its way to avoid setting off the accounts, but Lindley MR in the leading judgment
did not regard the bank's action as significant. He said[41] that the amount of the indebtedness secured by the bonds was:

> the amount, taking the deposit account[42] and current account together (you cannot separate
> them), which is due to the bankers on the two accounts. With that amount his bonds must
> stand charged. I do not care how the bankers may have manipulated their books or how
> many accounts they may have kept. When you come to ascertain what is the amount due
> from [the brokers] to the bankers the question admits of only one solution – it is the balance
> due on the loan account after deducting the 1362*l* 10*s*.

The amount due represented the debt on the basis of combination of accounts.[43] In
Halesowen Presswork & Assemblies Ltd v Westminster Bank Ltd,[44] Lord Denning sought to
explain *Mutton v Peat* on the ground that a customer has the right to call upon the bank

---

[37] [1930] 1 Ch 342.
[38] [1930] 1 Ch 342, 349.
[39] [1900] 2 Ch 79.
[40] The bank had sold the bonds. However, unknown to the bank, the bonds were not the property of the
stockbrokers but belonged to clients. Similarly, once again unknown to the bank, some of the money paid into
the current account was clients' money. The plaintiff was a client whose bonds had been deposited as security.
He sought a declaration that the balance remaining in the hands of the bank represented the net proceeds of
sale of the bonds, and that he was entitled to have paid to him so much of those moneys as represented the
purchase moneys received for his bonds. The money remaining would only have included money belonging
to him if the bonds were provided as security for the general indebtedness of the brokers to the bank, and not
merely the indebtedness on the loan account. The defendants, on the other hand, included a client whose
money had been paid into the current account. He argued, unsuccessfully, that the security related only to the
loan account, so that the current account, into which his money could be traced, remained untouched.
[41] [1900] 2 Ch 79, 85.
[42] This should refer to the loan account.
[43] See the discussion of *Mutton v Peat* in *Halesowen Presswork & Assemblies Ltd v Westminster Bank Ltd*
[1971] 1 QB 1, 22 (Roskill J, at first instance), 34 (Lord Denning MR), 42 (Winn LJ), 46 (Buckley LJ).
[44] [1971] 1 QB 1, 34.

to combine accounts, while on another occasion Mocatta J referred to it as a case in which the bank was obliged to combine.[45] In truth, the case was not decided on those grounds. Rather, Lindley MR proceeded on the basis that an act of combination was not necessary, since there was in any event only one debt for the balance. Consistent with that view, Rigby LJ in *Mutton v Peat* considered that the correct analysis was that the bank was bound to allow the credit balance in account in determining the indebtedness, rather than that they ought to have appropriated it in reduction of the loan.[46]

15.11   The next case is *Garnett v M'Kewan*.[47] A customer had an account in credit at one branch of a bank and another account in debit at another branch. The bank transferred the debit balance in reduction of the credit account, and refused to honour cheques drawn on that account. The Court of Exchequer held that the bank was entitled to do so. There was in this case an act of combination, but the later explanation of the decision by the Privy Council in *Prince v Oriental Bank Corporation*[48] suggests that it did not turn on that point. Sir Montague Smith, in delivering the judgment of the Privy Council,[49] said of *Garnett v M'Kewan* that:[50]

> [T]he Court held that money of the Plaintiff lodged at one branch, and being still there to the credit of his account, was to be treated as part of the customer's entire account with the bank, and that the whole account was to be looked at to see on which side as between him and the bank the balance stood.

Consistent with that observation, Bramwell B in *Garnett v M'Kewan*[51] said that: 'the customer has no claim, for he is indebted to the bank on his whole account in such an amount as to reduce his assets to almost nothing.' Martin B referred to the account in credit as an 'apparent balance'. He said that:[52] 'the mere existence of an apparent balance, if there is no real balance, is not enough to render the bank liable to pay a cheque at the branch where the apparent balance is.' Similarly Pigott B referred to the bank 'taking into account the state of the plaintiff's balance as a whole . . .'.[53] According to Kelly CB:[54] 'The question substantially raised by the pleadings is whether any money of the plaintiff's was in the hands of the London and County Bank', which captures the essence of the principle underlying combination.

---

[45] *Barclays Bank Ltd v Okenarhe* [1966] 2 Lloyd's Rep 87, 95–6. See also *Ellinger's Modern Banking Law* (4th edn, 2006), 248.

[46] Rigby LJ commented: 'I think we are bound to say that the bankers ought to have appropriated the 1362*l* 10*s* in reduction of the 7500*l* loan, or perhaps it would be more correct to say that they were bound to allow the 1362*l* 10*s* in account whether they appropriated it or not, and even if they endeavoured not to appropriate it. The security was given for the indebtedness of [the stockbrokers] to the bankers and for nothing else, and that indebtedness was the 7500*l* minus the 1362*l* 10*s*, and that only.' See [1900] 2 Ch 79, 86.

[47] (1872) LR 8 Ex 10.

[48] (1878) 3 App Cas 325.

[49] Sir James Colville, Sir Barnes Peacock, Sir Montague Smith and Sir Robert Collier.

[50] (1878) 3 App Cas 325, 333.

[51] (1872) LR 8 Ex 10, 15.

[52] (1872) LR 8 Ex 10, 13–14.

[53] (1872) LR 8 Ex 10, 14.

[54] (1872) LR 8 Ex 10, 12.

More recently, the view that combination is a matter of account rather than a set-off of **15.12** debts was emphasized by Buckley LJ in the Court of Appeal in the *Halesowen* case:[55]

> Where the relationship of the banker and customer is a single relationship . . . albeit embodied in a number of accounts, the situation is not, in my judgment, a situation of lien at all. A lien postulates property of the debtor in the possession or under the control of the creditor. Nor is it a set-off situation, which postulates mutual but independent obligations between the two parties. It is an accounting situation, in which the existence and amount of one party's liability to the other can only be ascertained by discovering the ultimate balance of their mutual dealings.

Millett J referred to that passage with evident approval in *Re Charge Card Services Ltd*,[56] as did Otton J in *Re K (Restraint Order)*.[57] In the latter case, Otton J said[58] that combination: 'is a means of establishing the indebtedness of the customer to the bank and the bank to the customer.' He went on to observe that the bank in exercising the right: 'is merely carrying out an accounting procedure so as to ascertain the existence and amount of one party's liability to the other. This can only be ascertained by discovering the ultimate balance of their mutual dealing.'[59]

A similar position has been adopted in other jurisdictions. In Scotland, Lord Dunedin in **15.13** *James Kirkwood & Sons v Clydesdale Bank*,[60] in a judgment with which Lord Kinnear, Lord M'Laren and Lord Pearson concurred, observed that, 'the state of affairs between a banker and his customer as at any given time must be taken to be the state of affairs upon all the accounts',[61] and that 'upon a true accounting between the parties concerned there were no funds in the hands of the Clydesdale Bank belonging to this gentleman'.[62] In Ireland, Sir Andrew Porter MR posed the question, 'Now what is the meaning of a No. 2 account? It no doubt often means that the account refers to another subject-matter or department of business for mere convenience, but is not otherwise legally separate from the No. 1 account of the customer . . .'[63] In Northern Ireland, Black CJ adopted a similar view in *Clark v Ulster Bank Ltd*,[64] commenting:[65] 'The balance at credit of No. 2 account was merely one of the elements to be taken into account in conjunction with the balance at debit of No. 1 Account in computing the indebtedness between Mr Clark and the bank.'

---

[55] [1971] 1 QB 1, 46. See also his earlier comments in *Re E J Morel (1934) Ltd* [1962] 1 Ch 21, 32.
[56] [1987] 1 Ch 150, 173–4. See also *Wade v Grimwood* [2004] EWCA Civ 999 at [12] (Sir Martin Nourse).
[57] [1990] 2 QB 298, 303. While Otton J referred (at 305) to the account in credit itself as a chose in action, that was in the context of a discussion of the bank's rights arising under a letter of set-off as opposed to common law combination.
[58] [1990] 2 QB 298, 304.
[59] The bank in this case had a letter of set-off empowering it to set off the accounts, but the comments related to the position apart from the letter. See [1990] 2 QB 298, 304–5.
[60] [1908] SC 20.
[61] [1908] SC 20, 24.
[62] [1908] SC 20, 25.
[63] *Re Johnson & Company Ltd* [1902] 1 IR 439, 442. Sir Andrew Porter continued: 'and in such cases the balance on the one account can be set off against the other.' Having made the point that the accounts are not legally separate, it is suggested that he meant by that comment an accounting exercise in order to ascertain the balance, as opposed to a set-off of independent debts.
[64] [1950] NILR 132, 142–3.
[65] [1950] NILR 132, 143.

15.14 This is also the position in Canada. Indeed, Middleton JA in the Ontario Court of Appeal in *Re Sutcliffe & Sons Ltd, ex p Royal Bank*[66] could not have expressed the principle in clearer terms when he said, in the context of a loan account with a debit balance in excess of the credit balance on a current account, that: 'the fact that there were two accounts kept by the bank is utterly immaterial. There was in law but one account to be ascertained by bringing all items into consideration. The bank is not and never was, in this case, a debtor in any sense. It was and is a creditor.'[67] Canadian courts have adopted this approach on other occasions.[68]

15.15 The principle has also been recognized in both New Zealand[69] and Australia,[70] with McPherson JA in the Queensland Court of Appeal in *Re Bank of Queensland Ltd*[71] referring to the principle described by Buckley LJ in *Halesowen* (above) as the 'single indebtedness' principle. Observations in the New South Wales Court of Appeal in *Cinema Plus Ltd v Australia and New Zealand Banking Group Ltd*[72] also support that view. Sheller JA in that case said that: 'Strictly the consolidation or combination may be regarded as a matter of account rather than set off. The balance of all such accounts represents the debt . . .'[73] Similarly, Giles JA commented in relation to combination that: 'It is necessary that there be "really but one account" . . .'[74]

(3) Cases supporting the contrary view

15.16 There are nevertheless statements to be found in the cases that support the contrary view.[75] In New Zealand, Conolly J suggested that, until the accounts were amalgamated, they had

---

[66] [1933] 1 DLR 562.

[67] [1933] 1 DLR 562, 569.

[68] *Ross v Royal Bank of Canada* (1965) 52 DLR (2d) 578; *Re T. C. Marines Ltd* (1973) 34 DLR (3d) 489. See also *Deep v Bank of Montreal* (1991) 47 OAC 319. Compare *Royal Trust Co v Molsons Bank* (1912) 8 DLR 478, in which it was assumed that an act of combination was required.

[69] *Re Shoreville Mandalay Ltd* [1993] MCLR 122, 135 (NZ CA). See also *Horton v Bank of New Zealand* (1889) 7 NZLR 582, 591 (although in that case the several accounts were opened at the instance of the bank for convenience of bookkeeping).

[70] In addition to the following, see Hood J in *Mercantile Bank of Australia Ltd v Weigall* (1895) 16 ALT 192, 193 ('As a matter of fact the two accounts were really one, though kept separate in the bank books'); *Re Tonkin* (1938) 6 ABC 197, 210; *Re Deague* (1951) 15 ABC 197, 202; *Matthews v Geraghty* (1986) 43 SASR 576, 580 *per* King CJ ('The allocation of moneys which the customer has advanced to the bank between various accounts is, in the absence of special contract, a mere matter of mutual convenience').

[71] [1997] 2 Qd R 129, 137–8.

[72] (2000) 49 NSWLR 513.

[73] (2000) 49 NSWLR 513 at [116], referring to *Re Charge Card Services Ltd* [1987] 1 Ch 150, 173–4 (where Millett J quoted with evident approval Buckley LJ in *Halesowen Presswork & Assemblies Ltd v Westminster Bank Ltd* [1971] 1 QB 1, 46 (see para. 15.12 above)). Earlier in his judgment in the *Cinema Plus* case (at [113]) Sheller JA commented that a banker 'has a *prima facie* right in law to combine the accounts of a customer and set off debits against credits', which is consistent with an accounting exercise in order to ascertain the balance of the account as between banker and customer, as opposed to a set-off of independent debts.

[74] (2000) 49 NSWLR 513 at [142], referring to *Re European Bank* (1872) LR 8 Ch App 41, 44 (see above).

[75] In addition to the cases referred to below, see *Barclays Bank Ltd v TOSG Trust Fund Ltd* [1984] BCLC 1, 23, in which Nourse J referred to 'the process of debits and credits which were necessary to combine the accounts', though one of the four accounts in that case related to a separate company, and so it could only have been combined with the other three as a result of the letter of set-off which contemplated an act of combination. Similarly, in *Royal Bank of Scotland Plc v Wallace International Ltd* [2000] EWCA Civ 16 the set-off involved accounts of a number of companies, and it appears (see at [8] and [48]) that a contractual right was

to be considered as separate,[76] and Hawkins J in *York City and County Banking Co v Bainbridge*[77] seemed to be of the same opinion. Reference also may be made to *Barclays Bank Ltd v Okenarhe*,[78] in which Mocatta J in an unreserved judgment assumed that an act of combination was required.[79] Further, the courts and text-writers have been accustomed to refer to combination as a right of set-off,[80] or a right in a bank to consolidate or combine accounts.[81] This includes Roskill J at first instance[82] and Lord Denning MR and Winn LJ in the Court of Appeal in the *Halesowen* case,[83] while in the House of Lords in that case Viscount Dilhorne, Lord Cross of Chelsea and Lord Kilbrandon each used language suggestive of a right or a power in the bank to consolidate or combine.[84] Expressions such as these may suggest that, in the absence of an exercise of the right or power, the accounts represent separate debts. It is true that Winn LJ in the *Halesowen* case doubted that a number of accounts could be said to give rise to a single account.[85] But apart from that, when it was said in the *Halesowen* case that a bank has a right to combine or consolidate accounts, there was no criticism of the explanation put forward by Buckley LJ in the Court of Appeal

---

in issue. In *Box v Barclays Bank* [1998] Lloyd's Rep Bank 185, 202 Ferris J assumed that an overdrawn No. 1 account was separate from other accounts in credit, but there was little discussion (see at 188) of the nature of the accounts and moreover the nature of the right of 'set-off' was not explored. In New South Wales, Hodgson J in *Hamilton v Commonwealth Bank of Australia* (1992) 9 ACSR 90, 106–7 assumed that an act of combination was required, although that view also seems to have been a consequence of an agreement between the parties. In particular, the loan was not repayable until 15 January 1989, and Hodgson J (at 107) referred to the 'understanding' between the customer (Skinnys) and the bank which would have enabled the bank to dishonour cheques prior to that date.

[76] *National Bank of New Zealand v Grace* (1890) 8 NZLR 706. Compare the comments of Richmond J in *Horton v Bank of New Zealand* (1889) 7 NZLR 582, 591, which accord with orthodoxy. The decision in *National Bank of New Zealand v Grace* in any event may be explained on another ground. The question was whether interest had to be calculated on the net position, but the single debt theory does not require that result before the bank has given effect to the combination in its books by an appropriate entry. See para. 15.20 below.

[77] (1880) 43 LT 732, 734.

[78] [1966] 2 Lloyd's Rep 87.

[79] See Mocatta J's discussion of events at [1966] 2 Lloyd's Rep 87, 90.

[80] See e.g. *Ex p Kingston, re Gross* (1871) LR 6 Ch App 632; *Garnett v M'Kewan* (1872) LR 8 Ex 10, 12, 13 (Kelly CB), 14 (Pigott B); *Bank of New South Wales v Goulburn Valley Butter Co Pty Ltd* [1902] AC 543, 550 (PC); *Re Morris, deceased; Coneys v Morris* [1922] 1 IR 136; *Re Shaw; ex p Andrew v Australia and New Zealand Banking Group Ltd* (1977) 31 FLR 118, 122; *Oceanica Castelana Armadora SA v Mineralimportexport* [1983] 1 WLR 1294; Pennington, Hudson and Mann, *Commercial Banking Law* (1978), 29; *Goode on Legal Problems of Credit and Security* (4th edn (ed. Gullifer), 2008), 295–7; Holden, *The Law and Practice of Banking* (5th edn, 1991) vol. 1, 71; Wood, *English and International Set-off* (1989), 93; *Ellinger's Modern Banking Law* (4th edn, 2006), 233; *Paget's Law of Banking* (13th edn, 2007), 713 (but see the explanation of the principle at 714–15 and 720–1).

[81] See e.g. *Re E J Morel (1934) Ltd* [1962] 1 Ch 21, 30; *Barclays Bank Ltd v Okenarhe* [1966] 2 Lloyd's Rep 87, 95; *Direct Acceptance Corporation Ltd v Bank of New South Wales* (1968) 88 WN (Pt 1) (NSW) 498, 504; *Matthews v Geraghty* (1986) 43 SASR 576, 580; *Welsh Development Agency v Export Finance Co Ltd* [1992] BCLC 148, 167. In *Inglis v Commonwealth Trading Bank of Australia* (1973) 47 ALJR 234, 234–5, Mason J referred to a right to consolidate accounts, but that was following termination of an agreement to keep the accounts separate. See paras 15.29–15.31 below.

[82] [1971] 1 QB 1, 19. Roskill J regarded combination as a manifestation of or a right analogous to the banker's right of lien. See, however, para. 15.03 above.

[83] [1971] 1 QB 1, 34, 35 (Lord Denning), 38 (Winn LJ).

[84] [1972] AC 785, 807 (Viscount Dilhorne), 810 (Lord Cross of Chelsea), 819–20 (Lord Kilbrandon).

[85] [1971] 1 QB 1, 40.

in that case, and in other cases which pre-dated the *Halesowen* case,[86] to the effect that the principle is based on the view that the debt at any particular time is the balance of all the accounts. In truth, the nature of the principle of combination was not considered by the House of Lords.

15.17 In so far as the cases may refer to a right or a power to set off or consolidate or combine, a number of points may be made. In the first place, they may in some instances have contemplated an accounting exercise, in other words a process of setting off debits against credits[87] as an accounting procedure for the purpose of calculating the amount owing, as opposed to a set-off of independent debts, together with the right to take action consequent upon the state of that account, for example the dishonouring of a cheque. Secondly, the bank may give effect to the principle of combination in its books,[88] and while that in itself does not involve a payment of one account by the use of another, because there was in any event one debt, it does have significance for some purposes, in particular for the calculation of interest and the application of *Clayton's Case*. In that sense, the entry made in the bank's books may be said to constitute the exercise of a 'right'. Thirdly, *Halesowen* was a case in which there was an agreement that the accounts should be kept separate, although the bank could put an end to the agreement in the event of a material change of circumstances. If there were materially changed circumstances, the question of termination of the agreement, and of a consequential combination or consolidation of the accounts, would have involved the exercise of a right or power by the bank.[89] While some of the comments in the House of Lords in the *Halesowen* case in relation to combination were expressed generally,[90] they should nevertheless be considered with these points in mind.[91]

C. Criticisms

15.18 This analysis of combination has been said to be inconsistent with many of the features of bank accounts,[92] although in truth any difficulty is more apparent than real. In particular, some of the criticisms assume that statements by judges to the effect that all the accounts constitute a single account were intended to refer to the operation of the accounts, and not just to the ascertainment of the debt at any particular time. The important point is that the accounts are not treated as one for all purposes. While the existence and the amount of the debt owing by the bank or the customer to the other can only be ascertained by looking at the balance of all the accounts together, for some purposes the accounts retain their separate identities until the bank effects a physical combination in its books.[93]

---

[86] See above.
[87] See the language used in *Matthews v Geraghty* (1986) 43 SASR 576, 580 and *Cinema Plus Ltd v Australia and New Zealand Banking Group Ltd* (2000) 49 NSWLR 513 at [113] (Sheller JA).
[88] See para. 15.05 above.
[89] See also para. 15.30 below.
[90] See Lord Cross of Chelsea and Lord Kilbrandon [1972] AC 785, 810, 819–20.
[91] In relation to the third point, see in particular Viscount Dilhorne at [1972] AC 785, 807.
[92] Wood, *English and International Set-off* (1989), 93; Salter, 'Remedies for banks: an outline of English law' in Blair (ed.), *Banks and Remedies* (2nd edn, 1999), 52.
[93] See para. 15.05 above.

As a preliminary point, one effect of the view that there is at any particular time a single **15.19** debt would be that an account could not be sued for separately if there is a second account which reduces or cancels the balance on the first,[94] unless it has been separated out by agreement. This is unlikely to have any practical significance, however. Neither the bank nor the customer is likely to suffer an action against it in such a case. Whether the defence is based upon the notion that there is only one debt or upon a set-off, the result would be the same. A similar comment may be made in respect of the argument that an account may be assigned or garnished.[95] The assignee or the creditor would take subject to equities,[96] including rights of set-off, so that the theory that combination operates as a set-off would produce the same result in any event as the view that it is simply an accounting exercise.

(1) Interest

Before accounts are combined in the bank's books,[97] interest is calculated ordinarily on the **15.20** balance of each account, without reference to the balance on any other account. This method of calculating interest, however, is not inconsistent with the suggested explanation of combination.[98] The parties can agree that interest is to be calculated on whatever basis they choose, and the bank and its customer ordinarily would contract on the basis that, while an account retains its separate identity in the bank's books,[99] interest is to be calculated by reference to the balance on that account.[100]

(2) *Clayton's Case*, and the order of combination

Nor is the notion that combination is a matter of accounting rather than of set-off incon- **15.21** sistent with the application of *Clayton's Case*[101] to each of the accounts. The accounting simply goes to the question whether, and to what extent, there is a debt owing at any particular time by one party to the other in their banking relationship. This does not impact upon how debits and credits are treated within an account. If a customer pays an amount to the credit of one of a number of current accounts, *Clayton's Case* operates so as to appropriate the payment to the earliest drawing on that account, as opposed to the earliest drawing on the accounts taken together.[102] Any other result would be contrary to

---

[94] Compare Wood, *English and International Set-off* (1989), 93.

[95] *Ibid.*

[96] See paras 17.02–17.98 below (assignment) and paras 17.136–17.145 below (third party debt (or garnishee) order).

[97] See para. 15.05 above.

[98] Compare *Pott v Clegg* (1847) 16 M & W 321, 327, 153 ER 1212, 1214 (Parke B, *arguendo*).

[99] Compare *Royal Trust Co v Molsons Bank* (1912) 8 DLR 478. Assuming that the promissory notes came to the bank as part of the banker/customer relationship (see paras 15.41–15.47 below), *Royal Trust Co v Molson* would have been correctly decided if (as Falconbridge CJKB postulated, at 480) the bank were regarded as having applied the deposit against the indebtedness on the notes.

[100] See *Barclays Bank Ltd v Okenarhe* [1966] 2 Lloyd's Rep 87, 98. Compare *National Bank of New Zealand v Grace* (1890) 8 NZLR 706 (esp. at 712), in which Conolly J, in holding that interest is payable on an overdrawn account without reference to a credit balance on another account, assumed that, until the accounts were closed and the balance sued for, the accounts had to be considered as separate accounts for all purposes.

[101] (1816) 1 Mer 572, 35 ER 781.

[102] *Horton v Bank of New Zealand* (1889) 7 NZLR 582, 593–4 (Richmond J having accepted (at 591) that the accounts in law were combined); *Re Yeovil Glove Co Ltd* [1963] 1 Ch 528, 543 (affirmed [1965] 1 Ch 148); *Re James R Rutherford & Sons Ltd* [1964] 1 WLR 1211, 1216–17. See also the formulation of the principle by

the presumed intention of the parties, which is the basis of *Clayton's Case*.[103] The parties nevertheless may have expressed an intention that *Clayton's Case* is not to be applied in that manner, or there may be special circumstances from which such an intention may be implied, in which case appropriation of payments will be dealt with in accordance with their intention.[104] An illustration is *Re E J Morel (1934) Ltd*.[105] In that case, drawings on a No. 3 account were regarded as having come from a credit balance on a No. 2 account. The circumstances were exceptional, however. A drawing could not be made from the No. 3 account unless the No. 2 account had a credit balance sufficient to cover it, so that they were interdependent and, in substance, were the one account.[106]

15.22 The question of how accounts are to be appropriated in relation to combination may arise in some circumstances.[107] Consider that two accounts, a No. 1 account and a No. 2 account, are in debit, while a third No. 3 account has a credit balance. At any particular time the customer's or the bank's debt to the other can be ascertained only by looking at the balance of all three accounts, and the ascertainment of the balance does not depend upon the order in which the accounts are set against each other. However, the bank is entitled to give effect to the principle of combination in its books by moving assets and liabilities from one account to another, unless there is an express or an implied agreement to the contrary,[108] and it is at that point that the question of the order of the combination may arise. In the example, does the credit balance on the No. 3 account reduce first the No. 1 account or the No. 2 account? While the bank's book entry itself would not constitute a payment, since there was in any event only one debt for the balance,[109] it could affect issues such as the calculation of interest and the application of *Clayton's Case* in relation to future debits and credits. In *Re E J Morel (1934) Ltd*,[110] Buckley J (as he then was) said that the bank can combine the accounts in whatever way it chooses, a view that was also accepted by Nourse J at first instance in *Barclays Bank Ltd v TOSG Trust Fund Ltd*.[111] That view would seem to be correct. It is consistent with the rules applicable to appropriation of payments. If a debtor makes a payment to a creditor to whom the debtor owes a number of debts, the debtor can appropriate the payment to which ever of the debts he or she chooses. But if the debtor does not make an appropriation, the right of appropriation devolves upon the creditor.[112] Similarly, when a customer has a number of accounts with a bank, the customer has the opportunity to appropriate the accounts in a particular way.

---

the Earl of Selborne in *Re Sherry* (1884) 25 Ch D 692, 702. Compare *Mutton v Peat* [1899] 2 Ch 556 (reversed [1900] 2 Ch 79).

[103] See *Re Hallett's Estate* (1880) 13 Ch D 696, 738–9.

[104] *Re Hallett's Estate* (1880) 13 Ch D 696, 738–9.

[105] [1962] 1 Ch 21. See para. 15.59 below.

[106] Compare the arrangement adopted in *Re James R Rutherford & Sons Ltd* [1964] 1 WLR 1211.

[107] See e.g. the discussion of time bars in paras 15.36–15.40 below.

[108] See para. 15.05 above.

[109] *Re Sutcliffe & Sons Ltd, ex p Royal Bank* [1933] 1 DLR 562 (esp. at 569); *Ross v Royal Bank of Canada* (1965) 52 DLR (2d) 578; *Re T. C. Marines Ltd* (1973) 34 DLR (3d) 489; *Re Plasky* (1981) 39 WWR 186.

[110] [1962] 1 Ch 21, 31–2.

[111] [1984] BCLC 1, 22.

[112] *Cory Bros & Co Ltd v The Owners of the Turkish Steamship 'Mecca' (The Mecca)* [1897] AC 286.

If the customer does not do so, the bank should be able to choose how to apply the accounts in a combination, given that *Clayton's Case* does not apply as between accounts.

It is true that Walton J in *Re Unit 2 Windows Ltd*[113] held that, when there is a claim going **15.23** one way and two cross-claims going the other, or, as in that case, one cross-claim which is partly preferential and partly non-preferential in the liquidation of the debtor, the set-off should occur rateably as between the cross-claims. *Re Unit 2 Windows*, however, was decided on the basis of the interpretation of the set-off section in the insolvency legislation. When common law principles of combination are in issue, as opposed to a question of statutory interpretation, the position at common law regarding appropriation of payments would appear to provide the appropriate analogy. Nor would the principles ever conflict. If, as a matter of the law of combination, there is only one debt for the balance, the insolvency set-off section would not apply. The set-off section requires mutual but independent obligations, whereas under the principle of combination there is only one obligation.[114]

(3) Guarantees and securities

A guarantee may be given in respect of a customer's indebtedness. If the customer has two **15.24** accounts with the bank, one in debit and the other in credit, it would be to the advantage of the guarantor if the two accounts were combined so as to produce a single debt for the balance. The guarantor's liability in such a case would be reduced.[115] Alternatively, a customer may have provided security to a bank for his or her indebtedness to the bank, and the customer has one account with a debit balance and another in credit. The question whether the debt secured is the balance of the two accounts taken together,[116] or whether regard is to be had only to the account in debit,[117] would depend principally on the terms of the security, but it could also depend on whether the accounts are combined.[118] In relation to these issues, a number of general comments may be made. In the first place, it may be relevant to consider whether the circumstances surrounding the provision of the guarantee or the security in relation to a particular account evidence an agreement that that account is to be separated from other accounts.[119] Alternatively, notwithstanding the principle of combination, there is no reason why a guarantee or a security in its terms

---

[113] [1985] 1 WLR 1383. See para. 6.171 above.

[114] See Buckley LJ in *Halesowen Presswork & Assemblies Ltd v Westminster Bank Ltd* [1971] 1 QB 1, 46.

[115] See e.g. *Re Tonkin* (1933) 6 ABC 197, 210–11. Compare *York City and County Banking Co v Bainbridge* (1880) 43 LT 732, in which a surety's liability in respect of a loan made to a customer was not reduced by a credit balance on the customer's current account, since the accounts were separate. In that regard, there is usually an implied agreement that a loan account and a current account are to be kept separate. See para. 15.54 below.

[116] As in *Re European Bank. Agra Bank Claim* (1872) LR 8 Ch App 41 and *Mutton v Peat* [1900] 2 Ch 79. See also *Horton v Bank of New Zealand* (1889) 7 NZLR 582; *Re Sherry* (1884) 25 Ch D 693, 706; *National Bank of Nigeria Ltd v Awolesi* [1964] 1 WLR 1311, 1316–17.

[117] See *Royal Bank of Canada v Bank of Montreal* [1976] 4 WWR 721, although it is unclear whether the current account in fact had a credit balance.

[118] In *Stannard v National Bank of New Zealand Ltd* (1986) 3 NZCLC 99,510 there were three accounts in debit (an overdrawn current account and two term loans), and the question was whether security provided to the bank was confined to the current account or whether it extended to all the accounts on the basis that the accounts were combined. See also *Bradford Old Bank Ltd v Sutcliffe* [1918] 2 KB 833 (below).

[119] This may apply in particular where an account in credit is charged back to the bank. See para. 16.89 below. The giving of separate securities to a bank in relation to two or more accounts may indicate that

could not be confined to a particular account, treating it for the purpose of the guarantee or the security as if it were a separate debt.[120] On the other hand, where the accounts would otherwise be regarded as separate, the terms of the guarantee or the security should be examined to see whether, as a matter of construction of the contract, it is in any event only intended to benefit the bank to the extent of any net balance on all the accounts[121] Further, if accounts are separate, and a guarantee is given in respect of the customer's indebtedness on one of the accounts, the customer as the principal debtor would have a defence of set-off under the Statutes of Set-off to the extent of the credit balance on the second account if he or she was sued for payment of the debit balance on the first account. The guarantor in that situation might also be able to rely on the principal debtor's defence in an action on the guarantee[122] (although the question whether a guarantor is entitled to rely on the principal debtor's defence under the Statutes remains uncertain[123]). It may also be the case that a guarantee in its terms contemplates a single unbroken account so that, if the bank permits the principal debtor to open a second account into which credit funds are deposited, the guarantor may be prejudiced so as to discharge him or her from the guarantee.[124]

15.25   The question of combination in the context of a guarantee arose in *Bradford Old Bank Ltd v Sutcliffe*.[125] A bank provided a fixed loan and a current account with an overdraft limit to a company, supported by a guarantee from the directors. One of the directors subsequently became insane. This had the consequence that the guarantee ceased to be continuing in relation to that guarantor, so that it only extended to debts in existence at that date. The company nevertheless continued to operate the current account for a number of years, when a demand was made on the guarantee. The current account was overdrawn, but in accordance with *Clayton's Case*[126] payments into the current account during the intervening period had had the effect of satisfying the debt on that account as it stood when the guarantee ceased to be continuing. The director, therefore, was no longer liable under the guarantee in relation to the current account. In so far as the loan account was concerned, the Court of Appeal held that there was an implied agreement that it was to be kept separate from the current account.[127] The amount owing on the loan account, therefore, was not satisfied by subsequent payments into the current account, and the guarantor remained liable for the debt on that account. A curious aspect of the case is that it seems to have been assumed that, if the accounts had not been separate, *Clayton's Case* would have operated on

---

the accounts are to be treated as separate. See *Lloyds Bank NZA Ltd v National Safety Council* [1993] 2 VR 506, 523.

[120] In *Re Bank of Queensland Ltd* [1997] 2 Qd R 129, 137 McPherson JA said that: 'the principle [of combination] applies in relation to cases in which the bank holds securities for one only of two accounts.'

[121] See the discussion of *Mutton v Peat* [1900] 2 Ch 79 in para. 15.10 above.

[122] Compare *York City and County Banking Co v Bainbridge* (1880) 43 LT 732.

[123] See paras 18.27–18.29 below.

[124] *National Bank of Nigeria Ltd v Awolesi* [1964] 1 WLR 1311. If the guarantee on its proper construction permits the opening of a second account, so as to cover all such accounts, the Privy Council in *National Bank of Nigeria v Awolesi* considered that the guarantor may still be discharged if the accounts are allowed to be operated so as to increase the burden on the guarantor, for example in the calculation of interest.

[125] [1918] 2 KB 833.

[126] (1816) 1 Mer 572, 35 ER 781.

[127] See para. 15.54 below.

the basis that payments into the current account would have reduced the loan account, but it is suggested that that would not have been the case. *Clayton's Case* ordinarily should be confined in its operation to an individual account notwithstanding the principle of combination.[128]

A similar situation occurred in *Re Sherry*.[129] A bank provided an overdraft to a customer **15.26** secured by a guarantee. The guarantor died, whereupon the guarantee was determined as to future advances. The bank accordingly closed the account, and opened a new account to which subsequent payments in were credited and drawings debited. When the guarantee was later enforced, it was held that *Clayton's Case* did not apply so as to appropriate the payments credited to the second account in reduction of the guaranteed debt on the first account. Nor was it a term of the guarantee that payments received from the debtor should be regarded as appropriated in that manner. *Re Sherry* is not inconsistent with the notion that combination is a matter of account.[130] The fact that *Clayton's Case* was applied only in relation to the second account does not show any inconsistency.[131] Further, the second account had a debit balance so that, even assuming that the case was one in which there was a single debt between banker and customer represented by the balance of both accounts, there was no account in credit which could have had the effect of reducing the guaranteed debt.[132]

A bank has a lien on cheques and other securities deposited with it,[133] which should include **15.27** a right to apply the proceeds against the customer's debt to the bank.[134] The lien is applicable in respect of the balance on all accounts between the bank and the customer, including a loan account.[135]

(4) Notice of combination

It has been suggested that the question may still be open as to whether a bank may be **15.28** required to give notice before exercising its combination rights, and that any such requirement would be inconsistent with the view that at any particular time there is only one debt.[136] The answer is that there is no requirement of notice for combination as such, and

---

[128] See para. 15.21 above. The current account was overdrawn, but if the current account had had a credit balance when the proceeding commenced which exceeded the loan, and if the current account and the loan account had not been separate so as to preclude combination, the principle of combination would have dictated that the company would not have been indebted to the bank, and the bank therefore could not have sued the director on the guarantee.

[129] (1884) 25 Ch D 692. See also *Kirby v Duke of Marlborough* (1813) 2 M & S 18, 105 ER 289; *Williams v Rawlinson* (1825) 3 Bing 71, 130 ER 440.

[130] Compare Wood, *English and International Set-off* (1989), 93 (referring to para. 10–223).

[131] See para. 15.21 above.

[132] Compare *Hollond v Teed* (1848) 7 Hare 50, 68 ER 20 (explained in *Re Sherry* (1884) 25 Ch D 692, 704–5). In that case there was a balance standing to the credit of an account at the date the guarantee determined. However, at that date the outstanding bills of exchange the subject of the guarantee had not matured, and the amount standing to the credit of the account was withdrawn before maturity. Accordingly, it could not have been a case of combination.

[133] *Re Keever* [1967] 1 Ch 182, 189.

[134] See para. 15.123 below.

[135] *Re Keever* [1967] 1 Ch 182, 190, citing *Re European Bank* (1872) LR 9 Ch App 41.

[136] Salter, 'Remedies for banks: an outline of English law' in Blair (ed.), *Banks and Remedies* (2nd edn, 1999), 52.

nor is the bank obliged to give notice of its intention to rely upon the principle.[137] Accordingly, there is no inconsistency.

15.29 There may, however, be a requirement of notice where there is an agreement between the parties to keep the accounts separate and the bank wishes to terminate the agreement. For example, when a customer has both a current account in credit and a loan account, the courts usually imply an agreement that the accounts are to be kept separate,[138] because otherwise the customer could not safely draw cheques on the current account. Consistent with the view that reasonable notice is required to close a current account in credit,[139] it may be that the agreement can be terminated if reasonable notice is given.[140] The question of reasonableness would depend upon the circumstances of the case,[141] but in any event provision would have to be made for outstanding cheques.[142]

15.30 A similar issue was the subject of discussion in the House of Lords in the *Halesowen* case.[143] The bank in that case had agreed that it would not require repayment of a frozen current account for a period of four months unless there was a material change in circumstances. This gave rise to an implied term that, during the period, the bank would not combine or consolidate the account with another current account in credit. Viscount Dilhorne left open the question whether the bank would have been required to give notice of termination in the event of a material change in circumstances,[144] but Lord Cross of Chelsea inclined to the better view, that notice was required, albeit notice having immediate effect as opposed to reasonable notice.[145] A requirement of reasonable notice would have enabled the customer to defeat the object with which it was given, by immediately withdrawing the funds standing to the credit of the current account. On the other hand, Lord Cross considered that the bank would still have been required to honour cheques drawn before notice up to the limit of the credit balance on the account. The bank's right to terminate the arrangement upon the occurrence of a material change of circumstances carried with it

---

[137] *Garnett v M'Kewan* (1872) LR 8 Ex 10; *Irwin v Bank of Montreal* (1876) 38 UCQB 375, 393; *Wallinder v Imperial Bank of Canada* [1925] 4 DLR 390, 392; *Deep v Bank of Montreal* (1991) 47 OAC 319. See also *Re Shaw* (1977) 31 FLR 118, 122 in relation to a contractual right to set off accounts. Compare *Krishell Pty Ltd v Nilant* (2006) 32 WAR 540 at [105]–[106] in relation to a court order expressed in terms that one party was 'entitled' to set off judgments, and see also para. 16.03 below in relation to a contractual right of set-off.

[138] *Bradford Old Bank Ltd v Sutcliffe* [1918] 2 KB 833. See para. 15.54 below.

[139] *Joachimson v Swiss Bank Corporation* [1921] 3 KB 110, 127; *Tai Hing Cotton Mill Ltd v Liu Chong Hing Bank Ltd* [1986] 1 AC 80, 105. Compare *Paget's Law of Banking* (13th edn, 2007), 213–14 with respect to an overdraft. The Banking Code 2008, para. 7.6 and the Business Banking Code 2008, para. 7.8 provide that, under normal circumstances, a bank will not close an account without giving at least thirty days' notice.

[140] See *Buckingham and Co v London and Midland Bank* (1895) 12 TLR 70, 72, and also *Cumming v Shand* (1860) 5 H & N 95, 157 ER 1114. Compare *Inglis v Commonwealth Trading Bank of Australia* (1973) 47 ALJR 234, in which the current account was overdrawn so that the bank was not obliged to honour further cheques. Mason J accordingly held that the bank could consolidate the accounts without notice, following breach of the agreement by the customer to maintain the working (current) account in credit. Compare also Roskill J at first instance in the *Halesowen* case. See para. 15.55 below.

[141] *Prosperity Ltd v Lloyds Bank Ltd* (1923) 39 TLR 372, 373.

[142] *Joachimson v Swiss Bank Corporation* [1921] 3 KB 110, 125.

[143] [1972] AC 785.

[144] [1972] AC 785, 807.

[145] [1972] AC 785, 810, referring to Buckley LJ in the Court of Appeal [1971] 1 QB 1, 47.

a consequential power to combine the accounts.[146] This would have differed from the ordinary case of combination which does not depend upon termination of an agreement to keep accounts separate, because combination ordinarily operates on the basis that the accounts are combined in a single debt without the exercise of a right or a power.[147]

In a case where an agreement to keep accounts separate is terminated, combination may **15.31** not require a book entry by the bank. An assertion that the accounts are combined may suffice.[148]

(5) The bank's right, and different branches

It is sometimes suggested that the right to combine accounts is a right possessed by the bank **15.32** only, and not the customer,[149] but that in some circumstances the bank may be obliged to combine.[150] The authority generally cited in support of the second of those propositions is *Mutton v Peat*,[151] though this is not an accurate description of the ground upon which the case was decided. In truth, the presence or absence of an act of combination was regarded as irrelevant, because it was considered that there was in any event only one debt for the balance.[152]

In so far as the view that only the bank may combine is concerned, it is based on what has **15.33** been described as the 'apparent anomaly'[153] that arises in relation to accounts at different branches of the same bank. A bank may look upon various accounts as combined notwith-standing that they are kept at separate branches. Thus, a bank may refuse to honour a cheque drawn by a customer on one branch at which the customer has an account in credit if there is a countervailing account in debit at another branch, such that the overall credit balance is insufficient to cover the cheque.[154] On the other hand, when a customer has two current accounts at separate branches, he or she may only draw upon either account to the extent of the balance on the account at the branch where the account is kept. If the customer draws on either account for an amount in excess of the credit balance on that account, or in excess of an agreed overdraft limit, he or she is not entitled to have the cheque honoured on the ground that the combined balance on both accounts is more than

---

[146] See also *Inglis v Commonwealth Trading Bank of Australia* (1973) 47 ALJR 234.
[147] See para. 15.04 above.
[148] See Roskill J at first instance in *Halesowen Presswork & Assemblies Ltd v Westminster Bank Ltd* [1971] 1 QB 1, 19, and also *Direct Acceptance Corporation Ltd v Bank of New South Wales* (1968) 88 WN (Pt 1) (NSW) 498, 502. This also accords with the bank's contention in *Neste Oy v Lloyds Bank plc* [1983] 2 Lloyd's Rep 658, 662–3.
[149] *Barclays Bank Ltd v Okenarhe* [1966] 2 Lloyd's Rep 87, 95; Herzberg, 'Bankers' rights of combination' (1982) 10 *Australian Business Law Review* 79, 82, 83.
[150] *Barclays Bank Ltd v Okenarhe* [1966] 2 Lloyd's Rep 87, 95–6; *Halesowen Presswork & Assemblies Ltd v Westminster Bank Ltd* [1971] 1 QB 1, 34; *Paget's Law of Banking* (13th edn, 2007), 716; *Ellinger's Modern Banking Law* (4th edn, 2006), 248.
[151] [1900] 2 Ch 79.
[152] See the discussion of *Mutton v Peat* in para. 15.10 above.
[153] *Barclays Bank Ltd v Okenarhe* [1966] 2 Lloyd's Rep 87, 95.
[154] *Garnett v M'Kewan* (1872) LR 8 Ex 10, approved by the Privy Council in *Prince v Oriental Bank Corporation* (1878) 3 App Cas 325. See also *Irwin v Bank of Montreal* (1876) 38 UCQB 375, 393; *Wallinder v Imperial Bank of Canada* [1925] 4 DLR 390, 392; *Barclays Bank Ltd v Okenarhe* [1966] 2 Lloyd's Rep 87; *National Bank of New Zealand v Heslop* (1882) NZLR 1 CA 47.

sufficient to cover it.[155] While this has been said to be inconsistent with the notion that combination is a matter of account rather than set-off,[156] it may be explained on the basis that a bank only promises to repay any part of the amount due on an account against the customer's written order if the order is addressed to the bank at the branch at which the account is kept.[157] It is not necessary to say that combination is a right only of the bank. If there is only one debt for the balance *vis-à-vis* the bank, there should also be only one debt *vis-à-vis* the customer,[158] although the customer's right to have cheques honoured is subject to the terms of the contract with the bank.

15.34   It may be that, instead of having two accounts in credit at different branches, both accounts are at the same branch. A cheque may be drawn on the first account for an amount which is in excess of the credit balance on that account, although it would be covered if both accounts were taken together. The question arises whether the bank is obliged to honour the cheque by transferring part of the balance on the second account to the first account. Ellinger, Lomnicka and Hooley considered the issue in the situation in which the second account is a savings account.[159] In their opinion, the maintenance of different types of accounts manifests an intention that they are to be kept separate, and accordingly the bank could dishonour the cheque. Their view would appear to be correct. If a cheque cannot be drawn on a savings account, it would be contrary to the parties' agreement to that effect if the bank were required to transfer a part of the balance on a savings account to a current account in order to honour a cheque. They went on to suggest that, in practice, the bank would permit the customer to overdraw the current account and leave the savings account intact as a form of security. This differs from a transfer of part of the savings account to the current account, because the customer would be debited with interest on the overdrawn account at a rate which exceeds the interest that would be earned on the savings account if it were left intact.

15.35   What if the second account is another current account rather than a savings account? The argument that the bank should honour the cheque is not without merit. In the situation in which a customer has two or more accounts at different branches, it has been said that the bank is not required to honour a cheque drawn on one account for an amount greater than the balance on that account, notwithstanding that the account at the second branch has sufficient funds to cover the shortfall, because each branch of a bank could not be expected

---

[155] *Garnett v M'Kewan* (1872) LR 8 Ex 10, 12 *per* Kelly CB ('if the plaintiff had had a balance in his favour at both places he could of course have drawn at either to the extent of the balance there'), 14–15 (Bramwell B); *Barclays Bank Ltd v Okenarhe* [1966] 2 Lloyd's Rep 87, 95. See also *National Bank of New Zealand v Grace* (1890) 8 NZLR 706, 710.

[156] Salter, 'Remedies for banks: an outline of English law' in Blair (ed.), *Banks and Remedies* (2nd edn, 1999), 52.

[157] See *Joachimson v Swiss Bank Corporation* [1921] 3 KB 110, 127; *Prince v Oriental Bank Corporation* (1878) 3 App Cas 325, 332; *Woodland v Fear* (1857) 7 El & Bl 519, 119 ER 1339.

[158] In *Re Bank of Queensland Ltd* [1997] 2 Qd R 129, 137 McPherson JA said that: 'where a customer has two accounts with a bank, either the bank or the customer is entitled to treat those two accounts . . . as one.'

[159] *Ellinger's Modern Banking Law* (4th edn, 2006), 247–8.

to know the state of the customer's account at every other branch.[160] This would not be the case in modern times, but in any event it could hardly apply when both current accounts are at the same branch. Moreover, when Atkin LJ in *Joachimson v Swiss Bank Corporation*[161] discussed the terms implied in the banker/customer contract, he referred to the bank's obligation to honour the customer's written orders addressed to the bank at the branch where the account is kept. The emphasis was on the branch, as opposed to a particular account. Nevertheless, the question of the bank's obligation when there is more than one account was not an issue in *Joachimson v Swiss Bank*, and indeed Bankes LJ in that case warned against placing too much reliance upon the language used in a judgment when the judge had not the precise point before him or her.[162] The better view is that the bank is not obliged to honour the cheque, notwithstanding that the accounts may be combined to form a single debt.[163] The opening of separate accounts is likely to be regarded as giving rise to an implied term in the banker/customer contract that the bank is only obliged to honour a cheque drawn on a particular account to the extent of the credit balance on that account.[164]

(6) Time bars

It has also been suggested that a debit balance may become statute-barred as a result of the expiration of a limitation period and hence ineligible for a set-off, and that this is inconsistent with the notion that only one amount is owing on all the accounts.[165] The proposed analysis of combination indeed suggests that an account that otherwise would have been time-barred if it had existed in isolation may be included in a combination. If at the same time there was a second account in credit, the first account to the extent of the credit balance will have been paid. This may not always be the case, however. If, for example, the second account only came into existence after the expiration of the limitation period for the first account, there may be an implied agreement that it is to be kept separate. The circumstances of each case would require consideration.   **15.36**

Two comments may be made in respect of the criticism of the view that an account that otherwise would be time-barred may be included in a combination.   **15.37**

The first is that there is nothing in the cases which is inconsistent with that result. The two cases which have been cited as authority to the contrary in fact were not concerned with combination. In *Pott v Clegg*[166] the assignees in bankruptcy of a bankrupt banker   **15.38**

---

[160] *Barclays Bank Ltd v Okenarhe* [1966] 2 Lloyd's Rep 87, 95. See also *National Bank of New Zealand v Grace* (1890) 8 NZLR 706, 710; *Joachimson v Swiss Bank Corporation* [1921] 3 KB 110, 129–30; *Prince v Oriental Bank Corporation* (1878) 3 App Cas 325, 332–3.

[161] [1921] 3 KB 110, 127.

[162] *Joachimson v Swiss Bank Corporation* [1921] 3 KB 110, 120.

[163] See *Paget's Law of Banking* (13th edn, 2007), 716 (though the case referred to, *Direct Acceptance Corporation Ltd v Bank of New South Wales* (1968) 88 WN (Pt 1) NSW 498, appears not to directly support that proposition).

[164] This would address the concern expressed in *Goode on Legal Problems of Credit and Security* (4th edn (ed. Gullifer), 2008), 296.

[165] Wood, *English and International Set-off* (1989), 93, and see also Salter, 'Remedies for banks: an outline of English law' in Blair (ed.), *Banks and Remedies* (2nd edn, 1999), 52.

[166] (1847) 16 M & W 321, 153 ER 1212.

sued the executor of William Turner for the balance owing on an account. The executor pleaded set-off based upon an account that had been opened in the joint names of Turner and one Mawdesley, the limitation period for which had elapsed. Mawdesley had died, and the account accordingly had vested in Turner, although it still remained in the bank's books in the joint names. It was held that Turner's executor could not employ the time-barred account in a set-off. The case turned on the availability of a set-off under the Statutes of Set-off, for which it is accepted that the debt sought to be set off must be enforceable by action.[167] It was not a case of combination, because the basis of that principle is a single relationship of banker and customer,[168] whereas in *Pott v Clegg* separate banker/customer relationships were in issue. A similar comment may be made in respect of *Re Morris; Coneys v Morris*.[169] A customer with a deposit account was liable as a surety on a promissory note given to the bank. After the limitation period for a claim on the note had expired the bank purported to set off the amount of the note against the deposit. It was held that the bank was not entitled to do this, given that an action could not have been brought on the note. Once again, however, this was not a case of combination, since the customer's liability on the note as a surety did not arise out of the banker/customer relationship.

15.39   The second comment is that, even if combination of accounts were properly characterized as a set-off rather than an accounting situation,[170] the fact that one of the accounts is time-barred should still not preclude an exercise of the right. In other words, the position should be the same whichever way combination is characterized. This conclusion should apply notwithstanding comments by Sir John Ross C in the Irish High Court of Appeal in *Re Morris* which suggest that an account in respect of which the limitation period has expired could not be the subject of combination.[171] A statute of limitation takes away the remedy of enforcing a debt in an action at law but commonly leaves the debt itself intact. Assume that combination indeed operates by way of set-off. The set-off would be effected by the bank without recourse to the courts, in which case the expiration of a limitation period should not affect the right. There are indeed a number of situations in which the courts have recognized that a creditor may exercise rights and remedies in relation to a time-barred debt in circumstances where recourse to the courts is not required.[172] For example, the common law has recognized that a possessory lien may be exercised in respect of a statute-barred debt,[173] and one would have thought that the same principle should apply

---

[167] See para. 2.46 above.
[168] See Buckley LJ in the Court of Appeal in *Halesowen Presswork & Assemblies Ltd v Westminster Bank Ltd* [1971] 1 QB 1, 46, and para. 15.04 above.
[169] [1922] 1 IR 136, affirming [1922] 1 IR 88.
[170] Compare para. 15.04 above.
[171] [1922] 1 IR 136, 137. Compare O'Connor MR, whose judgment consisted primarily of a rejection of the argument that the bank had a 'lien' on the deposit account. In relation to set-off, his only discussion was in the context of pleading set-off as a defence to an action at law, presumably pursuant to the Statutes of Set-off, for which an enforceable debt is required. See below.
[172] See *Commonwealth v Mewett* (1997) 191 CLR 471, 535.
[173] *Spears v Hartly* (1800) 3 Esp. 81, 170 ER 545; *Higgins v Scott* (1831) 2 B & Ad 413, 109 ER 1196. See also *Australia and New Zealand Banking Group Ltd v Douglas Morris Investments Pty Ltd* [1992] 1 Qd R 478, 497 (security for a statute-barred debt).

in relation to a common law right to combine accounts which, like a lien, takes effect extra-judicially. Consistent with that view, Mocatta J commented in *Barclays Bank Ltd v Okenarhe*[174] that a bank should not be in any worse position with respect to money deposited with it than it would be with respect to securities over which it had a lien. A similar stance has been adopted in equity in relation to both the substantive defence of equitable set-off[175] and the principle in *Cherry v Boultbee*.[176] Another illustration is the right that an executor formerly enjoyed to retain a sufficient amount from the estate in order to pay a debt owing to him or her by the deceased in priority to other creditors.[177] While the executor's right has now been abolished in England,[178] it was nevertheless held that the expiration of the limitation period for the debt did not affect the executor's right.[179] Further, reference may be made to the case of a debtor who makes a payment to the creditor without directing that it be paid in reduction of a particular debt. The right of appropriation in such a case devolves upon the creditor, and the creditor may apply the payment to a time-barred debt rather than to another debt that is still enforceable.[180] It is true that, in the case of set-off under the Statutes of Set-off, the common law courts have required that the cross-debt sought to be set off must be enforceable by action,[181] and that may well be what Sir John Ross C had in mind in *Re Morris*. This form of set-off, however, is a procedural defence to an action at law, which requires a court order to bring about a set-off.[182] It differs in that respect from combination of accounts.

How would combination work in practice in relation to an account that otherwise would be time-barred? Consider that there are two accounts, account No. 1 which is in credit, and account No. 2 which has a debit balance and in respect of which the limitation period has expired. In such a case the customer could only sue for the balance of the two accounts if the credit balance on account No. 1 exceeds the debit balance on account No. 2. If, on the other hand, the debit balance on account No. 2 exceeds the debit balance on account No. 1, the bank's claim for the ultimate balance would be unenforceable. It may be that there are two accounts with debit balances, account No. 2 which is time-barred and account No. 3 which is not. In such a case the principle should be that, in the absence of an appropriation by the customer, the bank could treat the credit balance on account No. 1 as reducing first the debit balance on account No. 2.[183] To the extent that any part of the balance on account No. 2 is not reduced in that manner, an action in respect of it, being an action founded upon simple contract, would be precluded by the Limitation Act 1980, s. 5. **15.40**

---

174 [1966] 2 Lloyd's Rep 87, 97.
175 See paras 4.51–4.54 above.
176 (1839) 4 My & Cr 442, 41 ER 171. See para. 14.17 above.
177 See paras 14.04–14.05 above.
178 Administration of Estates Act 1971, s. 10.
179 *Hill v Walker* (1858) 4 K & J 166, 70 ER 69.
180 *Mills v Fowkes* (1839) 5 Bing (NC) 455, 132 ER 1174.
181 See para. 2.46 above.
182 See paras 2.34–2.45 above.
183 See para. 15.22 above.

D. Banker and Customer Relationship

15.41 Combination only extends to obligations owing to a bank in its capacity as banker.[184] A debt due to it as a result of carrying on another business will not suffice.[185] Moreover, the obligations should relate to the same bank, a requirement that probably would not be satisfied where a bank uses separate corporate structures for its trading and savings bank functions.[186]

(1) Banking business

15.42 Combination is a common law concept, and it should apply in the case of institutions that are regarded at common law as carrying on the business of banking.[187] In Australia, Isaacs J in *State Savings Bank of Victoria v Permewan Wright & Co Ltd*[188] described the essential characteristics of the business of banking as:

> the collection of money by receiving deposits upon loan, repayable when and as expressly or impliedly agreed upon, and the utilization of the money so collected by lending it again in such sums as are required. These are the essential functions of a bank as an instrument of society.

In other words, the business of banking essentially is the borrowing and lending of money. Isaacs J went on to say that the methods by which the functions of a bank are effected, as by current account, deposit account at call, fixed deposit account, orders, cheques, secured loans, discounting bills, letters of credit, telegraphic transfers and other modes, are merely auxiliary circumstances, any of which may or may not exist in any particular case. In particular, he said that banks are not bound by law to open current accounts, but may confine themselves to deposit accounts. Subsequently, the English Court of Appeal in *United Dominions Trust Ltd v Kirkwood*[189] rejected Isaacs J's approach as not reflecting modern practice,[190] the court emphasizing instead the importance that cheques now play as a means of paying and receiving money.[191] Consistent with that view, Harman and Diplock LJJ regarded it as an essential characteristic of banking business that the bank

---

[184] See Roskill J in *Halesowen Presswork & Assemblies Ltd v Westminster Bank Ltd* [1971] 1 QB 1, 20 ('whenever a customer is indebted to a banker as a banker'), and the discussion in *Barclays Bank Ltd v Okenarhe* [1966] 2 Lloyd's Rep 87, 98–9 in relation to whether the loan was made in the ordinary course of banking business.

[185] See Pigott and Bramwell BB in their judgments in *Garnett v M'Kewan* (1872) LR 8 Ex 10, 14. Bramwell B gave as an example the business of brewer.

[186] Herzberg, 'Bankers' rights of combination' (1982) 10 *Australian Business Law Review* 79, 86.

[187] See also *Paget's Law of Banking* (13th edn, 2007), 137.

[188] (1913) 19 CLR 457, 470–1. See also *Melbourne Corporation v Commonwealth* (1947) 74 CLR 31, 54, 63 (Latham CJ), 64–5 (Rich J); *Mason v Savings Bank of South Australia* [1925] SASR 198, 204; *PP Consultants Pty Ltd v Finance Sector Union of Australia* (2000) 201 CLR 648 at [17].

[189] [1966] 2 QB 431. See also *Re Roe's Legal Charge* [1982] 2 Lloyd's Rep 370 (CA).

[190] [1966] 2 QB 431, 445–6 (Lord Denning), 464 (Diplock LJ).

[191] [1966] 2 QB 431, 446 (Lord Denning), 459 (Harman LJ), 465 (Diplock LJ).

conducts current accounts,[192] while Lord Denning described the keeping of current accounts as a characteristic 'usually' found in banks.[193]

In so far as it emphasized the role of cheques, the analysis in *United Dominions Trust v Kirkwood* is now of reduced significance given that major banks in the United Kingdom have announced that they intend to phase out the clearing of cheques.[194] But in any event, that analysis does not mean that banking business, and combination of accounts,[195] is confined to current accounts. The conduct of current accounts may be regarded as an essential characteristic of modern banking business, in that an institution is not considered to be a bank unless it provides current accounts, but the business of banking encompasses more than that. A bank conducts the business of banking with customers,[196] and the main criterion for determining whether a person is a customer of a bank is whether that person has an account with the bank through which transactions are passed.[197] It does not have to be a current account. It has been said, for example, that a deposit account will suffice.[198] Indeed, it has been suggested that a continued practice of getting bills discounted by a bank would probably be enough to establish a person as a customer,[199] but in such a case the discount proceeds usually would be credited to an account.[200]

Lease finance facilities

It is now common for banks to provide lease finance facilities to customers. Typically, this involves the bank acquiring items of equipment and leasing them to the customer. The question arises whether the customer's payment obligations pursuant to the lease, including as a result of early termination, may be the subject of combination with a credit balance

15.43

15.44

---

[192] [1966] 2 QB 431, 457–8, 459 (Harman LJ), 465 (Diplock LJ).

[193] [1966] 2 QB 431, 447. Lord Denning (at 453–4) said that there are other characteristics which go to make a banker, including stability, soundness and probity, and the reputation of the firm amongst ordinary commercial men. Diplock LJ (at 473–5) also thought that regard could be had to reputation (although for a reason different from that which commended itself to Lord Denning), though compare Harman LJ at 460–1.

[194] An end date of 31 October 2018 has tentatively been set.

[195] See paras 15.48–15.50 below. Compare Ireland, where it has been said that combination is confined to current accounts. See *Bank of Ireland v Martin* [1937] IR 189, 202–3; Earley, 'Set-off rights available to banks in Ireland' [1997] 4 *Journal of International Banking Law* 153, 154.

[196] In *Melbourne Corporation v Commonwealth* (1947) 74 CLR 31, 51 Latham CJ said that, 'A banker conducts a business of banking with customers. The customer of a banker does his banking business with the banker. That which the banker does as a banker is the business of banking, and that which the customer does as a customer of the banker is also the business of banking.'

[197] *Paget's Law of Banking* (13th edn, 2007), 141, and see also *Ellinger's Modern Banking Law* (4th edn, 2006), 118–21.

[198] *Dixon v Bank of New South Wales* (1896) 12 WN (NSW) 101 (fixed deposit); *Great Western Railway Co v London and County Banking Co Ltd* [1901] AC 414, 420–1; *Hart v Sangster* [1957] 1 Ch 329, 336, 337; *Warren v Colonial Catering Co Ltd* [1975] 1 NZLR 273, 276; *Paget's Law of Banking* (13th edn, 2007), 143; *Ellinger's Modern Banking Law* (4th edn, 2006), 119; Weaver and Craigie, *The Law Relating to Banker and Customer in Australia* (looseleaf) vol. 1, [3.8610]; *Halsbury's Laws of England* (4th edn, 2005) vol. 3(1), 159, para. 193.

[199] *Paget's Law of Banking* (13th edn, 2007), 143, and see also Weaver and Craigie, *The Law Relating to Banker and Customer in Australia* (looseleaf) vol. 1, [3.8590].

[200] In *Great Western Railway Co v London and County Banking Co Ltd* [1901] AC 414, 422–3, Lord Brampton left open the question whether the keeping of an ordinary bank account is essential to constitute a person a customer of a bank.

on another account. The issue came before the New South Wales Court of Appeal in *Cinema Plus Ltd v ANZ Banking Group Ltd*.[201] A customer defaulted under a lease facility, and the bank argued that the amount payable by the customer consequent upon the default could be combined with a credit balance on the customer's current account. Both Sheller and Giles JJA considered that combination did not apply. Sheller JA thought that the situation was governed by the principle that a loan account cannot be combined with a current account in credit,[202] while Giles JA said that, for combination to apply, there must be 'really but one account', and the current account and the lease finance facility served different functions which were inimical to their combination.[203] It is suggested that the same conclusion could have been reached by reference to a more fundamental principle, that combination only applies to amounts owing to a bank as banker. While it has been said that the meaning of 'banking business' can change from time to time,[204] when a bank leases equipment to a customer one would have thought that payments under the lease are due to it in its capacity as the owner and lessor of the equipment, as opposed to the capacity of banker. Thus, in *United Dominions Trust Ltd v Kirkwood*,[205] Lord Denning said of a facility whereby a finance house acquired goods and let them to a customer on hire purchase terms that it was not banking.

(2) Guarantor of another customer's debt

15.45 Combination should not apply when a person who has a deposit account with a bank gives a guarantee to the bank in respect of a second customer's indebtedness.[206] The guarantee in that circumstance would not be given in the capacity of a customer, but rather to assist the bank in its relationship with the second customer. If the bank wishes to be able to utilize the deposit in order to secure the liability under the guarantee, it should obtain an express contractual right of set-off from the guarantor.[207]

(3) Joint account

15.46 When two or more persons have a joint account with a bank, and one of those persons has another account in his or her own right, separate banker/customer relationships would be in issue so as to preclude a combination.[208]

---

[201] (2000) 49 NSWLR 513.

[202] (2000) 49 NSWLR 513 at [113] and [114]. See para. 15.54 below.

[203] (2000) 49 NSWLR 513 at [142].

[204] *Ellinger's Modern Banking Law* (4th edn, 2006), 69, referring *inter alia* to *Woods v Martins Bank Ltd* [1959] 1 QB 55, 70. See also *United Dominions Trust Ltd v Kirkwood* [1966] 2 QB 431, 464.

[205] [1966] 2 QB 431, 449.

[206] *Bank of Ireland v Martin* [1937] IR 189, although in any event it was said in that case (at 202–3) that combination is confined to current accounts. See, however, para. 15.48 below.

[207] See ch. 16 below in relation to set-off agreements.

[208] *Watts v Christie* (1849) 11 Beav 546, 50 ER 928, and see also *Ex p Morier, re Willis, Percival, & Co* (1879) 12 Ch D 491 (in which the joint executors in any event were not beneficial owners of the account). Compare *Ellinger's Modern Banking Law* (4th edn, 2006), 241–2 (referring to *Hill v Bank of Hochelaga* [1921] 3 WWR 430). *Quaere* whether a joint and several liability owing to a bank would give rise to a combination under general law. In *York City and County Banking Co v Bainbridge* (1880) 43 LT 732, 734, Hawkins J contemplated that possibility, but he assumed that the right in question took the form of a right in the bank to set one account against another, as opposed to a notion that the accounts in any event are combined. The better view is that combination does not apply in this situation. If a number of the joint and several debtors are

(4) Different names

Alternatively, the same person may open two or more accounts for his or her own benefit **15.47**
though under different names. While in this situation there is the same bank and the same
customer, it is doubtful whether it can be said that there is the one relationship. Nevertheless,
in *Barclays Bank Ltd v Okenarhe*[209] Mocatta J in an unreserved judgment allowed combination of accounts in this situation, and a similar view has been expressed in New South
Wales.[210] It is suggested that those views should be re-considered.

E. The Scope of Combination

(1) Not confined to current accounts

Combination may apply in the case of two current accounts.[211] Indeed, it has been said in **15.48**
Ireland that combination is confined to that context,[212] while in *Re E J Morel (1934) Ltd*,[213]
Buckley J suggested that combination does not apply where accounts are of a different
character,[214] for example when a customer has a current account and another account
which is not a current account.[215] Combination should not be so limited, however, but

---

customers of the bank, it could hardly be said that the liability is combined at one and the same time with all
the customers' individual accounts in credit. In the absence of an agreement for a set-off, the bank should be
confined to a set-off, either as a procedural defence to an action at law under the Statutes of Set-off or pursuant to the insolvency legislation. Combination may apply, however, in relation to joint accounts in the same
names. See *Houben v Bank of Nova Scotia* (1970) 3 NBR (2d) 366, 374.

[209] [1966] 2 Lloyd's Rep 87.

[210] *Commonwealth v Official Trustee in Bankruptcy* [2004] NSWSC 1155 at [9]–[10].

[211] *Garnett v M'Kewan* (1872) LR 8 Ex 10; *Re E J Morel (1934) Ltd* [1962] 1 Ch 21, 30, 31–2; *Clark v
Ulster Bank Ltd* [1950] NILR 132.

[212] *Bank of Ireland v Martin* [1937] IR 189, 202–3; Earley, 'Set-off rights available to banks in Ireland'
[1997] 4 *Journal of International Banking Law* 153, 154. In *National Westminster Bank Ltd v Halesowen
Presswork & Assemblies Ltd* [1972] AC 785, 819, Lord Kilbrandon referred to the case of two current accounts,
but that would seem to have been in the context of providing an example, as opposed to a definition, of
combination.

[213] [1962] 1 Ch 21, 31–2.

[214] See also *Stannard v National Bank of New Zealand Ltd* (1986) 3 NZCLC 99,510 at 99,515. The
question in that case was whether two term loans were combined with an overdrawn current account, in
circumstances where a debenture secured indebtedness on the current account. In giving the judgment of
the New Zealand Court of Appeal, Richardson J said that the accounts were not combined because they
were of a different character. He suggested, on the other hand, that, if the bank was both entitled to and had
demanded payment of the term loan indebtedness under default provisions applicable to the term loans, all
three accounts would have had a similar character.

[215] Compare Buckley LJ's later, and more general, discussion in *Halesowen Presswork & Assemblies Ltd v
Westminster Bank Ltd* [1971] 1 QB 1, 46, in particular his reference to *Re European Bank* (1872) LR 8 Ch
App 41 and *Mutton v Peat* [1900] 2 Ch 79 as examples of combination. Those cases each concerned a current
account and a loan account, as opposed to accounts of the same character (though see para. 15.54 below in
relation to current and loan accounts). In *Oceanica Castelana Armadora SA v Mineralimportexport* [1983]
1 WLR 1294, Lloyd J held that a Mareva injunction granted in relation to a defendant's assets, which included
a deposit with a bank, should be varied so as to allow the bank to exercise any right of 'set-off' that it may have
in respect of facilities afforded by the bank to the defendant prior to the injunction. See para. 15.83 below. In
particular, Lloyd J referred to a right of 'set-off' against the deposit in respect of interest accruing to the bank
on term loans provided to the defendant, and also in respect of payments made by the bank on letters of credit
opened at the request of the defendant. The judgment, however, was premised on the assumption that the
bank had such a right of 'set-off'. The nature of the right in that case was not explored. In particular, it is not

should be capable of applying accounts of a different character, including non-current accounts, unless there is an agreement, express or implied, to keep them separate.[216] Thus, when Roskill J (as he then was) at first instance in *Halesowen Presswork & Assemblies Ltd v Westminster Bank Ltd*[217] characterized combination as a manifestation of or a right analogous to the exercise of the banker's right of lien,[218] he said of the lien, and inferentially of combination, that it is: 'a right which is of general application and not in principle (apart from special agreement whether express or implied) limited to current or other similar accounts.' For example, there is authority for the view that an overdrawn current account and a deposit account may be regarded as combined,[219] at least when the deposit account is at call. If the deposit is withdrawable after a specified period of notice by the customer, Roskill J in the *Halesowen* case[220] considered that the deposit would be treated as separate until the expiration of the requisite period after the customer has given notice, whereupon combination may apply.[221] Similarly, the Ontario Court of Appeal in *Deep v Bank of Montreal*[222] accepted that a bank was entitled to apply the proceeds of a maturing term deposit against an overdrawn current account.

15.49 There have also been instances in which combination has been recognized in relation to a loan account and a current account in credit.[223] More recent cases suggest that combination ordinarily does not apply in that situation,[224] but the reason given is not that combination is confined to current accounts, or accounts of the same character, but rather that, in the circumstances, the courts usually imply an agreement that the accounts are to be kept separate. It is the implied agreement which results in their separation, as opposed to a view that the different nature of the accounts precludes combination.[225] Moreover, there is

---

clear if Lloyd J considered that the common law principle of combination applied, or whether it was based on set-off clauses in the facility documentation.

[216] See paras 15.52–15.65 below.

[217] [1971] 1 QB 1, 19.

[218] See, however, para. 15.03 above.

[219] *Re K (Restraint Order)* [1990] 2 QB 298. The bank in that case had a letter of set-off, but Otton J (at 304) considered the position in relation to combination apart from the letter. See also *Wallinder v Imperial Bank of Canada* [1925] 4 DLR 390, 392; *Houben v Bank of Nova Scotia* (1970) 3 NBR (2d) 366, 374; *O'Hearn v Bank of Nova Scotia* [1970] SCR 341 (savings account and loan account). In Ireland, compare *Bank of Ireland v Martin* [1937] IR 189, 203–4.

[220] [1971] 1 QB 1, 21–2. In Australia, see also Weaver and Craigie, *The Law Relating to Banker and Customer in Australia* (looseleaf) vol. 1, [3.7130], referring to *Marosvary v Bank of NSW* (WA District Court, Gunning DCJ, 23 May 1979).

[221] In relation to a term loan, the New Zealand Court of Appeal in *Stannard v National Bank of New Zealand Ltd* (1986) 3 NZCLC 99,510 at 99,515 suggested that it may be combined with another account if the bank has demanded payment of the term loan under default provisions applicable to the loan.

[222] (1991) 47 OAC 319.

[223] *Re European Bank* (1872) LR 8 Ch App 41; *Mutton v Peat* [1900] 2 Ch 79; *Re Tonkin* (1933) 6 ABC 197 (esp. at 210–11). See also *Hamilton v Commonwealth Bank of Australia* (1992) 9 ACSR 90, 106. In Canada, see *Re Sutcliffe & Sons Ltd* [1933] 1 DLR 562 and *Ross v Royal Bank of Canada* (1965) 52 DLR (2d) 578 (esp. at 587–90).

[224] See para. 15.54 below.

[225] Thus, Lord Denning MR and Buckley LJ in the Court of Appeal in *Halesowen Presswork & Assemblies Ltd v Westminster Bank Ltd* [1971] 1 QB 1, 34, 46 accepted the earlier cases as examples of combination.

authority which suggests that combination may apply to a loan account and a deposit account upon which the customer may not draw cheques, if the accounts are presently payable upon demand.[226]

(2) Bills of exchange and promissory notes

The broader view of combination is also reflected in some cases in which a bank held a bill of exchange or a promissory note upon which its customer was liable, and the courts recognized that the bank could appropriate the customer's account in credit towards satisfaction of the bill or the note.[227] It is not made clear in the reports of some of the cases whether the bank obtained the bill or the note as a result of discounting it for the customer, or whether the bank obtained it from a third party.[228] The discounting of bills of exchange has been described as a method by which the functions of a bank are effected,[229] so that it may take place as part of the banker and customer relationship. If, on the other hand, a bank obtains a bill or a note upon which the customer is liable as a result of a dealing with a third party, it would be difficult to say that the customer's obligation to the bank arises out of the banker/customer relationship,[230] when the negotiation of the bill or the note to the bank took place outside that relationship. In that circumstance, combination should not apply.[231]

15.50

---

[226] *Barclays Bank Ltd v Okenarhe* [1966] 2 Lloyd's Rep 87 (the sum paid to the customer being treated as a loan). See also *Pertamina Energy Trading Ltd v Credit Suisse* [2006] SGCA 27 at [43] (deposit and a drawdown under a credit facility, though in that case the Singapore Court of Appeal held that the bank was entitled to rely on a contractual right of set-off).

[227] *National Bank of New Zealand v Heslop* (1882) NZLR 1 CA 47 (in which the customer's claim against the bank was for damages, for failure to honour a cheque, so that it could not have been a case of set-off of mutual debts under the Statutes of Set-off); *Royal Trust Co v Molsons Bank* (1912) 8 DLR 478; *Re T. C. Marines Ltd* (1973) 34 DLR (3d) 489. See also *Ontario Bank v Routhier* (1900) 32 OR 67, *Coulls v English, Scottish and Australian Chartered Bank* (1872) 6 SALR 44 (in which the proceeds of the bill of exchange discounted by the bank for the customer were appropriated by the bank to the customer's earlier overdue bill held by the bank) and *Baker v Lloyd's Bank Ltd* [1920] 2 KB 322, 327 (the bank's right against the credit balance on the current account being described as a 'lien'). In *Pollard v Ogden* (1853) 2 El & Bl 459, 118 ER 839, it is not clear if the bank, having paid the bill as indorser, was entitled to debit its customer's account, or whether a defence of set-off under the Statutes of Set-off was in issue. Compare *Rogerson v Ladbroke* (1822) 1 Bing 93, 130 ER 39, in which the bank received notice of the customer's death before the promissory note matured. It is also necessary to distinguish cases such as *Rogerson v Ladbroke* (in relation to the bill of exchange) and *Roy v Canadian Bank of Commerce* (1917) 38 DLR 742, in which the bill was made payable at the bank. If a customer of a bank accepts a bill and makes it payable at the bank, that fact constitutes authority to the bank to apply the customer's funds in paying the bill. See *Kymer v Laurie* (1849) 18 LJQB 218.

[228] See *Royal Trust Co v Molsons Bank* (1912) 8 DLR 478, *Ontario Bank v Routhier* (1900) 32 OR 67 and *Coulls v English, Scottish and Australian Chartered Bank* (1872) 6 SALR 44. In *National Bank of New Zealand v Heslop* (1882) NZLR 1 CA 47, the report states that the bank discounted the bill, but it is not clear for whom. The bill was accepted by the customer, but it was drawn by third parties (Stratford and Coupe) and it was made payable at another bank.

[229] *State Savings Bank of Victoria v Permewan Wright & Co Ltd* (1913) 19 CLR 457, 471 (Isaacs J), but compare Lord Denning in *United Dominions Trust Ltd v Kirkwood* [1966] 2 QB 431, 448–9.

[230] See paras 15.41–15.47 above.

[231] In *Flanagan v National Bank Ltd* [1939] IR 352, a customer was liable to a bank on promissory notes otherwise than as a result of the bank having discounted them for her, and it was held that the bank could not appropriate the customer's deposit in satisfaction of the notes.

(3) Presently matured obligations

15.51   Combination may only occur in relation to accounts which are otherwise presently payable.[232] In this context, that includes presently payable on demand.[233] Thus, a combination may not be based upon an obligation to the bank that will only mature at a future date or an obligation that is merely contingent,[234] unless there is an agreement to the contrary.[235]

F. Express and Implied Agreements to Keep Accounts Separate

15.52   It is not necessary to show an agreement between the bank and the customer that the accounts should be combined. If combination would otherwise apply, the principle is that two or more accounts kept by a customer with a bank give rise to a single debt unless there is an agreement, express or implied, to keep them separate.[236] This is a conclusion of law[237] which follows from the circumstance that there is a single banker/customer relationship.[238]

15.53   The mere act of opening two or more accounts does not constitute an agreement to keep them separate.[239] On the other hand, there may be an agreement to separate out an account

---

[232]   *Matthews v Geraghty* (1986) 43 SASR 576, 580. Compare *Agra and Masterman's Bank v Hoffman* (1864) 34 LJ Ch 285, which concerned equitable set-off. In that case, bankers refused to honour cheques drawn by a customer on an account in credit because of an unmatured liability of the customer on some bills of exchange. The customer accordingly brought an action against the bank for damages and for payment of the balance of the account. After the action was commenced, several of the bills, to a larger amount than the balance, were dishonoured, whereupon the bankers filed a bill in equity for an account and for an injunction to restrain the action at law. Stuart VC granted the injunction, on the ground that the customer's legal right was impeached in equity. However, it is difficult to see what connection there was between the demands which would have been sufficient to give rise to an equitable set-off on that ground. See paras 4.02–4.28 above.

[233]   As in the case of a bank's liability to its customer on a current account in credit. Compare *Joachimson v Swiss Bank Corporation* [1921] 3 KB 110.

[234]   *Rogerson v Ladbroke* (1822) 1 Bing 93, 130 ER 39; *Bower v Foreign and Colonial Gas Co* (1874) 22 WR 740; *Stannard v National Bank of New Zealand Ltd* (1986) 3 NZCLC 99,510 at 99,515 (term loans). See also *Jeffryes v Agra and Masterman's Bank* (1866) LR 2 Eq 674, 680 *per* Sir William Page Wood VC ('you cannot retain a sum of money which is actually due against a sum of money which is only becoming due at a future time'), *Ontario Bank v Routhier* (1900) 32 OR 67, 68, and *Paget's Law of Banking* (13th edn, 2007), 709–10 (criticizing Abbott CJ in *Bolland v Bygrave* (1825) 1 Ry & M 271, 171 ER 1017 with respect to a banker's lien on securities, although Abbott CJ's judgment was cited with evident approval by Ungoed-Thomas J in *Re Keever* [1967] 1 Ch 182, 189–90). Compare *Baker v Lloyd's Bank Ltd* [1920] 2 KB 322, in which the declaration of insolvency was held to constitute a repudiation of the obligation to pay the bills of exchange at maturity.

[235]   See paras 15.73–15.77 below.

[236]   See Roskill J at first instance in *Halesowen Presswork & Assemblies Ltd v Westminster Bank* Ltd [1971] 1 QB 1, 20–1 (who incorrectly characterized the right as an aspect of the banker's lien: see para. 15.03 above), and Lord Denning in the Court of Appeal in the *Halesowen* case (at 35), each criticizing the *dictum* of Swift J in *W. P. Greenhalgh and Sons v Union Bank of Manchester* [1924] 2 KB 153, 164 suggesting that the customer's assent to a combination is required. See also Lord Kilbrandon in the House of Lords in the *Halesowen* case [1972] AC 785, 819 (in relation to two current accounts) and *Re Bank of Queensland Ltd* [1997] 2 Qd R 129, 137–8.

[237]   In *Ex p Morier* (1879) 12 Ch D 491, 498, James LJ said that, 'in point of law there was but one account.' Compare McCracken, *The Banker's Remedy of Set-off* (3rd edn, 2010), 28–32, who has sought to explain combination on the basis of an implied term.

[238]   See para. 15.04 above.

[239]   *Halesowen Presswork & Assemblies Ltd v Westminster Bank Ltd* [1971] 1 QB 1, 35 (Lord Denning MR).

after the accounts have been established. For example, a customer may have a number of accounts with a bank which otherwise would be regarded as combined, but the parties may agree to strike a balance on one or more of the accounts on the basis of an account stated,[240] so that the balance on that account may be sued for separately. In *Cumming v Shand*,[241] the course of dealing between the bank and the customer was held to give rise to an implied agreement that a current account would not be debited with the sums paid on the customer's behalf by the bank, and the bank was required to give reasonable notice of its intention to discontinue the arrangement. If a customer gives a cheque to the bank with instructions to cash it and pay him or her the proceeds, as opposed to crediting the proceeds to an account, the better view is that the instructions would preclude a combination in relation to the proceeds,[242] although there is authority in Australia which suggests the contrary. [243]

(1) Current account and a loan account

A customer may have a loan from a bank and at the same time have a current account **15.54** in credit. While there are cases which suggest that the accounts may be regarded as combined,[244] the generally accepted view is that there is an implied agreement that they should be kept separate.[245] The reason, as Scrutton LJ explained, is that: 'No customer could otherwise have any security in drawing a cheque on his current account if he had a loan account greater than his credit balance on current account.'[246] The accounts serve different functions inimical to their consolidation.[247]

---

[240] *Siqueira v Noronha* [1934] AC 332, 337, and see also *Opal Maritime Agencies Pty Ltd v 'Skulptor Konenkov'* (2000) 98 FCR 519, 568.

[241] (1860) 5 H & N 95, 157 ER 1114.

[242] *Rouxel v Royal Bank of Canada* [1918] 2 WWR 791.

[243] *Coulls v English, Scottish and Australian Chartered Bank* (1872) 6 SALR 44.

[244] *Re European Bank* (1872) LR 8 Ch App 41; *Mutton v Peat* [1900] 2 Ch 79; *Re Tonkin* (1933) 6 ABC 197, 210–11. See also *Hamilton v Commonwealth Bank of Australia* (1992) 9 ACSR 90, 106. In Canada, see *Re Sutcliffe & Sons Ltd* [1933] 1 DLR 562 and *Ross v Royal Bank of Canada* (1965) 52 DLR (2d) 578 (esp. at 587–90).

[245] *Buckingham and Co v London and Midland Bank* (1895) 12 TLR 70 (action for damages for failing to honour the customer's cheques); *Bradford Old Bank Ltd v Sutcliffe* [1918] 2 KB 833 (in which the Court of Appeal held that sums paid into a current account, in the period after a guarantee relating both to that account and a loan account had ceased to be a continuing guarantee, could not be considered as constituting satisfaction of the indebtedness on the loan account, with the result that the surety remained liable for the sum outstanding on the loan account); *Re E J Morel (1934) Ltd* [1962] 1 Ch 21, 30–1; *Halesowen Presswork & Assemblies Ltd v Westminster Bank Ltd* [1971] 1 QB 1, 20, 22 (Roskill J, at first intance), 34 (Lord Denning MR, CA), and in the House of Lords ([1972] AC 785), Lord Cross of Chelsea at 809 and Lord Kilbrandon at 819; *Bhogal v Punjab National Bank* [1988] 2 All ER 296, 300; *Cinema Plus Ltd v Australia and New Zealand Banking Group Ltd* (2000) 49 NSWLR 513 at [113]–[114]; *Fraser v Oystertec plc* [2006] 1 BCLC 491 at [16]. See also *York City and County Banking Co v Bainbridge* (1880) 43 LT 732; *Re Deague* (1951) 15 ABC 197, 202; *Barclays Bank Ltd v Okenarhe* [1966] 2 Lloyd's Rep 87, 96. Compare *Matthews v Geraghty* (1986) 43 SASR 576, in which the bank had an express contractual right of set-off. Compare also *Stannard v National Bank of New Zealand Ltd* (1986) 3 NZCLC 99,510 at 99,515 (referring to an overdrawn current account and two term loans in respect of which the bank has demanded payment of the indebtedness under default provisions).

[246] *Bradford Old Bank Ltd v Sutcliffe* [1918] 2 KB 833, 847. See also Pickford LJ at 839.

[247] *Cinema Plus Ltd v Australia and New Zealand Banking Group Ltd* (2000) 49 NSWLR 513 at [142].

15.55   The view that there is no combination is subject to an agreement to the contrary.[248] As Lord Cross of Chelsea commented in the House of Lords in the *Halesowen* case,[249] a loan account and a current account are regarded as separate: 'unless the bank makes it clear to the customer that it is retaining the right at any moment to apply the credit balance on the current account in reduction of the debt on the loan account.' Roskill J at first instance in the *Halesowen* case[250] postulated that, if a customer has a loan account on (say) seven days' call, and a current account in credit, it would be a term of the contract between the parties that the accounts may be 'set off' if the call is made and payment is not tendered within the requisite period.[251] As a general proposition, this is doubtful. Unless the terms of an agreement between the parties to keep accounts separate are such that the agreement is determinable by notice having immediate effect,[252] the better view is that any such implied term would require the bank to give reasonable notice of termination. This would be consistent with the view that reasonable notice is required to close a current account in credit.[253]

(2) Current account and other accounts

15.56   The justification for implying a term that a current account in credit is to be kept separate from a loan account should be equally relevant in relation to other debts owing to the bank, for example where the customer is indebted to the bank on a bill discount facility,[254] or where the customer has defaulted under a lease facility provided by the bank and is indebted for a termination amount.[255]

(3) Deposit account upon which cheques cannot be drawn

15.57   That justification would not be relevant, however, to a loan account and a deposit account upon which the customer may not draw cheques, and there is authority which suggests that those accounts may be combined, at least when the deposit and the loan are both presently payable on demand.[256]

---

[248] 'The critical question must always be, 'What was the contract?' and not whether a particular account or accounts bear one title rather than another': *Halesowen Presswork & Assemblies Ltd v Westminster Bank Ltd* [1971] 1 QB 1, 21 *per* Roskill J (at first instance). Thus Roskill J (at 22) distinguished *Re European Bank* (1872) LR 8 Ch App 41 and *Mutton v Peat* [1900] 2 Ch 79 on the ground that it was not part of the arrangements between the parties in those particular cases that the accounts should be kept separate.

[249] *National Westminster Bank Ltd v Halesowen Presswork & Assemblies Ltd* [1972] AC 785. 809. See also Roskill J at first instance [1971] 1 QB 1, 22.

[250] [1971] 1 QB 1, 21.

[251] See also *Stannard v National Bank of New Zealand Ltd* (1986) 3 NZCLC 99,510 at 99,515 in relation to term loans in respect of which the bank has demanded payment of the debts under applicable default provisions.

[252] See para. 15.30 above.

[253] See paras 15.29–15.30 above.

[254] See para. 15.50 above.

[255] *Cinema Plus Ltd v Australia and New Zealand Banking Group Ltd* (2000) 49 NSWLR 513 at [142] (Giles JA), and see also Sheller JA at [113] and [114] (the 'loan facilities' included the lease finance facility: see at [72]). In any event, it is suggested that amounts due to a bank under a lease may be precluded from combination on the more fundamental ground that they are not due to the bank in its capacity as banker. See para. 15.44 above.

[256] This would seem to be the effect of Mocatta J's decision in *Barclays Bank Ltd v Okenarhe* [1966] 2 Lloyd's Rep 87, in which the sum paid to the customer was treated as a loan. Compare *Rogerson v Ladbroke*

(4) Termination of the banker/customer relationship

Roskill J at first instance in the *Halesowen* case considered that the implied agreement to **15.58** keep separate a loan account and a current account in credit only subsists while the banker/customer relationship remains in existence.[257] The relationship terminates upon the death or insanity of the customer or upon his or her bankruptcy or its liquidation,[258] but not upon the appointment of a receiver.[259] When termination occurs, Roskill J accepted that the bank becomes entitled to combine the accounts.[260] He suggested that the judgment of Buckley J in *Re E J Morel (1934) Ltd*[261] constitutes authority to the contrary, but he said that on this point Buckley J should be regarded as wrong.[262] Two points may be made in relation to the general proposition, and Roskill J's criticism of Buckley J's judgment in *Re E J Morel*. The first is that both the *Morel* and *Halesowen* cases concerned a company in liquidation. If a banker/customer relationship is terminated as a result of the bankruptcy or liquidation of the customer, the question should not arise as to whether the accounts may be combined after the termination of the implied agreement to keep them separate. This is because of the prevailing view as to the operation of the insolvency set-off section, that it takes effect automatically upon the occurrence of the bankruptcy or liquidation.[263] There would not be any scope for combination after the set-off has occurred.[264] The second point is that, in any event, there is nothing in Buckley J's judgment which is inconsistent with the general proposition accepted by Roskill J.

(1822) 1 Bing 93, 130 ER 39, in which the bank had notice of the customer's death before the loan secured by the promissory note matured. See para. 15.122 below.

[257] [1971] 1 QB 1, 23–4, following *Re Keever* [1967] 1 Ch 182. See also *Thomas v Howell* (1874) LR 18 Eq 198, 202–3 (death of customer). The *Halesowen* case involved an express agreement between the bank and the customer to keep the accounts separate, but Roskill J's opinion evidently was also intended to encompass the implied agreement arising in the case of a loan account and a current account. See also Lord Kilbrandon in the House of Lords [1972] AC 785, 819. Compare *Re Johnson & Co Ltd* [1902] 1 IR 439, in which the agreement was entered into specifically in contemplation of a winding up.

[258] *Halesowen Presswork & Assemblies Ltd v Westminster Bank Ltd* [1971] 1 QB 1, 24 (Roskill J). A demand by a bank upon a customer for repayment does not terminate the banker and customer relationship. See *National Bank of Greece v Pinios Shipping Co (No. 1)* [1990] 1 AC 637, 684.

[259] *Direct Acceptance Corporation Ltd v Bank of New South Wales* (1968) 88 WN (Pt 1) (NSW) 498, 504 (in which there was an express agreement not to set off).

[260] *Quaere* whether combination in this circumstance would require an act, or at least an assertion, of combination, given that the banker/customer relationship has terminated. See also paras 15.30 and 15.31 above.

[261] [1962] 1 Ch 21.

[262] Conversely, Roskill J said (at [1991] 1 QB 1, 23) that it could not be contended that the accounts remain separate after bankruptcy or liquidation without also contending that *Re Keever* [1967] 1 Ch 182 was wrongly decided. That conclusion does not necessarily follow. In *Re Keever*, a customer had three accounts with a bank, one in credit and two in debit (being a 'private' account and a loan account). The bank received a cheque from the customer for collection. It collected the cheque the next day, and on that day the customer also became bankrupt. Ungoed-Thomas J held that the bank had a lien on the cheque for the amounts owing, and that it was entitled to set off the proceeds against the debit balances. However, that does not require a conclusion about combination of the accounts. The case is explicable on the ground that the indebtedness on the private and the loan accounts, whether combined or separate, was secured by the lien, and that upon receipt of the proceeds the bank was entitled to apply them against the amounts owing, as an incident of the security conferred by the lien. See para. 15.123 below.

[263] See para. 6.119–6.146 above.

[264] The contrary seems to have been assumed in the House of Lords in the *Halesowen* case [1972] AC 785, 807 (Viscount Dilhorne), 811–12 (Lord Cross of Chelsea), 820 (Lord Kilbrandon).

15.59 *Re E J Morel* concerned the Companies Act 1948, s. 319(4), which, subject to certain limitations, conferred a right of priority in the liquidation of a company in favour of a person who had advanced money for the payment of wages to an employee of the company.[265] A company's current account was substantially overdrawn. This account (the No. 1 account) was frozen, and a No. 2 account, being a normal business current account, and a No. 3 account, called a wages account, were opened. The company was allowed to draw on the No. 3 account in order to pay the wages of its employees. However, it was a term of the arrangement that the No. 2 account had to have at all times a credit balance in excess of the debit on the No. 3 wages account. Buckley J held that the credit balance on the No. 2 account should be treated as reducing the debit on the wages account, rather than the debit on the No. 1 account. Therefore, the bank had a reduced claim to priority for sums advanced for the payment of wages, and it was left with a right of proof on the No. 1 account for which no priority was accorded. In order for the bank to have succeeded in its claim to priority, it had to be shown that the bank had actually made advances for the purpose of paying wages. Buckley J said that, because of the agreement to freeze the No. 1 account so as no longer to be capable of being operated in the ordinary way as a current account, it had assumed the character of a loan account.[266] Therefore, the arrangement usually implied in the case of a loan account and a current account in credit was applicable, that the No. 1 frozen account and the No. 2 current account should be regarded as separate and distinct,[267] which in turn meant that payments credited to the No. 2 account could not be regarded as having operated to reduce the prior debit balance on the No. 1 account.[268] In so far as the No. 3 wages account was concerned, the parties had agreed that any debit balance on that account was always to be covered by a credit balance on the No. 2 account, which led Buckley J to conclude that those two accounts were not separate, but were interdependent. In substance, they constituted the one account. The bank itself therefore had not made any advances for the payment of wages, except to the extent that at the final date the debit on the wages account was greater than the credit on the No. 2 account. Rather, the wages had been paid from the customer's own 'money' in the No. 2 account. Buckley J was not concerned with the question whether a combination could occur after termination of the banker/customer relationship as a result of the liquidation. Indeed, this should not be an issue in any event if the insolvency set-off section takes effect automatically upon the occurrence of the liquidation.[269] The essence of his analysis was simply that the bank had not made an advance on each occasion when resort was had to the wages account for the purpose of paying wages. The source of the payment instead was the company's own 'money' in the No. 2 account. The point upon which the judgment proceeded was how the

---

[265] See now the Insolvency Act 1986, ss. 175 and 386, referring to Sch. 6 (in particular category 5).

[266] Similarly, the assertion by counsel in the *Halesowen* case [1971] 1 QB 1, 9, that once the overdrawn No. 1 account in that case was frozen it became for all practical purposes a loan account, was not disputed. See e.g. in the House of Lords [1972] AC 785, 809 (Lord Cross of Chelsea), 819 (Lord Kilbrandon).

[267] See also *Re Deague* (1951) 15 ABC 197, 202. Riley J's *dictum* in *Re Shaw* (1977) 31 FLR 118, 122, that independently of the letter of set-off the bank had a right to combine the working current account in credit with the frozen overdrawn current account, should be regarded as doubtful.

[268] Compare the arrangement adopted in *Re James R Rutherford & Sons Ltd; Lloyd's Bank Ltd v Winter* [1964] 1 WLR 1211.

[269] See para. 15.58 above.

accounts operated prior to the liquidation, as opposed to how they were to be dealt with after the liquidation.

Buckley J then went on to consider the position the would have applied if he was wrong in the view that he had taken in relation to the No. 2 account and the wages account, in other words if all three accounts were separate so that the debit balance on the wages account indeed represented sums advanced by the bank for the purpose of paying wages. In that circumstance he said that the insolvency set-off section would have operated on the basis that the claim which otherwise would be preferred in the winding-up should be the first claim to be brought into account with the creditor's own liability to the company. This would have had the effect that the debit balance on the wages accounts would have been paid by a set-off against the credit balance on the No. 2 account, and so the same result would have been achieved. This aspect of Buckley J's judgment would no longer appear to be good law, following *Re Unit 2 Windows Ltd*.[270] In that case, Walton J advocated a different approach to the question of set-off where a creditor of a company in liquidation has both a preferred and a non-preferred claim. He had recourse to the maxim that equality is equity, and accordingly considered that a set-off should occur rateably as between the claims.[271] On that analysis, *Re E J Morel* would be a case in which the operation of the principle of combination prior to the liquidation produced a different result to that which would have obtained after the liquidation under the insolvency set-off section on the assumption that the accounts were separate.

15.60

(5) Freezing an overdrawn account and opening a new account

An arrangement similar to that in *Re E J Morel* is sometimes adopted when a bank is concerned as to the solvency of a customer with a substantially overdrawn current account. The overdrawn account is frozen, and a new current account is opened through which the customer's current business henceforth is to pass. This second current account is required to remain in credit, the intention being that the customer's indebtedness on the frozen account should be reduced progressively by occasional payments into it from the credit balance on the operating current account. As Buckley J noted in the *Morel* case, the act of freezing an overdrawn current account converts it into a loan account so that, even apart from any express agreement between the parties that the bank should not have a right of set-off,[272] the courts would usually find an implied agreement to the effect that the accounts should not be combined during the subsistence of the banker/customer relationship. The presumption that the accounts are intended to be separate will not be rebutted by the agreement that the debit on the frozen account should be reduced progressively, as long as the intention is that any transfers from one account to the other should be made on the instructions of the customer rather than on the initiative of the bank alone, albeit at the insistence of the bank.[273] Nor would the presumption be rebutted by an agreement that interest due

15.61

---

[270] [1985] 1 WLR 1383.
[271] See paras 6.168–6.173 above.
[272] As in *Direct Acceptance Corporation Ltd v Bank of New South Wales* (1968) 88 WN (Pt 1) (NSW) 498.
[273] *Re E J Morel (1934) Ltd* [1962] 1 Ch 21, 26.

on the frozen overdraft may be debited to the new account.[274] It may be, however, that, prior to (or as part of) this arrangement, the customer had given a letter of set-off to the bank authorizing the bank at any time without notice to apply a credit balance on any of the customer's accounts as payment of any account in debit. In the absence of a later agreement negativing the operation of the letter, this may have the effect that the usual implied term precluding combination in such cases would not arise.[275]

(6) Agreement to exclude set-offs

15.62 The parties may wish to exclude set-off in the event of the customer's bankruptcy or liquidation. For example, a company in financial difficulty may have proposed a moratorium with its creditors, or it may intend to realize its assets as a means of paying its debts. In order to prevent a situation arising in which its bank alone is benefited by any payments deposited with it, the parties may agree that the company's overdrawn account should be frozen and that a new account should be opened which is to remain in credit, and moreover that the bank should not be entitled to set off the credit balance on this new account against the debit balance on the frozen account. The House of Lords in *National Westminster Bank Ltd v Halesowen Presswork & Assemblies Ltd*[276] struck down this form of arrangement in the event of the bankruptcy or liquidation of the customer, by holding that the operation of the set-off section in the insolvency legislation cannot be excluded by agreement between the parties.[277] As a result, it is necessary for the customer in this situation to open a working account with a different bank if it is intended that the first bank is not to be preferred by means of a set-off at the expense of the other creditors in the event of bankruptcy or winding up proceedings. The Cork Committee described this as 'an unnecessary and undesirable complication',[278] and recommended that a creditor should be permitted to agree in advance with a debtor to waive the operation of the insolvency set-off section, particularly given that the creditor is the party who otherwise would be benefited by a set-off. This is a salutary proposal, and it is regrettable that a provision giving effect to it was not included in the Insolvency Act 1986.

(7) Bank's conduct precluding combination

15.63 Roskill J at first instance in the *Halesowen* case[279] said that a bank by its actions may preclude itself from asserting a combination. That observation requires further comment. If the general principle is that accounts are combined in a single debt unless there is an agreement to the contrary, the bank's actions should not preclude a combination unless those actions have the effect of giving rise to an agreement with the customer that henceforth the accounts should be regarded as separate, or the bank is otherwise estopped from asserting that there is an agreement in those terms. For example, the fact that a bank debits and credits interest to each account separately is not sufficient to preclude the bank from

---

[274] This is apparent from the *Halesowen* case [1972] AC 785.
[275] See e.g. *Re Shaw* (1977) 31 FLR 118, and para. 15.74 below.
[276] [1972] AC 785.
[277] See paras 6.111–6.112 above.
[278] *Cork Committee Report*, 306.
[279] [1971] 1 QB 1, 19.

asserting that the accounts are combined.[280] Nor should separate bank statements have that effect. Separate statements merely reflect the undoubted fact that a bank has a number of accounts entered in its books, and, as Lindley MR noted in *Mutton v Peat*,[281] no matter how many accounts a bank may have entered in its books the amount due to the bank is the balance of all of them.

(8) Deposit for a specific purpose

If money is deposited with a bank for a specific purpose known to the bank, for example, in order to provide funds to meet a particular cheque or bill of exchange, the courts may imply an agreement that the money should not be combined with an overdrawn account.[282]   **15.64**

(9) Consequences of an agreement to keep accounts separate

Usually an express or an implied agreement that accounts are separate would simply mean that each account should be considered as giving rise to a separate debt. It would deprive the bank of the right to act unilaterally based upon an assumption that there is only one debt arising out of the banker/customer relationship. The bank could not, for example, dishonour a cheque on the basis of the customer's entire position with the bank. Depending on the terms of the agreement, however, it may not have the additional effect of negating a right of set-off under the Statutes of Set-off as a defence to an action at law by the customer for payment of the balance on an account in credit,[283] or indeed under the insolvency set-off section in the event that the recommendation of the Cork Committee that contracting out should be permitted is ever adopted.[284] The agreement would bring about the very situation necessary for a set-off, that is, mutual and independent cross-demands. In relation to the Statutes of Set-off, the defence is only available in the case   **15.65**

---

[280] See para. 15.20 above. Mocatta J, in expressing this view in *Barclays Bank Ltd v Okenarhe* [1966] 2 Lloyd's Rep 87, 98, postulated that, in certain circumstances, the crediting of interest on an account might be evidence that the parties had reached agreement that the accounts should be kept separate. He conceded, however, that: 'the circumstances would probably have to be somewhat exceptional since . . . the general practice is that interest is either credited or debited after calculation by reference to one account and not to all the accounts between a customer and his bank.'

[281] [1900] 2 Ch 79, 85.

[282] *Garnett v M'Kewan* (1872) LR 8 Ex 10, 13 (citing *Hill v Smith* (1844) 12 M & W 618, 152 ER 1346); *MPS Constructions Pty Ltd v Rural Bank of New South Wales* (1980) 4 ACLR 835, 841–2 (account opened for retention money under a building contract). See also *W. P. Greenhalgh and Sons v Union Bank of Manchester* [1924] 2 KB 153. Compare *Oceanica Castelana Armadora SA v Mineralimportexport* [1983] 1 WLR 1294, in which the customer had deposited money for the purpose of securing a guarantee intended to be given by the bank to a third party, though that purpose failed. In some cases there may also be a trust, as in *Barclays Bank Ltd v Quistclose Investments Ltd* [1970] AC 567. See para. 15.90 below.

[283] *Bank of Ireland v Martin* [1937] IR 189, 205; *Flanagan v National Bank Ltd* [1939] IR 352. See also *Hill v Smith* (1844) 12 M & W 618, 631, 152 ER 1346, 1351 (money deposited with a bank for a specific purpose).

[284] See para. 15.62 above. See also e.g. *Ex p Pearce, re Langmead* (1841) 2 Mont D & De G 142, and *Pedder v The Mayor, Aldermen, and Burgesses of Preston* (1862) 12 CB (NS) 535, 142 ER 1251, with respect to special-purpose local government accounts. The denial of a set-off in cases such as *Hill v Smith* (1844) 12 M & W 618, 631, 152 ER 1346, 1351 and *Bell v Carey* (1849) 8 CB 887, 137 ER 757, when the customer's assignees in bankruptcy sued for damages rather than for money had and received, may be explained on the ground that, before the Bankruptcy Act 1861, a damages claim could neither be proved in the bankruptcy nor set off. See para. 10.52 above.

of mutual debts.[285] The customer's action, therefore, would have to be for payment of a debt, in the form of the balance standing to the credit of an account. The bank would not have a defence under the Statutes if the customer is suing instead for damages, for example for failure to honour a cheque.

G. Combination and Nominee Accounts

15.66   An account may be opened in the name of A, who, unknown to the bank, is merely a nominee for B. If B also happens to be a customer who is separately indebted to the bank on another account, the bank, when it discovers the nomineeship, may wish to assert that a credit balance on A's account may be combined with a debit balance on B's account.

15.67   Nominee accounts were considered earlier in the context of equitable set-off.[286] In a number of cases the Court of Appeal has accepted that, if A (in the example) commences proceedings against the bank for payment of the credit balance on the account in A's name and seeks summary judgment, the bank will not be given leave to defend, based upon a defence of equitable set-off arising out of B's debt to the bank, unless the bank adduces clear and indisputable evidence that the account in A's name is held on trust for B.[287] Equitable set-offs can take various forms,[288] but since the accounts ordinarily would not be sufficiently connected to give rise to a substantive equitable set-off,[289] the equitable set-off in issue would be based upon equity acting by analogy with the right of set-off available at law under the Statutes of Set-off.[290] Set-off under the Statutes is limited in its effect. It is confined to the case of mutual debts.[291] Further, it merely provides a procedural defence to an action at law for payment of a debt. The set-off is brought about by an order of the court consequent upon the pleading of set-off as a defence. The set-off cannot be effected by one party acting unilaterally.[292] The Statutes applied to cross-debts at common law between the parties to an action at law.[293] However, equity may act by analogy with the Statutes when debts are mutual having regard to equitable rights.[294] This may include a situation where a debt owed by a bank to A is held by A on trust for B and B is separately indebted to the bank on another account. The debts in such a case are mutual having regard to B's equitable interest in A's debt. When equity acts by analogy with the Statutes, it gives the same construction to the Statutes as at law.[295] The Statutes therefore should be ascribed a similar procedural operation. In other words, the set-off should simply be a procedural defence to

---

[285] See para. 2.14–2.28 above.

[286] See paras 11.21–11.36 above.

[287] See para. 11.23 above, referring to *Bhogal v Punjab National Bank* [1988] 2 All ER 296, *Uttamchandami v Central Bank of India* unreported but noted in (1989) 139 *New Law Journal* 222 and *Saudi Arabian Monetary Agency v Dresdner Bank AG* [2005] 1 Lloyd's Rep 12.

[288] See ch. 3 above.

[289] See ch. 4 above.

[290] The Statutes of Set-off are discussed in ch. 2 above.

[291] See paras 2.04–2.06 and 2.14 above.

[292] See paras 2.34–2.39 above.

[293] See para. 11.18 above.

[294] See paras 3.07 and 11.18 above.

[295] See *Ex p Stephens* (1805) 11 Ves Jun 24, 27, 32 ER 996, 997 (Lord Eldon) and para. 3.08 above.

an action.[296] Nevertheless, it seems to have been assumed in the cases that, if a bank has clear and indisputable evidence that a credit account in the name of A in truth is a nominee account held for the benefit of B who is separately indebted to the bank, the bank's right of set-off may extend beyond a procedural defence to an action by A for payment. *Bhogal v Punjab National Bank*[297] involved two applications for summary judgment against a bank in separate actions for payment of the credit balances on accounts which the bank alleged were nominee accounts. Prior to the actions, the bank had dishonoured cheques drawn on the accounts in reliance on an equitable set-off as against the person for whose benefit the accounts were alleged to have been held. In affirming the necessity for clear and indisputable evidence of the nomineeship in order to obtain leave to defend, Dillon LJ commented:[298]

> It is one thing when the fact that a customer holds his accounts as nominee or bare trustee for a third party is clear and indisputable. It is quite another where the alleged nomineeship is very far from plainly made out and is strongly disputed. It would be wholly contrary to the rules of banking law, above indicated, if a bank could without warning dishonour a customer's cheque when there were funds to cover it in the account, on a tenuous, if just arguable, suspicion that the account was held by the customer as nominee for a third party who was indebted to the bank, and if the bank could then freeze the customer's account until it had been ascertained after full inquiry after a lengthy trial a year or more later whether the customer was indeed such a nominee.

This suggests an acceptance of the proposition that, if indeed there had been clear and indisputable evidence that the accounts were nominee accounts, the bank would have been entitled to freeze the accounts and dishonour cheques. A note of the unreported judgment of Lloyd LJ in *Uttamchandami v Central Bank of India*[299] suggests that he was of the same view, and it also finds support in *Saudi Arabian Monetary Agency v Dresdner Bank AG*.[300]

In *Saudi Arabian Monetary Agency v Dresdner*, the claimant (SAMA) instructed the defend‑ **15.68** ant bank to transfer a sum of money from SAMA's account to an account with another bank. The defendant bank had obtained an assignment from an affiliated bank (Dresdner Bank Luxembourg SA) of a debt owing by other entities which were emanations of the Saudi Arabian government, and it asserted that the funds in SAMA's account were also held on trust for the Saudi Arabian government. On that basis, the bank refused to comply with the instruction to the extent of the debt owing to it consequent upon the assignment. SAMA admitted that it was not the beneficial owner of the funds in the account,[301] but denied that the Saudi Arabian government was the beneficial owner. SAMA accordingly

---

[296] Before the Judicature Acts, equitable set-offs were enforced by means of an injunction to restrain the plaintiff in an action at law from either proceeding with the action or enforcing a judgment until credit had been given for a cross-claim, but since the Judicature Acts a defendant has been permitted to plead equitable set-off directly as a defence to an action. See para. 3.01 above.

[297] [1988] 2 All ER 296.

[298] [1988] 2 All ER 296, 301. This passage was referred to in *Saudi Arabian Monetary Agency v Dresdner Bank AG* [2005] 1 Lloyd's Rep 12, 17–18.

[299] See (1989) 139 *New Law Journal* 222, 223, referring to the freezing of an account.

[300] [2005] 1 Lloyd's Rep 12.

[301] SAMA pleaded that the moneys in the account were 'attributable' to the General Organisation of Social Insurance, which was taken as an admission by SAMA that it was not the beneficial owner of the moneys.

commenced proceedings against the bank, seeking a declaration that the bank was not entitled to block the account and an order requiring the bank to transfer the funds in accordance with SAMA's instruction. The Court of Appeal held that the correct approach was to look at the position on the basis of the material upon which the bank relied at the time when it refused to comply with the instruction. On that basis, the evidence that the Saudi Arabian government had an equitable interest in the account was not clear and indisputable, and summary judgment was accordingly given in favour of SAMA.

15.69 At first instance in that case it had been accepted as 'common ground' that, if the money in the SAMA account was clearly the property of the Saudi government, the bank would have been able to block the account,[302] and there was no dissent from that proposition in the Court of Appeal. This is consistent with the suggestions in the *Bhogal* and *Uttamchandami* cases (above) that, if there is clear and indisputable evidence that an account is a nominee account held for the benefit of another person who is indebted to the bank, the bank would be entitled to freeze the account and dishonour cheques on the basis of equitable set-off. Nevertheless, the justification for that view is not readily apparent. The Statutes of Set-off, including where equity applies the Statutes by analogy in the situation where there is mutuality by reference to equitable interests, merely provide a procedural defence to an action for payment.[303] *Prima facie*, that procedural defence would not justify the bank in refusing to honour cheques otherwise properly drawn on the account. If a bank were to dishonour cheques drawn within the credit balance on the account,[304] the bank could be liable in damages for breach of contract for any loss suffered by the customer,[305] notwithstanding that the bank would have had a defence of set-off to an action for payment of the account balance. This is a consequence of the procedural nature of the defence.

15.70 The bank would not be liable for dishonouring cheques if it could rely on combination of accounts.[306] But there is a difficulty with combination in this situation.[307] When an account

---

[302] See Chadwick LJ in the Court of Appeal [2005] 1 Lloyd's Rep 12 at [5]. The relief sought by SAMA was an order requiring the bank to follow the instructions given to it. As Longmore LJ noted (at [35]), this was a form of specific performance (or a mandatory injunction). He said that the existence of the cross-claim to recover the debt would not have provided a defence to an action for specific performance, but if the evidence of a trust was clear the court in its discretion may have refused to make the order. See the discussion of the relationship between set-off and specific performance at paras 2.58–2.61 and 5.81–5.85 above.

[303] See para. 15.67 above.

[304] Assuming that the bank had not given the requisite notice terminating the account. See para. 15.29 above.

[305] *Ellinger's Modern Banking Law* (4th edn, 2006), 412–14, 461–5; *Paget's Law of Banking* (13th edn, 2007), 479–80.

[306] Another possibility would be an implied term in the contract between the bank and its customer, being the nominee (see below), to the effect that the bank may dishonour cheques drawn on the account if the beneficial owner of the account is separately indebted to the bank. This is the converse of the implied term contemplated by Chadwick LJ in *Saudi Arabian Monetary Agency v Dresdner Bank AG* [2005] 1 Lloyd's Rep 12 at [23] and [31] and by Neuberger J at first instance in that case [2004] 2 Lloyd's Rep 19 at [44]. But if the customer's status as a nominee was unknown to the bank when the account was opened, it would be difficult to see the basis for any such term, in particular as to why it should be regarded as necessary to give business efficacy to the contract between them.

[307] Compare the cases referred to in para. 15.47 above in relation to accounts opened in different names, but those cases are distinguishable. They concerned the one person, albeit using different names. In the case of a nominee account, different persons are involved, being the nominee and the principal who is separately indebted to the bank. In *Uttamchandami v Central Bank of India*, unreported but noted in (1989) 139

is opened and, unknown to the bank at the time, it is a nominee account, the nominee would be the customer, not the person for whom the account is held. The banker/customer relationship is one of contract, and the nominee ordinarily would be the contracting party.[308] The same banker/customer relationship therefore would not be in issue in relation to the accounts for the purpose of a combination.[309] There may, however, be instances in which the person for whom the nominee has opened the account is disclosed to the bank,[310] so that that person is regarded by all parties as the customer. Depending on the circumstances, combination may be appropriate in such a case in relation to that account and another account possessed by the customer.

A similar analysis may apply in the case of a customer with a loan account and a current account in credit. In such a case, an agreement ordinarily is implied that the accounts are to be kept separate so as to preclude combination.[311] If the bank were to dishonour cheques drawn on the current account because of the debt on the loan account, in circumstances where there were sufficient funds credited to the current account to cover the cheques, the bank could be liable in damages to the customer.[312] If, on the other hand, the customer were to sue the bank for payment of the credit balance on the account, the bank may have a defence of set-off under the Statutes of Set-off in relation to the loan if the loan is presently payable,[313] the accounts constituting mutual debts for the purpose of the Statutes.[314] **15.71**

(1) Collecting a cheque for another person

Consider that a cheque payable to B is deposited into A's account for the purpose of collection on behalf of B, and B happens to be separately indebted to the bank. In *Abbey National plc v McCann*,[315] Carswell LJ in the Northern Ireland Court of Appeal suggested that, when a cheque deposited in those circumstances was collected and the proceeds credited to A's account, there was an arguable case that the part of A's account representing B's beneficial entitlement to the proceeds could be combined with B's debt.[316] Ordinarily, that should **15.72**

New Law Journal 222, it is unclear if Lloyd LJ's remarks (at 223) concerning a case in which the account is indisputably a nominee account were intended to apply to combination giving the bank a right to dishonour cheques (as discussed in the preceding paragraph) or only to the availability of equitable set-off as a defence to an action for payment of the balance on that account. In *Bhogal v Punjab National Bank* [1988] 2 All ER 296, the headnote refers to a 'right to combine or set off', but combination (as distinct from equitable set-off) was not discussed in the judgments in the Court of Appeal. On the contrary, Scott J at first instance said that: 'This is not a case . . . in which the bank is seeking to exercise its common law right as a banker of combining accounts.' See [1988] 2 All ER 296, 305.

[308] *Saudi Arabian Monetary Agency v Dresdner Bank AG* [2005] 1 Lloyd's Rep 12 at [22]–[23]. When an agent contracts on behalf of an undisclosed principal, the agent is the contracting party. See para. 13.77 above.

[309] See para. 15.04 above. In *Saudi Arabian Monetary Agency v Dresdner Bank AG* [2005] 1 Lloyd's Rep 12 there was the additional factor that the debt to the defendant was obtained by way of an assignment from an affiliated bank.

[310] As occurred in *Re Hett, Maylor, and Co* (1894) 10 TLR 412.

[311] See para. 15.54 above.

[312] *Buckingham and Co v London and Midland Bank* (1895) 12 TLR 70.

[313] See para. 15.65 above.

[314] See paras 2.04–2.06 and 2.14 above.

[315] [1997] Northern Ireland Judgments Bulletin 158, 172–3.

[316] Carswell LJ (at [1997] NIJB 158, 172) referred to this as 'equitable set-off', which he said was 'basically the right to combine accounts'. See also Hutton LCJ at 180. Compare Nicholson LJ, who said (at 183) that there was no right of 'equitable set-off'.

not be the case, however. The debt is owed to the bank by B, but the deposit is into A's account. The deposit does not occur in the course of B's banking relationship with the bank, but rather through the medium of A's relationship. Separate banker/customer relationships therefore are in issue, so that there should not be a combination.[317]

H. Agreements Permitting Combination

15.73   A customer may agree with his or her bank that the bank may set off or consolidate or combine all or any of the customer's accounts at any time without notice.[318] An agreement in those terms contemplates an act of combination by the bank.[319] In considering the effect of the agreement, however, two situations that should be distinguished.

15.74   In the first place, it may be that two accounts are in issue which *prima facie* come within the ambit of the law of combination, being accounts arising pursuant to the one banker/customer relationship,[320] but that in the circumstances the courts usually would imply an agreement that the accounts are to be kept separate. Thus, when a customer has a loan account and a current account in credit, a term is usually implied that the current account is to be separate from the loan account so that the customer can deal safely with third parties in the knowledge that he or she has an account in credit against which cheques can be drawn.[321] Yet, in such a case, an agreement empowering the bank to combine the accounts at any time without notice[322] would abrogate the very reason for implying a term to keep them separate.[323] Therefore, even though the agreement may seem to contemplate some form of act of combination by the bank, it may be that the fact that the customer has authorized the bank to effect a set-off at any time without notice would mean that the accounts in any event are combined in a single debt. Alternatively, it may be that the agreement contemplates that a credit balance on an account may be applied in satisfaction of a liability in circumstances in which a combination would not otherwise be recognized, not because of an implied agreement in order to safeguard a credit account against which cheques may be drawn, but because there are separate banker/customer relationships. Thus, the letter may allow the bank to appropriate a customer's separate credit balance as

---

[317] See para. 15.04 above.

[318] In *Voyer v Canadian Imperial Bank of Commerce* [1986] 1 WWR 174, a bank improperly exercised a contractual right of set-off against a deposit account, and the customer sued in conversion in respect of the sum removed from the account. However, conversion is an inappropriate form of action in this situation. Conversion relates to interference with the right to possession of a chattel (see *MCC Proceeds Inc v Lehman Bros International (Europe)* [1998] 4 All ER 675, 685–6), and a bank account is not a chattel. The appropriate remedy is a declaration that the account was improperly debited. See *Clerk and Lindsell on Torts* (19th edn, 2006), 1022, n. 51.

[319] Depending on the terms of the agreement, this may not require a book entry. It may suffice if the bank asserts that the accounts are combined. See para. 15.74 below.

[320] See para. 15.04 above.

[321] See para. 15.54 above.

[322] As in *Matthews v Geraghty* (1986) 43 SASR 576. See also the letters of set-off in *Re Shaw* (1977) 31 FLR 118, 120 and *Re K (Restraint Order)* [1990] 2 QB 298, 299–300.

[323] This may explain Riley J's comments in *Re Shaw* (1977) 31 FLR 118, 122, given that a closed overdraft account is regarded as a loan account and therefore it cannot be the subject of a combination with another current account in credit. See para. 15.59 above.

satisfaction of a joint liability,[324] or it may entitle the bank to consolidate the accounts of the various companies in a group. An appropriation of the credit balance could only arise as a result of an act by the bank which is authorized by the set-off agreement. If an act of combination is required, it may not necessitate an actual book entry.[325] Depending on the terms of the agreement, an assertion that the accounts have been consolidated or combined may suffice.[326]

(1) Contingent obligation

Whether a right of set-off conferred by a set-off agreement extends to an amount which is not presently due and payable depends on the construction of the agreement.[327] In that regard, a bank is sometimes empowered to set off an account in credit against a liability which is contingent. Professor Goode has suggested that an agreement in those terms may be interpreted in either of two ways.[328] The more likely construction is that the bank is entitled to suspend payment of the account in credit until such time as the liability may vest, followed, if it does vest, by a set-off. Alternatively, there may be cases where the effect of the agreement is that the bank's liability on the account in credit is immediately cancelled to the extent of the maximum contingent liability, with an obligation to re-credit the customer if and to the extent that the contingent liability does not become an actual liability. **15.75**

(2) Account subject to an assignment or a trust

An agreement authorizing a bank to set off accounts will not be effective in relation to an account where moneys credited to the account were the subject of a prior assignment or trust in favour of a third party, and the bank had notice of the assignment or trust.[329] If the bank did not have notice, it will obtain priority if it was a *bona fide* purchaser for value.[330] **15.76**

(3) Customer's liquidation

An exercise of a contractual right of combination or set-off in relation to a customer's credit account after the commencement of the customer's liquidation, in circumstances where the insolvency set-off section does not apply, would be struck down as contrary to the *pari passu* principle.[331] **15.77**

---

[324] See para. 15.46 above.
[325] There may be an express provision to that effect in the agreement. See e.g. the letter of set-off in *Re Shaw* (1977) 31 FLR 118 (the material terms of the letter are set out at 120).
[326] See Roskill J at first instance in *Halesowen Presswork & Assemblies Ltd v National Westminster Bank Ltd* [1971] 1 QB 1, 19, and also *Direct Acceptance Corporation Ltd v Bank of New South Wales* (1968) 88 WN (Pt 1) (NSW) 498, 502.
[327] Compare *Matthews v Geraghty* (1986) 43 SASR 576, 580.
[328] *Goode on Legal Problems of Credit and Security* (4th edn (ed. Gullifer), 2008), 287.
[329] *Re Marwalt Ltd* [1992] BCC 32.
[330] *Neste Oy v Lloyds Bank Plc* [1983] 2 Lloyd's Rep 658, 666; *Re Marwalt Ltd* [1992] BCC 32, 38. See paras 15.93–15.112 below.
[331] See para. 16.21 below.

I. Different Currencies

15.78 An issue that is yet to be determined is whether combination applies to accounts in different currencies.[332]

15.79 A discussion of the issue must begin with the fundamental point, that combination is an accounting situation in which the existence and amount of one party's liability to the other can only be ascertained by looking at the ultimate balance of all the accounts.[333] The concept is dynamic in nature. At any particular point in time there is, as a matter of law, only one debt for the balance. Therefore, for combination to apply to a foreign currency account, there should be a mechanism for converting the account into sterling such that at any point in time both parties could calculate the combined position. Further, since the basis of combination is the banker/customer relationship, the exchange rate should be the rate that the bank would make available to the customer for the account in question. In this sense it would differ from a currency conversion effected for the purpose of proof of debts in a bankruptcy or a liquidation, or for the purpose of enforcing a foreign currency judgment in accordance with the decision of the House of Lords in *Miliangos v George (Frank) Textiles Ltd*.[334] In those situations, a general objectively ascertainable market rate would suffice.[335] This would not be appropriate, however, in the case of combination, which should direct attention to the rate that would apply as between that bank and that customer.

15.80 What rate, then, would be applied for conversion if the parties have not expressly agreed a conversion mechanism? It could be said that there is an implied term in the contract between the bank and its customer that conversion would occur at the bank's published rate for the relevant currency applicable at the time, for example the rate quoted by the bank on its web site. There are problems with that view, however. In the first place, it is difficult to see why the customer should be taken to have agreed to accept that rate. Secondly, the quoted rate may be expressed to be applicable only to transactions up to a stated amount. Thirdly, the bank's published rate may only be used as a guide by the bank when it is asked to quote a rate in a particular case. Rates move during the day, and the rate that is quoted to a customer may vary from the published rate, depending on the bank's perception of the direction of the market and the standing of the customer. Therefore, at any point in time, a customer with a large foreign currency account may not be in a position to know with certainty what its combined position is. It could be said that the customer can request the bank at any time to advise the appropriate rate for conversion so that it may know the position at that time, but that would not be a convenient solution. Moreover, it may not be feasible outside banking hours. While the bank may continue to trade in foreign currencies

---

[332] For a discussion, see Horrigan, 'Combining bank accounts in different currencies – a conceptual analysis' (1991) 65 *Australian Law Journal* 14.

[333] See para. 15.04 above.

[334] [1976] AC 443.

[335] E.g. the Practice Direction published after the decision in *Miliangos v George (Frank) Textiles Ltd* referred to the rate current in London at the close of business on the day in question. See [1976] 1 WLR 83.

overnight, this may be limited to only some currencies, and the customer therefore may not be in a position to obtain advice in relation to a particular currency after hours.

In *Garnett v M'Kewan*,[336] Bramwell B justified the bank's right to dishonour a cheque **15.81** drawn on an account where there was another account in debit on the ground that: 'to limit [the customer's] drawing to the amount of his total actual balance is no hardship on him, for he always knows, or can know if he likes, the state of his account as a whole.' As a corollary, where the customer at any point in time cannot know the state of the accounts on a combined basis with certainty, it is suggested that combination should not apply.[337] In any event, the bank's applicable rate to an extent would be within the bank's discretion, which would hardly be a satisfactory basis for combination from the customer's point of view, particularly where large amounts of money are in issue. Having said that, there is authority in Canada to the effect that combination may apply in relation to foreign currency accounts. In *Deep v Bank of Montreal*,[338] the Ontario Court of Appeal held that a bank was entitled to apply a maturing Deutschmark term deposit against a Canadian dollar overdraft. The court simply assumed, however, that combination applies to foreign currency accounts. Further, there was no discussion of the conversion mechanism.

Alternatively, the bank may have an express contractual right to combine accounts, includ- **15.82** ing foreign currency accounts. Unlike for the common law principle of combination, an act of combination would be required in this situation.[339] In such a case the agreement should specify the mechanism for converting foreign currency accounts into sterling for the purpose of a combination.

J. Freezing Injunctions and Restraint Orders

In *Oceanica Castelana Armadora SA v Mineralimportexport*,[340] the plaintiff in a suit against **15.83** a foreign defendant had obtained a freezing (or, as it was then called, a Mareva) injunction restraining the defendant from removing or disposing of its assets situated within the jurisdiction up to a stated maximum amount. Barclays Bank held funds deposited with it by the defendant. However, the bank had also made substantial loans to the defendant, and so it applied to the court for an order to vary the injunction in order that it might exercise its right of 'set-off'. Lloyd J granted the variation on the grounds that a freezing injunction was not intended to interfere with the ordinary rights and remedies of a third party. He accepted that the funds held by the bank *prima facie* were covered by the wording of the injunction before him, and that therefore it was necessary that the bank should come to court for

---

[336] (1872) LR 8 Ex 10, 15.

[337] The point is unsettled, however, and other writers have expressed the contrary view. See Wood, *English and International Set-off* (1989), 97; McCracken, *The Banker's Remedy of Set-off* (3rd edn, 2010), 33; *Goode on Legal Problems of Credit and Security* (4th edn (ed. Gullifer), 2008), 297; *Ellinger's Modern Banking Law* (4th edn, 2006), 238. Compare *Paget's Law of Banking* (13th edn, 2007), 722–3.

[338] (1991) 47 OAC 319.

[339] See paras 15.73–15.74 above. Depending on the terms of the agreement, an assertion that the accounts are combined, without a book entry to that effect, may suffice. See para. 15.74 above.

[340] [1983] 1 WLR 1294.

a variation.[341] His Lordship said that this was unsatisfactory, and suggested that henceforth all freezing injunctions intended to be served on banks should contain a suitable proviso exempting the bank's right of 'set-off' from the operation of the injunction.[342] However, if the case is truly one of combination, it is not at all clear that a bank should be required to apply to the court for a variation in the absence of a specific proviso protecting its rights. In such a case a right to set off independent cross-demands is not in issue. Rather, the bank is entitled to say that there is only one debt owing by or to the customer for the balance of all the accounts arising in the course of the banker/customer relationship, unless a particular item has been separated out by agreement. Therefore, a particular account in credit with the bank should not be regarded as a separate asset of the customer coming within the ambit of a freezing injunction, if there are other accounts in debit which must be brought into account in order to ascertain the debt owing by the bank or the customer to the other. Thus, Canadian courts have recognized that, when a bank makes an entry in its books giving effect to the principle of combination, the entry itself does not constitute payment of an account in debit, since there was in any event only one debt for the balance.[343] Consistent with that approach, Otton J in *Re K (Restraint Order)*[344] held that a bank's assertion of a right of combination in relation to a deposit account and an overdraft account was not in conflict with the terms of a restraint order under s. 8 of the Drug Trafficking Offences Act 1986, which restrained all dealings with the accounts. As his Lordship noted,[345] combination in truth is merely an accounting procedure in order to ascertain the existence and amount of one party's liability to the other.

15.84 Alternatively, the 'set-off' asserted by the bank may not be in respect of accounts that are combined in that sense, but rather it may be based upon a contractual right of set-off in respect of separate debts. In that circumstance, the bank would require the protection contemplated by Lloyd J.

15.85 When an account in credit has been frozen as a result of a freezing injunction, Lloyd J considered that the bank's right of 'set-off' should be protected in relation to all liabilities of the customer arising in connection with facilities granted to the customer before the bank received notification of the injunction. Thus, he considered that the bank should be permitted to debit the account in respect of any liability which it may incur on confirmed letters of credit opened at the request of the customer before notice.[346] Further, he said that any right of set-off possessed by the bank may be exercised in respect of interest accruing

---

[341] See also *Project Development Co Ltd SA v KMK Securities Ltd* [1982] 1 WLR 1470.

[342] Lloyd J expressed approval of a clause suggested by counsel: 'Provided that nothing in this injunction shall prevent [the bank] from exercising any rights of set-off it may have in respect of facilities afforded by [the bank] to the defendants prior to the date of this injunction.' A similar exemption appears in the draft freezing injunction annexed to the Practice Direction supplementing CPR Part 25: 'This injunction does not prevent any bank from exercising any right of set off it may have in respect of any facility which it gave to the respondent before it was notified of this order.'

[343] *Re Sutcliffe & Sons Ltd, ex p Royal Bank* [1933] 1 DLR 562 (esp. at 569); *Ross v Royal Bank of Canada* (1965) 52 DLR (2d) 578; *Re T. C. Marines Ltd* (1973) 34 DLR (3d) 489; *Re Plasky* (1981) 39 CBR 186. For the same reason, the book-keeping entry does not constitute a seizure of assets. See *Deep v Bank of Montreal* (1991) 47 OAC 319.

[344] [1990] 2 QB 298.

[345] [1990] 2 QB 298, 304.

[346] See the *Oceanica Castelana* case [1983] 1 WLR 1294, 1301.

due both before and after notification, provided that the facility in question was granted to the customer before notification.[347]

K. Preferences

Given the true nature of the principle of combination, that in the absence of an express or implied agreement to the contrary an account in credit and another account with a debit balance are combined in a single debt, it should follow that the mere fact that the bank may make an entry in its books giving effect to the combination by itself should not constitute a preference, since there was in any event only one debt.[348] Rather, the question whether the preference section[349] applies should be ascertained by an examination of the circumstances surrounding the deposits made by the customer with the bank.[350]   **15.86**

It may be, however, that a customer has two accounts which, it has been expressly or impliedly agreed, are to be regarded as separate, but the bank is empowered by a letter of set-off to combine them.[351] The question whether the bank's action in doing so constitutes a preference is considered later in the context of a discussion of set-off agreements.[352]   **15.87**

L. Trust Accounts

(1) Introduction

A customer may be a trustee in respect of an account in credit opened in his or her name. This by itself would not preclude the application of the principle that all the accounts kept by a customer with a bank are combined in a single debt.[353] If, however, the bank has knowledge of the trust, the principle of combination would not apply.[354] Nor could the   **15.88**

---

347 [1983] 1 WLR 1294, 1301.

348 This has been held to be the case in Canada. See *Re Sutcliffe & Sons Ltd, ex p Royal Bank* [1933] 1 DLR 562 (esp. at 569); *Ross v Royal Bank of Canada* (1965) 52 DLR (2d) 578; *Re T. C. Marines Ltd* (1973) 34 DLR (3d) 489; *Re Plasky* (1981) 39 CBR 186. See also *Salter & Arnold Ltd v Dominion Bank* [1926] SCR 621, which nevertheless proceeded upon a different analysis, and *Re Shibou* (1983) 3 DLR (4th) 723, 726–7 (decision affirmed *Guttman v Toronto-Dominion Bank* [1984] 5 WWR 529). In Australia, Riley J in *Re Shaw* (1977) 31 FLR 118, 123 inclined to the view that a payment for the purpose of the preference section occurred when the cheque was deposited with the bank and presented for payment (13 September), or alternatively when the funds represented by the cheque were made available to the bank, as opposed to when the bank debited the account with a sum sufficient to cover the overdrawn account. See also *Matthews v Geraghty* (1986) 43 SASR 576; *Re Tonkin* (1933) 6 ABC 197, 210–11. In *Re Shaw, quaere* why the date of payment was not simply the date of deposit of the cheque (12 September).

349 See the Insolvency Act 1986, s. 340, and, for companies, s. 239.

350 As in *Hamilton v Commonwealth Bank of Australia* (1992) 9 ACSR 90 (following (at 109–10) *Matthews v Geraghty* (1986) 43 SASR 576), although in the circumstances of that case Hodgson J accepted (at 106) that the accounts at the date of the payment were separate.

351 This assumes that the giving of the letter of set-off does not have as a consequence that there is no implied agreement to keep the accounts separate. See para. 15.74 above.

352 See paras 16.06–16.20 below.

353 See *Union Bank of Australia Ltd v Murray-Aynsley* [1898] AC 693; *Bank of New South Wales v Goulburn Valley Butter Co Pty Ltd* [1902] AC 543, 550; *Clark v Ulster Bank Ltd* [1950] NILR 132. Compare *Garnett v M'Kewan* (1872) LR 8 Ex 10, 14 (Pigott B), 14–15 (Bramwell B).

354 *Bank of New South Wales v Goulburn Valley Butter Co Pty Ltd* [1902] AC 543, 550. See also *Re Branston & Gothard Ltd* [1999] Lloyd's Rep Bank 251; *Bodenham v Hoskyns* (1852) 2 De G M & G 903, 905,

bank in that circumstance rely on a set-off agreement entered into with the customer,[355] unless the beneficiaries of the trust had consented to it or the circumstances otherwise are such as to give rise to an estoppel.[356] If the customer becomes bankrupt or goes into liquidation, the fact of the trust would mean that there would be a lack of mutuality in equity,[357] which in turn would have the consequence that the bank could not set off the accounts under the insolvency set-off section. For that reason it may be crucial that, despite the trust, combination should apply.

15.89   The principle that an account in a customer's name which is known to be a trust account cannot be combined with another account held by the customer in his personal capacity potentially could be explained on either of two grounds. If, when the account was opened, the customer made it clear that it was a trust account, for example by specifically labelling it as such, the circumstances could be regarded as giving rise to an implied agreement that it is to be kept separate. In fact, that approach is not reflected in the cases.[358] Rather, the principle that combination does not apply has been based simply on the notion that the bank cannot use moneys which in equity are the property of a third party in order to satisfy the customer's personal debt. If, on the other hand, the bank did not know of the trust, it may obtain the benefit of the trust account in a combination where the defence of *bona fide* purchaser for value is available.[359]

(2) The requirement of a trust

15.90   The money deposited by the customer must have been impressed with a trust in the customer's hands. An important decision in that regard is *Barclays Bank Ltd v Quistclose Investments Ltd*,[360] in which the House of Lords held that a trust may arise when a sum of money is advanced by A to B for a specific purpose, for example, in order to pay B's creditors, or, as in the *Quistclose* case itself, in order that B may pay a dividend. The fact that the money is advanced by way of loan does not preclude the court from finding that it is

---

42 ER 1125, 1126; *Houben v Bank of Nova Scotia* (1970) 3 NBR (2d) 366, 381; *Law Society of Upper Canada v Toronto Dominion Bank* (1995) 36 CBR (3d) 220. In the latter case a bank employed a solicitor to act for it in relation to a loan, and credited the solicitor's trust account with the amount of the proposed loan. The trust account, although in credit, had a shortfall as a result of defalcations by the solicitor, and when the bank was informed of the shortfall it purported to debit the account with the amount that it had credited to it. It sought to justify the debit on the ground that it was entitled to revoke the trust and then to set off the solicitor's resulting debt to it against the part of the trust account constituted by its funds credited to the account. Farley J in the Ontario General Division held that the bank was not entitled to do so. He said that, when a trust account has a shortfall, it is held on trust on a *pro rata* basis for all persons whose moneys are in the account, and there was no separate part of it to which the bank alone was entitled, and which could be the subject of a set-off. Farley J's decision was affirmed by the Ontario Court of Appeal: *Law Society of Upper Canada v Toronto-Dominion Bank* (1998) 169 DLR (4th) 353.

[355] *Pannell v Hurley* (1845) 2 Coll 241, 245, 63 ER 716, 718; *Neste Oy v Lloyds Bank Plc* [1983] 2 Lloyd's Rep 658; *Royal Bank of Scotland Plc v Wallace International Ltd* [2000] EWCA Civ 16 (see at [8] and [48]). If the bank effects a set-off, it may be liable by reason of having dealt with trust property in a manner inconsistent with the trust of which it was congnizant. See *Lee v Sankey* (1872) LR 15 Eq 204, 211; *Soar v Ashwell* [1893] 2 QB 390, 396–7.

[356] Compare *Royal Bank of Scotland Plc v Wallace International Ltd* [2000] EWCA Civ 16.

[357] See para. 11.13–11.17 above.

[358] See paras 15.113–15.116 below.

[359] See *Re Marwalt Ltd* [1992] BCC 32, 38; *Neste Oy v Lloyds Bank Plc* [1983] 2 Lloyd's Rep 658, 666.

[360] [1970] AC 567.

subject to a trust. As Lord Wilberforce remarked in delivering the judgment of the Law Lords:[361] 'There is surely no difficulty in recognising the co-existence in one transaction of legal and equitable rights and remedies.'[362] Lord Wilberforce analysed the position in terms of a primary and a secondary trust. He said that there is a primary trust in favour of the persons intended to benefit from the payment, and A has an equitable right to see that the money in fact is applied to this designated purpose. If the purpose is carried out, B becomes a debtor to A. If, however, the purpose fails, it becomes necessary to see whether the parties intended that a secondary trust should arise in favour of A. In the instant case the purpose had failed,[363] and in the circumstances Lord Wilberforce said that it was clear that the parties had intended that there should be a secondary trust. Moreover, the bank with which B had deposited the money had been informed that the money had been raised by means of a loan advanced for the sole purpose of enabling B to satisfy its liability to pay the dividend. That was sufficient to give the bank notice that the money was impressed with a trust, notwithstanding that it may not have been aware of the identity of the lender[364] or of the detailed terms of the trust.[365] Because of the notice, the bank could not set off the account into which the trust money had been paid against B's overdraft. The nature of the trust in the *Quistclose* case has been much-debated. In *Twinsectra Ltd v Yardley*[366] Lord Millett rejected the suggestion that there are successive trusts. He favoured the view that the lender remains the beneficial owner of the money, but with a mandate given to the transferee to apply it for the stated purpose.[367] But, however it is characterized, the possibility of a trust in these circumstances is now widely accepted.

The justification for the trust in *Barclays Bank v Quistclose Investments* was the presumed **15.91** intention of the parties. It should be contrasted with the constructive trust found in *Neste Oy v Lloyds Bank plc*,[368] which was based upon a perception of what fairness and good conscience required. In *Neste Oy v Lloyds Bank*, a principal made a number of payments into its agent's general bank account, which was in credit, for the purpose of providing funds to meet expenses. One such payment was received after the directors of the agent's holding company had determined that the group and its members should cease trading and

---

[361] Lord Reid, Lord Morris of Borth-y-Gest, Lord Guest, Lord Pearce and Lord Wilberforce.
[362] [1970] AC 567, 581. Note also the comments of Dixon J in *Palette Shoes Pty Ltd v Krohn* (1937) 58 CLR 1, 30. The money may be advanced in accordance with an antecedent contractual obligation, rather than by way of loan. In *Carreras Rothmans Ltd v Freeman Mathews Treasure Ltd* [1985] 1 Ch 207, Peter Gibson J applied *Barclays Bank v Quistclose Investments* in a case in which the money was paid by A into a specially labelled bank account to be used by B solely for the purpose of paying C, when B was liable as a principal to C but with a right of reimbursement from A.
[363] Why had the purpose failed as a result of the resolution to wind up the company? See Goodhart and Jones, 'The infiltration of equitable doctrine into English commercial law' (1980) 43 MLR 489, 494, referring to the statement of facts by Harman LJ in the Court of Appeal [1968] 1 Ch 540, 549–51, and *Twinsectra Ltd v Yardley* [2002] 2 AC 164 at [98] *per* Lord Millett.
[364] See Lord Wilberforce in the House of Lords [1970] AC 567, 582.
[365] See Sachs LJ in the Court of Appeal in the *Quistclose* case [1968] 1 Ch 540, 567.
[366] [2002] 2 AC 164 at [77] *et seq*.
[367] See also Lord Hoffmann at [2002] 2 AC 164 at [13], whose opinion, though confined to the circumstances in issue, was consistent with Lord Millett's analysis. Lord Hutton at [25] agreed with Lord Hoffmann and Lord Millett that there was a trust, and Lord Slynn of Hadley at [2] agreed with Lord Hoffmann's reasons.
[368] [1983] 2 Lloyd's Rep 658.

that the group's bank should be requested to appoint a receiver.[369] Bingham J held that this gave rise to a trust, notwithstanding an absence of evidence of intention that payments received from the principal were to be kept separate from the agent's own funds, so that it was apparent that the parties had contracted on a debtor/creditor basis.[370] In the case of the payment credited to the agent's general account after the resolution to cease trading, the trust was justified on the ground that no honest person receiving money from another in that circumstance, when there was bound to be a total failure of consideration, could in good conscience retain it. Further, Bingham J accepted that the bank in all probability was aware of the decision to cease trading before the money was credited to the account.[371] Therefore, it had prior notice of the circumstances giving rise to the constructive trust, and so it was obliged to refund the money to the principal notwithstanding that the account was the subject of a contractual right of set-off in favour of the bank, which otherwise permitted set-off against other accounts in debit.

15.92   In some respects, *Neste Oy v Lloyds Bank* is similar to *Sinclair v Brougham*,[372] in which depositors with a building society were allowed to follow their money by reason of the fact that the purpose for which they had handed the money to the directors was incapable at law of fulfilment.[373] The cases are distinguishable, however. The 'purpose' in *Sinclair v Brougham* was that the money should be deposited with the building society on the basis of a banker/ customer relationship, and that it should be recoverable at a later date as a debt. That purpose failed because repayment was *ultra vires*. The depositors lacked the personal remedy against the building society for which they had bargained, and so the court found a proprietary remedy. On the other hand, the principal in the *Neste Oy* case still had the personal right of a creditor against the agent which had been the basis of their relationship. The justice of finding a constructive trust is by no means clear when the principal provided the money as an unsecured creditor and still retained the rights of a creditor.[374] The principal took the risk of the agent's insolvency, and the imposition of a constructive trust in such a case would seem to confer an unjustified priority in the event of the agent's liquidation.[375] *Sinclair v Brougham* has now been overruled by the House of Lords,[376] and it is suggested that *Neste Oy* similarly should be reconsidered.[377]

---

[369] The sequence of events is set out at [1983] 2 Lloyd's Rep 658, 662.

[370] [1983] 2 Lloyd's Rep 658, 664–5.

[371] See [1983] 2 Lloyd's Rep 658, 667.

[372] [1914] AC 398.

[373] See *Re Diplock. Diplock v Wintle* [1948] 1 Ch 465, 540–1.

[374] See Goff and Jones, *The Law of Restitution* (7th edn, 2007) 709; *Daly v Sydney Stock Exchange* (1986) 160 CLR 371, 379–80. Compare *Re Kayford Ltd* [1975] 1 WLR 279, in which the company had set up a separate trust account for its customers' moneys. Note the criticism of the decision in *Re Kayford* by Goodhart and Jones, 'The infiltration of equitable doctrine into English commercial law' (1980) 43 MLR 489, 494–7, but see *Re Branston & Gothard Ltd* [1999] Lloyd's Rep Bank 251, 258–9.

[375] The resolution in the *Neste Oy* case was merely to cease trading. There is no mention in the report of a subsequent liquidation, although the resolution was based upon the directors' perception that the group and its companies could not meet credit as it fell due.

[376] *Westdeutsche Landesbank Girozentrale v Islington LBC* [1996] AC 669.

[377] *Neste Oy v Lloyds Bank* was criticized by Ferris J in *Box v Barclays Bank* [1998] Lloyd's Rep Bank 185, 199–201, though it was referred to with approval by Harman J in *Kingscraft Insurance Co Ltd v H S Weavers (Underwriting) Agencies Ltd* [1993] 1 Lloyd's Rep 187, 195.

(3) The defence of *bona fide* purchaser for value

The bank in these cases asserts that it is entitled to look upon the credit balance on the trust **15.93** account as combined with the trustee's personal account in debit. The beneficiaries, on the other hand, say that the moneys deposited with the bank were subject to a trust in their favour, that those moneys can be traced into the bank's debt to the customer on the account in credit, that the account accordingly is held on trust for them, and that the fact of the trust therefore precludes combination in relation to the account. The bank may then respond by way of defence that it was a *bona fide* purchaser for value without notice of the moneys deposited with it,[378] so that it is not affected by the trust in relation to either those moneys or the account into which they can be traced. On that basis, the bank says that it should not be precluded by the trust from looking upon the accounts as combined.[379]

The defence of *bona fide* purchaser raises the issues of the bank's knowledge and whether it **15.94** gave value.

Knowledge of the trust

Sometimes the account will be headed in such plain terms that the bank cannot fail but to **15.95** know that it is a trust account, for example when a county treasurer opened accounts headed 'Superannuation Fund' and 'Police Account'.[380] If, on the other hand, there is nothing on the face of the account to show that it stood on any different footing from other accounts kept by the customer, or if there is nothing to indicate that the moneys deposited by the customer were impressed with a trust, the Privy Council in *Union Bank of Australia Ltd v Murray-Aynsley*[381] said that it is incumbent upon the *cestuis que trust* 'to prove that the moneys for which they now sue were, in the knowledge of the bank, trust funds'. In that regard, a bank would have knowledge if it wilfully shut its eyes to the obvious, since this is regarded as actual knowledge.[382] Moreover, it suffices if the bank has knowledge of the circumstances giving rise to a trust.[383] It is not necessary that the bank should appreciate the legal consequences of those circumstances.

The difference between knowledge and notice. When a prior equitable interest in **15.96** property is asserted against a transferee of the legal title to the property, the question whether the transferee takes free of the prior equitable interest traditionally is expressed in terms whether the transferee is a *bona fide* purchaser of the legal interest for value without notice. Notice includes the equitable doctrine of constructive notice.[384] But when money

---

[378] As to the onus of proof, see *Polly Peck International plc v Nadir (No. 2)* [1992] 4 All ER 769, 781.

[379] See *Neste Oy v Lloyds Bank Plc* [1983] 2 Lloyd's Rep 658, 666, and also *Re Marwalt Ltd* [1992] BCC 32, 38.

[380] *Ex p Kingston, re Gross* (1871) LR 6 Ch App 632. See also *Greenwell v National Provincial Bank* (1883) 1 Cab & El 56; *Re Branston & Gothard Ltd* [1999] Lloyd's Rep Bank 251 ('client money requirement' account).

[381] [1898] AC 693, 697.

[382] *English and Scottish Mercantile Investment Co v Brunton* [1892] 2 QB 700, 707–8; *John T Ellis Ltd v Walter T Hinds* [1947] 1 KB 475, 483; *Macquarie Bank Ltd v Sixty-Fourth Throne Pty Ltd* [1998] 3 VR 133, 163.

[383] *Barclays Bank Ltd v Quistclose Investments Ltd* [1970] AC 567, 582.

[384] Constructive notice is a wholly equitable doctrine. See *English and Scottish Mercantile Investment Co v Brunton* [1892] 2 QB 700, 708.

is paid into a bank account, 'knowledge' rather than 'notice' is considered to be the appropriate concept.[385] Those expressions are not synonymous.[386] Knowledge is a narrower concept. As Vinelott J remarked in *Eagle Trust plc v SBC Securities Ltd*:[387]

> However, 'notice' is often used in a sense or in contexts where the facts do not support the inference of knowledge. A man may have actual notice of a fact and yet not know it. He may have been supplied in the course of a conveyancing transaction with a document and so have actual notice of its content, but he may not in fact have read it; or he may have read it some time ago and have forgotten its content . . . So also by statute a man may be deemed to have actual notice of a fact which is clearly not within his knowledge.

In particular, the doctrine of constructive notice was developed in the field of property transactions in which a full and complete investigation of title is called for, and there is time to investigate title.[388] An investigation of that nature is inappropriate in the case of a commercial transaction involving the payment of money in the ordinary course of business,[389] and the courts have shown a marked reluctance to extend the doctrine to those circumstances.[390] On the other hand, where it is not the custom or practice to investigate title, and there is no recognized procedure for doing so, it has been said that an analogous concept may apply in a situation in which an honest and reasonable man would have made inquiry.[391] It has also been said, however, that in an ordinary commercial context it would be difficult to establish that the circumstances were such as to put a party to the transaction on inquiry.[392]

---

[385] *Union Bank of Australia Ltd v Murray-Aynsley* [1898] AC 693, 697 (PC) (referring to knowledge). See also *Polly Peck International plc v Nadir (No. 2)* [1992] 4 All ER 769, 781–2.

[386] *Mildred, Goyeneche & Co v Maspons y Hermano* (1883) 8 App Cas 874, 885; *Goodyear Tyre & Rubber Co (Great Britain) Ltd v Lancashire Batteries Ltd* [1958] 3 All ER 7, 12; *Cresta Holdings Ltd v Karlin* [1959] 3 All ER 656, 657 (Hodson LJ); *Carl Zeiss Stiftung v Herbert Smith & Co (No. 2)* [1969] 2 Ch 276, 296; *Re Montagu's Settlement Trusts* [1987] 1 Ch 264, 271, 285 (Megarry VC); *Eagle Trust plc v SBC Securities Ltd* [1992] 4 All ER 488, 497–8 (Vinelott J); *Polly Peck International plc v Nadir (No. 2)* [1992] 4 All ER 769, 781 (Scott LJ); *Westpac Banking Corporation v Adelaide Bank Ltd* (2005) 12 BPR 22,919, [2005] NSWSC 517 at [75]; *MCP Pension Trustees Ltd v Aon Pension Trustees Ltd* [2010] 2 WLR 268. In *Re Montagu's Settlement Trusts* Megarry VC said (at 285) that a person is not to be taken to have knowledge of a fact that he once knew but has genuinely forgotten, and that it is doubtful whether there is a general doctrine of 'imputed knowledge' that corresponds with 'imputed notice'. In relation to 'imputed knowledge' for the purpose of enforcing a constructing trust on the basis of knowing receipt, see *El Ajou v Dollar Land Holdings plc* [1994] 2 All ER 685, 701–5 and *Farah Constructions Pty Ltd v Say-Dee Pty Ltd* (2007) 230 CLR 89 at [123]–[129].

[387] [1992] 4 All ER 488, 497–8.

[388] See Vinelott J in *Eagle Trust plc v SBC Securities Ltd* [1992] 4 All ER 488, 507, referring to *Manchester Trust v Furness* [1895] 2 QB 539, 545. See also *Cowan de Groot Properties Ltd v Eagle Trust plc* [1992] 4 All ER 700, 759–60.

[389] *Eagle Trust plc v SBC Securities Ltd* [1992] 4 All ER 488, 507–8.

[390] *Greer v Downs Supply Company* [1927] 2 KB 28; *The Njegos* [1936] P 90, 103; *Northside Development Pty Ltd v Registrar-General* (1987) 11 ACLR 513, 523; *Polly Peck International plc v Nadir (No. 2)* [1992] 4 All ER 769, 782.

[391] See Millett J in *El Ajou v Dollar Land Holdings plc* [1993] 3 All ER 717, 739 and in *Macmillan Inc v Bishopsgate Investment Trust plc* [1995] 1 WLR 978, 1000, and also his extra-judicial discussion in 'Equity – the road ahead' (1995) 9 *Tolley's Trust Law International* 35, 40. See also *Neste Oy v Lloyds Bank plc* [1983] 2 Lloyd's Rep 658, 667, and Scott LJ's reference to 'constructive knowledge' in the context of an equitable proprietary tracing claim against a bank in *Polly Peck International plc v Nadir (No. 2)* [1992] 4 All ER 769, 776, 781–2.

[392] Millett, 'Equity's place in the law of commerce' (1998) 114 LQR 214, referring to *Sanders Bros v Maclean & Co* (1883) 11 QBD 327, 343 and *Barclays Bank plc v Quincecare Ltd* [1992] 4 All ER 363,

Trust moneys paid directly into an overdrawn account

The issue of a trust in relation to combination of accounts arises in the situation in which **15.97**
trust moneys are paid into an account in credit, so that they can be traced into that account,
and the beneficiaries of the trust assert that their consequent interest in the account precludes a combination in respect of it. A similar issue may arise in another context. Instead
of being paid into a separate account, the trust moneys may be paid in breach of trust
directly into the trustee's overdrawn private account,[393] and the bank in an action against
it for repayment of the trust moneys asserts that they are not repayable because they were
used to reduce or discharge the debit balance on the trustee's account.[394] In principle, this
should produce the same result. If combination is merely an accounting exercise in order
to ascertain what the debt is at any particular time,[395] it should not make any difference
whether trust funds are deposited in an account in credit where there is another overdrawn
account, or whether they are credited directly to the trustee's personal overdrawn account
in reduction of the debt on that account. It is relevant therefore to consider under what
circumstances a bank may be liable when trust moneys are paid in breach of trust directly
into the trustee's overdrawn account, and it is in that context that the question of payment
of trust moneys to a bank is considered below.

If trust moneys are paid to a person in breach of trust, and the recipient retains the money, **15.98**
or the trust money can be traced into other property held by the recipient, the beneficiaries
may have a proprietary remedy.[396] That would not be the case, however, if the money is
credited to an overdrawn bank account. In such a case, it becomes part of the bank's general
pool of assets and is not traceable into any particular asset.[397] The beneficiaries would have
to seek a personal remedy against the bank on the basis of a constructive trust, either
because the bank knowingly received trust property transferred to it in breach of trust or
because it was an accessory to a breach of trust.[398] The foundation of accessory liability

---

[377] *per* Steyn J ('trust, not distrust, is also the basis of a bank's dealings with its customers'). In particular,
Millett J warned in *Macmillan Inc v Bishopsgate Investment Trust plc (No. 3)* [1995] 1 WLR 978, 1014 that
bank officers are not detectives. See also *Lloyds Bank Ltd v Chartered Bank of India, Australia and China*
[1929] 1 KB 40, 73, and *Lipkin Gorman v Karpnale Ltd* [1987] 1 WLR 987, 1006. If an inquiry is made
and an answer is received which the inquirer may reasonably believe to be true, the inquirer is entitled to act
on it. See *Selangor United Rubber Estates Ltd v Cradock (No. 3)* [1968] 1 WLR 1555, 1607, and also *Baden v
Société Generale pour Favoriser le Developpement du Commerce et de l'Industrie en France SA* [1992] 4 All ER
161, 246.

[393] Compare cases in which payment into the trustee's personal overdrawn account is not in breach of
trust. See *Marten v Rocke, Eyton and Co* (1886) 53 LT 946.

[394] See e.g. *Thomson v Clydesdale Bank Ltd* [1893] AC 282; *British America Elevator Co Ltd v Bank of
British North America* [1919] AC 658; *Westpac Banking Corporation v Savin* [1985] 2 NZLR 41. See also
Bodenham v Hoskyns (1852) 2 De G M & G 903, 42 ER 1125.

[395] See para. 15.04 above.

[396] See generally *Boscawen v Bajwa* [1996] 1 WLR 328, 334–5.

[397] *Bishopsgate Investment Management Ltd v Homan* [1995] Ch 211; *Director of Serious Fraud Office v Lexi
Holdings plc* [2009] QB 376 at [50]. Compare the equitable charge or lien on a bank's assets contemplated
by the Privy Council in *Space Investments Ltd v Canadian Imperial Bank of Commerce Trust Co (Bahamas) Ltd*
[1986] 1 WLR 1072, 1074 and *Re Goldcorp Exchange Ltd* [1995] 1 AC 74, 108–10, which has been criticized. See the authorities referred to in *Lehman Brothers International (Europe) v CRC Credit Fund Ltd* [2009]
EWHC 3228 (Ch) at [184]–[192], but in Australia compare *Stephenson Nominees Pty Ltd v Official Receiver*
(1987) 16 FCR 536, 556.

[398] *Barnes v Addy* (1874) LR 9 Ch App 244, 251–2.

under English law is dishonesty,[399] which often would be difficult to prove, and so the beneficiaries may focus on the question whether the bank is personally liable as having received and dealt with trust property.[400]

The bank as 'recipient'

15.99 The bank will not be regarded as a recipient of the trust moneys deposited with it unless it received the moneys for its own use and benefit,[401] and for that to have occurred the moneys should have brought about a reduction or discharge in the trustee's debt.[402] In that regard, the mere continuation of a running account in overdraft would not suffice to render the bank liable as a recipient.[403] The bank in that situation would be acting simply as the customer's agent, and not as the recipient of the money for its own use and benefit.

The degree of knowledge required

15.100 Assuming that the bank is a recipient in that sense, the question is what degree of knowledge of the trust is required in order to impose personal liability on the bank for trust money credited to the trustee's personal overdrawn account. In *Thomson v Clydesdale Bank Ltd*,[404] a broker was instructed to sell shares and to pay the proceeds into a bank account in the principal's name, but instead he paid the proceeds into his own overdrawn account. The House of Lords held that the bank was not obliged to repay the money to the principal. Lord Watson emphasized that it was not enough to show that the bank had acted negligently. Rather, he said that it had to be shown that the bank knew that the money did not belong to the broker and that the broker had no authority from the true owner to pay it into his bank account.[405] Lord Herschell in his judgment said that 'under ordinary circumstances' a bank that takes money in discharge of a debt is not bound to inquire into the manner in which the person paying the debt acquired the money.[406] On the other hand, he

---

[399] *Royal Brunei Airlines v Tan* [1995] 2 AC 378; *Twinsectra Ltd v Yardley* [2002] 2 AC 164; *Barlow Clowes International Ltd v Eurotrust International Ltd* [2006] 1 WLR 1476. In Australia, compare *Farah Constructions Pty Ltd v Say-Dee Pty Ltd* (2007) 230 CLR 89 at [159]–[164].

[400] As in *Westpac Banking Corporation v Savin* [1985] 2 NZLR 41 (see in particular at 52–3, 60, 69–70).

[401] In *Trustor AB v Smallbone* [2001] 1 WLR 1177 at [19] Sir Andrew Morritt VC said that it is: 'necessary that the receipt by the defendant should be for his own benefit or in his own right in the sense of setting up a title of his own to the property so received . . .'

[402] *Agip (Africa) Ltd v Jackson* [1990] 1 Ch 265, 292; *Nimmo v Westpac Banking Corporation* [1993] 3 NZLR 218, 224–6 (criticizing the distinction drawn in *Polly Peck International plc v Nadir (No. 2)* [1992] 4 All ER 769, 777 between the sterling transfers and the currency exchanges); *Stephens Travel Service International Pty Ltd v Qantas Airways Ltd* (1988) 13 NSWLR 331, 361–6; *Cigna Life Insurance New Zealand Ltd v Westpac Securities Ltd* [1996] 1 NZLR 80, 86–7 (also criticizing the distinction drawn in the *Polly Peck* case); *Sansom v Westpac Banking Corporation* (1996) Aust Torts Reports 81–383 at 63,325–63,326; *Box v Barclays Bank* [1998] Lloyd's Rep Bank 185, 202 (it was assumed that the overdrawn No. 1 account, into which the funds in question were paid, was separate from other accounts in credit, though there was little discussion (see at 188) of the nature of the accounts); *Evans v European Bank Ltd* (2004) 61 NSWLR 75 at [165]–[175]; Millett, 'Tracing the proceeds of fraud' (1991) 107 LQR 71, 82–3. Compare Bryan, 'The liability of banks to make restitution for wrongful payments' (1998) 26 *Australian Business Law Review* 93, 106–9.

[403] Millett, 'Tracing the proceeds of fraud' (1991) 107 LQR 71, 83, n. 46; *Stephens Travel Service International Pty Ltd v Qantas Airways Ltd* (1989) 13 NSWLR 331, 361–6; *Evans v European Bank Ltd* (2004) 61 NSWLR 75 at [167]–[170].

[404] [1893] AC 282.

[405] [1893] AC 282, 290.

[406] [1893] AC 282, 287. Compare *Bank of New South Wales v Goulburn Valley Butter Co Pty Ltd* [1902] AC 543, 550.

indicated that the bank would not have succeeded if it had 'reason to believe' that the money was trust money, but in the circumstances he concluded that there was no such reason to believe.[407] Similarly, Lord Shand rejected the argument that the circumstances were such as to put the bank on inquiry.[408]

In *Baden v Société Générale pour Favoriser le Developpement du Commerce SA et de l'Industrie*   **15.101**
en France SA,[409] Peter Gibson J referred to a classification of knowledge suggested by counsel in terms of five different mental states. The use of these categories has been criticized on the ground that they do not have clear and precise boundaries, but may merge imperceptibly into one another.[410] Nevertheless, they have formed the basis of discussion of knowledge in many of the cases on knowing receipt, and it has been said that assistance may still be gained by reference to them.[411] The categories are:

1. actual knowledge;
2. wilfully shutting one's eyes to the obvious;
3. wilfully and recklessly failing to make such inquiries as an honest and reasonable man would make;
4. knowledge of circumstances which would indicate the facts to an honest and reasonable man;
5. knowledge of circumstances which would put an honest and reasonable man on inquiry.

The first three categories have been said to involve 'actual knowledge', as understood both at common law and in equity, and the last two 'constructive knowledge' as developed in equity, particularly in disputes respecting old system conveyancing.[412]

In *Re Montagu's Settlement Trusts*,[413] Megarry VC said that want of probity is essential for   **15.102**
the imposition of personal liability as a constructive trustee on the knowing receipt ground, and that accordingly it is necessary to establish knowledge in categories 1, 2 and 3. This view has substantial support.[414] It was favoured by Alliott J at first instance in *Lipkin Gorman v Karpnale Ltd*,[415] by Steyn J in *Barclays Bank plc v Quincecare*,[416] and by Arden J

---

[407] [1893] AC 282, 287–8.
[408] [1893] AC 282, 293.
[409] [1992] 4 All ER 161, 235.
[410] See e.g. *Polly Peck International plc v Nadir (No. 2)* [1992] 4 All ER 769, 777; *Koorootang Nominees Pty Ltd v Australia and New Zealand Banking Group Ltd* [1998] 3 VR 16, 105. In *Royal Brunei Airlines v Tan* [1995] 2 AC 378, 392 the Privy Council suggested, in the context of accessory liability, that the *Baden* scale of knowledge is best forgotten. See also *Twinsectra Ltd v Yardley* [2002] 2 AC 164 at [113] (Lord Millett).
[411] See e.g. *Bank of Credit and Commerce International (Overseas) Ltd v Akindele* [1999] BCC 669, 677 *per* Carnwath J (at first instance); *Equiticorp Industries Group Ltd v The Crown* [1996] 3 NZLR 586, 604. See also *Farah Constructions Pty Ltd v Say-Dee Pty Ltd* (2007) 230 CLR 89 at [174]–[175] (accessory liability).
[412] *Farah Constructions Pty Ltd v Say-Dee Pty Ltd* (2007) 230 CLR 89 at [174], referring to Nourse LJ in *Bank of Credit and Commerce International (Overseas) Ltd v Akindele* [2001] Ch 437, 454.
[413] [1987] 1 Ch 264, 285.
[414] In addition to the cases referred to below, see *Cowan v de Groot Properties Ltd v Eagle Trust plc* [1992] 4 All ER 700, 758–60 (in relation to a *bona fide* purchaser for value); *Hillsdown Holdings plc v Pensions Ombudsman* [1997] 1 All ER 862, 902–3. See also *Eagle Trust plc v SBC Securities Ltd* [1992] 4 All ER 488, 509 in relation to commercial transactions (in other contexts, compare at 506–7).
[415] [1987] 1 WLR 987, 1005.
[416] [1992] 4 All ER 363, 375.

in *Eagle Trust plc v SBC Securities Ltd (No. 2)*.[417] In *Dubai Aluminium Co Ltd v Salaam*,[418] Rix J commented that the test in knowing receipt cases is likely to be the same as that for knowing assistance, in other words based on dishonesty, and similarly Potter LJ, in delivering the judgment of the Court of Appeal in *Twinsectra Ltd v Yardley*,[419] seemed to regard honesty as the test for both knowing receipt and knowing assistance. Aikens J in *Bank of America v Arnell*[420] also shared that view. There are other opinions, however, that favour a more expansive approach.[421] In the House of Lords in the *Twinsectra* case[422] Lord Millett said that there is no basis for requiring dishonesty in this context, and that constructive notice of a breach of trust is sufficient. Similarly, in *Houghton v Fayers*,[423] Nourse LJ, with whose judgment Ferris J agreed, said that it is unnecessary for a finding of dishonesty to be made in a knowing receipt case. He said that it is enough for the claimant to establish that the recipient knew or ought to have known that money had been paid to him or her in breach of fiduciary duty. Subsequently, Nourse LJ adopted a different approach in giving the judgment of the Court of Appeal in *Bank of Credit and Commerce International (Overseas) Ltd v Akindele*.[424] He reiterated his view that dishonesty is not a necessary ingredient in knowing receipt liability, and he also said that he had grave doubts as to the utility of the *Baden* categorisation in this context. Rather than expressing the question in terms whether the recipient knew or ought to have known of the breach of trust, as in *Houghton v Fayers*, he suggested that there should be a single test of knowledge. He said that all that is necessary is that the recipient's state of knowledge should be such as to make it unconscionable for the recipient to retain the benefit of the receipt. In New Zealand, on the other hand, it has been said that all five categories of knowledge are relevant to the knowing receipt head of constructive trust,[425] while in Australia it has been suggested that the first four categories may result in liability.[426] Alternatively, consistent with the view that has

---

[417] [1996] 1 BCLC 121, 152. Arden J emphasized, however, that her view was confined to cases where the receipt occurs in the discharge of a lawful debt, or at least where the case arises out of a transaction which does not itself constitute a breach of trust.

[418] [1999] 1 Lloyd's Rep 415, 453.

[419] [1999] Lloyd's Rep Bank 438 (in particular at [101]–[108], and see the extract from the first instance judgment of Carnwath J at [46]). See also Aikens J's reference to the *Twinsectra* case in *Bank of America v Arnell* [1999] Lloyd's Rep Bank 399 at [15].

[420] [1999] Lloyd's Rep Bank 399 at [15].

[421] In *Polly Peck International plc v Nadir (No. 2)* [1992] 4 All ER 769, 777 Scott LJ expressed doubt as to the sufficiency of the fifth category, but left the question open. On the other hand, he accepted (at 781–2) that constructive knowledge would suffice. See also Millett J in *El Ajou v Dollar Land Holdings plc* [1993] 3 All ER 717, 739, and, writing extra-judicially, in 'Tracing the proceeds of fraud' (1991) 107 LQR 71, 80–2.

[422] *Twinsectra Ltd v Yardley* [2002] 2 AC 164 at [105].

[423] [2000] 1 BCLC 511, 516.

[424] [2001] Ch 437. See also *Pulvers v Chan* [2007] EWHC 2406 (Ch) at [377].

[425] *Westpac Banking Corporation v Savin* [1985] 2 NZLR 41, 52–3; *Equiticorp Industries Group Ltd v Hawkins* [1991] 3 NZLR 700, 728; *Powell v Thompson* [1991] 1 NZLR 597, 608–9; *Lankshear v ANZ Banking Group (New Zealand) Ltd* [1993] 1 NZLR 481, 493–4; *Springfield Acres Ltd v Abacus (Hong Kong) Ltd* [1994] 3 NZLR 502, 510. Compare *Equiticorp Industries Group Ltd v The Crown* [1996] 3 NZLR 586, 604–5 (summary), [1998] 2 NZLR 481, 636–8.

[426] *Koorootang Nominees Pty Ltd v Australia and New Zealand Banking Group Ltd* [1998] 3 VR 16, 85, 105; *Hancock Family Memorial Foundation Ltd v Porteous* (1999) 32 ACSR 124 at [79]; *Kalls Enterprises Pty Ltd v Baloglow* (2007) 63 ACSR 557 at [176] (referring to the *Hancock* case), [197]–[199] ('an honest and reasonable man with his knowledge would have seen a real and not remote risk'); *Bell Group Ltd v Westpac Banking*

been expressed that the liability of a recipient of trust property is restitution-based,[427] there is support for the proposition that the liability should be strict but subject to defences of *bona fide* purchase and change of position.[428]

The law in relation to liability as a knowing recipient of trust property awaits a definitive **15.103** treatment by the House of Lords. But however the issue ultimately may be determined, there is much to be said for the view that an analogous approach should be adopted when combination against a trust account is in issue, despite the difference in the way that the case is presented when combination rather than payment in reduction of an overdraft is in issue.[429] In the case of combination the beneficiaries assert their beneficial interest in the account as a reason for denying that the bank can regard the account as combined with another account of the trustee/customer, whereas when trust money is paid directly into an overdrawn account the issue arises in the context of an attempt to render the bank personally liable as a constructive trustee as a consequence of having received trust property. The analogy is suggested nevertheless given the nature of combination of accounts,[430] and notwithstanding that the courts have emphasized the distinction between the doctrines of purchaser without notice and constructive trusts.[431]

One thing that is clear, however, is that a mere request by a customer that the money be put **15.104** into a separate account by itself is not sufficient to constitute knowledge of a trust.[432] Nor generally is it sufficient that the bank is aware that the customer occupies a position in which he or she often receives money on behalf of others, for example as a solicitor or stockbroker. Thus, in *T and H Greenwood Teale v William Williams Brown and Co*[433] a solicitor paid clients' money into an 'office account', while in *Clark v Ulster Bank Ltd*[434] the money was paid by a solicitor into a 'No 2 Account'. In each case it was held that the bank did not have sufficient knowledge of the fiduciary nature of the account to prevent combination.[435] In that regard, the Solicitors' Act 1974, s. 85(b) prohibits a bank from having recourse against money standing to the credit of an account kept by a solicitor with the bank in

---

Corporation (No. 9) [2008] WASC 239 at [4743]–[4748]. See also *Macquarie Bank Ltd v Sixty-Fourth Throne Pty Ltd* [1998] 3 VR 133, 165.

[427] *Royal Brunei Airlines v Tan* [1995] 2 AC 378, 386; *Twinsectra Ltd v Yardley* [2002] 2 AC 164 at [105] (Lord Millett).

[428] *Twinsectra Ltd v Yardley* [2002] 2 AC 164 at [105] (Lord Millett); Lord Nicholls, 'Knowing receipt: the need for a new landmark', in *Restitution Past, Present and Future* (ed. Cornish, 1998), 231; Underhill and Hayton, *Law Relating to Trusts and Trustees* (17th edn, 2006), 1198–201. This view was criticized in *Bank of Credit and Commerce International (Overseas) Ltd v Akindele* [2001] Ch 437, 455–6 (CA) and it has been rejected in Australia. See *Farah Constructions Pty Ltd v Say-Dee Pty Ltd* (2007) 230 CLR 89 at [130]–[158].

[429] Indeed, this would follow if the courts were to accept that the liability of a recipient of trust property is restitution-based, and therefore liability *prima facie* is strict (see above), because the question then would be whether the bank could establish a defence of *bona fide* purchase, which is also the defence that the bank would assert in the case of combination. See para. 15.93 above.

[430] See para. 15.97 above.

[431] *Re Montagu's Settlement* [1987] 1 Ch 264, 272–3, 278 (Sir Robert Megarry VC); *Linter Group Ltd v Goldberg* (1992) 7 ACSR 580, 636; *Bank of Credit and Commerce International (Overseas) Ltd v Akindele* [2001] Ch 437, 452 (CA).

[432] *Barclays Bank Ltd v Quistclose Investments Ltd* [1970] AC 567, 582.

[433] (1894) 11 TLR 56.

[434] [1950] NILR 132.

[435] See also *Thomson v Clydesdale Bank Ltd* [1893] AC 282 (stockbroker).

pursuance of the rules applicable to solicitors' client accounts, other than in respect of a liability in connection with the account itself. This would preclude set-off against or combination with an overdrawn account of the solicitor. *Prima facie* it would not prevent combination in relation to an account into which clients' moneys have been paid if the account is not kept in pursuance of the rules, although in accordance with the principles discussed above the combination may be impugned if the bank in any event is aware that the account is a trust account.[436]

The relevant time for knowledge

15.105 The question arises whether it is necessary to show that the bank had the requisite knowledge (or notice) of the trust when it received the trust money and credited it to the customer's account, or whether knowledge at a later date would suffice. On the one hand, in *Grigg v Cocks*,[437] the bank became aware of the circumstances giving rise to the trust affecting the bill of exchange after the proceeds of the bill were received and credited to the customer's account but before the bank made a book entry combining the account with another. Sir Lancelot Shadwell held that the bank was entitled to consider itself as debtor for the balance of the accounts, notwithstanding the notice.[438] In Northern Ireland Black CJ adopted a similar approach in *Clark v Ulster Bank Ltd*.[439] On the other hand, the Privy Council, in *Union Bank of Australia Ltd v Murray-Aynsley*,[440] seems to have considered that notice of a trust conveyed to the bank after it received the money could still be relevant.[441] In *Barclays Bank Ltd v Quistclose Investments Ltd*,[442] Lord Reid left open the question whether subsequent notice could have effected the bank's position,[443] but that case proceeded on the basis that set-off under the insolvency set-off section was in issue as opposed to combination of accounts.[444]

15.106 When a customer has a number of accounts with a bank, and the requirements of combination are satisfied, the principle of combination dictates that the accounts constitute a single debt unless there is an agreement (express or implied) that they should be kept separate.[445] On that basis, notice of a trust received after money has been credited to an account should not affect the position in relation to combination.[446] The credit will already have been

---

[436] See *Clark v Ulster Bank Ltd* [1950] NILR 132, 141.

[437] (1831) 4 Sim 438, 58 ER 163.

[438] See in particular (1831) 4 Sim 438, 453–4, 58 ER 163, 169.

[439] [1950] NILR 132, 142–3.

[440] [1898] AC 693.

[441] Lord Watson, in delivering the advice of the Privy Council, commented that: 'there is nothing to prove or even to suggest that any notice was subsequently conveyed to the bank of the trust character of the funds which the respondents are claiming in this action.' [1898] AC 693, 698. See also *Taylor v Forbes* (1830) 7 Bligh NS 417, 5 ER 828, which is difficult to follow given that separate banker/customer relationships appear to have been in issue.

[442] [1970] AC 567, 578.

[443] Compare Russell LJ in the Court of Appeal [1968] 1 Ch 540, 556, 561, who approached the problem in terms whether the bank in that case had notice when it received the money and credited it to an account, and see also Lord Wilberforce in the House of Lords [1970] AC 567, 582.

[444] See para. 15.109 below.

[445] See para. 15.04 above.

[446] The contrary was assumed in *Houben v Bank of Nova Scotia* (1970) 3 NBR (2d) 366, 381 (Saint John County Court, New Brunswick). Compare the situation in which the accounts are separate, and the bank effects a set-off pursuant to a set-off agreement. See para. 15.111 below. Compare also the case of

subsumed into the debt constituted by the overall balance on all the accounts. Similarly, a later entry by the bank reflecting the combination in its books should not be characterised a dealing with trust property so as to give rise to liability as a constructive trustee. There was in any event only one debt for the balance, in which case the book entry itself would not have constituted an appropriation by the bank of the trust account in reduction of a debt owing to the bank on another account.[447]

Value

In order to obtain the benefit of the *bona fide* purchaser principle in relation to a trust account, so as to be able to rely on combination in relation to that account and the trustee's overdrawn personal account,[448] the bank must have given value. **15.107**

When money is paid into a bank account in credit in circumstances where combination is not in issue, the bank is not regarded as having given value merely because of the promise to repay a like amount.[449] On the other hand, when a bank receives money in reduction or discharge of a debt, the fact of the reduction or discharge does constitute value,[450] and that should also apply in a case of combination. The position should be the same whether the customer has one overdrawn account to which trust moneys are credited, or whether the customer has a number of accounts the balance of which at any particular time represents a debt owing to the bank.[451] Because there is only one debt in any event, payment into an account in credit, where there is a second account which is overdrawn to a greater extent than the credit balance on the first account, should have the same effect at law as a payment to the credit of the overdrawn account itself, in that it brings about a reduction in the customer's debt to the bank. **15.108**

The question of value was referred to in *Neste Oy v Lloyd's Bank Plc*.[452] The case was considered earlier[453] in the context of a payment made by a principal which was credited to its **15.109**

---

a constructive trust arising as a result of the transfer of trust property to a person in breach of trust, where the person received the property initially unaware of the trust but subsequently acquired knowledge of it. See Millett, 'Tracing the proceeds of fraud' (1991) 107 LQR 71, 80, and *Agip (Africa) Ltd v Jackson* [1990] 1 Ch 265, 290, 291.

[447] *Re Sutcliffe & Sons Ltd, ex p Royal Bank* [1933] 1 DLR 562.

[448] See *Re Marwalt Ltd* [1992] BCC 32, 38 and *Neste Oy v Lloyds Bank Plc* [1983] 2 Lloyd's Rep 658, 666. See para. 15.93 above.

[449] *Lipkin Gorman v Karpnale Ltd* [1991] 2 AC 548, 562, 576–7. See also Lord Wilberforce in *Barclays Bank Ltd v Quistclose Investments Ltd* [1970] AC 567, 582 (discussed below), although compare Harman LJ in the Court of Appeal in *Quistclose* [1968] 1 Ch 540, 555.

[450] *Taylor v Blakelock* (1886) 32 Ch D 560 (esp. at 570); *Thomson v Clydesdale Bank Ltd* [1893] AC 282, 289–90, 291–2; *P T Garuda Indonesia Ltd v Grellman* (1992) 35 FCR 515, 530–2 (an antecedent debt constitutes valuable consideration for a payment in discharge of that debt); *Kyra Nominees Pty Ltd v National Australia Bank Ltd* (1986) 4 ACLC 400, 407; Millett, 'Tracing the proceeds of fraud' (1991) 107 LQR 71, 82. See also *Thorndike v Hunt* (1859) 3 De G & J 563, 570, 44 ER 1386, 1388–9; *Re Leslie Engineers Co Ltd* [1976] 1 WLR 292, 299; *Barclays Bank Ltd v W J Simms Son & Cooke (Southern) Ltd* [1980] 1 QB 677, 695; *Australia and New Zealand Banking Group Ltd v Westpac Banking Corporation* (1988) 164 CLR 662, 673 (although compare at 677–8); *David Securities Pty Ltd v Commonwealth Bank of Australia* (1992) 175 CLR 353, 405–6. Where a customer pays money into an account in credit, in circumstances where there is a second account which is overdrawn, the customer may not intend to reduce or discharge the debt to the bank, but should nevertheless be bound by the consequences that follow at law from his or her act.

[451] See para. 15.97 above.

[452] [1983] 2 Lloyd's Rep 658.

[453] See para. 15.91 above.

agent's account after the bank was aware of a decision that the group of companies of which the agent was a member was to cease trading. In addition, there were five other payments credited to the agent's account prior to the decision, which Bingham J held could be applied by the bank against other accounts in debit. The primary reason was that the payments were not received subject to a trust, but if he was wrong on that point he accepted that the bank in any event was a *bona fide* purchaser for value without notice. He said that the bank gave value when the payments were credited to the account. He went on to comment that the bank certainly gave value when it continued lending in the belief that the overall debt was reduced by the sum of the payments,[454] without analysing the position where there was no continued lending. In the absence of that circumstance, value would be given where payment into an account brings about a permanent reduction in the customer's debt. It is true that in *Barclays Bank Ltd v Quistclose Investments Ltd*[455] Lord Wilberforce said that the bank in that case had not in any real sense given value when it received the money or thereafter changed its position.[456] In that case, however, the bank had agreed that the money paid into the account was only to be used for the purpose of funding the payment of a dividend, which would have precluded a combination in respect of it.[457] The question instead concerned set-off under the insolvency set-off section, the customer having gone into liquidation.[458] It was not therefore a case in which it could be said that the deposit itself operated to reduce the customer's debt to the bank so as to constitute the giving of value on that ground.

15.110 A deposit may result in a net credit to the customer, as opposed to operating in reduction or discharge of the customer's debt. If in such a case the bank subsequently acquires notice of the trust, it may be liable as a constructive trustee if it nevertheless assists the trustee in dealing with the money in a manner which is inconsistent with the trust.[459]

(4) Set-off agreement

15.111 A customer may have a number of accounts with a bank that are separate from each other, and which accordingly are not subject to the principle of combination, but the bank has

---

[454] His Lordship said ([1983] 2 Lloyd's Rep 658, 667) that: 'It appears to me that the bank gave value when these first five payments were credited to PSL's account, certainly when the bank continued lending in the belief that the group's overall debt was reduced by the sum of the payments . . .' Note, however, that the case concerned a set-off effected pursuant to a set-off agreement. See para. 15.111 below.

[455] [1970] AC 567. See para. 15.90 above.

[456] [1970] AC 567, 582. See also Russell LJ in the Court of Appeal [1968] 1 Ch 540, 563, although compare the view of Harman LJ (at 555) that, 'The bank stands . . . in the position of an assignee for value, the consideration being the promise to repay.'

[457] See Russell LJ in the Court of Appeal [1968] 1 Ch 540, 563.

[458] In the Court of Appeal, Harman LJ [1968] 1 Ch 540, 551 noted that the bank informed the board of the customer that it was exercising its 'statutory' right to combine accounts. See also the reference by Russell LJ (at 563) to the decision in *Rolls Razor Ltd v Cox* [1967] 1 QB 552, which concerned the question whether the operation of the insolvency set-off section could be excluded by agreement between the parties, and the reference by Sachs LJ (at 567) to the Bankruptcy Act 1914, s. 31, which was the set-off section then applicable to company liquidations under the Companies Act 1948, s. 317.

[459] See e.g. *Selangor United Rubber Estates Ltd v Cradock (No. 3)* [1968] 1 WLR 1555 and *Karak Rubber Co Ltd v Burden (No. 2)* [1972] 1 WLR 602. The test for liability as an accessory is dishonesty. See *Twinsectra Ltd v Yardley* [2002] 2 AC 164; *Barlow Clowes International Ltd v Eurotrust International Ltd* [2006] 1 WLR 1476. In Australia, compare *Farah Constructions Pty Ltd v Say-Dee Pty Ltd* (2007) 230 CLR 89 at [163].

a set-off agreement entitling it to combine the accounts and set them off.[460] If one of the accounts is a trust account in credit, and the trustee has a second account with a greater debit balance, the payment of money into the trust account by itself should not constitute the giving of value, since, if the accounts are separate, the payment in would not result in a reduction in or discharge of the debt to the bank.[461] Questions of knowledge of the trust and of the giving of value generally should be determined instead as at the date that the bank purports to effect a set-off in accordance with the agreement.[462] The discharge or reduction of the customer's debt to the bank as a result of the bank's exercise of the contractual right of set-off would constitute the giving of value, and the question then would be whether the bank had knowledge of the trust at that time.[463]

It may not always be the case, however, that the date of the set-off is the relevant date. If the **15.112** deposit was required as a condition to the grant of a loan or other facility, the making of the loan itself may constitute value, and the question of knowledge of the trust similarly should be determined as at that time. Alternatively, the provision of the loan in that circumstance may justify a defence to the bank of innocent change of position.[464]

(5) Labelling an account as a trust account, where the customer is not a trustee

An account kept by a customer with a bank may be labelled as a trust account, but despite **15.113** the label it is not a trust account but rather it contains the customer's own money. In that situation, the fact of the label might be thought to suggest an intention that the account is to be kept separate from the customer's other accounts, and that an agreement to that effect therefore should be implied so as to preclude combination, notwithstanding that the customer is beneficially interested in the credit balance. That approach is not reflected in the cases, however, and there is authority for the proposition that combination may occur in relation to the account.

Bailey v Finch[465] concerned an account opened by a customer in his capacity as executor of **15.114** an estate, and labelled as such. In the course of his judgment, Blackburn J contemplated the possibility that the account could have been combined with other accounts held by the customer in his personal capacity,[466] in circumstances where the customer was also the residuary legatee and there were other assets in the estate which were sufficient to satisfy the specific bequests and charges upon the estate. His comments on the point were *obiter*, however, and the position was not the subject of detailed consideration. The case itself concerned insolvency set-off, the bankers in that case having become bankrupt, and moreover, as an alternative to combination prior to the bankruptcy, Blackburn J suggested that

---

[460] See paras 15.73–15.77 above.

[461] See para. 15.108 above.

[462] The bank in such a case may be liable for dealing with trust property in a manner inconsistent with the performance of a trust of which it is cognizant. See *Lee v Sankey* (1872) LR 15 Eq 204, 211; *Soar v Ashwell* [1893] 2 QB 390, 396–7.

[463] See *Neste Oy v Lloyds Bank Plc* [1983] 2 Lloyd's Rep 658, 667, and also *Re Marwalt Ltd* [1992] BCC 32, 38, 43.

[464] See generally *Boscawen v Bajwa* [1996] 1 WLR 328, 334.

[465] (1871) LR 7 QB 34.

[466] See (1871) LR 7 QB 34, 41–2, 43.

the Statutes of Set-off may have provided a defence to the customer to an action at law by the bank to obtain payment of the customer's personal account in debit.[467] Set-off under the Statutes is premised on the assumption that there are independent debts, which is the consequence when there is an implied agreement that accounts are to be kept separate, and it applies in circumstances where there is mutuality at common law and there is no reason in equity as to why a set-off at law should not proceed.[468] An implied agreement to keep accounts separate, while it would preclude combination, ordinarily should not affect a set-off under the Statutes.[469]

15.115 Two other cases are relevant, one Canadian and the other from New Zealand. In *Bank of Montreal v R & R Entertainment Ltd*[470] an account was labelled as a trust account, although the customer in truth was not a trustee. The judgment is not altogether clear, but the New Brunswick Court of Appeal appears to have accepted the view adopted by the trial judge, that the bank was entitled to apply the account against a second overdrawn account possessed by the customer personally, so as to justify the bank's initial act in dishonouring cheques drawn on the 'trust' account.[471] The circumstances were peculiar, however.[472] It appears that both the bank and the customer had transferred funds from one account to the other from time to time, and had treated the trust account as an extension of the customer's general account. The trust account was overdrawn almost every month from the time it was established, and funds were transferred from one account to the other when either of the accounts was overdrawn. The question whether the labelling of the account gave rise to an implied term that it was to be regarded as separate was not considered, but it is apparent that the parties own conduct was inconsistent with that conclusion. Furthermore, notwithstanding the general nature of the discussion,[473] the right of set-off which the trial judge accepted and to which the Court of Appeal referred may have rested in contract rather than on the common law doctrine.[474]

---

[467] (1871) LR 7 QB 34, 43. See ch. 2 above in relation to the Statutes of Set-off.

[468] See the discussion of *Bailey v Finch* in para. 13.129 above. Blackburn J in *Bailey v Finch* (1871) LR 7 QB 34, 42 referred to *Ex p Kingston* (1871) LR 6 Ch App 632, in which a set-off seems to have been allowed to the bank in relation to the part of the 'Police Account' which represented the customer's own money. However, the set-off may be explained as having occurred under the insolvency set-off section, the customer having become bankrupt, for which different considerations apply. See para. 15.116 below. The customer in *Ex p Kingston* had indicated to the bank that the account was to be kept separate (see at 634), which ordinarily would preclude combination. Nevertheless the county court judge in the *Kingston* case, to whose judgment Blackburn J referred in *Bailey v Finch* at 42, evidently regarded the case as involving a bankers 'lien' on the account. See the judgment set out in a footnote in *Ex p Kingston* at 635–7.

[469] See para. 15.65 above.

[470] (1984) 13 DLR (4th) 726.

[471] The facts of the case were unusual. Because of the debit on the customer's account the bank dishonoured some cheques drawn on the trust account, whereupon the payee of the cheques threatened to sue the bank on the ground that the account was held on trust for it. The bank settled the claim, and sought in this action to recover from the customer and some guarantors. The Court of Appeal held that the account was not a trust account, and that therefore the bank was entitled to dishonour the cheques. Furthermore, the bank had withdrawn the credit balance from the trust account and credited it to another account in order to secure the customer's debt. Therefore, when the bank settled the action it did so with its own money. It had no claim against the customer.

[472] See (1984) 13 DLR (4th) 726, 734.

[473] See (1984) 13 DLR (4th) 726, 732.

[474] See the terms of the 'Authority to Charge Accounts' set out at (1984) 13 DLR (4th) 726, 734.

The second case is *McMillan v Bank of New Zealand*,[475] a decision of the New Zealand **15.116** Supreme Court.[476] A debtor executed a deed of assignment for the benefit of his creditors whereby he was to be permitted to carry on business, but paying one half of the gross takings for distribution among his creditors. Of his own accord he opened an account with his bank in his own name for that purpose but with the words 'trust account' added. The creditors refused to assent to the deed, whereupon the bank transferred an amount standing to the credit of the account in reduction of another account in debit held by the customer. The bank's action in doing so was upheld, since the account was not subject to a trust. Once again, however, there was no consideration given to the possibility that the accounts may have been separate as a result of an implied agreement arising out of the labelling of the account as a trust account, so as to preclude the principle of combination. If that view had been adopted in the *McMillan* case, the result may have been the same in any event. The customer had become bankrupt, and a set-off may have been available under the insolvency set-off section so as to bring about the same practical result as a combination. The insolvency set-off section was not considered in the judgment, but in that form of set-off one would look beyond the mere labelling of the account in order to ascertain the true beneficial interests, and if there is mutuality in equity a set-off ordinarily should proceed.[477]

(6) Account containing both trust and personal moneys

An account in credit may have had deposited into it both trust moneys and the customer's **15.117** personal moneys. In such a case Wood's view[478] would appear to be correct that, consistent with the principle applicable to tracing trust moneys into an account,[479] a combination would reduce first the part of the account in which the customer is personally interested. If another account in debit kept by the customer is more than sufficient to extinguish that amount on the basis of combination, the question whether combination will then apply in relation to the trust moneys should be determined by reference to the principles discussed above.

If, on the other hand, the account is specifically labelled as a trust account, there is much to **15.118** be said for the view that the label may give rise to an implied agreement that it is to be kept separate so as to preclude combination.[480] This approach, however, is yet to be reflected in the cases, which instead suggest that combination may apply to the extent that the customer is personally interested in the credit balance on the trust account.[481] But even if the accounts are not combined, if the customer sues the bank for payment of the balance on the account a set-off should be available to the bank in any event under the Statutes of Set-off to the extent of the customer's personal interest,[482] or alternatively the insolvency set-off section may apply to that extent if the customer is bankrupt or is in liquidation.[483]

---

[475] (1882) NZLR 1 SC 332.
[476] Prendergast CJ and Richmond J.
[477] See para. 11.13 above.
[478] Wood, *English and International Set-off* (1989), 1067.
[479] *Re Hallett's Estate* (1880) 13 Ch D 696.
[480] See para. 15.113 above.
[481] See paras 15.113–15.116 above.
[482] See para. 15.114 above.
[483] See para. 15.116 above.

(7) Overdrawn trust account

15.119   The preceding discussion concerned a trust account in credit. If, on the other hand, a trust account is overdrawn for some reason, the customer would be personally liable.[484]

15.120   If an account is labelled as a trust account, it was suggested above that this should give rise to an implied agreement that it is to be treated as separate from the customer's private accounts,[485] and an agreement in those terms should continue to be relevant when the trust account is overdrawn. In other words, it should still be a separate account.[486] In that circumstance combination should not apply, in which case the bank should be confined to a procedural defence of set-off in an action at law under the Statutes of Set-off, or alternatively insolvency set-off. In the case of the Statutes, the accounts would not be set against each other until such time as judgment for a set-off is given,[487] which would have the consequence that the bank could be liable for damages if, prior to judgment, it failed to honour a cheque drawn by the customer on his private account in credit because of the presence of a debit balance on the trust account. However, the proposition that an implied term arises from the labelling of the account as yet is unsupported by authority,[488] and the question of combination in relation to an overdrawn trust account therefore remains uncertain.

M. Assignments[489]

15.121   An assignment of an account in credit is governed by principles similar to those applicable in the trust cases, so that the assignee takes subject to a combination arising before the bank had notice (or knowledge) of the assignment.[490] Prior to notice there is still the one banker/customer relationship in relation to the accounts. Where one of the accounts is payable on demand, an assignee may be subject to a combination notwithstanding the absence of a demand before the bank had notice of the assignment.[491]

---

[484] *Daniels v Imperial Bank of Canada* (1914) 19 DLR 166, 169; *Bailey v Finch* (1871) LR 7 QB 34, 41 (in relation to an overdrawn executorship account). See also, and compare, *Coutts and Co v The Irish Exhibition in London* (1891) 7 TLR 313.

[485] See para. 15.113 above.

[486] There is some support for this view in the discussion of Walsh J in the Alberta Supreme Court in *Daniels v Imperial Bank of Canada* (1914) 19 DLR 166, 168–9. The judgment is not entirely clear, but it seems to have been concluded that the defendant was entitled to succeed on the basis of a defence of set-off (see below), as opposed to combination of accounts. On the other hand, the New Brunswick Court of Appeal in *Bank of Montreal v R & R Entertainment Ltd* (1984) 13 DLR (4th) 726, 733 referred to *Daniels v Imperial Bank* in the context of a 'bank's right of set-off', by which it was apparently meant combination.

[487] See paras 2.34–2.39 above.

[488] See paras 15.113–15.116 above.

[489] See also para. 15.19 above.

[490] *Roxburghe v Cox* (1881) 17 Ch D 520; *Jeffryes v Agra and Masterman's Bank* (1866) LR 2 Eq 674, 680. Compare *Re Jane, ex p The Trustee* (1914) 110 LT 556, in which the accounts would have been separate, being a current account in credit and a loan account (see para. 15.54 above), and *Re Marwalt Ltd* [1992] BCC 32, in which the bank had notice of the assignment.

[491] See para. 15.51 above.

N. Deceased Customer

A deceased customer in whose name there is a credit balance on an account may also have **15.122** a loan which matures after the date of death. Since a combination does not arise in relation to an account that is neither presently payable nor presently payable on demand,[492] the accounts at the date of death would not have been combined in a single debt. When the loan matures, the liability will still be the liability of the deceased customer, but from the moment of death the right to receive the credit balance will have been vested in the executor.[493] Nevertheless, consistent with the principle applicable to assignments, it was held in *Rogerson v Ladbroke*[494] that the estate will take subject to a combination if the loan matured before the bank had notice of the death.[495]

O. Banker's Lien Over a Negotiable Instrument

A bank has a lien on all bills of exchange and cheques coming into its possession as banker **15.123** for the general balance of moneys due from the customer.[496] The lien is not merely over the paper on which the order to pay is written, but extends to the chose in action which the order creates.[497] This should include a power to collect the proceeds upon maturity.[498] The bank's security rights derived from the lien should also entitle it to apply the proceeds in reduction of the debt secured by the lien,[499] unless there is an agreement to the contrary. A contrary agreement would arise, for example, where the bank had specifically agreed to account to the customer for the proceeds.[500]

---

[492] See para. 15.51 above.

[493] *Williams, Mortimer and Sunnucks on Executors, Administrators and Probate* (19th edn, 2008), 503.

[494] (1822) 1 Bing 93, 130 ER 39.

[495] In the absence of information as regards the date of death, *quaere* whether *Thomas v Howell* (1874) LR 18 Eq 198 was correctly decided. The case was distinguished, on other grounds, in *Halse v Rumford* (1878) 47 LJ Ch 559. In *Royal Trust Co v Molsons Bank* (1912) 8 DLR 478, the customer died before the promissory notes became due, although it is not clear when the bank received notice of the death. A similar comment may be made in respect of *Ontario Bank v Routhier* (1900) 32 OR 67.

[496] *National Australia Bank Ltd v KDS Construction Services Pty Ltd* (1987) 163 CLR 668, 678, referring to *Brandao v Barnett* (1846) 12 Cl & Fin 787, 809, 8 ER 1622, 1631. The lien is a common law lien. It is doubtful if it would apply when a trustee deposits a cheque for collection and the beneficiary rather than the trustee is indebted to the bank. See *Abbey National plc v McCann* [1997] Northern Ireland Judgments Bulletin 158, 171–2, 183.

[497] *Sutters v Briggs* [1922] 1 AC 1, 20; *Re Keever* [1967] 1 Ch 182, 189; *National Australia Bank Ltd v KDS Construction Services Pty Ltd* (1987) 163 CLR 668, 679.

[498] *Duke Finance Ltd v Commonwealth Bank of Australia* (1990) 22 NSWLR 236, 249.

[499] *Duke Finance Ltd v Commonwealth Bank of Australia* (1990) 22 NSWLR 236; *Re Keever* [1967] 1 Ch 182. See also *National Australia Bank Ltd v KDS Construction Services Pty Ltd* (1987) 163 CLR 668, 678–9; *Eide UK Ltd v Lowndes Lambert Group Ltd* [1999] QB 199, 214 (insurance broker's lien on a policy). Compare *Abbey National plc v McCann* [1997] Northern Ireland Judgments Bulletin 158, 172–3. Similarly, an insurance broker who has a lien over a policy is entitled to apply the proceeds collected under the policy in satisfaction of the debt secured by the lien. See *Eide UK Ltd v Lowndes Lambert Group Ltd* [1999] QB 199, 208–11.

[500] *Rouxel v Royal Bank of Canada* [1918] 2 WWR 791.

16

SET-OFF AGREEMENTS

A. Introduction

Parties dealing with each other may enter into an agreement for the satisfaction of their **16.01** cross-demands by bringing them into an account in a set-off. The set-off may be expressed to occur immediately or upon the happening of a specified future event, or it may be at the option of one of the parties. Generally, this is not objectionable.[1] It merely constitutes

---

[1] Unless a contractual deduction or set-off is precluded by statute. See e.g. *VHE Construction Plc v RBSTB Trust Co Ltd* [2000] BLR 187, 192, in relation to the Housing Grants, Construction and Registration Act 1996 where a notice of intention to withhold payment has not been given. See paras 5.51–5.57 above. In *MT Realisations Ltd v Digital Equipment Co Ltd* [2003] 2 BCLC 117, a set-off agreement was held not to give rise to a breach of the Companies Act 1985, s. 151 as constituting the giving of financial assistance by a company for the purpose of the acquisition of shares in itself. In Australia, the courts have rejected an argument that a contractual set-off in the context of a debt for equity swap in an insolvent company, where the debts were immediately payable, constituted an issue of shares at a discount. See para. 8.79 above.

an agreed method of payment.[2] The agreement may not be effective, however, where trust moneys are in issue.[3] Thus, if a customer has deposited trust moneys into an account with a bank, and the bank, acting pursuant to a set-off agreement with the customer, purports to set off the account against a second overdrawn account held by the customer in the customer's personal capacity, the bank may be liable to account to the person beneficially entitled to the trust moneys if the bank cannot rely on a defence of purchaser for value without notice or change of position.[4]

16.02 A contractual right of set-off can arise by custom or be inferred from conduct.[5] It can be bilateral or multilateral,[6] and it may be expressed to extend to debts owing to affiliates.[7] If a set-off agreement is terminated pursuant to a contractual right of termination, the termination may be on terms preserving the operation of the agreement in respect of items covered by it prior to the termination.[8]

16.03 When a set-off is at the option of one of the parties, the question arises how the set-off is effected. In Western Australia,[9] that issue was considered by reference to the principle that applies when a debtor pays money on account to the creditor without appropriating it to a particular debt. The creditor in that situation can elect to apply the money to

---

[2] See e.g. *Jeffs v Wood* (1723) 2 P Wms 128, 129, 24 ER 668, 669; *Kinnerley v Hossack* (1809) 2 Taunt 170, 127 ER 1042; *Cheetham v Crook* (1825) M'Cle & Yo 307, 148 ER 429; *Livingstone v Whiting* (1850) 15 QB 722, 117 ER 632; *Re Kelly* (1932) 4 ABC 258, 267; *Federal Commissioner of Taxation v Steeves Agnew and Co (Vic) Pty Ltd* (1951) 82 CLR 408, 420–1; *First National Bank of Chicago v West of England Shipowners Mutual Protection and Indemnity Association (The Evelpidis Era)* [1981] 1 Lloyd's Rep 54, 63; *Matthews v Geraghty* (1986) 43 SASR 576, 582; *Pro-Image Studios v Commonwealth Bank of Australia* (1991) 4 ACSR 586, 588–9; *Re Keith Bray Pty Ltd* (1991) 5 ACSR 450, 451; *SEAA Enterprises Pty Ltd v Figgins Holdings Pty Ltd* [1997] 2 VR 90, 103–4; *Opal Maritime Agencies Pty Ltd v 'Skulptor Konenkov'* (2000) 98 FCR 519, 562, 568; *Trans Otway Ltd v Shephard* [2005] 3 NZLR 678 at [23]–[31] (CA) (and see in the Supreme Court *Trans Otway Ltd v Shephard* [2006] 2 NZLR 289 at [83]). Set-off is regarded as payment in cash. See *Owens v Denton* (1835) 1 C M & R 711, 712, 149 ER 1266, 1267 ('the parties are in the same situation as if payment in cash had been made'); *Re Harmony and Montague Tin and Copper Mining Co (Spargo's Case)* (1873) LR 8 Ch App 407 (set-off against amount unpaid on shares); *Commissioner of Stamp Duties (NSW) v Perpetual Trustee Co Ltd* (1929) 43 CLR 247, 263–4, 269–70. However, a contractual set-off may not be treated as a payment in cash if at the time the cross-claim was not immediately payable. See *Spargo's Case* at 414; *Commissioner of Stamp Duties (NSW) v Perpetual Trustee Co Ltd* at 263–4, 269–70; *FCT v Steeves Agnew* at 420–1. Compare *Mellham Ltd v Burton* [2003] STC 441 at [16], which was concerned with the construction of particular provisions in tax legislation. At [19], the statutory provisions in issue in that case were distinguished from a set-off by agreement. The decision in any event was reversed on appeal. See *Burton v Mellham Ltd* [2006] 1 WLR 2820 (see in particular at [29]).

[3] See e.g. *P. C. Harrington Contractors Ltd v Co Partnership Developments Ltd* (1998) 88 BLR 44 (retention fund held on trust).

[4] See paras 15.93 and 15.111 above.

[5] *Southern Textile Converters Pty Ltd v Stehar Knitting Mills Pty Ltd* [1979] 1 NSWLR 692, 698 (course of dealing); *Commercial Factors Ltd v Maxwell Printing Ltd* [1994] 1 NZLR 724, 737–9 (cheque swapping arrangement held to constitute a contractual set-off).

[6] *Latreefers Inc v Tangent Shipping Co Ltd* [2000] 1 BCLC 805 (multi-party).

[7] *Sinochem International Oil (London) Co Ltd v Mobil Sales and Supply Corp* [2000] 1 All ER (Comm) 474.

[8] *Opal Maritime Agencies v 'Skulptor Konenkov'* (2000) 98 FCR 519, 563 (though compare *Opal Maritime Agencies Pty Ltd v Baltic Shipping Co* (1998) 158 ALR 416, 422).

[9] *Krishell Pty Ltd v Nilant* (2006) 32 WAR 540 at [105] (Buss JA).

whichever debt he or she chooses, and the creditor retains that right of election until such time as an election is communicated to the debtor.[10] That principle was said to apply by analogy to the exercise of a right of set-off, so that a person who wishes to exercise the right must communicate to the other party that he or she has elected to set off the debts.[11] This would be subject, however, to the terms of the contract. For example, a contractual right of set-off in favour of a bank may provide that the bank can set off the customer's accounts at any time without notice. In that situation, communication to the customer would not be necessary to effect a set-off. The bank could effect the set-off simply by book entries.

(1) Contingent debts

A set-off agreement may extend to contingent debts. Professor Goode has suggested that **16.04** an agreement in those terms may operate in either of two ways.[12] In the first place, it may be intended that the creditor is to have the right to suspend payment of his or her debt to the debtor until the debtor's contingent liability matures, with an ensuing right of set-off, or until it is clear that the contingency will not occur. Alternatively, the creditor may have an immediate right to set off the maximum potential liability of the debtor, upon terms of re-crediting the debtor with the appropriate amount if the actual liability proves to be less or if the contingency fails to occur. Professor Goode considered that in most cases the former construction is likely to prevail. However, this may not be the case if, for example, the creditor is a bank and the creditor's debt takes the form of a deposit which is subject to a contractual restriction on withdrawals, in other words a flawed deposit.[13] In that circumstance, a right to suspend payment until the occurrence of the contingency would not add anything to the existing arrangement, in which case the second construction may reflect more accurately the parties' intention.

B. Insolvency

Where one of the parties to a set-off agreement is insolvent, the validity of a set-off effected **16.05** pursuant to the agreement is subject to two limitations. The first relates to preferences and other impugned transactions under the insolvency legislation, and the second concerns the *pari passu* principle which governs distributions in insolvencies.

---

[10] *Cory Bros & Co Ltd v The Owners of the Turkish Steamship 'Mecca'* [1897] AC 286 at 293–4.
[11] Compare paras 15.28–15.31 above in relation to combination of accounts. In *Krishell Pty Ltd v Nilant* (2006) 32 WAR 540 at [105] Buss JA considered the issue in the context of orders made by a judge to the effect that a defendant was 'entitled to set-off' a sum awarded in favour of the defendant against a sum awarded in favour of the plaintiff. See at [7] for the orders. Nevertheless, the discussion of the point was expressed generally and it would appear to be pertinent also to the case of a contractual right of set-off.
[12] *Goode on Legal Problems of Credit and Security* (4th edn (ed. Gullifer), 2008), 287.
[13] See para. 16.108 below.

(1) Preferences and other impugned transactions

16.06 The first limitation is that a set-off of debts effected pursuant to a contract may be impugned[14] if it constitutes a voidable preference,[15] or if it is a transaction at an under-value[16] or a transaction defrauding creditors,[17] or if it is a disposition of the company's property after the commencement of its winding up.[18] But in considering the possible application of those principles a number of points should be noted. In the first place, if the subject of the set-off is two bank accounts which in any event would be regarded as combined in a single debt pursuant to the principle of combination of accounts,[19] a book-keeping entry by the bank setting off the debit and credit balances against each other should not constitute a preference, since there was in any event a single debt for the balance.[20] Secondly, a contractual set-off effected prior to the bankruptcy or liquidation or administration[21] of one of the parties will not be struck down as a preference if the cross-demands would have been set off in any event under the insolvency set-off section.[22]

---

[14] In Australia, an additional issue in a bankruptcy is the relation back of the trustee's title, in the case of a creditor's petition to the time of the act of bankruptcy. See the Bankruptcy Act 1966 (Cth), ss. 115 and 116. This applies to debts owing to the bankrupt, which constitute property of the bankrupt. See the definition of 'property' in s. 5. On the other hand, the trustee takes subject to equities to which the bankrupt was subject (see *Mitford v Mitford* (1803) 9 Ves Jun 87, 99–100, 32 ER 534, 439), and a set-off agreement may constitute an equity. See paras 17.51–17.59 below.

[15] Insolvency Act 1986, s. 340 and, for company liquidation and administration, s. 239 (referring to s. 238). See generally *Re Washington Diamond Mining Co* [1893] 3 Ch 95; *Re Land Development Association (Kent's Case)* (1888) 39 Ch D 259; *Re Atlas Engineering Co (Davy's Case)* (1889) 10 LR (NSW) Eq 179, 6 WN (NSW) 64; *Mitchell v Booth* [1928] SASR 367.

[16] Insolvency Act 1986, s. 238 and, for bankruptcy, s. 339.

[17] Insolvency Act 1986, s. 423.

[18] Insolvency Act 1986, s. 127. In Australia, there is a suggestion in *Couve v J Pierre Couve Ltd* (1933) 49 CLR 486, 494 that the exercise of a contractual right of set-off may constitute a void disposition (although the avoidance of the disposition of the goods the subject of the sale in that case meant that there was no debt for the price, and therefore no set-off against that debt). See also *Barclays Bank Ltd v TOSG Trust Fund Ltd* [1984] BCLC 1, 25–6 (though, in so far as the comments related to set-off under the insolvency set-off section, they cannot be supported – see para. 6.162 above); Goode, *Principles of Corporate Insolvency Law* (3rd edn, 2005), 494. There is other authority to the contrary, however. In *Re K (Restraint Order)* [1990] 2 QB 298, 305, Otton J considered that the exercise of a contractual right of set-off was not a 'disposing of' assets for the purpose of the Drug Trafficking Offences Act 1986. Compare also *Re Loteka Pty Ltd* [1990] 1 Qd R 322, 324; Armour and Bennett (eds), *Vulnerable Transactions in Corporate Insolvency* (2003), 343–4 [8.28]–[8.29].

[19] See ch. 15.

[20] See para. 15.86 above.

[21] The Insolvency Act 1986, s. 239 (referring to s. 238) extends to a company in administration. In Australia, compare the Corporations Act 2001 (Cth), Pt 5.7B, which confines recovery of an unfair preference to the case of liquidation. For set-off in relation to a company in administration, see paras 6.10–6.14 above.

[22] *Re Washington Diamond Mining Co* [1893] 3 Ch 95, 104, 111; *Re Mistral Finance Ltd* [2001] BCC 27 at [53] and [61]; *Jetaway Logistics Pty Ltd v DCT* (2008) 68 ACSR 226 at [14] (reversed on other grounds (2009) 76 ACSR 404). See also *Hamilton v Commonwealth Bank of Australia* (1992) 9 ACSR 90, 106–8; *Wily v Rothschild Australia Ltd* (1999) 47 NSWLR 555, 566; *Wily v St George Partnership Banking Ltd* (1999) 84 FCR 423, 435–6 (mutual payments); *Minister of Transport v Francis* (2000) 35 ACSR 584, 594. See generally ch. 6 above in relation to insolvency set-off. Compare *Wily v Bartercard Ltd* (2000) 34 ACSR 186 (decision affirmed ((2001) 39 ACSR 94), in which there would not have been a set-off had the transaction been set aside. In *Wily v Rothschild*, a bank had provided a 'gold loan' to a company, which obliged the company to repay to the bank an equivalent amount of gold. In addition, the bank held funds on deposit for the company. On the day that the directors of the company resolved to wind up the company, the bank used the funds on deposit to purchase gold and apply it in reduction of the gold loan. Windeyer J held that this was not a preference, since a set-off would have been available in any event, and the payment therefore did not have the effect of preferring the bank over other creditors. A difficulty with that view is that at the date of the payment the

When a payment is avoided as a preference, the parties, so far as possible, are put in the same position as if the payment had not been made.[23] Consistent with that principle, if a contractual set-off were set aside, the debts would revive,[24] and they potentially would be available for set-off pursuant to the insolvency legislation. If the insolvency set-off section would have applied to the debts in any event, the contractual set-off would not be a preference. As Vaughan Williams J once remarked: 'You cannot prefer a man, it seems to me, by merely putting him in the very position in which he would be if a bankruptcy followed.'[25] Furthermore, in considering whether the qualification to the set-off section[26] would have precluded a set-off, the question of notice is to be determined by reference to the circumstances at the time of the incurring of the obligations, as opposed to the time that the contractual set-off is effected. This is because the question whether there has been a preference, in other words whether there would have been a set-off in any event, is to be tested on the assumption that the contractual set-off is set aside.[27]

If the form of set-off agreement between two parties, A and B, is such that it entitles A to act unilaterally and in his or her discretion to bring about a set-off, and A effects a set-off within the preference period applicable in B's insolvency, A's act in doing so on its own should not constitute a preference under the English insolvency legislation.[28] For the preference section to apply, an individual or a company must do something or suffer something   **16.07**

---

demands were not commensurable, in that the bank was liable as a debtor on the account while the company's obligation was to deliver gold. Therefore, the circumstances at that date were not such as to give rise to a set-off in a liquidation. See ch. 9. The decision would nevertheless appear to be correct. If the bank had not purchased the gold and applied it in reduction of the gold loan, either of two things would have happened. Either the liquidator himself would have performed the contract by delivering gold, or the company would have defaulted, thereby giving rise to a liability in damages to the bank which could have been set off in the liquidation against the debt on the deposit. See paras 8.51–8.52 above. In either case the bank would have been protected, so that the bank's action did not put it in a better position than it otherwise would have been in the liquidation. In *Trans Otway Ltd v Shephard* [2006] 2 NZLR 289, the New Zealand Supreme Court held that a payment by way of set-off constituted a preference in circumstances where the qualification to the insolvency set-off section (see paras 6.66–6.99 above) would have operated to preclude a set-off in the liquidation.

[23] Insolvency Act 1986, ss. 239(3) and 340(2); *Hamilton v Commonwealth Bank of Australia* (1992) 9 ACSR 90, 107. In Australia, see also the Bankruptcy Act 1966 (Cth), s. 122(5).

[24] See e.g. the order in *Wily v Bartercard Ltd* (2000) 34 ACSR 186, 197–8, in which the circumstances were not otherwise such as to give rise to a set-off under the insolvency set-off section. The decision was subsequently affirmed by the NSW Court of Appeal. See *Bartercard Ltd v Wily* (2001) 39 ACSR 94.

[25] *Re Washington Diamond Mining Co* [1893] 3 Ch 95, 104. Professor Goode has made the point that payment by a company into an overdrawn account with its bank would not be a preference in the company's subsequent liquidation if the payment does not exceed the amount of a credit balance on another account held by the company which otherwise would have been available as a set-off against the first account, because the effect of the payment is to reduce the set-off so that the position of other creditors is unaffected. See Goode, *Principles of Corporate Insolvency Law* (3rd edn, 2005), 245. It is suggested that this conclusion is subject to a further condition, that the debit balance on the overdrawn account did not exceed the credit balance on the second account. If it did, the payment into the overdrawn account will have reduced the debt.

[26] Insolvency Act 1986, s. 323(3) and, for company administration and liquidation, the Insolvency Rules 1986, rr. 2.85(2) and 4.90(2). See paras 6.66–6.99 above.

[27] *Minister of Transport v Francis* (2000) 35 ACSR 584, 594.

[28] See also Wood, *English and International Set-off* (1989), 373–4, and Goode, *Principles of Corporate Insolvency Law* (3rd edn, 2005), 245. Compare the position in Australia. See paras 16.10–16.20 below. The preference provision in Australia differs from its English counterpart in that the question of a desire to produce a preference is irrelevant. See para. 13.12 above.

to be done which has the effect of putting a creditor in a better position, in the event of the individual's bankruptcy or the company's liquidation or administration,[29] than the creditor would have been in if the thing had not been done, and the individual or the company must have been influenced by a desire to produce that result.[30] If a debtor authorizes the creditor to sell the debtor's property and to apply the proceeds in reduction of the debt, the creditor in doing so may be acting as the debtor's agent.[31] But when a creditor is empowered by a prior agreement to act unilaterally to set off their mutual debts, the creditor would usually be acting on his or her own behalf and not as an agent.[32] Nothing would be done by the debtor,[33] and the debtor could not be said to have suffered anything to be done if the debtor had no means of preventing the occurrence of a set-off.[34] The act of effecting a set-off should not therefore be a preference, and the question whether there has been a preference should be determined instead by reference to the circumstances surrounding the incurring of the debts the subject of the set-off, or the entry into the set-off agreement.[35] It is at that point that the question of a desire to produce a preference should be determined.

16.08   The analysis of Millett J at first instance in *Derek Randall Enterprises Ltd v Randall*[36] supports this reasoning.[37] A director paid funds to which the company was beneficially entitled into his personal account with a bank. Some nineteen months later, he guaranteed the company's overdraft to the bank and transferred the funds in his personal account to a special blocked account which he charged to the bank. The agreement authorized the bank to apply the moneys in the account against the director's liability as guarantor. When the

---

[29]   In Australia, the Corporations Act 2001 (Cth), Pt 5.7B confines the avoidance of unfair preferences to company liquidation.

[30]   Insolvency Act 1986, s. 340(3)(b) and (4), and for company liquidation s. 239(4)(b) and (5).

[31]   See *Re Kelly* (1932) 4 ABC 258, 262–7, and also *Re Hamling* (1957) 18 ABC 121, 127. *Aliter* if the agreement operates as an equitable assignment of the proceeds. Compare *Re Kelly* at 262–7.

[32]   In *Cinema Plus Ltd v Australia and New Zealand Banking Group Ltd* (2000) 49 NSWLR 513 the New South Wales Court of Appeal held that a bank which exercised a contractual power to consolidate accounts was not acting 'on behalf of' the customer for the purpose of the Corporations Law, s. 437D. See para. 16.11 below.

[33]   Compare the situation in which a debtor is required by a prior agreement to do something, for example to execute a charge in favour of a creditor upon request. The execution of a charge may constitute a preference. See *Re Eric Holmes (Property) Ltd* [1965] 1 Ch 1052.

[34]   See Goode, *Principles of Corporate Insolvency Law* (3rd edn, 2005), 469 [11–89], referring, *inter alia*, to *Tophams Ltd v Sefton* [1967] 1 AC 50. Compare Millett J's passing reference to suffering a payment in *Derek Randall Enterprises Ltd v Randall* [1991] BCLC 379, 383. In *British Eagle International Air Lines Ltd v Compagnie Nationale Air France* [1975] 1 WLR 758 (see para. 16.22 below), the clearing house arrangement was considered not to involve a fraudulent preference, because it could not be said to have been made with a view of giving a preference within the terms of the Bankruptcy Act 1914, s. 44. See Lord Morris of Borth-y-Gest at 762, and also the Court of Appeal [1974] 1 Lloyd's Rep 429, 431. It was not suggested (compare the reference to counsel's argument in the House of Lords at 779) that the striking of a balance pursuant to the arrangement itself was a preference.

[35]   Compare *Re Deague* (1951) 15 ABC 197, although in that case the customer himself transferred funds from one account to another. See also the discussion of *Re Deague* in *Hamilton v Commonwealth Bank of Australia* (1992) 9 ACSR 90, 106.

[36]   [1991] BCLC 379, 383. The preference issue was not considered in the judgments in the Court of Appeal.

[37]   See also the cases referred to in paras 16.10–16.16 below in relation to the Australian bankruptcy preference provision.

company's position subsequently deteriorated, the bank transferred the money standing to the credit of the blocked account in reduction of the company's debt. This occurred a short time before the company went into liquidation. The liquidator argued that, by using the company's money instead of his own, the director had discharged not only the company's debt but also his own as guarantor and thereby he had obtained a preference over the other creditors of the company.[38] The argument was rejected by Millett J on the ground that the director had not caused or permitted the payment of the funds in discharge of the guarantee obligation when the bank effected the transfer. The payment was made by the bank pursuant to a security that had been given before the preference period, and the director was not in a position to prevent it.

When a company owes a debt to A, and as a result of a prior arrangement the company is entitled, without A's consent, to set off the debt against a separate debt owing to the company by another person, B, the company's act in effecting a set-off in accordance with the arrangement would not be a preference to A in the company's subsequent liquidation or administration. In *Katz v McNally*,[39] two directors of a company, GM and RM, had loan accounts with the company. GM's account had a credit balance in his favour of £135,001 but that of RM was in debit to the extent of £61,607. An administration order was made against the company, and subsequently went into liquidation. Within the preference period the company paid £73,394 to GM, representing the sum of £135,001 due to him less the amount of £61,607 owing by RM to the company, which amount was set off against RM's debt. One of the questions for determination was whether the preferential payment to GM was limited to the amount actually paid to him (£73,393), or whether it included also the sum of £61,607 the subject of the set-off. This was thought to depend on whether the company had a right to set off RM's debt to it against its debt to GM. The Court of Appeal accepted that, if the company was entitled to effect a set-off without GM's consent, the effect of such a set-off could not be treated as a preferential payment to GM. If, on the other hand, a set-off could not have been effected without GM's consent, the payment would fall to be treated as an application of £135,001 to or at the direction of GM. The evidence indicated that the company had a right of set-off and that it did no need the consent of GM. The preference to GM was accordingly limited to the amount actually paid to him.

16.09

(2) Preferences in Australia – bankruptcy

In Australia, the preference section in bankruptcy[40] applies where there was a 'transfer of property by a person who is insolvent ("the debtor")' within the preference period in the debtor's bankruptcy. A transfer of property is defined as including a payment of money.[41] The word 'transfer' has been described as one of the widest terms that can be used.[42]

16.10

---

[38] Presumably, this was on the basis of the Insolvency Act 1986, s. 239(4)(a). There is a similar provision in bankruptcy: s. 340(3)(a).

[39] [1999] BCC 291, affirming *Re Exchange Travel (Holdings) Ltd (No. 3)* [1996] 2 BCLC 524 (Rattee J).

[40] Bankruptcy Act 1966 (Cth), s. 122.

[41] Bankruptcy Act 1966 (Cth), s. 122(8). Apart from that, it has been said that the payment of money does not readily fall into the description of a conveyance or transfer of property. See *Anscor Pty Ltd v Clout* (2004) 135 FCR 469 at [2].

[42] *Gathercole v Smith* (1881) 17 Ch D 1, 7, 9; *Re Hardman* (1932) 4 ABC 207, 210.

Similarly, 'payment' has been said to be a very wide term, such that it may include a mere transfer of figures in an account without any money passing.[43] The exercise of a contractual right of set-off should therefore constitute a transfer of property for the purpose of the preference section.[44] In order to constitute a voidable preference, however, the payment must have been made *by the debtor*. This raises a similar issue to that considered above in relation to contractual set-offs under the English legislation.[45] If a creditor is empowered by a prior agreement to act unilaterally to set off mutual money obligations as between it and the debtor, is the creditor's act in effecting a set-off, in circumstances where the cross-demands otherwise would not have been set off in the bankruptcy,[46] properly characterized as a payment 'by' the debtor so as to be voidable as a preference?

16.11 *Cinema Plus Ltd v Australia and New Zealand Banking Group Ltd*[47] suggests that the creditor's act in effecting the set-off does not constitute a payment 'by' the debtor. One of the issues in the case concerned the meaning of s. 437D(1) of the Corporations Law,[48] which operated to avoid a transaction or dealing entered into by a person 'on behalf of' a company under administration which affected the property of the company. The New South Wales Court of Appeal held that a bank which exercised a contractual right to consolidate, or set off, the accounts of a company was not acting 'on behalf of' the company for the purpose of s. 437D(1). The clause in issue provided that the bank at any time could: 'consolidate . . . any of your accounts . . . towards payment of money which is then, or will become, due and payable by you to us . . .' Spigelman CJ said that the reference in the clause to 'payment' was not a reference to an act of the company, or an act on behalf of the company.[49] Sheller JA, with whose reasons Giles JA agreed, referred to an earlier discussion by Dixon J of the expression 'on behalf of'. In the context there under consideration, Dixon J said that it meant: 'for the purposes of, as an instrument of, or for the benefit and in the interest of . . .'[50] Sheller JA considered that, even giving the expression 'on behalf of' in s. 437D(1) that meaning, the bank was not so acting when it consolidated the accounts.[51] The clause empowered the bank to act independently and in no sense on behalf of the company. The bank acted on its own behalf. The *Cinema Plus* case concerned a company under administration, but the same reasoning should apply when the bank's customer is an individual. When a bank sets off an individual's accounts pursuant to a prior contractual right, the act

---

[43] *Re Hardman* (1932) 4 ABC 207, 210 (and see also *Re Kelly* (1932) 4 ABC 258, 267); *Ramsay v National Australia Bank Ltd* [1989] VR 59, 61; *Findlay v Trevor* (1993) 11 ACLC 483, 499; *Driver v Federal Commissioner of Taxation* (1999) 42 ATR 510, 513 (decision affirmed [2000] NSWCA 247).

[44] Similarly, the provision of property by a debtor to a creditor for sale and to retain the proceeds may be characterized as a 'payment made' by the debtor for the purpose of the preference section. See *Findlay v Trevor* (1993) 11 ACLC 483, 499; *Re Wade* (1943) 13 ABC 116; *Re McConnell* (1911) 18 ALR 90, [1912] VLR 102.

[45] See paras 16.07–16.09 above.

[46] See para. 16.06 above. For example, the creditor may have given or received credit after the creditor had notice of an act of bankruptcy, which would preclude a set-off in the subsequent bankruptcy. See the Bankruptcy Act 1966 (Cth), s. 86(2), and paras 6.84–6.86 above.

[47] (2000) 49 NSWLR 513.

[48] Now, the Corporations Act 2001 (Cth).

[49] (2000) 49 NSWLR 513 at [56].

[50] *R v Portus, ex p Federated Clerks Union of Australia* (1949) 79 CLR 428, 438.

[51] (2000) 49 NSWLR 513 at [118].

of effecting payment in that manner would not be an act of the individual through the bank as its instrument, and nor would it be an act on behalf of the individual in the other senses referred to by Dixon J. It should not then be a payment 'by' the individual for the purpose of the preference section in the individual's subsequent bankruptcy.

The judgments of King CJ and Bollen J in the South Australian Supreme Court in *Matthews* **16.12** *v Geraghty*[52] are consistent with that view. The case concerned s. 453(5) of the Companies (South Australia) Code, which applied in the situation in which a disposition of property made by a company within six months before the commencement of its winding up conferred a preference upon a creditor of the company, with the consequent effect of discharging an officer of the company from a liability as guarantor.[53] In those circumstances, the liquidator could recover from the officer an amount equal to the value of the property. In *Matthews v Geraghty*, a bank had made a loan to a company which was guaranteed by the directors. In addition, the company had executed a set-off agreement which entitled the bank to set off debit and credit balances. Some two weeks before the company went into liquidation the company deposited a sum of money to the credit of a current account, and four days later the bank, acting pursuant to the agreement, set off the resulting credit balance against the loan. The set-off had the effect of discharging both the company from its liability on the loan and the directors from their liability to the bank as guarantors. It was argued that the section did not apply because, while the deposit with the bank was a disposition of property, the deposit itself did not confer a preference, which occurred as a result of the subsequent act of the bank manager in setting off the accounts. However, King CJ said that it was a natural and reasonably foreseeable consequence of the deposit that the bank would apply the resulting credit balance in satisfaction of the loan. The deposit put it in the power of the bank to apply the money in that manner. In his opinion, therefore, the disposition of property consisting of the deposit conferred a preference on the bank as a creditor, and it also had the effect of discharging the guarantors from their liability under the guarantee. Accordingly, the section applied.[54] Bollen J adopted a similar analysis. Both King CJ and Bollen J regarded the deposit as the relevant disposition of property made 'by' the company, not the bank's act in setting off the credit balance against the debit balance pursuant to the prior set-off agreement.[55]

---

[52] (1986) 43 SASR 576.

[53] See now the Corporations Act 2001 (Cth), s. 588FH. In England, the preference section may apply to a guarantor by virtue of the Insolvency Act 1986, s. 239(4)(a) and, for bankruptcy, s. 340(3)(a). See also *West Mercia Safetyware Ltd v Dodd* [1988] BCLC 250, in which it was held to be a breach of duty by a director to cause a transfer of the company's funds when the company was known to be insolvent for the purpose of relieving the director of personal liability under a guarantee.

[54] See also the discussion of *Matthews v Geraghty* in *Hamilton v Commonwealth Bank of Australia* (1992) 9 ACSR 90, 109–10.

[55] See also Madden CJ's comment in *Re McConnell* [1912] VLR 102, 109, (1911) 18 ALR 90, 94, that the words of the preference section 'connote an active operation by the insolvent himself . . .'. A'Beckett J, with whom Hood J concurred, differed from Madden CJ, holding (at [1912] VLR 102, 112) that the appropriation by the agent of the insolvent's money in discharge of the insolvent's debt in that case was a 'payment made' by the insolvent. However, that view was premised on his Honour's assumption (at 111) that the creditor could not have sold the debtor's goods without the debtor's assent. Madden CJ, on the other hand, considered that the authority to sell was an authority coupled with an interest and therefore it was irrevocable by the debtor.

16.13   The third member of the Supreme Court, Cox J, similarly held that there was a disposition of property for the purpose of the section, but he described the transaction differently. In a short judgment, he said that, since the transfer from the current account to the loan account was authorized by the terms of the arrangement between the bank and the company, the 'whole transaction', in other words the deposit together with the set-off, was a relevant disposition of property by the company within the meaning of the section.[56] The set-off on its own, however, was still not regarded as a disposition of property made by the company.

16.14   In *Matthews v Geraghty* the subject of the set-off was a debt arising from a deposit. King CJ and Bollen J viewed the deposit as the relevant disposition of property by the company, while Cox J regarded the subsequent contractual set-off as part of the same transaction as the deposit. Those analyses would not be available if the debt the subject of the set-off is not the result of a disposition of property, for example in the case of a contract to perform work. There is nevertheless other authority which suggests that a creditor's act in effecting a set-off pursuant to a prior set-off agreement by itself could constitute a preference for the purpose of the bankruptcy legislation.

16.15   In *Driver v Federal Commissioner of Taxation*,[57] a company was assessed to pay amounts to the Commissioner of Taxation as income tax in respect of two tax returns. In each case the company lodged a request for an amended assessment, which resulted in a credit to the company. Pursuant to a power conferred by the income tax legislation, the Commissioner of Taxation applied the credits in reduction of the company's outstanding tax liabilities. The company went into liquidation, and the liquidator asserted that the application of the credits to the unpaid tax constituted a preference. Windeyer J rejected the argument. His decision turned on the language of the preference provisions set out in the Corporations Law for company liquidation,[58] the effect of which is considered below.[59] If, however, the question had arisen under the earlier Companies (New South Wales) Code, he said that the Commissioner's unilateral act in applying the credit to the outstanding tax liability would have been a preference. The preference section in the Code[60] applied in circumstances where there was: 'A settlement, a conveyance or transfer of property, a charge on property, a payment made, or an obligation incurred, by a company . . .' This was similar in effect to the current bankruptcy provision. Windeyer J said that the application of the credit in reduction of the outstanding tax would have been characterized as a 'payment' for the purpose of that section, and that it would have constituted a preference under the Code.[61]

16.16   Windeyer J's discussion of the earlier legislation was *obiter*. Furthermore, while he referred to the meaning of 'payment', accepting that this may include a mere transfer of figures in

---

[56] Hodgson J adopted Cox J's analysis as an alternative basis for his decision in *Hamilton v Commonwealth Bank of Australia* (1992) 9 ACSR 90, 109–10. See also *Re Emanuel (No. 14) Pty Ltd; Macks v Blacklaw & Shadforth Pty Ltd* (1997) 147 ALR 281 in relation to company liquidation. See para. 16.18 below.

[57] (1999) 42 ATR 510, affirmed [2000] NSWCA 247.

[58] Corporations Law, ss. 588FA–588FF. See now the Corporations Act 2001 (Cth).

[59] See paras 16.17–16.20 below.

[60] Section 451(1).

[61] Windeyer J found support for this view in comments by Tipping J in the New Zealand Supreme Court in *Re Peter Austin Ltd* [1990] 2 NZLR 245, 248 in relation to the equivalent New Zealand provision.

an account without any money passing,[62] the further requirement that the payment had to be made 'by' the company was not explored. Nevertheless, in a subsequent appeal to the New South Wales Court of Appeal, Sheller JA expressed agreement with Windeyer J's judgment, including, presumably, his Honour's assessment of what the position would have been under the earlier legislation.[63] If indeed the Commissioner's unilateral application of the credits in reduction of the tax liability pursuant to a power in the income tax legislation were properly characterized as a payment 'by' the company, the same conclusion *prima facie* would apply in cases where a creditor's unilateral act in effecting a set-off is derived from a power conferred by a prior set-off agreement with the debtor. However, the preferred view, which is consistent with the *Cinema Plus* case, is that, while the set-off constitutes a payment, it is not a payment 'by' the debtor. The creditor, acting on his or her own behalf and not on behalf of the debtor, pays him or herself from a designated asset of the debtor.[64] On its own, therefore, this should not be a preference. On the other hand, the circumstances surrounding the incurring of the debts the subject of the set-off,[65] or the entry into the set-off agreement itself, could give rise to a preference. This accords with the views expressed above in relation to the position under the English legislation.[66]

(3) Preferences in Australia – company liquidation

In Australia, a new scheme governing preferences and other voidable transactions in company liquidation was introduced into the Corporations Law in 1992, and subsequently it was re-enacted as part of the Corporations Act 2001 (Cth). An analysis of the question whether the exercise by a creditor of a contractual right of set-off prior to the debtor's liquidation may be a preference, in circumstances where the cross-demands otherwise would not have been set off in the liquidation,[67] involves a number of steps. **16.17**

Section 588FA provides that a transaction may be an unfair preference in a company's liquidation if the company and the creditor are parties to it, and it results in the creditor receiving more from the company in respect of an unsecured debt than the creditor would receive if the transaction were set aside. The first step is to identify the 'transaction'. Because of the requirement that the company be a party to the transaction, Windeyer J held in *Driver v Federal Commissioner of Taxation*[68] that the Commissioner of Taxation's action in applying a company's tax credits in reduction of its tax liabilities was not a preference in the company's liquidation, a view that was affirmed on appeal by the New South Wales Court **16.18**

---

[62] See para. 16.10 above.

[63] *Driver v Commissioner of Taxation* [2000] NSWCA 247 at [19] and [20].

[64] In *Sheahan v Carrier Air Conditioning Pty Ltd* (1997) 189 CLR 407, 437, Dawson, Guadron and Gummow JJ noted (referring to *Re Stevens* (1929) 1 ABC 90, 93) that there may be a payment made by a debtor within the meaning of the preference section in the bankruptcy legislation where the debtor directs a third party who holds funds at the direction of the debtor, or is otherwise obliged to the debtor, to account to the debtor, not by payment to the debtor, but to a creditor of the debtor. But the High Court went on to comment that the third party in that circumstance is to be treated as acting 'on behalf of' the debtor, whereas on the basis of the *Cinema Plus* case (see above) that explanation would not be available in the case of a set-off effected pursuant to a prior set-off agreement.

[65] Including as a result of a deposit of money, as in *Matthews v Geraghty* (1986) 43 SASR 576. See above.

[66] See paras 16.07–16.09 above.

[67] See para. 16.06 above.

[68] (1999) 42 ATR 510. See paras 16.15 above.

of Appeal.[69] The exercise of a contractual set-off differs from the circumstances in issue in the *Driver* case in that the set-off occurs as a result of a power conferred by the debtor on the creditor. Nevertheless, the debtor is still not usually a party to the ultimate act of effecting a set-off, and so ordinarily that act should not be a transaction for the purpose of s. 588FA.[70] In some cases the analysis in *Re Emanuel (No. 14) Pty Ltd; Macks v Blacklaw & Shadforth Pty Ltd*[71] may qualify that proposition. In *Re Emanuel*, the Federal Court[72] accepted that there may be a transaction to which a debtor (A) is a party, notwithstanding that it is made up of a composite of dealings in not all of which A participates. That view was expressed in the context of an agreement between A and B that, as part of a settlement of the claims between them, B would make a payment to C who was A's creditor. The court rejected an argument that, since the payment was made by B and not A, A was not a party to the transaction constituting the payment, and therefore the payment was not a preference in A's liquidation. The transaction consisted of a composite of dealings, and it did not matter that A did not participate in the final act of payment to C. But in discussing the point, the court emphasized that it was confining its observations for the purpose of that case to a course of dealing initiated by a debtor for the purpose, and having the effect, of extinguishing a debt. It referred to the situation in which the debtor 'procures the intended outcome' and to 'the intended purpose of extinguishing the debt'.[73] In the case of a set-off agreement, on the other hand, often it would not be the debtor's intention at the time of entering into the agreement that the creditor would exercise the right conferred by the agreement. The right commonly would be exercisable upon default, but the debtor would not expect to default. A general contractual right of set-off may have been given as a form of security in furtherance of a commercial relationship that was intended to be ongoing.

16.19 But whatever the position in that regard, the entry into the set-off agreement, or the incurring of an obligation the subject of the set-off, itself could be a transaction for the purpose of s. 588FA, given that the company was a party to those acts. Ordinarily, then, s. 588FA should initially direct attention to those matters as the foundation of a preference argument. Once a transaction is characterized as an unfair preference for the purpose of s. 588FA, s. 588FC provides that it may be an insolvent transaction, and therefore it potentially may be avoided, if it was entered into when the company was insolvent, or if an act was done for the purpose of giving effect to the transaction when the company was insolvent.[74] But what if the obligations the subject of the contractual set-off were incurred,

---

[69] [2000] NSWCA 247. See also *Macquarie Health Corp Ltd v Commissioner of Taxation* (1999) 96 FCR 238 at [124]–[134] in relation to a notice given by the Commissioner under the former Income Tax Assessment Act 1936 (Cth), s. 218.

[70] Compare Cox J in *Matthews v Geraghty* (1986) 43 SASR 576, 581–2, in relation to the expression 'a disposition of property is made by a company', where a company made a deposit with a bank which the bank set off against an overdrawn account. However, King CJ and Bollen J adopted a different analysis. See paras 16.12–16.13 above.

[71] (1997) 147 ALR 281.

[72] O'Loughlin, Branson and Finn JJ.

[73] (1997) 147 ALR 281, 288. See also *V R Dye & Co v Peninsula Hotels Pty Ltd* [1999] 3 VR 201, 215; *Macquarie Health Corp Ltd v Commissioner of Taxation* (1999) 96 FCR 238 at [129]–[130]; *Re Imobridge Pty Ltd (No. 2)* [2000] 2 Qd R 280, 295.

[74] It is not necessary that all the acts giving effect to an impugned transaction should have occurred during the preference period. See *New Cap Reinsurance Corporation Ltd v All American Life Insurance Co* (2004) 49 ACSR 417.

and the set-off agreement was entered into, before the company's insolvency, though the set-off was effected after insolvency? It suffices for s. 588FC that an act is done for the purpose of giving effect to the transaction, but the section does not stipulate who must perform the act. It is not limited in that regard to the company. If the transaction is characterized as the entry into the set-off agreement, the creditor's act in setting off the demands pursuant to the agreement may be characterized as an act done for the purpose of giving effect to the transaction. If the set-off was effected within the preference period[75] and while the company was insolvent, the set-off may be voidable.[76]

The creditor nevertheless will be protected if it can rely on s. 588FG(2). An examination of that issue directs attention to the transaction (entry into the set-off agreement or the incurring of the obligations), as opposed to an act done for the purpose of giving effect to it. Section 588FG(2) protects a creditor if a number of conditions are satisfied. In summary, these are: (a) that the creditor became a party to the transaction in good faith, (b) that, at the time when the creditor became a party, it had no reasonable grounds for suspecting that the company was insolvent at that time or would become insolvent as a result of an act done for the purpose of giving effect to the transaction, and moreover a reasonable person in the creditor's circumstances would have had no such grounds for so suspecting, and (c) that the creditor provided valuable consideration under the transaction or changed its position in reliance on the transaction. If those requirements are satisfied, the transaction would not be impugned as a preference.

16.20

C. Set-off Agreement Taking Effect Contrary to the *Pari Passu* Principle

(1) The '*British Eagle*' principle

There is a second limitation on the validity of a contractual set-off in an insolvency administration. Unless a set-off would otherwise be available under the insolvency set-off section,[77] or the agreement is effective to create a charge,[78] the statutory requirement of a *pari passu* distribution of the estate amongst the general body of creditors[79] has the consequence that

16.21

---

[75] Corporations Act 2001 (Cth), s. 588FE.

[76] In order to constitute a preference, the transaction must 'result' in the creditor receiving more from the company in respect of an unsecured debt than the creditor would receive if the transaction were set aside. When a creditor unilaterally effects a set-off pursuant to a prior set-off agreement, and a set-off would not otherwise have been available in the liquidation (see para. 16.06 above), it is the creditor's own action, rather than the earlier transaction to which the company was a party, which is the immediate cause of the creditor receiving more than it would have received in the liquidation. The connection should nevertheless be established, because the set-off is the natural and reasonably foreseeable consequence of the transaction. See *Matthews v Geraghty* (1986) 43 SASR 576 (which was referred to in *Hamilton v Commonwealth Bank of Australia* (1992) 9 ACSR 90, 109–10), and para. 16.12 above.

[77] *Re Charge Card Services Ltd* [1987] Ch 150, 177; *Re Bank of Credit and Commerce International SA (No. 8)* [1996] Ch 245, 257, 272–3; *Sinochem International Oil (London) Co Ltd v Mobil Sales and Supply Corp* [2000] 1 All ER (Comm) 474, 480. Compare *Sturdy v Arnaud* (1790) 3 TR 599, 100 ER 754 and *Hanford v Moseley*, unreported but referred to in *Jones v Mossop* (1844) 3 Hare 568, 572–4, 67 ER 506, 508–9. Compare also *Dobson v Lockhart* (1793) 5 TR 133, 101 ER 77, in which the agreement in question was interpreted as making the debt to the bankrupt conditional. See generally ch. 6 above in relation to insolvency set-off.

[78] See paras 16.93–16.107 below.

[79] See the Insolvency Act 1986, s. 107 (which is expressed to apply only to voluntary winding up, though the equivalent provision in earlier legislation was also applied in compulsory liquidation: see *Webb v Whiffin*

a contractual set-off which involves a claim in favour of the insolvent[80] will not be effective to the extent that the demands had not been set against each other, and a balance struck, before the commencement of the insolvency administration. As Rose LJ remarked in delivering the judgment of the Court of Appeal in *Re Bank of Credit and Commerce International SA (No. 8)*:[81] 'Once insolvency supervenes, rule 4.90 of the Insolvency Rules 1986 requires set-off in the situations in which it is applicable and public policy forbids it where it is not.' Thus, where a surety places a deposit with a creditor charged as security for the principal debtor's liability, and the creditor becomes bankrupt or goes into liquidation, lack of mutuality would prevent a set-off under the insolvency set-off section in relation to the deposit and the principal debt,[82] and a prior agreement that the deposit is to be set off against the debt in the event of default in payment would not be effective in the bankruptcy or the liquidation.[83]

16.22 The leading authority on this second limitation is *British Eagle International Air Lines Ltd v Compagnie Nationale Air France*.[84] The International Air Transport Association ('IATA') had established a clearing house system for the monthly settlement of debits and credits arising when members performed services for one another. A balance would be struck between the total sum owing to a particular member in respect of services supplied by it *for* all other members, and the total owing by that member in respect of services supplied *by* all other members. The clearance took effect within five days after the thirtieth day of each

---

(1872) LR 5 HL 711, 735 and *Attorney-General v McMillan & Lockwood Ltd* [1991] 1 NZLR 53), and r. 4.181 of the Insolvency Rules (which applies to winding up generally). For bankruptcy, see the Insolvency Act 1986, s. 328(3).

[80] Compare the discussion below of a set-off agreement where the set-off concerns only a *liability* of the bankrupt or the company.

[81] [1996] Ch 245, 272. In Australia, see also *Ansett Australia Ltd v Travel Software Solutions Pty Ltd* (2007) 65 ACSR 47 at [94] in relation to a deed of company arrangement pursuant to Part 5.3A of the Corporations Act 2001 (Cth). In both cases the statements were made in the context of an agreement for a set-off. Compare paras 6.25–6.32 above in relation to equitable set-off.

[82] *Re Bank of Credit and Commerce International SA (No. 8)* [1998] AC 214. See para. 12.41 above.

[83] *Re BCCI (No. 8)* [1996] Ch 245, 272 (CA).

[84] [1975] 1 WLR 758. See also *Re NIAA Corporation Ltd* (1993) 33 NSWLR 344, 359; *Stotter v Equiticorp Australia Ltd* [2002] 2 NZLR 686 at [41] (but see para. 8.16n above in relation to that case); *Hague v Nam Tai Electronics Inc* [2006] 2 BCLC 194 at [8] (PC) (amendment of a company's articles of association after the liquidation of a shareholder for the purpose of redeeming the shares and setting off the redemption price against a debt owing by the shareholder). In *Nationwide General Insurance Co v North Atlantic Insurance Co* [2004] EWCA Civ 423 the Court of Appeal held that, in the absence of a trust, an arrangement between members of an underwriting pool as to how the proceeds of reinsurance were to be dealt with once collected by the underwriting agent on behalf of members could not affect the right of a liquidator of a member to collect the asset for the benefit of the general creditors. See also *Attorney-General v McMillan & Lockwood Ltd* [1991] 1 NZLR 53 and *B Mullan & Sons Contractors Ltd v Ross* (1996) 86 BLR 1 in relation to a provision in a building contract between an employer and a contractor that in specified circumstances, for example default by the contractor in paying sub-contractors, the employer may pay sub-contractors directly and deduct the sums paid from sums due to the contractor. Compare in that regard *Hitachi Plant Engineering & Construction Co Ltd v Eltraco International Pte Ltd* [2003] 4 SLR 384 at [55]–[87] (Singapore CA) (scheme of arrangement outside liquidation). Compare generally *Carreras Rothmans Ltd v Freeman Mathews Treasure Ltd* [1985] 1 Ch 207, in which there was a trust. The application of the principle must be considered by reference to the effect of the arrangement in the insolvency of a particular party. See *Re SSSL Realisations (2002) Ltd* [2005] 1 BCLC 1 at [45] (decision affirmed [2006] Ch 610 (CA)). Debt subordination does not infringe the *pari passu* principle. See paras 6.114–6.116 above.

calendar month in relation to the month prior to that calendar month. Members with an overall debit balance would pay into the clearing house the amount of the debit, while the clearing house would pay to members with an overall credit balance the sums due to them. British Eagle went into liquidation. The House of Lords said that any clearance that had taken place before the commencement of the liquidation was binding on the liquidator,[85] since there was no question of a preference. The majority[86] held, however, that the clearing house system could not operate after the commencement of the liquidation in respect of debits and credits not cleared at that date, because this would be contrary to the statutory injunction that the property of a company is to be applied in its winding up in satisfaction of its liabilities *pari passu*.[87] It made no difference that the parties may have had good business reasons for entering into the arrangement, or that the arrangement was not designed specifically in order to evade the insolvency legislation.[88] Therefore, the liquidator was entitled to recover the uncleared credits owing to the company, while members with uncleared debits on the company's accounts were each remitted to a proof in respect of them. On the other hand, each member could set off the uncleared sums owing to it individually by the company against its individual indebtedness to the company.

The principle is not confined to bankruptcy and company liquidation, but should extend **16.23** to any formal insolvency administration which is subject to the *pari passu* principle.[89] Thus, it should apply in an administration under the English Insolvency legislation where the administrator has given notice to creditors of his or her intention to make a distribution to creditors in accordance with r. 2.95 of the Insolvency Rules.[90] Set-off is available in that

---

[85] As Lord Romilly MR remarked in *Re Smith, Knight, & Co, ex p Ashbury* (1868) LR 5 Eq 223, 226: 'The Act of Parliament unquestionably says, that everybody shall be paid *pari passu*, but that means everybody after the winding-up has commenced. It does not mean that the Court will look into past transactions, and equalise all creditors by making good to those who have not received anything a sum of money equal to that which other creditors have received.' See also *Carreras Rothmans Ltd v Freeman Mathews Treasure Ltd* [1985] 1 Ch 207, in which the money in the account was not an asset of the company at the date of the liquidation.

[86] Lord Cross of Chelsea, Lord Diplock and Lord Edmund-Davies concurring, Lord Morris of Borth-y-Gest and Lord Simon of Glaisdale dissenting.

[87] It has been pointed out that there were in fact two principles at play. First, a person cannot by contract divest him or herself of assets when bankruptcy occurs and, secondly, all creditors in the same class are to be treated alike. See *Goode on Legal Problems of Credit and Security* (4th edn (ed. Gullifer), 2008), 290, 292–3.

[88] Compare *Ex p Mackay* (1873) LR 8 Ch App 643 with respect to the agreement as to the royalties in a bankruptcy. Lord Cross of Chelsea rejected the argument that the parties to the clearing house arrangement in *British Eagle* had intended to give one another charges on some of each other's future book debts. Compare *Ex p Mackay* with respect to the right to half of the royalties.

[89] In Australia, see *International Air Transport Association v Ansett Australia Holdings Ltd* (2008) 234 CLR 151 in relation to a deed of company arrangement entered into pursuant to Part 5.3A of the Corporations Act 2001 (Cth), and also in that context *Ansett Australia Ltd v Travel Software Solutions Pty Ltd* (2007) 65 ACSR 47 at [94]. In *Perpetual Trustee Co Ltd v BNY Corporate Trustee Services Ltd* [2009] EWCA Civ 1160 at [43] and [112] it was accepted, for the purpose of an agreement governed by English law, that the principle applied where a company had filed for Chapter 11 protection in the United States (at least where the filing was for the purpose of maximizing the return on the insolvency and cessation of business). Compare *Charter Reinsurance Co Ltd v Fagan* [1997] AC 313, 351–2 (*per* Mance J, whose judgment was upheld by the Court of Appeal and the House of Lords) in relation to provisional liquidation, and *Hitachi Plant Engineering & Construction Co Ltd v Eltraco International Pte Ltd* [2003] 4 SLR 384 at [55]–[87] (Singapore CA) in relation to a scheme of arrangement outside liquidation.

[90] See the Insolvency Rules 1986, rr. 2.68 and 2.69 (debts of insolvent company to rank equally). In *Perpetual Trustee Co Ltd v BNY Corporate Trustee Services Ltd* [2009] EWCA Civ 1160 at [43], Neuberger MR said that it was common ground in that case that the *British Eagle* principle applies when a company goes into

situation pursuant to r. 2.85,[91] the date for determining what debts can be included in a set-off being back-dated to the commencement of the administration.[92] By reason of that back-dating, a debt incurred after the commencement of the administration would not be included in a set-off under r. 2.85. The exercise of a contractual right of set-off after the commencement of the administration but before a notice has been given under r. 2.95 should not be objectionable, including in relation to post administration debts. But once a notice is given under r. 2.95, a subsequent exercise of the contractual right would not be effective to the extent that it goes beyond the scope of r. 2.85, including in relation to post administration debts.

16.24 The difference in the opinions of the majority and the dissenting minority[93] in *British Eagle* fundamentally concerned the question whether debts remained owing as between airlines. The clearing house regulations provided that debits and credits were payable and receivable through the medium of the clearing house 'and not otherwise in any manner', and it was accepted as implicit that members could not enforce payment by legal proceedings.[94] The dissentients were of the view that, as a result of the clearing house rules, money was not payable by one member to another. Rather, the clearing house itself was the creditor or debtor, as the case may be. Therefore, the property of the company in liquidation did not include the right to receive money from the other members. The majority,[95] however, noted that the framers of the regulations had described the rights of the members *inter se* as debts, and concluded that, notwithstanding that one member could not have brought legal proceedings against another member, each member performing services for another obtained a species of chose in action against that other member which could be enforced against it separately in the liquidation.

16.25 If, on the other hand, the rules of a clearing house system have effect such that the clearing house itself is the debtor or creditor, and that members are not liable to each other, the system should not be objectionable in the insolvency of one of the members. This could occur by way of automatic novation of contracts before the insolvency, in other words, the replacement of a contract made between members with new contracts between each member and the clearing house.[96] Alternatively, the rules of a clearing house may provide that the clearing house from inception is the debtor or creditor. The efficacy of clearing house rules drafted in that manner was confirmed by the High Court of Australia in

---

administration, at least where the administration effectively is for the purpose of maximizing the return in the insolvency and will lead to a winding up order. See also Lightman and Moss, *The Law of Administrators and Receivers of Companies* (4th edn, 2007), 548.

[91] See para. 6.10 above. There is no equivalent provision in administration in Australia. See para. 6.12 above.
[92] See paras 6.49 and 6.50 above.
[93] Lord Morris of Borth-y-Gest and Lord Simon of Glaisdale.
[94] See [1975] 1 WLR 758, 773.
[95] [19751 1 WLR 758, 778 (Lord Cross of Chelsea).
[96] By way of example, *Goode on Legal Problems of Credit and Security* (4th edn (ed. Gullifer), 2008), 283–4, 293 refers to the General Regulations of the London Clearing House (LCH.Clearnet Limited). Regulation 3 provides that, upon registration of a contract by the Clearing House, the contract is replaced, by novation, by two open contracts, one between the seller and the Clearing House as buyer and one between the buyer and the Clearing House as seller, in each case as principals to the relevant contract.

International Air Transport Association v Ansett International Holdings Ltd.[97] Ansett was an Australian airline which was member of IATA. Administrators were appointed to IATA pursuant to Part 5.3A of the Australian Corporations Act 2001 (Cth) and subsequently it executed a deed of company arrangement under that Act. IATA brought proceedings challenging decisions by the deed administrators that IATA was not a creditor of Ansett in respect of monthly clearances effected in accordance with the rules. In addition, Ansett commenced proceedings against IATA seeking a declaration that the clearing house rules ceased to apply in relation to it upon execution of the deed. Ansett relied upon the decision in *British Eagle*. Following *British Eagle*, however, the IATA clearing house rules had been amended in an attempt to overcome the effect of that decision. In particular, reg. 9(a) provided:

> With respect to transactions between members of the Clearing House which are subject to clearance through the Clearing House as provided in Regulations 10 and 11 and subject to the provisions of the Regulations regarding protested and disputed items, no liability for payment and no right of action to recover payment shall accrue between members of the Clearing House. In lieu thereof members shall have liabilities to the Clearing House for balances due by them resulting from a clearance or rights of action against the Clearing House for balances in their favour resulting from a clearance and collected by the Clearing House from debtor members in such clearance . . .

As a consequence of that amendment, the majority of the High Court in the *Ansett* case[98] accepted that, as a matter of construction, no liability to effect payment arose as between member airlines. The only debt or credit which arose was between IATA and each member in relation to the final, single balance of all items entered for the relevant clearance.[99] Since the property of Ansett did not include claims against other member airlines, the rules did not affect a distribution contrary to the insolvency laws.

The Australian High Court considered a further argument that, even accepting that **16.26** construction, the IATA rules were contrary to public policy. The public policy was said to be that Australian courts should refuse to give effect to contractual provisions which purported to circumvent or dislocate the order of priorities that were set out in a deed of company arrangement and given statutory force and effect by Part 5.3A of the Corporations Act.[100] The substance of the argument was that, since the only claim that could be propounded was by or against IATA for a net balance remaining after the process required by the clearing house rules had been carried out, an airline to which Ansett had not provided services could have obtained satisfaction in full of its claim against Ansett.[101] However, that argument was also rejected. In the *British Eagle* case, the insolvent airline had property, in the form of claims against other member airlines, which was subject to a statutory requirement of a *pari passu* distribution, and a contractual provision negating that outcome could not prevail against the terms of the statute. The attempt to contract out of the

---

[97] (2008) 234 CLR 151. See Bridge, 'Clearing houses and insolvency in Australia' (2008) 124 LQR 379.
[98] Gleeson CJ and Gummow, Hayne, Heydon, Crennan and Kiefel JJ, Kirby J dissenting.
[99] (2008) 234 CLR 151 at [60]–[62] (Gummow, Hayne, Heydon, Crennan and Kiefel JJ).
[100] (2008) 234 CLR 151 at [72].
[101] (2008) 234 CLR 151 at [84] and [92].

legislation was said to be contrary to public policy,[102] but in truth that result flowed from the operation of the statute.[103] In the *Ansett* case, on the other hand, the effect of the rules was that Ansett's only property consisted of rights against IATA. The rules achieving that outcome were not contrary to the terms of the insolvency legislation, and the majority said that, if the clearing house rules did not operate in a manner contrary to the relevant legislation, public policy could not achieve what the statute did not otherwise achieve.[104]

(2) Legislation in relation to investment exchanges and clearing houses

16.27 The Companies Act 1989, Part VII introduced provisions designed to overcome the effects of *British Eagle*.[105] Their scope is limited, however. They relate to the rules of certain recognized investment exchanges and clearing houses.[106] The effect of the legislation is to modify the application of insolvency laws to the 'default rules' of the exchange or clearing house, and other rules of the exchange or clearing house relating to the settlement of market contracts.[107] Part VII provides that the rules are not invalid on the ground of inconsistency with the insolvency laws relating to the distribution of the assets of a person in bankruptcy, winding up or administration.[108] 'Default rules' are rules which provide for the taking of action in the event of a person appearing to be unable, or likely to be unable, to meet his or her obligations in respect of a market contract.[109] The application of the Act has been extended by regulation to include 'money market contracts'.[110] A money market contract is defined as a contract for the acquisition or disposal of currency of the United Kingdom

---

[102] *British Eagle v Air France* [1975] 1 WLR 758, 780–1. See also *Carreras Rothmans Ltd v Freeman Mathews Treasure Ltd* [1985] 1 Ch 207, 226.

[103] (2008) 234 CLR 151 at [76]–[78].

[104] See (2008) 234 CLR 151 at [71]–[93]. In a separate judgment, Gleeson CJ (at [24]–[29]) advanced a different reason for rejecting the public policy argument. He said that, while public policy may render a contractual provision invalid, it cannot create a contract to which the parties have never agreed. Members had agreed that they were not debtors or creditors of each other. If the clearing house rules were contrary to public policy in an insolvency, the court could not re-write the contract so that members were liable to each other when they had agreed that they would not be so.

[105] [1975] 1 WLR 758. See para. 16.22 above.

[106] Within the meaning of the Financial Services and Markets Act 2000, s. 285 (and see the Financial Services and Markets Act 2000 (Recognition Requirements for Investment Exchanges and Clearing Houses) Regulations 2001 (S.I. 2001 No. 995)). See the Companies Act 1989, s. 190.

[107] Defined in s. 155 as a contract connected with a recognized investment exchange or recognized clearing house, being a contract of the type described in that section. See also ss. 173–6 in relation to market charges, being a charge, whether fixed or floating, in favour, *inter alia*, of a recognized investment exchange or clearing house, for the purpose of securing debts or liabilities arising in connection with the settlement of market contracts or in connection with ensuring the performance of market contracts.

[108] See in particular the Companies Act 1989, s. 159, and generally ss. 155, 158–65, 188 and 190. See also the Financial Markets and Insolvency (Settlement Finality) Regulations 1999 (S.I. 1999 No. 2979) in relation to certain 'designated systems'.

[109] Companies Act 1989, s. 188.

[110] Financial Markets and Insolvency (Money Market) Regulations 1995 (S.I. 1995 No. 2049). See also regs 20–4 in relation to money market charges (being a charge granted in favour of a listed person for the purpose of securing debts or liabilities arising in connection with the settlement of money market contracts or related contracts), and the Financial Markets and Insolvency Regulations 1996 (S.I. 1996 No. 1469) in relation to system charges (being a charge granted in favour of a settlement bank for the purpose of securing various debts and liabilities). The 1995 Regulations were amended by the Financial Markets and Insolvency (Ecu Contracts) Regulations 1998 (S.I. 1998 No. 27) to include rights under a contract the value of which is determined by reference to the value of the ecu.

or elsewhere and which is a contract in relation to which a 'listed person' provides settlement arrangements. A 'listed person' is a person included in a list maintained by the Financial Services Authority. The regulations have the effect that the default rules of the listed person are not to be invalid by reason of inconsistency with insolvency laws relating to the distribution of assets.

Australia

A similar development has occurred in Australia, with the enactment of the Payment Systems and Netting Act 1998 (Cth). The Act gives effect to the rules of stock and futures exchanges and clearing houses approved by the Minister[111] which relate to the termination of obligations and the calculation and netting of termination values, including in the 'external administration' of a participant (which includes bankruptcy and liquidation).[112] The Act also applies to 'approved netting arrangements',[113] which include payment systems. To qualify, the system must provide for netting to occur at least once on each business day and be approved by the Reserve Bank.[114] In relation to approved netting arrangements, however, the efficacy of the netting is subject to a qualification. If a party to an approved netting arrangement goes into external administration, and an obligation owed by that party to another party has been netted under the arrangement, in circumstances where a direct payment by that party to the other would have been voidable in the external administration if it had been made to settle the obligation on the day on which the netting occurred, the liquidator (or the equivalent in other forms of external administration) may recover from the other party an amount equal to the amount of the obligation.[115] Thus, the effect of voidable preferences, and other such insolvency principles allowing for claw-back of payments, is preserved. **16.28**

(3) Contractual set-off against an insolvent's liability

The objection in *British Eagle*, in so far as that case may apply generally to multi-party set-off agreements, should only be relevant when the agreement provides for a set-off against a *claim* possessed by a person or a company the subject of a formal solvency administration, in circumstances where the insolvency set-off section does not apply. There is no reason why a set-off agreement which involves only a liability of the insolvent should be impugned. For example, A, B and C may agree that A's liability to B may be set off against B's liability to C, and A goes into liquidation before the set-off has occurred. Since A's liability, as opposed to property distributable amongst creditors, is in issue, the liquidation should not affect the agreement.[116] The agreement would have the effect that B would no longer be a proving creditor to the extent of the set-off, with a consequent increase in the **16.29**

---

[111] These are referred to in the Act as 'netting markets'.
[112] Payment Systems and Netting Act 1998 (Cth), Part 5.
[113] Payment Systems and Netting Act 1998 (Cth), Part 3.
[114] Payment Systems and Netting Act 1998 (Cth), s. 12.
[115] Payment Systems and Netting Act 1998 (Cth), s. 10(4).
[116] See also para. 13.78 above. Mance LJ's comments in *Sinochem International Oil (London) Co Ltd v Mobil Sales and Supply Corp* [2000] 1 All ER (Comm) 474, 480 with respect to the liquidation of the affiliate may support this view, although it is not clear if his Lordship was referring to a set-off of a debt owing by the insolvent affiliate against a debt owing to Sinochem London or another affiliate.

dividend payable to other creditors. Nevertheless, a comment made by Rose LJ in delivering the judgment of the Court of Appeal in *Re Bank of Credit and Commerce International SA (No. 8)*[117] suggests the contrary. Rose LJ said that: 'if A owes B £x and B owes C £y *and any of them becomes insolvent* the two debts cannot be set off even if there is an express agreement by the three of them that B may set them off; such an agreement is contrary to the scheme of distribution on insolvency and cannot prevail over the rules which require *pari passu* distribution . . .'[118] But why the agreement should be regarded as contrary to public policy when A is the insolvent party is difficult to understand. The decision in that case went on appeal to the House of Lords. In a speech with which the other Law Lords agreed, Lord Hoffmann observed:[119]

> In English law, it [i.e. insolvency set-off] is strictly limited to mutual claims existing at the bankruptcy date. There can be no set-off of claims by third parties, even with their consent. To do so would be to allow parties by agreement to subvert the fundamental principle of *pari passu* distribution of the insolvent company's assets . . .

Once again, however, to the extent that this may encompass an agreement which provides that a claim by B against an insolvent company in liquidation (the company's liability) is to be set off against a third party's (C's) claim against B, as opposed to an asset of the insolvent company in the form of a claim being utilized by way of a set-off against a third party's liability, it is difficult to understand why it should be objectionable. The agreement in this situation would not subvert the *pari passu* principle.

D. Close-out Netting

16.30   Close-out netting[120] is a contractual arrangement whereby the obligations of the parties under transactions between them are valued and replaced by an obligation to pay a net money amount.[121] Netting is commonly used in relation to contracts for the acquisition or disposal of currencies. However, it applies more generally, for example in relation to contracts for the delivery of commodities or securities.

16.31   Consider that a bank and a counterparty have entered into a number of foreign exchange contracts involving various currencies and settlement dates. Prior to the decision of the Court of Appeal in *Camdex International Ltd v Bank of Zambia*,[122] there was a considerable body of opinion to the effect that the foreign money obligation under a foreign exchange

---

[117] [1996] Ch 245 (Rose, Saville and Millett LJJ).

[118] [1996] Ch 245, 257 (emphasis added).

[119] [1998] AC 214, 223.

[120] Alternative forms of netting are payment netting and netting by novation, although neither is entirely satisfactory. See generally Derham, 'Set-off and netting of foreign exchange contracts in the liquidation of a counterparty – Part 2: netting' [1991] JBL 536, 536–9. The various forms of netting are discussed in *Enron Europe Ltd v Revenue and Customs Commissioners* [2006] EWHC 824 (Ch) at [19]–[22].

[121] See the definitions of 'netting' in the Financial Markets and Insolvency (Settlement Finality) Regulations 1999 (S.I. 1999 No. 2979), reg. 2(1), of 'close-out netting provision' in the Financial Collateral Arrangements (No. 2) Regulations 2003 (S.I. 2003 No. 3226), reg. 3 and, in Australia, of 'close-out netting contract' in the Payment Systems and Netting Act 1998 (Cth), s. 5.

[122] [1997] 6 Bank LR 43. See para. 9.19 above.

contract is not a money obligation.[123] That view in turn resulted in doubt as to whether, in the event of the liquidation of the counterparty, the various obligations under foreign exchange contracts between the counterparty and the bank could be set off.[124] The position in a liquidation, on the assumption that the foreign money obligation was not a money obligation, was considered earlier.[125] In an attempt to avoid that perceived difficulty, participants in foreign exchange and other markets have had recourse to close-out netting agreements.[126] In the *Camdex case*, the Court of Appeal considered that the foreign money obligation under an exchange contract is properly characterized as a money obligation,[127] which has added greater certainty to the question of set-off in relation to those contracts. But the difficulty in a liquidation referred to earlier, on the assumption that the foreign money obligation is not a money obligation, may still apply in relation to other contracts that provide for the delivery of commodities or securities or other non-monetary assets, which raises the issue of the efficacy of close-out netting in those contexts. Regulations have been made giving effect to EC Directives in relation to netting which have affected the position in certain situations. The regulations are considered later.[128] An outstanding issue is whether, apart from the regulations, a close-out netting agreement would be effective in a liquidation to avoid the difficulty which otherwise may arise in relation to set-off where contracts provide for the delivery of non-monetary assets. This issue is addressed below.

The essence of close-out netting is that, upon the occurrence of a liquidation, the various **16.32** contracts are 'closed,' and are replaced by an obligation to pay the net money value of the contracts based upon the market rates prevailing at the time. Because the obligation is simply to pay a net money amount, the perceived difficulty which otherwise may arise in a liquidation consequent upon the circumstance that the delivery obligation relates to a non-monetary asset would be avoided. There would be no danger of the solvent party being confined to a dividend in the liquidation of the counterparty in respect of contracts disclaimed by the liquidator, and at the same time having to perform contracts which are unprofitable from the solvent party's perspective.[129] However, a question which has generated considerable debate is whether a close-out netting agreement could be struck down as an attempt to evade the operation of the insolvency law, if a set-off otherwise would not have been available in the liquidation under the insolvency set-off section.

---

[123] See paras 9.14–9.16 above.
[124] See Derham, 'Set-off and netting of foreign exchange contracts in the liquidation of a counterparty' [1991] JBL 463.
[125] See paras 9.01 and 9.11–9.18 above.
[126] For an illustration, see *Enron Europe Ltd v Revenue and Customs Commissioners* [2006] EWHC 824 (Ch).
[127] [1997] 6 Bank LR 43, 51–2 (Simon Brown LJ), 55–7 (Phillips LJ). In Australia, compare *Daewoo Australia Pty Ltd v Suncorp-Metway Ltd* (2000) 48 NSWLR 692 at [33], where the traditional view was reiterated that the foreign money obligation under a foreign exchange contract is not a money obligation. Note also the criticism of the *Camdex case* in Brindle and Cox (ed), *Law of Bank Payments* (3rd edn, 2004), 35–41.
[128] See paras 16.45–16.51 below. See also para. 16.27 above in relation to certain investment exchanges and clearing houses. In Australia, see the Payment Systems and Netting Act 1998 (Cth), s. 5, considered in paras 16.28 above and 16.52–16.67 below.
[129] See paras 9.13 and 9.17–9.18 above.

16.33   The principle in question[130] has been referred to as a rule of public policy,[131] though in Australia that characterization has been criticized on the ground that in truth it rests upon an application of generally expressed provisions in the insolvency legislation, such as the requirement that all debts should rank equally and the rules in relation to the identification of the 'property' that is to be applied in satisfaction of the insolvent's liabilities.[132] In *Perpetual Trustee Co Ltd v BNY Corporate Trustee Services Ltd*,[133] Neuberger MR equated those views, commenting that the principle is based on public policy but only to the extent that one cannot contract out of the insolvency legislation.

16.34   The principle has also been expressed in different ways in the cases.[134] It has been said, for example, that 'there cannot be a valid contract that a man's property shall remain his until his bankruptcy, and on the happening of that event shall go over to some one else, and be taken away from his creditors',[135] and that a contract cannot 'provide for a different distribution of [a person's] effects in the event of bankruptcy from that which the law provides'.[136] It is commonly called the anti-deprivation rule.[137] The essence of it is that a company's property must be administered in its liquidation for the benefit of creditors, and the principle strikes down contracts which operate upon the occurrence of the liquidation[138] to take away assets from the creditors.

16.35   Consider the position in relation to close-out netting of contracts providing for delivery of non-monetary assets. Strictly, netting does not deprive the counterparty in liquidation of its profitable contracts. The counterparty retains the benefit of those contracts albeit that they are netted off against its unprofitable contracts. But in substance the counterparty's

---

[130] For recent discussions, see *Money Markets International Stockbrokers Ltd v London Stock Exchange Ltd* [2002] 1 WLR 1150; *Perpetual Trustee Co Ltd v BNY Corporate Trustee Services Ltd* [2009] EWCA Civ 1160.

[131] See e.g. *British Eagle International Air Lines Ltd v Compagnie Nationale Air France* [1975] 1 WLR 758, 780; *Money Markets International Stockbrokers Ltd v London Stock Exchange Ltd* [2002] 1 WLR 1150 at [88] and [117].

[132] *International Air Transport Association v Ansett Australia Holdings Ltd* (2008) 234 CLR 151 at [71]–[93]. That was in the context of a contractual provision which was said to be contrary to the policy of the insolvency legislation requiring equal treatment of creditors. Nevertheless, it would be wrong to suggest that public policy, operating outside the express terms of the insolvency legislation, has played no part in the development of insolvency law. An illustration is the development of the law relating to fraudulent preferences. Preferences were first made the subject of express enactment in the Bankruptcy Act 1869, s. 92. But even before then, payments by way of fraudulent preference were held to be void as being contrary to the spirit and principle of the bankruptcy law. See *Marks v Feldman* (1870) LR 5 QB 275, 279; *Butcher v Stead* (1875) LR 7 HL 839, 846; Williams and Muir Hunter, *The Law and Practice in Bankruptcy* (19th edn, 1979), 346. The principle is said (see *Marks v Feldman* at 283) to have had its origin in the judgment of Lord Mansfield in *Alderson v Temple* (1768) 1 Black W 660, 96 ER 384. In that case, a payment made to a creditor on the eve of the debtor's bankruptcy was avoided as an act to defeat the bankruptcy law.

[133] [2009] EWCA Civ 1160 at [54]. See also Patten LJ at [172].

[134] See *Perpetual Trustee Co Ltd v BNY Corporate Trustee Services Ltd* [2009] EWCA Civ 1160 at [1], and the cases referred to at [32]–[49].

[135] *Ex p Jay, re Harrison* (1880) 14 Ch D 19, 26 *per* Cotton LJ.

[136] *Ex p Mackay* (1873) LR 8 Ch App 643, 647 *per* James LJ.

[137] *Perpetual Trustee Co Ltd v BNY Corporate Trustee Services Ltd* [2009] EWCA Civ 1160 at [1] and [113].

[138] The principle has no effect upon a contract which has effect before liquidation and which is not a sham. See *Perpetual Trustee Co Ltd v BNY Corporate Trustee Services Ltd* [2009] EWCA Civ 1160 at [70]–[72], [88], [162].

creditors are deprived of the full benefit of those assets in that, as a consequence of the change in the nature of the obligations upon the occurrence of the liquidation so that there is only an obligation to pay a net money amount, the situation cannot arise where the solvent party, on the one hand, is required by the liquidator to perform contracts unprofitable to it but profitable to the counterparty and, on the other, is confined to a dividend in relation to the counterparty's unprofitable contracts.[139] As a consequence of that change in the nature of the obligations, the solvent party in effect obtains priority in the counterparty's liquidation over other creditors. In *Perpetual Trustee Co Ltd v BNY Corporate Trustee Services Ltd*,[140] an agreement which changed the respective priorities of parties to the proceeds of collateral held by a trustee upon the insolvency of one of the parties was held not to be objectionable. But in that case the solvent party, in whose favour the priority changed, had provided the funds for the purchase of the collateral. Were it not for that circumstance, the judgment of Neuberger MR suggests that he would have regarded the change in the order of priority as falling foul of the anti-deprivation rule.[141]

The better view is that close-out netting is not objectionable.[142] But before considering the issue, three points should be noted. **16.36**

In the first place, the situation is distinguishable from a floating security which is expressed to crystallize upon liquidation.[143] Crystallization alters priority. Nevertheless, a floating security is still a present security even before crystallization.[144] Moreover, it is of the essence of a floating security that it crystallizes upon liquidation even in the absence of an express provision to that effect, given that the company then ceases to carry on business other than for the purpose of its winding up.[145] Therefore, the stipulation for crystallization upon liquidation itself does not result in preferential treatment for the chargee. **16.37**

The second point is that the termination of the obligations on its own is not a ground for objection. There is nothing wrong with a contract providing for termination upon liquidation.[146] The termination does not operate to deprive the company's creditors of the benefit **16.38**

---

[139] See para. 16.32 above.

[140] [2009] EWCA Civ 1160.

[141] [2009] EWCA Civ 1160 at [62]–[68]. Longmore LJ (at [99]) agreed with the judgment of Neuberger MR.

[142] Close out netting was assumed to be effective in an administration in *Enron Europe Ltd v Revenue and Customs Commissioners* [2006] EWHC 824 (Ch). In any event, the principle in question could only apply if as a result of the relevant event the estate available for distribution amongst the general body of creditors is lessened. Compare the stock exchange close out rules considered in *Ex p Grant, re Plumbly* (1880) 13 Ch D 667, discussed in Derham, 'Set-off and netting' [1991] JBL 536, 545–6, and *Perpetual Trustee Co Ltd v BNY Corporate Trustee Services Ltd* [2009] EWCA Civ 1160 at [41], [83] and [170].

[143] Compare Coleman, 'Netting a red herring' (1994) 9 *Journal of International Banking and Financial Law* 391, 399.

[144] *Evans v Rival Granite Quarries Ltd* [1910] 2 KB 979, 999; *Smith v Bridgend County BC* [2002] 1 AC 336 at [61] and [62].

[145] *Re Crompton & Co Ltd* [1914] 1 Ch 954, 961–5; *Wily v St George Partnership Banking Ltd* (1999) 84 FCR 423 at [52]; *Goode on Legal Problems of Credit and Security* (4th edn (ed. Gullifer), 2008), 153–4 [4.32].

[146] *Whitmore v Mason* (1861) 2 J & H 204, 212–13, 70 ER 1031, 1034–5 (termination of lease consequent upon the tenant becoming bankrupt); *Perpetual Trustee Co Ltd v BNY Corporate Trustee Services Ltd* [2009] EWCA Civ 1160 at [81] and [143]–[146] (termination of a licence).

of an asset that otherwise would have been available to them in the liquidation, but rather it defines the scope of the rights flowing from the contract.[147] Nor is there anything objectionable *per se* in a clause in a standard loan agreement which accelerates a payment obligation in the event of liquidation,[148] since the clause merely crystallizes the position between the parties without changing the nature of the obligation. If there is an objection in the case of close-out netting, it would be in the replacement of the obligations upon liquidation, some of which may not be money obligations and therefore not susceptible to a set-off under the insolvency set-off section, with a net money obligation.

16.39   The third point is that it would be misleading to analyse the situation in terms of a single transaction. For this reason *Shipton, Anderson & Co (1927) Ltd v Micks, Lambert & Co*,[149] which is commonly cited as supporting the validity of close-out netting,[150] does not in fact do so. The totality of the arrangement must be looked at. When there is only one transaction, and that transaction is closed out in the liquidation of one of the parties so as to result in an obligation on one of them to pay the net market value to the other, depending on which way the market has moved, it cannot be said that there has been any substantive change in the insolvent party's overall position. This is because there is no question of set-off within the confines of a single transaction. Were it not for the close-out provision, the position would be that the liquidator would either disclaim or affirm the contract. If the liquidator disclaimed, the contract would be terminated and the solvent party would prove for its loss. If, on the other hand, the liquidator elected to keep the contract on foot, because it was considered profitable from the insolvent party's perspective, the liquidator would have to perform it,[151] in which case set-off within the contract would not be an issue. In substance, the result is similar to that in the case of a close-out. That scenario should be distinguished from close-out netting of contracts where there are a number of such contracts between the parties.[152] In that situation, the question of set-off assumes importance. In the absence of close-out netting each contract would either be affirmed or disclaimed by the liquidator.[153] The solvent party would be confined to a dividend for its losses as a result of the disclaimer of contracts unprofitable to the insolvent defaulter, and therefore profitable to the solvent party. However, in relation to contracts which the liquidator has elected to perform, the solvent party may not be entitled to a set-off in relation to its obligations to deliver non-monetary assets under those contracts.[154] In those circumstances, close-out netting may have a substantive effect upon the position of the general body of creditors, by changing the nature of the obligations and thereby effectively letting in a set-off where otherwise none would have been available. If the close-out provisions were considered in

---

[147] The contract is 'inherently limited'. See *Money Markets International Stockbrokers Ltd v London Stock Exchange Ltd* [2002] 1 WLR 1150 at [37] and [89] (Neuberger J).

[148] *Re Mistral Finance Ltd* [2001] BCC 27 at [57]; *Lamson Store Service Co Ltd v Russell Wilkins & Sons Ltd* (1906) 4 CLR 672; *Re South Brisbane Theatres Pty Ltd* [1940] QWN 18.

[149] [1936] 2 All ER 1032. See the discussion of the case in Derham, 'Set-off and netting' [1991] JBL 536, 549–50.

[150] See e.g. *Re Opes Prime Stockbroking Ltd* (2008) 171 FCR 473 at [19].

[151] See paras 9.05 and 9.17 above.

[152] See paras 9.11–9.20 above for the position in the absence of a close out netting agreement.

[153] See paras 9.13 and 9.17–9.18 above.

[154] See para. 9.18 above.

the context of each individual contract in isolation, they would not be objectionable.[155] When, however, the relationship is considered in its entirety, so that it is apparent that closure of the contracts pursuant to the close-out provisions would have the effect of changing the distribution in a liquidation, it becomes relevant to consider whether close-out netting is open to objection in a liquidation.

A significant consideration is that the solvent party's position could be protected by alternative mechanisms, which suggests that close-out netting itself is not contrary to public policy. **16.40**

For example, it could be made a term of each contract, amounting to a condition,[156] that the counterparty must not go into liquidation.[157] The parties to a contract are entitled to stipulate that any term is of a fundamental character going to the root of the contract, although in some circumstances clear language may be required.[158] If liquidation then occurred, the solvent party would be entitled under normal common law principles to terminate its future obligations under each contract and to claim damages.[159] When a contract is terminated pursuant to an express power contained in the contract, the party exercising the power ordinarily is confined to damages for any breaches that have occurred up to the date of termination, but (in the absence of a repudiation[160]) not thereafter.[161] When termination occurs as a result of a breach of condition, however, the measure of damages relates to the loss of the whole transaction. It includes compensation for loss of the opportunity to receive performance of the other party's outstanding obligations.[162] In the case of contracts which are wholly executory, this should equate to the cost of obtaining replacement contracts in the market, which would be similar to the close-out amount payable under a netting agreement. Indeed, if each contract is separate,[163] a breach of condition could produce a better result for the solvent party than netting, because the solvent party would have a claim for damages in respect of each contract in its favour, and could terminate contracts which were unprofitable from its perspective without having to credit the counterparty in liquidation with the market value of those contracts. The counterparty as the defaulter would not be entitled to damages from the solvent party. While close out netting provisions are not usually drafted in terms of breach of a condition, the fact that the parties by their contract have agreed that a result should follow which is similar to, or **16.41**

---

[155] This seems clear from *Shipton, Anderson & Co (1927) Ltd v Micks, Lambert & Co* [1936] 2 All ER 1032.

[156] As distinguished from a warranty. A condition in this sense should also be distinguished from the condition precedent to the performance of obligations referred to in para. 16.44 below.

[157] A similar condition would apply to the solvent party.

[158] *Schuler AG v Wickman Machine Tools Sales Ltd* [1974] AC 235, 251; *Bunge Corporation v Tradax Export SA* [1981] 1 WLR 711, 715–16; *Lombard North Central Plc v Butterworth* [1987] 1 QB 527, 535–6, 546.

[159] *Wickman Machine Tool Sales Ltd v L. Schuler AG* [1972] 1 WLR 840, 851; *Lombard North Central Plc v Butterworth* [1987] 1 QB 527, 535.

[160] Liquidation without more would not constitute a repudiation of foreign exchange contracts. See para. 9.05 above, and Derham, 'Set-off and netting' [1991] JBL 463, 481–4.

[161] *Lombard North Central Plc v Butterworth* [1987] 1 QB 527, 546.

[162] *Lombard North Central Plc v Butterworth* [1987] 1 QB 527 (esp. at 535). See also *Chitty on Contracts* (30th edn, 2008) vol. 1, 1690–1 [26–141].

[163] Compare the 'one contract' approach in relation to netting, referred to below.

indeed less advantageous for the solvent party than, that which would apply in the case of a breach of condition, suggests that netting itself should not be objectionable.

16.42 There are other protections that may be built into netting agreements with the aim of bringing about a situation in which the result obtained as a result of netting is similar to that which would follow in any event in the absence of the basic netting provisions.

16.43 A master netting agreement may provide that all the obligations of the parties that arise out of the transactions the subject of the netting agreement constitute a single contract. In other words, it is not a case in which a master agreement sets out terms that apply to each transaction, each of which is regarded as a separate contract. Rather, there is only one contract for the performance of all obligations that arise pursuant to outstanding transactions between the parties. The purpose of such a provision is to prevent a liquidator being able to 'cherry pick', in other words, being able to disclaim some transactions but not others.[164] The right of disclaimer applies to a 'contract'.[165] The liquidator could not enforce one part of the contract and disclaim another part. Therefore, if all the transactions constitute a single contract, the counterparty's liquidator could not 'cherry pick' by disclaiming some of the transactions and affirming others. The single contract could be analysed in either of two ways. In the first place, it could be said that entry into a new transaction takes effect as an amendment to a prior contract which governed their earlier transactions, so that the obligations of the parties under the contract henceforth consist of their obligations pursuant to their prior outstanding transactions together with the obligations arising under the new transaction.[166] Alternatively, when a new transaction is entered into, a new contract could be formed which includes also the rights and obligations under earlier transactions, so that those rights and obligations henceforth become rights and obligations under the new contract.

16.44 The 'single contract' approach is artificial, and it has its critics. An alternative solution, which is commonly used, is a condition precedent in the netting agreement by which the obligations of each party under transactions the subject of the agreement are expressed to be subject to a condition precedent that no event of default, including liquidation of the counterparty, has occurred. If the counterparty goes into liquidation after it has performed its side of a particular transaction, the solvent party might not be able to rely on the clause as a justification for not performing its own obligation pursuant to the transaction.[167] But in relation to transactions which are wholly executory, it is difficult to see, in the absence of a waiver by the solvent party, what basis the liquidator would have for arguing that the counterparty after the liquidation still has valuable enforceable rights against the solvent

---

[164] See paras 9.13 and 9.17–9.18 above.

[165] See the Insolvency Act 1986, s. 178(3)(a), and in Australia the Corporations Act 2001 (Cth), s. 568(1)(f).

[166] This should not entail changing the accounting procedures and records of the parties, since each transaction still remains distinct, although it does not constitute a separate contract in its own right. For that reason, it does not suffer from the same drawback as netting by novation. See Derham, 'Set-off and Netting' [1991] JBL 536, 537–9.

[167] See *A-G v McMillan & Lockwood Ltd* [1991] 1 NZLR 53 (CA), and note also the discussion in *British Eagle International Air Lines Ltd v Compagnie Nationale Air France* [1975] 1 WLR 758, 778.

party. An agreement for close out netting in such a case could hardly be struck down as an attempt to evade the operation of the insolvency law.[168]

E. Regulations Giving Effect to EC Directives in Relation to Netting

Regulations have been made implementing two EC Directives in relation to netting. The first, the Financial Markets and Insolvency (Settlement Finality) Regulations 1999,[169] implemented Directive 98/26/EC of the European Parliament and of the Council on settlement finality in payment and securities settlement systems. The Regulations apply to rules of certain 'designated systems' which provide for netting and the closing out of open positions. They provide[170] that the rules are not to be regarded as invalid on the ground of inconsistency with the law relating to the distribution of the assets of a person in insolvency. The second, the Financial Collateral Arrangements (No. 2) Regulations 2003,[171] implemented Directive 2002/47/EC on financial collateral arrangements. These Regulations are not confined to designated systems and accordingly have a more general scope. They are considered below.   **16.45**

Regulation 12 of the Financial Collateral Arrangements (No. 2) Regulations 2003 applies to 'close-out netting provisions'.[172] A close-out netting provision is defined (in reg. 3) in terms of a financial collateral arrangement, or of an arrangement of which a financial collateral arrangement forms part, under which, on the occurrence of an enforcement event: **16.46**

(a) the obligations of the parties are accelerated to become immediately due and expressed as an obligation to pay the estimated current value or replacement value of the original obligations, or the obligations are terminated and replaced by an obligation to pay such an amount; or

---

[168] This condition precedent would also provide a solution to the problem posed in Australia by the Banking Act 1959 (Cth), s. 13A(3), in relation to the situation in which the counterparty is another bank. Section 13A(3) provides that, in the event that an authorized deposit-taking institution becomes unable to meet its obligations or suspends payment, its assets in Australia are to be available to meet its deposit liabilities in Australia in priority to other liabilities (other then certain liabilities to APRA). This should not affect netting where the condition precedent applies, since in such a case foreign exchange contracts which are still wholly executory would not be valuable assets. In any event, see now the Payment Systems and Netting Act 1998 (Cth), discussed below.

[169] S.I. 1999 No. 2979.

[170] Regulation 14.

[171] S.I. 2003 No. 3226.

[172] For a discussion of some issues that have arisen in relation to reg. 12, see Fawcett, 'The financial collateral directive: an examination of some practical problems following its implementation in the UK' [2005] *Journal of International Banking Law and Regulation* 295. Mr Fawcett considered (at 296) whether reg. 12 requires mutuality (see ch. 11 above), an issue that he said could arise where one of the parties to the arrangement was acting as agent (see paras 13.75–13.117 above) or trustee (see paras 11.13–11.17 above) for a third party or in relation to multilateral netting. He referred to recital 15 of the EC Directive, which stated that the Directive was 'without prejudice' to any restrictions or requirements under national law on set-off, 'for example relating to their reciprocity'. Mutuality relates to reciprocity, and accordingly Mr Fawcett suggested that that it was unlikely that the regulations had altered the requirement for mutuality. That conclusion is supported by the statement of the focus of the Directive in recital 3 as being *bilateral* financial collateral arrangements, by the reference to bilateral close-out netting in recitals 5 and 14, and by the references in the regulations to 'the other party' (singular) in (b) of the definition of 'close-out netting provision' and in reg. 12(2).

   (b) an account is taken of what is due from each party to the other in respect of those obligations and a net sum equal to the balance of the account is payable by the party from whom the larger amount is due to the other.

A 'financial collateral arrangement' can be either a 'title transfer financial collateral arrangement' or a 'security financial collateral arrangement'.[173] Under the former,[174] a collateral-provider transfers legal and beneficial ownership in financial collateral[175] to the collateral-taker on terms that, when the relevant financial obligations secured or covered by the arrangement are discharged, the collateral-taker must transfer legal and beneficial ownership of equivalent financial collateral to the collateral-provider. In the case of the latter,[176] a collateral-provider creates or there arises a security interest in financial collateral to secure the relevant financial obligations owed to the collateral-taker, and the financial collateral is delivered, held or otherwise designated so as to be in the possession or under the control of the collateral-taker or a person acting on its behalf.

16.47   The relevant financial obligations referred to may consist of or include present or future, actual or contingent or prospective obligations, obligations owed to the collateral-taker by a person other than the collateral-provider or obligations of a specified class or kind.[177]

16.48   Pursuant to reg. 12(1), a close-out netting provision is to take effect in accordance with its terms[178] notwithstanding that one of the parties is subject to winding up proceedings[179] or reorganisation measures, which is defined[180] as including administration and a company voluntary arrangement within the meaning of the Insolvency Act. This is subject, however, to para. (2) of the regulation. In effect, para. (2) qualifies the effectiveness of netting in situations where there was notice of insolvency.[181] It provides that para. (1) does not apply[182] if at the time that a party to a financial collateral arrangement entered into the arrangement, or at the time that the relevant financial obligations came into existence, that party:

   (a) was or should have been aware that winding up proceedings or reorganisation measures had commenced in relation to the other party;[183]
   (b) had notice that a meeting of creditors of the other party had been summoned under the Insolvency Act 1986, s. 98 or that a petition for the winding up of the other party was pending;

---

[173] See the definition of 'financial collateral arrangement' in reg. 3.

[174] See the definition of 'title transfer financial collateral arrangement'.

[175] Defined as cash and financial instruments, which in turn is defined in terms of shares, bonds and other securities.

[176] See the definition of 'security financial collateral arrangement'.

[177] See the definition of 'relevant financial obligations' in reg. 3.

[178] Additional protection is provided by reg. 10(1), which provides that s. 127 of the Insolvency Act 1986 (avoidance of property dispositions) shall not apply to prevent a close-out netting provision taking effect in accordance with its terms.

[179] Defined in reg. 3 as a winding up by the court or a voluntary winding up.

[180] Regulation 3.

[181] Similar to the concept that applies in relation to the set-off section in the insolvency legislation. See paras 6.66–6.99 above.

[182] In other words, the guarantee of validity under para. (1) does not apply. This does not have the consequence that the netting provision is necessarily invalid. See Turing, 'New growth in the financial collateral garden' (2005) 1 *Journal of International Banking and Financial Law* 4, 5.

[183] See reg. 12(3) as to the commencement of winding-up proceedings and reorganization measures.

(c) had notice that an application for an administration order was pending or that notice of an intention to appoint an administrator had been given by any person; or

(d) had notice that an application for an administration order was pending or that notice of an intention to appoint an administrator had been given by any person and liquidation of the other party was immediately preceded by an administration of that party.

The restriction in para. (2), in terms that para. (1) does not apply if the party had the requisite notice at the time that the relevant financial obligations came into existence, presumably was intended to preclude the application of para. (1) only in relation to the relevant financial obligations which came into existence after notice.

Regulation 12(4) provides that rr. 2.85(4)(a) and (c) and 4.90(3)(b) of the Insolvency Rules 1986 (mutual credit and set-off) shall not apply to a close-out netting provision unless reg. 12(2)(a) applies. The references appear to be to the form of rule 2.85 as set out in Sch. 1, Part 3 of the Insolvency (Amendment) Rules 2003 (S.I. 2003 No. 1730), and to the form of r. 4.90(3) as set out in Sch. 1, Part 4 of those rules.[184] In substance, they correspond with rr. 2.85(2)(a) and (d) and 4.90(2)(c) of the current rules,[185] which were made in 2005. Regulation 12(4) assumes that, in its absence, those rules would have applied. However, reg. 12(1) provides that a close-out netting provision takes effect in accordance with its terms notwithstanding a liquidation or an administration, subject only to reg. 12(2). On its face, that leaves no room for the application of rr. 2.85(4)(a) and (c) and 4.90(3)(b). The purpose of reg. 12(4) is unclear.

16.49

Regulation 14 applies in the situation in which the collateral-provider or the collateral-taker is in liquidation or administration and a close-out netting provision provides for (or permits) either the debt owed by the party in liquidation or administration to be assessed or paid in a currency other than sterling, or the debt to be converted into sterling at a rate other than the official exchange rate prevailing on the date when that party went into liquidation or administration. In those situations, reg. 14 disapplies r. 4.91 (liquidation) or, as the case may be, r. 2.86 (administration) of the Insolvency Rules 1986 (debt in foreign currency) unless the arrangement provides for an unreasonable exchange rate or the collateral-taker uses the mechanism provided under the arrangement to impose an unreasonable exchange rate, in which case the appropriate rule will apply.

16.50

The scope of reg. 12 is confined. In the first place, the concept of 'close-out netting provision' applies in the case of a financial collateral arrangement or an arrangement of which a financial collateral arrangement forms part. It would not extend to ordinary contracts for the sale and purchase of foreign currencies where a financial collateral arrangement does not form part of the arrangement. Secondly, financial collateral arrangement is defined[186]

16.51

---

[184] See paras 6.06 (liquidation) and 6.10 (administration) above.

[185] See paras 6.74 (liquidation) and 6.81 (administration) above. Rule 2.85(2)(a) and (d) exclude from set-off in administration a debt arising out of an obligation incurred after the company entered administration and a debt arising out of an obligation incurred during a winding up which immediately preceded the administration. Rule 4.90(2)(c) excludes from set-off in a liquidation a debt arising out of an obligation incurred during an administration which immediately preceded the liquidation.

[186] Through the definitions of 'title transfer financial collateral arrangement' and 'security financial collateral arrangement'.

in terms of an arrangement in which both parties are 'non-natural persons'. 'Non-natural person' in turn is defined as a corporate body, unincorporated firm, partnership or body with legal personality except an individual. A close out netting agreement with an individual therefore is not protected by reg. 12.

F. Netting in Australia

(1) Payment Systems and Netting Act 1998 (Cth)

16.52 Legislation giving effect to the principle of close-out netting has also been enacted in Australia.[187]

16.53 Part 4 of the Payment Systems and Netting Act 1998 (Cth), which deals with close-out netting, resulted from a report prepared by a sub-committee of the Companies and Securities Advisory Committee.[188] The sub-committee included in its report a form of draft legislation which confined close-out netting to certain types of financial contracts, principally consisting of products such as swaps, foreign exchange contracts, and various forms of options and derivatives. The Act is not so confined, however. It allows netting in respect of a 'close-out netting contract', which is defined broadly in s. 5. Subject to a number of exclusions, a close-out netting contract essentially is a contract under which, upon the happening of a particular event, (a) particular obligations of the parties terminate or may be terminated,[189] (b) termination values of the obligations are calculated or may be calculated,[190] and (c) the termination values are netted or may be netted so that only a net cash amount is payable. In addition, a contract may be declared by regulation to be a close-out netting contract.

16.54 Close-out netting contracts need not relate to a particular subject, but may encompass obligations of any nature.[191] Thus, a simple contract debt, for example in relation to a bank account, potentially could be the subject of a close-out netting contract. The obligations, it would seem, need not be prospective, but could include obligations already incurred at the date of the close-out netting contract. Further, the legislation is not in its terms confined to bilateral netting, but would allow netting in relation to three or more parties.[192]

---

[187] In New Zealand, see the Companies Act 1993, ss. 310A–310O and the Insolvency Act 2006, ss. 255–263.

[188] Netting Sub-Committee of the Companies and Securities Advisory Committee, *Netting in Financial Markets Transactions – Final Report* (June 1997).

[189] This does not require an express statement that obligations are terminated. Termination for the purpose of the definition may include a situation in which obligations are expressed to come to an end by being accelerated and liquidated, in the sense that they are converted into money debts. See *Re Opes Prime Stockbroking Ltd* (2008) 171 FCR 473 at [40]–[41].

[190] For the valuation of claims for the purpose of voting at a meeting of creditors pursuant to the Corporations Regulations, reg. 5.6.23(2) before close out has occurred, see *Re Opes Prime Stockbroking Ltd* (2008) 171 FCR 473 at [43] and [63] *et seq.*

[191] The legislation has been held to apply to close out under a securities lending agreement. See *Re Opes Prime Stockbroking Ltd* (2008) 171 FCR 473.

[192] See para. 16.66 below.

Subject to a close-out netting contract having a sufficient nexus with Australia,[193] it is **16.55** provided in s. 14(1)(c) that 'obligations may be terminated, termination values may be calculated and a net amount become payable in accordance with the contract.' Further, s. 14(1)(d) stipulates that a disposal of rights by a counterparty, or the creation of a security interest over those rights, where it occurs in contravention of a prohibition in the close-out netting contract, will not defeat the netting. The efficacy of netting is further reinforced by s. 14(1)(e), which stipulates that, 'for the purposes of any law', the assets of a party to a close-out netting contract are taken to include any net obligation owed to the party under the contract, and are taken not to include obligations terminated under the contract. This would apply, for example, where a third party seeks to execute a judgment obtained against a party to a close-out netting contract by attaching a debt owing to that party which is subject to the contract. Termination and netting under the contract would defeat the execution creditor.

Section 14(2) governs the situation in which a counterparty goes into external administra- **16.56** tion, which is defined in s. 5 as including events such as company liquidation, receivership, administration, bankruptcy and the execution of a personal insolvency agreement under Part X of the Bankruptcy Act 1966 (Cth). In any of those circumstances, s. 14(2)(c), like s. 14(1)(c), provides that obligations may be terminated, termination values may be calculated and a net amount become payable in accordance with the contract. Obligations that have been terminated are to be disregarded in the external administration, and the net obligation is to be provable in the external administration or is to be payable to the external administrator, as the case may be. Section 14(2)(g) goes on to provide that the termination of obligations, the netting of obligations and any payment made to discharge a net obligation are not to be void or voidable in the external administration. This negates the effect of the decision in the *British Eagle* case.[194]

Netting in the event of liquidation (or other external administration) is subject to two **16.57** limitations. In the first place, s. 14(3) provides that a person may not rely on a close-out netting contract in relation to a right or obligation: 'if the person acquired the right or obligation from another person with notice that that other person was at that time unable to pay their debts as and when they became due and payable.' Close-out netting is also restricted by s. 14(5). This applies in relation to an obligation owed by a party to a close-out netting contract to another person, in circumstances where the first party goes into external administration and the obligation is, or has been, terminated under the contract. If the other person did not act in good faith in entering into the transaction that created the terminated obligation, or the other person had reasonable grounds to suspect insolvency

---

[193] This is satisfied if Australian law governs the close-out netting contract and the contract is entered into in circumstances that are within Commonwealth constitutional reach. See s. 14(1). Commonwealth constitutional reach is defined in s. 5 in terms of various matters which are recognized heads of Commonwealth power under the Australian Constitution. In addition, if a person who is a party to a close-out netting contract goes into 'external administration' (which is defined in s. 5 in terms that would include matters such as company liquidation, administration, receivership and bankruptcy), there is a sufficient nexus for the Act if Australian law governs the external administration. See s. 14(2).

[194] *British Eagle International Air Lines Ltd v Compagnie Nationale Air France* [1975] 1 WLR 758. See para. 16.22 above.

when the transaction that created the terminated obligation was entered into, or the other person neither provided valuable consideration nor changed its position in reliance on the transaction, s. 14 will not apply to the obligation. It cannot be netted in the liquidation (or other form of external administration), and similarly the protection provided by s. 14 will not apply where netting occurred prior to the external administration.[195]

16.58   A number of points may be made in relation to the legislation.

16.59   Section 14(1)(d), dealing with assignments and security interests, and s. 14(1)(e), which provides that the assets of a party to a close-out netting contract are taken, for the purposes of any law, to include the net obligation owed to the party under the contract, have not been specifically extended to s. 14(2) in relation to external administrations. This may be because s. 14(1) is intended to apply in all cases, but if that is the explanation it is unclear what purpose s. 14(2)(c) serves, given s. 14(1)(c). Alternatively, s. 14(1)(d) may not have been extended to s. 14(2) because it was thought that the principles set out in s. 14(2) would take effect in accordance with their terms, and on that basis they would override any assignment or other interest asserted by a third party. In its application to s. 14(1), however, para. (d) only subordinates the interest of the assignee or the encumbrancee where the assignment or the encumbrance is entered into in contravention of a prohibition in the close-out netting contract. This would not be the case, for example, if the assignment or the encumbrance occurred before the close-out netting contract. On the other hand, if in the case of s. 14(2) it is sought to rely on the general language of the subsection in order to defeat the interest of an assignee or the holder of an encumbrance, the qualification in s. 14(1)(d) would not appear to apply.

16.60   Section 14(2) gives supremacy to a close-out netting contract in the event of an external administration. The obligations may be terminated, termination values may be calculated and a net amount become payable in accordance with the contract, and obligations that have been terminated under the contract are to be disregarded in the external administration. The definition of external administration includes receivership.[196] On its face, s. 14(2) would seem to apply even where the security pursuant to which the receiver was appointed pre-dated the netting agreement. For example, a debt to the knowledge of the debtor may be charged in favour of a third party, and subsequently the chargor/creditor and the debtor may enter into a close-out netting contract in respect of their obligations, including the charged debt. In that circumstance, it seems unjust that, if the chargee later were to appoint a receiver and the receiver attempted to collect the debt, the close-out netting contract

---

[195] This appears from s. 14(5)(b), which refers to an obligation which 'has been' terminated under the contract. Apart from subsection (5), netting prior to an external administration is protected by s. 14(2) in a subsequent liquidation (or other external administration). Thus, s. 14(2) is expressed to apply (in (a)) where a party is, or 'has been', a party to a close-out netting contract, while, according to (d), obligations that are 'or have been' terminated under the contract are to be disregarded in the external administration (subject, however, to sub-s. (5)).

[196] The definition of 'external administration' in s. 5 includes (in (a)) the case of a body corporate that is an externally administered body corporate within the meaning of the Corporations Act 2001 (Cth), and in s. 9 of the Corporations Act 'externally-administered body corporate' is defined as including a body corporate in respect of property of which a receiver, or a receiver and manager, has been appointed (whether or not by a court).

should prevail. Nevertheless, this would seem to be the effect of s. 14(2). At general law the earlier charge, of which the debtor was aware, would have priority over a set-off agreement in this situation,[197] and it is difficult to see why close-out under the Payment Systems and Netting Act should produce a different result.

Section 14(3) also presents difficulties. It applies in an external administration. It provides **16.61** that a person may not rely on the application of s. 14(2) to a right or obligation if the person 'acquired the right or obligation' from 'another person' with notice that that other person at the time was unable to pay their debts as and when they became due and payable. The expression 'another person' also appears in s. 14(5), and its use in that context suggests that it includes a counterparty to a close-out netting contract. Subsection (3) seems intended to introduce into the netting legislation a concept similar to the qualification to the insolvency set-off section.[198] The Corporations Act 2001 (Cth), s. 553C(2) provides, as a qualification to the right of set-off conferred by s. 553C(1) in the case of company liquidation, that a person dealing with a company is not entitled to a set-off in the company's liquidation if at the time of giving or receiving credit from the company the person had notice of the fact that the company was insolvent. In bankruptcy, the corresponding provision[199] is expressed in terms of notice of an available act of bankruptcy. There is, however, an important distinction between, on the one hand, s. 14(3), and on the other the qualifications to the set-off in bankruptcy and company liquidation. The latter are drafted in terms of notice of insolvency, or of notice of an available act of bankruptcy, at the time of giving or receiving credit. Those provisions would apply, for example, to the case of a deposit made by an insolvent customer to the credit of an account with a bank, in circumstances where the customer is separately indebted to the bank. The deposit to the credit of the account would result in a debt owing by the bank to the customer, and would constitute the giving of credit by the customer to the bank. Therefore, if the bank had notice of the customer's insolvency at the time of the deposit, it could not employ the debt in a set-off in the customer's subsequent liquidation. Section 14(3), on the other hand, is not well expressed in that regard. It is drafted in terms of acquiring a right or an obligation from another person, as opposed to giving or receiving credit. When a customer makes a deposit with a bank, the bank receives credit from the customer, but it is a misnomer to say that the bank acquires an obligation from the customer. It certainly acquires the funds the subject of the deposit, and moreover it is correct to say that it *incurs* an obligation to the customer as a result of accepting the deposit. But the obligation itself is not acquired from the customer. It is simply a consequence of the deposit.

Furthermore, s. 14(3) on its face would not preclude netting in circumstances where one **16.62** party with notice of the other's insolvency buys up at a discount debts owing by the other to third parties. Consider that two companies, A and B, have entered into a close-out netting contract which applies to their respective obligations to each other, and B to the knowledge of A is insolvent. In addition, B is indebted to various third parties. In the hands

---

[197] See para. 17.59 below.
[198] See paras 6.66–6.99 above.
[199] Bankruptcy Act 1966 (Cth), s. 86(2).

of the third parties the debts would be of diminished value, given B's insolvency. Therefore, A may buy them from the third parties at a discount, on the assumption that A could obtain their full value in B's liquidation by netting them off against A's own indebtedness to B. Under the insolvency set-off section, the qualification to the section would preclude a set-off in that circumstance. When A purchased the debts, B would have become indebted to A, and A correspondingly would have given credit at that time to B. Because the giving of credit occurred at a time when A had notice of B's insolvency, s. 553C(2) would deny a set-off in B's liquidation in respect of the debts.[200] The insolvency, of which there must be notice in order to preclude a set-off, is that of the other party to the set-off, in the example, B. Section 14(3), on the other hand, is drafted in terms of notice of the insolvency of the person from whom the right or obligation was acquired. In the example, A has acquired the rights against B from the third parties, and so s. 14(3) *prima facie* directs attention to notice of the insolvency of the third parties, rather than of B. If s. 14(3) is intended to preclude netting in the liquidation of a counterparty to a close-out netting contract in respect of an obligation of the counterparty which was purchased at a discount from a third party with notice of insolvency, it has referred to the wrong party. The notice should relate to the insolvency of the counterparty. The insolvency of the third party from whom the obligation was acquired should not be of any consequence. Alternatively, if s. 14(3) is not intended to cover that situation, it should.

16.63   According to s. 14(4), sub-ss. (1) and (2) of that section, which give effect to close-out netting contracts both before and during external administration, are to have effect despite any other law, including the 'specified provisions'.[201] That expression is defined in s. 5 in terms of various matters, including Div. 2 of Part 5.7B of the Corporations Act 2001 (Cth) and ss. 120, 121 and 122 of the Bankruptcy Act 1966 (Cth). Division 2 of Part 5.7B deals with such matters as unfair preferences and uncommercial transactions,[202] and ss. 120, 121 and 122 of the Bankruptcy Act deal with similar matters (undervalued transactions, transfers to defeat creditors and preferences) in the context of bankruptcy. Those provisions do not therefore impugn netting under the Payment Systems and Netting Act.

16.64   On the other hand, s. 14(5) may apply to exclude netting.[203] The exclusion is limited, however. It only precludes netting in relation to an obligation owed *by* the party in external administration. It does not extend to an obligation owed *to* that party. Thus, for example, it would not preclude netting in relation to a deposit made by an insolvent customer with a bank in circumstances where the bank was aware of the insolvency, and the deposit was made in order to advance the bank's position in a subsequent liquidation of the customer

---

[200] See para. 6.99 above. If B is an individual, and has become bankrupt, a set-off would be denied in the bankruptcy if at the time of the purchase A had notice of an available act of bankruptcy committed by B. See the Bankruptcy Act 1966 (Cth), s. 86(2).

[201] If there is a conflict between s. 14 of the Payment Systems and Netting Act and the Corporations Act 2001 (Cth), s. 554, which relates to the computation of the amount of a debt or claim for the purpose of proof in a liquidation, s. 14 should prevail. See *Re Opes Prime Stockbroking Ltd* (2008) 171 FCR 473 at [74]–[75] (though Finkelstein J concluded that there was no conflict in that case). As to whether there may be a conflict between s. 14 and the provisions of the Corporations Act relating to deeds of company arrangement, see at [76]–[78].

[202] Corporations Act 2001 (Cth), ss. 588FA and 588FB.

[203] See para. 16.57 above.

by enabling the bank to set off the deposit against a separate debt owed to the bank by the customer (or indeed by another insolvent party to the close-out netting contract[204]). The deposit gives rise to an obligation owed to, as opposed to an obligation owed by, the customer, and *prima facie* s. 14(5) would not be relevant. Section 14(3), on the other hand, may apply. Subsection (3), it will be recalled, precludes a person from relying on the protection provided by sub-s. (2) where it acquired a right or obligation from another person with notice that that other person was unable to pay their debts as and when they became due and payable. The point is made above, however, that s. 14(3) is not well expressed.[205] When a deposit is made with a bank, the bank incurs an obligation to the customer, but it seems a misnomer to say that an obligation has been acquired from the customer.

Close-out netting, where a set-off would not otherwise have been available

A close-out netting contract could provide a means of bringing about a set-off in the **16.65** liquidation of a company against an obligation that otherwise is not susceptible to a set-off. For example, a liability for unpaid share capital may not be the subject of a set-off in the company's liquidation against a separate debt owing by the shareholder to the company.[206] On the contrary, the share capital must be paid in full before the shareholder is entitled to a dividend in the liquidation.[207] Further, an agreement for a set-off between the company and the shareholder would not be effective to avoid the rule if the set-off has not been effected pursuant to the agreement before the liquidation.[208] This has been explained on a number of grounds,[209] including that the insolvency legislation contemplates that the proceeds of a call for payment of unpaid share capital are to be used with the other assets of the company in the *pari passu* payment of the company's debts, and it would be contrary to that principle to allow a set-off against the call.[210] Similarly, a liability for misfeasance cannot be the subject of a set-off in a liquidation.[211] However, a close-out netting contract could provide a means of circumventing those principles. This assumes that there is a valid netting contract. Depending on the circumstances, the entry into the netting contract could constitute a breach of duty by the directors to the company, so as to enable the company to avoid the contract.

Multilateral netting

The Act does not confine close-out netting to bilateral arrangements, but in its terms would **16.66** extend also to multilateral close-out netting, in other words where there are three or more

---

[204] See para. 16.66 below in relation to multilateral netting.
[205] See paras 16.61–16.62 above.
[206] See paras 8.64–8.79 above.
[207] *Re Overend, Gurney, and Co (Grissell's Case)* (1866) LR 1 Ch App 528, 536; *Re China Steamship Co, ex p MacKenzie* (1869) LR 7 Eq 240, 244; *Ramsay v Jacobs* (1987) 12 ACLR 595, 597. See para. 8.64 above.
[208] *Re Law Car and General Insurance Corporation* [1912] 1 Ch 405; *Harding and Co Ltd v Hamilton* [1929] NZLR 338. See para. 8.64 above.
[209] See paras 8.65–8.66 above.
[210] *Re Overend, Gurney, and Co (Grissell's Case)* (1866) LR 1 Ch App 528, 535–6; *Re Paraguassu Steam Tramroad Co (Black & Co's Case)* (1872) LR 8 Ch App 254, 262, 265; *Re Auriferous Properties Ltd* [1898] 1 Ch 691, 696.
[211] See paras 8.81–8.87 above.

parties to the contract.[212] For example, if A is indebted to B, but A has a claim against C, B and C being related, and A becomes insolvent, a lack of mutuality would prevent a set-off in A's liquidation,[213] even if there were an express agreement for a set-off between the parties.[214] However, the parties could now achieve that result by the use of a close-out netting agreement in accordance with the Act.

16.67 In that situation A's creditors would obtain some benefit from the agreement, in that netting would result in the reduction or discharge of a provable debt in A's liquidation in the form of A's debt to B. Consider, however, that B is the party in liquidation. Netting in that circumstance would result in B's creditors losing the benefit of an asset otherwise available in the liquidation (the claim against A), without their obtaining any compensating benefit. Furthermore, the netting agreement would not be registrable, so that persons dealing with B may not be aware that an asset appearing in its books may not be available to satisfy B's debts in the event of a liquidation. Multilateral netting can also occur under Part 3 of the Act, dealing with payment systems,[215] as well as under Part 5, relating to the rules of financial markets and clearing and settlement facilities,[216] but the scope of those Parts is confined. Part 3 only applies to an 'approved netting arrangement', being an arrangement approved by the Reserve Bank, and in granting approval the Reserve Bank must be satisfied that systemic disruption to the financial system otherwise could result if a participant went into external administration.[217] Similarly, for Part 5, the arrangement must be approved by the Minister or declared by regulation to be within the Act.[218] However, no such restrictions apply in the case of close-out netting contracts, which are purely private arrangements between the parties to them. On the other hand, Parts 3 and 5 do not contain restrictions similar to those in ss. 14(3) and (5) (above) in relation to external administration, so that s. 14 to that extent is more confined. Moreover, while in the above example B's creditors are deprived of the benefit of B's asset in the liquidation, that would have been the case in any event if B had given a guarantee to A in respect of C's debt. B's claim against A on the debt, and B's liability to A on the guarantee, would have been mutual and could have been set off in B's liquidation without recourse to the Payment Systems and Netting Act.[219] The Act achieves the same result, but without requiring the use of a guarantee for the purpose of bringing about mutuality.

---

[212] The definition of close-out netting contract in s. 5 excludes from its scope an 'approved netting arrangement'. That term is defined in terms of a netting arrangement approved under s. 12, which applies to multilateral netting arrangements. See s. 11. But in order to be an approved netting arrangement, the arrangement must provide for netting to occur at least once on each business day. See s. 12(1)(b). That is not ordinarily the case in close-out netting. Therefore, the exclusion of an approved netting arrangement from the definition of close-out netting contract would not preclude a multilateral contract from coming within the definition in circumstances where netting is not to occur at least once on each business day.

[213] See generally ch. 11 above. For an analogous case, see *Re Bank of Credit and Commerce International SA (No. 8)* [1998] AC 214.

[214] *Re Bank of Credit and Commerce International SA (No. 8)* [1996] Ch 245, 257 (CA).

[215] See, in particular, the Payment Systems and Netting Act 1998, s. 12.

[216] See the definitions of 'market netting contract' and 'netting market' in s. 5, referring to the definitions of 'licensed market' and 'licensed CS facility' in the Corporations Act 2001 (Cth), s. 761A.

[217] Payment Systems and Netting Act 1998, s. 12(1)(a).

[218] See the definition of 'netting market' in the Payment Systems and Netting Act 1998, s. 5.

[219] See paras 8.10–8.34 above.

G. An Administrator's Indemnity and Lien in Australia

In Australia, an administrator appointed to a company pursuant to Part 5.3A of the **16.68** Corporations Act 2001 (Cth) is personally liable for certain debts incurred in the performance or exercise of his or her functions or powers.[220] On the other hand, the administrator is entitled to be indemnified out of the company's property for debts for which the administrator is liable and also for remuneration.[221] The right of indemnity is expressed to have priority over the company's unsecured debts,[222] and is secured by a lien over the company's property.[223] If the property in question consists of a debt owing to the company, and the debtor has a contractual right to set off the debt against a separate debt owing by the company to the debtor, the question may arise whether the administrator's lien on the company's property has priority over the contractual right of set-off.

In *Cinema Plus Ltd v Australia and New Zealand Banking Group Ltd*,[224] a company had **16.69** a current account with a bank with a substantial credit balance when administrators were appointed to it, and it was also indebted to the bank on a terminated lease facility. The lease documentation entitled the bank to set off the debt against the credit balance, but before it purported to do so the administrators incurred debts in the course of the administration for which they were personally liable. The account represented property of the company in the form of a debt owing to it, but if the bank could then set off the account against the company's liability on the terminated facility the account would have disappeared, and the administrators would not have been able to look to it in order to indemnify themselves. The administrators had a lien on the company's property to secure their right of indemnity, and a person taking an assignment of or a security over a debt ordinarily takes subject to a prior contractual right of set-off available to the debtor.[225] However, the New South Wales Court of Appeal[226] held that the administrator's lien had priority over the contractual right of set-off, and was not disturbed by it. Spigelman CJ[227] justified that conclusion by reference to the object of Part 5.3A of the Corporations Act,[228] as set out in s. 435A. The stated object is to provide for the business, property and affairs of an insolvent company to be administered in a way that maximises the chances of the company continuing in existence or, if that is not possible, that results in a better return for the company's creditors and members than would result from an immediate winding up of the company. The Chief Justice said that it would best serve the achievement of that object if the reference to 'the company's property' in s. 443D, which confers the right of indemnity, were understood as

---

[220] Corporations Act 2001 (Cth), s. 443A.
[221] Corporations Act 2001 (Cth), s. 443D.
[222] Corporations Act 2001 (Cth), s. 443E.
[223] Corporations Act 2001 (Cth), s. 443F.
[224] (2000) 49 NSWLR 513.
[225] See paras 17.51–17.59 below.
[226] Spigelman CJ, Sheller and Giles JJA.
[227] (2000) 49 NSWLR 513 at [57]–[69]. Sheller and Giles JJA (at [124] and [141]) agreed with Spigelman CJ on this point.
[228] The legislation at the time was the Corporations Law, which subsequently was replaced by the Corporations Act 2001 (Cth), although the relevant provisions are the same.

referring to the company's property as it existed at the time when the debts were incurred and the right to remuneration accrued. He suggested that persons would be reluctant to accept appointment as administrators if they could not determine in advance whether the statutory indemnity would cover their exposure. If the value of the indemnity could be reduced by subsequent conduct of creditors which retrospectively exposed an administrator to liability or loss of remuneration, the statutory scheme would not operate effectively.

16.70   The Court of Appeal rejected an argument that the set-off agreement in issue created a charge.[229] If it had operated as a charge, the bank would have been precluded from enforcing it during the administration without the administrators' consent or the leave of the court.[230] Since the agreement was not a charge the bank was an unsecured creditor, and a result in its favour would have run counter to the stipulation in the Corporations Act that an administrator's right of indemnity has priority over all the company's unsecured debts.[231] The decision would therefore appear to be correct.

16.71   On the other hand, the Court of Appeal emphasized that the bank's contractual right of set-off was only impaired to the extent that, at the date of the set-off, the account was subject to the lien. Apart from that, the bank's contractual right was not affected by the administration.[232] This had the consequence that the administrator's priority was limited to remuneration and debts incurred between the date of the appointment and the date of set-off. An administrator's lien attaches to the company's property when the right of indemnity arises, and after the company's account in credit has been consolidated with a debt owing by the company there is no longer any property existing to which a lien can attach for the purpose of *subsequently* incurred debts and *subsequent* remuneration.

H. Partnerships

16.72   One of a number of partners indebted in his or her personal capacity to a creditor, who in turn is indebted to the partnership, may authorize the creditor to set off the partner's separate debt against the debt due to the partnership. The agreement for a set-off may provide a defence to an action at law brought by the partnership for the recovery of the debt owing to the partnership if the creditor had no knowledge of the interest of the other partners in his or her indebtedness.[233]

---

[229] (2000) 49 NSWLR 513 at [47] (Spigelman CJ), [116] (Sheller JA) and [145] (Giles JA).
[230] Corporations Act 2001 (Cth), s. 440B.
[231] Corporations Act 2001 (Cth), s. 443E(1).
[232] (2000) 49 NSWLR 513 at [69] (Spigelman CJ), [124]–[128] (Sheller JA).
[233] *Gordon v Ellis* (1844) 7 Man & G 607, 135 ER 244; *Piercy v Fynney* (1871) LR 12 Eq 69. See also *Harper v Marten* (1895) 11 TLR 368 (see para. 12.18 above), and para. 12.02 above.

I. Taking a Charge Over One's own Debt

(1) The conceptual impossibility argument

Is it possible for a debtor to take a charge or other security over its own indebtedness?[234] **16.73**
Until the House of Lords opined on the issue in *Re Bank of Credit and Commerce Inter-national SA (No. 8)*,[235] that deceptively simple question gave rise to much debate. Typically
the issue may arise when a bank provides financial accommodation to a customer, for
example by way of a bank guarantee or a letter of credit facility, and as security for the customer's obligation to indemnify the bank in the event that the bank has to pay under the
guarantee or the letter of credit the customer deposits cash with the bank. The deposit gives
rise to a debt owing by the bank to the customer, which the customer purports to charge or
mortgage in favour of the bank. The question is whether a charge (or mortgage) in fact has
been created. The effectiveness of the security has been recognized in Canada,[236] but in
England[237] and in Australia[238] there developed a body of opinion of considerable standing
to the effect that a charge-back is conceptually impossible. According to this view, a 'charge-
back' is not without legal effect. It operates as a contractual right of set-off which, not being
a charge, would not require registration. But it is not regarded as conferring a proprietary
interest in the debt, in the form of a charge properly so-called.

If a charge-back were conceptually impossible, and the customer (in the example **16.74**
above) went into liquidation, the bank's rights would rest on the insolvency set-off section
as opposed to the security. In some circumstances, those rights could produce

---

[234] In some jurisdictions legislation has been enacted to specifically recognize the validity of a charge in
this situation. In Bermuda, see the Charge and Security (Special Provisions) Act 1990; in Singapore, s. 13 of
the Civil Law Act (c 43); and in Hong Kong, the Law Amendment and Reform (Consolidation) Ordinance,
s. 15A.

[235] [1998] AC 214.

[236] *Clarkson v Smith & Goldberg* [1926] 1 DLR 509 (Ontario Supreme Court, Appellate Division). Wood,
English and International Set-off (1989), 200 also refers to *Re Century Steel & Boiler Ltd* (1981) 94 APR 490,
36 NBR (2d) 490 as an example of the recognition of a charge-back. It is not clear, however, whether the New
Brunswick Court of Appeal in that case regarded the landlord as a trustee of the security deposit, in which
case the charge would have been over the proceeds of the deposit, including any bank account into which the
proceeds could be traced, or whether the landlord was entitled to mix the proceeds with its own funds and
therefore was simply a debtor, in which case the question would have involved a charge-back.

[237] The conceptual impossibility argument found favour with Millett J (as he then was) in *Re Charge Card
Services Ltd* [1987] 1 Ch 150, and subsequently with the Court of Appeal (which included Millett LJ) in
Re BCCI (No. 8) [1996] Ch 245. Professor Goode has been a distinguished supporter of this view. See *Goode
on Legal Problems of Credit and Security* (4th edn (ed. Gullifer), 2008), 102–3, and also 'Charges over book
debts: a missed opportunity' (1994) 110 LQR 592, 606.

[238] *Broad v Commissioner of Stamp Duties* [1980] 2 NSWLR 40; *Griffiths v Commonwealth Bank of
Australia* (1994) 123 ALR 111, 120; *First For Finance Pty Ltd v Westpac Banking Corporation* (Vic SC, Hansen
J, 7 May 1998, BC9801760 (esp. at 23)); *Wily v Rothschild Australia Ltd* (1999) 47 NSWLR 555. See also
Estate Planning Associates (Australia) Pty Ltd v Commissioner of Stamp Duties (1985) 2 NSWLR 495, in which
it was held that *Broad's* case applied in the case of a policy of insurance issued by an insurance company
which was deposited back with the company by way of security. In *Jackson v Esanda Finance Corporation Ltd*
(1992) 59 SASR 416 the principle was applied in the context of a purported charge over a debenture stock
certificate. Compare *Cinema Plus Ltd v Australia and New Zealand Banking Group Ltd* (2000) 49 NSWLR
513 at [7]–[30], discussed below.

different results. The distinction could be important, for example, in relation to the accruing of interest, or for currency conversions where one or both of the debts is in a foreign currency. In the case of an automatic set-off under the insolvency set-off section at the date of the liquidation,[239] interest would be determined as at that date[240] and foreign currency conversions similarly would take place as at that date or, if the liquidation was immediately preceded by an administration, as at the date that the company went into administration.[241] In the case of a charge, however, interest would continue to accrue until the debt is paid, and any foreign currency conversion ordinarily should also occur at that date in accordance with express or implied terms in the contract.[242] The distinction could also be important when a company has a contingent debt at the time of its liquidation which is not capable of acceleration. In the case of a set-off, the liquidator would value the contingent debt,[243] and that value, which may be less than its maximum potential amount, would be the subject of an automatic set-off. In the case of a charge, on the other hand, the creditor could retain the security until the contingency occurs, and apply it at that time against the debt which ultimately arises.[244] Richard Calnan has provided another example,[245] relating to the situation in which a guarantor has placed a deposit with a bank charged to secure the guarantee liability to the bank, recourse under the guarantee is limited to the amount of the deposit, both the guarantor and the principal debtor have gone into liquidation, and the deposit charged to the bank is less than the principal debt. Consider for example that the principal debt is £100 but the security deposit is only £60. If an automatic set-off occurred in the guarantor's liquidation, the debt would be reduced to £40 and the bank's proof in the principal debtor's liquidation would be limited to that amount.[246] If, on the other hand, the charge were effective in the liquidation, the bank could delay in enforcing the charge, and could prove for the full £100 in the principal debtor's liquidation.

16.75 The argument against the validity of the security is sometimes said to be stronger in the case of a mortgage than a charge. A mortgage is a form of security that takes effect by way of assignment. An argument sometimes presented is that, if a creditor were to assign the debt to the debtor, the debtor would become his or her own creditor. The interests would merge, so that there would no longer be a debt and consequently no security. Any document purporting to bring about an assignment could only take effect as a release of the debt or a

---

[239] See para. 6.123 above.

[240] Other than when the liquidation was immediately preceded by an administration. See para. 6.158 above.

[241] See para. 6.153 above.

[242] See also Calnan, 'The insolvent bank and security over deposits' (1996) 11 *Journal of International Banking and Financial Law* 185, 187 in relation to debts in different currencies.

[243] Pursuant to the Insolvency Rules 1986, r. 4.86, and for bankruptcy see the Insolvency Act 1986, s. 322.

[244] See Calnan, 'Security over deposits again: *BCCI (No. 8)* in the House of Lords' (1998) 13 *Journal of International Banking and Financial Law* 125, 127.

[245] Calnan, 'The insolvent bank and security over deposits' (1996) 11 *Journal of International Banking and Financial Law* 185, 189.

[246] This assumes that the guarantee is of part of the debt, as opposed to a guarantee of the whole debt but with liability limited. See para. 8.15 above.

covenant not to sue.[247] The tenor of Lord Hoffmann's brief reference to merger in *Re BCCI (No. 8)*[248] in the context of an equitable charge,[249] where he emphasized that in the case of a charge the depositor retains title, suggests that he may have regarded the question as open in relation to a mortgage.[250] It is suggested nevertheless that there would not be a merger in the case of a mortgage.[251] The equity of redemption that the debtor retains should prevent merger. In that regard, courts of equity, having regard to the intention of the parties, may treat an interest which merged at law as still subsisting in equity.[252] Thus, while the appointment of a debtor as executor of the creditor's estate has the effect at common law of extinguishing the debt, on the ground that at law the executor cannot sue him or herself, this is not so in equity, which fastens upon the executor an equivalent obligation to account to those interested in the estate for the amount of the debt.[253] Further, there is authority which supports the proposition that in equity a debtor can be a trustee of his or her own indebtedness.[254]

But whatever the position in relation to a mortgage, Lord Hoffmann in *Re BCCI (No. 8)*[255] **16.76** considered that merger is not a problem when an equitable charge is in issue. A charge does not involve an assignment of the subject-matter of the security. Rather, it arises when certain property is specifically made responsible for the discharge of an obligation, without any transfer of title or possession to the obligee.[256] It takes effect as an hypothecation rather

---

[247] *Broad v Commissioner of Stamp Duties* [1980] 2 NSWLR 40, 46; *Re Charge Card Services Ltd* [1987] 1 Ch 150, 175. See also *Street v Retravision (NSW) Pty Ltd* (1995) 56 FCR 588, 596; *Re Bank of Credit and Commerce International SA (No. 8)* [1996] Ch 245, 261–2 (CA). For the general proposition that a person cannot covenant with him or herself, or at the same time be both landlord and tenant, see *Rye v Rye* [1962] AC 496, 512, 513–14.

[248] [1998] AC 214, 227.

[249] See below.

[250] See also Segal, 'Conceptual implausibility in the Court of Appeal' [1996] 8 *Journal of International Banking Law* 307, 308.

[251] In *Clarkson v Smith & Goldberg* [1926] 1 DLR 509, 510 the Appellate Division of the Ontario Supreme Court commented that, by an hypothecation agreement, a bank's indebtedness on a deposit was 'in effect assigned to the bank', and treated it as a valid security. See also the discussion in *Banco Santander SA v Bayfern Ltd* [2000] 1 All ER (Comm) 776 in relation to an assignment of a joint and several debt to one of the joint and several debtors.

[252] *Capital and Counties Bank Ltd v Rhodes* [1903] 1 Ch 631, 652; *Cinema Plus Ltd v Australia and New Zealand Banking Group Ltd* (2000) 49 NSWLR 513 at [23]–[30]; *Meagher, Gummow and Lehane's Equity Doctrines and Remedies* (4th edn, 2002), 1101, 1103.

[253] *Commissioner of Stamp Duties (NSW) v Bone* (1976) 135 CLR 223, 227–8, [1977] AC 511, 518 (PC); *Commissioner of Taxation v Orica Ltd* (1998) 194 CLR 500, 544 (Gummow J); *Cinema Plus Ltd v ANZ Banking Group Ltd* (2000) 49 NSWLR 513 at [28] and [29] (Spigelman CJ).

[254] *Moore v Darton* (1851) 4 De G & Sm 517, 64 ER 938; *Paterson v Murphy* (1853) 22 LJ Ch 882 (the point appears more clearly in that report than in the report of the case at 11 Hare 88, 68 ER 1198); *Parker v Stones* (1868) 38 LJ Ch 46. See also Marshall, *The Assignment of Choses in Action* (1950), 97–9; Oditah, 'Financing trade credit: Welsh Development Agency v Exfinco' [1992] JBL 541, 557; *Scott and Ascher on Trusts* (5th edn, 2006) vol. 2, 580–2 (departing from the contrary view expressed in previous editions).

[255] [1998] AC 214, 227.

[256] *Re Bank of Credit and Commerce International SA (No. 8)* [1998] AC 214, 226; *Re Cosslett (Contractors) Ltd* [1998] Ch 495, 508; *Tancred v Delagoa Bay and East Africa Railway Co* (1889) 23 QBD 239, 242; *Morris v Woodings* (1997) 25 ACSR 636, 640–1; Gough, *Company Charges* (2nd edn, 1996), 18; *Fisher and Lightwood's Law of Mortgage* (12th edn, 2006), 63. However, the distinction between a charge and an assignment has not always been recognized. See e.g. *Roadshow Entertainment Pty Ltd v (ACN 053 006 269) Pty Ltd* (1997) 42 NSWLR 462, 482 ('fixed charge which operated as a completed equitable assignment') and *Hoverd*

than an alienation.[257] It is true that the primary remedies of an equitable chargee are the right to apply to the court for an order for sale or for the appointment of a receiver,[258] whereas a receiver would hardly be apt in the case of a charge-back, and nor would a sale be contemplated. The only remedy that the parties would have had in mind is that the bank itself, without recourse to the courts, would set one demand against another. This should not be an objection, however. There is no reason why the parties to a security contract cannot provide for their own remedies in the event of default,[259] the classic example being the appointment of a receiver out of court. It should not make any difference that the remedy contemplated may be in substitution for the traditional remedies available to an equitable chargee, as opposed to being in addition to them. For the same reason, the fact that the debtor cannot enforce the debt by suing him or herself is not an impediment.[260] It is not necessary for the debtor to do so.

16.77 In *National Westminster Bank Ltd v Halesowen Presswork & Assemblies Ltd*[261] a number of the judges in both the Court of Appeal and the House of Lords commented that a bank cannot have a lien on its own indebtedness,[262] and the statements to that effect have been referred to as supporting a like principle in the case of an equitable charge.[263] Those statements, however, should be considered in the context in which they were made. The courts in the *Halesowen* case were concerned to distinguish a bank's right to combine accounts[264] from the lien that a bank has on its customer's securities as a security for any indebtedness of the customer arising out of the banker/customer relationship. The lien is a common law possessory lien, which presupposes the existence of tangible property which may be retained and held in possession until the debt in question is paid. A credit balance on a bank account is not tangible property capable of being held in this manner. It is a debt. It was said therefore that the use of the word 'lien' in the context of combination of accounts is inappropriate. The statements in question are not authority for the proposition that it is not possible for a debtor to have a charge over its own indebtedness because, in contrast

---

Industries Ltd v Supercool Refrigeration and Air Conditioning (1991) Ltd [1995] 3 NZLR 577, 587 ('A fixed charge would operate as an equitable assignment . . .').

[257] In effect a shadow is cast over the property set aside as security for the debt until the debt is paid. See Sykes and Walker, *The Law of Securities* (5th edn, 1993), 18, referring to *Salmond on Jurisprudence* (12th edn, 1966), 430.

[258] Megarry and Wade, *The Law of Real Property* (7th edn, 2008), 1127 [25–050], referring to *Tennant v Trenchard* (1869) LR 4 Ch App 537 and *Re Owen* [1894] 3 Ch 220.

[259] As Wigram VC remarked in *Sampson v Pattison* (1842) 1 Hare 533, 535, 66 ER 1143: 'The only question is, what are the terms of the contract?'

[260] Compare *Re Charge Card Services Ltd* [1987] 1 Ch 150, 176.

[261] [1972] AC 785 (HL), reversing [1971] 1 QB 1 (CA).

[262] See Lord Denning MR and Buckley LJ in the Court of Appeal [1971] 1 QB 1, 34, 46, and Viscount Dilhorne and Lord Cross of Chelsea in the House of Lords [1972] AC 785, 802, 810. See also *MPS Constructions Pty Ltd v Rural Bank of New South Wales* (1980) 4 ACLR 835. In that case a customer had executed a 'lien' in favour of a bank over all moneys deposited by it with the bank. Helsham CJ in Eq, in following the *Halesowen* case, held that this did not encompass moneys standing to the customer's credit in a bank account in the customer's name. However, the question of the effect of a charge, as opposed to a lien, was not considered.

[263] *Broad v Commissioner of Stamp Duties* [1980] 2 NSWLR 40, 46–7; *Re Bank of Credit and Commerce International SA (No. 8)* [1996] Ch 245, 259–60 (CA).

[264] See ch. 15 above.

to the case of a common law possessory lien, intangible property may be the subject of an equitable charge.[265]

An argument of greater refinement has been proposed,[266] based on the distinction between property and obligation. The argument is that, while as between a creditor and a third party the debt is an asset, as between the debtor and the creditor it is not an asset but an obligation. In other words, the creditor does not own the debt, rather the debt is owed to it.[267] But, while it is true to say that the creditor is owed the debt, the creditor as against the debtor also has rights which are a species of property and which should be just as capable of being the subject of a security in favour of the debtor as a third party.[268]

16.78

There is, on the other hand, authority which supports the validity of a charge-back,[269] and consistent with that authority the House of Lords in *Re BCCI (No. 8)*[270] rejected the conceptual impossibility argument. While a determination of the point was not necessary for the decision in *BCCI (No. 8)*, Lord Hoffmann, with whose judgment the other

16.79

---

[265] See the discussion of the *Halesowen* case in *Re Bank of Credit and Commerce International SA (No. 8)* [1998] AC 214, 226.

[266] It has been suggested that the question whether an equitable charge may arise depends upon the availability of specific performance, and that accordingly a relevant issue in considering the validity of charge-backs is whether specific performance would be ordered. See Everett, 'Security over bank deposits' (1988) 16 *Australian Business Law Review* 351, 364, and McCracken, *The Banker's Remedy of Set-off* (3rd edn, 2010), 251–6, 258–61, 327–8. The better view, however, is that an equitable charge of present property (as distinct from a promise for valuable consideration to charge future acquired assets) does not depend on specific performance. See *Hewett v Court* (1983) 149 CLR 639 (esp. Deane J at 665–7) in relation to an equitable lien, which is a form of equitable charge (see 663). Indeed, it is difficult to see what the substance of the order against the chargor would be (although compare McCracken, *op. cit.* 261).

[267] *Re BCCI (No. 8)* [1996] Ch 245, 259 (CA); Millett (1991) 107 LQR 680; *Goode on Legal Problems of Credit and Security* (4th edn (ed. Gullifer), 2008), 102 (and see also, by Professor Goode, 'Security: a pragmatic conceptualist's pesponse' (1989) 15 *Monash University Law Review* 361, 368, 'Charges over book debts: a missed opportunity' (1994) 110 LQR 592, 606 and 'Charge-backs and legal fictions' (1998) 114 LQR 178, 179). 'A liability is not property of the person liable': *Cummings v Claremont Petroleum NL* (1996) 185 CLR 124, 133.

[268] Lindley LJ's comment in *Lister v Stubbs* (1890) 45 Ch D 1, 15, that the employer's claim in that case confounded ownership with obligation, does not assist the argument. An employee received money by way of secret commission which he invested in the purchase of land, and the employer sought to trace the money into the investment. The action failed on the ground that the relation between them was only that of debtor and creditor, rather than trustee and cestui que trust. While the employee had an obligation to the employer on a debtor/creditor basis, neither the money itself nor the property into which it could be traced was owned by the employer.

[269] *Ex p Caldicott, re Hart* (1884) 25 Ch D 716; *Ex p Mackay* (1873) LR 8 Ch App 643, 42 LJ Bcy 68 (esp. at 69); *Swiss Bank Corporation v Lloyds Bank Ltd* [1982] AC 584, 614; *Welsh Development Agency v Export Finance Co Ltd* [1992] BCLC 148, 166–7 (and see also Browne-Wilkinson VC in the Chancery Division [1990] BCC 393, 408). These cases were discussed in greater detail in the second edition of this book, at 554–5. See also Oditah, 'Financing trade credit: Welsh Development Agency v Exfinco' [1992] JBL 541, 557. A number of other cases are referred to in Wood, *English and International Set-off* (1989), 199–205, although some of them may be explained on other grounds. E.g. in *Webb v Smith* (1885) 30 Ch D 192, which is often cited as authority in support of charge-backs, the proceeds of sale would have been impressed with a trust, and the auctioneer's 'lien' would have attached to the trust fund. The auctioneer had paid the proceeds into a bank account, which the auctioneer would have held on trust, first to discharge his lien and then to pay to the vendor or to his order. It was not a simple case of a debt owing at common law by the auctioneer to the vendor. See the discussion of *Webb v Smith* in the Court of Appeal in *Re BCCI (No. 8)* [1996] Ch 245, 261.

[270] [1998] AC 214.

Law Lords agreed, considered that it should be dealt with given that it had been fully argued.[271]

16.80 Lord Hoffmann approached the issue by reference to basic principles rather than by undertaking a comprehensive analysis of the authorities.[272] He said that a debt is a chose in action, which the law has always recognized as property. A charge over a chose in action can validly be granted to a third party. He then asked, in what respects would the fact that the debtor is the beneficiary of the charge be inconsistent with the transaction having one or more of the features of a charge? The method by which the property is realized would differ, in that, instead of the beneficiary of the charge having to claim payment from the debtor, the realization would take the form of a book entry, by setting off one debt against the other. But in no other respect would the transaction have any consequence different from that which would attach to a charge given to a third party. It would still be a proprietary interest which, subject to questions of registration and a possible defence of purchaser for value without notice, would be binding upon an assignee, and upon a liquidator or a trustee in bankruptcy. Similarly, the chargor would retain an equity of redemption. In those circumstances, Lord Hoffmann said that he could not see why it could not properly be said that the debtor has a proprietary interest by way of charge over the debt.[273] He also noted that documents purporting to create such charges had been used by banks for many years,[274] and was of the view that the law should attempt to uphold a practice adopted by the commercial community, provided that there was no threat to the consistency of the law or an objection on grounds of public policy.[275] This reflects a sentiment earlier expressed by Hammond J in New Zealand, that 'good commercial law should follow good commercial practice (and not vice versa)'.[276]

16.81 Notwithstanding that the view expressed by the House of Lords on the validity of chargebacks strictly was *obiter*, it was nevertheless a considered opinion after full argument, and it would appear to have settled the law in England.[277] Indeed, the validity of the security interest is assumed in the Financial Collateral Arrangements (No. 2) Regulations.[278] The Regulations relate to a 'financial collateral arrangement', which includes a 'security financial collateral arrangement'. That term in turn is defined[279] as including an arrangement evidenced in writing where a collateral-provider creates a security interest in 'financial collateral' for the purpose of securing financial obligations owed to the collateral-taker, and the financial collateral is held by the collateral-taker. The term 'financial collateral' is

---

[271] [1998] AC 214, 225.
[272] See in particular the discussion at [1998] AC 214, 226–7.
[273] [1998] AC 214, 227.
[274] [1998] AC 214, 225–6, 227.
[275] [1998] AC 214, 228.
[276] *Commercial Factors Ltd v Maxwell Printing Ltd* [1994] 1 NZLR 724, 727.
[277] The judgment on this point has been both applauded and criticized. Compare the views of Richard Calnan, 'Fashioning the Law to Suit the Practicalities of Life' (1998) 114 LQR 174 and Professor Roy Goode, 'Charge-backs and legal fictions' (1998) 114 LQR 178. It was applied in *Fraser v Oystertec plc* [2006] 1 BCLC 491.
[278] S.I. 2003 No. 3226. See paras 16.45–16.51 above.
[279] Regulation 3.

defined[280] as including cash. The Regulations therefore implicitly accept the validity of security over cash deposited with a collateral-taker (a bank) securing obligations owed to the collateral-taker. Further, 'security interest' is defined as including a mortgage, so that the assumption of validity extends to a mortgage-back. Mortgages are dealt with expressly in reg. 17. This provides that, where a security collateral financial arrangement creates a legal or equitable mortgage on terms that include a power for the collateral-taker to appropriate the collateral, the collateral-taker may exercise that power in accordance with the terms of the arrangement, without any order for foreclosure from the courts.[281] However, 'security financial collateral arrangement' is confined to an arrangement where both the collateral-provider and the collateral-taker are 'non-natural persons'.[282] If, therefore, the collateral-provider is a natural person, reg. 17 does not apply.

In Australia, decisions of the House of Lords are not binding. They are persuasive, but only, **16.82** it has been said, to the degree of persuasiveness of their reasoning.[283] In New South Wales, Windeyer J in *Wily v Rothschild Australia Ltd*[284] declined to follow *Re BCCI (No. 8)* on this point. He preferred instead earlier Australian authority, including a decision of the Full Court of the South Australian Supreme Court,[285] in which it had been accepted that a charge-back is conceptually impossible,[286] commenting that he would leave it to an appeal court to determine that those cases should not be followed.[287] He noted that the views expressed in *Re BCCI (No. 8)* were not essential for the decision, and said that they seemed partly to have been brought about through a desire to make the law accord with the desires of commerce rather than through totally convincing reasoning.[288] Windeyer J adhered to that view at first instance in *Cinema Plus Ltd v Australia and New Zealand Banking Group Ltd*,[289] but Spigelman CJ later rejected it on appeal in that case.[290] The reasoning of the Chief Justice is not free of difficulty,[291] but *Re BCCI (No. 8)* has since been followed in

---

[280] Regulation 3.

[281] Regulation 17 is not expressed to apply to an equitable charge. This presumably is because an equitable chargee cannot foreclose. See *Fisher and Lightwood's Law of Mortgage* (12th edn, 2006), 682 [32.3].

[282] Defined in reg. 3 as: 'any body corporate, unincorporated firm, partnership or body with legal personality except an individual . . .'

[283] *Cook v Cook* (1986) 162 CLR 376, 390.

[284] (1999) 47 NSWLR 555.

[285] *Jackson v Esanda Finance Corporation Ltd* (1992) 59 SASR 416.

[286] In addition to *Jackson v Esanda Finance Corporation Ltd* (1992) 59 SASR 416, see *Broad v Commissioner of Stamp Duties* [1980] 2 NSWLR 40; *Estate Planning Associates (Australia) Pty Ltd v Commissioner of Stamp Duties* (1985) 2 NSWLR 495; *Griffiths v Commonwealth Bank of Australia* (1994) 123 ALR 111, 120; *First For Finance Pty Ltd v Westpac Banking Corporation* (Vic SC, Hansen J, 7 May 1998, BC9801760) (esp. at p 23)).

[287] (1999) 47 NSWLR 555, 564.

[288] See also McCormack, 'Charge-backs and commercial certainty in the House of Lords' [1998] *Company Financial and Insolvency Law Review* 111.

[289] (2000) 34 ACSR 621, 627.

[290] *Cinema Plus Ltd v Australia and New Zealand Banking Group Ltd* (2000) 49 NSWLR 513 at [7]–[30]. The other members of the Court of Appeal, Sheller and Giles JJA, did not consider the conceptual impossibility argument, determining the charge issue instead on the basis that the clause in question was not apt to create a charge. See Sheller JA at [116] and Giles JA at [143]–[145].

[291] Spigelman CJ ((2000) 49 NSWLR 513 at [24]) had recourse to the equitable maxim that 'equity looks to the intent rather than to the form' and said (at [30]): 'In my opinion, there is no reason why, in an appropriate case, equity could not find that the intention of the parties to create a charge between a debtor and creditor, over-rides what would be regarded, at common law, as a "conceptual impossibility".' This appears to concede

Queensland[292] and the validity of charge-backs is also now accepted in the Personal Property Securities Act 2009 (Cth), s. 12(4) and (4A).

(2) Charge-backs and mutuality

16.83   A charge-back could secure a third party's indebtedness, for example where a deposit held by a bank is charged by the depositor to secure financial accommodation provided to a related entity.[293] But in the situation in which there are only two parties, so that the debt secured by the charge-back is owing by the depositor, it has been suggested that, as a result of the analysis of the insolvency set-off section adopted in *Stein v Blake*,[294] the charge, accepting that it is otherwise valid, would not continue after the depositor's liquidation. In *Stein v Blake* the House of Lords held that a set-off takes effect automatically upon the occurrence of a bankruptcy, so as to bring about a cancellation of the cross-demands on that date to the extent of the set-off.[295] A similar principle applies in company liquidation.[296] It has been argued that, as a consequence, the cross-demands would no longer exist, and that a charge over one claim to secure payment of the other accordingly would not survive a winding-up order.[297]

16.84   The principal source of support for that view is *MS Fashions Ltd v Bank of Credit and Commerce International SA*.[298] A bank advanced money to a company, taking as security a deposit from a director which was charged to the bank. In addition, the director assumed a personal liability for the company's debt. Subsequently, the bank went into liquidation. It was held that the director's personal liability to the bank and the bank's debt to the director on the deposit were demands arising out of mutual dealings within the ambit of the insolvency set-off section, and accordingly were the subject of an automatic set-off upon the occurrence of the liquidation. As a result, the bank could not choose to sue the company for payment and confine the director to a proof in the liquidation in respect of the deposit. Counsel for the liquidator argued that, because of the charge, there was no set-off,

---

that at 'common law' a charge over one's own debt is conceptually impossible, but postulates that equity would have regard to the intention of the parties in order to override that result. But a charge is a creature of equity. There is no such thing as a legal charge, except as provided by statute. See *Goode on Legal Problems of Credit and Security* (4th edn (ed. Gullifer), 2008), 37 (though *Goode* notes an exception in relation to maritime liens, which have their roots in Admiralty law). It is not then a question of the common law maintaining that it is conceptually impossible to have a charge over one's own debt. If, on the other hand, his Honour used the expression 'common law' as including the doctrines of equity (see Spigelman CJ at [32] and [39]), and in contradistinction to statutory law, his Honour's comment would raise further questions. In particular, why would equity, on the one hand, regard something as conceptually impossible, and on the other suggest that that result could be avoided by looking to the intent rather than the form? If equity were to regard its own institution of a charge as conceptually impossible in a particular situation, that would be the end of the matter. The answer, as the House of Lords has determined, is that in fact there is no conceptual impossibility in the notion of a debtor taking a charge over its own debt.

[292]   *Emanuel Management Pty Ltd v Foster's Brewing Group Ltd* (2003) 178 FLR 1 at [1434]–[1438].
[293]   As in *Re Bank of Credit and Commerce International SA (No. 8)* [1998] AC 214.
[294]   [1996] AC 243.
[295]   See paras 6.119–6.122 above.
[296]   See para. 6.123 above.
[297]   For a discussion of the issue, see Berg, 'Charges over book debts: a reply' [1995] JBL 433, 465–7, and 'House of Lords clarifies liquidation netting', *International Financial Law Review*, August 1995, 20, 21.
[298]   [1993] Ch 425. See also the discussion of the *MS Fashions* case in paras 12.24–12.28 above.

but that argument received little sympathy from Hoffmann LJ in the Chancery Division. He said that, even if one ignored the question whether a charge-back is conceptually possible, the charge was over a debt owing by the bank to secure a debt owed to the bank. In that circumstance: '[t]he account to be taken by rule 4.90 must require an unwinding of that arrangement so that the deposit is set off against the debt it was intended to secure.'[299] On appeal the Court of Appeal similarly held that the fact of the charge over the deposit did not prevent a set-off.[300] While the issue was discussed in that forum primarily from a different perspective, as to whether the deposit was a special-purpose payment and therefore not available for a set-off on that ground,[301] the tenor of the judgment, and the result, suggest that the Court of Appeal agreed with Hoffmann LJ's analysis. That view is also consistent with earlier decisions of the Court of Appeal in *Sovereign Life Assurance Co v Dodd*[302] and *Re City Life Assurance Co Ltd (Grandfield's Case)*.[303] In those cases a loan made by an insurance company to an insured was set off in the company's liquidation against the insured's claim on a policy issued by the company, which policy had been mortgaged-back to the company as security for the loan.[304] Nevertheless, the effect of the mortgage-back on mutuality was not considered, other than by Bowen and Kay LJJ in *Sovereign Life v Dodd*[305] (see below), who referred to it only briefly. This lack of critical analysis diminishes the weight to be attached to those cases as authorities on this point.

It is difficult to support the proposition that, in the event of a charge-back, a set-off under **16.85** the insolvency set-off section would occur as between the charged debt and the debt owing by the chargor to the chargee for which it is security,[306] and it is suggested that the *MS Fashions* case is wrong on this point. The essence of Hoffmann LJ's analysis, that the account to be taken under the insolvency set-off section requires an unwinding of the arrangement, begs the question as to whether the requirements of the set-off section in fact have been satisfied so as to justify an account under it. As counsel argued before the Court of Appeal in the *MS Fashions* case,[307] the charge in that case had the consequence that there was no mutuality for the purpose of a set-off. The bank had a claim against the director, and it also

---

[299] [1993] Ch 425, 438.

[300] See the discussion at [1993] Ch 425, 448–51.

[301] See paras 10.47–10.58 above.

[302] [1892] 2 QB 573.

[303] [1926] Ch 191, 199, not following *Ex p Price, re Lankester* (1875) LR 10 Ch App 648 and *Paddy v Clutton* [1920] 2 Ch 554.

[304] See also *Re National Benefit Assurance Co Ltd* [1924] 2 Ch 339. In *Hiley v The Peoples Prudential Assurance Co Ltd* (1938) 60 CLR 468 an insured executed a 'memorandum of deposit' as collateral security for a loan from the insurance company (a mortgage of land also having been obtained), and deposited with the insurer a life policy issued by the insurer. The insurer expressly repudiated the policy, and the insured was allowed to set off his cross-claim for damages resulting from the repudiation against the loan. The terms of the 'memorandum of deposit' are not set out in the report, and the nature and ambit of the collateral security are unclear, in particular as to whether it would have extended to a damages claim for repudiation of the policy.

[305] [1892] 2 QB 573, 582, 585–6.

[306] In *Ex p Mackay* (1872) LR 8 Ch App 643, in which the right to retain the royalties in that case was treated as a charge on a debt, it is apparent that the companies' debt to Jeavons for the royalties and their rights against Jeavons in respect of the loan were not regarded as having been set off under the insolvency set-off section. It is unclear from the report, however, whether the debt for the royalties was joint or several for the purpose of determining mutuality, and accordingly whether the insolvency set-off section applied. See para. 12.02 above in relation to joint debts and para. 12.21 above in relation to joint and several debts.

[307] [1993] Ch 425, 440–1. See also Wood, *English and International Set-off* (1989), 195.

had a beneficial interest in the deposit as a result of the charge. Because of the charge, the director himself did not have an unimpeded beneficial interest in the deposit, which should have been sufficient to prevent mutuality arising.[308] A set-off under the insolvency set-off section therefore should not have occurred in that case. Under a charge-back the chargee is a secured creditor, and the chargee's position should be governed by the rules relating to the security,[309] including as to the timing of enforcement. It should not be a question of insolvency set-off. Subsequently, Lord Hoffmann again referred to the issue in the House of Lords in *Re Bank of Credit and Commerce International SA (No. 8)*.[310] He said that the argument that the charge destroyed mutuality 'was somewhat cursorily rejected in the *MS Fashions* case', though without expressing a concluded view on the subject.[311] It nevertheless suggests a willingness to reconsider the opinion that he had expressed in *MS Fashions*.[312]

16.86 Consider once again the case of a bank which provides a facility to a customer secured by a charge over a deposit made by the customer with the bank. Subsequently, the bank goes into liquidation. If, as suggested, the insolvency set-off section does not apply because of lack of mutuality, *prima facie* the liquidator could sue the customer for payment of the debt, and after it has been paid confine the customer to a proof in the liquidation in relation to the deposit. That seems an unjust result. When a customer provides a deposit as security for the customer's own debt, the intention usually would be that the deposit itself would provide the source of the payment to the bank. It is unlikely that the parties contemplated that the customer would have to find the sum in question twice – once to fund the deposit and a second time to pay the debt. In that circumstance, Richard Calnan has suggested that it would be unconscionable for the bank to insist on recovering the customer's liability in

---

[308] See para. 11.46 above.

[309] *Ex p Caldicott, re Hart* (1884) 25 Ch D 716, 722.

[310] [1998] AC 214, 225.

[311] Mokel, 'Resolving the *MS Fashions* "paradox"' [1999] *Company Financial and Insolvency Law Review* 106, 107–8 has supported Hoffmann LJ's initial stance in the *MS Fashions* case, *inter alia* on the ground that the charge over the deposit did not reduce its value, but simply affected the depositor's ability to apply it for any purpose other than to pay off the secured debt. That may be accepted, but the charge also had the effect of impeding the depositor's beneficial interest in the deposit. It is that which affects mutuality, not the value of the deposit in the liquidation.

[312] Richard Calnan has queried whether that aspect of *MS Fashions v BCCI* is consistent with *Ex p Caldicott, re Hart* (1884) 25 Ch D 716. See Calnan, 'The insolvent bank and security over deposits' (1996) 11 *Journal of International Banking and Financial Law* 185, 189. In *Ex p Caldicott*, a partner in a firm mortgaged his separate property to the firm's bankers in order to secure the firm's indebtedness. In addition, he gave a personal covenant to the bank that the firm would pay the balance due on the firm's current account. Subsequently, the partner entered into an agreement to sell the mortgaged property. The bank concurred in the sale on condition that the proceeds be placed on deposit with it, and that they should stand charged with the payment of the firm's debt. The firm later became bankrupt. The Court of Appeal regarded the deposit as a security held by the bank, but since it was not a security on an asset belonging to the firm it was held that it was not necessary that it be deducted from the proof lodged by the bank against the joint estate. As Calnan has pointed out, this assumes that the deposit was not set off in the partner's bankruptcy against his liability on the separate undertaking. In other words, it assumes that there was no mutuality. If a set-off had occurred in the partner's bankruptcy, the firm's debt to that extent would have been paid, in which case the bank's proof in the firm's bankruptcy would have had to be reduced. The only query in relation to that analysis is that the report of *Ex p Caldicott* simply states that the deposit was charged with payment of the firm's debt. It is not specifically mentioned that it was security also for the partner's separate liability on his undertaking.

full without taking account of the deposit, and that therefore an equitable set-off may be available.[313] There is a lack of mutuality, but (notwithstanding some recent statements in the Court of Appeal which suggest the contrary[314]) the better view is that equity does not in all cases regard mutuality as a strict requirement for an equitable set-off.[315] Calnan's argument is contrary to the view that is sometimes expressed, that equitable set-off is not available in bankruptcy or company liquidation in circumstances that are outside the operation of the insolvency set-off section,[316] but it is suggested that that proposition is doubtful, both as a matter of principle and as a matter of precedent.[317] There are other difficulties with Calnan's view, however. While the parties may indeed have assumed that the deposit would be applied in satisfaction of the debt, the agreement usually would be drafted in terms of giving the bank a discretion to effect a set-off, in which case the notion that equity may require a set-off *prima facie* would be contrary to the terms of their agreement.[318] The point is that insolvency does not give rise to an equity sufficient to support an equitable set-off.[319] Therefore, if equitable set-off were available, it should be available irrespective of the bank's insolvency. But if that were the case, the contractual stipulation for a discretion would be illusory. Further, the notion that equity would require a set-off is at variance with the view that a secured creditor is not obliged to resort to the security, but can claim repayment from the debtor personally and leave the security alone.[320]

But notwithstanding those difficulties, there is much to commend Calnan's view when a lender is insolvent. Moreover, it is supported by comments by Bowen and Kay LJJ in the Court of Appeal in *Sovereign Life Assurance Co v Dodd*.[321] An insurance company provided a loan to an insured customer, the company taking as security a mortgage of a life policy issued by the company to the insured. The company went into liquidation, and it was held that the loan to the insured could be set off against the insured's claim against the company

16.87

---

[313] Calnan, 'The insolvent bank and security over deposits' (1996) 11 *Journal of International Banking and Financial Law* 185, 187–8.

[314] See para. 4.69 above.

[315] See paras 4.67–4.83 above.

[316] *Brown v Cork* [1985] BCLC 363, 376 (CA); *Day & Dent Constructions Pty Ltd v North Australian Properties Pty Ltd* (1981) 34 ALR 595, 599, 601, 636–7 (Federal Court). See also *Re BCCI (No. 8)* [1996] Ch 245, 269–70 (CA), although the discussion in that case was confined to two cases (*Ex p Stephens* (1805) 11 Ves Jun 24, 32 ER 996 and *Jones v Mossop* (1844) 3 Hare 568, 67 ER 506) which were said to support a wider right of set-off in equity than under the insolvency set-off section. See para. 6.25 above.

[317] See paras 6.25–6.32 above.

[318] A similar point was made in *Lord v Direct Acceptance Corporation Ltd* (1993) 32 NSWLR 362, 369. See para. 4.87 above. Compare *Goldstar Finance Plc v Singh* [2005] EWCA Civ 1544, in which it was held that a security deposit for a loan was to be taken as 'netted off' against the loan at the end of the contractual repayment repayment period, but it was emphasized (at [62] and [69]) that the circumstances of the case were 'highly unusual', 'bizarre' and 'unique'.

[319] *Rawson v Samuel* (1841) Cr & Ph 161, 175, 41 ER 451, 457. See para. 4.03 above.

[320] *Re BCCI (No. 8)* [1998] AC 214, 222 (HL), referring to *China and South Sea Bank Ltd v Tan Soon Gin* [1990] 1 AC 536, 545 (PC).

[321] [1892] 2 QB 573. The analysis in *Clarkson v Smith and Goldberg* [1926] 1 DLR 509 would also support Calnan's view. See para. 12.42 above.

on the policy. Kay LJ considered an argument that there was no debt owing to the insured on the policy because of the mortgage.[322] He dealt with it shortly:[323]

> There was a clear debt due upon these policies when the present action was brought; and I think we may discard the argument founded upon the fact that there had been an assignment of the policies to the company, for there will be a set-off in equity in cases where, but for some such circumstance as this assignment, there would have been a legal set-off. The company were liable to the defendant for the amount of the policies, subject of course to their charge upon the policies for the advances, and I think that in this action the defendant probably had a set-off against the company wholly independent of the section.

Kay LJ went on to say that there were in any event mutual dealings for the purpose of the insolvency set-off section.[324] This would not appear to have been the case, because the mortgage would have destroyed mutuality. But whatever the position in that regard, he was of the view that a set-off 'probably' was available in equity and that this was independent of the insolvency set-off section. Nor was Kay LJ alone in that regard, Bowen LJ similarly commenting:[325]

> As far as I can see, this is a good set-off at law; but if it were not a good legal set-off by reason of the existence of an assignment of the policies to the secretary of the company, it would, at all events, be a good set-off in equity.

Those remarks support Calnan's view, that a set-off may be available in equity in the case of a charge-back, notwithstanding that the insolvency set-off section does not apply because of lack of mutuality.

16.88 On the other hand, an equitable set-off should not be available when the deposit is made by a third party, such as a director of the customer.[326] The effect of allowing an equitable set-off to the customer would be to require the bank to look to the deposit provided by the third party as a security, as opposed to seeking payment from the customer as principal debtor. That would make the surety primarily liable to discharge the debt. As the New South Wales Court of Appeal observed in *Lord v Direct Acceptance Corporation Ltd*,[327] there would be no equity in that result.[328]

(3) Charge-back and combination of accounts

16.89 When a customer has a number of accounts with a bank, the principle of combination may apply so that, unless a particular account has been separated out by agreement or it is separate as a matter of law, the balance of all the accounts represents the debt at any particular time.[329] If, however, a customer establishes a security deposit at the request of a bank and

---

[322] [1892] 2 QB 573, 584. See also counsel's argument at first instance [1892] 1 QB 405, 408.
[323] [1892] 2 QB 573, 585.
[324] [1892] 2 QB 573, 586.
[325] [1892] 2 QB 573, 582.
[326] This was the view also of Calnan, 'The insolvent bank and security over deposits' (1996) 11 *Journal of International Banking and Financial Law* 185, 189.
[327] (1993) 32 NSWLR 362, 369. See para. 4.87 above.
[328] See also *Re BCCI (No. 8)* [1996] Ch 245, 256 (CA) in relation to insolvency set-off.
[329] See ch. 15 above.

charges it to the bank, the security interest that the bank has in the account should have the effect of preventing a combination in respect of it, so that the bank's position should be governed instead by the security. In any event, combination would not be applicable where, as is often the case, the liability secured by the charge is contingent, for example where the deposit secures a contingent liability to the bank on a letter of credit provided by the bank, or a contingent liability under a guarantee of a related company's indebtedness.[330]

(4) Registration

Consider that a deposit with a bank has been charged in its favour by way of a charge-back. **16.90** The question arises whether the charge would require registration under companies legislation where the party granting the charge is a company.[331] If registration were required, failure to register the charge would render it void as against a liquidator or administrator of the company.[332]

The registration requirement in companies legislation commonly extends to a charge **16.91** on the company's book debts.[333] The term 'book debts' is not defined in the English legislation,[334] but in its generally accepted sense it refers to debts connected with and growing out of a person's trade or business which would ordinarily be entered in that person's books.[335] Opinions differ as to whether this would include a bank account.[336] The better view is that a bank account ordinarily is not a book debt, since it does not arise out of the company's trade or business but is merely the consequence of the deposit of

---

[330] See para. 15.51 above.

[331] Companies Act 2006, s. 860. In Australia, see the Corporations Act 2001 (Cth), s. 262. The mere possibility of a set-off under either the Statutes of Set-off or the insolvency set-off section is not registrable. One reason is that the possibility does not confer any form of security interest. See *Re John Ewing, A Bankrupt* (1906) 8 GLR 612; *Official Assignee of Reeves & Williams v Dorrington* [1918] NZLR 702, 706. In any event, the creditor's right arises by operation of law, as opposed to being created by the company itself.

[332] Companies Act 2006, s. 874. In Australia, see the Corporations Act 2001 (Cth), s. 266(1). See also in Australia the recently enacted Personal Property Securities Act 2009 (Cth). The Act extends to a charge over a bank deposit (termed an 'ADI deposit'). It also provides for registration of security interests in personal property. Pursuant to s. 267, a security interest granted by a company which is being wound up vests in the grantor (the company) if the security interest was not 'perfected' at the commencement of the winding up. A security interest may be 'perfected' by registration, but registration is not necessary. It suffices if the secured party has 'control'. See s. 21(2). In the case of an ADI account, s. 25(1) provides that the secured party has control if the secured party itself is the ADI, in other words a charge-back. Therefore, lack of registration should not trigger the operation of s. 267 in the case of a bank deposit charged back to the bank. The new system is due to begin operating in May 2011. For the transitional application of s. 267, see Divisions 4 and 5 of Part 9.4. Section 267 will apply also to administration, deeds of company arrangement and bankruptcy.

[333] See the Companies Act 2006, s. 860(7)(f). In Australia, see the Corporations Act 2001 (Cth), s. 262(1)(f).

[334] Compare Australia, where a charge on a book debt is defined in the Corporations Act 2001 (Cth), s. 262(4) in terms of a charge on a debt due: 'on account of or in connection with a profession, trade or business carried on by the company, whether entered in a book or not . . .' The term 'book debt' does not appear in the Personal Property Securities Act 2009 (Cth), but see the definition of 'account' in s. 10.

[335] *Shipley v Marshall* (1863) 14 CB (NS) 566, 143 ER 567; *Independent Automatic Sales Ltd v Knowles & Foster* [1962] 1 WLR 974. See also *Waters v Widdows* [1984] VR 503, 519–20.

[336] See generally McCracken, *The Banker's Remedy of Set-off* (3rd edn, 2010), 268–72, and McCormack, 'Charge-backs and commercial certainty in the House of Lords' [1998] *Company Financial and Insolvency Law Review* 111, 117–19.

surplus funds.[337] Consistent with that view, in *Re Brightlife Ltd*[338] Hoffmann J held that the expression 'all book debts and other debts' in a debenture did not encompass an amount standing to the credit of a bank account.[339] Some two years later, however, he commented in *Re Permanent Houses (Holdings) Ltd*[340] that *Re Brightlife* was concerned with the construction of a particular debenture, and that he did not express an opinion in that case as to whether a credit balance with a bank is a book debt for the purpose of registration of charges under the Companies Act. More recently, Lord Hoffmann again referred to the issue in delivering the judgment of the House of Lords in *BCCI (No. 8)*.[341] While emphasizing that he was not expressing a view on the point, he nevertheless referred to the judgment of Hutton LCJ (as he then was) in *Northern Bank Ltd v Ross*,[342] which suggested that an obligation to register is unlikely to arise in the case of bank deposits, in terms suggesting that he also inclined to that view.

16.92   In England, registration on this ground would no longer be an issue in most cases, following the making of the Financial Collateral Arrangements (No. 2) Regulations 2003.[343] Regulation 4(4) provides that the statutory requirement for registration of charges[344] does not apply in relation to a 'security financial collateral arrangement'. That term is defined[345] as an arrangement evidenced in writing where: (a) the purpose of the arrangement is to secure financial obligations owed to the collateral-taker; (b) the collateral-provider creates or there arises a security interest[346] in financial collateral (which includes cash) to secure those obligations; (c) the financial collateral is held or otherwise designated so as to be in the possession or under the control of the collateral-taker; and (d) the collateral-provider and the collateral-taker are both non-natural persons. This would cover the case of a cash deposit with a bank which is charged in favour of the bank. However, the concept of 'security financial collateral arrangement' (and therefore the exemption from registration)

---

[337] In addition to the cases referred to below, see *Goode on Legal Problems of Credit and Security* (4th edn (ed. Gullifer), 109; *Ellinger's Modern Banking Law* (4th edn, 2006), 810; *Re Stevens* [1888] WN 110, 116; *Watson v Parapara Coal Co Ltd* (1915) 17 GLR 791; *Perrins v State Bank of Victoria* [1991] 1 VR 749, 754–5; *Re Old Inns of NSW Pty Ltd; Millar v Leach* (1994) 13 ACSR 141, 143. See also *Cox v Smail* [1912] VLR 274, 285; *Re Grimsley* (1938) 10 ABC 88. For the contrary view, see Calnan, 'Security over deposits again: BCCI (No. 8) in the House of Lords' (1998) 13 *Journal of International Banking and Financial Law* 125, 128. However, there may be situations in which a bank account constitutes a book debt, such as where money is deposited by an investment company with a bank by way of investment. See Goode, *op. cit.* 109 (referring to sums deposited by a dealer in the money market), and Ellinger, *op. cit.* 810, n. 33.

[338] [1987] 1 Ch 200.

[339] In the context of the construction of a debenture, see also *Re Buildlead Ltd (No. 2)* [2006] 1 BCLC 9 at [119] (Etherton J).

[340] [1988] BCLC 563, 566–7.

[341] [1998] AC 214, 227.

[342] [1991] BCLC 504, [1990] BCC 883.

[343] S.I. 2003 No. 3226, amended by the Financial Collateral Arrangements (No. 2) Regulations 2003 (Amendment) Regulations 2009 (S.I. 2009 No. 317).

[344] Referring to the Companies Act 2006, ss. 860 and 874.

[345] Regulation 3.

[346] Defined in reg. 3 as including a mortgage or a charge, including a charge created as a floating charge where the financial collateral charged is delivered, transferred, held, registered or otherwise designated so as to be in the possession or under the control of the collateral-taker or a person acting on his or her behalf. The application of the Regulations to floating charges gives rise to difficulty. See Turing, 'New growth in the financial collateral garden' (2005) 1 *Journal of International Banking and Financial Law* 4, 5 and *Goode on Legal Problems of Credit and Security* (4th edn (ed. Gullifer), 2008), 263–5.

does not apply in the case of an arrangement not evidenced in writing. Further, the financial collateral must be in the possession or under the control of the collateral-taker.[347] If a company has the right to operate a bank account the subject of a charge-back without restriction until such time as the bank effects a set-off, a charge over the account would resemble a floating charge, in which case the agreement may be registrable on that ground.[348] Moreover, the circumstance that the company is free to operate the account may have the consequence that it is not in the possession or under the control of the bank, in which case the exemption from registration under the Regulations would not apply.

J. A Set-off Agreement as a Charge

Acceptance of the view that a debtor (typically a bank) can have a security over its own indebtedness leads to the question whether a set-off agreement is a charge. This is not intended to refer to a situation in which it is agreed that a set-off is to occur immediately or as a matter of course, since this is merely a method of payment.[349] Nor would it apply to a provision in a contract to the effect that the amount payable is the contract price less allowable deductions in respect of expenditure. Rather, the issue may arise when one party (referred to in the following discussion as the debtor) is given a power to set off debts in circumstances where the essence of the arrangement is to provide a form of security to the debtor. For example, it is common for banks to be given a power by contract to set off a customer's credit account against any debt owing by the customer, or a related company, to the bank as a result of the provision of financial accommodation. The question is whether the contractual right of set-off results in the creation of a charge over the credit account in favour of the bank as the debtor on that account. A contractual right of set-off would go beyond the right of set-off conferred by the Statutes of Set-off. The Statutes provide a procedural defence which requires an order of the court for its enforcement.[350] A set-off agreement, on the other hand, allows the debtor itself to effect a set-off and thereby obtain payment. 16.93

If the customer has gone into liquidation, and the circumstances in any event are such as to give rise to a set-off under the insolvency set-off section, it would often be of little practical consequence whether or not the set-off agreement has resulted in a charge in favour of the bank, because the same result would follow in any event. There may be cases, however, where the question would assume importance.[351] If a charge has been created, it would survive the insolvency of the person entitled to the credit account, and the bank could rely 16.94

---

[347] The circumstance that the collateral-provider is entitled to substitute equivalent financial collateral or to withdraw excess financial collateral does not prevent the financial collateral being in the possession or under the control of the collateral-taker. See the para. (c) of the definition of 'security financial collateral arrangement'.

[348] See the Companies Act 2006, s. 860(7)(g). In Australia, see the Corporations Act 2001 (Cth), s. 262(1)(a).

[349] This would include, for example, the clearing arrangement in *British Eagle International Air Lines Ltd v Compagnie Nationale Air France* [1975] 1 WLR 758. See para. 16.22 above.

[350] See paras 2.34–2.45 above.

[351] See also para. 16.74 above.

on it[352] notwithstanding that a set-off is not available under the insolvency set-off section. This may be important where, for example, the credit balance is held by one company in a group and banking accommodation is provided to another, because in such a case a lack of mutuality would prevent the operation of the set-off section. The issue could also arise in the context of a negative pledge which prohibits the granting of security. Further, if a company voluntary arrangement is proposed under Part I of the Insolvency Act, the arrangement must not affect the rights of a secured creditor without the concurrence of the creditor concerned,[353] and in that circumstance the question whether a set-off agreement is a charge may be crucial. When a company is in administration, Sch. B1, para. 43(2) of the Insolvency Act prohibits any step being taken to enforce 'security'[354] over the company's property except with the consent of the administrator or the permission of the court.[355] Pursuant to reg. 8(1)(a) of the Financial Collateral Arrangements (No. 2) Regulations 2003,[356] that restriction does not apply in the case of a 'financial collateral arrangement' (as defined[357]). But where the security does not arise under a financial collateral arrangement governed by the Regulations,[358] the question whether Sch. B1, para. 43(2) would prevent a bank exercising rights under a set-off agreement may depend on whether the agreement gives rise to a charge.[359]

---

[352] Subject to the question of registration. See paras 16.90–16.92 above.

[353] Insolvency Act 1986, s. 4(3) and Sch. A1 para. 39(4). In Australia, when it is proposed that a company execute a deed of company arrangement, or the company has executed such a deed, the court may order a secured creditor not to realize the security. See the Corporations Act 2001 (Cth), s. 444F(2). However, an order cannot be made under s. 444F(2) if the creditor has security over all or substantially all of the company's assets. See s. 441A. Clause 7(d) of Sch. 8A to the Corporations Regulations, which prescribes provisions to be incorporated into a deed of company arrangement save where the deed provides otherwise, provides that a creditor may not exercise any right of set-off to which the creditor would not have been entitled had the company been wound up. However, clause 7(d) is expressed to be subject to s. 444D, which (subject to the exceptions mentioned therein) preserves the position of secured creditors.

[354] Defined in the Insolvency Act, s. 248(b) as: 'any mortgage, charge, lien or other security.'

[355] See also the interim moratorium in relation to an administration application in Sch. B1, para. 44, and para. 12(1)(g) of Sch. A1 in relation to a moratorium under s. 1A of the Act in the case of a proposal for a company voluntary arrangement.

[356] S.I. 2003 No. 3226. See also reg. 8(5) in relation to the moratorium under para. 12(1)(g) of Sch. A1 of the Insolvency Act in the case of a proposal for a company voluntary arrangement.

[357] Regulation 3.

[358] This would be the case if the arrangement is not evidenced in writing, or if the subject of the charge is not in the possession or under the control of the deposit-taker (this could include a floating charge over a bank account which the customer is free to operate without restriction), or if the collateral-taker is a natural person, or in jurisdictions where the regulations do not apply.

[359] The term 'security' in this context has been interpreted broadly as including the exercise by a landlord of a right of re-entry for non-payment of rent. See *Exchange Travel Agency Ltd v Triton Property Trust plc* [1991] BCLC 396; *Re Olympia & York Canary Wharf Ltd* [1993] BCLC 453, 455, 456. On that basis, a 'security' could be said to include a set-off agreement, whether or not it is a charge. However, in *Re Lomax Leisure Ltd* [2000] Ch 502, Neuberger J declined to accept the view expressed in those cases in relation to the right of re-entry (though see now the Insolvency Act 1986, Sch. B1, para. 43(4), and also para. 12(1)(f) of Sch. A1 in relation to a moratorium under s. 1A of the Act, and ss. 252(2)(aa) and 254(1)(a) in relation to an interim order under Part VIII). In Australia the corresponding restriction in company administration, in s. 440B of the Corporations Act 2001 (Cth), is expressed to relate to enforcement of a 'charge', and the New South Wales Court of Appeal in *Cinema Plus Ltd v ANZ Banking Group Ltd* (2000) 49 NSWLR 513 held that the set-off agreement in issue in that case was not a charge for the purpose of s. 440B. Compare *Timbertown Community Enterprises Ltd v Holiday Coast Line Credit Union Ltd* (1997) 15 ACLC 1679, in which the issue was raised but not determined.

The view that a set-off agreement may give rise to a charge finds support in the judgment **16.95** of Harman J in *Re Tudor Glass Holdings Ltd, Franik Ltd and Thermal Aluminium Ltd.*[360] An officer of the BA group of companies referred in a letter to a director of the Tudor Glass group to the practice of 'contra accounting'. Harman J was prepared to accept that it was intended to provide security to the BA group in the event of a persistent delay in payment by the members of the Tudor Glass group, by allowing for a set-off of debts as between the two groups of companies. He doubted that the letter was effective to achieve that result, but if it had been he said that it would have constituted a floating charge, in which case it would have been void as against the receiver of the Tudor Glass group for want of registration under the companies legislation. More recently, it was accepted by the Canadian Supreme Court in *Caisse populaire Desjardins de l'Est de Drummond v Canada*[361] that a set-off agreement in some circumstances can constitute a security interest. Nevertheless, the contrary view has considerable support.[362] This includes comments by Lord Hoffmann in delivering the judgment of the House of Lords in *Re Bank of Credit and Commerce International SA (No. 8)*,[363] where a contractual right of set-off appears to have been contrasted with a proprietary interest. The comments were made in passing, however, and the issue was not analysed. What then is the basis of the view that a set-off agreement is not a charge? Statements to the effect that the agreement confers a purely personal right,[364] or that it gives no right over the creditor's asset,[365] do not advance the argument. They merely constitute different expressions of the conclusion. Why is the right is to be regarded as purely personal rather than proprietary?

The essence of an equitable charge is that specific property is appropriated to the discharge **16.96** of a debt or other obligation, without there being a change of ownership either at law or in

---

[360] (1984) 1 BCC 98,982.

[361] (2009) 309 DLR (4th) 323 (Rothstein J, McLachlin CJC, Binnie, Fish and Charron JJ concurring, Deschamps and LeBel JJ dissenting).

[362] See *Electro Magnetic (S) Ltd v Development Bank of Singapore Ltd* [1994] 1 SLR 734; *Griffiths v Commonwealth Bank of Australia* (1994) 123 ALR 111, 120; *Broad v Commissioner of Stamp Duties* [1980] 2 NSWLR 40, 48; *Bank of New Zealand v Harry M Miller & Co Ltd* (1992) 26 NSWLR 48, 54; *Commercial Factors Ltd v Maxwell Printing Ltd* [1994] 1 NZLR 724, 738; *Cinema Plus Ltd v ANZ Banking Group Ltd* (2000) 49 NSWLR 513 at [144]–[145] (Giles JA). Academic writers have also favoured the view that a set-off agreement is not a charge. See *Goode on Legal Problems of Credit and Security* (4th edn (ed. Gullifer), 2008), 13; Goode, *Commercial Law* (3rd edn, 2004), 610; Wood, *English and International Set-off* (1989), 148–50, 193–4; Hapgood, 'Set-off under the laws of England', in *Using Set-off as a Security* (ed. Neate, 1990), 32, 37. On the other hand, prior to *Re BCCI (No. 8)* [1998] AC 214, in which the House of Lords affirmed the conceptual validity of charge-backs, some writers had argued that, if the conceptual problem could be overcome, a set-off agreement could give rise to a charge. See Pollard, 'Credit balances as security – II' [1988] JBL 219, 220; Everett, 'Multi-party set-off agreements' [1993] *Journal of Banking and Finance Law and Practice* 180, 183–4 (in relation to a multi-party set-off agreement). See also Blair, 'Charges over cash deposits', *International Financial Law Review*, November 1983, 14; Yeowart, 'House of Lords upholds charge-backs over deposits', *International Financial Law Review*, January 1998, 7, 9.

[363] [1998] AC 214, 227.

[364] See e.g. *Goode on Legal Problems of Credit and Security* (4th edn (ed. Gullifer), 2008), 13.

[365] Goode, *Commercial Law* (3rd edn, 2004), 610.

equity.[366] A commonly cited definition is that of Atkin LJ in *National Provincial and Union Bank of England v Charnley*:[367]

> It is not necessary to give a formal definition of a charge, but I think there can be no doubt that where in a transaction for value both parties evince an intention that property, existing or future, shall be made available as security for the payment of a debt, and that the creditor shall have a present right to have it made available, there is a charge, even though the present legal right which is contemplated can only be enforced at some future date, and though the creditor gets no legal right of property, either absolute or special, or any legal right to possession . . .

No particular form of words is necessary in order to give rise to an equitable charge,[368] although there must be an intention to create a security.[369] The intention is not wholly subjective. As Buckley LJ observed in the Court of Appeal in *Swiss Bank Corporation v Lloyds Bank Ltd*,[370] an intention to create a security may be expressed or it may be inferred. An inference to that effect may be drawn from the construction of the agreement in the light of admissible evidence as to the surrounding circumstances, and if an agreement on its proper construction has the effect of creating a charge, it does not matter that the parties themselves did not realise that that was a consequence. They must be presumed to intend the consequences of their acts.[371] Brandon and Brightman LJJ agreed with Buckley LJ's judgment, and Browne-Wilkinson J commented to a similar effect at first instance.[372]

16.97 At first blush those principles seem apt to encompass some set-off agreements, for example where a bank as a condition to the grant of a facility requires that a deposit be made with it which the depositor is not permitted to access until all indebtedness under the facility has been paid, and the parties agree that the bank may set off the deposit against the debt in the event of default in payment. The essence of the arrangement is that the depositor's property, in the form of the account in credit resulting from the deposit, is to function as a security. Indeed, in the case of a charge-back in which express words of charge are used, a contractual set-off is the very remedy that would be contemplated,[373] and the House of Lords has now confirmed that a charge-back can be effective to create a proprietary interest

---

[366] *Carreras Rothmans Ltd v Freeman Mathews Treasure Ltd* [1985] 1 Ch 207, 227; *Re Bond Worth Ltd* [1980] 1 Ch 228, 248; *Re Charge Card Services Ltd* [1987] 1 Ch 150, 176; *Re Cosslett (Contractors) Ltd* [1998] Ch 495, 508; Megarry and Wade, *The Law of Real Property* (7th edn, 2008), 1092–3 [24–042]. See also *Bristol Airport plc v Powdrill* [1990] 1 Ch 744, 760. Compare *Palmer v Carey* [1926] AC 703, which is explained in *Re Gillott's Settlement* [1934] Ch 97, 109–10 and *Swiss Bank Corporation v Lloyds Bank* [1979] 1 Ch 548, 568.

[367] [1924] 1 KB 431, 449–50.

[368] *National Provincial and Union Bank of England v Charnley* [1924] 1 KB 431, 440 (Bankes LJ); *Gorringe v Irwell India Rubber and Gutta Percha Works* (1886) 34 Ch D 128, 134; Megarry and Wade, *The Law of Real Property* (7th edn, 2008), 1093 [24–042].

[369] *Re State Fire Insurance Co* (1863) 1 De G J & S 634, 641, 46 ER 251, 254; *National Provincial and Union Bank of England v Charnley* [1924] 1 KB 431, 449–50; *Swiss Bank Corporation v Lloyds Bank Ltd* [1982] AC 584, 595; Megarry and Wade, *The Law of Real Property* (7th edn, 2008), 1093 [24–042].

[370] [1982] AC 584, 595–6.

[371] See also *Smith v Bridgend County BC* [2002] 1 AC 336 at [42] and [53].

[372] [1979] 1 Ch 548, 569.

[373] Thus, when the Court of Appeal in *BCCI (No. 8)* [1996] Ch 245 held that a charge-back is conceptually impossible, it said (at 262) that the agreement would take effect as a contractual set-off, even if this were not expressly spelt out. Millett J expressed a similar view in *Re Charge Card Services Ltd* [1987] 1 Ch 150, 177.

in the indebtedness of the party asserting the right.[374] It would be odd in those circumstances if an express contractual stipulation for a set-off were to be regarded as inconsistent with a charge. In *Caisse populaire Desjardins de l'Est de Drummond v Canada*[375] the Supreme Court of Canada accepted that a set-off agreement in this situation would involve a security interest.

It has been suggested, however, that it is a characteristic of set-offs generally that they operate by way of the debtor (in the example, a bank) using its asset to pay its liability (on a deposit) to the creditor (being the bank's customer), as opposed to the debtor applying the creditor's asset (the claim against the debtor) in payment of the creditor's liability to the debtor.[376] That view forms the basis of a distinction that that has been drawn between contractual set-off and a charge. In the case of a charge, the debtor applies the creditor's asset over which the debtor has a charge to pay the creditor's liability to the debtor, whereas in the case of a contractual set-off it is said that the essence of the agreement is that the debtor applies the debtor's own asset to pay its liability.[377] Applying that analysis, when a bank has a contractual right of set-off against a customer's account in credit, the agreement does not operate by way of giving the bank a right to use the customer's asset, in the form of the account in credit, in order to satisfy the customer's debt to the bank. Rather, the bank satisfies its liability to the customer on the credit account by appropriating as payment its own asset in the form of the debt owing to it by the customer. On that basis, it is said that the agreement is not a charge. This reasoning suggests that the result may differ depending on whether a set-off agreement is drafted in terms of permitting A to set off B's debt to A (A's asset) against A's debt to B, as opposed to A setting off A's debt to B (B's asset) against B's debt to A.

16.98

In relation to the basic proposition as to how set-off functions, the various forms of set-off in truth operate differently and consequently it is difficult to generalize about them. In most forms of set-off, the setting of the demands against each other is not effected by the parties themselves. Thus, in the case of set-off in bankruptcy and company liquidation, the set-off occurs automatically at the date of the bankruptcy or the liquidation.[378] It is not profitable in that situation to consider which of the demands is set against the other. All that can be said is that the cross-claims are brought together, by force of statute, into an account. It is therefore difficult to reconcile the suggested definition of set-off with insolvency set-off. In relation to set-off under the Statutes of Set-off, the issue of set-off will arise when a debtor being sued for payment pleads as a defence a debt that the creditor owes to him or her, and in that sense it can be said that it involves the debtor using the debtor's own asset. But this is simply the means by which the issue is brought before the court. It is the judgment of the court which brings about the set-off,[379] not the act of the debtor, and the

16.99

---

[374] *Re Bank of Credit and Commerce International (SA) (No. 8)* [1998] AC 214.

[375] (2009) 309 DLR (4th) 323 at [24], [25] and [38].

[376] Wood, *English and International Set-off* (1989), 5.

[377] Wood, *English and International Set-off* (1989), 148–50, 193–4. See also *Krishell Pty Ltd v Nilant* (2006) 32 WAR 540 at [105]; Hapgood, 'Set-off under the laws of England', in *Using Set-off as a Security* (ed. Neate, 1990), 32, 37.

[378] See paras 6.119–6.146 above.

[379] See paras 2.34–2.45 above.

debts are merged in the judgment.[380] Where set-off is pleaded based on mutual debts, the first Statute of Set-off simply provided that 'one debt may be set against the other'.[381] There is no differentiation in the Statutes between the two debts in relation to the set-off. In the case of equitable set-off, the essence of the set-off is that a debtor has a cross-claim against the creditor which renders it unjust for the creditor to regard the debtor as having defaulted in payment. But once again, a right to an equitable set-off does not entitle the debtor to extinguish the debts at law. For that, a judgment of the court is still required.[382]

16.100 Contractual set-off differs fundamentally from those forms of set-off in that it is the act of the party possessed of the right which brings about the set-off. In that context, one can sensibly ask whether it is a case of the debtor paying its liability by the application of the debtor's own asset, or whether the essence of the agreement is that the contract allows the debtor to use the creditor's asset (the claim against the debtor) to discharge the creditor's liability to the debtor. Nevertheless, agreements drafted in the latter form are commonly described as conferring rights of set-off.[383] The term 'set-off' is not inapt in that context. As Rose LJ remarked in giving the judgment of the Court of Appeal in *Re BCCI (No. 8)*:[384]

> a debtor's right to appropriate a debt which he owes to his creditor and apply it in reduction or discharge of a debt which is owed to himself whether by the creditor or a third party is in our opinion accurately described as a right of set-off.

That proposition, in terms of the debtor appropriating the creditor's asset in reduction of the debt owed to the debtor, does not accord with the definition of 'set-off' that has been suggested, and brings that definition into question.

16.101 In the context of a set-off agreement which permits one party to set off cross-debts, there is no justification for limiting the term 'set-off' to a situation in which the debtor uses its asset to pay its debt, as opposed to using the creditor's asset to pay the creditor's debt. Both are appropriately described as set-offs. As a consequence, the question whether a particular agreement is a charge should not be determined by reference to whether it is labelled a 'set-off', but rather by an examination of the terms of the arrangement. The label itself means nothing. The true position is that some set-off agreements[385] are charges and some are not.[386]

16.102 A further observation may be made. Often, the view that in a set-off the debtor pays its liability using its own asset would not reflect the reality of the situation. Consider the

---

[380] *Stein v Blake* [1996] AC 243, 251.

[381] See para. 2.04 above.

[382] See paras 4.29–4.57 above.

[383] See e.g. the agreements in *Matthews v Geraghty* (1986) 43 SASR 576, 580–1, 582 ('letter of set-off'), *Lord v Direct Acceptance Corporation Ltd* (1993) 32 NSWLR 362, 364–5 ('Memorandum of Deposit and Set-off'), *Griffiths v Commonwealth Bank of Australia* (1994) 123 ALR 111, 115–16 (setting out the agreement), 121–4 (referring to set-off), and *Marathon Electrical Manufacturing Corp v Mashreqbank PSC* [1997] 2 BCLC 460, 468.

[384] [1996] Ch 245, 262. See also *Re Charge Card Services Ltd* [1987] 1 Ch 150, 177.

[385] Using the word 'set-off' in a sense which includes that referred to by the Court of Appeal in *Re BCCI (No. 8)* above.

[386] As recognized in the judgment of the majority in *Caisse populaire Desjardins de l'Est de Drummond v Canada* (2009) 309 DLR (4th) 323 (SC).

following scenario. A bank has provided a facility to a customer; as a form of security the bank is given the right to effect a set-off against a deposit in the customer's (or a related company's) name; the 'trigger' for doing so is the customer's default; the customer (or the related company) has not sought repayment of the deposit; and the bank required the deposit and the right of set-off as a form of security in the event of the customer's insolvency, in which case the bank's asset (the claim against the customer) may be worthless. It would be artificial to say that the substance of the transaction is that the bank in effecting a set-off pays its debt on the deposit by the application of its own asset, rather than that the debt owing by the customer in default is satisfied by the application of the customer's asset, in the form of the deposit. In other situations involving set-offs, the courts have shown a preparedness to have regard to the substance of the transaction.[387] Consider *Kent's Case*[388] in relation to preferences. Mr Kent held partly paid shares in a company. He took an assignment of a debt owing by the company, and wrote to the directors requesting them to transfer from the amount due in respect of the debt a sum sufficient to pay up his shares in full. The directors then passed a resolution that: 'the debt assigned by Mr Eichholz to Mr Kent as aforesaid should be applied in paying up in full the shares mentioned in Mr. Kent's letter of this date.' Shortly afterwards, an order was made to wind up the company. Assuming that the resolution would otherwise have constituted payment of the amount owing on the shares,[389] it was held that the transaction was void as a preference.[390] But for that result to follow, the transaction had to be regarded as a payment or a transfer of property *by the company* as a debtor in favour of Kent as a creditor,[391] notwithstanding that the directors' resolution was cast in terms that Kent's asset, in the form of the assigned debt, should be used to pay his liability. Plainly, given the company's insolvency, that was not the substance of the transaction. A similar situation occurred in New South Wales. In *Re Atlas Engineering Co (Davy's Case)*[392] a shareholder requested the company to apply a debt due to him from the company in settlement of the amount unpaid on his shares, and he was given a receipt acknowledging that the company had received the sum. As in *Kent's Case*, this was held to be a preference in the company's liquidation, Owen J regarding it as a payment by the company, notwithstanding that the request and the receipt suggested that the shareholder was using his asset to pay his liability.[393]

---

[387] This also accords with the approach of the majority in *Caisse populaire Desjardins de l'Est de Drummond v Canada* (2009) 309 DLR (4th) 323 (see esp. at [25]) (SC).

[388] *Re Land Development Association (Kent's Case)* (1888) 39 Ch D 259.

[389] It was held that the transaction did not support a plea of payment in cash since the debt due by the company was not presently payable and nor was the liability on the shares.

[390] See also *Re Washington Diamond Mining Co* [1893] 3 Ch 95.

[391] See the Bankruptcy Act 1883, s. 48, being the preference section in issue, which was made applicable to company liquidation by the Companies Act 1862, s. 164. Cotton LJ referred to the transaction as an agreement to anticipate payment of the debt owing on the assigned debt and to receive by anticipation the sum payable on the shares. See (1888) 39 Ch D 259, 266. Fry and Lopes LJJ, on the other hand, simply characterized the transaction as a fraudulent preference.

[392] (1889) 10 LR (NSW) Eq 179, 6 WN (NSW) 64.

[393] The question could also arise in relation to an allegation that a company's property has been disposed of after the commencement of its winding up, contrary to the Insolvency Act 1986, s. 127. Consider that a company's claim against a debtor is the subject of a contractual right of set-off in favour of the debtor, and a set-off is not available under the insolvency set-off section. After the commencement of the company's liquidation the debtor purports to effect a set-off. If the liquidator asserts that the set-off constituted a void

16.103 In New South Wales, Giles JA in *Cinema Plus Ltd v ANZ Banking Group Ltd*[394] offered a different explanation as to why a set-off agreement is not a charge. The case concerned an agreement which entitled a bank at any time to 'combine, consolidate, merge or apply any credit balance in any of [the customer's] accounts' towards payment of any moneys owing by the customer to the bank. The question was whether this was a charge for the purpose of s. 440B of the Corporations Law in Australia, which rendered a charge given by a company unenforceable while the company was in administration.[395] His Honour said that a charge, being proprietary in nature, must in its nature be assignable. In the case of the agreement in issue, he said that it could only be given effect by the bank by a book entry. Because it could only be given effect in that manner, he said that the agreement was of no use to anyone other than the bank, and effectively it was not assignable. On that basis, he concluded that it was a personal right, and did not confer a proprietary interest.[396] In *Caisse populaire Desjardins de l'Est de Drummond v Canada*,[397] the Canadian Supreme Court[398] rejected the suggestion that the circumstance that a set-off is given effect by means of a book entry detracts from the view that it is a security interest. But apart from that, the reasoning of Giles JA is questionable on a more fundamental ground.

16.104 Giles JA's analysis reflects one of the criteria which Lord Wilberforce in *National Provincial Bank Ltd v Ainsworth*[399] said must be satisfied before a right or interest can be admitted into the category of property, that it must be capable in its nature of assumption by third parties.[400] Millett LJ had recourse to this criterion in *Re Cosslett (Contractors) Ltd*[401] as a test for determining whether the circumstances in issue gave rise to an equitable charge. The case concerned a right possessed by an employer under a building contract to retain possession

---

disposition, it is unlikely that the court would be attracted to an argument that the company's property in truth was not disposed of, but rather it was a repayment of the debt owing to the company by an application of the debtor's asset. In *Barclays Bank Ltd v TOSG Trust Fund Ltd* [1984] BCLC 1, 24–6 Nourse J contemplated that a set-off taking effect after the commencement of a winding up could constitute a void disposition, and there was also a suggestion to that effect in *Couve v J Pierre Couve Ltd* (1933) 49 CLR 486, 494 (however, the avoidance of the disposition of the goods the subject of the sale in that case meant that there was no debt for the price, and therefore no set-off against that debt). See also Goode, *Principles of Corporate Insolvency Law* (3rd edn, 2005), 494. On the other hand, Otton J in *In re K (Restraint Order)* [1990] 2 QB 298, 305 considered that the exercise of a contractual right of set-off was not a 'disposing of' assets for the purpose of the Drug Trafficking Offences Act 1986. Compare also *Re Loteka Pty Ltd* [1990] 1 Qd R 322, 324. Nourse J's comment in the *TOSG* case (at 25–6) that, in the event of a conflict between the insolvency set-off section and the void disposition section the latter prevails, cannot be supported. See para. 6.162 above.

[394] (2000) 49 NSWLR 513 at [144] and [145].

[395] There is an exception in the case of a charge over the whole or substantially the whole of the company's property. See the Corporations Act 2001 (Cth), s. 441A.

[396] A more compelling reason is that there was no intention to create a security. See Spigelman CJ (2000) 49 NSWLR 513 at [46] and para. 16.107 below.

[397] (2009) 309 DLR (4th) 323 at [32].

[398] Rothstein J, McLachlin CJC, Binnie, Fish and Charron JJ concurring, Deschamps and LeBel JJ dissenting.

[399] [1965] AC 1175.

[400] Lord Wilberforce said: 'Before a right or an interest can be admitted into the category of property, or of a right affecting property, it must be definable, identifiable by third parties, capable in its nature of assumption by third parties, and have some degree of permanence or stability.' See [1965] AC 1175, 1247–8. Similarly, Plowman J in *Re Button's Lease* [1964] 1 Ch 263, 272 said that: 'It is inherent in the nature of a piece of property that the owner of it should be able to dispose of it.'

[401] [1998] Ch 495, 508.

of the contractor's equipment and to use it to complete the works. One of the reasons that Millett LJ gave for holding that this was not an equitable charge was that it did not create a 'transmissible interest'. Australian courts, however, have rejected the proposition that an interest must in its nature be assignable in order that it may be characterized as proprietary. Kitto J made that point in *National Trustees Executors and Agency Co of Australasia Ltd v Federal Commissioner of Taxation*:[402]

> It may be said categorically that alienability is not an indispensable attribute of a right of property according to the general sense which the word 'property' bears in the law. Rights may be incapable of assignment, either because assignment is considered incompatible with their nature, as was the case originally with debts (subject to an exception in favour of the King) or because a statute so provides or considerations of public policy so require, as is the case with some salaries and pensions; yet they are all within the conception of 'property' as the word is normally understood: *Ex parte Huggins; In re Huggins* (1882) 21 Ch D 85, at p 91; *Hollinshead v Hazleton* [1916] 1 AC 428, at p 447.

In *Federal Commissioner of Taxation v Orica Ltd*,[403] the High Court of Australia referred to those observations with evident approval. On another occasion, Mason J commented that, while it is generally correct to say that proprietary rights are capable in their nature of assumption by third parties, assignability is not in all circumstances an essential characteristic of a right of property.[404] The same point has been made on other occasions,[405] including by English text-writers.[406] On this view, it should not be fatal to the argument that a set-off agreement may be a charge that effectively it may not be assignable.

But even apart from the question whether assignability is necessary for a proprietary interest, the objection raised by Giles JA would not be relevant to all set-off agreements. The set-off agreement in issue in the *Cinema Plus* case referred to a right to 'combine, consolidate, merge or apply' a credit balance. In the case of a right to 'combine', 'consolidate' or 'merge' accounts, it is, as Giles JA pointed out, difficult to see how it could be given effect other than by way of a book entry by the bank holding the deposit. However, a set-off agreement may be drafted instead in terms of the bank being entitled to 'apply', or 'appropriate', a customer's account in credit in reduction or discharge of the customer's debt.[407]

16.105

---

402 (1954) 91 CLR 540, 583. See also Dixon J at 558.

403 (1998) 194 CLR 500, 537 (Gaudron, McHugh, Kirby and Hayne JJ), 542–3 (Gummow J).

404 *R v Toohey, ex p Meneling Station Pty Ltd* (1982) 158 CLR 327, 342–3.

405 *Dorman v Rodgers* (1982) 148 CLR 365, 374; *Australian Capital Television Pty Ltd v The Commonwealth* (1992) 177 CLR 106, 165–6; *Georgiadis v Australian and Overseas Telecommunications Corporation* (1994) 179 CLR 297, 311–12; *Wily v St George Partnership Banking Ltd* (1998) 84 FCR 423, 432 (criticizing the view of Lord Wilberforce in *National Provincial Bank Ltd v Ainsworth* [1965] AC 1175, 1247–8); *Meagher, Gummow and Lehane's Equity Doctrines and Remedies* (4th edn, 2003), 126–7 [4–015]. Jackson (*Principles of Property Law* (1967), 42) said that the ability to deal with an interest is not a criterion which should be adopted to decide the existence of a proprietary interest, but rather it should be treated as a *prima facie* right following from the classification of an interest as proprietary. See also in Canada *Delgamuuk v British Columbia* (1997) 153 DLR (4th) 193, 241 (Lamer CJC, with whom Cory, McLachlin and Major JJ concurred). Compare *Krishell Pty Ltd v Nilant* (2006) 32 WAR 540 at [73] and [75].

406 Gray and Gray, *Elements of Land Law* (5th edn, 2009), 98 [1.5.30]; Pettit, *Equity and the Law of Trusts* (11th edn, 2009), 21 ('a property right can exist without all of these elements being present').

407 See e.g. the agreements in *Matthews v Geraghty* (1986) 43 SASR 576 ('appropriate and transfer the whole or any part of any credit balance . . . to payment in whole or in part of any debit balance'), *Lord v Direct Acceptance Corporation Ltd* (1993) 32 NSWLR 362 ('redeem and/or appropriate the Deposit . . . in total or

In that regard, the Court of Appeal accepted in *Re BCCI (No. 8)*[408] that a right in a debtor to appropriate a debt which it owes to the creditor and apply it in reduction of a debt which is owed to the debtor (whether by the creditor or a third party) is accurately described as a right of set-off. A right to appropriate or apply differs from a right to 'combine', 'consolidate' or 'merge' accounts, in that those latter rights each contemplate the bringing together of two debts to produce a balance, as opposed to a dealing in relation to one of the debts by applying or appropriating that debt in satisfaction or reduction of the other. Further, in contrast to a consolidation or a combination or a merger, a right to appropriate or apply a credit balance could be given effect other than by way of book entry by the bank holding the deposit, in which case it should be capable of assumption by a third party. Thus, the debt representing the credit balance conceivably could be appropriated by way of a sale, a court-ordered sale and the appointment by the court of a receiver being the primary remedies of an equitable chargee.[409] Alternatively, consistent with the principle that security on an asset extends also to its products and proceeds,[410] a right to appropriate or apply a credit balance towards payment should also include a right to appropriate or apply the proceeds of the credit balance.[411] In other words, the credit balance could be repaid, and the proceeds used to pay the security holder. As Millett LJ remarked in *Royal Trust Bank v National Westminster Bank plc*:[412] 'I do not see how it can be possible to separate a debt or other receivable from the proceeds of its realisation.' An agreement in those terms therefore would not suffer from the difficulty suggested by Giles JA in the *Cinema Plus* case. Indeed, a charge is often defined in terms of an 'appropriation' of specific property to the discharge of a debt,[413] and it would be surprising if an agreement expressed in terms of an appropriation of a deposit were to be characterized differently to an agreement which referred instead to a charge.

16.106 Consider the case of a specific deposit made by a customer with a bank as a result of the bank's requirement for 'cash cover' for a facility provided either to the customer or to a third party, the deposit being on terms that it cannot be withdrawn until all amounts actually or

---

partial satisfaction of the Debt'), *Griffiths v Commonwealth Bank of Australia* (1994) 123 ALR 111 ('prepay and apply the whole or any part of the deposit . . . in or towards payment of the moneys owing'), and *Marathon Electrical Manufacturing Corp v Mashreqbank PSC* [1997] 2 BCLC 460, 468 ('set off transfer or apply all or any of the monies standing to the credit of any current account or deposit account').

[408] [1996] Ch 245, 262. See para. 16.100 above.

[409] Megarry and Wade, *The Law of Real Property* (7th edn, 2008), 1127 [25–050]; Sykes and Walker, *The Law of Securities* (5th edn, 1993), 198.

[410] Goode, *Commercial Law* (3rd edn, 2004), 583–4, 618 (and also *Goode on Legal Problems of Credit and Security* (4th edn (ed. Gullifer), 2008), 42); Oditah, *Legal Aspects of Receivables Financing* (1991), 25; *Re Cosslett (Contractors) Ltd* [1998] Ch 495, 508.

[411] Sometimes the clause itself makes this clear. In *Lord v Direct Acceptance Corporation Ltd* (1993) 32 NSWLR 362 the clause was in terms of '*redeem* and/or appropriate' the deposit (emphasis added), while in *Griffiths v Commonwealth Bank of Australia* (1994) 123 ALR 111 it referred to the right to '*prepay* and apply' the deposit (emphasis added).

[412] [1996] 2 BCLC 682, 704. See also *Agnew v Commissioner of Inland Revenue* [2001] 2 AC 710 at [46].

[413] *Carreras Rothmans Ltd v Freeman Mathews Treasure Ltd* [1985] 1 Ch 207, 227; *Re Bond Worth Ltd* [1980] 1 Ch 228, 248; *Re Cosslett (Contractors) Ltd* [1998] Ch 495, 508.

contingently owing under the facility have been paid, and in the event of a default the bank is given the right to appropriate or apply the deposit in reduction of amounts owing to it under the facility. Since it is not necessary to use any particular form of words in order to create a charge,[414] once the objection to a debtor taking a charge over its own debt is removed there is force in the argument that the agreement results in the creation of a security interest.[415] This should be so notwithstanding the contrary view expressed in Australia by Lee J in *Griffiths v Commonwealth Bank of Australia*,[416] which concerned an agreement in similar terms to those posited.[417] The agreement would appear to come squarely within Cotton LJ's definition of a charge over a debt in *Gorringe v Irwell India Rubber and Gutta Percha Works*:[418]

> When there is a contract for value between the owner of a chose in action and another person which shews that such person is to have the benefit of the chose in action, that constitutes a good charge on the chose in action. The form of words is immaterial so long as they shew an intention that he is to have such benefit.

Further, if, as the Court of Appeal has accepted,[419] an agreement for an appropriation in those terms is accurately described as a set-off, it should not make any difference that the agreement is expressed in terms of setting off the deposit against the amounts owing, as opposed to appropriating or applying the deposit. The reasoning of the majority in the Canadian Supreme Court in *Caisse populaire Desjardins de l'Est de Drummond v Canada*[420] supports this view.

Nevertheless, the applicable circumstances in the case of each contract would require consideration. The above scenario should be contrasted with a standard clause in a bank loan agreement to the effect that the bank can appropriate (or set off) any account in credit that the customer may have with the bank in discharge of the loan, but without a deposit specifically being required for the purpose of security, and without there being an obligation to maintain such an account and without imposing restrictions on withdrawals. Ordinarily, the clause should not result in the creation of a charge in favour of the bank. It is not a case of specific property being permanently appropriated to the discharge of a

16.107

---

[414] *National Provincial and Union Bank of England v Charnley* [1924] 1 KB 431, 440 (Bankes LJ); *Gorringe v Irwell India Rubber and Gutta Percha Works* (1886) 34 Ch D 128, 134.

[415] This conclusion is consistent with the reasoning of Spigelman CJ in *Cinema Plus Ltd v ANZ Banking Group Ltd* (2000) 49 NSWLR 513 at [46]. Compare Sheller JA at [113]–[116]. He said (at [116]) that the set-off agreement in that case was not a charge because it was 'no greater and no different in nature from the right enjoyed [by the bank] at law to combine current accounts'. That was not the case, however. Combination is entirely different from contractual set-off. Combination proceeds on the basis that the balance of all the accounts represents the debt. See para. 15.04 above. A contractual set-off, on the other hand, assumes that the accounts are separate debts which the bank may set off in order to produce a single debt. The set-off can only operate in a situation in which the accounts are not combined.

[416] (1994) 123 ALR 111, 120.

[417] The agreement in *Griffiths v Commonwealth Bank of Australia* provided that, so long as any moneys remained owing or payable to the bank, the bank was under no obligation to repay the deposit, and: 'the bank may without prior notice to me/us prepay and apply the whole or any part of the deposit and interest accrued thereon in or towards payment of the moneys owing or any part thereof.'

[418] (1886) 34 Ch D 128, 134.

[419] *Re BCCI (No. 8)* [1996] Ch 245, 262 (CA). See para. 16.100 above.

[420] (2009) 309 DLR (4th) 323 at [24], [25] and [34]–[39].

debt,[421] and it does not manifest an intention to create a present right over property of the customer.[422] Nor should it constitute a floating charge. It has been said to be a characteristic of a floating charge that it is a charge on fluctuating assets,[423] but that is not an apt description of a situation in which there may not be and may not ever be an account in credit. The agreement suggests an intention to provide the bank with a simple means of effecting payment to the extent of any cash that may be at hand, but without appropriating an account as security. Indeed, any charge which the agreement might be thought to create would be so precarious that, in the absence of clear language, no such intention ought to be imputed.[424] On that basis, the decision of the Singapore Court of Appeal in *Electro Magnetic (S) Ltd v Development Bank of Singapore Ltd*,[425] that an agreement in those terms was not a charge, would appear to be correct. It is distinguishable from *Re Tudor Glass Holdings*,[426] because in that case the essence of the arrangement was that there would be cross-demands, the purpose of the arrangement being to provide protection to the BA group of companies for an increase in the indebtedness of the Tudor Glass group.[427] It is also distinguishable from *Caisse populaire Desjardins de l'Est de Drummond v Canada*,[428] in which the deposit was required to be maintained for five years and it was expressed to be not assignable.

K. Flawed Asset

16.108 Consider that a bank wishes to provide financial accommodation to a customer secured by a cash deposit provided either by the customer or a third party. As an alternative to a charge-back or a set-off agreement, or as additional protection, the deposit may be on terms constituting it a 'flawed asset'. In other words, repayment of the deposit is expressed to be conditional, or contingent, upon the customer satisfying its obligations to the bank under the facility. Until the obligations are satisfied, the deposit is not repayable.[429] The condition on repayment of the deposit is not a charge,[430] and therefore it is not

---

[421] *Re Spectrum Plus Ltd* [2005] 2 AC 680 at [138].

[422] See Spigelman CJ in *Cinema Plus Ltd v ANZ Banking Group Ltd* (2000) 49 NSWLR 513 at [42] and [46], referring (at [41] and [42]) to *National Provincial and Union Bank of England v Charnley* [1924] 1 KB 431, 449–50 (Atkin LJ). See also *Southern Wine Corporation Pty Ltd v Frankland River Olive Co Ltd* (2005) 31 WAR 162 at [108]–[110].

[423] *Agnew v Commissioner of Inland Revenue* [2001] 2 AC 710 at [19]; *Re Cosslett (Contractors) Ltd* [1998] Ch 495, 510; *Smith v Bridgend County BC* [2002] 1 AC 336 at [41]. However, while this is a characteristic usually found in floating charges, it should not be a necessary requirement. Thus, Professor Goode has suggested that a floating charge can be made to cover any description of property, including land. See Goode, *Commercial Law* (3rd edn, 2004), 679.

[424] As in *Swiss Bank Corporation v Lloyds Bank Ltd* [1982] AC 584, 614.

[425] [1994] 1 SLR 734. See also *Caisse populaire Desjardins de l'Est de Drummond v Canada* (2009) 309 DLR (4th) 323 at [33], [36], [39] and [54] (SC).

[426] (1984) 1 BCC 98,982. See para. 16.95 above.

[427] See the discussion at (1984) 1 BCC 98,982, 98,984.

[428] (2009) 309 DLR (4th) 323.

[429] See *Fraser v Oystertec plc* [2006] 1 BCLC 491. A security deposit may be made on terms that it will mature and become payable if it is to be appropriated by the bank in discharge of a debt owing to the bank, and otherwise it is not repayable until the debt has been repaid in full. See e.g. *Lord v Direct Acceptance Corporation Ltd* (1993) 32 NSWLR 362, 365–6.

[430] This seems to have been assumed in *Re Bank of Credit and Commerce International SA (No. 8)* [1998] AC 214, 227. See also *Hoverd Industries Ltd v Supercool Refrigeration and Air Conditioning (1991) Ltd* [1995] 3 NZLR 577, 588.

registrable.[431] Nevertheless, it should still be effective in the bankruptcy or liquidation of the depositor.[432] After insolvency, the deposit remains a flawed asset subject to the same contractual restriction on repayment as before. That was the view of the Court of Appeal in *Re Bank of Credit and Commerce International SA (No. 8)*,[433] and observations on appeal in the House of Lords suggest that their Lordships were of the same opinion.[434] Moreover, if a flawed asset is used in conjunction with a charge-back and in a particular case the charge-back was registrable,[435] failure to register, while it would render the charge void as against a liquidator, should not affect the contractual restriction on the right to repayment.[436]

If the deposit is made by a third party, and the depositor is not personally liable for the debt,[437] lack of mutuality would prevent a set-off in the depositor's or the customer's bankruptcy or liquidation against the customer's debt to the bank. Because of the contractual restriction on withdrawal the bank would not have to repay the deposit, and to that extent it would be protected.[438] Nevertheless, the debts would retain their separate identities and would not be set off. Alternatively, the deposit may be made by the customer itself. In that circumstance, if the customer goes into liquidation, the Court of Appeal in *Re BCCI (No. 8)*[439] assumed that the deposit may be set off against the customer's debt to the bank under the insolvency set-off section. At the time when the case was decided, that assumption was doubtful. If the customer was in liquidation, its claim against the bank on the deposit would have been contingent upon satisfaction of its debt to the bank. But, unlike a contingent liability of a company in liquidation, at that time a contingent claim possessed by a company could not be set off in its liquidation until the contingency occurred.[440] Therefore, as long as the customer remained indebted to the bank, a set-off should not have been available in the customer's liquidation against the deposit. The position in company liquidation has changed, however, since *Re BCCI (No. 8)* was decided. Following amendments to the Insolvency Rules in 2005,[441] a contingent debt owing to a company in liquidation has been put in the same position for the purpose of set-off as

16.109

---

[431] In Australia, a flawed asset arrangement is a security interest for the purpose of the Personal Property Securities Act 2009 (Cth) (see s. 12(2)(l)) and may be registered under the Act. Registration is not necessary for the validity of the arrangement, but it constitutes a means of ensuring that it is enforceable against third parties. See ss. 20, 21 and 43. Where the subject of a flawed asset arrangement is a bank deposit (or 'ADI account'), the security will be 'perfected' without registration because the bank has control of the deposit. See ss. 21(2) and 25(1).

[432] Compare *Hoverd Industries Ltd v Supercool Refrigeration and Air Conditioning (1991) Ltd* [1995] 3 NZLR 577, 584, 587, in which the New Zealand Court of Appeal accepted that the condition linking the payment obligation with redemption of the preference shares was not intended to apply in a winding up, since it was not possible in a winding up to redeem the shares.

[433] [1996] Ch 245, 262–3.

[434] [1998] AC 214, 227.

[435] But see paras 16.90–16.92 above.

[436] See the analogous situation considered in *Re Cosslett (Contractors) Ltd* [1998] Ch 495, 511.

[437] As in *Re BCCI (No. 8)* [1998] AC 214.

[438] Compare Calnan, 'The insolvent bank and security over deposits' (1996) 11 *Journal of International Banking and Financial Law* 185, 190, and 'Security over deposits again: BCCI (No. 8) in the House of Lords' (1998) 13 *Journal of International Banking and Financial Law* 125, 127.

[439] [1996] Ch 245, 262–3.

[440] See para. 8.35 above.

[441] See para. 6.06 above.

a contingent debt owing by the company.[442] The liquidator may estimate the value of the contingent debt and that estimation may be included in a set-off.[443] However, a similar amendment has not been made to the bankruptcy set-off section,[444] and so in that context the criticism of the assumption made in *Re BCCI (No. 8)* remains valid. Moreover, the law has not changed in either bankruptcy or company liquidation in Australia, and so that criticism remains valid in that jurisdiction.

16.110   In any event, apart from the question of set-off, the condition on repayment should still have the consequence that the bank would not have to repay the deposit, and to that extent it would remain protected.[445]

---

[442] See para. 8.35 above.
[443] Insolvency Rules 1986, rr. 4.90(4) and (5), referring to r. 4.86.
[444] Insolvency Act 1986, s. 323.
[445] See above.

17

ASSIGNEES, AND OTHER INTERESTED THIRD PARTIES

A. Introduction

17.01 Consider that A is indebted to B, and that a third party, C, has an interest in the debt. This may arise, for example, because C is an assignee, or the holder of a security interest, or the beneficiary of a trust, or an undisclosed principal, or a person with subrogation rights, or a judgment creditor levying execution on B's asset in the form of the debt. If A has a cross-claim against B that would otherwise be eligible for a set-off against the debt, A would be concerned to know whether the set-off is still available notwithstanding the interest of C. Alternatively, if A has a cross-claim against C, the question may arise whether the cross-claim can be set off against A's debt to B, given C's interest in the debt. Some general principles were considered earlier in the context of a discussion of mutuality.[1] The purpose of this chapter is to consider the availability of a set-off in cases involving assignments, crystallized floating securities, trusts, execution creditors and subrogation rights. Undisclosed principals[2] were considered earlier, as were assignments in the context of the principle in *Cherry v Boultbee*[3] and combination of bank accounts.[4] In addition, the Contracts (Rights of Third Parties) Act 1999 in some circumstances permits a person who is not a party to a contract to enforce a term in the contract which purports to confer a benefit on him or her, and the chapter concludes with a brief discussion of set-off in that situation.

---

[1] See ch. 11 above.
[2] See paras 13.79–13.99 above.
[3] See paras 14.63–14.78 above.
[4] See paras 15.121 above.

B. Assignments[5]

When a debt is assigned,[6] a set-off may occur as between the assignee's beneficial interest in the assigned debt and a cross-claim that the debtor has against the assignee.[7] In addition, there is a general equitable principle[8] that, in some circumstances, an assignee takes subject to equities, which include rights of set-off,[9] that are available to the debtor as against the assignor.[10]   **17.02**

(1) Equitable assignment

Consider the case of an equitable assignment of a common law debt.[11] Commonly, the question of set-off will arise in the situation in which the assignor is indebted to the debtor on a cross-debt that is independent of the assigned debt. When the assignee sues for payment of the assigned debt, the debtor asserts that the debts should be set off under the Statutes of Set-off,[12] notwithstanding the assignment. The basic principle is that, if the cross-debt arose after the debtor had notice of the assignment, the debtor cannot set it off against the assignee, but that a set-off is available if the cross-debt arose before the debtor had notice.[13] In *N W Robbie & Co Ltd v Witney Warehouse Co Ltd*[14] the Court of Appeal sought to explain the denial of a set-off in relation to a post-notice cross-debt on the ground that the demands are not equitably mutual. The assigned debt is owned beneficially by the assignee, whereas the cross-debt constitutes a claim against the assignor. This is not a convincing explanation, however. It fails to explain why a set-off is allowed to the debtor when the cross-debt arose after the assignment but before the debtor had notice of the assignment, because in the period between assignment and notice mutuality determined   **17.03**

---

[5] For a critique of the rules governing set-off in the case of an assignment, see Tettenborn, 'Assignees, equities and cross-claims: principle and confusion' [2002] LMCLQ 485.

[6] This includes an assignment by way of mortgage and a sub-mortgage. See *Popular Homes Ltd v Circuit Developments Ltd* [1979] 2 NZLR 642 (sub-mortgage) and compare *Clairview Developments Pty Ltd v Law Mortgages Gold Coast Pty Ltd* [2007] 2 Qd R 501 at [42].

[7] See paras 3.07, 11.13 and 11.18 above. See e.g. *Moore v Jervis* (1845) 2 Coll 60, 63 ER 637; *Horrobin v Australia & New Zealand Banking Group Ltd* (1996) 40 NSWLR 89, 93. Compare *Society of Lloyd's v Leighs* [1997] 6 Re LR 289.

[8] Compare the pre-Judicature Acts, common law case of *Watkins v Clark* (1862) 12 CB (NS) 277, 142 ER 1149.

[9] It has been suggested that the rule that an assignee takes subject to equities is distinct from the rule that an assignee takes subject to defences. See *Goode on Legal Problems of Credit and Security* (4th edn (ed. Gullifer), 2008), 319. The better view is that it is the one rule albeit that the concept of 'equities' has a number of aspects or categories. See e.g. Smith, *The Law of Assignment* (2007), 91–2, 365–70.

[10] Save possibly in some situations involving equitable set-off (see para. 17.84 below), the debtor could not set off a debt owing by a person other than the assignor (or the assignee). See *First National Bank of Chicago v West of England Shipowners Mutual Protection and Indemnity Association (The Evelpidis Era)* [1981] 1 Lloyd's Rep 54.

[11] See para. 17.04 below in relation to an assignment which complies with the Law of Property Act 1925, s. 136(1).

[12] See paras 2.04–2.62 above. In Australia, see paras 2.63–2.86 above.

[13] See paras 17.13–17.15 below.

[14] [1963] 1 WLR 1324, 1339 (Russell LJ, with whose reasons Sellers LJ (at 1331) agreed). See also *Coba Industries Ltd v Millie's Holdings (Canada) Ltd* [1985] 6 WWR 14, 28–9; *Telford v Holt* (1987) 41 DLR (4th) 385, 394.

by reference to beneficial titles similarly would be lacking.[15] The preferred analysis[16] is that at common law mutuality for the purpose of the Statutes of Set-off is determined by reference to legal titles, so that if cross-debts are legally mutual there is a *prima facie* right to a set-off under the Statutes. The question then becomes whether equity regards it as unconscionable for the debtor to rely on this right of set-of otherwise available at law when the equitable title to one of the debts is in someone else.[17] This reflects the position that applied before the Judicature Acts. An assignment of a debt was not then generally recognized by the common law courts, in the sense that the assignee could not enforce the debt in a common law action brought in his or her own name.[18] The assignee was required to sue in the name of the assignor. If the assignor refused to allow his or her name to be used, the assignor could be compelled to do so by a court of equity. As far as the common law was concerned, however, the resulting action to enforce the debt was still the assignor's action, and unless equity intervened defences available to the debtor against the assignor, including pursuant to the Statutes of Set-off, could be asserted in that action. Equity would not enjoin the debtor at the request of the assignee from raising defences that arose before the debtor had notice of the assignment.[19] However, it was considered unconscionable for the debtor to diminish the rights of the assignee by relying on defences that accrued after the debtor had notice of the assignment,[20] and so in that situation the assignee could obtain an injunction to restrain the debtor from relying on the defence.[21] The Judicature Acts brought about a fusion of the courts of law and equity,[22] but the courts nevertheless have

---

[15] See para. 11.19 above.

[16] See paras 11.18–11.20 above.

[17] This draws on the analysis in *Meagher, Gummow and Lehane's Equity Doctrines and Remedies* (4th edn, 2002), 943–4 [28–335]. See also Blackburn J in *Wilson v Gabriel* (1863) 4 B & S 243, 247–8, 122 ER 450, 452, referred to in *Christie v Taunton, Delmard, Lane and Co* [1893] 2 Ch 175, 182, and *Hoverd Industries Ltd v Supercool Refrigeration and Air Conditioning (1991) Ltd* [1995] 3 NZLR 577, 587.

[18] The major reasons put forward for the non-assignability of choses in action at law are discussed in Marshall, *The Assignment of Choses in Action* (1950), 34 *et seq*. There were nevertheless a number of situations in which the common law recognized the transfer of a debt. See Warren, *The Law Relating to Choses in Action* (1899), 34–45 and Starke, *Assignments of Choses in Action in Australia* (1972), 10–11.

[19] This has been explained on the ground that equity will not intervene when the equities are equal. *Wilson v Gabriel* (1863) 4 B & S 243, 248, 122 ER 450, 452.

[20] This notion underlies the explanation in *Roxburghe v Cox* (1881) 17 Ch D 520, 526 (James LJ). See also *Meagher, Gummow and Lehane's Equity Doctrines and Remedies* (4th edn, 2002), 943–4 [28–335]; *Long Leys Co Pty Ltd v Silkdale Pty Ltd* (1991) 5 BPR 11,512, 11,519 (NSW CA).

[21] As Bramwell B expressed it, the question was: 'taking the set-off to be available at law, would equity restrain the defendants from relying on it?' See *Higgs v The Northern Assam Tea Co Ltd* (1869) LR 4 Ex 387, 394.

[22] It was suggested in *United Scientific Holdings Ltd v Burnley Borough Council* [1978] AC 904 that the Judicature Acts also brought about a fusion of the principles of law and equity. This view has been attacked as heretical. See Baker, 'The future of equity' (1977) 93 LQR 529; *Meagher, Gummow, and Lehane's Equity Doctrines and Remedies* (4th edn, 2002), 76–7 [2–295]; Martin, 'Fusion, fallacy and confusion; a comparative study' [1994] *The Conveyancer* 13. See also *MCC Proceeds Inc v Lehman Bros International (Europe)* [1998] 4 All ER 675, 690–1 (equitable title not sufficient to found a common law claim in conversion) and Sir Peter Millett, 'Equity – the road ahead' (1995) 9 *Tolley's Trust Law International* 35, 37. In *Bank of Boston Connecticut v European Grain and Shipping Ltd* [1989] 1 AC 1056, 1109 the House of Lords said that the Judicature Acts: 'while making changes to procedure, did not alter the rights of the parties.' Compare *Bank of Credit and Commerce International SA v Ali* [2002] 1 AC 251 at [17] *per* Lord Bingham ('More than a century and a quarter have passed since the fusion of law and equity . . .'), and Burrows, 'We do this at common law but that in equity' (2002) 22 OJLS 1, 4.

continued to apply the principle that an assignee is bound by equities arising before notice. Moreover, notwithstanding the fusion, and notwithstanding the modern view as to enforcement, that an equitable assignee may sue in his or her own name subject to a requirement (which can be dispensed with in exceptional circumstances[23]) of joining the assignor as a party to the action,[24] the explanation should still be the same.

(2) Statutory assignment

The Judicature Acts[25] also introduced a statutory form of assignment, the successor of which is set out in s. 136(1) of the Law of Property Act 1925.[26] In order to come within this provision, the assignment must be in writing, it must be absolute and not by way of charge only, and express notice in writing must be given to the debtor. When the section is complied with, the assignee obtains the legal title to the debt and may sue in his or her own name without joining the assignor. The operation of the section has a hybrid quality. It has been said that it enables an assignee to acquire a title that has all the procedural advantages of a legal title but so far as priorities are concerned the assignee's position is no better than if the assignment had been effected in equity.[27] The section preserves the equitable principle that an assignee takes subject to equities, so that a debtor can rely, as against a statutory assignee, on a right of set-off that would have prevailed against an equitable assignee before the Judicature Acts.[28] This includes a set-off at common law under the Statutes of Set-off.[29] On the other hand, because the assignor is not a party to the action, the debtor cannot counterclaim in the action for the excess of the assignor's indebtedness to him or her over and above the amount of the assigned debt.[30]

17.04

(3) Australia: Personal Property Securities Act 2009 (Cth)[30a]

In Australia, the Personal Property Securities Act 2009 (Cth) establishes a national law governing security interests in personal property. Section 12 defines 'security interest'

17.05

---

[23] Compare *Commercial Factors Ltd v Maxwell Printing Ltd* [1994] 1 NZLR 724; *Thomas v National Australia Bank Ltd* [2000] 2 Qd R 448, 458, 460.

[24] *Three Rivers District Council v Bank of England* [1996] QB 292, 313, 315 (Peter Gibson LJ); *Raffeisen Zentralbank Osterreich AG v Five Star Trading LLC* [2001] QB 825 at [60] (Mance LJ). In Australia, see also *Long Leys Co Pty Ltd v Silkdale Pty Ltd* (1991) 5 BPR 11,512, 11,517; *McIntyre v Gye* (1994) 51 FCR 472, 480; *Brookfield v Davey Products Pty Ltd* (1996) 14 ACLC 303, 305; *Chapman v Luminis Pty Ltd* (1998) 86 FCR 513, 519. Compare *Meagher, Gummow and Lehane's Equity Doctrines and Remedies* (4th edn, 2002), 285–7 [6–515].

[25] Supreme Court of Judicature Act 1873, s. 25(6).

[26] In Australia, see e.g. the Conveyancing Act 1919 (NSW), s. 12.

[27] *Pfeiffer GmbH v Arbuthnot Factors Ltd* [1988] 1 WLR 150, 162–3, adopting a submission by counsel in those terms. Therefore, in the case of a priorities dispute between a prior equitable assignment of a debt and a subsequent statutory assignment, the principle of *bona fide* purchaser of a legal title for value without notice does not apply. Rather, Phillips J accepted in the *Pfeiffer* case (at 163) that the dispute is to be determined on the basis of the rule in *Dearle v Hall* (1828) 3 Russ 1, 38 ER 475.

[28] *Lawrence v Hayes* [1927] 2 KB 111, 120–1; *Roadshow Entertainment Pty Ltd v (ACN 053 006 269) Pty Ltd* (1997) 42 NSWLR 462, 482.

[29] *Glencore Grain Ltd v Agros Trading Co* [1999] 2 Lloyd's Rep 410, 420.

[30] *Young v Kitchin* (1878) 3 Ex D 127; *Mitchell v Purnell Motors Pty Ltd* [1961] NSWR 165, 168; *Franks v Equitiloan Securities Pty Ltd* [2007] NSWSC 812 (appeal allowed in part *Equititrust Ltd v Franks* (2009) 256 ALR 388).

[30a] The new system under the Act is due to begin operating in May 2011.

broadly as including the interest of a transferee of an 'account' or a 'chattel paper', whether or not the particular transaction secures a payment or the performance of an obligation.[31] Therefore, an absolute transfer of an 'account' or a 'chattel paper' is governed by the Act. Those concepts are defined in s. 10. Essentially, an 'account' is a debt that arises from disposing of property (whether by sale, lease, licence or in any other way) or granting a right or providing services in the ordinary course of business, and a 'chattel paper' is a 'writing'[32] that evidences a monetary obligation and a security interest in, or a lease of, specific goods, or a security interest in specific intellectual property or a specific intellectual property licence. Section 80(1) sets out the 'taking subject to equities' principle in the case of those transfers. It provides that the rights of a transferee of an account or chattel paper are subject to:

(a) the terms of the contract between the debtor and the transferor and any equity, defence, remedy or claim arising in relation to the contract (including a defence by way of a right of set-off); and

(b) any other equity, defence, remedy or claim of the debtor against the transferor (including a defence by way of right of set-off) that accrues before the first time when payment by the debtor to the transferor no longer discharges the obligation of the debtor under s. 80(8) of the Act to the extent of the payment.

Section 80 preserves the basic rule, that a transferee takes subject to equities and defences, though it gives rise to a number of difficulties.[33] Apart from s. 80, the Act is expressed not to apply to rights of set-off or combination of accounts.[34] It should not therefore affect the application of the principles discussed below in relation to assignments of other forms of debt.

(4) Cross-demand must be available as a set-off against the assignor

17.06 An assignee takes subject to a cross-demand available to the debtor against the assignor only if the cross-demand would have been available as a set-off as between the assignor and the debtor in circumstances where neither was insolvent.[35] It has been suggested in Australia that in some cases a cross-demand that would not have given rise to a set-off in an action by the assignor against the debtor nevertheless may be asserted against the assignee.[36] This is

---

[31] Section 12(3).

[32] Defined broadly in s. 10 as including the recording of words or data in any way.

[33] See paras 17.11–17.12, 17.22–17.24, 17.31 and 17.35 below.

[34] Section 8(1)(d), but see s. 8(2).

[35] See paras 17.39 and 17.42 below. See e.g. the statement of the principle in *Norrish v Marshall* (1821) 5 Madd 475, 481, 56 ER 977, 980.

[36] *McDonnell & East Ltd v McGregor* (1936) 56 CLR 50, 60 (Dixon J). See also *Re K L Tractors Ltd* [1954] VLR 505, 508; *Bayview Quarries Pty Ltd v Castley Developments Pty Ltd* [1963] VR 445, 449; *Edward Ward & Co v McDougall* [1972] VR 433, 438–9; *Provident Finance Corporation Pty Ltd v Hammond* [1978] VR 312, 320; *James v Commonwealth Bank of Australia* (1992) 37 FCR 445, 461–2; *Re Partnership Pacific Securities Ltd* [1994] 1 Qd R 410, 423–4; *Walker v Department of Social Security* (1995) 56 FCR 354, 363–4, 367; *Roadshow Entertainment Pty Ltd v (ACN 053 006 269) Pty Ltd* (1997) 42 NSWLR 462, 482; *Franks v Equitiloan Securities Pty Ltd* [2007] NSWSC 812 at [25] (but compare at [38]) (appeal allowed in part *Equititrust Ltd v Franks* (2009) 256 ALR 388); Spry, 'Equitable Set-offs' (1969) 43 *Australian Law Journal* 265, 269–70 (although the treatment in Spry, *Equitable Remedies* (8th edn, 2010) 178 is more equivocal); *Meagher, Gummow & Lehane's Equity Doctrines and Remedies* (4th edn, 2002), 284 [6–500] (' 'equity' means in this context a defence, set-off or counterclaim'), 1060–2 [37–050]. In *Clyne v Deputy Commissioner of*

contrary to the view expressed by the House of Lords in *Bank of Boston Connecticut v European Grain and Shipping Ltd*,[37] and it should not be accepted as correct.

The origin of that suggestion is a statement by Lord Hobhouse in the Privy Council **17.07** in *Government of Newfoundland v Newfoundland Railway Co*[38] in the context of a claim by an assignee for payment of sums due under a construction contract:

> Unliquidated damages may now be set off as between the original parties, and also as against an assignee if flowing out of and inseparably connected with the dealings and transactions which also give rise to the subject of the assignment.

That statement was adopted by Lord Brandon of Oakbrook in the House of Lords in the *Bank of Boston* case as setting out the applicable test for an equitable set-off as between the original parties, to which an assignee also takes subject.[39] Traditionally, an equitable set-off was said to be available where the connection between the claimant's claim and the defendant's cross-claim was such that the claimant's title to sue was impeached.[40] Lord Brandon said that the concept of impeachment is not a familiar one today, and formulated the test instead by reference to whether the defendant's cross-claim could be characterized as 'flowing out of and inseparably connected with the dealings and transactions which also give rise to' the claimant's claim.[41] This was said to be merely a different version of the impeachment test,[42] but in truth it is broader. Thus, it is difficult to see how the formulation adopted in the *Bank of Boston* case could ever operate to deny an equitable set-off when the same transaction is the source of both demands, whereas in the context of the traditional impeachment test it has been said that it is not sufficient for an equitable set-off that the cross-demands arose out of the one transaction.[43] In Australia the courts have tended to be more rigorous than those in England in emphasizing impeachment of title as the basis of equitable set-off,[44] and in order to distinguish the statement in *Government of Newfoundland v Newfoundland Railway Co*, which formed the foundation of the test approved in *Bank of Boston v European Grain and Shipping*, it has been suggested that the *Government of Newfoundland* case in truth was not concerned with determining the availability of an equitable set-off as between the debtor and the assignor in that case. Rather, it was concerned with the question whether an assignee of a contract could recover moneys owing under it without being met by a counterclaim for breach by the assignor of the

---

Taxation (1981) 150 CLR 1, 20, Mason J (with whose judgment Aickin and Wilson JJ agreed) said that the word 'equities' in the context of the expression 'an assignment is subject to equities' comprehends 'set-off and counterclaims'. However, the point was not discussed in any detail, and Mason J proceeded (at 20–1) to express the principle in terms of an assignee taking subject to 'any defence or set-off available to the debtor at the time when notice of assignment is given', without referring to counterclaim.

[37] [1989] 1 AC 1056, 1105–6, 1109–11.

[38] (1888) 13 App Cas 199, 213.

[39] [1989] 1 AC 1056, 1106, 1110–11. The Appellate Division of the Alberta Supreme Court in *Kaps Transport Ltd v McGregor Telephone & Power Construction Co Ltd* (1970) 73 WWR 549, 552 similarly treated this as a test for set-off between original parties.

[40] See para. 4.02 above.

[41] [1989] 1 AC 1056, 1103.

[42] [1989] 1 AC 1056, 1102.

[43] See para. 4.14 above.

[44] See paras 4.19–4.28 above.

same contract.[45] It is said to have been assumed in the *Government of Newfoundland* case that Newfoundland legislation similar to s. 25(6) of the Supreme Court of Judicature Act 1873 (UK) applied to the assignment.[46] That legislation conferred a statutory power to assign debts,[47] and it provided that the assignee took 'subject to all equities which would have been entitled to priority over the right of the assignee if this Act had not been passed'. The argument proceeds that the equities to which the assignee took subject included not only claims which might have been set off in equity, but also cross-demands which, whilst affording no defence and giving rise only to a counterclaim, under the old system would have founded a common injunction against the enforcement of the plaintiff's claim.[48] By confining the case to assignments, the view has been expressed that *Government of Newfoundland v Newfoundland Railway Co* does not provide a good juridical root for any changed doctrine of equitable set-off.[49]

17.08   However, whether or not the Privy Council in the *Government of Newfoundland* case correctly stated the relevant test for equitable set-off, it is apparent, for reasons set out in greater detail elsewhere,[50] that it proceeded on the basis that a set-off can be asserted against an assignee only because it could also be asserted against the assignor.[51] The case does not support a proposition that a cross-claim that arises from the transaction which gave rise to the assigned debt may be asserted against the assignee in circumstances where it would not have supported a set-off as against the assignor. Indeed, it is difficult to find any pre-Judicature Acts authority for the proposition that a debtor being sued by an equitable assignee of the debt, but in the name of the assignor, could obtain a common injunction to restrain the action on the basis solely of a cross-demand that would not have given rise to set-off (in its various forms) against the assignor in the absence of an assignment. In the first edition of *Kerr on Injunctions*, published in 1867 only a short time before the enactment of the Judicature Acts, there is no mention of an injunction being available in that circumstance.[52] On the contrary, the principle is stated simply in terms that: 'The assignee of a chose in action takes subject to any equitable right of set-off existing as against the

---

[45]   *McDonnell & East Ltd v McGregor* (1936) 56 CLR 50, 60 (Dixon J). Thus, in *Roadshow Entertainment Pty Ltd v (ACN 053 006 269) Pty Ltd* (1997) 42 NSWLR 462, 482 the New South Wales Court of Appeal said that an assignee takes subject to cross-claims for unliquidated damages arising out of the contract which gave rise to the assigned debt, without requiring any other connection. See also *Parsons v Sovereign Bank of Canada* [1913] AC 160, 166 (PC). Yet the Privy Council in *Government of Newfoundland v Newfoundland Railway Co* (1888) 13 App Cas 199, 212 acknowledged that: 'There is no universal rule that claims arising out of the same contract may be set against one another in all circumstances.' This accords with the generally accepted view in relation to equitable set-off. See para. 4.91 above.

[46]   *James v Commonwealth Bank of Australia* (1992) 37 FCR 445, 461.

[47]   See now the Law of Property Act 1925, s. 136(1). See para. 17.04 above.

[48]   *James v Commonwealth Bank of Australia* (1992) 37 FCR 445, 461.

[49]   *James v Commonwealth Bank of Australia* (1992) 37 FCR 445, 462.

[50]   Derham, 'Recent issues in relation to set-off' (1994) 68 *Australian Law Journal* 331, 334–7.

[51]   See *Bank of Boston Connecticut v European Grain and Shipping Ltd* [1989] 1 AC 1056, 1110–11, approving of Hobhouse J's first instance discussion of the *Government of Newfoundland* case in *Colonial Bank v European Grain and Shipping Ltd (The Dominique)* [1987] 1 Lloyd's Rep 239, 254–7. See also *Geldof Metaalconstructie NV v Simon Carves Ltd* [2010] EWCA Civ 667 at [30] and [32].

[52]   In Ch 4, dealing with equitable grounds for relief against proceedings at law, or in ch. 3, dealing with injunctions to restrain proceedings at law.

assignor at the date of or before notice of the assignment . . .'[53] Further, if a common injunction would not have been available before the Judicature Acts, an argument that s. 25(6) of the 1873 Act[54] itself was the source of a debtor's right to assert the cross-demand against the assignee would not be tenable given that the Judicature Acts were purely procedural.[55] In so far as *Young v Kitchen*[56] has been referred to as a case in which an assignee took subject to a cross-demand that might not have been available as a set-off against the assignor,[57] it is relevant to note the central point made by counsel for the defendant (Bompas QC) in his successful argument in favour of the set-off. He is reported as having argued that: 'Whatever defence might be set up against the assignor may be set up against his assignee, for the assignee cannot be in a better position than his assignor.'[58] In other words, counsel for the debtor regarded it as a case in which the assignee took subject to a defence that was available against the assignor. It was not argued in the alternative that, even if the debtor's unliquidated cross-demand could not have been set off in an action brought by the assignor in his own right, the assignee nevertheless should still take subject to the cross-demand. Nor did Baron Cleasby make any such point in his judgment.[59]

The theory proposed in Australia originated in a discussion of *Government of Newfoundland v Newfoundland Railway Co* by Dixon J in *McDonnell & East Ltd v McGregor*.[60] Dixon J suggested in the *McDonnell* case that set-off is not available against a claim for damages.[61] That proposition has now been discredited in relation to equitable set-off,[62] but it may have influenced his view that the *Government of Newfoundland* case was not a case of equitable set-off. Moreover, in so far as it has been sought to justify the decision in the *Government of Newfoundland* case by reference to a notion that an assignee of a contract cannot take the benefit of the contract without also assuming the burden,[63] that explanation would be of doubtful validity in Australia following the rejection, by the Full Court of the Victorian

17.09

---

[53] *Kerr on Injunctions* (1867), 68.

[54] See paras 17.04 and 17.07 above.

[55] *Meagher, Gummow and Lehane's Equity Doctrines and Remedies* (4th edn, 2002), 1060 [37–050].

[56] (1878) 3 Ex D 127.

[57] *Meagher, Gummow and Lehane's Equity Doctrines and Remedies* (4th edn, 2002), 1060–1 [37–050].

[58] (1878) 3 Ex D 127, 129.

[59] See Hobhouse J's discussion of *Young v Kitchen* at first instance in the *Bank of Boston* case: *Colonial Bank v European Grain and Shipping Ltd* (*The Dominique*) [1987] 1 Lloyd's Rep 239, 253–4. Note also the explanation of *Smith v Parkes* (1852) 16 Beav 115, 51 ER 720 in Derham, 'Recent issues in relation to set-off' (1994) 68 *Australian Law Journal* 331, 335.

[60] (1936) 56 CLR 50, 59–60.

[61] (1956) 56 CLR 50, 62.

[62] See e.g. *Beasley v Darcy* (1800) 2 Sch & Lef 403n; *Galambos & Son Pty Ltd v McIntyre* (1974) 5 ACTR 10 (and the cases there referred to); *Knockholt Pty Ltd v Graff* [1975] Qd R 88; *United Dominions Corporation Limited v Jaybe Homes Pty Ltd* [1978] Qd R 111; *British Anzani (Felixstowe) Ltd v International Marine Management (UK) Ltd* [1980] 1 QB 137, 145–6.

[63] *Aries Tanker Corporation v Total Transport Ltd* [1977] 1 WLR 185, 193 (Lord Simon of Glaisdale). In *Government of Newfoundland v Newfoundland Railway Co* (1888) 13 App Cas 199, 212, Lord Hobhouse commented that: 'It would be a lamentable thing if it were found to be the law that a party to a contract may assign a portion of it, perhaps a beneficial portion, so that the assignee shall take the benefit, wholly discharged of any counter-claim by the other party in respect of the rest of the contract, which may be burdensome.' See also *Roadshow Entertainment Pty Ltd v (ACN 053 006 269) Pty Ltd* (1997) 42 NSWLR 462, 482; *Business Computers Ltd v Anglo-African Leasing Ltd* [1977] 1 WLR 578, 585 (referred to in *John Dee Group Ltd v WMH (21) Ltd* [1997] BCC 518, 530).

Supreme Court in *Government Insurance Office (NSW) v K A Reed Services Pty Ltd*,[64] of the broad benefit and burden principle advocated by Megarry VC in *Tito v Waddell (No. 2)*.[65] Indeed, the House of Lords in *Bank of Boston Connecticut v European Grain and Shipping Ltd*[66] specifically rejected the benefit and burden principle as an explanation for the *Government of Newfoundland* case.

Claim for freight, and claim on a negotiable instrument

17.10 If the claim assigned is such that as a matter of law it is not susceptible to a set-off as between solvent parties, not because of a lack of connection between the demands but because of its nature, the assignee similarly will take free of a set-off.[67] This includes a claim for freight under a charterparty in circumstances where the charterer has a cross-claim for damages against the shipowner,[68] and a claim on a negotiable instrument where the issuer has an unliquidated cross-claim arising out of the transaction in respect of which the instrument was issued.[69]

Australia: Personal Property Securities Act 2009 (Cth)

17.11 In relation to the principle that the cross-claim must have been available as a set-off against the assignor, further difficulty arises in Australia consequent upon the enactment of s. 80(1) of the Personal Property Securities Act 2009 (Cth) in the case of a transfer of an 'account' or a 'chattel paper' (as defined in the Act).[70]

17.12 Section 80(1)(a) provides that a transferee takes subject to 'any equity, defence, remedy or claim arising in relation to the contract (including a defence by way of a right of set-off).' The express references to both 'claim' and 'defence' (including a defence by way of a right of set-off) suggest that a 'claim' to which a transferee takes subject is not synonymous with a 'defence'. The only requirement in relation to a 'claim' is that it must have arisen 'in relation to the contract' between the debtor and the transferor, which is broader than the principle which governs the availability of equitable set-off.[71] Paragraph (1)(b) of s. 80 goes even further. It provides that the transferee's rights are subject to 'any other equity, defence, remedy or claim of the account debtor against the transferor (including a defence

---

[64] [1988] VR 829 (Brooking J, with whom O'Bryan and Nicholson JJ agreed). See also *Calaby Pty Ltd v Ampol Pty Ltd* (1990) 102 FLR 186, 205; *Ashton v Australian Cruising Yacht Co Pty Ltd* [2005] WASC 192 at [62]; *Meagher, Gummow and Lehane's Equity Doctrines and Remedies* (4th edn, 2002), 97 [3–100], 1187 [43–160]. The question was left open, however, in *Konstas v Southern Cross Pumps and Irrigation Pty Ltd* (1996) 217 ALR 310, 313–14. In England the 'pure principle of benefit and burden' was criticized in *Rhone v Stephens* [1994] 2 AC 310, 322, which in turn was referred to in *Gallagher v Rainbow* (1994) 179 CLR 624, 648 (McHugh J), and see also *Amsprop Trading Ltd v Harris Distribution Ltd* [1997] 1 WLR 1025, 1034–5 and *Thamesmead Town Ltd v Allotey* [1998] 3 EGLR 97. Compare Aughterson, 'In defence of the benefit and burden principle' (1991) 65 *Australian Law Journal* 319.

[65] [1977] 1 Ch 106, 289 *et seq.*

[66] [1989] 1 AC 1056, 1105–6.

[67] *Bank of Boston Connecticut v European Grain and Shipping Ltd* [1989] 1 AC 1056.

[68] See paras 5.02–5.24 above.

[69] See paras 5.25–5.49 above.

[70] See para. 17.05 above.

[71] Thus, it does not suffice for equitable set-off that cross-claims arise out of the same contract. See para. 4.91 above.

by way of a right of set-off)' that accrues before the time referred to in s. 80(8).[72] Apart from that temporal limitation, there is no required connection on the face of para. (1)(b) between the assigned claim and the debtor's cross-claim against the transferor. The lack of a required connection accords with the position under the Statutes of Set-off, which apply to mutual debts. The debts need not be connected.[73] The Statutes do not extend to damages claims. For that, reliance must be placed upon equitable set-off, but for that form of set-off the cross-claims must be connected.[74] Thus, there is no set-off under either the Statutes or the principles of equitable set-off in relation to an unconnected damages claim.[75] But, on a literal reading of s. 80(1), a transferee of an account or a chattel paper could take subject to a totally unrelated cross-claim in damages available to the debtor against the transferor that accrued before the relevant time, for example an unrelated claim in defamation. If correct, this could substantially affect the rights of transferees and would represent a significant departure from the general law position. Section 80(1) is headed '*Rights of transferee subject to contractual terms and defences*'. The heading suggests that the section is directed at claims which give rise to a *defence*, and s. 80(1) should be construed in that manner.[76] Though the section heading is not part of the Act,[77] consideration may be given to it if it is capable of assisting in the ascertainment of the meaning of the section in circumstances where the ordinary meaning would lead to a result which is manifestly absurd or unreasonable.[78]

(5) Statutes of Set-off

Date of notice

Mutual debts in existence between the debtor and the assignor at the date that the debtor receives notice of the assignment may give rise to a set-off under the Statutes of Set-off enforceable against the assignee.[79] This should also apply where the cross-debt owing by the assignor to the debtor was acquired by the debtor as a result of an assignment before notice,[80]

17.13

---

[72] Essentially, before the debtor has notice of the assignment. See paras 17.22–17.24 below.

[73] See para. 2.14 above.

[74] See ch. 4 above.

[75] Note, however, the position in Victoria. See paras 2.83–2.86 above.

[76] Section 80(1) specifically refers to a defence by way of a right of set-off, but *prima facie* that would not pick up a claim which gives rise to a common law defence of abatement. See para. 2.134 above.

[77] Acts Interpretation Act 1901 (Cth), s. 13.

[78] Acts Interpretation Act 1901 (Cth), s. 15AB(1)(b). For the application of the Acts Interpretation Act to the Personal Property Securities Act, see s. 11 of the latter Act.

[79] See e.g. *Smith v Parkes* (1852) 16 Beav 115, 51 ER 720; *Chick v Blackmore* (1854) 2 Sm & Giff 274, 65 ER 398; *Stephens v Venables (No. 1)* (1862) 30 Beav 625, 54 ER 1032; *Roxburghe v Cox* (1881) 17 Ch D 520; *Lawrence v Bell* (1866) 14 WR 753; *Biggerstaff v Rowatt's Wharf Ltd* [1896] 2 Ch 93; *Re Smith & Co Ltd* [1901] 1 IR 73. See also *Peters v Soame* (1701) 2 Vern 428, 23 ER 874, which was decided before the enactment of the Statutes of Set-off. *Contra* if the assignor becomes indebted to the debtor after the debtor received notice of the assignment. See *Wolfe v Marshall* [1997] EWCA Civ 1329, and also para. 17.15 below. The statement in *Glencore Grain Ltd v Agros Trading Co* [1999] 2 Lloyd's Rep 410, 420 (CA), that an assignment takes effect subject to any right of set-off which is available to the debtor against the assignor, should be read subject to the limitation relating to notice of the assignment. Compare para. 14.75 above in relation to the situation in which a trustee obtains an order for costs against a beneficiary as a result of a failed action brought by the beneficiary against the trustee, and the beneficiary assigned his or her interest in the trust after commencement of the action but before judgment.

[80] See e.g. *Tony Lee Motors Ltd v M S MacDonald & Son (1974) Ltd* [1981] 2 NZLR 281 (company receivership). Compare *N W Robbie & Co Ltd v Witney Warehouse Co Ltd* [1963] 1 WLR 1324 (see para. 17.105 below), in which the assignment occurred after notice.

including where there is an effective assignment without consideration.[81] In the case of set-off under the Statutes of Set-off, the debts are not set against each other until judgment for a set-off.[82] Notice of an assignment given to the debtor itself does not effect a set-off.[83] As a corollary, there must not only be mutual debts in existence at the date of notice but the set-off must also be available when the debtor is sued by the assignee and files his or her defence. If therefore the cross debt is not enforceable at that time,[84] or if the court in the assignee's action would not determine the cross-debt, for example because it is subject to an arbitration clause or a foreign jurisdiction clause,[85] the assignee will not be subject to the set-off.[86]

Presently payable

17.14 It is not necessary that the pre-existing cross-debt owing by the assignor to the debtor should have been presently payable before the date of notice.[87] It should suffice if it is payable when the defence is filed.[88] It has been said, however, that, if the assigned debt was not presently payable at the date of notice, in order that the cross-debt may be set off it should have become payable before the assigned debt became payable.[89] The reason for that limitation is unclear. The set-off in issue is the procedural defence provided by the Statutes of Set-off. If the cross-debt owing by the assignor is in existence before notice, it should be sufficient if it is payable at the date that the defence is filed regardless of when the assigned debt became payable. Indeed, it is difficult to reconcile the suggested limitation with *Christie v Taunton, Delmard, Lane and Co*.[90] The case concerned an assignment of debentures issued by a company. Notice of the assignment was given to the company on 6 November 1890. Prior to that date, on 3 November, a call was made on shares held by the assignor, which call was payable on 20 November. The debentures on their face were not payable until 31 December, but in the event of the winding up of the company the principal moneys secured by them were to become immediately due and payable. On 19 November the company went into voluntary liquidation. Both the company's liability on the debentures and the assignor's liability for the call constituted existing debts at the date of notice, although they were not payable until after that date. Stirling J held that the company could bring them into an account, notwithstanding that, because of the

---

[81] For a discussion of consideration in relation to assignments of choses in action, see Keeton and Sheridan, *Equity* (3rd edn, 1987), 239 *et seq.*

[82] See para. 2.35 above.

[83] *Glencore Grain Ltd v Agros Trading Co* [1999] 2 Lloyd's Rep 410, 417–19.

[84] See para. 2.46 above.

[85] See para. 2.51 above.

[86] *Glencore Grain Ltd v Agros Trading Co* [1999] 2 Lloyd's Rep 410.

[87] *Jeffryes v Agra and Masterman's Bank* (1866) LR 2 Eq 674; *Christie v Taunton, Delmard, Lane and Co* [1893] 2 Ch 175; *Re Pinto Leite and Nephews, ex p Visconde des Olivaes* [1929] 1 Ch 221. See also *Downes v Bank of New Zealand* (1895) 13 NZLR 723; *Business Computers Ltd v Anglo-African Leasing Ltd* [1977] 1 WLR 578, 585.

[88] *Stein v Blake* [1996] AC 243, 251. See paras 2.08–2.12 above.

[89] *Re Pinto Leite and Nephews* [1929] 1 Ch 221, 234–6, explaining *Jeffryes v Agra and Masterman's Bank* (1866) LR 2 Eq 674, 680. See also *Downes v Bank of New Zealand* (1895) 13 NZLR 723, 734; *Business Computers Ltd v Anglo-African Leasing Ltd* [1977] 1 WLR 578, 584.

[90] [1893] 2 Ch 175, discussed in *Clyne v Deputy Commissioner of Taxation* (1981) 150 CLR 1, 21–2.

occurrence of the winding up, the assignor's indebtedness for the call matured after the assigned debt became due and payable.[91]

Subsequent debt arising out of a prior contract

There must be an existing debt owing by the assignor to the debtor before notice.[92] It is not **17.15** considered sufficient for a set-off that a debt accrues in favour of the debtor from the assignor after notice as a result of a contract entered into before notice.[93] Thus, where a debtor had leased property to the creditor, and the creditor assigned the debt, it was held that the assignee was not subject to a set-off in respect of rent which accrued to the debtor/lessor after notice of the assignment, even though the lease was entered into before notice.[94] This is an undesirable result. Set-offs should be favoured in circumstances where there was a possibility of a perception of a form of security in the existence of cross-demands,[95] and this should be ascertained by reference to the state of affairs existing when a binding contractual relationship was entered into, as opposed to when a debt arose as a result of the contract. It should suffice that there are presently payable cross-debts at the date of the action which arose out of contractual obligations incurred before notice. Consistent with that approach, an exception to the established principle may arise in circumstances where there was a temporary suspension of mutuality.[96] For example, if a debtor before notice of an assignment of the debt by the creditor held a negotiable instrument upon which the creditor was liable, which the debtor indorsed to a third party before notice, and after notice the debtor was obliged to take up the instrument again as a result of the creditor's default, the assignee would take subject to the debtor's right to set off the resulting claim against the creditor/assignor on the instrument. The availability of a set-off in this situation

---

[91] In addition, calls were made in the winding up. See para. 8.69 above.

[92] Compare para. 17.25 below in relation to the debt assigned. Compare also equitable set-off. See para. 17.32 below.

[93] *Stephens v Venables (No. 1)* (1862) 30 Beav 625, 54 ER 1032; *Watson v Mid Wales Railway Co* (1867) LR 2 CP 593. See also *Woodhams v Anglo-Australian and Universal Family Assurance Co* (1861) 3 Giff 238, 66 ER 397 (call on shares made after notice); *Re China Steamship Co, ex p Mackenzie* (1869) LR 7 Eq 240, 243; *Christie v Taunton, Delmard, Lane and Co* [1893] 2 Ch 175, 181; *Re Bailey Cobalt Mines Ltd* (1919) 45 DLR 585 (judgment in misfeasance action obtained after notice); *Re Pinto Leite and Nephews* [1929] 1 Ch 221, 233–4; *Business Computers Ltd v Anglo-African Leasing Ltd* [1977] 1 WLR 578 (see esp. at 585). This is also consistent with *Unity Joint Stock Mutual Banking Association v King* (1858) 25 Beav 72, 79–80, 53 ER 563, 566, for which see para. 3.06 above. Compare *John Dee Group Ltd v WMH (21) Ltd* [1997] BCC 518, 530 (decision affirmed [1998] BCC 972 without reference to this point) in relation to the return of the initial down payment, although Neuberger J relied on a misstatement in *Business Computers Ltd v Anglo-African Leasing Ltd* [1977] 1 WLR 578, 585 of the facts in issue in *Rother Iron Works Ltd v Canterbury Precision Engineers Ltd* [1974] 1 QB 1 (the company rather than the debtor was the seller of the goods), and in any event the question in relation to that payment concerned the quantum and the timing of the obligation, as opposed to whether there was an existing debt. Compare also the exceptional fact situation in *Ralston v South Greta Colliery Co* (1912) 13 SR (NSW) 6. See paras 4.64 and 4.66 above.

[94] *Watson v Mid Wales Railway Co* (1867) LR 2 CP 593. See also *Stephens v Venables (No. 1)* (1862) 30 Beav 625, 54 ER 1032.

[95] See para. 6.20 above.

[96] See paras 6.105–6.107 above in relation to company liquidation.

has been recognized in the context of company receivership,[97] and questions of set-off in that context are governed by the same principles which apply to assignments.[98]

(6) Set-off in Australia[99]

New South Wales and Queensland

17.16 The Statutes of Set-off have been repealed in Queensland,[100] which should have as a consequence that the only form of set-off to which an assignee in that jurisdiction takes subject is equitable set-off, together with analogous rights such as pursuant to the principle in *Cherry v Boultbee*[101] and combination of bank accounts.[102]

Victoria

17.17 In Victoria, it has been suggested that SCR r. 13.14 has had the effect that any cross-claim, whether liquidated or unliquidated, may now be included in the defence and be the subject of a set-off.[103] That proposition may be debated,[104] but if the rule does operate in that manner *prima facie* it would have a corresponding effect on the position of an assignee. It could be said that an expanded defence under the rule would not apply in the case of a legal assignment by a creditor which complies with s. 134 of the Property Law Act 1958 (Vic).[105] The argument would be that r. 13.14 is expressed to apply where 'a defendant has a claim against a plaintiff for the recovery of a debt or damages . . .', and in the case of an assignment satisfying s. 134 the assignee is the plaintiff. The argument would proceed that the rule can have no application in relation to a cross-claim against the assignor, who is not the plaintiff, notwithstanding that, if the assignment had not occurred, so that the original creditor would have been the party suing, r. 13.14 would have provided a defence. Therefore, in this situation the set-offs that can be asserted against the assignee are those arising under established principles, rather than pursuant to r. 13.14. Section 134 nevertheless provides that the assignee takes subject to equities, and the point is that, if the assignor had sued, a defence would have been available to the debtor. The principle of taking subject to equities suggests that that defence should also be available against the assignee if it arose before notice.

17.18 But whatever the position in relation to a legal assignment, the same argument ordinarily would not be available in the case of an equitable assignment, because in such a case the

---

[97] See *Handley Page Ltd v Commissioners of Customs and Excise and Rockwell Machine Tool Co Ltd* [1970] 2 Lloyd's Rep 459, 464–5, referred to in *Business Computers Ltd v Anglo-African Leasing Ltd* [1977] 1 WLR 578, 585–6. See also para. 17.106 below.

[98] See paras 17.99–17.118 below.

[99] See paras 2.63–2.86 above. In Australia, note paras 17.11–17.12 above in relation to the Personal Property Securities Act 2009 (Cth).

[100] See paras 2.63 and 2.81–2.82 above. The Statutes have also been repealed in New South Wales but were re-enacted in the Civil Procedure Act 2005 (NSW), s. 21. See paras 2.63–2.80 above.

[101] See paras 14.63–14.78 above.

[102] See para. 15.121 above.

[103] See para. 2.83 above.

[104] See paras 2.83–2.86 above.

[105] This is in similar terms to the Law of Property Act 1925, s. 136. See para. 17.04 above.

action usually is brought in the name of the assignor as plaintiff.[106] If the debtor has an unrelated damages cross-claim against the plaintiff/assignor that arose before the debtor had notice of the assignment, an expanded defence in Victoria under r. 13.14 *prima facie* would allow the debtor to include it in its defence and set it off against the plaintiff's claim, notwithstanding the assignment, since it is not regarded as unconscionable for a debtor to rely, as against an assignee, on a defence available against the assignor that arose before notice.[107]

(7) Notice to the debtor

It is the date that the debtor receives notice of the assignment,[108] as opposed to the date of **17.19** the assignment itself, that determines whether an assignee takes subject to a set-off under the Statutes in relation to a cross-debt owing by the assignor to the debtor.[109] The notice need not be in any particular form.[110] It need not, for example, be in writing. Nor is it necessary that the notice should come from the assignee.[111] It would be unconscionable for the debtor to rely on a set-off otherwise available at law if the debtor knows of the assignment from whatever source. Moreover, there need only be notice of the fact that the debt has been assigned. The assignee need not be named.[112]

There is little direct authority as to what constitutes adequate notice to the debtor in order **17.20** to prevent set-offs arising as between the assignor and the debtor, but some guidance can be obtained by reference to the approach adopted in other situations in relation to the adequacy of notice, for example in the case of a priorities dispute between successive assignees of a debt. The relevant principle is the rule in *Dearle v Hall*,[113] which in essence accords priority to the assignee who is the first to give notice to the debtor. In this situation the courts have emphasized that it is in the interests of an assignee to give notice so as to prevent another assignee, whether earlier or later, obtaining priority. An assignee who does not give

---

[106] In the case of an equitable assignment of a legal chose in action it is said that the assignor should be a party to the action, either as claimant or defendant. See *McIntyre v Gye* (1994) 51 FCR 472, 480; *Three Rivers District Council v Bank of England* [1996] QB 292. See also para. 17.03 above.

[107] See para. 17.03 above.

[108] Notice given to an agent of the debtor may suffice. See *Moore v Jervis* (1845) 2 Coll 60, 69, 71–2, 63 ER 637, 641, 642.

[109] See e.g. *Moore v Jervis* (1845) 2 Coll 60, 63 ER 637; *Wilson v Gabriel* (1863) 4 B & S 243, 248, 122 ER 450, 452–3; *Watson v Mid Wales Railway Co* (1867) LR 2 CP 593, 601; *Canadian Admiral Corporation Ltd v L. F. Dommerich & Co Inc* (1964) 43 DLR (2d) 1; *Commercial Factors Ltd v Maxwell Printing Ltd* [1994] 1 NZLR 724, 735. See also *Brice v Bannister* (1878) 3 QBD 569, 578. The statement in *Dixon v Winch* [1900] 1 Ch 736, 742 (and see also *Turner v Smith* [1901] 1 Ch 213, 219), in so far as it appears to suggest the contrary, should be regarded as incorrect.

[110] *G & N Angelakis Shipping Co SA v Compagnie National Algerienne de Navigation (The Attika Hope)* [1988] 1 Lloyd's Rep 439, 442. For the position in relation to the notice necessary to effect a statutory assignment under the Law of Property Act 1925, s. 136(1), see Oditah, *Legal Aspects of Receivables Financing* (1991), 131.

[111] See e.g. *Lloyd v Banks* (1868) LR 3 Ch App 488 (notice in newspaper); *Ex p Agra Bank, re Worcester* (1868) LR 3 Ch App 555, 559; *Re Dallas* [1904] 2 Ch 385, 309; *Talcott Ltd v John Lewis & Co Ltd* [1940] 3 All ER 592.

[112] *Smith v Parkes* (1852) 16 Beav 115, 117–18, 51 ER 720, 721.

[113] (1828) 3 Russ 1, 38 ER 475. In Australia, compare the position under the Personal Property Securities Act 2009 (Cth).

notice acts at his or her peril. Accordingly, the duty is on the assignee to give notice.[114] Moreover, to be effective the assignee's notice should be clear and distinct.[115] To paraphrase Lord Cairns in *Lloyd v Banks*,[116] there must be proof that the mind of the debtor has in some way been brought to an intelligent apprehension of the assignment, so that a reasonable person, or an ordinary person of business, would act upon the information and would regulate his or her conduct by it. In particular, Lord Cairns indicated that proof of what would only be constructive notice would not suffice.[117] A similar approach has been adopted when the question concerns payment by the debtor. If the debtor has notice of the assignment, the debtor can only discharge his or her obligation by paying the assignee,[118] unless the assignee has agreed otherwise.[119] If the debtor ignores the assignment and pays the assignor, the debtor may be liable to pay a second time to the assignee.[120] Once again, because the debtor may obtain a good discharge by paying the assignor if the debtor does not have notice,[121] the assignee in failing to give notice acts at his or her peril, and accordingly the view is that the assignee must give clear notice in order to secure his or her position.[122] Thus, in *Talcott Ltd v Lewis & Co Ltd*,[123] the notice sent to the debtor was ambiguous, and it was held that it was insufficient to render the debtor liable to pay the assignee after having already paid the assignor. Nor was there a duty of inquiry imposed.

17.21 Set-off is equivalent to payment,[124] and the issue of notice for the purpose of whether a cross-debt owing by the assignor to the debtor can be set off against the assigned debt should be determined by like principles. In the case of an equitable assignment, where the legal title to the assigned debt remains with the assignor, the debtor *prima facie* has a right of set-off at law under the Statutes of Set-off in relation to any cross-debt, no matter when it arises. Equity, on the other hand, will protect the assignee against a set-off arising after the debtor has notice of the assignment.[125] An assignee therefore acts at his or her peril if he or she does not give notice[126] because the assignee may not be able to take advantage of the equitable rule. The courts have emphasized that it is up to an assignee to look after his or her own interests and to make inquiries as to prior equities,[127] and consistent with that

---

[114] *Willes v Greenhill* (1861) 4 De G F & J 147, 150, 45 ER 1139, 1140; *Ward v Duncombe* [1893] AC 369, 395. See also *Mangles v Dixon* (1852) 3 HLC 702, 732–3, 10 ER 278, 291.

[115] *Bence v Shearman* [1898] 2 Ch 582, 587.

[116] (1868) LR 3 Ch App 488, 490–1.

[117] (1868) LR 3 Ch App 488, 490.

[118] *Agnew v Commissioner of Inland Revenue* [2001] 2 AC 710 at [17].

[119] See e.g. *First National Bank of Chicago v West of England Shipowners Mutual Protection and Indemnity Association (The Evelpidis Era)* [1981] 1 Lloyd's Rep 54, in which it was agreed that insurance payments could be made directly to the insured mortgagor until such time as the mortgagee notified the insurer of a default.

[120] See e.g. *Brice v Bannister* (1878) 3 QBD 569.

[121] See e.g. *Norrish v Marshall* (1821) 5 Madd 475, 56 ER 977.

[122] *Bence v Shearman* [1898] 2 Ch 582, 587, 591.

[123] [1940] 3 All ER 592.

[124] See paras 12.34 and 16.01 above.

[125] See para. 17.03 above.

[126] *Parker v Jackson* [1936] 2 All ER 281, 289–90.

[127] *Mangles v Dixon* (1852) 3 HLC 702, 732–3, 10 ER 278, 291; *Canadian Admiral Corporation Ltd v L. F. Dommerich & Co Inc* (1964) 43 DLR (2d) 1, 2, 8–9; *Helstan Securities Ltd v Hertfordshire County Council* [1978] 3 All ER 262, 266. See also *Athenaeum Life Assurance Society v Pooley* (1858) 3 De G & J 294, 299, 44 ER 1281, 1283.

view, and with the attitude of the courts in relation to questions of payment and priorities, the onus should be on the assignee to give notice which is clear and unambiguous so as to prevent the debtor obtaining a subsequent right of set-off.[128] This should also be the case when the requirements for a statutory assignment set out in s. 136 of the Law of Property Act 1925 are in issue,[129] particularly given the commonly expressed view that the section relates to procedure only.[130] On the other hand, if sufficient notice is given to the debtor, the debtor cannot refuse to accept it.[131] Nor can the debtor shut his or her eyes to the obvious.[132] In *Cavendish v Geaves*,[133] a pass book issued by a banking firm from time to time to a customer showed changes in the firm, and principal and interest payments on some bonds given by the customer to the firm appeared as entries in the pass book. This was held to constitute notice that the bonds were assigned to the new firm whenever a change occurred.

Australia: notice under the Personal Property Securities Act 2009 (Cth)

In Australia, the Personal Property Securities Act 2009 (Cth) addresses the question of **17.22** notice in the context of both payment and set-off in relation to a transfer of an 'account' or a 'chattel paper' (as defined in the Act).[134] Pursuant to s. 80(7)(a), the debtor[135] may continue to make payments to the transferor until the debtor receives a notice that: (i) states that the amount payable, or to become payable, under the contract has been transferred; (ii) states that payment is to be made to the transferee; and (iii) identifies the contract (whether specifically or by class) under which the amount payable is to become payable. The notice must be in writing.[136] If a notice received was not from the transferor, s. 80(7(b) provides that the debtor nevertheless may continue to make payments to the transferor if the debtor requests the transferee to provide proof of the transfer and the transferee fails to provide proof within five business days after the request. Section 80(8) then provides that payment by the debtor to the transferee in accordance with a notice under para. (7)(a) (including in the circumstances described in para. 7(b)) discharges the obligation of the debtor to the extent of the payment.

Set-off is dealt with in s. 80(1). It provides, *inter alia*, in para. (1)(b) that the rights **17.23** of the transferee are subject to any defence by way of a right of set-off that accrued before the time when payment by the debtor to the transferor would no longer discharge the obligation of the debtor under s. 80(8). That point in time may thus determine

---

[128] Thus, when the third party interest takes the form of a fixed charge over a debt, as opposed to an absolute assignment, the better view is that registration of the charge by itself should not suffice to constitute notice to the debtor. Unless the debtor has undertaken a search of the register or is otherwise aware of the charge, the fact of registration should simply be constructive notice. See Lightman and Moss, *The Law of Receivers and Administrators of Companies* (4th edn, 2007), 558–9.

[129] See para. 17.04 above.

[130] *Tolhurst v Associated Portland Cement Manufacturers (1900) Ltd* [1902] 2 KB 660, 676–7.

[131] *Higgs v The Northern Assam Tea Co Ltd* (1869) LR 4 Ex 387, 396.

[132] *Mangles v Dixon* (1852) 3 HLC 702, 732, 10 ER 278, 290.

[133] (1857) 24 Beav 163, 53 ER 319.

[134] See para. 17.05 above.

[135] Termed the 'account debtor', which is defined in s. 10 as a person who is obligated under an account or chattel paper.

[136] Section 286.

whether a set-off which has accrued to the debtor against the transferor can be asserted against the transferee.

17.24 Pursuant to s. 80(7)(b), if a request for proof is made, the transferee must provide the proof within five days. If it is not provided within that time, the debtor can continue to pay the transferor and set-offs against the transferor can continue to accrue at the expense of the transferee. The transferee in that situation presumably would have to provide another notice under para. (7)(a), which seems an unnecessary complication. It is unclear why a time limit is imposed on the transferee. If the transferee was tardy in providing the proof, the debtor would be protected in that he or she could tender payment to the transferor.

(8) Assignment of a future debt

Prior contract

17.25 English law regards an unearned debt under an existing contract as an existing debt.[137] The principle has been expressed in terms that a legal right to be paid money at a future date is a present chose in action if it depends upon an existing contract on the repudiation of which an action could be brought for anticipatory breach.[138] This broad interpretation ascribed to the concept of existing debts has not been invoked in relation to set-off when the cross-debt owing by the assignor to the debtor is in issue. It is said that a debt which accrues to the debtor from the assignor after notice, albeit pursuant to a prior contract, cannot be set off against the assigned debt.[139] In New Zealand, the Court of Appeal in *Hoverd Industries Ltd v Supercool Refrigeration and Air Conditioning (1991) Ltd*[140] considered that the assigned debt is subject to a similar restriction, so that it has to be presently due when the assignment occurs[141] in order to be susceptible to a set-off.[142] However, there is other authority which supports the view that the restriction applicable to the cross-debt does not apply to the assigned debt when it arises out of a prior contract. In the context of a company receivership,[143] the Court of Appeal in *Rother Iron Works Ltd v Canterbury Precision Engineers Ltd*[144] allowed a set-off in circumstances where a company entered into a contract for the sale of goods, a receiver was subsequently appointed to the company, thereby crystallizing a floating charge, and after the appointment the company delivered

---

[137] Oditah, *Legal Aspects of Receivables Financing* (1991), 27–9, 135. See e.g. *Shepherd v Federal Commissioner of Taxation* (1965) 113 CLR 385 (assignment of royalties payable under a licence agreement). In *Marathon Electrical Manufacturing Corp v Mashreqbank PSC* [1997] 2 BCLC 460, 467 Mance J said that the principle embraces any contract under which payments may be received, provided at least that it is not terminable at will. Compare *Norman v Federal Commissioner of Taxation* (1963) 109 CLR 9 in relation to future interest payable on a loan which could be repaid by the borrower at any time without notice (see the explanation of the case in *Shepherd*).

[138] Oditah, *Legal Aspects of Receivables Financing* (1991), 28–9, referring to *Norman v Federal Commissioner of Taxation* (1963) 109 CLR 9, 26 (Windeyer J).

[139] See para. 17.15 above.

[140] [1995] 3 NZLR 577, 587–8.

[141] To be more precise, at the date of notice of the assignment. See para. 17.19 above.

[142] See also *Colvin v Hartwell* (1837) 5 Cl & Fin 484, 7 ER 488. In any event, the New Zealand Court of Appeal in the *Hoverd Industries* case concluded that a set-off would have been contrary to the intention of the parties, and therefore it was not permitted on that ground. See [1995] 3 NZLR 577, 588.

[143] See paras 17.99–17.118 below.

[144] [1974] 1 QB 1 (Russell, Cairns and Stamp LJJ). See para. 17.109 below.

the goods to the purchaser, whereupon the purchaser became indebted for the price. The Court of Appeal held that the secured creditor took subject to a set-off available to the purchaser in relation to a debt owing to it by the company before the appointment, notwithstanding that the debt for the price when it arose was embraced by a fixed charge as a result of the crystallization, and notwithstanding that it arose after notice of the appointment, albeit pursuant to a prior contract. It is commonly said that, when a floating charge crystallizes, any debt which is owing to the company and which comes within the ambit of the charge is assigned in equity to the chargee.[145] The case is therefore an authority in relation to assignments. The New Zealand Court of Appeal in the *Hoverd Industries* case made the point that *Rother Iron Works Ltd v Canterbury Precision Engineers Ltd* differed from the case before it, in that in *Rother Iron Works* the debt which the purchaser sought to set off was already due and payable before the company entered into the contract of sale, but the New Zealand court nevertheless acknowledged that the judgment did not turn on that point. Russell LJ in the *Rother Iron Works* case emphasized instead that, when the debt for the price first came into existence, on delivery of the goods after crystallization, it was subject to the set-off.[146]

More recently, Mance J followed the *Rother Iron Works* case in *Marathon Electrical Manufacturing Corp v Mashreqbank PSC*.[147] The case concerned a letter of credit issued in favour of a company, Munradtech, which in turn engaged Mashreqbank to collect moneys payable under the letter. Munradtech assigned the proceeds of the letter of credit to the plaintiffs, and on 2 April 1996 notice of the assignment was given to Mashreqbank. On 22 May 1996 Mashreqbank received the proceeds from the issuer of the letter of credit, whereupon it asserted that the assignees took subject to its right to set off a prior separate debt owing to it by Munradtech. Mance J accepted that the subject of the assignment was Munradtech's entitlement against Mashreqbank as collecting bank, as opposed to Munradtech's entitlement as against the issuer.[148] The date of notice was 2 April, whereas Mashreqbank did not receive the proceeds, and therefore it did not become indebted in respect of them, until later, on 22 May.[149] Nevertheless, its indebtedness arose out of

17.26

---

[145] *Rother Iron Works Ltd v Canterbury Precision Engineers Ltd* has been referred to in later cases with evident approval. In addition to *Marathon Electrical Manufacturing Corp v Mashreqbank PSC* [1997] 2 BCLC 460 (see below), see *George Barker (Transport) Ltd v Eynon* [1974] 1 WLR 462, 470, 473–4, 475 (CA) and *Business Computers Ltd v Anglo-African Leasing Ltd* [1977] 1 WLR 578, 585 (although the facts of the *Rother Iron Works* case were there incorrectly stated, in that the goods were not delivered *to* the company but *by* the company). See also *Caratti v Grant* (1978) 3 ACLR 322, 331; *Roadshow Entertainment Pty Ltd v (ACN 053 006 269) Pty Ltd* (1997) 42 NSWLR 462, 483 (CA); *John Dee Group Ltd v WMH (21) Ltd* [1997] BCC 518, 530 (and see also on appeal [1998] BCC 972, 976).

[146] See [1974] 1 QB 1, 6.

[147] [1997] 2 BCLC 460.

[148] See [1997] 2 BCLC 460, 464–5.

[149] Mance J accepted that the notice was effective, notwithstanding that it was given before the debt accrued, since Mashreqbank had been appointed prior to the assignment to act as collecting bank. He therefore considered that there was an existing debt at the date of notice, in accordance with the principle referred to in para. 17.25 above, and the notice was of an assignment of an existing debt. See [1997] 2 BCLC 460, 465–7. *Quaere* whether that was correct. It is not clear from the report why the authority to collect was not revocable, as opposed to constituting an existing contract on the repudiation of which an action could be brought for anticipatory breach.

a prior engagement, and Mance J held that the prior debt of Munradtech could be set off against it.

17.27 The approach adopted in the *Rother Iron Works* case and the *Marathon Electrical* case should be followed in preference to that favoured by the New Zealand Court of Appeal in *Hoverd v Supercool*. It is difficult to support the restriction on set-off in the case of a debt arising after notice but pursuant to a prior contract in context of the cross-debt owing to the debtor,[150] and there is no reason for extending that restriction to the assigned debt.

An expectancy not derived from a present contract

17.28 Alternatively, the subject of an assignment may be a future debt (or an expectancy) that is not the product of an existing contract. If value has been given the assignment will be effective in equity, so that the assignment attaches to the debt as soon as it is acquired.[151] The determinative date for a set-off is the date of notice of the assignment, as opposed to the date of the assignment itself, and a set-off would be denied to the debtor if the contract out of which the assigned debt arose was entered into after notice. But what constitutes notice in the case of an expectancy? In the context of a priorities dispute between successive assignees under *Dearle v Hall*,[152] notice of assignment of a future debt is regarded as ineffective while the debt remains an expectancy.[153] In *Roxburghe v Cox*,[154] Baggallay LJ considered that the principle applies also to set-off so that, until the assigned debt has become a present debt,[155] the assignee could not give notice which would prevent rights of set-off accruing to the debtor in relation to cross-debts which may become owing by the assignor. Similarly, the application of that principle to set-off was assumed by Mance J in *Marathon Electrical Manufacturing Corp v Mashreqbank PSC*,[156] although the debt in that case was held not to be a future debt since it arose out of a prior engagement. Those views are also consistent with descriptions of notice given before an assigned debt has become an existing debt as 'perfectly useless and idle' and 'void altogether'.[157]

17.29 But, notwithstanding those views, it is suggested that the principle which applies to *Dearle v Hall* should not extend to set-off. The fact that, as between successive assignees of an expectancy, notice to the debtor is ineffective while the assigned debt is still an expectancy is not to the point. As far as the debtor is concerned, his or her conscience should be affected

---

[150] See para. 17.15 above.

[151] *Tailby v Official Receiver* (1888) 13 App Cas 523; *Norman v Federal Commissioner of Taxation* (1963) 109 CLR 9, 20–2. If an assignee of future debts becomes bankrupt and the trustee in bankruptcy proceeds to earn the future debts by carrying on the bankrupt assignor's business, the assignee's title to the receipts is inoperative as against the title of the trustee in bankruptcy. See e.g. *Wilmot v Alton* [1897] 1 QB 17 and *Re Collins* [1925] Ch 556, and paras 13.51–13.52 above.

[152] (1828) 3 Russ 1, 38 ER 475.

[153] *Somerset v Cox* (1865) 33 Beav 634, 55 ER 514; *Re Dallas* [1904] 2 Ch 385; Oditah, *Legal Aspects of Receivables Financing* (1991), 133–5. Compare the circumstances in issue in *Marathon Electrical Manufacturing Corp v Mashreqbank PSC* [1997] 2 BCLC 460, 465–7.

[154] (1881) 17 Ch D 520, 527.

[155] In the sense referred to in para. 17.25 above.

[156] [1997] 2 BCLC 460, 465–7.

[157] *Re Dallas* [1904] 2 Ch 385, 395 (Buckley J).

as from the time that he or she becomes aware of the assignment.[158] There is support for that approach in Canada in the context of a debt factoring agreement. The Ontario Court of Appeal accepted that the agreement in question operated as a present assignment of future accounts receivable, and held that notice of it precluded the subsequent accrual of rights of set-off in relation to future debts.[159] In truth, notice for the purpose of establishing priorities serves a different function to notice for the purpose of set-off. In the case of priority under *Dearle v Hall*, notice is given to the debtor because it is regarded as the method by which the assignee gets in possession of the debt,[160] with the first to obtain possession in that sense having priority. But while a debt is still an expectancy, there is nothing in respect of which possession can be taken, and therefore notice at that time is ineffective.[161] In the case of set-off, on the other hand, notice defines the point beyond which the debtor's conscience is affected, which can occur whether the debt is present or future. It has nothing to do with obtaining possession of the debt.

This assumes that there is a present (although an inchoate[162]) assignment of a future debt. **17.30** If, on the other hand, an agreement contemplates a further agreement in order to effect the assignment of a future debt, as is often the case when book debts are factored, the first agreement itself would not constitute an assignment, in which case notice of it would not be notice of a present assignment which would prevent the accrual of rights of set-off as against future debts. It would be necessary to have regard instead to each subsequent agreement which effects a present assignment of a debt, and then to determine set-off rights in relation to each such debt by reference to the position as at the date of notice of the assignment of that debt.[163]

Australia: Personal Property Securities Act 2009 (Cth)

The position in relation to an assignment of an expectancy is unclear in Australia under the **17.31** Personal Property Securities Act 2009 (Cth), s. 80(1) in the case of a transfer of an 'account' or a 'chattel paper' (as defined).[164] The application of the 'subject to equities' principle set out in s. 80(1)(b) rests (through sub-s. (8)) upon the giving of a notice of transfer to the

---

[158] See para. 17.03 above, and *Meagher, Gummow and Lehane's Equity Doctrines and Remedies* (4th edn, 2002), 943–4 [28–335].

[159] *L. F. Dommerich & Co v Canadian Admiral Corporation Ltd* (1962) 34 DLR (2d) 530 (esp. at 537). The decision to refuse a set-off in the *Dommerich* case was reversed on appeal by the Supreme Court of Canada, not because of a principle that notice of an assignment of a future debt is ineffective to prevent set-offs accruing to the debtor, but because the agreement in question itself did not operate as a present assignment of future book debts. Rather, it contemplated a further agreement before a particular book debt was assigned, and it was by reference to notice of each such subsequent assignment of a debt that rights of set-off in relation to that debt were to be determined. See *Canadian Admiral Corporation Ltd v L. F. Dommerich & Co Inc* (1964) 43 DLR (2d) 1. See para. 17.30 below.

[160] See *Dearle v Hall* (1828) 3 Russ 1, 12, 14, 22–4, 38 ER 475, 479, 480, 483–4, and on appeal (1827) 3 Russ 48, 58–9, 38 ER 492, 494–5 (Lord Lyndhurst).

[161] See the discussion in Oditah, *Legal Aspects of Receivables Financing* (1991), 28, 134.

[162] *Goode on Legal Problems of Credit and Security* (4th edn (ed. Gullifer), 2008), 74–5.

[163] *Canadian Admiral Corporation Ltd v L. F. Dommerich & Co Inc* (1964) 43 DLR (2d) 1 (Supreme Court of Canada); *New Zealand Factors Ltd v Farmers Trading Co Ltd* [1992] 3 NZLR 703, 711. One may query Master Kennedy-Grant's view in the *New Zealand Factors* case (at 710–11) that the circumstances were such as to give rise to an equitable set-off.

[164] See para. 17.05 above.

debtor under s. 80(7)(a). Paragraph (7)(a) provides that, if an account or chattel paper is transferred, the debtor may 'continue to make payments under the contract to the transferor' until the requisite notice is received, and the notice must state that the amount payable or to become payable under 'the contract' has been transferred. It does not refer to future contracts. While sub-para. (7)(a)(ii) provides that the contract need only be identified in the notice by class, and not specifically, the section seems to contemplate an amount payable or to become payable under an existing and identifiable contract at the date of the notice. It should be clarified in the Act that the notice may extend to future accounts receivable from the debtor.

(9) Equitable set-off

17.32   The preceding discussion concerned the exercise of a right of set-off against an assignee based upon the Statutes of Set-off. For that form of set-off both demands must be liquidated. On the other hand, an unliquidated cross-claim possessed by the debtor against the assignor[165] may be set off against the assigned debt if the case is one in which the claims are sufficiently closely connected to give rise to an equitable set-off as between the debtor and the assignor.[166] In contrast to set-off under the Statutes, it is not necessary in this situation that the cross-claim sought to be set off should have arisen before notice of the assignment. The assignee may take subject to an equitable set-off where the cross-claim arose after notice, if the claims are otherwise sufficiently closely connected.[167]

---

[165] See also *Horrobin v Australia & New Zealand Banking Group Ltd* (1996) 40 NSWLR 89, 93 in relation to the situation in which the cross-demand is directly against the assignee, in that case for fraud inducing the contract subsequently assigned to the assignee.

[166] See ch. 4 above. In addition to the cases cited below, see *Popular Homes Ltd v Circuit Developments Ltd* [1979] 2 NZLR 642; *Lean v Tumut River Orchard Management Ltd* [2003] FCA 269 at [60]–[79] (cross-claim for misleading or deceptive conduct contrary to the Australian Trade Practices Act 1974 (Cth), s. 52). It is not sufficient for an equitable set-off that the claims arose out of the same contract. See *Government of Newfoundland v Newfoundland Railway Co* (1888) 13 App Cas 199, 212 (PC); *G and T Earle Ltd v Hemsworth RDC* (1928) 44 TLR 605, 609. Compare *Phoenix Assurance Co Ltd v Earl's Court Ltd* (1913) 30 TLR 50, 51. See also *Packer & Co Pty Ltd v Aksha Pty Ltd* (1995) 12 BCL 143 (South Australia) in relation to a subcontractor's lien under the Worker's Liens Act 1893 (SA).

[167] *Coba Industries Ltd v Millie's Holdings (Canada) Ltd* [1985] 6 WWR 14 (repudiation by assignor after notice); *Telford v Holt* (1987) 41 DLR (4th) 385; *Roadshow Entertainment Pty Ltd v (ACN 053 006 269) Pty Ltd* (1997) 42 NSWLR 462 (receivership). See also Bovill CJ in *Watson v Mid Wales Railway Co* (1867) LR 2 CP 593, 598 (referring to *Smith v Parkes* (1852) 16 Beav 115, 51 ER 720); *Business Computers Ltd v Anglo-African Leasing Ltd* [1977] 1 WLR 578, 585 (see below); *Re Wirragana Nominees Pty Ltd* (1991) 9 ACLC 1168, 1179–80; *Wolfe v Marshall* [1997] EWCA Civ 1329 (see the discussion of the case of a debtor incurring a liability to the assignor in a transaction in circumstances which might be expected to give rise to a liability of the assignor to the debtor). In relation to a court-appointed receiver, see *Parsons v Sovereign Bank of Canada* [1913] AC 160, and para. 17.120 below. In *Government of Newfoundland v Newfoundland Railway Co* (1888) 13 App Cas 199 (discussed below), the assignment occurred a number of years before the breach, although the report does not state when notice of the assignment was given. Given, however, that the assignee was a trustee for bondholders of the company, and the company was empowered to issue bonds by an Act of the Newfoundland legislature embodying the contract between the government and the company, it would seem unlikely that the government (the debtor) was unaware of the assignment. See also the reference to the *Government of Newfoundland* case in *John Dee Group Ltd v WMH (21) Ltd* [1997] BCC 518, 530 (appeal dismissed [1998] BCC 972) in relation to set-off against charges incurred after notice of the receivership. Reference also may be made to *Bank of Boston Connecticut v European Grain and Shipping Ltd* [1989] 1 AC 1056. The bank in that case gave notice of assignment on 14 July 1982, whereas the repudiation occurred after then, on 19 July, and the Court of Appeal accepted that an equitable set-off was available against the bank. The decision was reversed by the House of Lords, but on the separate ground that an

Using the traditional formulation of equitable set-off, the title to sue is impeached, and in that circumstance it should not matter when the cross-claim accrued. The title of an assignee to sue is equally affected.[168]

It has been suggested that the transaction out of which the cross-claims arose should have been entered into before the debtor had notice of the assignment.[169] However, there is no justification for any such limitation. Consider, for example, the case of a receiver appointed to a company under a crystallized floating charge. It is commonly (though sometimes inaccurately) said that crystallization of a floating charge brings about an equitable assignment to the secured creditor of any debt owing to the company and coming within the ambit of the charge.[170] Consider that the receiver enters into a contract on behalf of the company, which the company proceeds to breach, and the resulting damages claim against the company is such that it ordinarily would give rise to an equitable set-off against a debt due to the company under the contract. The debtor in that circumstance should not be denied a set-off on the ground that he or she was aware of the receivership, and of the consequent equitable assignment of the debt under the contract to the secured creditor. If the claims are such that the title to sue would be impeached, it should not matter that the contract was entered after the receivership.

17.33

In an often-quoted passage in *Business Computers Ltd v Anglo-African Leasing Ltd*,[171] Templeman J summarized the position in relation to set-off in the context of assignments in the following terms:

17.34

> The result of the relevant authorities is that a debt which accrues due before notice of an assignment is received, whether or not it is payable before that date, or a debt which arises out of the same contract as that which gives rise to the assigned debt, or is closely connected with that contract, may be set off against the assignee. But a debt which is neither accrued nor connected may not be set off even though it arises from a contract made before the assignment.

The reference to 'a debt which arises out of the same contract as that which gives rise to the assigned debt, or is closely connected with that debt', contemplates equitable set-off.[172] The statement suggests, correctly, that the cross-claim need not have accrued due before

---

equitable set-off is not available against a claim for freight. See para. 5.04 above. In New Zealand, compare *Popular Homes Ltd v Circuit Developments Ltd* [1979] 2 NZLR 642, 660 (and see also *Hoverd Industries Ltd v Supercool Refrigeration and Air Conditioning (1991) Ltd* [1995] 3 NZLR 577, 586 in relation to the relevance of the charge being fixed or floating), where it seems to have been assumed that the cross-claim should have accrued before notice. Compare also in Canada *Re Jason Construction Ltd* (1972) 29 DLR (3d) 623, 627–8.

[168] This accords with the better view (notwithstanding recent Court of Appeal authority to the contrary: see para. 4.69 below) that mutuality is not a strict requirement of equitable set-off. See paras 4.67–4.83 above.

[169] Wood, *English and International Set-off* (1989), 768, 793, 1056. Wood uses transaction set-off as a compendious term encompassing both equitable set-off and common law abatement. See *op. cit.*, 9–10.

[170] See para. 17.100 below.

[171] [1977] 1 WLR 578, 585. See also e.g. *Glencore Grain Ltd v Agros Trading Co* [1999] 2 Lloyd's Rep 410, 420–1.

[172] See the references in *Business Computers Ltd v Anglo-African Leasing Ltd* [1977] 1 WLR 578, 583–4 to *Government of Newfoundland v Newfoundland Railway Co* (1888) 13 App Cas 199 (as explained in *Bank of Boston Connecticut v European Grain and Shipping Ltd* [1989] 1 AC 1056, 1102–3, 1110–11) and *Hanak v Green* [1958] 2 QB 9, which concerned equitable set-off.

notice.[173] On the other hand, it is not necessary that the cross-claim be for a debt, and indeed in the majority of cases of equitable set-off a damages claim is in issue.[174] Moreover, notwithstanding the suggestion to the contrary in that passage, the courts have emphasized that it is not sufficient for an equitable set-off that the demands arose out of the same contract.[175] The question is whether there is a sufficiently close connection, which is to be determined by reference to principles canvassed earlier.[176]

17.35 In Australia, s. 80(1)(b) of the Personal Property Securities Act 2009 (Cth)[177] contemplates that a transferee of an account or a chattel paper (as defined) may take subject to a defence of set-off that accrued before notice. There is no such temporal limitation in s. 80(1)(a) in the circumstance where a defence arises 'in relation to' the contract between the debtor and the transferor, which is consistent with the above analysis. The language is unfortunate, however, because it does not accurately state the test for equitable set-off applied by Australian courts.[178] Nevertheless, it is suggested that it should be interpreted as incorporating the principles developed in relation to equitable set-off.[179]

17.36 In *Young v Kitchin*,[180] a sufficiently close connection provided the basis for a set-off against an assignee of a sum of money owing under a building contract when the debtor had a damages claim against the assignor for failure to complete and deliver the building by the specified date. Similarly, in *Government of Newfoundland v Newfoundland Railway Co*,[181] the Privy Council held that an assignee of a sum payable to a construction company under a railway construction contract took subject to a claim for damages against the company for not completing the line, while in *Lawrence v Hayes*,[182] the purchaser of a business was allowed to set off against an assignee's claim for the sums due to the vendor under the contract the amount of a judgment obtained against the vendor for damages for breach of warranty. The breach arose from the fact that chattels included in the sale either were not the property of the vendor or were the subject of a charge which had not been paid off. In Canada, a damages claim available to a mortgagor against the mortgagee for breach of an obligation to renew the insurance on the mortgaged premises was set off against the mortgage debt, notwithstanding that the debt had been assigned.[183]

17.37 Those cases should be contrasted with *Stoddart v Union Trust Ltd*.[184] In the *Stoddart* case, the defendant in an action brought by an assignee for payment of a debt due under a contract was not allowed to bring into account a claim for damages against the assignor

---

[173] See above.
[174] In *Business Computers v Anglo-African Leasing* itself, the debtor's cross-claim was based upon a repudiation of a contract, which sounds in damages, although in that case there was an 'agreed damages' clause.
[175] See para. 4.91 above.
[176] See ch. 4 above.
[177] See para. 17.05 above.
[178] See paras 4.19–4.28 above.
[179] But see paras 17.11 and 17.12 above.
[180] (1878) 3 Ex D 127. See also *Mitchell v Purnell Motors Pty Ltd* [1961] NSWR 165.
[181] (1888) 13 App Cas 199.
[182] [1927] 2 KB 111.
[183] *Campbell v Canadian Co-operative Investment Co* (1906) 16 Man LR 464.
[184] [1912] 1 KB 181. See also *Cummings v Johnson* (1913) 4 WWR 543; *Provident Finance Corporation Pty Ltd v Hammond* [1978] VR 312; *Birchal v Birch, Crisp & Co* [1913] 2 Ch 375, 379.

for fraud inducing the contract. The court reasoned that the damages claim was not a claim arising under the contract, or for breach of the contract,[185] but rather it was said to be a claim *dehors* the contract.[186] That analysis is not convincing,[187] and indeed there is an apparent conflict between the decision in that case, on the one hand, and on the other the principle applied in the context of insolvency set-off, that a claim for damages for misrepresentation inducing a contract with the representor is not a mere personal tort, but rather it constitutes a breach of the obligation arising under the contract so that, even apart from the reform set out in the Insolvency Act 1986 by which tortious demands became provable, it could be employed in a set-off in the event of a bankruptcy.[188] Both Vaughan Williams and Buckley LJJ in the *Stoddart* case[189] emphasized that the plaintiff was an assignee for value without notice of the fraud. However, that should not have affected the question whether there was an equitable set-off available as against the assignor, and if there was it should have been available against the assignee. The point was also made in the judgments that the debtor in such a case may be entitled to set aside the contract,[190] but if the contract has not been set aside the remedy of set-off should still be available[191] *Stoddart v Union Trust Ltd* should be compared to the decision of Mann CJ in the Victorian Supreme Court in *Sun Candies Pty Ltd v Polites*.[192] The fraudulent misstatement inducing the purchaser to buy the business in that case constituted a breach of a warranty which determined the amount of the purchase price. Since the cross-claim arose out of the contract, the Chief Justice held (following *Government of Newfoundland v Newfoundland Railway Co*) that it gave rise to an equitable set-off to which the assignee from the vendor took subject.[193]

---

[185] See Buckley LJ [1912] 1 KB 181, 192. On the other hand, a debtor sued by an assignee may set up the defence that the contract under which the debt arose ought to be set aside and cancelled for fraud.

[186] See Kennedy LJ at [1912] 1 KB 181, 194.

[187] In *Banco Santander SA v Bayfern Ltd* [2000] 1 All ER (Comm) 776 Waller LJ (at 780) noted that *Stoddart v Union Trust* has been the subject of criticism. In any event, the Court of Appeal in *Banco Santander* said that *Stoddart* does not apply where the fraud itself, as opposed to a cross-claim for damages for fraud inducing the contract, gives rise to a defence to an action for payment. In Australia, compare also *Lean v Tumut River Orchard Management Ltd* [2003] FCA 269 at [60]–[79] (cross-claim for misleading or deceptive conduct contrary to the Trade Practices Act 1974 (Cth), s. 52).

[188] See para. 8.53 above (and compare paras 8.57–8.61 above in relation to a contract entered into with a third party). The leading authority is *Jack v Kipping* (1882) 9 QBD 113. In Australia it has been questioned whether the claim for fraudulent misrepresentation inducing the contract in *Jack v Kipping* instead should be treated as illustrating the availability of equitable set-off. See *Re NIAA Corporation Ltd (in liq)* (NSW SC, McLelland CJ in Eq, 2 December 1994, BC9403369), referred to in *Aliferis v Kyriacou* (2000) 1 VR 447 at [48] (Charles JA). If that view were correct, the conflict between *Jack v Kipping* and *Stoddart v Union Trust* would be heightened. In *Jack v Kipping* itself, however, the set-off was treated as arising under the bankruptcy section (see e.g. the reference to *Peat v Jones & Co* (1881) 8 QBD 147), and it has been regarded in later cases as an authority on insolvency set-off. See e.g. *Re Mid-Kent Fruit Factory* [1896] 1 Ch 567, 571–2; *Tilley v Bowman Ltd* [1910] 1 KB 745, 751; *Gye v McIntyre* (1991) 171 CLR 609, 630–1; *Coventry v Charter Pacific Corporation Ltd* (2005) 227 CLR 234 at [38]–[50].

[189] [1912] 1 KB 181, 188, 192.

[190] [1912] 1 KB 181, 189, 192, 194–5. See also *Provident Finance Corporation Pty Ltd v Hammond* [1978] VR 312, 318.

[191] See *Tilley v Bowman Ltd* [1910] 1 KB 745, 751 in relation to insolvency set-off.

[192] [1939] VLR 132.

[193] Compare *Provident Finance Corporation v Hammond* [1978] VR 312, in which the damages claim for breach of warranty related to a different contract to that assigned. The action for the price was brought by an assignee of a bill of sale given by the purchaser of a business for the outstanding amount, rather than

17.38 Consider that a debtor has an unliquidated cross-claim against the creditor which is not sufficiently closely connected to give rise to an equitable set-off. If the cross-claim has been converted into a judgment before the debtor has notice of an assignment of the debt by the creditor, the judgment would constitute a debt which should be able to be set off against the assignee under the Statutes of Set-off, since the case would then be one of mutual debts in existence before notice.[194]

(10) Insolvency

Insolvent assignor

17.39 An assignee takes subject to a right of set-off that would have been available as a defence to an action brought by the assignor against the debtor, either pursuant to the Statutes of Set-off in the case of mutual debts or because of a defence of equitable set-off when the demands are inseparably connected. If the assignor becomes bankrupt or goes into liquidation[195] after the assignment, the assignee does not take subject to the wider right of set-off that would otherwise have been available under the insolvency set-off section.[196] The debt, having been assigned, will not have passed to the assignor's trustee in bankruptcy as property of the bankrupt or, in the case of a company, it will not constitute an asset of the company distributable amongst creditors. As a consequence, unless the assignment is set aside as a preference or on a similar ground, it may be enforced outside of the operation of the insolvency legislation.[197]

17.40 As Wood noted,[198] the bankruptcy of an assignor may give rise to a problem for the debtor.[199] The insolvency set-off section would not apply. Further, a set-off against the assignee, whether by way of equitable set-off or under the Statutes of Set-off, depends upon the continued existence of a claim against the assignor. But if the assignee delays in suing the debtor, so that in the interim the assignor is discharged from bankruptcy, the

---

on the contract of sale itself. Lush J considered (at 321) that one of the objects of the contract of sale in providing for the execution of a bill of sale was to give the debt aspects of the contract a separate existence in a separate contract, and that the rights embodied in the bill of sale were not intended to be 'intertwined' with the various other rights and obligations of the contract of sale. While that may have been true in the particular circumstances of that case, it should nevertheless be borne in mind that it is not a prerequisite to an equitable set-off that the demands should have arisen under the same contract. See paras 4.91 and 4.111 above.

[194] See para. 2.91 above.

[195] Or, in England, if the assignor is a company which has gone into administration and the administrator, being authorized to make a distribution, has given notice of his intention to do so. See para. 6.10 above.

[196] *Re Asphaltic Wood Pavement Co. Lee & Chapman's Case* (1885) 30 Ch D 216, 225. See also *De Mattos v Saunders* (1872) LR 7 CP 570; *Re City Life Assurance Co Ltd (Stephenson's Case)* [1926] 1 Ch 191, 214 (as explained in *Hiley v The Peoples Prudential Assurance Co Ltd* (1938) 60 CLR 468, 501–5); *Popular Homes Ltd v Circuit Developmnents Ltd* [1979] 2 NZLR 642. Note also *Boyd v Mangles* (1847) 16 M & W 337, 153 ER 1218; *Hunt v Jessel* (1854) 18 Beav 100, 52 ER 40 (assignment to a trustee under a deed of arrangement). In relation to equitable set-off, see also (in the analogous situation of an insolvent trustee) *Murphy v Zamonex Pty Ltd* (1993) 31 NSWLR 439 (referred to with approval in *Penwith District Council v V P Developments Ltd* [2005] 2 BCLC 607 at [20]–[23]) and *Doherty v Murphy* [1996] 2 VR 553, discussed at para. 17.122 below. Compare the situation in which the bankruptcy or liquidation occurred before the assignment. See *Stein v Blake* [1996] AC 243, and para. 6.122 above.

[197] See also para. 11.16 above.

[198] Wood, *English and International Set-off* (1989), 894–5.

[199] See also paras 4.35–4.36 above.

assignor would be released from liability.[200] The debtor would no longer have a cross-claim, and the House of Lords held in *Aries Tanker Corporation v Total Transport Ltd*[201] that a claim that has ceased to exist cannot be employed in a set-off. In the case of an equitable set-off, Wood has suggested that the debtor could avoid that result by exercising a 'self-help remedy', in the sense that the debtor could act unilaterally to bring about a set-off.[202] That view is doubtful, however. Equitable set-off admittedly a substantive defence,[203] but the judgment of Lord Wilberforce in the *Aries Tanker* case is authority against the view that the equitable defence entitles a debtor to extinguish the debts in that manner.[204]

Insolvent debtor

Consider that the debtor becomes bankrupt or is a company which goes into liquidation[205] after the assignment. **17.41**

A set-off would not be available in that circumstance under the insolvency set-off section, given that the assigned debt is held by the assignee and the insolvent debtor's claim is against the assignor. There would be a lack of mutuality.[206] The only possible rights of set-off are equitable set-off[207] and set-off pursuant to the Statutes of Set-off. If the cross-demands are sufficiently closely connected to give rise to an equitable set-off, the better view is that the fact of the bankruptcy or the liquidation does not affect the debtor's right, though there is authority which suggests that equitable set-off is not available in bankruptcy or company liquidation in circumstances which are outside the operation of the insolvency set-off section.[208] The position is more complicated when one considers the defence of set-off conferred by the Statutes of Set-off in the case of mutual debts. The Statutes provide a procedural defence to an action at law.[209] Therefore, when it is said that an assignee takes subject to an equity constituted by this form of set-off, it is meant that the assignee, when suing the debtor, takes subject to the procedural defence that would have been available to the debtor in an action at law brought against him or her by the assignor. If, however, the debtor is bankrupt or is in liquidation, the assignee could not sue the debtor without the leave of the court,[210] and so the issue ordinarily would not arise in the context of an action against the debtor. A set-off may be asserted instead by the debtor's trustee in bankruptcy or liquidator when a proof is lodged by the assignee, so as to reduce the proof by the amount of a debt owing by the assignor to the debtor.[211] If the trustee or **17.42**

---

[200] Insolvency Act 1986, s. 281.

[201] [1977] 1 WLR 185. See para. 4.31 above.

[202] Wood, *English and International Set-off* (1989), 895.

[203] See paras 4.29–4.57 above.

[204] See paras 4.31–4.32 above.

[205] Or, in England, if the debtor is a company which has gone into administration and the administrator, being authorized to make a distribution, has given notice of his intention to do so. See para. 6.10 above.

[206] See para. 11.13 above.

[207] Recent Court of Appeal authority suggests that mutuality is necessary for equitable set-off (see para. 4.69 above), but the better view is that it is not an inflexible requirement. See paras 4.67–4.83 above.

[208] See paras 6.25–6.32 above.

[209] See paras 2.34–2.45 above.

[210] See the Insolvency Act 1986, s. 130(2) in relation to a court-ordered winding up, and for bankruptcy s. 285(3).

[211] The trustee in bankruptcy or liquidator would only wish to assert a set-off if recovery from the assignor is unlikely, for example because of the assignor's own insolvency. Normally, it would be to the advantage of

the liquidator rejects the proof lodged by the assignee because of the assignor's debt, the assignee could apply to the court to reverse the decision,[212] but the question would still not arise in the context of pleading set-off as a defence to an action. On a strict analysis, therefore, the Statutes should not justify a set-off. There is nevertheless authority to the effect that a trustee in bankruptcy or a liquidator may reduce an assignee's claim in the debtor's bankruptcy or liquidation to the extent of a debt owing by the assignor before notice.[213] A similar approach was adopted in another situation. Prior to the enactment of the Supreme Court of Judicature Act 1875, the insolvency set-off section in the bankruptcy legislation did not apply to company liquidation. Set-offs had been enforced in liquidations,[214] but these were founded upon the right of set-off conferred by the Statutes of Set-off in the case of mutual debts as a defence to an action at law,[215] rather than upon the bankruptcy set-off section. In *Re South Blackpool Hotel Co, ex p James*,[216] Lord Romilly MR allowed a set-off in that context against a proof lodged by a creditor, as opposed to the set-off operating as a defence to an action. He said that: 'These cases are not to be decided on technicalities, but on principles of common sense.'[217]

Insolvent assignee

17.43 The bankruptcy or liquidation of the assignee will not affect the principle that an assignee takes subject to equities.

17.44 If the debtor's cross-demand against the assignor is not such as to provide a set-off under the Statutes or in accordance with the principles of equitable set-off, the debtor could not rely on the insolvency set-off section in the assignee's bankruptcy or liquidation. The debtor's liability to the assignee, and the claim against the assignor, would not be mutual. But if the assignee happens to be separately liable to the debtor, the insolvency set-off section may apply in relation to that liability and the assigned debt.[218]

(11) Agreement not to assert set-offs

17.45 If a term in the contract between a debtor and a creditor provides for payment without set-off,[219] the term is equally applicable when payment is sought by an assignee.[220] Alternatively, a debtor may have contracted with the creditor on terms that, in the event of

---

the debtor's estate to pay a dividend to the assignee on the assigned debt and proceed against the assignor for payment in full of what the assignor owes. Compare *Re Parker* (1997) 80 FCR 1.

[212] For company liquidation, see the Insolvency Rules 1986, r. 4.83, and for bankruptcy, the Insolvency Act 1986, s. 303.

[213] *Re Richard Smith & Co Ltd* [1901] 1 IR 73; *Re China Steamship Co, ex p MacKenzie* (1869) LR 7 Eq 240; *Re Pinto Leite and Nephews* [1929] 1 Ch 221. See also *Christie v Taunton, Delmard, Lane and Co* [1893] 2 Ch 175 (members' voluntary winding up).

[214] See para. 6.05 above.

[215] *Brighton Arcade Co Ltd v Dowling* (1868) LR 3 CP 175, 182, 184; *Sankey Brook Coal Co Ltd v Marsh* (1871) LR 6 Ex 185, 187, 189; *Ex p Price, re Lankester* (1875) LR 10 Ch App 648, 650.

[216] (1869) LR 8 Eq 225.

[217] (1869) LR 8 Eq 225, 226. *Quaere*, however, if this was a case of equitable set-off arising from closely connected cross-claims. See generally ch. 4 above.

[218] See para. 11.17 above.

[219] See paras 5.99–5.141 above.

[220] *John Dee Group Ltd v WMH (21) Ltd* [1998] BCC 972 (receivership). In Australia, see the Personal Property Securities Act 2009 (Cth), s. 80(2).

an assignment, the debtor will not assert against an assignee any equities which the debtor may possess against the creditor or any intermediate assignee.[221] This agreement will bind the debtor[222] as against an assignee who is a *bona fide* purchaser for value.[223] An agreement to that effect may arise by implication. In one case, a company issued debentures to a person who also became a shareholder. The articles of the company provided that the company was to have a lien on the debentures held by a member who was indebted to it, and that the company could sell the debentures in order to obtain payment of the debt. The shareholder assigned the debentures. The shareholder was also liable for unpaid calls, which the company asserted as a set-off against the assignee. Since, however, it was contemplated by the parties that the debentures could be sold and assigned, including possibly by the company through the lien, and since it would have been difficult to sell debentures if a transferee would have had to take subject to an uncertain set-off available to the company against the member, it was held that the company and the member must have intended that a transferee of debentures should take free from set-offs available to the company against the member.[224] A similar implication has been held to arise when a company issues bearer debentures,[225] and in one case where a bank issued an open letter of credit pursuant to which the bank held out to persons negotiating bills drawn by its customer upon the bank that it would honour the bills.[226] In the latter case the bank had gone into liquidation. The liquidator argued that the letter constituted a contract with no one but the customer, and that it did not preclude the bank from setting off the customer's debt to it against the claim of an indorsee of the bills. The argument to that effect was rejected by the Court of Appeal, Turner LJ commenting:[227]

> The whole effect of the letter is, that the Agra Bank held out to the persons negotiating the bills a promise that it would pay the bills; and it would be impossible, according to my view of the doctrines of Courts of equity, to allow the bank, after having sent that letter into

---

[221] See also *Society of Lloyd's v Leighs* [1997] 6 Re LR 289, in which the clause excluded set-off in respect of a cross-claim available directly against the assignee enforcing the assigned debt, although in that case the assignee itself was a party to the contract containing the exclusion.

[222] *Re Agra and Masterman's Bank, ex p Asiatic Banking Corporation* (1867) LR 2 Ch App 391, 397; *Re Blakely Ordnance Co, ex p New Zealand Banking Corporation* (1867) LR 3 Ch App 154, 159–60; *Phoenix Assurance Co Ltd v Earl's Court Ltd* (1913) 30 TLR 50; *Southern British National Trust Ltd v Pither* (1937) 57 CLR 89, 113; *Hilger Analytical Ltd v Rank Precision Industries Ltd* [1984] BCLC 301. See also *Re Goy & Co Ltd. Farmer v Goy & Co Ltd* [1900] 2 Ch 149 with respect to the rule in *Cherry v Boultbee* (1839) 4 My & Cr 442, 41 ER 171 (see para. 14.77 above), and compare *Re Rhodesia Goldfields Ltd* [1910] 1 Ch 239, in which the debentures did not contain a stipulation to the effect that they would be paid without regard to equities.

[223] *Re Goy & Co Ltd* [1900] 2 Ch 149, 153. See also *Re Blakely Ordnance Co* (1867) LR 3 Ch App 154, 159; *Re Brown & Gregory Ltd. Shepheard v Brown & Gregory Ltd* [1904] 1 Ch 627, affirmed [1904] 2 Ch 448; *Ghiradi v Allregal Corp Pty Ltd* [2001] WASCA 366 at [17] ('If the contracting parties agree that the contract may be assigned free from such equities, this can be done').

[224] *Higgs v The Northern Assam Tea Co Ltd* (1869) LR 4 Ex 387. See also *Re Northern Assam Tea Co, ex p Universal Life Assurance Co* (1870) LR 10 Eq 458; *Re South Essex Estuary Co, ex p Chorley* (1870) LR 6 Eq 157.

[225] *Re Blakely Ordnance Co* (1867) LR 3 Ch App 154. See also *Re General Estates Co, ex p City Bank* (1868) LR 3 Ch App 758 (payable to order). Compare *Re Natal Investment Co* (1868) LR 3 Ch App 355.

[226] *Re Agra and Masterman's Bank, ex p Asiatic Banking Corporation* (1867) LR 2 Ch App 391, explained in *Rainford v James Keith & Blackman Co Ltd* [1905] 1 Ch 296, 303. Compare *Graham v Johnson* (1869) LR 8 Eq 36.

[227] (1867) LR 2 Ch App 391, 395.

the world, addressed to the persons who were to negotiate the bills, and so held out to them that it would be answerable for their payment, to say that because there was a debt due to it from the persons to whom it had given the letter of credit, therefore it would not pay the bills.

17.46   On the other hand, a transferee who is not a *bona fide* purchaser for value cannot rely on the agreement. In *Re Brown & Gregory Ltd*,[228] a trustee under a creditors' deed was held not to be a purchaser of debentures assigned to the trustee under the deed, so that the trustee took subject to equities available against the assignor notwithstanding that the debentures in question contained a clause protecting transferees from equities. Similarly, neither a trustee in bankruptcy nor a judgment creditor is considered to be a purchaser.[229]

17.47   The principle is stated in the cases in terms whether the assignee or transferee is a *bona fide* purchaser for value. If those requirements are satisfied, notice of a prior right of set-off available to the debtor against the assignor should not affect the assignee's position.[230] The debtor has held out that it will not enforce equities against assignees, in which case notice of any such equities should not be relevant.

17.48   Debentures issued by a company may provide that, upon registration of a transfer, the transferee will take free from equities. The effect of this provision is that the company reserves the right to assert equities against a transferee prior to registration. However, the fact that the company has a right of set-off available to it against the transferor under the Statutes of Set-off should not entitle the company to refuse to register a transfer. For reasons given earlier,[231] this should be so notwithstanding the decision of Street J in New South Wales in *Stewart v Latec Investments Ltd*,[232] which stands as authority to the contrary when equity acts by analogy with the Statutes.

(12) Conduct of the debtor

17.49   A debtor may be precluded by his or her conduct from setting up equities against an assignee.[233] This does not mean that the debtor is bound to volunteer information to an assignee as regards any prior equities,[234] including as to the existence of a set-off agreement between the debtor and the assignor.[235] An assignee is expected to look after his or her own interests and to make inquiries as to prior equities which may affect the assignee's position.[236] If, on the other hand, the notice given to the debtor indicated that the assignee may have been deceived, and that the assignee was advancing money to the

---

[228] [1904] 1 Ch 627, affirmed [1904] 2 Ch 448.

[229] *Kilworth v Mountcashell* (1864) 15 Ir Ch Rep 565, 581; *Re Marquis of Anglesey* [1903] 2 Ch 727, 732,

[230] Compare *Hilger Analytical Ltd v Rank Precision Industries Ltd* [1984] BCLC 301, 304, in which the principle was discussed in terms of notice.

[231] See para. 3.08 above.

[232] [1968] 1 NSWR 432.

[233] *Athenaeum Life Assurance Society v Pooley* (1858) 3 De G & J 294, 299, 302, 44 ER 1281, 1283, 1284.

[234] *Canadian Admiral Corporation Ltd v L. F. Dommerich & Co Inc* (1964) 43 DLR (2d) 1, 2, 8–9; *Higgs v The Northern Assam Tea Co Ltd* (1869) LR 4 Ex 387, 396.

[235] *Mangles v Dixon* (1852) 3 HLC 702, 732–3, 10 ER 278, 291; *Rolt v White* (1862) 3 De G J & S 360, 46 ER 674; *Toronto-Dominion Bank v Block Bros Contractors Ltd* (1980) 118 DLR (3d) 311. See paras 17.51–17.59 below in relation to set-off agreements.

[236] See para. 17.21 above.

assignor upon a ground which he or she misunderstood, or if the debtor was otherwise aware of a deception but stood by and allowed the assignment to proceed, it may be inequitable to allow the debtor to rely on a right of set-off otherwise available at law under the Statutes if the debtor failed to inform the assignee of the true facts.[237] It is not sufficient to render it inequitable for the debtor to rely on the set-off that the debtor knew of the assignment, if there was nothing to indicate that the assignor was deceiving the assignee.[238] If, however, the debtor was aware of a deception and he or she did not inform the assignee, it may be unconscionable for the debtor to assert a set-off. This would also be the case if the assignee inquired of the debtor but the debtor concealed the truth.[239]

In the case of a transfer of debentures, the company may lose the right to set up prior equities if the company registers the transferee as the holder, and subsequently treats the transferee as such.[240]   **17.50**

(13) A set-off agreement as an equity

There is surprisingly little authority on the effect on an assignee of a set-off agreement entered into between the assignor and the debtor before the debtor had notice of the assignment.[241]   **17.51**

Set-off simply by virtue of the agreement

Consider first the situation in which the agreement contemplates that a set-off will occur, not at the option of the one of the parties, but simply by virtue of the agreement so as to constitute an agreed method of payment. This should be effective as against an assignee.[242] In *Watson v Mid Wales Railway Co*,[243] an assignor of a debt was also a lessee of property from the debtor. The Court of Common Pleas held that the debtor could not set off rent which accrued after the debtor received notice of the assignment, notwithstanding that it arose out of a prior contract.[244] On the other hand, the tenor of the judgments of Willes and Montague Smith JJ suggests that the result would have been different if it had been agreed that the rent was to be set off against the debt, so that only the balance was to be owing.[245]   **17.52**

---

[237] *Mangles v Dixon* (1852) 3 HLC 702, 733, 10 ER 278, 291; *Canadian Admiral Corporation Ltd v L. F. Dommerich & Co Inc* (1964) 43 DLR (2d) 1, 2–3. See also *Rolt v White* (1862) 3 De G J & S 360, 365, 46 ER 674, 676; *Wilson v Gabriel* (1863) 4 B& S 243, 247, 122 ER 450, 452; *Bank of Nova Scotia v Hellenic Mutual War Risks Association (Bermuda) Ltd (The Good Luck)* [1989] 2 Lloyd's Rep 238, 265.

[238] *Mangles v Dixon* (1852) 3 HLC 702, 734–5, 741, 10 ER 278, 291–2, 294. See also *Canadian Admiral Corporation Ltd v L. F. Dommerich & Co Inc* (1964) 43 DLR (2d) 1, 2, 8.

[239] See *Woodhams v Anglo-Australian and Universal Family Assurance Co* (1861) 3 Giff 238, 66 ER 397; *Athenaeum Life Assurance Society v Pooley* (1858) 3 De G & J 294, 299, 44 ER 1281, 1283.

[240] *Re Northern Assam Tea Co, ex p Universal Life Assurance Co* (1870) LR 10 Eq 458, following *Higgs v The Northern Assam Tea Co Ltd* (1869) LR 4 Ex 387.

[241] For the situation in which the set-off agreement is entered into after the debtor has notice of the assignment, see para. 17.59 below.

[242] In addition to the cases referred to below, see *Re Moss Bay Hematite Iron and Steel Co* (1892) 8 TLR 63, 475; *Bank of Montreal v Tudhope, Anderson & Co* (1911) 2 Man R 380. See also *Lambarde v Older* (1853) 17 Beav 542, 547, 51 ER 1144, 1146 in relation to a set-off against a deceased's estate. See paras 13.129–13.135 above.

[243] (1867) LR 2 CP 593.

[244] See para. 17.15 above.

[245] See (1867) LR 2 CP 593, 600 (Willes J), 601 (Montague Smith J).

This is consistent with the earlier decision of the House of Lords in *Mangles v Dixon*.[246] The owners of a vessel chartered it to merchants for a voyage, and later assigned the freight payable. Notice of the assignment was given to the charterers before the voyage was completed. There was a second contract between the owners and the charterers, of which the assignee was not aware, the effect of which was that the profit or loss resulting from the voyage was to be shared between them. The second contract was entered into at the same time as the first contract, and before the charterer had notice of the assignment. The voyage resulted in a loss, half of which accordingly was payable by the owners. When the assignees sought payment of the freight which was due upon termination of the voyage, the charterers sought to deduct the owners' share of the loss. Lord St Leonards held that the question was not one of set-off, strictly so called, because there were not cross-demands. Rather, he said that the effect of the agreement between the owners and the charterers was that freight never became due upon termination of the voyage to the extent that the owners were responsible for a part of the loss.[247] This was an equity to which the assignees took subject, notwithstanding that they were unaware of the second agreement. They should have inquired of the charterers before the assignment.[248]

Option to effect a set-off

17.53 A set-off agreement may take a different form, in that it gives one of the parties a right, or an option, to set off various cross-debts. This may apply not only bi-laterally, as between a debtor and creditor, but also in a multi-party situation, for example where a bank has an agreement with a group of companies entitling the bank to set off deposits of any of the companies against debts owing by that company or any other company in the group. The principle that an assignee takes subject to equities is sometimes referred to in terms suggesting that 'equities' means defences,[249] whereas in this form of set-off agreement a defence as such is not in issue. The right of a party to the agreement is positive in nature, to effect a set-off, and the question is whether an assignee of a debt who gives notice of the assignment will be bound by the debtor's positive right to effect a set-off after that date pursuant to the prior agreement. Certainly the suggestion that 'equities' is confined to defences is too narrow. The concept includes, for example, a right to rescind or rectify a contract.[250] It has been said that 'equities' should be given a wide meaning.[251] In *Mangles v*

---

[246] (1852) 3 HLC 702, 10 ER 278.

[247] (1852) 3 HLC 702, 729, 10 ER 278, 289–90.

[248] (1852) 3 HLC 702, 732–3, 10 ER 278, 291. See also *Toronto-Dominion Bank v Block Bros Contractors Ltd* (1980) 118 DLR (3d) 311.

[249] E.g. in *Roxburghe v Cox* (1881) 17 Ch D 520, 526 James LJ said that an assignee: 'takes subject to all rights of set-off and other defences which were available against the assignor.' Joyce J in *Edward Nelson & Co Ltd v Faber & Co* [1903] 2 KB 367, 375 remarked that, 'an assignee [of a chose in action] takes it subject to all equities – in other words, whatever defence by way of set-off or otherwise the debtor would be entitled to set up against the assignor's claim . . .'. *White & Tudor's Leading Cases in Equity* (9th edn, 1928) vol. 1, 136 states the principle in terms that an assignee 'takes subject to all defences existing in respect of the right assigned which would be available against the assignor seeking to enforce the right assigned'. See also *Clyne v Deputy Commissioner of Taxation* (1981) 150 CLR 1, 20–1.

[250] Smith, *The Law of Assignment* (2007), 91–2, 365–6, referring *inter alia* to *Smith v Jones* [1954] 1 WLR 1089, 1091 (rectification) and *Bristol and West Building Society v Mothew* [1998] Ch 1, 22 (rescission).

[251] *Re H Simpson & Co Pty Ltd* [1964–5] NSWR 603, 605 (Jacobs J); *Franks v Equitiloan Securities Pty Ltd* [2007] NSWSC 812 at [25] and [31] (appeal allowed in part *Equititrust Ltd v Franks* (2009) 256 ALR 388).

Dixon,[252] Lord St Leonards equated the principle that an assignee takes subject to equities with the notion that the assignees in that case 'took precisely the same interest, and were subject to the same liabilities' as the assignor.[253] He also said that: 'if a man does take an assignment of a chose in action he must take his chance as to the exact position in which the party giving it stands.'[254] In *Cockell v Taylor*,[255] Sir John Romilly MR expressed the principle in terms that: 'the purchaser of a chose in action takes the thing bought subject to all the prior claims upon it.' The principle has been expressed in similar terms on other occasions.[256] Those statements, on their face, would extend to a positive right to apply the assigned debt in reduction of another debt, whether owing by the assignor or another party, which is the preferred view.[257]

Transaction entered into before notice

An assignee should take subject to an agreement conferring a right to effect a set-off in so **17.54** far as it applies to a debt which has accrued and is owing to the debtor as a result of a transaction entered into before the debtor had notice of the assignment, whether the debt itself arose before or after notice.[258] In that regard, a set-off agreement may be expressed generally to extend to contingent debts. This should be effective against an assignee when the cross-debt sought to be set off by the debtor has its source in a transaction entered into before notice, but is still contingent at the date of the assignee's action.[259] Professor Goode's analysis of the operation of a set-off agreement in relation to contingent debts is instructive.[260] Depending on the circumstances, he suggested that the agreement may be interpreted in either of two ways. The more likely construction is that the debtor is entitled to suspend payment of the debt that he or she owes until such time as the assignor's contingent liability may vest, followed, if it does vest, by a set-off. Alternatively, there may be cases where the effect of the agreement is that the debtor's liability is immediately cancelled to the extent of the assignor's maximum contingent liability, with an obligation to re-credit the assignor if and to the extent that the contingent liability does not become an actual liability.

---

[252] (1852) 3 HLC 702, 10 ER 278.

[253] (1852) 3 HLC 702, 731, 10 ER 278, 290.

[254] (1852) 3 HLC 702, 735, 10 ER 278, 292.

[255] (1852) 15 Beav 103, 118, 51 ER 475, 481.

[256] See e.g. *Athenaeum Life Assurance Society v Pooley* (1858) 3 De G & J 294, 299, 44 ER 1281, 1283; *Re H Simpson & Co Pty Ltd* [1964–5] NSWR 603, 605; *Clyne v Deputy Commissioner of Taxation* (1981) 150 CLR 1, 20.

[257] See the concession by counsel in *First National Bank of Chicago v West of England Shipowners Mutual Protection and Indemnity Association (The Evelpidis Era)* [1981] 1 Lloyd's Rep 54, 57 with respect to the deduction allowed by the club rules, and also the cheque swapping arrangement in issue in *Commercial Factors Ltd v Maxwell Printing Ltd* [1994] 1 NZLR 724. See also *Fraser v Oystertec plc* [2006] 1 BCLC 491. In Canada, see *Toronto-Dominion Bank v Block Bros Contractors Ltd* (1980) 118 DLR (3d) 311.

[258] This assumes that an assigned debt would come within the terms of the set-off agreement. Compare the submission in *Marathon Electrical Manufacturing Corp v Mashreqbank PSC* [1997] 2 BCLC 460, 469, 471. In *Watson v Mid Wales Railway Company* (1867) LR 2 CP 593, 601, Montague Smith J seems to have considered that a set-off against subsequently accruing rent would have been permitted if there had been an agreement for a set-off. See also *Fraser v Oystertec plc* [2006] 1 BCLC 491 in relation to a debt which is not presently payable.

[259] Compare Oditah, 'Financing trade credit: Welsh Development Agency v Exfinco' [1992] JBL 541, 559.

[260] *Goode on Legal Problems of Credit and Security* (4th edn (ed. Gullifer), 2008), 287.

In either case, the agreement should be binding on the assignee given the assignee's duty of inquiry.[261]

Transaction entered into after notice

17.55 The more difficult question, about which academic writers have expressed differing opinions,[262] is whether a prior set-off agreement will be effective as against an assignee where the transaction out of which the cross-debt sought to be set off arose was entered into after notice. There are two competing views on this. The first, which is consistent with the tenor of Lord St Leonards' judgment in *Mangles v Dixon*,[263] is that an assignee takes the same interest and is subject to the same liabilities as the assignor at the date of notice, and the effect of the prior agreement is that the assigned debt is liable to be used in a set-off against cross-debts both present and future, including where they arise out of new transactions. Moreover, when a chose in action is assigned the courts have emphasized that it is up to the assignee to make inquiries as to prior equities so as to protect his or her position,[264] and the inquiry should extend to the terms of any set-off agreement in place which may affect the debt. The contrary view is that, when the debtor receives notice, the debtor should regulate his or her conduct accordingly[265] and, to paraphrase the language of James LJ in *Roxburghe v Cox*,[266] the debtor should not rely on debts arising out of new transactions to diminish the rights of the assignee as they stood at the time of notice. In the second edition of this book[267] it was suggested that the second approach was more likely to appeal to the court. After further reflection, my opinion on the matter has changed, and it is suggested that the first view should be preferred.[268]

17.56 This is consistent with the approach adopted in *George Barker (Transport) Ltd v Eynon*[269] in the context of a contractual lien. A carrier entered into a contract with a company to carry the company's goods, the contract being on terms that the carrier was to have a general lien on the goods for any money whatsoever due from the company to the carrier. In addition, the company had granted a floating charge over its assets to a debenture-holder. The charge crystallized as a result of the appointment of a receiver after the contract with the carrier but before the carrier obtained possession of some of the goods. Crystallization of a floating charge brings about, or at least it has an effect similar to, an equitable assignment of a

---

[261] See para. 17.21 above.

[262] Compare Wood, *English and International Set-off* (1989), 862, para. 16–36, with Oditah, (1990) 106 LQR 515, 518–19.

[263] (1852) 3 HLC 702, 731, 735, 10 ER 278, 292.

[264] See para. 17.21 above.

[265] *Lloyd v Banks* (1868) LR 3 Ch App 488, 490–1.

[266] (1881) 17 Ch D 520, 526. In *Brice v Bannister* (1878) 3 QBD 569, 578, Cotton LJ expressed it in terms that, after notice of an assignment, the debtor cannot defeat or prejudice the assignee's right. See also *Long Leys Co Pty Ltd v Silkdale Pty Ltd* (1991) 5 BPR 11,512, 11,519 (NSW Court of Appeal).

[267] *Set-off* (2nd edn, 1996), 588.

[268] This is subject to the assumption that the assigned debt would come within the terms of the set-off agreement. See para. 17.54n above. Note also *Commercial Factors Ltd v Maxwell Printing Ltd* [1994] 1 NZLR 724, in which a cheque swapping arrangement was held to be effective against an assignee of book debts. However, the question whether the cross-debts the subject of the arrangement in relation to each assigned invoice arose before or after notice of the assignment of that invoice was not considered.

[269] [1974] 1 WLR 462. See also *Re Diesels & Components Pty Ltd* [1985] 2 Qd R 456; *Mercantile Credits Ltd v Jarden Morgan Australia Ltd* [1991] 1 Qd R 407.

debt owing to the company which comes within the ambit of the charge.[270] The Court of Appeal held that the debenture-holder's charge took subject to the carrier's general lien. The court rejected the receiver's argument that the case involved a priorities dispute between a lien and a crystallized floating charge and that, since the lien was a possessory lien which did not come into existence until the carrier was in possession of the goods, the lien did not arise until after the charge had crystallized, and therefore it was subject to the charge. The carrier's rights did not simply come into existence at the time it took possession of the goods. The rights were created by the contract, albeit that they were not exercisable until a future event, and it was the prior contractual rights to which the debenture-holder took subject.[271]

George Barker v Eynon differed from the situation under discussion in a number of respects. **17.57** In the first place, the contract was for the creation of a security interest in the form of a contractual lien. A set-off agreement, on the other hand, may not constitute a security interest as such,[272] although it performs a similar function. In addition, the contract which gave rise to the lien was also the contract which authorized the carriage of the goods, and therefore it could be said that the debenture-holder should not take the benefit of the contract without at the same time accepting the liabilities under it.[273] Further, the lien in the *George Barker* case arose as a matter of course from a contract of carriage entered into before crystallization, and while in the situation under discussion the set-off agreement is entered into before the assignment, the transaction which gives rise to the cross-debt from the assignor to the debtor is not entered into until after notice of the assignment to the debtor. Nevertheless, the reasoning of Edmund Davies LJ in the *George Barker* case[274] is pertinent. He considered that the company could not simply shrug off the contract it had entered into for the creation of the lien, and he said that the debenture-holder could assert its position as assignee of the company's property and contractual rights only by itself recognizing and giving effect to the pre-appointment contractual rights of the carrier. Similarly, an assignee of a debt should not be able to assert its position as assignee of the assignor's contractual rights without itself recognizing and giving effect to the pre-assignment contractual right of set-off available to the debtor as against the assignor. The assignor's rights, and therefore the rights of the assignee, are circumscribed by the prior set-off agreement. If, on the other hand, the debtor is aware that the assignee is being deceived but fails to inform the assignee of the true facts, the circumstances may render it inequitable to permit the debtor to assert the set-off against the assignee.[275]

---

[270] See para. 17.100 below.
[271] See, in particular, the discussion by Stamp LJ at [1974] 1 WLR 462, 472–3, and also *Re Diesels & Components Pty Ltd* [1985] 2 Qd R 456, 461. Nor did it matter whether the carrier received notice of the appointment of the receiver before or after obtaining possession of the goods. See Stamp LJ at [1974] 1 WLR 462, 465. See also *Re Diesels & Components Pty Ltd* (above), in which the customs agent became aware of the appointment of the receiver before it received the bill of lading relating to the goods.
[272] See paras 16.93–16.107 above.
[273] See [1974] 1 WLR 462, 475 (Sir Gordon Willmer).
[274] [1974] 1 WLR 462, 470. See also Sir Gordon Willmer at 475.
[275] See para. 17.49 above.

Security over a debt

17.58 The notion that an assignee takes subject to a prior set-off agreement should also apply where a debt constitutes property the subject of a security.[276] The security-holder takes subject to equities, which should include prior contractual rights of set-off. In Australia, an exception has been recognized in the situation in which an administrator is appointed to a company under Part 5.3A of the Corporations Act 2001 (Cth), and the administrator has a lien over property of the company, consisting of a debt due to the company, out of which he or she is entitled to be indemnified for debts incurred in the performance or exercise of the functions and powers as administrator. This follows from the decision of the New South Wales Court of Appeal in *Cinema Plus Ltd v Australia and New Zealand Banking Group Ltd*,[277] which was considered earlier.[278]

Subsequent set-off agreement

17.59 A set-off agreement entered into by a debtor and an assignor after the debtor has notice of the assignment ordinarily would not be effective as against the assignee. On the other hand, the assignee may have agreed with the debtor that, notwithstanding the assignment, the debtor can pay the assignor until such time as the assignee notifies the debtor that payment must be made directly to the assignee. Ordinarily, payment to the assignor would be construed as including payment by way of an agreement for a set-off.[279] However, the set-off should have been carried into effect before the debtor receives notice from the assignee in accordance with their agreement. If the debtor and the assignor enter into an agreement for a set-off to occur in the future, and the settlement in account has not taken place when the assignee gives notice that payment is to be made directly to him or her, it would not be a case of a payment already having been made to the assignor, and (subject to the terms of the agreement with the assignee) the assignee should therefore be entitled to demand payment in full.[280] Further, the assignee's agreement that the debtor may pay the assignor ordinarily would not be interpreted as authorizing a set-off involving liabilities owing by parties other than the assignor to the debtor.[281]

(14) Successive assignments

17.60 Consider the case of successive assignments. For example, A may assign a debt to B, who in turn assigns it to C. The debtor in that circumstance should be entitled to a set-off in respect of a cross-debt owing to him or her by C as the ultimate assignee. However, would C take subject to a set-off in respect of a debt owing to the debtor by the intermediate assignee, B? A similar issue arose in *Re Milan Tramways Co, ex p Theys*.[282] The case concerned a number of debts for which proofs had been lodged in the liquidation of the debtor company. Subsequently, the creditors assigned the debts to H, who happened to be the

---

[276] See paras 17.99–17.118 below.
[277] (2000) 49 NSWLR 513.
[278] See para. 16.69 above.
[279] *First National Bank of Chicago v West of England Shipowners Mutual Protection and Indemnity Association (The Evelpidis Era)* [1981] 1 Lloyd's Rep 54, 63.
[280] [1981] 1 Lloyd's Rep 54, 64–5, 66 (and see also counsel's argument summarized at 62–3).
[281] [1981] 1 Lloyd's Rep 54, 65.
[282] (1884) 25 Ch D 587.

subject of an allegation of misfeasance in relation to the company. H then assigned the debts to T, who gave notice of the assignment to the liquidator. After this second assignment an order was made that H should pay £2,000 to the company on account of his misfeasance. The Court of Appeal held that the liquidator could not set off that sum against the assigned debts under the insolvency set-off section, because at the date of the liquidation the debts were held by the original creditors, and there was no right of set-off at that date available against them.[283] Alternatively, the liquidator argued that he could make a deduction from the dividend payable on the debts to the extent of H's obligation to contribute to the fund consisting of the company's assets available for distribution in the liquidation. Essentially, this was based on the principle considered in *Cherry v Boultbee*,[284] although the case was not mentioned in the judgments. The argument to that effect also failed. The order against H for payment of the £2,000 was made after the assignment to the ultimate assignee, T, and before the dividend was declared. Fry LJ considered that the principle could not be invoked unless at the time the dividend was declared the entitlement to the dividend belonged to a person who was indebted to the company.[285] It was not evidently regarded as sufficient that the liability arose out of conduct by H that occurred before the debts were assigned.[286] Cotton LJ reached the same conclusion but expressed his reasoning in different terms. He said that T, in seeking payment of the dividend, was not enforcing the rights of H, but rather the rights of the original creditors, and there was no equity available against the original creditors to which T could be made to take subject.[287] This was in the context of the *Cherry v Boultbee* principle, but the statement was expressed generally, in terms of 'equities', and it should be relevant also to set-off. If, in the *Milan Tramways* case, H had been an equitable assignee, it would have been a powerful argument.[288] It is consistent with the later discussion by Dixon J in the High Court of Australia in *Southern British National Trust Ltd v Pither*,[289] and it also accords with the view

---

[283] See paras 6.63–6.65 above.

[284] (1839) 4 My & Cr 442, 41 ER 171. See ch. 14 above.

[285] (1884) 25 Ch D 587, 594.

[286] It could not be said that H had a monetary liability before the assignment because the company had the right to elect to take the shares the subject of the misfeasance allegation rather than compensation. See Kay J at first instance (1882) 22 Ch D 122, 125–6. See also the similar case of *Re Bailey Cobalt Mines Ltd* (1919) 45 DLR 585. Note, however, the criticism of *Stephens v Venables* (1862) 30 Beav 625, 54 ER 1032 in paras 14.70–14.74 above.

[287] (1884) 25 Ch D 587, 593.

[288] In addition to the cases referred to below, see *Re Poulter; Poulter v Poulter* (1912) 56 Sol Jo 291.

[289] (1937) 57 CLR 89, 108–9. Dixon J commented: 'Confusion sometimes arises between the two very different applications of the statement that the assignee of a chose in action takes subject to all equities affecting the assignor. When this statement is made in relation to the rights and liabilities of the debtor or obligor, it means that every assignee takes subject to all defences available as between the original parties to the obligation up till the completion of the first assignment by notice. The debtor's liabilities may be discharged in whole or in part by some transaction with the immediate assignee, as for instance, by payment to him. In that case an assign of an assignee would take subject to that defence also. But it is not every defence open to the debtor against such an intermediate assignee that is available against a subsequent assignee. Set-off is an instance.' See also Latham CJ at 102–3. Dixon J distinguished set-off from an equity which affects the intermediate assignee's title as against the assignor, such as a right in the assignor to set the assignment aside for fraud. A second assignee takes subject to that equity, on the basis of the principle *nemo dat quod non habet*. See also Rich J at 105.

of Parker J in *The Raven*[290] that: 'The rule that an assignee takes subject to equities means, in my judgment, equities as against the assignor and does not include claims against an intermediate assignee.'[291] It is true that, in *Cavendish v Geaves*,[292] Sir John Romilly said that an ultimate assignee takes subject to rights of set-off available to the debtor against an intermediate assignee, and, in *Pellas v Neptune Marine Insurance Co*,[293] Bramwell LJ expressed agreement with the principles laid out in *Cavendish v Geaves*. However, the views of Cotton LJ, Dixon J and Parker J are to be preferred. The point is that, in the case of an equitable assignment, the assignor has the legal title to the assigned debt. The reason that an equitable assignee takes subject to a set-off available against the assignor under the Statutes of Set-off is that there is mutuality at law, and therefore there is a right of set-off at law, and if the debtor's cross-claim against the assignor arose before the debtor had notice of the assignment there is nothing unconscionable in the debtor asserting this legal right of set-off against the assignee.[294] On the other hand, when there are successive equitable assignments, and the debtor is owed a debt by the intermediate assignee, the position is different. There is no mutuality at law, given that the legal title to the debt being enforced is in the assignor whereas the debtor's claim is against the intermediate assignee, and therefore there is no right of set-off at law. Nor would an equitable set-off be available by analogy with the Statutes,[295] since the cross-demands are not equitably mutual. The beneficial title to the assigned debt is in the ultimate assignee, whereas the debtor's claim is against the intermediate assignee.

17.61 In the *Milan Tramways* case, however, it appears that H was not an equitable assignee, but had taken a statutory assignment of the debts in accordance with the Judicature Act 1873, s. 25(6),[296] so that he had the legal title. In Cotton LJ's opinion, this did not make any difference, because: 'there is nothing to prevent the ultimate assignee from suing in the name of the original creditors, free from any equities which only attach on the intermediate assignee.'[297] Yet Lord Esher MR later commented in *Read v Brown*[298] in relation to a statutory assignment, that: 'The debt is transferred to the assignee and becomes as though it had been his from the beginning; it is no longer to be the debt of the assignor at all, who cannot sue for it, the right to sue being taken from him.'[299] If, therefore, the assignment to the intermediate assignee complies with the statute and the ultimate assignee is an equitable

---

[290] *Banco Central SA v Lingoss & Falce Ltd (The Raven)* [1980] 2 Lloyd's Rep 266, 273.

[291] Compare the suggestion in Treitel, *The Law of Contract* (12th edn, 2007), 735 n 176, that this should be understood in the context of a cross-claim available to the debtor against the intermediate assignee which arose before the assignment to the intermediate assignee. Parker J's comments were not qualified in this manner, however, and indeed it is not expressly made clear in his judgment when the cross-claim in that case arose.

[292] (1857) 24 Beav 163, 53 ER 319.

[293] (1879) 5 CPD 34, 39 (*arguendo*).

[294] See para. 17.03 above.

[295] See paras 3.07–3.09 above.

[296] See (1884) 25 Ch D 587, 590, 593. See now the Law of Property Act 1925, s. 136(1), and para. 17.04 above.

[297] (1884) 25 Ch D 587, 593. See also *Southern British National Trust Ltd v Pither* (1937) 57 CLR 89, 109 (Dixon J).

[298] (1888) 22 QBD 128, 132.

[299] See also *Bennett v White* [1910] 2 KB 643; *Re Pain (Gustavson v Haviland)* [1919] 1 Ch 38, 45.

assignee, the ultimate assignee would sue in respect of the intermediate assignee's legal title, which should have as a consequence that the ultimate assignee takes subject to equities available against the intermediate assignee that arose before the debtor had notice of the second assignment.[300] It has been said that the statutory form of assignment relates only to procedure,[301] but at least in relation to the rights of a sub-assignee it may have a substantive effect.

It may be that the intermediate assignee and the debtor entered into an agreement to set off **17.62** the assigned debt against a debt owing by the intermediate assignee to the debtor. Provided that the agreement is entered into before the debtor has notice of the second assignment, it should bind the ultimate assignee, whether the first assignment was equitable or statutory.[302] The agreement is equivalent to payment, and payment by the debtor to the intermediate assignee before notice of the second assignment would be effective to discharge the debtor as against the ultimate assignee.[303]

The ultimate assignee would take subject to equities available against the original assignor **17.63** before notice. If the assignment to the intermediate assignee and the second assignment to the ultimate assignee were both merely equitable, the ultimate assignee would be enforcing the legal rights of the original assignor, and therefore the principle of taking subject to equities should apply in relation to the original assignee.[304] If the original assignment complied with the statute, the intermediate assignee would take subject to any equity available against the original assignor,[305] which in turn should constitute an equity available against the intermediate assignee to which the ultimate assignee takes subject, whether the ultimate assignment was statutory or equitable.

(15) Marshalling

Consider that a creditor is owed two debts by the one debtor.[306] One of the debts (debt 1) **17.64** is assigned to an assignee, and the other (debt 2) is retained by the creditor/assignor. In addition, the debtor is owed a cross-debt by the assignor. The debtor would appear to have a choice. He or she could employ the cross-debt either as a defence under the Statutes of Set-off to an action by the assignor for payment of debt 2, or alternatively as a defence to an action by the assignee to enforce debt 1 on the basis of the principle that an assignee takes

---

[300] *Re Richard Smith & Co Ltd* [1901] 1 IR 73 may support this view, given that the transfer of the debentures by Murphy and Smith (the original assignors) to Fitt (the intermediate assignee) was by deed, and the conditions attached to the debentures required that the transfer in writing be delivered to the company in order to be registered. For a valid legal assignment, express notice in writing of the assignment must be given to the debtor. However, there are no formal requirements for a valid notice (see *Van Lynn Developments Ltd v Pelias Construction Co Ltd* [1969] 1 QB 607, 613), and the delivery of a transfer ordinarily should suffice. On that basis the requirements for the statutory form of assignment may have been satisfied, this having been introduced into Ireland by the Supreme Court of Judicature Act (Ireland) 1877, s. 28(6).

[301] *Tolhurst v Associated Portland Cement Manufacturers (1900) Ltd* [1902] 2 KB 660, 676–7; *Torkington v Magee* [1902] 2 KB 427, 435. Compare Tolhurst, *The Assignment of Contractual Rights* (2006), 107–15.

[302] See para. 17.52 above.

[303] *Southern British National Trust Ltd v Pither* (1937) 57 CLR 89, 108–9.

[304] See above.

[305] See para. 17.04 above.

[306] For marshalling to apply there must be at least two separate debts. See *Re Bank of Credit and Commerce International SA (No. 8)* [1996] Ch 245, 271–2 (CA), [1998] AC 214, 230–1 (HL).

subject to equities. A similar analysis would apply if debt 2, instead of being retained by the assignor, was the subject of an assignment to a second assignee. The debtor *prima facie* could assert the set-off against either of the assignees. The result suggested in the cases is that, if the assignor has retained debt 2, any set-off in relation to the cross-debt should occur first as against debt 2 so as not to diminish the rights of the assignee in relation to debt 1,[307] while, if debt 2 similarly has been assigned to a second assignee, the set-off should operate rateably as against both debt 1 and debt 2.[308] This has been justified on the basis of the equitable doctrine of marshalling. It is argued elsewhere,[309] however, that marshalling is inappropriate to a situation in which a defence of set-off in relation to debts is in issue, as opposed to a positive right to have recourse to more than one fund. This is not to suggest that the assignee of debt 1 is without a remedy if the debtor asserts the cross-debt as a defence to the assignee's action. The assignee may be entitled to be indemnified by the assignor or, if debt 2 has also been assigned, to claim contribution from the second assignee. Alternatively, subrogation may provide relief, in the sense that the assignee may be entitled to be subrogated to the assignor's rights against the debtor on debt 2 or, if debt 2 has also been assigned, to a rateable proportion of the benefit of debt 2 as against the second assignee.

Different rights

17.65   There is in any event a limitation on the application of the doctrine of marshalling which is relevant to the question of set-off, and that is that marshalling cannot apply when different rights are in issue. In *Webb v Smith*,[310] the defendants were auctioneers who had sold a brewery for a customer. The proceeds of sale of the brewery remained in the auctioneers' hands subject to a particular lien for their charges incurred in connection with the sale. However, the customer had charged the proceeds of sale in favour of the plaintiff. In addition, the auctioneers had in their hands the proceeds of sale of some furniture which they had sold for the customer. The auctioneers had two courses of action open to them. They could have deducted their charges from the brewery proceeds pursuant to their lien, and delivered the furniture proceeds to the customer and the balance of the brewery proceeds to the plaintiff in accordance with the charge. Alternatively, they could have delivered all of the brewery proceeds to the plaintiff, and asserted a right to set off the customer's indebtedness for the charges against their own indebtedness for the furniture proceeds.[311] The auctioneers adopted the first approach, to the disadvantage of the plaintiff.

---

[307] *Cavendish v Geaves* (1857) 24 Beav 163, 53 ER 319; *Smit Tek International Zeesleepen Berginsbedrijf BV v Selco Salvage Ltd* [1988] 2 Lloyd's Rep 398.

[308] *Cavendish v Geaves* (1857) 24 Beav 163, 53 ER 319; *Moxon v Berkeley Mutual Benefit Building Society* (1890) 62 LT 250.

[309] Derham, 'Set-off against an assignee: the relevance of marshalling, contribution and subrogation' (1991) 107 LQR 126. Compare *Meagher, Gummour and Lehans's Equity Doctrines and Remedies* (4th edn, 2002), 425–6 in relation to the alternative remedies suggested below.

[310] (1885) 30 Ch D 192. Compare *Moxon v Berkeley Mutual Benefit Building Society* (1890) 62 LT 250, criticized in Derham, 'Set-off against an assignee: the relevance of marshalling, contribution and subrogation' (1991) 107 LQR 126, 138–40.

[311] There is authority for the view that an auctioneer is entitled to a set-off against proceeds of sale in his or her hands, and this would seem to apply notwithstanding that the proceeds may be impressed with a trust. See *Palmer v Day & Sons* [1895] 2 QB 618, and para. 10.20 above.

The plaintiff sued the auctioneers, arguing that because of the doctrine of marshalling the auctioneers should have acted in accordance with the second possible approach so as not to disappoint the plaintiff. The Court of Appeal held that marshalling was not applicable. Brett MR noted that the auctioneers had a lien upon the brewery proceeds and a right of set-off against the furniture proceeds, and said that marshalling is not applicable when different rights exist in respect of different funds. Similarly, Lindley LJ said that the auctioneers had a 'superior right of lien as to the fund produced by the sale of the brewery',[312] and they could not be deprived of this superior right.

(16) Assignment merely of the proceeds of a debt

When a debt is assigned the assignee obtains an equitable interest in the debt, and once the debtor has notice of this equitable interest it is unconscionable for the debtor to rely on subsequent events to diminish the rights of the assignee.[313] But what if the assignment is confined to the proceeds of the debt when received? It has been said that it is not possible to separate a debt from its proceeds,[314] but that was in the context of a charge on a debt. While a charge on or an assignment of a debt would extend also to the proceeds,[315] the converse does not always apply. There may be an assignment of the proceeds of a debt when received, but not of the debt itself.[316] Nothing would pass, even in equity, until the subject of the assignment, being the proceeds, comes into existence.[317] **17.66**

Where an assignment is confined to the proceeds of a debt when received, the assignee does not acquire an interest in the debt itself.[318] If the debtor has a defence to an action for payment, there would not be any proceeds received, and therefore there would not be anything to which the assignment could attach. Moreover, because the assignee's interest does not extend to the debt, it should not be unconscionable for the debtor to rely on a set-off **17.67**

---

[312] (1885) 30 Ch D 192, 202.

[313] See para. 17.03 above.

[314] *Royal Trust Bank v National Westminster Bank plc* [1996] 2 BCLC 682, 704 (Millett LJ). See also *Agnew v Commissioner of Inland Revenue* [2001] 2 AC 710 at [46].

[315] See *Buhr v Barclays Bank Plc* [2001] EWCA Civ 1223. In Australia, see the Personal Property Securities Act 2009 (Cth), s. 32(1) in relation to a security interest over a debt (which includes a transfer of an account or chattel paper (as defined): see s. 12(3)).

[316] *Glegg v Bromley* [1912] 3 KB 474; *Palette Shoes Pty Ltd v Krohn* (1937) 58 CLR 1, 13; *ANC Ltd v Clark Goldring & Page Ltd* [2001] BCC 479, 485; *Re SSSL Realisations (2002) Ltd* [2005] 1 BCLC 1 at [52]–[54] (charge over a sum of money once paid) (Lloyd J, whose views were referred to with approval on appeal: [2006] Ch 610 at [122]). See also *Maunder Taylor v Blaquiere* [2003] 1 WLR 379 at [20] in relation to a trust imposed on the proceeds of a debt but not on the debt itself. An assignment of proceeds may nevertheless be interpreted in a particular case as an assignment of the right to receive them. See e.g. *Marathon Electrical Manufacturing Corp v Mashreqbank PSC* [1997] 2 BCLC 460, 464–5 in relation to a letter of credit, and also *Re Emilco Pty Ltd* (2002) 20 ACLC 388 at [19]. See also Fealy, 'Can set-off prejudice a debt subordination agreement?' (2009) 24 *Journal of International Banking and Financial Law* 64.

[317] *Glegg v Bromley* [1912] 3 KB 474, 490.

[318] *ANC Ltd v Clark Goldring & Page Ltd* [2001] BCC 479, 485. Compare *Southern British National Trust Ltd v Pither* (1937) 57 CLR 89, 107–8 in relation to a charge on the proceeds of a chose in action. Dixon J said that the chargor in such a case comes under an equitable obligation in respect of the chose in action itself, in that the chargor is bound to exercise his or her rights in respect of the chose in action in such a way as will not defeat or impair the charge. He went on to comment that it may be a question whether the chargee obtains in consequence an equitable interest in the chose in action or an equity only against the person in whom it is vested, but did not decide the point. An equity against the chargor personally should not prevent the debtor from raising a defence.

or other defence to an action on the debt that accrues after notice of the assignment, notwithstanding the consequential effect that this would have on the assignee's position. A person who takes an assignment merely of the proceeds of a debt, and not of the debt itself, should take subject to all defences of set-off available against the assignor whether arising before or after notice.

(17) Assignment of part of a debt

17.68 A part of a debt may be assigned in equity.[319] In that case, if the debtor has a cross-claim against the assignor which, apart from the assignment, is eligible for a set-off against the debt, the cross-claim should be available as a set-off against the unassigned part of the debt.[320] Furthermore, if the cross-claim is also otherwise eligible for a set-off against the assignee, the better view is that the set-off should occur first against the part of the debt in which the assignor alone is beneficially interested, and after that as against the unassigned part. The assignor, as the party liable on the cross-claim, should be the first to bear the burden of a set-off which arises in relation to it. Nevertheless, that approach was not adopted in *Re South Blackpool Hotel Co, ex p James*.[321] Prior to its winding up, a company had issued seventeen debentures to a promoter of the company, three of which he assigned to the claimant. The promoter was also liable to the company, and Lord Romilly MR held that the promoter's liability should be set off pro rata against the debentures.[322]

(18) Debts transferable at common law in their own right

17.69 Prior to the Judicature Acts the common law did not generally recognize an assignment of a debt, in the sense that the assignee could not enforce the debt in a common law action brought in the assignee's own name. Assignments generally were recognized only in equity, which would compel the assignor to allow his or her name to be used in a common law action on the assigned debt.[323] But while that was the general position, there were nevertheless certain types of debts, such as bills of exchange and other negotiable instruments, which the common law accepted could be transferred and enforced by the transferee.[324] This distinction between common law and equity is significant. The principle that an assignee takes subject to equities is an equitable principle which historically applied only where there was a chose in action which, before the Judicature Acts, was assignable only in

---

[319] *Durham Brothers v Robertson* [1898] 1 QB 765, 769; *Brice v Bannister* (1878) 3 QBD 569; *Re Steel Wing Co Ltd* [1921] 1 Ch 349, 355.

[320] *Hiley v Peoples Prudential Assurance Co Ltd* (1938) 60 CLR 468, 497–8 (Dixon J), referring to *Re Asphaltic Wood Pavement Co. Lee & Chapman's Case* (1885) 30 Ch D 216, 222.

[321] (1869) LR 8 Eq 225.

[322] The liquidation in that case had occurred before the assignment, and it might be suggested that the result is explicable on the basis of automatic set-offs having occurred rateably at the date of the liquidation pursuant to the insolvency set-off section. See paras 6.119–6.146 above in relation to the automatic nature of insolvency set-off, and paras 6.168–6.173 above in relation to a pro rata set-off in insolvency. However, that explanation would not be available in relation to the *South Blackpool* case, given that it was decided before the insolvency set-off section was incorporated into the law of company liquidation. See para. 6.05 above.

[323] See para. 17.03 above.

[324] See Warren, *The Law Relating to Choses in Action* (1899), 34–45 and Starke, *Assignments of Choses in Action in Australia* (1972), 10–11.

equity.[325] It did not apply when a transferee was suing upon a debt which was transferable at common law in its own right.[326] While an assignee of a debt which otherwise was assignable only in equity may now sue in his or her own name if the requirements of s. 136(1) of the Law of Property Act 1925 are satisfied,[327] the section is merely procedural in its operation,[328] in the sense that it only applies where, prior to the Judicature Acts, the assignee would have had to proceed in the name of the assignor in a common law action for payment.[329] Where, however, a debt is transferable at common law in its own right, the transferee before the Judicature Acts could have sued in his or her own name and in respect of his or her own legal title. The transferee need not have relied on the legal title of the transferor. A mere personal equity such as a right of set-off under the Statutes of Set-off that could have been asserted against the transferor in an action brought by the transferor could not be asserted against the transferee suing in his or her own name, irrespective of when the transferor's indebtedness may have arisen. The reason for the distinction is plain enough. When an equitable assignee of a debt sues for payment through the assignor's legal title, there is mutuality at law in relation to that debt and a cross-debt owing by the assignor to the debtor, and the question is whether it is unconscionable for the debtor to rely on the consequent right of set-off available at law.[330] Where, however, the transferee of a debt can sue at common law in his or her own name and in respect of his or her own legal title, there is not mutuality at law in relation to the transferred debt and a debt owing by the transferor to the debtor, and accordingly the question does not arise as to whether it is unconscionable for the debtor to rely on a defence that would have been available if regard were had only to legal titles. Nor is there mutuality in equity to support an equitable set-off.[331] There is then no basis for a set-off, either at common law or in equity.

---

[325] Compare *Muscat v Smith* [2003] 1 WLR 2853, which is considered, and criticized, at paras 17.79–17.88 below.

[326] *Priddy v Rose* (1817) 3 Mer 86, 107, 36 ER 33, 41 *per* Sir William Grant ('The assignee for the annuitants, taking no legal interest in the funds, could only take subject to the same equity to which the assignor was liable'); *Ord v White* (1840) 3 Beav 357, 365–6, 49 ER 140, 143–4 *per* Lord Langdale ('the assignee of a chose in action, assigned by an instrument which is available only in equity, must take subject to all equities which subsist as against the assignor'); *Taylor v Blakelock* (1886) 32 Ch D 560, 567 *per* Cotton LJ ('But that rule applies only to a chose in action not transferable at law'); *Reeves v Pope* [1913] 1 KB 637, 642 *per* Bankes J ('the principle . . . has always been confined to the assignment of choses in action, rights which before the Judicature Act were assignable only in a Court of Equity; it has never been extended to the assignment of a reversion, an interest which was always assignable at law . . .'); *Southern British National Trust Ltd v Pither* (1937) 57 CLR 89, 109 *per* Dixon J ('choses in action formerly assignable at law are not within the doctrine'). See also *Rolt v White* (1862) 31 Beav 520, 523, 54 ER 1240, 1242, and the discussion of *David v Sabin* [1893] 1 Ch 523 in Derham, 'Equitable set-off: a critique of *Muscat v Smith*' (2006) 122 LQR 469, 486–7. Tudsbery, *The Nature, Requisites and Operation of Equitable Assignments* (1912), 88, n. (c) states: 'Where a debt is legally assignable apart from the Judicature Act, the assignee takes free from equities.' The principle is expressed in similar terms in *Ashburner's Principles of Equity* (2nd edn, 1933), 241, n. 1. Compare the discussion in *Byles on Bills of Exchange and Cheques* (28th edn, 2007) 233–4 [18–029].

[327] See para. 17.04 above.

[328] Compare Tolhurst, *The Assignment of Contractual Rights* (2006), 107–15.

[329] *Torkington v Magee* [1902] 2 KB 427, 435; *Tolhurst v Associated Portland Cement Manufacturers (1900) Ltd* [1902] 2 KB 660, 676–7.

[330] See para. 17.03 above.

[331] On the basis of equity acting by analogy with the Statutes. See paras 3.07–3.09 above.

Negotiable instruments

17.70 The principle is illustrated by the case of a holder in due course of a negotiable instrument, but the holder of a negotiable instrument takes free of the personal defence of set-off under the Statutes of Set-off even if he or she is not a holder in due course.[332] This appears from the overdue bill cases, such as *Oulds v Harrison*.[333] An indorsee of an overdue bill is not a holder in due course.[334] Nevertheless, it was confirmed in *Oulds v Harrison* that, while the indorsee of the bill takes subject to all equities that had attached to the bill[335] in the hands of the holder when it was due (this includes an agreement with the holder that the bill was to be satisfied by a set-off against a debt owing to the acceptor[336]), the indorsee does not take subject to claims arising out of collateral matters such as a right of set-off available to the acceptor against a prior holder pursuant to the Statutes.[337] Furthermore, it made no difference that the indorsee in that case was aware of the set-off available against the indorser,[338] that the indorsement was made solely in order to defeat the set-off, and that the indorsement had been made without consideration. If, on the other hand, an indorsee did not give value, it may be the case that he or she is a trustee for the indorser, and if the indorsee is simply a trustee he or she would take subject to any right of set-off available against the indorser.[339] The indorsee would also be subject to a set-off if he or she is merely an agent for collection.[340]

17.71 The view that a holder who is not a holder in due course takes free of a right of set-off available under the Statutes of Set-off as against a prior holder, is not universally accepted

---

[332] In addition to the cases referred to below, see *Williams & Glyn's Bank Ltd v Belkin Packaging Ltd* (1983) 147 DLR (3d) 577, 590 (Canadian SC) ('What then is the position of the Bank as a holder for value, not in due course? As such, the Bank is, as we have seen, subject to the equities attaching to the promissory notes but not to mere personal defences . . .').

[333] (1854) 10 Ex 572, 156 ER 566. See also *Burrough v Moss* (1830) 10 B & C 558, 109 ER 558; *Stein v Yglesias* (1834) 1 Cr M & R 565, 149 ER 1205; *Whitehead v Walker* (1842) 10 M & W 696, 152 ER 652; *Re Overend, Gurney & Co, ex p Swan* (1868) LR 6 Eq 344. Compare *Goodall v Ray* (1835) 4 Dowl 76, the accuracy of the report of which has been doubted. See Parke B in *Oulds v Harrison* at 576, 568.

[334] Bills of Exchange Act 1882, s. 29(1).

[335] This expression is synonymous with the term 'defect of title' in the Bills of Exchange Act 1882, s. 36(2). See *Chalmers and Guest on Bills of Exchange, Cheques and Promissory Notes* (17th edn, 2009), 326 [5–041]. For a non-exhaustive list of some defects of title, see the Bills of Exchange Act 1882, s. 29(2).

[336] *Oulds v Harrison* (1854) 10 Ex 572, 578–9, 156 ER 566, 569; *Ching v Jeffrey* (1885) 12 OAR 432 (promissory note). See also *Holmes v Kidd* (1858) 3 H & N 891, 157 ER 729, and *Merchants Bank of Canada v Thompson* (1911) 23 OLR 502, 514–15. Compare *Re Overend, Gurney, & Co, ex p Swan* (1868) LR 6 Eq 344, in which the agreement was with the drawer (that the funds remitted to the acceptor were to be used to satisfy the bills), as opposed to the holders when the bills were dishonoured.

[337] While the contrary view has been expressed (see e.g. Wood, *English and International Set-off* (1989), 700–1), the better view is that the issuer of a negotiable instrument being sued for payment can rely on a defence of set-off under the Statutes if the person suing on the instrument is indebted to him or her. See paras 5.35–5.41 above.

[338] Parke B in *Oulds v Harrison*, referring (at (1854) 10 Ex 572, 579, 156 ER 566, 569) to *Whitehead v Walker* (1842) 10 M & W 696, 152 ER 652.

[339] *Agra and Masterman's Bank Ltd v Leighton* (1866) LR 2 Ex 56, 65; *Churchill & Sim v Goddard* [1937] 1 KB 92, 103–4; *Barclays Bank Ltd v Aschaffenburger Zellstoffwerke AG* [1967] 1 Lloyd's Rep 387. See also *Watkins v Bensusan* (1842) 9 M & W 422, 152 ER 179; *Mayhew v Blofield* (1847) 1 Ex 469, 154 ER 199; *Tolhurst v Notley* (1848) 11 QB 406, 116 ER 529.

[340] *Re Anglo-Greek Steam Navigation and Trading Co (Carralli & Haggard's Claim)* (1869) LR 4 Ch App 174.

by text-writers.[341] However, it is consistent not only with a first-principles analysis,[342] but also with the overdue bill cases referred to above. The contrary view has been said[343] to be supported by the decision in Manitoba of Major J in *Del Confectionery Ltd v Winnipeg Cabinet Factory Ltd*,[344] but the circumstances were unusual and the case is distinguishable. The plaintiff had entered into a contract with a cabinet maker to install some fixtures in his business premises by a certain date. Attached to the contract was a promissory note which was expressed to be payable at a date after the agreed completion date. The promissory note was security for payment of the unpaid balance of the price, together with interest calculated from the date of delivery. Because the date from which interest was to be calculated depended upon delivery, which was uncertain, the note was undated. After the agreed completion date but before actual completion, the cabinet maker assigned the contract to a finance company. This included the promissory note attached to the contract. Major J held that the finance company's claim on the promissory note was subject to the plaintiff's claim for damages against the cabinet maker for non-completion by the fixed date. However, the case does not support a general proposition that a subsequent holder of a negotiable instrument takes subject to a set-off between prior parties. In the first place, Major J postulated that the note may not have been a promissory note, given that it encompassed the payment of exchange and collection charges and accordingly it may not have provided for payment of a sum certain in money.[345] But, in any event, the peculiar circumstances upon which the cross-claim was based, in particular that the note was attached to the contract, appear to have been regarded as giving rise to a defect in title to which the finance company took subject, as opposed to a mere personal equity.[346]

(19) Leases and mortgages

A similar issue may arise when rent is claimed by a mortgagee in possession or a purchaser of land.[347] Can a tenant rely on an equitable set-off that would have been available against the obligation to pay rent if the original landlord had been suing, in circumstances where the action for payment is brought instead by a mortgagee or a purchaser of the land?   **17.72**

---

[341] See Wood *English and International Set-off* (1989), 901, and also *Paget's Law of Banking* (13th edn, 2007) 569–70 [22.21], where it is suggested that a holder for value who is not a holder in due course takes subject to personal defences available to prior parties among themselves. On the other hand, for the preferred view see Crawford and Falconbridge, *Banking and Bills of Exchange* (8th edn, 1986) vol. 2, 1524 *et seq.* and *Chitty on Contracts* (30th edn, 2005) vol. 2, 320–1 [34–095]. See also *Chalmers and Guest on Bills of Exchange, Cheques and Promissory Notes* (17th edn, 2009), 255–6 [4–027] in relation to a holder for value. *Byles on Bills of Exchange and Cheques* (28th edn, 2007), 233–4 [18–029] also appears to support this view in relation to set-off of unconnected cross-debts under the Statutes of Set-off.

[342] See para. 17.69 above.

[343] Wood, *English and International Set-off* (1989), 901.

[344] [1941] 4 DLR 795, [1941] 2 WWR 636.

[345] See the discussion at [1941] 2 WWR 636, 641.

[346] See the discussion at [1941] 2 WWR 636, 641–2. Thus, Major J relied on the earlier decision in *Edie v Turkewich* [1940] 1 WWR 554, in relation to which he said (at 642): 'Here it was held that an uncompleted contract of which certain promissory notes formed a part *affected the title of a subsequent holder*; that such holder had notice of the uncompleted conditions which put him on inquiry and he made none. Under these circumstances he was not a holder in due course.' (emphasis added).

[347] See also para. 13.64 above in relation to the vesting of premises subject to a lease in a trustee in bankruptcy.

The law in this area has been affected by the enactment of the Landlord and Tenant (Covenants) Act 1995.[348] However, the legislation does not generally apply to leases entered into before 1 January 1996,[349] and there is no comparable legislation in Australia.

Mortgage of leased premises – Reeves v Pope

17.73 Contrary to views formerly expressed, it is now accepted that a personal claim for damages available to a tenant against the landlord may be employed by the tenant as an equitable set-off against a liability for rent if there is a sufficiently close connection between the demands.[350] Consider, however, that the landlord has mortgaged the premises, and the mortgagee, having gone into possession of the rents and profits, is the party seeking payment of the rent. In *Reeves v Pope*,[351] mortgagees of leased premises went into possession and sued the tenant for arrears of rent accrued since the date of the mortgage but before the taking of possession. The Court of Appeal held that a personal cross-claim available to the tenant against the landlord/mortgagor[352] could not be set off by the tenant against the mortgagees' claim. The principle has since been affirmed in Victoria[353] and in South Australia,[354] but it is not universally accepted by commentators.[355] The decision in *Reeves v Pope* has been said to constitute an attempt to confer a special insulation in favour of mortgagees from the application of the principle applicable in the case of an assignment of a debt, that the assignee takes subject to an equitable set-off available to the debtor against the assignor.[356] In truth, however, there is nothing special or exceptional about the mortgagee's position, and *Reeves v Pope* was correctly decided.

17.74 *Reeves v Pope* concerned the old form of mortgage which took effect as a conveyance.[357] The land was conveyed to the mortgagee subject to an obligation to re-convey upon satisfaction of the debt. Since the mortgagee had the legal title to the land, he or she had

---

[348] See paras 17.77, 17.88 and 17.90 below.

[349] Landlord and Tenant (Covenants) Act 1995, s. 1 and the Landlord and Tenant (Covenants) Act (Commencement) Order 1995 (S.I. 1995 No. 2963).

[350] See paras 5.67–5.71 above.

[351] [1914] 2 KB 284. See also *Mortgage Corporation Ltd v Ubah* (1996) 73 P & CR 500 in relation to a set-off agreement between a landlord/mortgagor and the tenant, but note para. 17.94 below in relation to a payment of rent in advance.

[352] In *Reeves v Pope*, for breach of contract for failure to complete the construction of a hotel on the leased land by the specified date.

[353] *Citibank Pty Ltd v Simon Fredericks Pty Ltd* [1993] 2 VR 168 (cross-claim for damages for loss of profits arising from breaches of the covenant for quiet enjoyment in an earlier lease); *Piazza Grande Pty Ltd v Portis Pty Ltd* (1993) V ConvR 54–460 (breach of covenant by the lessor to provide a manager for the shopping complex of which the leased premises formed part, and breach of covenant that only one restaurant would be operated in the complex). Compare *Westend Entertainment Centre Pty Ltd v Equity Trustees Ltd* (2000) V ConvR 54–619.

[354] *Ory & Ory v Betamore Pty Ltd* (1993) 60 SASR 393 (overpayment of rent to the landlord/mortgagor not able to be set off by the tenant against rent subsequently claimed by the mortgagee).

[355] See Wood, *English and International Set-off* (1989), 886–7, and also Waite, 'Disrepair and set-off of damages against rent: the implications of British Anzani' [1983] *The Conveyancer* 373, 384–6 in relation to an absolute sale of the reversion (see below). In a note in (1992) 66 *Australian Law Journal* 313, *Citibank Pty Ltd v Simon Fredericks Pty Ltd* [1993] 2 VR 168 was described as a good illustration of a situation whose solution is clear on the authorities but which might be reconsidered.

[356] Wood, *English and International Set-off* (1989), 886–7. See also Lightman and Moss, *The Law of Receivers and Administrators of Companies* (4th edn, 2007), 555, n. 14.

[357] See generally Sykes and Walker, *The Law of Securities* (5th edn, 1993) 39 *et seq.*

the legal entitlement to the rent. Prior to intervention by the mortgagee, the mortgagor had the 'tacit agreement' of the mortgagee to receive rent.[358] The mortgagor received the rent for his or her own absolute use, and not for the use of the mortgagee.[359] The mortgagee, however, could put an end to this tacit agreement at any time,[360] in which case, given the legal entitlement, the mortgagee could sue for future rent as it accrued, and also for any rent in arrears as from the date of the legal title.[361] Indeed, prior to 1873, a mortgagor's remedies at common law to enforce payment of rent before intervention by the mortgagee were limited. A landlord who subsequently mortgaged the reversion could not sue or distrain for rent accrued since the mortgage in his or her own name or bring proceedings for ejectment.[362] The mortgagor's position was ameliorated with the enactment of s. 25(5) of the Supreme Court of Judicature Act 1873, which empowered the mortgagor to sue in his or her own name for unpaid rent. A similar provision is now set out in the Law of Property Act 1925, s. 98, and it has also been adopted in all Australian states.[363] However, this applies only until such time as the mortgagee gives notice of intention to enter into the receipt of the rents and profits. Once the mortgagee gives notice, the mortgagor has no right to sue.

Real property mortgages in England no longer take effect by way of conveyance.[364] As a **17.75** result of reforms introduced by the Law of Property Act 1925, ss. 85 and 87, a mortgage of freehold could operate either as a demise to the mortgagee for a term of years absolute, subject to a provision for cesser on redemption, or alternatively as a charge by deed expressed to be by way of legal mortgage, in which case a mortgagee of an estate in fee simple is expressed to have the same protection, powers and remedies (including the right to take proceedings to obtain possession) as if a mortgage term of three thousand years had been

---

[358] *Moss v Gallimore* (1779) 1 Dougl 279, 283, 99 ER 182, 184.

[359] *Trent v Hunt* (1853) 9 Ex 14, 22–3, 156 ER 7, 10.

[360] *Moss v Gallimore* (1779) 1 Dougl 279, 283, 99 ER 182, 184.

[361] See e.g. *Burrows v Gradin* (1843) 12 LJQB 333 (referring to *Moss v Gallimore* (1779) 1 Dougl 279, 99 ER 182). The same principle applies when the lease is entered into after the mortgage. See *Re Ind, Coope & Co Ltd* [1911] 2 Ch 223, 231–2. Compare the position of an equitable mortgagee, discussed in *Finck v Tranter* [1905] 1 KB 427.

[362] *Doe d Marriott v Edwards* (1834) 5 B & Ad 1065, 110 ER 1086; *Trent v Hunt* (1853) 9 Ex 14, 156 ER 7; *Matthews v Usher* [1900] 2 QB 535, 538–9. A different principle applied if the mortgagor leased the premises *after* the mortgage. The lease was void as against the mortgagee, so that the tenant was liable to be ejected by the mortgagee, unless the mortgagee adopted or otherwise authorized the lease. If that occurred, the mortgagee upon giving notice to the tenant was entitled to all arrears of rent as well as rent which accrued due afterwards. See *Pope v Biggs* (1829) 9 B & C 245, 109 ER 91. If the lease was not adopted or authorized by the mortgagee, the tenant as against the mortgagor was estopped from disputing the validity of the lease. Accordingly, the mortgagor could enforce the covenants in the lease against the tenant, and could distrain for unpaid rent in his or her own name. See *Cuthbertson v Irving* (1859) 4 H & N 742, 157 ER 1034; *Trent v Hunt* at 22–3, 10. In England a mortgagor in possession now has a power to lease, pursuant to the Law of Property Act 1925, s. 99. For the position in the various Australian States, see Sykes, *The Law of Securities* (5th edn, 1993), 102–4. If a lease is granted pursuant to this power, the mortgagee is entitled to the rent on the same basis as for a prior lease. See, e.g., *Re Ind, Coope & Co Ltd* [1911] 2 Ch 223, 231–2 (power in mortgage document to create leases).

[363] See Sykes and Walker, *The Law of Securities* (5th edn, 1993), 99.

[364] In Australia, see also paras 17.91–17.92 below in relation to Torrens title mortgages.

created in his or her favour.[365] In the case of registered land, however, the Land Registration Act 2002, s. 23 has the effect that a mortgage by demise is no longer possible, so that a mortgage would be by way of a charge by deed.[366] This gives the mortgagee a legal estate in possession, and a consequent legal right to go into possession by receipt of the rents and profits,[367] so that the position with respect to rent should be the same as under the old form of mortgage.[368]

17.76 The position of a mortgagee suing for rent is not the same as that of an assignee of a debt. Unless the requirements of s. 136 of the Law of Property Act 1925 have been satisfied,[369] an assignment of a debt generally does not pass the legal title.[370] It is effective only in equity, and therefore the assignee generally can only enforce payment of the assigned debt in an action at law if the assignor as the legal owner of the debt is joined as a party.[371] On the other hand, a mortgagee in possession can sue for rent accruing after the mortgage in his or her own name and in respect of his or her own legal title.[372] The mortgagee is not a mere assignee from the mortgagor of the tenant's indebtedness for rent,[373] but rather has a legal entitlement to rent as a result of having a statutory legal estate.[374] Therefore, for the same reason that a transferee of a debt which is transferable at law does not take subject to rights of set-off that would have been available against the transferor,[375] a set-off otherwise available to a tenant against the landlord/mortgagor under the Statutes of Set-off or by way of equitable set-off should not be capable of being asserted against the mortgagee. Nor would a substantive defence of equitable set-off be available directly against the mortgagee independently of the 'taking subject to equities' principle.[376] Using Lord Cottenham's

---

[365] See the Law of Property Act 1925, s. 87 and Megarry and Wade, *The Law of Real Property* (7th edn, 2008), 1085–6 [24–025].

[366] See Megarry and Wade, *The Law of Real Property* (7th edn, 2008), 1083 [24–019]. The Land Registration Act 2002, s. 23(1)(b) also confers a power to charge a registered estate with the payment of money, but s. 51 provides that, upon completion of registration, the charge has effect as a charge by way of legal mortgage, so that the result would be the same.

[367] See Megarry and Wade, *The Law of Real Property* (7th edn, 2008), 1112 [25–024], 1136–7 [25–071] and [25–072].

[368] See generally *Fisher and Lightwood's Law of Mortgage* (12th edn, 2006), 591–3 [29.59].

[369] See para. 17.04 above.

[370] Save for certain types of debts. See paras 17.69–17.71 above.

[371] See para. 17.03 above.

[372] See e.g. *Burrows v Gradin* (1843) 12 LJQB 333 (referring to *Moss v Gallimore* (1779) 1 Dougl 279, 99 ER 182). See now the Landlord and Tenant (Covenants) Act 1995, s. 15(1)(b).

[373] *Reeves v Pope* [1914] 2 KB 284, 287, 289. The point is illustrated by *Re Ind, Coope & Co Ltd* [1911] 2 Ch 223. Leasehold premises were mortgaged to debenture-holders. The mortgagor then assigned the rent to a third party, who gave notice of the assignment to the tenants before the debenture-holders went into possession of the rents and profits. The dispute as to who was entitled to the rent was not determined by reference to the rule in *Dearle v Hall* (1828) 3 Russ 1, 38 ER 475, as one would have expected if the dispute was regarded as being between two assignees of a chose in action. Rather, the case was decided on the basis that it was not within the power of the mortgagor to assign the rents in priority to the debenture-holders.

[374] See *Reeves v Pope* [1914] 2 KB 284, 289–90 in relation to a mortgage by way of conveyance.

[375] See paras 17.69–17.71 above.

[376] This involves, on the one hand, a claim by the mortgagee against the tenant and on the other a cross-claim by the tenant against the mortgagor. There is an evident lack of mutuality. However, notwithstanding the contrary view that has been expressed in recent times (see para. 4.69 above), in exceptional circumstances equity may permit a set-off despite an absence of mutuality. See paras 4.67–4.83 above.

traditional formulation of the requirement for an equitable set-off in *Rawson v Samuel*,[377] a claim by a mortgagee for rent accrued since the date of the mortgage is not impeached by a damages claim available to the tenant against the mortgagor. Since the mortgagee's claim is based on his or her own title, and not that of the mortgagor, the cross-demands would not be inter-dependent.[378] Similarly, relief would not be available on the basis of the formulation endorsed by the House of Lords in *Bank of Boston Connecticut v European Grain and Shipping Ltd*,[379] that the cross-claim should flow out of and be inseparably connected with the dealings and transactions which gave rise to the claim. The mortgagee's claim is derived from his or her legal estate consequent upon the mortgage, whereas the tenant's cross-claim does not flow out of and is not inseparably connected with the mortgage. The circumstances do not support an equitable set-off.[380] *Reeves v Pope*, therefore, was correctly decided. In *Re Arrows Ltd (No. 3)*[381] Hoffmann J (as he then was) said that he could see no grounds upon which *Reeves v Pope* might be overruled, and the decision was approved by the Court of Appeal in *Edlington Properties Ltd v J H Fenner & Co Ltd*.[382]

Sale of leased premises

The Law of Property Act 1925, s. 141 provides that rent reserved by a lease 'shall be annexed **17.77** and incident to and shall go with the reversionary estate in the land'. Similar legislation exists in most Australian jurisdictions.[383] It permits a purchaser of the land to sue for unpaid rent whether accrued before or after the sale.[384] On the other hand, while s. 142 provides that the obligation under a covenant such as a covenant to repair runs with the land,[385] the purchaser is not liable for past breaches.[386] The position differs in the case of

---

[377] (1841) Cr & Ph 161, 41 ER 451. See para. 4.02 above.

[378] See *Grant v NZMC Ltd* [1989] 1 NZLR 8, 13, and para. 4.03 above.

[379] [1989] 1 AC 1056. See para. 4.13 above.

[380] This relates to a claim for rent accruing *after* the date of the mortgage. Compare the case of a purchaser of land suing to recover arrears of rent from the period before the sale. See paras 17.79–17.88 below.

[381] [1992] BCLC 555, 559.

[382] [2006] 1 WLR 1583 at [28]–[30], [56], referring to the discussion of *Reeves v Pope* in *National Provincial Bank Ltd v Ainsworth* [1965] AC 1175, 1225 (Lord Hodson), 1238 (Lord Upjohn) and 1260 (Lord Wilberforce).

[383] Conveyancing Act 1919 (NSW), ss. 117 and 118; Property Law Act 1958 (Vic), s. 141 and 142; Property Law Act 1974 (Qld), ss. 117 and 118; Property Law Act 1969 (WA), ss. 77 and 78; Conveyancing and Law of Property Act 1884 (Tas), ss. 10 and 11. For South Australia, Northern Territory and the ACT, see *Halsbury's Laws of Australia* vol. 16, at [245–355].

[384] *London and County (A & D) Ltd v Wilfred Sportsman Ltd* [1971] 1 Ch 764; *Arlesford Trading Co Ltd v Servansingh* [1971] 1 WLR 1080; *Muscat v Smith* [2003] 1 WLR 2853 at [12]; *Edlington Properties Ltd v J H Fenner & Co Ltd* [2006] 1 WLR 1583 at [47]. In Queensland, see *Ashmore Developments Pty Ltd v Eaton* [1992] 2 Qd R 1. Section 141 had the effect of reversing the decision of Shadwell VC in *Flight v Bentley* (1835) 7 Sim 149, 58 ER 793, that an assignee of a reversion was not entitled to arrears of rent which became due prior to the assignment. See also *Martyn v Williams* (1857) 1 H & N 817, 825, 156 ER 1430, 1434.

[385] Law of Property Act 1925, s. 142.

[386] *Duncliffe v Caerfelin Properties Ltd* [1989] 2 EGLR 38; *Edlington Properties Ltd v J H Fenner & Co Ltd* [2006] 1 WLR 1583 at [18]. See also Megarry and Wade, *The Law of Real Property* (7th edn, 2008), 942. In *Muscat v Smith* [2003] 1 WLR 2853 at [20] and [28] Sedley LJ left open the question whether *Duncliffe* was rightly decided, but see Buxton LJ at [41] and [52]. Compare *Lotteryking Ltd v AMEC Properties Ltd* [1995] 2 EGLR 13. Lightman J suggested in that case that an obligation to repair assumed by a landlord in a collateral contract ran with the reversion, with the consequence that a claim for damages for breach of the covenant could be set off against rent due to a subsequent assignee of the reversion. However, *Lotteryking v AMEC Properties* was disapproved in the *Edlington Properties* case at [55]–[60].

ases entered into on or after 1 January 1996. Leases entered into after that date are subject to the Landlord and Tenant (Covenants) Act 1995,[387] which disapplies sections 141 and 142 of the 1925 legislation in relation to leases which are subject to the Act.[388] Section 3(1) of the 1995 Act is similar to the 1925 Act in that it provides that the benefit and burden of all landlord and tenant covenants in a tenancy subject to the Act are annexed and incident to the premises and pass on an assignment of the premises. However, unlike the position under s. 141 of the 1925 Act, a transferee of the premises is not entitled to the benefit of a covenant in the lease, which includes the covenant to pay rent, in relation to any time falling before the assignment.[389] Similarly, the transferee does not have any liability under the lease covenants in relation to any time falling before the assignment, which accords with the position under s. 142 of the 1925 Act.

17.78   Given that the mortgage in issue in *Reeves v Pope*[390] took effect as a conveyance, the views expressed in that case in relation to the availability of a set-off to a tenant against a mortgagee should also be relevant when there is an absolute sale of the reversion.[391] The case suggests that the purchaser should be able to sue for rent which has accrued since the sale unaffected by an equitable set-off that the tenant could have asserted against the vendor (as the original landlord) as a result of the vendor's breach of contract. One writer has argued to the contrary.[392] The essence of his argument is that the tenant's right of set-off against the vendor/landlord is not a personal equity, but rather it has a proprietary character. The proprietary character is said to arise because the set-off impeaches the landlord's entitlement to rent, and therefore it is incidental to the tenancy. Further, the courts have said that a purchaser of land has constructive notice of any interest that a tenant in possession has in land,[393] so that the purchaser will have constructive notice of the tenant's right of set-off. Accordingly, the argument proceeds that the purchaser is not a *bona fide* purchaser for value without notice. There are a number of difficulties with that analysis. In the first place, it is not clear that the equitable doctrine of constructive notice would apply in the case of a set-off operating as a mere equity.[394] More importantly, the suggestion that the equity in question has a proprietary character was rejected by the Court of Appeal in *Edlington Properties Ltd v J H Fenner & Co Ltd*[395] and it is difficult

---

[387] Landlord and Tenant (Covenants) Act 1995, s. 1 and the Landlord and Tenant (Covenants) Act (Commencement) Order 1995 (S.I. 1995 No. 2963).

[388] Landlord and Tenant (Covenants) Act 1995, s. 30(4).

[389] Landlord and Tenant (Covenants) Act 1995, s. 23(1).

[390] [1914] 2 KB 284. See paras 17.73 and 17.74 above.

[391] See e.g. Buckley LJ's reported response during argument in *Reeves v Pope* [1914] 2 KB 284, 286 to counsel's statement regarding a purchase.

[392] Waite, 'Disrepair and set-off of damages against rent: the implications of British Anzani' [1983] *The Conveyancer* 373, 380–1 (where the question being considered is set out), 384–6. In addition to the argument set out below, Waite advanced an argument (at 385–6) based upon an assignment of the indebtedness for rent. As in the case of a mortgagee, however, a purchaser is not an assignee of the rent but rather has a right to sue for rent because of his or her own legal title.

[393] See e.g. *Jones v Smith* (1841) 1 Hare 43, 60, 66 ER 943, 950.

[394] See *Smith v Jones* [1954] 1 WLR 1089 (equity of rectification in relation to a lease), although compare *Downie v Lockwood* [1965] VR 257.

[395] [2006] 1 WLR 1583 *per* Neuberger LJ at [20] ('The very nature of an equitable set-off is that it is personal in nature, in that it is a claim raised against the claimant which impeaches his right to sue and does not run against third parties . . .'), [21] and [26]. In *Reeves v Pope* [1914] 2 KB 284, 288, 289, 290

to support. The suggestion to that effect was based, *inter alia*, on the proposition that the right is capable of transmission to a successor tenant by assignment.[396] The problem with this is that equitable set-off is a defence, albeit a substantive defence. It is unclear how a defence available to a tenant against his or her obligation to pay rent could be 'assigned' to a successor tenant in respect of the latter's own rental obligation. This is not to suggest that the fact that something cannot be assigned is a sufficient reason for concluding that it is not proprietary in nature.[397] Rather, the position is simply that it is difficult to see how a defence can be regarded as anything other than a personal equity. The kind of equity to which a purchaser of land with notice takes subject is an equity which is ancillary to or dependent upon an equitable estate or interest in land,[398] in the sense that it will involve an adjustment of the rights of the person possessed of the equity to the land in question.[399] Examples include the right of a tenant to have the lease rectified,[400] and the right of a mortgagor to have a sale by the mortgagee set aside on the ground that the mortgagee's exercise of the power of sale was fraudulent.[401] At common law a purchaser of land does not take subject to a personal obligation of the vendor which does not run with the land, even though it may relate to the use of the land.[402] In the case of a tenant's equitable set-off, while it may be said to relate to the leasehold interest, it does not involve any adjustments to the tenant's right to the land itself, and accordingly it is not an equity to which a purchaser of the land with notice may be obliged to take subject.

Sale of leased premises – both breach of covenant and accrued rent before the sale.   Consider the case of leased premises which are not subject to the Landlord and Tenant (Covenants) Act 1995. Where a purchaser of the premises claims rent which had accrued before the sale,[403] it would be unjust to deny a set-off to the tenant in relation to breaches of the lease by the vendor (as the original landlord) that similarly occurred during that period. In *Muscat v Smith*,[404] the Court of Appeal held that the tenant is entitled to a set-off in this situation. But while the decision to permit a set-off seems correct, it is suggested that the reasoning is unsound. **17.79**

---

the Court of Appeal emphasized that the tenant's damages claim in that case did not create an estate or interest in the land.

[396] Waite, 'Disrepair and set-off of damages against rent: the implications of British Anzani' [1983] *The Conveyancer* 373, 386.

[397] *R v Toohey, ex p Meneling Station Pty Ltd* (1982) 158 CLR 327, 342–3 (Mason J); *Federal Commissioner of Taxation v Orica Ltd* (1998) 194 CLR 500, 537, 542–3. Compare *National Provincial Bank Ltd v Ainsworth* [1965] AC 1175, 1247–8. See also para. 16.104 above.

[398] *National Provincial Bank Ltd v Ainsworth* [1965] AC 1175, 1238 (Lord Upjohn).

[399] See *Meagher, Gummow & Lehane's Equity Doctrines and Remedies* (4th edn, 2002), 146 [4.145].

[400] See *National Provincial Bank Ltd v Ainsworth* [1965] AC 1175, 1238 (Lord Upjohn), and compare *Smith v Jones* [1954] 1 WLR 1089.

[401] Compare *Latec Investments Ltd v Hotel Terrigal Ltd* (1965) 113 CLR 265, in which the purchaser did not have notice of the equity.

[402] *National Provincial Bank Ltd v Ainsworth* [1965] AC 1175, 1253–4 (Lord Wilberforce), referring to Buckley LJ in *London CC v Allen* [1914] 3 KB 642, 657.

[403] Compare the position under the 1995 Act. See para. 17.77 above.

[404] [2003] 1 WLR 2853. The following discussion of *Muscat v Smith* is based upon material that first appeared in an article published in the *Law Quarterly Review*: 'Equitable set-off: a critique of *Muscat v Smith*' (2006) 122 LQR 469. It is reproduced with the permission of the editor of the *Law Quarterly Review*.

17.80 In *Muscat v Smith*, the defendant was a tenant of a dwelling-house. The landlord had breached his obligation to repair, and so the tenant began to withhold rent. Later the landlord sold the property to the plaintiff. The plaintiff sued the tenant for unpaid rent, including for the period before the sale. The question was whether the tenant could set off his claim for damages against the original landlord for breach of the obligation to repair against his liability for arrears of rent from the earlier period.[405] If the original landlord had sued the tenant for the outstanding rent, the tenant would have been entitled to an equitable set-off in respect of his damages claim against the landlord for breach of the repair covenant.[406] But the action for payment of rent was brought by the plaintiff, as the purchaser of the reversion, pursuant to s. 141 of the Property Law Act 1925,[407] and the plaintiff was not liable for breaches of the lease before the sale.[408] For those breaches, the original landlord remained liable. There was, therefore, a lack of mutuality. It was argued that the claims nevertheless could be set off in equity, but Buxton LJ[409] rejected the proposition that an equitable set-off is available where the defendant has a claim against someone other than the plaintiff.[410] Because the parties were not the same, he considered that there could not be a direct set-off in equity between the tenant's liability to the plaintiff for rent in arrears from the period before the sale and the tenant's claim for damages against the original landlord. A set-off nevertheless was justified on another ground, which Buxton LJ referred to as an exception to the general doctrine of privity.[411] The plaintiff was said to be an assignee of the rent owing to the original landlord, and an assignee of a debt takes subject to equities which include rights of set-off available to the debtor against the assignor. Therefore, the plaintiff, in suing as assignee of the rent due to the original landlord, took subject to the tenant's right to a set-off against the original landlord for that landlord's breach of the covenant to repair.[412]

17.81 One can appreciate the justice of the result. As mentioned, if the tenant had been sued by the original landlord for the unpaid rent, the tenant could have set off in that action his damages claim for breach of the repair covenant.[413] Further, if the tenant had sufficient funds to undertake the repairs himself, his expenditure would have gone in reduction of the rent, on the basis of a separate common law principle of recoupment,[414] and this would

---

[405] Compare *Edlington Properties Ltd v J H Fenner and Co Ltd* [2006] 1 WLR 1583 in relation to rent accruing *after* the assignment. See paras 17.83 and 17.89 below.

[406] *British Anzani (Felixstowe) Ltd v International Marine Management (UK) Ltd* [1980] 1 QB 137. See para. 5.67 above. Because the tenant's cross-claim was in damages there was no question of a set-off under the Statutes of Set-off, which requires mutual *debts*. See para. 2.14 above.

[407] See para. 17.77 above.

[408] See para. 17.77 above.

[409] Buxton LJ's analysis was adopted by the other members of the court. See [2003] 1 WLR 2853 at [31] (Sedley LJ) and [56] (Ward LJ).

[410] [2003] 1 WLR 2853 at [42]–[45].

[411] [2003] 1 WLR 2853 at [50]. See also *R (on the Application of Burkett) v London Borough of Hammersmith and Fulham* [2004] EWCA Civ 1342 at [58].

[412] Referring ([2003] 1 WLR 2853 at [51]) to *Lotteryking Ltd v AMEC Properties Ltd* [1995] 2 EGLR 13, in which Lightman J accepted (at 15) that the 'taking subject to equities' principle may apply when a reversion is assigned in relation to a breach of a covenant which runs with the reversion. That case was criticized, however, in *Edlington Properties Ltd v J H Fenner & Co Ltd* [2006] 1 WLR 1583 at [55]–[60].

[413] See above.

[414] See paras 5.77–5.80 above.

have been effective as against the plaintiff as the purchaser of the reversion.[415] As Sedley LJ remarked in *Muscat v Smith*,[416] it is not easy to see why similar relief should be denied to a tenant who may not have had enough money to do the repairs. Nevertheless, the reasoning employed to justify the set-off is open to criticism.

The difficulty is in the assumption that the 'taking subject to equities' principle applied. In **17.82** *Muscat v Smith*, s. 141 of the Law of Property Act 1925 permitted the purchaser of the reversion to sue to recover the arrears of rent relating to the period before the sale.[417] However, this was not based upon an assignment of a debt that, before the Judicature Acts, would have been effective only in equity. Rather, pursuant to s. 141, the unpaid rent was annexed to and went with the reversionary interest in the land. The purchaser could sue for it in his own name and in respect of his own title, as the holder of the reversion.[418] There is no basis in such a case for the application of the 'taking subject to equities' principle.[419]

Muscat v Smith was distinguished by the Court of Appeal in *Edlington Properties Ltd v* **17.83** *J H Fenner & Co Ltd*.[420] The cases differed in that, unlike *Muscat v Smith*, which concerned rent accrued before the transfer of the reversion, the transferee of the reversion in the *Edlington Properties* case was seeking to recover rent which fell due after the transfer. This was pursuant to the Landlord and Tenants (Covenants) Act 1995, the lease having been entered into after 1 January 1996.[421] In that context (and unlike in the case of rent accrued prior to a transfer of the reversion[422]), the position is the same under the 1995 Act as under s. 141 of the Law of Property Act 1925.[423] In the case of rent accrued prior to a transfer, being the circumstance in issue in *Muscat v Smith*, Neuberger LJ in the *Edlington Properties* case[424] reasoned that the right to recover it, although it went with the reversion, was a chose in action which at the time it fell due was impeached by an equitable set-off, and the effect of s. 141 of the Law of Property Act was to effect an automatic assignment of that chose in action. He distinguished that situation from the claim in the *Edlington Properties* case for rent accruing after the transfer which, he said, was not a chose in action at the time of the transfer but simply an incident of the reversion.[425] The transferee could recover it in his own right, as opposed to through the original landlord.[426] The right to recover therefore was not subject to a set-off in relation to prior breaches by the original landlord, unless the

---

[415] See para. 17.93 below.
[416] [2003] 1 WLR 2853 at [16]. Compare *Edlington Properties Ltd v J H Fenner & Co Ltd* [2006] 1 WLR 1583 at [54].
[417] See para. 17.77 above.
[418] *Edlington Properties Ltd v J H Fenner & Co Ltd* [2006] 1 WLR 1583 *per* Neuberger LJ at [13] ('when the reversion to a lease is transferred the transferee, that is the new landlord, has the right to recover the rent under the lease in his own right, and does not need to claim through the transferor, that is the original landlord'), [15] and [26].
[419] See para. 17.69 above, and para. 17.76 above in relation to mortgages.
[420] [2006] 1 WLR 1583.
[421] See para. 17.77 above.
[422] See para. 17.77 above.
[423] *Edlington Properties Ltd v J H Fenner & Co Ltd* [2006] 1 WLR 1583 at [13].
[424] Pill and Scott Baker LJJ agreeing.
[425] [2006] 1 WLR 1583 at [15] and [47]–[48].
[426] *Edlington Properties Ltd v J H Fenner & Co Ltd* [2006] 1 WLR 1583 at [13].

lease had specifically provided for a set-off.[427] However, while the decision in the *Edlington Properties* case to disallow a set-off was correct, that analysis does not satisfactorily explain *Muscat v Smith*. In the first place, the impeachment of the right to the accrued rent before the transfer did not affect the existence of the debt for rent to the extent of the set-off. It simply affected the original landlord's conscience.[428] Secondly, the point remains that, where it applies, s. 141 permits the transferee of the reversion to recover prior accrued rent in an action at law. It is a statutory right to recover in the transferee's own name and right,[429] as opposed to an assignment of the transferor's chose in action. Moreover, unlike in the case of a statutory assignment pursuant to s. 136 of the Law of Property Act 1925,[430] s. 141 does not provide that the transferee is to take subject to equities.[431] As a consequence, there is no justification for applying the 'subject to equities' doctrine.[432]

17.84 The decision in *Muscat v Smith* nevertheless can be supported on another ground. While the reasoning in the case is open to criticism, the decision to permit a set-off may be explained on the basis of a principle that was rejected in that case, and also in later Court of Appeal judgments,[433] that in some circumstances a cross-claim against someone other than the plaintiff can be asserted by way of equitable set-off. Ordinarily, equity requires mutuality for a set-off but, unlike in the case of statutory-based set-offs,[434] there is substantial authority for the proposition that an absence of mutuality is not necessarily fatal to an equitable set-off if the circumstances otherwise are such as to justify equitable relief.[435] If a direct set-off were available as against the transferee of the reversion, it would not be necessary to rely on the 'taking subject to equities' principle. The question is whether the circumstances in issue in *Muscat v Smith* were such as to justify a direct equitable set-off despite the absence of mutuality.

17.85 The critical point is that the transferee of the reversion was seeking to obtain the benefit of the lease for the period before the transfer, at a time when the transferee had no interest in the land, by claiming unpaid rent from that period. In that situation, the transferee should expect to take subject to a claim based upon a breach of a covenant to repair in that period that otherwise would have impeached the title to the rent.

17.86 In the context of an assignment of a debt, the Privy Council in *Government of Newfoundland v Newfoundland Railway Company*,[436] justified its decision in that case, that an assignee of a debt took subject to a cross-claim for damages available to the debtor against the assignor

---

[427] *Edlington Properties Ltd v J H Fenner & Co Ltd* [2006] 1 WLR 1583 at [64].
[428] See paras 4.29–4.34 above.
[429] See the *Edlington Properties* case [2006] 1 WLR 1583 at [13].
[430] See para. 17.04 above.
[431] *Edlington Properties Ltd v J H Fenner & Co Ltd* [2006] 1 WLR 1583 at [15].
[432] See para. 17.69 above.
[433] *R (on the Application of Burkett) v London Borough of Hammersmith and Fulham* [2004] EWCA Civ 1342 at [58]; *Edlington Properties Ltd v J H Fenner & Co Ltd* [2006] 1 WLR 1583 at [20]. See para. 4.69 above. The comment in *Maunder Taylor v Blaquiere* [2003] 1 WLR 379 at [42], to the effect that set-off was not possible in that case because there was no mutuality, should be considered by reference to the circumstances there in issue, in particular that the justice of the case did not support an equitable set-off. See at [43] and [50].
[434] See ch. 11 in relation to insolvency set-off and the Statutes of Set-off.
[435] See paras 4.67–4.83 above.
[436] (1888) 13 App Cas 199, 212.

under the contract assigned, by reference to the notion that an assignee should not take the beneficial part of a contract wholly discharged from the burdens under it. In *Bank of Boston Connecticut v European Grain and Shipping Ltd*[437] the House of Lords rejected the proposition that this notion alone can justify a set-off against an assignee. The cross-claims in addition must be sufficiently closely connected to give rise to an equitable set-off. This accords with the courts' rejection[438] of the 'pure principle of benefit and burden' advocated by Sir Robert Megarry VC in *Tito v Waddell (No. 2)*.[439] But if the cross-claims are otherwise sufficiently closely connected, the notion of benefit and burden could provide a basis in some cases for permitting a set-off in equity where there is an absence of strict mutuality.[440]

This approach would have provided a more satisfactory basis for a set-off in *Muscat v Smith* **17.87** than the reasoning adopted by the Court of Appeal in that case.[441] But since it is not based on the principle that an assignee takes subject to equities, it would have the consequence that a transferee of the reversion would not take subject to an equity in the form of a right of set-off available to the tenant against the original owner under the Statutes of Set-off in relation to an unrelated cross-debt. Unlike in the case of equitable set-off, the absence of mutuality would be fatal to a set-off under the Statutes.[442] The availability of a set-off therefore would be considerably narrower than under the 'taking subject to equities' doctrine.

The decision in *Muscat v Smith* would not be relevant in England to leases entered into after **17.88** 1 January 1996 given that, under the Landlord and Tenant (Covenants) Act 1995, a transferee of leased premises does not have any rights under a covenant in the lease in relation to any time falling before the assignment.[443] This would include in relation to arrears of rent from the period before the assignment. On the other hand, the legislation provides that such rights may be expressly assigned.[444] If there is an express assignment, the principle of taking subject to equities would then apply. In any event, the 1995 Act generally does not apply to tenancies entered into before 1 January 1996,[445] and, moreover, the law remains

---

[437] [1989] 1 AC 1056, 1105–6.

[438] *Government Insurance Office (NSW) v K A Reed Services Pty Ltd* [1988] VR 829; *Rhone v Stephens* [1994] 2 AC 310, 322. See para. 17.09 above.

[439] [1977] Ch 106, 289–311.

[440] This occurred in New South Wales, in *Murphy v Zamonex* (1993) 31 NSWLR 439. In that case, Giles J in the New South Wales Supreme Court permitted an equitable set-off in relation to closely connected cross-claims arising between a trustee and a person dealing with the trust. He accepted that there was no mutuality in equity, since the trustee was personally liable for the damages claim against it whereas the debt owing to the trustee was held for the benefit of the beneficiaries of the trust. Nevertheless, he permitted an equitable set-off, on the basis that the beneficiaries should not take the benefit of the transaction without bearing the burden of the trustee's conduct. *Murphy v Zamonex* was referred to with approval in *Penwith District Council v V P Developments Ltd* [2005] 2 BCLC 607 at [21]–[23] (Laddie J).

[441] It would also explain Millett LJ's comment in *Mortgage Corporation Ltd v Ubah* (1996) 73 P & CR 500, 507–8, that an equitable set-off available to a tenant may bind successors in title to the land.

[442] See para. 2.13 above.

[443] See para. 17.77 above. See also *Edlington Properties Ltd v J H Fenner and Co Ltd* [2005] EWHC 2159 (QB) at [24]–[25] (Bean J).

[444] Landlord and Tenant (Covenants) Act 1995, s. 23(2).

[445] Landlord and Tenant (Covenants) Act 1995, s. 1 and the Landlord and Tenant (Covenants) Act (Commencement) Order 1995 (S.I. 1995 No. 2963).

unaffected in other jurisdictions such as in Australia where legislation similar to the English 1995 Act has not been enacted.

17.89   **Sale of leased premises – breach of covenant before the sale and rent accruing after the sale.**   Whatever the position in relation to *Muscat v Smith*, a set-off should not be available to a tenant as against a purchaser of the reversion where the tenant's claim relates to a breach of covenant by the original landlord before the sale but the transferee is claiming rent which fell due after the transfer. This was confirmed by the Court of Appeal in *Edlington Properties Ltd v J H Fenner & Co Ltd*,[446] to which reference has been made.[447] In this situation (and unlike in the circumstances in issue in *Muscat v Smith*[448]), there is no justification for a direct equitable set-off as between the tenant and the purchaser.

Breach of covenant by the mortgagee or purchaser

17.90   The preceding discussion concerned the situation in which a tenant seeks to set off a personal liability of the original landlord to the tenant against a claim for rent by a mortgagee in possession or a purchaser of the reversion. The position would be different if the mortgagee or the purchaser breaches a covenant in the lease which is binding on him or her personally, and thereby becomes liable to the tenant. Pursuant to the Landlord and Tenant (Covenants) Act 1995, the burden of all 'landlord covenants' (as defined in s. 28(1)) passes on an assignment of the reversion, and subject to some exceptions they bind the purchaser as from the assignment.[449] This is expressed to extend to a mortgagee in possession.[450] If the requirements for a set-off are otherwise satisfied, a breach of a landlord covenant by a mortgagee or a purchaser should be capable of being the subject of a set-off in a claim by the mortgagee or the purchaser for rent.[451]

Mortgages in Australia

17.91   The old form of mortgage no longer applies in Australia in relation to Torrens title land. The legislation of all Australian states provides that a mortgage under the relevant Act does not operate as a transfer of the land, but rather it takes effect as a security, or a statutory charge,[452] with the consequence that the legal estate remains in the mortgagor.[453] While the general approach is universal, there are nevertheless differences under the Acts as regards

---

[446]   [2006] 1 WLR 1583.

[447]   See para. 17.83 above.

[448]   See paras 17.79–17.87 above.

[449]   The Landlord and Tenant (Covenants) Act 1995, s. 3. A purchaser of the reversion is not bound by a covenant which is expressed to be personal to the vendor. See s. 3(6). In relation to leases not subject to the Act, see the Law of Property Act 1925, s. 142, and para. 17.77 above.

[450]   See s. 15(2).

[451]   In Australia, see *Westend Entertainment Centre Pty Ltd v Equity Trustees Ltd* (2000) V Conv R 54–619. It was argued in that case that the covenant in question, relating to the refurbishment of the leased premises, was not personal to the mortgagor/landlord but rather it ran with the land, so that the mortgagee in possession could not claim the benefit of the rent under the lease without accepting the burden of the covenant. Mandie J, while commenting that the argument faced substantial legal obstacles, nevertheless said that it raised a serious question to be tried.

[452]   See e.g. the Real Property Act 1900 (NSW), s. 57(1), and generally Sykes and Walker, *The Law of Securities* (5th edn, 1993), 227 *et seq*.

[453]   *Figgins Holdings Pty Ltd v SEAA Enterprises Pty Ltd* (1999) 196 CLR 245, 279 (McHugh J).

the rights and powers of the mortgagee, and as a result the decision in *Reeves v Pope*[454] may not be applicable in all states in so far as Torrens mortgages are concerned. Beach J, in *Citibank Pty Ltd v Simon Fredericks Pty Ltd*,[455] held that it applies in Victoria, and it has also been adopted in South Australia,[456] but its application to Torrens mortgages in Queensland was rejected in *Re Partnership Pacific Securities Ltd*.[457]

The facts of *Re Partnership Pacific Securities* were similar to those in *Reeves v Pope*. It **17.92** concerned a leased property registered under the Queensland Torrens legislation, the legislation current at the time being the Real Property Act 1861 (Qld). That Act has since been replaced by the Land Title Act 1994 (Qld), but the relevant principles remain the same. The lessor decided to re-develop the property, and agreed with the lessee that it would cause the work to be completed in a good workmanlike manner by a particular date. The lessee alleged a breach of this agreement, and claimed damages from the lessor. The applicant had a registered mortgage over the premises and, after default by the lessor/ mortgagor, went into possession by claiming all arrears of rent up to the date of possession together with all rental and other moneys coming due in respect of the lease. The question was whether the lessee was entitled to set off its damages claim against the lessor. The claim for rent was the subject of two actions, the first before de Jersey J.[458] His Honour held that, unlike the corresponding Victorian legislation considered in *Citibank v Simon Fredericks*, the Queensland Torrens legislation did not allow a mortgagee to sue for rent. In Victoria, s. 81 of the Transfer of Land Act 1958 provides that a first mortgagee has the same rights and remedies at law and in equity as he or she would have had if the legal estate in the mortgaged land had been vested in him or her as mortgagee, with a right of quiet enjoyment in the mortgagor until default. This has the effect that, following default, the mortgagee has the same entitlement to sue for rent as an old title mortgagee,[459] which would justify the application of the *Reeves v Pope* principle in relation to a Torrens title mortgage in Victoria. The Victorian legislation should be compared to the Real Property Act in Queensland, which did not have an equivalent of s. 81, and that remains the case under the Land Title Act 1994 (Qld). Section 60 of the Real Property Act provided that a mortgagee could enter into possession of the mortgaged land by receiving the rents and profits thereof.[460] However, de Jersey J held that this only entitled the mortgagee to receive the rents and profits as they were paid, in the sense that it was not wrongful for the mortgagee to do so, but without conferring an independent right to sue for them.[461] This accords with views expressed by

---

[454] [1914] 2 KB 284. See paras 17.73–17.76 above.

[455] [1993] 2 VR 168.

[456] *Ory & Ory v Betamore Pty Ltd* (1993) 60 SASR 393.

[457] [1994] 1 Qd R 410.

[458] Unreported, 12 May 1992.

[459] See the discussion in Sykes and Walker, *The Law of Securities* (5th edn, 1993), 260–2, and in Francis and Thomas, *Mortgages and Securities* (3rd edn, 1986), 146–7. In *Figgins Holdings Pty Ltd v SEAA Enterprises Pty Ltd* (1999) 196 CLR 245, 284 McHugh J said in relation to s. 81(1) that: 'the mortgagee must . . . have the same rights against any tenant of the mortgaged property as the mortgagor would have if there were no mortgage.'

[460] See now the Land Title Act 1994 (Qld), s. 78(2).

[461] In *Citibank v Simon Fredericks* [1993] 2 VR 168, Beach J justified the decision in that case by reference to s. 78 of the Transfer of Land Act, which is in similar terms to s. 60 of the Queensland Act, and not s. 81, as suggested by de Jersey J. Indeed. s. 81 was not referred to in the Beach J's judgment. This suggests a broader

text-writers.[462] De Jersey J nevertheless found another source of power for a mortgagee to sue for rent, in s. 117(2) of the Property Law Act 1974 (Qld), and said that this was sufficient to bring the case within *Reeves v Pope*. When it came to making his order, de Jersey J noted that the claims for declaration set out in the summons only related to the obligation to pay rent as from the date that the mortgagee went into possession. Accordingly, he declined to make declarations as to the mortgagee's entitlement to rent in arrears before that date. This was the subject of the second action, before Williams J.[463] In this action his Honour agreed with de Jersey J that the Real Property Act in Queensland did not confer upon a mortgagee an independent right to sue for rent,[464] a view with which Moynihan J also later expressed agreement.[465] Williams J disagreed, however, with de Jersey J's conclusion that the Property Law Act 1974 (Qld), s. 117(2) conferred a power to sue. Section 117(2) provides that: 'Any such rent, covenant, obligation, or provision shall be capable of being recovered, received, enforced, and taken advantage of, by the person from time to time entitled . . .' While s. 60 of the Real Property Act entitled a mortgagee to receive rents and profits, s. 117(2) had to be read in the light of s. 117(1), which provides that: 'Rent reserved by a lease . . . shall be annexed and incident to and shall go with the reversionary estate in the land.' As Williams J noted,[466] the section is concerned primarily with defining the rights of the owner of the reversionary estate from time to time,[467] and a mortgagee of Torrens title land is not the owner of the reversionary estate in the land. Accordingly, he concluded that the section did not assist the mortgagee.[468]

Tenant's right of recoupment against a mortgagee or purchaser

17.93 If leased premises have fallen into disrepair and responsibility for the repairs is on the landlord, the tenant may expend money in executing the repairs and recoup him or herself from future payments of rent.[469] This is sometimes described as a set-off,[470] but set-off is not an

---

operation for s. 78 than de Jersey J ascribed to s. 60 in Queensland. Subsequently, the Full Court of the South Australian Supreme Court in *Ory & Ory v Betamore Pty Ltd* (1993) 60 SASR 393, 406 referred with approval to Beach J's reliance on s. 78, although without referring to *Re Partnership Pacific Securities*. But whatever the position in relation to s. 78 following *Re Partnership Pacific Securities*, the decision in *Citibank v Simon Fredericks* would in any event appear to have been justified by s. 81. Compare *Westend Entertainment Centre Pty Ltd v Equity Trustees Ltd* (2000) V Conv R 54–619 at 64,431.

[462] Sykes and Walker, *The Law of Securities* (5th edn, 1993), 258–9; Francis and Thomas, *Mortgages and Securities* (3rd edn, 1986), 147–8.

[463] [1994] 1 Qd R 410.

[464] [1994] 1 Qd R 410, 420.

[465] *Re FAI Leasing Pty Ltd* [1994] 2 Qd R 482, 486. See also *Lensworth Properties Pty Ltd v Entera Pty Ltd* [1994] ANZ ConvR 564 [Ext]; *Permanent Trustee Australia Ltd v Jibali Pty Ltd* (Qld SC, Wilson J, 27 April 2001, BC200102641 at 6).

[466] [1994] 1 Qd R 410, 421.

[467] This includes an owner in equity who is entitled to the rent to the exclusion of all others. See *Schalit v Joseph Nadler Ltd* [1933] 2 KB 79, 82–3.

[468] See also *Re FAI Leasing Pty Ltd* [1994] 2 Qd R 482, 487; *Lensworth Properties Pty Ltd v Entera Pty Ltd* [1994] ANZ ConvR 564 [Ext]. While the mortgagee in *Re Partnership Pacific Securities* was entitled pursuant to a separate agreement with the lessee to sue for rent, Williams J held that the mortgagee's right to do so was only as an assignee from the lessor, and that in suing in that capacity the mortgagee took subject to equities available to the lessee against the lessor, including an equitable set-off. See [1994] 1 Qd R 410, 421–4.

[469] See paras 5.77–5.80 above.

[470] See *Waters v Weigall* (1795) 2 Anst 575, 145 ER 971; *Knockholt Pty Ltd v Graff* [1975] Qd R 88, 91, 92.

accurate description of the tenant's right.[471] Rather, it gives rise to a question of payment.[472] The money spent by the tenant on repairs is regarded as a payment *pro tanto* of future rent,[473] or of any arrears of rent.[474] The tenant's right to take this course of action is based upon a policy consideration, that: 'he shall be otherwise at great mischief, for the house may fall upon his head before it be repaired; and therefore the law alloweth him to repair it, and recoupe the rent.'[475] If the tenant's expenditure constitutes payment of rent in advance, it should be binding upon a mortgagee or purchaser of the land. This occurred in *Lee-Parker v Izzet*,[476] in which Goff J enforced as against a mortgagee a tenant's right to have expenditure on repairs regarded as a payment of future rent.

The decision in *De Nichols v Saunders*[477] is not inconsistent with this view. In that case the **17.94** Court of Common Pleas held that a payment by a tenant to the landlord, which was expressed to be and was accepted as a payment of rent in advance, was not effective as against a mortgagee who had obtained the mortgage before the payment. The mortgagee, on going into possession, was allowed to sue for the rent that, according to the terms of the lease, accrued after the tenant had notice of the mortgage,[478] and the tenant could not rely on the advance payment to the mortgagor/landlord as a defence. In this regard, if a landlord mortgages the premises after receiving an advance payment, the payment will be binding on the mortgagee as a discharge of the rent obligation, unless the mortgagee had enquired of the tenant as to the rent and the tenant answered incorrectly or failed to answer.[479] It is

---

[471] *Lee-Parker v Izzet* [1971] 1 WLR 1688, 1693; *British Anzani (Felixstowe) Ltd v International Marine Management (UK) Ltd* [1980] 1 QB 137, 148.

[472] This appears to have been accepted in *Edlington Properties Ltd v J H Fenner & Co Ltd* [2006] 1 WLR 1583 at [53].

[473] *Taylor v Beal* (1591) Cro Eliz 222, 78 ER 478 (Gawdy J); *Lee-Parker v Izzet* [1971] 1 WLR 1688, 1693; *British Anzani (Felixstowe) Ltd v International Marine Management (UK) Ltd* [1980] 1 QB 137, 148; *Connaught Restaurants Ltd v Indoor Leisure Ltd* [1994] 1 WLR 507, 511.

[474] *Asco Developments Ltd v Gordon* (1978) 248 EG 683.

[475] *Taylor v Beal* (1591) Cro Eliz 222, 78 ER 478 (Gawdy J).

[476] [1971] 1 WLR 1688. This decision was referred to without adverse comment in *Edlington Properties Ltd v J H Fenner & Co Ltd* [2006] 1 WLR 1583 at [52]–[54] (CA). See also *Muscat v Smith* [2003] 1 WLR 2853 at [16], where the proposition was assumed.

[477] (1870) LR 5 CP 589. See also *Lord Ashburton v Nocton* [1915] 1 Ch 274. In relation to a Torrens title mortgage in Australia, see *Figgins Holdings Pty Ltd v SEAA Enterprises Pty Ltd* (1999) 196 CLR 245 (reversing *SEAA Enterprises Pty Ltd v Figgins Holdings Pty Ltd* [1998] 2 VR 90, where *De Nicholls v Saunders* was considered).

[478] See *Cook v Guerra* (1872) LR 7 CP 132 in relation to rent accruing before notice. Prior to the statute (1705) 4 Anne, c. 16, the assignee of a reversion could not recover rent until the tenant had attorned to him or her. Section 9 of the Act took away the necessity for attornment, although s. 10 provided protection to a tenant who paid rent before he or she had notice that the premises had been assigned.

[479] *Green v Rheinberg* (1911) 104 LT 149. See also *Grace Rymer Investments Ltd v Waite* [1958] 1 Ch 831. Compare *Mortgage Corporation Ltd v Ubah* (1996) 73 P & CR 500, in which a landlord was indebted to the tenant and it was agreed that, pending repayment by the landlord, the tenant could set off that debt against rent as it accrued. It was held at first instance that the agreement was ineffective as against a subsequent mortgagee. The point was not pursued on appeal, but Millett LJ nevertheless said that he agreed with that view. *Green v Rheinberg* was not referred to, but in that case there was an actual payment of the rent. See *Edlington Properties Ltd v J H Fenner & Co Ltd* [2006] 1 WLR 1583 at [52]. The result may have been different in the *Mortgage Corporation* case if the agreement had been in terms that the debt was set off against future rent.

in the situation in which there was a prior mortgage that the principle in *De Nichols v Saunders* applies. Willes J explained the basis of the decision in the following terms:[480]

> The receipt of the rent could not be treated here as a discharge by the landlord, because by assigning the reversion before the rent was received by him he had parted with the power of giving such a discharge. The plaintiff [mortgagee] lent his money on a contract, which was under an implied condition that the landlord should continue entitled to the rent at the time it became due, and able, therefore, then to give the plaintiff a valid discharge.

He said that the payment was not a fulfilment of the obligation imposed by the lease to pay rent. Rather, he characterized it as an advance to the landlord, with an agreement that on the day when the rent became due the advance should be treated as a fulfilment of the rent obligation.[481] This could not be effective as against a prior mortgagee, because the mortgagee was the party entitled to the rent as it fell due.

17.95 *De Nichols v Saunders* essentially turned upon a question of power. The landlord, having assigned the reversion by way of mortgage, did not have power to give a discharge to the tenant before the due date. However, the principle that a tenant who expends money in repairs may treat it as an advance payment of rent if the landlord is responsible for the repairs is not based upon a question of power, or upon an agreement (express or implied) between the tenant and the landlord regarding the payment of rent. The tenant's right to treat the cost of repairs as an advance payment of rent arises as a matter of law. It is designed to encourage the tenant to effect repairs so as to protect against the possibility that 'the house may fall upon his head'. It is effective against the landlord whoever it may be, whether it is the person whom the tenant thinks is the landlord, or whether it is a prior assignee of the reversion of whom the tenant is unaware. In *Lee-Parker v Izzet*, it is unclear from the report whether the repairs were effected before or after the mortgage, but this was not important. The decision was correct, irrespective of when the mortgage was executed.

(20) Freight payable to a mortgagee or purchaser of a ship

17.96 The principle underlying *Reeves v Pope*[482] is also relevant when a mortgagee goes into possession of a ship. The mortgagee is entitled to the freight in the course of being earned, not because the mortgagee is an assignee of the debt, but because the mortgagee is the owner of the ship.[483] The mortgagee's right depends on property, not on contract.[484] In the same way, when a ship is sold, the right to freight in the course of being earned passes to the purchaser.[485] Therefore, when a mortgagee in possession or a purchaser of a ship sues for

---

[480] (1870) LR 5 CP 589, 594.

[481] See also *FCT v Steeves Agnew & Co (Vic) Pty Ltd* (1951) 82 CLR 408, 418; *Ory & Ory v Betamore Pty Ltd* (1993) 60 SASR 393, 403–4 (an overpayment of rent is not rent); *Altonwood Ltd v Crystal Palace FC (2000) Ltd* [2005] EWHC 292 (Ch) at [34] (payment of rent before it is due is not fulfilment of an obligation to make that payment).

[482] [1914] 2 KB 284. See paras 17.73–17.76 above.

[483] *Keith v Burrows* (1877) 2 App Cas 636, 646. See also *Kerswill v Bishop* (1832) 2 C & J 529, 149 ER 224; *Japp v Campbell* (1888) 57 LJQB 79; *Wilson v Wilson* (1872) LR 14 Eq 32 (mortgagee's right to freight has priority over an earlier assignment of freight of which the mortgagee did not have notice).

[484] *Rusden v Pope* (1868) LR 3 Ex 269, 276–7.

[485] See e.g. *Morrison v Parsons* (1810) 2 Taunt 407, 127 ER 1136. As Lord Ellenborough remarked in *Case v Davidson* (1816) 5 M & S 79, 82, 105 ER 980, 981: 'freight follows, as an incident, the property in the ship.'

ayment of freight, the charterer or shipper may not set off a debt which is owing by the mortgagor or, as the case may be, the vendor.[486] The principle of taking subject to equities does not apply.

(21) Transfer (or sub-mortgage) of a Torrens mortgage in Australia

In the case of a transfer of a mortgage and the mortgage debt relating to land registered **17.97** under the Torrens system in Australia,[487] the principle of indefeasibility of title is separate from and does not affect the principle that the transferee of the debt takes subject to set-offs available against the transferor.[488] Therefore, where an equitable set-off would have provided a defence to the mortgagor to an action for possession by the original mortgagee,[489] the defence should be equally available as against a transferee of the mortgage.[490]

(22) Judgments and orders

The courts commonly permit a set-off of judgments of orders for the payment of money.[491] **17.98** This has been characterized as an equitable set-off, but in truth it is derived from the court's inherent jurisdiction.[492] In the event of an assignment of the benefit of a monetary judgment or order, in circumstances where the judgment debtor has a cross-judgment or order against the assignor, a principle analogous to the taking subject to equities doctrine in an action at law may apply so as to permit the judgment debtor to assert against the assignee a set-off that otherwise would have been available against the assignor.[493]

C. Security Over a Debt

(1) Introduction

An intervening third party interest in a debt may take the form of a fixed security. The **17.99** issue commonly arises when a floating security over a company's assets and undertaking crystallizes. If the company continues to carry on business, a person dealing with the company may be concerned to know whether debts and credits arising before and after

---

[486] *Tanner v Phillips* (1872) 42 LJ Ch 125.

[487] In the context of old title land, see *Norrish v Marshall* (1821) 5 Madd 475, 481, 56 ER 977, 980.

[488] *Long Leys Co Pty Ltd v Silkdale Pty Ltd* (1991) 5 BPR 11,512, 11,519–20 (CA). See also *Fisher and Lightwood's Law of Mortgage* (2nd Aust edn, 2005), 128–9. Some comments in *Clairview Developments Pty Ltd v Law Mortgages Gold Coast Pty Ltd* [2007] 2 Qd R 501 at [8] (McMurdo P), [43] (Jerrard JA) may suggest the contrary, However, they should be considered in the context that the remedy sought was an injunction to restrain the transferees of the mortgages from exercising their powers of sale under the mortgages (see at [6]), and a mortgagee ordinarily will not be restrained from exercising a power of sale unless the amount due under the mortgage is paid into court or some other compensatory form of security is provided. See paras 4.137–4.140 above. Compare the dissenting judgment of Helman J at [53], who favoured the preferred view.

[489] See paras 4.142–4.146 above.

[490] *Long Leys Co Pty Ltd v Silkdale Pty Ltd* (1991) 5 BPR 11,512. This includes a sub-mortgage. See *Popular Homes Ltd v Circuit Developments Ltd* [1979] 2 NZLR 642, and compare *Clairview Developments Pty Ltd v Law Mortgages Gold Coast Pty Ltd* [2007] 2 Qd R 501 at [42].

[491] See paras 2.98–2.122 above.

[492] See paras 2.99–2.105 above.

[493] See paras 2.108–2.110 above.

crystallization can be set off. This includes debts and credits contracted by the company through the agency of a receiver appointed to the company by the secured creditor.[494]

17.100 When a floating security crystallizes, it is commonly said that any debts owing to the company and coming within the ambit of the security are assigned in equity to the secured creditor.[495] This would be the case when crystallization results in an assignment of the company's property by way of mortgage, but a floating security often is not expressed to bring about a mortgage. The terms of a floating security commonly provide for the company's property to become subject to a charge upon crystallization, the difference being that, unlike a mortgage, a charge does not take effect as a transfer of ownership.[496] Sometimes when a floating security is expressed to take effect by way of charge it is nevertheless interpreted as giving rise to an assignment,[497] but the distinction between a charge and a mortgage in any event should not be crucial to a set-off. A charge should have the same effect upon the availability of a set-off as a mortgage,[498] in that, after a debtor to the company has notice that a third party has a security interest in the debt, whether by way of charge or mortgage, it would be unconscionable for the debtor to rely on subsequent dealings with the chargor to diminish the rights of the third party.[499] Therefore, whether crystallization results in an assignment by way of mortgage or a charge, questions of set-off[500] should be determined by reference to the same principles that apply to assignments of choses in action, the relevant date being the date of notice of a fixed security over the company's property consequent upon the crystallization.[501] Mere notice of the existence of a floating security at a time when cross-debts are contracted, without notice of crystallization, does not preclude a set-off. In *Biggerstaff v Rowatt's Wharf Ltd*,[502] both demands were liquidated and arose before crystallization. It was held, correctly, that

---

[494] The receiver may be an administrative receiver as defined in the Insolvency Act 1986, ss. 29(2) and 251, in other words a receiver and manager of the whole (or substantially the whole) of a company's property appointed by or on behalf of the holders of debentures of the company secured by a charge which, as created, was a floating charge. The powers and duties of an administrative receiver are set out in ss. 42–49 of the Act and Part 3 of the Insolvency Rules 1986.

[495] See para. 11.49 above. The appointment of a receiver out of court under a floating charge does not of itself determine contracts previously entered into by the company in the ordinary course of its business. See *George Barker (Transport) Ltd v Eynon* [1974] 1 WLR 462, 468, 471. This is also the case when a receiver and manager is appointed by the court. See *Parsons v Sovereign Bank of Canada* [1913] AC 160.

[496] See para. 11.46 above. The distinction between a charge and a mortgage has not always been maintained. For example, Stamp LJ in *George Barker (Transport) Ltd v Eynon* [1974] 1 WLR 462, 471 referred to 'an equitable assignment (by way of charge)', and see also *Security Trust Co v Royal Bank of Canada* [1976] AC 503, 518 ('assigned to the respondent by way of equitable charge') (PC).

[497] See e.g. *Re ELS Ltd* [1995] Ch 11, 24–5; *National Mutual Life Nominees Ltd v National Capital Development Commission* (1975) 37 FLR 404, 409–10 (criticized in Sykes and Walker, *The Law of Securities* (5th edn, 1993), 960).

[498] See para. 11.46 above. Compare Goode, 'Centre Point' [1984] JBL 172.

[499] See para. 17.03 above.

[500] Set-off only provides a defence to a monetary demand. It may not be invoked when the receiver is suing for the return of goods or other specific things wrongfully detained. See *Tony Lee Motors Ltd v M. S. MacDonald & Son (1974) Ltd* [1981] 2 NZLR 281, and Ch 9 above.

[501] *Business Computers Ltd v Anglo-African Leasing Ltd* [1977] 1 WLR 578, 582; *B Hargreaves Ltd v Action 2000 Ltd* [1993] BCLC 1111, 1115. As opposed to the date of crystallization: compare *Steinberg v Herbert* (1988) 14 ACLR 80, 96 (WA, Full Court).

[502] [1896] 2 Ch 93.

the debenture-holders took subject to a set-off notwithstanding that the defendant knew of the floating security at the time when the debt due to it was contracted.[503]

The following discussion takes place in the context of a crystallized floating security. **17.101**
However, the principles discussed are equally relevant to a fixed security arising otherwise than by reason of crystallization of a floating charge, the relevant date being the date of notice of the security.

(2) Australia: Personal Property Securities Act 2009 (Cth)

In Australia, the Personal Property Securities Act 2009 (Cth) has established a national law **17.102**
governing security interests in personal property, and in doing so it has significantly altered the position in relation to fixed and floating charges. It provides that a reference to a floating charge in a law of the Commonwealth or in a security agreement is to be taken to be a reference to a security interest attached to a circulating asset.[504] The concept of crystallization itself has no relevance under the Act.[505] The Act states that it does not apply to rights of set-off except as provided in s. 80.[506] In relation to questions of set-off, attention is therefore directed to that section.[507]

Section 80(1) was referred to earlier in the context of assignments of debts.[508] It deals with **17.103**
'accounts' and 'chattel papers'. An 'account' is defined in s. 8 in terms of a monetary obligation arising from disposing of property (whether by sale, lease, licence or in any other way) or from granting a right or providing services in the ordinary course of business. Those debts ordinarily constitute circulating assets,[509] and they are also the form of obligation in relation to which questions of set-off typically have arisen in the context of crystallized floating charges.

---

[503] See also *Edward Nelson & Co Ltd v Faber* & Co [1903] 2 KB 367; *Commercial Factors Ltd v Maxwell Printing Ltd* [1994] 1 NZLR 724, 735; *Business Computers Ltd v Anglo-African Leasing Ltd* [1977] 1 WLR 578, 582 (in relation to the instalment due before notice of the appointment); *Fire Nymph Products Ltd v The Heating Centre Pty Ltd* (1992) 7 ACSR 365, 376; *Norgard v Deputy Federal Commissioner of Taxation* (1986) 79 ALR 369, 399; *Hoverd Industries Ltd v Supercool Refrigeration and Air Conditioning (1991) Ltd* [1995] 3 NZLR 577, 585. *A fortiori* a set-off is available against a cross-debt arising before notice of crystallization if the defendant did not know of the floating security. See *Tony Lee Motors Ltd v M S MacDonald & Son (1974) Ltd* [1981] 2 NZLR 281, in which the defendant, before crystallization, had obtained an equitable assignment of a debt owing by the company to a third party. Notice to the company was not necessary to complete the assignment.
[504] Section 339(5). The term 'circulating asset' is defined in s. 340.
[505] However, the Act does not derogate from the rights and remedies that the parties to a security agreement have, apart from the Act, in relation to a default under the agreement. See s. 110.
[506] See ss. 8(1)(d) and 8(2).
[507] See para. 17.05 above in relation to s. 80.
[508] See para. 17.05 above.
[509] See s. 340(5)(a) and (b), together with s. 340(1)(a). Section 340(5)(a) refers to an account (defined in s. 8 in terms of a monetary obligation) that arises from granting a right or providing services in the ordinary course of business. The extension of the definition of 'circulating asset' in s. 340(5) to a debt arising from the sale of property is more obscure. Paragraph (5)(b) refers to 'an account that is the proceeds of inventory', and 'proceeds' of collateral is defined in s. 31(1)(a) as including personal property that is derived directly or indirectly from a dealing with collateral. That personal property should include a debt arising consequent upon the sale of the collateral.

17.104 Section 80(1) is expressed to apply in relation to 'a transferee of an account or chattel paper (including a secured party or a receiver)'. Though there is no reference to a 'secured party' in sub-ss. (7) and (8) of s. 80, relating to payment by the debtor,[510] the intention appears to be that s. 80 is to apply generally to any person who holds a security interest in any form,[511] and that it is not confined to a person who takes an absolute transfer.[512] The drafting of s. 80 gives rise to a number of difficulties,[513] but, subject to those points, s. 80(1) would generally preserve the principles set out below as constituting equities and defences to which the secured party takes subject. The relevant time is that referred to in s. 80(1)(b),[514] being the time when payment by the debtor to the transferor (or security provider) would no longer discharge the debtor's obligation. This, in turn, refers to the giving of notice to the debtor that payment is to be made to the transferee (or, it would seem, the secured party) and, in some cases, the provision of proof of the transfer to the debtor.[515]

(3) Statutes of Set-off

The general principle

17.105 Consistent with the principle applicable in the case of assignments of debts,[516] a debtor to a company ordinarily will be denied a set-off under the Statutes of Set-off in an action for payment brought against him or her by the company where the subject of the claimed set-off is a cross-debt incurred by the company to the debtor after the debtor had notice of crystallization of a floating charge over the company's assets and undertaking. The leading authority is *N W Robbie & Co Ltd v Witney Warehouse Co Ltd*.[517] The plaintiff company had issued a debenture to a bank securing, by means of a fixed and floating charge over its assets, all moneys due from it to the bank. The bank subsequently appointed a receiver and manager under the debenture, whereupon the floating charge crystallized. Before the appointment, the company had sold goods on credit to the defendant. The company continued to carry on business after the appointment, during which time the defendant purchased more goods on credit. At a later date, the defendant obtained an assignment from a third party of a debt owing by the company. When the company sued the defendant for the price of the goods sold, the defendant sought to set off the assigned debt. The Court of Appeal held that a set-off was not available. The decision to deny a set-off seems

---

[510] But see s. 80(3).

[511] Whether fixed or floating.

[512] There is little attraction in an argument that s. 80(1) contemplates only a security interest that takes effect as a transfer, in other words a mortgage as opposed to a charge. See para. 11.46 above. This is consistent with the general approach of the Act, which is not to draw a distinction between different forms of security interest.

[513] See paras 17.11–17.12, 17.22–17.24, 17.31 and 17.35 above.

[514] As opposed to the date of notice of crystallization.

[515] See paras 17.22–17.24 above.

[516] See paras 17.13–17.15 above.

[517] [1963] 1 WLR 1324. See also *Lynch v Ardmore Studios (Ireland) Ltd* [1966] IR 133, which concerned a similar fact situation, and *United Steel Corporation Ltd v Turnbull Elevator of Canada Ltd* [1973] 2 OR 540.

correct[518] but, as Meagher, Gummow and Lehane in Australia explained,[519] the reasoning is questionable. Russell LJ (with whom Sellers LJ agreed) said that there was no right of set-off because there was no mutuality in equity. When the floating charge crystallized, the defendant's debt for the goods purchased before crystallization was assigned in equity to the debenture-holder while, in the case of purchases made after that date, each debt as it arose became the subject of an immediate equitable assignment in favour of the debenture-holder.[520] This meant that, at the later date when the defendant first obtained the assignment of the company's debt from the third party, there was no identity between the person beneficially interested in the claims (the debenture-holder) and the person against whom the cross-claim existed (the company). The assumption inherent in this analysis is that mutuality under the Statutes of Set-off is determined by reference to the equitable rather than the legal interests of the parties, and that, if the demands are not and never have been equitably mutual, a set-off is not available under the Statutes. However, the point was made earlier that this fails to explain why a debtor on an assigned debt is permitted a set-off when the cross-debt from the assignor to the debtor arose after the assignment but before the debtor had notice of the assignment, because in that circumstance there never has been mutuality in equity.[521] The preferred analysis is that the Statutes *prima facie* confer a right of set-off at law when there is mutuality at law, although a lack of mutuality in equity may render it unconscionable for a debtor to rely on the legal right.[522] *Robbie v Witney* is better explained on the ground that, since the cross-claim against the company was acquired after the defendant was aware of the crystallization of the charge, and the consequent equitable interest of the debenture-holder in the defendant's debt to the company, it was unconscionable for the defendant to rely on the right of set-off that otherwise was available at law.[523]

Cross-debt arising after notice pursuant to a prior contract

There is authority for the proposition that a defendant in an action brought by a company for payment of a debt which is the subject of a crystallized floating charge will be denied a set-off under the Statutes where the cross-debt owing by the company arose after the defendant had notice of the fixed security arising consequent upon crystallization, notwithstanding that the cross-debt may have had its source in a contract entered into between the defendant and the company before notice.[524] This is consistent with the principle applied in relation to assignments generally, and it was criticized earlier in that

17.106

---

[518] Compare Barwick CJ In *Ferrier v Bottomer* (1972) 126 CLR 597, 603, who left open the question whether *Robbie v Witney* was correctly decided.

[519] *Meagher, Gummow and Lehane's Equity Doctrines and Remedies* (4th edn, 2002), 943–4 [28–335].

[520] See also *Ferrier v Bottomer* (1972) 126 CLR 597; *Roadshow Entertainment Pty Ltd v (ACN 053 006 269) Pty Ltd* (1997) 42 NSWLR 462, 482.

[521] See para. 11.19 above.

[522] See paras 11.18–11.20 and 17.03 above.

[523] The report of the case does not establish when the defendant first became aware of the crystallization of the floating charge, but Russell LJ said that the defendant should be fixed with knowledge of crystallization before it acquired the cross-claim against the company. See [1963] 1 WLR 1324, 1338.

[524] *Business Computers Ltd v Anglo-African Leasing Ltd* [1977] 1 WLR 578, 585. Compare *West Street Properties Pty Ltd v Jamison* [1974] 2 NSWLR 435 (discussed below) in the situation in which the company instead is the party claiming a set-off.

context.[525] It suffices to say that, if there was a binding contractual relationship in existence before notice, it is unclear why it should be considered unconscionable for the defendant to rely on a right of set-off otherwise available at law under the Statutes when the company's debt arose under that contract but after notice. In any event, similar to the principle that applies in bankruptcy and company liquidation,[526] there is an exception in the case of a temporary suspension of mutual credit. Thus, if a person holding a negotiable instrument upon which a company is liable indorses it to a third party before crystallization, and after crystallization the person is obliged to take up the instrument again as a result of the default of the company, the resulting claim on the instrument against the company may be the subject of a set-off.[527]

Set-off asserted by the company

17.107   The preceeding discussion concerned the situation in which the debtor to the company is the party seeking to base a set-off upon a debt owing by the company that arose after the debtor had notice of a fixed security consequent upon crystallization. A set-off ordinarily is not available to the debtor. But this is not to say that a set-off similarly would be denied to the company.

17.108   The issue arose in New South Wales, in *West Street Properties Pty Ltd v Jamison*.[528] The plaintiff was a lessor of premises, and was claiming payment of arrears of rent from the lessee. Pursuant to a mortgage debenture the lessee had granted a floating charge to a creditor, which crystallized when the debenture-holder appointed a receiver to the lessee. The lease was entered into before the receivership, but the subject of the proceeding was the obligation to pay rent accruing after the appointment, the receiver having determined to continue the company's business for the benefit of the debenture-holder.[529] Jeffrey J was asked to determine a question of law, whether the company could set off against its rent obligation a debt owing to it by the lessor on an advance made before the receivership. He held that the company was entitled to the set-off. He acknowledged the existence of authority for the view that the defendant in an action brought against him or her by a company in receivership for payment of a debt could not set off a debt owing by the company which accrued after the defendant had notice of crystallization of the charge pursuant to which the receiver was appointed. But they were cases where the defendant, as an unsecured creditor, was seeking to obtain payment of the debt owing to him or her in priority to the secured creditor, by setting it off against a debt which the defendant owed to the company but which in equity belonged to the secured creditor.[530] The objection to a set-off

---

[525] See para. 17.15 above.

[526] See also paras 6.105–6.107 above.

[527] *Handley Page Ltd v Commissioners of Customs and Excise and Rockwell Machine Tool Company Ltd* [1970] 2 Lloyd's Rep 459, 464–5, discussed in *Business Computers Ltd v Anglo-African Leasing Ltd* [1977] 1 WLR 578, 585–6.

[528] [1974] 2 NSWLR 435.

[529] Jeffrey J (at [1974] 2 NSWLR 435, 439) considered that, whatever personal liability for rent the receiver may have incurred by virtue of the Companies Act 1961 (NSW), s. 188(1) (see now the Corporations Act 2001 (Cth), s. 419A(2)), it could not have been to the exclusion of the company's liability, given that the lease was entered into before the appointment.

[530] [1974] 2 NSWLR 435, 440–1.

in that circumstance is not relevant when the company, and inferentially the secured creditor, is the party seeking to assert a set-off. There is no countervailing equity in that case which renders it unconscionable for the company to rely on a right of set-off otherwise available at law. The cross-demands would not have been equitably mutual at any time, but lack of mutuality in equity will only deprive a defendant of a right of set-off otherwise available at law if in the circumstances it is unconscionable for the defendant to assert the legal right. As Jeffrey J remarked:[531]

> In a case where the debenture-holder elects after crystallization to cause the company to carry on its business, debts incurred to existing debtors of the company in so doing may be met by the *pro tanto* collection of the debts owed by them to the company by means of set-off. This is but a method of recovery alternative to the taking of proceedings at law in the name of the company, something which, as already observed, the debenture-holder has after crystallization, an undoubted right to do. For him to direct that a debt which he owns should be applied in reduction or extinction of an indebtedness which the company incurs is merely to exercise his dominion over it. It is one thing to say that a set-off at law cannot be availed of to defeat or postpone a prior equitable title to a debt, but quite another to say that it is not available to the equitable owner who wishes to employ the legal rights over which he has control in order to collect it.

In the *West Street Properties* case, the company's debt arose after crystallization pursuant to a prior contract, but the reasoning would appear to be equally relevant where the company's debt has its source in a contract entered into after crystallization.[532] *West Street Properties v Jamison* supports the view that, in the situation in which a company after crystallization of a floating charge over its assets becomes indebted to a person who in turn is indebted to the company, it is only unconscionable for the debtor to the company to assert a legal right of set-off otherwise available under the Statutes of Set-off. There is no countervailing equity which would preclude the company and the secured creditor from relying on a set-off available at law. There is merit in that view. On the other hand, a set-off should not be available where a receiver is personally liable for a debt[533] and the receiver is sued personally.[534] In that circumstance, there would not be mutuality at law or in equity, so that Jeffrey J's analysis would not apply.

Debt to the company arising after notice but pursuant to a prior contract

Consider the converse situation, in which the debt owing to the company, rather than the **17.109** company's debt to the debtor, arises after notice of crystallization as a result of a contract entered into before notice. It seems that a set-off may be available in that case at the instance of either party against a debt incurred by the company before crystallization.[535] In *Rother*

---

[531] [1974] 2 NSWLR 435, 441.

[532] See e.g. the discussion at [1974] 2 NSWLR 435, 439–40.

[533] As in the case of an administrative receiver in relation to a contract entered into by him or her in the carrying out of his or her functions, pursuant to the Insolvency Act 1986, s. 44(1)(b). In Australia, see the Corporations Act 2001 (Cth), s. 419.

[534] Compare *West Street Properties* [1974] 2 NSWLR 435, 439.

[535] Compare *T. R. Hillson Ltd v Beverley Trading Co Ltd* (1987) 3 NZCLC 100,026 (New Zealand HC). A company, prior to crystallization of a floating charge over its assets by the appointment of a receiver, had paid for some goods. It was therefore at the date of the appointment entitled to delivery of the goods. However, the right to delivery itself could not have been the subject of a set-off. The goods were not delivered,

Iron Works Ltd v Canterbury Precision Engineers Ltd,[536] a floating charge in a debenture granted by a company crystallized when a receiver was appointed to the company. Prior to the appointment, the company was indebted to the defendant for £124. In addition, it had entered into a contract to sell goods to the defendant for £159. The goods were not delivered until after the receiver was appointed, and it was only upon delivery that the defendant became indebted for the price. The Court of Appeal held that the defendant need only pay £35, after the deducting the company's debt. Russell LJ in delivering the judgment of the court[537] said that the obligation of the defendant to pay the £159: 'never . . . came into existence except subject to a right to set off the £124 as, in effect, payment in advance. That which became subject to the debenture charge was not £159, but the net claim sustainable by the plaintiff for £35.'[538]

17.110   *Rother Iron Works v Canterbury Precision Engineers* has been referred to with evident approval in later cases,[539] and Mance J followed it in *Marathon Electrical Manufacturing Corp v Mashreqbank PSC*[540] when he allowed a set-off against an assignee of a debt where the assigned debt arose after the debtor had notice of the assignment but pursuant to a prior engagement. On the other hand, the British Columbia Court of Appeal declined to apply the *Rother Iron Works* case in *CIBC v Tuckerr Industries Inc.*[541] A debenture-holder appointed a receiver to a lessor of premises, which crystallized a floating charge under the debenture. Notice of the appointment was given immediately to the lessee. Prior to the appointment,

---

and after the appointment the company accepted the failure to deliver as a repudiation and claimed the return of the price paid. McGechan J held that the circumstances were not such as to entitle the defendant to set off a pre-receivership cross-claim against the company.

[536] [1974] 1 QB 1. See also *State Bank of South Australia v Kralingen Pty Ltd* (1993) 172 LSJS 438, a decision of Cox J in the South Australian Supreme Court. A lease required the lessor to purchase the tenant's fixtures upon determination of the lease. The lessee granted a floating mortgage debenture over its rights under the lease to the plaintiff bank. The security crystallized and, after that, the lessor determined the lease. Cox J held that the lessor could set off the lessee's arrears of rent against its liability to pay the price of the fixtures. The *Rother Iron Works* case was not referred to, but it is consistent with that decision.

[537] Russell, Cairns and Stamp LJJ.

[538] [1974] 1 QB 1, 6.

[539] In addition to *Marathon Electrical Manufacturing Corp v Mashreqbank PSC* [1997] 2 BCLC 460 (see below), see *George Barker (Transport) Ltd v Eynon* [1974] 1 WLR 462, 470, 473–4, 475 (CA) and *Business Computers Ltd v Anglo-African Leasing Ltd* [1977] 1 WLR 578, 585 (although the facts of the *Rother Iron Works* case were incorrectly stated, since the company rather than the debtor was the seller of the goods). See also *Caratti v Grant* (1978) 3 ACLR 322, 331; *Roadshow Entertainment Pty Ltd v (ACN 053 006 269) Pty Ltd* (1997) 42 NSWLR 462, 483 (CA). In *John Dee Group Ltd v WMH (21) Ltd* [1997] BCC 518, 529–31, Neuberger J accepted that, were it not for a clause in the contract in issue which required payment without set-off, a set-off would have been available in relation to transport charges payable to a company in receivership for services performed after notice of the receivership but pursuant to a prior contract, notice of the receivership also constituting notice of crystallization. However, while Neuberger J referred to the *Rother Iron Works* case, it is unclear if the availability of a set-off was thought to be on the basis of a set-off under the Statutes of Set-off or an equitable set-off arising from closely connected claims, for which the date of notice is not determinative. See para. 17.113 below. See Neuberger J's reference (at 530) to *Government of Newfoundland v Newfoundland Railway Co* (1888) 13 App Cas 199 (which concerned equitable set-off), and (at 531) to the extract from *Business Computers Ltd v Anglo-African Leasing Ltd* [1977] 1 WLR 578, 585 in relation to closely connected claims. Neuberger J's decision was affirmed on appeal [1998] BCC 972 but without reference to this point.

[540] [1997] 2 BCLC 460.

[541] (1983) 149 DLR (3d) 172. See also *Re Associated Investors of Canada Ltd* (1989) 62 DLR (4th) 269, but compare *Clarkson Company Ltd v The Queen* (1988) 88 *Dominion Tax Cases* 6256.

the lessor was indebted to the lessee on a transaction independent of the lease. The question was whether the lessee could set off the prior debt against rent accruing after the appointment. The Court of Appeal held that there was a lack of mutuality, and therefore there was no set-off, since on the one hand the lessor was indebted to the lessee and on the other the subsequently accruing rent was owed to the debenture-holder as equitable assignee. While *Rother Iron Works* appears to have been a similar case, it was distinguished on the ground that it was an example of an equitable set-off,[542] the basis of which was said to be that the two companies in that case had traded with each other in such a way that every debt that arose between them in the course of their trade was subject, at the time it arose, to being set off against every subsequent cross-debt that arose within the trading relationship. That explanation is doubtful. There is nothing in Russell LJ's judgment in the *Rother Iron Works* case to suggest that there was an agreement for a set-off,[543] so as to support an equitable set-off on that ground,[544] and nor do the demands appear to have been sufficiently closely connected to give rise to a substantive equitable set-off.[545] The court in deciding against a set-off in *CIBC v Tuckerr* seems to have assumed that mutuality under the Statutes of Set-off is determined solely by reference to equitable titles, but that assumption does not accurately describe the position.[546] In *Rother Iron Works v Canterbury Precision Engineers*, there was mutuality at law, and therefore *prima facie* there was a right of set-off at law under the Statutes of Set-off, and the case is authority for the proposition that in the circumstances in issue there was nothing inequitable in the defendant relying on the legal right. This should be equally relevant to a case such as *CIBC v Tuckerr*.

In *Hoverd Industries Ltd v Supercool Refrigeration and Air Conditioning* (1991) Ltd[547] the New Zealand Court of Appeal noted that the debt which the defendant was permitted to set off in *Rother Iron Works v Canterbury Precision Engineers* was already due and payable before the company entered into the contract which gave rise to the receiver's later claim. However, that was not the basis of the decision in the *Rother Iron Works* case. The point that Russell LJ made was that, when the debt for the price first came into existence, it was already subject to the set-off,[548] and the debt came into existence when the goods were delivered. Whether the debt which the defendant was allowed to set off arose before or after the date of the contract which gave rise to the claim for the price was not significant. The New Zealand Court of Appeal was also critical of Russell LJ's comment that the set-off was 'in effect, payment in advance',[549] pointing out that set-off is a defence which can only be pleaded against a claim which is presently due.[550] That observation is true enough, but it does not detract from the decision. A set-off against an assignee does not occur at the date

17.111

---

[542] The better view (notwithstanding recent Court of Appeal authority to the contrary: see para. 4.69 above) is that mutuality is not necessary in all cases for equitable set-off. See paras 4.67–4.83 above.
[543] Indeed, the contrary is inherent in Stamp LJ's comment in *George Barker (Transport) Ltd v Eynon* [1974] 1 WLR 462, 474.
[544] See paras 3.03–3.04 above.
[545] See ch. 4 above.
[546] See paras 11.18–11.20 and 17.03 above.
[547] [1995] 3 NZLR 577, 587–8.
[548] See [1974] 1 QB 1, 6.
[549] [1974] 1 QB 1, 6.
[550] [1995] 3 NZLR 577, 588.

of notice of an assignment,[551] and so it should not suffice to deny a set-off that the assigned debt was not in existence at that date if it arose out of a prior contract. The debt must, of course, be in existence and be presently payable when it is sued upon, and the question then is whether it is unconscionable for the defendant to rely on a right of set-off which is available at law given the intervening equitable interest of the secured creditor. It is in the context of the question of unconscionability that the decision in *Rother Iron Works* should be considered.

Contract entered into after notice

17.112 Russell LJ emphasized in the *Rother Iron Works* case that the delivery of the goods in that case occurred pursuant to a contract made by the company before crystallization, and that the court was not concerned with a claim made by the receiver against the defendant which arose out of a contract made by the receiver subsequent to crystallization.[552] It would generally be unconscionable to allow a defendant to assert a set-off otherwise available at law when the defendant's liability to the company arose out of a dealing transacted after the defendant was aware that the company's assets were charged to a secured creditor, and that the dealing was being conducted for the benefit of the secured creditor. Thus, there are a number of cases in which a person who purchased goods from a company known to be in receivership was not allowed to set off the debt for the price against a pre-receivership debt owing to the person by the company,[553] the receivership having crystallized a floating security over the company's assets.[554] In New Zealand, Richmond J in *Felt and Textiles of New Zealand Ltd v R Hubrich Ltd*,[555] in denying the appellant a set-off against the price of goods sold to it after a floating charge over the vendor's assets crystallized upon the appointment of a receiver, emphasized that: 'the appellant had notice of the fact that it was buying an asset then charged in favour of the debenture-holder from a company empowered by the debenture to sell that asset through the agency of the receiver for the purpose, primarily, of discharging the company's indebtedness to the debenture-holder.'[556] The sale in the *Felt and Textiles* case arose in the course of the realization of the company's assets by the receiver after crystallization. Richmond J tentatively suggested that there may be a distinction between that case and a case in which the receiver was carrying on the company's business. Subsequently, however, Chilwell J in the New Zealand Supreme Court in *Rendell v Doors*

---

[551] *Glencore Grain Ltd v Agros Trading Co* [1999] 2 Lloyd's Rep 410, 417–19.

[552] [1974] 1 QB 1, 6.

[553] In addition to the cases discussed below, see *Leichhardt Emporium Pty Ltd v AGC (Household Finance) Ltd* [1979] 1 NSWLR 701; *Cheviot Australia Pty Ltd v Bob Jane Corporation Pty Ltd* (1988) 52 SASR 204. Compare *F Suter & Co Ltd v Drake and Gorham Ltd* (1910), unreported but noted in Weaver and Craigie, *The Law Relating to Banker and Customer in Australia* (looseleaf) vol. 2, [14.8470], in which it appears that the Divisional Court (Darling and Phillimore JJ) allowed a set-off in this situation.

[554] *Robbie v Witney* [1963] 1 WLR 1324 (see para. 17.105 above) is authority for the proposition that this also applies when the cross-claim against the company was acquired after notice through an assignment. While *Robbie v Witney* also concerned a sale of goods by a company, it is not stated in the report whether the defendant purchaser had notice of the appointment of the receiver, and therefore of crystallization, at the time of the sale of the goods. Russell LJ simply remarked ([1963] 1 WLR 1324, 1338) that the defendant should be fixed with knowledge of the assignment some time before it acquired the cross-claim against the company.

[555] [1968] NZLR 716.

[556] [1968] NZLR 716, 718.

and Doors Ltd,[557] rejected this as a ground for distinction, and held that a creditor of a company who purchased goods from a receiver known to be carrying on the company's business could not set off the price against the company's pre-receivership debt to him. There is nevertheless a suggestion in the judgment that, in some cases in which a company's business is being carried on after crystallization, an equity could possibly arise which would justify a set-off against the secured creditor.[558] The situation postulated by Chilwell J was one in which a person supplied material to a company after crystallization, which material was used in the manufacture of goods subsequently purchased by that person. The basis of any supposed equity was not explored further, but, as Jeffrey J remarked in New South Wales,[559] there is something to be said for the view that a secured creditor should expect to take subject to a set-off when both demands arose out of dealings with the company while the company's business was being carried on for the benefit of the secured creditor, notwithstanding that it is contrary to the generally accepted position in relation to assignments of debts, that the line is drawn at the date of notice.

(4) Equitable set-off[560]

When the argument for a set-off is based upon the procedural defence available under the Statutes of Set-off in the case of mutual debts, the availability of a set-off is generally determined by reference to the date of notice of a fixed security.[561] However, consistent with the principle applicable in the case of an assignment of a debt,[562] that date is not determinative when an equitable set-off is in issue based upon cross-demands which are inseparably connected.[563] The point is illustrated by *Parsons v Sovereign Bank of Canada*.[564]

17.113

---

[557] [1975] 2 NZLR 191.

[558] This would be better expressed in terms that in some cases it would not be unconscionable for the defendant to rely on a right of set-off which is available at law under the Statutes of Set-off.

[559] *West Street Properties Pty Ltd v Jamison* [1974] 2 NSWLR 435, 440. See also *Leichhardt Emporium Pty Ltd v AGC (Household Finance) Ltd* [1979] 1 NSWLR 701, 706–7, although compare *Business Computers Ltd v Anglo-African Leasing Ltd* [1977] 1 WLR 578, 585. An equitable set-off in any event should be available when both demands arose out of the same contract entered into by a receiver on behalf of the company and the demands are inseparably connected. This form of equitable set-off is considered below.

[560] In Australia, note the point made in para. 17.35 above in relation to the Personal Property Securities Act 2009 (Cth).

[561] In the case of a floating charge, this refers to the date of notice of crystallization.

[562] See para. 17.32 above.

[563] See ch. 4 above. The judgment of Mocatta J in *Handley Page Ltd v Commissioners of Customs and Excise and Rockwell Machine Tool Company Ltd* [1970] 2 Lloyd's Rep 459 is confusing in this respect. If indeed the demands arose under the same contract and were sufficiently closely connected to give rise to an equitable set-off (see at 465, in particular the reference to *Hanak v Green* [1958] 2 QB 9), a set-off should have been available without the need to have recourse to the principle of a temporary suspension of mutual credit (see para. 17.106 above) as a means of overcoming the perceived difficulty that the bills were returned to Rockwell after crystallization by the appointment of a receiver under the debenture issued by Handley-Page. In *Business Computers Ltd v Anglo-African Leasing Ltd* [1977] 1 WLR 578, 585–6 these were treated as alternative grounds for allowing a set-off in the *Handley Page* case.

[564] [1913] AC 160. See also *Forster v Nixon's Navigation Co* (1906) 23 TLR 138 (court-appointed receiver); *West Street Properties Pty Ltd v Jamison* [1974] 2 NSWLR 435, 439; *Re Wirragana Nominees Pty Ltd* (1991) 9 ACLC 1168, 1179–80; *Roadshow Entertainment Pty Ltd v (ACN 053 006 269) Pty Ltd* (1997) 42 NSWLR 462 (see esp. at 481 *et seq.*). In New Zealand, compare *Popular Homes Ltd v Circuit Developments Ltd* [1979] 2 NZLR 642, 660 and *Hoverd Industries Ltd v Supercool Refrigeration and Air Conditioning (1991) Ltd* [1995] 3 NZLR 577, 586 (in relation to the relevance of the charge being fixed or floating), where the contrary seems to have been assumed.

A company prior to the appointment of a receiver and manager at the instance of debenture-holders had entered into a number of contracts with the defendants for the supply of quantities of paper to them on a periodic basis. The receiver, immediately after his appointment, continued to supply paper under the contracts,[565] but subsequently repudiated the contracts. The receiver assigned the defendants' debt for the price of paper delivered after the appointment to the plaintiff, but when the plaintiff sued for payment it was held that the defendants could set off their unliquidated damages claim against the company for breach of contract.[566] The fact that the demands arose after the appointment of the receiver was not sufficient to deny a set-off as against either the debenture-holders or the assignee. The receiver in the *Parsons* case was appointed by the court as opposed to by the debenture-holders, but the principle should be the same for both forms of appointment.[567]

(5) Debt owing to the company exceeds the secured debt

17.114   In the preceding discussion of the circumstances in which a set-off is denied to a defendant in an action brought by a company for payment of a debt which arose after the defendant had notice of a fixed security consequent upon crystallization, it was assumed that the defendant's debt to the company is less than the debt for which the charge to the secured creditor constitutes a security. If the defendant's debt to the company exceeds the company's debt to the secured creditor, so that the company alone is interested in the excess, and the defendant is solvent,[568] the defendant may set off the excess against the company's debt to the defendant.[569]

(6) Liquidation

17.115   A company may go into liquidation after a floating charge over its assets has crystallized.[570] If at the commencement of the liquidation the secured creditor has not been paid in full, and the security operates as an equitable mortgage, any debts owing to the company and coming within the ambit of the security will be the subject of a prior equitable assignment in favour of the secured creditor. Since the secured creditor, rather than the company, has

---

[565] The Privy Council accepted that the paper was delivered under the old contracts with the company, and not pursuant to new contracts made with the receiver personally.

[566] When an equitable set-off is in issue based upon an inseparable connection, it is not necessary that the demands be liquidated. See para. 4.02 above and e.g. *Sun Candies Pty Ltd v Polites* [1939] VLR 132 (receivership). Compare *W Pope & Co Pty Ltd v Edward Souery & Co Pty Ltd* [1983] WAR 117. A company in receivership was suing for the price of goods supplied to the defendant. The defendant was not permitted to set off a claim for unliquidated damages arising out of defects in an earlier consignment under a separate contract, it being doubted whether set-off applies to damages claims. But in any event, there was not in that case a sufficiently close connection so as to give rise to an equitable set-off.

[567] See paras 17.119–17.120 below.

[568] See para. 11.40 above.

[569] See Dixon J in *Hiley v Peoples Prudential Assurance Co* (1938) 60 CLR 468, 497–8, referring to *Re Asphaltic Wood Pavement Co. Lee & Chapman's Case* (1885) 30 Ch D 216, 222. See also paras 11.39–11.40 above.

[570] Compare *Re Parker* (1997) 80 FCR 1, in which the liquidation was deemed to have commenced prior to the appointment of the receiver, as a result of the appointment of an administrator to the company pursuant to Part 5.3A of the Corporations Law, and Mansfield J held that the question of the application of the insolvency set-off section fell to be determined as at the earlier date. See paras 6.52–6.62 above.

the beneficial title to the debts, the set-off section in the insolvency legislation would not be relevant in the liquidation as between the company and the debtor to the company,[571] and rights of set-off should continue to be determined by reference to the principles outlined above.[572] Nor should the result differ if a charge rather than a mortgage is in issue,[573] even assuming that the stipulation for a charge is not interpreted as operating by way of assignment in any event.[574] If, on the other hand, the security is redeemed before the commencement of the liquidation by payment to the secured creditor, the secured creditor will no longer have an interest in the debts owing to the company. The company itself would be the beneficial owner of the debts, and so the insolvency set-off section should determine the existence of any right of set-off in its liquidation.[575] Alternatively, redemption of the security may occur after the liquidation. The question of set-off in that circumstance was considered earlier.[576] Further, a set-off may occur under the insolvency set-off section as between the company and the debtor if, and to the extent that, the debt owing to the company exceeds the company's debt to the secured creditor, but a set-off should not be permitted in that circumstance unless the debtor is solvent.[577]

(7) Preferential debts

When a receiver is appointed to a company on behalf of the holders of debentures secured by a charge which, as created, was a floating charge, the Insolvency Act 1986, s. 40(2)[578] accords preferential status to certain debts, so that they are required to be paid out of the assets of the company coming into the hands of the receiver in priority to any claims for principal or interest payable to the debenture-holders. The concept of preferential debts also applies in company liquidation.[579] If a creditor of a company in liquidation has two debts owing to it, one preferential and the other non-preferential, and at the same time the creditor is indebted to the company, the prevailing view in company liquidation is that a set-off under the insolvency set-off section occurs rateably as between the preferential and the non-preferential debts,[580] and it has been suggested that a similar principle should apply in receivership.[581] That proposition is doubtful, however.

17.116

The point is that different forms of set-off are in issue. In company liquidation, a set-off under the insolvency set-off section occurs automatically at the date of the liquidation.[582] In that situation, there is no difficulty in saying that a set-off may operate rateably as

17.117

---

[571] See para. 17.39 above, and also *Re Parker* (1997) 80 FCR 1, 16–18.
[572] See e.g. *Handley Page Ltd v Commissioners of Customs and Excise and Rockwell Machine Tool Company Ltd* [1970] 2 Lloyd's Rep 459; *Rendell v Doors and Doors Ltd* [1975] 2 NZLR 191; *Hoverd Industries Ltd v Supercool Refrigeration and Air Conditioning (1991) Ltd* [1995] 3 NZLR 577, 585 *et seq.*
[573] See para. 17.100 above.
[574] See *Re ELS Ltd* [1995] Ch 11, 24–5.
[575] See *Rendell v Doors and Doors Ltd* [1975] 2 NZLR 191, 202–3.
[576] See para. 11.51 above.
[577] See paras 11.39–11.41 above.
[578] In Australia, see the Corporations Act 2001 (Cth), s. 433(3).
[579] Insolvency Act 1986, s. 175. In Australia, see the Corporations Act 2001 (Cth), ss. 555–563AAA.
[580] *Re Unit 2 Windows Ltd* [1985] 1 WLR 1383. See paras 6.168–6.173 above.
[581] Lightman and Moss, *The Law of Administrators and Receivers of Companies* (4th edn, 2007), 377–8 [14–008], 707–8 [28–051].
[582] See paras 6.119–6.146 above.

between the debts. The same cannot be said, however, in the case of receivership. A set-off does not occur automatically upon the appointment of a receiver, and nor can the receiver act unilaterally to effect a set-off. Unless the circumstances are such as to give rise to an equitable set-off, the form of set-off in issue is the procedural defence provided by the Statutes of Set-off. A set-off under the Statutes is pleaded as a defence to an action, and the set-off is effected by a judgment of the court.[583]

17.118   Consider that a receiver wishes to make a payment to the debenture-holders before suing for a debt owing to the company by a person who is a creditor in relation to two debts, one of which is preferred. In that circumstance, the receiver could only make the payment by complying with the Insolvency Act, which requires that he or she must pay preferential debts first. The receiver could not reduce or extinguish the preferential debt by unilaterally effecting a set-off. Therefore, the receiver would have to pay the amount of the preferential debt to the creditor as that debt exists at the time. Alternatively, the receiver may commence an action against the creditor for payment of the debt owing to the company before making any payment to debenture-holders. In that circumstance, it would be up to the creditor as to which debt (or debts) is pleaded by way of defence under the Statutes. If the creditor relies only on the non-preferential debt as a set-off, it is difficult to see how a set-off could then occur rateably as against that debt and the preferential debt, when the preferential debt has not been pleaded as a defence.[584] The same result should therefore follow.

D. Court-Appointed Receiver on the Application of a Secured Creditor

17.119   A receiver may be appointed by the court. One situation considered later is an appointment by way of equitable execution,[585] but the court's power is not confined to that circumstance. The court has a broad jurisdiction to appoint a receiver in all cases in which it appears to be just and convenient to do so.[586] This includes the appointment of a receiver and manager of the company's business on the application of a secured creditor in order to protect the creditor's security.[587] Court appointments in this situation are rare, given that secured creditors usually now reserve the right to appoint a receiver out of court. It may nevertheless occur if in a particular case the security document does not empower

---

[583]   See paras 2.34–2.39 above.

[584]   Compare *Re South Blackpool Hotel Co, ex p James* (1869) LR 8 Eq 225. Set-off was applied rateably in that case as between a number of debentures issued by a company. The company was in liquidation, and the set-off occurred in the context of a proof of debt in the liquidation. The case was decided before the bankruptcy set-off section was extended to company liquidation, rights of set-off in company liquidation being founded instead at that time on the Statutes of Set-off. In that sense, it might be said to support the view that set-off under the Statutes of Set-off is applied pro rata when there are a number of cross-debts. However, the application of the Statutes in company liquidation was not without difficulty, in particular when applied in the context of a proof of debt lodged in the liquidation. See para. 6.05 above. In any event, the decision may be explicable on the basis of an equitable set-off arising from closely connected cross-claims. See ch. 4 above.

[585]   See paras 17.147–17.148 below.

[586]   Senior Courts Act 1981, s. 37(1).

[587]   See *Halsbury's Laws of England* (5th edn, 2009) vol. 15, 632, para. 1362.

the creditor to appoint a receiver, or the validity of an appointment made by the creditor is in dispute.[588]

In *Robbie v Witney*,[589] Russell LJ said that it should not make any difference in relation to questions of set-off whether a receiver has been appointed out of court under a crystallized floating security or whether the receiver is court-appointed. In both cases, he said, the receiver and manager is merely a piece of administrative machinery designed to enforce a security. This requires further comment. The incidents of the two forms of receivership in fact differ in a fundamental respect. A receiver appointed by a creditor pursuant to a power conferred by a security is usually expressed to be the agent of the company,[590] whereas a court-appointed receiver is the agent of neither the company nor the creditor on whose application he or she was appointed.[591] Any new contracts ordinarily are made by the receiver personally, in reliance on his or her right of indemnity from the company's assets.[592] When a receiver is appointed at the instance of a secured creditor, the same result usually would follow in relation to set-off whether the receiver is appointed by the court or out of court, not because of the incidents attaching to the appointment as such, but because the debtor to the company will have notice of a fixed security attaching to his or her debt, and once the debtor has notice he or she cannot rely on subsequent events to diminish the rights of the creditor.[593] In any event, in the case of a court appointment a debtor to the company could not rely by way of set-off on a debt which is incurred by the receiver pursuant to a contract entered into with the receiver personally, because there would be a lack of mutuality. On the other hand, contracts entered into by the company before the court appointment remain the company's contracts, and an equitable set-off against a liability of the company under the contract where there is a sufficiently close connection remains available to the debtor, even where the cross-claim accrued after notice of the security. This is the effect of the decision of the Privy Council in *Parsons v Sovereign Bank of Canada*,[594] and it is consistent with the principle applicable in the case of an assignment.[595]

17.120

(1) Manager appointed by a leasehold valuation tribunal

The position of a court-appointed receiver in relation to equitable set-off should be contrasted with that of a manager appointed by a leasehold valuation tribunal under s. 24 of the Landlord and Tenant Act 1987 to carry out functions in connection with the management of leasehold premises. The appointee carries out those functions

17.121

588 See generally Lightman and Moss, *The Law of Administrators and Receivers of Companies* (4th edn, 2007), 718–19 [29–005]. See also *Bank of Credit and Commerce International SA v BRS Kumar Brothers Ltd* [1994] BCLC 211.
589 [1963] 1 WLR 1324, 1340. See also *Roadshow Entertainment Pty Ltd v (ACN 053 006 269) Pty Ltd* (1997) 42 NSWLR 462, 483–4.
590 In relation to an administrative receiver, see the Insolvency Act 1986, s. 44(1)(a).
591 *Parsons v Sovereign Bank of Canada* [1913] AC 160, 167.
592 *Parsons v Sovereign Bank of Canada* [1913] AC 160, 167. See also *Burt, Boulton, & Hayward v Bull* [1895] 1 QB 276; *Moss Steamship Co Ltd v Whinney* [1912] AC 154.
593 See para. 17.03 above.
594 [1913] AC 160. See para. 17.113 above. See also the similar case of *Forster v Nixon's Navigation Co* (1906) 23 TLR 138.
595 See para. 17.32 above.

881

as a court-appointed manager. He or she does not carry on the landlord's business but acts in a capacity independent of the landlord. In a claim by the manager against a tenant for the tenant's share of costs expended by the manager for repairs and for the supply of services, the tenant cannot set off a damages claim against the landlord for breach of the lease.[596]

E. Trusts[597]

(1) Set-off between the trustee and a third party

Equitable set-off

17.122   A trust is not a legal entity separate from the trustee.[598] When a trustee incurs a debt in that capacity, the trustee is personally liable. The creditor does not have direct recourse either to the trust assets[599] or to the beneficiaries. On the other hand, when the trust property includes a debt owing to the trustee, the trustee, though possessed of the legal title to the debt, is not the beneficial owner. *Prima facie*, there would not be mutuality in equity as between, on the one hand, a debt incurred by a trustee, and on the other a cross-claim available to the trustee in his or her capacity as such against the creditor.[600] Consider, however, that a trustee has entered into a transaction with a third party out of which cross-demands arise which otherwise are sufficiently closely connected to give rise to an equitable set-off. Notwithstanding some recent judicial opinions suggesting the contrary,[601] the better view is that equity does not always insist upon mutuality as a strict requirement for equitable set-off.[602] On that basis, the apparent lack of mutuality should not be a sufficient reason for denying a set-off to the third party. In New South Wales, Giles J in *Murphy v Zamonex Pty Ltd*[603] held that set-off is available in equity in this situation, a view that was accepted by Laddie J in *Penwith District Council v V P Developments Ltd*.[604] Nor was Giles J persuaded to adopt a different view by an argument that the trustee in that case may have lost its right to an indemnity from the trust estate in respect of the liability because it was in breach of trust.[605] The equitable set-off was justified on the ground that the beneficiaries of a trust should not have the benefit of the transaction without also bearing the burden of the

---

[596] *Taylor v Blaquiere* [2003] 1 WLR 379.

[597] If a trustee is liable for distinct breaches of trust, one of which has resulted in a gain to the estate and the other a loss, it is said that the trustee cannot set off the gain against the loss unless they arise in the same transaction. See *Bartlett v Barclays Bank Trust Co Ltd* [1980] 1 Ch 515, 538; Underhill and Hayton, *Law Relating to Trusts and Trustees* (17th edn, 2006), 1079. However, this is not a case of set-off of cross-demands, but rather of fixing the amount of compensation payable.

[598] *Kemtron Industries Pty Ltd v Commissioner of Stamp Duties* [1984] 1 Qd R 576, 584.

[599] *Worrall v Harford* (1802) 8 Ves Jun 4, 8, 32 ER 250, 252; *Re Evans* (1887) 34 Ch D 597, 600; *Jennings v Mather* [1902] 1 KB 1, 5; *General Credits Ltd v Tawilla Pty Ltd* [1984] 1 Qd R 388.

[600] Compare the discussion below of the effect of the trustee's right of indemnity. In *Murphy v Zamonex Pty Ltd* (1993) 31 NSWLR 439, 464 Giles J left that question open.

[601] See para. 4.69 above.

[602] See paras 4.67–4.83 above.

[603] (1993) 31 NSWLR 439.

[604] [2005] 2 BCLC 607 at [20]–[23]. The analysis in *Murphy v Zamonex* was accepted as arguable in *Doherty v Murphy* [1996] 2 VR 553 (Appeal Division) in a summary judgment application.

[605] (1993) 31 NSWLR 439, 464.

trustee's conduct.[606] Moreover, while there had been a change in trustee in *Murphy v Zamonex*,[607] that did not affect the view expressed. The new trustee in such a case takes subject to equities, so that the defendant can assert the set-off notwithstanding that the action is brought by the new trustee.

Abatement

Similarly, the fact of a trust should not affect the availability of a common law defence of abatement.[608] This defence applies in an action for the agreed price of goods sold with a warranty or of work to be performed according to a contract. If the goods are delivered in a defective condition or the work is improperly performed, the purchaser on being sued for the price can defend the action by showing how much less the subject-matter of the action was worth by reason of the breach, and can obtain an abatement of the price accordingly. The rationale for the defence should not be affected by the circumstance that either the purchaser or the vendor is a trustee.

17.123

Statutes of Set-off, and insolvency set-off

What if the case is one of unrelated cross-debts, so that the question concerns the Statutes of Set-off or, in the event of a bankruptcy or liquidation, the insolvency set-off section?[609] In the first place, if the trustee is indebted to the third party in the trustee's personal capacity as a result of a dealing unrelated to the trust, lack of mutuality would preclude a set-off under either the insolvency set-off section[610] or the Statutes of Set-off[611] against a debt held on trust, unless in the case of the Statutes the principle of taking subject to equities applies.[612] Consider, however, that the trustee incurred the debt in the proper execution of the trust, so that the trustee has a right of indemnity from the trust assets, and at the same time the trustee is a creditor of the third party in respect of a debt which is held on trust for the beneficiaries. In *Nelson v Roberts*,[613] the defendant was an executor of an estate, and he had also been appointed receiver and manager. In his capacity as executor he had a claim against one Joseph Grimes. On the other hand, as receiver and manager he had incurred a debt to Joseph Grimes. While different representative capacities were involved, in that the claim was held in the capacity of executor and the debt was incurred in the capacity of receiver and manager, they both related to the same estate. Nevertheless, when the defendant was sued for payment of the debt incurred as receiver and manager, Mathew and Wright JJ held that he was not entitled to set off the debt due to the estate under the Statutes, not-withstanding that he may have had a right of indemnity from the estate in respect of his indebtedness. It was still his personal liability. Mathew J said that the same principle applies in the case of an executor, an agent and a trustee. However, the issue of an indemnity from

17.124

---

[606] (1993) 31 NSWLR 439, 465, 468.
[607] This had also occurred in *Doherty v Murphy* [1996] 2 VR 553.
[608] See paras 2.123–2.134 above.
[609] See also paras 6.10–6.11 above in relation to administration (in Australia, compare para. 6.12 above).
[610] See para. 11.13 above.
[611] See para. 11.18 above.
[612] See para. 17.128 below.
[613] (1893) 69 LT 352. See also *Rex v Ray, ex p Chapman* [1936] SASR 241, 249; *Kent v Munroe* (1904) 8 OLR 723.

the estate was not satisfactorily dealt with,[614] and where it is clear in a particular case that the trustee is entitled to be indemnified there is merit in the argument that a set-off should be available.

17.125 **Trustee's lien.** A trustee who properly incurs a debt in the execution of the trust is entitled to be indemnified from the trust assets,[615] and for the purpose of giving effect to the indemnity the trustee has an interest which has been described as a first charge or a lien over the assets.[616] This is not a mere right of retainer,[617] but rather it confers an equitable proprietary interest in those assets[618] which has priority over the interests of the beneficiaries.[619] In an appropriate case[620] the court may order a sale of trust property in order to satisfy the trustee's claim.[621] The trustee's first charge should extend to a trust asset in the form of a debt owing to the trustee in his or her capacity as such.[622] Furthermore, it is not necessary that the trustee should first have paid the debt before claiming against the trust assets.[623] If the trustee has not paid the debt from his or her personal assets, the trustee is entitled to apply the trust property in discharging it, in other words the trustee has a right to exoneration, and he or she has a charge on the trust property in that circumstance as well.[624]

---

[614] Mathew J simply commented that: 'It is clear that the debt of the defendant was a personal debt; it may be that the Court of Chancery will say that it was rightly incurred by him as receiver and manager of the estate of John Grimes, but as between himself and Joseph Grimes it was purely personal.' (1893) 69 LT 352.

[615] Underhill and Hayton, *Law Relating to Trusts and Trustees* (17th edn, 2006), 999, and the Trustee Act 2000, s. 31.

[616] *Re Exhall Coal Co Ltd* (1866) 35 Beav 449, 452–3, 55 ER 970, 971; *Re Pumfrey* (1882) 22 Ch D 255, 262; *Stott v Milne* (1884) 25 Ch D 710, 715; *Jennings v Mather* [1902] 1 KB 1, 6, 9; *Re Spurling's Will Trusts* [1966] 1 WLR 920, 930; *Octavo Investments Pty Ltd v Knight* (1979) 144 CLR 360, 367; *Chief Commissioner of Stamp Duties (NSW) v Buckle* (1998) 192 CLR 226, 247. In the *Buckle* case the High Court of Australia held that, while the trustee's right is referred to as a charge, it is not a security interest as such, but rather it confers a beneficial interest in the trust assets which has priority over the interests of the beneficiaries.

[617] The right nevertheless is sometimes discussed in terms of retainer. See e.g. *Jennings v Mather* [1901] 1 QB 108, 113–14, and on appeal [1902] 1 KB 1, 9.

[618] *Octavo Investments Pty Ltd v Knight* (1979) 144 CLR 360, 367, 369–70; *Chief Commissioner of Stamp Duties (NSW) v Buckle* (1998) 192 CLR 226, 246–7; *Penwith District Council v V P Developments Ltd* [2005] 2 BCLC 607 at [18]–[19]; *Bruton Holdings Pty Ltd v Commissioner of Taxation* (2009) 258 ALR 612 at [43]. See also *Re Byrne Australia Pty Ltd* [1981] 1 NSWLR 394, 398; *Re Suco Gold Pty Ltd* (1983) 33 SASR 99; *Murphy v Zamonex Pty Ltd* (1993) 31 NSWLR 439, 464; *Re Matheson, ex p Worrell v Matheson* (1994) 49 FCR 454.

[619] Underhill and Hayton, *Law Relating to Trusts and Trustees* (17th edn, 2006), 1008–9; *Octavo Investments Pty Ltd v Knight* (1979) 144 CLR 360, 367; *Chief Commissioner of Stamp Duties (NSW) v Buckle* (1998) 192 CLR 226, 246–7. Compare *Re Pumfrey* (1882) 22 Ch D 255, 262, which was criticized in *Re Staff Benefits Pty Ltd* [1979] 1 NSWLR 207, 213–14.

[620] Compare *Darke v Williamson* (1858) 25 Beav 622, 53 ER 774, in which a sale would have had the effect of destroying the trust.

[621] McPherson, 'The insolvent trading trust' in Finn (ed.), *Essays in Equity* (1985), 142, 149, referring to *Grissell v Money* (1869) 38 LJ Ch 312 and *Re Pumfrey* (1882) 22 Ch D 255, 261–2; *Chief Commissioner of Stamp Duties (NSW) v Buckle* (1998) 192 CLR 226, 247.

[622] For an analogous situation, where a claimant entitled to a proprietary remedy against the defendant elected to pursue that remedy by seeking a charge over the defendant's asset consisting of the claimant's own debt to the defendant for the purpose of facilitating a set-off against that debt, see *Clark v Cutland* [2004] 1 WLR 783.

[623] *St Thomas's Hospital v Richardson* [1910] 1 KB 271, 276; *Re Blundell* (1889) 40 Ch D 370, 376–7; *Savage v Union Bank of Australia Ltd* (1906) 3 CLR 1170, 1197; *Re Suco Gold Pty Ltd* (1983) 33 SALR 99, 104–5.

[624] In *St Thomas's Hospital v Richardson* [1910] 1 KB 271, 276 Cozens Hardy MR said that, 'A's [the trustee's] right of indemnity exists before payment . . . . In respect of this right of indemnity A has a first charge or lien upon the trust property . . .'. See also *Savage v Union Bank of Australia Ltd* (1906) 3 CLR 1170, 1197;

Accordingly, when a trustee is sued by a third party for payment of a debt properly incurred in the execution of the trust, and at the same time the trustee, as a result of a consequent right of indemnity, has a charge on a debt owing to the estate by the third party, there is much to be said for the view that the trustee's interest may suffice to bring about mutuality in equity[625] for the purpose of equity acting by analogy with the Statutes.[626] This should also be relevant to insolvency set-off.[627] It assumes, however, that the trustee has a right of indemnity. In a particular case the right may be restricted to certain assets, as where a testator has authorized the executor to carry on a business but only by utilizing those assets,[628] and in some jurisdictions it might be capable of being limited by the trust instrument.[629] Moreover, an executor or an administrator of an estate who carries on the deceased's business other than for the purpose of its realization or winding up may not be entitled to an indemnity at the expense of creditors of the deceased unless those creditors had authorized the executor or the administrator to carry it on.[630] Authority in the testator's will is not sufficient in that regard.[631] Further, the trustee may be in default or otherwise may have an obligation to contribute to the trust fund, so that the right to an indemnity out of the trust fund is subject to the principle in *Cherry v Boultbee*.[632] It has been suggested in Australia that a breach of trust will only debar the trustee from indemnity if the breach is related to the subject-matter of the indemnity.[633] However, the basic principle underlying

---

Re Matheson, ex p Worrell v Matheson (1994) 49 FCR 454; *Chief Commissioner of Stamp Duties (NSW) v Buckle* (1998) 192 CLR 226, 245–7.

[625] See para. 11.46 above in relation to an equitable charge.

[626] See para. 3.07 above.

[627] This may explain the set-off in *Re Last, ex p Butterell* (1994) 124 ALR 219. Rawilla Pty Ltd was indebted on a loan account to Last and had a cross-claim against Last for an indemnity consequent upon a payment under a guarantee. Last had become bankrupt. Rawilla was permitted a set-off in the bankruptcy in relation to the cross-claims notwithstanding that it was the trustee of a discretionary trust.

[628] *Ex p Garland* (1803) 10 Ves Jun 110, 32 ER 786. The corresponding passage (above) in the third edition of this book was adopted by Laddie J in *Penwith District Council v V P Developments Ltd* [2005] 2 BCLC 607 at [18].

[629] In England, the right of indemnity under the Trustee Act 2000, s. 31 cannot be ousted by contrary provision in the trust instrument. See Underhill and Hayton, *Law Relating to Trusts and Trustees* (17th edn, 2006), 1001–2. See also, in Queensland, the Trusts Act 1973 (Qld), ss. 65 and 72. In any event, the trustee's right of indemnity has been said to be inseparable from the office of trustee. See Underhill and Hayton, *op. cit.* 1001 [83.3], referring to *Worrall v Harford* (1802) 6 Ves Jun 4, 8, 32 ER 250, 252 and *Re The Exhall Coal Co Ltd* (1866) 35 Beav 449, 453, 55 ER 970, 971–2. As a consequence, it has been suggested that it might be incapable of being excluded. See *Kemtron Industries Pty Ltd v Commissioner of Stamp Duties* [1984] 1 Qd R 576, 585 (McPherson J); *JA Pty Ltd v Jonco Holdings Pty Ltd* (2000) 33 ACSR 691 at [87]; *Moyes v J & L Developments Pty Ltd (No. 2)* [2007] SASC 261 at [38]–[41]; McPherson, 'The insolvent trading trust' in Finn (ed.), *Essays in Equity* (1985), 142, 149–50. For the contrary view, see *Re German Mining Co* (1854) 4 De G M & G 19, 52, 43 ER 415, 427; *RWG Management Ltd v Commissioner for Corporate Affairs* [1985] VR 385, 395.

[630] *Dowse v Gorton* [1891] AC 190. Compare *Re Oxley* [1914] 1 Ch 604, and *Vacuum Oil Co Pty Ltd v Wiltshire* (1945) 72 CLR 319.

[631] *Vacuum Oil Co Pty Ltd v Wiltshire* (1945) 72 CLR 319, 335.

[632] (1839) 4 My & Cr 442, 41 ER 171. See ch. 14 above. In particular, see *Re Johnson* (1880) 15 Ch D 548; *Re Evans* (1887) 34 Ch D 597, 601–2; *Re British Power Traction and Lighting Co Ltd* [1910] 2 Ch 470; *RWG Management Ltd v Commissioner for Corporate Affairs* [1985] VR 385, 397–9. Compare the situation in which a defaulting trustee is a beneficiary under the trust, as opposed to claiming an indemnity for expenses and liabilities properly incurred on behalf of the trust. In that situation, slightly different formulations of the applicable principle have been proposed. See paras 14.79–14.91 above.

[633] *Re Staff Benefits Pty Ltd* [1979] 1 NSWLR 207, 214; *Jacobs' Law of Trusts in Australia* (7th edn, 2006), 567. See also the comment by Giles J in *Murphy v Zamonex Pty Ltd* (1993) 31 NSWLR 439, 464 regarding

Cherry v Boultbee, that the person entitled to participate in the fund already has an asset of the fund in his or her hands in the form of the obligation to contribute which should be appropriated in satisfaction of the right to participate,[634] in its terms would apply whether or not the breach is related to the subject matter of the indemnity.[635] Indeed, the contrary view sits uncomfortably with *Re Johnson*,[636] in so far as the right of indemnity in that case for debts incurred in running the Cambridge business was affected by the failure of the trustee to account for amounts in relation to the London business.

17.126 **Subrogation.** Where there are other trust creditors, an additional issue is whether the subrogation rights of those creditors would prevent mutuality in equity. A creditor whose debt was properly incurred in the execution of the trust is entitled to be subrogated to the trustee's right of indemnity from the trust assets, as well as to the charge consequent upon that right,[637] so as to give the creditor an indirect claim against the assets.[638] However, the circumstances in which the subrogation right may be enforced remain unclear.[639] A creditor may enforce the right if the estate is under the administration of the court,[640] or if the trustee is bankrupt or in liquidation.[641] The judgment of Byrne J in *Re Raybould*[642] suggests that the court in other circumstances may order that a trust creditor can claim directly against the trust estate, but in that case the creditor seeking the order may have

---

a 'breach of trust related to the indemnity', and note also the neutral reference to *Re Staff Benefits* in *RWG Management Ltd v Commissioner for Corporate Affairs* [1985] VR 385, 399.

[634] See para. 14.03 above, and also in this context *Re British Power Traction and Lighting Co Ltd* [1910] 2 Ch 470, 475. On this formulation of the principle, it is not accurate to say that the trustee loses or is deprived of his or her right of indemnity. Compare *Re Staff Benefits* [1979] 1 NSWLR 207, 214, and *Jacobs' Law of Trusts in Australia* (7th edn, 2006), 567. Rather, the trustee is required to satisfy the indemnity from a particular source. Thus, if the trustee's claim for an indemnity exceeds the amount due from the trustee by way of compensation, it has been said that the trustee may recover from the estate to the extent of the balance without first having to bring into the estate the whole of the amount for which he or she is liable. See *RWG Management Ltd v Commissioner for Corporate Affairs* [1985] VR 385, 397–8, criticizing statements suggesting the contrary in *Re Frith* [1902] 1 Ch 342, 346. Compare, however, *Staniar v Evans* (1886) 34 Ch D 470. See para. 14.14 above.

[635] See e.g. the formulations of the principle in *Jennings v Mather* [1902] 1 KB 1, 5 and *RWG Management Ltd v Commissioner for Corporate Affairs* [1985] VR 385, 398. See also para. 14.83 above in relation to a defaulting trustee who is a beneficiary under the trust. In relation to the rule in *Cherry v Boultbee* generally, see *Russell-Cooke Trust v Richard Prentis* [2003] EWHC 1206 (Ch), in which Mr Halsey's right to participate in the fund (as an investor) was unrelated to his obligation to contribute (in the form of an account of profits).

[636] (1880) 15 Ch D 548. See also *General Credits Ltd v Tawilla Pty Ltd* [1984] 1 Qd R 388, 389–90. A similar comment may be made in relation to *Re British Power Traction and Lighting Co Ltd* [1910] 2 Ch 470.

[637] *Re Johnson* (1880) 15 Ch D 548, 552; *Re Blundell* (1890) 44 Ch D 1, 11; *Vacuum Oil Co Pty Ltd v Wiltshire* (1945) 72 CLR 319, 335–33.

[638] Upon subrogation, the party subrogated has been said to acquire an equitable interest in the trust assets: See *Nolan v Collie* (2003) 7 VR 287 at [66], and see *Octavo Investments Pty Ltd v Knight* (1979) 144 CLR 360, 367–8. Nevertheless, the trustee's claim for an indemnity is not held on trust for the creditor. See para. 17.131 below.

[639] See McPherson, 'The insolvent trading trust' in Finn (ed.), *Essays in Equity* (1985), 142, 151.

[640] See e.g. *Re Evans* (1887) 34 Ch D 597 and *Re Frith* [1902] 1 Ch 342.

[641] *Octavo Investments Pty Ltd v Knight* (1979) 144 CLR 360, 367. See e.g. *Nolan v Collie* (2003) 7 VR 287 (liquidation).

[642] [1900] 1 Ch 199. See also *Re Enhill Pty Ltd* [1983] VR 561, 570; *Moyes v J & L Developments Pty Ltd (No. 2)* [2007] SASC 261 at [41].

been the sole trust creditor,[643] and, moreover, the trustee supported the creditor's claim to be paid directly out of the estate. If that approach is to be adopted generally, it may be a requirement that other trust creditors are not prejudiced.[644] It has been said that it is no longer necessary to have a full administration before a creditor can be paid out of the assets of a trust, but that in such a case there should be reliable evidence establishing that the judgment debt was a liability properly incurred by the trustee, who had an unqualified right to be indemnified out of the trust assets in priority to the claims of beneficiaries and perhaps of other trust creditors.[645] This in turn raises the issue of *Cherry v Boultbee*, to which reference was made above. If, however, the trustee is solvent, so that judgment at law against the trustee would not be fruitless, the traditional view is that a trust creditor should proceed against the trustee personally rather than have recourse to the trust assets by means of the right of subrogation.[646] In light of these principles, how would the subrogation rights of other trust creditors affect the availability of a set-off to the third party? Trust creditors are not equitable assignees or chargees of the assets the subject of the trustee's right of indemnity,[647] and the fact that there are other trust creditors apart from the third party *prima facie* should not be a sufficient reason for denying a set-off as between the trustee and the third party. On the other hand, the point has been made that the trustee's equitable charge to which a subrogation claim relates is available for the benefit of all trust creditors, and the consequence of allowing a particular trust creditor to enforce it may be to give that creditor an advantage over other creditors.[648] If, in the situation posited, the third party as a trust creditor could look upon the charge that the trustee has over the particular trust asset represented by the third party's own indebtedness to the trustee as sufficient to bring about mutuality as between that debt and the cross-debt in respect of

[643] See McPherson, 'The Insolvent trading trust' in Finn (ed.), *Essays in Equity* (1985), 142, 151.

[644] *Jacobs' Law of Trusts in Australia* (7th edn, 2006), 574–5. This may require that the claims of other creditors be before the court. See Mitchell, *The Law of Subrogation* (1994), 156. Compare *Moyes v J & L Developments Pty Ltd (No. 2)* [2007] SASC 261. In *Deancrest Nominees Pty Ltd v Nixon* (2007) 25 ACLC 1681 at [48] Newnes J said that: 'the right of subrogation is a right in equity of the creditor to enforce the trustee's right of indemnity from the trust assets, not a right of recovery in respect of a specific asset . . .' In *Nolan v Collie* (2003) 7 VR 287 at [62]–[68], the decision of the Victorian Court of Appeal, that the judgment creditor was entitled to stand in the shoes of the trustee (in liquidation) for the purpose of enforcing the trustee's right of indemnity, was regarded as separate from the issue as to how the liquidator proposed to administer the trust estate, including in relation to other trust creditors.

[645] *General Credits Ltd v Tawilla Pty Ltd* [1984] 1 Qd R 388, 390 (McPherson J), and see also Ford and Lee, *Principles of the Law of Trusts* (looseleaf), [14.6050].

[646] *Owen v Delamere* (1872) LR 15 Eq 134; *Re Morris* (1889) 23 LR Ir 333; *Deancrest Nominees Pty Ltd v Nixon* (2007) 25 ACLC 1681 at [49] (off-setting claim for the purpose of a statutory demand); *Zen Ridgeway Pty Ltd v Adams* [2009] 2 Qd R 298 at [13]; Underhill and Hayton, *Law Relating to Trusts and Trustees* (17th edn, 2006), 1017. See also *Murphy v Zamonex Pty Ltd* (1993) 31 NSWLR 439, 464. It is not necessary, however, that the trust creditor should pursue his or her common law claim against the trustee to judgment if the circumstances are such as to lead to the reasonable inference that a judgment would be fruitless. See *Re Wilson* [1942] VLR 177, 183.

[647] McPherson, 'The insolvent trading trust' in Finn (ed.), *Essays in Equity* (1985), 142, 156; *Staniar v Evans* (1886) 34 Ch D 470, 477. Compare *Napier v Hunter* [1993] AC 713, 736, 738 in relation to insurance subrogation.

[648] McPherson, 'The insolvent trading trust' in Finn (ed.), *Essays in Equity* (1985), 142, 151. See also *Jacobs' Law of Trusts in Australia* (7th edn, 2006), 574–5. Nevertheless, it has been held in Australia that a trustee who is not insolvent may charge or assign the right of indemnity from the trust assets to a creditor of the trust to the extent necessary to discharge the liability of that creditor in respect of which the right of indemnity arose. See *Custom Credit Corporation Ltd v Ravi Nominees Pty Ltd* (1992) 8 WAR 42, 52–7.

which he or she is a trust creditor, the third party, through a set-off, could obtain an advantage over other trust creditors if the trustee is insolvent or approaching insolvency. If that would be the case, and if other trust creditors have an enforceable right of subrogation, the indirect interest that they have as a result of subrogation may suffice to prevent mutuality in equity arising. The approach of the courts to the issue has yet to emerge, however.

17.127 **Debt owing to the trustee in his personal capacity.** Given that a trustee who incurs a debt in that capacity is personally liable, there should be mutuality as between that debt and a cross-debt owing by the creditor to the trustee in the trustee's personal capacity.[649]

(2) Taking subject to equities

17.128 The third party may not have been aware that he or she was dealing with a person who was a trustee. Notwithstanding that the beneficiaries of the trust have the equitable title to a debt which accrues to the trustee as a result of the dealing, the beneficiaries should take subject to equities available to the third party against the trustee on a similar basis to that described earlier in the context of assignments.[650] This should apply whether or not the cross-debt owing by the trustee was incurred in the trustee's private capacity or in his or her capacity as trustee. The general principle applicable to taking subject to equities is that, when there are unconnected cross-debts, the debts must have arisen before the third party had notice of the trust,[651] although there is no such requirement when a substantive defence of equitable set-off is in issue.[652]

(3) Receipt of trust moneys in breach of trust

17.129 The application of the principle of taking subject to equities assumes that the beneficiary's entitlement is to a beneficial interest in a debt which at law is owing to the trustee. Alternatively, a beneficiary may claim that another has knowingly received trust moneys in circumstances where the trustee paid the moneys to the recipient in breach of trust.[653] The beneficiary in that circumstance may assert an equitable tracing claim to recover the moneys. This gives rise to a proprietary remedy to recover trust property, and it cannot be the subject of a set-off.[654] But even if the moneys are no longer traceable so as to preclude a proprietary remedy, and the beneficiary's claim instead is that the recipient has a personal liability as a constructive trustee on the basis of knowing receipt of trust property,[655] the recipient could not assert a set-off in respect of a separate debt owing to him or her by the trustee. The principle that a beneficiary takes subject to equities available against the trustee is based on the notion that there is mutuality at law as between the debt held on trust and the cross-debt owing by the trustee, and the question is whether it is unconscionable for the

---

[649] *Daniels v Imperial Bank of Canada* (1914) 19 DLR 166.
[650] See paras 17.02–17.98 above.
[651] See para. 17.13 above.
[652] See para. 17.32 above.
[653] A similar question may arise in the context of combination of bank accounts, when a trustee has deposited trust moneys into an account with a bank and the bank asserts that the account may be regarded as combined with the trustee's personal overdrawn account. See paras 15.88–15.120 above.
[654] See ch. 10 above.
[655] See generally *Snell's Equity* (31st edn, 2005), 691–2.

debtor to rely on this defence at law, given the trust.[656] However, when a recipient of trust money has a personal liability as a constructive trustee to the beneficiary on the basis of knowing receipt, there is not mutuality either at law or in equity in relation to that liability and a debt owing by the trustee to the recipient. This should also be the case when the basis of liability as a constructive trustee is as an accessory to a breach of trust.[657] It is only when the beneficiary's claim is based on an equitable interest in a debt owing by the third party to the trustee that the principle of taking subject to equities becomes relevant. In some cases this may be the position when a trustee paid trust money to a third party in breach of trust under circumstances where the third party as a result is indebted to the trustee. If the beneficiary acquiesced in the breach an equitable proprietary remedy would not be available to him or her, and nor would the third party be personally liable to the beneficiary as a constructive trustee.[658]

(4) Set-off between a beneficiary and a third party

Beneficiary has a personal claim against a trust creditor

When a debt accrues to a trustee in his or her capacity as such the debt belongs in equity **17.130** to the beneficiaries, while a debt incurred by the trustee is the trustee's own personal liability. A trustee who has incurred a debt in the proper performance of his or her duties as trustee is entitled to apply the trust assets in discharge of the debt, and to that end the trustee has a first charge or lien on the trust assets which has priority over the interests of the beneficiaries.[659] It was suggested earlier that this interest may justify a set-off in relation to that debt, for which the trustee otherwise is personally liable, and a cross-claim possessed by the trustee against the creditor in the trustee's capacity as such.[660] This avenue for a set-off would not be available, however, when a beneficiary's claim against a trust creditor against which the trust creditor wishes to assert a set-off arose out of a dealing unrelated to the trust, so that it is not trust property over which the trustee has a charge. *Prima facie* the trustee's personal liability to the creditor and the beneficiary's separate claim against the creditor would not be mutual. It may nevertheless be possible in that circumstance to support a set-off on the basis of the trustee's right to an indemnity from the beneficiary personally.

A beneficiary who is *sui juris* and absolutely entitled ordinarily is personally liable to indem- **17.131** nify the trustee against debts properly incurred in the execution of the trust.[661] This applies

---

[656] See para. 17.03 above in relation to assignments.

[657] See *Royal Brunei Airlines Sbd Bhd v Tan* [1995] 2 AC 378 and *Twinsectra Ltd v Yardley* [2002] 2 AC 164.

[658] *Target Holdings Ltd v Redferns* [1996] AC 421, 433; *Blake v Gale* (1886) 32 Ch D 571. Acquiescence is used in the sense described by Lord Cottenham in *Duke of Leeds v Earl of Amherst* (1846) 2 Ph 117, 123, 41 ER 886, 888, that: 'If a party, having a right, stands by and sees another dealing with the property in a manner inconsistent with that right, and makes no objection while the act is in progress, he cannot afterwards complain.'

[659] See para. 17.125 above.

[660] See para. 17.125 above.

[661] Underhill and Hayton, *Law Relating to Trusts and Trustees* (17th edn, 2006), 1000, 1012–14. This applies not only in the case of a sole beneficiary (see *Hardoon v Belilios* [1901] AC 118), but also where there are a number of beneficiaries who between them are absolutely entitled and sui juris. See Underhill and Hayton, *op. cit.* 1000, 1013–14; *Balkin v Peck* (1998) 43 NSWLR 706; *Hurst v Bryk* [1999] Ch 1, 14–15

also while the debt is still outstanding, so that the trustee is entitled to be exonerated by the beneficiary. Furthermore, Underhill suggests that the right of indemnity against the beneficiaries personally should be the subject of the same right of subrogation as subsists in respect of the trustee's right of indemnity out of the trust property,[662] and indeed there is authority to that effect in Australia.[663] This right of subrogation is probably subject to restrictions similar to those applicable in the case of subrogation to a trustee's right of indemnity from the trust assets, for example that the trustee should be insolvent or the circumstances otherwise should be such as to suggest that judgment against the trustee would be pointless.[664] If a trust creditor is entitled to be subrogated to the trustee's claim for an indemnity against a beneficiary, it would open the possibility of a set-off against the beneficiary's cross-claim against the trust creditor. A difficulty is that, when a third party as a trust creditor is subrogated to the trustee's claim for an indemnity from a beneficiary, the trustee does not hold the claim on trust for the third party. This is apparent when one considers the position in the event that the trustee becomes bankrupt. In that circumstance the benefit of the trustee's claim for an indemnity passes to the trustee in bankruptcy,[665] whereas if it were trust property that would not be the case. The trustee in bankruptcy admittedly would be required to apply the proceeds received from the beneficiary in reduction only of the trust debts, as opposed to all debts provable in the trustee's bankruptcy,[666] but that is because the trustee is not permitted to profit from the trust, which would occur if the proceeds of the indemnity were used to pay his or her personal creditors.[667] If there is more than one trust creditor, the proceeds received by the trustee in bankruptcy would be divisible amongst all trust creditors.[668] In relation to the question of set-off, because the claim for an indemnity that the trustee has against the beneficiary is not held on trust for the third party, there is not mutuality in a strict sense as between that claim and the debt owing by the third party to the beneficiary. Nevertheless, when there is an enforceable right of

---

(decision affirmed *Hurst v Bryk* [2002] 1 AC 185); *Ron Kingham Real Estate Pty Ltd v Edgar* [1999] 2 Qd R 439. The indemnity obligation is in proportion to their beneficial interests. See *Matthews v Ruggles-Brise* [1911] 1 Ch 194. A trustee's right to indemnity from the beneficiaries personally can be excluded by the trust instrument. See *Hardoon v Belilios* at 127; *RWG Management Ltd v Commissioner for Corporate Affairs* [1985] VR 385, 394.

[662] Underhill and Hayton, *Law Relating to Trusts and Trustees* (17th edn, 2006), 1013, and see para. 17.126 above. See also *Re Richardson* [1911] 2 KB 705.

[663] *Ron Kingham Real Estate Pty Ltd v Edgar* [1999] 2 Qd R 439; *Belar Pty Ltd v Mahaffey* [2000] 1 Qd R 477, 487. In Australia, see Ford and Lee, *Principles of the Law of Trusts* (looseleaf), [14.6310].

[664] Underhill and Hayton, *Law Relating to Trusts and Trustees* (17th edn, 2006), 1017, and see para. 17.126 above. For a discussion of Australian authorities on point, see Ford and Lee, *Principles of the Law of Trusts* (looseleaf), [14.6310].

[665] *Re Richardson* [1911] 2 KB 705, 715 (Buckley LJ); *Octavo Investments Pty Ltd v Knight* (1979) 144 CLR 360, 367–8.

[666] *Re Richardson* [1911] 2 KB 705.

[667] *Re Richardson* [1911] 2 KB 705, 711 (Cozens-Hardy MR); *Re Suco Gold Pty Ltd* (1983) 33 SASR 99 (esp. at 106–7); Ford, 'Trading trusts and creditors' rights' (1981) 13 *Melbourne University Law Review* 1, 20.

[668] Ford and Lee, *Principles of the Law of Trusts* (looseleaf), [14.6310], and see also, with respect to the indemnity from the trust estate, *Re Byrne Australia Pty Ltd* [1981] 1 NSWLR 394, 399; *Re Suco Gold Pty Ltd* (1983) 33 SASR 79, 109, 111; *Re ADM Franchise Pty Ltd* (1983) 7 ACLR 987, 988–9; *Re Matheson* (1994) 49 FCR 454. In Victoria, on the other hand, the right of indemnity has been said to be an asset available for distribution amongst creditors generally, and not just trust creditors. See *Re Enhill Pty Ltd* [1983] VR 561 and also *Young v Murphy* [1996] 1 VR 279, 303.

subrogation and there are no other trust creditors,[669] so that no one other than the third party would benefit in any event from proceeds of the indemnity received from the beneficiary, there is much to be said for the view that a set-off should be permitted in equity notwithstanding the absence of strict mutuality.[670]

Beneficiary personally liable to a trust debtor

There is also the possibility of a set-off in the converse situation, of a debt owing by a third **17.132** party to the trustee in that capacity and a cross-debt owing by the beneficiary to the third party on another account. The beneficiary is personally liable on his or her separate debt and at the same time may have a sufficient equitable interest in the debt held on trust so as to bring about mutuality in equity, and therefore to justify an equitable set-off by analogy with the Statutes.[671] For a set-off to occur, however, the beneficiary's interest in the trust should be such that he or she has an interest in possession in the debt as trust property, in the sense that the beneficiary has a present right to claim the benefit of the debt.[672] This does not describe the entitlement of a residuary legatee under a will or a person entitled under an intestacy where the administration of the estate has not been completed.[673] Prior to completion of the administration, the legatee or the person entitled does not have a beneficial interest in the assets of the trust. Rather, the legatee or the person entitled only has an equitable chose in action to have the estate properly administered.[674] An object of a discretionary trust is in a similar position.[675] Furthermore, the beneficiary must be the sole party beneficially interested in the debt, unless, if the debt is held on trust for two or more beneficiaries, those beneficiaries are also jointly liable to the debtor. This is necessary in order to satisfy the requirement of mutuality.[676] It has been suggested that a set-off in this circumstance will not be permitted unless the beneficiary's interest in the debt is clear and ascertained without inquiry.[677] That proposition was considered earlier.[678]

A trustee who properly incurs costs and expenses in the administration of the trust is **17.133** entitled to be indemnified from the trust assets,[679] and for the purpose of enforcing the indemnity the trustee has a charge or lien over the assets.[680] The trust assets may include a

---

[669] This appears to have been the case in *Re Richardson* [1911] 2 KB 705.
[670] Notwithstanding recent judicial suggestions to the contrary (see para. 4.69 above), the better view is that mutuality is not an indispensable requirement of equitable set-off. See paras 4.67–4.83 above.
[671] *Bankes v Jarvis* [1903] 1 KB 549, 552. See paras 3.07–3.09 above.
[672] See *Gartside v IRC* [1968] AC 553, 607.
[673] *Bishop v Church* (1748) 3 Atk 691, 26 ER 1197; *Ex p Morier, re Willis, Percival, & Co* (1879) 12 Ch D 491; *Phillips v Howell* [1901] 2 Ch 773.
[674] *Commissioner of Stamp Duties (Queensland) v Livingston* [1965] AC 694. This applies equally in the case of a specific bequest. See *Official Receiver in Bankruptcy v Schultz* (1990) 170 CLR 306, 312. See also para. 13.124 above.
[675] *Gartside v IRC* [1968] AC 553; *Chief Commissioner of Stamp Duties v ISPT Pty Ltd* (1998) 45 NSWLR 639, 655.
[676] See ch. 12 above.
[677] Wood, *English and International Set-off* (1989), 779–80.
[678] See paras 11.21–11.36 above.
[679] The right of indemnity is restricted, however, when a testator has authorized the trustee to carry on a business though only by utilizing a certain part of the estate. See *Ex p Garland* (1803) 10 Ves Jun 110, 32 ER 786.
[680] *Stott v Milne* (1884) 25 Ch D 710; *Re Spurling's Will Trusts* [1966] 1 WLR 920, 930; *Octavo Investments Pty Ltd v Knight* (1979) 144 CLR 360, 367.

debt held on trust by the trustee. While the charge might be thought to have the effect of destroying mutuality as between that debt and a cross-debt owing to the debtor by the beneficiary otherwise entitled under the trust to the benefit of the first-mentioned debt, the better view is that a set-off nevertheless may still occur as between those parties if the trustee's position, and that of other trust creditors who are subrogated to the trustee's right, is otherwise sufficiently secured.[681]

(5) Set-off between trustee and beneficiary

17.134 There may be cross-claims between a trustee and a beneficiary, for example when the trustee is entitled to an indemnity from the beneficiary personally and at the same time is liable to the beneficiary on another account. The availability of a set-off in such a case should be determined according to normal principles. The beneficiary's claim may be for payment of the trust fund itself. Issues of set-off in that context were considered earlier.[682] Alternatively, the beneficiary's liability may not be to the trustee personally, but may take the form of an obligation to contribute to the trust fund. The question in that situation is whether the principle in *Cherry v Boultbee*[683] applies.

F. Execution of Judgments

(1) Introduction

17.135 Consider that a creditor has obtained judgment against the debtor, which the debtor has failed to satisfy, and the creditor accordingly wants to enforce the judgment against the debtor's assets. If one of the assets is a debt owing to the judgment debtor by a third party, and the judgment creditor obtains an order for the enforcement of the judgment against that asset, the question may arise whether the third party can set off a cross-claim that he or she has against the judgment debtor. The principal method of enforcing a judgment by execution against a debt owing to the judgment debtor is a third party debt order, although a charging order and the appointment of a receiver by way of equitable execution may also be relevant. The effect of each of these is considered below.

(2) Third party debt order

17.136 The procedure for obtaining a third party debt order (formerly called a garnishee order) is set out in CPR Pt 72.[684] When a creditor has obtained judgment and a debt is due or accruing due to the judgment debtor from a third party, the court may make an order (a 'final third party debt order') on the application of the judgment creditor requiring the third party to pay to the judgment creditor the amount of the debt, or so much of it as is sufficient to satisfy the judgment debt and the judgment creditor's costs of the

---

[681] See paras 11.39–11.41 above. This is consistent with comments by McPherson J in *Kemtron Industries Pty Ltd v Commissioner of Stamp Duties* [1984] 1 Qd R 576, 587.

[682] See ch. 10 above.

[683] (1839) 4 My & Cr 442, 41 ER 171. See ch. 14 above.

[684] While the terminology in CPR Pt 72 has changed from that in the former RSC O 49 dealing with garnishee orders, the nature of the procedure has not changed. See *Société Eram Shipping Co Ltd v Cie Internationale de Navigacion* [2004] 1 AC 260 at [12] and [33].

application.[685] Before applying for the final order, the judgment creditor must obtain an interim third party debt order.[686] This becomes binding on the third party when it is served on him or her. It directs the third party not to make any payment which reduces the amount that the third party owes the judgment debtor to less than the amount specified in the order, and it fixes a hearing to consider whether to make a final order.

Attachment only relates to a debt which is due or accruing due.[687] There is a considerable body of case law as to what this encompasses, for which reference should be made to specialist texts on the subject. One thing that is clear, however, is that it is not confined to debts which are presently payable. A debt which is presently existing but not payable until a future day may be attached,[688] although the third party cannot be required to pay before the contract date.[689]

17.137

Service of a third party debt order does not operate as a transfer of the property in the debt,[690] though English courts have nevertheless accepted that it gives rise to a proprietary interest in the form of a charge.[691] Australian courts, on the other hand, have rejected the view that a garnishee order results in a proprietary interest,[692] and indeed the notion that it gives rise to a proprietary interest does not sit easily with the proposition that the holder of a floating security granted by a judgment debtor has priority over a judgment creditor

17.138

---

[685] Payment by the third party in compliance with the order discharges his or her liability in respect of the debt to the extent of the payment. See *Société Eram Shipping Co Ltd v Cie Internationale de Navigacion* [2004] 1 AC 260.

[686] CPR rr. 72.2(2) and 72.4.

[687] CPR r. 72.2(1)(a).

[688] *Tapp v Jones* (1875) LR 10 QB 591; *Webb v Stenton* (1883) 11 QBD 518, 522–3; *O'Driscoll v Manchester Insurance Committee* [1915] 3 KB 499, 516–17; *Joachimson v Swiss Bank Corporation* [1921] 3 KB 110, 131.

[689] *Tapp v Jones* (1875) LR 10 QB 591.

[690] *Re Combined Weighing and Advertising Machine Co* (1889) 43 Ch D 99; *Norton v Yates* [1906] 1 KB 112; *Société Eram Shipping Co Ltd v Cie Internationale de Navigacion* [2004] 1 AC 260 at [15].

[691] *Emanuel v Bridger* (1874) LR 9 QB 286, 291; *Galbraith v Grimshaw and Baxter* [1910] 1 KB 339, 343 (decision affirmed [1910] AC 508); *Joachimson v Swiss Bank Corporation* [1921] 3 KB 110, 131; *Plunkett v Barclays Bank Ltd* (1936) 52 TLR 353; *Re Caribbean Products (Yam Importers) Ltd* [1966] 1 Ch 331, 343, 350, 353; *Choice Investments Ltd v Jeromninon* [1981] 1 QB 149, 155 (CA); *Fraser v Oystertec plc* [2006] 1 BCLC 491 at [5]; *Société Eram Shipping Co Ltd v Cie Internationale de Navigacion* [2004] 1 AC 260 at [14], [24] (Lord Bingham) and [86]–[88] (Lord Millett); *Masri v Consolidated Contractors International Co SAL* [2008] 2 Lloyd's Rep 128 at [47]. In *Re Combined Weighing and Advertising Machine Co* (1889) 43 Ch D 99, 104 Cotton LJ described it as a lien. An interim third party debt order does not afford priority over a prior equitable charge or a contractual restriction on payment (a flawed asset arrangement). See *Fraser v Oystertec plc*, though in Australia compare the Personal Property Securities Act 2009 (Cth), s. 74 in relation to an unperfected security interest (a flawed asset arrangement is a security interest for the purpose of the Act: see s. 12(2)(l)). Where the subject of a flawed asset arrangement is a bank deposit (or 'ADI account'), the security will be 'perfected' without registration because the bank has control of the deposit. See ss. 21(2) and 25(1).

[692] *Hall v Richards* (1961) 108 CLR 84, 92 (Kitto J); *Clyne v Deputy Commissioner of Taxation* (1981) 150 CLR 1, 27 (Brennan J); *Blacktown Concrete Services Pty Ltd v Ultra Refurbishing & Construction Pty Ltd* (1998) 43 NSWLR 484, 495–6, 502; *Macquarie Health Corp Ltd v Commissioner of Taxation* (1999) 96 FCR 238 at [116]; *Bruton Holdings Pty Ltd v Commissioner of Taxation* (2009) 239 CLR 346, at [14] (HC). Compare *Commissioner of Taxation v Donnelly* (1989) 25 FCR 432, 456; *Philippa Power & Associates v Primrose Couper Cronin Rudkin* [1997] 2 Qd R 266, 274.

with a third party debt order where crystallization occurs after the final order but before payment by the third party.[693]

17.139   Consider that the third party has a substantive defence of equitable set-off available against the judgment debtor. The nature of the judgment creditor's right as a result of the third party debt order should be immaterial to the question whether the set-off can be asserted against the judgment creditor. The judgment debtor's title to sue the third party is impeached,[694] and the judgment creditor cannot obtain a better title.[695] Similarly, the precise characterization of the nature of the right should not be crucial to the question whether a judgment creditor takes subject to a defence of set-off under the Statutes of Set-off in the case of mutual debts as between the judgment debtor and the third party. The relevant question is not so much what rights have priority according to the law of set-off, but rather the circumstances in which the court in its discretion will make a final order. The Statutes of Set-off strictly have no application in proceedings for a third party debt order. They provide a defence to an action at law for payment of a debt,[696] whereas, when a final third party debt order is made, the judgment creditor may proceed directly to execution without the necessity of bringing a separate action on the order.[697] Indeed, if the judgment creditor were to bring an action when there was no necessity to do so, he or she would run the risk of having the action stayed as an abuse of the process of the court.[698] CPR r. 72.2(1) provides that the court 'may' order the third party to pay the judgment creditor. The making of a final third party debt order is discretionary,[699] and the question is under what circumstances the court will make an order notwithstanding that the third party has a cross-claim against the judgment debtor. The applicable principle has been equated with that governing assignments of debts.[700] In other words, the judgment creditor should take subject to equities available to the third party against the judgment debtor before service of the interim order,[701] equities in this sense including rights of set-off, whether equitable[702] or contractual[703] or under the Statutes of Set-off, as discussed in the context of assignments.[704] Thus, when there is a cross-debt owing by the judgment debtor to the third party at the time that the interim order is served on the third party, there is support for the proposition the judgment creditor should take subject to a defence of set-off that the third

---

[693] *Cairney v Back* [1906] 2 KB 746.

[694] *Rawson v Samuel* (1841) Cr & Ph 161, 179, 41 ER 451, 458. See para. 4.02 above.

[695] *Hale v Victoria Plumbing Co Ltd* [1966] 2 QB 746.

[696] See paras 2.34–2.39 above.

[697] See *Société Eram Shipping Co Ltd v Cie Internationale de Navigacion* [2004] 1 AC 260 at [75] and *Kuwait Oil Tanker Co SAK v Qabazard* [2004] 1 AC 300 at [16].

[698] Compare *Pritchett v English and Colonial Syndicate* [1899] 2 QB 428.

[699] *Martin v Nadel* [1906] 2 KB 26.

[700] In addition to the cases referred to below, see *Wolfe v Marshall* [1997] EWCA Civ 1329.

[701] *Norton v Yates* [1906] 1 KB 112, 121 *per* Warrington J ('the right of the garnishor under the garnishee order nisi is subject to such rights and equities as already exist over it as the property of the debtor'). See also *Re Stanhope Silkstone Collieries Co* (1879) 11 Ch D 160; *Blacktown Concrete Services Pty Ltd v Ultra Refurbishing & Construction Pty Ltd* (1998) 43 NSWLR 484, 495.

[702] See *Hale v Victoria Plumbing Co Ltd* [1966] 2 QB 746.

[703] See *Rymill v Wandsworth District Board* (1883) Cab & El 92; *Fraser v Oystertec plc* [2006] 1 BCLC 491. See also *Hutt v Shaw* (1887) 3 TLR 354.

[704] See paras 17.02–17.98 above.

party otherwise would have had available in an action at law under the Statutes,[705] notwith-standing that a third party debt order generally does not result in an action. On the other hand, the third party does not take subject to a set-off where the cross-debt accrued after service of the interim order.[706] In the case of an assignment, the courts have denied a set-off against an assignee in relation to a cross-debt accruing after notice even when the cross-debt had its source in a prior contract.[707] But, notwithstanding the position adopted in relation to assignments, there is much to be said for the view that the court in its discretion should not make a final third party debt order where the judgment debtor became indebted to the third party after service of the interim order but before the final order if the debt had its source in a prior transaction. Nor should it be an objection to a substantive equitable set-off that the cross-demand arose after notice.[708]

Cross-debt payable at a future date

It may be that the cross-debt owing by the judgment debtor to the third party is in existence **17.140** at the date of service of the interim order, but it is not payable until a future date. In order to give rise to a set-off under the Statutes of Set-off, the cross-debt must be due and payable when the defence is filed.[709] A judgment creditor may proceed directly to execution against the third party without bringing an action, so that the question of filing a defence does not arise, but an analogous principle should apply. When a third party asserts that a set-off is available under the Statutes of Set-off against the attached debt, the cross-debt should not only be in existence at the date of the interim order, but it should also be presently payable when the final order is made, because at that point payment is to be made. If the attached debt itself is not payable at that date, it is suggested that the cross-debt should be presently payable before the attached debt becomes payable.[710]

Trust money

In *Stumore v Campbell & Co*,[711] a judgment creditor sought to attach money which the **17.141** third party garnishee held on trust for the judgment debtor. A sum held on trust is an equit-able debt which may be attached,[712] but generally it cannot be the subject of a set-off.[713] Accordingly, in *Stumore v Campbell*, the third party was required to account for the trust money without deduction in respect of a debt owing to him by the judgment debtor.

Debt owing by the judgment creditor

There is no procedure in CPR Pt 72 for giving effect to a set-off as between the third party **17.142** and the judgment creditor in relation to a separate debt of the judgment creditor to the

---

[705] *Tapp v Jones* (1875) LR 10 QB 591, 593; *Bishop v Woinarski* (1875) 1 VLR (L) 31. See also *Sampson v Seaton and Beer Railway Co* (1874) LR 10 QB 28, 30; *Fraser v Oystertec plc* [2006] 1 BCLC 491 at [6] and [20]. Compare *Fitt v Bryant* (1883) Cab & El 194, in which the debt attached, to the knowledge of the third party, was held by the judgment debtor on trust for the judgment creditor.
[706] *Tapp v Jones* (1875) LR 10 QB 591, 593. See also *Fraser v Oystertec plc* [2006] 1 BCLC 491 at [6].
[707] See para. 17.15 above.
[708] See para. 17.32 above.
[709] See paras 2.29–2.31 above.
[710] See also, and compare, para. 17.14 above in relation to assignments.
[711] [1892] 1 QB 314.
[712] *Webb v Stenton* (1883) 11 QBD 518, 526.
[713] See ch. 10 above.

third party, and accordingly the third party cannot set off the judgment creditor's debt against the attached debt,[714] at least where the third party has not yet proceeded to judgment against the judgment creditor. The courts have power to set off judgments and orders as part of their inherent jurisdiction,[715] and if the third party has a judgment against the judgment creditor it should be capable of set-off under the inherent jurisdiction against the amount payable under the third party debt order.[716]

Insolvency

17.143 If a bankruptcy petition is pending against a judgment debtor or if the debtor has been adjudged bankrupt, the court may stay execution or other legal process against the property or person of the debtor,[717] and similarly after the bankruptcy order a person who is a creditor in respect of a provable debt has no remedy against the property or person of the bankrupt in respect of that debt.[718] Further, the Insolvency Act 1986, s. 346 provides that, where a creditor of a person who is adjudged bankrupt has, before the commencement of the bankruptcy,[719] attached a debt[720] due to the person from a third party, the creditor is not entitled as against the official receiver or trustee of the bankrupt's estate to retain the benefit of the attachment[721] unless it was completed before the commencement of the bankruptcy. Similar principles apply in the case of a company liquidation.[722] The Act stipulates that an attachment is completed by receipt of the debt,[723] by which is meant receipt of the proceeds.[724]

17.144 Section 346 is not confined to attachment of debts, but extends to other forms of execution against the goods or land of the bankrupt. A creditor is not entitled to retain the benefit of the execution as against the trustee in bankruptcy unless the execution was completed before the bankruptcy. The corresponding provision in Australia[725] differs from s. 346 in that it captures executions which occurred six months before the bankruptcy. Where a creditor has issued execution against the property of a debtor within six months before the presentation of a petition against the debtor, and the debtor becomes bankrupt, the

---

[714] *Sampson v Seaton and Beer Railway Co* (1874) LR 10 QB 28.

[715] See paras 2.98–2.122 above.

[716] See *Walters v D Miles-Griffiths, Piercy & Co* (1964) 108 Sol Jo 561 in relation to the solicitors' costs of the appeal.

[717] Insolvency Act 1986, s. 285(1).

[718] Insolvency Act 1986, s. 285(3). This is expressed to be subject, however, to ss. 346 (enforcement procedures) and 347 (limited right to distress).

[719] A bankruptcy commences on the date on which the order is made. See the Insolvency Act 1986, s. 278.

[720] Attachment is not defined in the Insolvency legislation, although it was said in relation to the equivalent provision in the Bankruptcy Act 1914 (s 40) that it is not a term of art. See *Re Lupkovics* [1954] 1 WLR 1234, 1241. In Australia the Federal Court held in *Commissioner of Taxation v Donnelly* (1989) 25 FCR 432 that attachment in the context of s. 118 of the Bankruptcy Act 1966 (which in its terms is similar to s. 346 of the English Insolvency Act) means attachment by curial order, and it did not include a notice under (the former) s. 218 of the Income Tax Assessment Act 1936 (Cth).

[721] For a discussion of the meaning of this expression, see *Re Caribbean Products (Yam Importers) Ltd* [1966] 1 Ch 331.

[722] Insolvency Act 1986, ss. 126, 130 and 183. The commencement of a winding up is defined in s. 129.

[723] Insolvency Act 1986, s. 346(5)(c), and, for companies, s. 183(3)(b).

[724] *George v Tompson's Trustee* [1949] 1 Ch 322.

[725] Bankruptcy Act 1966 (Cth), s. 118.

creditor must pay to the trustee an amount equal to the amount received by the creditor as a result of the execution.[726] The creditor may then prove in the bankruptcy for his or her debt as an unsecured creditor as if the execution had not taken place. There is a similar provision in the Corporations Act 2001 (Cth), s. 569 in the context of company liquidation.[727]

The application of an earlier equivalent of s. 569 in Australia produced an unjust result in the circumstances in issue in *Findlay v Trevor*.[728] The owner of a farm, A, mortgaged it to B to secure a debt owing to B. In addition, B leased the farm from A. B breached the lease, as a result of which the lease was terminated and A sued B for damages. After A recovered judgment, a writ of *fi fa* was issued against B's asset in the form of the mortgage. The mortgage was offered for sale by the sheriff at a public auction, and A was the successful bidder. It was then agreed that the purchase price payable by A to B should be set off against the amount of the judgment debt owing by B, and that only the balance should be payable to B. This was a convenient course of action to adopt, but some two months later B went into insolvent liquidation, whereupon the liquidator challenged the arrangement. The Supreme Court of Western Australia[729] held that A had received an amount as a result of an execution issued within six months of B's liquidation, the reference to 'the amount . . . received' in the section being held to include satisfaction of a debt by way of set-off. As a result, A had to pay to the liquidator the amount of B's liability received in this manner, with a resulting right of proof in the liquidation for the amount paid. This seems unjust because, if A had not issued execution, the mortgage debt and the judgment debt would have been set off in the liquidation. The problem is that the legislation does not give the judge a discretion in the matter. Indeed, if there was a second debt owing by B to A, it would appear that this debt could not have been set off against A's obligation to account to the liquidator. The demands in such a case would not have been mutual, since the amount in question would have been payable to the liquidator in his or her own right as liquidator, and not because it was payable to B before the liquidation.[730] Moreover, in the circumstances the unwinding of the contractual set-off in relation to the debt for the price and the judgment debt may not have resulted in a set-off as between those debts in the liquidation. When the sale occurred, A may be said to have had notice of B's insolvency, in which case the qualification to the insolvency set-off section[731] would have operated to preclude a set-off. On the other hand, if A had a separate liability to B, and A paid the liquidator and therefore obtained a provable debt pursuant to s. 569, a set-off may have been available in relation to A's separate liability and A's provable debt.

17.145

---

[726] Less the taxed costs of the execution.

[727] The company liquidation and bankruptcy provisions are not identical. See *Findlay v Trevor* (1993) 11 ACLC 483, 488.

[728] (1993) 11 ACLC 483. The provision in issue was the Companies (Western Australia) Code, s. 455(1), which was in the same terms as the Corporations Act 2001 (Cth), s. 569(1).

[729] Malcolm CJ and Murray J, Pidgeon J dissenting on this point.

[730] See, in a different context, Fletcher Moulton LJ in *Re A Debtor, ex p Peak Hill Goldfield Ltd* [1909] 1 KB 430, 437. See also paras 13.07–13.31 above.

[731] Corporations Act 2001 (Cth), s. 553C(2). See paras 6.66–6.99 above.

(3) Charging orders

17.146 A charging order may be made in favour of a judgment creditor under the Charging Orders Act 1979. Its application to debts is limited, however. The only debts to which it extends are government debentures, or debentures issued by a body corporate that is either incorporated in England or Wales or has the register for the debentures in England or Wales.[732] When a charging order is made it operates as a charge securing payment of any money due or to become due under the judgment.[733] It has a like effect and is enforceable in the same manner as an equitable charge,[734] and it should be subject to the same principles as a third party debt order in relation to questions of set-off.[735]

(4) Appointment of a receiver by way of equitable execution

17.147 A receiver may be appointed by way of equitable execution in circumstances where execution at common law for some reason cannot be had,[736] and included amongst the property which the receiver is authorized to receive may be a debt owing to the judgment debtor by a third party.[737] The use of the term 'execution' in this context is a misnomer. The obtaining of a receivership order in truth is not execution, but rather it constitutes equitable relief on the ground that there is no adequate remedy by execution at law.[738] The appointment by itself does not create a charge or other security interest in favour of the judgment creditor, unless in a particular case the order in its terms has specifically charged the third party not to deal with the debt except by payment to the judgment creditor.[739] Rather, it operates as an injunction to restrain the judgment debtor from receiving the proceeds of the debt the subject of the order, and from dealing with the debt to the prejudice of the judgment creditor.[740] In addition, it would prevent the judgment debtor from using the debt as a set-off against a separate debt that he or she owes to the third party.[741] It confers upon the judgment creditor purely personal rights against the judgment debtor and gives the former no right over the property as such.[742] In so far as the third party is concerned, Greer J in *Giles v Kruyer*[743] considered that, if the third party is not a party to the order, his or her

---

[732] Charging Orders Act 1979, s. 2(2), 'stock' being defined in s. 6(1) as including debentures.

[733] See s. 1(1).

[734] See s. 3(4).

[735] See *Goodfellow v Gray* [1899] 2 QB 498 in relation to a set-off of judgments, for which see paras 2.98–2.122 above.

[736] *Re Shephard* (1889) 43 Ch D 131, 135–6, 137, 138.

[737] For an illustration of circumstances held sufficient to justify the appointment of a receiver in relation to debts owing to the judgment debtor, see *Goldschmidt v Oberrheinische Metallwerke* [1906] 1 KB 373. The court has power to appoint a receiver by way of equitable execution over future receipts from a defined asset. See *Masri v Consolidated Contractors International Co SAL* [2008] 2 Lloyd's Rep 128 at [174] and [184].

[738] *Re Shephard* (1889) 43 Ch D 131, 135, 137, 138; *Ideal Bedding Co Ltd v Holland* [1907] 2 Ch 157, 169.

[739] See *Re Pearce* [1919] 1 KB 354, 363 (Swinfen Eady MR), referring to *Re Potts, ex p Taylor* [1893] 1 QB 648, 659 (Lord Esher). See also *Re Whitehart* (1972) 116 Sol Jo 75.

[740] *Tyrrell v Painton* [1895] 1 QB 202, 206; *Re Marquis of Anglesey* [1903] 2 Ch 727, 730–1; *Ideal Bedding Co Ltd v Holland* [1907] 2 Ch 157, 169–70; *Stevens v Hutchinson* [1953] 1 Ch 299, 305. See also *Re Potts, ex p Taylor* [1893] 1 QB 648.

[741] See *Re A Debtor, ex p Peak Hill Goldfield Ltd* [1909] 1 KB 430, 437 (Farwell LJ).

[742] *Stevens v Hutchinson* [1953] 1 Ch 299, 305; *Masri v Consolidated Contractors International Co SAL* [2008] 2 Lloyd's Rep 128 at [51]–[58] and [71].

[743] [1921] 3 KB 23, referring to *Re Potts, ex p Taylor* [1893] 1 QB 648.

rights and duties are not affected and, while the order has the consequence as against the judgment debtor that the debtor cannot give a discharge, it does not prevent the third party from paying the debtor. That view has been criticized, however.[744] If the third party is aware of the order, and therefore of the injunction restraining the judgment debtor from receiving payment, it has been suggested that the third party will not obtain a valid receipt if he or she nevertheless pays the debtor.[745]

Consider that the judgment debtor becomes bankrupt after the appointment but before payment is received from the third party. Because the appointment does not generally give rise to a charge, the judgment creditor is not a secured creditor in the insolvency. Therefore, he or she does not have priority over other creditors, and the proceeds of the debt will form part of the estate available for distribution generally.[746] According to views expressed in the Court of Appeal in *Re A Debtor, ex p Peak Hill Goldfield Ltd*,[747] this does not have as a consequence that the third party will be entitled to a set-off under the insolvency set-off section in respect of a cross-claim that he or she has against the judgment debtor.[748] While after the bankruptcy the debt is payable to the trustee in bankruptcy, the problem is that, because of the appointment, the debt immediately before the bankruptcy was not payable to the judgment debtor. In the *Peak Hill Goldfield* case,[749] Fletcher Moulton LJ expressed the relevant principle in terms that: 'Moneys which under a bankruptcy became payable to the trustee . . . because they were payable to the debtor, come *prima facie* within the mutual credits clause, but not if they are moneys which, upon bankruptcy, become payable to the trustee in his right as trustee and not by virtue of their being payable to the debtor.' This nevertheless seems a harsh result.

G. Notice Under Section 260-5 of the Taxation Administration Act in Australia

In Australia, s. 260-5 in Sch. 1 to the Taxation Administration Act 1953 (Cth) deals with the collection and recovery of amounts in satisfaction of a debt to the Commonwealth for a tax-related liability. It provides that, where a tax-related liability is payable to the Commonwealth by an entity ('the debtor'), the Commissioner may give a notice to a third party who owes or may later owe money to the debtor, requiring the third party to pay to the Commissioner the lesser of the tax-related liability and the amount owed by the third party to the debtor.[750] Section 260-5 was inserted in the Tax Administration Act in 1999, replacing a similar provision in s. 218 of the Income Tax Assessment Act 1936 (Cth).

17.148

17.149

---

[744] *Kerr and Hunter on Receivers and Administrators* (19th edn, 2010), 156–7 [6–11] and [6–12], and in Australia O'Donovan, *Company Receivers and Administrators* (looseleaf), [22.2760]–[22.2810].

[745] *Kerr and Hunter on Receivers and Administrators* (19th edn, 2010), 156–7 [6–12], referring to *Eastern Trust Co v McKenzie, Mann & Co Ltd* [1915] AC 750. As Wood noted (*English and International Set-off* (1989), 963), *Eckman v Midland Bank Ltd* [1973] 1 QB 519, a case on sequestration, is consistent with this view.

[746] *Re Potts, ex p Taylor* [1893] 1 QB 648; *Ideal Bedding Co Ltd v Holland* [1907] 2 Ch 157, 169.

[747] [1909] 1 KB 430, in particular Cozens-Hardy MR at 434–5 and Fletcher Moulton LJ at 436–7.

[748] *Re A Debtor, ex p Peak Hill Goldfield Ltd* [1909] 1 KB 430.

[749] [1909] 1 KB 430, 437.

[750] The Child Support (Registration and Collection) Act 1988 (Cth), s. 72A is to a similar effect.

A recipient of a notice under s. 260-5 who fails to comply with it commits an offence, and where a person is convicted of an offence for failing to pay an amount under the notice the court may, in addition to imposing a penalty, order the person to pay to the Commissioner an amount not exceeding that amount.[751] A question which has yet to be determined is whether the Commissioner takes subject to a right of set-off available to the third party against the debtor.

17.150   The Commissioner should take subject to a substantive defence of equitable set-off.[752] The taxpayer's title to sue the third party would be impeached,[753] and the Commissioner could not have a better title. The position is more complicated in relation to the procedural defence of set-off under the Statutes of Set-off in the case of mutual debts.[754] A notice under s. 260-5 has been equated with a garnishee order,[755] and in that context there is authority suggesting that a statutory set-off that would be available to a third party garnishee as a defence to an action for payment of a debt owing to the judgment debtor can be asserted against the judgment creditor seeking to attach the third party's debt.[756] But there is a problem in applying that principle in the case of a s. 260-5 notice. Section 260-5 is expressed to apply where the third party 'owes' money to the debtor. The availability of a set-off under the Statutes does not mean that there is nothing owing by the third party to the debtor to the extent of the set-off. There is money owing, but the third party has a procedural defence to an action at law to enforce the debt, should the third party choose to plead the cross-debt as a defence to the action.[757] Because the debt is owing, s. 260-5 *prima facie* applies and an offence is committed if the notice is not complied with. Since the procedure which may result in the commission of an offence does not involve an action at law, the Statutes of Set-off do not apply. A similar issue in relation to the application of the Statutes arises in the context of a garnishee order, but there is a distinction between a garnishee order and a s. 260-5 notice. An application for a garnishee order involves a two-stage process, requiring

---

[751] Section 260-20. The section in its terms does not create an obligation on the recipient of the notice to comply with it, but it is an offence to fail to comply. See *Clyne v Deputy Commissioner of Taxation* (1981) 150 CLR 1, 17.

[752] See ch. 4 above.

[753] See paras 4.29–4.57 above in relation to the substantive nature of equitable set-off.

[754] For the application of the Statutes in Australia, see paras 2.63–2.86 above. This includes the re-enactment of the Statutes in New South Wales, pursuant to the Civil Procedure Act 2005, s. 21. See paras 2.64–2.73 above.

[755] *Clyne v Deputy Commissioner of Taxation* (1981) 150 CLR 1, 19 (Mason J); *Commissioner of Taxation v Donnelly* (1989) 25 FCR 432, 442, 456; *Macquarie Health Corp Ltd v Commissioner of Taxation* (1999) 96 FCR 238 at [117]; *Bruton Holdings Pty Ltd v Commissioner of Taxation* (2009) 239 CLR 346 at [14]–[15] and [51]. Garnishee orders (or, as they are now called under the English Civil Procedure Rules, third party debt orders) are considered at paras 17.136–17.145 above. It was said in relation to a notice under the former s. 218 that it created a charge in favour of the Commissioner over the debt owing to the taxpayer which was the subject of the notice. See *Commissioner of Taxation v Donnelly*; *Macquarie Health Corp Ltd v Commissioner of Taxation*. See also *Commissioner of Taxation v Government Insurance Office of New South Wales* (1993) 45 FCR 284, 292–4; *Deputy Commissioner of Taxation v Conley* (1998) 88 FCR 98, 99–100, 106; *Clyne v Deputy Commissioner of Taxation* at 17–18. However, Australian courts have rejected the view that a garnishee order gives rise to a proprietary interest (see para. 17.138 above), and the similarity between a notice under s. 260–5 and a garnishee order suggests that service of s. 260-5 notice would also be regarded as not giving rise to a proprietary interest.

[756] See para. 17.139 above.

[757] See paras 2.34–2.39 above.

an order nisi (or interim order) followed by an order absolute. The final order is discretionary, and the authorities which support the view that a judgment creditor takes subject to a statutory set-off available to the third party garnishee against the judgment debtor can be explained by reference to the judicial discretion which applies when application is made for the order absolute.[758] However, no such judicial discretion applies in the case of a s. 260-5 notice, and hence the justification for permitting a third party to rely on procedural defence under the Statutes as against a judgment creditor seeking a garnishee order is not available in the case of a s. 260-5 notice. On that basis, it is suggested that a third party upon whom a s. 260-5 notice is served could not rely on the statutory defence, notwithstanding that the set-off could have been asserted against a judgment creditor seeking a garnishee order.[759]

H. Subrogation

(1) Insurance subrogation

It was suggested earlier that a person who has an assignment merely of the proceeds of a debt should be in a different position to that of an assignee of the debt itself as regards set-off.[760] Unless a substantive defence of equitable set-off is in issue,[761] an assignee of a debt as a general rule takes subject to defences of set-off available to the debtor against the assignor which had accrued before the debtor had notice of the assignment,[762] whereas an assignee merely of the proceeds should take subject to a defence of set-off whenever it arose, notwithstanding that this would have the effect that nothing would be received to the extent of the set-off to which the assignment could attach. A similar issue arises in the context of insurance subrogation.[763] An insurer that has indemnified its insured is subrogated to any claim possessed by the insured against a third party that reduces the loss. This entitles the insurer to use the insured's name in order to sue the third party, and also to claim any moneys recovered by the insured from the third party in reduction of the loss. The insurer has an equitable proprietary interest in moneys recovered by the insured, in

17.151

---

[758] See para. 17.139 above.

[759] A similar issue may arise in relation to the availability of a contractual right of set-off. In *Fraser v Oystertec plc* [2006] 1 BCLC 491 the decision of Mr Terence Mowschenson QC, sitting as a deputy judge of the High Court, that the judgment creditor in that case took subject to the bank's contractual right, was based upon the court's discretion applicable in the case of a third party debt (or garnishee) order.

[760] See paras 17.66–17.67 above.

[761] See para. 17.32 above.

[762] See paras 17.03 and 17.13 above.

[763] In *Lewenza v Ruszczak* (1959) 22 DLR (2d) 167, a subrogated insurer's interest in a judgment obtained by the insured against the third party was held to preclude the third party from setting off a judgment that he had obtained against the insured. The set-off in issue was a set-off of judgments, which involves a question of the court's inherent jurisdiction, as opposed to a defence of set-off under the Statutes of Set-off. See paras 2.99–2.105 above. See also *Co-operators Insurance Association v Brown* (1989) 69 OR (2d) 135 (no counterclaim against the insured in a subrogation action, although in that case the insurer was suing in its own name). Compare *Page v Scottish Insurance Corporation* (1929) 140 LT 571, which concerned a claim for a set-off between the insurer and the third party. A set-off was denied for a number of reasons, including that the insurer had not indemnified the insured so that it was not entitled to be subrogated to the insured's right of action. Compare also *Re Casey; A Bankrupt* Irish High Court, Hamilton P, 1 March 1993, noted by O'Dell [1995] RLR 193. It is not clear from the note when the rates were due, and in any event the decision appears to have turned on the statutory right of set-off in the Local Government Act 1941, s. 58.

the form of an equitable lien or charge.[764] But what about the right of action itself? The issue was referred to in the House of Lords in *Napier v Hunter*,[765] albeit inconclusively. Lord Browne-Wilkinson declined to express a concluded view as to whether subrogation gives the insurer a proprietary interest in the claim, but the tenor of his judgment suggests that he doubted that it has that effect. If a subrogated insurer is without a proprietary interest in the claim, the insurer's subrogation entitlement should not affect a set-off available as between the insured and the third party, notwithstanding that the insurer would have had a proprietary interest in any sums that the third party would have paid to the insured were it not for the set-off. Lord Goff of Chieveley, on the other hand, said that he could see no reason in principle why an equitable proprietary interest should not be capable of attaching to the chose in action,[766] but he went on to say that he was reluctant to reach a conclusion on the point without a full examination of the authorities and that he reserved his opinion on the subject. Lord Templeman initially suggested that the insurer has an equitable interest in the right of action,[767] but later in his judgment he expressed himself more cautiously, commenting that, since reading in draft the speech of Lord Goff, he agreed that, if the point should become material, his initial view may require reconsideration in the light of further research.[768] Consistent with the interest that attaches to moneys recovered by the insured from the third party,[769] if the insurer has an interest in the right of action itself it probably would be characterized as an equitable charge or lien,[770] and the determination of set-off rights in the case of a fixed equitable charge is governed by the same principles as apply in the case of an equitable assignment.[771] On this view, if the third party obtained a cross-claim against the insured after notice of the insurer's interest and the demands are not sufficiently closely connected to give rise to an equitable set-off,[772] it would be regarded as unconscionable for the third party to rely on the right of set-off otherwise available against

---

[764] *Napier v Hunter* [1993] AC 713, 738, 744–5, 752. On the other hand, when the insurer obtains recoveries which exceed the sum to which it is entitled in order to recoup itself, the insurer holds the surplus on trust. See *Lonrho Exports Ltd v Export Credits Guarantee Department* [1999] Ch 158, 181–2.

[765] [1993] AC 713, 752–3.

[766] [1993] AC 713, 745.

[767] [1993] AC 713, 737–8. In Western Australia, this was referred to in *Insurance Commission of Western Australia v Kightly* (2005) 225 ALR 380 at [50] (CA).

[768] [1993] AC 713, 740.

[769] See above.

[770] Lord Templeman and Lord Goff seem to have assumed that this would be the case. See [1993] AC 713, 740, 745. Thus, it has been said that the interest of a subrogated insurer in the insured's right of action is not that of a *cestui que* trust. See *Linsley v Petrie* [1998] 1 VR 427, 445. On other occasions, however, the epithet 'trust' has been used. See *Hartford Fire Insurance Co v Hurse* [1962] WAR 187, 191; *Levesque v Co-operative Fire & Casualty Co* (1976) 68 DLR 553, 557. It has also been said that the insurer is not an assignee of the insured's claim. See *Linsley v Petrie* at 445 and *Esso Petroleum Co Ltd v Hall Russell & Co Ltd* [1989] 1 AC 643, 663, although Morison J in *Schiffahrtsgesellschaft Detlev von Appen GmbH v Voest Alpine Intertrading GmbH* [1997] 1 Lloyd's Rep 179, 186 described the effect of subrogation as a 'transfer' (on appeal [1997] 2 Lloyd's Rep 279, 286 Hobhouse LJ referred to counsel's characterization of the right in terms of a transfer without comment either way). Some of the effects of subrogation, on the other hand, have been said to be similar to an equitable assignment. See *Hobbs v Marlowe* [1978] AC 16, 39, *Linsley v Petrie* at 445.

[771] See para. 17.100 above. In the event that the insured's claim against the third party exceeds the insurer's subrogation entitlement, so that to the extent of the excess the insured alone is beneficially interested, the third party's set-off rights as against the excess should not be affected by the insurer's interest. See para. 17.68 above in relation to an assignment of part of a debt.

[772] See paras 17.32–17.38 above in relation to equitable set-off.

the insured to diminish the rights of the insurer.[773] This would be so notwithstanding statements to the effect that a subrogated insurer can only make such claim as the insured himself could have made,[774] and that a subrogated insurer takes subject to all defences available to the third party against the insured.[775]

However, in *Re Ballast Plc*[776] Lawrence Collins J rejected the view that a subrogated insurer **17.152** has a proprietary interest in the insured's right of action. Ballast was a civil engineering contractor. It entered into a contract to carry out certain works, and appointed MMD as a consultant. One of MMD's obligations was to design some slopes near a road. Cracking subsequently occurred on the road caused by shearing within a slope, and as a result Ballast was required to carry out remedial work. Ballast was insured for the project under a contractors' all risk policy. The insurer indemnified Ballast for the cost of the remedial work, less a deductible payable by Ballast. Ballast instructed MMD to carry out the necessary design work to deal with the problem, without prejudice to the question of who was responsible. MMD carried out that design work and rendered four invoices in connection with it. In addition, MMD had a number of other outstanding invoices, both for that project and for other projects. Ballast subsequently went into liquidation. The insurer contended that Ballast had a claim against MMD to which it was subrogated. The liquidators, on the other hand, considered that a claim by Ballast against MMD had no merit, and filed a notice of disclaimer under the Insolvency Act 1986, s. 178 disclaiming Ballast's interest in any claim that Ballast may have had against MMD.[777] The present application was issued by the insurer under s. 181 of the Insolvency Act seeking an order vesting in it Ballast's claim against MMD. An application under s. 181 may be made by 'any person who claims an interest in the disclaimed property'. MMD argued in response that a subrogated insurer only has a proprietary interest in any proceeds of litigation or of a settlement once they arise, and not in the antecedent claim itself. Hence, it said that the insurer had no standing to apply for a vesting order in relation to the claim. Further, if a vesting order otherwise might have been made, MMD contended that there was no utility in making the order.

---

[773] See para. 17.03 above. Ordinarily, a subrogation action would involve a claim for damages. Equitable set-off extends to damages claims but the Statutes of Set-off are confined to a case of mutual debts. See para. 2.14 above. Therefore, unless the case is one involving closely connected cross-claims giving rise to an equitable set-off, for which the date of notice is not determinative (see paras 17.32–17.34 above), it is likely that the question of set-off in the context of an action by a subrogated insurer would seldom arise.

[774] *Simpson v Thomson* (1877) 3 App Cas 279, 286; *Lister v Romford Ice and Cold Storage Co Ltd* [1957] AC 555, 600 *per* Lord Somervell of Harrow ('The insurer, when he has paid, succeeds to such rights as the assured possesses'); *Ross Southward Tire Ltd v Pyrotech Products Ltd* (1975) 57 DLR (3d) 248, 251 *per* Laskin CJC ('The subrogated insurer's position in this litigation against the tenant is, admittedly, no better than that of the landlord itself.').

[775] *Sydney Turf Club v Crowley* [1971] 1 NSWLR 724, 734 *per* Mason JA (the action 'is brought in the name of the insured and it is subject to all the defences which would be available if the action had been brought by the insured for his own benefit'). See also Mitchell, 'Defences to an insurer's subrogated action' [1996] LMCLQ 343, 356, 360.

[776] [2007] Lloyd's Rep IR 742. See Look Chan Ho, 'Of proprietary restitution, insurers' subrogation and insolvency set-off – the untenable case of *Re Ballast*' (2007) 23 *Insolvency Law & Practice* 103.

[777] Ballast's parent had agreed with the liquidators that it would pay a sum to the liquidators for distribution to Ballast's creditors provided that the dissolution of Ballast commenced by 31 March 2006. See [2007] Lloyd's Rep IR 742 at [19]. A subrogation action, on the other hand, required that Ballast remain in existence and on the register.

It submitted that it had cross-claims for unpaid invoices which were automatically set off by operation of the insolvency set-off section against the claim, and to that extent no asset remained which could be vested in the insurer.[778] Lawrence Collins J held that an applicant for a vesting order must have some form of proprietary interest in the property in respect of which the order is sought and that the insurer's right of subrogation did not suffice in that regard.[779] The issue in relation to 'utility' accordingly did not arise, but Lawrence Collins J said that, if the insurer had had a 'relevant' (in other words, a proprietary) interest, that interest would have been an interest in the claim subject to the cross-claims.[780]

17.153 The proposition that a subrogated insurer does not have a proprietary interest in the insured's right of action is unlikely to be regarded as having been settled.[781] On that basis, the issue in relation to 'utility' merits further consideration.

17.154 The set-off asserted in the case was insolvency set-off, pursuant to the Insolvency Rules 1986, r. 4.90,[782] and it is apparent that it was that form of set-off that Lawrence Collins J had in mind. In support of the view that set-off in any event would have applied if the insurer had had a proprietary interest, he referred to *Stein v Blake*.[783] In that case, the plaintiff had commenced proceedings against the defendant for damages for breach of contract, and the defendant counterclaimed for damages for misrepresentation. The plaintiff became bankrupt, and the trustee in bankruptcy purported to assign the claim back to the bankrupt. The House of Lords held that the cross-claims were set off automatically on the date of the bankruptcy pursuant to the insolvency set-off section, so that at that date the bankrupt's claim ceased to exist to the extent of the set-off. All that remained capable of assignment was the net balance after the set-off. In that case, the purported assignment occurred after the bankruptcy. In *Re Ballast*, the report does not state expressly when the insurer indemnified Ballast, but the recitation of the facts suggests that it would have occurred before the liquidation.[784] If that was the case, the circumstances were different to those applicable in *Stein v Blake*. On the assumption that subrogation gives an insurer a proprietary interest in the insured's claim,[785] the insurer would have had a proprietary interest in the claim against MMD *before* the liquidation of Ballast. That prior interest would have had the effect that there was no mutuality at the date of the liquidation, so as to preclude a set-off under r. 4.90.[786] But that would not have been the end of the matter. While the insolvency set-off section would not have applied, the insurer's interest in Ballast's

---

[778] [2007] Lloyd's Rep IR 742 at [34]. See paras 6.119–6.146 above in relation to the automatic nature of insolvency set-off.

[779] [2007] Lloyd's Rep IR 742 at [109].

[780] [2007] Lloyd's Rep IR 742 at [110].

[781] In *The 'WD Fairway'* [2009] 2 Lloyd's Rep 191 at [52]–[53] Tomlinson J agreed with a submission that none of the reasons given by Lawrence Collins J for denying a proprietary interest in the claim is necessarily inconsistent with a proprietary interest in the form of an equitable lien, but nevertheless said that he would be reluctant not to follow Lawrence Collins J's view.

[782] See the discussion of utility [2007] Lloyd's Rep IR 742 at [59]–[70], and at [71]–[72] and [84] (MMD).

[783] [1996] AC 243, 259. See para. 6.122 above.

[784] See [2007] Lloyd's Rep IR 742 at [3]–[14].

[785] Contrary to the view of Lawrence Collins J in *Re Ballast*.

[786] See para. 11.46 above in relation to a fixed equitable charge.

claim consequent upon the indemnification would have been subject to prior equities, on principles similar to those applicable in the case of an equitable assignment.[787] The prior equities would have included rights of set-off available as between solvent parties.[788] Ballast's claim against MMD was in damages. Therefore, the defence of set-off under the Statutes of Set-off in the case of mutual debts[789] would not have been available to MMD. Equitable set-off, on the other hand, is not confined to debts, but for that form of set-off to apply the cross-claims must be closely connected.[790] The damages claim against MMD would have impeached MMD's claim for payment for the remedial work so as to give rise to an equitable set-off. Similarly, other payment claims relating to that project probably would be regarded as sufficiently closely connected if there was a single contract and price for the performance of the work. On the other hand, a set-off would not have been available in respect of payment claims for other projects.[791]

The preceding discussion concerned the case of a subrogated insurer standing behind a claimant. Alternatively, a defendant raising a cross-claim by way of defence may have been indemnified by an insurer for the loss the subject of the cross-claim. This may arise, for example, where a claimant is suing for the price of equipment delivered to the defendant, and the defendant alleges that the equipment is defective so as to give rise to a defence either on the basis of equitable set-off or the common law defence of abatement.[792] If the defendant in that circumstance has been indemnified by an insurer, the insurer is entitled to insist that the defendant raise the cross-claim by way of defence, and if the defence succeeds the defendant must account to the insurer for the benefit that the defendant has obtained through the reduction or extinction of the liability for the price.[793]   **17.155**

(2) Subrogation in other situations

It has been said that insurance subrogation forms a category of its own,[794] and so considerations applicable to that form of subrogation may not be relevant to other forms.[795]   **17.156**

---

[787] See para. 17.151 above.

[788] See paras 17.39 and 17.115 above.

[789] See para. 2.14 above.

[790] See ch. 4 above.

[791] See para. 4.93 above.

[792] See paras 2.123–2.134 above. The better view is that strict mutuality is not always required for equitable set-off, though there is recent authority (see para. 4.69 above) suggesting the contrary. See paras 4.67–4.83 above.

[793] *National Oilwell (UK) Ltd v Davy Offshore Ltd* [1993] 2 Lloyd's Rep 582, 624.

[794] *Barclays Bank Ltd v TOSG Trust Fund Ltd* [1984] 1 AC 626, 639 (Oliver LJ). See also *Bofinger v Kingsway Group Ltd* (2009) 239 CLR 269 at [6], referring to *Orakpo v Manson Investments Ltd* [1977] 1 WLR 347, 357 (Buckley LJ).

[795] In relation to a trust creditor's right to be subrogated to the trustee's claim for an indemnity from the trust assets or the beneficiaries, see paras 17.126 and 17.131 above. In *Boscawen v Bajwa* [1996] 1 WLR 328, 333 Millett LJ said in relation to subrogation generally that it is concerned with the assignment by operation of law of a third party's rights. In *Secretary of State for Trade and Industry v Frid* [2004] 2 AC 506 at [2] and [34] the House of Lords referred to the Secretary of State's rights under the Employment Rights Act 1996, 167(3), which provided for a transfer and vesting of an employee's rights in the Secretary consequent upon the making of a payment to the employee, in terms of subrogation. Compare *Banque Financière De La Cité v Parc (Battersea) Ltd* [1999] 1 AC 221, 236 in relation to subrogation to securities.

17.157 *Jenner v Morris*[796] concerned a person who made loans to another's deserted wife for the purpose of purchasing necessaries. While a person who supplied necessaries to a deserted wife could sue the husband at common law for payment, the common law did not recognise a similar right in a person who merely lent money for the purpose of acquiring them. It was held in *Jenner v Morris*, however, that the person advancing money for this purpose was entitled to be subrogated to the claim that the supplier would have had against the husband, and further that this could be set off against a judgment debt owing by the person to the husband. The fact that a set-off was permitted suggests that the person who made the advance was regarded as having an equitable proprietary interest in the claim as a result of the right of subrogation, and indeed Lord Campbell LC suggested that the subrogation could possibly be explained as an equitable assignment of the supplier's claim against the husband.[797] A similar comment may be made in relation to the judgment of Powell J in the New South Wales Supreme Court in *A E Goodwin Ltd v A G Healing Ltd*[798] in the context of a surety's right of subrogation as against the principal debtor.[799] Powell J contemplated that the right of subrogation may bring about mutuality so as to allow a set-off in respect of the principal debtor's debt to the creditor to which the surety is subrogated and a separate debt owing by the surety to the debtor, which once again suggests that it was thought to confer an interest in the creditor's claim. On the other hand, Powell J also said that the right of subrogation is in the nature of a class right, so that if there is more than one surety subrogated to the creditor's claim there would be a lack of mutuality as between the subrogation claim and a debt owing by one of the sureties to the debtor.[800]

I. Contracts (Rights of Third Parties) Act 1999[801]

17.158 Subject to various qualifications and exceptions, the Contracts (Rights of Third Parties) Act 1999 permits a person who is not a party to a contract (referred to as a 'third party') to enforce a term of the contract in his or her own right if the contract expressly provides that he or she may, or if the term purports to confer a benefit on the third party.[802] If a third party brings proceedings pursuant to the Act to enforce a term of the contract, s. 3 sets out three circumstances in which the person against whom the term is enforceable ('the promisor'[803]) may avail him or herself of a set-off.

---

[796] (1860) 1 Dr & Sm 218, 62 ER 362, affirmed (1861) 3 De G F & J 45, 45 ER 795.

[797] (1861) 3 De G F & J 45, 52, 45 ER 795, 798.

[798] (1979) 7 ACLR 481, 488–9.

[799] Wood, *English and International Set-off* (1989), 943–4 also regards *Re Jeffrey's Policy* (1872) 20 WR 857 as authority for the proposition that subrogation in the context of suretyship affects mutuality, although the case may be explained on the ground that the payment of the money into court by the creditor constituted an admission that it was not entitled to retain the money but rather it was a trustee.

[800] (1979) 7 ACLR 481, 489. See also *Rowlatt on Principal and Surety* (5th edn, 1999), 157; Andews and Millett, *Law of Guarantees* (5th edn, 2008), 456–7; O'Donovan and Phillips, *Modern Contract of Guarantee* (looseleaf), [12.2450].

[801] See generally Stevens, 'The Contracts (Rights of Third Parties) Act 1999' (2004) 120 LQR 292.

[802] See, in particular, s. 1, and note the exceptions in s. 6.

[803] See s. 1(7).

In the first place, the promisor has available by way of defence or set-off any matter that **17.159** arises from or in connection with the contract and is relevant to the term being enforced.[804] However, this is subject to the qualification that the matter must have been available to the promisor by way of defence or set-off if the proceedings had been brought by 'the promisee', being the party to the contract by whom the term is enforceable against the promisor.[805] This would have the consequence that the third party takes subject to defences of equitable set-off and common law abatement that arise out of the contract. Secondly, the promisor may also invoke a defence or set-off against the third party if an express term of the contract provides for it to be available to the promisor in proceedings brought by the third party and, in addition, if it would have been available to the promisor by way of defence or set-off if the proceedings had been brought by the promisee. Thirdly, s. 3(4) provides that the promisor may rely on a defence or set-off that would have been available to him or her against the third party if the third party had been a party to the contract.[806] This picks up set-offs arising from the third party's own circumstances. If the third party's claim is for a debt under the contract, it confirms that the promisor may set off a separate debt owing to him or her by the third party under the Statutes of Set-off.

---

[804] This is subject to an express term of the contract as to matters that are not to be available to the promisor by way of set-off. See s. 3(5).

[805] See s. 1(7).

[806] This is subject to an express term to the contrary. See s. 3(5).

18

SURETIES

This chapter is concerned with contracts of suretyship, and the availability of rights of set-off as between a creditor, the debtor and a guarantor of the debt. **18.01**

A. Principal Debtor's Right to Require a Set-off

If a principal debtor has a cross-claim against the creditor which is available as a set-off **18.02** against the debt, equitable considerations dictate that the creditor should not be able to avoid the set-off by proceeding against a guarantor. If it were otherwise, and the creditor recovered from the guarantor, the guarantor would be entitled to be indemnified by the principal debtor. The debtor could still proceed separately against the creditor on the cross-claim, but he or she would have lost the benefit of the set-off. There is early authority which supports the principal debtor's right to relief in this situation.

In *Ex p Hanson*,[1] the assignees in bankruptcy of a creditor sued Hanson and Williamson on **18.03** a bond given by them jointly as security for a loan made to Hanson alone. Hanson therefore was the principal debtor, and Williamson had only joined in the bond as a surety. Hanson also had a separate claim against the creditor. Lord Eldon held, on Hanson's petition, that the assignees' action should be restrained, and that Hanson's separate claim should be

---

[1] (1811) 18 Ves Jun 232, 34 ER 305, affirming (1806) 12 Ves Jun 346, 33 ER 131.

deducted from and set off against the joint debt on the bond. The creditor in that case was bankrupt, but Lord Eldon's analysis did not turn on any peculiarity of insolvency set-off.[2] Rather, he invoked a general equitable principle that:[3] 'the joint debt was nothing more than a security for a separate debt; and upon equitable considerations a creditor, who has a joint security for a separate debt, cannot resort to that security without allowing what he has received on the separate account . . .' The set-off in issue was based upon 'equitable considerations'. Because of a lack of mutuality,[4] it was not a set-off of mutual debts pursuant to the bankruptcy set-off section. Subsequently, Lord Eldon adopted a similar approach in *Ex p Hippins, re Sikes*.[5] Hippins had accepted two bills of exchange for the accommodation of the drawer, one Harrison, who discounted them with a firm of bankers. The banking firm became bankrupt, at which time it was indebted to Harrison in an amount greater than the indebtedness on the bills. The firm's assignees in bankruptcy claimed to be entitled to sue Hippins as the acceptor, which would have had the consequence that Harrison would have been denied the benefit of the set-off that would have been available if he had been sued. Harrison and Hippens accordingly brought this petition to restrain the threatened proceedings. Lord Eldon affirmed an order of the Vice Chancellor[6] that the assignees should deliver up the bills and that all proceedings against Hippins in respect of the bills should be stayed. The important point was that the bills were accommodation bills. Therefore, as between Hippins and Harrison, equity considered that Harrison as the party accommodated was principally liable,[7] and if Hippins paid the bills he would have been entitled to be reimbursed by Harrison. If, on the other hand, a bill of exchange is not an accommodation bill, the acceptor rather than the drawer is principally liable, and the drawer is not entitled to restrain the holder from suing the acceptor despite a set-off that otherwise would have been available to the drawer.[8]

18.04   Consider also *Hamp v Jones*.[9] A tenant had obtained a verdict at law against the landlord and his bailiff for damages for trespass. The landlord had agreed to indemnify the bailiff, and the landlord also had a separate claim for rent against the tenant which exceeded the amount of the verdict. Sir Lancelot Shadwell VC granted an injunction to restrain the tenant from issuing out execution or taking other proceedings upon the judgment. In the course of his judgment, the Vice Chancellor commented that a set-off was not available at law, because there was a joint demand against the landlord and the bailiff and only a 'single' demand against the tenant. But if the landlord had agreed to indemnify the bailiff, the Vice Chancellor said that that seemed a reason for the interference of the Court of Chancery.

---

[2] Compare Lord Erskine in earlier proceedings (1806) 12 Ves Jun 346, 348, 33 ER 131, 132.

[3] (1811) 18 Ves Jun 232, 233–4, 34 ER 305.

[4] See paras 12.02–12.20 above.

[5] (1826) 4 LJOS Ch 195, 2 Gl & J 93.

[6] Sir John Leach.

[7] The common law, on the other hand, considered that the accommodation acceptor was principally liable. See *Coles Myer Finance Ltd v Commissioner of Taxation* (1993) 176 CLR 640, 657, 683–8.

[8] *Ex p Banes, re The Royal British Bank* (1857) 28 LTOS 296; *Ex p Burton, Franco and Corea, re Kensington* (1812) 1 Rose 320. In *Ex p Hippins* (1826) 2 Gl & J 93, 96 Lord Eldon confirmed, after an examination of the secretary's book, that *Ex p Burton* did not involve an acceptance for accommodation.

[9] (1840) 9 LJ Ch 258.

Lord Eldon in *Ex p Hanson* ordered that the action against the joint debtors be restrained **18.05** and that the securities given by them be delivered up, this being the method by which equitable set-offs were enforced before the Judicature Acts.[10] Since the Judicature Acts, an equitable set-off may be pleaded directly as a defence in the claimant's action. An order setting off cross-demands may occur when the principal debtor claiming the set-off is a party to the creditor's action, as was the case in *Ex p Hanson*. If, however, the principal debtor is not a party, he or she should still be entitled to apply to the court for a declaration as to the set-off entitlement and for an order restraining the creditor from proceeding against the guarantor without giving credit for the set-off. If the principal's cross-claim exceeds the debt, the action against the guarantor should be stayed and there should be a consequential order for delivery up of the guarantee.[11]

B. Set-off Available to the Guarantor

A guarantor being sued by the creditor for payment under the guarantee may base a set-off **18.06** upon a cross-claim that the guarantor has against the creditor, including in circumstances where the creditor gave warranties to the guarantor in relation to the transaction the subject of the principal obligation.[12] On the other hand, while a principal debtor should be entitled on equitable grounds to insist that the creditor not avoid a set-off available to the principal by proceeding against a guarantor,[13] a similar equity does not arise in the situation in which the creditor is liable to the guarantor. The creditor is not obliged to sue the guarantor so as to give effect to a set-off, but can look instead to the principal for payment.[14] But if the guarantor contracted on terms that he or she was to be liable as a principal debtor, and the creditor has become bankrupt or is a company in liquidation, the guarantor's liability and a cross-claim possessed by the guarantor against the creditor may be the subject of an automatic set-off under the insolvency set-off section, and the creditor's trustee in bankruptcy or liquidator could not avoid that result by commencing proceedings against the person who in substance is the principal debtor.[15]

---

[10] See para. 3.01 above.

[11] See also *Rowlatt on Principal and Surety* (5th edn, 1999), 106.

[12] *BOC Group plc v Centeon LLC* [1999] 1 All ER (Comm) 53; *Zeekap (No. 47) Pty Ltd v Anitam Pty Ltd* (1989) 14 Tas R 206 (see esp. at [31]). See also *Doherty v Murphy* [1996] 2 VR 535 (esp. at 561–2 (referring to the notice of appeal), 565 and 566) and *Young v National Australia Bank Ltd* (2004) 29 WAR 505 at [29] (in relation to a misrepresentation made to a guarantor). Note also *Murphy v Zamonex Pty Ltd* (1993) 31 NSWLR 439 (in which the guarantors, as well as the principal debtor, appear to have been regarded as having a cross-claim consequent upon the representation); *Harrison v Australian and New Zealand Banking Group Ltd* (Vic CA, 15 May 1996, BC9602140) (remedy in damages available to a guarantor against a mortgagee under the Property Law Act 1994 (Qld), s. 85 for failure to take reasonable care in selling the mortgaged property). Compare *Continental Illinois National Bank & Trust Co of Chicago v Papanicolaou* [1986] 2 Lloyd's Rep 441 (sale of mortgaged property at an undervalue) and *Capital Finance Australia Ltd v Airstar Aviation Pty Ltd* [2004] 1 Qd R 122, in which the guarantee excluded a defence of set-off. See para. 18.34 below.

[13] See paras 18.02–18.05 above.

[14] *Lord v Direct Acceptance Corporation Ltd* (1993) 32 NSWLR 362, 369. See also *Ex p Burton, Franco and Corea, re Kensington* (1812) 1 Rose 320 and *Ex p Banes, re The Royal British Bank* (1857) 28 LTOS 296, for which see para. 12.23 above.

[15] *MS Fashions Ltd v Bank of Credit and Commerce International SA* [1993] Ch 425. See paras 12.24–12.28 above. The set-off would also discharge the principal debtor. See the *MS Fashions* case at 448. In company

C. Guarantor's Right to Rely on the Principal Debtor's Set-off

18.07 Consider once again the case of a creditor who is suing a guarantor, and the principal debtor, who is not being sued, has a cross-claim against the creditor which would provide a defence if the creditor sued him or her. The principal debtor in that circumstance should be entitled to an order restraining the creditor's action so that the debtor's defence can be given effect.[16] If, however, the debtor fails to take the point, the question arises whether the guarantor can defend the creditor's action on the basis of the set-off available to the debtor.[17] This differs from the assignment cases discussed in the preceding chapter. In the case of an assignment of a debt, the question is whether the debtor can assert a set-off available against the assignor in an action brought against him or her by a third party assignee. In the guarantee cases, on the other hand, the third party surety is endeavouring to obtain the benefit of a set-off arising out of dealings between the principal debtor and creditor.

(1) Set-off agreement

18.08 A surety is entitled to the benefit of an agreement between the principal debtor and the creditor pursuant to which the debt was set off against a separate debt of the creditor to the debtor, since the set-off constitutes payment.[18]

(2) Solvent set-off – the various approaches

18.09 The position is more complex in relation to the availability of defences of equitable set-off, common law abatement and set-off under the Statutes of Set-off. On a general level, three distinct approaches to the question of set-off have been suggested. It is appropriate to set these out before considering each of the forms of set-off.

18.10 One view, which represents the preferred approach, is that the surety can defend him or herself on the basis of any defence of set-off or abatement available to the principal debtor,[19] subject possibly to a requirement that the debtor be joined as a party to the action.[20] This view is supported by a passage in *Halsbury*, to the effect that a surety can avail him or herself of any right of set-off or counterclaim that the principal debtor has against the creditor,[21]

---

liquidation and administration in England, that result would no longer depend on the guarantor having contracted as a principal debtor. See para. 12.28 above.

[16] See paras 18.02–18.05 above.

[17] Compare the exceptional fact situation in *R v Shaw* (1901) 27 VLR 70 (fidelity policy), in which the issue was not set-off as such but whether the guaranteed debt had been reduced by payment.

[18] See *Aurora Borealis Compania Armadora SA v Marine Midland Bank NA (The Maistros)* [1984] 1 Lloyd's Rep 646 (letter of undertaking given by bank); *Cheetham v Crook* (1825) M'Cle & Yo 307, 148 ER 429; *Wreckair Pty Ltd v Emerson* [1992] 1 Qd R 700, 708. See also *Re Bank of Credit and Commerce International SA (No. 8)* [1996] Ch 245, 268.

[19] In addition to the authorities referred to below, see *Diebel v Stratford Improvement Co* (1917) 33 DLR 296, 301. See also *Mann v Secretary of State for Employment* [1999] UKHL 29 in relation to a set-off available to a principal debtor pursuant to statute.

[20] See below.

[21] *Halsbury's Laws of England* (4th edn, 1978) vol. 20, 102, para. 190 ('On being sued by the creditor for payment of the debt guaranteed, a surety may avail himself of any right to set off or counterclaim which the principal debtor possesses against the creditor . . .'). In *Halsbury* (5th edn, 2008) vol. 49, 509, para. 1135 this is expressed in terms of a set-off or counterclaim which the principal debtor could set up against the creditor

which passage was quoted with evident approval by Roskill LJ in *Hyundai Shipbuilding and Heavy Industries Co Ltd v Pournaras*[22] and by Scott LJ in *Barclays Bank plc v Gruffydd*.[23]

A second view, which is favoured by some text-writers,[24] is that a surety can invoke an **18.11** equitable set-off available to the principal debtor arising out of a sufficiently close connection with the guaranteed debt (once again, possibly subject to a requirement that the debtor be joined[25]), but not a defence of set-off under the Statutes of Set-off. This is suggested by a comment by Willes J in *Bechervaise v Lewis*,[26] that: 'the plea is a special plea by a surety, of a set-off by the principal, arising out of the same transaction out of which the liability of the surety on the note arose.'

A third view, which has support in Victoria[27] and New South Wales,[28] and possibly also in **18.12** England in the judgment of Finlay LJ in *Wilson v Mitchell*,[29] is that a defence of set-off available to the principal debtor cannot be invoked by a surety. On the other hand, the rigour of this approach has been said to be ameliorated in two respects. In the first place, an exception has been recognized when the debtor is bankrupt or is a company in liquidation. This has been justified on the ground that the creditor might otherwise recover in full against the surety whereas the surety would only receive a dividend from the debtor,[30] but it could also be explained on the basis that the insolvency set-off section ordinarily would apply in that circumstance as against the principal debt, in which case a set-off would have occurred

---

in reduction of the guaranteed debt. In relation to a counterclaim which is not available as a set-off, see para. 18.30 below. See also *Enron (Thrace) Exploration and Production BV v Clapp* [2004] EWHC 1612 (Comm) at [56] *per* Langley J ('It is trite law that the general rule is that where the principal debtor has a right of set-off giving him a defence to the debt the subject of the guarantee the surety is entitled to raise it as a defence to the creditor's claim . . .'); *Marubeni Hong Kong and South China Ltd v Mongolian Government* [2004] EWHC 472 (Comm) at [232] *per* Cresswell J ('A guarantor can *prima facie* avail itself of any right of set-off possessed by the primary debtor against the creditor').

   [22] [1978] 2 Lloyd's Rep 502, 508. Stephenson LJ agreed with Roskill LJ's judgment.
   [23] Court of Appeal, 30 October 1992. Scott LJ said that the passage in Halsbury was a correct statement of the law. Compare *National Westminster Bank v Skelton* [1993] 1 WLR 72, 78–9 (Slade LJ, with whose judgment Anthony Lincoln J agreed).
   [24] Wood, *English and International Set-off* (1989), 641, 645; O'Donovan and Phillips, *The Modern Contract of Guarantee* (looseleaf), [11.670] and [11.800].
   [25] See O'Donovan and Phillips, *The Modern Contract of Guarantee* (looseleaf), [11.670] (though suggesting that this should not be required in a summary judgment application against the guarantor) and *Paget's Law of Banking* (13th edn, 2007), 838.
   [26] (1872) LR 7 CP 372, 377. See also *Sun Alliance Pensions Life & Investments Services Ltd v RJL* [1991] 2 Lloyd's Rep 410, 416.
   [27] *Indrisie v General Credits Ltd* [1985] VR 251, though compare *Doherty v Murphy* [1996] 2 VR 553. It appears from the report of *Indrisie* that the High Court refused special leave to appeal from the decision, but it is not clear whether this was because of a view that a set-off available to the principal debtor can never be invoked by the surety, or whether it was because the principal debtor was not a party to the action, or whether it was simply on the ground that the demands in any event were thought to be insufficiently connected to give rise to an equitable set-off.
   [28] *Cellulose Products Pty Ltd v Truda* (1970) 92 WN (NSW) 561; *Covino v Bandag Manufacturing Pty Ltd* [1983] 1 NSWLR 237, 240–1. In Queensland, see *Ansell Ltd v Coco* [2004] QCA 213 at [39] (but compare at [23]).
   [29] [1939] 2 KB 869, 871. Finlay LJ commented: 'There is here a cross-claim for damages, and this cannot be prayed in aid by a surety against the claim on the guarantee. Even if my view is wrong as to this, it certainly could not be prayed in aid without bringing in the principal debtor whose claim it was.'
   [30] *Cellulose Products Pty Ltd v Truda* (1970) 92 WN (NSW) 561, 585 (referring to *Alcoy and Gandia Railway and Harbour Co Ltd v Greenhill* (1897) 76 LT 542, 553). See also *National Westminster Bank plc v Skelton* [1993] 1 WLR 72, 79.

automatically upon the occurrence of the bankruptcy or the liquidation.[31] If the principal debt has been extinguished in a set-off, so should the surety's liability under the guarantee.[32] Secondly, while this third view would generally deny the surety a defence, it is said that the surety nevertheless may achieve a similar result by a procedural means. In New South Wales, Isaacs J in *Cellulose Products Pty Ltd v Truda*[33] explained this in the following terms:

> This review of the cases lends no support to the submission that a surety when sued is entitled to set up in equity or at law as an equitable plea any cross action for unliquidated damages which the debtor may have against the creditor in respect of the transaction, the performance of which the guarantor had entered upon his guarantee; that is, in the absence of the debtor being before the court in the proceeding so as to be bound by verdict and judgments. This of course does not mean that the guarantor is without remedy; when he is sued he has a right immediately to join the debtor as a third party and claim complete indemnity from him. The debtor has then a right to join the plaintiff as a fourth party, claiming damages for breach of warranty and so obtain indemnity either in whole or in part. All the actions would be heard together, the rights of all persons determined and appropriate set-off's made after verdict, and if there be any surplus of damages over and above that which is required to meet the guarantee, the debtor will have recovered that from the creditor who, in the result, will get no more than that to which he would be justly entitled.

Isaacs J referred generally to cross-actions for unliquidated damages, but the case itself was concerned with the common law defence of abatement, and it is evident that his statement was intended to encompass the availability of that defence to the debtor. Moreover, one of the proposed pleas related to equitable set-off, and it is clear that the discussion extended also to that defence.[34]

18.13 Isaacs J referred to an exception where the debtor is before the court, although by that he would appear to have had in contemplation the procedure he described of joining the principal as a party and setting off the judgments. That procedure, however, does not provide a defence, and as such it would not assist in a summary judgment application.[35] Moreover, because the guarantor does not have a defence, the procedure may have different costs consequences. It may also be the case that the debt and the guarantee have been assigned, and the assignee is suing, in which case it is difficult to see how the procedure of setting off judgments could apply. Furthermore, the approach suggested by Isaacs J may not be as advantageous when the debtor has available a substantive defence of equitable set-off. For example, the debtor's cross-claim may be unenforceable as a result of the expiration of a limitation period, although this would not preclude the debtor from relying on it as a defence of equitable set-off if it is sufficiently closely connected with the debt owing to the creditor.[36] But if instead the creditor could sue a guarantor and the guarantor could not invoke the debtor's defence, it would not be a case of the guarantor joining the debtor and the debtor in turn claiming from the creditor, because the creditor could assert the expiration of the limitation period as a defence to the debtor's claim. If Isaacs J's approach were adopted, the debtor

---

[31] See paras 6.119–6.146 above.
[32] See para. 18.31 below.
[33] (1970) 92 WN (NSW) 561, 588.
[34] See e.g. (1970) 92 WN (NSW) 561, 574–5, and also *Indrisie v General Credits Ltd* [1985] VR 251 and *Langford Concrete Pty Ltd v Finlay* [1978] 1 NSWLR 14, 18.
[35] As in *Indrisie v General Credits Ltd* [1985] VR 251.
[36] See para. 4.51 above.

would have to take steps to protect his or her position in that circumstance, by applying for an order restraining the creditor's action against the surety, on the basis referred to above.[37]

In *National Westminster Bank Plc v Skelton*,[38] Slade LJ, with whose judgment Anthony Lincoln J[39] agreed, commented that he found the reasoning of Isaacs J impressive. Nevertheless, he went on to say that he did not think it right, in a striking out application, to decide whether there is a general rule that a guarantor cannot avail him or herself of the remedies that otherwise may be open to the principal debtor as against the creditor. Subsequently, however, a differently constituted Court of Appeal in *Barclays Bank plc v Gruffydd*[40] was not as reticent. Scott LJ said that he had difficulty in accepting that the statements of principle to be found in *Wilson v Mitchell* and *Cellulose Products v Truda* correctly stated the law, and Purchas LJ similarly considered that those cases were either wrongly decided or they did not represent English law.   **18.14**

(3) Equitable set-off and common law abatement

Consider the case of an unliquidated damages claim available to the debtor as an equitable set-off against the creditor or, if it relates to a breach of warranty under a contract for the sale of goods or for the performance of work, as a common law defence of abatement.   **18.15**

In Australia, differing views have been expressed as to whether a guarantor can invoke the debtor's defence. There is on the one hand authority for the view that a surety cannot rely on a cross-claim for damages which may be available to the principal debtor as against the creditor.[41] This includes the judgment of the Full Court of the Victorian Supreme Court in *Indrisie v General Credits Ltd*.[42] Subsequent to the *Indrisie* case, however, the Appeal Division of the Victorian Supreme Court in *Doherty v Murphy*,[43] without referring to that case, allowed a guarantor leave to defend in a summary judgment application, *inter alia* on the basis of an arguable equitable set-off available to the principal debtor against the creditor.[44]   **18.16**

---

[37] See para. 18.05 above.

[38] [1993] 1 WLR 72, 79.

[39] Sitting in the Court of Appeal.

[40] Unreported, 30 October 1992 (Purchas, Nolan and Scott LJJ).

[41] In addition to *Cellulose Products Pty Ltd v Truda* (1970) 92 WN (NSW) 561 (see para. 18.12 above), see *Covino v Bandag Manufacturing Pty Ltd* [1983] 1 NSWLR 237 and *Ansell Ltd v Coco* [2004] QCA 213 at [39] (but compare at [23]), and the cases referred to below.

[42] [1985] VR 251, 253–4. See also *Australia and New Zealand Banking Group Ltd v Harvey* (1994) ATPR (Digest) 46–132 at p 53,643; *Australia and New Zealand Banking Group Ltd v Ringrong Pty Ltd* (Federal Court of Australia, Ryan J, 11 September 1995, BC9502889); *Citic Australia Commodity Trading Pty Ltd v Lau* (Vic SC, Byrne J, 11 November 1997, BC9706281); *Citic Commodity Trading Pty Ltd v JBL Enterprises (WA) Pty Ltd* (Federal Court of Australia, Heerey J, 16 March 1998, BC9800781); *Florgale Uniforms Pty Ltd v Orders (No. 1)* [2000] VSC 427 at [26]. The Full Court in *Indrisie v General Credits* (at 254) noted that the principal debtor was not before the court as a party, but that was said to provide an *additional* reason for deciding against the surety. Compare, however, the interpretation of the *Indrisie* case in *Elkhoury v Farrow Mortgage Services Pty Ltd* (1993) 114 ALR 541, 549, *Re Kleiss* (1996) 61 FCR 436, 439–40 and *Dougan v Conias* [2000] FCA 1556 at [18].

[43] [1996] 2 VR 553.

[44] This was subject to a condition that an application be made to join the principal debtor as a defendant. See paras 18.24–18.26 below. The principal debtor was in liquidation, so that the leave of the court would have been required to join it as a party. See the Corporations Act 2001 (Cth), s. 471B. In *Young v National Australia Bank Ltd* (2004) 29 WAR 505 at [29] it was suggested that the right of the guarantors in *Doherty v Murphy* to raise equitable set-off as a defence may have turned on the circumstance that the representation was made by the creditor to the guarantor and that it may not have depended merely upon the right of the guarantor to rely on an equitable set-off available to the debtor. However, the guarantors presented separate

This reflects more liberal formulations of the principle that have been expressed on other occasions in Australia, in terms suggesting that the surety can invoke the principal debtor's defence if the debtor has been joined as a party to the action,[45] which represent the preferred view. On the other hand, joinder has been said not to be necessary if the debtor is insolvent. That proposition is considered later.[46]

18.17 But whatever the position in Australia, English courts favour the view that a surety can rely on a defence of equitable set-off or abatement available to the debtor against the creditor.[47] On two occasions a passage in *Halsbury*[48] to that effect has been referred to with evident approval in the Court of Appeal.[49] In *BOC Group plc v Centeon LLC*,[50] Rix J held that a

---

arguments for a set-off based, on the one hand, on the debtor's claim against the creditor for breach of contract and, on the other, on the misrepresentations made directly to the guarantors. Both grounds were regarded as arguable. See [1996] 2 VR 553, 562, 565, 566.

[45] *Langford Concrete Pty Ltd v Finlay* [1978] 1 NSWLR 14, 18, 19 (CA); *Re Kleiss* (1996) 61 FCR 436, 438–41; *Elkhoury v Farrow Mortgage Services Pty Ltd* (1993) 114 ALR 541, 549 (Lockhart, Gummow and Lee JJ); *Dougan v Conias* [2000] FCA 1556 at [18]. See also *Commonwealth Development Bank v Windermere Pastoral Co Pty Ltd* [1999] NSWSC 518 (in which a guarantor successfully resisted a summary judgment application by the creditor on the basis of an arguable equitable set-off available to the principal debtor, without the imposition of a requirement that the debtor be joined as a party); *Electricity Meter Manufacturing Co Ltd v D'Ombrain* (1927) 44 WN (NSW) 131 (which was criticized in the *Cellulose Products* case (1970) 92 WN (NSW) 561, 582–3); *Tooth & Co v Rosier* (NSW SC, Wood J, 7 June 1985, BC8500768) (to the extent that Wood J referred to equitable set-off as well as insolvency set-off); *Lord v Direct Acceptance Corporation* (1993) 32 NSWLR 362, 368–9 (Sheller JA referring to a submission of counsel without adverse comment); *Young v National Australia Bank Ltd* (2004) 29 WAR 505 at [21]; *Ansell Ltd v Coco* [2004] QCA 213 at [23] (but compare Chesterman J at [39]); *Sansom Nominees Pty Ltd v Meade* [2005] WASC 9 at [189]; *Clambake Pty Ltd v Tipperary Projects Pty Ltd (No. 3)* [2009] WASC 52 at [196]–[197]. In *GE Capital Australia v Davis* (2002) 11 BPR 20,529, [2002] NSWSC 1146 at [84], Bryson J said that it is 'desirable' that the debtor should be party to the proceedings and bound by the result, but that if the guarantor takes the initiative and brings proceedings in which orders are sought establishing the amount of the guarantor's indebtedness, the court should not permit the guarantor to do so without joining the debtor as a party. However, the justification for the distinction between those situations in relation to joinder of the principal is unclear. In relation to the joinder of the principal, see paras 18.24–18.26 below.

[46] See para. 18.32 below.

[47] See also in Canada *420093 BC Ltd v Bank of Montreal* (1995) 128 DLR (4th) 488, 500–1 (Alberta Court of Appeal); *Diebel v Stratford Improvement Co* (1917) 33 DLR 296, 301 (Ontario Supreme Court, Appellate Division).

[48] See para. 18.10 above.

[49] *Hyundai Shipbuilding & Heavy Industries Co Ltd v Pournaras* [1978] 2 Lloyd's Rep 502, 508 and *Barclays Bank plc v Gruffydd* (30 October 1992, Scott LJ). See also the broad statement of the principle by Langley J in *Enron (Thrace) Exploration and Production BV v Clapp* [2004] EWHC 1612 (Comm) at [56] and by Cresswell J in *Marubeni Hong Kong and South China Ltd v Mongolian Government* [2004] EWHC 472 (Comm) at [232]. Compare *National Westminster Bank v Skelton* [1993] 1 WLR 72, 78–9, which pre-dated *Barclays Bank v Gruffydd*, and in which the Court of Appeal left the question open. In *Aliakmon Maritime Corporation v Trans Ocean Continental Shipping Ltd (The Aliakmon Progress)* [1978] 2 Lloyd's Rep 499, which was decided on the same day as *Hyundai v Pournaras*, it was not disputed that if an equitable set-off had been available to the charterer it would have provided a defence to the guarantor, but Lord Denning, with whom Geoffrey Lane LJ agreed, considered that the circumstances were not such as to give rise to an equitable set-off. *Murphy v Glass* (1869) LR 2 PC 408, a case which is also often cited as support for the surety's right to have recourse to the benefit of the set-off, may possibly be explained on an alternative basis, that the debt secured by the bills of exchange was regarded as having been reduced so that a possible set-off of cross-demands was not in issue. This appears to have been the view of the Victorian Supreme Court, whose decision was affirmed on appeal by the Privy Council. See Isaacs J in *Cellulose Products Pty Ltd v Truda* (1970) 92 WN (NSW) 561, 580–2.

[50] [1999] 1 All ER (Comm) 53.

guarantor could avail itself of the principal debtor's set-off, and in *Oastler v Pound*[51] Blackburn J accepted that the surety in that case could have relied on any defence of abatement that the debtor had against the creditor, although it was held that the circumstances were not such as to give rise to the defence. More recently, the House of Lords in *Trafalgar House Construction (Regions) Ltd v General Surety & Guarantee Co Ltd*,[52] accepted that the characterization of a bond as a guarantee had the consequence that an equitable set-off[53] that could have been relied upon by the principal obligor by way of defence could also be relied on by the guarantor in an action by the obligee for payment under the bond. Those cases should be contrasted with *Sun Alliance Pensions Life & Investments Services Ltd v RJL*.[54] Mr Anthony Colman QC (as he then was), sitting as a deputy judge, suggested that a set-off available to the principal debtor which arose out of the same transaction as the principal debt and which was for a 'limited amount' could be relied on by the guarantor to reduce or extinguish his personal liability on the guarantee. By 'limited amount', it appears that the deputy judge meant a liquidated sum, but if the circumstances are such as to give rise to an equitable set-off the nature of the debtor's cross-claim which the guarantor can invoke should not be restricted in that manner.

Bechervaise v Lewis[55] is also sometimes referred to in this context.[56] The plaintiff and a third **18.18** party, one Rowe, were in partnership. A number of debts were due to them as partners, and the plaintiff sold his interest in the debts to Rowe. As security for Rowe's obligation to pay the purchase price, the plaintiff was given a joint and several promissory note made by Rowe and the defendant, the defendant joining in only as a surety for Rowe. The plaintiff sued the defendant on the note, whereupon the defendant pleaded a defence on equitable grounds that the plaintiff was indebted to Rowe as a result of the plaintiff having received the proceeds of some of the assigned debts, so that the plaintiff could not have recovered from Rowe. The judgment of the Court of Common Pleas[57] was delivered by Willes J, who described the plea: 'as a special plea by a surety, of a set-off by the principal.'[58] He commented:[59]

> Thus we have a creditor who is equally liable to the principal as the principal to him, and against whom the principal has a good defence in law and equity, and a surety who is entitled in equity to call upon the principal to exonerate him.

> In this state of things, we are bound to conclude that the surety has a defence in equity against the creditor . . .

---

[51] (1863) 7 LT 852.
[52] [1996] 1 AC 199.
[53] While the House of Lords did not characterize the nature of the set-off in issue, since the liability of the obligor was in damages it could only have been an equitable set-off, and indeed counsel for the surety referred in his argument to equitable set-off.
[54] [1991] 2 Lloyd's Rep 410, 416.
[55] (1872) LR 7 CP 372.
[56] *Rowlatt on Principal and Surety* (5th edn, 1999), 103–4, para. 4–91. See also *Alcoy and Gandia Railway and Harbour Co v Greenhill* (1897) 76 LT 542, 552–3 (Stirling J commenting that the set-off in *Bechervaise v Lewis* arose out of the same transaction as that out of which the suretyship arose).
[57] Willes, Keating, Montague Smith and Brett JJ.
[58] (1872) LR 7 CP 372, 377.
[59] (1872) LR 7 CP 372, 377.

It is not clear what form of set-off was thought to be in issue between Rowe and the plaintiff. While the argument of counsel for the plaintiff centred on the right of set-off available at law under the Statutes of Set-off in the case of mutual debts, Willes J emphasized in his judgment that the set-off arose out of the same transaction out of which the liability of the surety on the note arose,[60] which suggests that it may have been regarded as an equitable set-off arising out of a sufficiently close connection between the demands.[61] Another interpretation of the case has been proposed, that in truth it was not concerned with set-off at all. In *Cellulose Products v Truda*[62] Isaacs J said that it was part of the arrangement in *Bechervaise v Lewis* that the plaintiff was to collect the debts, and that the proceeds received by the plaintiff had the effect of reducing the liability of Rowe which the defendant had guaranteed. However, the report does not mention that the plaintiff was intended to collect payment, and moreover the case was argued on the basis of set-off. Nor does the judgment suggest Isaacs J's analysis. On the contrary, Willes J commented that: 'in our law set-off is not regarded as an extinction of the debt between the parties,' and that 'we have a creditor who is equally liable to the principal as the principal to him.'[63] These comments indicate that subsisting cross-debts were thought to be in issue, which would not have been the case if the receipt of the proceeds by the plaintiff itself had the effect of reducing the debt.

Explanation of the set-off

18.19   However, *Bechervaise v Lewis* is regarded, a surety ordinarily[64] should be able to rely on the debtor's defence of equitable set-off or abatement.[65] The surety's right to invoke the defence may be explained on either of two grounds.

18.20   In the first place, the guarantee as a matter of construction may require that defences of set-off available to the principal be taken into account in determining the extent of the liability of the guarantor. Thus, in *Langford Concrete Pty Ltd v Finlay*[66] a guarantor guaranteed 'the payment . . . of all moneys which are now payable or may in the future

---

[60] (1872) LR 7 CP 372, 377.

[61] Willes J referred during argument to equitable set-off, although that possibly could be explained on the ground that the principal had a set-off at law under the Statutes of Set-off as against the creditor which could be invoked on equitable grounds by the surety.

[62] (1970) 92 WN (NSW) 561, 583–4, 586.

[63] (1872) LR 7 CP 372, 377.

[64] Unless the terms of the guarantee are such as to preclude reliance on the debtor's set-off. See paras 18.34–18.39 below.

[65] *Williston on Contracts* (3rd edn, 1967) vol. 10, 799, para. 1251 sets out five objections to allowing the defence, which were reproduced in *Cellulose Products v Truda* (1970) 92 WN (NSW) 561, 575 from an earlier edition. The first and the second are considered below. In relation to the third, Isaacs J in the *Cellulose Products* case (at 573) doubted, correctly, whether the plea would succeed. The fifth is cured by requiring joinder of the debtor (see below). Insofar as the fourth is concerned, regarding a number of sureties who are severally liable, this is more likely to arise when a set-off of unrelated debts under the Statutes of Set-off is in issue, and it is considered in that context below. In addition, the objection raised in Wood, *English and International Set-off* (1989), 636, 643, that the principal debtor as an alternative to equitable set-off may be entitled to rescind the guaranteed contract altogether because of the breach giving rise to the cross-claim, should not be a reason for denying a guarantor's right to invoke the defence generally. The debtor should retain the right to rescind, and (depending on the terms of the guarantee) if the debtor exercises the right the guaranteed obligation may fall away. As to the effect of a rescission consequent upon the acceptance of a repudiation, see *Hurst v Bryk* [2002] 1 AC 185, 193, referring to *McDonald v Dennys Lascelles Ltd* (1933) 48 CLR 457, 476–7.

[66] [1978] 1 NSWLR 14.

become payable' to the creditor by the principal.[67] The subject of the guarantee was moneys due under a contract for the performance of work, but it was alleged that the work was defective. The New South Wales Court of Appeal held that the guarantor could rely on the principal's cross-claim, commenting that:

> [T]his guarantee is so formulated that the guarantor can take advantage of the proposed cross-claim. All that the appellant undertook to pay was what was payable, that is, payable by the debtor. It was not a guarantee to pay the price, or the price without deduction, but to pay only what the debtor could have been compelled to pay.[68]

Similarly, if the guarantee is expressed to apply in the event of a default in payment by the principal, and the principal has a cross-claim giving rise to an equitable set-off for a sum which exceeds the debt, the substantive nature of the defence[69] should have as a consequence that there has not been a default by the principal, so that the creditor should not be entitled to proceed against the guarantor.[70] In *BOC Group plc v Centeon LLC*[71] the guarantor guaranteed the 'prompt payment when due of the obligations of Purchaser'. Rix J at first instance said that the guarantor had not guaranteed more than the purchaser was obliged to pay.[72] If at the time when the purchaser's payment obligation fell due the purchaser was entitled to a set-off, the purchaser would not have been obliged to pay anything, and nor should the guarantor.

But apart from the question of construction of the guarantee,[73] the surety's right to rely on the principal debtor's defence may be explained on equitable grounds, based upon the right **18.21**

---

[67] Compare a guarantee which is expressed in terms of guaranteeing the payment of any moneys advanced (see *Beri Distributors Pty Ltd v Pulitano* (1994) 10 SR (WA) 274 (WA DC)) or the payment of the contract price. See *Jinhong Design & Constructions Pty Ltd v Yi Nuo Xu* [2010] NSWSC 523 at [116].

[68] [1978] 1 NSWLR 14, 17. See also *Re Kleiss* (1996) 61 FCR 436, 440. *Langford Concrete v Finlay* should be compared to *Westco Motors (Distributors) Pty Ltd v Palmer* [1979] 2 NSWLR 93. The guarantee in that case related to amounts which were due and payable for goods supplied. The debtor's cross-claim did not relate to the goods supplied, but was for damages for breach of the Trade Practices Act (Cth) consequent upon allegations relating to restraint of trade, misuse of market power and resale price maintenance. Sheppard J said that the cross-claim was separate and distinct from the cause of action which the creditor had for the moneys it was owed, so that, in contrast to *Langford Concrete v Finlay*, the cross-demand as a matter of construction did not reduce the subject of the guarantee. Sheppard J went on to doubt whether the circumstances gave rise to an equitable set-off, but he said that that was not the real question. The real question was, what was it that was guaranteed by the guarantor? The subject of the guarantee was the amount owing on the creditor's cause of action, which was not reduced by the cross-claim. See also the explanation of the case in *Westpac Banking Corporation v Eltran Pty Ltd* (1987) 14 FCR 541, 559. Subsequently, Wood J in *Tooth & Co Ltd v Rosier* (NSW SC, 7 June 1985, BC8500768 at 16–18) doubted the applicability of the *Westco Motors* case when an equitable set-off is in issue. Moreover, the principal debtor in the *Westco Motors* case was in liquidation but there was no consideration given to the insolvency set-off section. See para. 18.31 below.

[69] See paras 4.29–4.57 above.

[70] For a similar argument in a different context, see *Ashley Guarantee plc v Zacaria* [1993] 1 WLR 62, 67–8, 71.

[71] [1999] 1 All ER (Comm) 53, decision affirmed [1999] 1 All ER (Comm) 970 (CA).

[72] [1999] 1 All ER (Comm) 53, 67. Rix J's analysis should not extend to a right of set-off under the Statutes of Set-off which, unlike equitable set-off (see paras 4.29–4.57 above), is merely a procedural defence. See paras 2.34–2.39 above.

[73] In Australia, Wood J in *Tooth & Co Ltd v Rosier* (NSW SC, 7 June 1985, BC8500768 at 18) commented that the ultimate question might not always turn on the construction of the guarantee alone. Compare *Westco Motors (Distributors) Pty Ltd v Palmer* [1979] 2 NSWLR 93, 99.

that the surety has in equity to be exonerated by the debtor.[74] The debtor, as the person principally liable to the creditor, should exonerate (or relieve) the guarantor from liability to the creditor through the defence of set-off that the debtor has against the creditor. The burden of the debt should be borne by the principal debtor,[75] and the surety's right to be exonerated should override the right that the debtor otherwise would have had to elect to waive the defence and to prosecute the cross-claim against the creditor in a separate action.[76] It is in a sense related to another principle considered earlier, that the creditor should not be able to avoid the set-off available to the principal by resorting to the guarantee. If the creditor sues the guarantor, the principal should be entitled to apply for orders restraining the action and for the court to give effect to the set-off.[77] The surety's right to be exonerated by the principal therefore should require the principal to relieve the surety by insisting that the set-off available to him or her be given effect.

An objection that has been raised

18.22   In *Indrisie v General Credits Ltd*,[78] the Full Court of the Victorian Supreme Court raised as an objection to the defence that it would involve a transference of the principal's claim in order to meet the surety's liability. That objection is without foundation, however.[79] As Willes J expressed the nature of the surety's defence in *Bechervaise v Lewis*:[80] 'the plea is a special plea by a surety, of a set-off *by the principal* . . .' The surety is not seeking to employ the principal's claim against the creditor in a set-off against the surety's own liability on the contract of guarantee. Rather, the surety's argument is that the principal has a cross-claim against the creditor which is available to the principal as a set-off against the debt to the creditor,[81] and because of the surety's right to be exonerated by the principal, it is appropriate that the principal rather than the guarantor should bear the burden of the debt through a set-off against the principal's cross-claim.

18.23   Because the guarantor's defence is based upon an equitable set-off available to the principal debtor against the creditor, it should not matter that the circumstances giving rise to the cross-claim against the creditor occurred after the contract of guarantee was entered into,

---

[74] *Bechervaise v Lewis* (1872) LR 7 CP 372, 377; *Alcoy and Gandia Railway and Harbour Co Ltd v Greenhill* (1897) 76 LT 542, 553; *Re Kleiss* (1996) 61 FCR 436, 440. This point was not considered in *Beri Distributors Pty Ltd v Pulitano* (1994) 10 SR (WA) 274 (WA DC).

[75] See generally *Rowlatt on Principal and Surety* (5th edn, 1999), 143.

[76] Compare the second objection in *Williston on Contracts* (3rd edn, 1967) vol. 10, 799, para. 1251. The equivalent passage in an earlier edition is referred to in *Cellulose Products Pty Ltd v Truda* (1970) 92 WN (NSW) 561, 575.

[77] See paras 18.02–18.05 above.

[78] [1985] VR 251, 254. See also the first objection referred to in *Cellulose Products Pty Ltd v Truda* (1970) 92 WN (NSW) 561, 572, 575.

[79] It was not apparently regarded as an objection by the Appeal Division of the Victorian Supreme Court in *Doherty v Murphy* [1996] 2 VR 553, 565.

[80] (1872) LR 7 CP 372, 377 (emphasis added). Similarly, Drummond J in *Re Kleiss* (1996) 61 FCR 436, 441 referred to the situation in which: 'a guarantor seeks to rely on an equitable set-off available to the principal debtor . . .'

[81] As Bryson J expressed it in *GE Capital Australia v Davis* (2002) 11 BPR 20,529, [2002] NSWSC 1146 at [83]: 'The substance of what the guarantor does by relying on a set-off is establishing the true amount of his own liability by showing that the debtor is entitled to a set-off.' See also *Ultimate Property Group Pty Ltd v Lord* (2004) 60 NSWLR 646 at [75]–[77].

and were in no sense contemporaneous with the guarantee. The contrary view expressed in Western Australia[82] is difficult to support.

Joinder of the principal

In *Bechervaise v Lewis*,[83] the Court of Common Pleas considered that the surety in that case **18.24** had a defence in equity against the creditor based upon the principal debtor's cross-claim, notwithstanding that the debtor was not a party to the proceeding. The question of the availability of a set-off arose upon a demurrer, but nevertheless the case is curious because the attitude of courts of equity[84] usually is that all parties materially interested in the subject of a suit should be made parties to the suit.[85] The debtor is the party who has the legal right to sue the creditor on the cross-claim, and so the debtor should be present so that he or she may be bound by a determination as to a set-off. The creditor would then be protected against a subsequent claim by the debtor.[86] On that basis, the debtor should be a party in these cases. The surety should be entitled to have the debtor joined as a defendant, since the debtor's presence would be necessary to enable the surety to set up a defence to the creditor's action.[87] Further, when a creditor is applying for summary judgment against the surety, it would be consistent with that view to impose a condition upon the grant of leave to defend that the debtor be joined.

That approach has support in both Australia[88] and in England.[89] On the other hand, **18.25** there have been suggestions to the effect that the principal debtor need not be a party to the action against the guarantor where the set-off operates directly to reduce the debt guaranteed.[90] A set-off effected between the principal debtor and the creditor pursuant to

---

[82] *Young v National Australia Bank Ltd* (2004) 29 WAR 505 at [34] (Barker J, Murray J agreeing).

[83] (1872) LR 7 CP 372, 377. See para. 18.18 above.

[84] *Bechervaise v Lewis* was decided by a common law court (the Common Pleas), but the Common Law Procedure Act 1854 (17 & 18 Vict c 125, ss. 83–86) made provision for equitable defences to be pleaded at law.

[85] See *Daniell's Chancery Practice* (8th edn, 1914) vol. 1, 147; *John Alexander's Clubs Pty Ltd v White City Tennis Club Ltd* (2010) 266 ALR 462 at [139].

[86] See *Daniell's Chancery Practice* (8th edn, 1914) vol. 1, 151.

[87] *Amon v Raphael Tuck & Sons Ltd* [1956] 1 QB 357, 386.

[88] *Cellulose Products Pty Ltd v Truda* (1970) 92 WN (NSW) 561, 588; *Indrisie v General Credits Ltd* [1985] VR 251, 254; *Doherty v Murphy* [1996] 2 VR 553 (summary judgment application); *Re Kleiss* (1996) 61 FCR 436, 441; *Clambake Pty Ltd v Tipperary Projects Pty Ltd (No. 3)* [2009] WASC 52 at [190] (where the requirement of joinder was explained by reference to the reasoning in *Cellulose Products Pty Ltd v Truda* (1970) 92 WN (NSW) 561, for which see para. 18.12 above). Compare *Commonwealth Development Bank v Windermere Pastoral Co Pty Ltd* [1999] NSWSC 518, in which a guarantor successfully resisted a summary judgment application by the creditor on the basis of an arguable equitable set-off available to the principal debtor, without any condition being imposed that the debtor be joined, and *Electricity Meter Manufacturing Company Ltd v D'Ombrain* (1927) 44 WN (NSW) 131 (which was criticized in the *Cellulose Products* case (1970) 92 WN (NSW) 561, 582–3) in relation to an application to strike out the guarantor's plea of set-off. When a creditor suing for a debt has joined both the principal debtor and the surety as defendants, both defendants may be granted leave to defend on the basis of a possible right of set-off available to the debtor. See *Petersville Ltd v Rosgrae Distributors Pty Ltd* (1975) 11 SASR 433.

[89] *Wilson v Mitchell* [1939] 2 KB 869, 871; *National Westminster Bank plc v Skelton* [1993] 1 WLR 72, 81 (which was argued on the basis of equitable set-off notwithstanding that the company was in liquidation); *Chitty on Contracts* (30th edn, 2008) vol. 2, 1691 para. 44–086.

[90] *Rowlatt on Principal and Surety* (5th edn, 1999), 103–104; *Halsbury's Laws of England* (5th edn, 2008) vol. 49, 509 para. 1135. In *Barclays Bank plc v Gruffydd* Court of Appeal, 30 October 1992, Scott LJ accepted

a set-off agreement between them would operate as a payment, and therefore it would reduce the debt.[91] Further, in an unreserved judgment in *Barclays Bank plc v Gruffydd*,[92] Scott LJ is reported to have commented, in the context of an application by a guarantor for leave to defend on the basis of the principal debtor's set-off, that: 'A set-off, whether legal or equitable, available to the principal debtor extinguishes, or reduces pro tanto, the amount of the creditor's claim.'[93] However, that statement inaccurately describes the position in so far as it refers to the period before judgment for a set-off. A debt is not reduced or extinguished merely by reason of an entitlement to an equitable set-off or to a defence of set-off under the Statutes of Set-off.[94] Admittedly, equitable set-off is referred to as a substantive defence. But by 'substantive defence' it is meant that, where circumstances exist which give rise to the set-off, the creditor is not permitted in equity to assert that any moneys are due to it, or to proceed on the basis that the debtor has defaulted in payment, to the extent of the set-off. Because of the substantive nature of the defence its effect in equity is similar to a discharge of the debt *pro tanto*, but it does not bring about a reduction in or an extinguishment of the cross-demands at law until judgment for a set-off.[95] In *Barclays Bank v Gruffydd* the principal debtor was in liquidation, and Scott LJ said that the insolvency set-off section rather than equitable set-off was in issue. Unlike equitable set-off, insolvency set-off does bring about an automatic extinguishment of the debts to the extent of the set-off, at the date of the liquidation.[96] Nevertheless, it was still accepted that a grant of leave to defend should be subject to a condition that an application be made to join the principal debtor as a party.[97] That should apply *a fortiori* to equitable set-off, which does not operate to extinguish the debts at law until judgment. On the other hand, the decision of the House of Lords in *Trafalgar House Construction (Regions) Ltd v General Surety & Guarantee Co Ltd*[98] suggests that joinder may not be required in the case of an equitable set-off. The House of Lords accepted that a consequence of characterizing the bond in issue in that case as a guarantee was that an equitable set-off[99] that could have been relied on by the principal obligor as a defence could also be relied on by the guarantor. The case concerned an application for

---

that the corresponding passage in an earlier edition of *Halsbury* correctly stated the law. See also *Hudson Investment Group v Mower Specialists Association of Australia* [2005] NSWSC 459 at [28] ('cross–claims . . . which reduce or extinguish the particular debt which has been guaranteed').

[91] See para. 18.08 above. The suggestion would extend to the circumstances in issue in *Murphy v Glass* (1869) LR 2 PC 408, as explained in *Cellulose Products Pty Ltd v Truda* (1970) 92 WN (NSW) 561, 580–2. See also the explanation of *Bechervaise v Lewis* (1872) LR 7 CP 372 in *Cellulose Products v Truda* at 583–4 and 586, for which see para. 18.18 above.

[92] Court of Appeal (Scott, Nolan and Purchas LJJ), 30 October 1992.

[93] In referring to 'legal set-off', Scott LJ may have had in contemplation the common law defence of abatement, which in England is regarded as a substantive defence (see para. 2.129 above), as opposed to set-off under the Statutes of Set-off, which is a procedural defence. See paras 2.34–2.39 above.

[94] *Langford Concrete Pty Ltd v Finlay* [1978] 1 NSWLR 14, 18. See also para. 2.35 above in relation to the Statutes of Set-off.

[95] See paras 4.29 and 4.34 above. See also para. 2.130 above in relation to abatement.

[96] See paras 6.119–6.146 above.

[97] See para. 18.32 below.

[98] [1996] 1 AC 199.

[99] Lord Jauncey of Tullichettle, in delivering the judgment of the House of Lords, referred simply to set-off, without commenting upon the nature of the set-off in issue. However, since the liability of the obligor was in damages, it could only have been an equitable set-off, and indeed counsel for the surety referred in his argument to equitable set-off.

summary judgment by a creditor on a bond against a guarantor. Their Lordships held that the guarantor was entitled to leave to defend on the basis of the principal's set-off entitlements, without imposing a condition that the principal be joined.[100] However, notwithstanding that it was not made a condition in that case, the better view is that the principal debtor should be a party when the action is tried.[101]

In Australia, where the weight of authority favours the view that joinder is necessary,[102] one **18.26** situation in which it nevertheless has been recognized that joinder is not required is in an application to set aside a bankruptcy notice. In *Re Kleiss*[103] a creditor issued a bankruptcy notice against a guarantor, whereupon the guarantor applied to set it aside on the basis of an equitable set-off available to the principal debtor against the creditor. Drummond J commented that, while joinder may well be necessary in an action for payment brought by a creditor against a guarantor, failure to comply with the procedural requirement would not prevent the Bankruptcy Court determining that, because of the debtor's entitlement to an equitable set-off, there was no debt truly owing by the guarantor.[104]

(4) Statutes of Set-off

It is sometimes said that, while a guarantor may be able to invoke the debtor's equitable **18.27** set-off as a defence to an action by the creditor, a similar right is not available when the debtor's set-off arises under the Statutes of Set-off.[105] However, there is no compelling reason for restricting the defences available to the guarantor in that manner.[106] Set-off under the Statutes admittedly differs from equitable set-off in that it is a procedural rather than a substantive defence.[107] But given that the right of the surety to invoke the debtor's defence of equitable set-off is not based upon the substantive nature of the defence, but rather the surety's right to be exonerated by the principal debtor and the construction of the guarantee,[108] the fact that set-off under the Statutes is procedural should not preclude the

---

[100] See also, in Australia, *Commonwealth Development Bank v Windermere Pastoral Co Pty Ltd* [1999] NSWSC 518 and *Electricity Meter Manufacturing Company Ltd v D'Ombrain* (1927) 44 WN (NSW) 131 (application to strike out the guarantor's plea of set-off).

[101] See also Phillips, 'When should the guarantor be permitted to rely on the principal's set-off?' [2001] LMCLQ 383, 387.

[102] See para. 18.24 above.

[103] (1996) 61 FCR 436.

[104] (1996) 61 FCR 436, 441. It has been suggested that a guarantor cannot rely on the principal debtor's equitable set-off as a basis for setting aside a statutory demand served on the guarantor for its winding up if judgment had been obtained against the principal debtor and the guarantor (*Remly Pty Ltd v Annis-Brown* [2010] NSWSC 397 at [16] – [19], explaining *Saratoga Integration Pty Ltd v Canjs Pty Ltd* (2010) 78 ACSR 600), but compare *Re Kleiss*).

[105] Wood, *English and International Set-off* (1989), 645; O'Donovan and Phillips, *The Modern Contract of Guarantee* (looseleaf), [11.750]; Andrews and Millett, *Law of Guarantees* (5th edn, 2008), 446–7 para. 11–011; *Re Kleiss* (1996) 61 FCR 436, 440–1 (where it was said that a guarantor can only rely on an equitable set-off available to the debtor against the creditor); Phillips, 'When should the guarantor be permitted to rely on the principal's set-off?' [2001] LMCLQ 383. See also the reference to cross-claims which reduce or extinguish the guaranteed debt in *Hudson Investment Group v Mower Specialists Association of Australia* [2005] NSWSC 459 at [28]. *Prima facie*, this would preclude reliance on a procedural defence of set-off under the Statutes.

[106] In Australia, in addition to the cases referred to below, see the submission to which Sheller JA referred without adverse comment in *Lord v Direct Acceptance Corporation* (1993) 32 NSWLR 362, 368–9.

[107] See paras 2.34–2.39 above, and compare paras 4.29–4.57 above in relation to equitable set-off.

[108] See paras 18.19–18.21 above.

surety from relying on it.[109] It is not a convincing argument that the debtor may owe other debts to the creditor which he or she may have preferred to set off against the cross-debt owing by the creditor,[110] since the surety's right to be exonerated should override the debtor's entitlement to utilize the cross-debt as he or she chooses. Nor is *Harrison v Nettleship*[111] contrary to this view.[112] In that case the surety's unsuccessful argument for a set-off was based upon cross-debts which it was said were owing by the creditor to the debtor 'at one time' during the course of their dealings, as opposed to presently existing debts. A right of set-off under the Statutes is a procedural defence which does not bring about an automatic extinction of the debts in question. A surety could only have a defence to the extent that a defence is still open to the debtor at the time of the creditor's action.

18.28   The argument in favour of the surety's right to rely on the defence is consistent with a broad statement in Halsbury,[113] which was quoted with evident approval in the Court of Appeal,[114] to the effect that a surety can avail him or herself of any right of set-off (or counterclaim[115]) that the principal debtor has against the creditor. The statement was not limited to any particular form of set-off.[116] A similar comment may be made in relation to the expressions of the principle by Langley J in *Enron (Thrace) Exploration and Production BV v Clapp*[117] and by Cresswell J in *Marubeni Hong Kong and South China Ltd v Mongolian Government*.[118] Further, since the Statutes do not require any connection between the debts the subject of a proposed set-off, it should not be necessary that the debt owing to the principal should have arisen out of the same transaction as the guaranteed debt.[119] On the other hand, for

---

[109] Compare *York City and County Banking Co v Bainbridge* (1880) 43 LT 732 in relation to the current account, assuming that the defendant was indeed a surety.

[110] See Steyn, 'Guarantees: The Co-extensiveness Principle' (1974) 90 LQR 246, 263.

[111] (1833) 2 My & K 423, 39 ER 1005.

[112] Compare Wood, *English and International Set-off* (1989), 645–6, and also Andrews and Millett, *Law of Guarantees* (5th edn, 2008), 446–7 para. 11–011. Andrews and Millett (*loc. cit.*) have also referred to *National Bank of Australasia v Swan* (1872) LR 3 VR (L) 168, but the issue in that case did not concern a set-off available to the principal debtor.

[113] *Halsbury's Laws of England* (4th edn, 1978) vol. 20, 102, para. 190. The formulation in the 5th edition in 2008, vol. 49, 509, para. 1135 is in similar (but not identical) terms.

[114] *Hyundai Shipbuilding and Heavy Industries Co Ltd v Pournaras* [1978] 2 Lloyd's Rep 502, 508 (Slade LJ, with whose judgment Stephenson LJ agreed). See also Scott LJ in *Barclays Bank plc v Gruffydd* Court of Appeal, 30 October 1992. Compare *National Westminster Bank v Skelton* [1993] 1 WLR 72, 78–9 (Slade LJ, with whom Anthony Lincoln J agreed). In Canada, see *Diebel v Stratford Improvement Co* (1917) 33 DLR 296, 301 *per* Hodgins JA ('equity would require that [the guarantor] should be allowed to set off that which the debtor himself could set off').

[115] But see para. 18.30 below in relation to a cross-claim not amounting to a set-off.

[116] In Story, *Commentaries on Equity Jurisprudence* (6th edn, 1853) vol. 2, 931, para. 1437, *Ex p Hanson* (1811) 18 Ves Jun 232, 34 ER 305 (see para. 18.03 above) is referred to as authority for the proposition that, if one of two joint debtors is only a surety for the other, he may in equity set off against the joint debt a separate debt owing to the principal by the creditor. The set-off was said to be available in equity, and was not limited to bankruptcy.

[117] [2004] EWHC 1612 (Comm) at [56]: 'It is trite law that the general rule is that where the principal debtor has a right of set-off giving him a defence to the debt the subject of the guarantee the surety is entitled to raise it as a defence to the creditor's claim . . .'

[118] [2004] EWHC 472 (Comm) at [232]: 'A guarantor can *prima facie* avail itself of any right of set-off possessed by the primary debtor against the creditor.'

[119] Compare *Sun Alliance Pensions Life & Investments Services Ltd v RJL* [1991] 2 Lloyd's Rep 410, 416–17. While in *Bechervaise v Lewis* (1872) LR 7 CP 372 the principal's cross-claim was for a liquidated sum, Willes J noted in his judgment that it arose out of the same transaction out of which the surety's liability arose, in which case the set-off in issue may have been regarded as an equitable set-off. See para. 18.18 above. In any

the reason set out earlier in the context of equitable set-off,[120] the debtor should be made a party to the proceedings. Set-off under the Statutes is a procedural defence,[121] and it could not be said that the entitlement to the set-off itself reduces the debt.[122]

Williston on Contracts has raised as an objection to the recognition of the defence that there may be a number of sureties severally liable.[123] However, this circumstance should not prevent the application of the principle. If the sureties are jointly and severally liable for the same debt, an order for a set-off in an action against one surety would give rise to a payment to the creditor to the extent of the set-off, which should provide a defence to other sureties as well.[124] Alternatively, a number of sureties each may be severally liable for distinct parts of the same debt, or there may be separate guarantees in place in relation to separate debts owing by the principal to the creditor. Since the right of a surety to rely on the principal's right of set-off is based on equitable grounds, the maxim that equality is equity may apply in relation to sureties who are the subject of an action at the time when the issue arises, so that each may be entitled to a defence to the extent of a proportionate part of the cross-debt owing to the debtor. But what if a particular surety is not the subject of a present action? Because the Statutes of Set-off do not result in an automatic extinction of cross-demands, the better view is that the surety not being sued should be disregarded. If instead the rule were adopted that the defence available to a surety the subject of an action must be reduced in order to take into account the possibility of a future action against another surety, the creditor could pay off the remainder of the cross-debt not set off in the first action before the second surety is sued, in which case the defence would be lost to the second surety in any event.

18.29

(5) Cross-action not available as a set-off

A statement in *Halsbury*,[125] to which the Court of Appeal has referred with evident approval,[126] suggests that a surety on being sued by the creditor can avail him or herself of a cross-action which the principal debtor could have asserted by way of counterclaim in an action on the guaranteed debt. That statement would appear to have been expressed in unduly wide terms in so far as it may extend to a mere counterclaim not available as a set-off.[127] The surety should only be entitled to a defence to the creditor's claim if the

18.30

---

event, it is doubtful whether the comment regarding the same transaction was intended to lay down a rule applicable generally whenever a surety seeks to rely on the debtor's set-off.

[120] See para. 18.24 above.

[121] See paras 2.34–2.39 above.

[122] See also para. 18.25 above in relation to equitable set-off. Scott LJ's comment in *Barclays Bank plc v Gruffydd* (Court of Appeal, 30 October 1992), to the effect that a legal set-off available to the principal debtor reduces the amount of the creditor's claim, may have been a reference to the common law defence of abatement, which in England is regarded as substantive in its operation. See paras 2.129–2.133 above.

[123] *Williston on Contracts* (3rd edn, 1967) vol. 10, 799, para. 1251. See also Steyn, 'Guarantees: the co-extensiveness principle' (1974) 90 LQR 246, 263.

[124] See para. 12.21 above.

[125] *Halsbury's Laws of England* (4th edn, 1978) vol. 20, 102 para. 190. See para. 18.10 above.

[126] *Hyundai Shipbuilding & Heavy Industries Co Ltd v Pournaras* [1978] 2 Lloyd's Rep 502, 508, and see also Scott LJ in *Barclays Bank plc v Gruffydd* Court of Appeal, 30 October 1992. Compare *National Westminster Bank v Skelton* [1993] 1 WLR 72, 78–9.

[127] While the House of Lords in *Trafalgar House Construction (Regions) Ltd v General Surety & Guarantee Co Ltd* [1996] 1 AC 199, 207 referred to the appellants (as guarantors) as having been entitled to raise

principal's cross-action in turn would have provided a defence to the principal against a claim on the guaranteed debt.[128] Indeed, this point is made in a later edition of *Halsbury*.[129] On the other hand, the procedure outlined by Isaacs J in *Cellulose Products*[130] should still be relevant in the case of a mere counterclaim, so that the surety could join the principal as a third party and claim an indemnity, and the principal in turn could join the creditor as a fourth party in relation to the cross-claim.

(6) Insolvency set-off

18.31 If the principal debtor is bankrupt or is a company in liquidation,[131] the surety ordinarily[132] should be entitled to assert a set-off under the set-off section in the insolvency legislation as between the debtor and the creditor.[133] In accordance with the accepted view as to the nature of insolvency set-off,[134] a set-off as between the debtor and the creditor would have occurred automatically upon the occurrence of the debtor's bankruptcy or liquidation. The debt to the extent of the set-off would have been paid, and a discharge of the principal debtor in that manner by way of a set-off should also discharge the surety.[135] If the debt to the creditor has been reduced by an automatic set-off so as to discharge to that extent the

---

'all questions of sums due and cross-claims' which would have been available to the principal debtor, it is apparent that a defence of set-off was thought to be in issue. See in particular [1996] 1 AC 199, 206, and also the argument of counsel for the appellant at 201.

[128] *Oastler v Pound* (1863) 7 LT 852; *Aliakmon Maritime Corporation v Trans Ocean Continental Shipping Ltd (The Aliakmon Progress)* [1978] 2 Lloyd's Rep 499. See also *Westco Motors (Distributors) Pty Ltd v Palmer* [1979] 2 NSWLR 93 (the principal debtor in that case was in liquidation, but the possible application of the insolvency set-off section was not considered: see para. 18.31 below), and the judgment of Hutley JA in *Covino v Bandag Manufacturing Pty Ltd* [1983] 1 NSWLR 237, 238. Compare *Sun Alliance Pensions Life & Investments Services Ltd v RJL* [1991] 2 Lloyd's Rep 410, 416–17, where it is suggested that a guarantor can rely on the debtor's unliquidated cross-claim not arising out of the same transaction to extinguish or reduce the guarantor's own liability if the principal debtor is joined as a party.

[129] *Halsbury's Laws of England* (5th edn, 2008) vol. 49, 510, para. 1135, n. 2, referring to *Aliakmon Maritime Corporation v Trans Ocean Continental Shipping Ltd (The Aliakmon Progress)* [1978] 2 Lloyd's Rep 499.

[130] (1970) 92 WN (NSW) 561, 588. See para. 18.12 above.

[131] Or, in England, where an administrator appointed to a company, being authorized to make a distribution, has given notice to creditors of his or her intention to do so. See the Insolvency Rules 1986, r 2.85.

[132] See para. 18.37 below in relation to the terms of the guarantee.

[133] In addition to the cases referred to below, see *Wreckair Pty Ltd v Emerson* [1992] 1 Qd R 700 (Full Court). In New South Wales, see also *Tooth & Co v Rosier* (NSW SC, Wood J, 7 June 1985, BC8500768). In *Westco Motors (Distributors) Pty Ltd v Palmer* [1979] 2 NSWLR 93 the principal debtor was in liquidation. In rejecting the surety's claim for a set-off, Sheppard J held that the cross-demands between the principal and the creditor were not sufficiently connected to give rise to an equitable set-off. However, the insolvency set-off section was not considered. A similar comment may be made in relation to *Re Kleiss* (1996) 61 FCR 436. *Beri Distributors Pty Ltd v Pulitano* (1994) 10 SR (WA) 274, 276–7 (WA DC) should also be considered in that context. Cockburn CJ in *Rouquette v Overmann* (1875) LR 10 QB 525, 541–2, in explaining *Allen v Kemble* (1848) 6 Moore 314, 13 ER 704, seemed to doubt that English law permits a surety to invoke a set-off as between a bankrupt creditor and the principal debtor, but that was before the courts adopted the automatic theory of insolvency set-off. See paras 6.126–6.127 above.

[134] See paras 6.119–6.146 above.

[135] *Re Bank of Credit and Commerce International SA (No. 8)* [1996] Ch 245, 268 (CA), referring to *Ex p Hanson* (1806) 12 Ves Jun 346, 33 ER 131 and see generally *McDonald v Dennys Lascelles Ltd* (1933) 48 CLR 457, 479–80. On the other hand, the Court of Appeal in *Re BCCI (No. 8)* suggested (at 268–9) that a discharge of the surety by way of a set-off under the insolvency set-off section may not discharge the principal debtor. That proposition is doubtful. See paras 12.29–12.39 above.

surety as well as the principal, the surety should be entitled to plead the discharge as a defence to an action by the creditor.[136]

In Australia, it has been said that the debtor need not be joined if it is insolvent[137] although **18.32** if the creditor wishes to have the debtor bound by the court's determination the creditor can join the debtor in the proceedings.[138] This was not justified on the basis of the automatic nature of insolvency set-off. Indeed, in most of the cases the insolvency set-off section was not referred to.[139] Rather, it was said that the requirement of joinder is one for the benefit of the creditor and that joinder can be of no practical benefit to the creditor where the debtor is in liquidation or insolvent. In England, on the other hand, the cases suggest that joinder is required.[140] This is the preferred view. The principal debtor should be a party so that it is bound by the determination in relation to set-off,[141] and that reasoning is just as valid when the debtor is insolvent as when it is solvent, though it may be noted that this conclusion sits uneasily with other views that have been expressed to the effect that the principal need not be joined if the set-off reduces the debt, which is the consequence of an automatic set-off under the insolvency set-off section.[142] In *Sun Alliance Pensions Life & Investments Services Ltd v RJL*,[143] the principal debtor was a company in liquidation and had a cross-claim for unliquidated damages against the creditor. Without referring to the insolvency set-off section, Mr Anthony Colman QC, sitting as a deputy judge, said that, in order for the guarantor to rely on the company's cross-claim as a defence, the guarantor would have had to join the company as a party, for which leave of the Companies Court

---

[136] A clause in a guarantee, to the effect that the liability of the guarantor is not to be affected by any act matter or thing that the creditor may do or omit to do which but for the clause might release the guarantor, would not assist when a set-off occurred automatically on the date of liquidation. See *National Mutual Royal Bank Ltd v Ginges* NSW SC, Brownie J, 15 March 1991.

[137] *Langford Concrete Pty Ltd v Finlay* [1978] 1 NSWLR 14, 18–19 (referring to *Cellulose Products Pty Ltd v Truda* (1970) 92 WN (NSW) 561, 585); *Re Kleiss* (1996) 61 FCR 436, 440; *GE Capital Australia v Davis* (2002) 11 BPR 20,529, [2002] NSWSC 1146 at [84]; *Jinhong Design & Constructions Pty Ltd v Yi Nuo Xu* [2010] NSWSC 523 at [113]–[114]. See also *Westco Motors (Distributors) Pty Ltd v Palmer* [1979] 2 NSWLR 93, 97 and *Tooth & Co Ltd v Rosier* (NSW SC, Wood J, 7 June 1985, BC8500768). Compare *Ansell Ltd v Coco* [2004] QCA 213 at [27]. Compare also *Elkhoury v Farrow Mortgage Services Pty Ltd* (1993) 114 ALR 541, 548–9, in which the creditor was in liquidation, but the court considered only equitable set-off and not insolvency set-off.

[138] *Langford Concrete Pty Ltd v Finlay* [1978] 1 NSWLR 14, 19.

[139] But see *Tooth & Co Ltd v Rosier* (NSW SC, Wood J, 7 June 1985, BC8500768).

[140] In addition to the cases referred to below, see *National Westminster Bank plc v Skelton* [1993] 1 WLR 72, 81. This has also been held in New Zealand. See *New Zealand Bloodstock Leasing Ltd v Jenkins* [2007] NZHC 336 at [156]–[163]. Compare *Alcoy and Gandia Railway and Harbour Co Ltd v Greenhill* (1897) 76 LT 542, the principal debtor being Murrietas Ltd which was not a party (although compare the discussion of the case in *Cellulose Products Pty Ltd v Truda* (1970) 92 WN (NSW) 561, 585).

[141] See para. 18.24 above.

[142] See para. 18.25 above.

[143] [1991] 2 Lloyds Rep 410.

would have been required given the liquidation.[144] *Barclays Bank plc v Gruffydd*[145] also concerned a corporate principal debtor in liquidation. The creditor applied for summary judgment against the guarantor, who sought leave to defend on the basis of a set-off as between the creditor and the company. Scott LJ noted that set-off under r 4.90 of the Insolvency Rules 1986 was in issue, as opposed to equitable set-off. He said that, if the company's claim could be regarded as having sufficient substance, leave to defend should be granted on terms that, unless the liquidator of the company agreed that the company would regard itself as bound by an adjudication on the claim in the company's absence, an application would have to be made for leave to join the company as a party. He went on to hold that the circumstances were not such as to justify leave to defend. Nolan and Purchas LJJ differed from Scott LJ on that issue, but Nolan LJ also said that leave to defend should be subject to the condition that an application be made to join the company.

Two debts owing to the creditor

18.33　Where the principal debtor owes two debts to the creditor, one of which is guaranteed and the other is not, and the creditor is separately liable to the debtor, a set-off under the insolvency legislation should take effect rateably as between the two debts.[146]

(7)　Contract excluding the defence

18.34　A guarantor's right to rely on the debtor's cross-claim as a defence may be excluded by contract. In the first place, if the contract between the debtor and the creditor is effective to exclude set-off as between those parties,[147] it should equally be effective as against the guarantor. If the debtor's cross-claim would not provide the debtor with a defence, the guarantor could not be in a better position. Alternatively, the contract of guarantee may be formulated in terms evidencing an intention that the surety is not to have the benefit of any defence of set-off that is available to the debtor.[148] This may be the case if the

---

　　[144] [1991] 2 Lloyds Rep 410, 418. Leave of the court is required to commence a proceeding against a company in liquidation. See the Insolvency Act 1986, s. 130(2). In the case of bankruptcy, see the Insolvency Act 1986, s. 285. Since the purpose of seeking to join the bankrupt or the company in liquidation would be to assist the surety in defending the action brought against him or her on the basis of a prior right of exoneration, rather than to determine a point in the insolvency, leave ordinarily should be granted. See *Re Hutton (A Bankrupt)* [1969] 2 Ch 201 with respect to an application to stay proceedings already commenced against a bankrupt.

　　[145] Court of Appeal (Purchas, Nolan and Scott LJJ), 30 October 1992.

　　[146] Consistent with *Re Unit 2 Windows Ltd* [1985] 1 WLR 1383, for which see para. 6.171 above. Compare para. 18.27 above in relation to the Statutes of Set-off.

　　[147] An agreement purporting to exclude rights of set-off will not be effective in a bankruptcy or a company liquidation. See paras 6.111–6.112 above.

　　[148] In addition to the cases referred to below, see *Continental Illinois National Bank & Trust Co of Chicago v Papanicolaou* [1986] 2 Lloyd's Rep 441 (although in that case cross-claims by the guarantors were in issue); *Coca Cola Financial Corporation v Finsat International Ltd* [1998] QB 43; *Try Build Ltd v Blue Star Garages Ltd* (1998) 66 Con LR 90. In Australia, see *Re Kleiss* (1996) 61 FCR 436, 439–40; *Dougan v Conias* [2000] FCA 1556; *GE Capital Australia v Davis* (2002) 11 BPR 20,529, [2002] NSWSC 1146 at [93] (see at [17] for the terms of clause 8.1); *Permanent Trustee Co Ltd v Gulf Import and Export Co* [2008] VSC 162 at [86]–[88]. In *Clambake Pty Ltd v Tipperary Projects Pty Ltd (No. 3)* [2009] WASC 52 at [182] and [184] a stipulation in a guarantee that precluded the guarantor from raising a set-off or counterclaim 'available to it' was held to extend to a set-off available to the principal debtor and asserted by the guarantor, *sed quaere*: see *Enron (Thrace) Exploration and Production BV v Clapp* [2004] EWHC 1612 (Comm) at [56]. A stipulation that a debtor is to pay 'without deduction' on occasions has been said to be insufficient

guarantor's liability is expressed to be primary,[149] and similarly the set-off would not apply if the instrument in question is an irrevocable letter of credit or a bank guarantee given in circumstances such that it is equivalent to an irrevocable letter of credit,[150] or if it takes the form of a bond which is not a guarantee.[151] On the other hand, a promise in a guarantee not in those forms to pay whatever is payable by the principal would not preclude reliance by the guarantor on the principal debtor's set-off. A guarantee in those terms only obliges the guarantor to pay what the principal debtor could have been compelled to pay, and if the principal could not have been compelled to pay anything because of a defence of set-off available against the creditor, the guarantor similarly should not be liable.[152]

The court may examine the factual or business background of the guarantee in order to **18.35** ascertain the intention of the parties in relation to the availability of a set-off.[153] In *Hyundai Shipbuilding & Heavy Industries Co Ltd v Pournaras*,[154] a shipyard had contracted to build a number of ships for a buyer, with the defendants guaranteeing: 'the payment in accordance with the terms of the contract of all sums due or to become due by the buyer to you under the contract, and in case the buyer is in default of any such payment the undersigned will forthwith make the payment in default on behalf of the buyer.' The buyer repudiated the contracts, and the yard, having accepted the repudiation, sued the guarantors for payment of instalments which had accrued and were unpaid. The buyer had paid an amount on account to the yard which may have exceeded the damages payable by the buyer consequent upon the repudiation, and the Court of Appeal[155] was prepared to assume that

to preclude the debtor from relying on an equitable set-off available against the creditor (see *Connaught Restaurants Ltd v Indoor Leisure Ltd* [1994] 1 WLR 501, and paras 5.101–5.106 above), and if that is the case it similarly should not suffice to preclude reliance by a guarantor on the debtor's set-off. In Australia, compare *Langford Concrete Pty Ltd v Finlay* [1978] 1 NSWLR 14, 17 and *Australia and New Zealand Banking Group Ltd v Harvey* (1994) 16 ATPR 46–132 at p 53,643. Note also the possible application of the Unfair Contract Terms Act 1977. See paras 5.114–5.120 above, and Phillips, 'When should the guarantor be permitted to rely on the principal's set-off?' [2001] LMCLQ 383, 384.

[149] *National Westminster Bank plc v Skelton* [1993] 1 WLR 72, 79–80. *Prima facie* a 'principal debtor' clause in a guarantee should have a similar effect. See *Elkhoury v Farrow Mortgage Services Pty Ltd* (1993) 114 ALR 541, 549. Compare *Langford Concrete Pty Ltd v Finlay* [1978] 1 NSWLR 14, 19 (where the guarantor was described as a principal debtor) and *Commonwealth Development Bank v Windermere Pastoral Co Pty Ltd* [1999] NSWSC 518 (see the terms of the guarantee at [28]–[29]), in neither of which was the point considered.

[150] *Intraco Ltd v Notis Shipping Corporation (The Bhoja Trader)* [1981] 2 Lloyd's Rep 256; *Power Curber International Ltd v National Bank of Kuwait SAK* [1981] 1 WLR 1233.

[151] Compare *Trafalgar House Construction (Regions) Ltd v General Surety & Guarantee Co Ltd* [1996] 1 AC 199.

[152] *Langford Concrete Pty Ltd v Finlay* [1978] 1 NSWLR 14, and compare *Westco Motors (Distributors) Pty Ltd v Palmer* [1979] 2 NSWLR 93, 98–9. See para. 18.20 above. Compare a guarantee expressed in terms of guaranteeing the payment of any moneys advanced, or of the contract price, as opposed to moneys which the debtor could be compelled to pay. See *Beri Distributors Pty Ltd v Pulitano* (1994) 10 SR (WA) 274 (WA DC); *Jinhong Design & Constructions Pty Ltd v Yi Nuo Xu* [2010] NSWSC 523 at [116].

[153] In *Barclays Bank plc v Gruffydd* Court of Appeal, 30 October 1992 Scott LJ commented that the terms of a guarantee, either express or to be implied from the commercial background to the transaction, may disentitle the surety from reliance on a set-off defence.

[154] [1978] 2 Lloyd's Rep 502. Compare *BOC Group plc v Centeon plc* [1999] 1 All ER (Comm) 53, and the letter in *Marubeni Hong Kong and South China Ltd v Mongolian Government* [2004] EWHC 472 (Comm) at [4], [134]–[136] (appeal dismissed [2005] 1 WLR 2497 (see at [35])).

[155] Stephenson and Roskill LJJ.

the buyer could have claimed back from the yard so much of the amount already paid as exceeded the yard's loss and damage.[156] On that assumption, the guarantors argued that they were entitled to take advantage of the buyer's right so as to reduce or extinguish the liability under the guarantees.[157] Their argument to that effect failed.[158] Roskill LJ, who delivered the judgment of the Court of Appeal, said that the guarantees could have been more clearly drafted, but that, having regard to the factual and business background of the guarantees,[159] the avowed object was to enable the yard to recover from the guarantors the amount due, irrespective of the position between the yard and the buyer, so that the yard could get the money from the guarantors without difficulty if they could not get it from the buyer. If the guarantors' argument were given effect, he said that the commercial utility of the guarantee would have been nullified.[160] In a later discussion of the *Pournaras* case,[161] Rix J emphasized that the guarantees in that case concerned shipbuilding contracts where the guaranteed instalments were necessary to give the shipbuilders cash flow necessary to complete the ships, that the guarantees were drafted in terms of a conditional agreement to pay forthwith (in other words, the guarantors would pay if the debtor failed to pay) as opposed to an undertaking by the guarantors that the debtor would carry out its obligations,[162] and that the guarantors' obligation to pay 'forthwith' accrued at a time when the principal debtor did not have an arguable set-off, since the debtor's right to the return of the amount paid on account did not accrue until the later repudiation.

18.36 The *Pournaras* case was referred to with approval in the House of Lords in *Hyundai Heavy Industries Co Ltd v Papadopoulos*,[163] which concerned a similar guarantee. In *Trafalgar House Construction (Regions) Ltd v General Surety & Guarantee Co Ltd*,[164] Lord Jauncey of Tullichettle commented that clear and unambiguous language must be used to displace the normal consequences of a contract of suretyship, but agreed that the language of the guarantees in *Pournaras* was sufficient to enable recovery from the guarantors irrespective of the position between the yard and the buyer.

Insolvency set-off in the debtor's bankruptcy or liquidation

18.37 If the principal debtor has become bankrupt or gone into liquidation, so that on the occurrence of the bankruptcy or the liquidation the insolvency set-off section operated automatically to extinguish the debt to the creditor to the extent of a cross-claim available to the debtor,[165] it is suggested that clear words would be required to preserve the guarantor's

---

[156] In accordance with *Dies v British and International Mining and Finance Corporation, Ltd* [1939] 1 KB 724. See, however, Andrews and Millett, *Law of Guarantees* (5th edn, 2008), 280–3, para. 6–030.
[157] See the discussion at [1978] 2 Lloyd's Rep 502, 507–8.
[158] For a criticism of the decision, see Andrews and Millett, *Law of Guarantees* (5th edn, 2008), 280–1, para. 6–030.
[159] See the discussion of the 'factual matrix' at [1978] 2 Lloyd's Rep 502, 506.
[160] [1978] 2 Lloyd's Rep 502, 508.
[161] *BOC Group plc v Centeon LLC* [1999] 1 All ER (Comm) 53, 63–7.
[162] See Lord Reid's discussion of the distinction in *Moschi v Lep Air Services Ltd* [1973] AC 331, 344–5.
[163] [1980] 1 WLR 1129, 1137–8 (Viscount Dilhorne), 1142–3 (Lord Edmund Davies), 1152 (Lord Fraser of Tullybelton).
[164] [1996] 1 AC 199, 208.
[165] See para. 18.31 above.

liability to the creditor.[166] This is because the effect of permitting recovery from the guarantor would be that the creditor would be paid twice, once by the principal debtor through a set-off in the liquidation[167] and a second time by the guarantor.

In *Rayden v Edwardo Ltd*[168] Gloster J held that a guarantor remained liable notwithstanding an asserted set-off between the creditor and the principal debtor in the debtor's liquidation. The decision is questionable, however. The contract between the debtor and the creditor obliged the debtor to pay the creditor without set-off. However, unlike the position in relation to other forms of set-off,[169] that provision was ineffective as between those parties to exclude insolvency set-off in the debtor's liquidation.[170] The guarantor guaranteed, as a primary obligation, the 'full, complete, due and punctual performance of all the obligations' of the debtor. For the guarantee to apply, there should have been a subsisting obligation in the principal debtor. But because the exclusion of set-off was ineffective in the liquidation, any set-off would have taken effect as between the debtor and the creditor automatically upon the occurrence of the liquidation. As a consequence, the principal debt to that extent would have been paid, notwithstanding the expressed obligation to pay without set-off, and the debtor would have had no remaining obligation to the creditor. Thus, the creditor could not have proved in the liquidation in respect of the debt. Further, there was nothing in the guarantee itself which expressly preserved the guarantor's liability notwithstanding payment of the principal debt through set-off.[171] Since the debtor had no remaining obligation to the extent that the debt had been paid by set-off, the guarantee as a matter of construction should not have applied. **18.38**

The subject of the asserted set-off in that case was a claim for damages for breach of warranties in a share purchase agreement. That claim had yet to be established. Gloster J said that, if and when the damages claim came to be established, the principal debtor's debt would be deemed to have been retrospectively *pro tanto* discharged as from the date of the winding up, but until that occurred the guarantor had a continuing and separate obligation to honour the payment obligation.[172] However, there would be nothing retrospective about the set-off. Any such set-off will have taken effect automatically upon the occurrence of the **18.39**

---

[166] On the basis that clear words would be required to impose on a surety a liability exceeding that of the debtor. See *Barclays Bank Plc v Kingston* [2006] 2 Lloyd's Rep 59 at [30]. As a general principle, but subject to some qualifications and exceptions, discharge of the principal debtor also discharges the surety. See *McDonald v Dennys Lascelles Ltd* (1933) 48 CLR 457, 479–80. Compare *Westco Motors (Distributors) Pty Ltd v Palmer* [1979] 2 NSWLR 93, although the possible application and effect of the insolvency set-off section was not considered. A similar comment may be made in relation to *National Westminster Bank plc v Skelton* [1993] 1 WLR 72, which was concerned with a claim for possession under a mortgage given by a third party as surety, as opposed to a personal claim against the surety for payment of the debt. See paras 4.133 and 4.134 above.

[167] Set-off is payment. See para. 12.34 above.

[168] [2008] EWHC 2689 (Comm). In Australia, see also *Jinhong Design & Constructions Pty Ltd v Yi Nuo Xu* [2010] NSWSC 523 at [115]–[116], in which the principal debtor was in liquidation. It does not appear to have been argued that the automatic occurrence of a set-off in the debtor's liquidation would have had the consequence that, to the extent of the set-off, the price had been paid.

[169] See paras 5.96 (equitable set-off and abatement) and 5.133 (Statutes of Set-off) above.

[170] See para. 6.111 above.

[171] Clauses 12.17 and 12.10 of the guarantee, to which Gloster J referred [2008] EWHC 2689 (Comm) at [25], did not touch upon the question of a set-off operating as a payment to the creditor.

[172] [2008] EWHC 2689 (Comm) at [25].

liquidation, without the necessity for a court order.[173] Subsequent proceedings, in which the damages claim was established, would simply confirm what the position was at the winding-up date.

D. Mortgage Given to Secure Another Person's Debt

18.40   A contract of suretyship may take the form of a mortgage given to secure a debt owing by another person to a creditor. The question whether the creditor is entitled to possession of the mortgaged premises, or to exercise security rights which are dependent upon default, in circumstances where the principal debtor is entitled to an equitable set-off, was considered earlier.[174]

E. Surety's Right to Rely on a Co-Surety's Set-off

18.41   A right of exoneration similar to that available to a surety as against the principal debtor[175] does not apply as between co-sureties on a joint and several covenant. If one of the sureties is sued by the creditor, that surety may not set off a debt owing by the creditor to a co-surety.[176]

F. Set-off Between the Surety and the Principal Debtor

18.42   As between a surety and the principal debtor, the surety after paying the creditor may employ his or her claim for an indemnity as a set-off under the Statutes of Set-off.[177] But since the Statutes extended only to the case of mutual debts which were both presently existing and payable at the date of the action,[178] a mere contingent right to an indemnity, where the surety has not paid the creditor, will not give rise to a defence under the Statutes.

18.43   The position with respect to insolvency set-off is more complex, and was considered earlier.[179]

---

[173] See para. 18.31 above.
[174] See paras 4.130–4.146 above.
[175] See para. 18.21 above.
[176] *Bowyear v Pawson* (1881) 6 QBD 540; *Lord v Direct Acceptance Corporation Ltd* (1993) 32 NSWLR 362, 371–2. However, see para. 12.21 above in relation to insolvency set-off.
[177] *Rodgers v Maw* (1846) 15 M & W 444, 153 ER 924.
[178] See para. 2.29 above.
[179] See paras 8.10–8.34 (contingent debt owing by the insolvent) above and paras 8.35–8.46 (contingent debt owing to the insolvent) above.

BIBLIOGRAPHY

1. BOOKS

Andrews and Millett, *Law of Guarantees* (5th edn, 2008), London: Sweet & Maxwell

Armour and Bennett (eds), *Vulnerable Transactions in Corporate Insolvency* (2003), Oxford: Hart Publishing

Arnould's Law of Marine Insurance and Average (17th edn, 2008), London: Sweet & Maxwell

Australian Law Reform Commission Report No 45, *General Insolvency Inquiry* (1988) ('the Harmer Report')

Babington, *The Law of Set-off and Mutual Credit* (1827), London: Henry Butterworth

Bacon's Abridgement of the Law (7th edn, 1832), London: J and W T Clarke

Beatson, *The Use and Abuse of Unjust Enrichment* (1991), Oxford: Clarendon Press

Benjamin's Sale of Goods (7th edn, 2006), London: Sweet & Maxwell

Birks, *An Introduction to the Law of Restitution* (1989), Oxford: Clarendon Press

Blackstone, *Commentaries on the Laws of England* (3rd edn, 1768), Oxford: Clarendon Press

Blagden Committee Report ('Report of the Committee on Bankruptcy Law and Deeds of Arrangement Amendment') (Cmnd 221, 1957)

Bowstead and Reynolds on Agency (18th edn, 2006), London: Sweet and Maxwell

Brandon, *The Customary Law of Foreign Attachment* (1861), London: Butterworths

Brindle and Cox (ed.), *Law of Bank Payments* (3rd edn, 2004), London: Sweet & Maxwell

Broom's Legal Maxims (10th edn, 1939), London; Sweet and Maxwell

Buckley on the Companies Acts (14th edn, 1981), London: Butterworths

Bullen and Leake and Jacob's Precedents of Pleadings (15th edn, 2004), London: Sweet & Maxwell

Burrows, *The Law of Restitution* (1993), London: Butterworths

Byles on Bills of Exchange and Cheques (27th edn, 2002), London: Sweet and Maxwell

Carver's Carriage by Sea (13th edn, 1982), London: Stevens and Sons

Chalmers and Guest on Bills of Exchange, Cheques and Promissory Notes (17th edn, 2009), London: Sweet & Maxwell

Chitty's Blackstone (1826), London: William Walker

Chitty's Practice (3rd edn, 1837)

Chitty's Precedents in Pleadings (2nd edn, 1847)

Chitty on Contracts (30th edn, 2008), London: Sweet & Maxwell

Christian, *Bankrupt Law* (2nd edn, 1818), London: W Clarke and Sons

Civil Procedure (2nd edn, 1999), London: Sweet & Maxwell

Clerk and Lindsell on Torts (19th edn, 2006), London: Sweet & Maxwell

Coke's Institutes (1648)

Comyns' Digest (5th edn, 1832), London: Butterworth

Cooke, *The Bankrupt Laws* (8th edn, 1823), London: Charles Hunter

Cooper's Parliamentary Proceedings (1828), London: John Murray

Coote on Mortgages (9th edn, 1927), London: Stevens & Sons Ltd

Cork Committee Report on Insolvency Law and Practice (Cmnd 8558, 1982)

Cousins, *The Law of Mortgages* (2nd edn, 2001), London: Sweet & Maxwell

Cranston, *Principles of Banking Law* (2nd edn, 2002), Oxford: Oxford University Press

Crawford and Falconbridge, *Banking and Bills of Exchange* (8th edn, 1986), Toronto: Canada Law Book Inc

Dal Pont, *Law of Agency* (2nd edn, 2008), Australia: LexisNexis Butterworths

Daniell's Chancery Practice (8th edn, 1914), London: Stevens and Sons

Derham, *Subrogation in Insurance Law* (1985), Sydney: Law Book Company

Dicey and Morris and Collins, *The Conflict of Laws* (14th edn, 2006), London: Sweet & Maxwell

Doria, *The Law and Practice in Bankruptcy* (1874), London: Law Times Office

Doria and Macrae, *The Law and Practice of Bankruptcy* (1863), London: John Crockford

Ellinger's Modern Banking Law (4th edn, 2006), Oxford: Oxford University Press

Farrands, *The Law of Options and Other Pre-Emptive Rights* (2010), Pyrmont NSW: Lawbook Co

Finn, *Fiduciary Obligations* (1977), Sydney: The Law Book Company

Fisher and Lightwood's Law of Mortgage (12th edn, 2006), London: LexisNexis Butterworths

Fisher and Lightwood's Law of Mortgage (2nd Aust edn, 2005), Australia: LexisNexis Butterworths

Ford and Lee, *Principles of the Law of Trusts* (looseleaf), Sydney: LBC Information Services

Francis and Thomas, *Mortgages and Securities* (3rd edn, 1986), Sydney; Butterworths

Fridman, *The Law of Agency* (7th edn, 1996), London: Butterworths

Goff and Jones, *The Law of Restitution* (7th edn, 2007), London: Sweet & Maxwell

Goode on Legal Problems of Credit and Security (4th edn (ed. Gullifer), 2008), London: Sweet & Maxwell

Goode, *Commercial Law* (3rd edn, 2004), London: Butterworths

Goode, *Principles of Corporate Insolvency Law* (3rd edn, 2005), London: Sweet & Maxwell

Goodinge, *The Law Against Bankrupts* (2nd edn, 1701), London: John Hartley

Gore-Browne on Companies (45th edn, looseleaf), Bristol: Jordans

Gough, *Company Charges* (2nd edn, 1996), London: Butterworths

Gray and Gray, *Elements of Land Law* (5th edn, 2009), Oxford: Oxford University Press

Halsbury's Laws of England, London: LexisNexis

Handley, *Estoppel by Conduct and Election* (2006), London: Sweet & Maxwell

Henley, *A Digest of the Bankrupt Law* (3rd edn, 1832), London: Saunders and Benning

Hill and Redman's Law of Landlord and Tenant (17th edn, 1982), London: Butterworths

Hogg and Monahan, *Liability of the Crown* (3rd edn, 2000), Canada: Carswell

Holden, *The Law and Practice of Banking* (5th edn, 1991), London: Pitman

Holdsworth, *A History of English Law*, London: Methuen

Houlden and Morawetz, *Bankruptcy Law of Canada* (1960), Toronto: The Carswell Company

Hudson's Building and Engineering Contracts (11th edn, 1995), London: Sweet & Maxwell

Jackson, *Principles of Property Law* (1967), Sydney: Law Book Company

Jacobs, *Security of Payment in the Australian Building and Construction Industry* (3rd edn, 2010), Pyrmont NSW: Lawbook Co

Jacobs' Law of Trusts in Australia (7th edn, 2006), Australia: LexisNexis Butterworths

Jones and Goodhart, *Specific Performance* (2nd edn, 1996), London: Butterworths

Keating on Construction Contracts (8th edn, 2006), London: Sweet & Maxwell

Keating, *Law and Practice of Building Contracts* (3rd edn, 1969), London: Sweet & Maxwell

Keeton and Sheridan, *Equity* (3rd edn, 1987), England: Kluwer Law Publishers

Kerr on Injunctions (1867), London: William Maxwell & Son

Kerr and Hunter on Receivers and Administrators (19th edn, 2010), London: Sweet & Maxwell

Lewin on Trusts (18th edn, 2008), London: Sweet & Maxwell

Lightman and Moss, *The Law of Administrators and Receivers of Companies* (4th edn, 2007), London: Thomson

Lindley & Banks on Partnership (18th edn, 2002), London: Sweet & Maxwell

Lindley on Companies (6th edn, 1902), London: Sweet & Maxwell

MacGillivray on Insurance Law (11th edn, 2008), London: Sweet & Maxwell

Macken, O'Grady, Sappideen and Warburton, *The Law of Employment* (5th edn, 2002), Sydney: Lawbook Co

Maddock, *Principles and Practice of the High Court of Chancery* (3rd edn, 1837), London: J & W T Clarke

Maitland, *Equity* (2nd edn (rev by Brunyate), 1936), Cambridge: Cambridge University Press

Mann on the The Legal Aspect of Money (6th edn (ed. Proctor), 2005), Oxford: Oxford University Press

Marshall, *The Assignment of Choses in Action* (1950), London: Sir Isaac Pitman & Sons

McCracken, *The Banker's remedy of Set-off* (3rd edn, 2010), England: Bloomsbury Professional

McPherson's Law of Company Liquidation (5th edn (by Gronow), looseleaf), Sydney: Thomson Lawbook Co

Meagher, Gummow and Lehane's Equity Doctrines and Remedies (4th edn, 2002), Australia: Butterworths LexisNexis

Megarry, *The Rent Acts* (10th edn, 1967), London: Stevens and Sons

Megarry and Wade, *The Law of Real Property* (7th edn, 2008), London: Sweet & Maxwell

Mitchell, *The Law of Subrogation* (1994), Oxford: Clarendon Press

Montague, *Summary of the Law of Set-off* (2nd edn, 1828), London: Joseph Butterworth and Son

New South Wales Law Reform Commission Report, No 94, *Set-off*, February 2000

Nussbaum, *Money in the Law National and International* (1950), Brooklyn: The Foundation Press, Inc

O'Donovan, *Company Receivers and Administrators* (looseleaf), Sydney: Thomson Lawbook Co

O'Donovan and Phillips, *Modern Contract of Guarantee* (looseleaf), Australia: Thomson Lawbook Co

Oditah, *Legal Aspects of Receivables Financing* (1991), London: Sweet & Maxwell

Paget's Law of Banking (13th edn, 2007), London: LexisNexis Butterworths

Palmer's Company Law (looseleaf), London: Stevens and Sons

Palmer's Company Precedents (16th edn, 1952), London: Stevens and Sons

Palmer, *The Law of Set-off in Canada* (1993), Ontario; Canada Law Book Co

Parry and Kerridge, *The Law of Succession* (12th edn, 2009), London: Sweet & Maxwell

Pennington, *Company Law* (7th edn, 1995), London: Butterworths

Pennington, Hudson and Mann, *Commercial Banking Law* (1978), Plymouth: MacDonald and Evans

Pettit, *Equity and the Law of Trusts* (11th edn, 2009), Oxford: Oxford University Press

Powell, *The Law of Agency* (1952), Sir Isaac Pitman & Sons

Rabel, *The Conflict of Laws* (2nd edn, 1964), Ann Arbor: Michigan Legal Publications

Robson, *The Law of Bankruptcy* (7th edn, 1894), London: William Clowes and Sons

Robson's Annotated Corporations Law (4th edn, 1999), Sydney: LBC Information Services

Rowlatt on Principal and Surety (5th edn, 1999), London: Sweet & Maxwell

Russell on Arbitration (23rd edn, 2007), London: Sweet & Maxwell

Salmond on Jurisprudence (12th edn, 1966), London: Sweet & Maxwell

Scott and Ascher on Trusts (5th edn, 2006), Boston: Aspen Publishers

Shelford, *The Law of Bankruptcy and Insolvency* (3rd edn, 1862), London: Sweet & Maxwell

Smith, *The Law of Assignment* (2007), Oxford: Oxford University Press

Smith's Leading Cases (12th edn, 1915), London: Sweet & Maxwell

Snell's Equity (31st edn, 2005), London: Sweet & Maxwell

Spencer Bower, *The Law Relating to Estoppel by Representation* (4th edn, 2004), London: LexisNexis

Spencer Bower and Handley, *Res Judicata* (4th edn, 2009), London: LexisNexis

Spencer Bower, Turner and Handley, *Actionable Misrepresentation* (4th edn, 2000), London: Butterworths

Spry, *Equitable Remedies* (8th edn, 2010), Australia: Lawbook Co

Starke, *Assignments of Choses in Action in Australia* (1972), Sydney: Butterworths

Stoljar, *The Law of Agency* (1961), London: Sweet & Maxwell

Story, *Commentaries on Equity Jurisprudence* (14th edn, 1918), Boston: Little, Brown and Co

Sykes and Walker, *The Law of Securities* (5th edn, 1993), Sydney: The Law Book Company

The Supreme Court Practice (1999), London: Sweet & Maxwell

Tidd, *The Practice of the Courts of King's Bench and Common Pleas in Personal Actions and Ejectment* (9th edn, 1828), London: Joseph Butterworth and Son

Tolhurst, *The Assignment of Contractual Rights* (2006), Oxford: Hart Publishing

Treitel, *The Law of Contract* (12th edn, 2007), London: Sweet & Maxwell

Tudsbery, *The Nature, Requisites and Operation of Equitable Assignments* (1912), London: Sweet & Maxwell

Underhill and Hayton, *Law Relating to Trusts and Trustees* (17th edn, 2006), London: LexisNexis Butterworths

Viner's Abridgment (2nd edn, 1741), London: G Robinson

Wadsley and Penn, *The Law Relating to Domestic Banking* (2nd edn, 2000), London: Sweet & Maxwell

Warren, *The Law Relating to Choses in Action* (1899), London: Sweet & Maxwell Limited

Waters, *The Constructive Trust* (1964), London: The Athlone Press

Weaver and Craigie, *The Law Relating to Banker and Customer in Australia* (looseleaf), Sydney: LBC Information Services

White and Tudor's Leading Cases in Equity (9th edn, 1928), London: Sweet & Maxwell

Wilken and Villiers, *The Law of Waiver, Variation and Estoppel* (2nd edn, 2002), Oxford: Oxford University Press

Williams on Wills (9th edn, 2008), London: LexisNexis Butterworths

Williams, Glanville, *Joint Obligations* (1949), London: Butterworth & Co

Williams, N, *Civil Procedure Victoria* (looseleaf), Sydney: Butterworths

Williams, W, *The Law Relating to Assents* (1947), London: Butterworth & Co

Williams and Muir Hunter, *The Law and Practice in Bankruptcy* (19th edn, 1979), London: Stevens & Sons

Williams and Williams, *The New Law and Practice in Bankruptcy* (1870), London: Stevens & Sons

Williams, Mortimer and Sunnucks on Executors, Administrators and Probate (19th edn, 2008), London: Sweet & Maxwell

Williston on Contracts (3rd edn, 1967), New York: Baker, Voorhis & Co

Withers on Reversions (2nd edn, 1933), London: Butterworth & Co

Wood, *English and International Set-off* (1989), London: Sweet & Maxwell

Woodfall's Law of Landlord and Tenant (looseleaf), London: Sweet & Maxwell

Yale, *Lord Nottingham's Chancery Cases* vol. 1, 73 *Selden Society* (1957), London: Bernard Quaritch

2. ARTICLES, NOTES ETC

Adams, '"No deduction or set-off" clauses' (1994) 57 *Modern Law Review* 960

Ames, 'Undisclosed principal – his rights and liabilities' (1909) 18 *Yale Law Journal* 443

Andrews, 'The proper limits of set-off' [1992] *Cambridge Law Journal* 239

Aughterson, 'In defence of the benefit and burden principle' (1991) 65 *Australian Law Journal* 319

Baker, 'The future of equity' (1977) 93 *Law Quarterly Review* 529

Bennetts, 'Voidable transactions: consequences of removing avoidance powers from the liquidator and vesting them in the court' (1994) 2 *Insolvency Law Journal* 136

Berg, 'Arbitration: legal set-off and enforcing admitted claims' [2000] *Lloyd's Maritime and Commercial Law Quarterly* 153

Berg, 'Charges over book debts: a reply' [1995] *Journal of Business Law* 433

Berg, 'House of Lords clarifies liquidation netting' *International Financial Law Review*, August 1995, 20

Berg, 'Contracting out of set-off in a winding Up' [1996] *Lloyd's Maritime and Commercial Law Quarterly* 49

Berg, 'Liquidation set-off: the mutuality principle and security over bank balances' [1996] *Lloyd's Maritime and Commercial Law Quarterly* 176

Bewick, Hertz, Marshall and Tett, 'Administration Set-off: A Commentary on the Paper of the FMLC Working Group' (2008) 23 *Journal of International Banking and Financial Law* 287

Birks, 'Equity in the modern world: an exercise in taxonomy' (1996) 26 *University of Western Australia Law Review* 1

Bishop, 'Set-off in the administration of insolvent and bankrupt estates' (1901) 1 *Columbia Law Review* 377

Blair, 'Charges over cash deposits' *International Financial Law Review*, November 1983, 14

Breslin, 'Set-off under Irish law' (1997) 18 *Company Lawyer* 198

Bridge, 'Clearing houses and insolvency in Australia' (2008) 124 *Law Quarterly Review* 379

Bryan, 'The liability of banks to make restitution for wrongful payments' (1998) 26 *Australian Business Law Review* 93

Bryson, 'Restraining sales by mortgagees and a curial myth' (1993) 11 *Australian Bar Review* 1

Burrows, 'We do this at common law but that in equity' (2002) 22 *Oxford Journal of Legal Studies* 1

Burton, 'Negotiability: set-offs and counterclaims' in Burton (ed.), *Directions In Finance Law* (1990), Sydney, Butterworths

Capper, 'Deceit, banker's set-off and Mareva undertakings – The Abbey's bad habits' [1999] *Lloyd's Maritime and Commercial Law Quarterly* 21

Calnan, 'The insolvent bank and security over deposits' (1996) 11 *Journal of International Banking and Financial Law* 185

Calnan, 'Security over deposits again: BCCI (No 8) in the House of Lords' (1998) 13 *Journal of International Banking and Financial Law* 125

Calnan, 'Fashioning the law to suit the practicalities of life' (1998) 114 *Law Quarterly Review* 174

Castles, 'The reception and status of English law in Australia' (1963) 2 *Adelaide Law Review* 1

Chorley, 'Del credere' (1929) 45 *Law Quarterly Review* 221, (1930) 46 *Law Quarterly Review* 11

Coleman, 'Netting a red herring' (1994) 9 *Journal of International Banking and Financial Law* 391

Dean, Luckett and Houghton, 'Notional calculations in liquidations revisited' (1993) 11 *Companies and Securities Law Journal* 204

Derham, 'Recent issues in relation to set-off' (1984) 68 *Australian Law Journal* 331

Derham, 'Set-off and netting of foreign exchange contracts in the liquidation of a counterparty' [1991] *Journal of Business Law* 463, 536

Derham, 'Set-off against an assignee: the relevance of marshalling, contribution and subrogation' (1991) 107 *Law Quarterly Review* 126

Derham, 'Some aspects of mutual credit and mutual dealings' (1992) 108 *Law Quarterly Review* 99

Derham, 'Set-off in Victoria' (1999) 73 *Australian Law Journal* 754

Duns, Note (1998) 6 *Insolvency Law Journal* 4

Earley, 'Set-off rights available to banks in Ireland' [1997] 4 *Journal of International Banking Law* 153

Everett, 'Security over bank deposits' (1988) 16 *Australian Business Law Review* 351

Everett, 'Multi-party set-off agreements' [1993] *Journal of Banking and Finance Law and Practice* 180

Farrar, 'Contracting out of set-off' (1970) 120 *New Law Journal* 771

Fawcett, 'The Financial Collateral Directive: an examination of some practical problems following its implementation in the UK' [2005] *Journal of International Banking Law* and Regulation 295

Fealy, 'Can set-off prejudice a debt subordination agreement?' (2009) 24 *Journal of International Banking and Financial Law* 64

Ford, 'Trading trusts and creditors' rights' (1981) 13 *Melbourne University Law Review* 1

Goode, 'Centre Point' [1984] *Journal of Business Law* 172

Goode, 'Security: a pragmatic conceptualist's response' (1989) 15 *Monash University Law Review* 361

Goode, 'Charges over book debts: a missed opportunity' (1994) 110 *Law Quarterly Review* 592

Goode, 'Charge-backs and legal fictions' (1998) 114 *Law Quarterly Review* 178

Goodhart and Hamson, 'Undisclosed principals in contract' (1932) 4 *Cambridge Law Journal* 320

Goodhart and Jones, 'The infiltration of equitable doctrine into English commercial law' (1980) 43 *Modern Law Review* 489

Grantham, 'The impact of security interest on set-off' [1989] *Journal of Business Law* 377

Gummow, 'Compensation for breach of fiduciary duty', in Youdan (ed.), *Equity, Fiduciaries and Trusts* (1989), Toronto: Carswell

Handley, 'Anshun today' (1997) 71 *Australian Law Journal* 934

Hapgood, 'Set-off under the laws of England' in Neate (ed.), *Using Set-off as a Security* (1990), London: Graham & Trotman

Harpum, 'Specific performance with compensation as a purchaser's remedy – a study in contract and equity' [1981] *Cambridge Law Journal* 47

Herzberg, 'Bankers' rights of combination' (1982) 10 *Australian Business Law Review* 79

Higgins, 'The equity of the undisclosed principal' (1965) 28 *Modern Law Review* 167

Ho, 'Of proprietary restitution, insurers' subrogation and insolvency set-off – the untenable case of *Re Ballast*' (2007) 23 *Insolvency Law & Practice* 103

Hoffheimer, 'The common law of Edward Christian' [1994] *Cambridge Law Journal* 140

Hogan, 'Set-off, members' rights and winding up' (1998) 19 *Company Lawyer* 16

Horack, 'Insolvency and specific performance' (1918) 31 *Harvard Law Review* 702

Horrigan, 'Combining bank accounts in different currencies – a conceptual analysis' (1991) 65 *Australian Law Journal* 14

Jones, Comment [1980] *Cambridge Law Journal* 275

Kleiner, 'Foreign exchange claims against banks in dispute' *International Financial Law Review*, May 1989, 204

Ladbury, 'Introduction to the law of contractual set-off in Australia' in Neate (ed.), *Using Set-off as a Security* (1990), London: Graham & Trotman

Loyd, 'The Development of Set-off' (1916) 64 *University of Pennsylvania Law Review* 541

Luckett and Dean, 'Cross-debts: notional calculations in liquidations' (1983) 11 *Australian Business Law Review* 69

McCormack, 'Charge backs and commercial certainty in the House of Lords' [1998] *Company Financial and Insolvency Law Review* 111

McPherson, 'The insolvent trading trust' in Finn (ed.), *Essays in Equity* (1985), Sydney: Law Book Company

Manire, 'Foreign exchange sales and the law of contracts: a case for analogy to the Uniform Commercial Code' (1982) 35 *Vanderbilt Law Review* 1173

Martin, 'Fusion, fallacy and confusion: a comparative study' [1994] *The Conveyancer* 13

Matthews, 'Restitution 0, Trusts 0 (after extra time) – a case of set-off' [1994] *Restitution Law Review* 44

Melville, 'Disclaimer of contracts in bankruptcy' (1952) 15 *Modern Law Review* 28

Millett, 'Tracing the proceeds of fraud' (1991) 107 *Law Quarterly Review* 71

Millett, 'Equity – the road ahead' (1995) 9 *Tolley's Trust Law International* 35

Millett, 'Equity's place in the law of commerce' (1998) 114 *Law Quarterly Review* 214

Millett, 'Restitution and constructive trusts' (1998) 114 *Law Quarterly Review* 399

Millett (Richard) 'Pleasing paradoxes' (1996) 112 *Law Quarterly Review* 524

Mitchell, 'Defences to an insurer's subrogated action' [1996] *Lloyd's Maritime and Commercial Law Quarterly* 343

Mokel, 'Resolving the *MS Fashions* "paradox"' [1999] *Company Financial and Insolvency Law Review* 106

Montrose, 'Liability of principal for acts exceeding actual and apparent authority' (1939) 17 *Canadian Bar Review* 693

Nicholls (Lord), 'Knowing receipt: the need for a new landmark' in *Restitution Past, Present and Future* (ed by Cornish, 1998), Oxford: Hart Publishing

Note, 'Set-off in case of mutual dealings' (1882) 26 *Solicitors' Journal* 575

Note, (1992) 66 *Australian Law Journal* 313

Oditah, 'Assets and treatment of claims in insolvency' (1992) 108 *Law Quarterly Review* 459

Oditah, 'Financing trade credit: Welsh Development Agency v Exfinco' [1992] *Journal of Business Law* 541

Phillips, 'When should the guarantor be permitted to rely on the principal's set-off?' [2001] *Lloyd's Maritime and Commercial Law Quarterly* 383

Pollard, 'Credit balances as security – II' [1988] *Journal of Business Law* 219

Pollock, (1887) 3 *Law Quarterly Review* 358

Pollock, (1893) 9 *Law Quarterly Review* 111

Pollock, 'Re wait' (1927) 43 *Law Quarterly Review* 293

Rank, 'Repairs in lieu of rent' (1976) 40 *The Conveyancer and Property Lawyer* 196

Reynolds, 'Practical problems of the undisclosed principal doctrine' (1983) 36 *Current Legal Problems* 119

Rose, 'Deductions from freight and hire under English law' [1982] *Lloyd's Maritime and Commercial Law Quarterly* 33

Russell, 'Defences by Way of Set-off, Counterclaim and Cross Action' (1928) 2 *Australian Law Journal* 80

Salter, 'Remedies for banks: an outline of English law' in Blair (ed.), *Banks and Remedies* (2nd edn, 1999), London: Lloyds of London Press

Segal, 'Conceptual implausibility in the Court of Appeal' [1996] 8 *Journal of International Banking Law* 307

Shea, 'Statutory set-off' (1986) 3 *Journal of International Banking Law* 152

Shea, 'Further reflections on statutory set-off' (1987) 3 *Journal of International Banking Law* 183

Shea, 'Foreign exchange contracts and netting in the UK' *International Financial Law Review*, January 1990, 19

Smart, 'International insolvency: banks and set-off' (1991) 1 *Journal of International Banking and Financial Law* 10

Spry, 'Equitable set-offs' (1969) 43 *Australian Law Journal* 265

Stevens, 'The Contracts (Rights of Third Parties) Act 1999' (2004) 120 *Law Quarterly Review* 292

Steyn, 'Guarantees: the co-extensiveness principle' (1974) 90 *Law Quarterly Review* 246

Taylor, 'The year in review – New Zealand insolvency law in 1999' [1999] *Insolvency Law Journal* 212

Tettenborn, 'Remedies for the recovery of money paid by mistake' [1980] *Cambridge Law Journal* 272

Tettenborn, Note (1997) 113 *Law Quarterly Review* 374

Tettenborn, 'Assignees, equities and cross-claims: principle and confusion' [2002] *Lloyd's Maritime and Commercial Law Quarterly* 485

Tigar, 'Automatic extinction of cross-demands: *compensatio* from Rome to California' (1965) 53 *California Law Review* 224

Treitel, 'Specific performance in the sale of goods' [1966] *Journal of Business Law* 211

Turing, 'Setting off down a new road' (2004) 19 *Journal of International Banking and Financial Law* 349

Turing, 'New growth in the financial collateral garden' (2005) 1 *Journal of International Banking and Financial Law* 4

Waite, 'Repairs and Deduction from Rent' [1981] *The Conveyancer* 199

Waite, 'Disrepair and set-off of damages against rent: the implications of British Anzani' [1983] *The Conveyancer* 373

Wallace, 'Set back to set-off' (1973) 89 *Law Quarterly Review* 36

Wallace 'Set fair for set-off' (1974) 90 *Law Quarterly Review* 21

Walters and Armour, 'The proceeds of office-holder actions under the Insolvency Act: charged assets or free estate?' [2006] *Lloyd's Maritime and Commercial Law Quarterly* 153

Weir, 'A tenant's right of set-off' (1994) 68 *Australian Law Journal* 857

Williams, Glanville, 'Mistake as to party in the law of contract' (1945) 23 *Canadian Bar Review* 380

Wood, 'Netting agreements in organised and private markets' in Kingsford-Smith (ed.), *Current Developments in Banking and Finance* (1989), London: Sweet & Maxwell

Wood and Terray, 'Foreign exchange netting in France and England' *International Financial Law Review*, October 1989, 18

Yeowart, 'House of Lords upholds charge-backs over deposits' *International Financial Law Review*, January 1998, 7

INDEX

Index

substantive equitable set-off (*cont.*)
asserted, action taken by creditors before set-off has
been 4.48–4.49
assignment 4.36
close connection between claims 4.03, 4.11,
4.17–4.18, 4.29, 4.58, 4.62
conduct of creditors affecting debtor's ability to
pay 4.97–4.102
contingent debts and debts not payable 4.65–4.66
contracts
different contracts, arising out of 4.91–4.96
fraud 4.113–4.115
misrepresentation inducing a contract
4.110–4.112
repudiation 4.103–4.109
damages 3.10, 4.01, 4.05–4.07, 4.31–4.34
discretion 4.60
estimation of value 4.50
freight 4.31–4.32
liquidated cross-claims 4.63–4.66
overriding agreements 4.96
repudiation 4.18
third parties 4.37
declarations 4.30, 4.34, 4.37
default, right to take action consequent
upon 4.45–4.49
definition of substantive 4.30–4.34
delay in prosecuting claim 4.58
different contracts, arising out of 4.91–4.96
discretion 4.58–4.62
extinguishment 4.30, 4.35, 4.38
foreign jurisdiction clauses 4.55, 4.62
fraud 4.113–4.115
freight, deduction from 4.31
hire, deductions from 4.46
impeachment, concept of 4.03–4.15, 4.43,
4.49, 4.65
injunctions 4.01, 4.04, 4.06, 4.14, 4.30,
4.37, 4.41
insolvency 4.37
instalment, default in payment of 4.46
insurance 4.16
interest 4.56
Judicature Acts 4.41
leases, forfeiture for non-payment of rent 2.62
limitation on liability 4.119
limitation periods 4.35, 4.51–4.54
liquidated cross-claims 4.63–4.66
litigation, whether set-off confined to defence
to 4.38–4.44
manifest injustice or fairness 4.11–4.12, 4.17
misrepresentation inducing a contract
4.110–4.112
mortgages 4.125–4.148
mutuality 4.67–4.90
new approaches 4.08–4.18
New Zealand 4.03

overriding agreements 4.94–4.96
periodic payments 4.120–4.124
quantum of cross-claim 4.61
repairing covenant, breach of 4.59
repudiation of contract 4.18, 4.103–4.109
retrospectivity 4.49
royalties 4.63–4.64
self-help remedy, set-off as 4.32–4.33, 4.38, 4.41,
4.43
substantive 4.29–4.57
meaning of 4.30–4.34
subrogation 2.54
summary judgments 4.62
third parties 2.54–2.55
traditional formulation 4.02–4.18
trustees 4.37
unconscionability 4.30, 4.33
value of cross-claims, estimating the 4.50
winding up petitions 4.57
substantive equitable set-off in Australia 4.19–4.28
abatement 4.24
assignment 4.27
close connection between claims 4.20, 4.22, 4.58
damages 4.20–4.23, 4.27–4.28
default, right to take action consequent
upon 4.47
defence, set-off as a 2.56
delay in prosecuting claims 4.58
impeachment 4.19–4.20, 4.24, 4.26, 4.47
manifest injustice and unfairness 4.28
misleading or deceptive conduct 4.116–4.118
New South Wales 2.76–2.79, 4.117
Trade Practices Act 1974 4.116–4.118
sub-tenancies 5.67, 5.75–5.76
summary judgment
arbitration clauses 2.51
building and construction contracts 5.56
counterclaims 1.05, 5.177
criticism of law of set-off 5.167–5.171, 5.177
foreign jurisdiction clauses 2.51
Statutes of Set-off 2.51
stay of enforcement 2.92–2.93
substantive equitable set-off 4.62
sureties 18.01–18.43 *see also* guarantees
abatement 18.09–18.10, 18.12, 18.15–18.26
assignment 18.03, 18.07
Australia 18.12, 18.16–18.17, 18.20–18.26,
18.32
automatic set-off 18.31–18.32
bailiffs 18.04
bankruptcy 18.06, 18.10–18.12, 18.31,
18.37–18.39
assignment 18.03
contingent debts and claims 8.20, 8.27–8.33
equitable set-off 6.28
joinder 18.26
notice 18.26

978